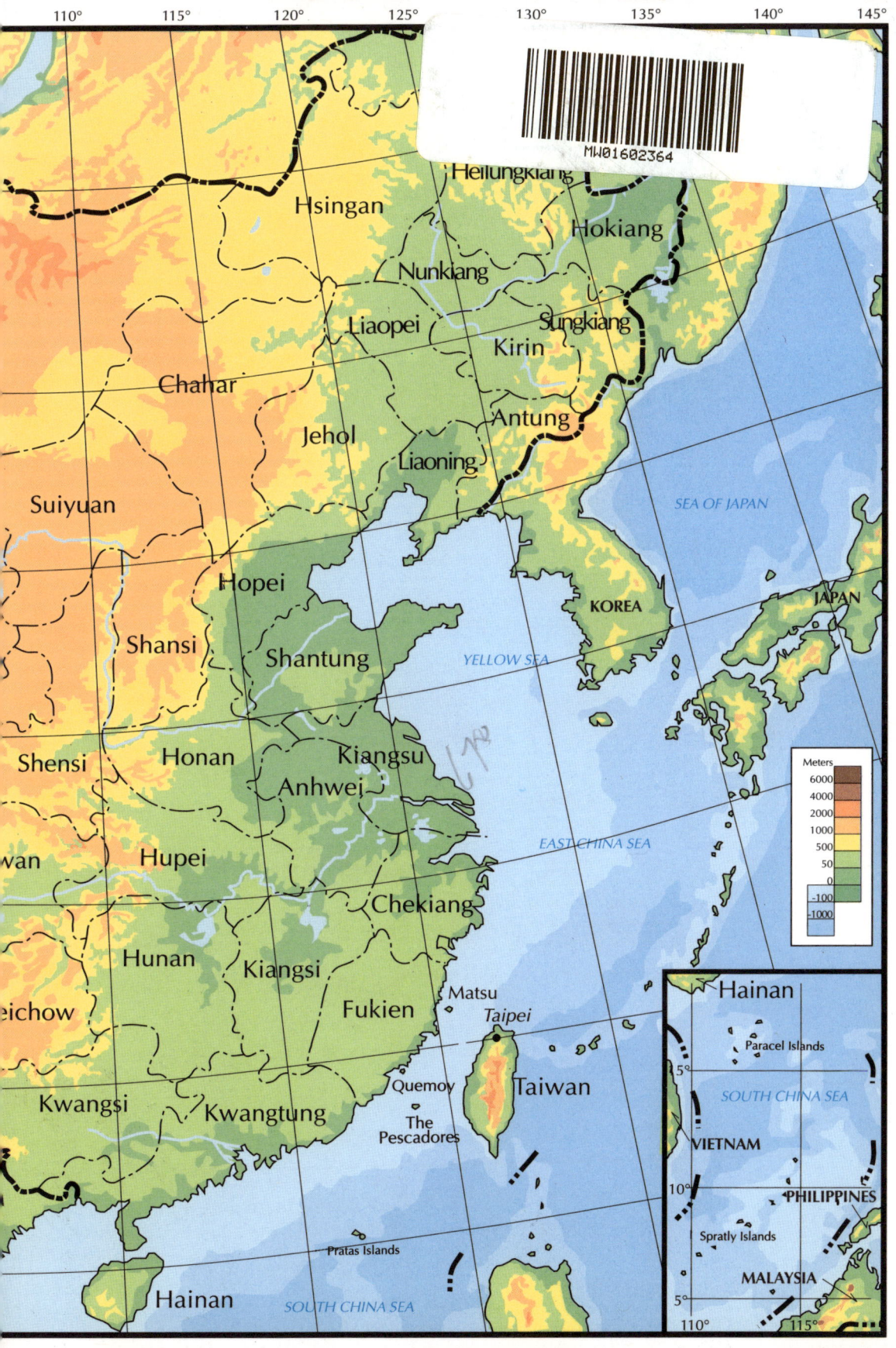

110° 115° 120° 125° 130° 135° 140° 145°

Hsingan

Heilungkiang

Hokiang

Nunkiang

Liaopei

Sungkiang

Kirin

Chahar

Jehol

Antung

Suiyuan

Liaoning

SEA OF JAPAN

Hopei

KOREA

JAPAN

Shansi

Shantung

YELLOW SEA

Shensi

Honan

Kiangsu

Anhwei

Meters
6000
4000
2000
1000
500
50
0
-100
-1000

wan

Hupei

EAST CHINA SEA

Chekiang

Hunan

Kiangsi

eichow

Fukien

Matsu

Taipei

Kwangsi

Kwangtung

Quemoy

Taiwan

The
Pescadores

Hainan

Paracel Islands

SOUTH CHINA SEA

5°

VIETNAM

Pratas Islands

10°

PHILIPPINES

Hainan

SOUTH CHINA SEA

Spratly Islands

5°

MALAYSIA

110° 115°

1997

The Republic of China Yearbook

The Republic of China Yearbook

1997

GOVERNMENT INFORMATION OFFICE

REPUBLIC OF CHINA

Published by the Government Information Office
2 Tientsin Street, Taipei 100, Taiwan, ROC

Printed by China Color Printing Co., Inc.
229 Pao Chiao Rd., Hsintien, Taipei County, Taiwan, ROC

1st edition, C75 May 1997
Catalog Card No.: GIO-EN-BO-86-009-I-1

ISBN 957-00-8992-X
ISSN 1013-0942

統 一 編 號
015039860340

Hardcover: US$45.00   NT$ 1,200
Paperback: US$30.00   NT$ 800

Cover: The snow-capped peaks of Mount Hohuan at daybreak. (Photo by Yeah Ming-yuan 葉銘源)

Back cover inset (top): The *Leontopodium microphyllum Hayata*, an indigenous species in Taiwan, blooms in summer at altitudes of 3,200 to 3,950 meters above sea level. (Photo by Elick Lee 李以德)

Back cover inset (bottom): The *Gentiana arisanensis Hayata* dots Taiwan's highlands at 2,000 meters above sea level between June and September. (Photo by Elick Lee 李以德)

Cover design: Wang Yueh-chin 王月琴

Contents

Preface

The year 1996 marked a milestone of singular significance for the Republic of China, as the nation held its first-ever presidential election by popular vote. The significance of this signal event this past year could be summarized in a single statement: The citizens of the Republic of China deftly demonstrated the will to determine their national destiny democratically— an exercise that assured their domestic welfare and affirmed their positive role in the international community. As the pages of this publication attest, the people of Taiwan have built their nation into an economic powerhouse far beyond what might be expected from its land, natural resources and population size, and have also built a political system of democracy and freedom many "experts" had assumed was beyond the capabilities of a Chinese society.

Accordingly, the *Republic of China Yearbook 1997* details what has been accomplished to date in this nation, and plans under development to build upon this base by carving out a pivotal niche for Taiwan in the coming century as an Asia-Pacific regional operations center. It also chronicles the continuing pragmatic diplomacy efforts, including the ROC's campaign for membership in international organizations and greater participation in international events, as well as its steps to develop an international profile commensurate with a nation of the Republic of China's economic and political stature. The ultimate dream, of course, is to see China reunited as a democratic, free and prosperous nation when the enormous political, social and economic gap between the Chinese mainland and Taiwan is significantly narrowed one day.

The *Republic of China Yearbook 1997* has been designed to help its readers comprehensively understand what is happening in the ROC today. With chapters devoted to foreign relations, mainland affairs and the environment, the reader can delve into the background of the current state of events or read about the cultural or historical backdrop to the way the people in the greater Taiwan area now live in the chapters on history, the economy, transportation, sports and the arts.

Throughout the text, an exchange rate of NT$27 to US$1 has been used in making financial statistics meaningful to the greatest number of non-Taiwan residents. With the exception of personal or already widely recognized non-standard spellings, Chinese terms are rendered in a modified Romanization based on the Wade-Giles notation generally employed in the ROC and many prestigious academic publications throughout the West today.

This year as last, the entire text and some charts of the *Republic of China Yearbook 1997* is available on the Internet at *http://gio.gov.tw*. Only this book form, however, contains the full complement of pictures, color charts and Chinese glosses. We welcome feedback from our readers about this book either via the enclosed questionnaire or E-mail by clicking the appropriate spot on the GIO home page or the opening page of the Internet yearbook edition.

Chi Su
Director-General
Government Information Office

Editorial Staff and Major Contributors

Contributing Government Agencies:

Academia Sinica
Atomic Energy Council
Central Election Commission
Control Yuan
Council for Economic Planning and
 Development
Council of Agriculture
Council of Labor Affairs
Department of Agriculture and Forestry,
 Taiwan Provincial Government
Department of Health, Executive Yuan
Directorate-General of Budget Accounting &
 Statistics
Directorate General of Telecommunications
Employment and Vocational Training
 Administration
Energy Commission
Environmental Protection Administration
Examination Yuan
Executive Yuan
Government Employees' Insurance Department,
 Central Trust of China
Industrial Development and Investment Center
Industrial Development Bureau
Judicial Yuan

Land Department, Taiwan Provincial Government
Legislative Yuan
Mainland Affairs Council
Median and Small Business Administration
Ministry of Economic Affairs
Ministry of Education
Ministry of Finance
Ministry of Foreign Affairs
Ministry of the Interior
Ministry of National Defense
Ministry of Transportation and Communications
Ministry of Personnel
National Assembly
National Police Administration
National Science Council
Taipei City Council
Taipei City Government
Taiwan Agricultural Research Institute
Taiwan Forestry Bureau
Taiwan Provincial Assembly
Taiwan Provincial Food Bureau
Taiwan Provincial Government
Taiwan Railway Administration
Tourism Bureau
Water Resources Planning Commission

National Symbols

National Designation

The Founding Father of the ROC, Dr. Sun Yat-sen, first proposed naming what was to ultimately become our country the "Republic of China" 中華民國 at the first official meeting of the T'ung-meng Hui 同盟會 (Revolutionary Alliance) in Tokyo in 1905. Dr. Sun said: "It was not until the day in autumn of 1905 when outstanding individuals of the entire country gathered to found the T'ung-meng Hui in Tokyo that I came to believe the great revolutionary task could indeed be achieved. Only at this point did I dare to propose the national designation of 'Republic of China' and announce it to the members of our party, so that each could return to his respective province and proclaim the message of the revolution and disseminate the ideas behind the founding of the Republic of China."

Dr. Sun's suggestion was officially adopted when the Provisional Assembly 臨時國民大會 was established in 1912.

ROC Year Designations

In official and most ordinary usages, years in the Republic of China are calculated from the year of the Republic's founding, 1912. Thus, 1912 was referred to as "the first year of the Republic of China," and 1997 is "the 86th year of the Republic of China," and so on. This is a continuation of the millennia-old system in China of beginning new year designations with the ascension of a new emperor.

National Anthem

The words of the ROC national anthem were first delivered as an exhortation at the opening ceremony of the Whampoa Military Academy 黃埔軍校 on June 16, 1924, by Dr. Sun Yat-sen. This exhortation was designated as the Kuomintang's (KMT) party song in 1928, after which the KMT then publicly solicited contributions for a tune to fit the words. The melody submitted by Ch'eng Mao-yün 程懋筠 was the undisputed winner out of 139 contenders.

In the late 1920s and early 1930s, the Ministry of Education held two separate competitions for lyrics for a national anthem, using the KMT party song in the meantime as a temporary national anthem. None of the entries reviewed by the Ministry of Education were deemed appropriate, so Dr. Sun's composition was finally adopted as the official national anthem of the Republic of China in 1937.

The anthem first declares the Three Principles of the People to be the foundation of the nation and guides to a world commonwealth of peace and harmony; and then calls upon the people to be brave, earnest and constant in striving to fulfill the nation's goals.

The piece was honored as the world's best national anthem at the 1936 Berlin Olympics.

National Flag

The "white sun in a blue sky" portion of the Republic of China's national flag was originally designed by Lu Hao-tung 陸皓東, a martyr of the Chinese revolution. Lu presented his design upon the founding of the Hsing-chung Hui 興中會 (Society for Regenerating China) in Hong Kong on February 21, 1895. It was redesigned to include a crimson background during the years just prior to the revolution. This design is still used today as the national emblem.

Before the Wuchang Uprising 武昌起義 in 1911, the revolutionary armies in different provinces had different flags: the one used in the Wuhan area had 18 yellow stars, representing the 18 administrative divisions of China at the time; the Shanghai army adopted a five-color flag of red, yellow, blue, white, and black, representing the five main ethnic groups of China; and Kwangtung, Kwangsi, Yunnan, and Kweichow provinces used the "white sun in a blue sky."

When the Provisional Government 臨時政府 was first established, the five-color flag was adopted as the national flag, the 18-star flag was used by the army, and the "white sun in a blue sky" by the navy. The current ROC national flag was officially adopted on May 5, 1921.

NATIONAL ANTHEM OF THE REPUBLIC OF CHINA

Dr. Sun Yat-sen
Translated by Tu Ting-hsiu
Maestoso

Music by Cheng Mao-yun
Accompaniment by Huang Tzu

The 12 points of the white sun in the emblem represent the 12 two-hour periods of the day, symbolizing unceasing progress. At one level, the three colors of blue, white, and crimson stand for the Three Principles of the People: nationalism 民族, democracy 民權, and social well-being 民生. At another level, the colors embody qualities that evoke other concepts enumerated in the Three Principles: the blue signifies brightness, purity, freedom, and thus a government that is of the people 民有; the white—honesty, selflessness, equality, and thus a government that is by the people 民治; and the crimson—sacrifice, bloodshed, brotherly love, thus a government that is for the people 民享.

National Flower

The plum blossom, *prunus mei*, was officially designated by the Executive Yuan of the Central Government to be the national flower on July 21, 1964. The plum blossom, which produces shades of pink and white and gives off a delicate fragrance, has great symbolic value for the Chinese people because of its resilience in harsh winter weather. The triple grouping of stamens (one long and two short) represents Dr. Sun Yat-sen's Three Principles of the People, while the five petals symbolize the five branches of the ROC government.

Sun Yat-sen 孫中山

Founding Father
Republic of China

D r. Sun Yat-sen, also known as Sun Chung-shan and Sun Wen, was born in 1866 in a coastal village of Hsiangshan County, Kwangtung Province. After receiving his early education in both Chinese and Western schools, he moved to Hawaii in 1879, where he attended Iolani and Oahu Colleges. In 1883, he returned to China to continue his studies, concentrating on the Chinese classics and history. He later moved to Hong Kong to attend Queen's College and in 1892 graduated from Hong Kong Medical College.

Seeing the weakness of the imperial Manchu court and the encroachment on China by foreign powers, Sun gave up his medical career to pursue political reform. In 1894, together with a group of overseas Chinese youths, Sun established his first revolutionary organization, the Hsing-chung Hui 興中會 (Society for Regenerating China), in Honolulu, Hawaii. His political ideals are summarized in a set of doctrines called the Three Principles of the People—nationalism, democracy, and the people's well-being—which were designed to build an independent, democratic, and prosperous China.

Over the next 16 years, Sun and his followers launched ten futile attempts to topple the corrupt imperial Manchu court. Finally, on October 10, 1911, forces loyal to Sun took over Wuchang, the capital of Hupei Province. Thereafter, other provinces and important cities joined the revolutionary camp and declared independence from the Manchu government. On December 29, 1911, Sun was elected provisional president of the new republic by delegates from 16 of the 17 provinces gathered in Nanking. He was inaugurated on January 1, 1912, the founding day of the ROC.

To preserve national unity, Sun relinquished the presidency on April 1, 1912, to military strongman Yuan Shih-k'ai 袁世凱, who declared himself emperor in 1915. Sun and other leaders moved the revolutionary effort to Japan until Yuan Shih-k'ai's death in 1916. In 1917, the Provisional Assembly elected Sun to lead the Chinese Military Government 軍政府 based in Canton, and in 1921 Sun assumed office as president of the newly formed government in Canton. He devoted the rest of his life to uniting China's feuding factions.

Dr. Sun denied the inevitability of communism in China. He believed that class struggle, an intrinsic element of communism, was not a requirement of human progress. He reiterated this point in a joint declaration issued with Soviet envoy Adolf Joffe in 1923, which stated that the communist system was not suitable for China. He also believed that cooperation rather than class struggle was the motive force for social development.

Sun died of illness on March 12, 1925, at the age of 59 in Peking. In 1940, he was posthumously declared the Founding Father of the Republic of China for his life-long contributions to the revolution.

Lee Teng-hui 李登輝

Ninth-term President
Republic of China

Lee Teng-hui was born on January 15, 1923 in Sanchih 三芝, a rural community on the outskirts of Taipei. After graduating from Taipei High School 臺北高等學校, he was admitted into Kyoto Imperial University in Japan as one of a very limited number of Chinese allowed to receive higher education during the Japanese occupation of Taiwan. After the war, he continued his studies at National Taiwan University 國立臺灣大學 (NTU), majoring in agricultural economics. In 1951, Lee studied agricultural economics at Iowa State University in the United States, then returned to Taiwan upon completion of the master's degree to work with the Taiwan Provincial Department of Agriculture and Forestry 臺灣省政府農林廳. He also taught part-time at NTU and served as a research fellow at the Taiwan Cooperative Bank 臺灣省合作金庫.

Lee received his Ph.D. in agricultural economics from Cornell University in 1968. His doctoral dissertation, "Intersectoral Capital Flows in the Economic Development of Taiwan," was cited as the best doctoral dissertation by the American Association for Agricultural Economics in 1969.

Lee began his career in public service in 1957 as a specialist for the [US-ROC] Joint Commission on Rural Reconstruction 中國農村復興聯合委員會 (JCRR). In 1961, he became a senior specialist at JCRR, and after completing graduate study at Cornell University, was appointed chief of the JCRR's Rural Economics Division 農業經濟組 in 1970.

When appointed a minister without portfolio in 1972 by then Premier Chiang Ching-kuo, Lee was then the youngest person ever to hold such an office. He served as mayor of Taipei between 1978 and 1981, and as governor of Taiwan Province from 1981 to 1984.

After Lee was elected vice president in 1984, he worked closely with then President Chiang Ching-kuo 蔣經國 to implement far-reaching political and economic reforms and visited South Africa, Paraguay, Uruguay, Costa Rica, Panama and Guatemala to promote foreign relations. On the sudden death of President Chiang on January 13, 1988, Lee filled out the remainder of President Chiang's term in accordance with the ROC Constitution. On March 21, 1990, Lee was elected in his own right by the National Assembly 國民大會 as eighth-term president of the Republic of China.

President Lee convened a National Affairs Conference 國是會議 in July 1990, then retired members of the parliament who had been in office for over four decades to make way for new elections. Later on, he proclaimed the end of the Period of National Mobilization for Suppression of the Communist Rebellion 動員戡亂時期, and repealed the *Temporary Provisions Effective During the Period of Communist Rebellion* 動員戡亂時期臨時條款.

The President has made quite a number of groundbreaking visits abroad. The earliest of these was in March of 1989, when he made a trip to Singapore. In February 1994, he visited the Philippines, Indonesia, and Thailand; in May of the same year, he paid an official visit to Nicaragua, Costa Rica, Swaziland and South Africa. In April 1995, he visited the United Arab Emirates and Jordan; and he visited the United States in the following June.

In 1990, the National Unification Council 國家統一委員會 was established under the Office of the President, and the *Guidelines for National Unification* 國家統一綱領 were promulgated in the following year to guide the ROC's mainland policy.

In 1994, the Second National Assembly adopted constitutional amendments stipulating the direct election of president and vice president starting with the ninth term. President Lee was nominated by the KMT's 14th National Congress in August 1995. On March 23, 1996, the Lee-Lien ticket won a landslide victory, garnering 54 percent of the vote. President Lee was sworn in as the ninth-term president of the Republic of China on May 20.

Lien Chan 連戰

Ninth-term Vice President
and Premier
Republic of China

Dr. Lien Chan, born in Sian 西安, Shensi Province 陝西省, on August 27, 1936, is the scion of a family hailing from Tainan City, Taiwan. Lien Chan graduated from National Taiwan University 國立台灣大學 in 1957 with a B.A. in political science, then earned a master's degree at the University of Chicago in international law and diplomacy in 1961, and a doctorate in political science at the same institution in 1965.

After teaching at what is now the University of Wisconsin-River Falls campus and the University of Connecticut, he returned to National Taiwan University in 1968, and served as chairman of the Department of Political Science and of the Graduate Institute of Political Science. In 1975, he was appointed ambassador to the Republic of El Salvador. A year later, he was reassigned as director of the Department of Youth Affairs of the Kuomintang Central Committee 中國國民黨中央委員會青年工作會. He was promoted to deputy secretary-general of the KMT Central Committee 中國國民黨中央委員會 in 1978. A few months later, he began serving as chairman of the National Youth Commission of the Executive Yuan 行政院青年輔導委員會.

Dr. Lien was appointed minister of transportation and communications in December 1981, vice premier in 1987, minister of foreign affairs in July 1988, and governor of Taiwan Province in June 1990. In February 1993, President Lee Teng-hui nominated Dr. Lien Chan to serve as premier. This nomination was confirmed by the Legislature 立法院 on February 23, 1993.

From 1993 to 1996, Lien Chan visited Malaysia, Singapore, Honduras, the Bahamas, El Salvador, Guatemala, Mexico, Austria, Hungary, the Czech Republic, the Dominican Republic, and Ukraine to cement closer international relations. Dr. Lien also promoted cross-Straits relations. In April 1993, the heads of the ROC's Straits Exchange Foundation 海峽交流基金會 and mainland China's Association for Relations Across the Taiwan Straits 海峽兩岸關係協會 met in Singapore and reached four breakthrough agreements. Lien also strongly promoted administrative reforms and set as his goal achieving clean and capable government. He set up an anti-corruption task force, presided over an Economic Revitalization Program 經濟振興方案 and a plan to develop Taiwan into an Asia-Pacific regional operations center, and promoted the ROC's southward investment policy 南向政策 and its application for WTO membership. He also launched a war on drugs and later, a National Health Insurance program 全民健康保險.

In August 1995, Lien Chan was chosen by KMT Chairman Lee Teng-hui to serve as his vice-presidential running mate for the nation's ninth-term presidential and vice presidential election. In the ROC's first-ever direct popular presidential election on March 23, 1996, the Lee-Lien team achieved a landslide victory, garnering 54 percent of the votes. Lien Chan was sworn in as vice president of the Republic of China on May 20, 1996. Vice President Lien continues to serve concurrently as premier, vowing that his government will undertake administrative reform and work to improve public services, the investment climate and the lives of citizens on Taiwan. He has overseen the formulation of a Development Plan for the 21st Century 跨世紀國家建設計畫, which aims to raise national competitiveness, improve the domestic quality of life, and ensure the sustainable development of the nation.

1.
Geography

Above: Visitors explore fissured and worn rock formations at Kenting National Park in southern Taiwan.

Right: Only an hour's drive from downtown Taipei, the billowing steam and acrid fumes of Yangmingshan National Park's Hsiaoyuk'eng draw many curious visitors from the capital and beyond.

Previous page: Wind-eroded landscapes and fantastical projections characterize the stark natural beauty of Taiwan's rugged coastline.

1 Geography

China is the second largest country in the world, with a total territorial area of 11.4 million sq. km (including Mongolia). Surpassed in size only by Russia, China is larger than the whole of Europe or Oceania. It occupies one-fourth of the land area of Asia and about one-twelfth the area of the entire world.

The easternmost boundary of the Republic of China, at longitude 135° 4'E, is the junction of the Amur and Ussuri rivers while its westernmost boundary, at longitude 71°E, falls along the Panja River of the Pamir Plateau. The southernmost point of China crosses latitude 4°N at James Shoal 曾母暗沙 in the Spratly Islands 南沙群島 (see section on Spratly Islands at the end of this chapter) while the northern-most point is at 53° 57'N on the Sayan Ridge in Tannu Tuva.

However, since the Chinese mainland is not presently being administered by the ROC government, this chapter will focus on the Taiwan area, which includes Taiwan proper, the Pescadores 澎湖, Quemoy 金門, and Matsu 馬祖, the major territories currently under the control of the Republic of China.

Taiwan

Off the eastern coast of Asia lie the mountainous island arcs of the Western Pacific. The island chain closest to the continent marks the edge of the Asiatic Continental Shelf. Taiwan, one of the islands of this chain, is the largest body of land between Japan and the Philippines.

The island of Taiwan is roughly shaped like a tobacco leaf. It is located between 21°53'50" and 25°18'20"N latitude and between 120°01'00" and 121°59'15"E longitude, straddling the Tropic of Cancer. It is 394 km long and 144 km broad at its widest point.

With a total area of nearly 36,000 sq. km, Taiwan is the smallest province of the Republic of China. (According to the current administrative divisions propounded by the communist authorities on the Chinese mainland, which the ROC does not recognize, Hainan Island became the smallest province in April 1988.) Taiwan is separated from the Chinese mainland by the Taiwan Straits, which is about 220 km at its widest point and 130 km at its narrowest. The island is almost equidistant from Shanghai and Hong Kong.

The surface geology of the island varies in age from very recent alluvial deposits to early sedimentary and crystalline rocks. The structure, relatively simple for the most part, is formed by a tilted fault block running roughly northeast to southwest along the entire length. The steep slope of this tilted block faces east and the rock mass slopes more gently to the west. This block is composed primarily of old rocks, some of which have been subjected to heat and pressure. Because of the terrain, scarcely more than one-third of the land area is arable. The mountains are mostly forested, with some minerals—chiefly coal—at the northern end.

On the east coast, the mountains fall away steeply to the Pacific. To the west, the level sediments lie just below the surface of the sea. As a result, river deposits have filled the shallow waters and extended the land 15 to 30 km westward from the foothills, giving Taiwan a larger proportion of useful level land than either Japan or the Philippines. Natural resources and agricultural potential make this coastal plain of great importance.

The shoreline of Taiwan is simple and fairly straight. The total length is 1,566 km (including the Pescadore Islands). Off the southern end of the island lie a number of coral reefs built up along the island's shores during the Pleistocene Period. However, the area covered by these reefs is small.

The fundamental topographic feature of Taiwan is the central range of high mountains running from the northeast corner to the southern tip of the island. Steep mountain terrain above 1,000 meters elevation constitutes about 32 percent of the island's land area; hills and terraces between 100 and 1,000 meters above sea level make up 31 percent; while alluvial plains below 100 meters elevation, where most communities, farming activities, and industries are concentrated, account for the remaining 37 percent. Based on differ-

Area of Taiwan			
Locality (km)	Number of Islands	Area (sq. km)	Coastline
Taiwan Area	86	35,961.21	1,566.34
Taiwan Proper & 21 offshore islands	22	35,834.35	1,239.58
Pescadore Islands	64	126.86	326.76

ences in elevation, relative relief character of rock formation, and structural pattern, the island can be divided physiographically into five major divisions: the Central Range, volcanic mountains, foothills, tablelands, and coastal plains and basins.

Mountain Ranges

Taiwan's five longitudinal mountain ranges occupy almost half of the island. As a group, they extend 330 km from north to south and an average of about 80 km from east to west. They include more than two hundred peaks with elevations of over 3,000 meters.

Central Range

The Central Range 中央山脈 extends from Suao 蘇澳 in the north to Oluanpi 鵝鑾鼻 in the south, forming a ridge of high mountains and serving as a major watershed for the island's rivers and streams. It is composed predominantly of hard rock formations resistant to weathering and erosion. Heavy rainfall has deeply scarred its sides with gorges and sharp valleys. The relative relief is usually great, and the forest-clad mountains with their extreme ruggedness are almost impenetrable. The east side of the Central Range is the steepest mountain slope in Taiwan, with fault scarps ranging in height from 120 to 1,200 meters.

Mount Snow Range

The Mount Snow Range 雪山山脈 lies northwest of the Central Range, beginning at Santiao Chiao 三貂角 in the northeast and gaining elevation as it extends toward the southwest. Mount Snow 雪山, the main peak, is 3,884 meters tall.

Mount Jade Range

The Mount Jade Range 玉山山脈 runs along the southwestern flank of the Central Range. It includes the island's tallest peak—3,952-meter Mount Jade 玉山.

Mount Ali Range

The Mount Ali Range 阿里山山脈 lies west of the Mount Jade Range, with major elevations between 1,000 and 2,000 meters. The main peak, Mount Tat'a 大塔山, towers 2,676 meters.

East Coastal Range

The East Coastal Range 東部海岸山脈 extends from the mouth of the Hualien River 花蓮溪 in the north to Taitung 台東 in the south. It consists chiefly of Miocene and Pliocene sandstones and shales. Although Mount Hsinkang 新港山, the highest peak, reaches an elevation of 1,682 meters, the whole range appears as hills. Small streams have developed on the flanks, but only one large river cuts across the range. Badlands have developed locally on the western foot of the range, where the ground water level is the lowest and rock formations the least resistant to weathering. Evidence of raised coral reefs along the east coast and the frequent occurrences of earthquakes in the rift valley indicate that the fault block is still rising.

Volcanic Mountains

Although igneous rocks are not commonly found in Taiwan, smaller outcroppings of extrusive bodies are scattered over the island, representing at least five periods of igneous activity, namely, pre-Tertiary intrusion of acid igneous rocks, pre-Oligocene intrusion of basic igneous rocks, Oligocene-Miocene volcanism, pre-

Pliocene intrusion of ultrabasic rocks, and Pleistocene volcanism.

The Tat'un mountain area 大屯山 is a prominent group of volcanic peaks. It lies at the promontory between Keelung Port 基隆港 and the Tamsui River 淡水河. The whole area is covered by lava that poured out of the volcanic craters which now stand as conical notches of over 1,000 meters. The area is unique for its hot springs and fumaroles.

Foothills

The physiographic division of the foothills is found in a narrow zone surrounding the Central Range. This zone, with an elevation of from 100 to 500 meters, is connected with the Central Range and linked with the tablelands in continuous slopes. It contains continuous mountain ranges and an unbroken series of ridges. Low hills with gentle slopes and longitudinal valleys woven with transverse gullies are characteristic topographic features of this zone, as are broad escarpments and short hogbacks formed on fault scarps or along rock formations.

Along the Central Range, the Keelung-Miaoli foothills and those extending from Chiayi 嘉義 to P'ingtung 屏東 are the broadest. The Keelung-Miaoli foothills start from the coast at Keelung 基隆 and end south of Miaoli 苗栗. The Chiayi foothills rise in front of Mount Ali, with their northern border on the Choshui River 濁水溪 and the southern border between Kaohsiung and P'ingtung. There is a shallow-faulted region between these foothills and the Fengyuan foothills, extending from Fengyuan 豐原, just north of Taichung, to Nant'ou 南投, some distance to the south. This is the widest section of western foothills in Taiwan. It is intersected by three rivers: the Tachia 大甲溪, Tatu 大肚溪, and Choshui. Included in this region is the Sun Moon Lake Basin 日月潭盆地, which lies about 765 meters above sea level and forms a graben basin. At the southern flank of the Central Range are the Hengch'un foothills that occupy most of the Hengch'un Peninsula 恆春半島. The topography is down-graded on the eastern and western sides.

Terrace Tablelands

From the foothills, the terrain is gradually reduced to tableland of 100 to 500 meters in height. These thick deposits of well-rounded sandstone gravel are accumulations of eroded material washed down from higher areas. The gravel beds may have been deposited near the sea and then raised into flat-topped tablelands by recent tilting. The broadest tableland is the one between T'aoyuan 桃園 and Hsinchu 新竹 in northern Taiwan. Next in size are the Houli Terrace 后里台地 in Taichung, the Tatu Terrace 大度台地 and the Pakua Terrace 八卦台地 in Changhua 彰化, and the Hengch'un Terrace 恆春台地 in southern Taiwan.

Coastal Plains and Basins

To the west, the physical character of Taiwan changes through the foothill zone to the alluvial

Position of Taiwan				
Locality	Longitude		Latitude	
	Aspect	Apex	Aspect	Apex
Total Taiwan Area	Eastern Point	124°34'09"	Southern Point	21°45'25"
	Western Point	119°18'03"	Northern Point	25°56'21"
Taiwan Proper	Eastern Point	121°59'15"	Southern Point	21°53'50"
	Western Point	120°01'00"	Northern Point	25°18'20"
Pescadore Islands	Eastern Point	119°42'54"	Southern Point	23°09'40"
	Western Point	119°18'03"	Northern Point	23°45'41"

Source: Department of Land Administration, MOI. Note: Reclaimed land is not included.

Major Rivers in Taiwan

River	Drainage (sq. km)	Length (km)	Passes Through
Tamsui River 淡水河	2,726	158	Taipei City, Taipei, Hsinchu and T'aoyuan counties
Tachia River 大甲溪	1,235	124	Taichung County
Wu River 烏溪	2,025	119	Taichung, Changhua, and Nant'ou counties
Choshui River 濁水溪	3,155	186	Nant'ou, Changhua, and Yünlin counties
Tsengwen River 曾文溪	1,176	138	Chiayi and Tainan counties, Tainan City
Kaop'ing River 高屏溪	3,256	171	Kaohsiung and P'ingtung counties
Peinan River 卑南溪	1,603	84	T'aitung County
Hsiukuluan River 秀姑巒溪	1,790	81	Hualien County
Hualien River 花蓮溪	1,570	57	Hualien County
Lanyang River 蘭陽溪	978	73	Ilan County

Source: *Historical and Geographical Annals of the Republic of China* 中華民國史地理志. National Museum of History, 1990.

plain. Topographically, the coastal plains and basins are monotonously flat, except near the foothills. All the larger rivers running through the plains have their sources in the high mountains. Flowing out of the western foothills, they divide into a number of channels and meander sluggishly to the ocean, forming large alluvial deltas. Many of them have been linked by irrigation and drainage canals.

The coastal plains are generally covered with gravel, sand, and clay, with an average slope of between 0.5 meters and one km. Slopes are gentle enough to eliminate the need for major terracing and are rarely subject to serious soil erosion. The western edge of the plain, where it meets the Taiwan Straits, is marked by wide tidal flats. The coast is swampy. Shore currents have built up a series of spits and offshore bars, and many lagoons have been formed through the shoreward shifting of the sandbars.

The Chianan Plain 嘉南平原 is the broadest in southwestern Taiwan, extending from Changhua to Kaohsiung. It is about 180 km long and 43 km wide at its broadest point, and makes up more than 12 percent of the total land area of Taiwan. Next are the P'ingtung Plain 屏東平原 and the Ilan Plain 宜蘭平原. There are three basins: the Taipei Basin 台北盆地, the Taichung Basin 台中盆地, and the East Longitudinal Valley 台東縱谷.

The East Longitudinal Valley is an extremely narrow fault valley in proportion to its length. It has a general elevation of about 120 meters above sea level and dips slightly toward the east. Coalescing alluvial fans have developed at the foot of both sides, and the river beds are full of gravel. Due to repeated movements along the fault line and frequent shocks, subordinate watersheds have developed in the valley.

Rivers

The Central Mountain Range is the major watershed for Taiwan's rivers and streams. For this reason, most rivers in Taiwan flow in either an easterly or westerly direction. They are short and steep, especially on the eastern side of the island, and become torrential during heavy rainstorms, carrying heavy loads of mud and silt. The riverbeds tend to be wide and shallow, making it difficult to manage and develop these water resources.

Taiwan has 151 rivers and streams. The Choshui River 濁水溪 is the longest (186 km) while the Kaop'ing River 高屏溪 has the largest drainage basin (3,256 sq. km).

High Peaks in Taiwan (meters)	
Mount Jade (Mt. Morrison)玉山:	
Main Peak 主峰	3,952
Eastern Peak 東峰	3,940
Northern Peak 北峰	3,920
Southern Peak 南峰	3,900
Mount Snow 雪山	3,884
Mount Siukuluan 秀姑巒山	3,860
Mount Wulameng 烏拉孟山	3,805
Mount Nanhu 南湖大山	3,740
Central Range Point 中央尖山	3,703
Mount Kuan 關山	3,666
Mount Ch'ilai 奇萊山:	
Northern Peak 北峰	3,605
Main Peak 主峰	3,559
Mount Hsiangyang 向陽山	3,600
Mount Tachien 大劍山	3,593
Cloud Peak 雲峰	3,562
Mount P'int'ien 品田山	3,529
Mount Tahsüeh 大雪山	3,529
Mount Tapachien 大霸尖山	3,505
Mount Tungchün 東郡大山	3,500
Mount Wuming 無明山	3,449
Mount Nengkao 能高山:	
Southern Peak 南峰	3,349
Main Peak 主峰	3,261
Mount Choshe 卓社大山	3,343
Mount Hsink'ang 新康山	3,335
Mount T'ao 桃山	3,324
Mount Paiku 白姑大山	3,341
Mount Taroko 太魯閣大山	3,282
Mount Tan 丹大山	3,240
Mount Hohuan 合歡山	3,146

Source: Department of Land Administrstion, MOI.

Natural Vegetation and Soils

Because of Taiwan's subtropical location, plant types are diverse and abundant. The high altitude of the island's mountains provides climatic and vegetation zones ranging from tropical to alpine. Except for the western coastal plain and Pescadore Islands, Taiwan was once entirely covered by forests. The forested area today is estimated at 1.9 million hectares.

Extensive stands of acacia occupy most sites. This tree is ubiquitous in lower hills. Bamboo groves and forests are found in central and northern Taiwan. Outside of forests, bamboo is ordinarily confined to relatively moist areas. In the south, most stands of bamboo are farm plantings. Bamboo can be planted almost anywhere.

The flora of Taiwan resembles that of the Chinese mainland. A wide range of Asian tropical elements is found in the lowlands. Low altitude flora is closely related to that of the southern Chinese provinces. Mountain flora is related to that of western China, and high alpine flora to that of the Himalayan region.

Taiwan has 15 families, 55 genera, and 537 species of ferns; and 175 families, 1,079 genera, and 3,305 species of seed plants. Endemic species are relatively numerous, amounting to about 40 percent of the total.

Soils vary in fertility. Many have been leached of their inherent fertility through centuries of irrigation and heavy rainfall. In the north, the soils of arable land are primarily acid alluvials and latosols of diluvial, some of which are residuals. In the southwest, where agricultural production is concentrated, most of the arable soils are alluvials of neutral to weak alkalinity and planosol-like alluvials. Upland soils of mountainous areas are mostly lithosoils, which are usually thin, immature, and infertile.

Climate

Situated off the east coast of Asia and in the path of warm ocean currents, Taiwan enjoys an oceanic and subtropical monsoon climate conspicuously influenced by its topography. Summers are long and accompanied by high humidity, while winters are short and usually mild. In the coldest months, a thin layer of snow is visible on the peaks of high mountains. Frost is rare in the lowlands, where most of the population live and work. The mean monthly temperature in the lowlands is about 16°C in the winter, and ranges between 24°C and 30°C the rest of the year. The relative humidity averages about 80 percent.

Taiwan is in the trade wind belt of the planetary wind system, and is greatly affected by the seasonal exchange of air masses between the continent and the ocean. Besides location and topography, the winter (northeast) and summer (southwest) monsoons are the main factors controlling the climate of Taiwan.

Because of the different direction of the winter and summer monsoons, seasonal distribution of rainfall in northern Taiwan is different from that in the south. In winter, the northeast monsoon 東北季風, which lasts about six months from October to late March, brings steady rain to the windward (northeast) side of the island. But the central and southern parts of the island, leeward of the northeast monsoon, have crisp and sunny winters with less than 30 percent of their annual precipitation falling during this season.

In summer, the southwest monsoon 西南季風 prevails for about five months, beginning in early May and ending in late September. During this period, southern Taiwan usually has wet weather, while northern Taiwan is relatively dry. The moisture, carried by the southwest monsoon and local terrestrial winds, falls largely in convectional form. Thundershowers and typhoons often bring Taiwan heavy rainfall in summer months.

Taiwan lies in the track of severe tropical cyclones known in East Asia as typhoons. With their violent winds and tremendous rainfall, these storms often cause heavy damage, especially to crops. However, they are the greatest source of water in the Taiwan area. An average of three to four typhoons hit Taiwan every year, usually coming in July, August, or September. During a typhoon, windward mountain slopes may receive as much as 300 mm of rainfall in 24 hours.

According to a statistical analysis by the Water Resources Planning Commission (WRPC) of the Ministry of Economic Affairs 經濟部水資源統一規劃委員會 based on data collected from 1949 to 1990 at 440 rainfall gauging stations, the mean annual rainfall in the Taiwan area is 2,515 mm, with the hills receiving more than 5,600 mm, and lowland areas at least 1,200 mm. Rainfall is most abundant in the north with mean annual rainfall at 2,934 mm, followed by the eastern region at 2,715 mm, the southern region at 2,501 mm, and the central region at 2,081 mm. The southern area of Taiwan receives 90 percent of its rainfall between May and October. In the north, the seasonal distribution of precipitation is more even, with 60 percent falling between May and October. Throughout the entire Taiwan area, the driest months occur between November and February.

Taiwan has seen lower than normal rainfall in recent years. In 1995, rainfall in the Taiwan area was only 1,921 mm, or 25 percent below average, making this the fifth-driest year since 1949 (1993 ranked the second driest year, receiving only 1,645 mm of precipitation). November and December of that year saw only 19 mm of precipitation fall on southern Taiwan, resulting in a serious water shortage in the region and making that the driest two-month period on record. The southwestern part of Taiwan averages a mild drought once every two years.

Climatic Statistics for Selected Taiwan Locations

City	Period	Average Temperature (°C)			Average Annual Rainfall (mm)	Average Rainy Days Per Year
		Annual	January	July		
Taipei	(1897-1992)	22.0	12.4	33.6	2134.6	182
Keelung	(1903-1994)	22.0	13.2	32.3	3338.4	210
Taichung	(1897-1994)	22.6	11.6	32.8	1711.5	123
Kaohsiung	(1932-1994)	24.4	14.9	31.8	1762.2	97
Hualien	(1911-1994)	22.8	14.5	31.6	2077.6	187

Source: Central Weather Bureau

Pescadore Islands

Lying between 119°18'03" and 119°42'54" E, the Pescadore (P'enghu) Islands 澎湖群島 consist of 64 islets situated in the Taiwan Straits, midway between the Chinese mainland and Taiwan proper. They form a natural demarcation between the East China Sea and the South China Sea. In the past they were a key stop for ships sailing throughout the Far East and crossing the Pacific. P'enghu is Taiwan's only county that is an archipelago.

Only 20 of the islands are inhabited. P'enghu proper, Yüweng 漁翁島, and Paisha 白沙島 are the main islands. They are connected by two causeways and the Cross-sea Bridge 跨海大橋. With 76 spans, this is the longest inter-island bridge in the Far East.

The total area of the islands is 126.86 sq. km. P'enghu, the largest island of the archipelago, accounts for half of the total area, and is home to 70 percent of the population.

The islands were formed by a mass of basalt rising from the sea through volcanic action. Due to long-term underwater erosion, the islands have a relatively flat terrain. Their highest elevation, located on Tamao Yu 大貓嶼 (Greater Cat Islet), is only 79 meters above sea level. There is some arable land on the three main islands, with altitudes varying from three to five meters above sea level. The islands have no rivers and are marked by winding coastlines forming numerous natural harbors. The shallow, warm water around the Pescadores favors the growth of coral. Numerous reefs provide the coral with shelter from sea waves.

Climate

The Pescadore Archipelago's climate is characterized by hot summers, cold winters, and strong winds. From October to March, the northeasterly wind (known as the northeast monsoon) blows with a mean velocity of nine meters per second. This often brings sea water to the islands in the form of so-called "salt rain." From June to October, the southwesterly wind is mild. Typhoons frequently hit the islands during the summer.

Annual rainfall in P'enghu County is about 1,000 mm, only half the rainfall of the plains of Taiwan. Moreover, the strong monsoon winds cause a high rate of evaporation. Over 1,800 mm of water, or 1.8 times the annual rainfall, evaporates every year. Therefore, maintaining water supplies is a high priority. Currently there are five reservoirs in the P'enghu area: Ch'engkung 成功, Hsingjen 興仁, Tungwei 東衛, Paisha Ch'ihk'an 白沙赤崁 (an underground reservoir with a capacity of 1,761,774 cubic meters) and Hsian 西安. Virtually every household has its own well.

Quemoy (Kinmen)

The 12 Quemoy islands 金門 are located off the southeastern coast of Fukien Province, covering an area of 150.45 sq. km. They lie at approximately 118°24'E longitude and 24°27'N latitude, a key position in the Taiwan Straits that blocks the mouth of the Amoy Bay and protects Taiwan and the Pescadores.

The Quemoy Islands are 82 nautical miles west of the Pescadore Islands and 150 nautical miles from Kaohsiung in southern Taiwan. The shortest distance from the main island, Quemoy, to communist-held territory is only 2,310 meters.

Although the satellite islets are low and flat, Quemoy itself is a hilly island. Mount T'aiwu 太武山 marks the highest point of the island, rising to 253 meters in the eastern part of the island. Mount Shuhao 菽蒿山 stretches into the sea where precipitous cliffs have formed as a result of sea wave erosion. Most rivers in Quemoy are short and narrow with unsteady flows, so it is necessary to construct reservoirs for water supply and irrigation.

Due to the hilly terrain, there are quite a few harbors around Quemoy. Liaolo Bay 料羅灣 on the south of the island is the most famous. Tzukan Harbor 子感港 of Liaolo Bay is deep enough to accommodate ships of several thousand tons.

Rain showers in the Quemoy area usually occur from April to August, and typhoons often strike the islands in July and August. East winds last for about eight months a year. The average temperature varies from 19°C to 25°C. The average absolute humidity is 16 mm, and the average relative humidity is 79 percent.

Matsu

Situated outside the mouth of the Min River 閩江, the Matsu Islands form the northern anchor of the offshore defense line commanding the Min River. The main island of the complex is Nankan 南竿, more commonly known as Matsu 馬祖, from the name of the major port of the island. It is 114 nautical miles northwest of Keelung, the port city on the northern tip of Taiwan, and is the same distance north of the Quemoy Islands. There are two harbors in Nankan: Fuwo 福沃 and Matsu. Other major islands of the group are Peikan 北竿, Kaoteng 高登, Tungyin 東引, Hsiyin 西引, Tungchü 東莒, and Hsichü 西莒. Nankan is the largest, with an area of 10.4 sq. km. Kaoteng is located only 5.5 nautical miles (9,250 meters) from the Chinese mainland.

The islands are composed of an uplift of igneous rock. Granite is the Matsu area's major natural resource. The climate is characterized by monsoon rains from August to December and typhoons during the summer.

Although the hilly terrain is not well suited for agriculture, 26 reservoirs, nine sea dikes, and 113 ponds have been constructed and 480 irrigation wells drilled to facilitate farming. Vegetable production has reached the point of self-sufficiency.

South China Sea

The South China Sea, with a surface area of nearly 3.5 million sq. km, is under the jurisdiction of the Republic of China. The ROC has all rights and privileges in this sea. Any type of activity conducted in the South China Sea requires the approval of the ROC government. Four groups of coral reef archipelagoes are scattered over this immense area. They are the Pratas Islands 東沙, the Spratly Islands 南沙, the Paracel Islands 西沙, and the Macclesfield Bank 中沙. All are part of the territory of the Republic of China.

In April 1993, the ROC Executive Yuan Council 行政院院會 approved the *South China Sea Policy Guidelines* 南海政策綱領, which affirm the ROC's sovereignty over the islands and other islets in the South China Sea. The guidelines also express the ROC's desire to step up the exploitation and management of resources in the South China Sea, to promote cooperation with littoral states, to peacefully resolve disputes arising over the South China Sea, and to protect the ecology of this vast ocean expanse. Furthermore, these guidelines mandate a comprehensive survey of the South China Sea and stepped-up naval patrols to protect the legal rights of ROC fishermen operating in the region.

Pratas Islands

The Pratas Islands comprise Tungsha Island 東沙島 and two coral reefs, North Vereker Bank 北衛灘 and South Vereker Bank 南衛灘. The archipelago is located in a strategically important position along the major sea route connecting the Pacific and Indian oceans, between 116°40' and 116°55'E longitude, and 20°35' and 20°47'N latitude. The group is 140 nautical miles south of Swatow 汕頭 in Kwangtung Province, 400 nautical miles northwest of Manila, 170 miles southeast of Hong Kong, and 240 nautical miles southwest of Kaohsiung. Tungsha Island is a coral atoll with a land area of 2.4 sq. km. Shaped like a horseshoe, it extends 0.9 km from east to west, and 2.7 km from north to south. Among these islands, only Tungsha is always above water. North and South Vereker Banks are completely submerged at high tide. On June 30, 1989, the ROC government set up a national monument on Tungsha Island to assert its sovereignty over the archipelago.

The Pratas Islands enjoy a subtropical climate, which is influenced by northeast winds during the winter. They experience their warmest weather in June, with an average temperature of 29.5°C. Temperatures are lowest in December, when the average is 22.2°C.

The areas around the Pratas provide excellent fishing grounds, and ROC fishermen visit the region during March and April. In addition to being a source of salt, fish, and minerals, the islands are an outpost for the ROC navy in the South China Sea. A hospital, power station, and runway have been set up on Tungsha Island. A fishermen's service center also provides fishermen operating in the South China Sea with emergency shelter. There are three jetties and an onshore service center which gives directions to fishing boats.

Spratly Islands

The Spratly Islands comprise 104 islands, reefs, cays, and banks. The area containing the islands stretches 810 km from north to south and 900 km from east to west. T'aip'ing Island 太平島, the major island of the group, is located at their center. Six hundred and eighty miles to its north lies Hong Kong; 700 miles to its northeast is Kaohsiung; and Singapore is located 880 miles southwest of the island. James Shoal at the south of the island complex is the southernmost territory of China.

T'aip'ing Island is located at 114°22'E longitude and 10°23'N latitude. The island has a land area of only 489,600 sq. meters. It stretches 1,360 meters from east to west and 350 meters from north to south. Its average altitude is 3.8 meters above sea level. Its cross-island highway runs about one km long and a trip round the island can be completed in 30 minutes. The area has abundant fishing, mineral, and petroleum resources.

The Spratly Islands have strategic importance; ROC marines are currently stationed on T'aip'ing Island. Facilities on the island include a radar station, meteorological center, power plant, library, and activities center.

Pacific Coast Islands

The two major islands located off the Pacific coast of Taiwan are Green Island 綠島 and Orchid Island 蘭嶼. (For further information on these islands, see Chapter 22, Tourism.)

To the northeast of Taiwan are the Tiaoyut'ai Islets 釣魚台列嶼, a tiny archipelago comprising Tiaoyu Islet 釣魚嶼, Huangwei Islet 黃尾嶼, Chihwei Islet 赤尾嶼, Nan Hsiao-tao 南小島, Pei Hsiao-tao 北小島, and three neighboring reefs. The group have a total area of 6.3 square kilometers, and lie just 120 nautical miles northeast of Keelung 基隆. These islets were officially included in China's territory as early as the Ming 明朝 and Ch'ing 清朝 dynasties.

Further Reading (in Chinese):

Nei-cheng T'ung-chi T'i-yao 內政統計提要 (Statistical Abstract of the Interior of the Republic of China). Taipei: Ministry of the Interior, annual. The Ministry of the Interior also publishes numerous maps, atlases, and local gazetteers of the Republic of China and Taiwan Province.

Wang Lu 王魯. *Chung-kuo Ti-li T'ung-lun* 中國地理通論 (General Introduction to the Geography of China). Taipei: New Learning Publishing Center, 1988.

2.
People

Above: Chinese culture on Taiwan is enriched by the performance in stage dress of traditional *ch'e-ku* 車鼓 drama, sung in Southern Fukienese to folk and *nan-kuan* 南管 tunes.

Right: As more families opt for only one child, Taiwan's population is rapidly graying.

Previous page: Taiwan's younger generation dresses, thinks and acts far differently than those that came before.

2 People

China's total population is estimated at just under 1.2 billion, about one-fifth of humanity. In this chapter, we present synchronic views of the nation's population distribution and ethnic composition, as well as a diachronic summary of the emergence of the majority Han group, which forms the cultural core of the Chinese nation. The latest available population figures for the Taiwan area are current through December 1996.

Taiwan's Population Distribution

According to census figures based on household registration released in 1996 by the Ministry of the Interior 內政部, the population of the ROC on Taiwan numbered over 21.4 million as of December 1996. The population density of the Taiwan area was, at 590 persons per square kilometer, the second highest in the world after Bangladesh. Taipei City is the most crowded urban area in Taiwan, with 9,600 persons per square kilometer, and is followed by Kaohsiung City, with 9,200 persons per square kilometer. In some parts of the island, such as downtown Taichung City, population density is as high as 32,000 persons per square kilometer. While about 60 percent of the population of Taiwan resides in the four metropolises of Taipei, Kaohsiung, Taichung, and Tainan, this trend towards concentrated urbanization has slowed down over the last decade. By the end of 1995, Taipei City had experienced negative population growth for seven consecutive years, and around the city proper, highly populated urban areas have emerged. Seven cities and 22 townships in Taipei County, with a total population of 3.31 million, form an interdependent economic and industrial network. In 1995, Taoyuan County 桃園縣, which lies south of Taipei, earned the distinction of being the county with the most rapidly growing population.

The earliest census taken in Taiwan put the island's population at 3.12 million in 1905. After 40 years, the figure had doubled to 6.02 million. The population further increased to 7.39 million in 1949 due to the influx of migrants from the Chinese mainland. The next year, the natural rate of increase peaked at 38.4 percent. A baby boom in the post-war years put excessive population pressure on Taiwan's economy, and the ROC government began implementing family planning and other demographic measures. By 1995, the population growth rate had dropped to 0.85 percent, and the death rate had fallen below 0.56 percent. Clearly, the population structure has undergone great changes over the last few decades. As those born during the baby boom matured, the economically productive 15-to-64 age group increased to account for 68.6 percent of the total population, while the ratio of dependents dropped from 64 percent in 1975 to 46 percent in 1995.

Longer education, later marriages, the rise of nuclear families, and comparatively fewer potential mothers between the ages of 20 and 34 have reduced the birth rate. Since 1984, the population replacement rate has remained below one, and it dropped to 0.8 in 1994.

Population Policy

In 1994, more than 7.6 percent of the population was over 65 years of age, and the average life expectancy was 74.5 years. The index of aging, which is calculated by dividing the number of people over 65 years of age by the number under the age of 15, stood at 29.2 percent. A national population policy and policy guidelines to cope with Taiwan's gradually aging population were approved by the Ministry of the Interior on October 23, 1992. Contrary to past family planning programs aimed at curtailing population growth, the ministry now proposes a moderate increase. "Two are just right" 兩個恰恰好 is the new family planning slogan, in contrast to the former slogan, "One is not too few; two are just right" 一個不嫌少, 兩個恰恰好.

Gender Imbalance

In 1995, there were 108.9 boys born in the Taiwan area for every 100 baby girls, according to the Taiwan Provincial Family Planning Institute 臺灣省家庭計劃中心. The global ratio of males to females at birth is about 105:100.

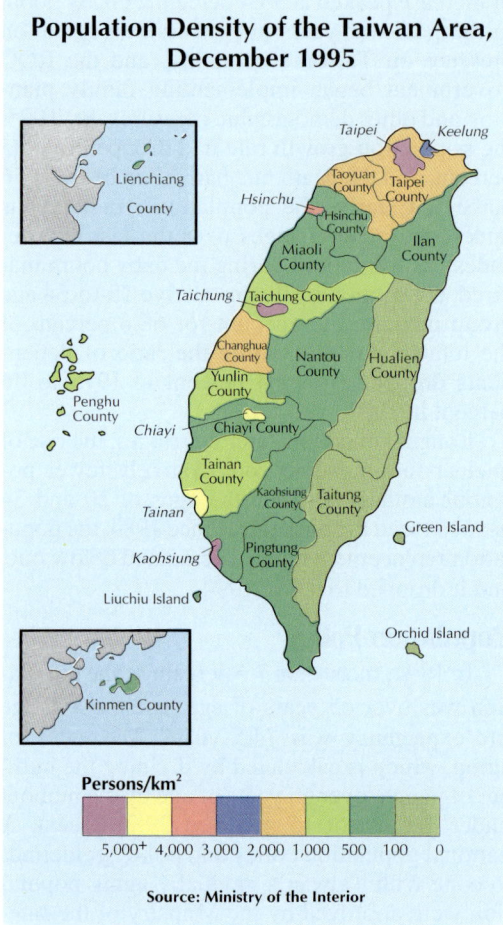

Population Density of the Taiwan Area, December 1995

Taipei
Keelung
Lienchiang County
Hsinchu
Taoyuan County
Taipei County
Hsinchu County
Miaoli County
Ilan County
Taichung
Taichung County
Changhua County
Nantou County
Hualien County
Yunlin County
Penghu County
Chiayi
Chiayi County
Tainan County
Tainan
Kaohsiung County
Taitung County
Green Island
Kaohsiung
Pingtung County
Liuchiu Island
Orchid Island
Kinmen County

Persons/km²

5,000⁺ 4,000 3,000 2,000 1,000 500 100 0

Source: Ministry of the Interior

The ratio in Taiwan reflects the traditional preference among parents in Asia for baby boys over baby girls. This preference has led to an imbalance between the numbers of boys and girls. Many young Taiwan newlyweds plan to have only one child for economic and lifestyle reasons. In 1965, a full 72 percent of parents wanted two children, but the percentage had decreased to 24 by 1991. Traditional requirements for a male descendant dictate that parents want an only child to be a boy. In 1965, only 6 percent of potential mothers preferred their first child to be a baby boy; but by 1991, some 52 percent preferred boys.

According to 1994 figures, among families having more than one child, the male-to-female ratio was 108:100 for the firstborn; 107:100 for the second child; 113:100 for the third; and 120:100 for the fourth. The figures reveal artificial manipulation to affect the gender of newborns. Private hospitals and small clinics in Taiwan ignore the ban on using chorionic villus sampling as a means of determining fetus gender and perform abortions for women who do not prefer the gender of their unborn child.

Some medical professionals have even suggested that the situation is a result of the 1985 promulgation of the *Genetic Health Law* 優生保健法, which allows abortion 24 weeks into pregnancy if the fetus is found to have a congenital defect. The law may have been used by some doctors as a pretext for performing otherwise illegal abortions. However, according to a survey by the Family Planning Institute, the abortion rate in Taiwan increased only slightly after the *Genetic Health Law* was enacted.

China's Ethnic Composition

The Han 漢, the largest ethnic group in China, represents more than 95 percent of the Chinese people. In addition to the Han, present-day China is home to a wide array of minority groups that display varying degrees of divergence from mainstream Han culture. There are about 60 such minority groups, including the Manchu 滿, Mongolian 蒙, Uighur 維吾爾, Tibetan 藏, Miao 苗, Yi 夷, Gerbao (Yao) 傜, and Chuang 羗 peoples, as well as the nine aboriginal peoples of Taiwan Province. The term "Chinese" includes all these peoples, and is mainly a cultural designation. Throughout China's long history, numerous ethnic groups from diverse areas came to be united by a set of complex and generally consistent national characteristics. But still, the origins of some of these groups remain unidentified. What is today called the majority Han people has, from the outset, been an aggregate ethnic group named after the Han dynasty. The ancient predecessors of the Han people were the Hua-Hsia 華夏 people. Similarly, *Cina* was an Indian transliteration of the name of the influential state of Ch'in 秦 during the Warring States Period. *Cina* was later transformed into the word "China," which still serves as a general western name for the nation.

The Emergence of the Han Culture

Members of the ethnic majority group in China have, for most of the Christian era, traditionally referred to themselves as the Han race. This may well be because of the relatively long period of social, political, economic, and military consolidation and stability enjoyed by the Chinese nation during the Han dynasty, its first sustained incarnation as a centralized imperial state with a coherent culture. The name "Han" recalls the glory of the dynasty which spanned from the latter part of the second century B.C. through the second century A.D., and roughly paralleled the ancient Roman empire in stature and cultural legacy throughout Asia.

The term "Han," however, does not fully account for the cultural and ethnic origins of the Chinese people. It is, instead, an inclusive name for the various peoples that lived together on the central plains of China at least two millennia prior to the time of Christ. Chinese today refer to themselves as the descendants of Emperor Yen 炎帝 and Emperor Huang 黃帝, who were the legendary founders of the Hua-Hsia nation. The imperial Huang clan was later divided into ten tribes that became the main components of the Hua-Hsia people. The people who first settled in the region of the sacred Mt. Hua 華山 in China's western mountain range, together with the Hsia people, who established themselves near the Hsia River 夏水 (the upper course of the Han River 漢水, a tributary of the Yangtze River), were referred to as the Hua-Hsia people. Both areas were located in the central southern region of Shensi Province.

The Hsia tribe formed the backbone of the Han people. In those days, the Hsia tribe lived in an area that comprises modern-day northern Shensi Province, northwestern Kansu Province, parts of Tsinghai Province, all of Szechwan Province, and

southwestern Shansi Province. Little by little the Hsia migrated eastwards into the border areas of what is presently Honan Province.

The Hsia were not the only tribe living in the central plains. All those ethnic groups with distinct tribes and territories in areas adjacent to the domains of the Hua-Hsia people—such as the Eastern Yi 東夷 group, who lived along the Huai and Yangtze rivers and contiguous areas, the Ch'u-Wu 楚吳 group, who lived along the middle and lower reaches of the Yangtze, and the Pai-Yueh 百越 group, who made their homes along the southeastern coast and southwestern mountains—assimilated with the Hua-Hsia people. Over the ages, various ethnic groups throughout the region seem to have had extensive contact in one form or another with neighboring areas: the Eastern Hu 東胡 tribes with the Eastern Yi tribes, the Miao-Yao 苗瑤 tribes with the Ch'u-Wu tribes, and the Miao-Yao and Po-Shan 僰撣 tribes with the Pai-Yueh tribes.

Recent archaeological findings throughout the Chinese mainland have spawned conflicting theories about the ultimate origin of Chinese Han culture. The concept expounded above of a nascent culture in the Central Plains that spread outward has been challenged by discoveries of cultural development taking place simultaneously all over the mainland area. Remnants of Paleolithic civilizations can be found in both northern and southern China, while Neolithic implements have been unearthed in various areas beyond the Central Plains, such as the lower reaches of the Yangtze River, Lake T'ai, the Han River delta, Manchuria, Kansu and Tsinghai provinces, the coastal region of southeastern China, and Taiwan. Just what picture of early Han culture will emerge from recent anthropological research and debate is still unclear at this time.

Cultural Amalgamation and Assimilation

The trend over the ages was for many ethnic groups living adjacent to the Hua-Hsia people to be assimilated at different times and to different degrees into what ultimately the Chinese have termed Han culture. The original ethnic stock for this amalgam seems to have primarily included the Hua-Hsia, the Eastern Yi, the Ch'u-Wu, and the Pai-Yueh groups mentioned above.

Other non-Han peoples were assimilated into the evolving culture of the Han group at different points in China's history: the Huns 匈奴 and Hsienpei 鮮卑 of Tungusic origin between the second and third centuries A.D., the Eastern Hu (a northern tribe) and the Jurchen (女真, ancestors of the Manchus) from the tenth through the early 13th centuries, later the Mongolians toward the end of the 13th century, and the Manchus through their conquest of the Chinese central plains in the 17th century. While the latter two groups retain a separate ethnic identity to a greater or lesser extent, all have fused with and become key elements of Han culture, which most Chinese regard as the cultural mainstream of the Chinese nation. Thus today, the Chinese are a pluralistic people: the geographical area they occupy encompasses a wide variety of land types; many diverse ethnic groups combine to form one people; languages belonging to distinct families and branches coexist side by side; and the national culture incorporates elements from a wide range of differing ethnic traditions.

Mainland Minorities

The Chinese nation boasts a large array of ethnic minorities that are distinct today from China's mainstream Han culture, both in terms of cultural practice and historical tradition. They include the Manchus of the nine provinces of northeastern China (Manchuria); the Mongolians north of the Great Wall; the Uighurs and other Islamic peoples in Sinkiang Province; the Tibetans living in Tibet, Sikang, and Tsinghai provinces and surrounding areas; and the Miao, Yi, Gerbao (Yao), Chuang, Kelao 仡佬, Li 黎, and others in the southern provinces of Szechwan, Sikang, Yunnan, Kweichow, Hunan, Kwangsi, and Kwangtung, and the mountain areas of Hainan Island. Many of these "minorities" in fact outnumber Han Chinese in a given province. A total of 57 different ethnic groups on the Chinese mainland have been identified.

The ethnic diversity of the Chinese people is demonstrated in the differences in economic lifestyle and religious practices. For instance, since the dawning of China's neolithic period, agriculture has been the economic mainstay of the Han people. In the embryonic stages of their ethnic development, the Han group lived primarily along the banks of China's three main rivers: the Yellow River; the Yangtze River along with its major tributaries, the Huai River and the Han River; and the Pearl River. The Yellow River region was characterized by a semi-arid climate, with loose, fertile soil that was suited for growing millet in the appropriate season. The subtropical climate of the Yangtze and Pearl rivers, however, was mild and the rainfall plentiful year-round. Rice was an appropriate crop for these river valleys, and could be planted every season in the southernmost part of the country. Thus millet and rice could be said to be the staple crops that delineated early Han culture.

As Han culture continued to develop, the use of hydraulics, canal-fed irrigation, and water-borne transportation facilitated agriculture and commerce. Thus, while agriculture was the mainstay of the vast majority of the Han people, commerce, industry, education, and government service were also viable livelihoods. Today, agriculture remains the dominant economic activity of the Chinese people, although the demands of modern nationhood are drawing larger and larger numbers of the populace from the countryside to urban areas to engage in non-agricultural activities.

The Tibetans and other peoples of western China, on the other hand, have traditionally had a mixed economy of agriculture and nomadism. The Uighurs of Sinkiang, or Chinese Turkestan, have historically engaged in either agriculture or nomadism, supplemented by commerce. The minority peoples of Kirin and Heilungkiang provinces rely on either fishing and hunting or nomadism, while the Mongolians have been mainly nomads.

A large proportion of Han Chinese engage in folk religious practices, often mixed with elements of Taoism and Buddhism (see Chapter 25, Religion). Moslems constitute a significant minority who are scattered across the whole country. With the exceptions of the worshipping conventions of Islam, Christianity, and Judaism, there are no set patterns to how most Han Chinese worship. It is not unusual for each member of a given Han family to have his or her own religious beliefs. The father might believe in Buddha, while the son believes in God. The husband might go to mass, while the wife recites the Goddess of Mercy Mantra 觀世音. Each family member is free to worship as he or she pleases, and many choose not to take part in any religious worship at all.

Such religious pluralism has not hindered the development of a unified and consistent set of ethics in Han society over the ages. Ethical conventions have consistently remained within the bounds of a set of orthodox principles: loyalty, filial piety, benevolence, righteousness, love, faith, harmony, and peace. These principles have applied to all strata of society since the founding of the Han dynasty in the third century before the Christian era.

Tibetans and Mongolians are mostly followers of the sect of Buddhism known as Lamaism, and minority peoples of southwestern China such as the Tai 傣 tend to be adherents of the Hinayana school of Buddhism prevalent in Thailand and Burma. Some minority peoples of Kirin and Heilungkiang provinces subscribe to shamanism, and other ethnic groups living in the valleys of the southwestern mountain ranges embrace animistic beliefs. There are also a number of Protestants and Roman Catholics as a result of western missionary efforts.

Taiwan's Aboriginal Peoples

An excellent place to get a comprehensive first-hand introduction to Taiwan's nine major aboriginal peoples is the Formosan Aboriginal Culture Village 九族文化村, located near Sun Moon Lake 日月潭 in Taiwan's Nant'ou County 南投縣. Designated areas of the village are devoted to displaying and explaining the common traditional dwellings, utensils, clothing, activities, and customs of the nine major peoples. Performances of traditional aboriginal music and dance are held daily.

In historical records, Taiwan's aboriginal peoples were unflatteringly called the Eastern T'i 東鯷 or Eastern Fan 東番, terms which translate as "savages." In the Ch'ing 清 dynasty, the indigenous peoples underwent Sinification, or Han assimilation, to different degrees (for details see Chapter 4, History).

Archaeologists have found evidence of prehistoric human habitation in Taiwan that dates back 12,000 to 15,000 years and proves that Taiwan's aborigines came from at least two places: southern China and Austronesia. In general, early settlers from southern China located in northern and central Taiwan, while Australoid settlements were mainly in southern Taiwan and along the eastern coast.

There are currently nine major aboriginal peoples in Taiwan Province: the Atayal 泰雅族, Saisiyat 賽夏族, Bunun 布農族, Tsou 鄒族, Paiwan 排灣族, Rukai 魯凱族, Puyuma 卑南族, Ami 阿美族, and Yami 雅美族. Early plains-dwelling aborigines, or the P'ingp'u 平埔 peoples (including the Ketagalan, Luilang, Favorlang, Kavalan, Taokas, Pazeh, Papora, Babuza, Hoanya, Siraya, and Sao), have ceased to exist as distinct groups due to assimilation with Han Chinese over the last three centuries. The mountain peoples have been better able to maintain their cultural identities by resisting intermarriage with the Han. In 1995, the population of Taiwan's indigenous people was just under 370,000, including both plains and mountain dwellers. More than one-third were Ami people, while the Yami accounted for less than 4,000. Many indigenous people live on land in mountainous regions zoned as reservations, which cannot be sold to non-aborigines.

Each indigenous group has its own family of aboriginal languages. The aboriginal languages are called "Formosan" to avoid confusion with "Taiwanese," which is the Southern Fukienese dialect of Chinese spoken widely in Taiwan. The aboriginal languages belong to the Proto-Austronesian linguistic family, an agglutinative language type, to which Malaysian and Hawaiian also belong. The Austronesian language that is spoken in Taiwan can be subdivided into three branches: Atayalic, Tsouic, and Paiwanic. There is, however, a greater diversity among the Formosan aboriginal languages than, for example, among those Philippine languages and dialects that are related to the Formosan languages. For this reason, some scholars believe that Taiwan may have been the original homeland of the vast Austronesian speech community.

Characteristics formerly common to all or most of the groups include a belief in animism; a lack of shrines or sanctuaries of any kind within tribal settlements (except for the *kuba* of the Paiwan people); a lack of written language; horizontal back-strap loom weaving and in-woven design; bark cloth making *(tapa)*; ironsmithing to make knives, spearpoints, and other implements; slash-and-burn cultivation; cultivation of millet and tuber crops such as sweet potatoes and taro; production of fermented-grain wine (except among the Yami); treatment of disease by trained female shamans; the hunting of deer, wild boar, and other animals with bow and arrow, harpoon-like spears, snares, and traps; and head-hunting (except among the Yami). Below are listed some of the distinctive historical traits of the nine main aborigine groups in Taiwan.

Atayal

The Atayal are distributed over a large area in the northern part of Taiwan's central mountain regions: northern Nant'ou 南投 and Hualien 花蓮, Ilan 宜蘭, and Taipei counties. They can also be found in Taoyuan, Hsinchu 新竹, Miaoli 苗栗, and Taichung counties. Their language is divided into the Atayal and Sedeg branches, and is apparently not closely related to any other aboriginal language. In the past their staple foods were corn, rice, sweet potatoes, and taro. The typical Atayal house was semi-subterranean and made of stacked branches and cordwood of varying lengths placed between upright roof supports, with gable roofs made of thatch, bark shingles, or slate. Clothing design was typified by rectilinear woven and beaded motifs. Facial tattooing among both men and women for personal adornment and to ward off harm was a special feature of this people. Their traditions of tattooing, head-hunting, and burial of the dead under dwelling structures vanished almost a century ago.

The Atayal kinship system is ambilineal, with a tendency for nuclear families preferring patrilocal residence. All three Atayal branches, the Segoleg, Tseole, and Sedeg, have patriarchal social systems. Several leaders from community ritual groups, or *gaga*, usually controlled the political authority and economy. Atayal society was relatively closed and did not readily accept outsiders. The Atayal believe in spirits and unnamed supernatural powers, which they call *utux*, as well as spirits of the dead.

Saisiyat

The Saisiyat are the second smallest of the island's aboriginal peoples in terms of population. Their language is divided into northern and southern dialect groups. The Saisiyat of the northern branch lived in the mountainous region of Hsinchu County. Most of the Saisiyat of the southern branch live and cultivate on Miaoli's highland. The gentle Saisiyat were long threatened by their aggressive Atayal neighbors, and their culture has been strongly influenced by the Atayal. The early Saisiyat practiced crop rotation, slash-and-burn mountain cultivation, hunting, and river fishing. As the amount of available land diminished, they turned to settled agriculture and forestry.

The Saisiyat were among the first to be acculturated by the Han Chinese and adopt Chinese surnames that were transliterations of the Saisiyat totemic surnames such as bee, spider, and crab. The basic structural unit of Saisiyat society is the totemic clan linked by geographical and family ties. Three or four households of the same clan name or totem constitute a settlement and clan worship group. Several neighboring settlements might unite to form a village with shared farmland, fishing zones, and mutual assistance units.

Distribution of Aboriginal Tribes in Taiwan

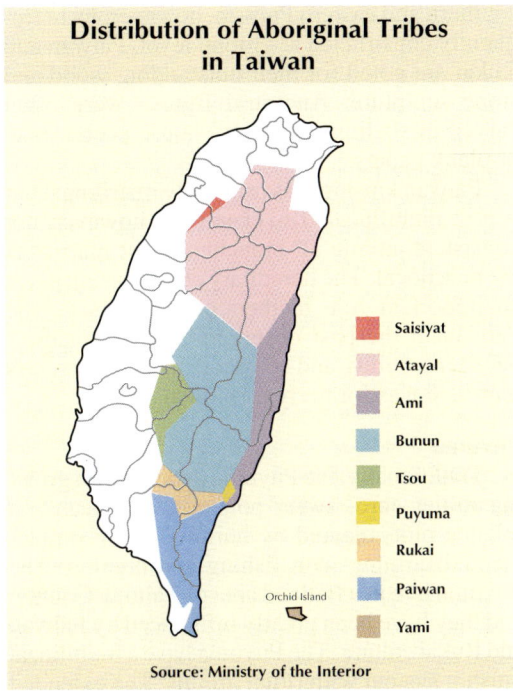

Saisiyat

Atayal

Ami

Bunun

Tsou

Puyuma

Rukai

Paiwan

Orchid Island

Yami

Source: Ministry of the Interior

As with the Atayal, the Saisiyat habit of tattooing disappeared long ago. However, the Saisiyat continue to observe a unique rite, the Ceremony of the Dwarfs, or *Pastáai,* once every two years in November in Miaoli County. According to legend, a group of three-foot tall, dark-skinned dwarfs once taught the Saisiyat to farm, sing, and dance, but also harassed and threatened the Saisiyat women. The Saisiyat retaliated by inviting the dwarfs to a ceremony and then pushing them into a ravine as they crossed a narrow footbridge. The original purpose of the ceremony was to appease the souls of these dwarfs.

Bunun

The Bunun live in mountainous regions of central Taiwan, including Hualien, Taitung 台東, and parts of Nant'ou, Kaohsiung, and P'ingtung 屏東 counties. Six cognate groups are included under the designation "Bunun": the Taketodo, Takebaka, Takevatan, Takbanuath, Isibukun, and Takopulan. Alternating cultivation of corn and beans by slash-and-burn agriculture was typical of the Bunun. Corn was their staple food, and beans were an economic crop. Brewing wine made of corn was also typical of the Bunun. Hunting was a key occupation, and it figures importantly in the Bunun oral literary tradition. Traditional houses were made by digging into the slope of a hillside and constructing an earth and stone terrace in front to provide a level or split-level foundation for the house and a large courtyard.

The Bunun are patrilineal, with extended family households grouped in small villages. Usually, these extended families have more than 20 members living in the same house. Patriarchal rule is absolute regarding familial division of labor, but every member has fair access to the settlement's resources, such as arable land and hunting grounds. Their production-consumption mode of living and the group sharing norm made accumulation of wealth quite impossible, and thus social stratification did not emerge in Bunun society. Close family ties imbue Bunun communities with greater cohesion than exists in some of the other aboriginal groups. They have been relatively accepting of outsiders and have incorporated cultural traits such as clothing styles and facial tattooing from other peoples, including the Atayal, Tsou, Rukai, and Paiwan. The Bunun practiced the extraction of certain teeth as a sign of social identity and adulthood.

Bunun pottery features impressed geometric designs. The Bunun have a strong musical tradition, which evolved partly through the use of song to communicate over long distances. Early Bunun religious beliefs are mentioned in oral literature as including periodic offerings to the moon. The Bunun also believe in the existence of *hanido,* or a guarding spirit. This spirit determines the inborn ability of a person. The Bunun had male as well as female shamans, who were responsible for sorcery and treating illnesses.

Tsou

The Tsou depend mainly on mountain agriculture for their livelihood, but supplement it by hunting, fishing, and raising animals. Traditional

Tsou houses had rounded corners and a dome-shaped roof of thatch which extended nearly to the ground-level packed-mud floor. The men's meeting hut, or *kuba,* serves as a religious and political center. The activities carried out in the *kuba* enhance clan social solidarity. The coming-of-age ceremony takes place in these meeting huts, which also once housed the cage for enemy heads and the box of fire-striking implements. The *hosa* was the basic political unit and was composed of several small tribes or clans which established the hierarchy of power and distributed wealth.

The Tsou are patrilineal. High positions, such as chiefs, war leaders, and elders, are differentiated. The former prominence of hunting among the Tsou is demonstrated by the extensive use of leather in their clothing. Their pottery, like that of the Bunun, is also adorned with impressed geometric designs.

The Tsou speak one of three languages: Tsou, Kanakanabu, or Saaroa. They are found in Chia-yi 嘉義 (Mt. Ali 阿里山), Nant'ou (Sun Moon Lake), and Kaohsiung counties. Of all aboriginal tongues, the Tsou language has the least in common with the other Formosan languages, suggesting that it separated from the common ancestral language in the very distant past. Spirits are called *hicu, ucu,* and *i'icu* in the three language groups, but unlike the Atayal and Bunun, the Tsou also have many particularized names for gods and spirits.

Paiwan and Rukai

The Paiwan, closely related in material culture to the Rukai, are divided into the Raval and Butaul peoples. The Butaul can be further subdivided into the Paumaumaq, Chaoboobol, Parilarilao, and Pagarogaro groups. The main occupation of the Paiwan and Rukai is agriculture. The traditional houses of the Paiwan and Rukai are similar to those of the Bunun. A site was leveled by digging into a slope, and then an earth and stone terrace was extended outward to provide a slightly lower than ground level floor and a slightly higher courtyard. Houses of the southern and eastern Paiwan, however, were frequently constructed at ground level. Paiwan and Rukai are noted for their outstanding wood and stone sculpture. Ancestral figures were often carved in shallow relief into house posts, slate, or plank panels.

Paiwan kinship was originally matrilineal but is now ambilineal. The custom is, however, not consistent among all branches. Most marriages are matrilocal. The hereditary chieftainship plays an important role in their oral literature. The Paiwan in the past observed class distinctions between nobility and commoners, and interclass marriage was formerly forbidden.

Puyuma

Traditionally, the Puyuma depended on growing millet, taro, sweet potatoes, and beans on hillside plots cleared by burning. They supplemented farming with fishing and hunting. The Puyuma live in a flatland area of Taitung County, and they have been greatly influenced by Paiwan and Rukai culture. The Puyuma have a multilineal kinship system with ritual groups. The extended family inheritance goes to the eldest daughter, but the kinship system is ambilineal. The positions of chieftains and shamans are patrilineal. Like the closely-related Paiwan, Puyuma society is stratified into "chiefly," or noble, families and commoners. Marriage between the two classes is, however, not prohibited. The more prominent ritual groups in each village cluster around the various "chiefly" families.

The clergy come from the leading clans' ancestral worshipping groups, which are called *karumangan.* Since 1964, there have been only three groups, which are responsible for performing ceremonies during harvests twice a year. The largest basic unit of a Puyuma settlement is called a *samawan.* Each *samawan* has a *karumahan,* or center of ancestor worship, and a *parakoang,* or men's meeting house. *Karumahan* of the same name belong to the same ancestor. Men's meeting houses accept members at age 15.

Samawan are divided into *saja munan.* The latter are composed of groups of families which share the same ancestor and bear the collective name of their leading clan. A chief's power is symbolized by his role in ancestor worship and the transfer of tribal knowledge, not from monopolization of land as in the Paiwan and Rukai.

Ami

The Ami, who are the largest aboriginal group in terms of population, are mainly plains dwellers, living in the valleys of the Hualien-Taitung area. The Ami can be divided into five groups based on geography, customs, and language: the northern Ami are also known as the Nanshih 南勢 group; the central Ami belong to the coastal and Hsiukuluan 秀姑巒 groups; and the southern Ami can be classified into the Peinan 卑南 and Hengch'un 恆春 groups. The Ami began to use oxen to cultivate paddy fields relatively early. They continue to fish, but now hunt only for recreation.

Ami houses are traditionally built flat on the ground, with the main beams and posts made of hard wood, and subsidiary beams usually of bamboo or betel palm. Walls were made of double layers of plaited dwarf bamboo with grass thatch in between to keep out the cold wind. Due to a comparatively advanced level of agriculture capable of supporting considerable numbers of people, traditional Ami villages were relatively large, with populations of between 200 and 1,000 people each.

The Ami are the only aboriginal group on the island of Taiwan (thus excluding the Yami) to preserve the art of pottery making. Pottery in the form of food vessels, water ewers, rice pots, and earthenware steamers is made by women. Sacrificial vessels in varying sizes are also made, and these are buried with their owner at death. Ami society is matrilineal, and the oldest woman in the extended family is generally the household head. Men, however, exercise authority when village councils of leading men from each village ward are held in the men's meeting houses. A rigid system of authority based on age is enforced. The Ami have elaborate cosmogonic myths, which may be recited only by trained male "lineage priests" and are subject to strict recitation-related taboos.

Yami

The Yami live almost exclusively on Orchid Island, which is called Lanyü 蘭嶼 in Chinese. The island is 44 sea miles off the eastern coast of Taitung County. Culturally, the Yami are closely related to the inhabitants of the Batan Islands of the Philippines, and the Yami language and Ivatan dialect of the Batanes are mutually intelligible. The Yami language also seems to be quite closely related to the Paiwanic languages on Taiwan.

Fishing is central to the Yami economy, and many of the fish caught are dried for later use. The basic cooperative and distributive units of the Yami are fishing groups formed by kinsmen in villages from the same region. Ceremonies related to fishing have become part of the Yami culture. The Yami grow taro extensively, as well as sweet potatoes, yams, and millet. Men are responsible for laying out fields, building boats, fishing, constructing the home, and making baskets, pottery, and metalwork. Women tend the fields, gather taro, cook, and weave cloth.

Yami dwellings are somewhat similar to those of the Paiwan, Rukai, and Bunun: a rectangular pit is first dug, then low stone walls line the top of the house pit as protection against frequent and fierce typhoons. Elevated "rest houses" called *tagakal* are used for sleeping or working when it is too hot to work in the house. The Yami live in nuclear families and tend towards patrilocality. Inheritance is patrilineal.

The Yami are constantly haunted by fear and hatred of ghosts. They think ghosts exercising evil influence are the cause of all mischief. The Yami do not have regular shamans, but do believe magical amulets to be effective in protecting one from mischief.

The Yami are known for their unique and beautifully decorated dugout canoes, which can carry eight to ten people at a time. The Yami are the only aborigine group of Taiwan known to practice silversmithing, and the only people that has never practiced headhunting or made alcohol. There is no chieftainship. One of the more notable of the many colorful Yami celebrations is an elaborate ceremony held upon the first launching of a newly-completed boat.

Aboriginal Life in Taiwan Today

Changes are taking place in aborigine culture and lifestyles as the descendants of Taiwan's earliest inhabitants struggle to adjust to rapid modernization. Young people are leaving traditional occupations such as farming, hunting, and fishing and are taking up factory jobs in the cities.

The vigor of aborigine languages varies according to area; on Orchid Island, for example, Yami is still widely spoken. However, throughout Taiwan native speakers are dwindling in number, and young people are usually not as fluent in their ancestral language as in Mandarin or Taiwanese. Bilingual education is being promoted and the publication of stories and legends is being undertaken as oral literary traditions attenuate (see Chapter 3, Language). A six-year program, starting in 1993, to reconstruct a comprehensive history of Taiwan's aborigines is being undertaken by the Historical Research Commission of Taiwan Province 臺灣省文獻會. The program aims to trace the languages, customs, living environments, legends, art, and religious beliefs of Taiwan's original inhabitants from prehistoric times to the present.

Some native traditions are still maintained, such as periodic tribal harvest festivals that celebrate a rich crop with singing and dancing. Most aborigines have switched to Western attire; however, loincloths are still common attire on Orchid Island. By adopting Han Chinese di-

Aborigine Population in Taiwan, 1995

	Individuals	Households
Plains Dwellers	172,081	41,830
Mountain Dwellers	197,601	46,989
Total	369,682	88,819

Source: Ministry of the Interior

Minority Studies in Taiwan

Scholarly research on China's minority peoples and cultures is conducted by the Institute of Ethnology at the Academia Sinica 中央研究院民族學研究所.

Courses on the languages, histories, and cultures of the Mongolian, Tibetan, Manchu, Uighur, and Taiwan aboriginal peoples are offered in both the Department and Graduate School of Ethnology at National Chengchi University 政治大學民族學系暨研究所. The Tibetan language is offered at National Taiwan Normal University 師範大學. Some courses on China's minorities are offered through the Department of Archaeology and Anthropology at National Taiwan University 臺灣大學人類學系 and the Institute of Sociology and Anthropology at National Tsinghua University 清華大學社會人類學研究所.

Missionaries and others serving in the United Bible Societies in Taiwan have compiled numerous materials on aborigine languages, and continue their work of translating the Bible and religious materials into these languages.

etary habits, most aborigines now eat a much more varied diet than did their forefathers. Animistic and shamanistic beliefs have largely given way to Christianity, due to intensive missionary efforts among the aborigines.

Education is increasingly providing a way for young aborigines in Taiwan to participate in mainstream Han Chinese culture. During Taiwan's period of Japanese occupation, only 19 aborigines graduated from middle school. The figure for 1994 approached 50,000. More than 2,500 graduated from a university or technical college, and a significant number participated in master's and doctoral programs in foreign countries.

Aborigines are also increasingly participating in local and national politics. In 1995, seven aborigines were elected to the National Assembly 國民大會 and seven to the Legislature (Legislative Yuan) 立法院; six serve in the Taiwan Provincial Assembly 臺灣省議會; 52 are county councilmen; 30 are magistrates of rural townships, and

366 are delegates to township and rural township councils. More than 6,000 serve in government agencies of various levels, and the number is growing. However, the 30 rural townships headed by aborigine magistrates throughout Taiwan have predominately aborigine constituents. Taitung County, which has a high percentage of aborigine inhabitants, is currently headed by a county magistrate of aborigine descent.

The overall educational and income levels of Taiwan's aborigines, however, still lag behind those of Han Chinese, and many aborigines face acute social problems such as alcoholism, unemployment, and adolescent prostitution. Therefore, in 1992 the Ministry of the Interior began implementing a six-year Living Guidance Plan for Aborigines Residing in Cities 都市原住民生活輔導計畫. The plan calls for spending approximately US$8 million to promote aboriginal culture and to provide urban-based aborigines with subsidized medical care, legal advice, educational guidance for adolescents, employment counseling, and loans for setting up businesses. By the end of June 1996, some 8,500 cases had been handled. Additionally, a construction plan drawn up by the Taiwan Provincial Government 臺灣省政府 to improve the roads which link aboriginal villages with nearby metropolitan communities was begun in 1992, further shortening the gap in living standards between aborigines and the general citizenry of Taiwan. The cabinet-level Council of Aboriginal Affairs under the Executive Yuan 行政院原住民委員會 is the agency responsible for aboriginal affairs at the central government level. Corresponding organizations at the provincial and municipal levels of government are the Taiwan Provincial Government's Council of Aboriginal Affairs 臺灣省政府原住民事務委員會, the Taipei City Government's "Commission for Native Taiwanese Affairs" 原住民事務委員會, and the Kaoshiung City Government's Aboriginal Affairs Council 原住民事務委員會. In addition to government agencies, over 40 private organizations, including World Vision of Taiwan 臺灣世界展望會 and the ROC Aborigine Tribal Welfare Promotion Association

中華民國山胞福利策進會, are also devoted to aboriginal welfare.

Search for an Appropriate Name

Heated controversy flared in Taiwan during the constitutional amendment process in the Second National Assembly session of 1992 over the official name to be used when referring to the island's aboriginal peoples. For years, the various aboriginal peoples were collectively called *shan-pao* 山胞 "mountain compatriots." The term is also incorporated into the Constitution of the Republic of China, which many aborigines want to see changed by way of amendment. Claiming that the term conveys a certain degree of discrimination, they instead assert that *yuan-chu-min* 原住民 (aborigines or indigenous peoples) is more suitable.

Parliamentarians representing aborigines said that they seek appropriate wording in the Constitution as a step toward giving these citizens the "dignity and justice" they seldom experience in today's society. Aborigines are looking forward to gaining greater social status via a constitutional amendment, which they feel would enhance their legal protection and lead to an increase in assistance from the government. Such benefits would in turn improve the overall standard of living among the aboriginal population.

During the fourth extraordinary session of the Second National Assembly at its 32nd plenary meeting in July 1994, National Assembly members adopted the more suitable term *yuan-chu-min* to replace the expression *shan-pao* when they passed a series of *Additional Articles of the ROC Constitution* 中華民國憲法增修條文. According to the articles, "The state shall accord to the aborigines in the free area [the Taiwan area] legal protection of their status and the right to political participation. It shall also provide assistance and encouragement for their education, cultural preservation, social welfare, and business undertakings. The same protection and assistance shall be given to the people of the Kinmen and Matsu areas."

Mongolian and Tibetan Affairs

The ROC government has an agency which serves Mongolians and Tibetans worldwide, the Mongolian and Tibetan Affairs Commission 蒙藏委員會 under the Executive Yuan. The commission has organizations in many foreign countries, including the United States, Canada, Germany, Switzerland, India, and Nepal, to serve local Mongolian and Tibetan communities. The commission's goals are to build up and maintain a worldwide liaison network for Mongolians and Tibetans. It offers programs to improve their living conditions and to raise the level of their educational and vocational training. The commission also provides regular Mongolian and Tibetan language broadcasts.

The commission puts out a colorful monthly pictorial, *Mongolian Tibetan Friendship* 蒙藏之友, which carries articles in Chinese, English, Mongolian, and Tibetan on current political affairs as well as features on Mongolian and Tibetan culture, history, and art.

The Tibetan Children's Home in Taiwan 西藏兒童之家 provides a supportive home environment to Tibetan children, mainly from Nepal, sent to Taiwan to receive an education. The home, established in 1980, has helped more than 100 children over the years. The children attend regular Chinese schools in Taipei, but receive special instruction in Tibetan language, culture, and religion at the home. In 1991, the home was moved from Taipei City to the more rural town of Sanhsia 三峽. The Chinese Refugees Relief Association 中國災胞救助總會 helps exiled Tibetans and Mongolians to come to Taiwan for various programs held by the Mongolian and Tibetan Affairs Commission.

Further Reading (in Chinese unless otherwise noted):

Ch'en, Ch'i-lu 陳奇祿. *Material Culture of the Formosan Aborigines* (in English). Taipei: Taiwan Provincial Museum, 1968.

Ch'en, Ch'ien-wu 陳千武. *T'ai-wan yüan-chu-min te mu-yü ch'uan-shuo* 台灣原住民的母語傳說 (Native Tongue Legends of Taiwan's Aborigines). Taipei: Taiyuan Publishing Co., 1991.

Ferrel, Raleigh. *Taiwan Aboriginal Groups: Problems in Cultural and Linguistic Classification* (in English). Taipei: Institute of Ethnology, Academia Sinica, 1969.

T'ai-wan kao-shan-tsu yü tsu-kuo chih yüan-yüan 台灣高山族與祖國之淵源 (The Historical Origins of Taiwan's Aborigines). Taipei County: Taiwan Aborigines' Association for Cultural and Economic Development, 1992.

Huang, Ying-kuei 黃應貴 (ed.). *Bibliography of Anthropological Works Published in Taiwan, 1945-82* (Chinese and English entries). Taipei: Ethnological Society of China and Resource Center for Chinese Studies, 1983.

Huang, Ying-kuei (ed.). *T'ai-wan t'u-chu she-hui wen-hua yen-chiu wen-chi* 台灣土著社會文化研究文集 (Studies on Aboriginal Society and Culture in Taiwan). Taipei: Linking Publishing Co., 1986.

Kano, Tadao, and Segawa, Kokichi. *An Illustrated Ethnography of Formosan Aborigines: The Yami* (in English). Tokyo: Maruzen Company, Ltd., 1956.

Li, I-yuan 李亦園. *T'ai-wan t'u-chu min-tsu te she-hui yü wen-hua* 台灣土著民族的社會與文化 (Society and Culture of Taiwan's Aboriginal Peoples). Taipei: Linking Publishing Co., 1982.

Tu-shih shan-pao sheng-huo fu-tao chi-hua 都市山胞生活輔導計畫 (Living Guidance Plan for Aborigines Residing in Cities). Taipei: Ministry of the Interior, 1992.

Ming, Li-kuo 明立國. *T'ai-wan yüan-chu-min te chi-li* 台灣原住民的祭禮 (Rituals of Taiwan's Aborigines). Taipei: Taiyuan Publishing Co., 1989.

Shepherd, John R. "Plains Aborigines and Chinese Settlers on the Taiwan Frontier in the Seventeenth and Eighteenth Centuries." (in English) Ph.D dissertation, Stanford University, 1991.

Shi, Wan-shou 石萬壽. *T'ai-wan te pai-hu min-tsu* 台灣的拜壺民族 (Worshipers of the Urn: the Pingpu Aborigines of Taiwan). Taipei: Taiyuan Publishing Co., 1990.

Starosta, Stanley. "A Grammatical Typology of Formosan Languages," *Bulletin of the Institute of History and Philology* (in English), Vol. 59, Part 2. pp. 541-576, Taipei: Academia Sinica. 1988.

Studies on Taiwan Plains Aborigines: a Classified Bibliography, 1988 (Chinese and English entries). Taipei: Institute of Ethnology, Academia Sinica.

Yao, Te-hsiung 姚德雄. *Formosan Aboriginal Culture Village* (九族文化村; 2nd English ed.). Taichung: Yin-shua Publishing Co, 1988.

Cheng-fu wei shan-pao tso shen-ma 政府為山胞做什麼 (What is the Government Doing for the Aboriginal People). Taipei: Ministry of the Interior, 1992.

TAIWAN

In the world of high-technology, everything looks a little like Taiwan.

Because with years of production expertise, and with world-class designers and engineers, Taiwan has risen to the top rung of Asian development. Take PCs, for example. Taiwan makes and exports more motherboards than any other country.

But the best part is, for all this cutting edge technology and quality, you still get great pricing. It's called VALUE. And it's what every buyer looks for.

At the Taipei World Trade Center, you can see the dynamos of Taiwan under one roof, especially at world-class Taipei Trade Shows. And at TWTC's International Trade Mart, you can see more than 300,000 product samples from Taiwan manufacturing networks spread from Bangkok to Beijing.

So get a byte of Asia. Get to TWTC.

Operated by:
China External Trade Development Council
5 Hsinyi Rd., Sec. 5, Taipei, Taiwan, R.O.C.
Tel: 886-2-725-1111, Fax: 886-2-725-1314
http://www.cetra.org.tw
http://www.taipeitradeshows.org

Taipei World Trade Center
Exhibition Hall
Grand Hyatt Taipei
International Trade Building
Taipei International Convention Center

TAIPEI WORLD
TWTC
TRADE CENTER

WHERE HIGH-TECH
GETS ITS BYTE

3.
Language

Previous page: Timeless Chinese characters woodblock-printed some time after the 14th century in the Regular Script 楷書 calligraphic style developed during the second century A.D.

Right: The art of Chinese calligraphy continues to give individual expression to the uniquely artistic aspect of Chinese writing.

Below: Tortoise shells inscribed with crude characters were commonly used to predict the future in the second millennium B.C. at the behest of ancient Chinese rulers [courtesy of Professor Chi Hsiu-sheng 季旭昇].

3 Language

More people speak a Chinese language natively than any other tongue in the world. Phonetic diversity within the Chinese language family is manifested in its extreme by a large number of mutually unintelligible dialects, creating a historical need for a common language through which speakers from the various dialectical regions might readily communicate. In the Chinese-speaking world of today, most educated people share a *lingua franca*, usually referred to as the National Language 國語 in Taiwan, the "Common Language" 普通話 on the Chinese mainland, and Mandarin in English.

The Chinese language group 漢語 is regarded as a major branch of the Sino-Tibetan family of languages, which includes Tibetan, Burmese, and numerous minority languages. Some of the outstanding characteristics of this group are monosyllabicity and a relatively simple phonological system, the use of tones to distinguish different meanings, and a word order-dependent syntax that lacks inflection, grammatical gender, and pluralization.

Written Chinese, which has historically provided a link among the various Chinese dialects, is unique in that it is the only major modern writing system that uses thousands of semantically meaningful characters 漢字 rather than a phonetic alphabet or syllabary of a few dozen symbols. The traditional Chinese writing system has inspired and profoundly influenced other writing systems of East Asia, and Chinese characters are still used extensively in modern Japanese and, to a much lesser extent, in modern Korean. In terms of its origin and underlying linguistic characteristics, however, Chinese is totally unrelated to Japanese, Korean, Vietnamese, and Thai; any apparent similarities are due to extensive borrowing.

A Chinese language is spoken by most of China's minority peoples as well as nearly all Han Chinese. Many though not all (for example, the Hui and Manchu) minority peoples also speak languages outside the Chinese language group. Much work remains to be done in classifying and describing the many minority languages of China.

Linguistic Features of the Chinese Language Family

The Chinese languages and their dialects are characterized linguistically as isolating or analytic, in that word units do not change due to inflection. Each Chinese character generally corresponds to exactly one syllable and one morpheme. The phonological structure of Chinese syllables is subject to strict limitations. In Mandarin, for example, it may consist of from one single vowel to up to five phonemes (the smallest unit of sound), and end in either a vowel, *-n*, *-ng*, or *-r*. With all these restrictions, the number of possible syllables in Chinese has a clear maximum limit. In practice, there are a total of only 1,277 different syllables in Mandarin, including the tonal variances, and 261 of these possible pronunciations correspond to only one word each. The number goes down to around 400 different syllables if tone distinctions are omitted. Since each of the Chinese languages has as rich a vocabulary as any other living language, this results in a tremendous number of homophones, with Mandarin demonstrating the greatest number.

There has been a strong tendency in the Chinese language family over the last 2,000 years for single morpheme words to develop into compounds of two or more morphemes. This has reduced ambiguity and enriched the language. The flexibility of Chinese compound formation patterns also makes it easy to invent new vocabulary items as needed. Thus, *airplane* in Mandarin is 飛機 or "flying machine," *shampoo* is 洗髮精 "wash-hair essence," and *automobile clutch* is 離合器 or "separate/combine device."

Tones (i.e., variations in vocal pitch while pronouncing each morpheme) go a long way to reducing the number of homophones. Homophonous words pronounced in different tones are as dissimilar to the ear of a native Chinese speaker as *bat*, *bet*, *bit*, and *but* are to a native English speaker, and are easily distinguished. Mandarin has four tones. The first is a high, level tone. The second starts mid-range and rises; the third starts mid-low, falls, then rises; and the fourth starts high and falls sharply. Some functional particles and unstressed syllables are pronounced in a fifth, or "neutral" tone.

Except for certain tone sandhi (predetermined tonal changes in the environment of adjacent tones), the tone of a word is invariable. In Mandarin, for instance, a third tone is changed to a second when it occurs before another third tone; and some tones become "neutralized" in certain environments. The dynamic effect of these tonal variations in the voice pitch of Chinese language speakers is a distinctly different phenomenon from the emotion-colored intonation patterns of any language, including Chinese itself. For example, a question asked in Chinese is not necessarily indicated by a rise of the voice at the end of a phrase or sentence. Instead, a final interrogative particle or other grammatical means may be used. A word given particular stress in English by a vocal pitch rise could be emphasized in most Chinese languages by stretching out the length of utterance.

Grammatically, the Chinese languages display a basic subject-verb-object word order, as does English. Some linguists have proposed the topic-comment syntactic model as a more appropriate one for Chinese, where a topic is introduced, and then some comment is made on it. There is some logic to champion this model, since a common Chinese sentence pattern is "As for . . . , it . . . ." exemplified by the Chinese sentence 衣服我已經洗好了, "As for the clothes, I have already washed them." Many Chinese subscribe to the popular notion that Chinese languages have no grammar, partly because grammar is not taught as a subject in schools, and also because of the lack of inflection in Chinese. It would be more accurate to say that the Chinese languages have an uninflected, highly word order-dependent grammar.

Rather than adding, for example, an ending (such as -ed in English) to indicate a past tense, Chinese speakers use particles (such as le 了, which indicates completion or a new situation) and context (words like yesterday or next year) to place ideas in time. The same applies to plurals.

Classifiers, or measure words, are a notable feature of modern Chinese and most Sino-Tibetan and Southeast Asian languages. Measure words, comparable to piece in a piece of cake and sheet in a sheet of paper in English, are required for almost all nouns in Mandarin when preceded by a number or demonstrative pronoun. Thus "a table" is 一張桌子 "one sheet of table." "Two cats" are 兩隻貓 "two one-of-a-pair cats." And, "this person" is 這個人 "this unit of person." Classifiers often describe the shape of the noun they modify: strip, piece, drop, and so forth. One classifier, 位, conveys respect, as in 一位教授 "one respected professor."

Traditional Chinese grammarians only divided the words of their language into two categories: substantial or "meaningful" words 實詞, and functional or "empty" grammatical particles 虛詞. This sparse distinction may reflect the fact that, even today, words in the Chinese language family cannot be definitively classed as nouns, verbs, adjectives, adverbs, and so forth except as they are used in specific contexts. They can serve as one part of speech or another with no external change in form or pronunciation, although not every word occurs as every part of speech. For example, in Mandarin the word 書 can be a noun meaning "book" or a verb meaning "write." Depending on context, 分 can be a verb, "to divide," an adjective, "branch" (as in branch office), and a measure word, "minute" or "cent."

The Dialects
Terminology Defined

Dialect distinctions are common in any language extending over a relatively large area, or even a relatively small one where geographic features traditionally have precluded easy communication, and a geographically large nation such as China is no exception to this rule. However, in addition to a large number of dialect differences throughout the nation, certain regional groups of some dialects, mostly concentrated in the southeastern part of China, are for the most part so mutually unintelligible that they could be considered different languages of the same fam-

The Regions of Chinese Dialects

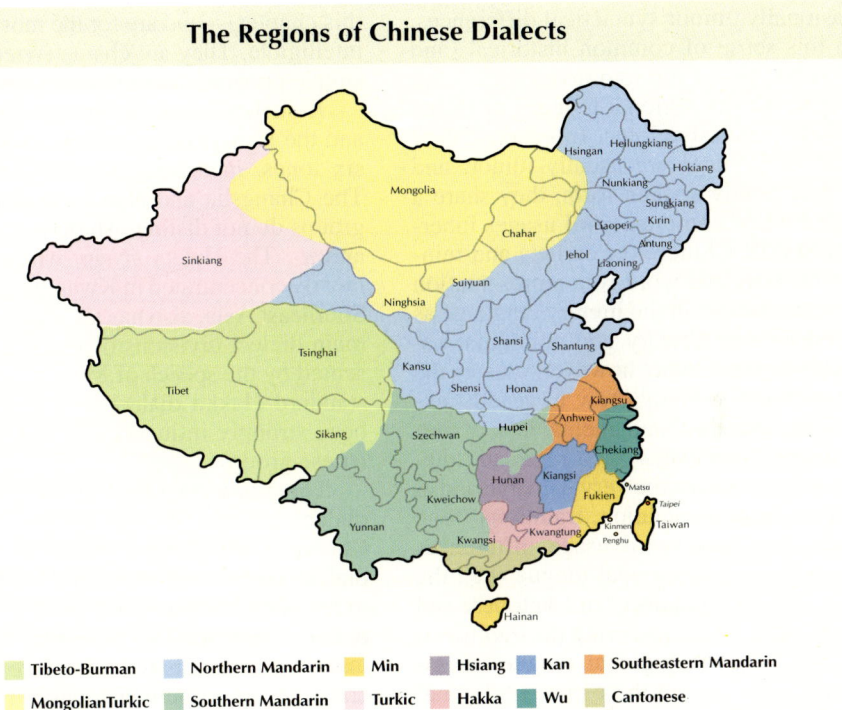

Tibeto-Burman	Northern Mandarin	Min	Hsiang	Kan	Southeastern Mandarin
MongolianTurkic	Southern Mandarin	Turkic	Hakka	Wu	Cantonese

ily. Phonetically, Fukienese, for example, is about as distinct from Mandarin as Dutch is from German, or French is from Italian. The reader therefore has to be prepared for a certain amount of confusion caused by the various descriptions of differences between such dialects stemming from the fact that such English terms as "language" or "dialect" seem to imply either too much or too little of a linguistic difference than actually is felt to exist. The customary translation of the Chinese term for these regional languages 方言, is often rendered into English as "dialect" from its literal meaning of "regional speech." It is common to regard the term "language" as a marker of political boundaries or ethnic identity, even when historical linguistic evidence might suggest otherwise. At times, this connotation of the term "language" may even run counter to common sense: A particular dialect of the Eng-

lish language is spoken natively by inhabitants of India, the Philippines, and certain Caribbean island nations; as is a dialect of Spanish by non-European inhabitants of various North, Central and Latin American nations; and a dialect of French in Haiti and Francophone Africa, yet the speakers of these areas today share no common political or ethnic identity with England, Spain or France. The language shared by such geographically disparate regions may primarily reflect a historical link of long-term cultural cross contact dating from earlier periods of colonial rule. Hence, our concept of language surpasses the traditional connotation of the term.

From a historical perspective, these disparate dialects of English, Spanish or French share common roots with other dialects of the language in question and are more or less mutually intelligible, despite pronunciation, word usage and occasionally, minor syntactical differences. Thus, in this sense of common historical (and cultural) roots, use of the traditional term "dialect" to describe the regional tongues of China has a certain persuasive logic. In general, their syntactical differences are usually minor, and even in their purely spoken form, they share a very large base of common word usages inherited from Middle Chinese (or earlier) and reinforced by the semantic word-root representation of Chinese characters in the literary language as it appeared in semi-literary and colloquial usages. Following this logic, however, creates the opposite problem, namely, how to readily express the long-standing fundamental lack of mutual intelligibility between such regional "dialects" and to account for the very palpable and at times extensive pronunciation, traditional tone class distinction, and word usage differences that exist *within* each regional tongue (i.e., the Chaochow and Amoy dialects, or Cantonese and Taishan dialects). Thus, reserving the traditional term "dialect" for the regional tongues themselves forces us to express these more traditional dialect differences within each tongue through an arcane term like "sub-dialect," a term distinction generally lost on the non-specialist. Accordingly, we refer to these regional tongues here as dialect groups which can be generally classed into the Mandarin, Hsiang 湘, Kan 贛, Hakka 客家, Wu 吳, Fukienese 閩, and Cantonese 粵 groups. Because each different group preserves different features of Middle Chinese (dating back to early or even pre-T'ang times), they have proven to be valuable research tools in the phonological reconstruction of Middle and even to some extent its ancestor, Old Chinese.

Dialect Group Characteristics

The Mandarin group is subdivided into Northern, Northwestern, Eastern, and Southwestern Mandarin. Dialects of the Mandarin group are spoken in three-quarters of the country by two-thirds of the population—one important reason why Mandarin was chosen for the national language (see section on the National Language in

this chapter)—and are for the most part mutually intelligible. They are characterized by relatively simple phonological and tone systems.

Both the Hsiang group as spoken in Changsha and the Kan group as spoken in Nanchang have six tones, including the 入聲 "entering tone." The Changsha and Nanchang dialects of these groups do not distinguish between the sounds *l*- and *n*-. The Hakka group, whose speakers are mostly concentrated in Kwangtung, Taiwan, and Southeast Asia, also has six tones. There are two main dialect divisions of Hakka: Sixian, represented by the speech of Meixian, considered the standard Hakka dialect; and Hailu, which has been strongly influenced by the Southern Fukienese group.

There is a great deal of variation among the dialects of the Wu group, spoken mostly in Chekiang and Kiangsu provinces. The Soochow dialect, representative of northern Wu, has seven tones, with complex tone sandhi; the Wenchow dialect, representing southern Wu, has eight tones; and Shanghainese has five tones. In general, the group demonstrates a rich variety of nasality and voicing in its vowels.

The main dialect of the Yue group, Cantonese, is extensively spoken throughout Kwangtung Province, Hong Kong, and in many overseas Chinese communities as a *lingua franca* when it is not a given speaker's native Chinese language. Some Yue dialects display perhaps more tones than any other dialect, a total of nine. The Yue group has been most faithful of all the regional groups in preserving the full range of Middle Chinese final consonants into modern times, and special Chinese characters have been devised over the centuries for Cantonese to a greater extent than the dialects of other groups to record spoken forms not shared by standard written Chinese. Extensive contact with Western culture has led to the coinage, especially in Hong Kong, of new words based on foreign loan words to a far greater extent than by any other regional group.

The Fukienese group traditionally includes the Southern Fukienese group (one dialect of which is often called Taiwanese) spoken natively by perhaps 70 percent of the people of Taiwan. Fukienese dialects are also spoken on Hainan Island, and many areas of Southeast Asia, including Singapore, southern Thailand and the Philippines. Most Southern Fukienese dialects have seven tones, each of which (with some exceptions) assumes the contour of a different tone when it is not the final word of a phrase or sentence. Distinctions between nasalized and non-nasalized vowel finals, as well as voiced and unvoiced initial consonants are another notable feature of dialects in this group. The Northern Fukienese group of dialects, found in the Foochow region, and the Southern Fukienese group are for the most part mutually unintelligible.

The National Language

Mandarin, the national language of the Republic of China and of the Chinese mainland, is based on the Peking dialect. Formerly referred to as Official Speech 官話, the Peking dialect has had an approximately 1,000-year-long history of use as the koine of politics and commerce in China, particularly in the north.

The Choice of Mandarin

The need to establish an official national language was felt as early as the 17th century when the Ch'ing dynasty established a number of "correct pronunciation institutes" to teach standard Peking pronunciation, particularly in the Cantonese and Fukienese-speaking southern provinces. The success of these schools, however, was extremely limited.

The concept of a national language coalesced around 1910. In 1913, the Ministry of Education 教育部 convened a Commission on the Unification of Pronunciation 讀音統一會 to establish a standard national tongue. Delegates with linguistic backgrounds from all of China's provinces voted to decide on official pronunciations for each individual Chinese character. Wu Ching-heng 吳敬恆 (also known as Wu Chih-hui 吳稚暉), a philosopher and one of the founders of the ROC, was chosen to direct the task of creating a truly national language that would transcend lo-

cality and dialect. The Peking dialect was the general foundation of the new national language, but features of various local dialects were also incorporated. This hybrid is now known to English speakers as Mandarin.

Phonetic Symbols

There was a great deal of disagreement as to the best way to notate the sounds of Mandarin. The three main options were modified Chinese characters, a new set of phonetic symbols, or Romanization. The system that was eventually adopted and developed was the predecessor of today's Mandarin phonetic symbols 注音符號. This collection of 39 symbols (later 40) plus four tone marks and a voicing symbol was designed by Chang Ping-lin 章炳麟 (also known as Chang T'ai-yen 章太炎).

Once the phonetic alphabet was approved and promulgated by the Ministry of Education in November 1918, primary school textbooks were required to use it alongside Chinese characters. In April 1919, the Ministry of Education formally established the Preparatory Committee for the Unification of the National Language. Mandarin became the required language of instruction in elementary and middle schools. Gramophone records recorded by Wang Pu 王璞 in Shanghai and Y.R. Chao 趙元任 in the US in 1920 and 1921 were used as a standard reference for correct pronunciation. The tonal system used was basically that of the Peking dialect, but a fifth tone marker for words originally pronounced in the "entering" tone of Middle Chinese (i.e., syllables ending in a -p, -t, or -k stop) was added, based on the Nanking dialect. Since the Peking dialect had not preserved this distinction for more than 500 years, this latter feature was eliminated in 1924. In 1932, a new system was devised for indicating the tone of a word, and three initials which were not used in standard Pekingese were dropped, bringing the total number of Mandarin phonetic symbols to today's 37.

Romanization

In 1928, the Ministry of Education promulgated a system of Romanization for Mandarin, the *Gwoyeu Romatzyh*, dubbed the National Phonetic Alphabet II 國音字母第二式. This intricate system incorporated the tone of each character into its Romanized spelling. In spite of the system's official status, it has never been widely studied or used because of its complexity, and the dominance of the Wade-Giles Romanization system, which predates it. In 1984, the Ministry of Education announced the adoption of a modified form of the *Gwoyeu Romatzyh*, in which tone spellings were replaced by tone marks. This, however, did not succeed in improving public acceptance of the system. Wade-Giles is currently the de facto standard in Taiwan, despite official use of the Postal Standard by the Directorate General of Posts under the Ministry of Transportation and Communications 交通部郵政總局, and occasional utilization in the public and private sectors of spellings based on other Romanization standards. Simultaneously using different Romanization systems to represent the same Chinese pronunciation confuses non-Chinese speakers attempting to identify street or place names in Taiwan. Concerns were voiced that this might add to the woes of Taiwan's already weak incoming foreign tourism industry and slow globalization of the ROC. Consequently, in April 1996, the Council for Economic Planning and Development, Executive Yuan 行政院經濟建設委員會 met with pertinent government agencies and achieved policy consensus that the *Gwoyeu Romatzyh* system adopted by the Ministry of Education in 1984 will be the official Romanization system for place names in the Taiwan area except for those widely known and used worldwide, such as Taipei, Taiwan, and Kaohsiung. However, the Pinyin system of Romanization promoted by the Chinese communists is used virtually everywhere else in the world. [See Appendix VI to find a comparison table of the most common Romanization systems and the Mandarin phonetic symbols.]

The Written Language

The main unifying force of China's many diverse dialect groups and the link with the Classical Chinese language of the ancients has always been the written system comprising tens of thousands of ideographic characters. While speakers of different Chinese dialects may assign differing pronunciations to a given character, the meaningful content of the character is, for the most part, the same for all. This explains why a speaker of one dialect may not be able to understand what a speaker of another dialect says but can still understand what that person writes. In theory, a well-educated Cantonese speaker and a well-educated Southern Fukienese speaker could both understand an article written in the now virtually obsolete literary language 文言 with Chinese characters by a Shanghainese speaker, but if the three people took turns reading the same article aloud, listeners would hear three completely different pronunciations. If our putative Shanghainese speaker wrote in the manner of contemporary speech, word usage differences among these three dialect groups might still preclude complete communication, so modern written Chinese has evolved a standard modern vernacular 白話 (see section on the Written/Venacular Split in this chapter). Thus, literate Chinese, no matter which dialect they speak natively, share the same writing system.

Evolution of Chinese Writing

The evolution and gradual institutionalization of the Chinese writing system can be traced back to the fifth and fourth millennium B.C. when the earliest extant ancestors of modern Chinese characters were painted or engraved on ancient clay potsherds. In comparison, the earliest Egyptian hieroglyphics and the earliest Sumerian cuneiform writings have been dated to the sixth millennium B.C. and 3100 or 3200 B.C., respectively. The potsherds were first unearthed in Banpo 半坡, Shensi Province in the 1950s, and have already been partially deciphered. The numerals one through eight have been conclusively identified and scholars believe that symbols identifying the artisan or owner of the pot were also inscribed on the pieces.

Although most of the potsherd markings were only symbols and not true writing, they were significant in the development of Chinese writing. The later the period of the potsherds, the more the markings on them resembled the tortoise and oracle bone inscriptions soon to follow. The inscribed clay pots were almost certainly not the only materials of their time used for writing. Writing on the clay pots was in fact very limited in scope and was somewhat incidental to the pots. It is extremely possible that wood, bamboo, and silk were already widely used as writing materials by this time; but since they decompose relatively quickly, none have yet been found dating back to this early period.

Oracle Bone and Tortoise Shell Inscriptions

Ox bones and tortoise shells inscribed with primitive Chinese characters were first discovered in 1899 in Xiaotun, Honan Province, at the site of a capital of the Shang dynasty (1766-1122 B.C.). Of the 2,000 or so different characters found on the bones and tortoise shells, about 1,300 have been definitively deciphered. The bones and tortoise shells were used in making divinations for the king. For simplicity's sake, these inscribed bones and tortoise shells are now known collectively as oracle bones.

Judging by the ancient inscriptions, an oracle would be consulted, for example, to predict whether or not it would rain on a certain day. The oracle would then inscribe on the bone or tortoise shell questions and possible answers, one set affirmative and the other negative. The inscribed bone or tortoise shell was then heated in a fire. The oracle would make his predictions based on the pattern of the cracks in the bone produced by the heat. The oracle inscriptions were extremely limited in content, and many of the characters used were simplified since the materials used did not allow for elaborate flourishes. Characters often had several alternate forms, and could be written in reverse.

Despite a certain lack of consistency, the oracle inscriptions reveal that a Chinese grammar and writing system strikingly close to the modern one

had already taken shape. Furthermore, a number of trends in the development of Chinese characters had emerged by the conclusion of the oracle inscription period: colored-in solids were replaced by lines; straight lines supplanted rounded ones; characters were gradually simplified, squared off, and standardized; and a set of stylized radicals (meaningful graphical classifying elements) was developed to be added to characters in order to distinguish among homophones.

Bronze Inscriptions

The next stage in the development of Chinese writing is represented by the inscriptions on bronzes which date back to at least the 15th century B.C. In the bronze inscriptions, meaningful pictures (radicals) began to be added onto characters borrowed purely for their sound. The addition of a radical to distinguish between two homophonous characters with different meanings is somewhat similar to having different spellings for homophones in English, such as *two*, *to*, and *too*. In Chinese, the addition of a radical suggested exactly which one of a series of homophones was being referred to. For example, if the intended object was a plant, the radical for "grass" or "wood" could be added. Since such characters give clues both to the meaning and pronunciation of a character, and reduced ambiguity to a minimum, they gradually came to comprise the largest category of Chinese characters. In modern Chinese, between 80 and 90 percent of all characters are phonetic ideographs.

By the end of the Bronze Age, Chinese writing began its trend from monosyllabicity to polysyllabic compounds. Another notable feature of writings at the end of the Bronze Age is the increasing use of functional grammatical particles. Few such particles had been used or needed in the elliptical oracle inscription style.

Types of Chinese Characters

Writing almost a thousand years after the end of the Bronze Age, China's first lexicographer, Hsu Shen 許慎, completed his compilation of the *Shuo-wen Etymological Dictionary* 說文解字 in 121 A.D. In the work, Hsu Shen noted six types of Chinese characters: (1) pictographs such as 日 "sun" and 月 "moon"; (2) ideographs such as 上 "above" and 下 "below" (indicating points above and below a line); (3) compound ideographs such as 信 "believe" (made up of character components for "person" plus "speech"); (4) characters with both a phonetic and pictographic or ideographic element such as 江 and 河 both meaning "river" (a phonetic element is added in each case to the radical indicating water); (5) characters borrowed to represent other homophones unrelated in meaning such as 而 "furthermore" or "however" (a borrowed character originally meaning "hair"); and (6) *chuan-chu* 轉注 which modern scholars have yet to exactly define.

The pictograph category was the earliest to appear; Chinese writing, like the Egyptian hieroglyphics, originated with increasingly stylized drawings of concrete objects. It is natural that many of the characters used in this early form of Chinese writing were pictographs, along with some ideographs of more abstract notions, a more advanced phase of character development. Phonetic borrowings and phonetic ideographs were also used, to a lesser extent. The pictographic category reached a point of maturity and saturation with the oracle inscriptions; very few new pictographs appeared after this point, though simplifications and modifications in established pictographs were later made.

Calligraphic Styles

Before the tyrannical first emperor of the Ch'in dynasty 秦始皇 seized power in 221 B.C., various nation-states in China had begun to develop their own individual—and sometimes outlandish—calligraphic styles. This ended with the unification of the written language during the Ch'in dynasty.

The standard script of the Ch'in dynasty is referred to as the large seal script 大篆, suggesting its use in name chops. The Ch'in dynasty Prime Minister Li Szu 李斯 later developed the small seal style 小篆, based on a combination of the ancient and large seal script

styles. The small seal style is characterized by thin, meticulously-rendered lines. The invention of the official script style 隸書 is attributed to the Ch'in dynasty prison warden Ch'eng Miao 程邈, but it would be more accurate to say that he organized and standardized a script that had already developed over a period of time.

Although the clerical script was easier and faster to write, and sped up the processing of official documents, the cursive script 草書 emerged as a faster alternative some time later. The regular script 楷書 was developed in the second century A.D., based on the official script style. The regular script shed the wavy, thickened brush strokes of the earlier style, and established a standard in the face of increasingly fanciful cursive scripts. It is the standard script used today.

The invention of the running script 行書 is attributed to Liu Te-sheng 劉德昇 of the second century A.D. The name of the script is self-explanatory: It is a flowing style that falls somewhere between the regular and cursive scripts.

Simplified Versus Standard Characters

The Chinese communists have promoted the use of a simplified form of Chinese characters, based on a list of 515 characters issued in 1956, and 2,236 characters published in 1964, in an effort to help alleviate widespread illiteracy in China. It is difficult to assess the pedagogical efficacy of the simplified characters 簡體字 in teaching, reading and writing. However, the simplified characters themselves produced a new kind of cultural illiteracy: the inability to read materials written in standard characters 繁體字. This has resulted in the alienation of a people from their own literary tradition. An additional list of 200 simplified characters released in 1977 was later removed from use. People had begun inventing new simplified characters as they pleased, to the point where there was no longer a commonly observed standard. The traditional, standard forms of Chinese characters are the only ones in general use in the Taiwan area, thus providing everybody with full access to China's classics and other writings in standard script.

The Written/Vernacular Split

Into the second decade of the 20th century, most literate Chinese wrote in classical Chinese 文言, which was far removed from their vernacular tongue. In 1917, Hu Shih 胡適, a professor of philosophy at National Peking University, and others launched a movement to promote a written vernacular 白話. The attempts to encourage a new vernacular literature became an important focus of the May Fourth Movement 五四運動 of 1919 and went on to spark a revolution in Chinese writing. This has not meant the complete end of the classical Chinese language. Today, classical Chinese is still used for certain kinds of formal writing and survives in the spoken language in the form of proverbs, idioms, and occasional sentence patterns in much the way Latin graced learned English prior to World War II.

Language in Taiwan Today

Though Mandarin is standardized nationwide, each region speaks its own local version of it, usually reflecting influence from the native dialects of the area. These regional variations of Mandarin are perhaps not even as great as the differences between British and American English, but are definable. Typical Taiwan Mandarin, for example, exhibits four major differences from the Mandarin spoken in Peking:

- The retroflex series of initials *tṣ-, tṣ'-, ṣ-* has generally merged with the dental sibilants *ts-, ts'-, s-* .
- The retroflex *-ʁ* suffix common in Peking is rarely used in Taiwan.
- The neutral tone is used much less often than in Peking.
- The third tone, which in Peking falls sharply and then rises back up, tends in Taiwan to conclude as a "creaky" tone, i.e., at a speaker's lowest voice pitch, without rising.

These characteristics are likely attributable, at least in part, to influence from the Southern Fukienese 閩南 dialect widely spoken throughout the Taiwan area. There are also some relatively minor vocabulary and grammatical differences between Mandarin as spoken in Taiwan and on the Chinese mainland, but perhaps not as much as those between British and American English today.

For many years, Chinese dialects like Southern Fukienese and Hakka 客家, and the aborigine languages, were not given much official attention in Taiwan. In the process of making sure everyone mastered the common national language, the importance of other dialects and languages was played down. The benefit of this policy was the dismantling of language barriers between different linguistic and cultural groups; the drawback was the neglect of rich language traditions.

While Southern Fukienese is still widely spoken in Taiwan, especially outside of the Taipei area, there is little understanding of its structure, history, and folk traditions among the general population. Hakka is being spoken less and less by younger generations in favor of Mandarin and Southern Fukienese. And many aboriginal tongues now face extinction.

Bilingual Education

Bilingual education has been introduced in the Taiwan area as a way of reversing the previous neglect of Chinese dialects other than Mandarin. The central government has been several steps behind proponents of bilingual education. The magistrates of three counties, making good on campaign promises, chose to "jump the gun" and institute programs in the areas under their jurisdiction prior to any decision by the central authorities.

Ilan County 宜蘭縣 was the first to initiate Southern Fukienese courses in elementary and junior high schools. The program was heralded by a county order in June 1990 that students should no longer be discouraged from or punished for speaking dialect at school. Pingtung County 屏東縣 followed suit in September 1991, and elective courses in Southern Fukienese, Hakka, and the Paiwan 排灣 and Rukai 魯凱 aboriginal languages are now taught in selected county schools. Additional activities, such as speech and

Mandarin Language Instruction for Non-Chinese Speakers

International interest in Chinese languages is growing, and Taiwan continues to be a popular place to study Mandarin. Government-approved programs are offered through the Mandarin training center of National Taiwan Normal University 國立台灣師範大學, Fu Jen Catholic University 私立輔仁大學, Tunghai University 私立東海大學, National Chengchi University 國立政治大學, National Cheng Kung University 國立成功大學, Tamkang University 私立淡江大學, Chinese Culture University 私立中國文化大學, Feng Chia University 私立逢甲大學, and the Mandarin Daily News Language Center 國語日報語文中心. The Language Training and Testing Center 財團法人語言訓練測驗中心, located on the National Taiwan University 國立台灣大學 campus, has begun offering Mandarin classes since August 1992 as well. Mandarin and Southern Fukienese are also taught at the four branches of the Taipei Language Institute 中華語文研習所, and at numerous other private language institutes, some of which help students with resident visa applications.

A selected number of foreign university students come to Taiwan to improve their language skills at the Inter-University Program for Chinese Language Studies in Taipei 美國各大學中國語文聯合研習所 administered by Stanford University on the National Taiwan University campus. Admission to the program requires passing a qualifying exam and submitting letters of recommendation. The Graduate Institute of Translation and Interpretation of Fu Jen Catholic University 私立輔仁大學翻譯學研究所 began accepting students into its rigorous M.A. program in September 1988.

singing contests, have also been held to further motivate students. These events led to the production of a full multicultural program of music and dance which was performed islandwide.

Extracurricular Atayal language lessons made their debut in 1990 at Taipei County's Wulai elementary and junior high schools 烏來國民小學和烏來國民中學, where the majority of students are Atayal 泰雅 aborigines. In the absence of ready-made teaching materials, teachers depended almost solely on a blackboard and their own ingenuity. Some were not very fluent in their ancestral language, and had to learn it themselves as they went along. Materials were compiled as courses were developed, and now three volumes of Atayal language lessons with accompanying cassette tapes have been published.

Parents were not always as supportive as might have been expected. They were concerned that the language lessons would take away class time from the regular curriculum. Some felt that the usefulness of their own native language was limited. "Outside of mountain areas where aborigine populations were concentrated, what use could it have? Wouldn't it be better to teach English or Japanese instead?" they reasoned. For aborigines who are less well off, economic and social advancement is much more urgent; bilingual education may be a luxury they feel they just can't afford at this time.

In response, the school made an active effort to communicate with parents, stressing the importance of preserving their native culture and language. The school eventually succeeded in allaying parental concerns by conducting the lessons outside of regular class time. Posters teaching Atayal vocabulary now adorn school walls, and a small museum of Atayal culture has been set up near the school. Even an Atayal language version of the school song is now sung regularly. Evening classes in Atayal are also being offered to the entire community.

Buoyed by the initial success of the Atayal dialect programs, the Taipei County Government 台北縣政府 in 1992 commissioned its Bureau of Education 台北縣政府教育局 and the Taipei County Cultural Center 台北縣立文化中心 to compile teaching materials for the two most prevalent Chinese dialects in Taiwan, Southern Fukienese and Hakka, and two aboriginal languages, Ami 阿美 and Atayal. The center was also asked to publish a county periodical on bilingual education; sponsor community and campus activities; establish a teacher consultation center; and conduct teacher training programs, teaching workshops and Romanization contests. Teaching textbooks compiled by linguistic specialists include content concerning the geography, history, famous people, religion and arts of Taiwan. So far, nearly 700 teachers have been trained to teach Southern Fukienese, 260 to teach Hakka and 56 to teach the Ami language. Instruction in both Chinese dialects and the two aforementioned aboriginal languages has been offered to Taipei County elementary and junior high school students as extracurricular classes since 1992. Such classes average 6,000 students a semester in Southern Fukienese, 1,800 in Hakka, 280 in Atayal, and 80 in Ami.

However, not all parents support such bilingual instruction programs. Some, for example, worry that instruction time spent gaining competence in a chosen Chinese dialect or aboriginal language might negatively affect a student's ability to compose in standard written Chinese (see section on the Written Language, above), and possibly result in a lower score on senior high school or college entrance exams.

Other obstacles stem from the fact that bilingual education has been left to local governments more or less by default, rather than being centrally planned. In the absence of generally agreed-upon standard written forms for each of the Chinese dialects and aboriginal languages, different phonetic systems have been proposed and tried out, sometimes in the same school.

These choices for representing aboriginal languages in the written content of textbooks range from a number of Romanization schemes to a phonetic symbol-based system similar to that for Mandarin; while for Southern Fukienese and Hakka, the use of Chinese characters with no phonetic alphabet is a third option. However, simply using currently standard Chinese characters is problematic, since they may only indirectly indicate pronunciation and some dialect words lack a known written character.

Mandarin phonetic symbols have sometimes been adapted to represent some Chinese dialects and the aboriginal languages. But because the Mandarin phonetic symbols are a part-alphabet, part-syllabary system created primarily for the relatively simple phonological and tonal structure of Mandarin, they are not particularly well-adapted for use with other dialects, and especially not for multisyllabic Austronesian languages like Taiwan's aboriginal tongues.

Romanization systems are perhaps the most flexible and precise, and thus are well suited to serve as the primary writing system for aboriginal languages, and additionally as at least an auxiliary system for teaching Chinese dialects. In the case of Southern Fukienese, for example, the Romanization system used in Christian churches has a long history and is currently in widespread use, so it would seem a natural candidate as a standard phonetic alphabet. Yet as things stand, each area tends rather to start from scratch and contribute yet another idiosyncratic system to the existing jumble. The solution adopted for the Taipei County dialect materials is a combination of regular Chinese characters, new Chinese characters invented expressly to represent dialect words not found in Mandarin, and Romanization for words for which a suitable Chinese character has yet to be found.

Progress is often held back simply due to indecision about which system to adopt in education. Orchid Island is in just such a situation. Although Yami is the dominant language of the island, failure to make a clear choice between the local church's and the Ministry of Education's Romanization systems has retarded the development of bilingual education.

Accordingly, the Ministry of Education has stepped up revision of relevant guidelines and has proposed research projects. The ministry has amended its *Curriculum Standards for the Elementary and Junior High Schools* 國民中小學課程標準, granting schools more leeway to work out teaching schedules that allow students to receive bilingual instruction as an extracurricular or elective course. Participation by students in such courses is voluntary. The government underwrites pertinent school expenses according to the following order of priority: compiling teaching material, publishing teacher handbooks, holding teacher workshops, producing audio and video cassettes, as well as collecting teaching materials. In order to establish standard instructional materials, the ministry has commissioned the Department of Education under the Taiwan Provincial Government 台灣省政府教育廳 and seven counties to review and compile teaching materials for the Southern Fukienese and Hakka dialects; as well as the Atayal, Ami, Yami 雅美, Paiwan, Rukai, Puyuma 卑南, Tsou 鄒, Bunun 布農, Saisiyat 賽夏, Kavalan 噶瑪蘭, and Sedeka 賽德克 aboriginal languages. So far, 25 textbooks totaling 59 volumes have been developed by 11 counties.

Southern Fukienese has in the meantime very much entered the mainstream of popular culture. Taiwanese dialect pop songs tended in the past to be stereotyped and relegated to a subordinate position in the market. Now singers are often expected to produce at least a few songs or an album in Southern Fukienese. Use of Southern Fukienese in advertising and business—from TV commercials to restaurant names—is considered fashionable. Bookstores now offer entire sections of literature written in a style reflecting spoken Southern Fukienese. To encourage research on Southern Fukienese, Hakka, other Chinese dialects and non-Han languages of China, the Ministry of Education offers various levels of financial support in the form of awards for scholarly publications in these areas.

Further Reading (in Chinese unless otherwise noted):

Chao, Yuen Ren 趙元任. *A Grammar of Spoken Chinese*. Berkeley (in English). University of California Press, 1970.

Cheng, Robert L. 鄭良偉. *Yen-pien-chung ti Tai-wan she-hui yü-wen: to-yü she-hui chi shuang-yü chiao-yü* 演變中的臺灣社會語文：多語社會及雙語教育 (Taiwan's Society and Language in Transition: A Multilingual Society and Bilingual Education). Taipei: Independence Evening News 自立晚報出版社, 1990.

Forrest, R. A. D. *The Chinese Language* (in English). London: Faber and Faber, 1973.

Huang Tung-chiu 黃東秋, ed. *Tai-wan yüan-chu-min yü-yen min-su yen-chiu* 臺灣原住民語言民俗研究 (A Study of Taiwan Aborigine Customs and Languages). Taipei: Crane Publishing 文鶴出版社, 1993.

Hung Wei-jen 洪惟仁. *Tai-wan fang-yen chih lü* 臺灣方言之旅 (An Excursion into the Dialects of Taiwan). Taipei: Ch'ien Wei 前衛出版社, 1992.

Kuo-wen t'ien-ti 國文天地 (The World of Chinese Language and Literature). Taipei: monthly.

Kuo-yin hsüeh 國音學 (A Study of Mandarin Phonology). National Taiwan Normal University, Committee for the Compilation of Mandarin Phonology Teaching Materials, ed. Taipei: Cheng Chung 正中 Bookstore, 1982; 1993.

Li, Charles N. and Sandra A. Thompson. 'Chinese.' in Bernard Comrie (ed.), *The World's Major Languages* (in English). New York and Oxford: Oxford University Press, 1990: pp. 811-833.

Lo Chao-chin 羅肇錦. *K'e-yü yü-fa* 客語語法 (A Grammar of the Hakka Dialect).Taipei: Student Book Store 學生書局, 1985.

Lo Chao-chin 羅肇錦. *Kuo-yü hsüeh* 國語學 (A Study of the National Chinese Language).Taipei: Wunan Publishers 五南出版社, 1990.

Norman, Jerry. *Chinese* (in English). Cambridge: Cambridge University Press, 1988.

Ramsey, S. Robert. *The Languages of China* (in English). Princeton: Princeton University Press, 1989.

Tai-yü wen-chai 臺語文摘 (Taiwanese Digest). Taipei, monthly.

Yang Hsiu-fang 楊秀芳. *Tai-wan Min-nan-yü yü-fa kao* 臺灣閩南語語法稿 (A Grammar of the Southern Min Dialect in Taiwan). Taipei: Tah-an Publishers 大安出版社, 1991.

TSMC
Where technology, quality and service push market windows wide open.

Semiconductor technology is entering the deep sub - micron era. Where production at 0.5μm pushed the envelope one year ago, radically new designs based on 0.35μm and 0.25μm are becoming a reality today. All of which means, TSMC can be more valuable than ever as we drive down the technology curve and provide early access to leading - edge processes in support of future product development. ◆ Fast - turns on prototype lots backed by rich technical support are hallmarks of our service - so customers won't miss a beat getting product to market. ◆ As always, we prize and protect intellectual property. With TSMC as a partner, customers are able to focus on design, free from concerns about manufacturing limitations. ◆ We are investing $2 billion over a two year period. With six fab facilities in Taiwan and a seventh being built in the United States through a joint venture, we continue to grow to address the future now. ◆ TSMC. Forging a future in the information age.

TSMC, 121 Park Avenue III, Science Based Industrial Park, Hsin-chu, Taiwan, R.O.C. (Ph: 886-3-5780221, Fax: 886-3-5781546)

TSMC-Europe, World Trade Center, Strawinskylaan 1145, 1077 XX, Amsterdam, The Netherlands (Ph: 31-20-3059900, Fax: 31-20-3059911)

TSMC-USA, 1740 Technology Drive, Suite 660, San Jose, CA 95110 (Ph: 408-437-8762, Fax: 408-441-7713)

4.
History

Previous page: Reminders of Japanese colonial rule can still be found in Taipei, such as this structure, which now houses the Taiwan Railway Administration 台灣省鐵路管理局 .

Right: A veteran of Taiwan's turbulent past—Fort San Domingo 紅毛城 , built by the Spaniards in 1629 at Tamsui 淡水 , and later occupied at various times by the Dutch, Ming loyalist Koxinga 鄭成功 and the British.

Below: The striking architecture of a memorial to the February 28 Incident 二二八事件 of 1947, erected in Taipei's New Park 新公園 , combines remembrance of the past with hope for the future.

4 History

Since the appearance of writing in China some 6,000 to 7,000 years ago, Chinese people have been recording the history of their families, clans, and dynasties. As time passed, many Chinese rulers and the large bureaucracies under them collated these various historical materials to create macro histories that highlighted the ruler's place in Chinese history. Despite the fact that many Chinese rulers have challenged each other's legitimacy, that many times China was not being ruled by any central authority at all, and that non-Chinese peoples occasionally conquered Chinese states, Chinese historians filled in any blanks and thus linked China's present firmly together with her past. The resulting histories showed a cycle that began with the fall of a corrupt ruler and a weak dynasty followed by the rise of a new moral ruler and a strong dynasty. This historical pattern is called a "dynastic cycle," and all traditional Chinese histories were written in accordance with this formula. Many of these traditional histories are still extant and intelligible to readers of Chinese today. The Chinese people are thus the proud inheritors of the world's longest unbroken historical tradition.

The historical focus on political legitimacy and continuity was a powerfully conservative force in China. Traditional histories provided successive dynasties and governments with a set of precedents by which to rule. So, even though ruling power passed hands quite often in China, the way the country was ruled remained roughly the same. This lent a degree of stability (some would say inertia) to Chinese culture that was absent in the cultures bordering on China.

One common explanation of the phenomenal endurance of Chinese civilization is that China was actually governed by an aristocracy of intelligentsia which had been continuously revitalized by the introduction of new personnel. A civil service examination system, first implemented in the Sui dynasty over 1,000 years ago, allowed young men who were well schooled in China's historical and literary traditions to enter the government bureaucracy, regardless of their family's social, political, or economic status. Theoretically, even the son of a farmer, butcher, or blacksmith could become prime minister one day as long as he could pass a series of imperial examinations. When an emperor was deposed, it mattered little who took his place, since the Chinese bureaucratic system continued to function.

Equally insulated from political infighting was the village economy, upon which China's agricultural civilization was based. Peasants seldom troubled themselves with national affairs unless war or imperial mismanagement threatened the livelihood of the village and its ability to raise grain, produce goods, and render the services of labor.

China's modern history begins when the three pillars of Chinese stability—rule by historical precedent, bureaucratic conservatism, and village-based economics—were shaken by contact with the West. This chapter seeks to shed light on China's modern history, show Taiwan's place in this history, and then provide enough background information on the history of the Republic of China so that materials mentioned in other chapters of this book can be viewed in perspective.

East Meets West

For thousands of years, China maintained close relations with nation states on its periphery. These border states often served as intermediaries between China and other major civilizations in India and the Middle East. As far back as the Han dynasty (206 B.C.-221 A.D.), China was exporting silk, porcelain, and other trade goods to the Roman Empire. During the Yuan dynasty (1279-1368), China's Mongolian rulers, especially Kublai Khan 忽必烈, brought a significant number of Persians, Turks, and other peoples from Central Asia to work in the Mongolian administration. The great Italian traveler, Marco Polo, visited China during this time and actually worked for the Mogolians as the Superintendent of Trade in Lanchow 蘭州.

Early in the 15th century, an ambitious Ming monarch, Ch'eng Tsu 成祖 (commonly referred to as the Yung Lo Emperor 永樂大帝), showed

Chinese Dynastic Chronology

Dynasty	Divisions	Dates	Capital
Hsia 夏		2205–1766 B.C.	Anyi
Shang 商 (or Yin 殷)		1766–1122 B.C.	Anyang
Chou 周	Western Chou	1122–770 B.C.	Hao (Sian)
	Eastern Chou	770–221 B.C.	Loyi (Loyang)
	(Spring and Autumn Period)	770–476 B.C.	
	(Warring States Period)	475–221 B.C.	
Ch'in 秦		221–206 B.C.	Hsienyang (West of Sian)
Han 漢	Western Han	206 B.C.–8 A.D.	Changan (Sian)
	Hsin	8–25	Changan
	Eastern Han	25–221	Loyang
Three Kingdoms 三國	Wei	221–265	Loyang
	Shu	222–263	Chengtu
	Wu	222–280	Nanking
Chin 晉	Western Chin	265–316	Loyang
	Eastern Chin	317–420	Nanking
Southern Dynasties 南朝	Sung	420–479	Nanking
	Ch'i	479–502	Nanking
	Liang	502–557	Nanking
	Ch'en	557–589	Nanking
Northern Dynasties 北朝	Northern Wei	386–534	Pincheng (Loyang)
	Eastern Wei	534–550	Yeh (Honan)
	Western Wei	535–557	Changan
	Northern Ch'i	550–557	Yeh
	Northern Chou	557–581	Changan
Sui 隋		581–618	Changan Loyang Yangchow
T'ang 唐		618–907	Changan Loyang
Five Dynasties 五代	Later Liang	907–923	Kaifeng
	Later T'ang	923–936	Loyang
	Later Chin	936–946	Kaifeng
	Later Han	947–950	Kaifeng
	Later Chou	951–959	Kaifeng
Sung 宋	Northern Sung	960–1127	Kaifeng
	Southern Sung	1127–1279	Hangchow
Yuan 元		1279–1368	Peking
Ming 明		1368–1644	Nanking Peking
Ch'ing 清		1644–1911	Peking

an intense interest in overseas exploration. He equipped scores of seafaring ships, manned by tens of thousands of sailors, and placed them under the command of one of his closest advisors, the eunuch Cheng Ho 鄭和. In the years between 1406 and 1433, Cheng Ho made seven voyages through the South China Sea, past the Malaysian Peninsula, into the Indian Ocean and to the east coast of Africa. His travels to more than 50 countries constituted the greatest overseas venture in Chinese history.

Two main sea routes linking the East and West were discovered during the Ming dynasty, and, by the early 16th century, Portugal, Spain, Holland, and England were sending powerful fleets to Asian waters. The Portuguese were the first Europeans to reach China by sea. With the permission of Ming officials, the Portuguese set up an entrepôt in Macau in 1535. In the following years, many Christian missionaries came to China on Portuguese ships. In 1601, the Italian Jesuit Matteo Ricci was granted an imperial stipend to reside in Peking. Other missionaries soon followed in his footsteps. Julius Aleni, Johannes Terrens, Didacus de Pentoja, Johannes Adam Schall von Bell, and Ferdiandus Verbiest brought not only their religion but also new concepts of arts, medical science, and water conservancy, not to mention mathematics, geography, astronomy, and the Gregorian calendar. Like in the Yuan dynasty, some of these intrepid Christians even served as officials in the imperial bureaucracy.

China's Closed-door Policy

The Manchus established the Ch'ing 清 dynasty in 1644. During their rule over China, the Manchus subdued the remnants of Mongol resistance in the northwest, and conquered the Khalkhas, the Kalmuks, and the Turks. They also formally annexed Outer and Inner Mongolia, Sinkiang, Tsinghai, and Tibet, thereby fixing the modern boundaries of China. In 1683, Ch'ing forces took over Taiwan.

At the height of Ch'ing power, the Manchus utilized the best minds and richest human re-

sources of the country, regardless of race, to carry out many scholarly projects. However, Western missionaries—active in China since the end of the Ming—lost the trust of the Yung Cheng Emperor 雍正 due to their role in a power struggle for the throne. Christianity was banned in 1724, and the flow of Western technology into China slowed to a trickle thereafter. During the entire 18th century and the early 19th century, the Ch'ing court adopted a virtual closed-door policy toward the Western world while Europe was being transformed and invigorated by the rise of rationalism, nationalism, colonialism, and ultimately the industrial revolution.

Breaking Down the Door

The Western powers, however, were not content to leave China isolated, as they coveted Chinese markets and resources. They were dissatisfied with perennial trade deficits with China, unhappy about being treated unequally by the royal court of China which viewed trade as bestowing a favor, and chafed at being restricted to doing business in several small ports. High productivity in light and heavy industries drove European countries (especially England) outward in a search for markets and resources. By the early 18th century, England dominated overseas trade, having gained dominance of the seas over Spain and Holland. During the next century, colonialism and resource exploitation backed by military force went hand in hand with the push to develop overseas markets by major European nations.

The seeds of the Opium War of 1839-42 were sown in a worsening trade relationship between Great Britain and the Ch'ing court. The Ch'ing government was desperate about the loss of the 1.8 million silver taels its populace was spending on 30,000 chests (each containing more than 100 catties) of opium each year. In January 1839, Ch'ing Commissioner Lin Tse-hsü 林則徐 was made responsible for stamping out the opium trade. He closed down 13 guilds in Kwangtung after foreign merchants such as Lancelot Dent refused to yield all the opium stored on Lingting Island 伶仃島. The foreign merchants finally gave in and handed more than 20,000 chests of opium to Lin who, to the great dismay of the drug dealers, promptly burnt it. In July 1840, British warships occupied Tinghai 定海 and headed for Tientsin. In August, Taku 大沽 was attacked. A Ch'ing official Ch'i Shan 琦善 gave way to English demands for indemnity and ceded Hong Kong to England. But England was not satisfied with the agreement. So the British government sent a new plenipotentiary, Henry Pottinger, who attacked Amoy in 1841, Shanghai in 1842, and then set off for Nanking. The Treaty of Nanking 南京條約 was then signed on August 29, 1842. It has proved to be the most important treaty in China's modern history, for it was the first of a series of unequal treaties signed with Western powers. The Treaty of Nanking also marked the beginning of a long period of internal turmoil and external concession for China over the next 150 years. The 13 articles in the treaty stipulated that five ports were to be opened for British trade and consulates were to be established there; Hong Kong was ceded to England; 21 million silver taels were to be paid in four installments. Supplementary clauses signed later further stipulated consulate jurisdiction over Englishmen residing in China.

After the signing of the Treaty of Nanking, Belgium, Holland, Prussia, Spain, Portugal, the United States, and France also asked to establish consulates in China. In 1844, the Treaty of Wanghsia 望廈條約 was concluded with the United States, stating that the US would enjoy whatever privileges China granted to other nations. This was equivalent to China granting most-favored nation status to the US. Later that year, the Treaty of Whampoa 黃埔條約 was signed with France.

By signing the Treaty of Nanking, China agreed to open five ports, including Kwangtung, to foreign trade. However, the residents of Kwangtung at first refused to allow Englishmen to enter the city and then attacked the Englishmen already there. In early 1856, a French missionary was killed in Kwangsi. Later that year the Arrow Incident 亞羅號事件 occurred, in which

a Hong Kong-registered ship (i.e., under the protection of the English government), the Arrow, was searched in Kwangtung by Ch'ing soldiers and 12 of its sailors were arrested. All these incidents finally led to an Anglo-French expedition against Peking in 1858 and the burning of the imperial summer palace by invading troops. The Ch'ing court was thus compelled to make further concessions in the 1860 Treaty of Peking 北京條約.

The signing of these treaties led to a flood of Western merchants with their foreign goods—better, cheaper textiles, kerosene and lamps, cigarettes and opium. Consequently, the old Chinese system collapsed and the village economy—the backbone of China's agricultural society that had sustained Chinese civilization for millennia—lay in tatters.

The proud imperial bureaucracy and the mandarin elite became useless this time. They were entirely ignorant of the new forces to which China was being subjected. Their training had been in the old Chinese classics, and their experience had not prepared them to meet the new challenge. The scholarly elite were no more capable of dealing with the situation than the eunuchs who served the wives and concubines of the imperial families in the Forbidden City.

Reformers in the Ch'ing court, however, were aware of the superiority of Western armaments. In 1861, the Han generals Tseng Kuo-fan 曾國藩, Li Hung-chang 李鴻章, and Tso Tsung-t'ang 左宗棠 were able to convince the Ch'ing court to initiate a 30-year "self-strengthening" program. Under the new program, the Ch'ing dynasty began to train translators, import Western military technology, and set up armories. The Tsungli Yamen 總理衙門 was set up to manage foreign affairs. The self-strengthening program, however, came too late. Further controversies with Russia in the northwest and with England and France in the southwest jeopardized the stability of the Ch'ing dynasty. A war with France ended with the signing of the Treaty of Tientsin 天津條約 in 1885. In the later half of the 19th century, China lost its suzerain rights and sovereignty over the Indo-China Peninsula and large areas of the northwest.

Chinese and Japanese spheres of influence overlapped in Korea, and Japan was showing interest in taking over Taiwan. The Ch'ing court sent Liu Yung-fu 劉永福 and his armies to safeguard the island. Unfortunately, the military modernization undertaken during the self-strengthening program proved to be a complete failure when war between China and Japan finally broke out in 1894. Japan quickly breached the Chinese defenses and sank most of her northern navy. The Treaty of Shimonoseki was signed the next year, compelling the Ch'ing to pay a huge indemnity, open its seaports, recognize the independence of Korea, and cede the Liaotung Peninsula, Taiwan, and the Pescadores to Japan.

The repeated defeats that China suffered at the hands of foreign powers, the weakness and incompetence of the Ch'ing court, and the success of the Meiji Reformation in Japan prompted many thinking Chinese to take action. Under the leadership of K'ang Yu-wei 康有為 and Liang Ch'i-ch'ao 梁啟超, a reform movement was initiated in 1898. The Kuang Hsü Emperor 光緒 sympathized with this movement, but met with strong opposition from his aunt, the Empress Dowager Tz'u-hsi 慈禧太后, and other conservative elements in the Ch'ing court. The movement came to an inglorious end after only 100 days and was followed by a coup d'état in which the Kuang Hsü Emperor was imprisoned by the Empress Dowager. Those who had played leading parts in the movement were executed or exiled.

Popular discontent with internal misgovernment and anti-foreign sentiment aroused by the unequal treaties combined to spark the Boxer Uprising 義和拳之亂 in 1900. The Boxers laid siege to the foreign legation in Peking, where a combined force of Japanese, French, British, Russian, and American troops held out for over a month. The siege was broken when the forces of eight foreign powers marched from Tientsin and scaled the walls of Peking. The foreign powers then took the opportunity to loot Peking in one of the most disgraceful episodes of modern diplomatic history. In the signing of the Treaty of Peking the following year, China was disarmed and forced to pay large indemnities. This treaty was regarded as the most humiliating of all the unequal treaties.

One of the foreign powers sacking Peking, Russia, also took the opportunity to occupy Manchuria. When the troops of the other foreign powers withdrew from Chinese territory, Russia refused to leave Manchuria. This led to conflicts of interest with Japan and to the outbreak of the Russo-Japanese War in 1904. Through the Treaty of Portsmouth signed in 1905, a victorious Japan obtained complete control over Korea and rights and interests in southern Manchuria, leaving the north to Russia. Thereafter, Manchuria and Mongolia became flash points of further conflict between Japan and Russia, with China as the only loser.

Birth of a New China

After decades of pain and frustration brought about largely by the weakness of the Ch'ing government, the Chinese people were totally disillusioned with the Ch'ing dynasty, and began to take a keen interest in the revolutionary movement launched by Dr. Sun Yat-sen 孫中山 in the late 19th century. Dr. Sun set up a series of secret societies that operated in inland Chinese cities as well as overseas. In 1887, Dr. Sun even set up a secret society in Japanese-controlled Taiwan, from where he directed an uprising in Hueichow 惠州.

In 1905, Dr. Sun Yat-sen, who had been exiled for his involvement in the anti-Ch'ing movement, organized the Revolutionary Alliance 同盟會 in Tokyo. This organization sponsored an entire network of revolutionaries inside China. On October 10, 1911, Dr. Sun's supporters in Wuchang 武昌, fearing their cover was blown by the recent arrest of one of their agents, seized the initiative and raised the standard of revolt in Hupei Province. Drawing on a wellspring of popular support and the defection of numerous officers in the local garrison, the revolutionaries soon captured Wuhan 武漢. Two months later, revolutionaries fought and won a pitched battle in Nanking. On January 1, 1912, the Revolutionary Alliance, which by that time controlled 16 of the Ch'ing dynasty's 22 provinces, established a provisional parliament in Nanking and elected Dr. Sun Yat-sen to the provisional presidency of Asia's first democratic republic—the Republic of China.

Northern China, however, was effectively controlled by Yuan Shih-k'ai 袁世凱, who had served the Ch'ing dynasty in a variety of high posts. To break the deadlock and unify China, a three-way settlement was reached between revolutionaries in the south and the military strongman Yuan in the north. The last Ch'ing emperor abdicated. Dr. Sun Yat-sen agreed to relinquish the provisional presidency of the Republic of China to Yuan Shih-k'ai, and Yuan promised to establish a republican government. On February 12, 1912, the last Ch'ing ruler, the Hsüan T'ung 宣統 emperor, gave up his throne. The rule of the Manchus had lasted 268 years and spanned the rule of ten emperors.

Shaky Beginnings

The first half of the 20th century in China saw the gradual disintegration of the old imperial order. Foreign political philosophies had halted the traditional dynastic cycle, and nationalism became the dominant force in China. Externally, China was still confronted by strong foreign powers and subject to the terms of unequal treaties. Domestically, the new democracy was severely tested by its nominal leader, Yuan Shih-k'ai.

As the former governor-general of Chihli 直隸, Yuan had trained the Peiyang Army 北洋軍, which was an elite Western-style army. He coerced the newly established parliament into formally electing him to the presidency, and was inaugurated on October 10, 1913. Upon his ascension to China's highest political office, Yuan sought to disband Dr. Sun Yat-sen's Revolutionary Alliance, which had been reorganized into the Kuomintang 國民黨. Yuan Shih-k'ai also dissolved the parliament and then assumed dictatorial powers. In an effort to appease China's

rapacious neighbor in the northeast, Yuan Shih-k'ai agreed to Japanese demands—known as the Twenty-one Demands 二十一條款—for special rights and privileges in Shantung in May 1915. As time passed, it became obvious that Yuan was planning to restore the imperial system with himself on the throne. Unmoved by the advice of foreign governments and the opposition of the Kuomintang, Yuan Shih-k'ai declared himself emperor on December 12, 1915.

That month, Ch'en Ch'i-mei 陳其美 led a revolt against the incipient restoration of monarchy in China. More significant was a military revolt in Yunnan Province, led by the governor of Yunnan, T'ang Chi-yao 唐繼堯 and General Ts'ai O 蔡鍔. Joined by Lee Lieh-chün 李烈鈞 and other revolutionary generals, these men established a National Protection Army 護國軍 and demanded that Yuan cancel his plan to reestablish monarchal rule in China. During the spring and early summer of 1916, one after the other, provinces and districts declared independence from the Yuan regime. Faced with intense and mounting opposition, Yuan Shih-k'ai fell gravely ill and died on July 6, 1916. General Li Yuan-hung 黎元洪, vice president of the democracy that Yuan Shih-k'ai had sought to dismantle, succeeded the presidency, and General Tuan Ch'i-jui 段祺瑞 retained his post as premier.

Highly ambitious and supported by many senior commanders from the old Peiyang Army clique, Tuan Ch'i-jui quickly began to gather power in his own hands. In February 1917 when the American government severed diplomatic relations with Germany and pressed China to do the same, President Li Yuan-hung strongly opposed the move, but Premier Tuan and his supporters were able to push through China's declaration of war on Germany on August 14, 1917. Despite sending over 100,000 men to France during World War I, China reaped little benefit from its entry into the war. It was assured a seat at the Versailles Peace Conference, but the Chinese delegation to that meeting of world leaders was stunned to discover that Germany's holdings in China were not going to be returned to the Chinese people. Rather, the Western powers had agreed to Japanese claims to the German concession in Shantung Province. Major portions of Shantung were to be held by another foreign colonial power, Japan.

On May 4, 1919, students in Peking protested the decision at the Versailles Peace Conference. A riot ensued and many students were arrested. Waves of protest spread throughout the major cities of China. Merchants closed their shops, banks suspended business, and workers went on strike to pressure the government. Finally, the government was forced to release the arrested students and discharge some of the Chinese officials who had collaborated with Japan. Ultimately, the Chinese government refused to sign the Treaty of Versailles.

An intellectual revolution sparked by the events of May 4, 1919, and often referred to as the May Fourth Movement 五四運動 gained momentum during the first decade of the Republic of China. The movement was led by a new generation of intellectuals who scrutinized nearly all aspects of Chinese culture and traditional ethics. This new intelligentsia emerged in China after the traditional civil service examination system was suspended in 1905 and educational reform enabled thousands of young people to study science, engineering, medicine, law, economics, education, and military science in Japan, Europe, and the United States. The "overseas students" returned to modernize China and, through their writings and lectures, exercised a powerful influence on the next generation of students. Guided by concepts of individual liberty and equality, a scientific spirit of inquiry, and a pragmatic approach to the nation's problems, the new intellectuals sought a more profound reform of China's institutions than what was accomplished by the self-strengthening movement of the late Ch'ing dynasty or the republican revolution. National Peking University, China's most prestigious institution of higher education, was transformed by its chancellor, Ts'ai Yuan-p'ei 蔡元培, who had spent many years in advanced study in Germany. Ts'ai made the university a center of scholarly research, and inspired educators all over China. A proposal by Professor Hu Shih 胡適, that literature be written in the vernacular language rather than in the classical style, won quick acceptance.

Important economic and social changes occurred during the first years of the Republic. With the outbreak of World War I, foreign economic competition against native industries abated, and state-run light industries experienced brisk development. By 1918, the industrial labor force numbered 1.8 million workers. A large portion of capital flowed from the agricultural sector to new industries in China's coastal provinces, and modern Chinese banks with growing capital resources were able to meet expanding financial needs.

In the 1920s the United States, Great Britain, and Japan seemed to be moving toward a new postwar relationship with China. At the Washington Conference, the major powers agreed to respect the sovereignty, independence, and territorial and administrative integrity of China; to give China opportunity to develop a stable government; to maintain the principle of equal opportunity in China for the commerce and industry of all nations; and to refrain from taking advantage of conditions in China to seek exclusive privileges. The powers also agreed to steps leading toward China's tariff autonomy and the abolition of extraterritoriality.

Warlord Era

For a few years after the Washington Conference, the foreign powers refrained from aiding particular Chinese factions in the recurrent power struggles. But China was in turmoil, and regional militarism was in full swell. During the first two decades of the republic, China had been fractured by rival military regimes to the extent that no one authority was able to subordinate all rivals and create a unified and centralized political structure. The powerful Peiyang Army had split into two major factions: the Chihli faction led by Feng Kuo-chang 馮國璋 and the Anhui faction under Tuan Ch'i-jui. These factions controlled provinces in the Yellow River and Yangtze River valleys and competed for control of Peking. In the Manchuria, Chang Tso-lin 張作霖 headed a separate army. Shansi Province was controlled by Yen Hsi-shan 閻錫山.

Having witnessed the collapse of the fledgling central government he had worked so hard to create, Dr. Sun Yat-sen turned south to his home province of Kwangtung, where he established a military government in August 1917. In 1919, Dr. Sun reorganized his party into the present-day Chinese Kuomintang (KMT, also known as the Nationalist Party), and in 1921 Dr. Sun Yat-sen assumed the presidency of the newly formed southern government in Kwangtung. When war between the northern warlords erupted the next year, Dr. Sun issued a manifesto urging the reunification of China by peaceful means. However, the political idealist, Dr. Sun Yat-sen, was to be disappointed by more years of sporadic fighting between warlords. Finally in 1924, Dr. Sun Yat-sen and his southern government moved to set up a military academy which would train an officer corps loyal to the Kuomintang and dedicated to the unification of China. Dr. Sun appointed Chiang Kai-shek 蔣中正 as commandant of the Whampoa Military Academy 黃埔軍校.

On November 10, 1924, Dr. Sun Yat-sen called for the early convocation of a National People's Convention to bring each of China's regional leaders to the conference table. Two weeks later, Tuan Ch'i-jui became the provisional chief executive of the Peking-based government and Dr. Sun Yat-sen, as head of the southern government, traveled north to hold talks with Tuan. While in Peking, Dr. Sun succumbed to liver cancer and died on March 12, 1925 at the age of 59. His dream of a unified and democratic China freed of foreign constraint had yet to be realized.

Dr. Sun's untimely demise left the southern government in the hands of a steering committee. This 16-member committee established a national government in July 1925 and some 11

months later appointed Chiang Kai-shek commander-in-chief of the National Revolutionary Army 國民革命軍. In this capacity, Chiang Kai-shek launched a military expedition northward to eradicate various feuding warlords in central and northern China. This military campaign lasted three years and came to be known as the Northern Expedition 北伐. On March 22, 1927, the first troops of the National Revolutionary Army entered Shanghai. Two days later, Nanking fell. Despite a split between the right and left wings of the Kuomintang, Chiang Kai-shek was able to establish a new National Government in Nanking on April 18, 1927, and the Northern Expedition continued without interruption.

Japanese Provocations

By the spring of 1928, the National Revolutionary Army was approaching Chinan 濟南, the provincial capital of Shantung Province. Japan dispatched 3,000 soldiers to the city under the pretext of protecting Japanese residents. On May 3, two days after the National Revolutionary Army moved into Chinan, Japanese soldiers killed the Chinese negotiator Ts'ai Kung-shih 蔡公時. Thousands of Chinese soldiers and civilians were slaughtered by Japanese regulars in the ensuing massacre. Less than a month later, the Japanese followed this atrocity with the assassination of the Chinese warlord in northeast China, Marshal Chang Tso-lin, after he had expressed his intention to surrender Manchuria to the National Government. Manchuria was a huge and rich area of China in which Japan had extensive economic privileges. Japan dominated much of the southern Manchurian economy through a monopoly of the Southern Manchuria Railway 南滿鐵路. Manchuria's impending unification with the rest of China threatened Japan's economic privileges in central China and its domination in Manchuria.

The Chinese government realized the Chinan massacre and the assassination of Chang Tso-lin were premeditated actions designed by the Japanese militarists to provoke war while China was still divided. Chiang Kai-shek thus ordered the National Revolutionary Army to continue its northward march but to avoid Japanese controlled areas in northern China. This strategy frustrated the Japanese schemes and effectively unified China under the National Government based in Nanking.

Japanese militarists remained undaunted. Believing Manchuria to be strategically and economically vital to their plans for the conquest of all Asia, Japanese officers in Shenyang (Mukden) sabotaged the Southern Manchuria Railroad on September 18, 1931, and ambushed the Northeastern Chinese Armies. On January 28, 1932, following a wave of murders and arson by their agents in Shanghai, Japanese armies attacked that city. Chinese defenders resisted heroically, and thereby drew international attention. To deflect world opinion which condemned their actions, the Japanese installed a puppet regime known as Manchukuo 滿洲國 in 1932. The "land of the Manchu" proved to be no more than another stepping stone for the extension of Japanese aggression. In 1933, a humiliating Tanggu Truce 塘沽協議 was signed, which in effect yielded eastern Hopei Province to the Japanese-controlled Manchukuo.

After long negotiations, Japan acquired the Soviet interests in the Chinese Eastern Railway 中東鐵路, the last legal trace of Russian influence in Manchuria. In 1935, Japanese armies attempted to detach Hopei and Chahar provinces from Chinese control and threatened Shansi, Suiyuan, and Shantung provinces. The Japanese then set up a so-called East Hopei Anti-Communist and Self-Government Council 冀東反共自治會, another move after the Tanggu Truce to extend Japanese control over northern China.

Rise of the Chinese Communists

The Japanese were not the only threat to the integrity of Chinese democracy. The Chinese communists, who had rebelled against the National Government, established a provisional Soviet "government" in Kiangsi on November 7, 1931, and created 15 rural bases in central China. The National Government launched five successive military campaigns to eradicate the communist threat to central authority. The communist armies were, in the end, forced to abandon their bases and retreat. Communist troops led by Mao Zedong 毛澤東, Zhu De 朱德, Zhou Enlai 周恩來, and Lin Biao 林彪 marched and fought their way across Western China on the 6,000-mile Long March. By mid-1936, Nationalist forces had cornered the remnants of several communist armies in the impoverished area of Yennan in northern Shansi.

At this point, the Chinese communists opted for a new "united front" strategy against Japan. In effect the communist leaders suggested that the National Government fight the Japanese instead of the communist armies. The National Government, however, argued that the communists must capitulate to central authority before China could effectively repel Japanese encroachment. The National Government's policy, therefore, was one of "unity before resistance against foreign aggression." While further Japanese transgressions made this policy a costly one, Generalissimo Chiang Kai-shek was determined to carry on the anti-communist campaign. He ordered the Northeastern and Northwestern Armies to attack the communist forces in northern Shansi Province. When the Northeastern Army, commanded by Chang Hsüeh-liang 張學良, disobeyed the order to pursue the war against the communists, Chiang Kai-shek flew to Sian 西安 on December 12, 1936, to confront Chang Hsüeh-liang. Chang's army subordinates, however, shot Chiang Kai-shek's bodyguards and arrested the generalissimo. After a series of behind-the-scenes negotiations, Chang Hsüeh-liang freed the generalissimo and escorted him back to Nanking on Christmas day of 1936. The Sian Incident was a severe setback to Generalissimo Chiang's efforts to subjugate the communists.

War Against Japan

On the eve of China's all-out war against Japan, the Japanese nation had a total of over 4.5 million soldiers. The total tonnage of its navy came to nearly 2 million, while its air force had

2,700 planes of various models. In comparison, the Chinese army had 1.7 million men, and its navy a total tonnage of 110,000, and its air force 600 aircraft, only 305 of which were fighters.

On July 7, 1937, a minor clash between Japanese and Chinese troops near Peking finally led China into war against Japan. (In Chinese this conflict is called the Eight-Year War of Resistance Against Japan 八年抗日戰爭.) From this point on, Chinese resentment of over half a century of Japanese barbarism was expressed in the form of overt, concerted, and armed resistance. The war against Japan unfolded in three stages: a first stage of undeclared war beginning with the Marco Polo Bridge Incident 七七事變 (or 蘆溝橋事變) on July 7, 1937; an intermediate stage beginning in late 1938; and a third stage that began with China joining the Allied Forces after the Japanese bombing of Pearl Harbor and ended with the surrender of Japan in 1945.

During the first stage of the war, Japan won successive victories. Tientsin was occupied in July 1937 and Peking in August. After three months of fierce fighting, Shanghai was captured by the Japanese on November 11, 1937. The ROC's capital, Nanking, fell in December. The fall of the capital is now known as the Rape of Nanking because Japanese forces occupying the city killed some 300,000 people (defenseless civilians and Chinese troops that had already laid down their arms) in seven weeks of unrelenting carnage. The loss of Nanking forced the ROC government to move its capital up the Yangtze River to the city of Chungking, which was shielded by a protective mountain screen. By the end of this initial phase of the war, the ROC government had lost the best of its modern armies, its air force and arsenals, most of China's modern industries and railways, its major tax resources, and all the Chinese ports through which military equipment and civilian supplies might be imported. However, China had won the battle in T'aierchuang 台兒莊 on April 6, 1938.

In 1940, Japan set up a puppet government in Nanking under Wang Ching-wei 汪精衛. But the Chinese people would not submit. Hundreds of thousands of patriotic Chinese continued to attempt the difficult trek to Chungking. Students and faculties from most colleges in eastern China traveled by foot to makeshift quarters in distant inland towns. Factories and skilled workers were re-established in the west.

The government rebuilt its scattered armies and tried to purchase supplies from abroad. But the supply lines were long and precarious. When war broke out in Europe, shipments became even more scarce. After Germany's conquest of France in the spring of 1940, Britain bowed to Japanese demands and temporarily closed Rangoon, Burma, to military supplies for China. In September 1940, Japan seized control of northern Indo-China and closed the supply line to Kunming 昆明. While Japan had more than 1,000 planes, China had only 37 fighter planes and 31 old Russian bombers that were not equipped for night flying. The United States, however, had by then sold the Republic of China 100 fighter planes—the beginning of an American effort to provide air protection to the ROC.

By the summer of 1941, the United States knew that Japan hoped to end the undeclared war in China and was preparing for a southward advance toward British Malaya and the Dutch Indies, planning first to occupy southern Indo-China and Thailand, even at the risk of war with Britain and the United States. On July 23, 1941, President Roosevelt of the United States approved a recommendation that the US send large quantities of arms and equipment to China, along with a military mission to advise on their use. The military mission arrived in October 1941. By December 1941, the United States had implicitly agreed to help create a modern Chinese air force, to maintain an efficient line of communication into China, and to arm 30 divisions of soldiers. The underlying goal was to revitalize China's war effort as a deterrent to Japanese military and naval operations in the south. The logistics line for all foreign aid depended on the 715-mile Burma Road, which extended from Chungking to Lashio, the Burmese terminus of the railway and highway leading to Rangoon.

The third phase of the war against Japan began on December 7, 1941, when the Japanese bombed Pearl Harbor, and shortly afterwards the United States and Britain declared war on Japan. China, which also formally declared war against Japan after four years of staunch resistance, joined the Allies in waging the Pacific War. On January 2, 1942, Generalissimo Chiang assumed the office of Supreme Commander of the China Theater of War. This escalation of the Sino-Japanese conflict raised Chinese morale but did damage to China's strategic position. With the Japanese conquest of Hong Kong on December 25, 1941, China lost its air link to the outside world and one of its principal routes for shipping supplies. By the end of May 1942, the Japanese held most of Burma, and China was almost completely blockaded.

Following an initial grant of US$630 million in lend-lease supplies, the United States granted China a loan of US$500 million in February 1942, and Great Britain stated its willingness to lend £50 million. This helped to stabilize the Chinese currency and provided China with better terms of trade. A solution to the supply problem was found in an air route from Assam, India, to Kunming in southwest China—the dangerous "Hump" route along the southern edge of the Himalayas. In March 1942, the China National Aviation Corporation 中國航空公司 began freight service over the Hump, and the United States began a transport program the next month. It was not until December 1943 that cargo planes were able to equal the tonnage carried over the Burma Road by trucks two years before, but China's needs for gasoline, arms, munitions, and other military equipment were still not adequately met.

Both air force development and army modernization were pushed in early 1943. A training center was created near Kunming and a network of airfields was built in southern China. By the end of 1943, the China-based American Fifteenth Air Force had achieved tactical parity with the Japanese over central China, and began to bomb Yangtze River shipping. The Fifteenth Air Force even successfully raided Japanese airfields on Taiwan. China's determination was beginning to pay off. During November and December of 1943,

the leaders of the Allied countries met in Cairo, Egypt. In the December 1st Cairo Declaration, the return of Manchuria, Taiwan, and the Pescadores was promised to China. The prewar system of extraterritoriality—whereby Chinese courts had no jurisdiction over any foreigner residing in China—was abolished. In addition, the Allies pledged themselves to "persevere in the prolonged operations necessary to procure the unconditional surrender of Japan."

On August 6, 1945, the United States dropped the first atomic bomb on Hiroshima. Three days later, a second atomic bomb was dropped on Nagasaki. The subsequent Japanese decision to surrender was delivered to the Allies through Switzerland the next day. On August 14, Japan announced its formal surrender in accordance with the terms of the Potsdam Declaration of July 1945 and declared that "the terms of the Cairo Declaration shall be carried out." The Japanese government accepted this in the instrument of surrender concluded on September 3, 1945, between Japan and the Allies. The Japanese armies in mainland China surrendered to the ROC government on September 9, 1945, in Nanking.

Communist Rebellion

Even before Emperor Hirohito's announcement of Japan's surrender was known, the commander of the Chinese communist armies, Zhu De, ordered his troops to move into Japanese-held territory and seize Japanese arms. The American general, Douglas MacArthur, then ordered all Japanese forces in China to surrender their arms only to forces of the ROC Government. Despite MacArthur's request, the Chinese communists sent tens of thousands of political cadres and soldiers into Manchuria. The Chinese communists got most of the arms of the 600,000-strong Japanese army in Manchuria which had previously been confiscated by the Russians. The Soviet army dismantled most of the industrial machinery in Manchuria. The valuable equipment, so crucial to China's postwar revival, was shipped to the Soviet Union while immovable objects were mostly destroyed. The situation in northeastern China was clearly alarming.

The government and the Chinese communists held peace talks which culminated in an agreement on October 10, 1945. The agreement called for the convening of a multiparty Political Consultative Council 政治協商會議 to plan for a liberalized postwar government and to draft a constitution for submission to a National Assembly 全國代表大會. When the Chinese communists continued to accept the surrender of Japanese garrisons, occupy cities, and confiscate property, Chiang Kai-shek ordered an offensive against them in November. Hostilities lasted throughout December and the early part of January 1947. At this point, US President Harry S. Truman dispatched George Marshall to China. Marshall was able to negotiate several cease-fires during 1947, but a pattern of non-cooperation between the government and the communists soon escalated into open conflict.

While ROC troops were busily suppressing the incipient communist rebellion, the many citizens were working to implement true democracy. On January 1, 1947, the Constitution of the Republic of China was promulgated. Within the year, members of the National Assembly, Legislature (Legislative Yuan) 立法院, and Control Yuan 監察院 had been democratically elected. In April 1948, the new National Assembly elected Chiang Kai-shek to the presidency of the Republic of China. These moves toward democratic government, however, were overshadowed by a communist offensive that cut Manchuria off from the rest of China.

The military setback was compounded by serious economic problems. Inflation continued unabated, caused principally by government financing of military and other operations, particularly for maintaining large garrison forces. Apart from the loss of millions of Chinese lives, the war against Japan had generated huge war debts, not to mention serious financial distress in the private sector. The government had run a budget deficit every year since 1928. Alarmingly, the money supply in China increased by 500 times between 1937 and 1945. Retail prices of daily necessities were so inflated that even middle-class families tottered on the brink of abject poverty. This unrestrained inflation triggered a national recession and alienated the public from its elected representatives.

By 1948, communist forces had cut lines of communication and destroyed vital outposts along the Longhai 隴海 and Pinghan 平漢 railways, isolating many cities. In December, the pivotal battle for Hsüchow 徐州 was lost. This defeat was followed by the fall of Tientsin and Peking on January 19, 1949. Other cities in northeastern China were lost by March. In early 1949, Chiang Kai-shek began deploying a force of 300,000 troops in Taiwan backed by a few gunboats and some planes. After the Chinese communists successfully crossed the Yangtze River, the government of the Republic of China began relocating its offices to Taiwan. As the mainland was falling to the communist forces, some two million people (both soldiers and civilians) accompanied the ROC government to the island of Taiwan. However, they were not the first people to reach the island.

History of Taiwan

Taiwan's first inhabitants have left no written records of their origins. Anthropological evidence suggests that Taiwan's indigenous people were proto-Malayans. Their vocabulary and grammar belong to the Malayan-Polynesian family of Indonesia, and they once shared many Indonesian customs such as tattooing, using identical names for father and son, gerontocracy, head-hunting, spirit worship, and indoor burials. Over 500 prehistoric sites in Taiwan, including many dwelling areas, tombs, shell mounds, and megaliths, have provided more, and sometimes seemingly contradictory, clues to origins of Taiwan's aborigines. The majority of the prehistoric artifacts unearthed so far (e.g., flat axes, red unpolished pottery, decorated bronze implements, megalithic structures, and glass beads) indicate an Indonesian connection. Other items (e.g., painted red pottery, red polished pottery, chipped stone knives, black pottery, pottery tripods, stone halberds, bone arrowheads), however, would suggest that Taiwan's earliest settlers might have come from the Chinese mainland. Other questions remain unanswered. Were the prehistoric remains left by the ancestors of the modern aborigines in Taiwan? The question is a complex one, but many anthropologists have suggested that the prehistoric cultural remains discovered so far have no proven connection to the present indigenous cultures in Taiwan.

What is known for certain is that large groups of indigenous peoples plus many people from the Chinese mainland were already living in Taiwan when the Europeans first arrived off the coast of Taiwan in 1590.

Buffeted by Colonial Winds

When Portuguese navigators came upon the island of Taiwan, they were struck by the tremendous beauty of its green mountains rising steeply out of the cobalt waters of the Pacific. The Portuguese navigator named the island *Ilha Formosa*, or "beautiful island," and under this name Taiwan was introduced to the Western world. Portuguese interest in the island was only moderate, however, since they left soon after establishing a settlement in the north.

The next Europeans to occupy Taiwan were the Dutch. The Dutch East India Company established a military base on the Pescadore Islands in 1622. The next year they were forced out of the Pescadores by the Chinese and moved to Taiwan. At the end of 1624, the Dutch landed on the southwestern coast of Taiwan and started building Fort Zeelandia and the town of Anp'ing 安平. In 1630, a number of Dutch merchants, technicians, and missionaries, as well as sailors, soldiers, and officials, settled on Taiwan to trade, develop virgin land, plant sugar cane, produce camphor, tax the Chinese immigrants already living on the island, and convert the natives to Christianity.

The news of the Dutch success in Taiwan so alarmed the Spaniards in the Philippines that they hurried to send a fleet from Manila to the northern part of Taiwan, which in 1626 was still not occupied by the Dutch. The Spaniards soon took control of the northeastern cape of the island, naming it Santiago. Before long, however,

they gave up this location and moved to a more desirable area, which they named Santisima Trinidad and which is known now as Keelung harbor. In Keelung 基隆 they built a fort and named it Fort San Salvador. In the summer of 1629, the Spaniards entered what is now Tamsui 淡水. They named this place Castillo, and built Fort San Domingo. In Castillo, the Spaniards set up a government, appointed civil officials, and prepared to occupy the colony permanently.

The Dutch in southern Taiwan made many attempts to drive the Spaniards out of the north. In 1630 and 1641, the Dutch attacked Castillo and Fort San Domingo, but their efforts were in vain. Finally, in the summer of 1642, when the Spaniards, threatened by a native rebellion in the Philippines, were forced to recall three-quarters of their troops from Taiwan, the Dutch landed at Castillo and conquered it.

Dutch Rule

In 1650, the Dutch moved the capital of their colony on Taiwan from Fort Zeelandia to the newly completed Fort Provintia (some sources say Providentia). Although this fort ultimately became known in Chinese as 赤崁樓, it seems to have been called a number of different names in the 17th century, including "edifice of the red-haired barbarians" 紅毛樓, signifying the presence of the Dutch. On the southwestern coast, where the city of Tainan is now located, the new fort accommodated as many as 600 Dutch officials and other civilians as well as a garrison of 2,200. This settlement continued to be the main base of colonization throughout the Dutch period.

After 1642, the Dutch, freed from all European competitors, began to strengthen their hold on Taiwan through the Dutch East India Company. The governor was appointed by the company and for 38 years the company used the island as a trading center. The Dutch government gave the company full power to tax the aborigines and Chinese on Taiwan. The few Dutch civilians on the island were greatly outnumbered by the aborigines and Chinese who had immigrated there prior to the arrival of the Europeans.

The company divided the indigenous people's territory into seven districts, each of which was governed by an aborigine elder chosen by his own people. The company established an advisory council made up of the elders, to whom they gave badges of honor, and through which company orders were carried out. In 1650 nearly 300 Chinese villages were under the direct jurisdiction of the Dutch East India Company. The Dutch organized the Chinese immigrant tenant farmers 佃農 into farm groups 結. As many as 50 tenant farming households were placed under one head 小結首 and every 30 or 40 heads elected a captain 大結首, who was responsible to the governor for keeping local peace and order. This arrangement proved very efficient for agricultural production, and the area of land under cultivation continued to increase.

Foreign Trade

Recent plans announced by the ROC government to develop Taiwan into an Asia-Pacific Regional Operations Center are, in a way, returning to a recognition of the fundamental advantages of Taiwan's pivotal geographical position for regional trade first apparent as long ago as the period of Dutch rule. Under the Dutch administration, Taiwan in the early 17th century became a trading and transshipment center for goods between a number of areas, such as Japan, China, and Batavia, as well as Holland. Taiwan's exports to China included rice, sugar, rattan, deer hides, deer horns, and medicine. The island's imports from China included raw silk and silk textiles, porcelain, and medicine. Some of the products after reaching Taiwan were again shipped either to Japan or to Batavia, or even to Holland. Imports to Taiwan from Batavia included spices, amber, tin, lead, cotton, and opium, some of which were later traded to China. Before the Dutch arrived on the island, the Chinese on Taiwan had enjoyed free trade with the Japanese without taxation. The Dutch subsequently established a tax on exports, at that time mainly on deer hides and sugar. The annual deer hides export amounted to 50,000 pieces and the sugar export to 5,000 tons.

Taiwan, even then a bustling area, proved to be one of the most profitable branches of the Dutch East India Company in the Far East. In a typical year, 1649 for example, the Ceylon and Siam 暹羅 branches were not profitable at all, while those in Japan and Taiwan did very well. The company's most profitable branch was in Japan, which accounted for 39 percent of all corporate profits worldwide, with the Taiwan branch second, at 26 percent. Actually the profit made in Japan derived mainly from goods that the Dutch carried from China to Japan via Taiwan, clearly underscoring the importance of Taiwan's position in the Dutch East India Company.

Frontier Missionaries in Taiwan

The Dutch were interested in Taiwan not only as a colony or commercial enterprise, but also as a field for missionary work. Protestant missionaries endeavored to convert the aborigines, and established schools where the Dutch language and religion were taught. By 1650 the Dutch had converted 5,900 inhabitants on the island.

The first Dutch missionary, the Reverend Georgius Candidius, who went to Taiwan in 1627, wrote a work entitled *Short Account of the Island of Formosa*, describing the manners, customs, and religion of the inhabitants. This account was published in 1627 in Germany. In the first 16 months of his stay, Candidius instructed 120 natives in the Christian religion. So inspiring were his teachings that the other Dutch missionaries and the aboriginal converts gave his name to what is now Sun Moon Lake 日月潭. Some maps in Western countries still call it Lake Candidius.

Another missionary, the Rev. Robertus Junius, spent 13 years, from 1629 to 1641, on the island and converted several thousand aborigines. In 1636 he founded the first Western style school in Taiwan.

Chinese Immigration

Chinese settlement in Taiwan dates back as far as the 12th century A.D., but large-scale immigration did not begin until the 17th century during the period of Dutch administration. While the Dutch were colonizing Taiwan, China was going through a period of strife. In 1644 the country was invaded by the Manchus, who overthrew the Ming dynasty in the north. The struggle continued for many years in the south, affecting many people, while Japanese pirates constantly ravaged Chinese coastal towns. Consequently, thousands of people, especially from the coastal provinces of Fukien and Kwangtung, began to migrate across the Taiwan Straits to Taiwan. They found the soil of Taiwan much richer than that of the mainland, and crops grew twice as abundantly. During the twenty years from 1624 to 1644, more than 25,000 Chinese households—some 100,000 people—immigrated to Taiwan.

The Dutch and Chinese Conflict

This mass migration to Taiwan changed the character of the island. At first the Dutch welcomed the new settlers warmly. Since most of the land in Taiwan was still covered with heavy growth and jungles and sparsely populated by aborigines who still practiced primitive farming methods. Recognizing the urgent need for industrious farmers, the Dutch employed the Chinese immigrants, providing them with oxen, seeds, and agricultural implements. Every new settler was promised an annual subsidy of cash and an ox. In the hands of the Chinese toilers, the farms of the island flourished. Thus, the Dutch profited tremendously from collecting heavy rents from the Chinese tenants.

However, the roots of the Chinese go deep into the earth. Agriculture has always been their essential means of life. To own a piece of land has always been the hope and ambition of the Chinese farmer. However, the Dutch did not allow farmers to own any real estate. All the land belonged to the Dutch East India Company. The Chinese settlers petitioned to be allowed to buy and own the land they were tilling so that they could pay taxes on it instead of rent, but the Dutch ignored these pleas. In addition, Chinese peasants were frequently mistreated by the Dutch.

The friction mounted when the Dutch decided to collect a poll tax for every Chinese over the age of six. In September 1652, frustrated Chinese farmers, led by Kuo Huai-yi 郭懷一, revolted against the Dutch. Although the rebellions were violently suppressed by the Dutch, who slaughtered nearly 6,000 poorly armed Chinese peasants, Dutch rule soon came to an end.

Cheng Ch'eng-kung

As Manchu troops poured into northern China, many Ming loyalists escaped southwards, where they resisted the foreign invasion for over 20 years. One of these celebrated resistance fighters was Cheng Ch'eng-kung 鄭成功 (also known as Koxinga 國姓爺), son of the pirate Cheng Chih-lung 鄭芝龍 and his Japanese mistress. Cheng Ch'eng-kung sailed with his troops to Quemoy 金門 in 1661 in hopes of returning to the mainland one day to restore the Ming dynasty. Though he never realized this dream (dying at the early age of 38), he did succeed in opening up Taiwan to greater numbers of Chinese settlers. A local guide for the Dutch, Ho Pin 何斌, provided Cheng Ch'eng-kung with a coastal map of Taiwan marking the ports and roads of the Dutch. Cheng Ch'eng-kung claimed Taiwan from the Dutch in 1662 and chose Anp'ing 安平 (present-day Tainan) as his capital. Dutch control over parts of Taiwan had lasted for only 38 years.

An Anti-Manchu Base

Cheng Ch'eng-kung, with the assistance of a capable advisor, Ch'en Yung-hua 陳永華, set up schools for the young, introduced Chinese laws and customs and transplanted Chinese traditions to the island. He also built the first Confucian temple in Taiwan to symbolize the introduction of Chinese culture to the island.

Cheng drilled his soldiers intensively for a planned attack on the mainland and had strong fortifications erected on the islands off the Fukien coast to bar the Manchus from crossing the straits to Taiwan. The Manchu rulers feared him so much that they forced people living within 15 kilometers of the mainland coast to move further inland lest Cheng received supplies and other assistance from them. As a result, many civilians fled to Taiwan to join Cheng's forces. During his rule, an unending stream of Chinese continued to pour into Taiwan and settlements sprang up in increasing numbers along the Western coast.

During the 23 years of the Cheng family's rule, agriculture was limited to southern Taiwan. There were three kinds of farms: official farms 官田, semi-official farms 私田, and military farms 營盤田. The official farms were constituted from land confiscated from the Dutch. The semi-official farms were owned by Cheng's military or civilian officials and other loyal supporters. The owners paid the taxes and the farming was done by tenants. Cheng Ch'eng-kung also designed a military camp farming system under which soldiers participated in farm work during their spare time in order to support themselves. Such military farms were established in about 40 locations.

Industry on Taiwan at the time consisted of refining sugar and manufacturing tiles. The efficiency of salt production improved by replacing the older baking methods with sun-drying methods. Shipbuilding also began at this time.

Brisk trade was carried on with neighboring areas, such as the Philippines, Japan, and Okinawa. Cheng's efficient administration laid a solid foundation for Taiwan's economy, so Cheng began to consider territorial expansion. He sent a Spanish Dominican friar, Riccio, to the Philippines demanding that the Spanish government pay him a yearly tribute. But Riccio's mission was a total failure, and many Chinese living in the Philippine capital were killed. Cheng then set about organizing an expedition to take the Philippines. At that time, however, he succumbed to a serious illness and died in 1662 at only 38 years of age.

Defeat by the Ch'ing

Cheng's son, Cheng Ching 鄭經, succeeded his father as ruler for the next twenty years until his death. His son, aged only 12, was placed on the throne. The next year, 1683, the Manchu court sent Shih Lang 施琅, a general under Cheng Ch'eng-kung who had defected to the Manchu Emperor, to attack Taiwan. Cheng's navy was defeated near the Pescadore Islands and the Cheng family unconditionally surrendered to the Ch'ing dynasty. Thus, after just over two decades of governance by Cheng's family, Taiwan was brought under Ch'ing rule and became a part of China's Fukien Province.

Despite the decisive Manchu victory in Taiwan, the resistance of the Chinese people against the "foreign" rulers continued underground. Secret societies were organized both on the island and in the mainland. The Hung Men 洪門 Society established by Ch'en Yung-hua was most famous and active, attracting hundreds of thousands of Ming loyalists under its flag. It instigated innumerable uprisings, first in Taiwan and then in the southeast coast of the mainland, during the following 200 years of the Ch'ing dynasty rule in China. No wonder Manchu officials claimed that Taiwan was an unstable place, subject to "a putsch every three years, and a general uprising every five years" 三年一小亂，五年一大亂.

Ch'ing Dynasty Rule

After the Manchus took over Taiwan in 1683, many officials advocated the immediate abandonment of the island because of its wildness and remoteness. However, the Ch'ing court finally adopted Shih Lang's suggestion to retain its rule over Taiwan and established the counties of Tainan, Fengshan 鳳山, and Chulo 諸羅 (present-day Tainan, Kaohsiung, and Chiayi).

Agriculture

During the Ch'ing dynasty, farming in Taiwan expanded northward. The official, semi-official, and military farm system was abolished, leaving only private farms. More and more Chinese left the mainland to settle on the island. Camphor, a major cash crop, became a cause of conflict between the new arrivals and the aborigines. Bamboo was planted widely; rice and tea, typical Chinese crops, were planted for the first time in Taiwan.

Taiwan's camphor comes from a beautiful tree with a shapely trunk and widespread branches. Exploiting this island resource brought with it conflicts between aborigines and Chinese, for the aborigines lived in the mountain forests where the trees were found. Since the Chinese method of collecting camphor required destroying the trees, the camphor workers had to go further and further inland, where they often encountered hostility from the natives. Despite the ensuing bloody conflicts, the Chinese were willing to risk their lives for the lucrative profits generated by the camphor trade. As a result, the aborigines were forced to retreat deeper into the mountains.

According to a report submitted by Huang Shu-ching 黃叔璥, an imperial censor who inspected Taiwan, the island produced more rice than it needed and sold the excess to the mainland. During the reign of the Tao Kuang Emperor 道光 (1821-50), more than 140,000 piculs of rice were transferred to Tientsin annually. Sugar production was second to rice in its importance as a commercial crop. It had been exported to Japan and Persia since the 1630s and workshops for sugar manufacture were established in the early 18th century. Tea was the third most important commercial product. During the reign of the Tao Kuang Emperor, Taiwan tea was sold to the mainland, and Taiwan camphor extract was sold to international manufacturers of celluloid.

The Japanese, as well as other foreign powers, deeply coveted in Taiwan's wealth. During the Opium War, British warships patrolled the Taiwan coast to check for any moves by Ch'ing forces stationed on the island in 1854. Commodore Matthew Perry, commander of the US East Indian Fleet, sent warships to Keelung to measure water depth and mineral reserves. Four years later, Prussian ships fired on indigenous people in southern Taiwan. After the conclusion of the Treaty of T'ientsin in 1858, four Taiwanese ports, Anp'ing, Tamsui, Takou 打狗 (modern day Kaohsiung) and Keelung, were opened to foreign trade. In 1866, American warships bombarded aborigines in southern Taiwan to punish their slaughter of two shipwrecked American sailors. In 1869, British warships attacked Anp'ing and demanded better terms for the camphor trade. In 1874, Japan's Meiji government sent troops to attack aborigines in Mutan She 牡丹社 to force the Ch'ing court into dropping its opposition to the Japanese annexation of Okinawa. In 1884, France attacked and shut down Keelung, Tamsui, and the Pescadores to curb Ch'ing power. All this made the Manchu court realize Taiwan's importance as a gateway to the seven provinces along the southeastern coast. Capable Ch'ing officials such as Shen Pao-chen 沈葆楨 and Liu Ming-ch'uan 劉銘傳 were appointed to develop Taiwan's infrastructure and strengthen its defenses.

Shen Pao-chen, the administrator of shipping affairs, was put in charge of Taiwan's defense in 1874. Shen recommended lifting the ban on immigration from the mainland, exploring Taiwan's eastern coast, and developing the island's northern area. He worked to educate the indigenous peoples, organized local militias, constructed cannon emplacements along the coast, and petitioned for a full-time governor to be solely responsible for Taiwan instead of placing the island under the jurisdiction of the governor of Fukien Province. The exploitation of coal in Keelung began under his administration and foreign specialists were employed to prospect for coal in 1868. Surveys of the island's crude oil and sulphur resources were also made. Aware of the need for better communications, Shen Pao-chen also recommended the construction of telegraph lines linking the central and southern parts of Taiwan, as well as connecting Taiwan with Fukien Province across the Taiwan Straits.

Ting Jih-ch'ang 丁日昌 was another important figure in Taiwan's development. Arriving in Taiwan in early 1876, Ting oversaw the construction of railroad and telegraph lines, and during his term in office, some 47 kilometers of telegraph cable were installed in southern Taiwan. Due to budget limitations and other restrictions, however, he never realized his dream of constructing a railroad on the island. After Ting was transferred, Wu Tsan-ch'eng 吳贊誠 and Ts'en Yü-ying 岑毓英 were successively appointed to be responsible for Taiwan's defense. Again, budget and priority considerations of the central government restrained their programs to develop a modern infrastructure on Taiwan.

Short-lived Provincial Status

In 1885, the Ch'ing dynasty made Taiwan its 22nd province. The following year, Liu Ming-ch'uan was appointed the first governor of Taiwan. Liu modernized Taiwan's defenses against foreign aggression, implemented tax reforms to make Taiwan financially independent, and educated its indigenous peoples. Under Liu's rule, Taiwan was divided into three prefectures 府, one autonomous prefecture 州, three offices 廳, and 11 counties. Telegraph lines linking Taipei, Keelung, Tamsui, and Tainan, as well as submarine lines between Tamsui and Foochow in Fukien Province and between Anp'ing and the Pescadores, were completed in 1888. A post office was set up in the same year, nine years before China formally established its own postal system. A land survey was completed in 1889, and a railroad connecting Keelung and Hsinchu 新竹 was completed in 1893. An irrigation system was planned to increase agricultural production. A general trade office was established to encourage foreign trade, and Western-style schools were set up.

When Taiwan was ceded to Japan in 1895 under the terms of the Treaty of Shimonoseki, Manchu officials stationed in Taiwan, such as T'ang Ching-sung 唐景崧 and Liu Yung-fu 劉永福, and local notables, such as Chiu Feng-chia 丘逢甲, declared independence on May 25, 1895, and formed the Democratic Taiwan Nation 台灣民主國 to resist the Japanese take-over. Armed resistance took place mainly in northern Taiwan until June 6 when Japanese troops formally entered Taipei. Once Taipei fell, the Taiwan nationalists shifted their base to Tainan under the command of General Liu Yung-fu, but their efforts were to no avail. On October 21, Japanese troops entered Tainan, and organized resistance against Japanese occupation of Taiwan ceased for the time being. A total of 7,000 Chinese soldiers were killed in the conflict and civilian casualties numbered in the thousands.

Japanese Rule of Taiwan

Unlike the Dutch, who in the 17th century colonized Taiwan more for immediate commercial gains than for establishing political sovereignty, the Japanese at the start of the 20th century gave priority to establishing effective political control over the island. Thus, the Japanese policeman, rather than the Protestant missionary of Dutch times, became the most important tool in the exercise of colonial aims.

During its 50-year rule of Taiwan, Japan developed programs designed to supply the Japanese empire with agricultural products, create demand for Japanese industrial products, and provide living space for emigrants from an increasingly overpopulated home country. In other words, Japan was intent on building an industrial homeland and an agricultural Taiwan.

The period of Japanese colonization can be roughly divided into three stages. The first, from 1895 to 1918, involved establishing administrative mechanisms and militarily suppressing armed resistance by local Chinese. During this stage, the Japanese introduced strict police controls, carried out a thorough land survey, standardized measurements and currencies, monopolized the manufacture and sale of important products, began collecting census data, and made an ethnological study of the island's indigenous peoples.

During the second stage, from 1918 to 1937, Japan consolidated its hold over Taiwan. Compulsory Japanese education and cultural assimilation were the focus of this stage, while economic development was promoted to transform the island into a secure stepping stone from which Japan could launch its southward aggression.

The third stage, from 1937 to 1945, entailed the naturalization of Taiwan residents as Japanese. The Chinese on Taiwan were forced to adopt Japanese names, wear Japanese-style clothing, eat Japanese food, and observe Japanese religious rites. Also during this stage, Japanese developed Taiwan into an area of heavy industry and foreign trade.

Modernization of Infrastructure

Recognizing the importance of transportation to Taiwan's economy and the Empire's expansion in Southeast Asia, the Japanese soon set out to increase Taiwan's transportation facilities by developing steamship lines, improving harbors, and building railroads and highways. Modernizing the island's 17 harbors, the largest of which were in Keelung, Kaohsiung, and Hualien, involved installing new piers and other facilities, and dredging shallow harbors.

The Japanese government rebuilt the old railroad connecting Keelung and Hsinchu to eliminate its numerous hairpin curves and steep gradients. They then built a new line within ten years (1898-1908), 250 miles long, linking Keelung on the northern coast with Kaohsiung on the southwestern tip and passing through a number of other major cities. At the same time, many Japanese sugar manufacturers built private lines for both general traffic and transporting sugar cane. By the end of Japanese rule, the private and government lines totaled 2,857 miles in length. The mountain railroad on Mt. Ali 阿里山 was a brilliant Japanese engineering feat, taking 12 years to accomplish. With this line the Japanese began to conquer the steep slopes of Taiwan's mountainous center and to tap its abundant timber resources. The railroad, 45 miles long and only 30 inches wide, still functions to this very day as a major tourist attraction.

The first highway was completed in 1913, and thereafter highway building proceeded rapidly. At the end of the Japanese period, Taiwan had about 2,500 miles of highways.

Chianan Irrigation System

Irrigation was the key to further developing Taiwan's agriculture, which had been plagued by uneven rainfall. The Japanese provided that key when they learned to use cement for building dams. The Japanese started to build the great Chianan Irrigation System 嘉南大圳 in 1920, and completed it in 1930. This irrigation system conducts the water of the Tsengwen River 曾文溪 through a 10,168-foot-long aqueduct into the artificial Coral Reservoir 珊瑚潭. The reservoir is formed by a dam that is 4,260 feet long and 1,284 feet high. With a depth of 525 feet, it is one of the largest reservoirs in the Far East. The Chianan Irrigation System converted 68,050 acres of poor land on the west coast of Taiwan, which constitutes about 60 percent of the total plain area, into the most fertile farmland of the island. After the system went into operation, arable land for growing rice increased by more than 74 percent and sugar cane by 30 percent.

During Japanese rule, Taiwan's agricultural production was vitally important, for Japan imported from Taiwan about 60 percent of the rice and nearly 90 percent of the sugar the Empire needed. To increase rice production, the Japanese introduced Japanica rice into Taiwan in 1922. This round-grain type of rice produced a higher yield than the original long-grain type of Taiwan Indica rice. As a result, the yield per acre increased by one-third, and total rice production doubled.

Intensification of Agriculture

The great increase in the production of sugar cane is also considered to be one of the most spectacular achievements of the Japanese occupation of Taiwan. From as early as 1896, the Japanese imported various cane cuttings and seedlings of improved sugar varieties from Java, Cuba, Louisiana, and Australia, as well as from Hawaii. *Lahaina* and *Rose Bamboo*, the varieties obtained from Hawaii, were found best suited to the local climate and soil, yielding two or three times as much as the indigenous varieties. A special sugar bureau was established in 1902. Over a period of 30 years (1905-1935) the area planted in sugar cane increased 500 percent, and total production skyrocketed. In 1939, Japanese-controlled Taiwan was the seventh largest producer of sugar in the world, ranking only after Cuba, India, the USSR, Germany, the United States, and Java.

Banana and pineapple production also attained record highs during the Japanese occupation. The banana tree is indigenous to Taiwan, but only after Japanese rule began did bananas become an important export item. Pineapple cultivation began to expand after canning techniques were introduced in 1923.

Industrial Development

The Japanese policy of "an agricultural Taiwan and an industrial Japan" did not call for developing Taiwan's industry to a high degree. However, industrial production began to increase after 1907, when sugar refining advanced noticeably. By 1939, industrial output had pulled slightly ahead of agricultural production. Nonetheless, the factories then were rather small in general; 95 percent had fewer than 30 workers each. Not until World War II, when military necessities forced the Japanese to develop aluminum, chemical, oil-refining, metal, shipbuilding, and other strategic industries, did Taiwan's industrial sector reach a high level of output. Many large-scale state-run factories still operating today in Taiwan were constructed by the Japanese.

Hydroelectric Power

Long before World War II began, the Japanese realized that the key to the island's industrial development was cheap hydroelectric power. Heavy rainfall and swift mountain streams on the island permitted the establishment of large hydroelectric plants. A project to utilize Sun Moon Lake and the Choshui River 濁水溪 to generate power was worked out in 1931 and completed in 1937. The Sun Moon Lake power plant stands out as one of the greatest achievements of the Japanese period in Taiwan. In terms of impact and scope, it can be considered the Tennessee Valley Authority (TVA) of the Far East. Through this power project, it was possible for the island to support aluminum, chemical, and steel alloy plants.

Enforced Economic Dependence

In order to exercise effective political control over Taiwan and make it a supplier of raw materials as well as a market for Japanese goods, Japan imposed a high tariff system on Taiwan's trade with other countries, especially with the Chinese mainland. Thus, 90 percent of Taiwan's foreign trade was with Japan. Of course, exports from Taiwan to Japan were mostly agricultural products, while manufactured goods were imported from Japan to Taiwan. If a trade involved the same kind of goods, the better-quality goods went from Taiwan to Japan, while the inferior-quality ones were imported from Japan to Taiwan. The Japanese monopolized camphor, opium, tobacco and alcoholic beverages, ultimately setting up a customs system that diverted all foreign trade from the island to Japan.

Resistance Against Japanese Rule

Despite the Japanese success in transforming Taiwan into a society that, economically, was rather modern in comparison with its neighbors, resistance against alien rule never ceased on the island. The Japanese colonial rulers issued numerous edicts to check Chinese resistance. The *Bandit Penalties and Punishments Decree* 匪徒刑罰令 was the most infamous of these. According to Japanese records, more than 10,000 "bandits" were executed between 1898 and 1920. Lo Fu-hsing 羅福星, leader of the Miaoli Incident 苗栗事件 (1913), who had participated in Dr. Sun's overthrow of the Ch'ing dynasty, and Yü Ch'ing-fang 余清芳, leader of the Tapani Incident 噍吧哖事件 (1915)—the largest-ever revolt organized by Taiwan residents, were all executed in accordance with the decree.

The Tapani Incident, in which more than 10,000 local Taiwanese lost their lives, marked a turning point in Taiwan's resistance against Japanese rule. After the revolt was finally put down, armed resistance was replaced by political movements that focused on building a national consciousness. To proselytize the cause of Taiwanese nationalism, overseas Taiwanese students established the Shengying Society 聲應會, the Ch'ifa Society 啟發會, and the Hsinmin Society 新民會 between 1919 and 1920 and petitioned for legal and political reforms by the Japanese rulers in Taiwan. On the island itself, such associations as the Society for Promoting the Establishment of a Taiwan Council 台灣議會設置期成會, the New Taiwan Alliance 新台灣聯盟, the Taiwan Culture Association 台灣文化協會, the Taiwan Civilian Party 台灣民眾黨, and the Local Self-governance Federation 台灣地方自治聯盟 were established. Many of these groups published their own magazines and newspapers and were active until the surrender of Japan at the end of World War II.

The ROC on Taiwan

Japanese forces surrendered the island of Taiwan to the Allied Forces on October 25, 1945. The Allies then placed the island under the sovereignty of the Republic of China in accordance with the Cairo Declaration. Thus, Taiwan, which had been occupied over the centuries by the Portuguese, Dutch, Spanish, Manchus, and Japanese, was finally ruled by Chinese.

Prior to this turnover, the president of the Republic of China, Chiang Kai-shek, had already appointed a committee headed by Ch'en Yi 陳儀 to take over the island's administration in 1945. As the first administrator of Taiwan, Ch'en worked with the Taiwan Garrison Command 警備司令部 to ensure a smooth transition of power. After Emperor Hirohito announced Japan's surrender, and before the ROC's administration could be put into place, a dangerous political vacuum ensued. Nonetheless, Taiwan's social order was well maintained under the temporary self-governance committee composed of local leaders and members of the intelligentsia. In late September 1945, before the Japanese formally surrendered Taiwan, ROC armies arrived at Keelung, Tsoying 左營, Kaohsiung, Tamsui, and Taipei and were heartily welcomed. However, the first group of ROC troops sent to take over Taiwan were poorly trained and undisciplined while the major fighting component of Nationalist troops remained on the Chinese mainland to fight the growing communist insurgency. Government inefficiency in Taiwan was a serious problem. Opportunists and carpetbaggers tried to seek financial and political advantages. Smuggling was rampant. Taiwan residents, both long-time natives and new arrivals from the mainland, were upset by the unjust appropriation of personal property, shortages of daily necessities, galloping inflation and unchecked profiteering.

It was under such conditions that the February 28 Incident 二二八事件 took place in 1947. An old woman had been injured while protesting against the expropriation of untaxed cigarettes she was selling in the T'aip'ing Ting 太平町 section of Taipei. The public was deeply angered when a passerby was shot in the commotion and the assailant was given shelter in a nearby police station. Early the next morning, the Tobacco & Wine Monopoly Bureau 煙酒公賣局 was besieged by thousands of people demanding the punishment of the murderer. When it became apparent that no official response was forthcoming, the crowd attacked the bureau and rioting soon spread throughout the island.

Lin Hsien-t'ang 林獻堂, a public opinion leader, and other prominent members of the Taiwan elite organized the February 28 Incident Management Committee 二二八事件處理委員會 on March 2, 1947, and proposed democratic elections for county chiefs and city mayors; the abolition of government monopolies; government guarantees for human life and property; and protection of the freedom of speech, publication, and assembly. Governor Ch'en Yi, who had proposed the formation of the Committee in the first place, turned to the Chinese mainland for help. On March 9, 1947, the 21st division of the Nationalist army landed at Keelung. By March 14, many local leaders and the members of the Management Committee had been arrested. These people included landowners, entrepreneurs, doctors, and teachers. A considerable number of them were executed, but some escaped overseas. Ch'en Yi was later replaced by a moderate administrator.

In 1949, the communists launched an all-out offensive on the Chinese mainland. On May 19, the Taiwan Garrison Command proclaimed the *Emergency Decree* 戒嚴令 (martial law) throughout Taiwan Province. By early 1949, a force of about 300,000 Nationalist troops was stationed in Taiwan. As the ROC government refused to compromise on the Chinese communists' eight-point program, fierce fighting broke out in Kwangtung and Amoy in October, and the ROC government was forced to move to Taiwan in December.

At first the situation on Taiwan was very tenuous, but, with the outbreak of the Korean War in late June 1950, US President Harry S. Truman ordered the US Seventh Fleet to protect Taiwan against Chinese communist attack. The US also provided Taiwan with economic aid. On March 3, 1954, Foreign Minister George K.C. Yeh 葉公超 and US Secretary of State John Foster Dulles exchanged instruments of ratification of the Sino-American Mutual Defense Treaty in Taipei to formally substantiate the neutralization of the Taiwan Straits. The international community sided with Taiwan and the internal situation began to stabilize. On August 23, 1958, the Chinese communists began shelling Quemoy in the Battle of the Taiwan Straits 八二三戰役. The communist attack was repulsed, and, on October 23, 1958, the US and the Republic of China issued a joint communiqué reaffirming solidarity between the two countries.

The ensuing decade brought a period of relative stability to the ROC. President Chiang Kai-shek used the time to re-invigorate Taiwan's economy. Land reform and a series of four-year plans undertaken during the 1950s and 1960s drastically reduced the inflation of wartime years and rapidly increased the island's productivity. When government leaders realized the economic bottleneck presented by the narrow base of Taiwan's domestic economy, they quickly opted for an export promotion strategy. As a resource-poor but labor-rich country, the ROC began with various light manufactured exports produced by labor-intensive industries. Like many other developing countries, the ROC suffered from a shortage of capital at the early stage of economic development and relied on US aid. Yet by 1965 Taiwan's economy was doing so well that foreign assistance was no longer required. When the US aid program was terminated, the ROC's savings rate was a tremendous 19.5 percent of the GNP. Between 1962 and 1985, Taiwan's economy grew by an average of 9.3 percent per year, over two times the average economic growth rate of industrialized countries during this period. (For detailed information on the economic development in the ROC in recent years, please see Chapter 10, Economy, and Chapter 11, Finance and Banking.)

The 1970s were a period of continued economic growth but political and diplomatic challenge. The ROC economy managed to ride out global recessions sparked by two oil embargoes but the global political environment was changing quickly. At the end of 1970, a campaign was launched to prevent the US from transferring the Tiaoyüt'ai Islets 釣魚臺列嶼 to Japanese sovereignty together with the Ryukyu Islands. As the campaign was under way, the US signaled a sudden change in its relationship with the ROC by stating that the "status of Taiwan remained undecided." In 1971, President Chiang Kai-shek announced that the ROC would withdraw from the United Nations rather than share a seat with the Chinese communists. The next year the ROC severed diplomatic relations with Japan when it recognized communist China, and, in the same year, US President Richard Nixon visited the Chinese mainland. President Chiang passed away on April 5, 1975, and was succeeded by the vice president Yen Chia-kan 嚴家淦. In the next presidential elections, held on March 21, 1978, Chiang Kai-shek's son Chiang Ching-kuo 蔣經國 was elected president of the ROC. He had been in office less than eight months when, in December 1978, President Jimmy Carter announced that the United States would shift diplomatic recognition from the Republic of China to the "People's Republic of China."

As the turbulent 1970s drew to a close, few international observers would have predicted that the ROC would continue to prosper, and yet, President Chiang Ching-kuo was able to stabilize the situation by implementing major infrastructure projects, expanding trade ties with other countries, and modernizing the ROC's defensive arsenal. President Chiang will be best remembered, though, for his commitment to rejuvenating the democratic functions of the ROC polity. Before passing away due to heart failure on January 13, 1988, President Chiang oversaw the lifting of the *Emergency Decree*, which had been the legal basis for the enforcement of martial law in the ROC for over three decades.

President Chiang's successor, President Lee Teng-hui 李登輝 has sworn to uphold his predecessor's legacy of democratic reform. After taking office, President Lee abolished the *Temporary Provisions Effective During the Period of Communist Rebellion* 動員勘亂時期臨時條款 adopted in 1948 to give the government more power during politically unstable periods. The abolishment of these provisions, in effect, reinstated parts of the ROC Constitution that had been frozen during the period of communist rebellion. Since then certain articles of the ROC Constitution have been amended and new articles added to facilitate further political reforms. Among other things, these amendments have paved the way for the direct election of the entire National Assembly 國民大會 and Legislature 立法院 as well as the president and vice president of the republic.

The ROC's efforts at democratization have borne fruit in recent years. Scores of new political parties have sprung up since the ban on their establishment was lifted in 1989. All members of both the National Assembly and the Legislature have been chosen by direct popular election since 1991 and 1992, respectively. On December 3, 1994, the governor of Taiwan Province and the mayors of Taipei and Kaohsiung cities were directly elected for the first time. And with the first direct popular presidential election in the history of China, held on March 23, 1996, full-fledged democracy was achieved in Taiwan. (For more information on the ROC government and its political system, please see Chapter 5, Government, and Chapter 6, Political Parties and Elections.)

The ROC is the inheritor of a historical tradition stretching back continuously for thousands of years. Those familiar with Chinese history will recognize that the Republic of China is a sovereign nation. And yet, the degree of economic prosperity and political democracy enjoyed in Taiwan are, in many ways, unprecedented in Chinese history. The process by which the ROC arrived at its present level of achievement is often referred to as a "quiet revolution."

Further Reading (in Chinese unless otherwise noted):

Erh-erh-pa shih-chien wen-hsien chi-lu 二二八事件文獻集錄 (The Historiographical Records of the February 28, 1947 Event). 2 vols. Taichung: The Historical Research Commission of Taiwan Province, 1991.

Fairbank, J.K. *China: A New History* (in English). Cambridge, Mass.: Belknap Press of Harvard University Press, 1992.

Hsieh Chiao-min. *Taiwan—Ilha Formosa* (in English). Washington: Butterworths, 1964.

Huang Ta-shou 黃大受. *Chung-kuo chin-tai shih-kang* 中國近代史綱 (Essentials of Modern Chinese History). Taipei: Wu Nan Publishing Company, 1991 edition.

———. *T'ai-wan shih-kang* 台灣史綱 (Essentials of Taiwan History). Taipei: San Min Bookstore, 1990 edition.

Liu Ning-yen 劉寧顏, ed. *T'ai-wan shih-chi yüan-liu* 臺灣史蹟源流 (The Roots of Taiwan's History). Taichung: The Historical Commission of Taiwan Province, 1981.

Ronning, Chester. *A Memoir of China in Revolution—From the Boxer Rebellion to the People's Republic* (in English). New York: Pantheon Books, 1974.

Shêng Ch'ing-yi 盛清沂, Wang Shih-lang 王詩琅, Kao Shu-fan 高樹藩, and Lin Heng-tao 林衡道. *T'ai-wan-shih* 臺灣史 (A History of Taiwan). Taichung: The Historical Research Commission of Taiwan Province, 1977.

Spence, Jonathan D. *The Search for Modern China* (in English). New York: W.W. Norton & Company, 1990.

Tai Kuo-hui 戴國煇. *T'ai-wan-shih yen-chiu* 臺灣史研究 (Studies in Taiwan History). Taipei: Yuan Liu Publishing Company, 1985.

Twitchett, Denis. *The Cambridge History of China* (in English). London: Cambridge University Press, 1980.

Weiss, H., & B.J. Weiss. *Hsien-min te tsu-chi* 先民的足跡 (The Authentic Story of Taiwan; Chinese-English bilingual). Taipei: Mappamundi Co., Ltd. Taiwan, 1991.

Yeh Chên-hui 葉振輝. *Ch'ing-chi T'ai-wan k'ai-pu chih yen-chiu* 清季臺灣開埠之研究 (The Opening of Formosa to Foreign Commerce). Taipei, 1985.

5.
Government

新任部會首長聯合記者會

Above: Cabinet members hold a joint press conference on June 10, 1996, after being appointed to their new posts by the ROC's first popularly elected president.

Right: The Executive Yuan Council 行政院會 in its weekly Thursday morning session, presided over by Vice President Lien Chan 連戰 in his additional capacity as Premier.

Previous page: The pomp and circumstance of the annual presidential address on the ROC's Double Tenth National Day makes for a memorable mid-Autumn holiday.

5 Government

Freedom and democracy are more than just slogans in the Republic of China. They are the tangible results of creatively applying constitutional government through the rule of law. In this chapter, we set forth a general outline of the ROC Constitution and the government which embodies its spirit. First, the essential concepts of the Constitution are explained, followed by a description of various parts of the highest level of government, the central government. This chapter concludes with a brief sketch of the workings of government at the provincial, municipal, and local levels. Readers may locate information on a specific government agency most quickly by first referring to the Index at the back of this book.

The Constitution

The Republic of China, founded on the Three Principles of the People, shall be a democratic republic of the people, to be governed by the people, and for the people. (Article 1, *Constitution of the Republic of China*)

The ROC Constitution is based on the Principles of Nationalism, Democracy, and Social Well-being formulated by Dr. Sun Yat-sen, the Founding Father of the Republic of China. His political doctrine is known as the Three Principles of the People 三民主義.

The first Principle of Nationalism 民族 advocates not only equal treatment and sovereign status for the Republic of China in the interdependent commonwealth of nations but also equality for all ethnic groups within the nation. The Principle of Democracy 民權 assures each citizen the right to exercise the political and civil liberties due to him or her. The Principle of Democracy is the guiding doctrine behind the organization and structure of the ROC government. The Principle of Social Well-being 民生 states that the powers granted to the government must ultimately serve the welfare of the people by building a prosperous economy and a just society. The three principles have extensively shaped current policies and legislation in areas ranging from education to land reforms, from social welfare to relations with mainland China, and more recently, in increasingly extensive political and economic liberalization.

The Constitution spells out the rights, duties, and freedoms of the people, the overall direction for political, economic, and social policies, and the organization and structure of the government. (The full text of the Constitution and its ten *Additional Articles* can be found in Appendix II.)

Constitutional Rights and Freedoms

The ROC Constitution guarantees various rights and freedoms to its people. Modeled after American constitutional concepts, the rights include equality, work, livelihood, and property, as well as the four political powers of suffrage, recall, initiative, and referendum. In return, the people have the duty to pay taxes and perform military service as prescribed by law. Obtaining an education is considered both a right and a duty of the people.

The people are also endowed with the basic freedoms of speech, residence, travel, assembly, confidential communication, religion, and association. Personal freedom is also guaranteed. Rights and freedoms not specified in the Constitution are also protected if they do not violate social order and public interest.

The law may not restrict freedoms stipulated in the Constitution unless the freedoms are abused, the freedoms of others are infringed upon, or public order is threatened. Even in these situations, the Constitution permits restrictions on constitutional rights and freedoms only under certain circumstances. This is designed to prevent legislative bodies from making laws that overstep the limits set down in the Constitution. Restrictions on constitutional freedoms are valid only if contained in legislation necessary to prevent restrictions against the freedom of others, to respond to emergencies, to maintain social order, or to enhance social interest. In any case, arrest, trial, and punishment must be implemented in strict accordance with proper legal procedures. If human rights are violated by the gov-

ROC Constitutional Amendment

On May 1, 1991, the ROC president promulgated ten *Additional Articles of the Constitution of the Republic of China* 中華民國憲法增修條文 that had just been passed by the First National Assembly. The articles were designed to reflect the fact that Taiwan and the Chinese mainland are administered by two separate political entities. The *Additional Articles* also provided the legal basis for the election of the Second National Assembly and the Second Legislative Yuan, which would be representative of Taiwan, a nationwide constituency covering the mainland, and overseas Chinese.

After the Second National Assembly assumed office on January 1, 1992, its delegates adopted *Additional Articles* 11 through 18. These articles were promulgated on May 28, laying the groundwork for the popular election of the president and vice president of the Republic, the transformation of the Control Yuan from a parliamentary body to a quasi-judicial organ, and the implementation of provincial and local self-governance.

Then, on July 28, 1994, the Second National Assembly revised the 18 *Additional Articles*, reducing the number to ten. Under the newly revised *Additional Articles of the Constitution:*

- The president (beginning with the ninth-term president since the Constitution went into effect in 1947) will be directly elected by the entire voting population in the Taiwan area.
- The presidential and vice presidential candidates will run on a single ticket.
- Overseas nationals may vote in the election for the president and vice president.
- The president can appoint and dismiss without the countersignature of the premier those officials who were appointed with the consent of the National Assembly or the Legislature.
- The National Assembly may have a speaker and a deputy speaker.
- The dismissal of the premier may take effect only after the new nominee to this office has been confirmed by the Legislature.

ernment, the victims are entitled to compensation by the state.

Government, Economic, and Social Policies

The ROC Constitution contains directives for formulating legislation and procedures addressing important government, economic, and social issues. Chapter XIII of the Constitution, titled "Fundamental National Policies" 基本國策, contains articles on national defense, foreign policy, national economy, social security, education and culture, and frontier regions. The policies outline the government's responsibility to provide necessary support for the welfare and well-being of the people and also to foster an environment that will enable them to engage in various business and professional activities. Article 9 of the *Additional Articles of the Constitution* prescribes specific policy orientations on several modern issues including scientific development, industrial upgrading, environmental and ecological pro-

tection, national health insurance, and the elimination of sexual discrimination.

Governmental Structure

The ROC government is divided into three main levels: central, provincial/municipal, and county/city, each of which has well-defined powers. The central government consists of the Office of the President 總統府, the National Assembly 國民大會, and five governing branches (called "yuan" 院), namely the Executive Yuan 行政院, the Legislative Yuan 立法院, the Judicial Yuan 司法院, the Examination Yuan 考試院, and the Control Yuan 監察院.

At the provincial level, the provincial governments exercise administrative responsibility. Since the ROC government administers only Taiwan Province and two counties in Fukien Province, only two provincial governments are currently operational—the Taiwan Provincial Government 台灣省政府 and the Fukien Provincial Government 福建省政府. The Fukien Provincial Government oversees the regional affairs of Kinmen

Organization of the Central Government

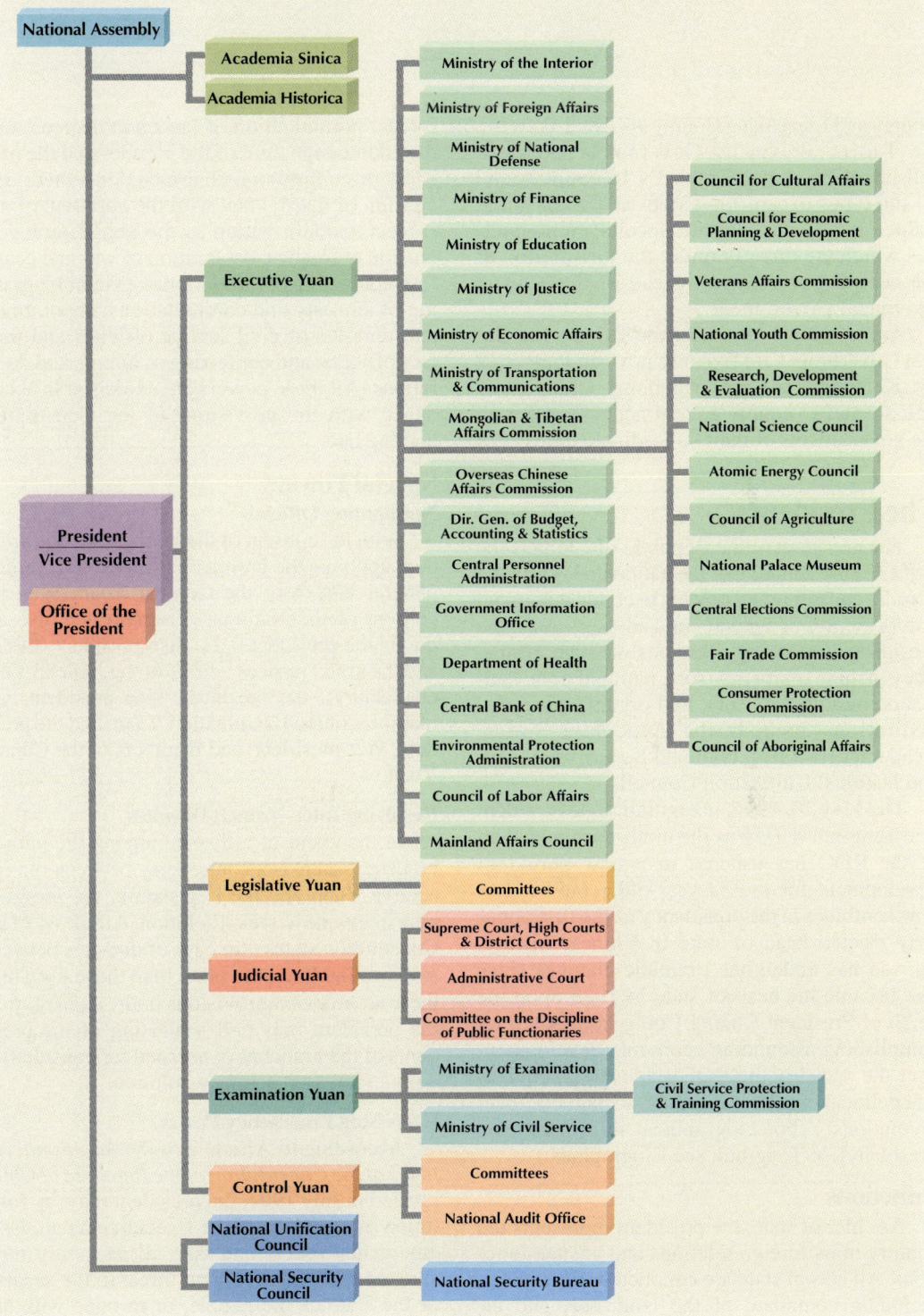

National Assembly

Academia Sinica

Academia Historica

President / Vice President

Office of the President

Executive Yuan
- Ministry of the Interior
- Ministry of Foreign Affairs
- Ministry of National Defense
- Ministry of Finance
- Ministry of Education
- Ministry of Justice
- Ministry of Economic Affairs
- Ministry of Transportation & Communications
- Mongolian & Tibetan Affairs Commission
- Overseas Chinese Affairs Commission
- Dir. Gen. of Budget, Accounting & Statistics
- Central Personnel Administration
- Government Information Office
- Department of Health
- Central Bank of China
- Environmental Protection Administration
- Council of Labor Affairs
- Mainland Affairs Council

- Council for Cultural Affairs
- Council for Economic Planning & Development
- Veterans Affairs Commission
- National Youth Commission
- Research, Development & Evaluation Commission
- National Science Council
- Atomic Energy Council
- Council of Agriculture
- National Palace Museum
- Central Elections Commission
- Fair Trade Commission
- Consumer Protection Commission
- Council of Aboriginal Affairs

Legislative Yuan
- Committees

Judicial Yuan
- Supreme Court, High Courts & District Courts
- Administrative Court
- Committee on the Discipline of Public Functionaries

Examination Yuan
- Ministry of Examination
- Ministry of Civil Service
  - Civil Service Protection & Training Commission

Control Yuan
- Committees
- National Audit Office

National Unification Council

National Security Council
- National Security Bureau

County and Lienchiang County 連江縣. Likewise, the Taiwan Provincial Government exercises full jurisdiction over Taiwan's 16 counties and all the cities except for Taipei and Kaohsiung. Taipei and Kaohsiung are special municipalities which are directly under the jurisdiction of the central government instead of the Taiwan Provincial Government.

At the local level, under the Taiwan Provincial Government are five city governments 市政府: Keelung, Hsinchu, Taichung, Chiayi, and Tainan; and 16 county governments 縣政府 with the governments of their subordinate cities 縣轄市.

The Presidency

The president of the Republic of China is the highest representative of the nation and is granted specific constitutional powers to conduct national affairs. Scores of agencies and advisors assist the president in reaching decisions on state affairs. They include senior advisors, national policy advisors, military advisors, and organizations and institutions such as the Academia Sinica, Academia Historica, National Security Council, and National Unification Council.

The May 20, 1996, inauguration of President Lee Teng-hui 李登輝 as the ninth-term president of the ROC has ushered in a new period of development for the 84-year-old republic. Lee now continues in the presidency as the first popularly elected head of state in Chinese history. Taiwan has undergone dramatic changes since Lee became the head of state in 1988 upon the death of President Chiang Ching-kuo. After accomplishing astounding economic development over the decades, the ROC achieved an equivalent political miracle—the much acclaimed "quiet revolutions." (For biographical information on President Lee Teng-hui, see Biographies.)

Functions

As chief of state, the president represents the country in its foreign relations and at state functions. All acts of state are conducted in his name, including command of the land, sea, and air forces; promulgation of laws and decrees, with the countersignature of the premier and the ministers or commission chairmen concerned; declaration of martial law with the approval of and subject to confirmation by the Legislature; conclusion of treaties; declaration of war and cease-fire; convening of the National Assembly; granting of amnesty and commutations; appointment and removal of civil service officials and military officers; and conferring of honors and decorations. All these powers are exercised in accordance with the provisions of the Constitution and the law.

Special Powers
Nominating Officials

With the consent of the Legislature, the president appoints the premier as well as the auditor-general 審計長 of the Control Yuan. With the consent of the National Assembly, he also appoints the president 院長, vice president 副院長, and the grand justices 大法官 of the Judicial Yuan (Judiaciary); the president, vice president, and members of the Examination Yuan; and the president, vice president, and members of the Control Yuan.

Resolving Inter-Branch Disputes

In the event of a dispute among the various branches, such as a controversy between the Executive Yuan and the Legislature, the president may intervene to seek a solution. Article 44 of the Constitution states: "In case of disputes between two or more branches other than those for which there are relevant provisions in the Constitution, the president may call a meeting of the presidents of the branches concerned for consultation with a view to reaching a solution."

Exercising Emergency Powers

According to Article 2 of the *Additional Articles of the Constitution of the Republic of China* revised in July 1994, the president may, by resolution of a council of the Executive Yuan, issue emergency orders and take all necessary measures to avert an imminent threat to the security of the state or the people, or to cope with any serious financial or economic crisis, without being subject to the restrictions prescribed in Article 43 of the Constitution. However, such orders must, within 10 days of issuance, be presented to the Legislature for confirmation. Should the Legislature withhold confirmation, the said emergency orders immediately cease to be valid.

The Office of the President

Administration

The secretary-general to the president takes general charge of the affairs of the Office of the President and directs and supervises staff members. He is assisted by two deputy secretaries-general.

The bureaus and offices under the Office of the President perform the following functions: The First Bureau 第一局 is in charge of promulgation of laws and decrees, drafting and safekeeping of confidential documents, and other general political affairs, while the bureau director also serves as chancellor of the national seal; the Second Bureau 第二局 is in charge of information systems and transmission of documents; the Third Bureau 第三局 is in charge of protocol and awarding honors, making and distributing official seals, publications, and other administrative and technical affairs; the Code Office 機要室 is in charge of telegraphic correspondence and national archives; the Office of the Guards 侍衛室 is in charge of security. A Department of Public Affairs 公共事務室, set up in January 1996, is in charge of public relations.

Subordinate Offices

There are four institutions under the direct administrative supervision of the Office of the President: Academia Sinica, Academia Historica, the National Unification Council, and the National Security Council.

The Academia Sinica 中央研究院, the leading research institution in the ROC, was established in Nanking on June 9, 1928. Its two basic missions are to conduct scientific research, and to direct, coordinate, and promote scientific research throughout the ROC. Although it is an organic unit of the government, the Academia Sinica enjoys virtually independent status. The most important body of the Academia Sinica is the Assembly of Members 院士會議. Members, commonly known as "Academicians" 院士, are elected for life from among Chinese scholars of distinction. Their duties include formulating national policies on research and pursuing specific research at the request of the government. As of mid-1996, the Academia Sinica had 22 institutes (four of them still preparatory offices) staffed by approximately 800 full-time research fellows.

The Academia Historica 國史館 is responsible for preserving documents and conducting research in modern Chinese history, particularly that of the republican period. The academy has a collection of 7.5 million publications and national records, mainly from the Office of the President, the Executive Yuan, provincial and local governments, plus some personal and other archives. Most of the records are open to the staff of Academia Historica and researchers.

Founded in 1990, the National Unification Council 國家統一委員會 now consists of 32 leaders in various fields, from both the government and private sectors, organized into task groups. The NUC recommends national unification policies to the president, helps the government to devise a national unification framework, and builds consensus at all levels of society and in all political parties concerning the issue of national unification. The NUC has already approved the *Guidelines for National Unification* 國家統一綱領, which are the highest directives governing ROC mainland policy.

The National Security Council 國家安全會議, established in 1967 and chaired by the president, is an advisory body to the president. The main functions of the National Security Council and its subsidiary organ, the National Security Bureau 國家安全局, are to determine the ROC's national security policies and to assist in planning the ROC's security strategy.

The National Assembly

The National Assembly 國民大會 is more limited in scope than the parliament or congress of a western democracy. In the Republic of China, the role of "parliament" is jointly filled by the National Assembly and the Legislature.

The functions of the National Assembly are: (1) to elect the vice president when the said office becomes vacant; (2) to recall the president and the vice president; (3) to pass a resolution on the impeachment of the president or vice president instituted by the Control Yuan; (4) to amend the Constitution; (5) to vote in the exercise of its rights of referendum on proposed constitutional amendments submitted by the Legislature; (6) to exercise the power of consent to confirm the appointment of personnel nominated by the president of the ROC.

The president may issue a notice of convocation when the National Assembly is to exercise its powers prescribed in item (1) or items (4) through (6), or when requested by no less than two-fifths of its members. The speaker of the National Assembly (or the president of the Legislature prior to the establishment of this office) may convoke a session for exercising the powers prescribed in item (2) or (3). The National Assembly is required to implement initiatives and referendums decided by the people of the Republic of China in accordance with Article 17 of the Constitution.

Another unique power of the National Assembly is spelled out in Article 4 of the Constitution: "The territory of the Republic of China within its existing national boundaries shall not be altered except by resolution of the National Assembly."

The assembly is led by a speaker and deputy speaker, both of whom are chosen by the assembly from among its members.

Delegates

Members of the National Assembly are elected according to Article 1 of the *Additional Articles of the Constitution* without being subject to the restrictions in Articles 26 and 135 of the Constitution. (1) Two members are elected from each special municipality 直轄市, and each county or city in the free area of the nation. However, where the population exceeds 100,000 persons, one member is added for each additional 100,000 persons.

(2) Three members each are elected from among lowland and highland aborigines in the free area of the nation. (3) Twenty members are elected from among Chinese citizens who reside abroad. (4) Eighty members are elected to represent the nationwide constituency.

Delegates representing overseas Chinese or the nationwide constituency are elected in accordance with a party-list proportional representation system. If the number of seats allotted to a special municipality, county or city covered under item (1) above, or if the number of seats won by a political party under item (3) or (4) above is between five and ten, then one of the seats stipulated in the pertaining paragraph is reserved for a female candidate.

In 1996, an election for the Third National Assembly was held in accordance with the old version of the *Additional Articles of the Constitution of the Republic of China*. Of the 334 members elected, 234 delegates were from the Taiwan area, with an additional 80 members representing a nationwide constituency and 20 representing overseas Chinese.

The four-year tenure for the Third National Assembly began on May 20, 1996. The Assembly convened on July 4, 1996, and met for 40 days, electing a speaker, Fredrick Chien 錢復, and a deputy speaker, Shieh Lung-sheng 謝隆盛, listening to a report on the State of the Nation by President Lee, and voting on presidential nominations for positions in the Examination Yuan and Control Yuan.

Five Government Branches

The ROC Constitution provides for a central government with five "yuan" (branches)—the Executive Yuan, the Legislative Yuan (Legislature), the Judicial Yuan (Judiciary), the Examination Yuan, and the Control Yuan.

Executive Yuan

The Executive Yuan 行政院 has a president, usually referred to as the premier of the ROC; a vice premier; a number of ministers and chairmen of commissions; and five to seven ministers of state. The premier is nominated by the president of the Republic. If the premier resigns or if his office becomes vacant during the recess of the Legislature, his functions are temporarily exercised by the vice premier but the president of the Republic must, within 40 days, request a meeting of the Legislature to confirm his nominee for the vacancy. The vice premier, ministers, and chairmen are appointed by the president of the Republic on the recommendation of the premier. In addition to supervising the operations of the various subordinate agencies of the Executive Yuan, the premier is also responsible for the following: (1) performing the duties of the president of the Republic in the event of vacancies in both the presidency and the vice presidency. This caretaker duty is limited to three months; (2) presenting administrative policies and reports to the Legislature and responding, either orally or in writing, to the interpellations of legislators; (3) countersigning laws and decrees proclaimed by the president of the Republic; and (4) requesting, with the approval of the president, the Legislature to reconsider its resolutions.

Dr. Lien Chan 連戰 has served as ROC premier since February 23, 1993. The Lien Cabinet resigned in January 1996. Dr. Lien was then renominated by the president and confirmed by the newly-elected Third Legislative Yuan on February 23. After his March 23 election and May 20 swearing-in as ROC vice president, Dr. Lien continued to serve as premier. This is the third time in the history of the ROC that one man has concurrently held the positions of vice president and premier.

There are three levels of subordinate organizations under the Executive Yuan: the Executive Yuan Council 行政院院會; executive organizations, i.e., the eight ministries, the Mongolian and Tibetan Affairs Commission 蒙藏委員會 and the Overseas Chinese Affairs Commission 僑務委員會; and subordinate departments, including the Directorate General of Budget, Accounting and Statistics 主計處, the Government Information Office 新聞局, and other special commissions and ad hoc committees.

Executive Yuan Council

The Executive Yuan Council is a policymaking organization that comprises the premier, who presides over its meetings, the vice premier, ministers of state, the heads of the ROC's eight ministries, and the heads of the Mongolian and Tibetan Affairs Commission and the Overseas Chinese Affairs Commission. According to Article 58 of the Constitution, the Council discusses and decides on statutory and budgetary bills and bills concerning martial law, amnesty, declarations of war, conclusion of peace or treaties, and other important affairs, which are to be submitted to the Legislature, as well as matters of common concern to the various ministries and commissions. The Council may invite heads of other organizations under the Executive Yuan to attend council meetings to answer any questions that may arise pertaining to the affairs under their jurisdiction. The secretary-general and the deputy secretary-general may attend the meetings, but only as observers.

Ministries and Other Organizations

There are eight ministries under the Executive Yuan. They are the ministries of the Interior 內政, Foreign Affairs 外交, National Defense 國防, Finance 財政, Education 教育, Justice 法務, Economic Affairs 經濟, and Transportation and Communications 交通.

In addition to the Mongolian and Tibetan Affairs Commission and the Overseas Chinese Affairs Commission, a number of commissions and subordinate organizations have been formed with the resolution of the Executive Yuan Council and the Legislature to meet new demands and handle new affairs. Examples include the Environmental Protection Administration 環境保護署, which was set up in 1987 as public awareness of pollution control rose; the Mainland Affairs Council 大陸委員會, which was established in 1990 to handle the thawing of relations between Taiwan and the Chinese mainland; the Fair Trade Commission 公平交易委員會, which was established in 1992 to promote a fair trade system; and the Consumer Protection Commission 消費者保

護委員會, which was set up in July 1994 to study and review basic policies on consumer protection.

Relationship with the Legislature

The consent of the Legislature is essential to the appointment of the premier by the president of the Republic. The Executive Yuan has the duty to present the Legislature with an annual policy statement and a report on administration. When the Legislature is in session, its members have the right to interpellate the premier, ministers, and chairmen of commissions of the Executive Yuan.

If the Legislature disagrees with an important policy of the Executive Yuan, it may, by resolution, request the Executive Yuan to alter it. Confronted with the Legislature's resolution, the Executive Yuan may, with the approval of the president of the Republic, request the Legislature's reconsideration. If, after reconsideration, two-thirds of the attending members of the Legislature uphold the original resolution, the premier must either abide by the same or tender his resignation. Similar procedures apply if the Executive Yuan deems a resolution on a statutory, budgetary, or treaty bill passed by the Legislature difficult to execute. The Executive Yuan shall, three months prior to the end of each fiscal year, present to the Legislature the budgetary bill for the following fiscal year.

Relationship with the Judicial Yuan

If problems arise in the enforcement of provincial self-governance regulations, the premier organizes a committee with the presidents of the Legislature, Judiciary, Examination Yuan, and Control Yuan in a joint effort to solve them.

Relationship with the Examination Yuan

Public functionaries to be appointed by the Executive Yuan must be qualified by examinations held by the Examination Yuan.

Relationship with the Control Yuan

The Control Yuan may, in the exercise of its powers of control, request the Executive Yuan and its ministries and subordinate organizations to submit for its perusal original orders issued by them.

The Control Yuan may set up a number of committees to investigate the activities of the Executive Yuan and its ministries and subordinate organizations to determine whether they are guilty of violation of the law or dereliction of duty. It may propose corrective measures and forward them to the Executive Yuan and the agencies concerned.

The Executive Yuan shall, within four months after the end of each fiscal year, present final accounts of revenues and expenditures to the Control Yuan for auditing.

Prosecutorial Arm

The Ministry of Justice 法務部 handles legal affairs for the Executive Yuan, including prosecution procedures, investigation of crimes, and management of prisons and rehabilitation programs. It consists of departments of Prosecution 檢察司, Prison and Detention House Administration 監所司, Rehabilitation and Civil Liberties 保護司, and Legal Affairs 法律事務司. The Investigation Bureau 調查局 is also under its jurisdiction.

Legislative Yuan

The Legislative Yuan 立法院 (Legislature) is the highest legislative organ of the state, comprising popularly elected representatives who serve for three years and are eligible for re-election. Elections for the Third Legislative Yuan were held in December 1995.

Functions and Powers

In accordance with the Constitution, the Legislature has the following functions and powers:

• General legislative power: The Legislature exercises legislative power on behalf of the people. The term "law" as used in the Constitution denotes any legislative bill passed by the Legislature and promulgated by the president of the Republic.

• Confirmation of emergency orders: Emergency orders and measures proclaimed by the president in the case of an imminent threat to national security or a serious financial or economic crisis during the recess of the Legislature are presented to the Legislature for confirmation within ten days of issuance.

- Hearing reports on administration and revision of government policy: The Executive Yuan presents to the Legislature a statement of its administrative policies and a report on its administration. If the Legislature does not concur in any important policy of the Executive Yuan, it may, by resolution, request the Executive Yuan to alter such a policy.

- Examination of budgetary bills and audit reports: The Legislature has the power to decide by resolution upon budgetary bills, which the Executive Yuan is required to present to the legislature three months before the beginning of each fiscal year. The auditor-general, within three months after presentation by the Executive Yuan of the final accounts of revenues and expenditures, completes the auditing thereof in accordance with the law and submits an auditing report to the Legislature.

- Right of consent: The premier and the auditor-general in the Control Yuan are nominated and, with the consent of the Legislature, appointed by the president of the Republic.

- Amendment of the Constitution: Upon the proposal of one-fourth of the members of the Legislature, and by a resolution of three-fourths of the members present at a meeting having a quorum of three-fourths of the members of the Yuan, a bill for amendment of the Constitution may be drawn up and submitted to the National Assembly by way of referendum.

- Settlement of disputes concerning self-governance: The Legislature settles any disputes over items and matters of self-governance in provinces, special municipalities, counties/cities, or other administrative units.

Election and Tenure of Office

According to Article 3 of the *Additional Articles of the Constitution of the Republic of China*, members of the Legislature after 1992 are elected according to the following provisions without being subject to the restrictions in Article 64 of the Constitution. (1) Two members are elected from each province and each special municipality in the free area. Where the population exceeds 200,000 persons, however, one member is added for each additional 100,000 persons; and where the population exceeds one million persons, one member will be added for each additional 200,000 persons. (2) Three members each are elected from among lowland and highland aborigines in the free area of the nation. (3) Six members are elected from among Chinese citizens who reside abroad. (4) Thirty members are elected to represent the nationwide constituency.

The members covered under item (3) or four (4) above are elected by way of party-list proportional representation. If the number of seats allotted to a province or special municipality covered under item (1) above; or if the number of seats won by a political party under item (3) or (4) above is between five and ten, then at least one of the seats stipulated in the pertaining item must be filled by a female candidate. Where the number exceeds ten, at least one seat out of each additional ten must be awarded to a female candidate.

Procedures pertaining to the election of members are conducted openly by universal, equal, and direct suffrage, and by single and secret ballot. The election is completed three months prior to the expiration of the current term. If the voters in a member's precinct feel that their elected representative has not duly performed his or her function, they may, after the member has been in office for six months, file a petition for recall (Article 133 of the Constitution and Article 40 of the *Public Officials Election and Recall Law* 公職人員選舉罷免法).

Immunity and Restrictions

According to Article 73 of the Constitution, "No member of the Legislature shall be held responsible outside the Yuan for opinions expressed or votes cast in the Yuan." This is to protect members from outside threats or disturbances, so that they can express their views and cast ballots freely.

Article 74 of the Constitution stipulates: "No member of the Legislature shall, except in case of *flagrante delicto*, be arrested or detained without the permission of the Legislature." This is to provide members with physical freedom and prevent unlawful arrest or detention, so as not to influence ongoing sessions of the Yuan.

Article 75 of the Constitution reads: "No member of the Legislature shall concurrently hold a government post." This provision is quite different from that which functions in other cabinet systems. Its purpose is the complete separation of legislative from executive power to avoid a monopolization of power by members of the Legislature.

Organization and Functioning

The Legislature operates through sessions of the Yuan, committees, and the secretariat. The Yuan holds two sessions each year and convenes on its own accord. The first session lasts from February to the end of May, and the second from September to the end of December. Whenever necessary, a session may be prolonged. An extraordinary session may be held at the request of no less than one-fourth of its members. Regular sittings of the Legislature require a quorum of one-third of the total membership. Unless otherwise stipulated in the Constitution, resolutions at sittings of the Legislature are adopted by a simple majority vote. In case of a tie, the chairman casts the deciding vote.

In exercising the power of consent in accordance with Article 55 or 104 of the Constitution, the Legislature, after hearing the report of the committee of the whole Yuan, may put the matter to vote. The chairman is elected by and from among the members present at a meeting of the committee of the whole Yuan.

The Legislature has the following ten standing committees: Home and Border Affairs 內政及邊政委員會, Foreign and Overseas Chinese Affairs 外交及僑政委員會, National Defense 國防委員會, Economics 經濟委員會, Finance 財政委員會, Budget 預算委員會, Education 教育委員會, Transportation and Communications 交通委員會, Judiciary 司法委員會, and Organic Laws 法制委員會. Each of the committees is composed of not more than 18 members, and no member may serve on more than one committee. Registration for committee membership may not be withdrawn. The Legislature has also set up the following five special committees: Discipline 紀律委員會, Rules 程序委員會, Accounts 經費稽核委員會, Publications 公報指導委員會, and Constitutional Amendment 修憲委員會.

Judicial Yuan

The Judicial Yuan 司法院 (Judiciary) is the highest judicial organ of the state. It has a president, a vice president, and 15 to 17 grand justices, all appointed by the president of the Republic with the consent of the National Assembly. The subordinate organs of the Judiciary are the Supreme Court, the high courts, the district courts, the Administrative Court, and the Committee on the Discipline of Public Functionaries. The Judiciary exercises administrative supervision of the ROC court system while enforcing compliance by ROC court personnel with constitutionally mandated strictures for juridical independence from the other branches of government.

The Council of Grand Justices

The sixth Council of Grand Justices, 大法官會議 comprising 16 members, assumed office on October 3, 1994, following confirmation by the National Assembly. The grand justices will serve nine-year terms. The Council interprets the Constitution and unifies the interpretation of laws and ordinances. The Council meets thrice a week and holds additional meetings as necessary. Oral proceedings may be held whenever the need arises. After an interpretation of the Constitution or unified interpretation of a law is made, the Judiciary publishes the text of the interpretation, the reasons supporting it, and dissenting opinions, if any. The petitioner and persons concerned are also notified.

Interpretation of the Constitution

From 1948 to mid-September 1996, the Council of Grand Justices rendered 412 interpretations of the Constitution at the request of government agencies, individuals, juridical persons and political parties. Constitutional interpretations are made when there are doubts concerning or disputes over:

• the application of the Constitution;

• the constitutionality of laws, regulations or decrees; and

• the constitutionality of laws governing provincial or county self-governance, and laws and regulations promulgated by provincial or county governments.

Unified Interpretation of Laws and Ordinances

A petition for a unified interpretation of a law or ordinance may be filed with the Council of Grand Justices if:

• a government agency, when applying a law or ordinance, has an interpretation that is different from that already expressed by itself or another government organ, unless it is legally bound to obey the expressed opinion or has the authority to revise it;

• an individual, a juridical person, or a political party whose rights have been infringed upon and who or which believes that the final decision of the court of last resort was based on an interpretation of the applicable law or regulation that is different from that previously adopted in precedents by other courts, but such requests will not be accepted if the petitioner has not yet exhausted all judicial remedies or the opinion adopted in an earlier decision has been altered by a later decision.

The Constitutional Court

In December 1993, the Judiciary formally established a Constitutional Court 憲法法庭 in accordance with Article 13 of the old version of the *Additional Articles of the Constitution* and the revised *Organic Law of the Judicial Yuan* 司法院組織法 to adjudicate cases concerning the dissolution of political parties that have violated the Constitution. The Constitutional Court is composed of the Grand Justices and presided over by its most senior member.

The Ministry of the Interior may, as the agency overseeing political parties, petition the Constitutional Court for the dissolution of a political party whose objectives and activities are found to endanger the existence of the ROC or its free and democratic constitutional order.

Public Functionary Disciplinary Committee

The Control Yuan may impeach a public functionary for malfeasance, dereliction of duty, or any other neglect of duty, or if the head of any of the various branches, ministries or commissions or the highest local administrative head requests a disciplinary measure against a public functionary for the same reasons. The Committee on the Discipline of Public Functionaries 公務員懲戒委員會, under the Judiciary, exercises jurisdiction over such cases.

The committee comprises 9 to 15 senior members, one of whom serves as the chairman. Cases are decided without any outside interference. The committee orders the impeached functionary to submit a written reply within a prescribed period of time and, when it deems necessary, may summon him to appear before the committee to defend himself. Such a conference is not open to the public and its proceedings are kept strictly secret.

There are six disciplinary measures which the committee may order: dismissal, suspension from office, demotion, reduction of salary, demerit, and reprimand. Only dismissal and reprimand are applicable to political appointees.

The ROC Court System

The judicial hierarchy in the Republic of China comprises three levels: district courts and their branches at the lowest level that hear civil and criminal cases in the first instance; high courts and their branches at the intermediate level that hear appeals, as the court of second instance, against judgments of district courts or their branches; and the Supreme Court at the highest appellate level which reviews judgments by lower courts as to their compliance with or violation of pertinent laws or regulations. Thus, issues of fact are decided in the first and second instances, while only issues of law are considered in the third instance. However, there are exceptions to this "three-level and three-instance" system. Criminal cases relating to rebellion, treason, and offenses against friendly relations with foreign states are handled by high courts as the court of first instance; and appeals may be filed with the Supreme Court.

District Courts

There are at present in the Taiwan area 17 district courts 地方法院 and two branch district courts. Each district court has a president, appointed from among the judges, who takes charge of the administrative work of the court. Each court is divided into civil 民事庭, criminal 刑事庭, and summary divisions 民刑事簡易庭. Currently there are 44 summary divisions in the Taiwan area to adjudicate cases that may be disposed of in a prompt and simple manner in comparison to regular proceedings. Summary proceedings are conducted by a single judge in the first instance. Appeals may be filed with the civil or criminal division of the district court for review by a three-judge panel in the second instance.

Specialized divisions may also be set up by district courts to deal with juvenile, family, traffic, financial, and labor cases as well as motions to set aside rulings on the violations of the *Statute for the Maintenance of Social Order* 社會秩序維護法. Cases to be tried and decided by a district court are heard before a single judge, though more important cases may be heard before three judges sitting in council.

High Courts

At present there is one high court 高等法院 in Taipei serving all of Taiwan including the Pescadores, with four branch courts in Taichung, Tainan, Kaohsiung, and Hualien. In the part of Fukien Province under the control of the ROC there is the Kinmen Branch Court of the Fukien High Court 福建高等法院金門分院, which exercises jurisdiction over cases of appeal against judgments or rulings in Kinmen County and Lienchiang County.

A senior judge of the High Court is appointed to serve concurrently as president of the court to take charge of the administrative work of the court and to supervise the administrative work of its subordinate organs.

The High Court is divided into civil, criminal, as well as specialized divisions dealing with juvenile, traffic and labor cases. Each division is composed of a presiding judge and associates. Cases to be tried and decided by the High Court are heard before three judges sitting in council. However, one of the judges may conduct the preliminary proceedings alone.

The High Court and its branches exercise jurisdiction over the following cases:

- civil, criminal, and election cases of appeal against judgments of district courts or their branches as a court of the first instance;
- motions to set aside rulings of district courts or their branches;
- criminal cases relating to rebellion, treason, and offenses against friendly relations with foreign states, acting as a court of the first instance; and
- other lawsuits prescribed by law.

The Supreme Court

Although it lies under the administrative supervision of the Judiciary, the entire ROC court system has juridical independence in criminal and civil matters of law. The Supreme Court 最高法院 is the final level of appeal in the ROC court system.

The Supreme Court has a president, who is responsible for the administrative work of the Court and acts concurrently as a judge. The Supreme Court is divided into seven civil divisions and ten criminal divisions. An appeal may be made to the Supreme Court only on grounds that the decision made is in violation of a law or ordinance. Since the Supreme Court does not decide questions of fact, documentary proceedings are the rule, while oral proceedings are the exception. Cases before the Supreme Court are tried and decided by five judges sitting in council.

The Supreme Court exercises jurisdiction over the following kinds of cases:

- appeals against judgments in civil and criminal cases rendered by high courts or their branches as court of second instance;
- appeals against judgments of high courts or their branches in criminal cases as court of first instance;
- motions to set aside rulings of high courts or their branches in civil and criminal cases;
- appeals against or motions to set aside rulings of district courts or their branches as court of second instance in civil summary proceedings; and
- cases of extraordinary appeal.

The Administrative Court

The Administrative Court 行政法院 has a decidedly different sphere of juridical authority from that of the other courts in the system. Any person who deems that his rights are violated by an administrative action rendered by a government agency may institute administrative proceedings before the Administrative Court. He is entitled to this right if he objects to the decision on an administrative appeal submitted by him in accordance with the *Law of Administrative Appeal* 行政訴訟法, or if no decision is rendered over three months after the submission of his administrative appeal, or over two months of extension after the prescribed period for decision has expired. An administrative action which exceeds the legal authority of the government agency that rendered it or which results from an abuse of power is considered unlawful.

In administrative proceedings, the plaintiff is a private person and the defendant is a governmental agency, both being equally bound by the adjudication of the Administrative Court. Cases before the Administrative Court are tried and decided by five judges sitting in council. The Administrative Court decides questions of both fact and law; it may make investigations and hold oral proceedings. Since the cases have gone through appeal proceedings before the institution of administrative proceedings, adjudication by the Administrative Court is final. However, where there are legitimate grounds, retrial proceedings are permissible. Should a decision by the Administrative Court set aside or alter the original administrative action or decision, under no circumstances will such a decision be less favorable to the plaintiff than the original action or decision.

Examination Yuan

The Examination Yuan 考試院 is responsible for the examination, employment, and management of all civil service personnel in the Republic of China. Specifically, the Examination Yuan oversees all examination-related matters; all matters relating to qualification screening, security of tenure, pecuniary aid in case of death, and the retirement of civil servants; and all legal matters relating to the employment, discharge, performance evaluation, scale of salaries, promotion, transfer, commendation, and reward of civil servants.

The examination system is applicable to all Chinese civil servants, high- or low-ranking, appointed or elected. The system is also applicable to specialized professionals and technicians of Chinese and foreign nationality. The examination function, being exercised solely by the Examination Yuan at the level of the central government, is separated from the executive power and thereby free from partisan influence.

Organization and Functions

The Examination Yuan has a president, a vice president, and 17 members, all of whom are appointed for six-year terms by the president of the ROC with the approval of the National Assembly. The Examination Yuan consists of a council, a secretariat, the Ministry of Examination 考選部, the Ministry of Civil Service 銓敘部, and the Civil Service Protection and Training Commission 公務員保障暨培訓委員會. It also supervises the operations of the Central Personnel Administration 人事行政局 established under the Executive Yuan in 1967.

The Council of the Examination Yuan 考試委員會 is a policymaking organ that decides on all significant matters within the jurisdiction of the Examination Yuan. It is composed of the president, vice president, and 17 members of the

Yuan, the minister of examination, and the minister of civil service.

Various examination boards are formed each year under the chairmanship of either the president, the vice president, or a member of the Examination Yuan. Members of examination boards formulate questions for and grade the examinations. They also determine the number of successful candidates in each examination. In addition, committees may be set up to facilitate the administration of examination and personnel projects.

The Ministry of Examination oversees all civil service, professional, and technological examinations. The Ministry of Civil Service is in charge of the government personnel system throughout the nation.

Examinations

The two main types of government examinations in the ROC are Civil Service Examinations 公務人員考試 and Examinations for Professionals and Technologists 專門職業及技術人員考試. Civil Service Examinations are divided into the following types:

- Senior-grade Civil Service Examinations 高等考試: Divided into Level I, for holders of Ph.D.; Level II, for holders of M.A. and M.S. degrees; and Level III, for holders of B.A. and B.S. degrees and for people who have passed the Senior Qualifying Examinations or those who passed the Junior-grade Civil Service Examinations at least three years prior to taking the exam;
- Junior-grade Civil Service Examinations 普通考試: Primarily for graduates of senior high schools or senior vocational schools and secondarily for those who passed the Junior Qualifying Examinations or those who passed Special Examination D at least three years prior to taking the exam;
- Special Examination A 特種考試（一等）: Corresponding to the Senior-grade Civil Service Examination Level I;
- Special Examination B 特種考試（二等）: Corresponding to the Senior-grade Civil Service Examination Level II;

- Special Examination C 特種考試（三等）: Corresponding to the Senior-grade Civil Service Examination Level III;
- Special Examination D 特種考試（四等）: Corresponding to the Junior-grade Civil Service Examination;
- Special Examination E 特種考試（五等）: Primarily for ROC citizens 18 years of age or older;
- Promotion Examinations 升等考試; and
- Qualifying Examinations 檢定考試.

Examinations for Professionals and Technologists are divided into the following types:

- Junior Examinations 普通考試;
- Senior Examinations 高等考試; and
- Special Examinations 特種考試: including tests for seafarers, harbor pilots, ship surveyors, crew of fishing boats, ship radiogram operators, doctors of Chinese medicine, and nutritionists.

The Ministry of Examination also screens qualifications for candidates running for elected posts, military personnel transferring to the civil service, and Chinese nationals and non-nationals for their technical skills.

Examinations for senior and junior civil servants are conducted every year, every other year, or whenever necessary. Categories of personnel needed, subjects to be tested, and dates are announced by the Ministry of Examination two months before the examination.

Civil Service

At the end of 1995, there were more than 618,100 civil servants in the ROC, 34.2 percent of whom worked in the central government, and about 78 percent of whom were college graduates.

Unlike the political appointees under whom they serve, civil servants are classified into senior (grades 10-14), intermediate (grades 6-9), or junior (grades 1-5) levels. The 14-grade scheme for administrative officials is designed to reflect an employee's abilities, experience, and seniority.

Pay and Benefits

Civil servants receive a salary on a monthly basis. They also recieve annual merit pay and allowances for special duties. An average pay raise of 3 percent for all government employees has been set for fiscal 1997. The government offers subsidies for the education of its employees and their dependents, and for special and emergency financial needs, such as maternity, marriage, funerals, sickness, hospitalization, and injury while on official duty. Health insurance is also available to all government workers under the new National Health Insurance program (see Chapter 15, Public Health).

Retirement from public service may be either voluntary or mandatory. Voluntary retirement is approved if one has reached the age of 60 and served in a government agency for at least five years or, for those under the age of 60, if one has served for 25 full years. Mandatory retirement applies to a civil servant who has served in a government agency more than five years and has reached the age of 65 or is mentally or physically unable to continue to fulfill his duties.

Pensions are calculated on the basis of base pay and years of service. A pension payment may be disbursed either in one lump sum, for those who have served from five to 15 years, or on a monthly basis. Compensation to the bereaved family of a civil servant is provided in the case of death due to disease or accident, or while on official duty.

Control Yuan

The Control Yuan 監察院 is the highest control body of the state, exercising the powers of impeachment, censure, and audit. The Control Yuan was formerly a parliamentary body, with its members elected by provincial and municipal councils. However, constitutional amendments in May 1992 transformed it into a quasi-judicial organization. The new Control Yuan started operations on February 1, 1993. It now has 29 members, including a president and a vice president, all of whom were nominated and, with the consent of the National Assembly, appointed by the president of the ROC, as stipulated in the *Additional Articles* of the Constitution. The term

of office for all members is six years. The president of the Yuan takes overall charge of its affairs and serves as chairman at meetings.

Organization

The Control Yuan Council, which is composed of the president, vice president and 27 other members, is the policymaking body of all the Yuan's significant matters. Meetings are held monthly with the president acting as chairman. The Control Yuan has ten committees that handle cases on domestic affairs, foreign affairs, national defense, finance, economic affairs, education, transportation and communications, judicial affairs, frontier affairs and overseas Chinese affairs. Each Control Yuan member may join three of the ten committees and participate in other committees as a non-voting member. Each committee elects a convener from among its members to handle day-to-day affairs.

Members

Control Yuan members are responsible for correcting government officials at all levels and generally monitoring the government. Members of the Control Yuan must be beyond party affiliation and independently exercise their powers and discharge their responsibilities in accordance with the law. Article 103 of the Constitution also stipulates that "no member of the Control Yuan shall concurrently hold any other public office or engage in any other profession."

Functions

The Constitution defines the Control Yuan as the highest control organ of the Republic. It is vested with the following powers:

The Control Yuan is empowered to institute impeachment proceedings against a public functionary of the central or local government, up to and including the president of the Republic, if it deems that individual to be guilty of dereliction of duty or violation of law. A decision concerning a motion for impeachment requires the concurrence of nine Control Yuan members other than those who initiated the motion. If the case is passed in the Control Yuan it goes to the appropriate authority for action—the Committee on the Discipline of Public Functionaries in the case of a civil servant, the Ministry of National Defense for military personnel, or the National Assembly for the president or vice president of the Republic.

A Control Yuan member may, with the support of three other members, file a written censure against a functionary whose offense he feels requires immediate suspension of duty or penalty. Pending legal proceedings, the superior of a censured functionary must deal with the matter in accordance with the *Law on Discipline of Public Functionaries* 公務員懲戒法 within one month of receiving the written censure.

The Control Yuan may investigate the operations of the Executive Yuan and its subordinate organizations and propose corrective measures, which are examined by relevant committees and referred to the ministry or commission concerned. This body must take appropriate action and report to the Control Yuan in writing.

By provision of the *Control Law* 監察法, the people are empowered to initiate proceedings against public functionaries by filing a written complaint with the Control Yuan. The complaint and any supporting evidence is taken into consideration by the member on duty, who will decide on investigation or other appropriate action.

The members of the Control Yuan or their designated personnel may conduct field investigations of public or private organizations based on people's complaints or press reports regarding dereliction of duty or violation of law. They may also initiate investigations.

The Control Yuan exercises its power of audit through its National Audit Office 審計部, which establishes audit departments in provinces and special municipalities, and sets up county and city audit offices. Audit departments or offices may be established in special government agencies, state-run enterprises, or public institutions.

According to the Constitution, the auditor-general is nominated by the president of the Republic and appointed with the consent of the Legislature. He is responsible for auditing central government expenditures.

The National Audit Office monitors public affairs, properties, institutions, as well as enterprises in which the state owns at least a 50-percent share. Auditing duties and functions include supervision over the execution of all government organization budgets, approval of receipts and disbursements, investigation of cases concerning irregularities and abuse of power in property and financial administration, evaluation of the efficiency of financial administration, decisions on financial responsibilities, and other auditing functions prescribed by law. The audit agencies also monitor the opening of bids, the awarding of contracts, and proceedings concerning the redemption of bonds, and conduct random inspections of ongoing construction projects.

The Control Yuan also established the Department of Assets Disclosure for Public Functionaries 公職人員財產申報處 in August 1993. In accordance with Article 4 of the *Public Functionary Assets Disclosure Law* 公職人員財產申報法, the Control Yuan receives assets disclosure reports from the president and vice president of the Republic, the presidents and vice presidents of the five Yuan, political appointees, paid advisors to the president of the Republic, elected officials at the level of township magistrates or above, and elected representatives of counties and cities under provincial jurisdiction and higher administrative units.

Provincial Government

A provincial government is the highest administrative organ of local self-governance prescribed by the *Constitution of the Republic of China*. Altogether, the ROC Constitution designates 35 provinces (see map on the inside of the front cover), but there is only one complete province under the effective control of the ROC. Thus, the Taiwan Provincial Government is the ROC's only fully active provincial government. The Fukien Provincial Government, headquartered in Kinmen County, enjoys fewer powers than its Taiwan counterpart as some of its powers have been relegated to the Kinmen and Lienchiang county governments.

The Taiwan Provincial Government

The Taiwan Provincial Government 台灣省政府 was established in May 1947. It replaced the Office of the Governor-General, which had been established after the Japanese returned Taiwan to Chinese control in 1945.

The provincial government is headed by a governor, who, prior to December 1994, was nominated by the premier and appointed by the president of the Republic after confirmation by the Taiwan Provincial Assembly. However, following the implementation of the *Self-governance Law for Provinces and Counties* 省縣自治法 in 1994, James C.Y. Soong 宋楚瑜 was elected Taiwan governor in the first-ever popular election for this office in December of the same year. He is assisted by two deputies, one in charge of political affairs and the other administrative affairs. The governor is eligible for re-election to a second term.

The principal responsibilities of the governor include: (1) handling the general administrative affairs of Taiwan; (2) promulgating provincial laws and regulations; (3) supervising the self-governance of the counties/cities under his jurisdiction; (4) repealing or suspending actions by organizations under his jurisdiction or by county/city governments if their actions are against the law, improper, or beyond their authority.

The Taiwan Provincial Government employs some 124,000 people in 13 departments, 13 subordinate agencies, and 20 business operations (see Appendix III, ROC Government Directory).

The Taiwan Provincial Assembly

The legislative power of a province is exercised by the provincial assembly as prescribed by the Constitution and its *Additional Articles*. For the Taiwan Provincial Assembly 台灣省議會, specific functions are stipulated in Article 18 of the *Self-governance Law for Provinces and Counties*:

• to pass provincial statutes;

• to approve the provincial administrative budget;
• to approve the levying of provincial special taxes, temporary taxes, and surtaxes;
• to decide on the disposal of provincial properties;
• to approve the organic laws of the provincial government and provincially-owned enterprises;
• to approve the provincial government's proposals;
• to screen the auditor's reports on provincial accounts;
• to approve proposals made by assembly members;
• to accept petitions from the people; and
• to exercise other powers prescribed by law or endowed by the laws promulgated by the central government.

The ninth and present Taiwan Provincial Assembly convened on December 20, 1994. Its 79 assemblymen, including 16 female members and four aboriginal members, were directly elected by citizens of the 16 counties and the five cities directly under the jurisdiction of the Taiwan Provincial Government. The members of the provincial assembly are elected to a four-year term and eligible for re-election. The assembly elects its speaker and deputy speaker from among its members.

Organization and Functioning

The assembly holds regular sessions not more than 80 days long once every six months. If the proposals and motions cannot be processed during this period, or if it is otherwise necessary, the session may be extended at the request of the provincial governor and the speaker (or over one-third of the membership) and with the approval of the assembly, but the extension may not be longer than ten days. In addition to the regular sessions, the assembly may hold provisional meetings, which may not last more than 20 days.

The Taiwan Provincial Assembly has six screening committees in charge of civil affairs, finance, construction, agriculture and forestry, education, and transportation and communications. The committees are responsible for processing the proposals made by assembly members and the government, petitions made by the people, and other cases referred to them by the assembly. The assembly also has procedural, public enterprise, disciplinary, statute research, and standing committees. The standing committee convenes during the assembly's recess, meeting once a week to listen to government administrative reports and to supervise the execution of the assembly's resolutions.

Relationship between the Taiwan Provincial Government and Assembly

According to Article 28 of the *Self-governance Law for Provinces and Counties*, Taiwan's governor presents administrative reports to the Taiwan Provincial Assembly during its regular sessions. The assembly has the right to interpellate the governor and departmental chiefs of the provincial government and may ask the provincial government to present reports on specific topics of concern.

The provincial government executes resolutions made by the assembly, which may demand explanations if its resolutions are not carried out or are improperly implemented. However, if the provincial government deems the assembly's resolutions difficult to execute, it may submit a statement of explanations to the assembly and ask for a reconsideration. But if two-thirds of the attending members of the assembly uphold the original resolution, the provincial government must abide by their decision.

The provincial government submits a budgetary bill to the assembly for review three months prior to the beginning of each fiscal year. The assembly may not propose any increase in expenditure. Any provincial joint ventures to be set up with other provinces or cities also require the approval of the provincial assembly.

The Fukien Provincial Government

The ROC government administers only two counties in Fukien Province: Kinmen County, which encompasses Kinmen, and Lienchiang County, which encompasses Matsu. In July 1956, the ROC military assumed full administrative responsibility for these two counties. Military administration lasted until August 7, 1992, when President Lee Teng-hui promulgated the *Statute for the Security and Guidance of Kinmen, Matsu, and the Pratas and Spratlys Areas* 金門、馬祖、東沙、南沙地區安全及輔導條例. The return of local autonomy to Kinmen County and Lienchiang County is part of the ROC's recent constitutional reforms. The residents of these counties now have the same rights and freedoms as all people in Taiwan. However, the *Self-governance Law for Provinces and Counties*, passed in July 1994, does not apply to the Fukien Provincial Government because of the small area under its jurisdiction.

Like its Taiwan counterpart, the Fukien Provincial Government has a council consisting of 11 members who are nominated by the premier and appointed by the president. Fukien governor Wu King-tsan 吳金贊, who is also a council member, presides over the council when it convenes once in June and once again in December.

The Kinmen County Government is responsible for the administration of six rural and urban townships, which are subdivided into 37 villages and boroughs. There is also a consultation delegation, composed of urban/rural township magistrates and village mayors and local leaders, which holds regular meetings and functions as a county council. Elections for township magistrates and village mayors as well as for representatives of the local and central governments have been held regularly since 1971. The first popular election for county magistrate took place in November 1993, followed by an election for county council in January 1994.

Lienchiang County contains four urban and rural townships, subdivided into 22 villages and boroughs. Like Kinmen County, Lienchiang County held its first popular election for county magistrate in November 1993, followed by an election for county council in January 1994. This newly elected council took office on Febru-

Organization of the Taiwan Provincial Government

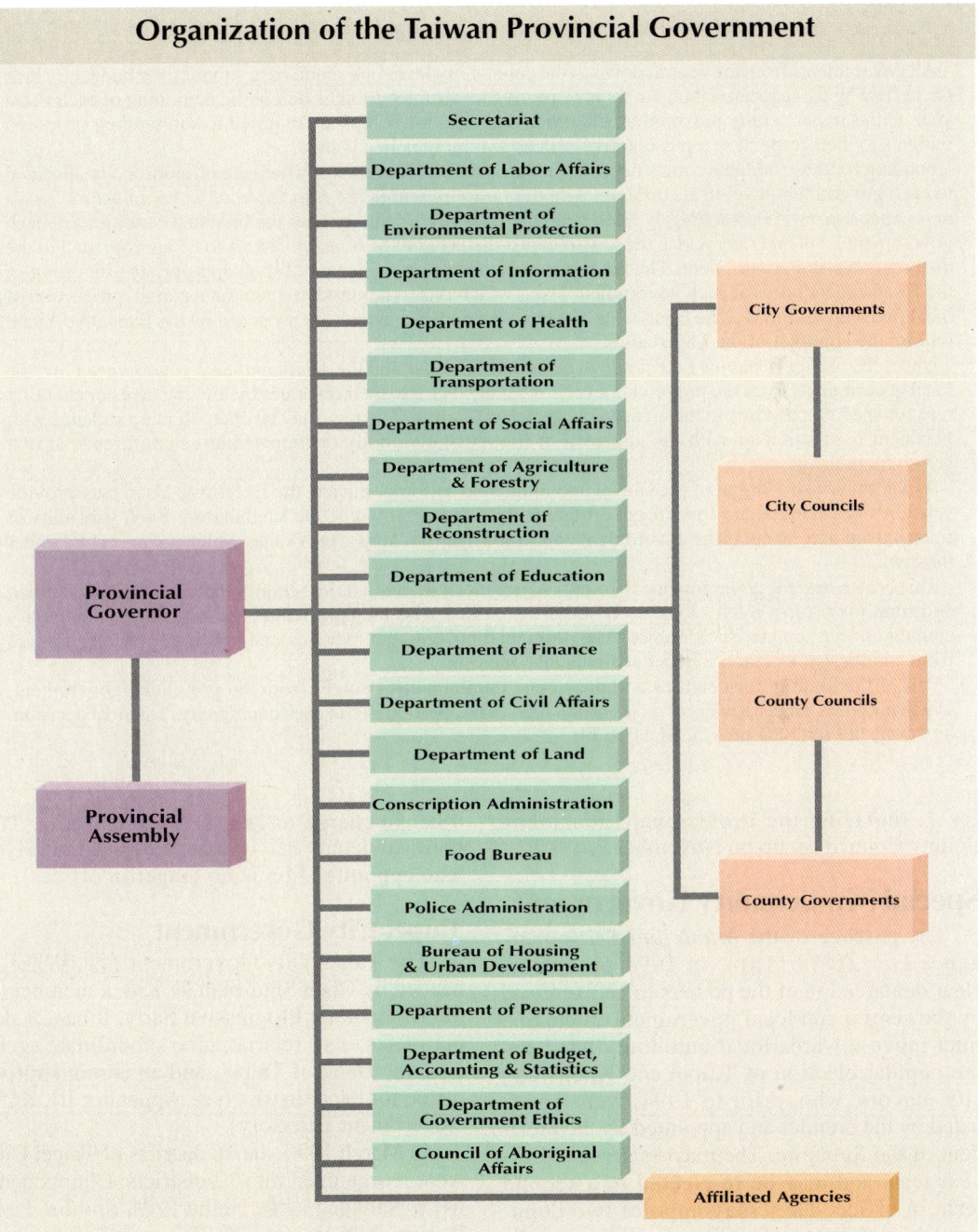

Budget Allocation

All governments from the central down to the county/city levels are required to submit their budgetary bills for review by the legislative body at their respective levels three months before the beginning of each fiscal year. Cities under county jurisdiction and urban and rural townships are required to submit their proposed budgets to their respective representative offices two months in advance.

Funding for these budgets comes mainly from national and local taxes, which are proportionally allocated to each government level in accordance with the *Law Governing the Allocation of Government Revenues and Expenditures* 財政收支劃分法. Each year, the Executive Yuan reviews the financial conditions of each government level and may revise the law to adjust the percentage of tax revenues to be appropriated to the different levels of government. The tax revenues shall, however, account for an appropriate proportion of the fiscal expenditures at each government level, which is also required to maintain a certain proportion of local financial resources. The figures for these two proportions, which are proposed by the Executive Yuan, require the approval of the Legislature.

Under the *Self-governance Law for Provinces and Counties* and the *Municipal Self-governance Law*, the local governments from the provincial level down may increase their revenues by levying taxes or charging fees for specific purposes in the areas under their jurisdiction. The fees may be charged in accordance with pertinent regulations or with the approval of the legislative body or representative conference at that government level.

As the supervisory organ of provincial and municipal self-governance, the Executive Yuan may provide subsidies or financial aid to said governments with the approval of the Legislature. Such subsidies or financial aid may be cut if the government concerned does not levy taxes or fees which are permitted under the law.

This is also true for governments of counties, provincial municipalities, county municipalities, and urban and rural townships. Such subsidies or aid are provided with the approval of the respective county/city council or representative conference. The provincial government may demand funding for such purposes from counties/cities that are in better financial conditions.

Part of the funding for counties and provincial municipalities comes from the provincial government, which proposes the percentage of a composite fund to be appropriated to each county/city. The final decision, however, lies with the provincial assembly.

ary 1, replacing the Provisional Lienchiang County Council set up on November 7, 1992.

Special Municipality Government

The passage of the *Municipal Self-governance Law* 直轄市自治法 in 1994 provides a clear demarcation of the powers to be exercised by the central and local governments. One distinct move towards local autonomy has been the popular election of Taipei and Kaohsiung city mayors, who, prior to 1994, were nominated by the premier and appointed by the president of the Republic. The mayors serve a four-year term and may be re-elected to a second term in office. They may appoint two deputies, one in charge of political affairs and the other in charge of administrative affairs. The political deputy mayor must resign if the mayor who appointed him is no longer in office.

Taipei City Government

The Taipei City Government 台北市政府 is headed by Chen Shui-bian 陳水扁, a member of the Democratic Progressive Party. It has 21 departments, a secretariat, nine subordinate agencies, the Bank of Taipei, and an administrative office for each district (see Appendix III, ROC Government Directory).

In March 1990, the 16 districts of Taipei City were reorganized into 12 districts: Chungcheng 中正, Nankang 南港, Neihu 內湖, Shihlin 士林, Peit'ou 北投, Hsinyi 信義, Ta-an 大安, Sungshan

松山, Chungshan 中山, Wenshan 文山, Tat'ung 大同, and Wanhua 萬華. These districts encompass a total of 435 boroughs.

Kaohsiung City Government

The mayor of Kaohsiung City, Wu Den-yih 吳敦義, won the December 1994 election as an incumbent. He is a member of the Kuomintang. The Kaohsiung City Government 高雄市政府 comprises 18 departments, a secretariat, four subordinate agencies, the Bank of Kaohsiung, and an administrative office for each of its 11 districts (see Appendix III, ROC Government Directory).

The 11 districts in Kaohsiung City are Yench'eng 鹽埕, Kushan 鼓山, Tsoying 左營, Nantzu 楠梓, Sanmin 三民, Hsinhsing 新興, Ch'ienchin 前金, Lingya 苓雅, Ch'ienchen 前鎮, Ch'ichin 旗津, and Hsiaokang 小港. The districts comprise 466 boroughs.

City Councils

According to Article 15 of the *Municipal Self-governance Law*, the main functions of the Taipei and Kaohsiung city councils are:
• to adopt municipal statutes and regulations;
• to approve the municipal budget;
• to approve the levying of special taxes, temporary taxes and surtaxes in the special municipality;
• to approve the disposal of municipal properties;
• to approve the organic laws of the municipal government and municipally owned businesses;
• to approve proposals made by the city government;
• to screen the auditor's reports on municipal accounts;
• to approve proposals made by the councilmen;
• to hear petitions from citizens; and
• to carry out other functions as prescribed by law or endowed by laws promulgated by the central government.

The term of office for a city councilor is four years. Councils meet for 60 days every six months. A session may be extended by ten days at the request of the mayor, council speaker, or one-third of the council members. In each session, various committees are formed to scrutinize proposals. A councilor may join only one committee.

In December 1994, the citizens of Taipei and Kaohsiung elected councils of 52 and 44 members, respectively.

City Government and Council Relationship

The municipal council sends its resolutions to the city government for implementation. In case of delay or otherwise unsatisfactory performance on the part of the city government, the municipal council may ask for an explanation and, if necessary, request that the Executive Yuan invite pertinent agencies to a consultation for a resolution to be reached.

If a municipal council resolution is considered impracticable, the municipal government may send it back for reconsideration. If two-thirds of the council members present uphold the previous resolution, the municipal government is obliged to abide by their decision.

When the municipal council is in session, the mayor must periodically submit an oral or written report on the city government's administrative policies, on how the resolutions of the previous session of the municipal council have been carried out, and on other major activities of the municipal government. Directors of departments in the municipal government must also submit reports on matters under their jurisdiction. The members of the council may interpellate the mayor and his subordinates. The mayor or officials concerned may be asked by the municipal council to submit special reports on matters of vital concern to the special municipality.

Every year the municipal government submits an administrative budget for the next fiscal year to the municipal council. Details of expected revenues and projected expenditures must be listed, but the council cannot propose spending increases.

County and Provincial Municipality Governments

Taiwan Province has 16 counties 縣: Taipei, Taoyuan, Hsinchu, Miaoli, Taichung, Changhua,

Yunlin, Chiayi, Tainan, Kaohsiung, P'ingtung, Taitung, Hualien, Nant'ou, Ilan, and P'enghu; and five provincial municipalities 省轄市: Keelung, Hsinchu, Taichung, Chiayi, and Tainan. Each county/city has a county/city government and a county/city council, which is an important check and balance against the county/city government. County governments are headed by magistrates and city governments are headed by mayors popularly elected for up to two four-year terms. County and city councilors are elected by popular vote for four-year terms of office. The number of county or city councilors is determined by the population of each given county; several county and city council seats are reserved for women and aborigines.

City Rankings

There are three levels of cities in the Taiwan area: special municipalities 直轄市, which, like provinces, fall under the direct jurisdiction of the central government; provincial municipalities 省轄市, which are under direct provincial jurisdiction; and county municipalities 縣轄市, which are under direct county jurisdiction.

The Taiwan area presently has two special municipalities: Taipei City, which was elevated to this status in 1967, and Kaohsiung City, which gained similar status in 1979 when its population exceeded one million. The *Municipal Self-governance Law* passed in July 1994 raised this population requirement to 1.5 million.

Under the *Self-governance Law for Provinces and Counties*, an area with a population of over 600,000 and which is politically, economically, and culturally important shall be considered a provincial municipality. There are five such cities directly under Taiwan Province: Keelung City 基隆市, Hsinchu City 新竹市, Taichung City, Chiayi City 嘉義市, and Tainan City. These cities are equivalent to counties in status.

There are 28 county municipalities in the Taiwan area. According to the *Self-governance Law for Provinces and Counties*, an area with a population of over 150,000 may become a county municipality if it is industrially and commer-

cially developed, and has ample financial resources, convenient transportation links, and complete public facilities. These population requirements are, however, not retroactive.

Special and provincial municipalities are subdivided into districts 區. Each district has an office headed by a chief administrator, who is appointed by the mayor. Districts and county municipalities are subdivided into boroughs 里. Each borough has a borough office headed by a warden who is elected by popular vote for a four-year term. The warden is assisted by an executive officer. Boroughs are subdivided into neighborhoods 鄰, which are the most basic unit of urban governance. Each neighborhood is represented by a chief who is nominated by the borough warden and contracted to a four-year term by the district office.

Cities and Townships under County Governments

Counties are subdivided into county municipalities 縣轄市, rural townships 鄉, or urban townships 鎮, depending on population density. Each city, rural township and urban township has a magistrate who is popularly elected for up to two four-year terms of office. Taiwan currently has 28 county municipalities, 221 rural townships, and 60 urban townships under county jurisdiction.

Villages and Boroughs

Rural townships are subdivided into villages 村, and urban townships are subdivided into boroughs 里. The residents of each village or borough elect their own wardens for four-year terms of office. The wardens work with executive officers to handle the administrative affairs of their village or borough. Villages and boroughs are subdivided into neighborhoods 鄰. Heads of neighborhoods are routinely recommended by wardens for appointment to the rural township or urban township office.

Further Reading (in Chinese unless otherwise noted):
Chung-hua min-kuo hsing-cheng kai-k'uang 中華民國行政概況 (*Annual Review of Government Administration of the*

Republic of China; in Chinese and English editions). Taipei: Research, Development and Evaluation Commission, Executive Yuan, annual.

Chung-hua min-kuo fa-lü hui-pien 中華民國法律彙編 (Compendium of Laws in the Republic of China). 10 vols. Taipei: Legislative Yuan.

Chung-hua min-kuo hsien-hsing fa-kui hui-pien 中華民國現行法規彙編 (Compendium of Current Laws and Regulations in the Republic of China). 1981– . Taipei: Compendium Compilation Steering Committee 中華民國現行法規彙編編印指導委員會印行.

This is a looseleaf edition with supplementary editions issued quarterly.

Control Yuan, Republic of China (in English). Taipei: Secretariat, Control Yuan.

1997 Directory of Taiwan, Republic of China (in English). Taipei: China News.

The Examination Yuan of the Republic of China (in English). Taipei: Examination Yuan.

T'ai-wan sheng yi-hui chien-chieh 台灣省議會簡介 (A General Introduction to the Taiwan Provincial Assembly). Taichung: Taiwan Provincial Assembly.

T'ai-pei shih yi-hui chien-chieh 台北市議會簡介 (*A Guide to the Taipei City Council*; Chinese-English bilingual). Taipei City Council.

Chien-ch'a-yüan kai-k'uang 監察院概況 (An Introduction to the Control Yuan). Taipei: Control Yuan.

Kao-hsiung shih hsing-cheng kai-k'uang 高雄市行政概況 (An Introduction to Kaohsiung Municipal Administration). Kaohsiung: Kaohsiung Municipal Government.

Chung-hua min-kuo k'ao-hsüan hsing-cheng kai-k'uang 中華民國考選行政概況 (An Introduction to the Examination Administration in the Republic of China). Taipei: Ministry of Examination.

Chung-hua min-kuo cheng-fu tsu-chih yü kung-tso chien-chieh 中華民國政府組織與工作簡介 (An Introduction to ROC Government Organizations and Their Tasks). Taipei: Research, Development and Evaltion Commission, Executive Yuan.

Chung-hua min-kuo shih-fa-yüan 中華民國司法院 (The Judicial Yuan of the Republic of China). Taipei: Judicial Yuan.

Legislative Yuan, Republic of China (in English). Taipei: Legislative Yuan.

Li-fa-yüan kung-pao 立法院公報 (Legislative Yuan Gazette). Taipei: Legislative Yuan, semiweekly.

Chung-hua min-kuo kuo-min ta-hui 中華民國國民大會 (*The National Assembly of the Republic of China*; Chinese-English bilingual). Taipei: Secretariat of the National Assembly.

T'ai-wan sheng t'ung-chi chi-k'an 台灣省統計季刊 (Statistical Quarterly of Taiwan Province). Nant'ou: Department of Budget, Accounting and Statistics, Taiwan Provincial Government, quarterly.

Statistics on Chinese Examination and Personnel Administrations (Chinese-English bilingual). Taipei: Examination Yuan, annual.

Taiwan: An Island Province of the Republic of China. Nant'ou: Taiwan Provincial Government.

Chung-hua min-kuo nien-chien 中華民國年鑑 (Yearbook of the Republic of China). Taipei: ROC Yearbook Publishers, annual.

6.
Political Parties and Elections

Above: The spectacle of multiparty politics—supporters of the opposition New Party gather for a spirited rally at the Dr. Sun Yat-sen Memorial Hall in downtown Taipei.

Right: Making Very Sure—votes cast in the 1996 presidential election are carefully tabulated in view of representatives from the public and contending political parties.

Previous page: Ultimately successful KMT presidential candidate Lee Teng-hui, with running mate Lien Chan, appear on stage at a political rally during the 1996 election campaign.

6 Political Parties and Elections

The Republic of China has, in the past decade or so, moved quite rapidly toward a full-fledged democracy. Vigorous opposition parties compete in regular and frequent elections, allowing citizens of the ROC a greater say in the future of their nation. While the United States may still hold the record for the frequency of elections and the number of elected offices, more posts are filled by election than ever before in the ROC today. Taiwan voters, however, differ from their American counterparts in at least one important respect—voter participation. Turnout rates in ROC elections consistently hover around 70 percent of eligible voters, slightly lower than in some European countries, but much higher than in the United States.

Voting eligibility is defined broadly: the minimum age is 20, and there are no gender, property or educational qualifications requirements. Registration is automatic. The government notifies every enrolled voter of an impending election and distributes a bulletin or gazette that identifies and describes all candidates.

Normally, voting is scheduled for Saturdays, which are usually made holidays of sorts in places where elections are held. A large retinue of workers, typically teachers and other dedicated locals, administer paper ballots at convenient polling stations. The workers count the votes reliably and quickly, and report the results just a few hours after the polls close. By any standard, election administration in Taiwan is efficient.

Electoral Systems

The election mechanism varies, depending upon the type of office. For such executive posts as president and vice president, provincial governor 省長, special municipality mayors 直轄市市長, county magistrates 縣長 and provincial municipality mayors 省轄市市長, and rural and urban township magistrates 鄉鎮長 and county municipality mayors 縣轄市市長, each voter casts only one vote in a single-seat constituency, and the candidate who receives the most votes, not necessarily an absolute majority of votes, gets elected.

For the election of members of the National Assembly 國民大會, Legislative Yuan 立法院, Taiwan Provincial Assembly 台灣省議會 and special municipal councils 直轄市議會, county or city councils 縣市議會, and township councils 鄉鎮市民代表會, what has been dubbed the single nontransferable vote (SNTV) is employed. Normally, several representatives are elected from a single constituency. Constituencies are demarcated by election commissions on the basis of existing administrative districts, population distribution, geography, and transportation accessibility. In a given constituency, each voter casts only one vote, and the leading candidates get elected.

Since the National Assembly election of 1991 and the Legislative Yuan election of 1992, a certain number of seats have been reserved for a national constituency and the overseas Chinese communities. These seats are allocated by proportional representation (PR). Before the election, each party submits two lists of candidates, one for the national constituency and the other for overseas Chinese representatives. After voters cast their ballots, votes gained by candidates are aggregated according to party affiliation, and the seats for the national constituency and overseas Chinese representatives are then distributed proportionally among the parties which obtain 5 percent of total valid votes nationwide. At present, 22 percent of the seats in the Legislative Yuan and 30 percent of those in the National Assembly are filled this way.

Both the SNTV and PR systems generally benefit the smaller parties, for as long as they are able to win a certain number of votes, they are able to secure at least a few seats. But in elections for administrative offices, the situation is quite different. Normally, only the two largest parties emerge victorious in these single-seat contests, and third parties are very much at a disadvantage.

As of 1996, a total of 82 political parties have registered with the Ministry of the Interior, but most are insignificant in electoral politics. The three significant parties are the Kuomintang (KMT), the Democratic Progressive Party (DPP), and the New Party (NP). All three of these parties have won seats in various legislative bodies, but only the

Central Election Commission

Founded in 1980, the Central Election Commission 中央選舉委員會 (CEC) under the Executive Yuan 行政院 is responsible for holding and supervising national and local elections, screening candidate qualifications, recalling elected officials, and drafting or amending laws concerning elections. The CEC is led by a chairman, and composed of 11 to 19 commissioners who, after nomination by the premier and then approval by the president, serve for a term of three years. To guarantee the impartiality of the CEC, the *Public Officials Election and Recall Law* 公職人員選舉罷免法 rules that commissioners from any single political party may not constitute more than two-fifths of the whole commission.

KMT and the DPP have been able to secure administrative offices.

In the past few years, the National Assembly has amended the ROC Constitution three times, changing electoral politics in Taiwan. First, the terms of office for the ROC president and for National Assemblymen were shortened from six to four years. (The term for Legislative Yuan members remained three years.) Second, it was stipulated that the president and the vice president would be elected directly by the citizens eligible to vote in the territory under the effective jurisdiction of the ROC, rather than indirectly by the National Assembly as in the past, and that a presidential and vice presidential ticket had only to win a plurality, not a majority, to be elected. Third, the mechanism through which members of the Control Yuan 監察院 are selected was changed. Previously, Control Yuan members were elected by provincial assemblies and special municipal councils. Now, they are nominated by the president and approved by the National Assembly. This reform has transformed the Control Yuan from a parliamentary body to a semijudicial institution.

Political Parties
The Kuomintang

The current ruling party of the ROC is the Kuomintang 中國國民黨, also known as the Na-

tionalist Party. Having celebrated its one hundredth anniversary on November 24, 1994, the KMT today boasts a membership of approximately 2.1 million, one-third of whom are technocrats and specialists. At the grassroots level, members are organized into cells. Moving upwards, there are district congresses and committees, county congresses and committees, provincial congresses and committees, and finally the National Congress 全國代表大會 and the Central Committee 中央委員會.

The National Congress is the highest authority of the party, and delegates are selected to serve four-year terms. The congress amends the party charter, determines the party platform and other important policies, elects the party chairman and 210 Central Committee members, and approves candidates nominated by the chairman to serve as vice chairmen and members of the Central Advisory Council 中央評議委員會. When the National Congress is in recess, the supreme party organ is the Central Committee, which holds a plenary session every year.

The Central Standing Committee 中央常務委員會, which represents the Central Committee when that body is not in session, is the most influential organ in the KMT. It meets every Wednesday morning to deliberate and approve important policies for the party and the government, and to nominate people for important party and government positions, including ministers, vice ministers, and various commissioners.

The day-to-day affairs of the party are managed by a secretary-general 秘書長 and three deputy secretaries-general. The current secretary-general is Wu Poh-hsiung 吳伯雄. Under his command, career staff run the various party departments and commissions. At lower levels, party organizations have their own secretariats and administrative staffs. All these organizations, from the national to the local levels, are funded to a large extent by profits from party-owned and operated business enterprises, ranging from newspapers and TV stations to electrical appliance companies and computer firms.

The Kuomintang held the first meeting of its 14th National Congress in August 1993. The Congress approved significant changes to the way party affairs would be conducted. It was decided that the party chairman would be elected by the National Congress by secret ballot. ROC President Lee Teng-hui 李登輝, won 83 percent of the votes cast and was re-elected chairman of the party. In addition, four vice-chairmen were added to the Central Committee after being nominated by the chairman and approved by the National Congress. It was also decided that the chairman would appoint only 10 to 15 of the 31 members of the Central Standing Committee, with the remaining members elected by the Central Committee. Finally, it was decided that the National Congress, which had been held every four years, would instead meet every two years.

The second meeting of the 14th National Congress was held in August 1995 to nominate the party's presidential candidate for the election held in March 1996 (see section on Presidential Elections in this chapter). The Central Standing Committee was also slightly reshuffled. At the fourth plenary session of the 14th Central Committee held in August 1996, Yu Kuo-hwa 俞國華, senior advisor to the president, and Chiu Chuang-huan 邱創煥, former president of the Examination Yuan, were named acting vice chairmen after former vice chairmen Lin Yang-kang 林洋港 and Hau Pei-tsun 郝柏村 were expelled from the KMT due to their decision to team up and run for president and vice president as independents.

Democratic Progressive Party

The Democratic Progressive Party 民主進步黨, formed on September 28, 1986, now has approximately 84,000 members. The party's organizational structure closely resembles that of the Kuomintang. The DPP's National Congress elects 31 members to the Central Executive Committee 中央執行委員會 and 11 members to the Central Advisory Committee 中央評議委員會. The Central Executive Committee in turn elects the 11 members of the Central Standing Committee 中央常務委員會. The members of these committees all serve two-year terms.

The chairman of the party is also directly elected by the National Congress, but only members of the Central Standing Committee are qualified for candidacy. The present chairman, Hsu Hsin-liang 許信良, was elected to a two-year term at the party's seventh National Congress held in June 1996. The chairman nominates a secretary-general, two deputy secretaries-general, and a number of department directors. These nominations are subject to the approval of the Central Standing Committee. Chiou I-jen 邱義仁 is the current secretary-general of the DPP.

At the party's sixth National Congress, held in April and May of 1994, a two-tier primary system was initiated under which ordinary members of the DPP vote for candidates in one primary election and party cadres vote in a second primary. The results of the two would then be combined, with equal weight given to both.

At the second plenary meeting of the sixth National Congress held in March 1995, the nomination process for the presidential and gubernatorial candidates was modified to add open primaries for DPP members and non-members alike. It was also decided that candidate slots on the party's list of national constituency representatives for the Legislative Yuan and National Assembly would be allotted equally among three groups: scholars and experts, representatives of disadvantaged groups, and politicians.

At the seventh National Congress, held in June 1996, further changes were made to the nomination of candidates for public offices. It was decided that the primary reserved for the party leadership would be abolished, and that for the nomination of candidates for such offices as president, provincial governor, special municipality mayors, county magistrates, provincial municipality mayors, Legislative Yuan members, National Assemblymen, and provincial assemblymen and special municipal councilmen, a two-stage process involving a closed primary for party members and an open primary for all eligible voters, each given equal weight, would be employed.

Perhaps what most distinguishes the DPP from the two other major parties is its support of Taiwan independence, or the permanent political separation of Taiwan from the Chinese mainland. Although the DPP has incorporated Taiwan independence into its official platform, the urgency accorded to its realization is a source of factional contention within the party. In more recent elections, the mainstream DPP leadership has tended to downplay the party's independence theme in an attempt to broaden voter support. This treatment of the issue, as well as the DPP's recent warming to interparty cooperation, has led to dissatisfaction among the more radical advocates of independence for Taiwan. Several of these disaffected DPP members thus left the party, and together with other independence supporters, officially established the Taiwan Independence Party 建國黨 (TAIP) on December 10, 1996.

New Party

In August 1993, shortly before the Kuomintang's 14th National Congress, a group of KMT Young Turks, including six Legislative Yuan members and one former lawmaker, broke away from the ruling party to establish the New Party 新黨. According to their common statement, the seven quit in protest against the "undemocratic practices of the KMT" as well as due to ideological differences. Such prominent personalities as the former Finance Minister Wang Chien-shien 王建煊 and former head of the Environmental Protection Administration Jaw Shau-kong 趙少康 were among the founders of the party, which adopted an anti-corruption platform and championed social justice. The goal of the NP is to attract voters who are dissatisfied with the performance of the ruling KMT and opposed to the DPP's advocacy of Taiwan independence. The NP now claims a registered membership of nearly 72,000.

The New Party differs from the KMT and the DPP in organizational structure, stressing the leadership of those holding public office. At the head of the party is the National Campaign and Development Committee 全國競選暨發展委員會. The convener of the committee, a position currently filled by Chen Kui-miao 陳癸淼,

serves as the leader of the party. Yok Mu-ming 郁慕明 is the secretary-general of the party and is in charge of day-to-day affairs.

Elections

There has been a long history of elections in the ROC. Even during the period of martial law, elections for county magistrates, municipality mayors, provincial assemblymen, and county and city councilmen were held quite regularly. Since 1969, supplementary elections for the members of the Legislative Yuan, Control Yuan, and the National Assembly have also been held regularly, with the exception of 1978, when the United States severed diplomatic ties with the ROC.

In 1986, under the leadership of President Chiang Ching-kuo 蔣經國, political reform was accelerated. After Chiang passed away, his successor, current president Lee Teng-hui, carried on with this liberalization. One result of these reforms was the retirement of all the senior members of the First National Assembly, Control Yuan, and Legislative Yuan, who had remained in office since the late 1940s, when they were elected both on the Chinese mainland and Taiwan as representatives of all of China.

The following sections begin with a brief review of recent elections for county magistrates and city mayors, as well as county and city councilors and town magistrates. We then move on to discuss the contests for the governorship of Taiwan Province and the mayoralities of Taipei and Kaohsiung cities, and seats in the Taiwan Provincial Assembly and Taipei and Kaohsiung city councils. The election of representatives to the Third Legislative Yuan is also covered. The final sections summarize the ROC's historic first-ever direct presidential election and the contest for seats in the Third National Assembly.

County Magistrates and City Mayors

The ruling Kuomintang shrugged off predictions of an election setback and won a majority of the 23 seats at stake on November 27, 1993, in an election for 18 county magistrates (16 counties of Taiwan Province and two counties of Fukien

Province) and mayors of the five cities under the jurisdiction of the Taiwan Provincial Government (Keelung 基隆, Hsinchu 新竹, Taichung, Chiayi 嘉義, and Tainan; see sections on City Rankings and County and City Governance in Chapter 5, Government). This was the first election in Taiwan strongly contested by three parties. The KMT defied pessimistic opinion polls by winning 15 seats. Contrary to its own optimistic predictions, the DPP won only six seats, one less than it had held before the election. One independent was elected as mayor of Chiayi, and another as magistrate of Miaoli 苗栗. The defection of a senior KMT member three days before the election proved to be of little help to the New Party, which earned no seats. However, by siphoning off some votes, the then 4-month-old NP kept the KMT from scoring a greater victory.

County and City Councilors and Township Magistrates

On January 29, 1994, more than 73 percent of all eligible voters cast ballots in local elections for 858 members of county and provincial municipality councils and 309 rural and urban township magistrates and county municipality mayors. The results demonstrate how Taiwan remains, at the local level, a one-party state (see section on Cities and Township under County Government in Chapter 5, Government).

Kuomintang candidates, including 42 who ran without party endorsement, captured 67.4 percent of the county and city council seats in Taiwan. They also won all 25 council seats in the counties of Kinmen and Lienchiang 連江縣 (the offshore islands of Quemoy and Matsu). KMT and affiliated candidates won 82.2 percent of the elections for township magistrates and county municipality mayors in Taiwan. However, these results were worse than in 1990 when the ruling party won 77 percent and 92 percent of the council seats and the magisterial and mayoral seats, respectively.

The Democratic Progressive Party won 10.7 percent of council seats and 7.4 percent of the

magisterial positions. While the results represent an increase from the party's 6 percent and 2 percent showings in 1990, the DPP has yet to win a majority of seats in a single county or city council.

The New Party competed in its first election for county councilors and township magistrates with the slogan, "Give the new guys a chance and teach the old guys a lesson." Its candidates won slightly less than 1 percent of council seats and no magisterial positions.

The remaining 180 council seats went to independent candidates, who outperformed DPP nominees and were the KMT's main competitors. Independents also won 10.4 percent of the magisterial and mayoral seats. Many independents were actually staunch KMT members who had failed to receive their party's nomination.

Gubernatorial and Mayoral Elections

It is difficult to describe the elections of December 3, 1994, without resorting to hyperbole. They involved the first ever direct election of the governor of Taiwan Province in history, and the first direct election of the mayors of Taipei and Kaohsiung municipalities since 1964 and 1977, respectively. The entire electorate of Taiwan was eligible to vote for one of these three positions, and voter turnout was a towering 76.8 percent.

Five candidates ran in the nation's first gubernatorial race: KMT candidate James C.Y. Soong 宋楚瑜; DPP candidate and former Ilan County Magistrate Chen Ting-nan 陳定南; New Party Legislative Yuan member Ju Gau-jeng 朱高正 and two independents, Wu Tzu 吳梓 and Tsai Cheng-chih 蔡正治. The KMT incumbent governor of Taiwan Province, James Soong, who had been appointed to that office, won 56.2 percent of the vote, easily beating both the DPP candidate, who came in second with 38.7 percent of the vote, and the NP candidate who ran a distant third with 4.3 percent. The two independent candidates together garnered less than 1 percent of the vote.

The gubernatorial race in Taiwan Province was the most significant of all the elections held on December 3. With a constituency of 11 million eligible voters (about 80 percent of total eligible voters in the ROC), Taiwan Province was a test for Lee Teng-hui, who chose mainland-born James Soong to be the KMT's candidate in a constituency where more than 85 percent of the voters were native Taiwanese.

As predicted, the election for Taipei mayor was a close race between DPP Legislative Yuan member Chen Shui-bian 陳水扁, New Party Legislative Yuan member Jaw Shau-kong, and KMT incumbent Huang Ta-chou 黃大洲. The only other candidate, independent Chi Jung-chih 紀榮治, was largely overshadowed by the race between the big three. In the end, Taipei voters gave DPP candidate Chen 43.7 percent of the vote. Surprisingly, the NP candidate came in second with 30.2 percent, outstripping the KMT incumbent, who could garner only 25.9 percent.

Meanwhile, the 80.6 percent of Kaohsiung voters who went to the polls on December 3 elected the incumbent mayor and KMT candidate, Wu Den-yih 吳敦義. Winning 54.5 percent of the vote, Wu topped DPP legislator Chang Chun-hsiung 張俊雄 (39.3 percent), New Party candidate Tang Ah-ken 湯阿根 (3.5 percent), and two other independents Sy Chung-sang 施鍾响 and Cheng Te-yao 鄭德耀, who together won less than 3 percent of the vote.

Taiwan Provincial Assembly and Taipei and Kaohsiung City Councils

On December 3, 1994, the same day as the gubernatorial and Taipei and Kaohsiung mayoral elections, voters also elected delegates to the Taiwan Provincial Assembly and the Taipei and Kaohsiung city councils.

Altogether, 79 members of the Taiwan Provincial Assembly were elected from the 16 counties and five cities under the jurisdiction of the Taiwan Provincial Government. Of the 79 seats, eight of the seats were reserved for women and four were filled by aboriginal representatives. The KMT won 48 seats, down from the previous 54. The DPP gained seven seats, winning a total of 23, while the New Party won only two seats. Independents and party members running without party endorsement won the remaining six seats.

Voters in Taipei City elected 52 members to the Taipei City Council. Of the 52, one member was to be elected from among the aborigines in Taipei City, and six of the seats were reserved for women. The KMT suffered a major drop in representation, winning only 20 seats compared to its previous 36. The DPP earned a net gain of four seats, moving from 14 to 18. The big winner was the New Party. Virtually unrepresented in the old city council, the NP saw 11 of its 14 candidates win. Independents and party members running without their party's endorsement won three seats.

Independents and party members running without party endorsement did much better in the elections for the Kaohsiung City Council, winning 17 of the 44 seats in that assembly. (One of the members was elected from among the aborigines in Kaohsiung City and five of the seats were reserved for women.) The KMT also fared well, taking six more seats for a total of 24. The DPP won 11 seats, while the New Party won only two.

Third Legislative Yuan

The election for the Third Legislative Yuan was held on December 2, 1995. Compared to the previous elections, the campaigning and election-related activities surrounding this vote were relatively subdued, as the upcoming presidential election had by that time already become the major focus of attention. In the weeks preceding the election, Chinese communist military exercises in the region pushed national security concerns into the spotlight. Another widely discussed question was whether or not the KMT would lose its majority in the new Legislative Yuan. Indeed, the New Party adopted this possibility as a theme of its Legislative Yuan campaign.

While the results of the voting did not live up to the opposition parties' expectations, the KMT found its majority in the Legislative Yuan trimmed to a mere three seats. Of the 164 seats contested, the KMT captured 85, its worst performance ever. The party's overall share of the vote dwindled to 46.1 percent. Unfortunately for the DPP, the KMT's loss did not translate into a resounding victory for its own candidates. The DPP won 54 seats with 33.2 percent of the vote. The outcome was similar to the party's performance in previous legislative elections and was a major disappointment for DPP leaders and supporters.

The New Party was probably the biggest winner. With 13 percent of the vote, it captured 21 seats and thereby tripled its size in the Legislative Yuan. Also encouraging to the NP was the fact that it won quite a few seats in southern Taiwan, indicating that it was no longer a party confined only to Taipei and the surrounding areas.

The remaining four seats were won by independents, who taken together garnered 7.8 percent of the vote.

Presidential Election

Democratic reforms in the ROC have been gathering momentum over the last decade. Ever since steps were first taken to liberalize and expand the political process, each election has carried politics on Taiwan closer to the goal of full democracy. On March 23, 1996, this evolution reached yet another milestone when voters went to the polls to cast their ballots in the ROC's first-ever direct presidential election.

As mentioned earlier in this chapter, the legal foundation which provides for the direct popular election of the president and vice president can be found in recent amendments to the ROC Constitution. These amendments also specify that the winning candidate need only a plurality rather than an outright majority. In addition to changes to the Constitution, a number of supporting laws have been passed to ensure that presidential elections are carried out smoothly and fairly. In July 1995, the Legislative Yuan passed the *Presidential and Vice Presidential Election and Recall Law* 總統副總統選舉罷免法, which legislates that presidential and vice presidential candidates may be nominated by any political party gaining at least 5 percent of the vote in the most recent provincial-level or higher election, or by collecting the signatures of no less than 1.5 percent of the eligible voters in the most recent parliamentary election. The law also requires that the Central Election Commission provide no less than 30

minutes of national television time for each candidate. Furthermore, when two or more candidates agree to participate, the committee will provide funding for nationally televised presidential debates.

As the race to become the first popularly elected president unfolded, four teams of candidates emerged. The ruling KMT nominated incumbent President Lee Teng-hui, who picked Premier Lien Chan as his running mate. The DPP, after a fierce primary process, nominated a long-time political refugee and professor, Peng Ming-min 彭明敏, as its presidential candidate. Peng then chose prominent legislator Hsieh Chang-ting 謝長廷 as his running mate.

While the KMT and DPP candidates were both nominated, the two other candidates entered the race via petition. One was Lin Yang-kang. He and his running mate Hau Pei-tsun were both vice chairmen of the KMT, but decided to run as independents. They were endorsed by the New Party. The fourth team was Chen Li-an 陳履安 and Wang Ching-feng 王清峰. Chen was also a member of the KMT and the president of the Control Yuan, but gave up both of these positions when he announced his candidacy. He picked up Wang, a female member of the Control Yuan, as his running mate.

The KMT ran a very successful campaign. Almost from the very beginning, Lee-Lien ticket was well ahead of the other three. Lee Teng-hui, as the ROC's first native Taiwanese president, not only received the backing of traditional KMT supporters, but was also supported by some in the DPP camp. The military exercises and missile tests which the mainland staged off the coast of Taiwan prior to the election further increased support for Lee by motivating people to "rally round the flag."

On March 23, slightly over 76 percent of eligible voters turned out to cast their ballots and re-elected Lee Teng-hui, giving him an impressive 54 percent of the vote. He was trailed by the DPP's Peng Ming-min, who captured 21.1 percent. Lin and Chen obtained 14.9 percent and 10 percent of the vote, respectively.

Third National Assembly

Voters at the polls on March 23, 1996, were not only deciding who would become the ROC's first popularly elected president, they were also electing members to the Third National Assembly. Although this contest was largely overshadowed by the much more prominent presidential election, many parties fielded candidates, and several constituencies saw hotly contested races.

In the end, the KMT captured 49.7 percent of the vote and remained the largest party in the new Assembly. Of the 334 seats that had been up for grabs, ruling party candidates won 183, or 54.8 percent. While the KMT kept its majority, the result represented a significant decline from the 75.4 percent of the seats it had held in the previous Assembly. As for the DPP, it added considerably to the 66 Assembly seats it won in 1991. DPP candidates walked away with 29.9 percent of the vote on March 23 and captured 99 seats, or 29.6 percent of the total. For the New Party, the 1996 election was its first National Assembly race. The party's candidates captured 46 seats, or 13.8 percent of the total, and 13.7 percent of the vote—a result similar to the NP's performance in the Legislative Yuan election in December 1995. Of the remaining seats, one went to a candidate backed by the newly-formed Green Party 綠色本土清新黨, while five others went to independents.

The ROC Constitution states that a constitutional amendment must be passed by at least three-fourths of the delegates present at a meeting attended by a quorum of two-thirds of the entire National Assembly. Thus in the new National Assembly, no political party is now able to single-handedly amend the Constitution.

Recalls and Referendums

According to the Constitution, ROC citizens have the rights of election, recall, initiative, and referendum. In practice, however, only the right of election has been frequently exercised. Indeed, legislation to regulate the exercise of the rights of initiative and referendum has yet to be passed. Nevertheless, there have been occasional attempts to recall elected officials and representatives, and even referendums have been held in certain areas despite the lack of supporting laws. Obviously, without a detailed legal framework, the results of these referendums are advisory at best.

The most recent attempts at recall occurred in November 1994 and January 1995 in Taipei County and the southern district of Taipei City, respectively. In both incidents, the targets of recall were KMT members of the Legislative Yuan who were accused of reneging on campaign promises by voting in favor of the construction of a nuclear power plant. Turnout rates in both incidents were very low. In Taipei County, only 21.4 percent of eligible voters turned out to vote, and in the southern district of Taipei City, the turnout rate was 8.6 percent. As the *Public Officials Election and Recall Law* requires that a majority of eligible voters must turn out to vote in order to recall elected officials or representatives, both attempts failed.

As for referendums, three recent attempts were centered around the construction of a new nuclear power plant. The first was held in May 1994 in Taipei County's Kungliao Township 台北縣貢寮鄉, the proposed site of the new plant. More than 58 percent of Kungliao's eligible voters went to the polls, and a whopping 96.1 percent expressed disapproval of the plan to construct the plant in their township. Another nuclear power plant referendum was held by the government of Taipei County in November of the same year, and while 87.1 percent of the ballots cast were against the power plant, only 18.5 percent of eligible voters participated. The most recent referendum held on the issue was undertaken by the government of Taipei City in March 1996. Fifty-eight percent of eligible voters cast their ballots, and 51.5 percent opposed the construction of the new nuclear power plant.

Another referendum was held in March 1995 by the government of Hsichih Township in Taipei County 台北縣汐止鎮 to decide on public works proposals. The turnout rate was only 17 percent, but 95 percent of the ballots cast were in favor of the local government's proposals.

Winbond is on the move

Winbond is a world class semiconductor
company supplying high-quality semiconductor
products to the computer, communications, and
consumer electronics industry. In less than a decade,
Winbond has earned a well deserved reputation
for high quality products and services.

11F, No.115, Sec.3, Ming Sheng E. Rd., Taipei, Taiwan, R.O.C.
TEL: 886-2-7190505   FAX: 886-2-7197502
WWW:http://www.winbond.com.tw/

7.
Mainland Affairs and
National Unification Policy

Previous page: A visiting kun opera troupe from the Chinese mainland performs in Taipei as part of ongoing cultural exchanges between the two sides.

Upper: Contributing color and grace to cross-Straits exchanges, a Shanghai ballet troupe performs at Taipei's Dr. Sun Yat-sen Memorial Hall.

Lower: Koo Chen-fu (right), chairman of the ROC's Straits Exchange Foundation, shakes hands with Tang Shubei, vice chairman of the Association for Relations Across the Taiwan Straits.

7 Mainland Affairs and National Unification Policy

The development of relations between Taiwan and the Chinese mainland since 1995 might be likened to a welcome and gradually-warming spring suddenly interrupted by a frigid and blustery tempest. The year opened on a promising note, with Chinese communist "president" Jiang Zemin introducing an eight-point proposal calling for continued cross-Straits economic exchange and cooperation. On April 8, 1995, President Lee Teng-hui 李登輝 responded by setting forth six principles to guide relations with the mainland. Although neither side found the other's proposals entirely acceptable, the gestures were deemed positive, and arrangements were made to hold a second round of high-level, semi-official talks (see section on Koo-Wang talks in this chapter). The first preparatory meeting for these talks took place on May 27 and 28, 1995, in Taipei, and it was decided that they would be held in Peking on July 20. The stage seemed set for substantial progress.

However, there were storm clouds on the horizon. On June 7, 1995, President Lee Teng-hui left Taiwan for a historic six-day trip to the United States. Shortly after his return, Peking announced that it was postponing indefinitely the talks which had been scheduled for July 20, citing President Lee's trip to the US as the major factor behind the decision. Although the president's US visit was of a private nature, Peking issued what was to become a standard charge: that the ROC was attempting to create "two Chinas," or "one China and one Taiwan." They claimed that the trip had "poisoned relations between the two sides" and launched a vitriolic propaganda campaign aimed at cowing Taiwan and discrediting President Lee.

The chill in Taipei-Peking relations soon deepened and took on a biting edge when the mainland began conducting live-fire military exercises and missile tests in the waters near Taiwan. Between July 21 and 28, 1995, mainland military units lobbed six surface-to-surface guided missiles into a small patch of the East China Sea approximately 140 kilometers north of Taiwan. A little less than three weeks later, from August 15 to 25, Peking again test-fired guided missiles and artillery in a larger area of ocean 135 kilometers north of Taiwan.

Most certainly the tensest period came in March of 1996, immediately before the ROC's historic first-ever direct presidential election. In what many characterized as an attempt to intimidate the voters of Taiwan and influence the outcome of the election, Peking launched a new wave of military exercises which included missile tests and live-ammunition maneuvers involving sea, air, and ground forces. The first of these exercises involved the test-firing of guided missiles into waters near Kaohsiung and Keelung 基隆, Taiwan's two largest ports. A total of four missiles were launched, and the closest of the target zones was only 35 kilometers off the northeastern tip of Taiwan. A second exercise conducted by naval and air force units in the Taiwan Straits began on March 12, and this was followed by an even more comprehensive round of maneuvers beginning on March 18. The third exercise, involving ground, air, and naval forces, was held in an area a mere 18.5 km from the ROC-administered Matsu 馬祖 island group.

In addition to their inherently threatening message, the exercises were also militarily significant. Analysts indicated that the exercises allowed mainland forces to practice for a staged invasion of Taiwan and its outlying islands. The first round simulated a missile attack on Taiwan and its harbors, while the second round involving live-fire drills by warplanes and warships demonstrated maneuvers necessary to control the Taiwan Straits by air and sea. The third exercise simulated a full-scale assault by combined forces, including ground troops, on either the Pescadore Islands 澎湖群島 or Taiwan.

The successful completion of the ROC's presidential election and the conclusion of the mainland's military exercises in the Taiwan Straits did not lead to a thaw in Taipei-Peking relations. Nevertheless, the ROC has continued to seek a resumption of semi-official talks in spite of the frosty attitude of the authorities on the Chinese mainland. As 1996 progressed, however, the two sides remained divided on the conditions under which such a dialogue might be pursued. Relations between Taipei and Peking thus have yet to return to the warmer and more genial season experienced in the opening months of 1995.

Of course, while it is true that cross-Straits relations have deteriorated since the beginning of 1995, viewing the development of the relationship between Taiwan and the Chinese mainland from such a narrow prospective gives the mistaken impression that little has been accomplished. To obtain a more accurate picture of how far relations have actually progressed, it is necessary to go back to the historical roots of the present situation.

Evolution of the State of Division

The Republic of China was founded in 1912. From the beginning, it maintained sovereignty over the territories that had been administered by a succession of Chinese governments down through the ages. The international community referred to these territories as "China."

Ten years after the founding of the Republic of China, the Chinese Communist Party was established under the aegis of international communist activists. In 1949, the Chinese communists gained control of the Chinese mainland through military force, and on October 1, 1949, they proclaimed the establishment of the People's Republic of China. The ROC government was compelled to move to the island of Taiwan, and China was divided into two. Since that time, two distinct societies, with different ideologies and contrasting political, economic, and social systems, have existed simultaneously on opposite sides of the Taiwan Straits.

For a long time after gaining control of the Chinese mainland, the Chinese communists sought to "liberate" Taiwan by force. Beginning in the early 1950s, they launched a series of military attacks against areas controlled by the ROC government in an effort to achieve reunification by force: the artillery bombardment of Quemoy 金門 (Kinmen) in 1958 is one of the most well-known of these incidents. Peking changed its policy toward Taiwan after establishing diplomatic relations with the United States in 1979 and began pursuing a course of peaceful confrontation. However, although references to "liberation" in propaganda concerning Taiwan were dropped in favor of the term "peaceful reunification," Peking has to this day refused to renounce the use of military force to solve the reunification problem.

In Taiwan, the pace of economic liberalization, social pluralization, and political democratization picked up speed throughout the 1980s, and with the lifting of martial law in July 1987, the government adopted a more open policy toward the Chinese mainland. In November 1987, the ROC government, out of humanitarian considerations, began to allow people residing in the Taiwan area to visit relatives on the Chinese mainland. This decision moved cross-Straits relations out of a state of complete estrangement and opened the door for personal-level exchanges.

The people-to-people exchanges, the indirect trade and investment, and the cultural exchanges between the two sides of the Taiwan Straits that blossomed in the wake of this thaw have engendered a range of issues that necessitate a more systematic approach to bilateral contacts. The ROC government has thus established a legal and organizational foundation on which to pursue the development of relations between Taiwan and the Chinese mainland.

Reunification Guidelines

The ROC government and the majority of the people of Taiwan earnestly hope for the peaceful reunification of China. Taipei's fundamental policies toward Peking can be summed up as "one China, two political entities." Under the ROC Constitution, the Republic of China regards itself as the national government of China while the "People's Republic of China" is a political entity that controls the Chinese mainland. Since Peking disagrees with Taipei on this point, Taipei's design of using the neutral term "political entity" instead of "state" or "government" is a pragmatic characterization of the political reality across the Taiwan Straits, allowing sufficient "creative ambiguity" for both sides. The termination of the Period of National Mobilization for Suppression of the Communist Rebellion 動員戡亂時期 by President Lee Teng-hui on May 1, 1991, signifies the ROC government's determination not to use force to achieve national reunification. Peking, however, has pointedly refused to respond in kind to this friendly gesture.

To articulate its position as clearly as possible, the ROC government has devised a blueprint for this process, the *Guidelines for National Unification* 國家統一綱領, which outline the principles and positive steps that both sides can take to expedite China's reunification. According to this gradual, sequential plan, China's reunification is imperative not only for the sake of territorial unity, but also for the political freedom and equitable distribution of wealth for all Chinese.

The guidelines state that China's reunification should be achieved in three phases: a short-term phase of exchanges and reciprocity, a mid-term phase of mutual trust and cooperation, and a long-term phase of consultations and reunification. The phased approach was chosen with the full realization that the reunification of China will be a long and arduous process. China's reunification will not be achieved overnight, because the two sides have divergent social, political, and economic systems, not to mention vast differences in lifestyles. However, there is no fixed time frame for each stage. Progress may be slow or fast, depending on the pace with which the mainland authorities respond to the ideas outlined in the guidelines.

In the short-term phase, it is hoped that neither side will deny the other's existence as a political entity, and that both sides will expand unofficial people-to-people contacts. In addition, the guidelines also call for Peking to renounce the use of force against Taiwan and allow Taiwan enough room to maneuver in the international community.

The first task in the medium-term phase is to set up channels for official communication between the two sides on the basis of parity. The goals of the second-term phase also include the establishment of direct postal, commercial, and transportation links across the Taiwan Straits, as well as for ranking officials from both sides to exchange visits. Only after the goals of this phase have been achieved can the process of national reunification be brought into the picture.

In the long-term phase, a bilateral consultative body will be established to jointly discuss the grand political and economic structure of a reunified China, in accordance with the wishes of the people on both sides of the Taiwan Straits. A China that realizes peaceful democratic reunification and prosperous growth will have a significant stabilizing effect on the Asia-Pacific region in particular and on world peace in general.

Currently, relations between the two sides are in the short-term phase, although exchanges in many areas have already moved into the second stage.

Statute Governing Relations

The ROC is a constitutional democracy, and all major governmental policies are formulated in accordance with due legal process. The evolving policy toward the Chinese mainland and the mainland authorities is no exception. At present, the most significant piece of legislation in this regard is the *Statute Governing the Relations Between the People of the Taiwan Area and the Mainland Area* 台灣地區與大陸地區人民關係條例. The statute, which was implemented in September 1992, covers administrative, civil, and criminal affairs, and recognizes the rights of the people living under the control of the authorities in the mainland. Thus, with certain exceptions necessary to maintain the economic and social stability of Taiwan, the people living on the Chinese mainland are basically the same as those living in Taiwan in the eyes of the law.

Organizational Structures

In addition to a clear set of principles and laws to guide the development of relations, appropriate channels of communication are also an obvious necessity. This has led to the birth of a set of institutions authorized to handle relations with the Chinese mainland. In 1990 and 1991, the ROC government set up a three-tier network of government and private sector institutions. In September 1990, the National Unification Council (NUC) was established. Then, in January 1991, the Executive Yuan's Mainland Affairs Council (MAC) was formed. In February 1991, the MAC approved the formation of a private non-profit organization, the Straits Exchange Foundation (SEF).

National Unification Council

The National Unification Council 國家統一委員會 functions as an advisory board and provides the president with research findings and ideas. The NUC is currently headed by the president himself, with the vice president and two opposition party members as deputies. The president has also invited respected civic leaders in Taiwan to sit on the NUC. The tenure for NUC members is one year, renewable at the president's discretion. As a non-partisan board, the NUC forges consensus among various interest groups regarding the reunification of China.

Mainland Affairs Council

The Mainland Affairs Council 行政院大陸委員會 is a formal administrative agency under the supervision of the ROC premier. It is responsible for the overall planning, coordination, evaluation, and partial implementation of the ROC government's policy toward the Chinese mainland. As a decision-making body, it also oversees rules and measures proposed by various ministries concerning cross-Straits relations. The MAC is headed by a chairman and three vice chairmen and is organized into seven departments and three divisions. Members of the Council include most of the ROC cabinet ministers and related commissioners or council chairmen.

Straits Exchange Foundation

The Straits Exchange Foundation 海峽交流基金會 is the only private organization empowered by the government to handle relations with the mainland. Nevertheless, the SEF so far only treats matters of a technical or business nature that might involve the government's public authority but would be inappropriate for the ROC government to handle under its policy of no official contacts with the mainland authorities. Accordingly, the SEF is not authorized to deal with political issues. "Policy dialogue," as exemplified by talks concerning the establishment of direct postal, commercial, and transportation links, is however an area of relations that the MAC is considering commissioning the SEF to conduct on its behalf.

The SEF is headed by a chairman and draws its funds from both the private sector and the government.

Koo-Wang Talks

On December 16, 1992, a little over ten months after the establishment of the SEF, the Peking government set up its Association for Relations Across the Taiwan Straits 海峽兩岸關係協會 (ARATS), with Wang Daohan as its chairman. In April 1993, Koo Chen-fu 辜振甫, chairman of the SEF, and the ARATS chairman met in Singapore and held talks in what was the first contact between Taipei and Peking since 1949. This first round of Koo-Wang talks resulted in several agreements dealing with document authentication, the handling of mail, and future meetings. Provisions were made for regular and non-periodic meetings between SEF and ARATS officials.

Following the meeting in Singapore, the two sides, through the SEF and the ARATS, held seven rounds of functional talks and three rounds of secretary-general-level talks. These meetings largely focused on practical issues and led to a number of agreements in areas such as the repatriation of hijackers, illegal entrants, and fishing disputes. Dates for future talks were also settled. At a preparatory meeting held in May 1995, it was decided that a second round of Koo-Wang talks would be held on July 20, 1995, in Peking. Both sides agreed that the talks would cover issues such as the implementation of accords signed during the first round of Koo-Wang talks, Taiwan investment rights on the Chinese mainland, and a wide range of unofficial exchanges.

Unfortunately, the mainland authorities postponed indefinitely this second round of Koo-Wang talks in June 1995, and began test-firing missiles into the Taiwan Straits the following month. Predictably, relations between Taiwan and the Chinese mainland at the semi-official level suffered. Thus, as of the end of 1996, the prospects that the second round of Koo-Wang talks would be held in the near future remained dim at best.

Unofficial Exchanges

Peking's bluster and military exercises certainly won it no friends in Taiwan. Compared to the first half of 1995, private-sector exchanges between Taiwan and the Chinese mainland dropped 24 percent in the second half of the year. The most precipitous drop was in the number of students, performing artists, athletes, and personnel accompanying cultural exhibits. Public opinion in Taiwan was also affected. A poll commissioned by the MAC in February 1995 indicated that roughly 58 percent of respondents felt Peking's attitude toward Taipei to be "hostile or unfriendly." In a similar MAC-sponsored poll conducted in July of the same year, this figure jumped to over 73 percent.

Nevertheless, the rapid expansion of exchanges between the two sides since 1987 seems to have imparted a certain momentum to their continuing development. For the year of 1995 as a whole, exchanges in almost all areas were up over 1994 levels (see inset, next page). One of the most actively growing areas was investment and trade. According to mainland statistics (as opposed to the lower figure recorded by the ROC's Investment Commission 經濟部投資審議委員會), Taiwan ranked as the second largest investor on the Chinese mainland in 1995, registering US$3.16 billion in direct investment that year. And despite the tensions between Taipei and Peking, indirect cross-Straits trade managed to grow by nearly 26 percent (see chart, next page). There were also several notable programs in the area of cultural exchanges. An exhibition of bronze wares from a Shanghai museum and the paintings of Qi Baishi 齊白石 came to Taiwan, while residents of the Chinese mainland were treated to "Living in Taiwan," a traveling photographic exhibition organized by the Chinese Photographic Culture Association 中華攝影文化協進會. A joint performance by Taiwan's ARS Formosa Company 傳大藝術公司 and the Shanghai National Music Orchestra, entitled "Experimental Chinese Orchestra," was another memorable production among the many valuable activities which enriched cross-Straits cultural exchanges in 1995. Educational exchanges included a visit by the presidents of Shanghai Jiaotong University and ten other universities on the mainland, as well as a donation of books to major universities on the mainland organized by the Chinese Comparative Education Society in Taipei 比較教育學會. The ROC government also provided scholarships for mainland postgraduates to conduct research in Taiwan.

Hong Kong and Macau

Chinese reunification cannot be discussed without mentioning Hong Kong and Macau, which are also integral parts of the Chinese nation. The ROC government realizes that the people of Hong Kong and Macau have carved remarkable niches for themselves in the East Asian economy and have contributed to positive change on the Chinese mainland. The ROC will therefore do everything in its power to preserve the rights and achievements of these two areas.

History of Hong Kong

Hong Kong has had a history separated from that of the rest of the Chinese nation for over 150 years. After losing the Opium War, the Ch'ing dynasty government was compelled to sign the unequal Treaty of Nanking in 1842 and to cede Hong Kong Island to Britain. Another military defeat ended with the 1860 Convention of Peking, under which the Ch'ing rulers leased the New Territories and 255 offshore islands to Brit-

Exchanges Between Taiwan and the Chinese Mainland in 1995

Category	Quantity	Annual change
Total cross-Straits trade[1]	US$22.53 billion	+25.97%
Mainland trade dependence on Taiwan[1]	10.46%	—
Taiwan trade dependence on the mainland[1]	8.02%	—
Taiwan investment in the mainland[2]	US$1.09 billion	+13.56%
Cross-Straits remittances[3]	US$620.92 million	+15.17%
Remittances to the mainland[3]	US$542.76 million	+20.48%
Remittances to Taiwan[3]	US$78.16 million	-11.8%
Cross-Straits postal exchanges[4]	17.19 million	-10.00%
Letters to the mainland[4]	6.25 million	-9.17%
Letters to Taiwan[4]	10.94 million	-10.48%
Cross-Straits telephone exchanges[5]	188.28 million min.	—
Calls to the mainland	134.17 million min.	—
Calls to Taiwan	54.11 million min.	—
Cross-Straits travel[6]	1.31 million	+13%
Taiwan visits to the mainland	1.27 million	+10%
Mainland visits to Taiwan	42,634	+80.9%

[1] MAC estimates based on ROC and Hong Kong customs data
[2] Investment Commission, Ministry of Economic Affairs, ROC 經濟部投資審議委員會
[3] Foreign Exchange Department, Central Bank of China, ROC 中央銀行外匯局
[4] Directorate General of Posts, Ministry of Transportation and Communications (MOTC), ROC 交通部郵政總局
[5] Directorate General of Telecommunications, MOTC 交通部電信總局
[6] China Travel Service 中國旅行社 in Hong Kong and the Bureau of Entry and Exit, National Police Administration, Ministry of the Interior, ROC 內政部警政署入出境管理局

ain for 99 years. The New Territories were leased to Great Britian for 99 years under the Convention for the Extension of Hongkong signed in Peking on June 9, 1898. In this chapter, the term Hong Kong refers to Hong Kong Island proper, southern Kowloon, the New Territories, and the offshore islands, that is, the whole area administered by the British since 1860.

In 1982, Britain opened negotiations with the authorities on the Chinese mainland to discuss the return of Hong Kong. On September 24, 1984, London and Peking signed a joint declaration in which they agreed that Hong Kong, after 150 years of British rule, was to be handed over to the mainland authorities on July 1, 1997. Peking made plans to establish the Hong Kong Special Administrative Region and promised to keep Hong Kong's capitalist system intact for 50 years after 1997. In April 1990, the mainland authorities drew up and promulgated the *Basic Law of the Hong Kong Special Administrative Region*. More recently, a provisional legislature was selected in March 1996 to take the place of Hong Kong's popularly elected Legislative Council, and the selection of a new governor followed in December of the same year.

History of Macau

Like Hong Kong, Macau has also experienced a history separate from that of the rest of China for over a century. Macau comprises a small peninsula projecting from the province of Kwangtung, as well as the islands of Taipa and Coloane, with a total area of only 16 square kilometers and a population of 4,000,000 mostly Chinese residents. The Portuguese leased Macau from China during the 16th, 17th, and 18th centuries and used the port as an entrepôt for trade with China and Japan. Under a treaty signed in 1887, the Ch'ing rulers deeded Macau to the Portuguese. In August 1979, Portugal established diplomatic relations with the authorities on the Chinese mainland and redefined Macau as a part of China temporarily administered by Portugal. In 1987, Lisbon and Peking issued a declaration stating that Macau will be returned to China on December 20, 1999. Starting in October 1988, the mainland authorities began drafting the *Basic Law of the Macau Special Administrative Region*. The first draft was completed in March 1992 and approved the following year.

ROC Government Policy

The ROC maintains very close ties with Hong Kong and Macau. In terms of the flow of people alone, Taiwan residents made 1.9 million trips to Hong Kong in 1995, while residents of Hong Kong took 174,000 trips to Taiwan. To handle this traffic, there are 250 flights from Taiwan to Hong Kong each week. Financial and investment ties are also strong: there are more than 3,000 Taiwan businesses registered in Hong Kong, and investors from Taiwan have sunk a total of over US$4 billion in the territory. In addition to Hong Kong's importance as a site for direct investment, the territory also serves as a transshipment point for cross-Straits trade. Hong Kong customs officials estimated that in 1995, US$11.46 billion worth of Taiwan-mainland trade passed through Hong Kong. Property and capital bound for investment on the Chinese mainland is also typically transferred through the territory.

In light of such close and comprehensive links, it should come as no surprise that policy concerning Hong Kong and Macau is a high priority of the ROC government. The ROC responded to the negotiations between Britain and the mainland authorities by forming a special Hong Kong Affairs Task Force in August 1983. After London and Peking signed their joint declaration, the Task Force was upgraded to a coordination panel under the direct supervision of the vice premier of the ROC government. Fol-

lowing the signing of the *Sino-Portuguese Joint Declaration* in July 1987, the name of the Hong Kong Affairs Task Force was changed to the Hong Kong and Macau Affairs Task Force 行政院港澳小組. At the end of January 1991 when the ROC government set up the MAC, the Task Force was incorporated into the new organization as its Department of Hong Kong and Macau Affairs 港澳處 to coordinate ROC government policies toward the two areas.

Due to the changes in the legal and political status of Hong Kong and Macau after 1997 and 1999, the ROC government plans to make some parallel adjustments in its Hong Kong and Macau policy. The goals are to preserve democracy, freedom, stability, and prosperity in Hong Kong and Macau; to promote understanding and cooperation between the people of Taiwan and the people of Hong Kong and Macau; to expand reciprocal bilateral exchanges and cooperation; and to respect the wishes of the people of Hong Kong and Macau and to continue to provide on-the-spot services in the two territories.

The ROC government has thus stated that it will retain its agencies in Hong Kong and Macau, and the MAC has been making plans regarding the post-handover names, status, structures, and functions of these agencies. It is hoped that the number and types of services provided by these agencies will not change. Responsibility for Hong Kong and Macau affairs will be redistributed to reflect the change in the two territories' legal and political status. The MAC will take charge of the overall planning and administration of Hong Kong and Macau affairs after responsibilities currently handled at the Ministry of Foreign Affairs 外交部 are transferred to it following the handovers. While administratively significant, this change should not have much impact on day-to-day affairs.

In order to establish a legal basis for the ROC's relations with Hong Kong and Macau after Peking assumes control, the MAC has drafted the *Statute on Relations with Hong Kong and Macau* 港澳關係條例. The operative principle behind the statute is that as long as the two territories retain a high degree of autonomy, the ROC government will regard them as special regions separate from the rest of the Chinese mainland. The statute addresses a number of issues, including travel, finance, trade, and transportation. According to the statute, people from Taiwan entering Hong Kong and Macau will follow normal regulations and will not be subject to special restrictions, while residents of Hong Kong and Macau may enter Taiwan after receiving approval. Calling for "free transportation links in principle; restriction or prohibition in exceptional cases," the statute also aims to preserve direct transportation and trade links. As for business and finance, the statute permits direct investment in Hong Kong and Macau by individuals and corporations from the ROC, and provides for such investment to be handled according to existing foreign investment and technical cooperation measures. The statute also indicates that investment in Taiwan by individuals and corporations from Hong Kong and Macau is to be handled according to existing laws on investment and technical cooperation by overseas Chinese.

Looking to the Future

A stable and democratic China is in the interest of both the Chinese people and the world as a whole. The Republic of China recognizes this fact and is firmly committed to the goal of reunification. However, the ROC is equally firm in its belief that reunification must be achieved peacefully, equitably, and democratically. Only by gradually expanding the scale and scope of exchanges and maintaining a continuous dialogue can success in this endeavor be assured.

'97 TAIPEI
INTERNATIONAL TRADE SHOWS

Taipei International Toy Show   Jan. 10-13

ENPROTECH '97   Feb. 26-Mar. 1

Taipei International   Mar. 6-10
Furniture Show

TIMTOS '97   Mar. 18-23
Taipei Int'l Machine Tool Show

Taipei International   Mar. 28-Apr. 1
Electronics Spring Show

GIFTIONERY TAIPEI '97   Apr. 8-11
Taipei Int'l Gift & Stationery
Spring Show

Taipei International Cycle Show   Apr. 16-19

TAISPO '97   Apr. 24-27
Taipei Int'l Sporting Goods Show

TAIPEI BUILD '97   May 2-5
Taipei Int'l Building Materials,
Hardware & Construction Show

SOFTEX TAIPEI '97   May 2-6
(Local Market Oriented)
Taipei Computer Software Show

Taipei Int'l Auto/Motorcycle   May 17-20
Parts & Accessories Show

Macworld Expo Taipei '97   May 24-28
(Local Market Oriented)

TIDEX '97   May 24-28
Taipei Int'l Design Exhibition

Celebration of Excellence-   May 24-28
Taiwan Product Showcase

COMPUTEX TAIPEI '97   June 3-7
Taipei Int'l Computer Show

Taipei Int'l Food Industry Show   June 12-16

Taipei Computer Applications Show   Aug. 4-8
(Local Market Oriented)

Taipei Aerospace Technology   Aug. 14-17
Exhibition

Taipei Int'l Jewelry &   Sept. 5-9
Timepiece Show

TITAS '97   Sept. 5-9
Taipei International Textile &
Apparel Show

TAIPEI PLAS '97   Oct. 6-10
Taipei Int'l Plastics &
Rubber Industry Show

Taipei Int'l Electronics Show   Oct. 16-21

GIFTIONERY TAIPEI   Oct. 27-30
Taipei Int'l Gift & Stationery
Autumn Show

Taipei Int'l Medical Equipment   Nov. 8-11
& Pharmaceuticals Show

TAIPEI PACK '97   Nov. 17-21
Taipei Int'l Packaging Industry Show

Subject to change without notice.

Organizer:
China External Trade
Development Council

Sponsor:
Taipei World
Trade Center

Official Carrier:

Organizer: China External Trade Development Council (CETRA).
    5 Hsinyi Road, Section 5, Taipei, Taiwan, R.O.C. Tel: 886-2-725-1111, Fax: 886-2-725-1314
    http://www.taipeitradeshows.org
Venue: Taipei World Trade Center Exhibition Hall (TWTC)

8.
National Defense

Above: The Harpoon Missile-like Hsiung-feng anti-ship surface-to-air missile, a mainstay in the defense arsenal of ROC ground forces.

Right: A female ROC naval officer—one tangible indicator of the increasing role of women in the armed forces of the Republic of China.

Previous page: A key component of the ROC Air Force operational unit—the S-70C helicopter is used extensively in emergency rescue operations throughout the Taiwan area.

8 National Defense

The primary objective of the ROC's defense policy is to defend the area currently under ROC control, which includes Taiwan, the Pescadores, Kinmen, and Matsu. This entails establishing a fighting force of sufficient readiness to guard the nation and protect its people. The direct and most serious threat to the ROC's national security remains the unwillingness of Peking to renounce the use of military force against Taiwan. Thus, while ROC national defense strategy calls for balanced development of the three Armed Forces, naval and air supremacy receive first priority. In addition to current defensive preparations, a long-term policy of developing an elite fighting force and self-sufficiency in defense technology is also being strictly followed. This calls for restructuring the Armed Forces, streamlining command levels, renovating logistical systems, merging or reassigning military schools and upper-ranking staff units, as well as reducing the total number of men in uniform.

Budgetary Reduction Trend

The defense budget for the ROC military has generally been trimmed each year over the past decade, and an increasing percentage has become open to public scrutiny. For fiscal 1996, the defense budget amounted to US$9.57 billion, or 22.76 percent of the total national budget, down from 24.51 percent in fiscal 1995. This latter percentage was actually 0.33 percent higher than fiscal 1994, due to the need to build new warships and replace outdated fighters. Thus, the overall downward budgetary trend has been resumed.

Doing More with Less

The thinking behind changes to the ROC's Armed Forces over the past few years reflects a shift from equal stress on offense and defense to assuring defense. This strategic principle, as implemented under the Ten-Year Troop Reduction Plan 十年兵力精簡方案, has led to a targeted force of less than 400,000 troops by the year 2003 and an increase in the ratio of combat troops to overall military manpower.

The allocation of resources among the three services will give priority to air superiority and control of the seas in defensive operations, as well as to coastal defense. Accordingly, a ten-year program is to be implemented in three phases, including the development of a practicable table of organization for the three services to facilitate training and carry out peacetime missions, elimination of overlapping staff units in the three major services, and consolidation of the General Staff Headquarters of the Ministry of National Defense (MND) and the general headquarters of the three services, transferring non-military tasks to organizations outside the MND.

Second-generation weapon systems used by the three armed services are also being actively updated. These include the inception of four E-2T air defense warning systems, the formation of the first Ching-kuo indigenous defense fighter 經國號戰機 (IDF) squadron, the commissioning of the Cheng-kung 成功號 and Knox-class missile frigates, and taking delivery of a second batch of AH-1W attack helicopters and OH-58D reconnaissance helicopters.

Command Structure

Article 36 of the ROC Constitution stipulates that the president of the republic "shall have supreme command of the land, sea and air forces of the whole country," and Article 3 of the *Organic Law of the Executive Yuan* 行政院組織法 states that "the Executive Yuan shall establish (among others) a Ministry of National Defense." According to the *Organization Law of the MND* 國防部組織法, the ministry shall be in charge of the defense affairs of the whole country, and the minister shall be a civilian. The current defense minister is Chiang Chung-ling 蔣仲苓.

Within the Ministry of National Defense is the General Staff Headquarters (GSH), under which are the various services, including the Army, Navy, Air Force, Combined Services Forces, Armed Forces Reserve Command/Coast Guard Command, and Military Police Command. In charge of military affairs, the GSH is headed by a chief of the general staff, who acts, in the military command system, as chief of staff to the president for operational matters; while in the administrative system, he serves as chief of staff to the minister of national defense. The current chief of the general staff is General Lo Pen-li 羅本立.

Ministry of National Defense

The Ministry of National Defense 國防部 is responsible for formulating military strategy, setting military personnel policies, devising draft and mobilization plans, delineating supply distribution policies, arranging for the research and development of military technology, compiling data for the national defense budget, setting military regulations, conducting court martial proceedings and administering military law. The ministry itself has a Minister's Office 部長辦公室; Departments of Manpower 人力司, Materials 物力司, and Law 法制司; a Bureau of the Comptroller 主計局, and the Judge Advocates Bureau 軍法局.

General Staff Headquarters, MND

In charge of the planning and supervision of joint war activities, political warfare, personnel, military intelligence, operations, education and training, logistics, organization and equipment calibration, communications, military archives management, and medical services, the General Staff Headquarters, MND 國防部參謀本部 contains the Office of the Chief of the General Staff 參謀總長辦公室; the Department of Supervision and Inspection 督察部; the General Political Warfare Department 總政治作戰部; Offices of the Deputy Chiefs of the General Staff for Personnel 人事參謀次長室, Intelligence 情報參謀次長室, Operations 作戰參謀次長室, Logistics 後勤參謀次長室, and Planning 計劃參謀次長室; the Bureau of Communications and Electronics 通信電子局; the Military History and Translation Bureau 史政編譯局; the Military Medical Bureau 軍醫局; and the General Affairs Bureau 總務局.

On July 1, 1995, various military purchasing units were integrated into a Procurement Bureau, MND 國防部採購局, responsible for overall plan-

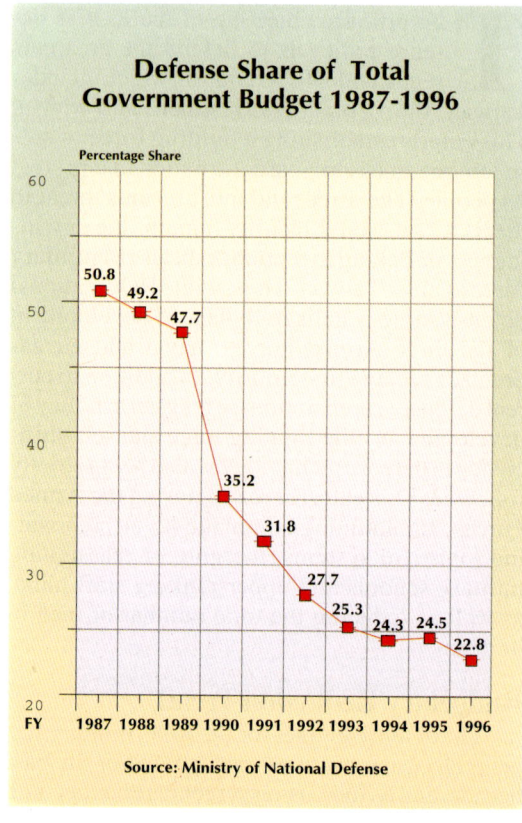

Defense Share of Total Government Budget 1987-1996

Percentage Share

FY	Value
1987	50.8
1988	49.2
1989	47.7
1990	35.2
1991	31.8
1992	27.7
1993	25.3
1994	24.3
1995	24.5
1996	22.8

Source: Ministry of National Defense

ning and purchasing major weapon systems and equipment required by the ROC Armed Forces. The Bureau consists of five departments, two offices, and one overseas procurement section.

General Headquarters of Each Service

Army General Headquarters

The Army General Headquarters 陸軍總部 is responsible for developing and maintaining the Army's combat power, commanding and supervising all subordinate troops and units. Under its command are the Army Logistics Command 後勤司令部, Army Commands 軍團司令部, and the Airborne and Special Operations Command 空降特戰司令部. Also under its command are the various Army units (in descending order) of army 軍團, division 師, brigade 旅, battalion 營, company 連, and platoon 排.

Navy General Headquarters

The Navy General Headquarters 海軍總部 is in charge of developing and maintaining the Navy's combat readiness, as well as commanding and supervising all its subordinate fleets and ground units. Under its command are the Naval Fleet Command 艦隊司令部, the Marine Corps Headquarters 陸戰隊司令部, the Navy Logistics Command 後勤司令部, Headquarters of the Naval Area Command 軍區司令部, the Area Service Office 地區勤務處, the Naval Base Command 基地指揮部, and the Bureau of Maritime Survey 海洋測量局. The subordinate Navy units are under the direct supervision of the Naval Fleet Command 艦隊司令部 and are organized into the fleet 艦隊, group 戰隊, and ship 艦 levels. The Marine Corps units, like those of the Army, extend from the Marine Corps Headquarters 陸戰隊司令部, through division 師, regiment 團, battalion 營, company 連, and platoon 排.

Air Force General Headquarters

The Air Force General Headquarters 空軍總部 is responsible for the Air Force's combat strength and commands and supervises all subordinate troops and units. The units include the Air Force Operations Command 作戰司令部, the Air Force Logistics Command 後勤司令部, the Air Defense Artillery Command 防砲警衛司令部, and various tactical wings 聯隊. Under the wing in descending order are the group 大隊, squadron 中隊, and flight 分隊.

Combined Services Force General Headquarters

The Combined Services Force General Headquarters 聯勤總部 is in charge of ordinance, military maps, and communication equipment for the ROC Armed Forces. It also provides support and services commonly needed by all Armed Forces services, such as finance, surveying, engineering, rear echelon administration, purchase and procurement, and armament appraisal and testing.

Armed Forces Reserve Command

Shortly after the ROC government announced the lifting of the *Emergency Decree* 戒嚴令 and the termination of the Period of National Mobilization for Suppression of the Communist Rebellion 動員戡亂時期, the Taiwan Garrison General Headquarters 警備總部 (TGGH) was deactivated, and two new commands were created to assume partial responsibility for tasks formerly performed by the TGGH. The first of these is the Armed Forces Reserve Command 軍管區司令部 (AFRC), which is mainly in charge of reservist management and mobilization affairs. For more detailed descriptions of AFRC tasks, see the sections on Manpower Structure and Military Mobilization below.

Coast Guard Command

The second new command to be formed from the TGGH, the Coast Guard Command 海岸巡防司令部 (CGC), is responsible for eight local coast guard commands and 25 coast guard battalions. These secure and protect the coastline from intrusion and smuggling by carrying out coastal patrol and defense through such activities, such as air patrols, inshore patrols, harbor inspections, and inland inspections.

The primary mission of Coast Guard forces is to safeguard coastal areas but in peacetime, they also detect and interdict, in conjunction with the military authorities, police units, custom houses, and/or other law enforcement units, smuggling and infiltration. In wartime, the Coast Guard forces have a ground-fighting mission.

Military Police Command

The Military Police 憲兵 guard military and certain governmental installations, enforce military law, maintain military discipline, support combat troops, and serve as supplementary police when necessary to maintain public security. The Military Police have five sub-commands and one training center. The Military Police Command 憲兵司令部 has a Department of Political Warfare 政治作戰部 and offices of Personnel 人事署, Intelligence 情報署, Police Affairs 警務署, Logistics 後勤署, Planning 計畫署, Comptroller 主計處, Judge Advocates 軍法處, and General Affairs 總務處.

Manpower Structure

A person in the ROC military may be an officer 軍官, a noncommissioned officer (NCO)

士官, or an enlisted man 士兵. He may be serving on either a volunteer 志願役 or a conscript 義務役 basis, and may be on active duty 常備 or reserve 後備 status.

Officers

Officers in the ROC military generally come from three backgrounds. They might be graduates of military academies who become career officers 正期軍官, graduates of different specialized military schools who serve shorter terms of duty 專科軍官, or college graduates who have passed a written test to become reserve officers 預官.

Approximately 15 percent of the officers commissioned each year are graduates from different military academies; another 45 percent are graduates of specialized military schools; and the remaining 40 percent are reserve officers.

The ratio of officers to NCOs is currently 1:2.4, while that to enlisted men is 1:2.6. Thus, the ratio of officers to soldiers as a whole in the ROC Armed Forces is around 1:5, which is close to the 1:6 ratio of the US Armed Forces, and almost equals that of the Japanese Self-Defense Force (1:4.98).

Noncommissioned Officers

NCOs constitute the backbone of basic units of the Armed Forces, and are increasingly depended upon to train troops and develop their combat performance. In recent years, however, most senior NCOs have retired, leaving the current proportion of career NCOs too low and the percentage of NCO reservists in service too high. Reservists are on active duty for a very limited period of time, making it difficult for them to keep up with changes in the operation and maintenance of ever-more sophisticated weapons and equipment. Solutions to this problem lie in reconfiguring the NCO organizational structure and recruiting new NCOs.

Conscripts

The *Military Service Law* 兵役法 of the ROC stipulates that all males in the Republic of China shall fulfill military service. Article 3 of the law states: "Male persons shall be liable for military service on January 1 of the year immediately following the year during which they reach the age of 18, and shall no longer be drafted for service beginning on December 31 of the year during which they reach the age of 45." Citizens who have been sentenced to imprisonment for longer than seven years are prohibited from entering the military.

Under the *Military Service Law*, military conscription is administered jointly by the Ministry of National Defense and the Ministry of the Interior 內政部. The former is responsible for securing an adequate number of conscripts and training them, while the latter determines the sources of the conscripts and ensures their rights and benefits. Generally, conscripts undergo a minimum of two months of basic training before receiving their 22-month unit assignments.

Male senior high, vocational high, and college students whose studies would be interrupted by military conscription can defer their induction until after graduation. Students who are admitted to a university or college undergo two months of basic training in the summer before their freshman year. Upon graduation, they re-enter the military to fulfill the remainder of their two-year commitment.

Young men in poor health are exempt from military conscription. Those in average health may serve in the National Guard 國民兵. Draftees from impoverished families may apply for service in this unit, giving them reserve status and allowing them to stay with their families. In addition, the only son of parents who are over seventy may also apply for National Guard service to fulfill his military obligation.

Manpower and Equipment
Ground Forces

Ground forces in the ROC, mainly those of the Army and the Military Police, number some 250,000. The Army is organized into combat, combat support, and service support troops—all under the command of the Army GHQ, and is organized into the following units:

* 3 armies;

- Quemoy 金門, Matsu 馬祖, P'enghu 澎湖, and Hualien 花蓮-T'aitung 台東 Headquarters;
- Tungyin Island Command 東指部 and Chükuang Island Command 莒指部;
- Airborne and Special Operations Command (2 airborne brigades and 2 aviation groups);
- 2 mechanized infantry divisions;
- 10 infantry divisions;
- 6 armored brigades;
- 1 tank group;
- 7 reserve divisions;
- 3 mobile divisions; and
- 2 air defense missile groups.

The primary weapon systems of the ROC ground forces include M48H and M60A3 tanks; M109 and M110 self-propelled artillery; M113, V-150, and CM-21 armored personnel carriers; UH-1H helicopters; Kung-feng 工蜂 6A rocket systems; TOW-type anti-tank guided weapons; Chaparral SP, Hawk, Tien-kung 天弓 (Sky Bow), and Tien-chien 天劍 (Sky Sword) air defense missile systems; as well as Hsiung-feng 雄蜂 I and Hsiung-feng II anti-ship missile systems.

Navy

The ROC Navy is charged with maintaining control and surveillance of the waters that surround Taiwan. The Navy also takes part in joint operations with the Army and Air Force. Including some 30,000 marines, the ROC Navy forces number around 68,000 officers and men. Navy GHQ oversees operational and land-based forces. The former consists of:

- 2 destroyer fleets and 1 frigate fleet;
- 1 amphibious landing fleet and 1 amphibious landing vessel fleet;
- 1 submarine group;
- 1 mine vessel fleet and 1 mine-sweeper/layer fleet;
- 1 logistical service fleet and 1 logistical rescue group;
- 1 Hai-chiao 海蛟 speedboat group;
- 1 anti-submarine helicopter group;
- 1 Hai-feng 海鋒 shore-based missile group; and

- 2 marine divisions, 1 landing tank regiment, and 1 operational service regiment.

Logistical support is carried out by one fleet of auxiliary craft while another fleet of auxiliary craft is assigned to disaster relief duties. The Navy's coastal SAM batteries employ Hsiung-feng missiles which resemble US Harpoon missiles.

Air Force

Taiwan's geographical location makes air defense critical for overall defense of the nation. At present, the ROC Air Force has some 68,000 officers and men. Personnel are divided into operational and logistical support systems under the command of the Air Force GHQ.

The main operational units in the ROC Air Force include the following:

- 6 tactical combat aircraft wings;
- 1 transport/anti-submarine wing;
- 1 tactical control wing;
- 1 communication and ATC wing;
- 1 weather forecasting wing; and
- 1 air-defense artillery guards command, comprising 4 commands, 14 air defense artillery battalions, and 11 guard battalions.

Units in the operational system are equipped with aircraft that include F-104 and F-5E fighter-interceptors, C-130 and C-119 transports, AT-3 trainers, and S-70C helicopters. In addition, the United States and France have respectively agreed to sell 150 F-16 fighters and 60 Mirage 2000 fighters to the ROC Air Force to counter moves by the Chinese mainland to buy advanced Russian fighters. These purchases are budgeted at US$11.6 billion to be paid for in the nine-year period from 1993 to 2001.

The ROC Army will spend over US$385 million to deploy 200 fourth-generation Patriot missiles—the most improved version. The only surface-to-air radar-guided anti-missile system ever tested in combat, Patriot missiles were used in the 1991 Persian Gulf War to defend against Scud missile attacks. The 200 Patriot missiles will be installed in three missile batteries in northern Taiwan.

Military Mobilization

The ROC defense strategy calls for maintaining a minimum force in peacetime and mobilizing a large number of troops in the event of war. In peacetime, the primary mobilization missions are to test the preparedness of reservists for instant action when needed.

At present, registered reservists in the ROC number about 3.8 million, or more than 18 percent of the general population. After a man is discharged from active duty, he must report to his local military reserve unit, a subunit under the Armed Forces Reserve Command. Reservists are organized into different units according to their military occupational specialty 軍職專長 (MOS). Of the total, about 800,000 to one million serve annually in the reserve for testing the muster to ensure mobilization for war can be realized. In 1995, some 58,000 men were called for muster and training. For 1996, almost 100,000 men have been called up.

Since a prolonged mobilization recall might adversely affect both the livelihood of a reservist and the overall economic development of the country, annual reservist training is usually conducted through recalls. An MOS refresher training course is conducted, and each reservist is notified of his unit combat mission and relative location.

The purpose of muster call is to maintain reserve readiness by practicing good habits of reporting immediately upon being called, and to keep reserve data up-to-date. Ways to streamline call-up procedures and maximize the public convenience of the workload are reviewed from time to time. In 1995, 762,000 men were called up, with 757,000 men, or 99 percent of them, reporting instantly. In 1996, some 800,000 men were called.

Military Education

Military education of officers is conducted along two developmental lines: the universal track 通才發展路線 for career soldiers and the professional track 專業發展路線 for specialized military personnel. The universal track is the general military education for career soldiers provided at the three service academies. Graduates of the three receive a bachelor's degree, which is considered the basic educational level for career soldiers. Career soldiers may then receive additional intermediate training on a short-term basis at a number of the military branch schools, such as the infantry, armor, and artillery branch schools of the Army. Candidates for full colonel (captain) 上校 or major general (rear admiral) 少將 have to receive advanced military education at the Armed Forces University 三軍大學.

The professional track is for specialized military personnel, including medical personnel, engineers, and technicians. Training for specialized military personnel is dispensed at various specialized military schools, such as Fu Hsing Kang College, the Chung-Cheng Institute of Technology, and the National Defense Medical College.

Military Academies

The Chinese Military Academy 陸軍軍官學校 (CMA), founded by Dr. Sun Yat-sen in 1924 at Whampoa 黃埔, Kwangtung Province, relocated to Fengshan 鳳山, Kaohsiung County, Taiwan in 1950. The large campus features modern educational facilities and equipment to cultivate future army officers and develop military science. The CMA has a tradition of stringent educational requirements, accepting and training only the most qualified candidates.

In 1954, the CMA began placing increased emphasis on education in scientific, technical, and other non-military fields. Cadets are required to complete 130 university-level credits in subjects such as political science, social science, mathematics, physics, chemistry, mechanics, civil engineering, electrical engineering, information management, and foreign languages over a period of four years. Right after graduation, the young lieutenants receive further training in a branch specialty, such as infantry, armor, artillery (missiles), engineering, transportation, communications (electronics), chemistry, or the military police.

The Chinese Naval Academy 海軍軍官學校 (CNA) offers cadets courses similar to those in civilian colleges of science and engineering. During a four-year training period, they take special military courses, including navigation, marine engineering, equipment maintenance, and serve an apprenticeship aboard ship.

Just prior to graduation, CNA cadets sail abroad in an armada dubbed the "Fleet of Friendship" 敦睦艦隊 for two months of hands-on training. In recent years, the "Fleet of Friendship" has sailed as far as the Middle East and South Africa. During the long voyage, future naval officers are given a chance to practice their combat skills and tactics and to enrich their navigational experience.

The Chinese Air Force Academy 空軍軍官學校 (CAFA) trains pilots for jet fighters and other combat and transport aircraft. Cadets learn aeronautic navigation, combat tactics, and related skills in a program that lasts four years. They participate in supervised flight operations during their second year. At the beginning of their junior year, cadets are divided into five sections to receive specialized training in flight skills, aeronautic machinery, electronic communication, antiaircraft warfare, and air control.

Fu Hsing Kang College 政治作戰學校 (FHKC), located in the Peit'ou 北投 district of Taipei, was established in 1951 to train competent political warfare cadres for the Armed Forces. There are three levels of education at FHKC: basic, advanced, and graduate. The college has 11 departments and a graduate school offering both master's and doctoral degree programs.

The National Defense Medical College 國防醫學院 (NDMC) trains military medical specialists, providing a basic college education plus medical training in such fields as dentistry, pharmacology, nursing, and public health. It also has 11 graduate-level, including master's and doctoral programs. The Tri-Service General Hospital 三軍總醫院 is the main teaching hospital of the NDMC.

The Chung-Cheng Institute of Technology 中正理工學院 conducts research and development of weapon systems, maintains arms and equipment, and educates technical military officers. It has one doctoral and six master's degree programs, and 11 undergraduate departments.

The National Defense Management College 國防管理學院 is responsible for educating the planning, decision-making, and management personnel of the Armed Forces. It has a Graduate School of Information Management 資訊管理所, a Graduate School of Law 法律研究所, and departments of accounting, statistics, business management, information management, and law.

The Chung-Cheng Armed Forces Preparatory School 中正國防幹部預備學校, founded in 1976, provides senior high school education to young students who wish to continue in one of the three service academies or FHKC following graduation. It combines the ordinary education of a senior high school with basic military training and innovative teaching methods.

The ROC Armed Forces also operate a number of branch schools, such as the Infantry 陸軍步兵學校, Armor 陸軍裝甲兵學校, and Artillery 陸軍炮兵學校 branch schools of the Army, as well as specialized schools, such as the Air Technical School 空軍機械學校 and the Air Communications and Electronics School 空軍通信電子學校.

The Armed Forces University, formerly the Army Officers School, was founded in 1906, six years before the establishment of the Republic of China. It is now the highest-level institution in our military education system. It is responsible for training strategic-level command and staff officers, as well as specialists in national defense administration and military intelligence. It also conducts research into the development of war strategies and political warfare. The university includes four colleges: the War College 戰爭學院, and the Command and Staff Colleges for the Army 陸軍指參學院, Navy 海軍指參學院, and Air Force 空軍指參學院.

Defense R&D

Research and development of national defense technology is crucial to national modernization. While the ROC industrial sector has made considerable progress over the past decade, most of it has in fact been confined to machining components and light manufacturing. The MND has long made use of the National Defense Industrial Development Fund 國防工業發展基金 to assist public and private enterprises in cultivating qualified technical personnel and purchasing facilities, transferring advanced technology, and developing a more sophisticated production base that one day promises a fully self-reliant defense industry.

The MND has issued the *Defense Science and Technology Development Plan* 國防科技發展方案 to strengthen cooperation between the academic and industrial sectors, and has, along with several cabinet-level institutions such as the National Science Council 國家科學委員會, the Ministry of Education 教育部, and the Ministry of Economic Affairs 經濟部, set up the Executive Committee for the Development of Defense Science and Technology 國防科技發展推行委員會 (ECDDST). With its two subdivisions, the Academic Cooperation Group 學術合作小組 and the Industrial Cooperation Group 工業合作小組, the ECDDST taps academic resources for researching defense technology and makes use of the industrial sector to develop and manufacture weaponry and armaments.

Chungshan Institute of Science and Technology

As the leading institution for the research, development, and design of defense technology in the ROC, the Chungshan Institute of Science and Technology 中山科學研究院 (CIST) contains some 6,000 scientists and more than 8,000 technicians.

With its headquarters in Lungt'an 龍潭, Taoyuan County 桃園縣, the CIST has facilities stretching over nearly 6,000 acres scattered throughout Taiwan, and is divided into four major research divisions: aeronautics, missiles and rockets, electronics, and chemistry. The CIST has six centers for systems development, systems maintenance, quality assurance, materials R&D, aeronautic development, and missile manufacturing. Each research division or research center has a director in charge of the research and

development of its specialty, while planning units have project chairmen responsible for R&D program management and system integration. The CIST jointly conducts independent research and development of weapon systems with the Aero Industry Development Center 航空工業發展中心, which is now under CIST supervision; some manufacturing units of the Combined Services Force; academic institutions; and public and civilian industries.

To date, a number of weapon systems have been domestically designed, tested, and produced on a mass scale by the CIST. These include the Kung-feng 6A rocket, the Hsiung-feng I and Hsiung-feng II SAMs, artillery fire control systems, naval sonar systems, naval electronic warfare systems, and the Tzu-chiang trainer aircraft 自強訓練機. The CIST has produced or plans to produce Tien-kung I and Tien-kung II SAMs, and Tien-chien AAMs. The institute is also developing the Tien-chien II AAM system.

The ROC Navy has been developing a second generation of missile frigates and missile patrol boats. The first domestically built missile frigate (FPG-2) was built and handed over to the ROC Navy in May 1993, with the expectation that one such frigate would be produced every 11 months from then on.

Aerospace Development

A proposal to privatize the Aero Industry Development Center was approved by the Legislature 立法院 on May 16, 1995. This conversion from military to private status, under the supervision of the Ministry of Economic Affairs, is intended to facilitate the transfer of ROC military aeronautic know-how to the private sector while enabling the center to form joint ventures with high-tech foreign manufacturers. This in turn is expected to bring advanced aviation technology into Taiwan to accelerate the growth of the nation's aerospace industry. A period of three-and-a-half years has been granted to the center to carry out full privatization.

THE GRAND HOTEL

The Grand is the only hotel in the world built in a truly Chinese-palace style. It has over 530 distinguished guest rooms and facilities that include 6 restaurants, the Golden Coin Bar, banquet rooms, and a ballroom to accommodate over 1,000 people for a sit-down banquet in grandeur. Recreational facilities include an Olympic-size swimming pool, tennis courts, billiards, and bowling alleys.

Above: Vice President Lien Chan accompanies King Mswati of Swaziland on a visit to Taipei's Chiang Kai-shek Memorial Hall.

Right: Technical training exchange programs play an important part in the ROC's relations with its diplomatic partners.

Previous page: ROC President Lee Teng-hui and President Yahya Jammeh of the Republic of the Gambia sign a communiqué in Taipei on November 25, 1996.

9 Foreign Relations

The Republic of China is a sovereign nation. As such, it conducts foreign relations with other countries and seeks a clearly defined status within the ever changing world order. For historical and political reasons, however, the ROC occupies a relatively amorphous position in the international community. The ROC is among the world's 20 largest trading nations, and in addition to sharing formal diplomatic ties with 30 countries, also maintains substantive relations with over 140 countries and territories around the globe. Nevertheless, the Republic of China is not yet seated in the United Nations. This situation is unacceptable to the government and people of the Republic of China.

The ROC, founded in 1912, weathered foreign invasions and a civil war in the middle of this century, and remains to this day the democratic and representative government on Chinese land. The international community should not ignore the fact that the Republic of China is a viable nation which rules a defined territory and has its own constitution, flag, legal system, and military. Furthermore, the ROC government represents the 21.4 million people living in the Taiwan area, who cannot be represented by any other government in the world.

Continued exclusion of the Republic of China from the realm of formal diplomacy is unrealistic and costly. Foreign relations in the post-Cold War era are characterized by multilateralism and the development of regional alliances to promote economic and security issues. Exclusion of any single nation in the Asia-Pacific region severely compromises the integrity and effectiveness of multilateralism in this area. Unable, in many cases, to join international bodies, to participate in multilateral forums, or to sign international conventions, the ROC has to resort to a roundabout form of bilateralism that duplicates effort and wastes time. The ROC could deal much more effectively with issues ranging from the provision of international aid to the conservation of endangered species if it were a signatory to relevant international conventions and

were allowed to attend the multilateral forums within the United Nations framework.

Obstruction

For many years, the authorities on the Chinese mainland have sought to obstruct the ROC's relations with the world community because they assert that China is united under the rule of their Marxist-Leninist party in Peking and that the ROC government is merely a local government. Peking insists that the people in the Taiwan area accept rule by a communist dictatorship and may not have their own foreign policy. Peking threatens to sever or downgrade relations with any country establishing or strengthening relations with the ROC. Insisting that Taiwan is a renegade province, the Chinese communists have fomented controversies over issues such as the right of representation, membership, and name to obstruct ROC participation in international organizations and activities, whether they are political, economic, or cultural in nature.

The ROC realistically acknowledges the fact that Taiwan is currently separated from the Chinese mainland and that the ROC government and the Chinese communists must coexist peacefully (see Chapter 7, Mainland Affairs and National Unification Policy). Worldwide diplomatic recognition of the political entities on both sides of the Taiwan Straits is a crucial step toward true reconciliation and, eventually, peaceful reunification. It will also help to preserve regional peace in Southeast Asia.

Multilateralism

Over the past year, the ROC's efforts to take part in world organizations produced significant results. To date, the Republic of China enjoys membership in a number of intergovernmental organizations such as the Asian Development Bank (ADB), the International Cotton Advisory Committee (ICAC), the Asian Productivity Organization (APO), the Afro-Asian Rural Reconstruction Organization (AARRO), and the Central American Bank for Economic Integration (CABEI). The ROC also holds membership in 893 international non-governmental organizations.

Reinvolvement in the United Nations

The Republic of China was one of the founding members of the United Nations. Delegates from the ROC signed the UN Charter on June 26, 1945 in the US city of San Francisco, and the ROC served for over 20 years as a permanent member of the Security Council. From 1950 to 1971, the UN attempted to handle the dispute over a UN seat for China, which was divided into two mutually antagonistic political entities, each having its own territory, people, and government. Although the 26th General Assembly of the UN did eventually pass Resolution 2758, allowing the People's Republic of China to take over China's UN seat and forcing the Republic of China out in October 1971, the ROC did not simply disappear at that moment. On the contrary, the ROC has become a very active member of the international community and now maintains close ties and friendly relations with many nations.

The government and people of the Republic of China are seeking to participate in the UN so that they can contribute to the international community. Even though efforts to work together with other nations under the umbrella of the UN have met with opposition, the ROC has not given up on fulfilling its international responsibilities. The ROC set up the International Economic Cooperation and Development Fund, now known as the International Cooperation and Development Fund 國際合作發展基金, in 1988 and the International Humanitarian and Relief Fund 國際人道救濟基金 in 1989. By March 1996, these two funds had disbursed a total of US$613 million. In addition to financial aid, the Republic of China had as of March 1996 sent 45 technical cooperation teams to 37 countries to help with development-related tasks. The ROC offers vocational training courses in the areas of agriculture, trade, taxation, small and medium-size enterprise development, and scientific technology as part of its efforts to assist developing countries.

ROC Membership in International Nongovernmental Organizations

Nature of Organization	Number
Science and Technology	78
Medicine and Hygiene	186
Agriculture, Forestry, and Fisheries	37
Religion	61
Charity and Social Welfare	53
Education	12
Journalism	3
Culture and Arts	28
Law and Police Administration	8
Labor	72
Transportation and Tourism	18
Leisure and Recreation	23
Women, Family, and Youth	7
Business, Finance, and Economics	61
Engineering	18
Industrial Technology	27
Electronics and Mechanical Science	13
Mining and Energy	12
R&D and Management	70
Wildlife Conservation and Environmental Protection	17
Sports	89
Total	893

Increasing Support for ROC's UN Bid

During the 50th session of the UN General Assembly, which was held from September 25 through October 11, 1995, a total of 29 countries, including seven that did not have diplomatic ties with the ROC, voiced direct or indirect support for the ROC's UN bid. Of these friendly countries, 20 expressed explicit support for the ROC, namely the Bahamas, Burkina Faso, the Central African Republic, the Dominican Republic, Fiji, the Gambia, Grenada, Guatemala, Guinea-Bissau, Liberia, Malawi, Nicaragua, Niger, Panama, Paraguay, Saint Christopher and Nevis, Saint Lucia, Saint Vincent and the Grenadines, Solomon Islands, and Swaziland. Nine other countries—Belize, Costa Rica, the Czech Republic, Jordan, Latvia, Papua New Guinea, the Philippines, El Salvador, and Togo—spoke about the UN principle of universality or expressed concern about relations across the Taiwan Straits. In 1995, 20 countries, five more than in 1994, endorsed a proposal requesting that the UN discuss the ROC's participation in the UN, and the proposal itself received considerable attention from other UN members. During the special commemorative meeting of the General Assembly held on the occasion of the 50th Anniversary of the UN in October 1995, 20 countries spoke in support of the ROC's participation in the UN: they were the Central African Republic, Costa Rica, the Ivory Coast, Dominica, Fiji, the Gambia, Grenada, Guatemala, Guinea-Bissau, Liberia, Malawi, Nicaragua, Niger, Panama, Saint Christopher and Nevis, Saint Lucia, Saint Vincent and the Grenadines, El Salvador, Solomon Islands, and Swaziland. Building on the efforts of 1995, representatives from 28 nations voiced their support of a proposal asking the UN General Assembly to discuss the ROC's bid to participate in UN activities. These countries were the Bahamas, Belize, Burkina Faso, the Central African Republic, Costa Rica, the Czech Republic, Dominica, the Dominican Republic, El Salvador, Fiji, the Gambia, Grenada, Guatemala, Guinea-Bissau, Honduras, Jordan, Latvia, Malawi, Nicaragua, Panama, Papua New Guinea, Paraguay, Saint Christopher and Nevis, Saint Lucia, Saint Vincent and the Grenadines, Senegal, Solomon Islands, and Swaziland. The ROC has also received support from the European Parliament, which passed a resolution in July 1996 asking the European Union to back the ROC's efforts to be represented in international organizations such as the United Nations.

Economic Organizations

The Republic of China is already an active member of many international economic organizations, and to further demonstrate its commitment to the world community, the ROC is working to expand its role in many more. One such example is the WTO. Although the ROC was one of the founding members of the WTO's predecessor, the GATT, it lost its membership following the communist takeover of the Chinese mainland. The ROC returned to the GATT as an observer in 1965, but was forced out again in 1972, shortly after the Chinese mainland replaced the ROC in the United Nations. In 1987, the ROC began seeking re-entry to the GATT, and in 1990 filed a formal application for membership under the name of the Separate Customs Territory of Taiwan, Penghu, Kinmen and Matsu. On September 29, 1992, the GATT established a working party to examine the ROC's Foreign Trade Memorandum and to draft a protocol of accession. Meanwhile, the GATT offered the ROC observer status, which allowed the ROC to participate in related meetings before becoming a full member. The working party held its first meeting in Geneva on November 6, 1992. Since April 1994, the ROC has been engaged in bilateral trade negotiations with various GATT members. By the end of 1995, seven formal working party meetings, one informal meeting, and 137 rounds of bilateral trade negotiations had taken place. On January 1, 1995, the World Trade Organization (WTO) was established to replace the GATT, and the ROC was granted WTO observer status on January 31, 1995. On December 1, 1995, the ROC applied for WTO membership. The ROC hopes to expedite the procedures for its accession to the WTO and has aggressively pursued negotiations with WTO member states to further this goal.

The ROC also played an extensive role in various other multilateral economic activities. From April 1995 through March 1996, the ROC was invited to participate in nine informal dialogues and workshops held between the Organization for Economic Cooperation and Development (OECD) and dynamic nonmember economies. In addition, the ROC is an active participant in the Pacific Economic Cooperation Council (PECC) and the Pacific Basin Economic Council (PBEC). As a full APEC (Asia-Pacific Economic Cooperation) member, the ROC plays an active role in the various forums and conferences sponsored by this organization. In November 1995, the ROC sent a representative to the third APEC Economic Leaders Meeting in Osaka, Japan. This year the ROC has attended almost all APEC meetings and activities. Senior advisor to the president Koo Chen-fu 辜振甫 represented the ROC at the APEC summit meeting held in November 1996 at Subic Bay in the Philippines.

Bilateralism

The Republic of China continues to strengthen formal relations with countries which recognize the ROC and to establish or enhance substantive relations with non-hostile nations that do not recognize the ROC. Pragmatism requires that the ROC maintain representative offices in non-hostile nations. Representative offices offer some but not all of the services usually provided by embassies or consulates. The ROC now has one consulate-general, 64 representative offices, and 30 administrative offices in 65 countries with which it does not share diplomatic relations. Of these, 17 offices are identified as representing the Republic of China, while 73 use names containing "Taipei."

Most of the ROC representative offices in Europe now use either Taipei Economic and Cultural Office or Taipei Representative Office. The names of those in the United States have also undergone revision. In September 1994, the ROC's head representative office in Washington, D.C., changed its name from the Coordination Council for North American Affairs (CCNAA) to the Taipei Economic and Cultural Representative Office (TECRO). Branch offices in other US cities made similar changes. The ROC mission in Colombia was renamed the Taipei Commercial Office. The ROC's representative office in France, the Association for the Promotion of Commercial and Tourist Exchanges with Taiwan, was renamed the Taipei Representative Office in France. Similarly, 42 countries that do not have diplomatic relations with the ROC have set up 45 representative offices, associations, or visa-issuing centers in Taiwan (for a complete listing of ROC representative offices abroad and foreign representative offices in the ROC, please see appendices IV and V).

Ministry of Foreign Affairs On-line

In August 1996, the ROC Ministry of Foreign Affairs 外交部 set up its own World Wide Web site to provide users access to information on the organization of the MOFA; the ROC's diplomatic relations; ROC embassies, consulates, and representative offices overseas; and the ROC's participation in APEC activities. While most of the information is in Chinese, a memorandum on the ROC's participation in the UN is provided in both Chinese and English. The site is located at *http://www.mofa.gov.tw*.

Asia and the Pacific

The Republic of China is an Asian nation located on the Pacific Rim. Given its geographical and cultural proximity to other Asia-Pacific countries, it is not surprising that the ROC attaches great importance to expanding and upgrading ties with the nations in this region. The Ministry of Foreign Affairs has divided the task of handling relations with the large number of important countries in the region between its Department of West Asian Affairs 亞西司 and Department of East Asian and Pacific Affairs 亞東太平洋司. The Department of West Asian Affairs manages relations with such major powers as the former Soviet Republics and Saudi Arabia, while the Department of East Asian and Pacific Affairs oversees relations with Japan and South Korea in the north, the ASEAN nations in the south, and Australia, New Zealand, and the island nations of Oceania.

In the past few years, substantive relations between the ROC and countries in Southeast Asia have been greatly reinforced. Since the ROC government initiated a Southern Investment Strategy 南向政策 in 1993, trade with ASEAN member states has intensified dramatically. In 1995, the value of the ROC's trade with Southeast Asia exceeded US$25 billion, making this the ROC's third largest overseas market after Hong Kong and the United States. As of the end of 1995, the ROC had invested US$21.6 billion in Southeast Asian countries, making the region the top destination for ROC outbound investment.

Australia

The Republic of China's economic achievements have encouraged the Australian government and private enterprises in the country to intensify their economic and trade relations with the ROC in recent years. Since 1992, the ROC and Australian governments have signed five important bilateral agreements (including memorandums of understanding) pertaining to scientific cooperation, the protection of industrial property, the promotion of investment and technology transfers, the avoidance of double taxation and the prevention of income tax evasion, and the temporary admission of goods.

Two-way trade between the ROC and Australia totaled US$4.33 billion in 1995, up from US$3.86 billion in 1994. This made the ROC Australia's sixth largest market for exports and seventh largest supplier of imports. Australia was the ROC's seventh largest supplier of imports and twelfth largest export market. Direct air links between Taipei and Sydney were inaugurated in October 1991. Today there are five international airlines providing direct services with continuing flights to major Australian cities. The number of ROC tourists visiting Australia reached a record 160,000 in 1995, and the exchange of visits by high-ranking government officials has encouraged both sides to strengthen cooperative bilateral relations.

Japan

Relations with Japan have grown substantially in recent years. In September 1994, the ROC and Japan signed an aviation agreement allowing EVA Airways and Air Nippon, a subsidiary of All-Nippon Airways, to fly the Taipei-Fukuoka route. The continual growth in bilateral trade, investment, cultural exchanges and tourism is also reflected in the flow of people between the two countries: some 1.41 million trips were made back and forth in 1995 alone.

Though bilateral trade has increased steadily, the Republic of China's trade deficit with Japan remains a chronic and growing problem. In 1995, the value of two-way trade between the ROC and Japan totaled US$43.5 billion, but the ROC trade deficit rocketed to a new high of US$17.1 billion. Bilateral economic and trade talks have been held annually to resolve this problem. The ROC Ministry of Economic Affairs 經濟部 (MOEA) and other governmental trade and economic units are also carrying on with plans aimed at improving the trade deficit situation between the ROC and Japan and promoting technology transfers from Japan to upgrade ROC industries.

Along with changes in the international state of affairs, Japan has raised the level of official visits to the ROC in recent years. The ROC's Legislature 立法院 and the ruling party maintain close relations with both the Liberal Democratic Party and the Social Democratic Party in Japan. Various Japanese counties and cities have also established Japan-ROC friendship groups to promote relations between the two countries.

The ROC's four representative offices in Japan are located in the cities of Tokyo, Yokohama, Osaka, and Fukuoka. On May 20, 1992, the name under which these offices operate was changed from the Association of East Asian Relations to the Taipei Economic and Cultural Representative Office. The new name refers to the ROC more specifically and concretely than the vague East Asian designation and marks another step towards stronger relations with Japan.

Malaysia

The Republic of China maintains very close relations with Malaysia. In 1995, the ROC invested US$565 million in Malaysia, pushing total ROC investment in the country up to US$7.6 billion and making the ROC the second largest foreign investor there after Japan. The value of two-way trade in 1995 reached US$5.8 billion, an increase of 28.6 percent over the previous year.

New Zealand

Direct air links between Taipei and Auckland were initiated in September 1992, and in December 1992, the Republic of China and New Zealand held their first trade talks since severing diplomatic relations in 1972. Since the talks, trade activities between the two countries have intensified. In 1995, bilateral trade amounted to US$698 million, an increase of 19 percent over the previous year.

Oceania

Relations between the Republic of China and the island nations of Oceania are developing steadily. Currently, the ROC maintains diplomatic ties with four island countries in this region: Solomon Islands, Tonga, Tuvalu, and Nauru. The ROC has sent nine agricultural and technical delegations to assist with development in these countries. In May 1995, the ROC and Papua New Guinea signed a joint communiqué recognizing each other and aiming to improve cooperation on the basis of reciprocal benefits.

The Philippines

Bilateral relations between the Philippines and the Republic of China moved a step forward with the conclusion of the Fourth Joint ROC-RP Economic Conference in July 1995. The Filipino delegation announced that an investment working committee comprising members from several government agencies would be set up to help ROC investors solve problems in the Philippines. Bilateral relations have also been strengthened significantly as a result of frequent exchanges and visits by high-ranking officials.

Singapore

Relations between the Republic of China and Singapore were further strengthened as the result of frequent interaction between high-ranking government officials from both sides. In February 1995, the two countries held their fifth round of ministerial-level economic talks in Taipei, during which they discussed joint investment projects in third areas, including mainland China. The ROC Ministry of Economic Affairs has also set up a task force to promote bilateral cooperation.

South Korea

In March 1995, the ROC and Republic of Korea held their first talks on direct air links since South Korea switched diplomatic recognition from Taipei to Peking in 1992. However, the two sides were unable to reach an agreement due to South Korea's insistence on referring to the Republic of China as an "area" instead of a sovereign nation. Despite this problem, the ROC-ROK Fruit Trade Conference held in Taipei in September 1995 successfully produced an agreement. Delegations representing the Republic of China and the Republic of Korea also reached an agreement on bilateral agriculture negotiations concerning Taipei's accession to the GATT/WTO. In the meantime, trade between the ROC and the ROK remained brisk throughout the entire year. The value of two-way trade soared 45 percent over the previous year to total US$6.9 billion in 1995. However, the ROC's trade deficit with South Korea also jumped to a new high of US$1.7 billion.

Thailand

In 1995, the ROC ranked as the third largest foreign investor in Thailand, accounting for US$1.8 billion. The value of two-way trade between the two nations surpassed US$4.5 billion. ROC investors pumped funds into a number of industries, including electronics, plastic latex, textiles, and chemicals. An investment protection agreement was initialed in October 1994, but has yet to be formally signed. By the end of 1995, the ROC had invested a total of US$6.7 billion in Thailand, making the ROC Thailand's fourth largest foreign investor overall.

Vietnam

Relations between the Republic of China and Vietnam grew rapidly after Hanoi established a representative office in Taipei in 1992 and the ROC reciprocated in 1993. The ROC has since then also set up a branch office in Ho Chi Minh City. In July 1995, the two countries held their second ministerial-level economic conference in Hanoi to discuss investment and trade cooperation, and plans to develop industrial areas in Hanoi, Haiphong, and Ho Chi Minh City are now under way. In 1995, the ROC invested a total of US$1.2 billion in Vietnam, maintaining its position as the leading foreign investor in the country, with an accumulated investment amounting to US$3.58 billion as of the end of 1995.

India

Relations between the ROC and India blossomed in 1995, when the two nations exchanged representative offices under the names of the Taipei Economic and Cultural Center in New Delhi and the India-Taipei Association in Taipei, respectively. The New Delhi office represents the ROC's first diplomatic foothold in South Asia.

Bilateral trade has intensified gradually in recent years as well. In 1995 it totaled nearly US$935 million, and ROC enterprises invested US$200 million in India the same year. To further enhance two-way trade, a trade mission led by the MOEA's Board of Foreign Trade 經濟部國際貿易局 officials visited India in March 1996, followed by a team of representatives from the Chinese National Association of Industry & Commerce 中華民國工商協進會 in April.

West Asia and the Middle East

Former Soviet Republics

From the early 1950s to the late 1980s, contacts between the Republic of China and the USSR were completely prohibited by the two governments. However, this changed when the drastic ideological and political transformation which occurred in the Soviet Union prior to its disintegration convinced the ROC government to lift its bans on direct trade with and investment in the Soviet Union in March and April of 1990. The ROC also relaxed limitations on nongovernmental exchanges between the two countries. Since then, a number of high-ranking ROC officials, legislators, and citizens' groups have exchanged visits with counterparts in the former USSR. In 1995, trade between the ROC and the former Soviet republics amounted to well over US$1.8 billion.

The ROC government is currently in the process of developing substantive relations with the former Soviet republics through all available channels, placing particular emphasis on Russia,

Belarus, Ukraine, and Kazakhstan. Most recently, Vice President and Premier Lien Chan 連戰 visited Ukraine in August 1996.

Jordan

Relations between the ROC and Jordan leapt forward when, in April 1995, an ROC president visited Jordan for the first time in 18 years. While in Jordan, President Lee Teng-hui 李登輝 met with Crown Prince Hassan Bin Talal as well as Deputy Prime Minister and Minister of Education Abdul Raouf al-Rawabden.

In recent years, the Republic of China's support of science and technology-based activities in Jordan, including contributions to the development of mechanical engineering and the Princess Sumaya University College of Technology at the Royal Scientific Society, has strengthened cooperative ties between the two countries.

United Arab Emirates

Substantive relations between the ROC and the UAE were further strengthened after President Lee Teng-hui visited the UAE in April 1995 as part of the first tour of the Middle East by an ROC president in 18 years. During his stay, President Lee met with the UAE's Minister of State for Foreign Affairs Hamdan Bin Zayed Al-Nahyan and Sheikh Khalifa Bin Zayed Al-Nahyan, the Crown Prince and Deputy Supreme Commander of the Armed Forces of Abu Dhabi.

The two countries signed an air traffic agreement on September 19, 1995, in Taipei, and China Airlines began flying the Taipei-Abu Dhabi route on October 29, 1995.

Africa

The Republic of China maintains diplomatic relations with nine African countries: South Africa, Malawi, Swaziland, Liberia, Guinea-Bissau, the Central African Republic, Burkina Faso, the Gambia, and Senegal. In addition to its official embassies and consulates on the continent, the ROC has set up representative offices in Angola, Libya, Madagascar, Mauritius, Nigeria, Zaire, and Congo, with the aim of promoting bilateral trade and economic relations.

South Africa

The Republic of China and the Republic of South Africa (RSA) had shared strong and friendly relations since formal ties were established in 1976. However, in November 1996, Pretoria announced that official diplomatic relations between the ROC and the RSA would be abandoned on December 31, 1997, in favor of unofficial substantive ties. In response, the ROC has decided to recall its ambassador from the RSA, and to suspend some of the 36 cooperative agreements that have been signed between the two countries, pending negotiations on future bilateral relations.

The ROC was the RSA's seventh largest trading partner in 1995, and the US$1.87 billion in trade between the two countries was US$180 million in South Africa's favor. Investors from Taiwan have been pursuing projects in areas including garments, shoes, radios, and plastic products, setting up a total of 285 factories in the RSA. In 1995 alone, ROC investors put US$400 million into South Africa and created 40,000 jobs. While in the past the ROC government has played a very active role in Taiwan investment in South Africa, this is not expected to continue, and the intensity of ROC-affiliated economic activity in the country is likely to be affected by the severance of Taipei-Pretoria ties in 1997.

Swaziland

Diplomatic relations between the ROC and Swaziland were further strengthened when King Mswati III paid a state visit to the ROC in May 1995. Two sessions of a Joint Ministerial Conference on Economic and Technical Cooperation were held in 1995, one in Taipei and the other in Mbabane, and the ROC and Swaziland have agreed to hold regular joint ministerial economic and technical cooperation conferences in the future. The ROC and Swaziland have also signed a joint communiqué and a cooperative agreement on handicrafts.

The Gambia

The ROC re-established full diplomatic relations with the Republic of the Gambia in July 1995. Official visits were exchanged, and in October 1995 the two countries signed a medical cooperation agreement. Relations between the ROC and the Gambia continued to grow closer and stronger throughout 1996.

Senegal

The ROC resumed diplomatic relations with the Republic of Senegal in January 1996 with the signing of a communiqué and a medical cooperation agreement by the foreign ministers of the two countries. Both governments are now promoting bilateral cooperation plans.

Assistance and Cooperation

The ROC has extended assistance to African countries in the fields of agriculture, medicine and handicrafts. As of the end of 1995, the ROC's assistance program was represented by agricultural technical missions in Malawi, Swaziland, Guinea-Bissau, Burkina Faso, the Central African Republic, and the Gambia; medical missions in the Central African Republic, Burkina Faso, and Guinea-Bissau; and one handicraft mission in Swaziland.

To strengthen cooperative ties, the ROC held bilateral economic and technical conferences with the Central African Republic, Guinea-Bissau, Burkina Faso, Swaziland, and Niger, respectively, from January 1995 to January 1996. The ROC also signed an investment guarantee agreement with Malawi in April 1995, an agricultural technology cooperation agreement with Burkina Faso in September 1995, a medical cooperation agreement with the Gambia in October 1995, and a communiqué and medical cooperation agreement with Senegal in January 1996.

Europe

On the European continent, the Republic of China maintains full diplomatic relations only with the Holy See. However, at present, 25 offices represent the ROC in 21 European countries, while 17 European countries have set up 18 representative offices in the ROC. These offices have facilitated the expansion of economic, cultural, and technological relations with European countries. Europe is the ROC's third largest trading partner after the United States and Japan. In 1995, the value of the ROC's two-way trade with Europe totaled US$34.43 billion.

In 1995, ROC Premier Lien Chan made a trip to Austria, Hungary, and the Czech Republic to strengthen bilateral relations. He was the highest ROC official to visit Europe since the ROC government relocated to Taiwan in 1949. In Vienna, Lien met with Gunther Winkler, chairman of the Austria-Taiwan Culture Exchanges Association, to discuss greater academic interaction between the ROC and Austria by increasing exchanges of professors and students and by establishing scholarship programs. In Prague, Lien was received by President Vaclav Havel and Prime Minister Vaclay Klaus. Lien and Havel agreed to enhance trade and academic exchanges between Taipei and Prague. The Czech Republic was the ROC's second largest eastern European trading partner after Poland in 1995.

In addition to Premier Lien Chan's trip, many ministerial-level officials from the ROC met with their counterparts in Europe, and numerous ministerial-rank officials from individual countries visited Taipei. The ROC also reached a number of agreements with European partners. In September 1995, the ROC and Norway signed an agreement concerning environmental protection, and in November the ROC and Poland signed an agreement pertaining to the avoidance of double taxation and the prevention of income tax evasion. Protocols for the mutual exemption of maritime transportation taxes have also been signed with Germany, the Netherlands, the European Union, Sweden, and Norway.

In view of the dynamism of the European market, the ROC adopted a series of measures in the last few years to further strengthen its relations with the European Union. The ROC established bilateral economic committees with France, the Netherlands, Belgium, Poland, Spain, Germany, Sweden, and Ireland. These committees held regular meetings to study commercial, economic and trade cooperation. Many countries signed technological cooperation agreements with the ROC, covering environmental protection techniques, computer technology, industrial planning, and biotechnology.

In addition, the ROC signed agreements covering educational cooperation and air links with the Netherlands, Austria, Luxembourg, Bulgaria, Latvia, the United Kingdom, Germany, and France. The ROC maintains direct air links with Austria, the Netherlands, Luxembourg, Italy, Switzerland, the UK, Germany, and France.

The ROC's substantive relations with countries in eastern Europe and the Baltic States continue to improve, especially in the areas of trade, culture, technology transfer, and tourism. The ROC has engaged in a number of shipping, telecommunications, aviation, educational, and cultural exchanges with these countries. In cooperation with the European Bank for Reconstruction and Development, the ROC also finances the Taipei China-European Bank Cooperation Fund to assist with the development of eastern European countries and the Baltic States.

North America
The United States of America

Relations between the Republic of China and the United States have moved rapidly forward over the past two years. In September 1994, the Clinton administration gave a boost to bilateral relations by agreeing to allow higher-level contacts and dialogues between officials of the two countries and by permitting a change in the name of the ROC's representative offices in the United States. The new name identifies the ROC more clearly, thus providing a more visible indication of our national presence (for details, see section on bilateralism in this chapter). At the same time, the US government also decided to support Taipei's efforts to enter nongovernmental international organizations. These adjustments provide the Republic of China with more flexibility to achieve a substantial upgrade in ROC-US relations and to cultivate Washington's support for the drive to enhance the ROC's international profile.

In 1995, the US Congress passed several resolutions to demonstrate its friendliness toward the ROC. The House of Representatives in May 1995 passed a resolution welcoming President Lee Teng-hui to visit his alma mater, Cornell University, by a vote of 396 to 0. Within one week, the Senate passed a similar resolution by a vote of 97 to 1. Also in 1995, the House and the Senate approved the *American Overseas Interest Act* and the *Foreign Relations Revitalization Act*, which included a provision amending the 1979 *Taiwan Relations Act* to ensure that US arms sales to the ROC not be affected by the Washington-Peking joint communiqués of 1982. Such friendly moves as these by the US Congress facilitated President Lee's visit to the US in June 1995 and ensured continued US arms sales to the ROC.

The United States continued defensive arms sales to the ROC to ensure the security of the Taiwan Straits. In August 1994, the US agreed to an initial sale of 600 Stinger missiles to the ROC, and in October 1994, US President Bill Clinton signed into law a bill that authorized the US Navy to lease two Newport-class tank landing craft to the ROC. Also in October, the ROC Navy purchased four ocean minesweepers. In January 1995, the ROC bought 160 M60A3 tanks from the US. Finally, an air defense system and the first batch of F-16 fighters are scheduled to be delivered to the ROC in 1996 and 1997, respectively.

The ROC and the US have also forged very close relationships at the local government level as well. Currently, 16 American states have formally established trade offices in the ROC, including Idaho, Indiana, Louisiana, Maryland, Missouri, Montana, Oregon, Utah, Washington, Arizona, Connecticut, Florida, Hawaii, California, Massachusetts, and Wyoming. In addition, 39 states and 123 counties and cities in the US have concluded sisterhood agreements with Taiwan Province and its various counties and cities.

Over the last 20 years, the ROC and the US have signed more than 100 agreements, covering education, customs duties, postal administration, air transportation, and technological cooperation. In September 1994, the ROC and the US signed a trade and investment framework agreement, the first time that the US had signed such a pact with a country with which it has no diplomatic relations. The United States is the ROC's single largest trading partner, while the ROC presently ranks eighth among US trading partners. Throughout the early 1990s, the ROC has enjoyed a large trade surplus with the United States, which is now sixth in size behind those of Japan, the Chinese mainland, Canada, Mexico, and Germany. In 1995, the ROC built up a US$5.64 billion trade surplus with the United States, a significant decrease from the 1987 figure of US$18.7 billion.

Canada

Relations between the Republic of China and Canada were held up for 20 years following Canada's establishment of diplomatic ties with the mainland government in 1970. However, substantive relations between the ROC and Canada have been developing steadily ever since agreements which paved the way for the exchange of representative offices and the establishment of air links were signed in 1990. At present, the ROC maintains three representative offices, in Toronto, Vancouver, and Ottawa, under the name Taipei Economic and Cultural Office.

Canada was the ROC's 14th largest trading partner in 1995, with the total two-way trade volume rising from US$2.7 billion in 1994 to US$3.02 billion. However, the balance of trade tilted in Canada's favor for the very first time in 1995, allowing Ottawa to build up a surplus of US$160 million. This was mainly the result of a powerful 27 percent surge in imports from Canada in 1995. Major imports from Canada included pulp, chemical products, lumber and wood products, machinery and parts, and mineral fuel. Major exports to Canada were items such as machinery and parts, electrical equipment, toys, auto parts, furniture, and machine tools.

In June 1995, ROC Vice Premier Hsu Li-teh visited Canada. Hsu was the highest-ranking ROC official to visit Canada since Ottawa switched recognition from Taipei to Peking in 1970.

Latin America and the Caribbean

Most of the countries with which the Republic of China has formal diplomatic relations are located in Central and South America and the Caribbean region. At present, the ROC maintains diplomatic relations with 16 countries in this region: the Bahamas, Belize, Costa Rica, Dominica, the Dominican Republic, El Salvador, Grenada, Guatemala, Haiti, Honduras, Nicaragua, Panama, Paraguay, Saint Christopher and Nevis, Saint Lucia, and Saint Vincent and the Grenadines.

Leaders from the ROC and friendly countries in Central and South America and the Caribbean region exchanged many high-level official visits in 1995. The visitors included Dominican Prime Minister Mary Eugenia Charles in February; Prime Minister James Mitchell of Saint Vincent and the Grenadines in March; Paraguayan President Juan Carlos Wasmosy, who attended the Eighth ROC-Paraguay Economic Cooperation Conference in August and during whose visit several bilateral agreements on economic cooperation were signed; Prime Minister Keith Mitchell of Grenada in September; and President Ernesto Perez Balladares of Panama in the same month as head of a 63-member delegation of officials and industrialists. On the part of the ROC, Vice President Lien Chan led a delegation to the inauguration ceremony of President Leonel Fernandez of the Dominican Republic.

Overseas Chinese

Aside from pragmatic diplomatic endeavors and attempts to participate in international organizations, the ROC government has in recent years stepped up contacts with overseas Chinese around the world and strengthened efforts to serve their interests. By tradition, any person of Chinese descent living outside the borders of the Republic of China is considered a *hua ch'iao* 華僑, or literally an overseas Chinese. Earlier overseas Chinese consisted mainly of emigrants who left China to make their fortunes or pursue higher studies abroad during the 19th and early 20th centuries. In the past few decades, emigrants from Taiwan have increased, initially for academic reasons and more recently for business as the ROC has continued to experience rapid economic growth and growing prosperity. These relatively new overseas Chinese 新僑, comprising mainly intellectuals and businessmen, face different challenges in their new environment compared with those encountered by the old overseas Chinese 舊僑.

Therefore, while equal attention will still be given to both old and new emigrants, the ROC government has adjusted its overseas Chinese policy to meet new demands arising from this demographic change in the overseas Chinese population. Previously, the emphasis was on preserving ethnic ties with the overseas Chinese by maintaining contact, providing education to new generations born overseas, offering economic assistance to overseas Chinese businessmen, and encouraging investment in the ROC. However, recent trends have led to a policy shift toward planned and guided emigration by Taiwan residents, as well as the integration of the business interests of old, and thus established, overseas Chinese with those of recent emigrants who are completely unfamiliar with their new adopted cultures. Meanwhile, the earlier focus on keeping overseas Chinese informed of domestic developments has been replaced by an effort to increase domestic understanding of Chinese residing overseas.

Immigration Trends and ROC Policy

There is historical evidence of Chinese people emigrating from China prior to the 14th century A.D. It was not until the early 19th century, however, that a population explosion, famines, and political instability within China swelled the ranks of people seeking greener pastures elsewhere. As more and more Chinese began arriving in places like Hanoi, Malacca, and San Francisco, communities of overseas Chinese sprang up and gradually became more prosperous than the hometowns left behind.

By the end of the 19th century, overseas Chinese communities had become havens for young

Overseas Chinese Affairs Commission

In 1926, the ROC government established the Overseas Chinese Affairs Commission (OCAC) 僑務委員會 to ensure the welfare and interests of overseas Chinese, and it was placed under the Executive Yuan in 1932. The OCAC is organized into eight divisions: an overseas Chinese student center, an overseas Chinese passport and visa office, four departments, and two subsidiaries—the Overseas Chinese News Agency 華僑通訊社 and the Chung Hwa Correspondence School 中華函授學校.

The student center is known as the Office for Overseas Chinese Students Guidance 僑生輔導室 and is in charge of overseas Chinese studying in the ROC. The center also provides guidance, counseling, and post-graduation services. Areas handled by the passport and visa office, known as the Overseas Passport and Visa Service Office 華僑證照服務室, include the approval and transfer of entry and exit applications, applications to travel or settle in Taiwan, matters relating to military service, applications for re-entry visas, and the issuance of overseas Chinese ID cards and name chop certificates.

As for the OCAC's four departments, the first department is in charge of keeping track of the number of overseas Chinese and providing services to overseas Chinese communities and to overseas Chinese on homecoming visits. The second department is responsible for fulfilling the formal educational, social service, and mass communication needs of overseas Chinese, as well as for promoting cultural and educational programs. Assisting overseas Chinese to invest in the ROC and providing economic and banking assistance to overseas Chinese enterprises are included in the third department's duties. The fourth department takes care of general affairs.

The Overseas Chinese News Agency provides news and media services pertaining to overseas Chinese affairs. The Chung Hwa Correspondence School provides educational services for overseas Chinese.

Chinese intellectuals escaping persecution at the hands of the Ch'ing dynasty. The Founding Father of the ROC, Dr. Sun Yat-sen 孫中山, who himself had been educated at a mission school on the Hawaiian island of Oahu, was able to garner financial support from influential overseas Chinese for his efforts to overthrow the Ch'ing dynasty. From among the thousands of overseas Chinese students in Japan, Dr. Sun Yat-sen formed his Revolutionary Alliance 同盟會. This organization, which was the forerunner of today's ruling Kuomintang 中國國民黨, organized several uprisings against the Ch'ing dynasty. Thirty-nine of the 72 valiant young men martyred in the abortive Canton uprising 廣州起義 in the spring of 1911 were overseas Chinese who had returned to China to help establish Asia's first democratic republic, the Republic of China. It was overseas Chinese such as these who earned Dr. Sun's praise as "the vanguard of the national revolution" 華僑為革命之母. Throughout the eight-year war of resistance against Japan 抗日戰爭, the communist rebellion, and the development of the Taiwan area, overseas Chinese communities have been a source of unfailing support for the Republic of China.

According to OCAC statistics, some 8.7 million Chinese were living overseas in 1948. By 1968, the number exceeded 18 million. By 1988, it had exploded to 30 million. The latest figures indicated that over 38.6 million Chinese resided outside China at the end of 1995. About 85 percent make their homes in Asia, mainly in Indonesia, Thailand, Hong Kong, Malaysia, and Singapore. A little over half of the 11 percent of overseas Chinese who live in North or South America are concentrated in the United States. Europe is home to a little less than 2.3 percent, while Oceania and Africa are home to about 1.3 percent and 0.3 percent, respectively. Most overseas Chinese come from Kwangtung and Fukien, followed by Taiwan and Shantung. By profession, the majority are engaged in engineering or business.

Statistics show that nearly 800,000 people have emigrated from Taiwan since 1950. Prior to 1961, the ROC government prohibited emigration from Taiwan, and only students pursuing advanced studies abroad were permitted to travel overseas. Between 1962 and 1989, the emigration policy was relaxed and citizens could accept employment or emigrate to live with relatives in foreign countries. In 1989, the ban was completely lifted and ROC citizens could travel overseas without being subject to regulation. In view of this open policy and other factors such as the ROC's pragmatic diplomacy, Taiwan residents have shown a greater interest in emigrating overseas. The past five years have seen between 20,000 and 25,000 ROC citizens emigrate annually. A survey shows that 27 percent of new Taiwan emigrants to the US thought it would benefit their business interests to do so.

Among the 9,255 overseas Chinese associations which were registered with the OCAC as of December 1995, about 28 percent maintain close contact with the commission. Approximately 55 percent of the associations were formed by old immigrants, while the rest have been established by new immigrants from Taiwan. Interestingly enough, the number of associations formed by emigrants from Taiwan has increased rapidly over the past 20 years.

These developments have prompted the ROC government to make adjustments in the selection of the 176 delegates to the OCAC who are chosen from among overseas Chinese to serve as a bridge between the ROC government and Chinese residing abroad. Younger and more educated delegates have been chosen, and Taiwanese and women emigrants are better represented. Guidance is provided to potential emigrants to help them make plans for their settlement overseas. Overseas Chinese and emigration lawyers have been invited to OCAC-sponsored seminars dealing with emigration to a number of countries to address issues such as living environments, education, business opportunities, investment markets, and emigration laws.

Cultural Solidarity

Maintaining cultural solidarity among overseas Chinese is one of the Overseas Chinese Affairs Commission's primary missions. The OCAC has 16 overseas Chinese cultural and educational centers in major US cities, Toronto, Manila, Sydney, Melbourne, Paris, and Bangkok.

Top Five Destinations for ROC Emigrants

	1991	1992	1993	1994	1995
USA	10,626	9,588	7,834	6,380	7,605
Canada	4,488	7,427	9,472	6,500	6,700
New Zealand	436	2,310	2,501	4,984	3,955
Austraila	3,219	1,943	774	626	1,115
South Africa	1,219	312	1,500	288	9
Total	19,988	21,580	22,081	18,778	19,384

The Overseas Chinese Culture and Education Foundation 海華文教基金會, set up with a US$15 million fund provided by the OCAC, subsidizes outstanding overseas Chinese youths in the areas of education, arts, and culture. In 1995, arts festivals were sponsored in 21 cities and areas with large populations of overseas Chinese.

The OCAC also subsidizes the establishment and management of Chinese TV and radio stations overseas. Its subsidiary, the Overseas Chinese News Agency, provides the latest information on current events in the Taiwan area to over 300 overseas Chinese publications. The agency also puts out press releases to local news agencies to keep Taiwan residents well-informed of overseas Chinese affairs.

Education

Traditionally, overseas Chinese education has been aimed at teaching cultural traditions—particularly Chinese customs, the Chinese family system, and Chinese literature—to new generations of foreign-born Chinese. For as long as Chinese have been emigrating and establishing themselves in new areas, they have set up schools to pass on this cultural heritage. In recent years, the OCAC has helped set up Chinese-language schools in Malaysia, Indonesia, Thailand, and Vietnam for the children of Taiwan businessmen who have accommodated the ROC's Southern Investment Strategy by investing in Southeast Asia. These "Taipei schools"

台北學校 differ from other overseas Chinese schools in that they hire teachers from Taiwan and employ the educational system and teaching materials used in Taiwan.

Another alternative form of Chinese education for overseas Chinese is the Chung Hwa Correspondence School, which was formally established in 1940. Instruction in Mandarin, vocational training, and general education is provided free of charge. In 1995, more than 10,183 students from 63 countries and areas registered for courses. Educational programs are broadcast via two international short-wave broadcast stations—the *Voice of Free China* 自由中國之聲 and the *Voice of Asia* 亞洲之聲.

Over the years, many overseas Chinese high school student graduates have returned to the ROC for further studies. In the 1995 academic year, about 3,000 of these students enrolled in universities throughout Taiwan.

Economic Integration

For many decades, overseas Chinese have been contributing financially to the development of the ROC. As the world moves towards economic alignment, and more and more Taiwan businessmen invest overseas, the OCAC has become aware of the need to integrate the business strength of Taiwan entrepreneurs. Toward this end, the OCAC has guided the establishment of Taiwan chambers of commerce, the number of which now stands at 61 worldwide. In order to help coordinate the activities of regional Taiwan chambers of commerce, a continental council was set up in North America in 1987, and in 1994, a World Taiwanese Chambers of Commerce 世界台灣商會聯合總會 was also established. Four additional continental councils were set up between 1994 and 1995 to coordinate regional Taiwan chambers of commerce in Asia, Europe, Africa, and Central and South America. Any businessman from the Taiwan area who has invested overseas may participate in these chambers of commerce. Because most Taiwan investments are in export-oriented areas, and as the earlier emigrant Chinese are largely engaged in local trade, the integration of these two groups could foster economic strength among overseas Chinese, which in turn could help the ROC achieve further economic growth.

The scope of the Overseas Chinese Credit Guarantee Fund 華僑貸款信用保證基金 has been expanded in the last few years to enhance the economic status of overseas Chinese. Originally set up to encourage overseas Chinese investment in the Taiwan area and to offer credit guarantees to overseas Chinese businesses which lacked collateral and bank credit lines, the fund has extended its services to include Taiwan investors overseas.

The Fund now has 67 service stations serving North and South America, Europe, Asia, Australia, and Africa. From its inception to the end of 1995, the fund had concluded 1,071 credit guarantee cases involving guarantees worth a total of US$165 million. The fund also helped overseas Chinese to obtain US$243.2 million from various financial institutions to develop their businesses during the same period. In 1995 alone, the number

Schools for Overseas Chinese

	Taipei School	Senior High	Vocational School	Junior HIgh	Elementary School
Asia	6	224	18	277	3,000
N./S. America	-	3	1	2	85
Europe	-	-	-	4	9
Oceania	-	-	-	-	16
Africa	-	2	-	3	31
Total	6	229	19	286	3,141

of cases handled by the fund rose 3 percent from 1994 to 279 cases.

Overseas Chinese have continued to invest in Taiwan. According to the Investment Commission under the Ministry of Economic Affairs 經濟部投資審議委員會, 43 new overseas Chinese investment projects worth a total of US$168 million were approved in 1995. These projects were concentrated primarily in Taiwan's service, financial, and insurance sectors, as well as electronics and electrical appliances, textiles, and the paper industry. Between 1952 and 1995, a total of 2,482 overseas Chinese investment projects in Taiwan, worth a total of US$2.8 billion, have been approved. To encourage the greater participation of overseas Chinese investors and professionals in the ROC's Asia-Pacific Regional Operations Center 亞太營運中心 plan, the government has improved the overall investment environment in Taiwan by amending the *Regulations Governing the Investment of Returning Overseas Chinese* 華僑回國投資條例.

Political Participation

Article 18 of the *Additional Articles of the ROC Constitution* 中華民國憲法增修條文 states that "the state shall accord to Chinese nationals residing overseas protection of their rights to political participation." Article 1 and 2 of the *Additional Articles* provide that 20 overseas Chinese (who must, however, retain ROC citizenship) shall be elected to the National Assembly 國民大會 and another six shall be elected to the Legislature 立法院. In accordance with these articles, overseas Chinese currently occupy six (three Kuomintang, two Democratic Progressive Party, and one New Party) of the 164 seats in the Legislative Yuan and 20 (11 KMT, 6 DPP, 3 NP) of the 334 seats in the National Assembly. Overseas Chinese who no longer hold an ROC passport can participate indirectly in ROC politics by becoming advisory members of the Overseas Chinese Affairs Commission. In addition, overseas Chinese have the right to take local exams to serve in government posts, and to vote. The right to vote is regulated by the ROC *Public Officials Election and Recall Law* 公職人員選舉罷免法 and the *Nationality Law* 國籍法. A special clause was also included in the *Presidential and Vice Presidential Election and Recall Law* 總統副總統選舉罷免法 to allow overseas Chinese to return to vote in the direct popular election of the ROC president.

客户滿意

是 **中華電信** 的責任

**Chunghwa Telecom exerts every effort
to ensure customer satisfaction.**

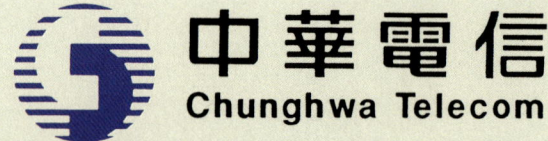

Chunghwa Telecom

31 Ai-Kuo E. Rd., Taipei, 106 Taiwan, R.O.C.

NEW CENTURY
NEW POWER

50

CHINESE PETROLEUM CORPORATION
THE 50TH ANNIVERSARY

NESE PETROLEUM CORPORATION is stepping toward its fiftieth year. From the
ntiness of its early stage to today's prosperity, CHINESE PETROLEUM CORPORA-
N has never ceased efforts to provide the best service and quality products to its
tomers. As it moves forward to the 21st century, CHINESE PETROLEUM CORPO-
TION will contribute its rich experiences and sincere devotion to create a new era
rogress for the people of Taiwan.

中國石油股份有限公司
CHINESE PETROLEUM CORP

10.
The Economy

Above: Catching up on the latest innovations—the display area of the Taipei World Trade Center features every conceivable Taiwan-manufactured product.

Right: The flag-ringed Taipei World Trade Center—symbol of the ROC's trading prowess, and a central focus of the plan to build Taiwan into an Asia-Pacific regional operations center.

Previous page: The premier port of the world's 14th largest trading nation, Kaohsiung Harbor in southern Taiwan now ranks as the third largest in the world.

10 The Economy

A prolonged slowdown in domestic private consumption, stagnant real estate and a sluggish stock market, and a series of bank runs all dampened the ROC's economic growth in 1995. Heightened tensions between mainland China and Taiwan further depressed the growth rate to 6.06 percent, the lowest in five years. But a reviving global economy helped boost Taiwan's foreign trade, with export and import values both exceeding US$200 billion. In general, export-related sectors, including manufacturing and the information technology industry, performed extremely well, while sectors aimed primarily at the domestic market, such as the automobile industry, housing construction, restaurants, and many other service businesses, all suffered slowdowns.

Taiwan's economy was one of only eight worldwide that the 1997 Heritage Foundation/Wall Street Journal Index of Economic Freedom classifies as "free." The ROC shares this distinction with Hong Kong, Singapore, Bahrain, New Zealand, Switzerland, the United States and the United Kingdom. The Index scores the relative freedom of economies from 150 nations based on trade policy, tax policy, government consumption of economic output, monetary policy, foreign investment, wage and price controls, property rights, regulations, and the size of the black market. This chapter profiles the ROC's economy in five sections: macroeconomic indicators, trade, services, industry, and energy. An introduction to the ROC's small and medium-sized enterprises, which have contributed so much to the economy over the past few decades, is also included.

Macroeconomic Indicators

Taiwan's economy grew by a moderate 6.06 percent in 1995, down from last year's 6.5 percent. This decline was attributed to increasingly high expenditures on social welfare, a relative low investment rate in the public and the private sectors, and a declining savings rate. In the past, especially in the 1970s and 1980s when the economy averaged double-digit growth, social

costs generally took a small percentage of all government expenditures. But as society became more affluent, people started demanding increased social welfare and services. In 1995, over 11 percent of the total government outlay was allocated for social expenditures.

In 1987, the savings rate was just short of 40 percent of the gross national product (GNP), but it dropped to 25 percent in 1995, the lowest among Asia's "Four Little Dragons." The ROC's GNP topped US$263.6 billion in 1995, ranking it the 20th in the world. Per capita GNP also hit the highest level to reach US$12,439 during the same year. The nation's gross domestic product (GDP) amounted to US$260.8 billion in 1995. Agriculture continued to take a smaller share of the GDP, accounting for 3.5 percent. Industry also dropped further to 36.3 percent, down from 37.3 percent in 1994, while the service sector continued to boom, topping 60.2 percent of the GDP in 1995.

Private consumption, which constituted the major force behind Taiwan's GDP growth over the past few years, suffered large-scale shrinkage in 1995. The continuing slump in both the global and domestic economy in the last couple of years has encouraged local consumers to become more conservative about spending their money. Uncertain relations between the two sides of the Taiwan Straits also deterred local people from making further investment in the domestic financial market and led to massive outflow of capital from Taiwan. Furthermore, frequent travel abroad by an increasingly large percentage of the populace accelerated the outflow of ROC foreign reserves, which led to a plunge in domestic private consumption. The 1995 average growth rate of private consumption slipped to 5.09 percent from last year's 8.58 percent. The third quarter of the year was in particular severely hit by the global recession, with the growth rate slipping to below 5 percent, the lowest point since 1982. Government expenditures increased slightly by 0.35 percent in 1995 in the wake of the implementation of the National Health Insurance program 全民健康保險.

Trade

Foreign trade climbed to US$215.3 billion in 1995 to break all previous records. Exports and imports both performed splendidly in terms of aggregate value. Over the last few decades, foreign trade—in particular exports—has played a vital role in the economy. A lack of natural resources and a relatively small domestic market have made Taiwan all the more dependent on foreign trade, which generally constitutes about 70 percent of the annual GNP.

Brisk foreign trade in the 1970s and 1980s enabled the ROC to amass huge surpluses that swelled the island's foreign exchange reserves to among the largest in the world. Annual trade surpluses peaked at US$18.7 billion in 1987. Taiwan's perennial trade surpluses soon evoked protests from major trading partners, in particular the United States, which demanded that the ROC remove trade barriers and allow more foreign products to enter the domestic market at reduced import tariffs. In 1992, Taiwan's trade surplus plunged to only US$9.5 billion, down nearly 30 percent from the preceding year, and the downward trend has continued. In 1995, the trade surplus stood at US$8.1 billion.

Exports

Exports topped US$111.7 billion in 1995, up 20 percent over 1994. The United States, Hong Kong, and Japan absorbed nearly 60 percent of Taiwan's exports. In 1995, exports to the United States rose by 8.5 percent to US$26.41 billion. Electronics and electrical appliances, personal computers and peripherals, metal products, and garments comprised the bulk of Taiwan's exports to the United States. The US market has been for decades the most important export destination, and this has resulted in huge trade surpluses in the ROC's favor. The importance of the US market decreased dramatically, however, after the ROC government began liberalizing its market in the early 1990s. Over a decade ago, nearly half of Taiwan's total exports were destined for the United States, but today only one quarter of the island's products go to the US

ROC Economy Statistical Profile	
Economic Growth Rate (%)	
1996	5.89f
1997 1st quarter	6.21f
2nd quarter	6.25f
GNP (at current prices, US$ million)	
1996	275,874f
1997 1st quarter	73,308f
2nd quarter	71,637f
Per Capita GNP (US$)	
1996	12,896f
1997 1st quarter	3,407f
2nd quarter	3,322f
Foreign Trade (US$ million)	
Exports	
1996 April	10,095r
May	9,552p
June	9,697p
July	9,478p
Imports	
1996 April	9,248r
May	7,768p
June	9,290p
July	8,124p

Notes: f–forecast; r–revised; p–preliminary

market. The ROC's trade surplus with the United States dropped from nearly US$9 billion in 1991 to less than US$5.5 billion in 1995. Nonetheless, Uncle Sam remained one of Taiwan's major trading partners in 1995.

ROC exports to Hong Kong continued to climb in 1995, growing by 22.9 percent over the previous year, for an aggregate value of US$26.1 billion. Hong Kong has since 1990 supplanted Japan to become the second-largest export destination for Taiwan products. Successful implementation of the ROC government policy to diversify its export market, as well as the burgeoning trade with mainland China (which is carried out via third areas such as Hong Kong), have further increased Hong Kong's importance in Taiwan's foreign trade.

During the first half of 1995, Hong Kong replaced the United States as the largest market for Taiwan exports. But tensions between the two sides of the Taiwan Straits, which heightened in the latter half of the year, caused Taiwan's trade volume with the British colony to fall below that with the United States. Nevertheless, Hong Kong still absorbed 23.37 percent of Taiwan's exports, lagging only slightly behind the 23.65 percent of Taiwan's US exports. In 1995, Taiwan enjoyed a US$24.3 billion trade surplus with Hong Kong, 23 percent higher than in the previous year. Major items included raw textile materials, electronics products, machinery, and raw plastic materials and wares.

Exports to Japan, mostly agricultural products, electronics and information technology products, and metal wares, registered a new record high in 1995, peaking at US$13.2 billion, a 29 percent growth. The steep appreciation of the Japanese yen and the increase in the export of Taiwan-made information products were major causes of this growth. The perennial deficit with Japan has prompted the ROC government to take a series of concrete measures to help redress the balance. These include encouraging the export of more Taiwan-made products to the Japanese market and attracting more Japanese investment and joint-ventures to Taiwan. Output from such cooperative projects can then be shipped back to Japan to improve the trade imbalance. In 1995, household appliances and electronics and information products were among the most important items recording strong growth, each over 120 percent. Overall exports to Japan have increased in the last few years, and in 1995 Taiwan supplanted Germany to become Japan's fifth largest imports supplier. Nevertheless, these exports are still growing much more slowly than Taiwan's imports from Japan.

Europe is another potential target for the ROC's market diversification policy. In 1995, exports to Europe rebounded after two consecutive years of decline, to reach US$15.73 billion, up 21 percent over the preceding year. ROC trade with Germany and France registered deficits for the fourth straight year, and the total trade deficit with this region amounted to

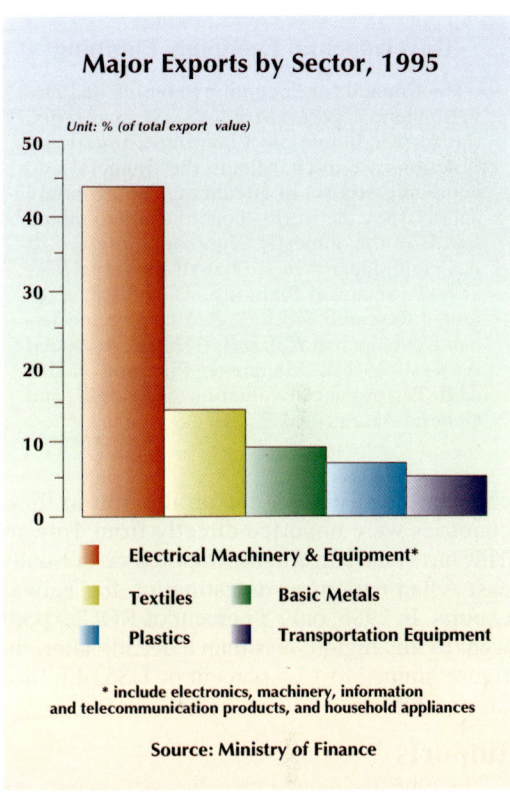

Major Exports by Sector, 1995

Unit: % (of total export value)

Electrical Machinery & Equipment*

Textiles   Basic Metals

Plastics   Transportation Equipment

* include electronics, machinery, information and telecommunication products, and household appliances

Source: Ministry of Finance

US$2.97 billion in 1995. To cope with the trade barriers created by the European Union's single market, a dozen of Taiwan's largest firms have already established a foothold in the EU by establishing factories or by merging companies in the United Kingdom, the Netherlands, and Germany. Because investment is mostly centered on electric appliances, electronics, and information technology products, once the EU market for such products is saturated, Taiwan's trade will be severely affected.

Southeast Asia has emerged as a trade alternative, and the second-most-favored place for Taiwan foreign investment, after the Chinese mainland. Many Taiwan enterprises have tried to establish a second foothold in this region to take advantage of abundant and cheap labor, raw materials, and significantly lower land prices. The key components of the products and ma-

Governmental Economic Planning

The Council for Economic Planning and Development 行政院經濟建設委員會 succeeded the former Economic Planning Council. Its functions are to coordinate the financial and economic sectors in advancing the economy and to study the world economic situation and trends in the domestic economic structure. It has eight departments: Overall Planning 綜合計劃處, Sectorial Planning 部門計劃處, Economic Research 經濟研究處, Housing and Urban Development 都市及住宅發展處, Financial Analysis 財務處, Manpower Planning 人力規劃處, Performance Evaluation 管制考核處, and General Affairs 總務處.

chinery (mostly used) for production in these countries were imported directly from Taiwan. This has contributed to the importance of Southeast Asian nations as a destination for Taiwan exports. In 1986, only 5 percent of ROC exports went to this region; less than a decade later, the figure jumped to 12.5 percent or US$14 billion (as of 1995).

Imports

In 1995, the aggregate value of Taiwan's imports was US$103.6 billion, up 21 percent over the previous year. Raw materials registered 24 percent growth, as did capital goods and equipment in terms of import value. Conversely, import of consumer goods recorded a growth rate of only 6.1 percent, the lowest in four years, a result of the continuing slump in the domestic economy.

Nearly 30 percent (US$30.3 billion) of Taiwan's 1995 imports were from Japan. Major import items included machinery, auto parts, and electrical appliances, electronics, chemicals, and metal products. Many of Taiwan's industries rely heavily on the supply of key parts and the transfer of cutting-edge technology from Japan, in particular the information and automotive industry (see the sections on Information Technology Industry and Automotive Industry). Each year, much of Taiwan's hard-earned trade surplus with other nations is offset by its deficit with Japan. Unabated growth (over 10 percent annually) in Japanese imports has led to a serious trade deficit with Japan. This has quintupled in less than 16 years, from US$3.18 billion to US$17.1 billion (as of 1995).

The second largest source of Taiwan's imports was the United States. American products comprised 20 percent (US$20.8 billion) of Taiwan's imports in 1995, up 15 percent over the preceding year. Imports from Europe and Southeast Asia recorded double-digit growth, rising by 17 percent and 27 percent, respectively. In the last few years, South Korea has also gained importance in Taiwan's imports. Although its export value still lags far behind that of Japan and the United States, it became the ROC's fifth-largest supplier and now runs a favorable trade balance with Taiwan.

Government Oversight of the Economy

The Ministry of Economic Affairs 經濟部 oversees the nation's economic administration and development. It has the departments of Mines 礦業司, Commerce 商業司, Water Resources 水利司, International Cooperation 國際合作處, Industrial Technology 技術處, and an International Trade Committee 貿易調查委員會. Also under its jurisdiction are the Industrial Development Bureau 工業局, Board of Foreign Trade 國際貿易局, National Bureau of Standards 中央標準局, Bureau of Commodity Inspection and Quarantine 商品檢驗局, Energy Committee 能源委員會, Water Resources Planning Commission 水資源統一規劃委員會, Medium and Small Enterprise Administration 中小企業處, Export Processing Zone Administration 加工出口區管理處, Central Geological Survey 中央地質調查所, Commission of National Corporations 國營事業委員會, Investment Commission 投資審議委員會, Committee for Aviation and Space Industry Development 航太工業發展推動小組 and an Industrial Development and Investment Center 投資業務處.

China External Trade Development Council

The principal organization in Taiwan designed to facilitate closer cooperation between government and industry as well as between Taiwan and its trading partners is the China External Trade Development Council (also known as CETRA) 中華民國對外貿易發展協會, which is co-sponsored by the government and private industrial and business organizations. The council maintains 38 branch offices, design centers, and trade centers in 30 countries.

CETRA gathers trade information, conducts market research, promotes made-in-Taiwan products, organizes exhibitions, promotes product and packaging designs, offers convention venues, and trains business people. Under CETRA's encouragement, 13 American states, San Francisco, and the American Institute in Taiwan maintain trade offices at the Taipei World Trade Center 台北世界貿易中心 (see Appendix V). An additional 11 nations—Bolivia, Canada, Chile, Finland, France, Indonesia, Ireland, Oman, the Philippines, Spain, and Thailand—have also set up trade offices at the Taipei World Trade Center to further promote trade relations with the ROC.

Economic Ties with Mainland China

Economic ties between Taiwan and mainland China have never been closer. Although the ROC government still bans direct cross-straits trade, in recent years Taiwan has shipped semifinished products, raw materials, and machinery worth billions of US dollars via Hong Kong to the mainland. According to the ROC's Mainland Affairs Council, the value of two-way trade between Taiwan and mainland China amounted to US$22.5 billion in 1995. Over 86 percent of the indirect trade was composed of exports from Taiwan, which totaled US$19.43 billion, up 21 percent from 1994. The bulk of the exports to the mainland were industrial raw materials and components. Textile fibers, including woven fabrics, polyester filament yarn, and knitted or crocheted fabrics, took up 24.3 percent of Taiwan's exports, while industrial machinery and equipment, electrical and electronics parts, and plastic raw materials accounted for 14.2 percent, 13.6 percent, and 11.9 percent, respectively.

Imports from the Chinese mainland rose by over 66 percent to US$3.09 billion over 1994. Major items were Chinese herbal medicines, semifinished footwear products, polyester, cotton, fur and down feathers.

Investment in the Mainland

Between 1991 and 1995, the ROC government approved some US$5.64 billion of investment in the mainland by Taiwan businessmen, covering over 11,200 applications, making the mainland the number one recipient of Taiwan investment. A large number of Taiwan manufacturers in labor-intensive industries have set up factories there to take advantage of the cheap labor and low overhead costs. Many of these manufacturers receive orders in Taiwan, produce their goods in the mainland, and ship the goods from the mainland to their overseas buyers.

As the China market becomes more open and lucrative, more of Taiwan's large enterprises, including firms in the information technology, plastics, and food and beverage industries, are beginning to undertake large-scale mainland projects. Furthermore, Taiwan investment is spreading beyond the eastern coast of Fukien and Kwangtung provinces. Taiwan businessmen are also beginning to invest in activities other than export manufacturing, setting up mainland outposts to handle real estate, insurance, banking, and tourism.

A worry looms large for Taiwan: trade dependence on the mainland is rising. Approximately 10.46 percent of Taiwan's 1995 trade was with the mainland, 4.4 percent higher than the previous year. Export dependency stood at 17.40 percent, and import dependency at 2.98 percent, up from the 1994 figures of 17.2 percent and 2.2 percent, respectively.

Services

The government defines the service sector as comprising wholesale, retail, international trade, transportation and storage, telecommunications, finance, insurance, real estate, and individual and governmental service businesses. In 1988, the service sector first surpassed the industrial sector in attracting more of the total work force. By the end of 1995, over 50 percent of the island's nine million employers were working in the service sector.

The service sector accounted for 60.2 percent of Taiwan's GDP in 1995. The percentage was similar to that of many advanced nations (see chart, next page). Total GDP value of service sector reached US$158.16 billion in 1995. Of this, over 31 percent was achieved by the finance, insurance, and real estate sectors, 26.4 percent by commerce, and 10.8 percent by transportation and storage. The combined GDP value of the transportation, storage, and telecommunications sector and the finance, insurance, and real estate sector have grown substantially in recent years, partly a result of their links with the manufacturing and construction sectors.

In addition to the government's ambitious plan to develop Taiwan into an Asia-Pacific regional operations center (see inset, next page), its efforts to join the World Trade Organization constituted another major factor that kept these sectors recession-resistant. In order to be admitted to the WTO, the government has adopted a series of measures to liberalize the domestic finance and insurance sectors, further reduce import tariffs, and open up the domestic telecommunications market (see Chapter 16, Mass Media) to foreign competitors.

Finance and Insurance Sectors

In 1995, the finance, insurance, and real estate sectors made up nearly one-fifth of the GDP, second only to manufacturing. The total production value of the same year reached US$49 billion, of which nearly half came from the finance and insurance sectors. By the end of 1995, over 5,000 banking institutions and

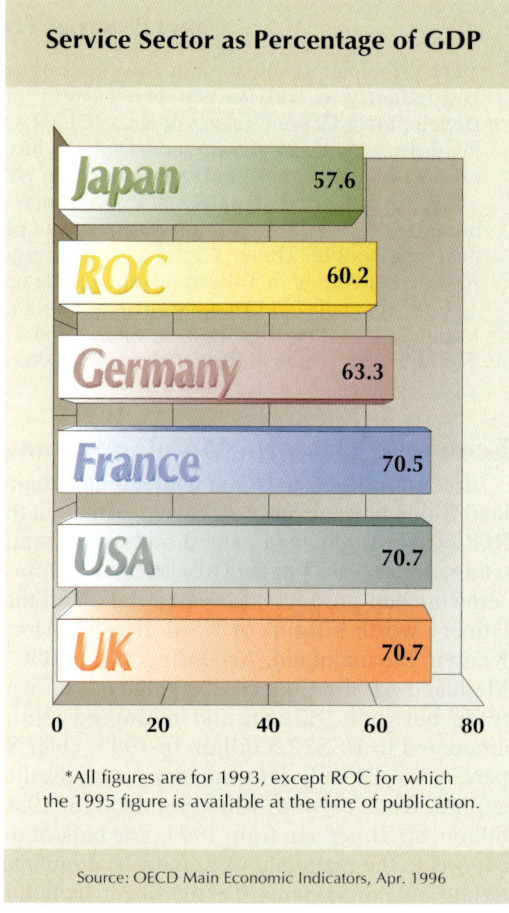

Service Sector as Percentage of GDP

Japan	57.6
ROC	60.2
Germany	63.3
France	70.5
USA	70.7
UK	70.7

0   20   40   60   80

*All figures are for 1993, except ROC for which the 1995 figure is available at the time of publication.

Source: OECD Main Economic Indicators, Apr. 1996

branches were operating in the Taiwan area, 40 of them foreign bank branches. (For more information on the financial sector, see Chapter 11, Finance and Banking.)

A decade has passed since the ROC opened its insurance market to foreign companies. Today, over 50 life and non-life insurance companies (foreign and domestic combined) with more than 200,000 qualified sales persons compete in the market. Taiwan's life insurance rate, which was slightly over 60 percent in 1995, still lags far behind that of the United States (142 percent) and Japan (544 percent). In other words, out of every 100 people in Taiwan, only 60 have a life

insurance policy, while in the United States each
citizen has an average of 1.4 and in Japan 5.4 life
insurance policies. It is not surprising that foreign insurance companies are anxious to penetrate the Taiwan market, and that domestic firms
are gearing up to keep their market share by
offering a wider variety of products and improving their customer services.

In 1995, collected life insurance premiums
totaled US$11 billion, up 13.5 percent over the
previous year. Foreign life insurance companies
garnered less than 6 percent of this amount, yet
they registered over 37 percent growth, compared to 12 percent by domestic companies. In
the area of non-life insurance, some US$2.7 bil-
lion in premiums have been registered in 1995,
14 percent higher than in 1994.

Industry

Industry has long been outpaced by the service sector in terms of GDP percentage. In 1986,
industry still accounted for nearly half of
Taiwan's GDP, but the following year it dropped
to slightly over 40 percent. The downward trend
has continued. In 1995, industry accounted for
36.3 percent of GDP, down from 37.3 percent
the previous year. Production of processed foods,
textiles, garments, leather products, and wood
and bamboo products, which once dominated
exports, continued to decrease in 1995. These
labor-intensive industries have gradually been
replaced by capital- and technology-intensive
industries, such as chemicals, petrochemicals,
information technology, electrical equipment,
and electronics—all of which experienced strong
growth in 1995.

In the 1960s, abundant, well-trained local
workers and inexpensive manufacturing sites
were two major factors that attracted many foreign companies to set up production branches in
Taiwan. These helped the island establish a solid
foundation for its own manufacturing and other
industries. By 1987, however, the stock market
was overheated because of excessive savings in
the private sector and a lack of investment channels. A large portion of the population started

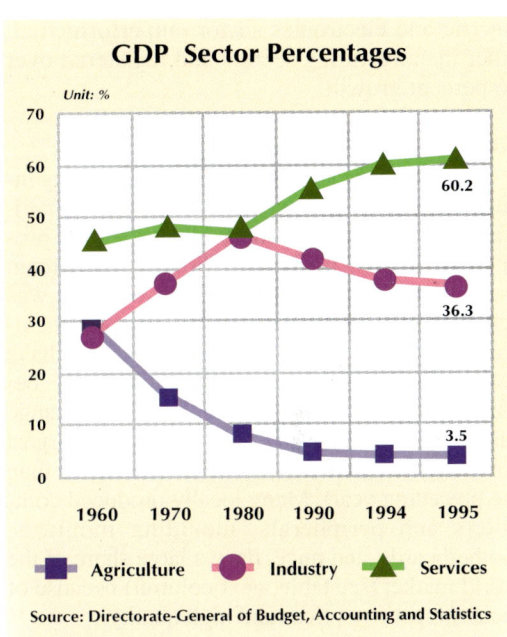

GDP Sector Percentages

Source: Directorate-General of Budget, Accounting and Statistics

playing the market, which resulted in a shortage
of manpower, especially blue-collar workers, in
nearly all industrial and business sectors. A steep
hike in land prices further exacerbated the overall manufacturing environment, forcing many
small and medium-sized firms and labor-intensive enterprises to scale down or even close their
businesses. Many firms went offshore to mainland China or Southeast Asia. The transplanta-
tion of these companies led to the shrinkage of
their relevant sectors.

Fortunately, the establishment of overseas
production sites by such technology- and capital-intensive industries as machinery, chemicals,
precision equipment, and electronics and information technology products, has not created the
side effect of reducing the growth of their parent
companies in Taiwan. These companies have
sharpened their international competitiveness by
streamlining operations, making them more effective in management and production. In 1995,
manufacturing output constituted nearly 80 percent of the total industrial production and engaged 27 percent of the national work force. The

electric and electronics sector outperformed all other manufacturing sectors and registered over 26 percent growth.

Information Technology Industry

In 1995, Taiwan's information technology industry (domestic and overseas production of hardware and software included) yielded a total production value of US$21.3 billion, up 33 percent over 1994. Three-fourths of the amount was achieved by the approximately 890 computer hardware manufacturers that dot the island. They have helped the information technology industry become the ROC's most important foreign exchange earner. Today, Taiwan is the world's third-largest computer hardware supplier (one rank higher than the preceding year). Many locally produced computers and peripherals, including monitors, motherboards, and mice, have a large share of the world market (see table, next column) because of their competitive prices and high quality.

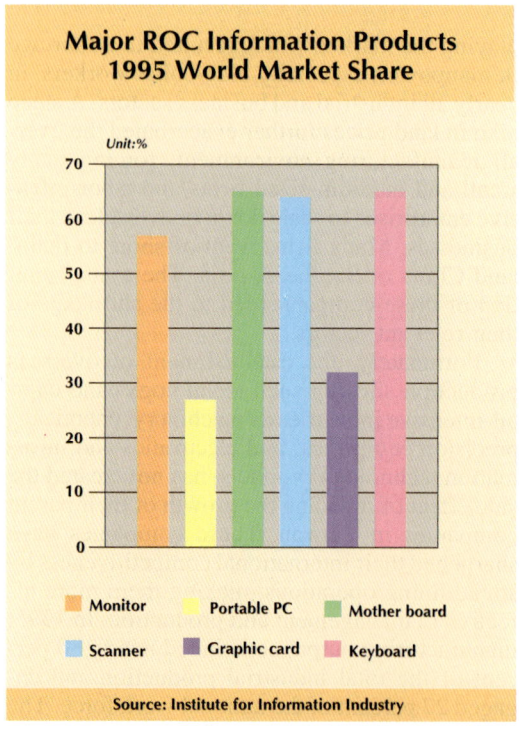

Major ROC Information Products 1995 World Market Share

Unit:%

Source: Institute for Information Industry

Monitor   Portable PC   Mother board

Scanner   Graphic card   Keyboard

Amid the generally lackluster performance of the domestic economy, Taiwan's information technology industry still managed to register 30 percent growth. This can be attributed to many factors, including the rapid growth of Internet use around the world, the increased popularity of multimedia computers, and the expansion of production by local PC manufacturers. Taiwan's information technology industry has grown from a minor role to become a major contributor to the island's flourishing exports, partly a result of governmental inducement and partly because domestic small and medium-sized enterprises are capable and flexible enough to follow latest market trends and adjust production accordingly. Nonetheless, the industry faces problems that also trouble many other manufacturing sectors. Foremost are labor shortages and high overheads.

The structure of Taiwan's information technology industry is pyramidical: a handful of companies at the top committing themselves to product innovation through costly and time-consuming R&D (see Chapter 18, Science and Technology), and small and medium enterprises (SMEs) forming the vast majority (85 percent) of the information technology industry. The latter comprise a weak and unstable downstream foundation. As in other manufacturing sectors, SMEs generally produce goods on an OEM (original equipment manufacturer) and ODM (original design manufacturer) basis. They spend a negligible percentage of their annual turnover on R&D. This has led to the inability of these companies to make in-depth assessments of investment, production, and marketing of innovative products. Moreover, heavy reliance upon the imports of key parts and cutting-edge technology from the United States and Japan has tied Taiwan's information technology industry to the economic strength of these countries and also offsets a good portion of Taiwan's trade surplus each year.

In 1995, Taiwan's information technology service sector grew by 16 percent to reach US$1.62 billion, partially a result of the government's National Information Infrastructure 國家資訊通信基本建設 (NII) program (see

Asia-Pacific Regional Operations Center

Global economic activity is becoming increasingly oriented toward the Asian-Pacific region as it emerges as a counterpart to the North American and European markets. With an eye toward capitalizing on this trend, the ROC government has declared its intention to develop Taiwan into an Asia-Pacific Regional Operations Center 亞太營運中心, promoting Taiwan as the location of choice for multinational enterprises wishing to set up headquarters from which to manage their operations in the Asia-Pacific.

Six sub-operations centers—including manufacturing, sea transportation, air transportation, financial, telecommunications, and media centers—have been envisioned within the regional operations center. While the Council for Economic Planning and Development (CEPD) [see earlier inset] is responsible for the overall planning and coordination of the project, the sub-operations centers are being handled by the Ministry of Economic Affairs 經濟部, the Ministry of Transportation and Communications 交通部, the Ministry of Finance 財政部, the Central Bank of China 中央銀行, and the Government Information Office 新聞局.

In March 1995, the Coordination and Service Office for Asia-Pacific Regional Operations Center under the CEPD 經濟建設委員會亞太營運協調服務中心 was set up to serve international companies that are interested in taking advantage of the opportunities created by this project. Globally renowned DuPont has announced plans to expand its Taiwan branch into the company's product hub for Asia. Chemical giant Bayer is also eyeing an 80-hectare industrial plot near Taichung Harbor as a site for its new Toluene Di-isocyanate (TDI) production facilities, which are slated to be built in Taiwan. The facilities will have an annual production capacity of 10,000 metric tons, 20 percent of which will be for domestic consumption, with the remaining 80 percent for export. Other specific ROC governmental measures for transforming Taiwan into a regional operations center include reducing import tariffs from the current average of 6.5 percent to 5 percent by 1999 and further opening Taiwan's service sector to foreign companies.

Chapter 18, Science and Technology), the thriving Internet, and continuing large-scale growth of the multimedia industry. Tailor-made software still dominates the market, although profits are not high. Over the long run, the potential of the local software market is considered quite limited, and observers urge the domestic software industry to establish a global sales network to promote its products and retain its leading position in Chinese-language software. Taiwan is already facing severe challenges from mainland China in this market segment.

Automotive Industry

Taiwan's auto makers and importers found 1995 a particularly bitter year. A sluggish domestic economy and mainland China's missile exercises in the Taiwan Straits caused a major slump in the island's automobile industry. The government's vigorous efforts to join the World Trade Organization, which will relax or remove trade barriers to the imports of foreign auto products, also cast a shadow over the industry's future.

Total automobile demand in Taiwan in 1995 decreased nearly 6 percent, to approximately 542,000 units. In the first half of 1996, sales dropped by 19 percent, compared to the same period the previous year. Taiwan is currently home to 11 automobile manufacturers, all of which have contracted joint ventures with foreign makers, mostly from Japan. The production value of this sector reached US$10.62 billion in 1995, the equivalent of 5.17 percent of Taiwan's aggregate manufacturing production value that year. Some 409,000 automobiles were produced in Taiwan in 1995.

Automobile sales in Taiwan during 1995 totaled 542,339 units, 90 percent of which were produced by the 11 companies mentioned above. These companies both produce and import automobiles. In 1995, nearly 70 percent of the 275,000 domestically made vans were supplied by Ford Lio Ho Motor Co., Ltd. 福特六和汽車股份有限公司 (29.5 percent), Yulon Motor Co., Ltd. 裕隆汽車製造有限公司 (19.4 percent), and the Kuozui Motors Ltd. 國瑞汽車股份有限公司.

China Motor Corporation 中華汽車工業股份有限公司 maintained its traditional top position in the commercial vehicle market, producing nearly 60 percent of the 117,000 commercial vehicles sold. Domestically produced models with 1301-1600 cc engines were most popular (54 percent), while imported sedans with 2001 cc and larger engines (38.2 percent) also enjoyed high sales.

Although the ROC still bans auto imports directly from Japan, vehicles with Japanese heritage have, like many other commercial products, successfully penetrated the market and built a solid base in consumer's hearts. In 1995, nearly one-third of the imported vans were American-made with Japanese brand names. Worries have long been looming among domestic automobile manufacturers that once Taiwan's door for imported cars is officially opened with reduced tariffs, when Taiwan is admitted to the WTO, foreign vehicles will flood the market and threaten the survival of domestic manufacturers.

Even today, Taiwan's automobile industry, with decades of governmental protection, is short on R&D. It needs to develop its own technology in engines, computerized gearing systems, and several other components, and step up its design capability. For years, Taiwan's reliance on foreign support for engines has hampered its plan to export vehicles. In light of this, the Ministry of Economic Affairs has helped China Motor Corp., San Yang Industrial Co., Ltd. 三陽工業股份有限公司, Yeu Tyan Machinery MFG Co., Ltd. 羽田機械股份有限公司, and Yulon Motor Co., Ltd. jointly develop an engine that can be utilized by all four manufacturers. A prototype has been built, and mass production is scheduled to begin in 1997.

Energy

Taiwan lacks sufficient energy resources. Its coal reserves amount to only 170 million tons, most of which are distributed throughout the northern part of the island. Oil and natural gas reserves total 0.61 million kiloliters and 14.2 billion cubic meters, respectively, and are found mostly in the northern Taiwan counties of Hsinchu and Miaoli, and near Kaohsiung. Total hydropower reserves have been estimated at 5,048 megawatts, of which 1,592 megawatts have been developed, primarily along several major rivers. Given such limited natural resources, Taiwan must import fossil fuels to meet the bulk of its energy needs.

Supply

The total energy supply in Taiwan increased from 17 million kiloliters of oil equivalent in 1974 to 79 million kiloliters in 1995, with an average annual growth of 7.7 percent. Over the past two decades, indigenous energy supplies have accounted for a progressively smaller portion of annual use, dropping from 30 percent in 1974 to 4 percent in 1995; the imported energy share has risen correspondingly. Oil as a relative share of the energy supply stood at 54 percent in 1995, and nuclear power accounted for 11 percent.

Expenditures for imported energy totaled US$6.8 billion in 1995, of which imported oil accounted for 71 percent or US$4.88 billion. Imported energy accounted for 6.6 percent of the total value of imports in 1995 and 2.6 percent of GDP, with per capita energy imports at US$314.

Consumption

Taiwan's energy consumption increased from 14 million kiloliters of oil equivalent in 1974 to 70 million kiloliters in 1995, an average annual growth rate of 7.9 percent. By comparison, GDP grew by an average of 8.1 percent during the same period, with an energy demand elasticity of about 0.97. Per capita energy consumption increased from 905 liters of oil equivalent in 1974 to 3,304 liters in 1995, an annual growth rate of 6.4 percent.

Over the past 20 years, the industrial sector has been the greatest energy consumer. However, its share of total energy consumption dropped from 65 percent in 1974 to 56 percent in 1995. Energy consumption for transportation increased from 10 percent in 1974 to 18 percent in 1995;

for agriculture, it declined from 5 percent to 2 percent; for residential use, it increased from 10 percent to 12 percent; for commercial use, it increased from 2 percent to 5 percent; for other sectors, it dropped from 8 percent to 6 percent. Non-use of energy was 1 percent in 1995.

Since the second worldwide energy crisis, coal has accounted for a growing percentage of Taiwan's overall energy consumption, rising from 8 percent in 1979 to 14 percent in 1995. By contrast, petroleum products accounted for only 43 percent of overall energy consumption in 1995, down from 51 percent in 1979.

Oil and Natural Gas

Taiwan is heavily dependent on imported oil. In 1995, approximately 69 percent of imported crude oil came from the Middle East. The other 31 percent came from Indonesia, the Congo, and Australia. Consumption of petroleum products totaled 37.6 million kiloliters of oil equivalent in 1995, of which 37 percent was for industrial use, 32 percent for transportation, 19 percent for power generation, 3 percent for agriculture, 4 percent for residential use, and 5 percent for other use.

The state-owned Chinese Petroleum Corporation 中國石油股份有限公司 (CPC) is solely responsible for exploring, producing, importing, refining, and marketing petroleum and natural gas in Taiwan. The CPC owns two oil refineries with a total capacity of 720,000 barrels per day, and recently has made considerable investment to increase the output of low-sulfur fuel oil to improve air quality.

In 1987, the government began allowing the installation of privately operated gas stations to sell gasoline and diesel oil. At the end of 1995, there were 1,243 gas stations, 648 (52 percent) of which were privately owned. In 1995, domestic petroleum production amounted to 62,310 kiloliters of oil condensate and 941.6 million cubic meters of gas respectively.

To diversify energy uses, the CPC has imported 1.5 million tons of liquefied natural gas (LNG) every year since 1990 under a long-term contract. Natural gas consumption in 1995 to-taled 4,260 million cubic meters, of which 46 percent was for industrial use, 33 percent for power generation, 17 percent for residential use, and 4 percent for commercial use.

In July 1996, the Overseas Petroleum Investment Co. 海外石油及投資公司 (OPIC), an affiliate of the CPC signed an agreement with mainland China's National Offshore Oil Corp. 中國海洋石油總公司 to jointly explore oil reserves in the Taiwan Straits. The target area lies just off the Pearl River delta 珠江三角洲 and is expected to produce ten million tons of petroleum for the first year.

Coal

Coal production dropped further in 1995 to 0.24 million tons from five million tons in 1968. Indigenous coal was once the prime source of energy, constituting over 60 percent of industrial energy use in the 1950s. During its heyday, some 65,000 coal miners were employed in over 400 mines. Due to the high costs of coal production under increasingly difficult mining conditions, as well as competition from imported coal, the number of coal mines and miners has decreased dramatically. Today the less than ten coal mines with one thousand workers are facing an even tougher time to find new blood for the industry, because the younger generation prefers white collar occupations. When the ROC is admitted to the World Trade Organization, the government will have to annul rules that protect local coal production, which means the remaining coal mines will most likely close within five years.

Coal supply totaled 29 million tons in 1995. Of this, 1 percent was domestically produced, while the remaining 99 percent was imported from Australia, Indonesia, South Africa, mainland China, and the United States. Some 53 percent of the total coal consumption of 26 million tons in 1995 went to power generation, 11 percent to the cement industry, 15 percent to steelworks, and 21 percent to other industries and users.

Electricity

Gross power generation by the Taiwan Power Company 台灣電力公司 in 1995 totaled

122.4 billion KWH, a 6.8 percent increase over 1994. Of the total, 7.3 percent was generated by hydropower, 33.7 percent by burning coal, 25.7 percent by burning oil, 4.5 percent by burning LNG, and the remaining 28.8 percent by nuclear fission. Power co-generation by auto producers totaled 11.4 billion KWH in 1995. Electricity consumption in 1995 came to 120.2 billion KWH, a 6.9 percent rise over the preceding year. At present, 99.7 percent of the population has electricity service.

The Taiwan Power Company, commonly known as Taipower, is solely responsible for developing, generating, supplying, and marketing electric power for the entire Taiwan area. By the end of 1995, the Taiwan area had 12 EHV substations (345/161 KV) with a capacity of 21,000 MVA; 45 primary substations (161/69 KV) with a capacity of 22,700 MVA; and 33 primary distribution substations (161/22-11 KV) with a capacity of 6,100 MVA. A total of 38 hydropower, 18 thermal, and three nuclear plants supply power to these stations. Total Taipower installed capacity was 21,898 megawatts, of which 19.1 percent was hydropower, 27 percent coal-fired, 9 percent gas-fired, 21.4 percent oil-fired, and 23.5 percent nuclear. By the end of l995, the installed capacity of auto producers was 3,432 megawatts, equivalent to 15 percent of Taipower's total installed capacity.

Owing to the continuous growth of the domestic economy, the peak load in 1995 reached 19,933 MW, up 7.1 percent over 1994. The average load was 13,454 MW, a 6.9 percent increase, compared with the previous year. In 1995, Units Two and Four of the Mingtan Pumped Storage Hydro Plant 明潭抽蓄水力發電廠 and the combined cycle units of the Nanpu Thermal Power Plant 南部火力發電廠 have been put into operation, generating an additional 933 megawatts. Furthermore, the government promulgated the *Independent Power Production Liberalization Guidelines* 開放發電業作業要點 in September 1994 to encourage the private sector to take part in power production and to alleviate an increasingly worsening power supply capabil-

ity. In 1995, 11 bidders were granted permission to generate electricity and operations will begin between 1997 and 2002, depending on the contract terms with Taipower.

Nuclear Power

The six nuclear units in Taiwan shared 23.5 percent of the total installed capacity (5,144 megawatts out of 21,898 megawatts) but produced 28.8 percent of Taiwan's total electrical output in 1995. The six nuclear units are housed in three nuclear power stations, all of which are owned and operated by Taipower. In light of the increasing demand on electricity, especially for industrial use, the government began planning a fourth nuclear power plant in 1980. But growing awareness of environmental protection among the general public and increasingly vehement protests against nuclear power have gradually undermined the support of many legislators who must approve the project's budget. In particular, legislators representing constituencies where the plant is slated to be built are being pressured to reject the plant.

The Legislative Yuan blocked the entire budget for the plan on May 24, 1996, primarily due to the opposition parties. Five months later, however, the ruling Kuomintang, which still constitutes the majority in the legislative body, was able to revive the project when members of the opposition Democratic Progressive Party and the New Party unanimously boycotted another vote on the plant (see inset, next page).

Alternative Energy Sources

Because Taiwan is in the subtropics, it has the potential to develop solar energy resources. A number of solar, thermal, and photovoltaic testing systems are in service in Taiwan. The total area of solar collectors reached 600,000 square meters by the end of 1995. Two 100-kilowatt wind power units are presently in service on Ch'imei Island 七美嶼. In addition, more than 100 thermal springs are active on Taiwan. One geothermal power plant, at T'uch'ang 土場 (a 300 KW binary process type) is currently

Fourth Nuclear Power Project Chronology

1980 Taipower first broaches the plan to build a fourth nuclear power plant, scheduled to be completed by 2004. Total budget for the project is US$6.3 billion.

1983 A 480-hectare land at Yenliao 鹽寮 in Kungliao Rural Township 貢寮鄉, Taipei County, in the northern part of Taiwan is acquired for the six-unit plant.

1985 The Executive Yuan 行政院 instructs Taipower to postpone the plan and step up public relations for the project.

1987 The Legislature 立法院 freezes budget for the plan passed between 1982 and 1986.

1992 The Budget Committee 預算委員會 of the Legislature releases the budget upon the request of the Executive branch.

1995 Taipower opens bidding for the contracts. No successful result is achieved because quotations submitted by international contractors exceed the set price cap by 20 percent or more.

1996 On May 24, the Legislature votes to overturn the budget for the nuclear power plant. On the same day, General Electric Company of the United States wins the US$1.8 billion contract for the plant's two reactors. On October 18, the Legislature votes to revive the project.

in service. Over the last decade, technologies for biogas purification and the assembly of biogas power generators have been investigated, and a number of pig farms have biogas power generators. They produced 6 megawatts in 1995.

Energy Prices

The price structure for electrical power is configured to reflect the cost of supplying energy at different seasons (seasonal rates) and different times of the day (TOU rates). Seasonal rates and TOU rates are designed to encourage peak clipping, valley filling and/or load shifting. Currently, the electrical service is divided into three categories: lighting, combined lighting and power, and power (metered and flat-rated). Seasonal rates are necessarily applied to all customer classes except flat-rated customers. TOU rates are mandatory for those with a contracted capacity of 100 KW, and are voluntary for those with a contracted capacity below 100 KW. At present, TOU rates are applied to all customer classes except lighting customers.

Low-tension metered lighting service is applicable to residential and small non-commercial and commercial customers. Charges for metered lighting service are calculated solely upon the KWH consumed. Low tension combined lighting and power service is applicable to medium non-commercial and commercial customers. Low tension metered power service is applicable to small and medium-sized industrial/agricultural customers. High or extra-high tension service is applicable to customers with a contracted capacity of around 100 KW. Charges for power service and combined lighting and power service are separated into demand charge and energy charge (a two-part rate). Demand charge is billed on the contracted KW and energy charge is calculated according to the KWH consumed.

In order to reduce the summer peak load directly, Taipower also offers a menu of interruptible rates (six options) on a voluntary basis to customers taking high or extra-high tension service. Interruptible rates are designed to reflect capacity cost savings for customers' interruptible loads. The rates require that customers reduce their peak demand to a pre-determined level in accordance with the contract in return for demand credits. The latest rate schedules for electrical service came into effect on June 1, 1995.

Domestic oil prices have been allowed to reflect the cost of imported oil as world prices fluctuate. The government also routinely considers the substitutability and heating values of petroleum products and natural gas before setting their prices. On July 1, 1995, the Chinese Petroleum Corporation adjusted its prices for petroleum products in accordance with the

Project to Improve and Safeguard Air Quality in Taiwan 台灣地區空氣品質改善維護計畫 and its *Air Pollution Control Fee Levy Plan* 空氣污染防制費收費辦法, passed in March of that year. Oil prices are as follows: US$0.62 for most tanked premium gasoline, US$0.61 for 95-octane unleaded gasoline, US$0.57 for 92-octane unleaded gasoline, US$0.43 for premium diesel oil, and US$0.46 for kerosene.

Energy Conservation

Energy conservation is a major part of energy policy. The *Measures for Energy Conservation* 節約能源措施 and the *Energy Management Law* 能源管理法 mandate a set of incentives for energy customers to conserve energy. So far, energy productivity has risen from US$2.07 per kg of oil equivalent in 1985 to US$3.37 in 1995—a 5 percent increase every year since 1991.

SMEs

For decades, small and medium-sized enterprises have been the backbone of the ROC's economic development. According to the Ministry of Economic Affairs, over 95 percent of Taiwan's 930,000 registered companies are SMEs. They employ nearly 80 percent of the total work force and account for half of the island's aggregate export value.

SMEs began emerging after World War II, when Japanese conglomerates withdrew from Taiwan and the local market fell into the hands of state-run enterprises and large private companies. The island's SMEs focused on foreign markets to survive. At first, agricultural products and agricultural processed goods made up the bulk of exported items. These were eventually replaced by light industrial products, especially after the government set up several export-processing zones to spur the economy. An export-oriented policy in the 1960s also created a favorable environment for SMEs to penetrate international markets. SME entrepreneurs are characterized by high adaptability to market trends, hard work, thrift, and a tendency to pass their businesses on to their children.

The 1995 revision to the *Small and Medium-sized Enterprise Development Statute* 中小企業發展條例 defines small and medium-sized enterprises by sector, paid-in capital/annual turnover, and the number of employees. Industries, including manufacturing, construction, and mining and quarrying, that have a paid-in capital not exceeding NT$60 million (an equivalent of US$2.2 million) or hire less than 200 regular workers, are categorized as SMEs.

Companies in commercial, service, and transportation sectors with an annual turnover not exceeding NT$80 million (an equivalent of US$3 million) or that hire less than 50 employees are also considered SMEs. Most SMEs (60 percent) are in the commercial sector, followed by manufacturing (17 percent). In terms of sales turnover, manufacturing accounted for over 37 percent of SME aggregate turnover, while the commercial sector took up 35 percent in 1994. The two, though distinguished by sector, are complementary in that many SMEs in the commercial sector rely on manufacturers to supply goods. At the same time, a large number of manufacturers also work closely with trading companies to export products.

For decades, Taiwan has been an Asian production outpost for many renowned multinational conglomerates, proof that Taiwan can produce high-quality goods. Today, made-in-Taiwan products, ranging from cans to toys and garments to personal computers, are found in shops around the world. A large number of Taiwan's SMEs still rely heavily on OEM and ODM orders, because these companies have been reluctant to invest in R&D and product innovation themselves. On average, SMEs spend no more than 3 percent of their annual operating income on R&D, because they tend to avoid relatively long-term investments and arduous R&D processes that have no guarantee of successful results.

Another factor that influences SME investment willingness lies in their difficulty in acquiring bank loan. Although banks generally consider many SMEs financially unstable, they still provide 40 percent of the capital resources for SMEs. Roughly 82 percent of the SMEs fund R&D projects on their own, while only 13 percent comes from bank loans.

Because of the worldwide economic slump, Taiwan's SMEs have encountered many hardships in exporting goods. A shortage of laborers, increases in wages, and prohibitive prices for land acquisition have also plagued both large-scale firms and SMEs. Fluctuating exchanges rates and keen competition from other nations are other major factors that have had direct impact on SME operations.

In light of the continuing importance of SMEs in Taiwan's overall economy, the government has made five revisions to the *Small and Medium-sized Enterprise Guidance Regulations* 中小企業輔導準則, first stipulated in 1967. The revisions are geared to create a sounder environment for SMEs to increase productivity. Other government measures to assist SMEs include a development fund that provides assistance in case of recession and indemnification for damages caused by natural disasters; programs to promote automation and computerization; seminars to cultivate marketing and managerial expertise; and strengthening the functions of the SME service centers located in 21 cities and counties around the island.

11.
Finance
and Banking

Previous page: The Central Bank of China is charged with promoting financial stability, ensuring the soundness of banks, maintaining price stability, and fostering economic development.

Upper: This branch of Dai-Ichi Kangyo Bank is one of the 44 branch offices which foreign banks have set up in Taiwan.

Lower: A paucity of domestic futures hasn't dampened the enthusiasm of local investors—here traders track the movement of foreign contracts.

11 Finance and Banking

The last two years have been a rough-and-tumble ride in the Republic of China's financial sector. The Mexican peso crisis, Kobe earthquake, and Barings collapse were just a few of the crises which shook the world economy in 1995, and financial markets in Taiwan suffered along with their global counterparts. The economic situation in the ROC improved in the second quarter, but after Peking held its first round of massive military maneuvers and missile tests off the coast of Taiwan in July 1995, the financial sector began to sink quickly. Severe panic-selling on the stock market, massive capital outflows, and a series of bank runs and other crises at financial institutions put considerable pressure on Taiwan's financial system.

Fortunately, monetary authorities adopted appropriate stabilizing measures to minimize the damage, and these efforts proved fairly successful. As if signalling that the worst was over, the Taiwan Stock Exchange index rose by over 800 points, or almost 16 percent, in the two months following the ROC's March 1996 presidential elections, and it has continued to climb since then. While trouble spots remained, the financial sector as a whole seemed to be on the road to recovery as 1996 was drawing to a close.

Public Finance
Government Expenditures

Total expenditures at all levels of government were up 8.3 percent from the fiscal 1994 level of US$70.9 billion to US$76.9 billion in FY1995 (July 1, 1994, to June 30, 1995). Current expenditures also rose, by 14.4 percent, from US$43.1 billion in FY1994 to US$49.3 billion in FY1995. Thanks to a national five-year administrative expenditure trimming program, increases in current expenditures by the central government contributed only slightly to this growth. However, such expenditures at the local government level shot up due to increased welfare spending. Capital expenditures fell 0.9 percent from US$27.8 billion in FY1994 to US$27.5 billion in FY1995.

Most categories of government expenditures decreased in fiscal 1995. Government spending on economic development in FY1995 fell 6.7 percent to US$16.2 billion, reflecting the fact that a number of major national development projects were nearly completed while others lagged behind schedule. Meanwhile, funding for education, science, and culture, which accounted for 17.3 percent of total government spending in FY1995, was cut from the FY1994 level of US$14.2 billion to US$13.3 billion. Although military purchases have accelerated recently as a result of higher tensions in the Taiwan Straits, national defense spending shrank 16.1 percent in fiscal 1995, from US$11.9 billion to US$10 billion. Only spending on general administration—which rose 2.7 percent to US$8.2 billion—and social welfare—which jumped 18 percent—grew in FY1995. The surge in social welfare expenditures, which rose from US$13 billion in FY1994 to US$15.3 billion in FY1995, came as a result of the initiation of the ROC's National Health Insurance program on March 1, 1995.

Government Revenues

Total revenues for all levels of government grew 9.1 percent, from US$71.3 billion in FY1994 to US$77.9 billion in FY1995. Of the total, tax and monopoly revenues accounted for 58.6 percent, while the share contributed by state-owned enterprises fell from the fiscal 1994 level of 9.6 percent to 6.7 percent in FY1995 due to the combined effects of a slowdown in the privatization process and lower revenues since privatization began. Borrowing accounted for an additional 22.2 percent, and assorted other sources of revenue made up the final 12.5 percent.

The composition of tax and monopoly revenues continued to shift in FY1995, with revenues from indirect taxes now accounting for over 52 percent of the total, up from the previous 48 percent. Direct tax revenues contributed a little less than 43 percent of the total. The percentage coming from monopoly revenues, which in the past exceeded 20 percent of the total, has fallen in recent years as the government contin-

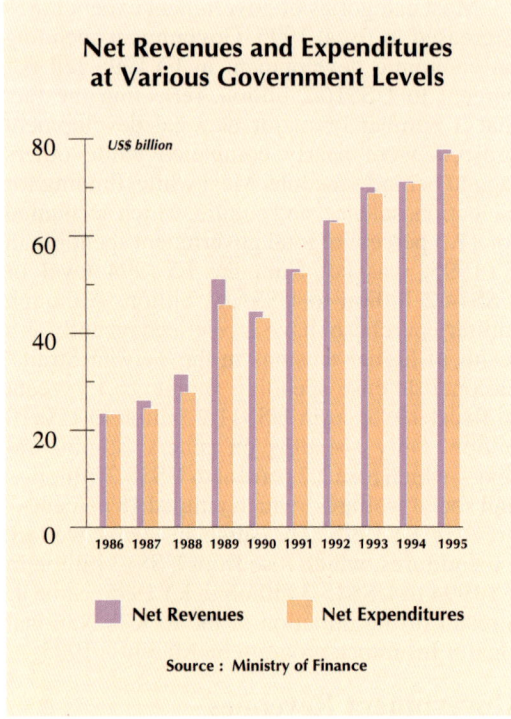

Net Revenues and Expenditures at Various Government Levels

US$ billion

80

60

40

20

0

1986 1987 1988 1989 1990 1991 1992 1993 1994 1995

■ Net Revenues   ■ Net Expenditures

Source : Ministry of Finance

ues to open up formerly closed markets. They now make up about 5 percent. Of the indirect taxes, commodity tax revenues rose 9 percent from US$5.3 billion in fiscal 1994 to US$5.8 billion in FY1995, and revenues from business tax (i.e. sales tax) increased 9.2 percent to US$7.9 billion over the same period. Thanks to the 20 percent increase in imports in FY1995, customs duties jumped 12 percent, from the FY1994 figure of US$3.8 billion to US$4.3 billion.

As for direct taxes, income tax revenues shot up 25.9 percent, from US$9.9 billion in FY1994 to US$11.8 billion in FY1995. This jump came despite an increase in the personal income tax exemption. However, land tax revenues, reflecting the sluggish state of the real estate market, fell another 6.1 percent in fiscal 1995.

Debt Obligations

The government deficit widened to US$19.2 billion in FY1995, a 26.4 percent increase, while net borrowing at all levels of government reached US$17.2 billion in the same year. This borrowing included US$2.8 billion in government bonds and US$14.4 billion in loans from postal savings and labor retirement funds. Meanwhile, total government debts were up 11.1 percent, reaching US$59.3 billion in fiscal 1995. The outstanding balance of public debt as a percentage of gross national product also increased in FY1995, to 22.6 percent. More than one-sixth of FY1995 expenditures were directed towards debt repayments and interest payments, with the obvious result that less resources were available for other projects.

Money & Banking
Money Supply

Money supply growth slowed in 1995. High-powered money, which increased 10.54 percent in 1994, grew at a much slower rate of 6.04 percent in 1995. As a result, the annual growth rate of the M2 money supply continued to shrink, declining from 13.11 percent in January to 8.46 percent in December 1995 and thus falling out of the target range set by the Central Bank of China 中央銀行. The growth rates of the narrowly defined M1b and M1a monetary aggregates fell even more drastically: the annual growth rate of M1b dropped from 12.12 percent to 0.74 percent, while M1a growth fell through the floor, from 8.89 percent to -4.30 percent. Both growth rates were far below Central Bank targets.

This sluggish monetary performance can be largely attributed to two factors. The first is slow growth in the non-financial sector, which in 1995 was reflected in a flagging real estate market, slower growth in private consumption, and a contraction in bank deposits associated with a bearish stock market. The second major factor was tensions across the Taiwan Straits. Peking held its first military exercises off the coast of Taiwan in July 1995, and in the second half of 1995 alone, total capital outflow reached US$12.5 billion. Although foreign direct investment in

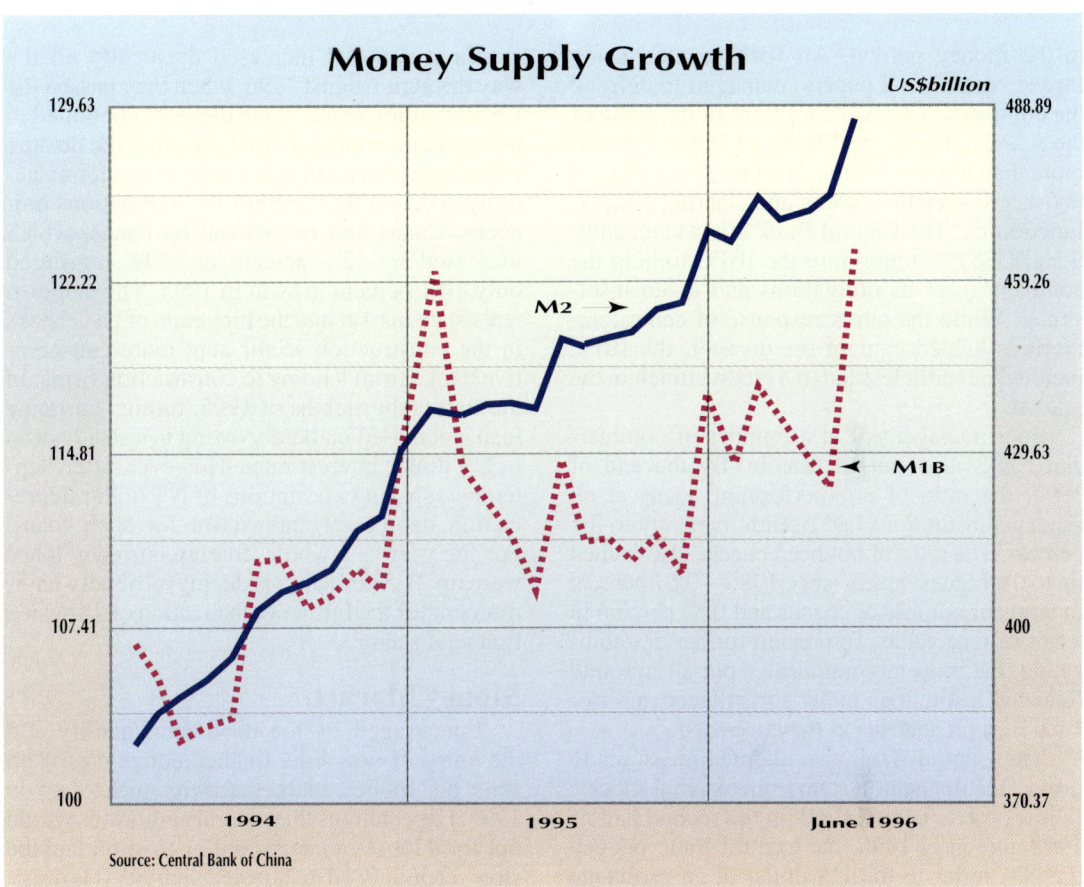

Money Supply Growth

US$billion

Source: Central Bank of China

the stock market rose by US$2.2 billion during the same period, the net effect on foreign reserves was still considerable. Capital continued to pour out of Taiwan as the crisis wore on, and by March 1996, total outflow topped US$19.2 billion. Only in June 1996 did the monetary situation begin to show signs of improvement.

A number of major scandals put further pressure on Taiwan's financial system. On July 29, 1995, the general manager of the Fourth Credit Cooperative of Changhua 彰化第四信用合作社 embezzled US$104 million to cover his personal stock market losses. Panicked depositors responded to the news by withdrawing US$370 million, and the run spread over to other credit cooperatives nearby. The monetary authorities quickly adopted a number of measures to restore confidence, including arranging for the Taiwan Cooperative Bank 台灣省合作金庫 to take over the troubled Changhua cooperative. The crisis nevertheless sparked a series of runs at other rural financial institutions such as farmers' associations 農會 and credit cooperatives 信用合作社, and as of August 1996, a total of 32 institutions had experienced runs on deposits. Predictably, this wave of runs seriously eroded confidence in basic depository institutions. Fortunately for the financial system, most of the funds withdrawn made their way into the postal savings system and commercial banks, and thus the withdrawals did not lead to a wider crisis.

Another serious incident involved the International Bills Finance Corporation 國際票券金融股份有限公司 (IBFC), a leading underwriter in the money market. An IBFC dealer, using forged commercial papers, managed to defraud the company of US$370 million. In the wake of the scandal, the Central Bank of China pumped more than US$1.1 billion into the money market in order to keep the trading and clearing systems functioning. The Central Bank injected an additional US$1.5 billion into the IBFC to help the company meet its obligations and avoid insolvency. While the quick response of central authorities helped contain the disaster, the IBFC incident nevertheless led to a credit crunch in the market.

Poor management at a number of commercial banks also caused trouble. By the end of 1995, the ratio of non-performing loans at all financial institutions had risen remarkably to 3.1 percent. The ratio of bounced checks also inched up to the highest levels since 1986—0.67 percent in terms of number of checks and 0.52 percent in terms of face value. To prevent further destabilization, the monetary authorities put all unsound financial institutions under surveillance and isolated runs on deposits as they occurred.

The Central Bank also adopted measures to protect the financial system from external shocks. In response to capital flight in the second half of 1995 and early 1996, the Central Bank pegged the NT dollar to the US dollar at an exchange rate of NT$27.5 to US$1. This put speculation off and rebuilt confidence in the local currency. The Central Bank also lowered the required reserve ratio on five occasions, reducing the cost of banking as well as increasing high-powered money and scaling up the money multiplier in order to fill in the liquidity gap caused by capital outflow.

As a result, the total assets of depository institutions grew by 8.3 percent in 1995 to reach US$596.3 billion by the end of the year—a lower rate of growth than the 15.1 percent recorded in 1994. The bearishness of the real estate and stock markets together with strong expectations of NT dollar depreciation was reflected in changes in the composition of deposits and the pattern of funding in the banking sector. Foreign currency deposits increased drastically all the way through August 1996, when they passed the US$10 billion mark. Time deposits continued to be the major source of funds because the decline in asset markets and slowdown in economic activity reduced the demand for transactions balances. Loans and investment by banks, which increased by 12.7 percent in 1994, registered only 10.1 percent growth in 1995. The sluggish real estate market and the high ratio of bad checks in the construction sector kept more conservative banks from lending to construction firms. In the first eight months of 1995, foreign currency loans increased markedly owing to a steady drop in US dollar interest rates. However, after September, strong expectations of NT dollar depreciation dampened enthusiasm for such loans. For the year as a whole, foreign currency loans were up 21.5 percent, producing a friendly environment for the further globalization of Taiwan's financial sector.

Money Market

Encouraged by the adequate liquidity and the entry of new bills finance companies from June on, money market activity picked up in 1995. Expectations that central authorities would opt for a loose monetary policy to stimulate the slow economy also boosted activity, as businesses, anticipating lower interest rates in the future, turned to short-term financing. Money market issues came more frequently, and the volume of issues thus increased remarkably. The primary market saw a total of US$333.3 billion in new issues in 1995, an increase of 22.1 percent over the previous year. At the end of December 1995, the value of outstanding short-term monetary instruments totaled US$51.9 billion, up 19.3 percent year-on-year. Money market interest rates generally remained stable throughout 1995, except for August and September 1995, when they experienced relatively large fluctuations due to runs on deposits at nonbank depository institutions, the scandal at the IBFC, and huge capital outflows caused by cross-Straits tensions.

In the secondary market, transactions in short-term monetary instruments were up 16.9 percent in 1995, to US$1.6 trillion. Of this total, commercial paper (CPs) accounted for 61.8 percent, negotiable certificates of deposit (NCDs) for 19.2 percent, and banker's acceptances (BAs) for 15.5 percent. The size of the Taipei market has made it the second largest money market in Asia.

Transactions in the interbank call-loan market expanded to US$481.5 billion in 1995, up 7.3 percent from the previous year. Overnight loan transactions, which made up 69.9 percent of transactions in 1994, accounted for 87.3 percent in 1995. This increase was due to expanded liability management by banks to meet reserve requirements after the Central Bank adjusted the counting basis from ten days to a monthly term. Seven-day call loans accounted for 9.41 percent of the total, and transactions involving call loans of other maturities accounted for less than 4 percent.

The foreign currency call-loan market (TIBOR market) grew impressively in 1995. Total turnover for the year reached US$535.2 billion, a dramatic increase of 88.7 percent from 1994. Of this total, US dollar transactions jumped 91.6 percent to account for US$528.2 billion, Japanese yen deals edged up 4.3 percent to ¥503 billion, and deutschemark transactions fell 43 percent to DM2.1 billion.

Foreign Exchange Market

Large capital outflows and NT dollar speculation in the second half of 1995 made the year a busy one on the foreign exchange market. The trading volume of major products on the forex market averaged approximately US$4.7 billion daily in 1995, yielding a total turnover of US$1.1 trillion for the entire year. Transactions between banks and customers accounted for 36.6 percent of the total, while the remaining 63.4 percent represented interbank transactions.

The ROC government is committed to liberalizing Taiwan's financial markets. At the beginning of 1995, the Central Bank had already approved margin trading, forward trading between NT dollars and foreign currencies settled by non-principal delivery, third currency swap trading, and third currency options and futures. Turnover for the year reflected this mix: spot market transactions accounted for 67.6 percent of the total, currency swap transactions made up 17.9 percent, forward transactions represented 5.9 percent, options transactions accounted for 1.9 percent, and financial future transactions contributed 0.7 percent. At the end of 1995, the Central Bank also approved foreign currency interest rate swaps, foreign currency forward rate agreements, foreign currency interest rate options, and trust funds for foreign securities investment. However, NT dollar-related forex futures and options remain off-limits.

Bond Market

In 1995, central authorities pursued a number of important initiatives to reform the issuance of government bonds. First, the government issued fewer new bonds throughout the year, and in July 1995, it began spacing new issues at regular intervals, with the value of each issue falling between US$370 million and US$740 million. This change is aimed at facilitating bond trading and establishing a benchmark interest rate in the market. Second, following the first issue of zero-coupon bonds by Chiao Tung Bank 交通銀行 in November 1994, the government released its first trench of zero-coupon bonds through a Dutch auction in October 1995. For the entire year of 1995, total government bond issuance fell 15.5 percent to US$4.6 billion, reflecting the government's expanded use of postal savings and labor retirement funds as sources of funding. Total outstanding central government bonds amounted to US$32.1 billion at the end of 1995.

While the issuance of government bonds slowed in 1995, corporate bonds saw tremendous growth. Due to low interest rates in the bond market and bearishness in the stock market, corporations turned to the bond market as a major funding source. In the primary market, a total of US$1.6 billion in corporate bonds were issued, a

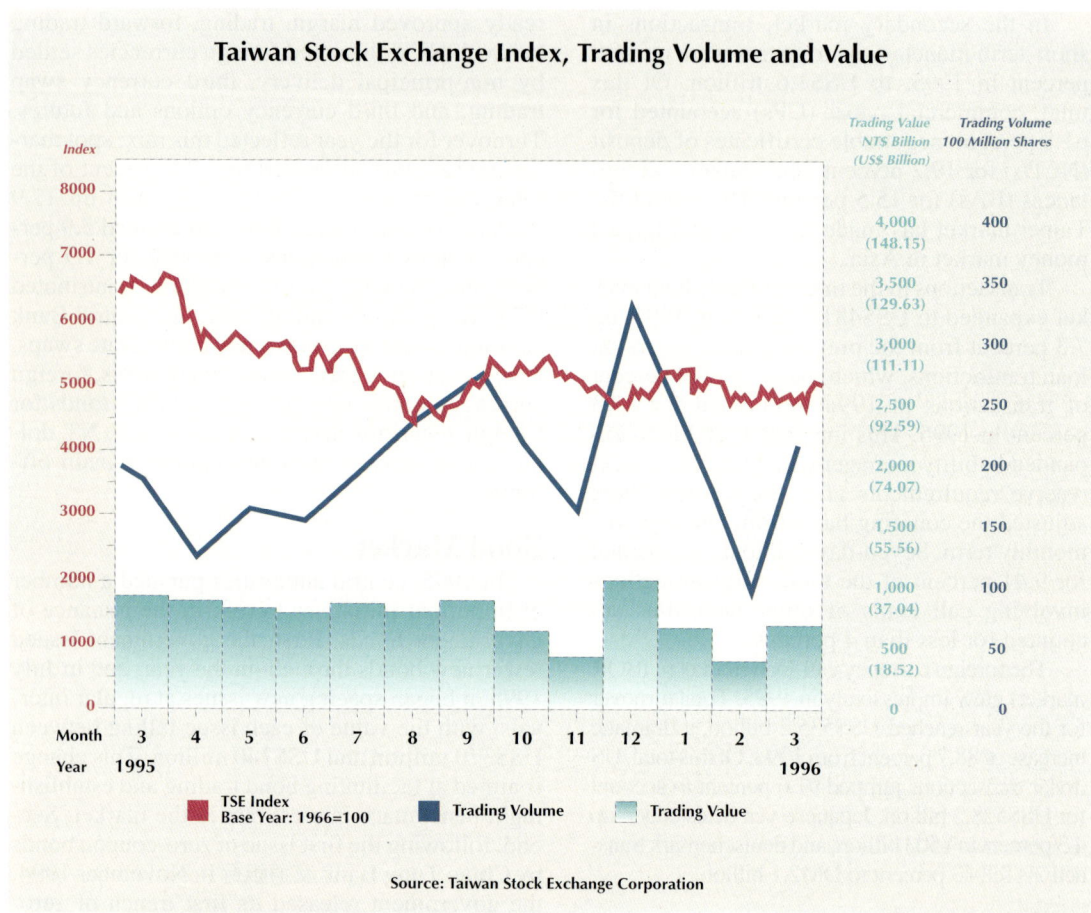

Taiwan Stock Exchange Index, Trading Volume and Value

Trading Value *Trading Volume*
NT$ Billion *100 Million Shares*
(US$ Billion)

Index

8000

7000   4,000
                                           (148.15)   400

6000   3,500
                                           (129.63)   350

                                            3,000
                                           (111.11)   300
5000
                                            2,500
                                           (92.59)   250
4000
                                            2,000
                                           (74.07)   200
3000
                                            1,500
                                           (55.56)   150

2000
                                            1,000
                                           (37.04)   100

1000
                                            500
                                           (18.52)   50

0   0   0

Month   3   4   5   6   7   8   9   10   11   12   1   2   3
Year   1995   1996

■ TSE Index   ■ Trading Volume   Trading Value
  Base Year: 1966=100

Source: Taiwan Stock Exchange Corporation

44.2 percent jump from the previous year. Introduced into the market were a variety of new issues, including callable bonds, floating rate bonds, and mortgage-backed bonds. This proliferation of debt instruments highlights the trend toward a more sophisticated bond market.

Also in 1995, banks issued almost US$1.7 billion in bank debentures, a significant increase over the previous year's US$1.2 billion. Among the new issues were the four trenches of "small dragon bonds" issued in Taiwan by the Asian Development Bank 亞洲開發銀行. The first three trenches, denominated in US

dollars, amounted to US$164 million. The fourth trench was denominated in NT dollars and totaled US$96.3 million. Chiao Tung Bank agreed to handle the NT dollar-US dollar conversion for the Asian Development Bank and thus take the exchange rate risk. At present, these "small dragon bonds" are the only foreign bonds to have been issued in Taiwan's primary bond market.

In the secondary market, total turnover for the entire year of 1995 reached US$770.2 billion, up 32.5 percent from 1994. Trading is dominated by government bonds. Only US$287 million of the total turnover represented transactions involving corporate bonds. The majority of all transactions—US$704 billion worth—were repurchase agreements, indicating that investors were trading for short-term liquidity purposes rather than long-term investment.

Stock Market

Although stock market performance in 1995 left much to be desired, the market nevertheless continued to grow. At the end of 1995, there were 347 companies listed on the Taiwan Stock Exchange, up from 313 listed last year. Total capitalization expanded by 22.5 percent to stand at US$49.6 billion. The average weighted price index, which began the year at 7,051.49 and fell almost steadily before recovering slightly to end December at 5,173.73, averaged 5,543.75 points for the whole of 1995. In the face of the mainland's renewed military threats in early 1996, the index dropped to a low of 4,692 in March before finally beginning to recover after the successful conclusion of the presidential election on March 23, 1996. Total turnover in the secondary market in 1995 hit US$380 billion, a 46 percent drop from 1994.

Stock Trading Value and Stock Price Index

The reasons behind the stock market's poor performance in 1995 and early 1996 included the tense state of Taipei-Peking relations, the numerous crises involving financial institutions, the tight liquidity created by massive outflows of capital, and the general sluggishness of the overall economy. When the mainland authorities announced in late February that they would conduct another round of missile tests and military exercises near Taiwan in late February 1996, confidence in the stock market collapsed and panic selling ensued. In order to avoid a stock market crash, authorities established a US$3.7 billion stock market stabilization fund and began buying into the market to bolster prices and rebuild market confidence. After the tensions wound down and the market rebounded in late March and early April 1996, the stabilization fund was dissolved and the banks and other

institutions which had taken part walked away with handsome profits.

Beginning in 1995 and continuing through early 1996, central authorities also relaxed restrictions on inward remittances of foreign capital. Foreign institutional investors took advantage of this to buy into the market when prices were low, pushing total inward remittances in 1995 to US$3.51 billion. The relaxation of restrictions on foreign capital inflow thus not only helped stabilize the stock market by stimulating demand, but also reduced the balance of payment deficit caused by capital outflow.

Financial Restructuring

The ROC economy grew at a phenomenal pace throughout the 1970s and 1980s. The rapid accumulation of assets which accompanied this growth has led to a tremendous increase in financial activity and brought about profound structural changes in the local financial market. Increasing labor costs and the appreciation of the NT dollar in the 1980s sped up the globalization of Taiwanese capital by encouraging investment and other financial involvement in overseas financial markets. This trend has in turn exerted competitive pressure on the domestic financial system and spurred the ROC to open up to attract foreign investors and financial institutions.

The financial system in the ROC has been undergoing restructuring since 1987. Among the many changes which have been made is the further relaxation of restrictions on inward and outward capital flows. Indeed, at the end of 1995, the annual ceiling on remittances for individuals stood at US$5 million, while for corporations the amount was US$20 million. The trading system in the foreign exchange market has also been updated from a mid-rate trading system to a regular quoting system. And in March 1994, the Central Bank approved most foreign exchange derivative products.

Interest rates have also been gradually liberalized, beginning with discount rates on CDs and bank debentures in 1980 and extending on to include deposit interest rates. Finally, in 1989, the revised *Banking Law* 銀行法 lifted all restrictions on interest rates, bringing an end to a long history of interest rate controls. In addition to interest rate liberalization, another important requirement to allow market forces to play a major role in the financial system is the development of short-term money markets and long-term capital markets where surpluses and shortages can be adjusted through market-driven mechanisms.

When the ROC set up its money market in 1975, the market was segregated among inter-bank call loans and other short-term monetary instruments. It has since evolved into the second largest money market in Asia, with an annual turnover exceeding US$1.6 trillion. The size of the bond market also expanded drastically after 1989 due to the heavy issuance of government bonds for national development. As for the stock market, the revised *Securities Transaction Law* 證券交易法 of 1989 allowed new entries to the brokerage business and loosened restrictions on inward remittances of foreign capital for the purpose of investing in the stock market, making Taiwan's financial markets more competitive internationally.

The financial re-regulation and supervisory enhancements underway in Taiwan are in response to changes in the financial environment. The rapid expansion of financial markets, the deregulation of financial activities, new financial innovations, and new entries in the financial sector, together with the disorder associated with financial realignment, all make re-regulation a necessary move. In line with the Bank of International Settlements, the ROC has set the capital adequacy ratio at 8 percent of risk assets. The government also established the Central Deposit Insurance Corporation 中央存款保險公司 in 1985 to provide a better safety net for depository institutions. The *Banking Law* of 1989, while allowing new entrants into the banking industry, also tightens up regulations dealing with problem banks. Re-regulating some areas while deregulating others has been the most important task in the financial restructuring of Taiwan.

PROTECTING THE EARTH IS EVERYONE'S RESPONSIBILITY

Conservation is a global effort, and the Republic of China on Taiwan is doing its part to conserve nature's bounty. The government agency in charge of the nation's wildlife conservation program is the Council of Agriculture. We at the Council of Agriculture look forward to working with you to protect our planet.

**COUNCIL OF
AGRICULTURE
EXECUTIVE YUAN**
37 NANHAI RD.
TAIPEI,TAIWAN 100
REPUBLIC OF CHINA
TEL:886-2-312-4065
FAX:886-2-312-5857

12.
Agriculture

Above: The catch unloaded at Kaohsiung's Chienchin fishing harbor helps feed a population that consumes a per capita average of 45 kilograms of fish per year.

Right: Watermelon, a summer favorite of local fruit lovers, was Taiwan's eighth most valuable crop in 1995.

Previous page: Attracted by growing local demand and high profits, many farmers in Taiwan have begun cultivating tea.

12 Agriculture

Brilliant green rice paddies set against a misty backdrop of bamboo and banana, cicadas droning loudly under the heat of the noontime sun—these are the images of old Taiwan, where once over 90 percent of the island's residents lived in farming villages growing rice, sugar, tea, camphor, and other crops. This picture has rapidly faded in the wake of industrialization, and today Taiwan's farmers make up only 11 percent of the work force and produce less than 4 percent of the island's GDP. Farmers in Taiwan today confront falling incomes, rising costs, and increased foreign competition. They are becoming fewer and older as the younger generations abandon farming for city life. As Taiwan gears up for entry into the World Trade Organization (WTO), the farmers' predicament will worsen before it gets better.

If the sector is to avoid becoming an anachronism in the margins of Taiwan's modern economy, it must completely re-invent itself. Farming operations must become smarter, and the commitment of farmers to professional full-time farming must be increased. Working together, the ROC government, farmers' associations and other organizations have begun to make many of the structural reforms needed to put Taiwan agriculture on track for a profitable and growing future.

Farmers

In 1995, there were about 873,000 hectares of farmland worked by more than 807,000 farming households, meaning that each household on average tills a plot of only 1.08 hectares (2.67 acres). For the past decade, Taiwan farmers have derived over 60 percent of their annual income from non-farming activities. The rise of part-time farming households, which have accounted for over 80 percent of all farming households since 1980, concerns economic planners, who argue that full-time farmers are more likely to make the capital and training investment needed to develop large and profitable businesses.

Efficient farming is also hindered by the rapidly aging agrarian workforce. In the Taiwan area the rural population over the age of 65 has increased from 326,000 in 1985 to 398,000 in 1994; that is, from 6.9 to 9.9 percent of the total farming population. Many youths are choosing to leave their parents' farms for better wages in the city. Farming incomes have grown, but they have not kept pace with gains in other sectors.

To plug the youth drain, the Council of Agriculture 農業委員會 (COA) is trying a number of measures to persuade graduates of agricultural institutes and young members of farming families to stay on the farm. Local agriculture authorities encourage young farmers to improve farm management and raise farm income after determining that they are capable of farming on their own. Rural development projects are also in the works to make rural life more compatible with young people's lifestyles and needs.

Invariably though, the only long-term solution is to gradually downsize the farming workforce as older farmers retire, and raise the efficiency of those that remain. To help farmers displaced by this trend, the COA and Council of Labor Affairs 行政院勞工委員會 in accordance with the *Agricultural Development Act* 農業發展 條例 have been conducting training programs and job counseling over the past several years. Recognizing the difficulty of training farmers advanced in age, and the need to provide alternative forms of assistance to this group, the government promulgated on May 31, 1995, a temporary statute to grant elderly Taiwan farmers a US$111 monthly stipend. Eligible farmers include those who:

- have attained the age of 65;
- have been covered by the farmers' health insurance program for more than six months;
- are not receiving any old-age pension from social insurance (such as labor insurance), living allowances, or other kinds of allowances from the government;
- are solely employed in the agricultural sector;
- have lands and houses (private farmlands and farmhouses excluded) with value not in excess of US$185,185; and

187

Government Agricultural Agencies

The principal governmental organization over-seeing agricultural development in the ROC is the Council of Agriculture. Agencies at the provincial level of government include the Taiwan Provincial Department of Agriculture and Forestry 台灣省農林廳, the Taiwan Provincial Food Bureau 台灣省糧食局, the Taiwan Provincial Water and Soil Conservation Bureau 台灣省水土保持局, the Taiwan Provincial Water Conservancy Bureau 台灣省水利局, the Taiwan Agricultural Research Institute 台灣省農業試驗所, and the Taiwan Provincial Land Administration 台灣省政府地政處. In addition, the government of each city and county in the Taiwan area, with the exception of Lienchiang County 連江縣 and Kinmen County 金門縣, has a department of agriculture. Under the supervision and guidance of the government, there are 304 local farmers' associations 農會, 17 irrigation associations 農田水利會, 456 agricultural cooperatives and stations 農業合作社、場, and 38 local fishermen's associations 漁會.

- have an individual consolidated income not exceeding the annual basic wage.

As of March 1996, more than US$319 million had been granted to some 336,000 farmers, and applications for this stipend were still being accepted and reviewed.

Land

In mountainous Taiwan, farming is largely restricted to the island's arable western slope lands and alluvial plains. Farming plots tend to be small: 75 percent of farming households have less than one hectare of cultivable land. The small average size of farming plots has created a huge obstacle to modernizing Taiwan's agricultural sector, since advanced methods of farm mechanization and management depend on scale to be cost-efficient. As a result, advances in farming efficiency have not kept pace with other sectors, and in many cases, the land has ceased to be profitable for farming. About 10 percent of total farmland in Taiwan is left fallow because it is no longer profitable.

To address this situation, the government has been working in cooperation with farmers' organizations and other agencies to convert unprofitable farmland to other uses, consolidate plots into more easily farmed divisions, and gradually reduce excess farmland. On July 11, 1996, the Executive Yuan passed amendments to the *Agricultural Development Act*, lifting restrictions on the transfer, inheritance, and division of farmland. Farmland heirs no longer need be farmers, and if agricultural activities are continued on the inherited farmland, the inheritance is tax-exempt. Farmland may now be divided into plots as small as 0.25 hectares. The number of farmland co-owners can now be increased, and there is no longer a minimum size requirement for share-cropped farmland: even a 0.1-hectare plot can be registered as share-cropped.

Farmland Rezoning

Some economists feel that the large amount of valuable land used for farming in Taiwan is out of proportion to agriculture's relatively small contribution to the economy. This usage not only limits the space for expanding industry, housing, recreation, and other purposes, they argue, but also impedes economic growth by driving up the price of land. Due to rezoning restrictions and other factors, however, farmers are often unwilling or unable to sell their land, even though it is no longer productive for farming.

On July 27, 1995, the Executive Yuan passed the Farmland Release Program 農地釋出方案 to ease restrictions on farmland rezoning. Some 160,000 hectares of farmland have been targeted for release, including 78,000 hectares of coastal subsidence area, 50,000 hectares of polluted area, and 27,000 hectares of low productive farmland. Fish farms in subsidence areas are given priority for release with the goal of reducing the present 50,000 hectares by 40 percent over the next ten years.

The minimum area for plots released for the construction of laborer housing is five hectares;

for industrial and commercial use, at least ten hectares; and for residential use, at least 30 hectares. If farmland transferred to industrial use is not developed within two years after the transfer, the transfer is automatically invalidated. To ensure safe and efficient land use, all development on rezoned farmland must be in line with the government's environmental and development policies.

To prevent windfall profits, those who transfer farmland to industrial or commercial use are required to pay a usage fee of 12 percent of the current assessed price of the transferred land, half of which is donated to government agriculture agencies, and half to local governments. At the same time, 30 percent of the land must be donated to the government for "green belts or infrastructure projects." To encourage businesses to move to eastern Taiwan and to accelerate offshore island development, farmland released in Ilan 宜蘭, Hualien 花蓮, Taitung 台東, the Pescadores 澎湖群島, Kinmen 金門, and Matsu 馬祖 is exempted from usage fees. As of February 1996, some 896 hectares had been released under the Farmland Release Program, and an additional 1,562 hectares were in the process of being released.

Farming Households

A farming household is a family of which at least one member grows agricultural products or raises domesticated animals, honey bees, or silk worms. Such a family must meet at least one of the following five criteria. It must:

- manage at least 0.05 hectares of cultivated land, which need not be owned by the family, but may be rented, borrowed, or share-cropped;
- raise at least one large animal such as a dairy cow, a head of beef cattle, or a deer;
- raise at least three medium-sized animals such as pigs or goats;
- raise at least 100 poultry such as chickens, ducks, geese, pigeons, or quail; or
- sell or consume agricultural products worth more than US$740 annually.

Farmland

According to Article 3, Item 10 of the *Agricultural Development Act,* farmland includes property necessary to farming, forestry, animal husbandry, and aquaculture—such as farm houses, animal stalls or coops, storage facilities, drying areas, collection areas, farm roads, irrigation ditches, catchment areas—and other land used for warehouses, refrigeration facilities, equipment centers, silkworm houses, and collection centers provided by farmers' associations or agricultural cooperatives and stations.

Farmland Consolidation

The farmland consolidation 農地重劃 program is designed to combine scattered, odd-shaped plots of farmland into one large "pie" which is then cut into easily farmed slices. The re-shaped plots of land are then re-distributed, giving each farmer a plot of land exactly the same size as the one he formerly owned but much better proportioned. Under the program, some 378,000 hectares of farmland were consolidated between 1958 and 1996, and an additional 1,800 hectares are slated for consolidation in 1997. Farm roads and irrigation ditches that serve these areas are also being improved, rebuilt, and repaired. This program is helping to overcome some of the shortcomings of small-scale farming, reduce production and marketing costs, and increase operational efficiency.

Farmland Utilization Project

The COA in cooperation with the Taiwan Provincial Department of Agriculture and Forestry enacted a long-term general farmland utilization project 農地利用綜合規劃 in 1992. The project guides county and city governments and grass-roots organizations in setting up collective agricultural production districts that match local environmental, economic, and technical conditions and farmers' actual needs. In fiscal 1995, the COA spent US$5.8 million in carrying out the project in districts encompassing over 60,000 hectares of farmland. For fiscal 1996, the budget was reduced to US$5.1 million.

Water

One cannot farm without large quantities of clean water. While Taiwan seems to be fairly rainy, with annual precipitation averaging 2,500 millimeters, water resources are unevenly distributed. Regional and seasonal water shortages necessitate careful planning and conservation. The Water Resources Planning Commission 水資源統一規劃委員會 (WRPC), an agency under the Ministry of Economic Affairs, estimated Taiwan's water usage in 1994 at 17.6 billion cubic meters (bcm). The agricultural sector used the lion's share, consuming 13.2 bcm, or about 75 percent of the total water usage that year. Irrigation consumed 9.9 bcm, aquaculture used 3.1 bcm, and animal husbandry accounted for the remainder of agricultural water usage. That year, 51 percent of Taiwan's farmland was irrigated, mostly by local irrigation associations.

Crops

The types and quantities of crops produced in Taiwan are changing rapidly. The ROC's pending acceptance into the WTO has given farmers impetus to diversify away from some traditional crops which cannot be competitively farmed in an unprotected market, and into horticulture, agritourism, exotic fruits and vegetables, chemical-free organic produce, new cultivars, and other high-value products. These moves are also in response to Taiwan's changing diet. People in Taiwan are eating more wheat-based foods and dairy products and less rice, and Taiwan's rising standard of living has boosted the demand for luxury products such as exotic flowers and processed foods.

Rice ranked as Taiwan's most valuable crop in 1995, followed by betel nuts, sugar cane, corn, mangoes, peanuts, grapes, watermelon, tea, and pears. In terms of harvested area, the rice crop again ranked first, followed by bananas, corn, sugar cane, betel nuts, peanuts, bamboo shoots, tea, mangoes, and watermelon.

Rice

According to the Taiwan Provincial Food Bureau (TPFB), there were 363,000 hectares of ricefields in Taiwan in 1995. Some 1.68 million tons of brown rice were produced during the island's two crop seasons, which outstripped the island's annual demand by over 220,000 tons. This surplus is largely attributable to Taiwan's changing eating patterns which have caused per capita rice consumption to plunge by over half between 1974 and 1994 from 134 kilograms to 60 kilograms. As Taiwan opens its doors to rice imports in preparation for entering the WTO, foreign competition will further exacerbate the problem of oversupply and intensify the downward pressure on rice prices.

To help Taiwan rice growers adapt to these trends, the government is working to bring rice supply in line with falling demand through the Rice Production and Ricefield Diversion Program 稻米生產及稻田轉作計畫, and has initiated several programs for rice purchasing, storage, and transport. These measures are discussed in greater detail below.

Ricefield Diversion Program

Since July 1984, the ROC government has been implementing the Rice Production and Ricefield Diversion Program to reduce the amount of rice grown in Taiwan. The program encourages farmers, through subsidies and other incentives, to leave rice paddies fallow, rotate crops, or fully convert them to more profitable uses. By 1995, nearly 177,000 hectares of paddies had been diverted, of which about 62,000 hectares were laid fallow and the remainder were planted with other crops. Nearly 365,000 farming households have participated in the program at a cost of about US$160 million in government subsidies. The total area of rice cultivation was reduced from 429,000 hectares in 1991 to about 363,000 hectares in 1995, and yields during the same period dropped by 130,000 metric tons to 1.68 million metric tons. The program is scheduled to terminate at the end of fiscal 1997.

Rice Purchasing Program

Since April 1974, the government has been buying rice from farmers by means of the Food

Stabilization Fund 糧食平準基金. In 1995, some 454,000 metric tons of rice were purchased in this manner for US$344 million, directly increasing growers' income by nearly US$37 million. From 1974 to 1995, the government purchased 13.4 million metric tons of rice for US$8.1 billion and increased growers' income by US$1.5 billion. Because the government sold the rice at a loss, by fiscal 1995 the Food Stabilization Fund had accumulated a deficit of US$4.5 billion.

Rice Storage Plan

The high expense of the rice purchasing program has motivated the government to pursue less costly ways of stabilizing rice prices. In May 1995, the COA began to implement the Rice Storage Plan 稻穀寄倉計畫, which provides free rice storage to farmers, allowing them to store rice when prices are low and sell when the market recovers. The program aims to reduce the price volatility of rice by regulating seasonal supply. If the plan succeeds, guaranteed rice purchases will be phased out in 1998, and rice prices will then be dictated entirely by market forces. According to the plan, after 1998 further government rice purchases will be strictly for maintaining safety reserves.

Anticipating the need for more storage space as the plan gets underway, the TPFB is constructing new granaries and repairing existing ones. Funding for the work is allocated by the provincial government and through annual subsidies from the central government. In fiscal 1995, some 17 granaries were built or repaired, increasing storage capacity by almost 6,000 metric tons. The following year, the central government allocated US$270,000, the provincial government US$920,000, and the TPFB US$1.85 million for farmers' associations to build or repair granaries and to automate public granaries and equip them with vacuum capabilities, which improve warehousing and storage while helping prevent environmental pollution.

Free Rice Transportation

Since the second crop season of 1980, the TPFB has arranged for free trucking of rice from field to granary and from granary to rice drying center. This door-to-door service is provided islandwide with the exception of Taipei and Taitung counties, and has become very popular because it saves time, effort, and transportation costs. In the two crop seasons of 1995, more than 299,000 farming households took advantage of the service, and nearly 470,000 metric tons of rice were transported. The program saved farmers about US$6.1 million in time and effort, according to the TPFB.

Rice Exports

Exporting is one effective way for Taiwan to manage its rice surplus. Rice exports are handled together by the COA, the Central Trust of China (CTC), and the TPFB. The COA determines the amount of rice to be exported, when it can be exported, and the conditions for the transaction. The CTC handles the financial end by overseeing the bidding process for would-be rice exporters, accepting bills of lading, and holding deposits placed by foreign buyers. The TPFB is responsible for processing the rice, and makes all shipping arrangements from granary to vessel lading. In 1995, the COA approved the export of 180,000 metric tons of rice. About 250,000 metric tons of brown rice (including that for international relief) were actually exported.

Rice Quality Improvement

The High-quality Rice Production and Marketing Program 良質米產銷計畫 was enacted in fiscal 1986 and included in the Six-Year National Development Plan 國建六年計畫 in fiscal 1992. In fiscal 1995, 26 farmers' associations participated in this program to improve rice quality, and 56 grain traders contracted with farmers to produce high-quality rice. In addition, since the first crop season of 1995, the TPFB and the Taiwan Provincial Department of Agriculture and Forestry have jointly implemented a program for the collective cultivation of high-quality rice on 42,000 hectares of land in 11 rural and urban townships.

Betel Nuts

According to the Taiwan Provincial Department of Agriculture and Forestry, betel nuts, with a production value of US$491 million in 1995, ranked as the Taiwan area's fourth most valuable farm product, behind hogs, rice, and chickens. Betel nuts became a popular crop in the 1980s, with cultivated area rising from 4,400 hectares in 1982 to 36,000 hectares in 1989. The 1990s have seen further expansion: in 1995, some 54,000 hectares of land were planted in betel nuts, mainly in P'ingtung 屏東, Nant'ou 南投, and Chiayi 嘉義 counties, with production weighing in at almost 156,000 metric tons, having more than doubled in the preceding decade. This explosive growth has been fueled by the high income that can be earned from growing betel nuts, which is on average more than two times, and as much as ten times, higher than from growing rice.

Vegetables

Taiwan's tropical-to-subtropical climate is ideal for cultivating vegetables. During the 1960s, processed mushrooms, asparagus, and vegetable seed products were among Taiwan's most important export items. The income from these products not only improved the rural economy, but also contributed to the rapid development of Taiwan's economy as a whole. Today, although their significance for the national economy has diminished, vegetables remain an important agricultural product.

In 1995, some 173,000 hectares of land were devoted to vegetable cultivation, down from a high of 240,000 hectares in 1986, but still considerably higher than the 1945 figure of 35,000 hectares. The leading vegetables in terms of planted area in 1995 were bamboo shoots, watermelon, vegetable soybeans, cabbage, cantaloupe, Chinese cabbage, garlic, radishes, scallions, and tomatoes. Due to international trade liberalization, most vegetables produced in Taiwan are now for domestic consumption.

Since vegetables are highly perishable, farms are located near consumption and distribution centers. Taiwan's main vegetable producing areas are concentrated in Changhua 彰化, Yünlin 雲林, and Tainan counties.

The production of vegetables is part of the multi-cropping system in Taiwan. Vegetables are often grown during the winter or between two rice crops, when more land and labor are available. Consequently, there is often a glut of vegetables in winter, resulting in a significant drop in price. However, prices soar during the summer when low production and typhoon damage dampen supply.

Vegetable production in 1995 was 2.85 million metric tons. Through technological improvements such as new cultivars, growth regulators, and mechanization, the yield per hectare jumped from 8,600 kilograms in 1945 to 16,000 kilograms in 1995. Taiwan's biggest vegetable crops by value in 1995 were watermelon, bamboo shoots, garlic, cantaloupe, water bamboo, cabbage, radishes, scallions, Chinese cabbage, and tomatoes. Currently more than 100 kinds of vegetables are produced in Taiwan. In northern Taiwan, radishes, Chinese cabbage, leaf-mustard, and garlic thrive in the cooler climate. In southern Taiwan, a medley of tomatoes, cauliflower, bamboo shoots, and beans are cultivated. Ginger is grown in central Taiwan.

Fruit

Around 50 types of fruit are cultivated in Taiwan. Deciduous varieties like apples, pears, and peaches thrive at high elevations, while citrus fruits, bananas, pineapples, lychees, longans, mangoes, papayas, persimmons, loquats, and guavas dot the lower plains and undulating slope lands. The main crops are bananas, pineapples, wax apples, mangoes, and citrus fruits. In 1995, almost 2.5 million metric tons of fruit were grown in Taiwan on a total planted area of nearly 229,000 hectares. Processed products enjoy stable domestic and international markets; canned pineapples and lychees are exported while a wide selection of fruit juices satisfies local taste.

Fruit growers have suffered as imports of foreign produce have flooded the domestic market in response to the reduction, and in some

Asian Vegetable Research and Development Center

The Asian Vegetable Research and Development Center 亞洲蔬菜研究發展中心, an international non-profit organization, was established at Tainan County's Shanhua Township 台南縣善化鎮 in October 1973. Its mission is to help farmers in the tropics raise more and better vegetables by developing varieties that resist insects and diseases and tolerate heat and flooding. This mission is carried out at the 98-hectare research farm through three programs: crop improvement, production systems, and international cooperation. Its research and development programs are led by internationally recruited professionals from 11 countries, who are backed by over 300 mid-level researchers and technical and administrative staff.

The center's gene bank, with over 43,000 accessions, is one of the world's largest for tropical germplasm and focuses on such globally and regionally important vegetables as tomatoes, peppers, eggplant, onions, garlic, shallots, soybeans, mungbeans, and Chinese and common cabbages. Researchers collect seeds, grow new varieties, document their results, and share the findings with other researchers and organizations worldwide. As of the end of 1994, a total of 197 breeding lines had been officially released in 87 countries. The center had also sent out about 290,000 seed samples to cooperators in 180 countries and territories.

Meanwhile, the AVRDC is assisting Taiwan farmers in managing insects and diseases, in intercropping, in making more efficient use of agricultural inputs, and in developing technologies to overcome seasonal stresses in vegetable production. Among the improved techniques developed by the center are raised beds to enhance drainage and improve soil aeration during the monsoon season; straw mulching to suppress weeds and retain soil moisture; and fertilization and composting to improve the fertility of tropical soils.

The center can look back on a number of triumphs. One of the biggest involved tomatoes. Over the last decade, researchers have increased the summer tomato yield for Taiwan farms from 5 to 40 metric tons per hectare. The center has produced 80 high-yielding, heat-tolerant, disease-resistant, high-quality tomato varieties for release in 34 countries. Nearly 87 percent of Taiwan's vegetable soybean fields are planted with strains developed at the center—Kaohsiung Nos. 1, 2, and 3. Much of the island's Chinese cabbage production also can be credited to the AVRDC.

---

cases elimination, of tariffs on imported fruit. To face this growing competition, Taiwan fruit growers have applied advanced horticultural technology to modernize their operations. Controlling disease effectively, adjusting fruit maturation periods, cultivating improved varieties, and carrying out multiple annual harvests have all contributed to the profitability and growth of the fruit sector. Orchards are also diversifying into the lucrative agritourism business (see section on Agritourism below).

Sugar Cane

Taiwan's sugar industry is losing some of its former sweetness as global sugar prices sour and imported sugar pours into the opening domestic market. All this spells "transition" for the state-run Taiwan Sugar Corporation 台灣糖業公司 (TSC), which is expanding its product line and diversifying into biotechnology, land develop-

ment, and overseas investment to remain competitive.

Taiwan used to be one of the world's leading sugar exporters. In the 1950s and 1960s, the island boasted some 100,000 hectares of cane fields, producing over one million metric tons of sugar annually. However, by 1995 farm labor shortages and a steady decline in world prices had reduced those fields to 59,000 hectares, half of which were owned by the TSC, and lowered sugar production to 410,000 metric tons. Since local demand was about 510,000 metric tons, Taiwan had to import 100,000 metric tons of sugar that year.

According to the Council for Economic Planning and Development 經濟建設委員會, Taiwan sugar prices rank 12th highest in the world and third highest in the Asia-Pacific region, behind Japan and Korea. For many years private enterprises have complained about high sugar prices and urged the government to open the market to imports. In June 1996, the Executive Yuan passed the Sugar Industry Management Policy and Sugar Price Adjustment Program 糖業經營策略與糖價調整方案 to progressively reduce domestic production and increase imports so as to bring down sugar prices. The government has also declared that by fiscal year 2003, Taiwan's sugar production will be lowered to 310,000 metric tons. To effect this production decrease, sugar cane acreage will be decreased, with most reductions coming from TSC-owned farms. On July 1, 1996, the domestic sugar price was lowered from US$0.91 to US$0.85 per kilogram, and the government budgeted US$56 million to compensate sugar cane farmers for resulting loss.

Tea

Tea, an age-old Chinese product, was one of the mainstays of Taiwan's early economy. At one time, Taiwan exported 80 percent of its tea production, and tea exports topped 21,000 metric tons in 1973. The situation has changed, however; since 1991 the island has been a net importer. More than 10,000 metric tons of tea were imported annually in both 1993 and 1994 at a cost of over US$13 million per year. The transformation from seller to buyer has been driven by local demand, which has risen along with incomes from 330 grams per person in 1973 to 1,440 in 1994. Customers think nothing of spending US$40 to US$80 per catty for medium-to-high-grade tea or three to five times that amount for exotic or award-winning varieties. High-quality tea from the mountain regions can bring a farmer an annual net profit of over US$19,000 per hectare. Even medium-to-low-grade teas bring about US$4,000. It is no surprise that many farmers have abandoned traditional crops like rice in favor of tea, which is five times more profitable. Between 1991 and 1995, the value of Taiwan's tea output increased from US$3,100 to US$6,700 per metric ton.

According to the Taiwan Provincial Department of Agriculture and Forestry, since the government opened the market to Southeast Asian tea in 1990,

Taiwan Area Tea Industry

(unit: metric tons)

Year	Local Production	Imports	Exports
1990	22,299	2,604	6,194
1991	21,380	6,045	5,696
1992	20,164	6,752	5,577
1993	20,515	10,237	5,606
1994	24,485	10,685	4,948
1995	20,892	8,354	4,150

Source: Taiwan Provincial Department of Agriculture and Forestry

Taiwan's annual tea imports have nearly tripled in weight. In 1995, tea imports totaled 8,300 metric tons while local production was almost 21,000 metric tons (see chart). Taiwan's tea processing techniques are being transferred to Vietnam, Indonesia, and Thailand, where low-cost tea is being produced for the Taiwan market. Even tea from the Chinese mainland has found its way to Taiwan's stores.

To compete with these imports, Taiwan producers are concentrating on raising quality. The Taiwan Tea Experiment Station 台灣茶業改良場 has also been working to develop new processes and products to add more value to medium- and high-grade tea. Agritourism is seen as another way to boost domestic tea consumption. Taiwan now has seven tourist tea fields to promote sales (see section on Agritourism below).

Flowers

With a wide variety of fresh, beautiful flowers to choose from, it is no wonder that Taiwan's floriculture industry has been smelling like roses in recent years. Between 1986 and 1995, output value ballooned from about US$74 million to nearly US$335 million, and export value from US$3.7 million to US$36 million. As sales soared, farmland planted in flowers expanded from 3,500 to 9,700 hectares during the same period. On average, each person in Taiwan spent US$9.13 on flowers in 1992, nearly five times higher than a decade earlier, but still only one-seventh the per capita sales in Japan, Europe, and the US, showing that the industry still has huge growth potential.

Floriculture has become the seventh largest industry in the Taiwan area, and it is estimated that the sector can maintain an annual growth rate of 10 to 12 percent over the next ten years. Despite this optimistic picture, Taiwan's flower industry faces a formidable distribution bottleneck which threatens to choke the industry's future growth. According to the ROC *Agricultural Products Market Transaction Act* 農產品市場交易法, flower wholesalers must be approved by the government, and can only conduct trade at certified markets. Before 1995, only one such government-approved wholesale flower market existed in Taiwan to accommodate the bidding of about 220 registered dealers. To speed up and expand distribution, three modern flower wholesale markets were constructed during 1995 in Tienwei Township of Changhua County 彰化縣田尾鄉, Taichung City, and Annan District of Tainan City 台南市安南區.

Recreational Agriculture

Agritourism

In the 1980s, as economic growth enriched Taiwan residents, tourism took off. Enterprising farmers, eager to cash in on affluent urbanites' nostalgia for the simpler, less cosmopolitan days of yore, spawned Taiwan's agritourism industry. Initially, farmers simply opened their fields to visitors on weekends, allowing tourists to pick their own fruit and other farm produce in a natural setting. Gradually, restaurants and other entertainment facilities sprang up around the farms, catering to the needs of the visitors. By the early 1990s several farming resort areas had developed in more picturesque agricultural regions of the island, complete with hotel accommodations, entertainment facilities, and even night-life attractions. This brought environmental and cultural consequences to the surrounding farming communities.

The government has been regulating agritourism in Taiwan since 1981. From 1982 to

1995, over 1,800 hectares of land yielding 23 crops were officially converted into "you-pick" tourist farms 觀光農園. And between 1989 and 1992, an additional 2,700 hectares were designated as recreational farms 休閒農場 intended to offer visitors picnicking, bird watching, and other similarly low-impact activities in addition to the opportunity to harvest agricultural products. However, in the early 1990s it became clear that the agritourism industry was developing to an extent and in a direction that violated environmental protection and land utilization laws and regulations.

In an effort to bring these farms under the rule of law, the Ministry of the Interior promulgated in May 1996 the *Non-urban Land Utilization Control Rules* 非都市土地利用管制規則. The COA also drew up a revised set of *Recreational Agriculture Guidance Measures* 休閒農業輔導辦法 in August 1996 for review by the Executive Yuan. These rules and measures aim to ensure that the environment is protected and that land is utilized wisely and appropriately, as well as to promote agricultural, educational, and recreational activities that will increase farmers' incomes and improve farming communities.

Urban Farming

Currently, as a result of industrialization, much of Taiwan's rural population has moved to the cities. This has led to extremely high urban population densities, and has created an environment in which most urban land is dedicated to non-agricultural uses. The few tracts of suburban agricultural land that still remain command extremely high prices, and only high-tech, high-quality, and high-value agricultural products can be farmed on this land for a reasonable return on the landowner's investment.

To provide owners of urban farmland with an alternative to cultivating such capital-intensive crops and at the same time meet urbanites' demand for opportunities to grow their own agricultural products, in 1993 the COA began designating urban farming plots 都市農園 in the suburbs.

Tracts of farmland are divided into small plots and then leased to city dwellers for the cultivation of fruit, vegetables, trees, or flowers. This enables urbanites who wish to dabble in farming to do so conveniently and brings rental income to the landowners.

Fishing Industry

Over the past half-century, the island's fishing industry has developed from small-scale coastal fishing to deep-sea commercial fishing. Whereas in 1945 only a hundred or so trawlers tied up at Taiwan's piers unloading an annual catch of about 40,000 metric tons, by 1995 Taiwan's fishing fleet totaled almost 30,000 (of which 14,000 were powered craft) and brought home a haul of about one million metric tons. This was slightly less than in 1993, when Taiwan's oceanic fishery production peaked at more than 1.1 million metric tons and the United Nations listed the ROC as the sixth largest tuna fishing country on the high seas.

In 1995 Taiwan produced US$3.7 billion worth of fish. Of this, 42 percent came from deep-sea fishing, 36 percent from aquaculture, 17 percent from offshore fishing, and 4 percent from coastal fishing. More than 30 percent of the catch was exported, with the biggest items being tuna and eel.

The expanding role of deep-sea fishing in Taiwan's fishing industry is largely a product of declining fish stocks close to home. Overfishing and pollution from industrial and household waste have severely depleted coastal and offshore fish stocks, and until a few years ago, coastal and offshore fishing yields were falling by more than 10 percent a year. The government has been working since 1990 to conserve fisheries, and in 1995 budgeted US$12 million to set up 25 fishery conservation zones and 70 artificial reefs along the Taiwan coast and around the Pescadores 澎湖群島. More than 1.7 million fry of sea bream, 430,000 fry of abalone, and three million fry of kuruma shrimp were released in this area in an effort to restore depleted fish stocks.

The COA is also working to reduce the Taiwan fleet size through a boat buy-back program, under which 2,338 old boats have been bought since initiation, and displaced fishermen have been trained for other occupations. Furthermore, the ROC government has played an active role in international fishery management organizations and worked to promote international fishery cooperation. As of 1995, the ROC had signed official or private fishery agreements with 25 countries.

Aquaculture

The role of aquaculture in Taiwan's overall fishing industry has been growing steadily over the years, and now accounts for more than a third of Taiwan's total seafood production. Taiwan's geography and climate are ideal for aquaculture, offering fish farmers tropical, temperate, and frigid conditions to raise a wide variety of fish. Even the North American rainbow trout can be cultivated in some of Taiwan's mountains.

Taiwan's most important farmed fish is eel, the annual production of which fluctuates between 26,000 and 56,000 metric tons, and is worth more than US$400 million. Taiwan also grows a considerable amount of grass shrimp, although disease has drastically reduced output from a high of 80,000 metric tons in 1987 to 11,000 metric tons in 1995. The land area under aquacultural cultivation has expanded from about 38,000 hectares before 1968 to a peak of 76,000 hectares in 1990, including 27,000 hectares of saltwater ponds and 26,000 hectares of freshwater ponds.

Aquacultural development has not come without environmental cost. Freshwater aquaculture operations draw off huge amounts of groundwater, sometimes causing land to shift or cave in (for details, see section on Land Subsidence in Chapter 13, Environmental Protection). To tackle this problem, the COA has promoted recycling systems that use fresh water more efficiently. Aquaculturists are encouraged to switch to forms of mariculture, such as cage culture, or high-tech fish hatchery, and to internationalize their operations in Southeast Asia. By 1995, Taiwan's aquacultural area had been reduced to 64,000 hectares.

Livestock Industry

Starting from backyard, scavenger-type farming in poverty-stricken villages in the 1950s, the livestock industry in Taiwan has grown into a multi-billion dollar business and become a mainstay of the agricultural sector. In 1995, livestock production was valued at more than US$5.2 billion, accounting for 34 percent of Taiwan's total agricultural production value. Taiwan's livestock industry not only produces enough animal protein to satisfy the domestic demand, it also exports large amounts of surplus. Taiwan pork has dominated the Japanese market for 13 consecutive years, and the market share rose from 51,000 metric tons in 1984 to nearly 270,000 metric tons in 1994. Taiwan hog exports totaled more than 6.7 million head in 1995. In terms of value, hog production ranks first in the livestock industry, followed by chickens, chicken eggs, and milk.

In recent decades, farmers have dramatically expanded herd sizes and automated operations to increase income. The expanded scale of farming, especially the swine industry raising more than 10.5 million head of hogs per year, has led to a serious animal waste pollution problem. To address this threat to the environment, the Taiwan Livestock Research Institute 台灣省畜產試驗所 initiated a hog waste treatment program in 1990. By the end of 1995, a full 95 percent of pig farms raising 200 head or more had installed waste treatment facilities. About 6,800 hog farms were operating their waste treatment systems properly and meeting effluent standards. Similar programs are also being implemented to handle poultry and cattle farm waste.

Agricultural Prospects

Perhaps the single biggest challenge confronting Taiwan farmers today is the increased competition they will face after the ROC is admitted to the World Trade Organization (WTO). To meet WTO requirements, the ROC government has been systematically reducing the trade barriers to its traditionally heavily protected agricultural goods market. Taiwan's current tariff on agricultural imports is on average 20.6 percent; the ROC government has agreed to reduce this to 14.3 and 12.3 percent by the first and the sixth year after its accession to the WTO, respectively. Area restrictions will be eliminated in full with substantial tariff cuts, and products currently subject to import control will be subject to tariff-based conversion measures after accession.

Currently, 90 percent of agricultural products consumed in Taiwan are open to import. According to the Taiwan Provincial Department of Agriculture and Forestry, tariff reductions caused Taiwan's trade deficit in agricultural products to climb to US$3.1 billion in 1995. That year, agricultural exports grew 17 percent to US$3.9 billion and imports rose 13 percent to US$7 billion. More than US$74 million of the central government's US$2.9 billion fiscal 1995 agricultural budget was set aside to compensate farmers for loss due to imports. The government has also taken legal steps to soften the impact of imports on local farmers, with the COA promulgating the *Agricultural Producer Import Damage Compensation Guidelines* 農產品受進口損害救助基金管理運用辦法 on January 31, 1996.

Creating a Better Life

The Formosa Plastics Group has played a considerably important role in fibers, textiles, dyeing and finishing, education and medical facilities, in addition to its backbone industry, plastics. In recent years, our group has also expanded its hi-tech operations with a particular emphasis on the electronics industry.

We firmly believe that natural beauty and high technology can co-exist. We are dedicated to enhancing people's lives while maintaining harmony with nature.

We abide by the 3Rs' principle and work hard to protect the environment. All people on this planet are responsible for protecting its beautiful natural environment so as to create better tomorrow for the future generations.

FORMOSA
PLASTICS
GROUP

201 Tun Hwa North Road.
Taipei, Taiwan, R O C
Tel:886-2-7122211
Telex:11246, 22260, 22603, Taipei
Cable:"Plasticorp" Taipei
Fax:886-2-7129211 886-2-7129233

13.
Environmental
Protection

Above: This wastewater treatment plant in northern Taiwan plays an important role in alleviating the island's serious pollution problem.

Right: A growing awareness of the negative consequences of the ROC's rapid development is propelling the environmental protection movement in Taiwan.

Previous page: The government has established 50 nature preserves to protect wild plant and animal species, including these rare mangroves.

13 Environmental Protection

Growing popular and governmental awareness of the severe extent and ultimate cost of pollution is propelling the environmental protection movement in the Taiwan area today, following four decades of rapid industrial development. A number of factors have conspired to shift the policymaking center of gravity. The predominant concern for stimulating economic growth of the 1960s and 1970s has given way to a more balanced consideration over the last decade or so of the needs for additional growth against the short- and long-term environmental costs. As Taiwan today approaches developed-nation status, its people are starting to demand a quality of life commensurate with their level of economic achievement. The move toward democracy in the Republic of China has accelerated over the past few years, heightening the Taiwan public's awareness of its environmental responsibilities and prerogatives.

Although the fight to clean up and preserve Taiwan's environment has brought about improvements in recent years, the ROC government has put new urgency into a major initiative for 1996. The demands on Taiwan's environment stem from a dense population of more than 21 million people on 36,000 square kilometers of land and the impact of the race over the last couple of decades to become an industrialized nation. Effective environmental protection measures have taken on added significance in recent years because Taiwan, now a major world trader, faces greater international pressure to protect the environment and step up its wildlife conservation efforts.

In all respects, the key to continued improvement is strict enforcement of already existing laws, coupled with a sustained campaign to inculcate a positive environmental protection and wildlife conservation ethic among the public of Taiwan. This chapter details the mandates of the various government agencies that work to preserve the environment, conserve Taiwan's natural resources, and protect wildlife, describes the legal and financial resources at their disposal, and recounts the vicissitudes of environmental protection and wildlife conservation in Taiwan.

Air Quality

Air pollution is one of the most serious problems in Taiwan, chiefly because of the heavy traffic and high concentration of industrial plants on the island. The Environmental Protection Administration (EPA [see inset, next page]) reported that in 1995, there were three registered factories and 367 motor vehicles for every square kilometer in the Taiwan area. Overall, there were some 13.2 million vehicles (4.6 million cars and 8.6 million motorcycles) registered in the Taiwan area, nearly three for every five people. According to the EPA, vehicular exhaust comprises more than 95 percent of the air pollution in Taipei, Taiwan's largest city.

While strengthened cleanup efforts over the past few years have reduced air pollution, Pollution Standard Index (PSI) readings in Taiwan are about six times higher than those recorded in the United States and Europe. According to EPA measurements of air quality in the Taiwan area in 1995, suspended particles topped the list of air pollutants, accounting for nearly 70 percent. Ozone was next at nearly 27 percent. Taiwan's dirtiest air can be found in Kaohiung County's Linyuan 林園 and Taliao 大寮, followed by P'ingtung 屏東.

In an effort to determine the effects of such conditions on local children, the EPA is funding the Student Respiratory System Screening Project 學童呼吸系統健康檢查計畫. By the end of June 1996, a little over one million junior high school students throughout Taiwan had responded to a respiratory health questionnaire, and roughly 200,000 had been given physical examinations. Preliminary results from the survey show that 13 percent of Taipei students are asthmatic, making Taipei the asthma capital of Taiwan. In Tainan and Kaohsiung, the results show that 11.3 and 11.1 percent, respectively, of students are asthmatic. These high rates of asthma are apparently directly related to vehicular exhaust.

To more effectively monitor air pollution, the EPA set up the Taiwan Area Air Quality Monitoring Network 台灣地區空氣品質監測網, which began formal operations in September 1993. By 1995, the network comprised 69 automatic air quality monitoring stations, three mobile monitoring vans,

Environmental Protection Administration

The only government agency at the national level that is devoted solely to protecting the environment is the Environmental Protection Administration under the Executive Yuan 行政院環境保護署. The EPA sets standards by which to measure the pollution of Taiwan's environment and drafts laws to elicit environmentally friendly behavior. The EPA had a budget of almost US$71.8 million in fiscal 1996, while the total ROC budget for environmental protection in fiscal 1996 amounted to US$195.6 million. As of 1996, the EPA was employing 606 full-time employees, 283 environmental investigators charged with collecting evidence in pollution cases, and 70 lab technicians responsible for analyzing test samples of pollutants brought back to the EPA's National Institute of Environmental Analysis 環境檢驗所.

one air quality laboratory, five remote work stations, and 59 airport noise remote monitoring sites. The EPA also divided Taiwan into eight air quality prediction areas and began issuing next-day air quality forecasts islandwide in January 1996.

In 1993, the EPA established a permit system for the emission of air pollutants by stationary sources. Prior to establishing a new source or modifying an existing facility, the operator must submit air pollution control plans to local authorities for approval. According to the EPA's Bureau of Air Quality Protection and Noise Control 空氣品質保護暨噪音管制處, there are over 3,200 factories which are required to apply for permits under the system.

In addition to the regulation of stationary pollution sources, the Legislature 立法院 approved a broad surcharge on fuel in the form of an air pollution control (APC) fee. Under this fee scheme, a per-liter tax of US$0.0075 was imposed on unleaded gasoline and high-grade diesel fuel, and an additional US$0.015 was tacked on to the price of leaded gasoline. Taxes of US$5.56 per kiloliter on fuel oil and US$6.3 per metric ton on fuel coal were also levied. The EPA began collecting APC fees on July 1, 1995.

In its first year, the APC fee system generated almost US$256 million, more than half of which was collected from factories. In August 1995, the EPA set up guidelines under which factory owners can apply to have APC fees reduced. The rules allow for APC fees to be discounted by 60 percent if sulfur oxide emissions at a factory are lowered by more than 60 percent. A factory can exempt itself from up to 85 or 95 percent of APC fees if sulfur oxide emissions are cut by more than 80 or 90 percent, respectively. As of May 1996, about 20 factories had applied for such reductions and were able to avoid US$3.7 million in APC payments.

The funds collected as APC fees are earmarked for carrying out air pollution control programs, such as implementing air quality improvement plans at the local level, establishing environmental conservancy parks, funding respiratory checkups for elementary and junior high school students, and subsidizing electric motorcycles and automobiles converted to run on liquefied petroleum gas. The EPA estimates that if 80 percent of Taipei's taxicabs were modified to run on LPG, 24,000 fewer metric tons of carbon monoxide and 1,100 fewer metric tons of hydrocarbons would be released into the city's air. The first LPG station in Taipei City was opened on March 15, 1996, and Taipei City's Office of Motor Vehicle Inspection 台北市監理處 has begun accepting applications from taxi owners for LPG conversion subsidies. The Bureau of Transportation under the Taipei City Government 台北市交通局 has budgeted sufficient funds to provide subsidies of US$740 for each of 1,000 LPG-fueled taxis.

Despite its promise, the air pollution control fee system has run into trouble. The EPA had set aside US$100 million in APC funds to finance local efforts to improve air quality, and by May 1996 local governments had proposed 223 air pollution control plans. However, the EPA approved only 140 plans and appropriated a mere US$37 million to fund the programs. In fiscal 1996, the EPA also budgeted US$74 million to establish environmental conservancy parks. Although the EPA approved 115 parks totaling 253 hectares in area, US$33.3 million of the budgeted

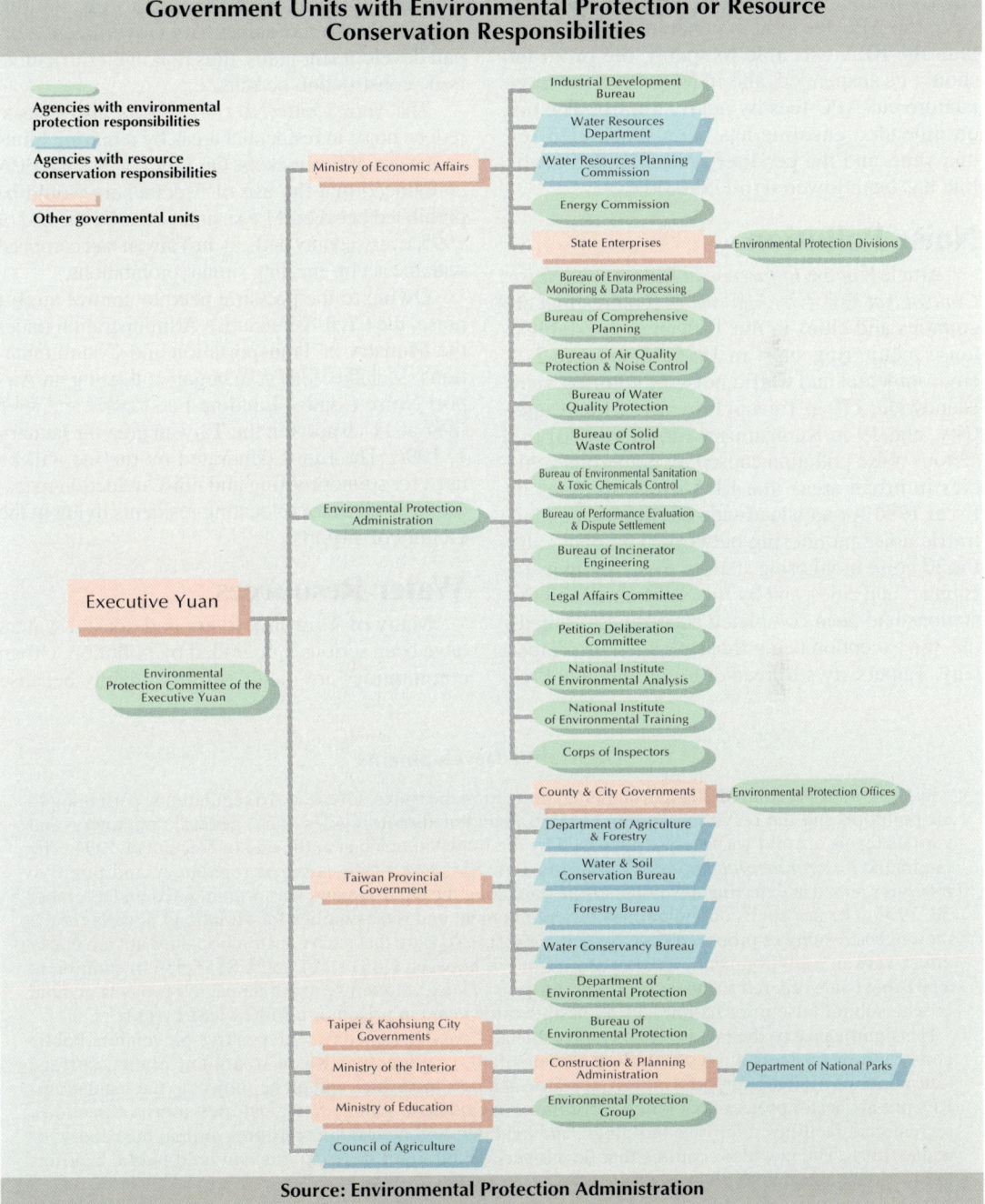

Government Units with Environmental Protection or Resource Conservation Responsibilities

Agencies with environmental protection responsibilities

Agencies with resource conservation responsibilities

Other governmental units

Executive Yuan

Environmental Protection Committee of the Executive Yuan

Ministry of Economic Affairs
- Industrial Development Bureau
- Water Resources Department
- Water Resources Planning Commission
- Energy Commission
- State Enterprises — Environmental Protection Divisions

Environmental Protection Administration
- Bureau of Environmental Monitoring & Data Processing
- Bureau of Comprehensive Planning
- Bureau of Air Quality Protection & Noise Control
- Bureau of Water Quality Protection
- Bureau of Solid Waste Control
- Bureau of Environmental Sanitation & Toxic Chemicals Control
- Bureau of Performance Evaluation & Dispute Settlement
- Bureau of Incinerator Engineering
- Legal Affairs Committee
- Petition Deliberation Committee
- National Institute of Environmental Analysis
- National Institute of Environmental Training
- Corps of Inspectors

Taiwan Provincial Government
- County & City Governments — Environmental Protection Offices
- Department of Agriculture & Forestry
- Water & Soil Conservation Bureau
- Forestry Bureau
- Water Conservancy Bureau
- Department of Environmental Protection

Taipei & Kaohsiung City Governments
- Bureau of Environmental Protection

Ministry of the Interior
- Construction & Planning Administration — Department of National Parks

Ministry of Education
- Environmental Protection Group

Council of Agriculture

Source: Environmental Protection Administration

funds went unused. As a result, several private environmental protection groups protested that since the APC fee system generated more funds than the EPA was able to spend, the program should be suspended, and in May 1996 the Legislature cut APC fees by nearly a third. The tax on unleaded gasoline has been suspended for one year, and the per-liter tax on leaded gasoline has been lowered to US$0.0075.

Noise Pollution

Article 8 of the *Enforcement Rules of the Noise Control Act* 噪音管制法施行細則 requires that all counties and cities in the Taiwan area establish noise monitoring sites. In 1995, there were 210 environmental and traffic noise monitoring sites islandwide: 170 in Taiwan Province, 21 in Taipei City, and 19 in Kaohsiung City. In view of the serious noise pollution caused by numerous vehicles in urban areas, the EPA drew up plans in fiscal 1996 for an islandwide environmental and traffic noise monitoring network. The plan calls for 26 noise monitoring stations to be set up in 16 counties and cities, and by July 1996 almost all the stations had been completed according to schedule, the exception being those planned for Taipei City. Taipei City's Bureau of Environmental Protection 台北市環境保護局 explained that the design and positioning of the monitoring stations conflicted with the Taipei City Government's urban development plans, thus making it difficult to issue construction permits.

The *Noise Control Act* 噪音管制法 also seeks to reduce noise in residential areas by requiring limits on the use of firecrackers. On July 1, 1995, the EPA announced that the use of firecrackers would be prohibited between 11 P.M. and 5 A.M. By the end of 1995, every county and city in Taiwan had complied with the act by enacting similar prohibitions.

Owing to the pressing need to control airport noise, the Civil Aeronautics Administration under the Ministry of Transportation and Communications 交通部民用航空局 began collecting an Airport Noise Control Landing Fee 機場噪音防制降落費 at 11 airports in the Taiwan area on January 1, 1996. The funds generated by the fee will be used for soundproofing and noise reduction measures as well as for relocating residents living in the vicinity of airports.

Water Resources

Many of Taiwan's rivers and coastal waters have been seriously degraded by pollution. Urban communities are major culprits, mainly because

Legislative Developments

In 1994, the EPA drafted 30 environmental protection measures. Of these, 16 regulations, pertaining to air pollution and the recycling and disposal of abandoned motorcycles, cars, general containers, and various forms of solid waste, were approved by the Legislative Yuan at the end of December 1994. The landmark *Environmental Impact Evaluation Law* 環境影響評估法, a set of regulatory and punitive measures aimed at deterring developers from damaging the environment, was promulgated on December 30, 1994. The law spells out guidelines for enforcement and sets penalties for violations. It calls for the thorough screening of proposed development projects to ensure that such construction does not adversely affect Taiwan's environment. Violators face fines of between US$11,111 and US$55,556 in addition to a possible court-ordered suspension of their projects. Those who refuse to put damaging projects on hold or who submit false information face a possible three years in prison or a fine of US$11,111.

The significance of the law lies in its replacement of passive remedies with positive prevention. Public construction projects such as nuclear power plants, radioactive waste treatment plants, surface transportation systems, airports, industrial zones, and new townships will all be subject to the regulations. Key private-sector projects that will be scrutinized include new golf courses, factories, tourist attractions, recreational facilities, high-rise buildings, and land that will be used for farming, animal husbandry, or aquaculture. The law also requires that developers solicit input from experts and hold public hearings before going ahead with planned projects.

Condition of Taiwan's Primary and Secondary Rivers

	Primary		Secondary	
	km	%	km	%
Unpolluted	1,297.7	62.1	584.9	69.2
Lightly Polluted	262.9	12.6	75.0	8.9
Moderately Polluted	205.1	9.8	114.5	13.5
Heavily Polluted	322.7	15.5	71.3	8.4
Total	2,088.3	100.00	845.7	100.0

Source: Environmental Protection Administration, 1995

of the island's failure to develop its sewage system. Most industrial, agricultural, and residential wastewater drains directly into rivers, seriously polluting downstream water sources. According to the EPA, most advanced nations have completed 95 percent of their sewage systems, while Taiwan has built only 3.8 percent, far behind most East Asian countries and some African countries. Even in Taipei City, where the ROC government began building a sewage system in 1972, only 160,000 households (25 percent) had been connected by April 1996. Taiwan thus urgently needs to build an adequate sewage system in order to stem the deterioration of water quality as a result of the growth of urban communities.

Taiwan has 129 rivers, and as of 1995 there were 238 river and stream water quality sampling stations and 50 ocean water quality sampling stations in Taiwan Province. Thirty-one river water quality sampling stations have been set up in Taipei's Tamsui 淡水 river basin alone. Environmental protection agencies have regularly monitored the water quality of primary and secondary rivers, measuring levels of dissolved oxygen, biochemical oxygen demand, suspended solids, and ammonia nitrogen. According to the EPA, 54 percent of primary and secondary rivers are polluted to various degrees, and the Peikang River 北港溪 tops the list of the 12 rivers that are most heavily polluted downstream. Industrial wastewater and waste are the main pollutants. Rivers are also threatened by trash; garbage dumps have been set up at 44 sites along primary rivers. The quantity of

refuse dumped daily at each of these locations ranges from ten to 300 metric tons.

To more effectively control water pollution, the EPA in May of 1991 promulgated amendments to the *Water Pollution Control Act* 水污染防治法 that stipulate daily fines of between US$2,222 and US$22,222 for polluting water. July 1994 saw the enactment of two major water pollution laws: the *Oceanic Effluent Standards* 海洋放流水標準 and the *Supervisory Guidelines for Industrial Wastewater Pollution Control Measures and Urban Effluent Discharge* 事業水污染防治措施及排放廢（污）水管理辦法. Furthermore, the EPA renewed the Integrated Environmental Protection Project for River Basins 流域整體性環保計畫 for fiscal years 1996 through 2001, and allocated just over US$7.4 million to dredge ten primary rivers in fiscal 1996. The Taiwan Provincial Government's Department of Environmental Protection 台灣省政府環境保護處 drew up a pollution treatment program for river basins in July 1995 and budgeted US$1.85 billion to manage pollution control in the Kaop'ing River 高屏溪 and the Tungkang River 東港溪. Thirty river-quality monitoring stations have already been set up on these two rivers to take monthly measurements.

There are 40 reservoirs in the Taiwan area, and the water quality at 20 primary reservoirs is regularly monitored. In 1994, 12 of the 20 primary reservoirs were heavily polluted and eutrophic. However, the EPA's May 1995 "Report on Water Quality at Taiwan's Reservoirs" 水庫水質監測檢

Environmental Nuisance Complaints

In 1995, environmental protection agencies in the Taiwan area registered more than 117,780 complaints about environmental nuisances, most of which concerned waste disposal. The number of environmental nuisance complaints has risen steadily since 1992. The public is increasingly intolerant of companies that do not offer environmentally-friendly products or services, and is more willing to do something about pollution control now that the government has set up channels for handling complaints and resolving disputes.

The *Public Nuisance Dispute Settlement Law* 公害糾紛處理法, promulgated in February 1992, and its enforcement rules, which were announced in February 1993, provide a legal basis for the Public Nuisance Arbitration Panel 公害糾紛裁決委員會 under the EPA as well as subordinate public nuisance mediation committees 公害糾紛調處委員會 in every city, county, and provincial government in the Taiwan area. These committees are open to public participation and are usually made up of academics and environmental specialists in order to insure objectivity. Decisions reached by the mediation committees and/or the EPA's arbitration panel are reviewed by the courts and thus carry the weight of legal judgments.

Yearly Tabulation of Selected Environmental Nuisance Complaint Categories

	Waste Disposal	Noise	Air Pollution	Noxious Odors	Total* Complaints
1991	31,322	15,726	12,966	3,814	67,438
1992	29,805	20,328	16,916	5,603	77,547
1993	32,319	19,165	18,676	8,186	84,273
1994	34,855	20,265	12,957	10,049	86,517
1995	52,462	21,149	12,277	11,950	117,788

*Includes categories not listed

Source: Environmental Protection Administration

驗報告 indicates that the situation at eight of the heavily polluted reservoirs improved, going from eutrophic to dystrophic. The following three reservoirs remained heavily polluted for two consecutive years: Akungtien Reservoir 阿公店水庫, Fengshan Reservoir 鳳山水庫, and Ch'eng Ch'ing Lake Reservoir 澄清湖水庫. The Sun Moon Lake Reservoir 日月潭水庫 and the Feits'ui Reservoir 翡翠水庫 had the best water quality, while the Fengshan Reservoir suffered most heavily from pollution due to livestock.

The development of industrial zones, golf courses, and real estate presents yet another challenge. Mountain deforestation has severely damaged watersheds. Soil in upstream areas washes away and silt fills the reservoirs downstream, reducing both the quantity and quality of water available for use. According to statistics compiled in April 1996, silt accumulation has reduced the storage capacity of Akungtien Reservoir by 76 percent, and storage volumes at Paiho Reservoir 白河水庫 and Wushant'ou Reservoir 烏山頭水庫 have fallen by 49 and 47 percent, respectively. There seems to be no quick fix for such upstream pollution beyond spending more money on downstream water cleanup or finding new water sources.

With this in mind, the Ministry of Economic Affairs 經濟部 (MOEA) plans to add 16 new reservoirs to the island's current 40. However, environmentalists worry about environmental degradation resulting from reservoir construction, and reservoir proposals almost always provoke public protest. Such resistance has thwarted the construction of both the Meinung 美濃 and the Machia 瑪家 reservoirs. To win over the public, the MOEA in April 1996 drafted the *Water Resource Development and Conservation Incentive Regulations* 水資源開發保育回饋條例, which establish an incentive fund for residents near the new reservoirs. Furthermore, the MOEA and Taiwan Provincial Water Conservancy Bureau 台灣省水利局 will jointly implement a five-year, US$1.55 billion integrated reservoir conservation program to clean up 38 reservoirs in the Taiwan area between 1997 and 2001. The EPA has also provided funds for local governments to carry out reservoir pollution control programs.

Besides adopting responsive measures to protect water resources and strengthen river and reservoir conservation, the EPA also stresses tap water quality and has helped the Taiwan Provincial Water Supply Corporation 台灣省自來水股份有限公司 to manage the aeration of the Ch'eng Ch'ing Lake Reservoir, Fengshan Reservoir, and Lant'an Reservoir 蘭潭水庫. To keep groundwater clean, the EPA commissioned the Taiwan Provincial Government's Department of Environmental Protection (DEP) to investigate the risk of pollution in the island's ten groundwater resource areas. Based on the result of this investigation, the EPA decided to establish an islandwide groundwater monitoring network by increasing the number of monitoring wells from 99 to 431. In the initial stage, from 1996 to 1999, a total of 215 monitoring wells will be dug with a budget of US$2.6 million.

The EPA and the DEP also assist local governments to supervise wastewater treatment at river-side factories as well as encourage owners of livestock to install waste treatment facilities. To encourage investment in pollution control systems, a program to provide low-interest loans to the private sector for the purpose of purchasing or improving such facilities was established in February 1988. Over US$444 million has been budgeted for the loans, 25 percent of which will come from the Executive Yuan Development Fund 行政院開發基金 and the remaining 75 percent from 29 banks. Factories, environmental protection companies, medical institutions, and other private enterprises that want to establish or improve pollution control facilities may apply for the loans.

Land Subsidence

Lured by profits, many farmers in the coastal areas of Yünlin 雲林, Changhua 彰化, P'ingtung, Chiayi 嘉義, and Ilan 宜蘭 have expanded into aquaculture. Because groundwater is cheap and has the advantages of stable temperature and quantity, aquaculturalists have dug 170,000 illegal wells and pumped excessive amounts of this precious resource. In addition to being used in aquaculture, groundwater is also pumped for industrial, residential, and standard agricultural uses. Recent data shows that while 7.14 billion cubic meters of groundwater is being pumped annually, only four billion cubic meters is replaced. This deficit has caused land in many areas to subside, especially along the southwestern coast and on the Ilan Plain 宜蘭平原. Overall, almost 1,190 square kilometers of Taiwan's plains, or a full 11 percent, have been affected. The most serious subsidence has occurred around Chiatung 佳冬 in P'ingtung County, where sites have sunk by as much as 2.82 meters. The average rate of subsidence in the coastal areas is between five and 15 centimeters each year.

In November 1995, the Executive Yuan 行政院 passed a land subsidence control program drawn up jointly by its Council of Agriculture 行政院農業委員會 and the MOEA. The program calls for US$56 million to be spent from July 1995 to June 2000 to control land subsidence in seven counties and cities. Efforts in Yünlin, Chiayi, and P'ingtung will be given the priority in

---

1995 Water Pollution Control Act Enforcement

According to the Ministry of Justice 法務部, there were 61 cases related to violations of the *Water Pollution Control Act* in 1995. Of the 53 persons prosecuted in connection with these cases, 32 were found to have discharged wastewater that contained hazardous material in excess of allowable limits, and 15 ignored orders to suspend work or cease operations.

Cases brought to trial	61
Persons prosecuted	53
Persons sentenced	39
between two and six months	35
less than two months	4
Persons found not guilty	1

Source: Ministry of Justice

the first two years. The essentials of the program include the designation of land use, the promotion of land recovery and conservation, guidance for the aquacultural and industrial sectors, groundwater monitoring, and the revision of pertinent laws to more effectively curb illegal practices.

Solid Waste Disposal

There has been a great increase in solid waste as a result of the rapid development of industry and the economy in the Taiwan area. The amount of household garbage produced in Taiwan has nearly doubled in a decade, according to the EPA, from 0.67 kilograms per person per day in 1984 to 1.14 kilograms in 1995. Just over 23,850 metric tons of household garbage was collected per day in 1995, or 8.7 million metric tons for the year. On top of this, domestic industries produce on average 12 million metric tons of waste each year, only 30 percent of which is properly treated. Overall, nearly 26,200 metric tons of garbage is treated properly in landfills or by incineration every day. The rest is dumped into landfills that do not meet the EPA's standards.

Another problem facing Taiwan is that many landfills are either full or nearing capacity, and constructing replacements is difficult since land is extremely scarce. In 1996, 178 of the island's 292 garbage treatment sites had reached full capacity, leaving more than half of Taiwan's rural and urban townships with no place to dump their garbage. The third stage of the Taiwan Area Solid Waste Disposal Project 台灣地區垃圾處理第三期計畫, which was initiated in July 1996, calls for the construction of 27 regional landfills, 172 ordinary dumping sites, and 19 large-scale incinerators. At the close of the second stage of the program at the end of 1995, 22 regional landfills, 131 ordinary dumping sites, and two incinerators had already been completed.

However, most new dump sites and expansion proposals have come under fire from residents of nearby communities. Since 1994, Taiwan has seen numerous serious conflicts between residents and local authorities over the issue of waste management. For example, in June 1994 the construction

of an incinerator near the coast in Tainan City's Annan District 台南市安南區 sparked public resistance. Only after the local government promised to provide over US$2.2 million in development funds annually was the conflict settled. Similar instances of resistance and confrontation have occurred again and again around the island. Protests against an incinerator project in Kaohsiung County's Jenwu Township 高雄縣仁武鄉 turned violent on September 14, 1995, and twelve policemen were wounded. A few days later, 234 primary school students boycotted classes, also to protest the Jenwu incinerator. Local governments that decided to continue using landfill sites where the lease had expired or that were already full also faced strong public resistance. In January 1996, local residents protested against continued dumping and improper waste treatment at Kaohsiung City's Hsich'ingp'u Sanitary Landfill 高雄市西青埔垃圾場 and at Taoyuan City's Hut'oushan Dump Site 桃園市虎頭山垃圾場. A plan to build a landfill in Ilan City 宜蘭市 also brought out over 200 protesters.

To mollify public resistance, in July 1996 the DEP doubled the amount of compensation paid to the communities where dumps are constructed. The compensation is calculated based on the size and type of the dump. The village and borough where the dump site is located share 70 percent of the compensation, and the surrounding communities through which dump trucks drive receive 30 percent. Funding for the increased compensation is provided for as part of the Taiwan Area Solid Waste Disposal Project.

Recycling

While pollution control measures are crucial to solving the problem, the most basic method of reducing environmental damage is to avoid producing pollutants and recycle resources. Recycling is, by necessity, a vital part of the ROC's efforts to manage solid waste and is also the primary concern of many environmental groups. About 40 percent of refuse in the Taiwan area is recoverable; paper alone makes up between 24 and 34 percent of the total, plastics about 17 to 18 percent, rubber from 0.05 to 2.4 percent, glass between 4.2 and 8.6 percent, and metals account for 6.8 to 8.1 percent. Recycling programs are now in place for PET bottles, metal cans, EPS containers, tires, batteries, agricultural chemical containers, abandoned vehicles, and other materials. The EPA-subsidized Foundation for Reduction, Reuse, and Recovery 一般廢棄物回收清除處理基金會 (3R Foundation) has 130 recycling sites around the island to oversee aspects of recycling and refuse disposal.

On July 19, 1995, the EPA revised the *Standards Governing the Methods and Facilities Used to Store, Clean, and Treat Industrial and Commercial Waste* 事業廢棄物貯存、清除、處理方法及設施標準, which regulate not only refuse disposal but also resource recycling. The EPA requires manufacturers of aluminum containers, glass, plastics, paper, and certain other products and materials to recycle at least half of their output.

The Ministry of Transportation and Communications 交通部 (MOTC) estimates that at least 240,000 motor vehicles are abandoned in Taiwan every year. However, in 1992, only 50,000 derelict vehicles were reported. In October 1994, the EPA, the MOEA, the Ministry of the Interior 內政部, and the MOTC jointly promulgated regulations under which the 3R Foundation began to take charge of vehicle recovery operations in January 1995. A special toll-free telephone line was set up for the public to report abandoned motor vehicles, and in 1995 nearly 160,000 derelict vehicles were collected. To encourage citizens to properly dispose of their old motor vehicles, the reward paid by the government for each automobile collected was raised on February 1, 1996, from US$18.50 to US$26.90, and from US$1.85 to US$7.47 for each motorcycle or scooter. Together with the value of the vehicle itself, up to US$88.90 can now be collected for an old car and US$25.90 for a motorcycle.

Hazardous Waste Disposal

In 1995, nearly 430,000 metric tons of hazardous industrial waste were produced by factories, farms, ranches, power plants, waterworks, and medical facilities in the Taiwan area. In 1989, the EPA

1995 Manufacturer Claimed Recycling Rates

	Legislated	Claimed
PET	65	80.47
Steel Cans	60	61.37
Aluminum Cans	60	62.00
Polystyrene Foam Containers	50	12.82
Tires	80	82.24
Mercury Cells	40	46.95
Agricultural Pesticide Containers	60	60.14
Lead Acid Batteries	60	61.90
Sanitation Chemical Containers	60	69.09

Source: Environmental Protection Administration

recognized the need to dispose of hazardous waste properly and proposed the establishment of a waste disposal center inside Kaohsiung's Tafa Industrial Zone 大發工業區. In September 1994, the Ministry of Economic Affairs decided to invest US$74 million to establish the center. An environmental impact assessment was carried out and the project received EPA approval, but public protests have prevented timely implementation of the plan.

Nearly 20,000 chemical substances are used regularly in the Taiwan area, of which 6,000 are highly toxic. In May 1996, the EPA, pursuant to the *Toxic Chemicals Control Act* 毒化物管理法, released a list of 106 toxic chemicals; any production, import, export, sale, or use of chemicals on the list must first be approved. Under another EPA program aimed at gathering information on pollution sources, all enterprises that use toxic substances or discharge waste gas, wastewater, or industrial waste are required to file plans covering the proper disposal of all toxins. Companies are then assigned deadlines for setting up disposal systems. A company that has filed a report and received a deadline is off the hook until the deadline passes. A company that does not file a plan and is found to be polluting the environment is subject to the heaviest fine under the law, which ranges from US$11,111 to US$37,037. Under the *Solid Waste Disposal Act* 廢棄物清理法, manufacturers must assume responsibility for managing waste, and violators face fines of between US$2,222 and US$5,556. Those who dump hazardous waste re sulting in the loss of life may be sentenced to life imprisonment. So far, however, the ROC government has yet to carry out any such punishment.

Wildlife Conservation

Over the past decade, the ROC government and private environmental groups in Taiwan have been acting to stop international traffic in outlawed wildlife products. Beginning with the promulgation of the *Wildlife Conservation Law* 野生動物保育法 in 1989 and continuing through 1995 with the formation of an interministerial wildlife conservation investigation and supervisory task force to crack down on the smuggling of wildlife products, Taiwan has repeatedly demonstrated its commitment to domestic conservation and support for global wildlife protection efforts. However, some well-intentioned environmental groups have felt that Taiwan's conservation efforts came "too little, too late."

Criticism of Taiwan's conservation record came to a head on March 25, 1994, when the Convention on International Trade in Endangered Species (CITES) concluded at its standing committee meeting in Geneva that Taiwan's proposed actions "toward meeting minimum requirements have not yet been" carried out. Following the decision by CITES, the United States invoked the Pelly Amendment to impose trade sanctions on Taiwan in April 1994, and went on to announce a ban on imports of wildlife and wildlife products from Taiwan, effective August 19, 1994. To avert international trade sanctions, the ROC legislature pushed through amendments to the *Wildlife Conservation Law* and toughened penalties against violators. The government also made an even greater and more visible effort to abide by international agreements to halt the trafficking of endangered species and illegal wildlife products.

Taiwan has enacted legislation which, as closely as possible, complies with CITES requirements. Close contact is maintained with officials at CITES, the Worldwide Fund for Nature, the Trade Records Analysis of Flora and Fauna in Commerce, the Environmental Investigation Agency, and numerous other international conser-

vation groups. As a result, Taiwan has won recognition for its efforts and progress in policing illicit trade in wildlife and wildlife products over the past three years, and on June 30, 1995, the United States lifted its trade sanctions on Taiwan. A little over a year later, on September 11, 1996, Taiwan's achievements were further confirmed when the US announced that Taiwan was being removed entirely from the Pelly Amendment "watch list." The United States cited the ROC government's comprehensive efforts and cooperation with international endeavors as being behind the decision.

Legal Framework

Trafficking in certain wildlife products in Taiwan is proscribed by the *Cultural Heritage Preservation Law* 文化資產保存法, enacted in 1981, and the *Wildlife Conservation Law*. The former mandates the creation of a system of nature reserves and designates 11 species of rare plants and 23 species of rare animals for protection. The latter classifies another 1,045 species of rare flora and fauna into three levels of protection. Species listed either as "endangered" 瀕臨絕種 (meaning that their population size is at or below a critical level) or as "rare and valuable" 珍貴稀有 (referring to endemic species or those with a very low population) may not be disturbed, abused, hunted, captured, traded, exchanged, owned, killed, or processed. Species considered to "require conservation measures" 應予保育 may be utilized once the population has reached a sustainable level as determined by the Council of Agriculture (see inset, next page).

The original *Wildlife Conservation Law* had a number of shortcomings. It lacked provisions for effective punishment of holders of unregistered rhino horns or tiger bones, mandated no punishments for people who falsely claim that their products contain materials derived from endangered species, and was lax on wildlife smuggling. A newly revised *Wildlife Conservation Law* went into effect on October 29, 1994. The revised law is among the most severe in Asia: the trade or display for commercial purposes of protected, en

Council of Agriculture

As opposed to the EPA, which is in charge of environmental protection, the Executive Yuan's Council of Agriculture 行政院農業委員會 (COA) is the highest government agency responsible for enforcing Taiwan's conservation laws, devising the nation's conservation policies, and overseeing implementation. The COA spent approximately US$9.09 million of its budget on wildlife conservation in fiscal 1996, and has allocated US$8.55 million for fiscal 1997. A Wildlife Conservation Investigation and Supervisory Force 野生動物保育查緝督導小組 was set up in September 1993 to coordinate conservation activities at various national and local government agencies, boost conservation awareness, train conservation personnel, and strengthen crackdowns on illicit traffic in wildlife products. The task force is composed of vice ministerial officials from selected government ministries and convened by the chairman of the COA. Currently, the task force meets regularly to coordinate a three-year government work plan to strengthen wildlife conservation. The government has allocated US$38.5 million to ensure the success of the program, which it launched in 1995.

dangered, or rare and valuable wildlife products, as well as the unauthorized import or export of live protected wildlife or products made from protected wildlife, is punishable by a prison term of between six months and five years and/or a fine of between US$11,111 and US$55,556. Habitual offenders face prison terms of between one and seven years and/or fines of between US$18,518 and US$92,593. A person who falsely labels merchandise as containing protected wildlife or protected wildlife products shall be subject to a fine of between US$5,556 and US$27,778.

Further progress was achieved with the promulgation of the *Wildlife Conservation Law Implementation Regulations* 野生動物保育法施行細則 on April 29, 1995. The regulations stipulate that the Wildlife Conservation Advisory Committee 野生動物保育諮詢委員會 shall review the classification of endangered species at least once a year.

Enforcement of Wildlife Conservation Laws

The ROC government has redoubled its efforts to investigate and punish violators of the *Wildlife Conservation Law* and other conservation-related legislation. A six-member Wildlife Protection Unit 野生動物保護小組 (WPU), set up on November 26, 1993, is in charge of investigations. The WPU is assisted by more than 350 police officers who have completed special training in wildlife conservation. Since it was established, the unit has conducted extensive undercover operations and overseen investigations into more than 9,700 traditional Chinese pharmacies.

The Taiwan Provincial Government has continued to coordinate the implementation of the *Wildlife Conservation Law* at the local government level by maintaining frequent contact and organizing training workshops and conservation-related activities. All local governments have established joint enforcement task forces, which coordinate affairs among different agencies at the county level and hold review meetings to improve enforcement efforts.

In 1995, local governments investigated more than 3,330 wildlife-related cases, and customs officials uncovered 34 cases of wildlife product smuggling. From December 1994 to December 1995, local police investigated 132 violations of the *Wildlife Conservation Law*, all of which were referred to the prosecutor's office for prosecution. During the same period, the WPU investigated 49 wildlife-related cases. In one case, the WPU seized dead and butchered dolphins in the town of Peikang 北港 in Yünlin County 雲林縣 on January 11, 1996. The dolphin meat, totaling more than 10,500 kilograms, was the largest amount ever seized in one raid in Taiwan. In June of the same year, one of the violators was sentenced to three years and fined US$37,037.

The Coast Guard Command 海岸巡防司令部, local police officers, customs agents, and state investigators are working together to enforce the *Wildlife Conservation Law* and to interdict the smuggling of wildlife and wildlife products at airports, seaports, along the coast, and in open waters. The Keelung Customs Bureau 基隆關稅局 seized 272 ivory tusks and 139 pieces of ivory tusk on October 3, 1994. After an investigation by the Ministry of Justice's Investigation Bureau 法務部調查局 (MJIB), the owner of the ivory was found, and the case was referred to the prosecutor's office for prosecution on July 4, 1995. In another case, the MJIB seized 2,100 kilograms of smuggled pilose antler 鹿茸 in Tainan County on February 25, 1995. The case was referred to the prosecutor's office for further investigation and went to trial in June of that year.

Wildlife Products in Traditional Chinese Medicine

Although tigers became extinct in Taiwan long ago, and rhinos have never inhabited the island at all, tiger parts and rhino horn have been used for thousands of years by Chinese pharmacists as ingredients in traditional remedies. Because of their scarcity, tiger and rhino products were seen as prestige items and demand for them in Taiwan was high. After the import of tiger parts and rhino horn was outlawed in August 1985, a black market in these goods and in counterfeit copies began to flourish. Some traditional Chinese pharmacies in Taiwan were still selling such products in the early 1990s. As a result, international environmental groups became alarmed and began a public relations campaign against Taiwan. Some environmentalists called for a boycott of products produced in Taiwan until the authorities passed tougher legislation and began devoting more manpower to enforcement.

In response, the ROC government revised the *Wildlife Conservation Law*, beefed up enforcement, and established a registration system for rhino horn. By December 1994, a total of 459 kilograms of rhino horn had been accounted for and marked with tamper-proof identification labels. Photographs and other measurements were also taken, and all registration information has been entered into a computer database to facilitate future reviews. This system has significantly strengthened the position of conservation officials. In March 1994, 6.5 percent of the tradi-

1995 Wildlife Conservation Law Enforcement

Cases brought to trial	88
Persons involved	114
Persons sentenced	92
one to two years	2
six months to one year	22
two to six months	48
less than two months	14
fine	6
Persons found not guilty	13
Persons not prosecuted	8
Persons whose cases have not been decided	1

Source: Ministry of Justice

tional Chinese pharmacies investigated were found to have violated conservation laws. This figure dropped to nil in August and September of that year. Throughout 1995, local governments conducted over 2,300 regular and random checks on such shops and found no evidence of illegal sales of rhino horns or tiger parts.

Despite recognizing the ROC government's overall effort to crack down on illegal imports of endangered wildlife products, some US wildlife conservation institutions have listed Taiwan among the world's major consumers of bear parts. In April 1996, the Humane Society of the United States estimated that pharmacies in Taiwan had a 710-kilogram supply of bear gall bladders, a stockpile representing 12,000 dead bears. However, the COA noted that a survey by the China Medical College 中國醫藥學院 indicates that the local supply of bear gall bladders is equal to only 1,000 bears. Moreover, the survey found that only about 11.5 percent of products sold as bear gall bladder in pharmacies in the Taiwan area are genuine; that is, most of them contain no bear gall bladders at all. All bear species, including American black bears, are listed as protected species under the *Wildlife Conservation Law*, and since May 1993, ROC customs officials have handled five cases involving suspected bear gall bladders. Analysis of the 154 pieces seized revealed that 37 pieces were from Asiatic bears, and 117 pieces were pig gall bladders.

Private Environmental Protection Groups in Taiwan

The Animal Protection Association of the ROC
中華民國保護動物協會
TEL: (02) 931-8464

Beautiful Taiwan Foundation 美化環境基金會
TEL: (02) 362-1823

Chinese National Park Society 中
華民國國家公園學會
TEL: (02) 944-9259

Environmental Greenery Association of the ROC
中華民國環境綠化協會
TEL: (02) 367-6616

The Environment Protection Foundation
財團法人中華民國環境保護文教基金會
TEL: (02) 366-0054

Green Consumers' Foundation 綠色消費基金會
TEL: (02) 773-9077

Homemakers' Union and Foundation
主婦聯盟環保基金會
TEL: (02) 368-6211

Life Conservationist Association of the ROC
關懷生命協會
TEL: (02) 715-0079

MOA International Foundation of Natural Ecology
財團法人國際美育自然生態基金會
TEL: (02) 781-9420

New Environment
Foundation 新環境基金會
TEL: (02) 396-9522

The Orangutan Foundation Taiwan
財團法人保護人猿基金會
TEL: (02) 362-6786

Society for Wildlife and Nature, ROC
中華民國自然生態保育協會
TEL: (02) 936-2801

Taiwan Pheasant Birds Conservation
Association 台灣省雉類動物保育協會
TEL: (02) 263-3317

TRAFFIC Taipei (Trade Records Analysis of
Flora and Fauna in Commerce)
台北野生動物貿易調查委員會
TEL: (02) 362-9787

Wild Bird Society of the ROC
中華民國野鳥學會
TEL: (02) 706-7219

The Zoological Society of Taipei
台北市動物園之友協會
TEL: (02) 939-0663

Nevertheless, the value of traditional Chinese medicine is recognized and has a strong impact on the public. It is thus still necessary to instill a conservation ethic within the traditional Chinese medical community. In 1995, the Department of Health 衛生署 (DOH) and the COA held many activities to boost public awareness of bear conservation; for instance, bear conservation spots were aired in 1995 on the nation's three broadcast TV stations. At the same time, the DOH distributed 15,000 bear conservation stickers throughout the traditional Chinese medical community, urging the public not to use bear gall bladders. In October 1995, the DOH further spread the word by producing 400,000 "Protect Bear Species" phone cards and posting conservation messages at Taipei bus stops from September through December of the same year. The COA produced posters and calendars concerning bear protection and held a workshop on the identification of bear gall bladders. Investigations into the smuggling of bear gall bladders as well as crackdowns on such activities are regular responsibilities of customs and law enforcement agencies.

Habitat Conservation

One of the best ways to protect wild animals is to preserve their natural habitat. Unfortunately, this is not easily done in Taiwan, which with 590 people per square kilometer and nearly as many motor vehicles as people is one of the most crowded places in the world. While the ROC government has been able to put a cap on serious pollution problems, the fact remains that much of Taiwan's unique habitat has suffered from human encroachment.

Taiwan's location between three major climatic zones and its diverse topography have, however, endowed the area with a wide range of flora and fauna. Some 60 species of mammals, around 450 species of birds (40 percent of which are resident), 94 species of reptiles, 30 amphibian species, nearly 130 species of freshwater fish, and 15,000 named insect species (including 400 butterfly species) are known to exist in the Taiwan area.

The different land forms, climates, and forest types, not to mention the impact of large-scale human development, have combined to create ecological islands within the physical entity that is Taiwan. To protect these ecological islands, the ROC government has set aside nearly 10 percent of the land in the Taiwan area as part of a multitiered conservation system that includes six national parks 國家公園, 18 nature preserves 自然保留區, 24 natural forest reserves 國有林自然保護區, and eight wildlife refuges 野生動物保護區.

Three laws specifically authorize the designation and protection of natural areas and wildlife refuges: the *Cultural Heritage Preservation Law*, which authorizes the creation of nature preserves and identifies endangered species of flora and fauna; the *Wildlife Conservation Law*, which establishes wildlife refuges; and the *National Park Law* 國家公園法, which allows for the designation of national parks. The central government agencies that supervise Taiwan's refuges are the Ministry of Interior's Department of National Parks 內政部國家公園組 and the Council of Agriculture. Answerable to the COA are the Taiwan Forestry Bureau 台灣省林務局 and the Taiwan Forestry Research Institute 台灣省林業試驗所 under the Taiwan Provincial Government, the bureaus of reconstruction 建設局 under the Taipei and Kaohsiung city governments, and the agriculture bureaus 農業局 of city and county governments in the Taiwan area.

National Parks

The government of the Republic of China has been trying to do in ten years what has taken some countries more than 100 years to do—create a comprehensive national park system that balances conservation, recreation, and research. Taiwan didn't begin to establish national parks until the island's population density was already very high. As a result, park officials have faced a constant tug of war over the use of park land—with businesses that predated the parks, with aborigines who want to keep or regain their ancestral land, with landowners who want to build hotels or other businesses for park visitors, and even with a veterans' agency that runs a farm in the middle of one park.

Constraints of time and space did not allow Taiwan to build its park system gradually. Instead, it has done the best it could, pushing through an ambitious parks program that has placed 8.4 percent of its land area under protection (see map, next page). Additional land acquisitions together with the 50 existing protected nature and wildlife areas will eventually push the proportion of Taiwan's territory under protection to over 12 percent.

Taiwan's national park system was inaugurated in 1984 with the establishment of Kenting National Park 墾丁國家公園 at the southern tip of the island.

Whale Conservation

In line with the world trend towards protecting whales, the Ministry of Economic Affairs licensed whaling and prohibited uncontrolled hunting in 1981. Whalers who returned their licenses to the government received assistance with establishing alternative businesses, and the COA bought and disassembled the decommissioned whaling ships. Pursuant to the *Wildlife Conservation Law*, the COA classified 23 species of whales as endangered. From 1990 through 1995, this list grew to include all species of whales. During the same period, the government investigated several cases involving violations of conservation laws, and about 40 people were charged with whaling and selling whale meat in connection with these cases. In February 1996, the COA launched a national whale conservation campaign, distributing posters and pamphlets to relevant agencies which in turn distributed them among the public. Currently, no whaling activities are conducted in Taiwan.

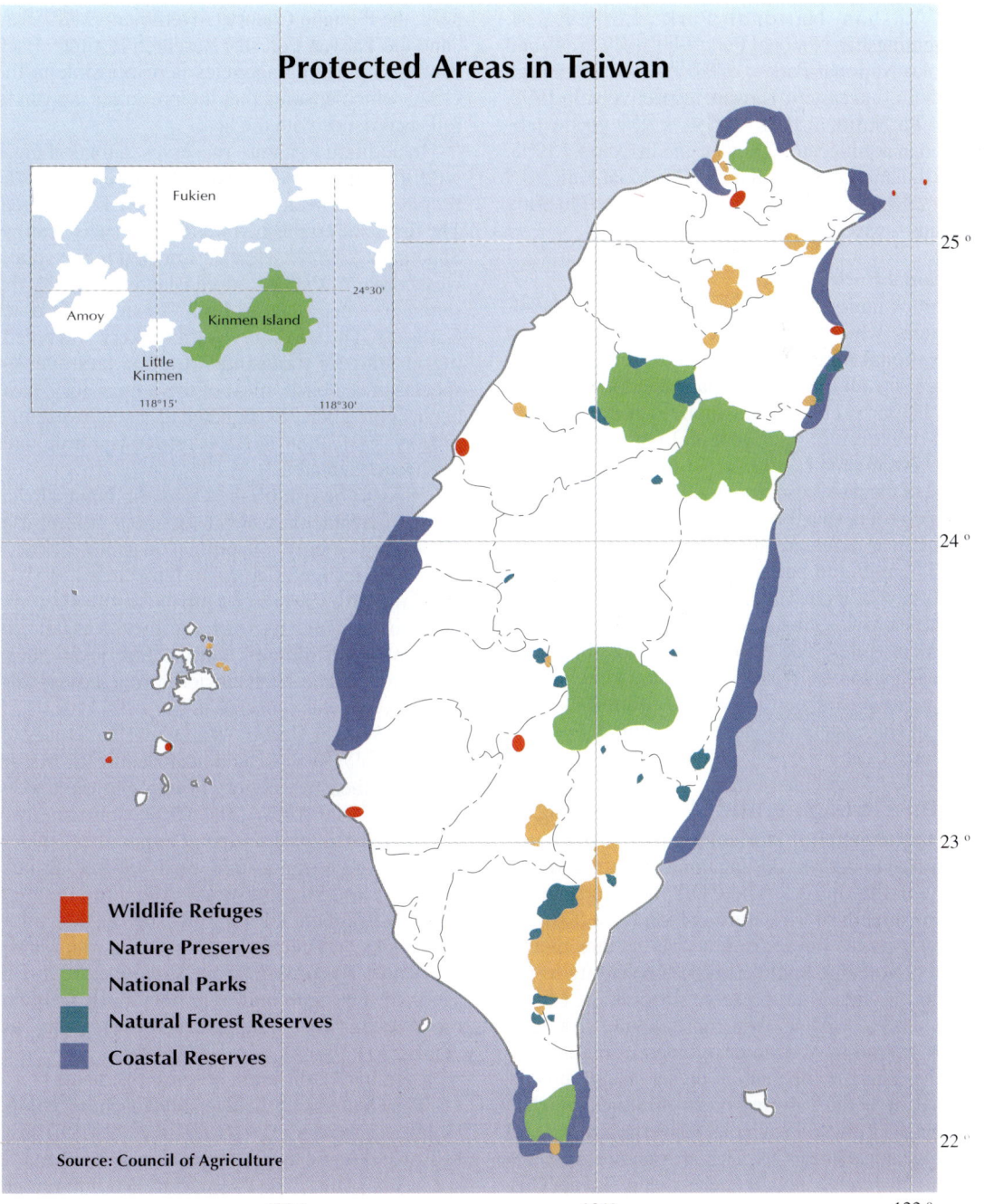

Protected Areas in Taiwan

Fukien

Amoy

Kinmen Island

Little
Kinmen

24°30'

118°15'   118°30'

25°

24°

23°

22°

Wildlife Refuges

Nature Preserves

National Parks

Natural Forest Reserves

Coastal Reserves

Source: Council of Agriculture

120°   121°   122°

In 1985 and 1986, Taiwan moved swiftly to set up the Yüshan National Park 玉山國家公園, Yangmingshan National Park 陽明山國家公園, and Taroko National Park 太魯閣國家公園 in central, northern, and eastern Taiwan, respectively. In 1992, Shei-Pa National Park 雪霸國家公園 was established in north-central Taiwan, and in October 1995, a sixth national park—Kinmen National Park 金門國家公園, occupying 25.5 percent of the Quemoy islands—was opened to the public.

National Park Facilities

Each national park has a national park headquarters, which is supervised by the Department of National Parks. In fiscal 1996, the combined budget for all the national park headquarters and the Department of National Parks exceeded US$100 million. Each national park has at least one visitor center and one nature display center. Most of the parks also have trailhead nature centers. Guided tours may be arranged by contacting the park headquarters in advance.

The national parks received more than 7.43 million visitors in 1995. To minimize the impact of these crowds, the parks were divided into management zones. The zones identify the best uses for each area of the parks, including general protection areas, recreational areas, cultural and historical sites, scenic areas, and ecological protection areas.

Nature Preserves and Wildlife Refuges

The Council of Agriculture administers land protected under two designations: nature preserves and wildlife refuges. The COA has overseen the establishment of 18 nature preserves in Taiwan. The preserves range from a five-hectare plot to protect volcanic land forms in Kaohsiung to the 47,000-hectare forest preserve surrounding Mount Tawu 大武山. Altogether, more than 63,200 hectares of land have been designated as nature preserves. Eleven of the nature preserves are directly managed by the Taiwan Forestry Bureau, which is under the Taiwan Provincial Government yet still accountable to the COA. The other nature preserves are managed by such agencies as the Taipei City

Government's Bureau of Reconstruction 台北市建設局, the P'enghu County Government 澎湖縣政府, and the Taiwan Forestry Research Institute. Each of these managing agencies is responsible to the COA, which ensures that the preserves are run in full accordance with the law.

In addition to nature preserves, a total of eight wildlife refuges, encompassing more than 4,020 hectares, have been established in the Taiwan area. The first to be established was the Cat Islets Seafowl Sanctuary 貓嶼海鳥保護區. Located in the southwest corner of the Pescadore islands 澎湖群島, the sanctuary encompasses both Greater and Lesser Cat Islets. The islets serve as a rookery and breeding ground for thousands of terns, and over 44 species of sea birds, most of them migratory, have been sighted here. Designated as a seafowl refuge in May 1991, the Cat Islets refuge is a little over ten hectares in area.

Next to be established was the Nantsehsien River Fish Sanctuary 楠梓仙溪溪流魚類保護區 in Kaohsiung County's Sanmin Township 高雄縣三民鄉. The refuge is home to ten species of river fish and 30 species of birds, including the plumbeous water redstart, the little forktail, the gray-throated minivet, and the Formosan whistling thrush. The Nantsehsien refuge covers 274 hectares and was set aside in May 1993.

The Wuwei Harbor Waterfowl Sanctuary 無尾港水鳥保護區 is located near Suao 蘇澳 in Taiwan's northeastern county of Ilan. Surrounded by diverse coastal forests, the 102-hectare site was designated as a bird refuge in September 1993 to protect its wetlands and bird habitat. Lakes, marshes, and streams within the site create an ideal environment for wildfowl such as the migratory ducks and geese that stop in Taiwan during the winter. According to one survey, close to 140 kinds of mountain and migratory birds frequent the Wuwei Creek site. Every winter, from November to February, some 3,000 ducks and geese, representing 12 different species, rest here.

The Chunghsing Bridge and Huachung Bridge Wildlife Sanctuary 中興橋華中橋野生動物保護區 in Taipei is home to 79 species of waterfowl and 41 species of plants. The 203-hectare wildlife refuge,

Nature Preserves

Alishan Taiwan Pleione Nature Preserve
阿里山台灣一葉蘭自然保留區

Chatienshan Nature Preserve 插天山自然保留區

Chuyunshan Nature Preserve 出雲山自然保留區

Hahpen Nature Preserve 哈盆自然保留區

Kenting Uplifted Coral Reef Nature Preserve
墾丁高位珊瑚礁自然保留區

Kuantu Nature Preserve 關渡自然保留區

Miaoli Sanyi Huoyenshan Nature Preserve
苗栗三義火炎山自然保留區

Nanao Hardwood Forest Nature Preserve
南澳闊葉樹林自然保留區

P'enghu Columnar Basalt Nature Preserve
澎湖玄武岩自然保留區

Pinglin Taiwan Keteleeria Nature Preserve
坪林台灣油杉自然保留區

Taitung Honye Village Taiwan Cycas Nature
Preserve 台東紅葉村台灣蘇鐵自然保留區

Tamsui River Mangrove Nature Preserve
淡水河紅樹林自然保留區

TawushanTaiwan Amentotaxus Nature
Preserve 大武山事業區台灣穗花杉自然保留區

Tawushan Nature Preserve 大武山自然保留區

Watzuwei Nature Preserve 挖子尾自然保留區

Wushanting Mud Volcano Nature Preserve
烏山頂泥火山自然保留區

Wushihpi Coastal Nature Preserve
烏石鼻海岸自然保留區

Yuanyang Lake Nature Preserve
鴛鴦湖自然保留區

set up in November 1993, serves as a natural classroom for Taipei citizens during the bird-watching season. Another urban area refuge is the Ssuts'ao Wildlife Sanctuary 四草野生動物保護區 in Tainan City. The sanctuary is an important wetland site in southern Taiwan where 40 species of wild birds are resident and 21 endangered and rare species of birds have been sighted. Designated as wildlife refuge in November 1994, the 515-hectare site also contains three kinds of rare mangroves.

In addition to the Cat Islets refuge, P'enghu County also contains the Wangan Island Green Turtle Sanctuary 望安島綠蠵龜產卵棲地保護區. As the number of green turtles in the Taiwan area is falling due to environmental degradation and poaching, the 23-hectare sanctuary was set aside in January 1995 to serve as a breeding ground and refuge for nesting green turtles. Wangan Island is one of the few green turtle habitats that remain largely untouched by human intrusion.

The Tatu River Waterfowl Sanctuary 大肚溪口水鳥保護區, which straddles the border between Taichung County and Changhua County 彰化縣, is a diverse collection of coastal waters, rivers, sandbanks, tidal flats, farmland, and fish farms. The wide plains and abundance of nourishing organisms brought in by the tides attract an enormous number of migratory birds, and 24 protected species have been sighted here. Established in February 1995, the 2,670-hectare sanctuary serves as an outdoor classroom for the residents of central Taiwan.

The Mienhua Islet and Huap'ing Islet Wildlife Sanctuary 棉花嶼花瓶嶼野生動物保護區 is located in the waters north of Keelung City 基隆市. Home to rare bird species and characterized by fascinating geology, the two uninhabited islets were classified as primary wildlife habitat in June 1995 and then upgraded to wildlife sanctuary status in March 1996.

Natural Forest Reserves and the Taiwan Forestry Bureau

According to the most recent survey, nearly 74 percent of the 1.56 million hectares of national forestland in Taiwan is virgin forest. The Taiwan Forestry Bureau (TFB) has classified the forests under its jurisdiction into 448 management and inspection zones based upon forest distribution, traffic conditions, and the degree to which the forests were damaged in the past. Over 850 rangers patrol these zones to prevent people from illegally felling trees, dumping refuse, or otherwise damaging the forests. These rangers also work to prevent and fight forest fires.

Natural forest reserves are national forest lands recognized as possessing unique natural charac-

Natural Forest Reserves

Alishan Coniferous and Hardwood Reserve
阿里山針闊葉樹林自然保護區

Chachayalaishan Formosan Amentotaxus
Reserve 茶茶牙賴山台灣穗花杉自然保護區

Chiahsien Ssute Fossil Reserve
甲仙四德化石保護區

Chiaohsi Taiwan Keteleeria Reserve
礁溪台灣油杉自然保護區

Chinshuiying Hardwood Forest Reserve
浸水營闊葉樹林自然保護區

Erhshui Formosan Rock-monkey Reserve
二水台灣獼猴自然保護區

Hsuehshankenghsi Reserve 雪山坑溪自然保護區

Juiyenhsi Forest Reserve
瑞岩溪自然保護區

Kuanshan Taiwan Juglans Reserve
關山台灣胡桃自然保護區

Kuanshan Taiwan Phoenix Reserve
關山台灣海棗自然保護區

Kuanwu Taiwan Sassafras Reserve
觀霧台灣檫樹自然保護區

Kuanyin Coastal Reserve 觀音海岸自然保護區

Liukuei Shihpalohanshan Landscape Reserve
六龜十八羅漢山自然保護區

Lulinshan Coniferous and Hardwood Forest
Reserve 鹿林山針闊葉樹林自然保護區

Peitawushan Coniferous and Hardwood Forest
Reserve 北大武山針闊葉樹林自然保護區

Sheipa Reserve 雪霸自然保護區

Shuangkuei Lake Reserve 雙鬼湖自然保護區

Taitung Coastal Range Hardwood Forest Reserve
台東海岸山脈闊葉樹林自然保護區

Taitung Coastal Range Taiwan Cycas Reserve
海岸山脈台灣蘇鐵自然保護區

Taitung Formosan Rock-monkey Reserve
台東台灣獼猴自然保護區

Takuanshan Reserve 達觀山自然保護區

Tawu Taiwan Keteleeria Reserve
大武台灣油杉自然保護區

Wulin Formosan Salmon Reserve
武陵櫻花鉤吻鮭自然保護區

Yuli Wildlife Reserve 玉里野生動物自然保護區

teristics. While these reserves are subject to the multiple-use policies of the TFB, managers of these areas are expected to emphasize preservation over development. In the past, several natural forest reserves have been promoted to refuge status, and this practice is expected to continue.

The basic law regulating the preservation of ROC's forests is the *Forest Law* 森林法. In accordance with this law, the TFB began a forest conservation program in 1965. The program includes surveying and studying rare plants and animals as well as drafting plans for long-term studies, experimentation, and educational tourism within protected nature areas. TFB workers are continuing to survey the forests of Taiwan to identify different kinds of representative ecosystems and rare flora and fauna. In addition to entering all data into a computer network and setting up management survey stations for researching and protecting wild plants and animals, the TFB also posts educational information along the perimeters of natural forest reserves.

The management plans for Taiwan's 24 natural forest reserves call for forest rangers and relevant staff to patrol these areas to crack down on the illegal hunting, trapping, and killing of wildlife as well as the illegal collection of protected plant species. They are also responsible for tearing down illegal snares, nets, and other traps. For example, the management authority of the Tawushan Nature Preserve 大武山自然保留區 devoted more than 3,050 man-hours to patrolling forest reserves in fiscal 1995, and during that period, 60 illegal hunting and trapping devices were torn down by forest rangers.

Until 1989, the TFB was financed through logging operations; however, forest management programs are no longer tied to timber harvest receipts. With a staff of more than 3,800, the TFB spent over US$192 million in fiscal 1995, yet the administration's income during the same period was just under US$4.4 million. Eighty-seven percent of the difference in funding was provided by the central government and 13 percent came from the Taiwan Provincial Government. The TFB also operates a network of hostels in forest areas beyond a day's journey from any city, increasing the accessibility of these relatively isolated regions. Such hostels are open to the public for a fee that depends on the quality of services available and the length of stay.

Creating a Conservation Ethic

Many government agencies and private conservation groups are working to carry out a massive educational campaign aimed at creating a conservation ethic in Taiwan. At the forefront of conservation education is the COA, which sponsors research projects, hosts international symposia, and subsidizes publicity campaigns. The COA also commissions other government agencies to provide conservation-related publications. Meanwhile, the Ministry of Education 教育部 (MOE) has introduced wildlife conservation into the public school curriculum in Taiwan. In less than a year, 16 new textbooks introducing conservation concepts have been written for students of all ages. The MOE is now training 5,000 teachers to teach courses on wildlife conservation.

Targeting the general public, the Government Information Office under the Executive Yuan 行政院新聞局 has made wildlife conservation a major part of its informational campaigns. In July 1995, the GIO went on the Internet with a new database, available in both Chinese and English, with facts and figures about Taiwan, including Taiwan's efforts in the area

Conservation on the Web

An environmental protection network, Taiwan EcoWeb 台灣環境網, was jointly founded by Taiwan's private environmental protection groups on April 23, 1996. The network allows users to obtain and exchange information about Taiwan's environmental protection groups, up-to-date environmental protection issues and campaigns, Earth Day activities, and other environmental issues. The network can be accessed at the address *http://pristine.com.tw/~ecoweb*.

of wildlife conservation. The World Wide Web address of the database is *http://www.gio.gov.tw*. Together with the Department of Health and the COA, the GIO also produced some 30 wildlife conservation films to be aired on Taiwan's three broadcast TV stations as well as cable TV channels. The three agencies also put out more than 232,000 copies of conservation-related booklets and pamphlets.

International Cooperation

The ROC has an established record of cooperation with international conservation organizations. From January to November 1995, the ROC donated US$540,000 to support international conservation activities and projects, such as the Decision Support-2001 Conference held in Canada, Israel's roe deer reintroduction project, Swaziland's rhino conservation project, the 1995 International Training Seminar for Wildlife Enforcement Officers in the USA, funding for daily operations at the CITES Standing Committee Asian Regional Office in Thailand, and light observation aircraft for a Wilderness Conservancy anti-poaching project in Africa. The ROC government's donations towards international wildlife conservation efforts have continued into 1996.

Like an endless summer,
EVA Air, the wings of Taiwan

Bask in EVA Air's service, as inviting as it is relaxing

After only five years, EVA Air has gained a reputation for remarkable comfort and friendly service. In the process, it has also earned numerous international honors and awards. This is no surprise to the savvy and selective frequent flyers who enjoy EVA Air's superior amenities, flight after flight. These travelers appreciate EVA Air's attention to the finer details, from a comforting pillow adjustment to an irresistible game no child can resist. And, more and more travelers are discovering EVA Air every day.

Isn't it about time you experienced EVA Air's service for yourself? From its home in Taiwan, EVA Air takes tropical warmth and tradition to new heights.

EVA Air, the wings of Taiwan.

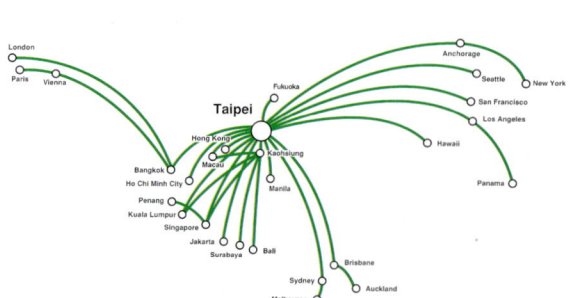

THE WINGS OF TAIWAN

EVA AIR

EVERGREEN GROUP

For reservations please call Taipei(02)501-1999 Taichung(04)329-9566
Kaohsiung(07)330-9301or contact your local travel agent.

14.
Transportation

Above: The Mucha Line of the Taipei Rapid Transit Systems allows passengers to travel quickly and conveniently above the crush of downtown traffic.

Right: Over 50 percent of Taipei's rapid transit system will run underground, like this section of the 10.3 km-long Hsintien Line.

Previous page: Thirty-nine airlines, including four based in the ROC, offer scheduled international passenger flights to an increasingly globalized Taiwan.

14 Transportation

A well-developed transportation network is essential to national development and an export-oriented economy. Transportation has therefore been an important priority, from the Ten Major Construction Projects 十大建設 of the 1970s through the Six-Year National Development Plan 國家建設六年計畫 of the 1990s. With the official approval of the Asia-Pacific Regional Operations Center plan 亞太營運中心計畫 on January 5, 1995, the expansion and improvement of the island's transportation infrastructure is even more critical. The plan—which targets the six major sectors of manufacturing, air transportation, sea transportation, finance, telecommunications, and media—aims to transform Taiwan into a center of business and investment in the Asia-Pacific. Thus, not only are considerable resources being devoted to achieving the plan's sea and air goals in particular, but also underway are many projects designed to ensure that businesses in Taiwan enjoy the advantages of an extensive and efficient transportation network. This chapter reviews the organization of the Republic of China's railways, harbors and shipping, civil aviation, freeways and highways, and urban transportation systems, as well as discusses recent developments that are shaping the new face of transportation in the ROC.

Railways

Taiwan has a modern railway system which provides frequent and convenient passenger service between all major cities on the island. As of December 1995, Taiwan's railway network totaled 2,363 kilometers, an equivalent of 1.11 km per 10,000 people, or 66 meters per sq. km of land. These 2,363 km of rail transported 30.1 million tons of freight in 1995, for a total of 1.9 billion ton-km, 3.56 percent less than in 1994. The number of passengers carried also fell 0.04 percent to total 161 million. Railways in Taiwan are operated by the Taiwan Railway Administration 台灣省鐵路管理局 (TRA), the Taiwan Sugar Corporation 台灣糖業公司, and the Taiwan Forestry Bureau 台灣省林務局. The TRA provides passenger and freight services to the general public, while the Taiwan Sugar Corporation and the

Taiwan Forestry Bureau haul their own products and offer only limited passenger service.

Several types of passenger train services are available: the fastest express class is the Tzu-chiang service 自強號, which only stops at the most major stations; the next fastest express class, with more frequent stops at lesser, but still mainly large stations, is the Chü-kuang service 莒光號. The third class of trains, at the Fu-hsing service 復興號 level, includes older trains that only exclude the smallest stops, and electric commuter trains 通勤電車 which stop at every station on a designated commuter route. Finally, local trains—both with air conditioning 平快車 and without 普通車—serve mostly long routes, stopping at every station, and generally yielding to higher-priority Tzu-chiang, Chü-kuang and Fu-hsing trains.

The TRA has started to upgrade some equipment and facilities. In October 1995, the administration purchased 68 EM500 commuter cars—each of which has three doors and a special compartment for disabled passengers—and began putting them in operation in December 1995. The TRA also completed a computerized ticketing system linking 41 stations in June 1995. In July of the same year, the TRA implemented an automated phone ticketing system at the Taichung, Keelung 基隆, Patu 八堵, Sungshan 松山, Taipei, Wanhua 萬華, Panchiao 板橋, Chiayi 嘉義, Tainan, Kaohsiung, Ilan 宜蘭, Hualien 花蓮, and Taitung 台東 stations. This new phone system has eliminated the hours-long lines common in the past, especially during long holidays and festivals. Plans are now being made to implement this automated phone ticketing system at all 41 of the stations linked by computer. Furthermore, to allow for the operation of new trains, platforms at all stations have been raised to 86 centimeters, and all but the smallest of stations have been paved with special guiding tiles for the sight-impaired.

While recent modernization projects have definitely resulted in a higher level of service, several areas await improvements. Routing and switching is still manually accomplished along

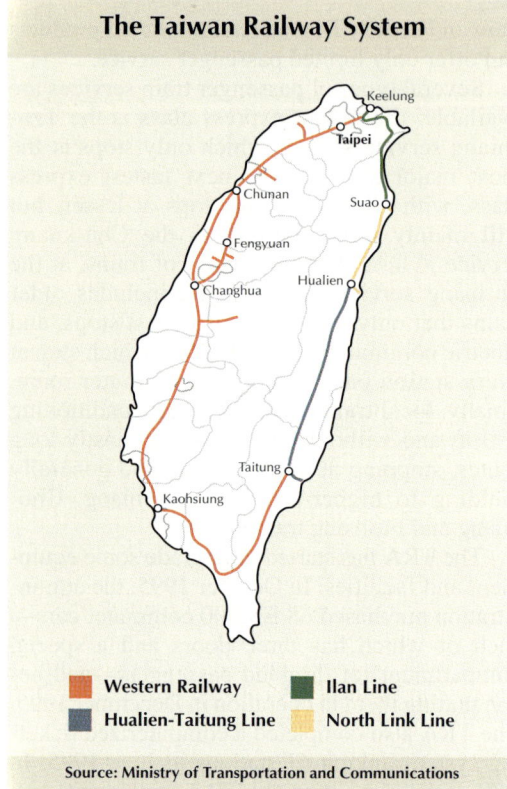

The Taiwan Railway System

Keelung

Taipei

Chunan

Suao

Fengyuan

Changhua

Hualien

Taitung

Kaohsiung

■ Western Railway   ■ Ilan Line
■ Hualien-Taitung Line   ■ North Link Line

Source: Ministry of Transportation and Communications

most of the rail network, and even at major stations, delays in arrivals or departures are often only disclosed at the last minute. The TRA is attempting to expedite commuter ticket purchases by installing additional ticket dispensing machines at major stations. However, passengers are still confronted by a confusing number of buttons to push (none are marked in English) before a ticket is issued. With the installation of such machines, the requirement that a ticket be bought before boarding is increasingly being enforced, despite often slow-moving lines at attended ticket booths and automated machines.

Nonetheless, younger station personnel are generally making an effort to serve passengers with more positive and courteous attitudes. Non-Chinese speakers almost always will find most personnel on the train and at information and ticket booths very willing to help them with scheduling questions and ticketing problems.

Round-island travel in just one day has been possible since December 1992, when the TRA completed the South Link Railway 南迴線 and finished broadening the gauge between Hualien and Taitung. Travel between Taipei near the northern tip of the island and Kaohsiung in the south takes just four-and-a-half hours by express train and six hours by regular train, with 39 round-trip services a day. At the end of 1996, a one-way ticket from Taipei to Kaohsiung by express train costs a little less than US$32. Information on current fares can be obtained by calling the Taipei Railway Information Desk 台灣鐵路局台北站服務台 (02-371-3558, 02-381-5226) or the Kaohsiung Railway Information Desk 台灣鐵路局高雄站服務台 (07-221-2376, 080-711-333).

High-speed Railway

The ROC government has already begun planning the construction of a high-speed railway (HSR) along Taiwan's western corridor. The Provisional Engineering Office of High Speed Rail 交通部高速鐵銘工程籌備處 (POHSR) under the Ministry of Transportation and Communications 交通部 (MOTC) is responsible for the planning, construction, and privatization of the project. Estimates put the cost of the project at US$16.37 billion, with a line capacity of over 300,000 passengers per day. Plans call for a 345-km line beginning in Taipei and passing through five intermediate stations—in Taoyuan 桃園, Hsinchu 新竹, Taichung, Chiayi, and Tainan—before ending in Kaohsiung. A proposal to add stations in Miaoli 苗栗, Changhua 彰化, and Yünlin 雲林 is currently under consideration.

Once completed, the HSR will be able to operate at speeds of up to 300 kilometers per hour, and it will take less than 90 minutes to go from Taipei to Kaohsiung. In April 1995, the Legislative Yuan 立法院 approved a budget of nearly US$3.23 billion for high-speed railway construction in fiscal 1996 and 1997. The *Incentive Measures for Private-sector Participation in Transportation Construction* 獎勵民間參與交通

Transportation Administration

Transportation facilities are administered by several government agencies, including the national Ministry of Transportation and Communications (MOTC), the provincial Department of Transportation 台灣省交通處, and various municipal-level agencies. Each agency has varying responsibilities depending on the type of transportation.

The MOTC has eight offices, departments, and divisions, three of which are devoted to various modes of transportation: Railways and Highways 路政司, Post and Telecommunications 郵電司, and Aviation and Navigation 航政司. Numerous other MOTC committees are responsible for making and administering policy in the transportation and communications fields. The Taiwan Provincial Government is especially active in the highway and railway portion of land transportation. Local municipal units are primarily responsible for developing adequate municipal transportation facilities but wield significant power over provincial and national transportation facilities located within their city limits.

Private sector participation can be found in many areas of transportation, but it is especially prominent in the airline, airport, and shipping sectors at this stage of development. Its influence is certain to expand as the government moves toward greater privatization and encourages increased private investment.

建設條例, which took effect in December 1994, should allow both the government and private sector to participate in the construction of the high-speed railway project.

Moving Underground in Taipei

Currently, two underground railway lines, both originating from the Taipei train station, are open to public traffic: the line westward to Wanhua (opened in 1989) and the line eastward to Sungshan train station (opened in 1994). Two additional sections have yet to be put underground: An extension from Wanhua to Panchiao, is under construction and scheduled for completion in June 1999, and a similar extension from Sungshan to Nankang 南港 is now in the integrated planning phase. An east-west expressway is being constructed over the subterranean links.

Double-Tracking

Rail travel between Changhua and Chunan 竹南 in western Taiwan follows two routes, one along the coast and the other through the mountains. Since 70 percent of the traffic takes the mountain route, bottlenecks have been created. Double tracks have already been laid between Changhua and Fengyuan 豐原, and the TRA is scheduled to finish double-tracking the Fengyuan-Chunan section by July 1998.

Upgrading Eastern Railways

Government plans to industrialize the eastern coast and to balance urban and rural development necessitate considerable improvements in the railway facilities in eastern Taiwan. An Eastern Railway Improvement Project 東部鐵路改善計畫, drawn up by the TRA and submitted through the Taiwan Provincial Government 台灣省政府, was approved by the Executive Yuan 行政院 in January 1991 and became part of the Six-Year National Development Plan. The project focuses on revamping the 337 km of railway comprising the Ilan line, the North Link line, and the Hualien-Taitung line. Construction started in July 1991 and is scheduled to be completed in June 2001 at a total cost of US$1.87 billion. Improvements will include electrification, double tracks, heavy rails, a centralized traffic control system, new locomotives and repair facilities, and the relocation of the Hualien maintenance yard.

Harbors and Shipping

Oceanic transportation is vital to the trade-oriented economy of Taiwan. As of December 1995, the ROC's shipping industry had a fleet of 245 vessels over 100 gross tons, for a total of 9.15 million dead weight tons. The ROC's fleet of cargo container ships is one of the largest in the world. In addition to two state-owned shipping corporations, Yangming Marine Transport Corporation 陽明海運公司 and Taiwan Navigation Company 臺灣航業公司, there are 111 private companies. The largest of the private operators, Evergreen Marine Corporation 長榮海運公司, now ranks as the second largest container forwarder in the world. The total freight handled by both state-owned and private corporations exceeded 123.6 million tons in 1995.

Yangming Marine Transport Corporation currently owns 31 vessels totaling 1.25 million dead weight tons. In 1995, it transported 26.38 million tons of cargo for a total of 231.87 billion nautical mile-tons. Meanwhile, the Taiwan Navigation Company's six vessels total 164,000 deadweight tons, and in 1995 they transported 16.18 million tons of cargo.

Taiwan has five international harbors—Keelung, Kaohsiung, Hualien, Taichung, and Suao 蘇澳. Waterborne imports and exports handled by these ports amounted to 141.2 million metric tons in 1995.

Kaohsiung Harbor

Kaohsiung Harbor 高雄港 handled nearly 5.1 million TEUs (Twenty-foot Equivalent Units; cargo measured in terms of standardized 20-foot long containers) in 1995, making it the third largest harbor in the world (after Hong Kong and Singapore) in terms of the volume of container cargo processed. Kaohsiung Harbor has 83 operating piers totaling 18,946 meters in length. With a water area of about 12.4 sq. km, the port can accommodate 145 ships at a time. The harbor has four container terminals, 18 container wharves, 46 gantry cranes, and 188.5 hectares of container yard. The harbor handled 80.9 million metric tons of cargo in 1995.

The government has built an 80,000-ton grain silo at Kaohsiung Harbor. A ten-year development project is underway to construct Container Terminal Number 5 第五貨櫃中心, including eight container wharves, in the Tajen Commercial Harbor Area 大仁商港區 of Kaohsiung Harbor. This project is scheduled to be completed by 1998 at an estimated cost of nearly US$420 million.

Keelung Harbor

Located near the northern tip of Taiwan, Keelung Harbor 基隆港 has 40 deep-water piers and three mooring buoys, capable of handling vessels up to the 30,000-ton class. Three container terminals with 14 berths and 24 gantry cranes have been built to accommodate 14 container ships of the 20,000-ton class. Storage capacity, including open storage, totals over 530,602 tons. The warehouses are equipped with conveyers and elevators. A 50,500-ton capacity grain silo has been outfitted with three pneumatic suckers. The container terminal consists of 14 berths with a total length of 3,235 meters. It has a 185,844-sq. meter marshalling yard, which can accommodate 8,374 TEUs. The government is now designing a new port and reconstructing container wharves in this natural harbor. More than 30.5 million tons of imports and exports passed through Keelung Harbor in 1995.

Taichung Harbor

Taichung Harbor 台中港 is a man-made port located on Taiwan's central west coast. In addition to meeting the shipping and fishery needs of central Taiwan, Taichung Harbor was also designed to share the shipping traffic burden of the heavily-used Keelung and Kaohsiung ports. Taichung Harbor currently has an annual cargo-handling capacity of 39.8 million revenue tons. With navigation lanes as deep as 13 meters below low-tide water level, Taichung Harbor can accommodate ships of the 60,000-ton class.

At present, 33 deep-water wharves have been completed: five for containers, 15 for general cargo, two for bulk cargo, four for liquid cargo, three for cement, two for grain, and two for coal. The warehousing facilities include 14 transit sheds, two grain silos, 20 cement silos, nine storage areas, five container yards, and 224 liquid cargo storage tanks. Taichung Harbor handled more than 36 million tons in 1995. Stevedoring and warehousing operations at the terminals equipped with automated facilities are open to investment by private firms.

Hualien Harbor

Located on Taiwan's east coast, Hualien Harbor 花蓮港 is a relatively small port with 25 deep-water berths totaling 4,742 meters in length. With the completion of the fourth extension in 1991, Hualien Harbor is capable of simultaneously berthing one 100,000-ton class vessel in a special terminal for unloading coal, six 60,000-ton ships, two 30,000-ton ships, fourteen 5,000- to 15,000-ton ships, and two ships under 5,000 tons. It has 504-meters of shallow-water wharves that are capable of accommodating fishing boats and other small vessels. In 1995, the harbor handled 9.5 million tons of cargo.

Suao Harbor

Suao Harbor 蘇澳港 is situated on the northeastern coast of Taiwan. The total water area of the harbor is about 1.7 sq. km. Currently, the harbor has 13 deep-water berths with an annual capacity of 11.2 million tons. In 1995, imports and exports passing through Suao Harbor totaled over 5.4 million metric tons.

Civil Aviation

As of 1995, a total of 53 airlines were providing flight services to destinations in the ROC. Of these, 35 foreign carriers and four ROC-based airlines (EVA Airways, Mandarin Airlines, China Airlines, and Transasia Airways) operate scheduled international flights into Taiwan. UNI Airways Corporation and Far Eastern Air Transport—also ROC-based carriers—offer international charter services. As for domestic air travel, there are ten companies running domestic passenger flights in the ROC.

There are currently two international airports in the Taiwan area: Chiang Kai-shek International Airport 中正國際機場 at Taoyuan in northern Taiwan, and Kaohsiung International Airport 高雄國際機場 in the south. In addition, there are several domestic airports: in Taipei, Hualien, Taitung, Taichung, Tainan, Chiayi, P'ingtung 屏東, Makung 馬公, Ch'imei 七美, Orchid Island 蘭嶼, Green Island 綠島, Wangan 望安, Quemoy 金門, and Peikan 北竿. As it is estimated that over the next

ROC Domestic Airlines

Asia Pacific Airlines 亞太航空公司
China Airlines 中華航空公司*
Chung Hsing Airlines 中興航空公司
Daily Air 德安航空公司
Emerald Pacific Airlines 凌天航空公司
EVA Airways 長榮航空公司*
Far Eastern Air Transport 遠東航空公司*
Formosa Airlines 國華航空公司*
Golden Eagle Airlines 金鷹航空公司
Great China Airlines 大華航空公司*
Mandarin Airlines 華信航空公司*
Taipei Airlines 台北航空公司
Taiwan Airlines 台灣航空公司*
Tapeng Airlines 大鵬航空公司
Transasia Airways 復興航空公司*
U-Land Airlines 瑞聯航空公司*
UNI Airways Corporation 立榮航空公司*

*passenger service

five years domestic air traffic will grow by over 10 percent annually, work is currently under way to expand capacity. Expansion of airport facilities and the addition of navigational equipment have been carried out at the Tainan, Hualien, Chiayi, Orchid Island, and Green Island airports. Also being planned are new airports at Quemoy, Hengchun 恆春, and Hsinchu 新竹; an expansion at P'ingtung; and a new domestic terminal at the CKS airport. In 1995, night flights were opened at the Taipei, Taichung, Chiayi, Tainan, Hualien, Taitung, Makung and P'ingtung airports.

It is not just domestic air traffic that is growing rapidly. The number of inbound and outbound international passengers exceeded 44 million in 1995, up more than 18 percent over the 1994 figure of 37 million. The amount of air freight handled also increased, from around 880,000 tons in 1994 to more than 1.1 million tons in 1995. In addition to passengers and cargo, the number of flights also grew by more than 97,000 to total over 633,000 in 1995.

To accommodate this heavier air passenger and cargo traffic, a US$800 million expansion project at the Chiang Kai-shek International Airport was

International Airlines Serving Taiwan

Airasia SDN BHD*
Air Charter*
Air Macau*
Air Micronesia*
Air New Zealand*
Air Nippon*
American International Airways
Ansett Australia*
Australia Asia Airlines*
British Asia Airlines*
Canadian Airlines*
Cargolux Airlines
Cathay Pacific Airways*
China Airlines*
Continental Micronesia*
Dragon Air*
EVA Airways*
Far Eastern Air Transport Corp.
Federal Express Airways
Garuda Indonesian Airways*
Grand International Airways*
Great China Airlines
Japan Asia Airways*

KLM Royal Dutch Airlines*
Malaysian Airlines*
Mandarin Airlines*
Martinair Holland
Northwest Airlines*
Pacific Airlines*
Pacific East Asia Cargo Airlines
Philippine Airlines*
Polar Air
Royal Brunei Airways*
Saudi Arabia Airlines
Sempati Air*
Singapore Airlines*
South African Airways*
Swiss Air*
Thai Airways*
Tower Air
Transasia Airways*
UNI Airways Corporation
United Airlines*
United Parcel Service
Viet Air*

*Scheduled passenger service

begun in 1989. The project includes a second passenger terminal, aircraft parking bays, airport connection roads, car parks and the expansion of air freight facilities. It is scheduled for completion in June 1999. The planned facilities are designed to allow the airport to handle an additional 14 million passengers annually by the year 2010.

In addition to work at the CKS airport, a new passenger terminal and an air cargo terminal complex will be constructed at the Kaohsiung International Airport. The new facilities will include a new international terminal building, aircraft parking hangars, a cargo terminal and maintenance areas. The two projects, which together will cost US$375 million, are scheduled for completion in December 1996 and December 1997, respectively. The project is designed to increase capacity at the airport by 4.83 million international passengers and 200,000 tons of international air freight per year by 2005.

ROC authorities have been working to open up additional routes for ROC carriers operating international air services. During 1995, the ROC signed agreements on air traffic rights with Italy, Switzerland, Belgium, Costa Rica, Abu Dhabi and Macau, as well as revised or renewed agreements with Indonesia, Singapore, Malaysia, Vietnam, Thailand and the Netherlands. As a result, China Airlines began flying new routes to Italy and Switzerland, while EVA Airways started offering flights to Amsterdam as the second designated carrier of the ROC. Direct flights between Taiwan and Macau were inaugurated by EVA Airways, Transasia Airways and Air Macau respectively in December 1995. The ROC also plans to pursue aviation accords with Spain, Turkey, Poland, India and other countries with market potential. As of the end of December 1995, the ROC had obtained air traffic rights from 34 countries and areas.

Highways and Freeways

Highway traffic, both in terms of passengers and cargo, was down in 1995. Traveling on Taiwan's 20,200 km of highways were a total of 1.22 billion passengers, or roughly 87 million less than in 1994. Passenger-kilometers fell 9.99 percent to 19.74 billion, and the 292 million tons of freight carried on highways in 1995 represented a 6.83 percent decrease from the previous year. Although these figures may give the impression of an improving traffic situation, the opposite is generally true. With more than 13.4 million vehicles and 21.3 million people packed on Taiwan, major highways are often congested, particularly during weekends and long holidays. The sections below describe existing highways and discuss new and future projects aimed at making highway travel faster and more convenient.

Sun Yat-sen Freeway

Inaugurated in 1978, the Sun Yat-sen Freeway 中山高速公路 (also called the North-South Freeway) was the ROC's first national freeway. The 373-km long route connects Kaohsiung in the south with Taipei in the north, and then continues northward to its terminus in Keelung. The freeway is still the island's primary north-south thoroughfare, and the rapid rate at which the traffic load has grown since the opening of the freeway has taken its toll both in terms of congestion and wear and tear. Thus a number of recent transportation projects and plans focus on ensuring that the Sun Yat-sen Freeway remains a safe and efficent road.

To relieve congestion along the section of the freeway running through Taipei, two 21-km long viaducts are being constructed to run parallel along both sides of the Sun Yat-sen Freeway from the Hsichih 汐止 interchange in the north to the Wuku 五股 interchange in the south. The southernmost 7.5 kilometers were opened to traffic in June 1996, and the middle seven kilometers were opened in August of the same year. The final 6.5-km section ending in Hsichih is scheduled to be completed in June 1997.

Several sections of the freeway running through northern and central Taiwan are becoming congested, and bottlenecks have developed. A 27.6-km long section of the four-lane freeway running from Yangmei 楊梅 in the north to Hsinchu in the south is one such stretch. A lane will thus be added on each side, and interchanges, toll stations and service areas will be improved. Bidding began in March 1996, and the project is scheduled to be completed at the end of 1998 at a cost of US$162 million. Another heavily used section of the freeway is the 112 kilometers from Hsinchu in the north to Yuanlin 員林 in the south. One lane is therefore being added on each side. The US$995 million project, which began in November 1994, is scheduled to be completed in June 1998.

The Sun Yat-sen Freeway is also becoming saturated in southern Taiwan, and preliminary plans have already been drawn up to widen the section between Yuanlin and Kaohsiung. The US$1.27 billion project will begin at the Yuanlin interchange in the north and run 158 kilometers to the Wuchia interchange 五甲交流道 in Kaohsiung in the south. One lane will be added to each side of the freeway, and two lanes are under consideration for a 4.3-km stretch running through the Kaohsiung metropolitan area. For some sections, bidding and construction will start as early as the beginning of 1997.

Taiwan Highway Classifications

Highways in Taiwan are classified according to what level of government has jurisdiction over them. Thus, highways are either national 國道, provincial 省道, county 縣道, township 鄉道, city 市道, or special highways 專用公路. There are six different kinds of highways: the freeway 高速公路, the round-the-island highway 環島公路, the cross-island highway 橫貫公路, the longitudinal highway 縱貫公路, the coastal highway 濱海公路, and the connecting highway 聯絡公路. The Taiwan Highway Bureau 台灣省交通處公路局 under the Taiwan Provincial government's Department of Transportation is responsible for the construction and maintenance of Taiwan's highway system.

Taiwan Highway Network

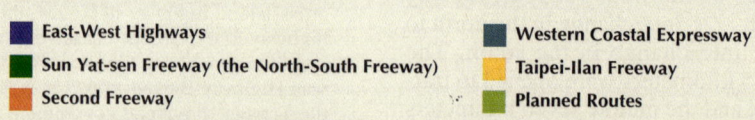

■ East-West Highways   ■ Western Coastal Expressway
■ Sun Yat-sen Freeway (the North-South Freeway)   ■ Taipei-Ilan Freeway
■ Second Freeway   ■ Planned Routes

Source: Ministry of Transportation and Communications

The volume of traffic on the Sun Yat-sen Freeway has grown by an average 11 percent annually since its opening. This heavy traffic load, coupled with a hot tropical climate, abundant rainfall, and overloaded trucks and trailers, causes considerable wear on the freeway's surface. To maintain the quality of the road, the first five-year road surface repair project was initiated in 1982. The second five-year project was formulated in May 1990 and was undertaken beginning in fiscal year 1992. The project's FY1995 budget stood at US$15.4 million.

In addition to expansion and maintenance projects, some major repair work has also been undertaken. The Sino-Saudi Arabian Bridge 中沙大橋 carries the Sun Yat-sen Freeway across central Taiwan's Choshui River 濁水溪. The river bed has subsided over the years due to excessive removal of gravel and flooding following typhoons. Pier protection and the stabilization of the river bed have thus become paramount concerns. As part of the project, a 2,300-meter submerged weir is being built and is expected to be completed by the end of 1996 at an estimated cost of US$27.78 million.

New Freeways

The Sun Yat-sen Freeway is particularly congested along the northern section. Statistics show that in the past the freeway handled more than 70 percent of the traffic between Keelung and Hsinchu. This heavy traffic load has since been somewhat alleviated by the construction of the Northern Second Freeway 北部第二高速公路. With a planned total length of 117 km including connecting roads, this new freeway is being constructed to connect with the Sun Yat-sen Freeway at Hsichih, extend southward, and rejoin the Sun Yat-sen Freeway at Hsinchu.

US$6 billion has been budgeted to construct the Northern Second Freeway. In August 1993, the southern 65 km between Chungho 中和 and Hsinchu were opened for traffic, and the opening of the northernmost section running between Hsichih and Mucha 木柵 followed in March 1996. The final middle section, which will link Mucha to Chungho, will be completed in mid-1997. While the construction of the

Northern Second Freeway will undoubtedly improve the regional traffic situation, the joining of the freeway with the Sun Yat-sen Freeway at Hsinchu has created a bottleneck. The MOTC therefore extended the northern section of the Second Freeway southward to Chunan 竹南, and this section was opened to traffic in February 1996. The Taipei Connection Route 台北聯絡道, which serves to link metropolitan Taipei with the Second Freeway was completed and opened to traffic in March 1996.

To facilitate traffic flow in Central Taiwan, a central section of the Second Freeway 中部第二高速公路 has now been mapped out along the coastline. It will connect with the northern section at Chunan and run southward to Nant'ou County 南投縣. If financial problems can be solved, it will be completed in 2003 at the earliest.

Construction of a Taipei-Ilan Freeway 北宜高速公路 commenced in July 1991. Beginning at Nankang 南港 with a tunnel to the picturesque Ilan, the freeway is scheduled for completion by the middle of 2003, when a three-hour drive from Taipei to Ilan should only take 40 minutes. In addition, a new east-west expressway in Taipei City is slated for completion in June of 1998.

The Ministry of Transportation and Communications is planning to expand the Western Coastal Expressway 西部濱海快速公路 currently under construction by building 12 additional east-west highways 東西向快速道路 that will connect the expressway with local transportation systems. Two of the 12 east-west lines, the northernmost and southernmost, will not link directly with the Western Coastal Expressway, but will instead hook into the larger highway network and provide express

Traffic Control

Traffic control is the joint responsibility of the Traffic Division of the National Police Administration 內政部警政署交通組, the Highway Police Bureau 公路警察局, the Taiwan Provincial Highway Police Corps 公路警察大隊, and all local police departments. The Airborne Squadron 空中警察隊 assists when necessary.

east-west routes in their respective localities. The 12 projected links, from north to south, are Wanli 萬里 to Juipin 瑞濱, Pali 八里 to Hsintien 新店, Kuanyin 觀音 to Tahsi 大溪, Nanliao 南寮 to Chutung 竹東, Houlung 後龍 to Wenshui 汶水, Changpin 彰濱 to Taichung, Hanpao 漢寶 to Ts'aot'un 草屯, T'aihsi 台西 to Kuk'eng 古坑, Chiayi to Tungshih 東石, Peimen 北門 to Yüching 玉井, Tainan to Kuanmiao 關廟, and Kaohsiung to Ch'aochou 潮州.

Freeway Traffic Control

During holidays, the volume of traffic is generally between 30 and 50 percent above normal traffic loads. Accordingly, the Taiwan Area National Freeway Bureau (TANFB) under the Ministry of Transportation and Communication 交通部台灣區國道高速公路局 has adopted a ramp metering control system 匝道儀控管制系統 to maintain an acceptable flow of traffic. This system was introduced on four national holidays in 1993, and as it proved fairly effective, the TANFB gradually extended the system to include long holidays, weekends and normal weekdays. The TANFB has also decided to implement a fully automated ramp metering control system over the entire 380-km length of the Sun Yat-sen National Freeway and the link to the CKS International Airport. The system is expected to be completed in early 1997 at an estimated cost of US$14.1 million.

To increase the effectiveness of the ramp metering control system and smooth the flow of traffic on the freeway during long holidays, High

Taipei Taxi Cabs

At the end of 1995, there were over 46,600 registered taxi cabs cruising the streets of Taipei City. Of these, almost 26,000 were operated by a total of 1,438 taxi companies. On top of this were another 10,000 individually-owned and operated taxis, 5,500 radio-dispatch taxis, and 5,116 cabs associated with but not operated by taxi companies.

The last fare increase approved by the Taipei City Government in October 1995 involves adding an NT$15 (US$0.55) surcharge to the old base fare of NT$50, making the effective base fare NT$65, or about US$2.40. Since this increase did not involve a recalibration of taxi meters (i.e., the other factors affecting the fare were not changed), the fare taxi passengers should pay at the end of a ride is always NT$15 higher than the total indicated on the meter.

Many major hotels now record the number of the taxicab on a card for their guests. This ensures that should there be any problem with the trip, the passenger has meaningful information to report to the passenger hotline listed below.

Effective Taipei Taxi Fares (with surcharge figured in the base rate) as of October 3, 1995

	Daytime (6 A.M.–11 P.M.)	Nighttime (11 P.M.–6 A.M.)
Base fare	NT$65 (1,650 meters)	NT$65 (1,375 meters)
Distance Increment	NT$5 (350 m)	NT$5 (290 m)
Time Increment	NT$5 every 3 min. under 5 km/hr.	NT$5 every 2.5 min. under 5 km/hr.

Regular additions to total fare:
    NT$10 for a dispatched cab
    NT$10 for luggage placed in the taxi trunk.
The nighttime fare is charged all day during the Chinese New Year's holiday.

Complaints about Taxi Service

Passenger Hotline—Taipei City Police Headquarters 台北市警察局 394-9007
Bureau of Transportation 台北市交通局 725-6888
Office of Motor Vehicle Inspection 台北市監理處 767-8217

Islandwide Parking Problem

The number of motorcycles and cars has continued to soar in recent years as strong overall economic growth and rising personal incomes have made the purchase of motor vehicles commonplace. By 1995, there were 13.2 million motor vehicles in the Taiwan area, a little less than 3.8 million of which were passenger cars. By way of comparison, there were only 7.95 million vehicles and 830,000 passenger cars ten years ago. With such skyrocketing growth, parking is already a problem, and it will become increasingly serious in the near future. Accordingly, the MOTC has recommended in its revision of the *Highway Law* 公路法 (which has been submitted to the Legislature 立法院 for approval) that every car buyer should be required to have a personal parking space. Even so, alleviating the serious shortage of parking spaces in the ROC will take time.

Government construction of over 90 public parking lots with a total of more than 24,000 parking spaces, at an expense equivalent to US$146 million, was expected to be completed by the end of 1996. A five-year (1995-1999) public parking lot construction plan 政府興建公共停車場五年投資計畫 calls for adding just under 360 parking lots during the time period in question, thereby generating nearly 104,000 new parking spaces, by providing central government matching grants for funds appropriated by the pertinent local government for each project. The central government share will amount to US$94.1 million, while the total cost of the project is estimated at roughly US$2.44 billion.

Occupancy Vehicle Control 高乘載車輛專用通行時段管制 has been in force since the 1995 Chinese New Year holiday. The system involves allocating different time slots during which vehicles of various carrying capacities are allowed onto freeways. High occupancy vehicles (HOV), such as buses and cars carrying at least four people, are given priority. As a result, congestion on the freeways during holidays has been reduced.

Toll differentials have also employed on a trial basis to encourage the public to take buses or share vehicles. HOV lanes, which are toll free, were designated for buses and vehicles carrying at least four people, whereas all autos and trucks carrying only a single person must pay double the standard toll. The system was implemented twice: once during the Dragon Boat Festival 端午節 on June 2, 1995, from 7:00 A.M. to 2:00 P.M. and June 4, 1995, from 12:00 P.M. to 7:00 P.M., and a second time during the New Year holiday on December 30, 1995 and January 2, 1996 from 12:00 P.M. to 7:00 P.M. However, due to impracticalities related to having to determine the number of people in each vehicle, this program has been suspended indefinitely.

Tolls

There are ten toll stations along the Sun Yat-sen Freeway and two on the Northern Second Freeway. Standard tolls are NT$40 (US$1.48) for cars, NT$50 (US$1.85) for buses and small trucks, and NT$65 (US$2.41) for trailer trucks. The number of vehicles passing through toll stations in 1995 grew by 4.98 percent, pushing toll revenues up 4.28 percent to US$578.9 million for the same year.

To help vehicles pass through quickly, there are "No Change" toll lanes at every toll station. Drivers are also encouraged to use coupons which can be conveniently purchased at post offices, gas and toll stations, rest areas, the Land Bank of Taiwan 台灣土地銀行, and the Medium Business Bank of Taiwan 台灣中小企業銀行.

Telephone Service System

An automated telephone system, which provides round-the-clock freeway information, has been in operation since November 1995. Drivers can access this information by calling (02) 297-5063, (02) 297-5064, or (02) 909-6141 at extension 552 or 553. There are also roadside emergency telephones set up one kilometer apart on each side of the freeway.

Traffic Accidents

Traffic accident figures for 1995 revealed both good news and bad news. The good news is that the total number of accidents was down. In 1995, there were 261 accidents on the ROC's freeways, which resulted in 192 deaths and 338 serious injuries, slightly less than in 1994. As for accidents on roads other than freeways, police handled a total of 3,528 in 1995. Although this figure represents a 2.08-percent decrease from 1994, these accidents nevertheless claimed 3,065 lives and left 2,933 injured.

The bad news is that despite the falling numbers of accidents, deaths, and injuries, roads in the ROC remain more dangerous than those in many advanced nations. Statistics compiled by the Executive Yuan's Department of Health 行政院衛生署 show that every year in the Taiwan area, 54.9 persons out of every 100,000 are killed in motorcycle and auto accidents. This rate lies above those recorded in Japan, the USA, England, France, Germany, Sweden, Hong Kong and Singapore.

Reckless driving and tailgating continued to be the major causes of accidents on the freeways, together accounting for over 51 percent of the total. As for the roads, the Car Accident Appraisal Committee 車輛行車事故鑑定委員會 listed the top five causes of accidents as speeding, drunken driving, illegal parking, illegal left turns, and careless driving.

Urban Traffic

Traffic in Taiwan's major cities is very congested. Urban planners in all of Taiwan's metropolitan areas must cope with a similar set of challenges: a soaring number of new motorcycles and cars, a limited number of streets, and the complexities of acquiring very scarce space for improvements. Fortunately, countermeasures such as the mass rapid transit systems and swift and convenient bus services are finally on the way.

Taipei's Traffic Challenge

Traffic in Taipei City and the greater Taipei metropolitan area is considered the worst among Taiwan's major cities. Growing numbers of private cars and numerous construction projects are placing an increasingly intolerable burden on Taipei's already clogged streets. Competing for lane space in 1995 with the estimated 617,000 automobiles operating in Taipei were approximately 735,000 motorcycles and scooters. An average of 5,460 additional automobiles and motor scooters take to Taipei's streets each month. Added to this are the public bus fleets operated by the Taipei City Bus Administration 台北市公共汽車管理處 and nine private bus companies.

To encourage increased use of public bus lines, the Taipei City Government has reserved certain lanes along sections of eight major metropolitan thoroughfares exclusively for use by authorized public buses, and has widened lane dividers and constructed bus stop shelters for those awaiting buses. Although the lanes are generally strictly reserved for city buses, the city government has agreed to accept applications to allow commuter buses owned by schools, businesses, and other organizations to use such lanes provided such vehicles have at least a 20-person seating capacity.

Taipei Rapid Transit

Preparations for the Taipei Rapid Transit Systems 台北大眾捷運系統 (TRTS) got under way back in early 1986, when the Executive Yuan 行政院 completed preliminary plans for the network and approved their implementation. The systems, comprising five lines with a total length of 88 km, are scheduled to be completed by 2005 at a cost of US$18 billion. French contractor MATRA started work on the first TRTS line—the Mucha Line—in July 1988. The Mucha Line began revenue service on March 28, 1996.

These mass transit systems were initially designed to alleviate urban traffic in downtown Taipei and to encourage people to move from the metropolitan area to the outlying areas. Not unexpectedly, property values along the five routes have skyrocketed. Housing prices have more than tripled in the suburbs of Mucha, Peit'ou, and Nankang since 1987, when the Taipei City Government formally established the Department of Rapid Transit Systems 台北市政府捷運工程局 (DORTS) to begin construction.

Taipei Rapid Transit Systems Lines (2005 Completion)

Tamsui Line 淡水線
Runs on surface, elevated and underground tracks from Tamsui to the Taipei Railway Station 台北車站, passing Peitou 北投, Shilin 士林, and Yuanshan 圓山—22.8 km, 20 stations, Mass Rapid Transit (MRT)

Hsintien Line 新店線
From the terminus of the Tamsui Line at the Taipei Railway Station, runs underground along Roosevelt Road 羅斯福路 and Peihsin Road 北新路 to Hsintien—10.3 km, 11 stations, MRT

Mucha Line 木柵線
Runs on elevated tracks from the Taipei City Zoo 台北市立動物園 in Mucha to the intersection of Hoping East Road 和平東路 and Fuhsing South South Road 復興南路, and then along Fuhsing South Road to Minchuan East Road 民權東路—10.9 km, 12 stations, Medium Capacity Transit (MCT)
An extension route runs from the Minchuan East Road terminus through Sungshan Airport 松山飛機場 to Nankang—13.1 km, 11 stations, MCT

Nankang Line 南港線
Runs underground along Chunghsiao (E. and W.) Road 忠孝東西路 from Nankang Railway Station 南港車站 to Chunghua Road 中華路, and then on to Hsimen Station 西門站—11.5 km, 12 stations, MRT

Panchiao Line 板橋線
Runs underground from the terminus of the Nankang Line at Hsimen Station to Hoping W. Road, then under the Hsintien River 新店溪 to Panchiao—12.4 km, 9 stations, MRT

Chungho Line 中和線
Runs underground from Chungho and Yungho 永和 roads under the Hsintien River to join the Hsintien Line at Kuting Station 古亭站—5.4 km, 4 stations, MRT

Maintenance Link 維護軌
Runs underground from Hsimen to the Chiang Kai-shek Memorial Hall 中正紀念堂 and provides a route for Nankang- and Panchiao-line cars to reach the Peitou depot—1.6km, 1 station, MRT

The TRTS lines all share the common feature of being able to transport a large number of passengers. With the exception of the Mucha Line, which runs four-car trains, all lines will operate six-car trains, giving each train a maximum capacity of 2,200 passengers. Hourly capacity will thus vary between 20,000 and 60,000 people per direction per hour, depending on the frequency of trains. In the case of the already-operating Mucha Line, the automatically guided trains currently have a carrying capacity of 10,000 to 20,000 passengers per direction an hour, and if trains were six cars long, the line would be able to transport roughly 30,000 passengers an hour. The frequency of trains on present and future lines can be controlled to account for heavy-use periods, but service is fast regardless of the time of day, with trains pulling into stations every one to ten minutes. Train speeds range from 25 to 80 kilometers per hour, and the distance between stations varies from between 800 and 1,000 meters downtown to between 1,000 and 2,000 meters in the suburbs.

Rapid Transit in Other Cities

Following Taipei's lead, many other cities in Taiwan, including Kaohsiung, Taichung, Tainan, and Taoyuan, began making plans for their own metropolitan rail transit systems. A feasibility study for a rapid transit system in Hsinchu has also been undertaken. However, the only project to have made it past the planning stage so far is Kaohsiung's.

Kaohsiung City is Taiwan's largest harbor and second-largest city. Rapid industrial devel-

Taipei Rapid Transit Systems

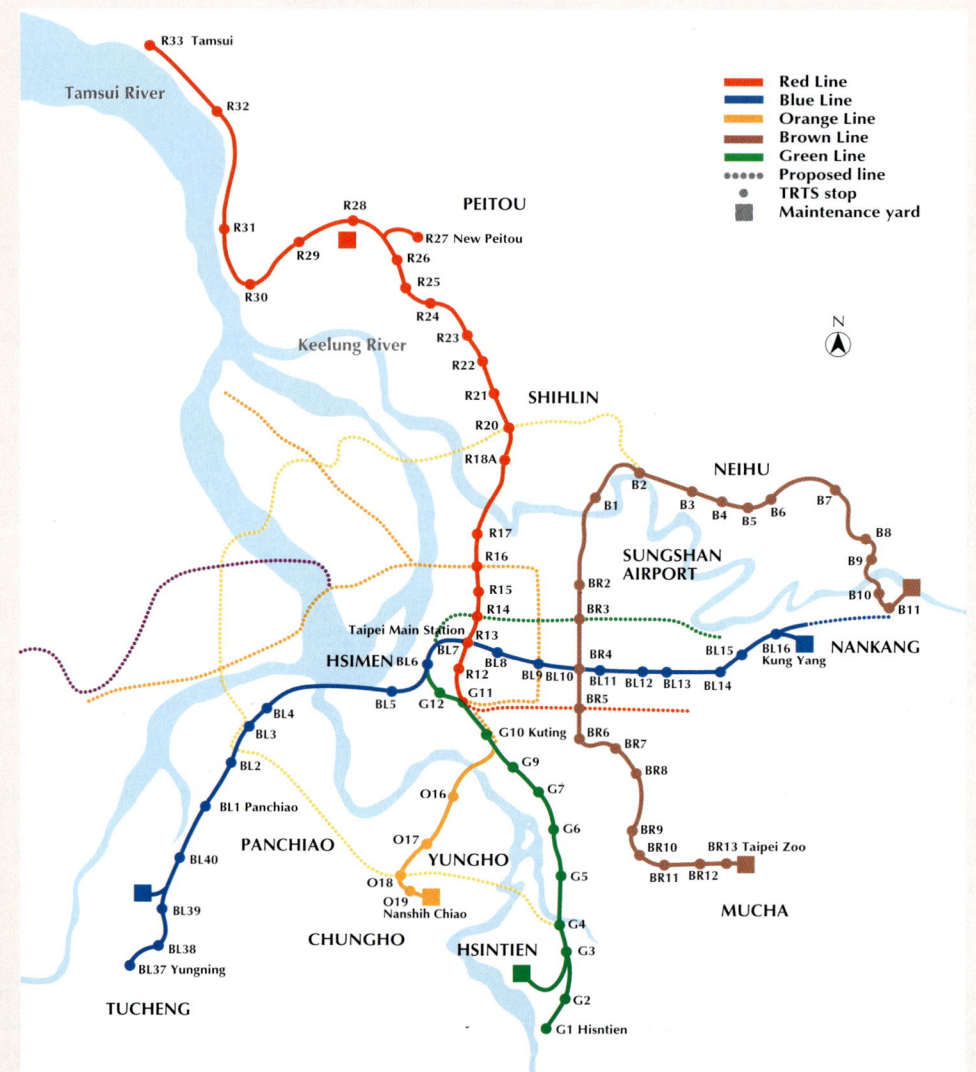

Legend:
- ▬ Red Line
- ▬ Blue Line
- ▬ Orange Line
- ▬ Brown Line
- ▬ Green Line
- ••••• Proposed line
- • TRTS stop
- ■ Maintenance yard

Red Line
R12 NTU Hospital
R13 Taipei Main Station
R14 Chungshan
R15 Shuanglien
R16 Minchuan W. Rd.
R17 Yuanshan
R18A Chientan
R20 Shihlin
R21 Chihshan
R22 Mingte
R23 Shihpai
R24 Chili An
R25 Chiyen
R26 Peitou
R27 Hsin Peitou
R28 Fuhsing Kang
R29 Chungyi
R30 Kuandu
R31 Chuwei
R32 Hung Shulin
R33 Tamsui

Blue Line
BL37 Yungning
BL38 Tucheng
BL39 Haishan
BL40 Nantzu
BL1 Panchiao
BL2 Hansheng Rd.
BL3 Hsinpu
BL4 Chiangtzu Tsui
BL5 Lungshan Temple
BL6 Hsimen
BL7 Taipei Main Station
BL8 Shantao Temple
BL9 Chunghsiao Hsinsheng
BL10 Chunghsiao Fuhsing
BL11 Chunghsiao Tunhua
BL12 Sun Yat-sen Memorial Hall

BL13 Taipei City Hall
BL14 Sungshan
BL15 Houshan Pi
BL16 Kunyang
BL17 Nankang

Orange Line
O16 Tinghsi
O17 Yung-an Market
O18 Ching-an
O19 Nanshih Chiao

Brown Line
BR2 Chungshan Middle School
BR3 Nanking E. Rd.
BR4 Chunghsiao Fuhsing
BR5 Ta-an
BR6 Technology Building
BR7 Liuchang Li
BR8 Linkuang

BR9 Hsinhai
BR10 Wanfang Hospital
BR11 Wanfang Community
BR12 Mucha
BR13 Taipei Zoo

Green Line
G1 Hisntien
G2 Hsintien City Hall
G3 Chichang
G4 Ta Pinglin
G5 Chingmei
G6 Wanlung
G7 Kungkuan
G9 Taipower Building
G10 Kuting
G11 CKS Memorial Hall
G12 Hsiao Nanmen

*The section of Brown Line from station B1 to station B11 has yet to receive final approval.
Source: Department of Rapid Transit Systems, Taipei City Government.

opment and population growth have accentuated the need for efficient metropolitan transportation. The Kaohsiung City Government 高雄市政府 has accordingly mapped out the Kaohsiung Metropolitan Area Mass Rapid Transit System Development Plan (First Term) 高雄都會區大眾捷運系統第一期發展計畫, which was passed by the Executive Yuan in January 1991. The Kaohsiung system is being designed to integrate the high-speed and regular railway and city bus systems, and thus provide a comprehensive mass transportation network.

Already finalized plans call for the construction of a Red Line and an Orange Line—with 37 stations and a total length of 42.7 km—at an estimated cost of US$7.6 billion. Two additional lines and extensions to the Red and Orange lines are currently in the planning stage. Although according to the original project schedule, bidding for the construction of the Orange Line was to have taken place in 1996, the Kaohsiung City Council 高雄市議會 has cut funding for the system two years in a row, putting the entire project behind schedule.

From a family bakery making delicious cakes to a world-famous corporation producing various succulent and high-quality pastries, Kuo Yuan Ye Foods Co., Ltd. has created a legend in Taiwan's pastry history. Whenever you bite a Kuo Yuan Ye cake, you will experience the change in bakery over the past one hundred years on the island.

The spokesman of Taiwan pastry tastes and treats: The 130-year-old Kuo Yuan Ye Foods Co., Ltd.

Stop by Kuo Yuan Ye to start enjoying Taiwan's sumptuous cakes and biscuits. Over the past one century, the Kuo Yuan Ye flavor has rooted in people's minds and spread the local specialty outward into the world community. The Hereditary Pastry Shop, Kuo Yuan Ye, is a good representative reflecting the growth and development of Taiwan through perfecting baking materials and techniques to provide people in Taiwan with healthy and good-taste pastries. Besides, Kuo Yuan Ye cherishes nature and our living environment. We hope all people in Taiwan, both the natives or the offspring of mainland immigrants, to hold the same attitude to strive hard for the better future of our country.

郭元益食品股份有限公司
KUO YUAN YE FOODS CO., LTD.

Head Office: 99, MEI DER ST., SHIN LIN, TAIPEI, TAIWAN, R.O.C.
TEL: 886-2-838-2700, 886-2-834-5211
Special Customers Service Line:
TEL: 886-2-832-2069

The National Health Insurance

has been implemented
in Taiwan, R.O.C. since March 1, 1995.
Foreigners legally employed
in Taiwan may also join
the NHI program.

For further information please call:

886-02-7029959

BUREAU OF NATIONAL HEALTH INSURANCE
DEPARTMENT OF HEALTH

No.140, Sec, 3, Hsin-Yi Road, Taipei, Taiwan, R.O.C.
FAX: 886-02-7025834 http://www.nhi.gov.tw

15.
Public Health

Previous page: Health authorities at the local government level conduct the inspection, sampling, and testing of foodstuffs and sanitation throughout the Taiwan area.

Right: The often high hospitalization expenses incurred with prematurely born babies are now cushioned by the ROC National Health Insurance program.

Below: The Department of Health had a contractual agreement with over 1,000 community pharmacies in 1995, stipulating that they would adhere to "Good Dispensing Practice."

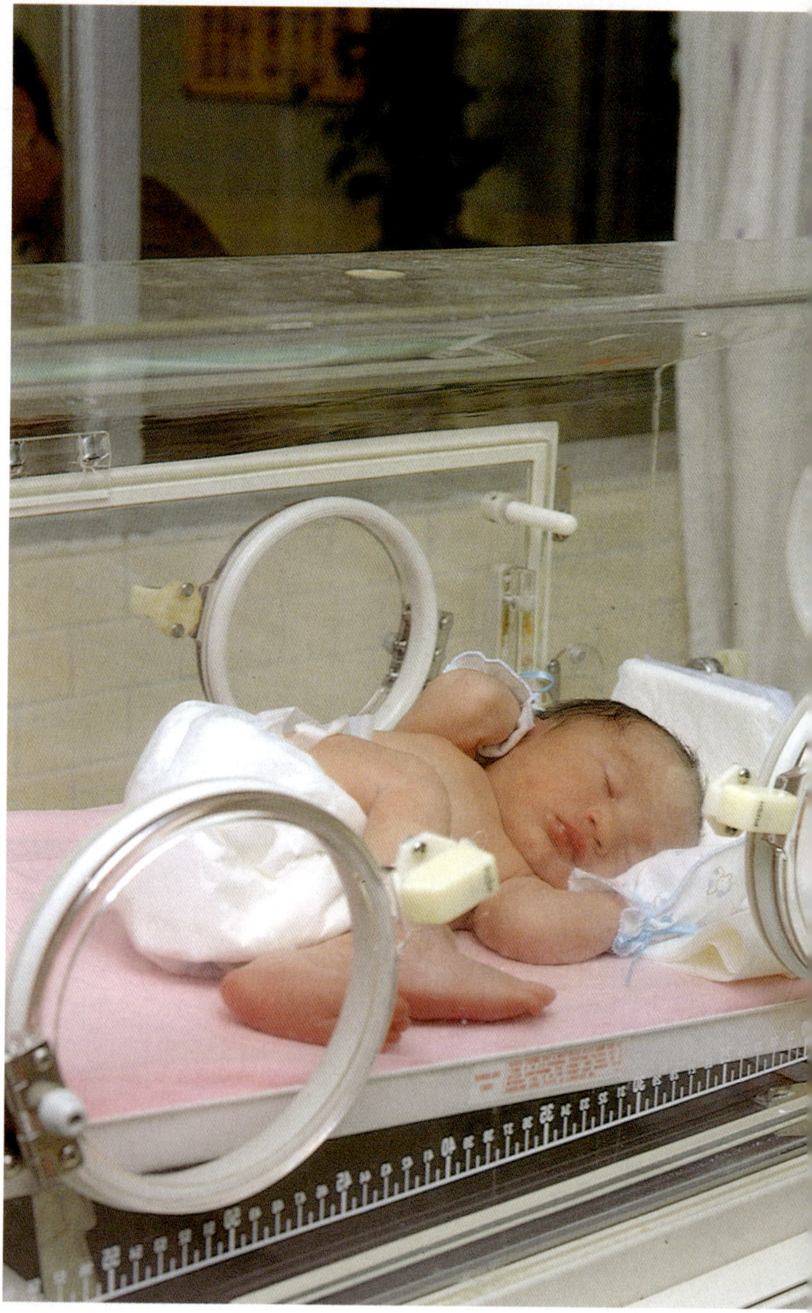

15 Public Health

Shifting demographic patterns and changes in modern lifestyles have modified health care in Taiwan. The graying of the population has highlighted pension issues and long-term care for the elderly. A recent influx of foreign laborers has exacerbated the problem of providing health care for foreign workers. Serious pollution and smoking problems have triggered a high rate of lung cancer, especially in the urban areas of Taipei, Kaohsiung, Keelung 基隆, and Tainan. Industrial development and growth in urban traffic have resulted in an alarming rate of occupational and traffic accidents. In 1995, a total of 12,983 fatal accidents were recorded, with transportation-related fatalities constituting the leading cause of death for people under the age of 44. Accidental falls were the second leading cause for those aged over 45. An unprecedented number of students are using amphetamines. Health authorities are also concerned about the sanitation standards of Taiwan's many unregulated eateries, roadside stalls, box lunch caterers, and galleries of food vendors. According to Chang Po-ya 張博雅, director-general of the Department of Health 衛生署 (DOH), future policy is seeking to further enlarge the National Health Insurance 全民健康保險 (NHI) program to include all residents of the ROC. By mid-1996, more than 93 percent of the 21 million people in the Taiwan area were insured.

The health of ROC citizens has greatly improved. Just 40 years ago, acute infectious diseases were the number one killer in the Taiwan area. Today they are no longer among the top ten causes of death in Taiwan. Bubonic plague, smallpox, and cholera were eradicated long ago. Not a single case of rabies has been discovered since 1959. In 1965, the World Health Organization of the United Nations declared malaria non-existent in Taiwan. Other infectious diseases such as diphtheria, pertussis, neonatal tetanus, poliomyelitis, Japanese encephalitis, and tuberculosis are now under strict control. Major immunization drives in 1995 focused on eradicating poliomyelitis, measles, congenital rubella, and neonatal tetanus.

The increasing economic prosperity of the Taiwan area has brought greater access to health care resources and enabled the government to launch the National Health Insurance program, which officially began on March 1, 1995. The health situation in Taiwan has already made impressive gains over the past 40 years: life expectancy for males has jumped from 53.38 years in 1951 to 71.93 years in 1995; and for females, from 56.33 years to 77.79 years. The crude death rate has also dropped from 18.15 per 1,000 persons in 1947 to 5.6 per 1,000 persons in 1995. The infant mortality rate dropped from 44.71 per 1,000 live births in 1952 to a low of 4.80 in 1993. However, in 1995 it rose to a ten-year high of 6.43 due to increased reporting and registration efficiency.

Medical Infrastructure
Manpower

As of the end of 1995, there were more than 118,000 medical personnel in the Taiwan area (see chart next page). On average, there was one physician every 873 persons, one doctor of Chinese medicine every 7,049 persons, and one dentist per 3,040 persons. There are currently 11 medical schools, 12 paramedical junior colleges, and 17 paramedical vocational schools in the ROC. In 1995, these institutions produced 1,091 physicians, 283 dentists, 859 medical technicians, 997 pharmacists, and 11,917 nurses and midwives. Physicians may apply for a medical specialist license after being certified in such specialties as family medicine, internal medicine, pediatrics, obstetrics and gynecology, orthopedics, neurology, neurosurgery, urology, ENT, ophthalmology, dermatology, psychiatry, rehabilitation medicine, anesthesiology, radiology, pathology, and nuclear medicine. A specialist license is only valid for five to six years. By the end of 1995, the system had certified nearly 21,000 specialists since it was set up in 1988.

Manpower imbalances pose major problems for the ROC's medical care system. A shortage of qualified nurses is especially serious, given the growing medical needs of an aging popula-

Medical Personnel in the Taiwan Area
(as of the end of 1995)

Type	Number in Service
Physicians	24,465
Doctors of Chinese Medicine	3,030
Dentists	7,026
Dental Assistants	105
Pharmacists	11,438
Pharmacist Assistants	7,786
Medical Technologists 醫檢師	4,370
Medical Technicians 醫檢生	352
Registered Nurses	56,725
Midwives	842
Radiography Technologists (Technicians) 醫用放射線技術師（士）	1,793
Nutritionists	298
Total	118,230

Source: Department of Health

tion. The number of medical technicians has not kept up with the increasing sophistication of specialized medical equipment. In contrast, the number of pharmacists has exceeded the number of physicians in Taiwan. The oversupply of pharmacists has brought about unemployment and prompted schools to cut down on the number of pharmacology students admitted each year.

Rural and remote areas suffer from a particularly acute shortage of qualified medical personnel. The government therefore offers incentives such as increased pay and commuting subsidies to medical personnel serving in these areas. The Taiwan Provincial Government is now holding its third ten-year program to train doctors and supporting staff who will work in rural hospitals and clinics.

Foreign nationals with licenses recognized by the ROC government can practice medicine on Taiwan as well. To obtain a license to practice, foreign doctors must pass an exam written in Chinese.

Medical Facilities

As of the end of 1995, there were more than 16,000 public and private hospitals or clinics in the ROC, with over 112,000 acute and long-term care beds, averaging nearly 53 beds per 10,000 people. A wide network of hospitals and clinics serves the people in the Taiwan area. Public medical care institutions consist of 94 hospitals and 496 clinics (including provincial, municipal, county and city hospitals, medical school hospitals, veterans hospitals and clinics, clinics affiliated with government institutions, and civil departments of military hospitals). Private medical care institutions number 692 hospitals and 14,826 clinics (including proprietary hospitals, hospitals affiliated with private medical schools, corporate hospitals and clinics, and private clinics). Medical institutions in the Taiwan area provide a total of more than 112,000 beds, about 53 percent of which are provided by private medical institutions.

Accreditation and Licensing

A hospital accreditation system has been in operation since 1978 to assure quality hospital in patient care and serve as a first step toward a service-quality ranking of Taiwan area hospitals. Currently, hospitals are evaluated on the basis of the quality of personnel, facilities, hospital management and community services, as well as the quality of medical care in various departments including internal medicine and surgery, radiological diagnosis and therapy, laboratory tests, nursing care, pharmaceutical services, ward management, infection control in hospitals, emergency care, and psychiatric care. The accreditation is valid for three years, after which a hospital must apply for re-assess-

Teaching Hospitals in Taiwan

Of the 547 hospitals with three-year accreditation in Taiwan (see chart next page), 128 are teaching hospitals 教學醫院. Teaching hospitals are classified into five categories: medical centers 醫學中心, regional hospitals 區域醫院, district hospitals 地區醫院, specialty teaching hospitals 特殊功能醫院, and psychiatric teaching hospitals 精神專科教學醫院.

Number of Accredited Hospitals in the Taiwan Area

Category	Year			Total*
	1994	1995	1996	
Hospitals Accredited for a Three-Year Term				
Medical Centers	9	1	2	12
Regional Hospitals**	39	0	5	43
District Teaching Hospitals***	34	7	25	63
District Hospitals****	131	41	261	401****
Specialty Teaching Hospitals	3	0	0	3
Psychiatric Teaching Hospitals	7	0	0	7
Psychiatric Hospitals	18	0	0	18
Hospitals Accredited for a One-Year Term				
District Teaching Hospitals			5	5
District Hospitals			24	24
Psychiatric Hospitals			2	2
Others				110

*Includes four units separated from main hospitals; **Excludes one hospital upgraded to a medical center in 1995; ***Includes three hospitals not shown separately, one of which became a regional hospital; ****Excludes seven closedowns, 19 double-counted hospitals, and seven hospitals upgraded to district teaching hospitals.

Source: Department of Health

ment. By the end of 1996, a total of 547 hospitals in the Taiwan area had received three-year accreditation.

Clinics are not subject to accreditation procedures, but instead must apply to the local health station for an operating license. The requirements for issuing such a license are set by the local health station. These include standards for the quality of medical care facilities and for the level of medical staff professional credentials. Once clinics obtain their operating licenses, they are subject to periodic inspections by local health station personnel to be able to renew their licenses.

Information Exchange

The DOH commissioned the Institute for Information Industry 資訊工業策進會 to set up an information exchange network among local hospitals. The National Health Information Network 全國醫療資訊網 began as an experimental project conducted between 1991 and 1993 to improve medical services in Hsinchu 新竹. The regional project was extended in 1993 to cover the entire Taiwan area, and by August 1995, regional centers had been established in Hsinchu, Taipei, Kaohsiung, and Taichung. At the end of 1997, the network will allow all health stations to exchange information concerning patients' medical records and insurance histories, medical personnel résumés, and the latest medical discoveries.

Medical Care Network

Rapid industrialization and urbanization, as well as the aging of the population in recent years, have highlighted the need for better health care and medical services. Health and medical care resources in the Taiwan area, however, are unevenly distributed. To balance medical resources, the DOH in July 1985 launched a 15-year project titled the Establishment of Medical Care Network 醫療保健計畫—籌建醫療網計畫 in the Taiwan area. The three-phase project divides the Taiwan area into 17 medical care regions 醫療區域. Each region serves as the basic unit for developing medical manpower, facilities, and emergency care network.

The 17 medical regions are further sub-divided, based on population size, geographic conditions and transportation facilities, into 63 sub-regions islandwide. Each sub-region is equipped with regional or district hospitals, as well as primary medical care units (i.e., private practitioners, group practice centers, and health stations). Under the project, 174 group practice centers had been established as of December 1995.

Under the project, the DOH restricts the establishment or expansion of hospitals in medical regions with plentiful medical resources. In regions lacking sufficient medical facilities, a Medical Care Development Fund 醫療發展基金 has been set up to encourage the private sector to establish health care institutions there. The Fund subsidized a total of 147 hospitals and 79 clinics between fiscal 1992 and 1995, thus cutting the number of regions lacking sufficient medical facilities from 37 to five.

Following the completion of the first phase in 1990, the second phase of the national medical care network project, scheduled for completion in December 1996, targets primary medical care in the mountain areas and outlying islands by expanding the emergency medical care network and developing health services for the chronically and mentally ill.

Health Stations

Residents in mountain areas and offshore islands rely heavily on the medical services provided by the local health stations 衛生所. Health stations and health rooms 衛生室 provide general outpatient treatment and emergency medical care. Educational programs provided by the

Public Health Administration

Public health administration in the ROC is organized at four distinct levels: national, provincial/special municipality, county and city, as well as township. At the national level, the Department of Health under the Executive Yuan is the highest authority. The DOH determines national health policies, formulates programs, and both supervises and coordinates health services at all levels. The DOH consists of five bureaus which oversee medical affairs 醫政處, pharmaceutical affairs 藥政處, food sanitation 食品衛生處, communicable disease control 防疫處, and health promotion 保健處. It also has an office of health planning 企劃室, and eight subordinate agencies: the National Institute of Preventive Medicine 預防醫學研究所, the National Laboratories of Foods and Drugs 藥物食品檢驗局, the Narcotics Bureau 麻醉藥品經理處, the National Quarantine Service 檢疫總所, the Bureau of National Health Insurance 中央健康保險局, the National Health Insurance Supervisory Committee 全民健康保險監理委員會, the National Health Insurance Dispute Review Committee 全民健康保險爭議審議委員會, and the Chinese Medicine and Pharmacy Committee 中醫藥委員會. The National Health Research Institute 財團法人國家衛生研究院 was established in 1996 as a new DOH-affiliated center.

At the provincial/special municipality government level are the Taiwan Provincial Department of Health 臺灣省政府衛生處, and its subordinate health bureaus 衛生局, which administer health programs for each of the 21 cities and counties of Taiwan Province; and the Taipei City Department of Health 臺北市政府衛生局 and Kaohsiung City Health Department 高雄市政府衛生局, along with their subordinate district health stations in each district within Taipei and Kaohsiung cities. These agencies are all responsible for implementing health and medical care programs in their respective administrative areas.

A health station is set up in each township. In mountain areas and outlying islands, smaller-scale health posts 山地離島衛生所 have been set up. Since 1983, group practice centers 群體醫療執業中心 have been organized in the remote areas to provide primary health services and to improve the health conditions and the medical care service quality at the grassroots level.

health stations include courses on maternal and child health, family planning, and the prevention and control of geriatric diseases and acute and chronic diseases. Surveys show that 70 to 90 percent of visits to community health stations are for infant and child immunizations. In 1945, there were only 15 health stations in the Taiwan area. By the end of 1995, there were 369 health stations and 498 health rooms throughout the Taiwan area, among which 12 health stations are located in Taipei City and 11 in Kaohsiung City.

Health stations form the basis of primary health care in the Taiwan area. As of December 1995, these health centers were staffed with nearly 4,900 medical personnel, including physicians, dentists, pharmacists, nurses, and laboratory technicians. In general, two doctors serve at each health station. But only 15 percent of the health stations are staffed with a dentist and 37 percent have a pharmacist. Even in remote areas, health stations and rooms feature basic medical equipment. As of December 1995, a full 249 of the health stations in Taiwan were equipped with X-ray machines, 128 with dental X-ray machines, and almost all of the group practice centers were equipped with automatic biochemical analyzers.

A health station has been set up in each township in areas with relatively limited medical resources, including 30 aboriginal townships in 12 counties in Taiwan proper, the Pescadores, Liuchiu 琉球鄉 in P'ingtung County 屏東縣, and Green Island 綠島 off the coast of Taitung 台東. Since 1979, the government has been sending mobile medical teams to remote villages on a regular basis. In the Pescadores, where there is no health station, a telecommunications medical care program was initiated in 1988 to provide emergency care. Later, 145 points of service in mountainous areas and offshore islands also joined this program.

To provide prompt and accurate information for the health stations around the island, a health station information system was inaugurated in 1983. At the end of 1995, a total of 218 health stations had implemented this computerized system.

Public Health Policy Report

The ROC released its first-ever *White Paper on Health Care* 衛生白皮書 on August 17, 1993. The 220-page document, consisting of 22 chapters, spells out the government's health care policies for the rest of the decade, which should be directed toward preparing for an aging society.

Currently, 7.6 percent of Taiwan's population is over 65 years of age. According to the white paper, by the year 2030 this figure will reach 18.5 percent. The document therefore spells out steps the government should take to reduce high blood pressure, cancer, diabetes, and other health problems associated with the elderly. Every five years, the department will revise the document to ensure that ROC citizens continue to receive the best health care possible.

Health Insurance

Prior to March 1995, only 59 percent of Taiwan's population were covered under 13 public health insurance plans. In view of the rapidly growing medical care costs and the increasing number of elderly, the ROC government launched the National Health Insurance program on March 1, 1995, to provide universally medicalible care. This new system incorporates the medical insurance coverage provided by the 13 health care plans and extends its coverage to the 7.5 million citizens, who were formerly uninsured. The main beneficiaries are the elderly, children, students, and housewives. Participation in the program is mandatory under the *National Health Insurance Law* 全民健康保險法.

An initial estimate put the total cost of the program—to employees, employers, and the government—at US$9.6 billion a year. Under the schedule for premiums and rates that was approved in July 1994, employees pay 30 percent of the premium, employers 60 percent, and the government 10 percent. A typical worker, earning just over US$943 a month, with a spouse and two children, paid about US$42 a month. The law specifies a first-year

National Health Insurance Premium Shares

Insured Status	Rate Shared %		
	Government	*Employer*	*Insurant*
Professional Groups			
Government employees, dependents	—	60	40
Private school employees, dependents	30	30	40
Wage & salary workers, dependents	10	60	30
Multiple jobholders*, dependents	40	0	60
Farmers & fishermen, dependents	70	0	30
Dependents of servicemen	—	60	40
Employers, self-employed, dependents	0	0	100
Regional Groups			
Low-income households, dependents	100	0	0
Veterans	100	0	0
Dependents of veterans	70	0	30
Others, dependents	40	0	60

*Persons with two or more employers.

Source: Department of Health

premium rate pegged at 4.25 percent of the monthly wage, which can be raised to no more than 6 percent thereafter. People aged 70 and older and the moderately and severely disabled pay no premium.

The new health care program pays 70 percent to 95 percent of costs for patients admitted to hospitals. Insurants have to pay for outpatient care with a flat rate copayment. Outpatients pay only a registration fee of US$2 at clinics and local hospitals, and less than US$4 at regional hospitals and medical centers. By mid-1995, more than 90 percent of the medical institutions in the Taiwan area had joined the program.

All ROC citizens who reside in Taiwan for more than four months of the year are eligible for the insurance except servicemen and inmates, who receive free government medical care. Foreign nationals with valid Alien Resident Certificates 外僑居留證 employed in Taiwan and their family members can also be insured.

The *National Health Insurance Law* requires that the Cabinet present an evaluation of the health insurance program within two years, especially concerning the source of funds to finance it. In the first half of the third year, the Cabinet must draft a revision of the law.

Integration with Existing Programs

Before the National Health Insurance Program was implemented, the pre-existing 13 public insurance plans under three main systems—government employee insurance, labor insurance, and farmers' insurance—were the primary sources of medical insurance. Although the medical coverage portions of these programs have been subsumed by the National Health Insurance program, the original programs still continue to provide cash benefits for various categories of extraordinary financial hardship. For instance, the Labor Insurance Program 勞工保險 still covers workers under 60, such as industrial workers, journalists, employees in nonprofit organizations, government employees and teachers not eligible for civil servants' or teachers' insurance, fishermen, persons receiving vocational training in institutes registered with the government, and workers under 15 years of age. The Executive Yuan's Council of Labor Affairs 行政院勞工委員會 is currently drafting the *Implementation Policies for Unemployment Insurance* 失業保險實施立案要點. Potential beneficiaries must be in good health and unwillingly unemployed.

The benefit packages in each of the nine Government Employees' Insurance programs vary in content, but generally include cash benefits for disability, old age, and death, as well as funeral allowances for dependents. The *Government Employees' Insurance Law* 公務人員保險法 entitles all present and retired civil servants and their dependents, as well as private school teachers, administrative staff, and their spouses, to coverage. As of December 1996, a total of 646,000 people were covered under a GEI program. All GEI programs are under the purview of the Examination Yuan's Ministry of Civil Service 考試院銓敘部 and insured by the Central Trust of China 中央信託局, a government-owned financial enterprise.

As of June 1995, the Comprehensive Farmers' Health Insurance program 農民健康保險 covered 1.78 million farmers. The insurance program is currently administered at the national level by the Ministry of the Interior 內政部, and at the local level by provincial, county, and city governments. Members of farmers' associations over 15 years of age who engage in agricultural work more than 90 days a year are eligible for coverage that provides compensation in the event of illness, injury, disability, or death.

Military officers pay special low premiums, and enlisted men receive free coverage. Professional groups are eligible for group life insurance sponsored by the Central Trust of China. Each professional group forms an insurance unit that pays two-thirds of the premium, while those insured pay the rest.

The government also offers comprehensive accident insurance for students 學生團體保險. The insurer, the Taiwan Life Insurance Co., Ltd.

台灣人壽保險股份有限公司, is supervised by the Taiwan Provincial Government and the Taipei and Kaohsiung city governments, according to the area of implementation. The government partially subsidizes the program, and students pay a token premium every semester. The government subsidizes the full cost of premiums for aboriginal and offshore island students.

Health Promotion Programs
Maternal and Child Health

Since the first health programs for mothers and children began in 1952, infant deaths caused by birth trauma and infection have decreased, yet the number of accidents, injuries, and congenital anomalies have increased. It is, therefore, vital that comprehensive health services cover all the stages of a child's development from conception through childhood.

The current health program provides prenatal and postnatal care for early detection and treatment of pregnancy-related diseases, ensures safe deliveries, and maintains the health of infants and mothers. As a result, the health of mothers and children in the Taiwan area has improved greatly. In 1965, the number of women who died in childbirth was 75 per 100,000. This figure had dropped to 9.41 by 1986, and to 7.59 by 1995.

The infant mortality rate has also fallen. In 1965, it was 24 per 1,000. By 1994 the rate had decreased to 5.06 per 1,000, but it rose a little to 6.43 per 1,000 in 1995. Prior to 1994, infant and neonatal mortality rates were underestimated. The situation has since been corrected through the implementation of a more efficient birth registration system.

Over 99.9 percent of all deliveries were assisted by qualified personnel in 1995, a marked improvement in health service over past years. That year, a surprising 35 percent of deliveries were by Caesarean section. Only 20 percent of these operations were performed out of medical necessity. It is thought that many women are asking for this procedure simply because the expense is covered by the NHI program. Hospitals may also be promoting C-sections out of a desire to increase their operation fee income.

Comprehensive health programs and health examinations for infants and children up to four years of age are available at clinics islandwide. Growth and development norms, as well as daily recommended dietary allowances for infants, have been charted. For preschool-age children, health care management in kindergartens and nurseries is now available to detect growth anomalies at an early stage. Comprehensive measures have also been taken to educate preschool teachers, parents, and expectant mothers on the merits and techniques of oral hygiene. From July 1994 to June 1995, over 653,500 preschool children were examined for oral hygiene and visual acuity. To prevent accidents and injuries, educational activities on accident prevention are conducted on Children's Day (April 4) each year. Health stations around the island offer free vaccinations for infants and children against hepatitis B, polio, measles, mumps, rubella, Japanese encephalitis, tuberculosis, diphtheria, pertussis, and tetanus.

Genetic Health Program

Congenital defects were the most common cause of infant death in 1994. Although the infant mortality rate has declined as a result of improved health services, the percentage of babies born with congenital abnormalities has risen. In 1994, nearly 35 percent of all infant deaths were caused by congenital defects, and 3 to 4 percent of newborns were categorized as severely deformed, adding more than 10,000 to the group annually. If organic or metabolic abnormalities were included, the rate would be much higher. In 1980, the government initiated the Congenital Defect Registration and Follow-Up Project 先天性缺陷兒登記計畫 to study the incidence, causes, and care of birth defects.

Genetic health counseling centers have been set up at the National Taiwan University Hospital 國立台灣大學附設醫院, Tzu-Chi Buddhist General Hospital 佛教慈濟綜合醫院 (Hualien), the Taipei Veterans General Hospital 台北榮民總醫院, and the Kaohsiung Medical College Hospital 高雄醫學院附設醫院. There are 15 certified cytogenetic laboratories operating in Taiwan. In 1995, approximately 98 percent of newborns were screened for congenital metabolic disorders.

The *Genetic Health Law* 優生保健法 provides a legal basis for health services, such as premarital health examinations, prenatal diagnosis, neonatal screening for congenital metabolic disorders, and genetic counseling. In 1995, there were 856 institutions providing these services. Under the law, a Medical Genetic Advisory Committee 優生保健諮詢委員會 promotes genetic health programs.

In 1995, some 25,000 persons received genetic health examinations, 16,000 persons received premarital health examinations, 8,400 prenatal diagnoses were conducted, and 316,000 neonatal screening were performed. In the same year, some 361,000 potential mothers received rebella vaccinations as a measure to prevent birth defects.

Family Planning

The contraceptive usage rate for married women between 22 and 39 years of age in the Taiwan area has increased from 24 percent in 1965 to 82 percent in 1993. Surveys also show that the average number of children for women between the ages of 40 and 49 has declined from 6.1 in 1975 to 3.1 in 1992. The proportion of women having four or more children has also declined from 18.8 percent in 1975 to 4 percent in 1994; the number of women having only one or two children increased from 61.8 percent to 80 percent in the same period. The number of children per family dropped from 5.75 in 1960 to 1.7 in 1995. Furthermore, the proportion of women married between the ages of 20 and 34 years has declined from 67.3 percent to 55.1 percent; the average age at first marriage for women increased from 22.7 to 27.6 years, and for men, from 27.1 to 29.8 years. These factors have lowered the birth rate in the Taiwan area. By 1995, the population growth rate had slowed down to 9.91 in 1,000 persons.

The aging of the population and the lower marriage rate among women aged between 20 and 34, coupled with a falling birth rate, have caused worries about a population gap. Starting in 1990, the government adjusted its family planning policy to encourage a moderate increase in the birth rate (see section on New Population Policy in Chapter 2, People).

Teenage Pregnancy

Pregnancy among adolescents between ages 15 and 19 in the Taiwan area is higher than in some other Asian countries. In 1994, teen pregnancy in this age group was 17 per 1,000. More than 15,000 children are being born annually to teenage mothers in Taiwan. According to a study conducted by the Taiwan Provincial Government comparing the results of a 1984 survey with those of the latest study in 1995, there has been a 264 percent increase in premarital sexual activities among teens. In 1995, about 10 percent of Taiwan teenagers had sex. Two-thirds of the teens who had sex for the first time did not take any contraceptive measures, and 11 percent of them became pregnant. Eight percent of the pregnant girls chose to abort and the rest became teenage mothers. As society becomes more open, the problem of unwed teenage mothers may worsen.

The DOH therefore offers sex education and counseling services in schools, factories, and communities. The Taiwan Provincial Institute of Family Planning 臺灣省家庭計畫研究所 also conducts surveys on family planning and population trends in the Taiwan area. By 1995, over 95,500 adolescents had attended almost 1,300 sexual educational symposia arranged by the Taiwan Provincial Government. Telephone consultation services were provided to more than 100,000 persons. Civic organizations like the ROC Public Health Association 中華民國公共衛生學會, the School Health Association 中華民國學校衛生學會, the Mercy Memorial Foundation 財團法人杏陵醫學基金會, the Youth Guidance Foundation 中國青少年輔導基金會, and the Maternal and Child Health Association 中華民國婦幼衛生協會 have cooperated with the DOH to develop educational materials, train professional counselors and provide consultation services for teenagers. The Mercy Memorial Foundation and the Family Life and Sex Education Center 家庭生活與性教育中心 provide sex education training to school administrators and teachers.

In 1995, some 15 youth health promotion clinics 青少年保健門診 were established in city medical centers and teaching hospitals to provide counseling services and sex education for young people.

Adult and Geriatric Health

The graying of the population has increased the need for adult and geriatric health care. In 1995, persons aged 65 and over constituted 7.6 percent of the population, or 1.63 million people, an increase of 3.5 percent over the previous year. Yet, the young population aged 15 and below dropped by 2.6 percent over the past decade. It is estimated that by the year 2000, people aged 65 and over will account for 8.4 percent of the population, thus qualifying the Taiwan area as an "aged society" in United Nations parlance.

As the ratio of elderly people in society increases, chronic cardiovascular diseases have replaced infectious diseases as the major causes of death among adults. In 1995, for instance, cerebrovascular diseases, heart diseases, diabetes mellitus, and hypertensive diseases were the second, fourth, fifth, and ninth leading causes of death, representing just under 30 percent of all deaths that year.

Currently, all persons over 65 are entitled to free blood pressure and blood sugar tests at local health stations. Family health records are kept at all health stations for efficient follow-up. Cases of cardiac disease, diabetes, and hypertension are generally referred to adult or chronic disease clinics in public hospitals for treatment. After discharge from public hospitals, patients are usually referred to local health stations for follow-up care. The primary health centers also provide home nursing services to persons aged 65 and over.

Local governments have specially appropriated funds to subsidize medical expenditures for the aged. Guidelines on the control and treatment of hypertension, diabetes, and hyperlipidemia have been derived to provide a standard treatment procedure for medical groups in the Taiwan area. Likewise, a series of educational materials on the control of stroke have also been developed for circulation among clinics.

Altogether 41 diabetes education centers have been established in medical centers islandwide to provide comprehensive care for diabetic patients.

Long-term Care

For many elderly people who are discharged from hospitals or who are chronically ill, home health care is provided by 70 hospital-based and nine free-standing home care institutions in the Taiwan area. For less than US$56 per visit, elderly people can receive the medical care they need on a regular basis. Most elderly people receive two visits a month. Nine nursing homes provide 450 beds for long-term care patients. Five hospitals in Kaohsiung and Taipei, Taichung, Nant'ou 南投, and Hualien 花蓮 counties provided 240 beds for day-care service. The DOH has commissioned the Christian Hospital 嘉義基督教醫院 (Chiayi), the Hualien Tzu-Chi Buddhist General Hospital, and the Kaohsiung Medical College Hospital to provide out-of-hospital services. The Sun Yat-sen Cancer Center 孫逸仙治癌中心醫院 provides home care specially for cancer patients. (Information on other welfare services for the elderly can be found in Chapter 19, Social Welfare.)

Health Control Programs
Myopia Control

Taiwan has the highest incidence of myopia in the world. A DOH survey conducted between mid-1995 and early 1996 revealed that while only 12.1 percent of first graders in elementary schools suffered from nearsightedness, the figure jumped to 55.4 percent for sixth graders, and 85 percent for twelfth graders. Vision screenings are now conducted in schools a month after school starts. By 1995, some 179 hospitals and clinics were providing special outpatient services for students experiencing vision problems. The DOH has implemented a vision protection and screening program that includes preschool children and special occupational groups. Since 1995, visual screening for preschool children from four to six years old has been conducted in 19 cities and counties.

Since 1986, visual health centers have been set up in major hospitals around the island, including the National Taiwan University Hospital, the Taipei and Taichung Veterans General hospitals, the Kaohsiung Medical College Hospital, and the Hualien Tzu-Chi Buddhist General Hospital.

Cancer Control

Cancer has been the leading cause of death in the Taiwan area since 1982. In 1995, over 25,800 people died of cancer—21.9 percent of all deaths. The five most common forms of cancer for men in Taiwan are liver, lung, colorectal, stomach, and oral cancer. For women, they are cervical, breast, colorectal, lung, and liver cancer. The DOH has initiated cancer control programs targeting the prevention and control of the more common cancers, including cervical, liver, colorectal, and breast cancer. Major medical research organizations, such as National Taiwan University's College of Public Health, are conducting studies on the early detection of some common cancers.

The chances of incurring cervical cancer have increased. In 1994, nearly ten out of every 100,000 women had cervical cancer, with almost 1,000 deaths that year. If detected and treated at an early stage, however, cervical cancer can be cured in 95 percent of the cases. Screenings are subsidized by the government. In 1995, some 1,000 medical care institutions provided screening services to around 420,000 women. Since July 1, 1995, the National Health Insurance program has covered pap smear tests for women aged 30 and over.

Similarly, breast cancer programs focus on prevention measures, especially increasing the current rate of self-examinations, which is 8.6 percent in Taipei city and county. The rate is even lower in the rest of the country.

The DOH offers free screenings for family members of liver cancer patients to detect liver cancer in its early stages. If family members are diagnosed as having chronic hepatitis and liver cirrhosis or carrying hepatitis B or hepatitis C antibodies, free re-screening is available once every six to 12 months. Some 5,300 family members of liver cancer patients received screenings in 1995 at the nine medical centers in Taiwan that offer screenings for liver cancer. The government also offers free colon cancer screening for people in high risk groups. The program covered screenings for approximately 2,800 patients in fiscal 1995.

Occupational Disease Prevention

In Taiwan, the most common diseases or disorders attributable to work environment include blood poisoning by heavy metals, gas narcosis, black lung disease, skin disorders, trauma, and dysbarism. Blood lead content over 40 µg/dl and 30 µg/dl for males and females, respectively, is considered excessive, and must be reported to the DOH monitoring system. In 1994, a total of 9,807 cases of lead poisoning were reported. An additional 6,420 cases were recorded by September 1995. Between January and September 1995, cases of hearing loss numbered 14,132, and 1,705 were deemed serious. According to the Council of Labor Affairs, the occupational disease mortality rate reached a new low of 0.01 per 10,000 persons in 1995, but the number of cases in which occupational disease went on to cause permanent disability remained high; indeed, this occurred in 4,585 of the 22,878 occupational disease cases reported in 1995.

Six hospitals have been designated standard facilities for the prevention and treatment of occupational disease: the National Taiwan University Hospital, National Defense Medical College Hospital 國防醫學院附設醫院, Taipei Veterans General Hospital, China Medical College Hospital. National Cheng Kung University Hospital 國立成功大學附設醫院, and Kaohsiung Medical College Hospital. The occupational disease centers provide diagnosis, treatment, follow-up assessment, referral, and consultation services. Twenty-four medical institutions, including 17 at public hospitals, provide special outpatient services for occupational disease patients. In 1995, more than 400 medical institutions were qualified to detect black lung disease and to conduct ordinary and special health examinations for workers. The DOH also holds occupational disease seminars to improve the quality of medical services and the knowledge of medical personnel. In 1995, some 158 doctors and 207 nurses attended such seminars.

Anti-Smoking Campaign

The smoking rate in Taiwan is alarmingly high: about 30 percent of the population over 18 years of age smokes; and about 55 percent of all male adults smoke tobacco products regularly. While only 3.4 percent of women smoke, this proportion is rising. Studies show that in 1989, among the population above 35 years of age, one of every five deaths was related to smoking. A recent survey of public health conducted by National Taiwan University revealed that an average of over 10,000 Taiwan residents die each year from smoking, including more than 4,490 who die of lung cancer. By Sex, smoking causes 12 percent of male deaths and 8 percent of female deaths in Taiwan.

According to the survey, 43.7 percent of the smokers consume between half a pack and one pack each day; 37.4 percent smoke less than half a pack and 15.3 percent smoke more than one pack a day. Since the government lifted the ban on the importation of foreign cigarettes to Taiwan in 1987, the smoking population has increased by 4.6 percent and has broadened to include a large portion of the teenage and female populations. A 1994 survey estimated that more than 16 percent of junior high school students and 10 percent of senior high school students smoke.

In July 1990, the DOH launched an anti-smoking campaign, which is now scheduled to last until June 1997. Under the project, free distribution of cigarettes in the army was terminated in July 1991, and more warnings against the health hazards of smoking have been printed on cigarette packs. Anti-smoking literature and films have also been distributed nationwide.

Despite these government measures, concern over smoking hazards rose in 1994. The Taiwan Tobacco and Wine Monopoly Bureau's 臺灣省菸酒公賣局 loss of its 40-year monopoly over alcohol and tobacco sales in June 1995 (to speed up Taiwan's entry into the World Trade Organization) has raised fears that the influx of foreign cigarettes will exacerbate an already grave health problem. Health authorities have thus submitted to the legislature a draft of the tough *Tobacco Hazards Act* 菸害防制法, which will outlaw the sale of cigarettes to minors (under the age of 18), ban all advertising and promotion (including handing out samples) by cigarette companies, and require the labeling of nicotine and tar contents on cigarette products. Currently, cigarette ads are still allowed in magazines and stores. Revisions to the law now under review will ban smoking in most public places, including theaters, libraries, museums, and public transport. Smoking areas will be designated in schools, department stores, train stations, and government offices. Smoking has already been banned in medical institutions and on express trains since January 1993. Tobacco advertisements have also been banned in the airports.

Anti-smoking consumer-interest groups like the John Tung Foundation 董氏基金會 have taken a more active role in increasing public awareness about smoking hazards. The foundation has initiated a "Dear Legislator" campaign to ask lawmakers to support revisions to the *Tobacco Hazards Act*. The first reading of the Act passed the legislature in 1994. The law includes restrictions on tobacco promotion ads, smoking areas, and ages of smokers, and a requirement that written warnings and the nicotine content be printed on cigarette packs. The Department of Health has awarded a large grant to the John Tung Foundation for an anti-smoking campaign. The campaign centers on a cartoon character named Hsü Tse-lin 徐則林 (a pun on Lin Tse-hsü 林則徐, the name of a Ch'ing dynasty official who fought the import of opium into China some 150 years ago). The cartoon character is drawn as a "hip" guy sporting a ponytail reminiscent of the long braids Chinese men wore during the Ch'ing dynasty. He can be spotted carrying an anti-smoking sign in made-for-TV videos, and on stickers, pamphlets, and placards in public places around Taiwan.

With so many smokers in Taiwan, it should come as no surprise that more than 96 percent of the non-smoking female and child population were exposed to secondhand smoke. According to a survey conducted by the Academia Sinica 中央研究院, 22 percent of female lung cancer victims are frequently exposed to secondhand smoke, although they themselves are not smokers. Around 75 percent of the pregnant women are unable to avoid secondhand smoke. By June 1995, all Taiwan-based airlines had forbidden smoking on their planes during both domestic and international flights.

The Betel Nut Problem

The seed of the betel palm has long been used by Chinese doctors to treat parasitic infections and other intestinal disorders. Only when taken in excess does this pulpy nut have negative side effects. However, the betel nut chewed widely in Taiwan as a stimulant often contains unhealthy additives.

Experts estimate that 96 percent of oral cancer patients and 88 percent of mucous membrane fibrosis patients in the Taiwan area are habitual betel nut chewers. Statistically, the likelihood of contracting oral cancer is 28 times higher for betel nut chewers than for non-chewers. The risk is 90 times higher for people who both chew betel nuts and smoke. And those who chew, smoke, and drink heavily are 123 times more likely to contract nasopharyngeal cancer than people who maintain none of these habits. Annual oral cancer deaths in the ROC have increased from 1.25 per 100,000 people in 1976 to

Ten Leading Causes of Death by Illness in the Taiwan Area, 1995

Cause of Death	% of All Deaths	Mortality per 100,000
All Causes	100.00	554.62
Malignancies	21.91	121.50
Cerebrovascular Diseases	11.98	66.45
Accidents and Adverse Effects	11.01	61.05
Heart Diseases	9.54	52.93
Diabetes Mellitus	6.12	33.97
Chronic Liver Diseases & Cirrhosis	3.78	20.95
Nephrites, Nephrotic Syndrome & Nephrosis	2.98	16.55
Pneumonia	2.60	14.44
Hypertensive Diseases	2.22	12.30
Bronchitis, Emphysema & Asthma	1.69	9.37
Subtotal	73.83	409.51
Other Causes	26.17	145.11

Source: Department of Health

2.25 in 1991. In 1995, there were an estimated 2.3 to 2.8 million betel nut chewers in the Taiwan area.

Especially worrisome to health officials is the increasing popularity of betel nuts and the changing demographics of the betel nut chewing population. In the past, most betel nut chewers were adult laborers concentrated in eastern and southern Taiwan. Today, young and educated urbanites and suburbanites are taking to the nut in unprecedented numbers. In response to this shift, the government is now targeting anti-betel nut campaigns at the younger generation. The hazards of betel nut chewing are being publicized in the form of TV ads, video programs, and leaflets distributed among high school and college students.

Communicable Diseases

An islandwide surveillance system involving a network of some 700 physicians has been set up for the physicians to report diseases. All the physicians hooked up to the network provide weekly updates by phone. The latest information and medical updates are then available to other physicians in the monthly *Epidemiology Bulletin* 疫情報導, which is circulated to medical centers islandwide. Currently, ten disease surveillance centers and quarantine stations under the National Quarantine Service have been set up in the central, southern, and eastern parts of the Taiwan area to administer the control and prevention of communicable diseases.

The *Communicable Disease Control Act* 傳染病防治條例 requires that communicable diseases be reported, patients treated, and all epidemic areas disinfected. Diseases that must be reported include cholera, bacillary and amoebic dysentery, typhoid fever and paratyphoid fever, yellow fever, meningococcal meningitis, diphtheria, scarlet fever, plague, typhus fever, relapsing fever, rabies, and acquired immune deficiency syndrome(AIDS). Most of these diseases have been either eradicated or brought under control in the Taiwan area. However, in 1995 a total of 78 cases of amoebic dysentery, 84 cases of bacterial dysentery, 57 cases of typhoid and paratypoid, seven cases of meningococcal meningitis, and 116 cases of scarlet fever were reported.

Other diseases and conditions which are not specified, but must nonetheless be reported, include malaria, poliomyelitis, acute flaccid paralysis, Japanese encephalitis, tetanus, neonatal tetanus, pertussis, tsutsugamushi disease, tuberculosis, meningitis, acute hepatitis, measles, rubella, congenital rubella syndrome, mumps, leprosy, syphilis, gonorrhea, dengue fever, rheumatic fever, and botulism. Some 11,422 cases of TB and 124 cases rubella were reported in 1994, and by 1995 more than 3,000 cases of syphilis, 780 cases of acute hepatitis, and 242 cases dengue fever had been recorded by the DOH. In addition, the DOH requires that any disease, parasitic infection, or unusual symptom related to pets be reported, especially in cases in which both the owner and pet become ill.

Local health authorities routinely carry out vaccination programs for smallpox, polio, measles, mumps, rubella, diphtheria-pertussis-tetanus (DPT), tuberculosis, Japanese encephalitis, and hepatitis B. The coverage rates for these vaccinations, with the exception of measles, have reached approximately 85 percent. In 1992, the DOH initiated the first stage (1992-1996) plan for polio, tetanus, measles, and rubella eradication, with excellent results. No cases of polio and tetanus were reported in 1995, but there were sporadic occurrences of rubella (121) and measles (42) that year. In order to stamp out polio by the year 2000 in accordance with World Health Organization policy, the DOH decided to continue with the second stage of the plan targeted at attaining vaccination coverage rates of 95 percent, strengthening the disease reporting network, and computerizing vaccination records to minimize the discontinuation of diptheria-pertussis-tetanus (DPT) and Sabin oral polio vaccination series. Other health measures include education on disease and sanitation, and vector control.

Poliomyelitis

Free vaccinations against communicable diseases are available for infants and preschool children. In May 1994, the DOH launched the largest immunization drive ever: an islandwide campaign to administer Sabin oral polio vaccine to the estimated 1.8 million children under six years of age in Taiwan. All such children were required to be inoculated, and the polio immunization coverage rate reached 102.5 percent in 1995.

AIDS

The *Acquired Immune Deficiency Syndrome (AIDS) Control Act* 後天免疫缺乏症候群防治條例 was promulgated in December 1990 to provide for screening and free treatment of patients, and to deal with cases of those who are HIV-infected knowingly transmitting the disease to unsuspecting others. As of May 1996, over 13 million blood tests had been conducted to screen for the human immune deficiency virus (HIV) antibody. By July 1996, a total of 1,144 people had tested HIV positive; and among these, 1,018 were ROC nationals. More than 44 percent were thought to have been infected through sexual contact with an HIV carrier. According to the DOH, the typical male HIV carrier in Taiwan is a single worker aged 31 who has visited prostitutes. Female HIV carriers are typically married and aged 34; many are housewives infected by their husbands. By mid-1996, male HIV carriers outnumbered female carriers 12 to 1.

Despite its efficiency, the screening procedure has brought about a new problem. For fear of social discrimination, people who suspect they may have AIDS shy away from going to hospitals to ask for testing. Instead, they resort to blood donation as an indirect method of determining their status. The DOH is therefore strongly urging high-risk groups to refrain from donating blood. Likewise, DOH is calling for legislation that would impose strict penalties on people who donate their blood as a means of AIDS detection. People who suspect they might have AIDS are encouraged instead to go to public health centers across the island, or to the 19 hospitals authorized by the DOH for free AIDS detection services. Specimens can also be mailed in for testing. AIDS screening is compulsory for servicemen, inmates, and alien workers.

The DOH also publishes pamphlets, booklets, and manuals on AIDS, which are distributed to medical personnel and the general public, and at airports or seaports. The government also produces TV programs and films to educate the public.

Hepatitis

Around 90 percent of the people in the Taiwan area are infected with hepatitis B viruses by the time they reach the age of 40, and between 15 and 20 percent of the total population are estimated to be hepatitis B carriers. A program to control the spread of hepatitis B, now in its third phase, is expected to last until 1997. The immunization program covers all newborns, preschool children, primary school children, young adults, medical personnel, and family members of carriers. Around 1,600 hospitals and clinics in 1995 administered 983,000 doses of hepatitis B vaccines (three being required for each vaccination) to preschool and elementary school children. During the same period, some 277,000 underwent an antenatal test for hepatitis B. Nearly 14,000 doses of hepatitis B immunoglobulin were provided to newborns of carriers, and 945,000 doses of hepatitis B vaccine (HBV) were used to immunize non-carriers' newborns. For the rest of the population, vaccinations are available at a reasonable cost. Immunization services are offered at health stations and clinics islandwide.

Hepatitis C is post-transfusion hepatitis transmitted 80 percent of the time by body fluids, especially blood or blood products. It can also be transmitted through the sharing of needles in tattooing or drug injection. The DOH requires that blood used for transfusion must be tested for hepatitis C antibodies.

Tuberculosis

Tuberculosis was one of the leading causes of death in the 1950s. In 1947, the TB death rate was 294.44 per 100,000 people. Accordingly, a TB prevalence rate survey has been taken once every five years since 1957. That year, TB was the third leading cause of death by illness in Taiwan, and the prevalence rates of pulmonary tuberculosis and bacteriologically infectious tuberculosis were 5.15 and 1.02 percent. By 1982, they had dropped to 0.88 and 0.15 percent. However, by the 1987 survey, the rate for pulmonary TB had risen back up to 1.29 percent while bacteriologically infectious TB continued to fall to 0.11 percent. Although the TB death rate was only 7.52 per 100,000 in 1995 with 1,574 reported deaths and 10,815 patients, it was still high compared with that of advanced nations.

A five-year project running between 1994 and 1998 aims to step up TB control by refurbishing treatment facilities, controlling chronically active cases, and implementing a surveillance system for TB risk groups, especially in the aboriginal communities, where TB was the sixth leading cause of death in 1995. Starting from April 1995, the DOH implemented the Mountain Area TB Inpatient Subsidy Plan 山地鄉結核病人住院治療補助計畫 and the Chronic TB Patient Accommodation Plan 慢性開放性結核病人收容管理計畫, with 13 hospitals participating.

Dengue Fever

A center for the control of dengue fever, which is caused by a mosquito-borne virus, was set up in December 1988 with the joint effort of DOH and the Environmental Protection Administration 環境保護署. The joint taskforce is responsible for the formulation and implementation of preventive measures, a surveillance system, vector surveying, insecticide spraying, and eliminating the breeding ground of mosquitoes. It also supervises local governments carrying out the disease control measures and at the same time provides medication.

In 1995, there was a small-scale outbreak of dengue fever in Taipei County, with 369 confirmed cases (329 domestic, 40 imported). As compared to the 1,938 cases in 1988, the disease has been brought under control. To prevent transmission of the virus, the results of a monthly density index of vector mosquitoes and larvae have to be recorded and reported to the relevant units for evaluation. Frequent checking of the vector index and intensive environmental sanitation education are the most important work of the taskforce after typhoons and floodings.

Quarantine

Quarantine procedures prevent the entry and spread of communicable diseases from abroad. Travelers, aircraft crew members, airport workers, and imported produce are targeted for scrutiny at ports of entry. International health regulations stipulate that all interference with modern transportation be minimized during the screening procedures, and the DOH makes every effort to do so while rendering efficient service.

The DOH consolidated the nation's seven quarantine stations and two sub-stations into the National Quarantine Service in 1989. The service includes quarantine, port sanitation management, and disease surveillance divisions.

Since April 1995, travelers entering Taiwan from highly infected areas in Southeast Asia have been required to submit a Health Declaration Form to monitor for cholera, plague, yellow fever, malaria, dengue, and other major infectious diseases. Travelers with symptoms are followed up by public health workers to identify cases for prompt treatment and to prevent further transmission. Through December 1995, some 1,439 suspected cases had been followed up and 15 confirmed. All of the confirmed cases were diarrheal infections such as shigellosis, salmonellosis, and vibrio parahemolyticus.

Field Epidemiology

The DOH administers a two-year field epidemiology instruction program at the National Institute of Preventive Medicine in collaboration with the US Center for Disease Control and Emory University. Physicians, dentists, and researchers in related fields are chosen annually for training in hands-on epidemiological investigations and long-term study projects. Since its inception, the program has trained 21 physicians, 18 dentists, and 40 public health specialists. Fifty-six of these graduates now serve in public institutions. Some 97 long-term projects had been completed.

Food Standards

Chinese people love to eat out. To make sure this enjoyable pastime is also a safe one, the Department of Health is campaigning to monitor sanitary standards in the ubiquitous eating places on the island. On a day-to-day basis, local health authorities equipped with 13 basic diagnostic devices test food and conduct routine spot checks of all food establishments on the island, as well as distribute educational materials. More than 237,000 spot checks were conducted in 1995, with 8.6 percent of food establishments failing to meet sanitary requirements. Less than 1 percent were fined, and only six establishments had their licenses suspended. Those that do pass are issued a plaque to display on the restaurant wall, and the restaurant names are published to help consumers locate safe eating places.

The DOH, in collaboration with the Council of Labor Affairs, is also promoting a licensing system for food technicians. In 1994, the DOH defined new requirements for chefs at six types of restaurants to be licensed within the next five years to ensure better hygiene. The plan will affect about 80 percent of the chefs at hotel restaurants, school cafeterias, banquet halls, catering services, airline caterers, and public cafeterias in the Taiwan area. Currently, there are more than 16,500 licensed chefs in Taiwan.

Widespread sanitary practices have cut down on the cases of food poisoning and hepatitis. Disposable tableware is now available in many restaurants. Consumers can purchase inspected processed food products labeled as meeting the Chinese Agricultural Standard 中國農業標準 (CAS) and general food products labeled with the seal of Good Manufacturing Practice 優良藥品製造標準 (GMP). By January 1996, nearly 300 factories producing some 2,200 food products had been authorized as GMP factories, while 30 factories were producing nearly 400 frozen food products bearing the CAS seal. Similarly, over 1,600 meat products qualified for the CAS label. Almost 5,400 licenses were issued for imported food additives and over 1,200 licenses for domestically produced additives.

The DOH Bureau of Food Sanitation oversees the amendment of laws and regulations, the review and approval of special dietary foods, and the registration and pre-market approval of food additives as well as domestically produced low-acid canned foods. Inspection, sampling, testing and supervision of foods and food sanitation is handled by local health authorities.

Pharmaceutical Regulation

All medicines and medical devices, both imported and locally produced, must be registered and issued product licenses by the DOH before they are marketed in the Taiwan area. Local health authorities conduct regular and unscheduled inspections and sample medicines and cosmetics that are manufactured, imported and sold in their areas. Manufacturers and purveyors of medicines and cosmetics that are found unqualified are punished according to the *Pharmaceutical Affairs Law* 藥事法 and the *Cosmetics Sanitary Control Law* 化妝品衛生管理條例.

By December 1995, the DOH and the Ministry of Economic Affairs 經濟部 had jointly issued the GMP seal to 225 certified pharmaceutical factories. An ongoing GMP monitoring program maintains the integrity of the ROC pharmaceutical industry as well as the quality of drug products in the market. All GMP drug manufacturers are inspected at least once every two years. Factories which do not meet the GMP standards are fined between US$1,100 and US$5,600. Factories which fail to improve as directed within a determined time may also be shut down by health authorities, and their applications for registration and market permits suspended during the probation period.

The DOH monitors the products of the domestic pharmaceutical industry for safety. During the monitoring period, manufacturers should submit records of safety monitoring in designated teaching hospitals for their newly licensed drugs and immediately report any side effects observed. Test results of domestic clinical trials are also required. As of July 1995, some 241

new chemical substances and 412 new pharmaceutical formulations were being monitored.

The DOH is currently conducting a truth-in-advertising campaign. Provincial and municipal health authorities strictly review applications for advertisements. According to the newly amended *Pharmaceutical Affairs Law*, media that run advertisements exaggerating the efficacy of medical products are subject to heavy fines.

The differentiation of the medical and pharmaceutical professionals is one of the most important task in restructuring the health services landscape in Taiwan. By mid-1995, over 1,000 community pharmacies were contracted with the DOH to be part of the health care delivery system. These pharmacies have to adhere to "Good Dispensing Practice." The DOH is helping to upgrade the quality of pharmaceutical personnel through on-the-job education and by helping to set up computerized patient profiles.

Drug Abuse

Until fairly recently, Taiwan's drug problem was no worse than that of Europe or America 20 years ago, and was also well behind neighboring areas like Japan and Hong Kong. But all that began changing in the early 1990s, when the number of drug-related criminal arrests started rising—from a fairly steady 5 percent or less of arrests each year to 13 percent in 1991, some 19 percent in 1992, and nearly 32 percent in 1993. By December 1994, drug offenders had replaced burglars as the largest group in Taiwan prisons, accounting for 63 percent of Taiwan's inmate population. However, there was a 7 percent decrease in drug-related criminal arrests in 1995.

Drug abuse on Taiwan is unfortunately trending toward harder drugs. In the 1970s, sporadic cases of glue sniffing were reported, and, in the 1980s, incidences of sedative abuse were occasionally uncovered. By the early 1990s, the drug of choice was amphetamines, with the addition recently of heroin. Although there were fewer than 34,000 addicts on record in the Taiwan area in 1995, it is estimated that more than 200,000 people (or nearly 1 percent of the total population) are currently abusing at least one substance, primarily methamphetamine or heroin. In contrast to the more than 3,760 kilograms of amphetamines (including raw materials and semi-products) seized in 1995, only 204 kilograms of illegal narcotics were confiscated, 70 percent less than during the same period last year. Thus amphetamine abuse has moved to the fore of current health care concerns in Taiwan.

Currently, there are four drug detox centers and 132 hospitals with a total of 722 beds. Arrested drug addicts are sent there for treatment before serving their sentences. There are also four special jails for inmates with drug-related offenses. Following the US DAWN model, a network for the survey of the prevalence of drug abuse and case reporting for the Taiwan area has been set up. All these detoxification, rehabilitation and medical care facilities, however, need to be expanded to deal with the estimated 200,000 drug addicts in Taiwan.

Traditional Chinese Medicine

Chinese medicine, just as valued today by Chinese people as it has been for thousands of years, is enjoying new-found respect from modern western medical researchers. In Taiwan, the main research body specializing in tradi-

tional Chinese medicine is the Committee on Chinese Medicine and Pharmacy (CCMP), members of which are selected from the ranks of the nation's most distinguished doctors of Chinese medicine. As of December 1994, there were 7,738 licensed doctors of Chinese medicine in the Taiwan area, but only 2,833 of them were actually practicing. There were 1,985 Chinese medicine hospitals and clinics, 9,812 licensed dealers of herbal medicines, and 250 manufacturers of herbal medicines.

In Taiwan today, treatment through Chinese medicinal practices—including acupuncture, moxibustion 艾灸 (burning of a medicinal plant close to pressure points to restore the body's "energy flow" 行氣 throughout what Chinese medicine refers to as the 12 meridians 經絡), and herbal remedies—is readily available. Treatment through Chinese medicine is also covered by the National Health Insurance program.

Chinese medicine is shaking off the stigma of being unscientific by combining age-old practices with high technology. At the Foundation for East-West Medicine 國際醫學科學研究基金會 in Taipei, doctors are using an electro-dermal screening device (ESD) to pinpoint the source of an illness. The ESD measures what traditional Chinese medicine refers to as the "energy flow"

Training in Chinese Medicine

Doctors of Chinese medicine can receive training at China Medical College Hospital 中國醫藥學院附設醫院, which offers a seven-year Chinese medicine program and a four-year post-baccalaureate Chinese medicine program to train modern Chinese medicine doctors. Candidates can then take the national examination offered by the Examination Yuan to qualify as Chinese medicine doctors. Candidates who have passed the written examination must also receive eight months of training in basic medical sciences, followed by ten months of clinical practice before they can be certified as doctors of Chinese medicine. Other hospitals with a Chinese medicine department include the Taipei Municipal Hoping Hospital 台北市立和平醫院, Taipei Municipal Chunghsiao Hospital 台北市立忠孝醫院, Taipei Municipal Chungshing Hospital 台北市立中興醫院, Taipei Municipal Jen-ai Hospital 台北市立仁愛醫院, Taipei Municipal Yangming Hospital 台北市立陽明醫院, Kaohsiung Municipal Chinese Medicine Hospital 高雄市立中醫醫院, Taiwan Provincial Keelung Hospital 台灣省立基隆醫院, Taiwan Provincial Hualien Hospital 台灣省立花蓮醫院, Taiwan Provincial Hsinying Hospital 台灣省立新營醫院, Taiwan Provincial Chiayi Hospital 台灣省立嘉義醫院, Tainan City Hospital 台南市立醫院, Hsiu Chuan Memorial Hospital 秀傳紀念醫院 (Changhua), Cardinal Tien Center 耕莘醫院, Mennonite Christian Hospital 門諾會醫院 (Hualien), Tzu-Chi Buddhist General Hospital (Hualien), St. Mary's Hospital 羅東聖母醫院 (Lotung), and the Min-Shen General Hospital 敏盛綜合醫院 (Taoyuan).

Number of Chinese Medicine Hospitals and Clinics, December 1995

	Hospitals	Clinics	Total
Overall Taiwan Area	109	1,876	1,985
Taiwan Province	88	1,461	1,549
Taipei City	10	277	287
Kaohsiung City	11	138	147

Source: Department of Health

in a patient's body by probing the acupuncture points 穴脈. Acupuncture is applied in the dentistry department, for example, to locate problems by tracking the places of energy stasis in the mouth. Once the problem area is detected, dental instruments are used to determine the problem.

The ROC is on the front lines of medical research on acupuncture and Chinese medicine. Various research projects have been conducted to evaluate the effects of Chinese medicine and acupuncture on various types of illnesses and diseases. The China Medical College 私立中國醫藥學院, for instance, has undertaken studies on the effects of Chinese medicine and acupuncture on hepatitis, sciatica, and other chronic diseases. Similar research studies have also been done on the effects of Chinese medicine on nephrosis. Chinese herbal remedies have also been developed for diseases like systemic lupus erythematosus, intestinal ulcers, and bronchial asthma. Between 1989 and 1994, the DOH underwrote 89 research projects in Chinese medicine. Several research projects have examined the tranquilizing effects of acupuncture. Such efforts are helping incorporate Chinese acupuncture techniques into the mainstream of modern medicine. In addition, important but abstruse Chinese medicine classics

have now been interpreted with modern research findings and published. The CCMP has also made other classics, such as the *Huang-ti Nei-ching* 黃帝內經 and *Chin-yuan Ssu-ta-chia* 金元四大家, available to the public in a computer-software format.

The Department of Health and the China Medical College study the distribution and cultivation of medicinal plants in the Taiwan area. With the assistance of the agriculture and forestry agencies, some rare medicinal plants of high economic value have been cultivated on a trial basis. If the results of the trials are satisfactory, these plants will be farmed on a large scale to safeguard the supply of raw materials. In the meantime, Kaohsiung Medical College and the China Medical College have been requested to evaluate and assess the efficacy of the available Taiwan-grown herbs to establish a data base on raw materials for Chinese medicine. An eight-year program to standardize some 200 Chinese medicine prescriptions was also started in July 1990. The program also authorizes factories to produce Chinese medicine. The China Medical College is hosting a project to promote the cross-Straits exchange of Chinese medicine doctors and pharmacists.

From romantic Paris to diverse Sydney,
Yang Ming Line supplies every possible service
to bring the whole world closer together.
Your trust is our honour.
"Punctual, Speedy, Reliable, and Economical"
is our quality commitment.

Yes, We can.

Taiwan's first shipping company awarded both the ISO 9002/ISM
CODE accreditation and the National Outstanding Quality Case

YANG MING LINE
陽明海運股份有限公司

4-6th Fl.,No.53 Hwai Ning St., Taipei, Taiwan, R.O.C. Tel:(02)3812911 Telex:1157
YANGMING Fax:(02)3148058 Keelung Tel:(02)4230149 Kaohsiung Tel:(07)83105
Internet web address http://www.yml.com.tw. E-mail address cs@hp720.yml.com.t

Metropolitan Rapid Transit Systems

❀ The initial Taipei Rapid Transit Systems (TRTS) network will meet the transportation needs of eight major corridors in metropolitan Taipei, strengthen the link between downtown Taipei and satellite towns and cities, and promote the overall development of the Taipei metropolitan area.

❀ The inital network will span 88 kilometers in Taipei City and Taipei County.

DEPARTMENT OF RAPID TRANSIT SYSTEMS, TMG.

7, Lane 48, Sec. 2, Chung Shan N. RD., Taipei Taiwan R.O.C.

Tel: 886-2-521-5550   Fax: 886-2-511-5335

16.
Mass Media

Previous page: The media has both benefited from and played a part in the democratic reforms and liberalization of society that have transformed Taiwan over the last decade.

Upper: The modernization of infrastructure is a crucial part of Taiwan's efforts to transform itself into an telecommunications center for the Asia-Pacific region.

Lower: The extensive incorporation of high technology in production has invigorated Taiwan's media industry.

16 Mass Media

Virtually all media markets in the Republic of China have changed dramatically in recent years, partly in response to technological advances, but perhaps more in concert with the lightning pace of democratization. New cable service authorizations and broadcast spectrum allocations have greatly increased the diversity of radio and television stations available to domestic audiences. Taiwan enjoys a flourishing multimedia and information industry. The domestic publishing industry is also thriving, and more than a few foreign publishers are joining Taiwan's magazine market. With increasing joint use of resources and global competition, more and more media operators are engaging in cross-media as well as international cooperation. This chapter discusses the most significant of recent changes in the ROC media industry, which include the proliferation of print media, the growth of cable TV, the release of new broadcast allocations, and the governmental and private-sector efforts to strengthen the industry.

Print Media
News Agencies

As of December 1996, there were 241 domestic news agencies in the Taiwan area, compared to 36 before the lifting of the ban on new press agencies in 1988. Concentrated in Taipei and generally small in scale, most of them focus on economic and financial news and developments in the stock market. They serve the print and electronic media, government agencies, financial organizations, the industrial and commercial sectors, and local schools.

The oldest and largest news agency is the Central News Agency 中央通訊社. In January 1996, the agency was reorganized as a state-run corporation, with the ROC government allocating just over US$370,000 to facilitate the reorganization process. The CNA is now the only nationwide news agency in the ROC. It operates on a 24-hour basis and employs more than 400 people in 15 departments. The agency also maintains 27 overseas offices and 40-plus overseas correspondents.

Every day the CNA provides 200,000 words of general-interest news over the Internet to more than 100 Chinese- and English-language newspapers. The agency's business wire transmits another 120,000 words to business-oriented clients. It also provides an audio-visual news service for local radio stations and cable TV operators, and supplies news photographs. It has amassed more than 1.3 million historical news photos since its establishment in 1924. In addition, the CNA maintains a database of around one million newspaper clippings collected over the years.

The Liberty News Agency 自由新聞社 focuses on financial and economic news as well as stock market information. It often sponsors courses, lectures, and panel discussions on stock investment. The Overseas Chinese News Agency 華僑通訊社 provides information on overseas Chinese affairs to the domestic and international media. The agency is an affiliate of the Overseas Chinese Affairs Commission 僑務委員會. The Military News Agency 軍事新聞通訊社 (MNA), which is under the Ministry of National Defense 國防部, is the only domestic news agency that specializes in military news. Besides news releases, the MNA also provides video programs for television.

There is also a long list of other professional news agencies that serve domestic subscribers. The China Youth News Agency 幼獅通訊社 emphasizes youth activities and educational reports. The China Economic News Service 中國經濟通訊社, an affiliate of the *United Daily News* 聯合報, provides domestic and foreign economic news and international financial updates in English to foreign businessmen in Taiwan. The Commercial and Industrial News Agency 工商徵信通訊社 targets the business sector with Chinese-language market information on various Taiwan industries. The China Labor News Service 中國勞工通訊社 offers reports on labor organizations, factory workers, and business. And the Ming Pan News Agency 民本通訊社 provides

Government Information Office

The existing *Organizational Statute of the Government Information Office under the Executive Yuan* 行政院新聞局組織條例 was promulgated in January 1981, stipulating the structure and functions of the ROC Government Information Office 新聞局. The GIO's departments include Domestic Information Services 國內新聞處, International Information Services 國際新聞處, Publication Affairs 出版事業處, Motion Picture Affairs 電影事業處, Radio and Television Affairs 廣播電視事業處, Compilation and Translation 資料編譯處, Audio-Visual Services 視聽資料處, and Planning and Evaluation 綜合計畫處. There is also a Division of Information and Protocol 聯絡室, a Regulations Committee 法規會, and an Appeals Committee 訴願會. In addition, the GIO oversees the Chinese Taipei Film Archive 國家電影資料館, the Broadcasting Development Fund 廣播電視事業發展基金, Kwang Hwa Publishing Company 光華書報雜誌社, and the preparatory committee for the ROC public television system 公共電視籌備委員會. The GIO is on-line to Internet users around the world, providing information on the Republic of China, its culture, latest developments, and challenges at *http://gio.gov.tw.*

information on Buddhist activities and articles about Chinese medicine.

Newspapers

The proliferation of the electronic media in many countries has had an adverse effect on the print media. Taiwan's newspaper industry, however, has expanded in the face of competition from cable TV. Major threats come not from the electronic media but from competitors in the newspaper market itself. The ROC government's lifting of restrictions in January 1988 on newspaper licensing and number of pages per issue, in effect, produced a more vocal press as major newspapers worked to maintain their lead in the market and new entrants tried to find their own target readers. The dramatic increase in the number of newspapers from 31 in 1987 to 371 by December 1996 has been accompanied by a steep rise in circulation.

Despite enjoying rapid growth, the ROC newspaper industry faces many challenges. The rising cost of newsprint, up 70 percent in the past three years, is the most serious problem facing today's newspaper publishers. Besides increasing their prices to boost business income, Taiwan's newspaper publishers have also reexamined their operational strategies to carve out market niches. The print media has had to keep pace with technological advancements by going on-line in order to compete with other

media. Most of Taiwan's major newspapers have installed modern printing equipment and computerized their editorial and printing processes. Moreover, they manage their own distribution and marketing systems and affiliated publishing companies, and have established various funds for sponsoring cultural activities and encouraging literary creation. What follows is a look at several Taipei-based, Chinese-language newspapers which together show the diversity of the ROC newspaper industry.

Representative Publications

The *China Times* 中國時報 is part of a chain of publications, including the *China Times Weekly* 時報週刊, the *China Times Express* 中時晚報, the *Commercial Times* 工商時報, and the Taiwan edition of the French magazine *Marie Claire* 美麗佳人. Its affiliated publishing companies include the China Times Publication Company 時報文化出版公司, the Infotimes Company 時報資訊公司, the Shih Kuang Company 時廣企業有限公司, and the Jih Fa 吉發 marketing firm. In September 1995, the enterprise went digital with the China Times Web site 中國時報系全球資訊網, providing daily electronic newspapers through the Internet to Chinese-language readers worldwide. According to the Chicago-based Audit Bureau of Circulation, the daily circulation of the *China Times* was over 1.28 million copies in 1986, while the *China Times* itself disclosed a daily circulation of 1.21 million in 1996.

The *United Daily News* 聯合報 is the flagship publication of another major family of publications, including the Taiwan-based *Economic Daily News* 經濟日報, *Min Sheng Daily* 民生報, *United Evening News* 聯合晚報, *Unitas* 聯合文學 literary monthly, and *Historical Monthly* 歷史月刊, in addition to the *World Journal* 美洲世界日報 in New York, the *Europe Journal* 歐洲日報 in Paris, and the *Universal Daily News* 世界日報 in Thailand. Its affiliated companies include the China Economic News Service, the Linking Publishing Company Ltd. 聯經出版事業公司, United Information Inc. 聯經資訊公司, and the World Television Corporation in New York. The current global circulation of the UDN chain of newspapers is said to be more than three million copies per issue.

The *Liberty Times* 自由時報 registered a daily circulation of 930,000 copies as of April 1996, up from 185,000 copies in 1988. The company publishes a US edition through its Los Angeles branch. The *Central Daily News* 中央日報, the official news organ of the Kuomintang 中國國民黨, is known for its comprehensive coverage of ROC politics. In contrast to the *Central Daily News*, the Independence Post group assumes a liberal approach in its news coverage. The *Independence Evening Post* 自立晚報, and its sister publication, the *Independence Morning Post* 自立早報, also have an international edition, the *Independence Weekly* 自立週刊.

While Taipei's major papers provide extensive coverage of national issues and approach the news more objectively, local dailies based in Kaohsiung perhaps reflect a stronger sense of the local identity of the people in southern Taiwan. Aggressive and provocative, the Kaohsiung press places a heavy emphasis on political news as well as the culture, literature, and history of the southern region. The *Commons Daily* 民眾日報 and the *Taiwan Times* 台灣時報, two leading Kaohsiung papers, are peppered with expressions unique to the Taiwanese dialect.

Other major locally focused newspapers include the *Taiwan Daily News* 台灣日報 in the central part of the island, the *China Daily News* 中華日報 in Tainan, the *Keng Sheng Daily News* 更生日報 in Hualien 花蓮, and the *Chien Kuo Daily News* 建國日報 on the offshore Pescadore Islands 澎湖群島.

The *Mandarin Daily News* 國語日報 and the *Children's Daily News* 兒童日報 are two children's papers published regularly. They carry news features and fictional stories written for elementary school students. Their texts feature Mandarin phonetic symbols as pronunciation glosses for each Chinese character.

Taiwan has two English-language dailies, the *China Post* and the *China News*. Although originally targeted at Taiwan's foreign community, they have become popular learning tools among students of the English language; today Chinese

Other Government Agencies Overseeing the Media

With the promulgation of the revised *Organic Law of the Presidential Office* 總統府組織法 in January 1996, the Department of Public Affairs 公共事務室 (DPA) was established under the Office of the President. The DPA combined the old presidential spokesman's office and appeals department. The DPA's three sections are in charge of clarifying and publicizing government policies, releasing news, collecting and reflecting public opinion, and managing appeals from the citizenry. However, it is the Military Spokesman's Office 軍事發言人室 under the Ministry of National Defense that oversees the release of military news and arranges visits of domestic and foreign journalists to the ROC armed forces. Other government information agencies include the Taiwan Provincial Department of Information 台灣省政府新聞處 and the information departments/bureaus 新聞處 of city and county governments.

All of the government information agencies are responsible for clarifying and publicizing national policy, government ordinances and administrative achievements, and regulations governing publications and the broadcast and movie industries. They also strengthen cultural communications with the Chinese mainland.

people form the bulk of readers for these two newspapers.

The Government Information Office publishes the *Free China Journal* (*FCJ*) in English once a week, and French and Spanish journals every ten days. The *FCJ* can also be accessed via the Oklahoma-based DataTimes International Online Network.

Magazines

The government's policy to liberalize and globalize Taiwan's economy and trade system has accelerated the development of the ROC magazine industry. In May 1983, *Newton* became the first foreign magazine authorized for publication in Taiwan with a Chinese translation. Since then, the number of Chinese editions of American and Japanese science magazines available locally has skyrocketed. International magazines that introduce new fashions and feature movie stars are also popular. In 1995, Taiwan imported 9.15 million magazines, representing a total market value of US$74 million.

The lifting of restrictions on the licensing and page limits of newspapers has had a strong impact on magazine publishers as well. Newspapers can now offer lengthy, in-depth coverage of hot news topics on a daily basis, compared with the monthly cycle of most magazines, so companies producing magazines have had to look beyond the domestic market to boost revenues. Confronted with the strong competition, many Taiwan magazine publishers are promoting sales in Hong Kong, the Chinese mainland, and elsewhere abroad. Moreover, as with all publishing sectors, the magazine industry has come under the mounting pressure of higher production costs and encroachment by the electronic media.

Nevertheless, the ROC magazine industry is witnessing substantial growth. The 1988-94 period averaged 700 new magazines and 500 discontinued magazines, according to GIO statistics. In other words, about 200 new publications were being launched and prospering on an annual basis. The number of registered magazines increased from 3,922 in 1988 to nearly 5,500 by

National Press Council

The National Press Council of the ROC 中華民國新聞評議委員會 (NPC), founded in 1974, currently consists of eight news groups 新聞團體: the News Editors Association 中華民國新聞編輯人協會, the News Agency Association 中華民國新聞通訊事業協會, the National Association of Broadcasters, ROC 中華民國廣播電視事業協會, the ROC Television Association 中華民國電視學會, Taiwan Province Press Association 台灣省報紙事業協會, Taipei Press Guild 台北市報業公會, Kaohsiung City Press Association 高雄市報紙事業協會, and Taipei Journalists Association 台北市新聞記者公會, to safeguard press freedom, promote press discipline, and raise the standards of media ethics. The NPC review board comprises veteran journalists, scholars of journalism, legal experts, and prominent civic figures. The panel regularly assesses the quality of media production in the Taiwan area in accordance with the Code of Ethics for Chinese Journalists 中國新聞記者信條, the Code of Ethics for the ROC Press 中華民國報業道德規範, the Code of Ethics for ROC Radio Broadcasting 中華民國無線電廣播道德規範, and the Code of Ethics for ROC Television 中華民國電視道德規範. The NPC reviews complaints raised by the public or other concerned parties and announces its conclusions after exhaustive investigations and hearings.

The NPC publishes a monthly magazine and numerous books exploring news issues. The council cooperates with the electronic and print media to promote the exchange of public views, and produces a ten-minute news evaluation program, *News Bridge* 新聞橋, which is simulcast on Taiwan's three television stations every Sunday evening. In 1990 the council began presenting the Outstanding Journalist Award of the ROC 中華民國傑出新聞人員研究獎. Each recipient obtains a research scholarship equivalent to as much as US$18,500 to study abroad for a period of three to six months. The council also offers programs for advanced studies at home to encourage professional journalists currently employed in the news media.

Foreign Correspondents in the ROC

As of December 1996, 43 foreign mass media organizations had correspondents and photographers stationed in the Republic of China. The accredited foreign correspondents were from the following enterprises:

- AFX-Asia Financial News Service (Hong Kong)
- Agence France-Presse (France)
- AP-Dow Jones News Service (United States)
- ARD German Television (Germany)
- *Asia Inc. Magazine* (Hong Kong)
- *Asia Times* (Thailand)
- *Asian Equities Report* (United States)
- *Asian Wall Street Journal* (Hong Kong)
- Associated Press (United States)
- Associated Press Television (United States)
- Black Star Photographic Agency (United States)
- *Bloomberg Business News* (United States)
- *Business Watch* (Nigeria)
- *Business Week* (United States)
- Chinese Television Network Ltd. (Hong Kong)
- *CommsNews Asia* (Australia)
- *Economist* (United Kingdom)
- *Far Eastern Economic Review* (Hong Kong)
- *Financial Review* (Australia)
- *Financial Times* (United Kingdom)
- *Hobby Japan* (Japan)
- Hong Kong Commercial Broadcasting Co. Ltd. (Hong Kong)
- *Inflight Entertainment* (Hong Kong)
- Knight-Ridder Financial News (United States)
- *Lianhe Zaobao* (Singapore)
- *Ming Pao Daily News* (Hong Kong)
- *Nachrichten für Aussenhandel* (Germany)
- *Nanyang Siang Pau* (Malaysia)
- *Nihon Kogyo Shimbun* (Japan)
- *The Nineties Monthly* (Hong Kong)
- Pan-Asia Newspaper Alliance (Japan)
- Reuters (United Kingdom)
- Reuters Television (United Kingdom)
- *Sankei Shimbun* (Japan)
- *Shipping and Trade News* (Japan)
- *Sin Chew Jit Poh* (Malaysia)
- *Sing Tao Daily* (Hong Kong)
- *South China Morning Post* (Hong Kong)
- *Straits Times* (Singapore)
- *Time* (United States)
- United Press International (United States)
- Voice of America (United States)
- *Yazhou Zhoukan* (Hong Kong)

December 1996. These publishers promote their sales through advertisements, direct marketing, telemarketing, discounts, giveaways, and by offering lotteries.

Financial Magazines

Since 1982, financial journals have outpaced Taiwan's other kinds of magazines in sales and advertisement revenues. According to a fiscal 1996 survey by *Brain Magazine* 動腦雜誌, Taiwan's top three magazines in terms of circulation are *Common Wealth* 天下雜誌, *Wealth* 財訊雜誌, and *Money* 錢雜誌. Fifteen-year-old *CommonWealth* is highly respected for its attractive design, excellent business image, and concern for the well-being of society. Its coverage of macroeconomic trends and modern man-

agement concepts carries much prestige in the commercial sector. For many years, *Common-Wealth* has maintained a sales figure of about 67,500 copies per issue and a subscriber-renewal rate of around 65 percent. In fiscal 1996, the magazine's sales increased to 68,392 copies per issue, up from 67,645 the previous year. The company attributed the jump in sales largely to its two-year promotion of markets overseas, particularly in Southeast Asia.

Wealth is considered a "must read" by many stock investors, entrepreneurs, and politicians in Taiwan because of its insightful articles. Even though the magazine seldom employs any means of sales promotion, it still maintains a subscriber-renewal rate of around 30 percent. The company places a heavy emphasis on sales at the news stand, and operates a wide-ranging distribution system to secure market share. *Wealth* averages newsstand returns of below 20 percent. In each of fiscal 1995 and 1996, the magazine averaged sales of about 47,850 copies per issue.

With personal finance as its focus, *Money* frequently sponsors lectures on managing finances for housewives and employees of leading enterprises. *Money* maintains about 50 percent of its subscribers each renewal period. The magazine's per-issue circulation averaged 46,110 copies in fiscal 1995, but slipped to 44,480 copies the next year.

Success 成功雜誌 is an international commercial magazine which appears in Taiwan in a Chinese edition. While most of the Taiwan edition's editorial content is staff-generated, 30 percent of its articles are solicited from instructors in educational training and another ten percent are translated from stories written in foreign languages. Since its establishment in October 1994, *Success* has spotlighted numerous prosperous industries in Taiwan, with particular attention given to direct-sales businesses. It is not unusual for the direct-sales sector alone to buy thousands of copies of a single issue of the magazine. Each month *Success* averages holding 36 lectures islandwide on personal training and marketing techniques, again selling large quantities of its issues at the events. Moreover, the contents of the lectures are turned into profitable tapes and books. As a result, the business income from these activities is even higher than the magazine's advertising revenues. The magazine's monthly advertising income averages US$25,925, while the activities can bring in as much as US$185,000 per month. In 1995, *Success* began to cooperate with some 30 radio and TV programs, expanding its market presence. The company also promotes sales through membership cards. In fiscal 1996, *Success* averaged sales of more than 15,600 copies per issue in Taiwan.

Women's Magazines

In recent years, as major cosmetics companies from abroad have penetrated the Taiwan market, international women's magazines also have launched Chinese editions on the island. *Harper's Bazaar, Cosmopolitan, Elle*, and *Vogue* are among them. Despite the influx of foreign competition, locally owned women's journals remain the leaders in domestic market sales. In fiscal 1996, the most popular women's journal in Taiwan was *Beauty* 美人誌, a local quarterly founded in June 1994. The magazine's sales have climbed to around 171,000 copies per issue. With scant effort spent on selling advertising, *Beauty* relies on the retail sales of its issues for more than 90 percent of its revenues. Subscriptions account for another 5 percent.

Likewise, the eight-year-old *Lady Ann* 安少女 magazine does not emphasize the selling of ad space among its pages. Also similarly, a hefty 95 percent of the publication's business income comes from newsstand sales and subscriptions. The magazine has about 5,000 subscribers in Taiwan, 3,000 in the combined market of Hong Kong, Singapore, and Malaysia, 2,000 in mainland China, and a smattering of subscribers in each of 30 other countries around the globe. *Lady Ann* has increased its print run from 12,000 copies for its first issue to around 60,000 copies for each of its current issues. Since its contents are mainly about movie stars, fashion, romance, fortune-telling, and the daily routines of young people, the magazine largely attracts a young female readership. When students take a break from their studies during the summer and winter recesses, the retail sales of *Lady Ann* magazine soar by as much as 88 percent.

Nong Nong 儂儂雜誌, another leading Taiwan magazine, has long maintained stable subscriptions and lively retail sales, owing to the company's aggressive promotional campaigns. Promotions range from advertising and discounts to giveaways, VIP membership cards and lotteries. *Nong Nong*'s readers are mostly unmarried women aged between 25 and 35. Currently, however, the company has embarked on a campaign to boost circulation among students. *Nong Nong*'s per-issue circulation hit 21,100 copies in fiscal 1996.

The 30-year-old *Mademoiselle* 女性雜誌 attracts readers with articles on fashion, famous personalities, cultural activities, travel, and food. A substantial portion of the magazine's revenues—60 percent—comes from the copious advertisements run in each issue. The monthly advertising income usually totals between US$55,500 and US$74,000. *Mademoiselle* promotes its sales by working in tandem with private and governmental organizations on special campaigns. It also encourages beauty parlors and trade unions to purchase group subscriptions. *Mademoiselle* averaged sales of 13,164 copies per issue in fiscal 1996.

General-interest Journals

General-interest journals in Taiwan mainly cover current events, social morals and political issues. In the past decade, the release of new radio frequencies and television channels has diversified information outlets on the island. In turn, this has reduced the sales of general-interest magazines. For example, the circulation of the Taiwan edition of *Reader's Digest* 讀者文摘 had hovered at around 190,000 copies per issue before falling to 160,000 in 1993 and 1994. But in June 1995, the magazine began offering a 50 percent discount on subscriptions, which helped circulation return to and even exceed previous heights. In fiscal 1996, its local sales averaged 207,819 copies per issue. The content of the Taiwan edition includes translations from the original English edition, supplemented by original Chinese-language essays of particular interest to Taiwan readers.

The *Better Life Monthly* 講義 places an even stronger emphasis on articles about social morals than does *Reader's Digest*. Last year, the circulation figure for *Better Life* averaged around 47,500 copies per issue. Sales dipped slightly to 37,500 copies per issue in fiscal 1996.

With its hard-hitting writing style, *The Journalist* 新新聞週刊 weekly magazine has sculpted an image for itself as a sharp critic of ROC political matters. Currently, the magazine is waging a campaign to cultivate more student subscribers by offering them special discounts. In another promotion move, *The Journalist* lowered its newsstand price to US$2.20. Sales of the magazine reached 22,764 copies per issue in fiscal 1996.

Business affairs from across Asia are the focus of the Hong Kong-based *Yazhou Zhoukan* 亞洲週刊 magazine. More than 80 percent of the publication's readers are businessmen aged between 30 and 40. In the past two years, *Yazhou Zhoukan* has made a strong effort to secure a foothold in the local market by establishing a branch on the island, launching a Taiwan edition, and increasing its coverage of Taiwan news. Local sales of the magazine in fiscal 1996 averaged 18,855 copies per issue.

Special-interest Magazines

With the flourishing of the ROC computer industry and the arrival of the Internet in Taiwan, computer science magazines have become very popular among local readers. Launched in February 1996, *PC Home* 電腦家庭 has witnessed a lightning-fast rise to prominence. The publication already has a circulation of 90,000 copies per issue, 50,000 of which are sold on the newsstand and the rest by subscription.

The Third Wave 第三波 is published by Taiwan computer giant, the Acer Group 宏碁關係企業集團. As the magazine targets people who are new to computers, more than 30 percent of its readers are students. Even though the publication raised its cover price from US$5.50 to US$7.40, sales have not been affected. It averaged a circulation of 27,000 copies per issue in fiscal 1996.

PC Magazine 微電腦傳真 provides information on industrial computerization and also reviews new products and emerging technologies. The publication has maintained sales of around 25,000 copies per issue in each of the past two years.

Amazing Computer Entertainment 電腦玩家, a Chinese-language publication licensed by the US *PC Gamer* magazine, introduces and analyzes new computer games and software. A free CD-ROM is included inside each issue. The magazine averaged sales of 20,042 copies per issue in fiscal 1996. *Style Game*

Magazine 新遊戲時代 also evaluates new computer-game software, and naturally most of its readers are students. Its circulation in fiscal 1996 was 18,640 copies per issue.

There are many other specialized magazines from which to choose as well. Convenience stores and corner newsstands in Taiwan carries periodicals on baseball, golf, cars, stereo equipment, religion, pets, gourmet cooking, the film industry, broadcasting, travel, leisure, and more.

English-language periodicals and magazines which juxtapose Chinese and English texts are an entertaining way for Taiwan readers to learn a foreign tongue. Currently, nine such periodicals are published in Taiwan. Among them, *Studio Classroom* 空中英語教室, which is also available on CD/ROM, had a sizable print run of 105,683 copies per issue in fiscal 1996. Half of its readers are college students.

Another such publication, *Let's Talk in English* 大家說英語, boasts more than 100,000 readers. A fast-rising bilingual magazine, *Time Express* 解讀時代, attracted 41,000 readers to its debut December 1995 issue. Other English or bilingual magazines in Taiwan include the *Free China Review* (available in English, French, German, Russian, and Spanish editions), *Sinorama* 光華 (available with English, Spanish, or Japanese texts juxtaposed with Chinese), *Taiwan International Trade*, and *This Month in Taiwan*.

Books

The ROC has a lively book publishing industry, with political and economic titles enjoying particularly large markets. Between 1988 and 1996, the number of registered book publishers in the Taiwan area increased from 3,190 to 5,286. The expansion of the book market has paralleled the rising affluence and purchasing power of the Taiwan public. Also, the government's campaign to promote a more culture-conscious and literary society in Taiwan has added fuel to the growth of the publishing industry. In 1995, total book sales in Taiwan climbed to around US$1.48 billion. Currently, local publishers are printing about 20,000 books each month.

Electronic Data Interchange

In December 1995, the Government Information Office commissioned the Institute for Information Industry 資訊工業策進會 to implement a nationwide program of electronic data interchange (EDI) as a means of promoting circulation growth in the book publishing sector. By April 1996, book publishers, wholesalers, retailers, exchange centers, and distribution services were linked to the EDI network. Information on new books, acquisition outlets, and delivery and return systems can be obtained through the EDI. As such, the EDI system can strengthen publishers' internal management and accounting systems, improve their delivery services, and save time and cost by minimizing labor and errors.

Book publishers in Taiwan can be classified into three groups: governmental, semi-governmental, and private. The Taiwan Book Store 臺灣書店 is a government agency under the Taiwan Provincial Department of Education 台灣省教育廳 responsible for editing and publishing elementary and high school textbooks. Semigovernmental units include the Cheng Chung Book Co. Ltd. 正中書局, which is run by the Kuomintang, and the Youth Cultural Enterprise 幼獅文化事業 of the China Youth Corps 中國青年反共救國團. As for the private publishers, about 80 percent of them are located in northern Taiwan. Most are small or medium-sized businesses with 10 to 50 employees; only a few have more than 100 full-time workers. Large-scale private firms have public affairs departments for developing marketing strategies, and frequently send new releases to book reviewers and media programmers. Their standard promotional methods involve sending news releases to and advertising through the mass media. Many newspapers and magazines have special columns introducing and critiquing new books. The opinions expressed in these columns are used as a benchmark by readers and publishers alike. Information on Taiwan's book market is also available from the National Central Library's International Standard Book Number Center 國家圖書館國際標準書號中心 and ISBN newsletter and by accessing the GIO's Internet address: *http://crab.ccl.itri.org.tw/newbooks*.

The demand for a tremendous number of textbooks over the past 50 years has nurtured the development of the printing industry as well as the publishing industry in Taiwan. Cheng Chung has long been a leader in this market, and about ten private publishers have also played important roles. Since 1996, the government's market liberalization policy has enabled private publishers to grab a bigger share of the textbook market. As Taiwan society stresses the importance of academic entrance examinations, the market for elementary and high school reference materials will remain profitable and keenly competitive in the years to come. Several large-scale companies that publish reference books operate their own printing and binding factories as a means of reducing production costs and raising competitiveness. One of them, the Tainan-based Nan I Book Enterprise Co. Ltd. 南一書局, began publishing high school reference books in 1957. Today its annual business income (excluding in-store sales) from primary and high school reference books exceeds US$4.6 million.

The pirating of college textbooks from overseas was common in Taiwan from the 1950s through the 1970s. But the revised ROC *Copyright Law* (see insert, below) promulgated on July 11, 1985, forced such publishers to change this business practice. Local publishers who once relied on unauthorized editions now strictly seek reprint permission from copyright holders, and many of them also have turned into importers. With Taiwan focusing on globalization and appropriating vast sums of money for research purposes, the market for imported Western books is poised for solid growth. Many foreign publishers are actively promoting their books in

Copyright Law

The ROC faced possible US trade sanctions starting in 1989, when it was first placed on the "Special 301" watch list of countries accused of violating American copyrights. But over the past few years, the ROC government has made big strides toward eliminating commercial piracy and the infringement of intellectual property rights (IPR) in Taiwan. The crackdown on pirated software has greatly reduced the amount of unauthorized exports. As evidence of this, in 1993 local authorities uncovered 879 incidents of software piracy, while in 1995 there were only 95 cases.

Furthermore, the government has revised the ROC *Copyright Law* to meet IPR safeguards previously set forth by the United States. In April 1993, the amended *Law* went into effect in Taiwan. The revised law grants copyright protection for up to 50 years after the death of a work's author and imposes a maximum fine of US$16,667 and a jail term of one to seven years on copyright violators. Then on January 16, 1996, the Ministry of the Interior called for a retroactive clause to be built into a subsequent amendment. The draft of this revision, which grants retroactive protection of copyrights going back 50 years prior to the law's implementation, is currently under legislative review.

The Ministry of the Interior's Copyright Committee 內政部著作權委員會 has launched several campaigns calling the public's attention to the importance of IPR protection. On April 11, 1996, Taiwan CD manufacturers signed a self-regulation pledge at the start of a "Copyright Week" that ran through April 17. Then on April 21 at a "Copyright Carnival" 著作權博覽嘉年華會, top ROC government officials led the general public in taking a pledge to support the protection of copyrights.

At the end of April 1996, the United States finally removed Taiwan from the Special 301 watch list in recognition of the ROC government's progress in protecting copyrights, trademarks, and patents. The US decision is expected to improve Taiwan's image in the world market. In particular, Taiwan manufacturers of electronics and information products are expected to benefit by obtaining more export orders and by gaining greater access to foreign technical expertise.

Taiwan. Among them, Simon & Schuster, Oxford, Longman, Thomson, and McGraw-Hill have set up Taiwan branches and sent representatives to manage their sales on the island. In 1995, Taiwan imported nearly 13 million foreign books.

Books on finance, trade and business management are at the top of the production schedules of local publishing houses. But easier access to overseas destinations and a stronger New Taiwan Dollar also have given rise to more books on foreign countries, unfamiliar cultures, and self-help travel tips. In addition, publishers have responded to the growing public concern for better health and spiritual growth amid Taiwan's ever-more-hectic lifestyles and increasing materialism. Also in recent years, the production of electronic books and CD-ROM products has expanded rapidly, further diversifying Taiwan's publishing sector. As an example of this, the Kwang Toong Book Department Store 光統圖書百貨公司, a major wholesaler of electronic books, operates seven outlets in Taipei and Kaohsiung. The company supplies electronic books to 120 retailers island-wide.

One of the major goals of the ROC publishing industry is to integrate the Chinese-language publications printed in Taiwan, Hong Kong, and mainland China. However, there are numerous barriers to overcome, not the least of which is the rising cost of production, contributor, translation, and royalty expenses for works from abroad. Furthermore, with the global supply of paper pulp plummeting from 1.4 million to 200,000 metric tons, prices of paper stock in Taiwan for books and newspapers have shot through the roof. And as Taiwan is totally dependent on imported paper, with no local pulp resources, prices will inevitably continue to rise. In 1995 Taiwan imported 342,000 metric tons of paper stock for use by newspapers and another 140,000 metric tons for general use.

Bookstores and Bestsellers

When Kingstone Book Store 金石堂書店 enterprise launched its chain of stores in 1983, it marked the first remarkable change in Taiwan's retail book market. Since then, Q Book Center Corporation 永漢國際書局, New-Schoolmate Book Co. Ltd. 新學友書局, and Caves Books Ltd. 敦煌書局 have followed suit and opened fleets of spacious, bright, and comfortable chainstores to attract customers. The Eslite corporation 誠品書局 arrived on the scene in 1989, representing another innovation in the marketing of books in Taiwan. Presenting a highly professional image, Eslite extended its cultural function beyond the selling of books to include the holding of art exhibitions, lectures, and musical performances in its stores.

By December 1995, Kingstone had expanded operations to include 51 chainstores. For Eslite, the number had increased to 12. The aggregate business income of Kingstone's stores reached US$92.59 million that year, about 12 percent of the total income of Taiwan's entire bookstore industry. The large-scale chains have changed the purchasing habits of Taiwan consumers and have become a major retail force. In 1984, Kingstone again broke new ground by compiling for customers a regular list of its 100 best-selling books, and other retailers soon followed suit. Most bookstores in Taiwan today promote self-compiled "top 100" lists. Taiwan's convenience stores also display bestsellers on their racks. The promotion of bestsellers has helped make books fast-moving commodities in Taiwan.

Besides fiction and non-fiction titles, comic books also appear frequently on the store's bestseller lists. Taiwan produces more than 4,000 kinds of comics each year. Convenience stores, supermarkets, newsstands, and bookstores share the estimated US$185 million market for comic books. Since the 1960s, Japanese comic books have been the market mainstay. Even after the promulgation of the strengthened *Copyright Law*, the authorized versions of Japanese comic books still occupy 95 percent of the market in Taiwan. Daran Culture Enterprise Co. Ltd. 大然文化事業股份有限公司 and Tong Li Publishing Co. Ltd. 東立出版社有限公司 are the sector's two biggest publishers. Daran's 1995 business income from comic books was US$7.1 million. For Tong Li, revenues totaled US$4.22 million.

In Taiwan, sales of the most popular Japanese comic books can exceed 100,000 copies per issue. *Crayon Little Hsin* 蠟筆小新 and *Bow Wow* 家有賤狗 often enjoy such numbers. Moreover, the added-value market of comic books in Taiwan is estimated at around US$185 million per year. This would include sales of cartoon cards, posters, cassette tapes and videotapes as well as the royalties for movies and TV programs. Though Japanese imports control a dominant share of the local market, many domestic comic books are witnessing lively sales as well. The per-issue sales of *Wu Lung Yuan* 烏龍院 have topped 80,000 copies, and the byproducts, such as films and TV programs based on the Taiwan comic book, also do a brisk business.

Direct Book Sales

Despite the advent of chainstores, only 20 percent of the book consumers in Taiwan go to bookstores to purchase their reading materials. Publishers have found that direct marketing can be a highly effective technique locally. The method was first used by Formosan Magazine Press Ltd. 台灣英文雜誌社 in the mid-1970s when the company marketed large sets of books through door-to-door sales, direct mail, and telemarketing. Since then numerous publishers have followed the example, including the US company Grolier, which has established a Taiwan branch and trained its salesmen to sell imported English-language encyclopedias by calling on households directly. From 1975 to 1985, sales of book sets on the island enjoyed a boom period, and the massive direct-marketing campaign involved hundreds of salespeople. Sales of encyclopedias averaged 3,000 sets per year, and annual revenues during the period were between US$3.7 million and US$5.6 million.

In 1980, Taiwan publishers started translating sets of foreign books and selling them locally through direct marketing. But due to a lack of professional management know-how, at the outset the sales of the translated books were

Book Fairs

From 1987 to 1996, the Taipei International Book Exhibition was held five times, with the number of participating nations increasing from 11 to 34 over the period. The Fifth Taipei International Book Exhibition, held January 19-24, 1996, was Asia's biggest and the world's fourth-largest book fair. In all, 588 publishers from 34 countries took part. One of the exhibition's principal functions was to facilitate copyright exchange. With "East Meets West" as its theme, the 1996 book show promoted Taiwan as a gateway to publishing industry exchanges between nations around the globe. Since 1988 the Government Information Office has sponsored Taiwan publisher participation in such international book shows as the Frankfurt Book Fair, the London International Book Fair, the Singapore World Chinese Book Fair, the Malaysia International Book Fair, the Hong Kong International Book Fair, and the Bologna Children's Book Fair.

slow. By the early 1990s, however, the direct-sales book market had grown to about 30 companies and 3,000 salespeople. Taiwan currently has about ten large-scale publishers that rely almost exclusively on direct-sales systems, the most prosperous of which have annual business revenues as high as US$74 million. The sales personnel of direct-marketing publishers are generally between the ages of 20 and 35. The gender ratio is 6.5 women to 3.5 men. Seventy percent of Taiwan's direct-sales personnel are engaged in the promotion of books for children and young students.

Children's Books

Over the past ten years, the market for children's books in Taiwan has witnessed substantial growth. In 1988 and 1989, the lifting of restrictions on publications stimulated the exchange of children's literature between Taiwan and the Chinese mainland. Taiwan publishers began purchasing reprint authorization from mainland publishers in addition to cooperating with mainland authors and translators. Around that time, about 20 children's periodicals put out their first issues in Taiwan. Also, popular comic strips started appearing in book form, covering subjects ranging from science and history to biographies and languages. In 1990, local writers became interested in writing books for children. Within a short time, children's books created in Taiwan were winning recognition on the world stage. In 1991 and 1992, Taiwan illustrators of children's books received awards at competitions in Bologna, Italy, and Catalonia, Spain, respectively.

Since 1993, the quality of Taiwan's *hui-pen* 繪本, or illustrated books, has improved rapidly. Several of these publications have won international prizes, while others have even sold copyrights to publishers in other countries. In view of such favorable acclaim, Taiwan publishers are actively encouraging local writers to create new novels or retell historical stories for children. Even so, at present more than 70 percent of the children's books on the Taiwan market are foreign publications. Taiwan and mainland China publications share the rest of the market. Many private organizations and government agencies, including the Government Information Office, Ministry of Education 教育部, and Taiwan Provincial Government 台灣省政府 have established funds and awards to encourage more local writers and publishers to create children's literature.

Broadcasting
Radio

After the ROC government's relocation to Taiwan, the radio industry in the Taiwan area expanded rapidly. However, due to military and telecommunications needs, only a limited number of frequencies were available for commercial broadcasting until the late 1980s. In 1987, the Government Information Office, Ministry of Transportation and Communications 交通部, and Ministry of National Defense began consultations on the release of new broadcast channels. But as the first of these were not opened until 1993, the delays in legislation led to the emergence of underground radio stations at the end of 1990. By 1994, there were an estimated 40 unlicensed stations operating throughout the Taiwan area. The majority of the illegal radio stations openly criticized government policies, and their call-in programs on political issues attracted considerable audiences. From April to August of 1994, the GIO, supported by the Ministry of Justice 法務部 and 6,000 local policemen, began a major crackdown on unlicensed radio broadcasts. In some instances, supporters of the programs staged large-scale public protests.

Since 1993, the GIO has accepted 169 applications for new AM and FM radio stations. Many of the applications have been filed by opposition groups and activist organizations. The large demand for channels prompted the GIO to reallocate the frequency spectrum so that it could accommodate three classes of FM stations: community, regional, and national. Community stations were limited to a maximum transmitter output of 250 watts and a service area of five kilometers. The limitations for regional-class stations were 3,000 watts and a service area of 20 kilometers, while national-class stations were allotted 30,000 watts and an unlimited service area. AM stations were limited to a maximum output of 1,000 watts and a service area of 40 kilometers. To encourage underground radio stations to become legal, the GIO reduced the minimum required capital for applicant community stations to an equivalent of US$37,000. As a result, many of the underground stations have applied for licenses. By September 1996, the GIO had issued 118 radio broadcasting licenses, with the application review process still ongoing.

Programming

The broadcast industry in Taiwan has come a long way since the 1950s, when dramatic, cultural, educational and children's programs on the radio were the mainstays of household entertainment. The advent of TV broadcasting in Taiwan in the 1960s brought revolutionary change to local entertainment habits. But another major change occurred in the 1980s, when radio stations adopted policies to specialize in order to secure target audiences. Currently, many radio stations focus almost exclusively on such specialty areas as current news, light music, traffic updates, stock market reports, or agricultural news. Throughout the 1990s, news stations have diversified their programming to include regular features and studio and telephone interviews. Also, newspapers, with their vast resources, have started working in cooperation with radio stations to bring the latest news into local homes as quickly as possible.

The ROC's increasing social diversity and growing public assertiveness have led to a proliferation of radio call-in programs. Listeners are eager to express their views on the air about national developments and to put questions to government officials who visit the studios to answer inquiries about government policy. Call-in programs cover a wide range of topics, everything from health care to traffic laws. A radio station in Taoyuan even airs a call-in program for Thai laborers who are working locally. Radio broadcasting in Taiwan includes regular domestic programming by medium-wave AM and VHF FM stations, medium- and short-wave broadcasts to the Chinese mainland, and specialized programming via short-wave transmissions to other countries. Programs in various Chinese dialects and English are also available.

Station Facilities and Services

The Broadcasting Corporation of China 中國廣播公司 (BCC) operates a flagship station in Taipei, nine regional stations, and two professional stations which specialize in agricultural programs and traffic reports. The BCC has six national and five regional simulcast programming streams. These networks offer popular music, national news, industrial and commercial services, educational and religious programs, stock market reports, and programs in the Southern Fukienese 閩南語 dialect. The news and popular music programs are simulcast to the Chinese mainland. In addition, the BCC transmits programs overseas via The Voice of Free China 自由中國之聲 in 14 languages along 31 short-wave frequencies. Through The Voice of Asia 亞洲之聲, it broadcasts in seven languages over two medium-wave

frequencies. In January 1996 the BCC signed a memorandum with the Radio Corporation of Singapore for the exchange of programming and personnel.

The Central Broadcasting System 中央廣播電臺 operates six stations equipped with 24 short- and medium-wave transmitters across Taiwan. Its broadcasts also reach most of the Chinese mainland. Through four simulcast programming streams, the CBS broadcasts to the mainland news about political, economic, cultural, educational, and social developments in Taiwan. These programs are broadcast mainly in Mandarin, but a few are presented in the Southern Fukienese, Cantonese and Hakka dialects, as well as in such borderland languages as Mongolian, Tibetan and Uigur. In January 1996, the ROC Legislature 立法院 passed the *Central Broadcasting System Establishment Statute* 中央廣播電臺設置條例, merging the CBS and the BCC's Voice of Free China into a single corporation. Though reorganized, the CBS continues to shoulder the responsibility of broadcasting to the global community and the mainland news of developments in the ROC's governmental policies, business activities, tourism, and education.

The Cheng Sheng Broadcasting Corporation Ltd. 正聲廣播公司 (CSBC) operates one FM, eight AM, and nine relay stations islandwide. The stations gear their programming to the needs of Taiwan's agricultural, fishing, and labor communities. Programs are broadcast in the Southern Fukienese and Hakka dialects as well as in Mandarin. In October 1994, CSBC launched a new service called the Information Broadcasting Company 生活資訊調頻台. Since October 1995, the company has been using an Integrated Services Digital Network (ISDN) to broadcast its "Super Sound" music program and simulcasts with KAZM AM 1300, a Chinese-language radio station in Los Angeles. The ISDN is also used to facilitate audience call-ins on the CSBC's news program aired in cooperation with the *China Times*.

The Public Radio System 警察廣播電臺 (PRS) specializes in traffic reports and social services. Besides its headquarters station in Taipei, the PRS has seven regional stations and eight relay stations across the island. Its traffic-news networks are located in the cities of Taipei, Taichung, Kaohsiung, and Hualien. The PRS also operates an Evergreen Network 長青網 to provide middle-aged and elderly citizens with cultural programs and information on medicine, health, and retirement. Through a computerized network, PRS stations receive and distribute round-the-clock reports on road conditions and traffic snarls in local areas and on the freeways. The traffic news is interspersed with music and special features.

International Community Radio Taipei (ICRT), owned and operated by the Taipei International Community Cultural Foundation, is Taiwan's only predominantly English-language radio station. Its FM and AM channels broadcast separate programming, including popular Western music, talk shows, and community service segments. ICRT is available via audio streaming on its 24-hour Internet home page at *http://www.icrt.com.tw*. A preparatory committee for the International Cultural Radio Corporation Ltd. was issued a construction permit in December 1995 for the first nationwide radio station in the ROC. A search is currently in progress for a sight on which to start construction of the new station.

Television
Over-the-air

The three major commercial television services in the ROC are the Taiwan Television Enterprise 台灣電視事業股份有限公司 (TTV), the China Television Company 中國電視股份有限公司, and the Chinese Television System 中華電視股份有限公司 (CTS). CTS is the only television station telecasting on both VHF and UHF, the latter being used mainly for its educational programs. The three commercial TV stations will soon be joined by a Kaohsiung-based Formosa Television corporation 民間全民電視股份有限公司, which in June 1995 won the license to set up Taiwan's fourth nationwide TV station. Formosa TV, which is affiliated with the opposition Democratic Progressive Party 民主進步黨, will most likely telecast on VHF low-band channels in the 76 to 88 MHz range, starting in 1997.

Golden Bell Awards

Since 1965, the Government Information Office has presented the Golden Bell Awards 金鐘獎 to outstanding radio and television programming. In fiscal 1996, the GIO spent US$98,520 on Golden Bell Awards for outstanding radio programming and US$240,740 on the awards for outstanding video programming and cable broadcasting systems. The awards aim to raise the standards of radio and television programming in the ROC.

TV programming in Taiwan makes effective use of digital networks and the latest video and filming techniques. The TV movies are transmitted along satellite TV and cable TV systems. The satellite and cable TV systems are highly sophisticated, as their facilities are convertible through uplink equipment to telecommunications usage. As such, the three commercial TV stations are facing a major threat with a growing number of viewers tuning in to satellite and cable TV. Because the ROC's *Cable Television Law* (see section below) does not permit over-the-air enterprises to operate cable systems, the three commercial stations are feeling intense pressure to preserve market share by improving their programming and technical facilities. In January 1992, the three stations began to use MTS/SAP stereo broadcast systems to allow viewers a bilingual selection of the audio portions of certain foreign-language programs. The sub-channel selection is primarily between English or Japanese. The commercial stations also started using satellite technology to improve reception of live remote transmissions and retransmitting programs on a second sub-carrier. The stations have enhanced their reporting of news by establishing bureaus in central and southern Taiwan and stepping up international exchanges.

Cable

Regulated cable television operation arrived relatively late on Taiwan. In 1976, illegal cable stations known collectively as the "fourth channel" began to operate in Keelung, and before long had spread islandwide to serve a growing market demand. After the government eased media restrictions, operators throughout Taiwan began openly competing for both cable and over-the-air broadcast channels. The cable TV stations attracted an enormous number of subscribers by offering a wide selection of Chinese and foreign movies, serial dramas from Hong Kong, variety shows, and cartoons. When KU-band and C-band receivers were legalized in Taiwan, the viewing options further expanded to include satellite TV.

Prior to November 1993, Taiwan's cable systems operated outside the law, forcing the government to step up legislation of the ROC's *Cable Television Law* 有線電視法. When the law was passed in August 1993, the Government Information Office began working out details on a legal framework for authorized cable systems. The existing illegal operators were required to register with the GIO. They will have to cease operations when authorized cable systems begin providing programming in the service area concerned. By the deadline of November 1, 1994, the GIO had received 204 applications for cable TV operation in Taiwan's 51 designated service areas. In September 1996, the application review process was completed and 126 operators had obtained construction permits.

In 1996, there were 150 cable TV systems and more than 1,000 programming and videotape suppliers. Today the cable operations offer some 60 channels, including satellite-based programming by NHK from Japan, HBO, CNBC and the Disney channel from the United States, as well as local sports, home-shopping services, music video channels, and talk shows. Approximately 75 percent of the satellite TV programming in Taiwan reaches more than two million households. One of the most popular channels is TVBS 無線衛星電視台. In its first year of operation, the channel attracted three million Taiwan households, or nearly 90 percent of all cable viewers. TVIS 歡樂放送台, which offers live telecasts of Taiwan's professional baseball and basketball leagues, is also high on cable subscrib-

ers' viewing lists. Other popular satellite channels include the American cable channel, ESPN, which features sports programs with Chinese subtitles, and MTV, featuring rock music videos. In addition, the Hong Kong-based Star Chinese Channel, Star Plus (cartoons and TV serials), Star Movie Prime Sports, and Channel V (music videos) are available. The major news and information channels that appeal to Taiwan viewers include the Chinese Television Network 傳訊電視中天頻道, which offers news round-the-clock, CNN, NBC Asia, and the Discovery Channel (which features Chinese subtitles). The programming distributed by satellite TV services through cable TV operators continues to eat away at the viewership and advertising profits of the three commercial TV stations in Taiwan.

Public TV

Since the currently three over-the-air stations are commercially oriented, the viewing public expressed an interest in having a full-fledged national public television station (PTV) with high-quality programs free from commercial interruption. Accordingly, the Legislature 立法院 in 1982 revised the ROC's *Radio and Television Broadcasting Law* 廣播電視法, stipulating that a portion of the annual profits of the commercial stations must be earmarked for a public television fund. The Broadcasting Development Fund was thus founded, and in May 1984 noncommercial programs were first broadcast on airtime allocated by the three commercial channels. In June 1990, a 22-member public television organization committee was set up to draft a *Public Television Bill* 公共電視法草案. The bill is meant to serve as public television's blueprint for hardware facilities, programming policies, and long-term allocations of financial resources. The bill calls for PTV to have its own channels and telecasting facilities instead of relying on a mere 15 hours of airtime per week presently allocated by the three local VHF television stations. The plan is for PTV to telecast exclusively on UHF channels 50 to 53 throughout Taiwan. Programming would be relayed from studios in Taipei via

Asia-Pacific Media Center

In 1995, the ROC government began to step up a project to build Taiwan into an Asia-Pacific media center. The primary goals of the project are to globalize the ROC media industry and develop Taiwan into a regional center for the production of Chinese-language movies and TV programming. From a commercial standpoint, the project aims to encourage private investment, spur the production of quality high-tech movies and TV programs, and create a lively market for such Chinese-language productions.

To realize the Asia-Pacific media center project, the Government Information Office has been working to improve Taiwan's environment for media growth, complete legislation of the ROC's *Satellite Television Bill* 衛星電視法, and liberalize cable TV operations. The GIO is drawing up plans for cultivating and training media professionals; setting up a consultation committee comprising the business, government and academic sectors; soliciting plans that could be incorporated into a "media park" project; and coordinating land tax incentives, lower tariff rates, and preferential loans with the appropriate governmental agencies.

satellite on KU-band uplink frequencies of 14.1-14.5 gHz and downlink frequencies of 12.2-12.75 gHz to UHF stations at ten sites around Taiwan. Viewers in Taiwan, the offshore islands of Quemoy, Matsu, and the Pescadores, as well as much of Southeast Asia should be able to receive the UHF PTV signals. PTV has conducted a number of trial broadcasts since 1995 to prepare for regular broadcasting, and PTV programming is currently available in the evening on selected cable TV systems around the island. In September 1992, the *Public Television Bill* was submitted for review by the Legislature; however, it has yet to be passed.

Motion Pictures

Chinese films made in Taiwan, as well as those from Hong Kong and mainland China, have stepped into the international limelight in the 1990s. Movies from the three areas have become the new favorites of judges at international festivals, winning numerous awards. In one example, at the 46th Berlin International Film Festival in February 1996, directors from Taiwan and the Chinese mainland won the Jury Prize while one from Hong Kong won the Silver Bear Award for best director.

Despite winning many awards of late at international festivals, Taiwan movies are suffering a period of decline here at home. Production in the local movie industry has decreased and

box office sales have shrunk noticeably. Applications for production licenses have fallen sharply, from 82 in 1990 to only 28 in 1995. Movies made in Hong Kong were the market leaders in Taiwan during the early 1990s, accounting for most of each year's highest-grossing films. But since 1993, foreign movies have outperformed their Chinese counterparts both in terms of films screened and box office sales. Foreign movies are expected to soon become the mainstream at Taiwan cinemas.

Over the past few years, the government has made a number of attempts to reinvigorate the Taiwan film industry. One such step was approval by the Executive Yuan 行政院 of the *Tax Deductions for the Purchase of Equipment or Investment in Technology by Private Movie and Television Enterprises* 民營影視事業購置設備或技術適用投資抵減辦法. Passed on February 1, 1996, the tax deductions are applicable to any private movie or TV enterprise

Number of Films Screened in Taiwan

Origin	1990	'91	'92	'93	'94	'95
Taiwan	82	33	40	23	*29	*28
Hong Kong	166	182	198	188	137	133
Other	258	285	296	223	211	261
Total	506	500	534	434	377	422

* One film renewed its license

Source: Department of Motion Pictures Affairs, GIO

that purchases in a particular taxation year automation equipment or technology worth more than US$22,222. The deductions also apply to purchases by such firms of the same amount of equipment or technology for controlling pollution or recycling resources. The investments are eligible for tax exemptions of between 5 percent and 20 percent. The tax incentive is regarded as an important measure for bolstering the development of ROC media industries.

Despite such positive steps, Taiwan filmmakers have had to branch out by investing in Hong Kong and mainland Chinese movies. (For details, see the Cinema section in Chapter 21, The Arts.) Financial assistance from the Government Information Office has given Taiwan's filmmaking industry a shot in the arm. In order to boost local film production, the GIO doubled its fiscal 1996 budget for local film assistance.

Film Imports

In October 1994, restrictions on the import of mainland Chinese movies and videotapes were lifted. Eight categories of mainland films were allowed for release in Taiwan: science and technology, business management, nature and animals, geography and scenic locations, culture and the arts, sports, language instruction, and medicine and health. In February 1995, variety and dramatic films were added to the list. The GIO's Department of Motion Picture Affairs on February 7, 1996, promulgated guidelines on the import quota, categories, and viewing hours allotted to Chinese mainland movies and videotapes in the Taiwan market. The annual import of mainland Chinese films is limited to ten different titles and 36 copies of each. Chinese mainland TV and radio programs are not counted as domestically produced programs. As such, their broadcast hours may not exceed 16 percent of the total airtime of channel operators in Taiwan.

In October 1994, quota restrictions on Japanese films were eliminated in line with the principle of free trade. Further, in June 1995 the permitted number of copies of each foreign film was increased from 24 to 28, and each foreign

Domestic Film Grants (US$)	
Fiscal 1995	*Fiscal 1996*
Film Production Grants:	
8 films	17 films
$1.85 million	$3.7 million
Outstanding Screenplay Awards:	
10 scripts	10 scripts
$111,111	$111,111
Outstanding Distribution:	
5 companies	5 companies
$18,518	$22,222
Outstanding Screening:	
22 cinemas	28 cinemas
$814,814	$1.04 million
Golden Harvest Awards:	
23 works	19 works
for Short Films and Videotapes:	
$74,074	$109,260
Golden Horse Awards:	
$237,037	$237,037

film imported into Taiwan was allowed to be screened simultaneously at 11 city cinemas and six county cinemas.

Telecommunications
Networking

To meet growing demands for a stronger national information infrastructure in the ROC, an Asynchronous Transfer Mode virtual path switch multiplexer and local area network has been established. The National Information Infrastructure 國家資訊通信基本建設 (NII) was launched on July 14, 1995, at the Hsinchu Science-based Industrial Park 新竹科學工業園區 in northern Taiwan. The initial services of the NII include a multimedia database, cable TV services, electronic data interchange, automated customs clearance, distance learning, and distance medical treatment. The NII also renders technical assistance to domestic research organizations and the private sector for the development of a broadband network, video on demand, multimedia applications, network security, and field trials.

Promotion of the information infrastructure has helped to usher in Internet services, enormously increasing the operational ranges and incomes of domestic networks. By November 1996, the TANet 台灣學術網路 had 400,000 local users; the HiNet 網際資訊網路, 166,000 users; and the SEEDNet 種子網路, 40,000 users. The growth of Internet applications themselves have been truly amazing. While there were only 35 World Wide Web home pages in Taiwan in 1994, the number had skyrocketed to 485 by December 1995.

Telecommunication Sector Reconfigured

Before July 1996, telecommunications services in the ROC fell under the jurisdiction of the Directorate General of Telecommunications 電信總局 (DGT), which is supervised by the Ministry of Transportation and Communications. The arrangement was very effective in achieving unified operations and optimal utilization of resources at a time when both Taiwan's telecommunications technology and economic development were in their early stages. However, the trend toward economic liberalization in recent years revealed that the original telecommunications structure could no longer meet social and consumer needs. Consequently, a regulatory reform process was initiated, ultimately resulting in the promulgation of an amended ROC *Telecommunications Act* 電信法 on February 5, 1996. The new legislation mandates the privatization of the huge government telecommunications monopoly within five years. The new act empowers the DGT to censor telecommunications companies and opens up five categories of services to private-sector investment. These include mobile data communications, very-small-aperture terminals (VSAT), trunking radio services, and pager and cellular phone services.

In accordance with the *Telecommunications Act*, Chunghwa Telecom Co. Ltd. 中華電信股份有限公司 (CHT), a fully state-run enterprise, was inaugurated to assume all the functions of providing telecommunications services. The CHT has six subordinate business groups responsible for daily business operations in dif-

Statistical Profile of Chunghwa Telecom
As of July 1, 1996

Total Assets	US$14.9 billion
Total Revenues (FY1996)	US$ 5.8 billion
Total Expenses (FY1996)	US$ 4.1 billion
Employees	35,719
Telephone Subscribers	9,575,918
Telephone Density	44.7 lines/100 persons
Mobile Phone Subscribers	
GSM	284,412
AMPS	590,748
Mobile Phone Density	4.1/100 persons
Radio Pager Subscribers	2,212,516
Pay Station Density	5.74/1,000 persons
HiNet Subscribers	95,323
Local Switches	12,416,883
Digitization Rate	95.89%
Toll Switches	863,000
Digitization Rate	100%
Toll Trunks	719,458
Digitization Rate	99.79%
International Direct Circuits	12,020

Source: Chunghwa Telecom Co. Ltd.

ferent regions of Taiwan and in different kinds of services. As a step toward globalization, the CHT has set up a Global Development Business Group 電信開發分公司 to coordinate domestic resources and speed up efforts to cultivate telecommunications markets abroad.

Telecommunications Services

Over the past four decades, the DGT has undertaken a number of telecommunications development projects to meet Taiwan's steadily growing information needs. Taiwan's local communications networks have been modernized with digitized telephone switches. The DGT also plans to develop the Integrated Services Digital Network (ISDN) to significantly enhance the quality and diversity of services. Taiwan's first ISDN field trials were conducted in 1989, and ISDN commercial service made its local debut on May 16, 1995, providing end-to-end voice and non-voice transmissions in Taipei, Taichung, Tainan, and

Kaohsiung along the No. 7 Common Channel Signaling System 第七號信號系統 for network interconnection. By September 1996, more than 10,000 ports had been set up to popularize ISDN services islandwide.

Mobile telephone services in Taiwan have been growing at a tremendous pace since their inauguration in July 1989. Because the analog Advanced Mobile Phone System was almost fully loaded, the DGT started a new Global System for Mobile Communication (GSM) cellular telephone service in July 1995 to accommodate the pressing demand. The DGT has also set up international GSM roaming services with Hong Kong, Macau, Singapore, Switzerland, the United Kingdom, Australia, and Malaysia. Negotiations with other countries are ongoing to further expand the coverage of international roaming services.

The first phase of the project to develop the Intelligent Network 智慧型網路 was completed on April 27, 1996, to promptly offer advanced free phone, mass calling, and credit telephone services. The DGT's Telecommunications Laboratories 電信研究所 has developed ATM VPX prototypes and will further develop an ATM/BEX-VCX. These products form the backbone of the broadband service trial network. The services to be provided include: point-to-point video-conferencing, LAN interconnection, video on demand, multimedia database retrieval, and E-mail.

Asia Pacific Cable Network

Asia Pacific Cable Network (APCN) System One, part of a shore-end submarine cable that will eventually connect Taiwan with most of East Asia, came ashore at the Toucheng 頭城 beach in Ilan County 宜蘭縣 on February 5, 1996. In fact, APCN System Two domestic fiber-optic submarine cable systems, one linking Tainan, the Pescadores, and Quemoy as well as another between Taiwan and Matsu are currently in operation to facilitate communication between Taiwan proper and the offshore islands. APCN is an international submarine fiber-optic cable network that is the joint investment of 48 telecommunications companies from 24 countries and regions, including the ROC's International Telecommunications Administration 國際電信管理局 (ITA) under the Ministry of Transportation and Communications. The ITA participates in the APCN project under the name of the International Telecommunication Development Corporation 國際電信開發公司. The ITA's investment requirement is about 8.3 percent of total contractual costs.

The APCN is the eighth international submarine cable system in Taiwan. The others include the Okitai 台琉, Tailu 台呂, Taiguam 台關, and Sinhontai 台港新 coaxial analog cable systems and the GPT 台菲關, Hontai-2 台港2號, and APC fiber-optic digital cable systems. APCN includes a synchronous digital hierarchy and submersible optical amplifiers. The total system length is about 12,000 kilometers, including seven switchable branching units. Based on the power feeding arrangement for the submersible plants, the APCN system can be generally divided into three subsystems, two of which involve Taiwan. One subsystem covers Korea, Japan, Taiwan, and Hong Kong, while another covers Taiwan, Hong Kong, the Philippines, Malaysia, and Singapore. Since the APCN reaches the most affluent and fastest-growing Asian areas, the introduction of the system is expected to expedite the development of Taiwan into an Asia-Pacific regional operations center.

Internet 1996 World Exposition

Internet Expo '96, the first world's fair to be held on the World Wide Web, kicked off February 9 with a ceremony at the Taipei International Convention Center 臺北國際會議中心. The fair began with a demonstration of the "Pavilion of Taiwan, Republic of China," the island's promotional feature on the Internet. Included in the ongoing pavilion program are seven basic categories of information about Taiwan. Internet users can access the program by keying in *http://expo96.org.tw* using Netscape 2.0 or more recent versions. The exhibition itself, which ran until the end of 1996, enabled participating countries to load information about their societies onto the Internet for viewing by over 50 million users of the global computer network.

17.
Education

Above: Something for Everyone—Taiwan's mentally challenged students receive special music training at National Taiwan Normal University's affiliated senior high school.

Right: Educational reform in Taiwan is resulting in an increasing number of extra curricular activities to develop skills and interests outside the mainstream.

Previous page: Preschoolers visiting the Chiang Kai-shek Memorial Hall—part of a growing number of Taiwan children getting an early start on their education.

17 Education

Education is strongly emphasized in the Republic of China, as it has been throughout Chinese history. Article 164 of the ROC Constitution states: "Expenditures of educational programs, scientific studies and cultural services shall not be, in respect of the Central Government, less than 15 percent of the total national budget; in respect of each province, less than 25 percent of the total provincial budgets; and in respect of each municipality or county, less than 35 percent of the total municipal or county budget." In fiscal 1995, more than US$16.75 billion, or 17 percent, of net government expenditures were allocated to education, science, and culture. This was about 6.75 percent of the GNP. That is, the government spent US$642 per citizen in FY1995.

Nine years of education has been compulsory since 1968, and there is a wide range of other educational options for citizens of all ages (see chart, next page). In the 1995-1996 school year from August 1, 1995 to July 31, 1996 (hereafter, SY1995), more than 99 percent of all school-age children (age six to 11) were in school. The enrollment rate of the population aged between six and 21 was 84.96 percent, and more than one-quarter of the total population was attending an educational institution of some type. In 1995, there were 7,228 registered schools, with an average of 39 students per class. A larger proportion of the population now receives higher education. In 1995, the national illiteracy rate was 6 percent.

Even though the education system has provided a large pool of skilled and informed young citizens, it has been criticized for inflexibility and for failing to address the needs of Taiwan's rapidly changing society. As a result, educational reform has become a major issue.

The Educational Mainstream
Preschooling

In 1950, there were only 28 kindergartens in Taiwan and preschool education was uncommon. Although the number of preschools and pupils between four and six years old has increased tremendously since then, limited financial resources have kept two-year preschool education an optional part of the educational system. Only in 1981 was the *Preschool Education Law* 幼稚教育法 promulgated to set basic standards for preschools, and thereby formally protect pupils' rights. The law covers kindergarten organization, the permitted number of pupils, required personnel qualifications, minimum standards for facilities, and financial penalties for violations.

According to the Ministry of Education (MOE), more than 240,360 children attended 2,581 registered preschools in SY1995. Of the registered schools, 883 were public schools, and the remaining 1,698 were private. Registered kindergartens accommodated 21.77 percent of the three- to five-year-olds eligible for schooling. Another 229,600 children attended 3,660 creche and nursery schools, raising the total enrollment to 40 percent or more of the age group. Nevertheless, the preschool enrollment rate is still lower than the 80 to 90 percent found in many developed nations.

About two-thirds of registered kindergartens are private institutions, and have higher tuition. Roughly 400, about one-sixth, of Taiwan's kindergartens are in Taipei; 70 percent of these are private. Private kindergartens in metropolitan areas usually have fewer problems recruiting pupils, because most parents want their children to get a head start in the highly competitive educational system. Outside the larger cities, however, private preschool fees prove to be a burden for most average-income families.

The MOE has recognized the widespread desire among parents to send their children to preschool, and it has tried to increase the number of these schools by affiliating them with existing elementary schools, oftentimes using the same school facilities. Public kindergartens set up by local governments are also encouraged. The central government estimates that preschool enrollment will reach 80 percent of the age group by 2000.

Educational Tracks in the ROC

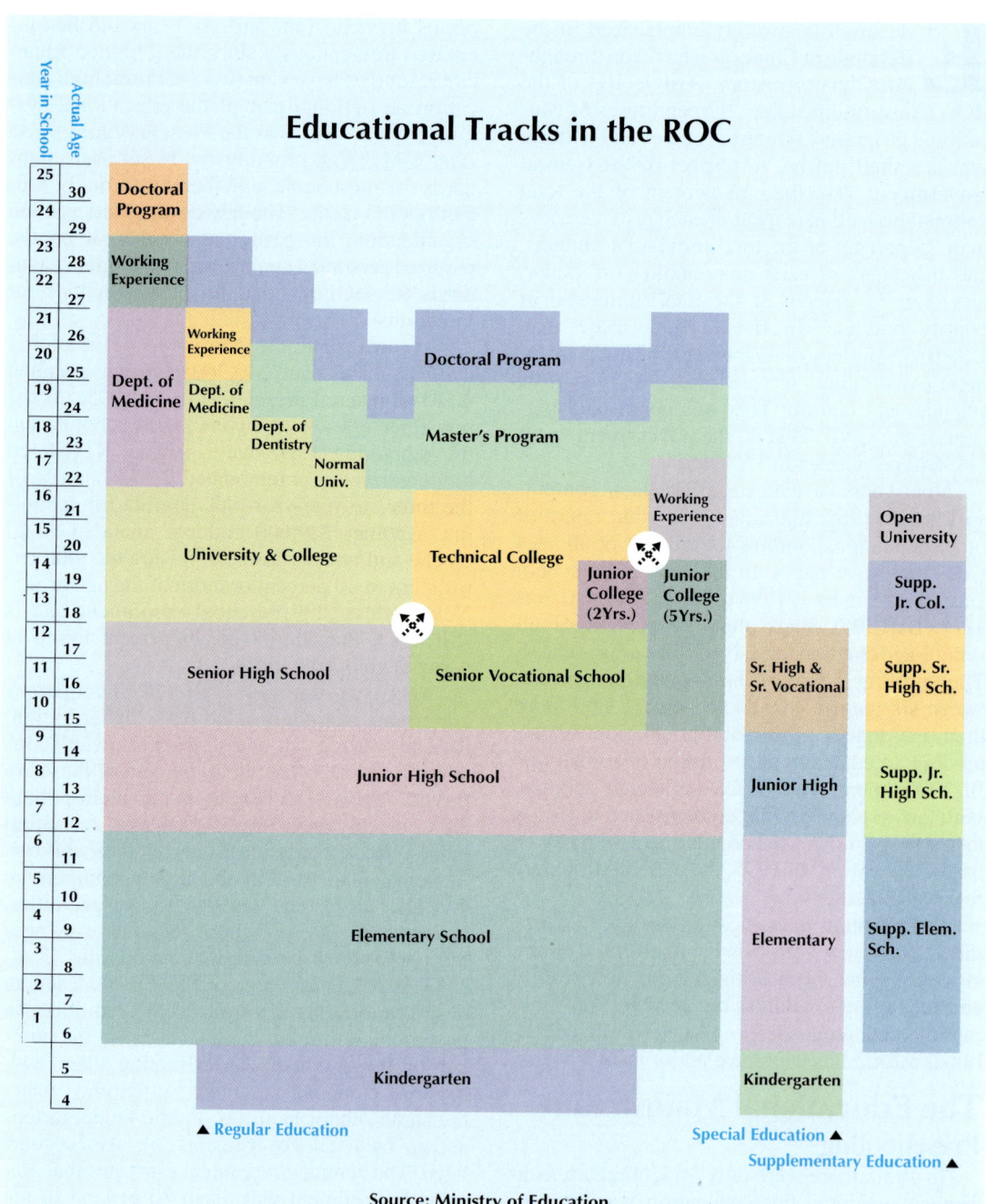

Source: Ministry of Education

Administrative Framework

Education in Taiwan is centrally managed. The Ministry of Education 教育部 sets national education policy, and directly oversees departments and bureaus of education at the provincial and local levels. The Ministry of Education, headed by a cabinet minister, has departments of higher education 高等教育司, technological and vocational education 技術及職業教育司, secondary education 中等教育司, elementary and junior high school education 國民教育司, physical education 體育教育司, and social education 社會教育司; bureaus of international cultural and educational relations 國際文教處, and of student military training 學生軍訓處; as well as a committee on school discipline and moral education 訓育委員會. Provincial and municipal governments have a department 教育廳 or bureau of education 教育局. County governments have education bureaus or sections 教育局.

As noted in *A Report on ROC Education* 中華民國教育報告書 published in 1995 by the MOE, about 20 percent of the operating private kindergartens are not registered, and therefore unregulated. Although they help overcome the shortfall in needed schools, many have poor teaching quality and learning conditions that can jeopardize the rights and safety of their pupils. To redress the situation, the MOE is planning to help private preschools restructure in accord with the law.

In 1983, the MOE first formulated the *Measures for Encouraging Private Preschool Development* 私立幼稚園獎勵辦法 to stimulate positive growth of well-established preschools. Over the past ten years, the number of preschool teachers has risen dramatically, while the number of pupils has stayed roughly the same. This has greatly improved the pupil-teacher ratio (14.9 pupils to one teacher in SY1995-1996). Furthermore, the government adjusted the preschool system in several ways, such as restricting the number of pupils to 30 in one class (less than 28 pupils per class in 1995) and providing more on-the-job training programs for teachers.

In 1995, the MOE promulgated the *Establishment Standard for Universities and Colleges Offering Teacher Education* 大學校院教育學程師資及設立標準, which created a regular channel for training teachers in the preschool system. The MOE is reviewing preschool curricula to ensure they fulfill the purposes stipulated in the

Preschool Education Law. Preschool education is supposed to foster good habits, promote basic physical and mental development, and enrich children's living experience.

Fundamental Education

The Constitution of the Republic of China entitles all children to at least six years of basic education. Building on this constitutional requirement, the *National Education Law* 國民教育法, promulgated in 1979, stipulates that all school-age children (between six and 15) will attend six years of public elementary school and three years of junior high school. Exceptions to this rule are children with special educational needs, students who spend time in the supplementary education track, and a small number of students in experimental schools (all discussed elsewhere in this chapter).

In 1982, when the *Compulsory School Attendance Statute* 強迫入學條例 was revised, the law expressly stated that parents or guardians of children between six and 15 are obliged to send them to school or be subjected to fines and other penalties. To enforce this statute, the Compulsory Attendance Committee 強迫入學委員會 was set up at different levels of local governments.

In 1995, according to compulsory attendance committee reports, about 12,000 school-age children were not attending school and had not completed the compulsory education requirements or received a general equivalence degree. Poor health conditions, poverty, runaways,

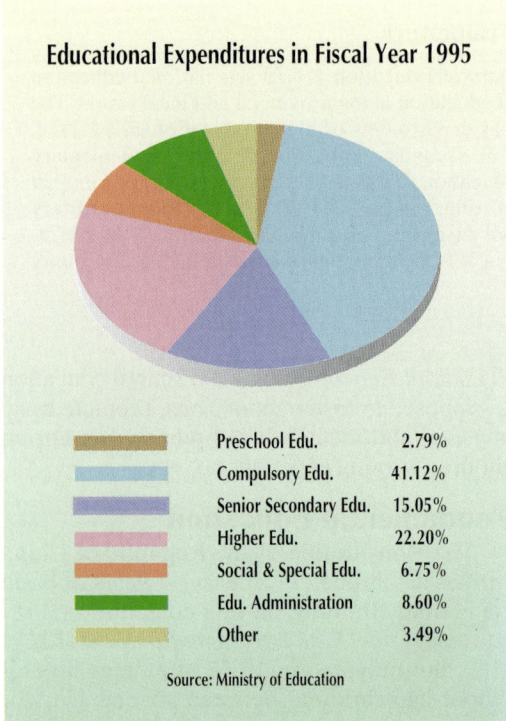

Educational Expenditures in Fiscal Year 1995

	Preschool Edu.	2.79%
	Compulsory Edu.	41.12%
	Senior Secondary Edu.	15.05%
	Higher Edu.	22.20%
	Social & Special Edu.	6.75%
	Edu. Administration	8.60%
	Other	3.49%

Source: Ministry of Education

cation system is the training ground for all children, a larger percentage of students are now continuing their education. In 1950, about 94 percent of students were in elementary or junior high school; in 1995, only 59.86 percent were.

After taking exams open to all students, slightly more than 89 percent of those who completed their compulsory education pursued their studies further, either entering senior high or vocational schools. Even though the remaining students are expected to enter the unskilled labor market or work at marginal jobs, the MOE has designed a program to help these former students acquire more skills (see section below on junior high school).

Elementary Education

Elementary schooling is the first formal education children receive, and the paramount aim is literacy. In 1952, about 42 percent of the Taiwan population could not read and write. Elementary school graduates comprised 77.5 percent of the total number of graduates that year. During the following 15 years, the population's general educational attainment improved as a larger share of children went on to secondary education. The illiteracy rate dropped to 5.99 percent in 1995, and is still falling.

The implementation of universal elementary education has been a success. In 1967, about 97.52 percent of the students aged six to 12 were enrolled. By SY1995, the enrollment rate was 99.91 percent, with an average of less than 36 students per class.

In 1968, when the government introduced nine-year compulsory education, elementary school graduates accounted for 57.35 percent of Taiwan's total graduates. By SY1994, it accounted for only one-third of the total, an indication of elevated general educational attainment. In 1994, the government spent US$2,029 (ranging from US$1,054 to US$2,943) on each elementary student, slightly more than a 10 percent increase over the previous year. There were 1,971,439 students in 2,523 elementary schools in SY1995.

and other personal reasons were the main causes for leaving school. Only about one-tenth of these students have resumed schooling, while 3,200 of them are still missing. But many who resume schooling discontinue their study for a second and even a third time. According to government statistics, Taipei County has the most dropouts, and Hualien County has the highest per capita dropout rate.

In SY1995, the net enrollment rate of students eligible for universal public education was 96.06 percent. Almost all (99.75 percent) the elementary school graduates were promoted to junior high schools as part of the compulsory system. During the same school year, Taiwan had 1.97 million students attending 2,523 elementary schools, more than 1.15 million students in 714 junior high schools, and small numbers attending experimental elementary and junior high schools. Although the compulsory edu-

1995-96 Mainstream Primary and Secondary Educational Resources

	Preschool	Elementary School	Junior High	Senior High	Senior Vocational
Schools	2,581	2,523	714	206	203
Students	240,368	1,971,439	1,156,814	255,387	523,412
Faculty	16,129	87,934	55,201	21,361	19,660

Source: Ministry of Education

Junior High School

In the ROC educational system, the three-year junior high school program is similar to grades seven through nine in the United States. Before 1968, junior high education was optional. Students at this level accounted for less than 15 percent of the total graduates in 1950, and less than one-quarter in 1968.

Junior high school, often referred to as "intermediate education" in Taiwan, is divided into academic and vocational tracks. The future of each child is profoundly affected by the decisions made by educational authorities during these intermediate years, for it is difficult for students to transfer from one track to another. After completing the three-year junior high courses, graduates of both tracks have to pass open examinations to enter senior high school or senior vocational school, both three-year programs.

According to the *National Education Law*, any ROC citizen between 12 and 15 years of age is eligible for public junior high school education. Students also have the option to attend private schools. In SY1995, there were 1,156,814 students attending the 714 junior high schools. Of these, only 1,074 students were registered in the nine private schools. Most classes have 30 students or less.

In SY1995, about 89 percent of the graduates went on to senior high or vocational schools. About 216,000 people sat for the joint public senior high-school entrance examinations 公立高中聯招, and roughly 38 percent were accepted, 12 percent more than in SY1994.

The junior high vocational program was abolished in 1970, after the implementation of nine-year compulsory education two years earlier. Some of the vocational courses were merged into the junior high curriculum, in line with Article 7 of the *National Education Law*, which states that the junior high school curriculum has to cater to both the academic and vocational needs. The law also stipulates that technical courses should be included in junior high schools. Specialized preparation for college or career usually begins at this level, although specific vocational training is not emphasized.

In 1992, the MOE implemented the "Prolonged National Education Based Upon Vocational Education" 延長以職業教育為主的國民教育. The special program was developed to increase work skills of youths who do not want to study further in a general education curriculum. The volunteers who participate in this program expect to enter the work force after graduation, so they have the option of taking technical training courses in their third year of junior high school. After graduation, they may also enroll in vocational schools that provide a minimum of one more year of vocational training, thus prolonging their compulsory education to ten years. After that, a student can take a job or continue studies for another one or two years in vocational school. In 1995, the prolonged educational program was transformed into the Practical Technical Program 實用技能班. Some 36,650 junior high graduates attended the program in SY1995.

In an attempt to reduce the pressure caused by keen competition in the entrance examinations, the MOE is planning to introduce the *Implementation Policies for Pedagogic Innovations at*

the Elementary and Secondary Levels 加強輔導
中小學正常教學實施要點. These policies will set
up alternatives to the entrance exams by establishing experimental bilateral (combined vocational and academic) high schools 綜合高中 and
comprehensive junior-senior high schools 完全
中學, as well as a program entitled the "Voluntary Promotion Scheme for Junior High School
Graduates Entering Senior High Schools" 國民
中學畢業生自願就學高級中等學校方案. These
alternatives will give students a more diversified
educational system with different channels for
completing their junior high and senior high
education.

Secondary Education

The secondary school in the ROC is a comprehensive institution that provides students with
various types of educational programs for their
intellectual development and career interests. The
system of schooling after the nine-year compulsory curriculum is a multilateral system in which
students are assigned to different types of schools
based on a range of factors. After junior high
school, students in the mainstream educational
system may enter one of three types of institutions. Programs vary in length. Those geared for
college entrance are the most difficult, terminat-
ing with rigorous examinations in the student's
late teens.

Among the 382,720 junior high graduates in
SY1994, about 91,000, or 23 percent of the total,
entered senior high school. High schools focus
primarily on training students who expect to
enter college by taking the Joint University Entrance Examinations 大學聯考 (JUEE) after 12th
grade. In FY1994, more than 185,300, about 40
percent of the total junior high graduates, went
into three-year senior vocational schools. Another 39,960 students, or 10.44 percent of the
total junior high graduates, went directly into
five-year "junior colleges" 五專, which also cover
a student's high school years. Entrance into all
of these institutions (except in a few experimental cases) is by competitive examinations. Yet
another 17,000 graduates went on to attend the

Higher Education Institutional Growth 1988–1995		
	1988	*1995*
Schools	109	134
Students	496,530	751,347
Faculty	23,809	36,348

Source: Ministry of Education

Practical Technical Program. Only about 10 percent of students who complete nine years of
compulsory education fail to continue their
schooling.

Senior High School

The three-year senior high school program
prepares students 15 to 18 years old for learning
special fields of knowledge and preparing them
for college study. In 1950, there were 62 senior
high schools serving 18,866 senior high students
islandwide. Beginning with the '70s, senior high
schools entered a period of phenomenal growth.
By 1972, there were 203 senior high schools
with an enrollment of 197,151, almost ten times
more than the 1950s.

From 1971 to 1982, the number of students
admitted to senior high was gradually reduced,
while the number of senior vocational school
students increased. This was done in order to
meet the growing demand for skilled workers
needed to sustain the rapid economic development of the time. Later, demands for high-quality professional laborers increased, and this led
to an educational policy change that cut down
the supply of senior vocational school students
by increasing the number of students admitted to
senior high schools.

By SY1995, senior high school students totaled 255,387, and the ratio of senior high school
students to those in senior vocational schools
was 33:67. Under the current education system,
senior high graduates have several options: to
pursue study at a university or college, or to
attend a two year junior college after one year of

work experience, provided they have passed the relevant entrance examinations. About 57 percent of senior high graduates chose to pursue further education in 1995.

In line with the policy of providing universal opportunity for secondary education, the ROC has made an effort to democratize the educational system so that all levels of training can be harmonized, yet vary enough to meet the many needs of students. A program entitled the "Voluntary Promotion Scheme for Junior High School Graduates Entering Senior High Schools" calls for a unitary system of schools in which experimental classes or schools can provide students with the option of attending a comprehensive junior-senior high school, or allow students to progress uninterruptedly from the first year of junior high through senior high without taking the competitive entrance examinations.

Senior Vocational School

The purpose of the senior vocational schools is to equip youths between 15 and 22 with vocational knowledge and skills. In 1950, there was only one senior vocational school and 32 junior-senior vocational schools with a total of 11,226 students. The number of junior vocational schools and students dropped in the subsequent years. By 1968, all junior vocational schools stopped enrolling new classes. All vocational schools are now senior vocational schools.

In SY1995, a total of 523,412 students attended 203 senior vocational schools and 87 senior high schools with vocational classes. Specialized high schools include those particularly designed for the study of art, music, business, agriculture, specific trades and industrial occupations, as well as paraprofessional occupations such as nursing and midwifery. About 42.5 percent of the students majored in engineering, 38 percent in commerce, 3.7 percent in agriculture, and 15.7 percent in maritime and marine products, medicare and nursery, home economics, and arts. A senior vocational school graduate may choose to take a job or go on to further study at an institute of technology, university, or independent college, at a two-year junior college, or at a three-year junior college, after passing the relevant entrance examinations.

In 1995, about 17.84 percent of senior vocational school graduates entered an institution of advanced education or noncollegiate postsecondary schools. In some vocational schools, 60 to 70 percent of their graduates chose to further their studies.

Current wisdom has it that the ideal proportion of senior high students to vocational high students is 3:7, and that admissions and facilities should be adjusted accordingly. Some vocational classes are already being affiliated with senior high schools; there has been considerable expansion in the vocational courses offered in all secondary schools. In 1996, experimental bilateral high schools first combined vocational and academic programs under the same roof. This development has enabled the students to select from a much wider range of courses. Nevertheless, all students must fulfill the same general requirements for graduation, as do students of other high schools.

Higher Education

Higher education, also called post-secondary education or tertiary education, includes a variety of programs beyond secondary schools. In the ROC, such education is offered at junior colleges, colleges, universities, and graduate programs. College and university enrollment in SY1995 was 35.18 per 1,000 of the total population, ranking the ROC comparatively high in the world.

Junior colleges focus primarily on applied sciences, providing well-trained technicians for the labor market. Besides five-year junior colleges (which some students enter straight out of junior high), there are two-year junior colleges, technical and other colleges, and universities. All colleges and universities are entered through the JUEE. Students enter junior college engineering programs through a nationwide joint examination, and business programs are entered through regional joint examinations.

In theory, students can test into any of these institutions out of either senior high or senior vocational schools. Moreover, students who complete any junior college program may retake the JUEE to enter college or university as freshmen, or they may transfer into college or university through tests held by the individual departments of each college and university, and enter as sophomores or juniors. Private medical colleges enroll transfer students through a joint entrance examination.

Finally, ROC universities and colleges offer a wide variety of master and doctoral programs. These are also entered through competitive examination. Students may go directly from university or college into these programs.

In 1950, seven institutions offered higher education programs serving 6,665 students. One university had three graduate-level departments. Since then, the government has established additional colleges and universities, and has allowed the private sector to set up such institutions. Twelve public higher education institutions have opened since 1974. Seventeen private institutions were added in the same period. By SY1995, the number of higher education institutions reached 134, including 24 universities, 36 independent colleges, and 74 junior colleges; some 751,347 undergraduates were enrolled in these institutions. More than 660 graduate programs were attached to these universities.

Junior Colleges

Fifty-eight of Taiwan's 74 junior colleges are private. They are categorized according to their specialization; the three main ones are science and technology, humanities, and social sciences. These fields are divided into sub-categories, including natural science, math and computer science, crafts and industry, mechanical and civil engineering, transportation and communication, agriculture, commerce, maritime affairs, home economics, pharmacy, medical technology, physical and preschool education, arts, humanities, and performing arts. By

Overseas Study

Over the past 40 years nearly a quarter of a million students from the Taiwan area have gone abroad to study. Although the exact numbers are not certain (except for government-funded students, the government no longer keeps statistics on the number going abroad each year since special permission to do so is no longer required), it is clear that at any given time there are well over 10,000 Taiwan students studying overseas. In recent years it has become increasingly popular for parents to send their elementary-school or junior-high aged children abroad. Between 1983 and 1993, more than 23,200 elementary school students and nearly 12,800 junior high students moved overseas to new schools.

SY1995, about 15 percent of the students were in junior college, a dramatic contrast with 0.63 percent in 1950.

Five-year Junior Colleges

A junior college under this category admits junior high school graduates for five years of specialized or paraprofessional training. SY1995 had 195,144 students enrolled in 3,977 classes; 32,736 graduated in SY1994. Some 193,737 students were enrolled in regular five-year junior colleges, while the rest (less than 1 percent) were in branch campuses of independent colleges. Less than 14 percent of the total number of students studied in public institutions. Those majoring in pharmacy, veterinary medicine, marine engineering, and navigation are required to take one more year of training.

Three-year Junior Colleges

Three-year junior colleges have shrunk in number and importance. They stopped enrolling freshmen in SY1994. Except for two that specialize in physical education, most are being upgraded to become independent colleges. In SY1995, a total of 86 classes in this category served 4,486 students. After SY1996, there will be no more three-year junior colleges in operation.

Two-year Junior Colleges

This category admits senior vocational school graduates majoring in sciences, relevant to the different curricula offered by specific colleges. Students with job experience can also seek admission. In SY1995, there were 195,121 students studying in 3,797 classes; and 63,785 students graduated in 1994.

University, Graduate School and Other Options

Most college and university programs last four years, but normal universities, teachers colleges, and departments of civil engineering all require five years, and undergraduate law and medical programs last from five to seven years. In 1995, nearly 246,000 students were registered in 24 universities, 16 of them national institutions. There are 36 independent colleges with 115,938 students.

Usually, institutes of technology recruit students through examinations. Two-year institutes of technology admit junior college graduates while four-year institutes admit senior vocational school graduates.

Unversity graduates must undergo an additional five years of training in departments of medicine and departments Chinese medicine. Graduate programs usually admit students after they pass relevant examinations. Junior college graduates with relevant work experience are also allowed to take graduate school entrance examinations.

Master's degree programs last one to four years. Doctorate programs admit master's degree holders or college graduates majoring in medicine. Such programs require at least two to seven years to accomplish. In 1995, there were 42,097 students studying in 664 graduate schools; 8,897 were studying for doctorates. In SY1994, 848 doctorates, 11,706 master's degrees, and 68,274 bachelor's degrees were awarded.

Alternatives to the Mainstream
Special Education

This category includes programs and facilities for gifted children as well as those with special needs because of handicaps or learning disabilities. Special schools in the latter category focus on blind, deaf, physically handicapped, and mentally retarded students. For the most part, these schools are run by the government and they parallel the mainstream educational system, from preschool through senior vocational school. In SY1995, there were 4,822 students in 17 such schools. In addition, 1,735 mainstream schools offered 3,332 classes for another 63,999 special students.

In SY1995, three schools for the blind had 504 students enrolled; four schools for the deaf had 1,291 students; nine schools served 2,647 mentally retarded pupils; and one school had 380 physically handicapped students. The mainstream system had another 932 special classes with professionals teaching more than 30,000 students who had speech, sight, or learning disabilities, or especially delicate health.

At the undergraduate level, roughly 400 resource rooms 資源班 provide facilities for 733 special-need students in 54 colleges and universities. Some of these resource rooms also provide support to gifted or especially talented students.

In SY1996, a total of 132 schools had classes for "gifted" students 資賦優異生 and 254 schools

---

Non-ROC Students in Taiwan

Overseas Chinese are offered places in Taiwan's educational system. In the 1995-1996 school year, there were over 10,000 overseas Chinese at various levels in the system, including 25 elementary school, 141 junior high, 243 senior high school, and 312 senior vocational school students. However, most overseas Chinese students come to the ROC on Taiwan for higher education. There were 765 overseas Chinese in junior colleges and 6,525 in colleges and universities in 1995. (The remaining 1,393 or so overseas Chinese were in special preparatory or technical training classes.)

There were 5,197 foreign students in the Taiwan area in 1995, the overwhelming majority (4,845) of whom were studying the humanities, mainly Chinese language.

Taiwan Area Libraries

(As of 1994)

National Library	1
Public Libraries	412
College Libraries	147
Senior High & Vocational School Libraries	374
Junior High School Libraries	718
Elementary School Libraries	2,286
Professional Libraries	448
Total	4,386

Source: National Central Library

for "talented" students 才藝優異生. Most gifted children are still educated in regular schools, but have special provisions made for their needs. Those who have superior ability in mathematics and sciences are classified as gifted. Children identified as "talented" can take special classes in such areas as music, fine arts, dance, sports, and computer science.

Social Education

The Ministry of Education supports a number of social education programs in line with the *Social Education Law* 社會教育法. These include supplementary education, adult education, and other services such as museums, libraries, exhibition centers, social education centers, and cultural centers. Social education programs include training in Mandarin Chinese (for native speakers of regional dialects), family education, support for folk arts, support for libraries and cultural centers islandwide, and the designation of Folk Art Heritage Award 民族藝術薪傳獎 winners in traditional arts.

Supplementary Education

Supplementary schools may be private or public. Private institutions, which parallel the mainstream educational system, numbered 3,680 in SY1995, more than half of the total of 6,858. Students receive certificates upon graduation, and may receive diplomas for equivalent levels in the mainstream system by passing examina-

tions. At the top of the supplementary system is the National Open University 國立空中大學.

Supplementary education can be divided into three types: compulsory, advanced, and short-term. Supplementary schools are attached to regular schools at their corresponding levels in the mainstream either as correspondence or night schools. Besides night classes, students can attend on weekends.

Supplementary compulsory education, also known as continuing education, is formal educational activity for adults. It includes elementary through junior high courses. Supplementary advanced education, or extension education, enrolls attendants at three levels: senior high school and vocational school; junior college, and college. After completing the prescribed courses of study and passing the qualification examinations, graduates earn mainstream-equivalent diplomas. The supplementary system does not include courses with university equivalence. Those enrolled in short-term supplementary education are either in general or technical educational courses.

In SY1995, some 323,500 students attended nearly a thousand supplementary schools: Approximately 48,500 were in elementary schools, 6,900 in senior high schools, 168,000 (the majority) in senior vocational schools, 32,200 in junior colleges, and 30,700 with National Open University. In addition, another 36,000 students participated in the Practical Technical Program.

Short-term Supplementary Classes

Large numbers of private cram schools 補習班 exist to prepare students for the senior high school and university entrance examinations. Other cram schools specialize in such subjects as foreign languages, children's classes, preparation for the civil service exams, and preparation for TOEFL and other exams required for study abroad. At last report in 1994, there were nearly 3,900 such schools registered with the government (a much larger number operate without licenses). About 22 percent were in Taipei City and 13 percent in Taipei County,

National Central Library

By the end of 1994, there were 4,386 libraries and information centers in the Taiwan area. The National Central Library (NCL) under the Ministry of Education handles the collection, storage, and review of ROC books and literature, as well as general research and guidance for all Taiwan's libraries. By 1996, the NCL had a collection of 1.24 million books, 25,000 periodicals, and 490,000 non-book documents. The NCL has large collections of rare books, Chinese calligraphic writings, governmental publications, and microfilms.

In 1981, the NCL established a Sinology Research Center 漢學研究中心, collecting global information on Chinese studies. In 1988, the NCL implemented a library information network program and established a national catalog center. Since 1991, its network has connected Taiwan's college and university libraries. In August 1993, the NCL began to issue its Chinese catalogue and Chinese-language periodicals. Recently, due to the frequent cross-Straits exchanges, the NCL has set up a Mainland China Information Center.

On January 9, 1996, the Legislature passed an amended *National Central Library Organizational Statute* 國家圖書館組織條例 and changed the Chinese name of the NCL into *Kuo-chia t'u-shu-kuan* 國家圖書館, but the English name has not changed. Since July 1989, the NCL has provided a free-of-charge ISBN system to publishers. As of May 1996, 2,700 publishers were using the system. To integrate the ROC publishing industry further internationally, the NCL helps ROC publishers participate in major international book fairs.

the metropolitan area with the largest market for short-term supplementary education.

Well over a million students study in these schools; some 700,000 students attended review classes to gain academic assistance in general subjects, with the aim of passing entrance examinations. These schools fulfill definite needs, and the government is exercising closer supervision of their safety and educational standards.

Since 1993, each year more than 6,000 students return to Taiwan after obtaining a master's or doctor's degree overseas. Over 83 percent study in the United States, and 6 percent in the United Kingdom.

Other Educational Options

Adult education classes are offered on writing skills, practical mathematics, and civics. Technical classes on basic job skills are available at training centers. In addition, the National Open University offers classes via radio and correspondence that can lead to a bachelor's degree. The university is open to qualified senior high school graduates and non-high school graduates after they pass an entrance exam. The Educational Broadcasting Station 教育廣播電台, Chinese Television System 中華電視股份有限公司, and school-on-the-air 空中教學 also offer educational classes.

ROC Educational Reform
Mixed Success

The ROC educational system is, by many standards, a success. Literacy is high and educational opportunities are varied and widely accessible. A full quarter of the total population is in some form of educational institution or program. Students generally emerge from the mainstream system skilled, well-informed, and self-disciplined.

Nevertheless, calls for sweeping reform of the educational system are common. In particular, the Joint University Entrance Examinations come in for regular criticism. At present, the MOE is investigating ways to reduce the pressure of examinations, as well as give more room to colleges and universities to govern themselves and set their own curricula.

Institutional reform has been under study for some time. In July 1994, the Seventh National Education Conference 第七屆全國教育會議 pointed out the need for pluralized cultural development and improved education. Among the highlighted issues are the distribution of educational resources, increasing the structure and flexibility of the curriculum, improving teacher quality, enhancing life-long education, beefing up physical education courses, and promoting cross-Straits academic exchanges.

Educational reform received a boost with the formation of a Commission on Educational Reform 教育改革審議委員會 (CER) in late 1994, headed by Nobel laureate Lee Yuan-tseh 李遠哲. The commission is responsible for diagnosing the problems of the present education system and is to suggest possible reforms. The commission's report should be made public by the end of 1996. The key concept underlying all reform efforts is flexibility, as the existing system is considered too rigid. Areas being examined include the optimal allocation of educational resources, adult education and retooling people to work in a high-tech environment, revised teacher training and teaching methodology, and curriculum changes.

Inordinate Emphasis on Examinations

There is growing dissatisfaction with the emphasis on examinations, especially the university entrance exam system. Currently, students are offered uniform national examinations depending upon the type of institution of higher education and field (social science, medicine, etc.) the student hopes to enter.

A major criticism is that the highly competitive system places tremendous stress on young people. A typical college-bound 17-year-old will devote at least a year or two of his or her life to test preparation, often attending both regular senior high school and cram schools. Many students who fail to score high enough to gain admission to the school or field they want choose to spend another full year preparing in cram schools to retake the exam.

Moreover, the exams emphasize rote memorization of a fixed catechism of texts. Critics of the system and many students feel that exam-takers merely fill their heads with vast amounts of disconnected trivia which they regurgitate during their exams and then forget. The emphasis on preparation for examinations based on rote memorization is, in fact, a problem that permeates the entire school system. Reformers say that students are denied the opportunity to develop their imagination and capacity for independent thinking, arguing that these skills, rather than the self-discipline for memorization and the deference to authority taught by the existing system, are more suited to contemporary needs.

Shortage of Resources and Opportunities

Many of the problems of the school system center around the inadequacy of resources, especially complaints about high student to teacher ratios and high student to classroom ratios.

The state of intense competition for entry into high schools and universities is fundamentally the result of a demand for far more places than currently exist in these institutions. In recent years the government has allowed many colleges to expand and upgrade to university status. Moreover, plans are currently being discussed to restructure the ratio of students in senior high schools as compared to senior vocational schools. Currently, the ratio is roughly 3:7; reformers wish to adjust it to 1:1. (For related data, see the section on Fundamental Education and Junior Colleges.)

Reform Measures
New Paths of Advancement

A few experimental programs to provide alternative routes to higher education are now being tested. In some junior high schools, advancement to successive levels is determined by each student's cumulative grades at the ratio of 20 percent for first-year grades and 40 percent for each of the next two years. Other experimental methods combine grades with examinations. Finally, a small number of spots are being made available so that students may be advanced by special recommendation.

Curriculum Revisions

New teaching methods and textbooks are also being introduced. In 1992, the MOE introduced an experimental interactive teaching method for mathematics designed by a group of math teachers and other educators interested in reform. The program should include all elementary schools by 1996-1997. Social science and history textbooks are also being greatly reworked. One important change is that there is less emphasis on Chinese history, with more attention being devoted to Taiwan's culture and history as well as world topics. Discussions are going on about phasing out those parts of the JUEE system dealing exclusively with the Three Principles of the People and the thought of Dr. Sun Yat-sen. While Dr. Sun remains a revered historical figure, it is thought that the time has passed for schools to promote only a single political ideology.

Greater Number of Choices

Students are starting to have more opportunities to choose electives, rather than be rigidly limited to a single curriculum. In perhaps the most extreme example of this increased flexibility, the MOE recently announced that it is selecting schools for an experimental program in which students would not have to define their major fields of study for their first year or two in university, thereby avoiding being locked into the department they had to choose while still high school seniors. This reform should also make schools more responsive to market demands for various fields, and better meet the needs of society.

The MOE is continuing its policy, begun in 1993, of gradually reducing class sizes for all schools to 40 pupils or less by the year 1998 (subject to the availability of resources for new schools and teachers and the availability of land for school construction).

Non-governmental reform efforts are also underway. Two well-known experimental elementary schools, the Forest School 森林小學 and the Caterpillar School 毛毛蟲學苑, have been established with small class sizes, low student-teacher ratios, and a curriculum that stresses creativity, personal growth and dignity, independent thinking, and harmony with nature. Civic reform groups are also currently lobbying the government to make it easier to establish such private educational institutions below the university level.

Mixed Reform Outlook

The demand for increased educational resources will inevitably compete with other demands on the state budget, such as increased social welfare and environmental protection. While alternative schools may come close to providing ideal, flexible, humanistic, and pluralistic education, they are also very expensive. Moreover, despite the flaws of the monolithic exam system with its demands for rote memorization, its universality and uniformity does create a level playing field for all higher education aspirants. Nonetheless, it is clear that reform is the wave of the future.

The Beauty of Taiwan Crafts

CRAFTS EXHIBITION CENTER
573, Chung-Cheng Rd., Tsao-Twen, Nan-Tou
9AM-5PM, Tuesday-Sunday, Closed on National Holidays
TEL: (049) 333544 FAX: (049) 356593

TAIWAN CRAFTS CENTER
7F, 110 Yeng-Ping S. Rd., Shin-San News Building, Taipei
10AM-6PM, Closed on Mondays
TEL: (02) 3315701-3 FAX: (02) 3315705

 臺灣省手工業研究所
TAIWAN PROVINCIAL HANDICRAFT RESEARCH INSTITUTE

18.
Science and
Technology

Above: Portable satellite telecommunications products on display at the World Trade Center attest to the increasing presence of Taiwan manufacturers in this global market.

Right: Fabrication of sub-micron DRAM 8" wafers, as well as ASEM and MCM foundry services, constitute the major business thrust of Hsinchu Science-based Industrial Park firms.

Previous page: Taiwan's pre-eminent role worldwide in computer manufacturing is evident from the wide variety of notebook computers on display at the Taipei World Trade Center.

18 Science and Technology

News of that handy device, the wheelbarrow, took almost 1,000 years to reach Europe from China. Similarly, fourteen centuries elapsed before something as simple as a screw was brought to China from the West. The tremendous lag in the diffusion of fundamental technology slowed the economic and intellectual growth of both East and West. Such a sluggish pace of technology transfer would be unpardonable in the late 20th century when the ability to design, develop, and produce state-of-the-art technology is a crucial component of economic progress and national strength.

The Republic of China is certainly aware of the need to stay abreast of scientific development. The ROC government has allocated an ever increasing portion of its budget and manpower to the research and development of new technologies. Indeed, the government's education, national defense, and economic policies all focus, to some extent, on the development of scientific expertise. The absolute and relative amounts of funding for R&D in both the public and the private sectors have grown rapidly over the last decade.

This commitment is born of pragmatism. Land and natural resources, two essential factors of production, are limited in the Taiwan area. A third factor of production, labor, is increasingly expensive. Where does Taiwan turn for comparative advantage? Brain power.

More people in Taiwan than ever before are graduating with bachelor of science degrees, master of science degrees, or Ph.D.s in hard sciences. More ROC scientists are traveling abroad and more non-Chinese scientists are visiting Taiwan. There are more R&D institutes, more experiments, and more scientific publications in Taiwan than ever before.

Direct scientific research in Taiwan is motivated first by profit—Taiwan's freewheeling market economy provides plenty of incentives for R&D in profitable technology; and second, by the National Science Council—the highest ROC government office charged with coordinating national science and technology policy—which closely coordinates all R&D activities, and funds public-sector scientific and technological research projects through grants and subsidies (see inset, next page).

Public Sector Research
NSC-supported

The National Science Council's fiscal 1997 (July 1, 1996, through June 30, 1997) budget registered moderate growth of 1.9 percent to US$514.8 million. The lion's share of the budget, some US$333 million, or 65 percent, is to be spent on basic and vanguard research projects in cooperation with academic institutions, and building construction and facility procurement for selected advanced technologies. To support academic research, a total of US$164 million worth of grants have been appropriated to projects ranging from natural sciences to humanities and social sciences. In 1995, almost the same amount was given to support 8,267 research projects (see chart, next page). For the National Science Council and its subsidiary research centers, some US$135 million has been allocated for the following expenses: US$8.6 million for administration, US$58.3 million for aerospace technology R&D, US$21.1 million for synchronous radiation technology R&D, US$11.3 million for the management of the Science and Technology Information Center 科學技術資料中心, US$3.2 million for experimental animal research, US$7.3 million for the development of precision instruments, and US$11.3 million for the Center for High-performance Computing 高速電腦中心. Furthermore, the NSC has appropriated US$46.7 million for the management of the Hsinchu Science-based Industrial Park 新竹科學工業園區. Any additional amounts have been deposited in a preparatory fund.

MOEA-supported

While a large portion of the NSC's annual budget goes to financing academic research, the Ministry of Economic Affairs 經濟部 is committed to industry-oriented scientific advancement in order to maintain continuous growth of manufacturing, expedite the transformation of traditional industries and promote technology-intensive indus-

National Science Council

The National Science Council 國家科學委員會 (NSC) is the highest government organ responsible for promoting and planning overall scientific and technological development in the ROC; setting national science policies; recruiting experts in scientific fields; providing stipends and incentives for researchers; coordinating the scientific and technological research and development projects of other government ministries; reviewing the annual science and technology reports of these ministries; and developing science-based industrial parks.

The National Science Council consists of the heads of government offices that have science or technology projects, the ministers without portfolio 政務委員 in charge of reviewing scientific or technological development, the president of Academia Sinica 中央研究院, the secretary-general of the Executive Yuan 行政院, and noted scientists. The chairman of the National Science Council is Dr. Liu Chao-shuan 劉兆玄.

tries. In 1995, the MOEA allocated some US$485 million to public and private non-profit research institutes for industrial applied research. Of this amount, over 63 percent, or US$305 million, was earmarked for the Industrial Technology Research Institute 工業技術研究院 (see ITRI section), with special emphasis on electronic and information technology research. Another 9 percent went to the Chungshan Institute of Science and Technology 中山科學研究院 (CSIST, see also Chapter 8, National Defense) and 7 percent to the Institute for Information Industry 資訊工業策進會 (see inset, next page). The MOEA expects that the CSIST will take an increasingly larger share of its annual expenditure for sci-tech projects because plans are underway to integrate defense technology into economic development and to open up CSIST R&D and production facilities to the private sector. The MOEA also set up an Industrial Technology Information Services office 產業技術資訊服務推廣計畫專案辦公室 in 1990 to provide a wide range of information covering

products, technology, and companies in the following industries: aerospace, electronics, mechanics, automation, food, metal, biochemistry, industrial materials, optoelectronics, chemistry, industrial safety, semiconductors, consumer electronics, information technology, shipbuilding, communications, measurement instrumentation, and textiles. Users may access the database at *http://140.96.1.11.*

Close Public/Private-sector R&D Cooperation

Overall ROC government economic policy in recent years has increasingly stressed a cooperative and complementary relationship between government and the private sector in developing Taiwan's economic future. In the area of technology, this generally involves specific, goal-oriented and time-limited government subsidies, and in some cases, the concerted commitment of government-founded research facilities and organizations, to develop further technologies considered key to national development and increased global competitiveness. For the most part, the goal of such government-subsidized research is to develop competitive technology in sufficient time for transfer to the private sector to allow Taiwan-based companies to produce increasingly competitive high-tech products and services, until the private sector can ultimately shoulder more of the R&D burden itself.

For an illustrative case, in 1995, the MOEA allocated US$431.3 million for its broad-ranging Sci-tech R&D Project 科技研究發展專案計畫 to

NSC Research Appropriations in 1995

	Support
Natural Sciences & Mathematics	21%
Engineering & Applied Sciences	30%
Life Sciences	29%
Humanities & Social Sciences	13%
Science Education	7%

Source: National Science Council

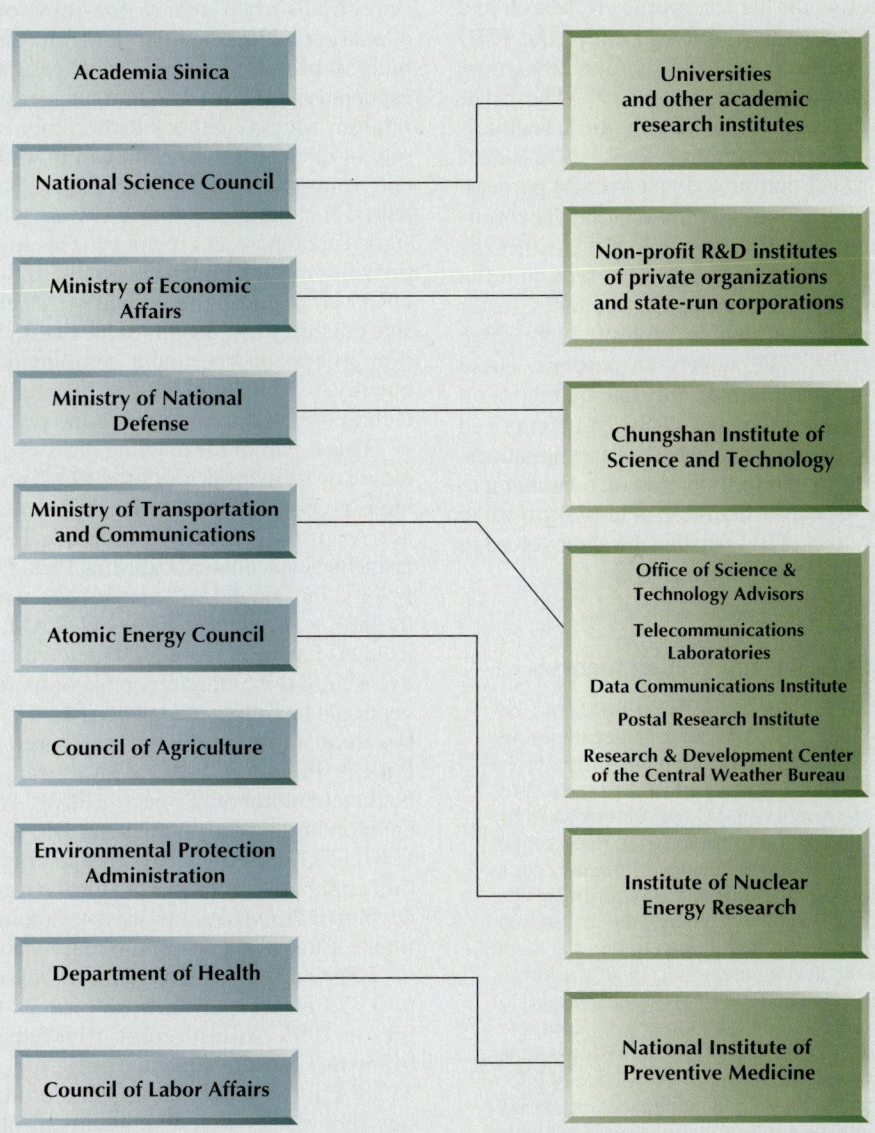

Scientific Research Institutions and Agencies

Academia Sinica

National Science Council

Ministry of Economic Affairs

Ministry of National Defense

Ministry of Transportation and Communications

Atomic Energy Council

Council of Agriculture

Environmental Protection Administration

Department of Health

Council of Labor Affairs

Universities and other academic research institutes

Non-profit R&D institutes of private organizations and state-run corporations

Chungshan Institute of Science and Technology

Office of Science & Technology Advisors

Telecommunications Laboratories

Data Communications Institute

Postal Research Institute

Research & Development Center of the Central Weather Bureau

Institute of Nuclear Energy Research

National Institute of Preventive Medicine

Source: Directorate-General of Budget, Accounting and Statistics

promote research programs involving more than 4,750 researchers in a variety of public and private industrial technology-oriented research entities, including the MOEA's own ITRI. MOEA appropriations for the Electronics Research and Service Organization (ERSO) under the ITRI umbrella (see inset, page 317) amounted to more than US$58 million for fiscal 1995. The Five-year Sub-micron Memory Production Technology Development Program 次微米記憶體製造技術發展五年計畫 comprised just over 34 percent, the Four-year Liquid Crystal Display Technology Development Program 液晶顯示器技術發展四年計畫 comprised nearly 33 percent, and the Four-year Microelectronics Component Cluster Technology Development Program 微電子零組件技術發展四年計畫, nearly 18 percent. These three programs represented only one-quarter of all programs conducted by the ERSO, yet comprised nearly 85 percent of the total budget appropriations, reflecting the high priority placed on continuing to develop these fields of high-tech industrial growth in the ROC. A total of 511 personnel were involved in the overall ERSO part of the project.

Institute for Information Industry

Founded in 1979 under the Ministry of Economic Affairs, the Institute for Information Industry (III) serves to develop and promote the information industry as part of the overall process of spurring economic development in the ROC. With 1,200 employees (over 55 percent of whom have a master's degree or higher education in a pertinent field), the III coordinates the efforts of government agencies, the private sector, and academic institutions to build a sound base for the development of Taiwan's information industry. The III also provides a variety of training courses for school teachers, computer professionals, and employees of private companies to increase their overall knowledge of information technologies and facilitate computerization in both the public and private sectors. In the past 14 years, over 134,000 people have benefited from the III's training programs.

Focusing on one of the specific R&D programs mentioned above that was funded from the ERSO allocation, the Sub-micron Memory Production Technology Development Program (which absorbed nearly one-third of ERSO's allocation within the total Sci-tech R&D Project budget) produced some notable results in 1995, especially in 0.5μm 4 and 16 megabyte dynamic random access memory technology. A success rate of over 50% was achieved in 4mb DRAM, and volume production techniques were established for 4 and 16mb DRAM, as well as 4mb static random access memory. This involved improvement and development of 0.5μm 16mb DRAM 8" fabrication techniques, as well as extensive reliability evaluations of the 0.5μm 8" fabrication process and pertinent components. Consequently, 0.5μm 16mb DRAM fabrication process technology was transferred to the private sector.

This is part of the ongoing process of developing a key growth sector of the ROC's technology industry. For example, among the Innovative Product Awards 創新產品獎 issued in 1995 by the Hsinchu Science-based Industrial Park, Etron Technology, Inc. 鈺創科技股份有限公司, was cited for its 256K x 16 extended data out DRAM, for which it claims having achieved a 60 percent reduction in cycle time to 45 nanoseconds compared to conventional fast-page-mode DRAMs. The company began operation in the Science-based Industrial Park in February 1991, with a grant from the National Submicron Project 次微米計畫 to jointly develop high-speed SRAM and DRAM with the ITRI. ITRI subsequently built upon the results of this collaboration in joint efforts with ERSO to develop 0.7μm/0.5μm process technology for ultimate transfer to consortium members.

ERSO research efforts moved beyond 0.5μm to 0.35μm and even 0.25μm process technologies in 1995. At last report, trial fabrication of 0.35μm CMOS, such as polycide gate and MOSFET components and a gate-oxide technology module, as well as assessment of process-related equipment were being carried out, while 0.25μm fabrication technology was still at the CMOS component simulation and design stage.

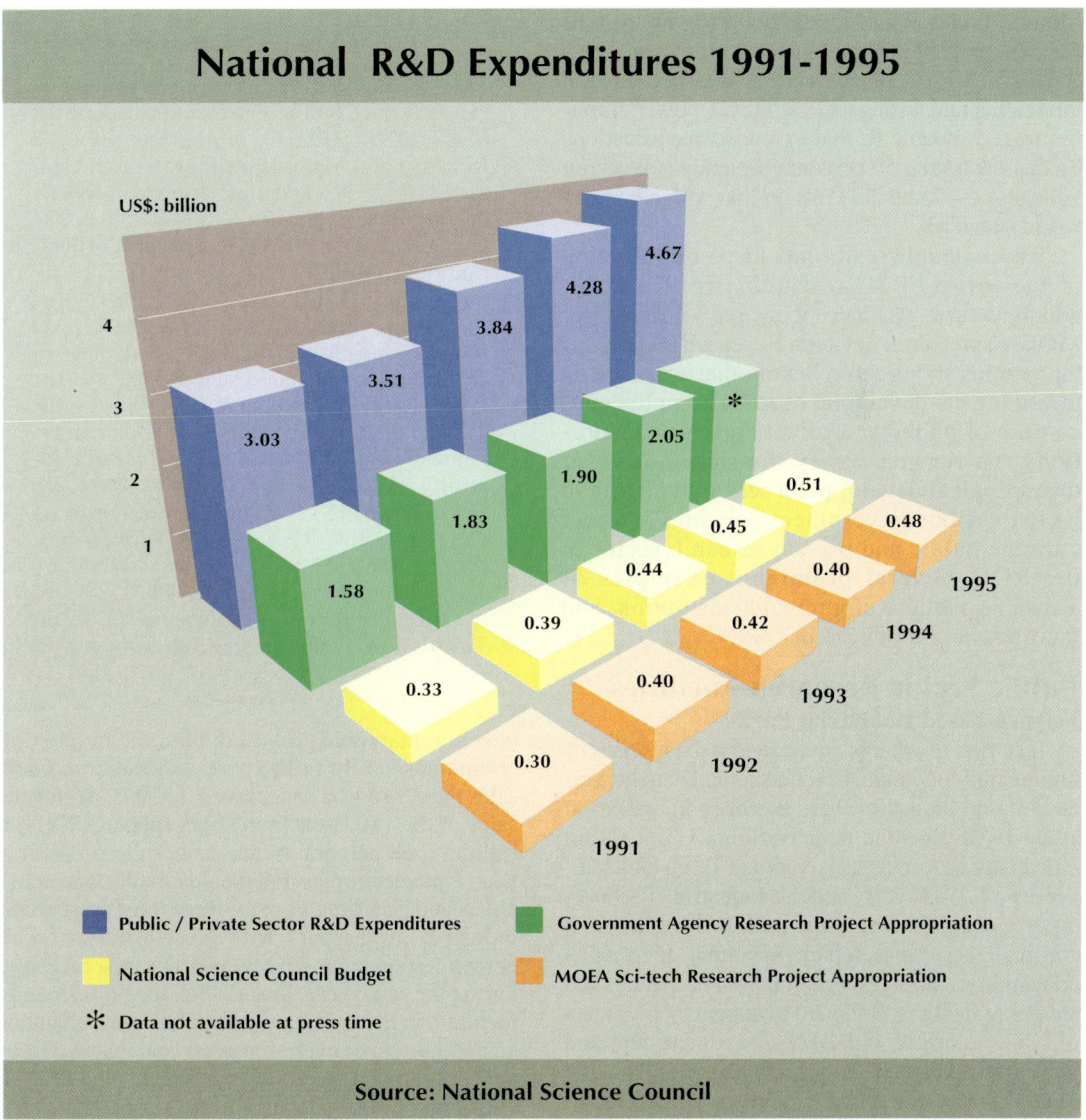

National R&D Expenditures 1991-1995

US$: billion

3.03	3.51	3.84

4.28
4.67

1.58
1.83
1.90
2.05
*

0.33
0.39
0.44
0.45
0.51

0.30
0.40
0.42
0.40
0.48

1991
1992
1993
1994
1995

■ Public / Private Sector R&D Expenditures   ■ Government Agency Research Project Appropriation

■ National Science Council Budget   ■ MOEA Sci-tech Research Project Appropriation

✳ Data not available at press time

Source: National Science Council

Similarly, the ERSO's four-year Microelectronics Component Cluster Technology Development Program produced a number of promising designs during 1995 in such areas as 10 bit 20-80mHz video analog-to-digital and digital-to-analog conversion, receiver and 0.5 watt power amplifier ICs for the Digital European Cordless Telecommunication (DECT) and Global System for Mobile communication (GSM) mobile telephone systems, and UHF phase-locked loop and voltage-controlled oscillator ICs. As of last report, first-cut designs have been completed for these projects, as well as the component fabrication for a 240 x 180 four-step gray-scale driver circuit. Another program, the RF

Module Technology Introduction Program 射頻模組技術引進計畫 (accounting for barely over 2 percent of the ERSO allocation in 1995), succeeded in fabricating and testing a GSM/DECT power amplifier mixed-module IC that exceeded specifications by demonstrating 50 percent efficiency at working voltages of 4.7 and 2.3 volts, in line with advanced world standards.

This example represents just a tiny fraction of the entire ERSO research effort in 1995, which, in turn, was merely one part of the larger MOEA-sponsored Sci-tech Research Project for the year involving a number of other areas of key technological development and a complex consortium of public and private research institutions. To further clarify the rich mosaic of technological development research efforts in which various government agencies interact with the public and private research sector in the ROC, several prominent examples of Taiwan's public-sector research institutions and facilities are introduced below:

Public Sector Research Facilities
Science-based Industrial Parks

The first of what is envisioned to be a series of high-technology industrial parks, the Hsinchu Science-based Industrial Park, has been in operation since 1980. Located near National Chiao Tung University 國立交通大學, National Tsing Hua University 國立清華大學, and the Industrial Technology Research Institute, the park is designed as a comprehensive research environment. It contains educational, sports, entertainment, residential, and shopping facilities designed to appeal to engineers of Chinese origin with overseas educational and working experience—especially that gained in the United States. Financial incentives are offered to induce companies to set up operations in the park.

Administered by a division of the National Science Council, the Science-based Industrial Park Administration 科學工業園區管理局, the Hsinchu Science-based Industrial Park has put Taiwan on the world map of such high-tech industries as IC manufacturing and key information industry components. Over the past decade, the park has wit-

Public Research Enterprises

One of the largest government-run enterprises is the Chinese Petroleum Corporation 中國石油股份有限公司, which has set up a Refining and Manufacturing Research Center 煉製研究中心 and an Exploration Development Research Institute 探採研究中心. The China Petrochemical Development Corporation 中國石油化學工業開發股份有限公司 conducts applied research as does the China Steel Corporation 中國鋼鐵公司. The Taiwan Power Company 台灣電力公司, usually known as Taipower, has one research institute, the Power Research Institute 電力綜合研究所. The Taiwan Sugar Corporation has two such organizations, the Taiwan Sugar Research Institute and the Animal Industry Research Institute 畜產研究所. The Taiwan Fertilizer Company 臺灣肥料公司, the Taiwan Salt Works 台灣製鹽總廠, the Taiwan Machinery Manufacturing Corporation 台灣機械公司, and the China Shipbuilding Corporation 中國造船股份有限公司 all run research laboratories.

nessed remarkable growth in both the number of companies set up in the park and the combined sales these firms have achieved. In 1995, aggregate sales of the 180 firms in the park topped US$11.3 billion, a 68 percent increase over the preceding year. Optoelectronics, integrated circuits, and computers and peripherals are the three most prosperous industries in the park with growth rates of 112 percent, 76 percent, and 69 percent, respectively, during the same year. Since 1992, the 56 IC manufacturers in the park have been able to maintain an annual growth of over 50 percent and major efforts are concentrated on producing DRAM, and SRAM chips, and developing Application Specific Electronic Module (ASEM) and Multichip Module (MCM) foundry services. IC manufacturing has been aided by a full range of support industries that handle materials, design, testing, and packaging. Today, these companies achieve a production value that takes up 4 percent of the world total and thereby make Taiwan the fourth largest supplier of IC products worldwide, after the United States, Japan, and

Korea. Computers and computer peripherals have gained importance in Taiwan's foreign trade over the past decade. For more information on this aspect, please see Chapter 10, Economy.

Growth of the Hsinchu facility has run up against the realities of land acquisition in Taiwan today. For the third phase of the project's expansion, basic infrastructure on a 190-hectare site has been completed and the park administration has begun planning the fourth phase which will involve a land area of 300 hectares in the proximity of Hsinchu. The National Science Council has designated a site in southern Taiwan for a second science-based industrial park. The location is a 600-hectare farm between Hsinshih rural township 新市鄉 and Shanhua urban township 善化鎮 in Tainan County owned by the state-run Taiwan Sugar Corporation 台灣糖業股份有限公司. Initially, 360 acres will be developed, starting in July 1996. The choice of locality is meant to capitalize on the agricultural resources of Taiwan's south, and the technological support of institutions nearby, such as the Asian Vegetable Research Center 亞洲蔬菜研究發展中心 and the Taiwan Sugar Research Institute 台灣糖業研究所.

Presently, plans are for the park to initially focus on serving companies from four major sectors: agriculture, biotechnology, micro-electronics, and precision machinery. Efforts are being made to avoid the crowding experienced with the first park by selecting a much larger initial area, and to develop the surrounding neighborhood to accommodate the potential 60,000 personnel who are projected to eventually work in the new park. Coordination with the Tainan municipal government is under way to assure that there will be an adequate transportation network to handle the expected traffic in and out of the area.

Industrial Technology Research Institute

The Industrial Technology Research Institute (ITRI), the largest of Taiwan's non-profit research institutes, has its headquarters in Hsinchu near the Science-based Industrial Park and branch offices throughout Taiwan. ITRI has about 5,900 employees, 80 percent of whom are engineers or scientists.

Founded in 1973 by the Ministry of Economic Affairs, ITRI serves primarily to develop industrial technologies and transfer them to domestic private enterprises to sharpen their competitive edge in the international market. ITRI's research projects cover a broad spectrum of industries from traditional to the emerging ones, and from labor-intensive to high-tech. One example is the integrated circuit industry. During the mid-1970s, ITRI began to provide Taiwan's IC manufacturers with the technology transfers necessary to acquire seven micron CMOS technology. Today, Taiwan is a major producer of eight-inch DRAM chip wafers. Taiwan's declining textile industry is another beneficiary of ITRI's R&D commitment. With ITRI's micro-fiber technology, local textile manufacturing has been able to improve polymerization and high-speed spinning processes to raise productivity.

ITRI generated US$537 million in revenue during 1995; 57 percent of ITRI funding came from government-sponsored projects, while 43

Organizations under the ITRI Umbrella

Underneath ITRI are the Union Chemical Laboratories 化學工業研究所, the Mechanical Industrial Research Laboratories 機械工業研究所, the Electronics Research and Service Organization 電子工業研究所, the Computer and Communications Research Laboratories 電腦與通訊工業研究所, the Energy and Resources Laboratory 能源與資源研究所, the Materials Research Laboratories 工業材料研究所, the Optoelectronics and System Laboratories 光電工業研究所, the Center for Measurement Standards 量測技術發展中心, and the Center for Pollution Control Technology 污染防治技術發展中心. ITRI has also established a Center for Industrial Safety and Health Technology 工業安全衛生技術發展中心 and a Center for Aviation and Space Technology 航空與太空工業技術發展中心.

Private Sector Research Institutes

The numerous private research institutes in the Taiwan area focus mainly on experimental development and commercialization of science and technology. Some of the more active private research institutes in the Taiwan area include the Industrial Technology Research Institute, the Food Industry Research and Development Institute 食品工業發展研究所, the Development Center for Biotechnology 生物技術開發中心, the Metal Industries Development Center 金屬工業發展中心, the United Ship Design and Development Center 聯合船舶設計發展中心, the China Textile Institute 中國紡織工業研究中心, the Taiwan Textile Federation 紡織業外銷拓展會, the Automotive Research Testing Center 車輛研究測試中心, the Electronics Testing Center, Taiwan 台灣電子檢驗中心 , and the China Technical Consultants Institute 中國技術服務社.

percent was received from the industrial sector for contract research, joint development, and technical services. ITRI aims to reach a one-to-one ratio of funding from government projects to revenue from contracts and services by 1997. In fiscal 1995, ITRI transferred new technology to 418 scientific and technical companies in Taiwan, hosted over 880 conferences and exhibits, and published 553 reference papers and 667 conference papers. Most indicative of its success was the number of patents it was awarded in fiscal 1995—a total of 381, of which 183 were foreign patents. In the same year, the institute provided technical services to over 27,000 scientific and technical companies in Taiwan.

Patents

More than 43,000 applications for patents were received by the National Bureau of Standards under the MOEA 經濟部中央標準局 (NBS) in 1995. Of these, ROC citizens filed nearly 67 percent, while foreign nationals submitted the remainder. The NBS approved nearly 30,000 applications in 1995, up 50 percent from the previous year. Approximately 70 percent of these were awarded to ROC citizens.

The NBS distinguishes between patents for new inventions, for new designs, and for new models. Foreign nationals have consistently filed several times as many successful patent applications for new inventions as ROC citizens have. In 1995, some 13,900 patent applications were made for new inventions. ROC citizens accounted for 2,216 of these applications, while foreign nationals submitted 11,721 applications. Of the 6,977 approved patent applications for new inventions in 1995, ROC citizens garnered 1,138, or 16 percent.

Research Work Force

At publication time, the latest available ROC research work force figures were from 1994. That year, over 92,000 people in Taiwan were working on R&D related projects. More than 55,000 were researchers, i.e., persons presently engaged in R&D activities, who hold B.S., M.S., or Ph.D., or associate degrees, and have more than three years of research experience outside the classroom.

The number of researchers rose by 6 percent over 1993. The corporate sector employed over 31,000 in 1994, up 8 percent over the previous year. Colleges and universities employed nearly 13,000, an increase of 4 percent from 1993, while research institutes employed just over 11,000 in 1994, or 3 percent more than a year earlier.

ROC researchers in 1994 were assisted by more than 24,000 technicians, i.e., people who perform technical tasks under the supervision of scientists and engineers, and are typically high school, vocational school, or junior college graduates with less than three years of working experience. Both researchers and technicians rely heavily on supporting personnel (administrators, accountants, secretaries, and maintenance workers), nearly 13,000 of whom were employed at scientific or technical institutes in 1994.

National Information Infrastructure

An ad hoc inter-ministerial steering committee meets monthly to monitor the development of the ROC's national information infrastructure. Minister without Portfolio 政務委員 Dr. Yang Shih-chien 楊世緘 is chairman. There are five sub-committees: resources planning (run by the Council for Economic Planning and Development 行政院經濟建設委員會), network construction (Ministry of Transportation and Communications 交通部), applied technology and promotion (Ministry of Economic Affairs), manpower development and basic applications (Ministry of Education 教育部), and general administration (Science and Technology Advisory Group [see inset, next column]). A civilian consultative committee with 24 members from leading private companies has also been formed to facilitate the plan.

The information industry today is the ROC's largest industry as well as its most prolific foreign exchange earner. New information industry products are to be developed, utilized and promoted by private businesses. The government's role is primarily to encourage investment and innovation through suitable tax and legislative measures. Tariff rates on data leased-lines will be lowered to encourage private investment. The project plans to give advance notice of major-item equipment procurement in large-scale computer and communication development projects to allow the private sector sufficient time to prepare bids.

Results to Date

The first concrete result from the project has been the Experimental Hsinchu Broadband Network Region 新竹寬頻試驗網路, which began operation on July 14, 1995. A similar network began operation in Taipei during September 1995. This project has required the cooperation of a number of government agencies. The Chunghwa Telecommunications Co. Ltd. 中華電信公司 (formerly known as the Directorate General of Telecommunications 交通部電信總局) under the Ministry of Transportation and Communications is laying a

Science and Technology Advisory Group

The Executive Yuan established the Science and Technology Advisory Group 行政院科技顧問組 in 1979. The group, which consists of scientists with administrative experience from around the world, serves as advisors to the Executive Yuan and evaluates R&D policies for applied science. Currently, there are 11 foreign advisors.

nationwide fiber-optic cable network. More than the equivalent of US$3.7 billion will be invested by Chunghwa Telecom. As of mid-1996, over 99 percent of all toll trunk circuits had been converted to optical fiber and the remainder was scheduled for completion within a year. Meanwhile, Chunghwa Telecom continues to deploy optical fiber cable for subscriber loops. The plan also calls for integrating existing narrow-band networks, including an AT&T No. 5 ESS, an Alcatel System 1240, a Taicom-T (Siemens EWSD) digital switching system, and Taiwan's recently established ISDN (see Chapter 16, Mass Media).

One application of the network to date is a remote tele-medicine pilot system to transmit medical history images and data, as well as remote medical instructions. Developed jointly by National Taiwan University Medical College 國立台灣大學醫學院, National Cheng Kung University Medical College 國立成功大學醫學院, Veterans General Hospital 台北榮民總醫院 (Taipei), and Taichung Veterans General Hospital 台中榮民總醫院, the system may ultimately be extended to provide medical consultation to the more remote parts of the Taiwan area.

Another example of applying the network to everyday life is E-mail service between the public and government inaugurated in July 1995. A Home-page E-mail Box Service system for communicating with the office of Premier Lien Chan, head of the Executive Yuan, is now up and running on the World Wide Web. Similar Home-page systems have already been operated by other government agencies at every level. According to a survey conducted by the Institute of Information Industry in March 1996, E-mail is the most used function by over 300,000 active Internet users in the Taiwan area. Currently, three networks are competing for Taiwan's Internet market, namely HiNet (run by the MOTC's Chunghwa Telecom), SEEDNet (run by the Institute of Information Industry), and TANet (run by the Ministry of Education). HiNet leads the market with over 100,000 subscribers while SEEDNet is attempting to catch up after signing a lease contract with American Global One Co. in June 1996 to provide users with high-speed access to the Internet.

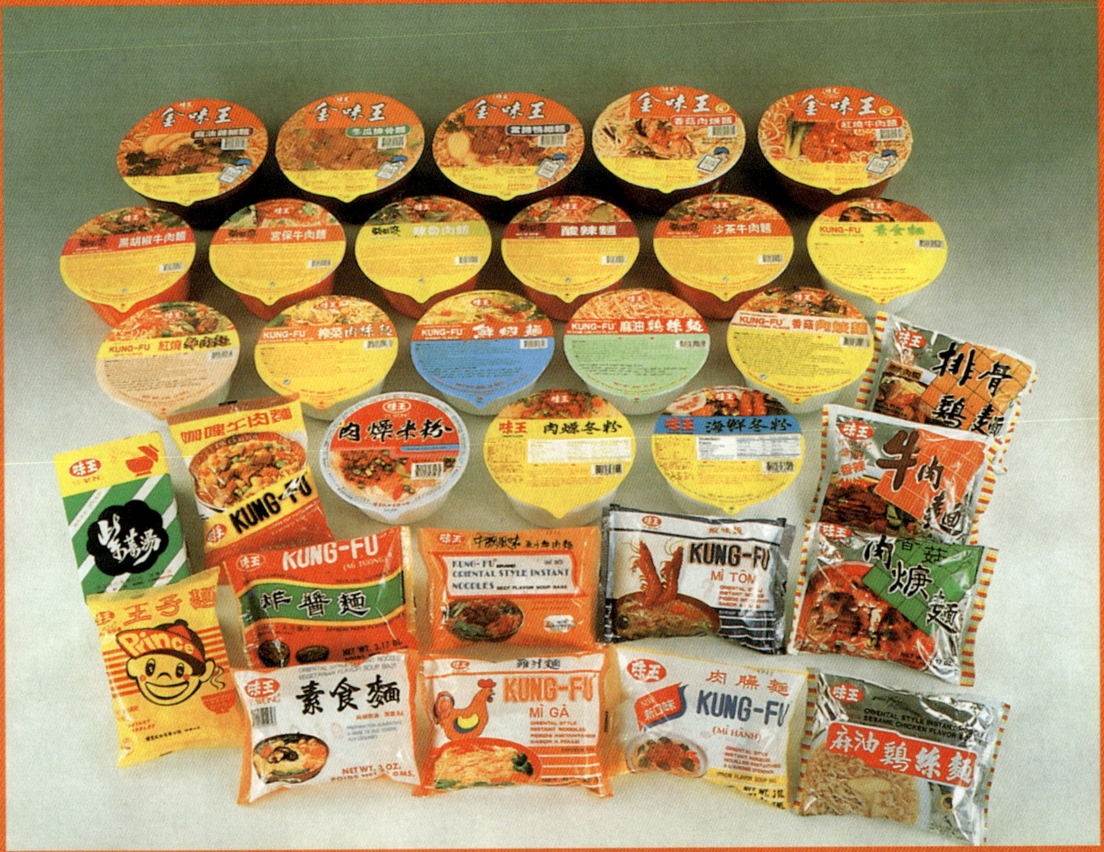

19.
Social Welfare

Previous page: Organized group activities provide the elderly with a socially stimulating way to pass their leisure time.

Right: To help alleviate the pressure of high property prices, the government has constructed public housing and offers low-interest loans to aspiring homeowners.

Below: Social welfare in Taiwan includes generously subsidized health care under the National Health Insurance program, which was launched on March 1, 1995.

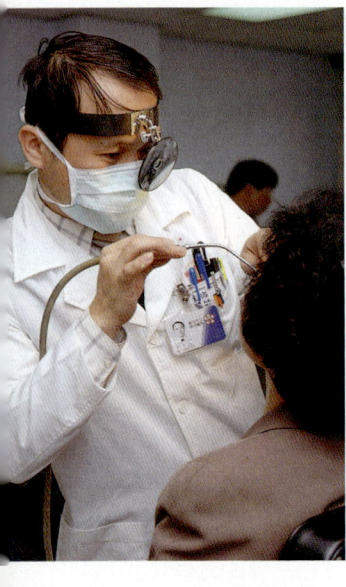

19 Social Welfare

The vast majority of the ROC people in the Taiwan area now enjoy a greater quality of life than ever before, such as equal access to education, jobs, housing, medical care, travel, and political participation. These are the result of profound social and political changes accompanying the astounding economic success of recent years that has capped Taiwan's transformation over the past four decades from a traditional agricultural economy into a modern industrial entity. However, this restructuring of society has also given rise to new social ills, which have made life more hazardous in many ways, especially for disadvantaged groups. This chapter highlights services provided by the government and private sector in Taiwan to children, juveniles, women, the elderly, people with mental and/or physical handicaps, and the poor.

Changing Welfare Sources

Extended families were once the fundamental source of welfare services in Chinese society. Traditionally, all members of a farming family lived together in one household, caring for each other's needs. Three generations cohabiting was common, and five generations together was seen as ideal. Each family member had certain responsibilities according to his or her age and gender. Young men worked in the field. Their wives cooked, managed the home, and took care of the family elders. Grandparents provided wisdom, guidance, and childcare. And children did light chores. When all members fulfilled their duties, everyone's needs were met, and the family was said to be in harmony.

The classical conception of family-based support has been challenged by the emergence of a modern, post-agricultural economy in Taiwan. By 1995, less than 11 percent of the working population were employed in agriculture. Many young people have left the farming households in which they grew up and established nuclear families in urban areas (50 percent of the population lives in either Taipei, Taichung, Tainan, or Kaohsiung). It is now common for both husband and wife to work full-time outside the home.

Children are often cared for by the school system. Grandparents are visited during major holidays.

The metamorphosis of extended farming families into nuclear urban families has resulted in growing numbers of children, juveniles, women, handicapped people, and senior citizens who require assistance from non-family sources. Coinciding with this increased need for outside assistance are two new phenomena: heightened demand for government services and the proliferation of private organizations that provide welfare services.

In fiscal 1996, the ROC central government spent US$11.8 billion, or 26.7 percent of its total expenditures, on what it broadly defines as "social services," a budget heading that includes social welfare expenses (13.2 percent), community development and environmental protection (1.4 percent), and pensions (12.1 percent). The social services portion of the budget was up 1.2 percentage points from the previous year. Although the social services budget is large, the ROC government is not attempting to be the sole source of welfare services in Taiwan. Instead, the government sees its role as a facilitator and coordinator of welfare activities in local communities.

As can be imagined, communication between various government agencies, academic institutions, private charities, and care recipients is of crucial importance. In a typical scenario, the Ministry of the Interior's Department of Social Affairs 內政部社會司 (DSA) formulates welfare policies and drafts related legislation. The DSA then briefs local welfare offices on the latest policies. These offices commission universities or individual scholars to survey the actual demand for specific services in the local community. Once community demand has been assessed, local welfare officials invite representatives from each of the private charities active in the area to attend seminars in which the new government guidelines are explained, community needs discussed, and responsibilities and priorities set. For their part, special interest groups, charities, the media, and the more than 500 professional social workers in Taiwan provide constant feedback to policymakers at the highest levels of government.

Over the last decade, a vast array of public and private agencies has arisen to assist disadvantaged people in Taiwan. While all of these Samaritan groups face shortages of manpower and funding, the number of people, the amount of media attention, and the total value of services devoted to helping people in need are continuing to rise rapidly. In addition, charitable organizations are now learning to form coalitions in which each member group provides a specific service. These coalitions of care are increasingly organized, focused, and effective.

Children's Welfare

Nearly one-fifth of the people in Taiwan are children (as defined in the *Children's Welfare Law* 兒童福利法, i.e., under 12 years of age). Experts agree that the pressures faced by most children in Taiwan, while not extreme, nevertheless demand immediate attention. For instance, children today have fewer siblings and less outdoor space to play in, but face increased pressure from academic competition at an early age. More often than ever, they are raised by a single parent who must spend most of his or her time working outside the home.

The *Children's Welfare Law* was promulgated in 1973. In 1993 it was revised in light of the 1989 UN Convention on the Rights of the Child. Under the law, a pregnant woman may not smoke, drink, take drugs, chew betel nuts (see section on betel nuts, Chapter 15, Public Health), or engage in any other activity that might endanger her fetus. The law also mandates subsidies for the medical care of premature babies and seriously ill children. Health care professionals, daycare workers, teachers, and the police are required to report cases of child abuse. The revised *Children's Welfare Law* also prohibits parents from leaving children who are under the age of six or who require special attention unattended. Parents violating this regulation must attend a minimum of four hours of classes on parental responsibilities. Fines of US$44 to US$222 are charged for each refusal to attend the classes. Under the revision, courts are able to assign a child to another

guardian if both parents are deemed incompetent. As an added measure, the revised *Children's Welfare Law* empowers authorities to make public the name of anyone who violates provisions of the law and to fine them up to US$11,111.

Child Protection

According to the Department of Social Affairs, reported cases of child abuse have increased steadily from 1,400 in 1993 to over 3,000 in 1995. Article 18 of the *Children's Welfare Law*, mandates that child abuse cases must be reported within 24 hours of discovery. At the end of 1995, a toll-free round-the-clock telephone hotline was set up in Taiwan Province in order to promptly uncover cases of child abuse. Taking Taipei as an example, among the 372 cases reported to the children's protection hotline in 1995, physical abuse was the most common complaint (28 percent), followed by neglect (21 percent), and substandard parenting (15 percent).

According to the law, all reports of child abuse must be investigated. A social worker is dispatched to the site, sometimes accompanied by police. When a serious child protection case is confirmed, and if the parents are unable to guarantee the safety of the child, he or she is then removed to a safe place. According to the *Children's Welfare Law,* the protective custody may not exceed 72 hours in duration without a direct court order. In 275 out of the 372 child protection cases discovered in Taipei in 1995, the children in question were able to remain with their families. Of the remaining 97 children, 34 were placed with relatives, six in temporary foster homes, 25 in children's homes, and one in permanent foster care.

Medical Care

All children are covered under the National Health Insurance 全民健康保險 (NHI) program, which came into effect on March 1, 1995. In addition to standard medical services, this comprehensive health program provides six free health examinations for children up to four years old.

On December 25, 1995, children below the age of three who are members of households registered in Taipei City started to enjoy extra medical care subsidies in addition to those provided under the NHI program. The Taipei City Government began paying for medical expenses not covered by the program. However, the granting of this subsidy is subject to budgetary limitations.

Childcare

The demand for childcare has risen rapidly in the ROC with the increase in the number of single parent families and nuclear families in which both parents work outside the home. The *Children's Welfare Law* and its enforcement rules, the *Nursery Establishment Measures* 托兒所設置辦法 and the *Foster Care Measures* 兒童寄養辦法, mandate the establishment of child welfare centers in all cities and counties in Taiwan. As of December 1995, there were a total of 21 public nurseries, approximately 1,300 private nurseries, and nearly 2,000 community nurseries in the Taiwan area. The number of children accommodated by these institutions fell slightly from the previous year to 220,000, due in part to an increase in the number of elementary schools providing services for preschool-age kids. Though few, some private corporations and government organizations also provide nurseries for staff children.

A program initiated on July 5, 1995, called for strengthening the professional training of kindergarten teachers. During fiscal 1996, 13 public kindergartens were under construction. In addition, as of December 1995, some 18 child welfare centers were serving the Taiwan area, while 39 homes for foundlings and orphans were caring for about 2,500 children.

To match the schedules of working mothers, elementary schools hold after-school classes for children up to eight years of age. Full-day childcare centers must meet legally mandated standards for basic facilities, personnel qualifications, space allotted, and staff size. To accommodate children from low-income families, all daycare centers must admit at least 10 percent of their students free of charge. Under the *Social Service Promotion Incentive Guidelines* 加強推展社會福利獎助作業要點, local social welfare bureaus offer grants and awards to outstanding daycare centers.

Juvenile Services

At the end of 1995, one in every nine people (about 2.39 million) in the Taiwan area was aged from 12 to 17. Most ROC citizens graduate from the nation's nine-year compulsory education system by age 15. These young people face abrupt and difficult choices. Will they take the competitive examinations to enter a senior high school or senior vocational school, enroll in a cram school to prepare for the exams (see Chapter 17, Education), or look for employment? Young people who are unable to pass the competitive examinations or who purposely forsake educational opportunities realize that life without a high school diploma will be difficult. Not surprisingly, rates of petty crime, drug dependence, and suicide are rising among this group.

Juvenile delinquency is a growing problem. The MOI's National Police Administration 內政部警政署 (NPA) statistics indicate that 18.8 percent of all crime suspects in 1995 were juveniles aged between 12 and 18, up from 17.5 percent in 1991. The juvenile crime rate has also risen, from 111 per 10,000 juveniles in 1991 to 122.4 per 10,000 in 1995. The most prominent categories involving juveniles were burglary, violent crimes, and drug violations. The proportion of juvenile suspects arrested for burglary and violent crime in 1995 rose to 57.4 and 12.5 percent, respectively. That same year, 12.6 percent of all juvenile delinquents were drug suspects, down from 28.7 percent in 1993.

The mean age of delinquents is falling. In the past, most juvenile delinquents were either 17 or 18 years of age, but since 1986 the number of 14- and 15-year-old delinquents has been rising quickly. In 1995, of all suspects in Taiwan, 18.4 percent received only an elementary-school education, 45.3 percent were graduates of junior high school, and 27.3 percent were senior high school graduates.

The NPA reports that in 1995, police charged 8,394 people with drug violations (excluding amphetamine-related charges). Among them, 6,441 were charged with drug abuse, 1,860 with drug dealing, and the remaining 93 with possession and/or transportation. Nineteen percent of those charged were young people between the ages of 12 and 23.

The rate of amphetamine and other drug abuse has reached major proportions over the past several years. The abuse of amphetamines (usually in the form of crystal methamphetamine) by youngsters in Taiwan appears to be even more common than in Japan, Korea, Singapore, or Hong Kong. About 40 percent of the people charged with amphetamine use in Taiwan were between the ages of 12 and 24.

Campaign Against Drug Abuse

To combat the increase in drug usage and drug-related crimes, Premier Lien Chan 連戰 formally declared war on drugs on May 12, 1993. As almost all drugs used on the island come from overseas, the government has mobilized every available force, including the military, to protect the island from the influx of illegal drugs. In addition to law enforcement agencies, customs authorities, and the judiciary, agencies working in such diverse areas as health, education, finance, and agriculture also contribute to the common effort to attack this scourge on all fronts. The government is running advertisements to convince youngsters to stay away from drugs. These ads feature movie stars and other famous celebrities, and appear in print, television, and radio formats. Large concerts by celebrities popular among teenagers have been held in major cities to drive home the anti-drug message. Taiwan's three TV stations have also aired prime-time shows centering on this theme.

Youth Counseling and Guidance

Young people in need do have somewhere to turn. Counseling and psychiatric services for youths are readily available at community health centers and psychiatric health clinics at major hospitals. The government subsidizes 40 youth welfare centers in the Taiwan area which provide youths with counseling, psychiatric advice, emer-gency aid, school and employment assistance, and recreational opportunities.

Hotlines in north, central, and south Taiwan also serve people in need. One such hotline is named "Teacher Chang" 張老師. Set up by the China Youth Corps (see inset) in 1969, the Teacher Chang hotline is a free counseling service that recruits volunteers from all walks of life to provide professional phone counseling to youths.

In 1995 alone, Teacher Chang handled over 44,000 counseling cases. Their problems ranged from family, personal relationship, problems with the other sex, studies, jobs, life prospect and so on.

Teenage Prostitution

According to the *Penal Code* 刑法, any person who has sexual intercourse with an individual aged 14 or under is guilty of statutory rape and is subject to a mandatory sentence of at least five years' imprisonment. A person who has sex with an adolescent aged 15 or 16 is also guilty of rape and must be sentenced to one to seven years in jail. But these provisions are based on the condition that a complaint must be filed either by the victim or the victim's guardian, not just by the public prosecutor. Most parents of young victims are reluctant to seek redress in a public court of law, usually preferring out-of-court settlements.

In July 1995, the Legislative Yuan passed the *Child and Youth Sexual Transaction Prevention Act* 兒童及少年性交易防治條例. This law targets teenage prostitution, supplementing the *Penal Code* and compensating for its inadequacy with respect to sexual exploitation of adolescents. Pursuant to the new law, public prosecutors can now independently press charges against pimps or patrons. The act stipulates that a sexual patron of a prostitute aged under 16 can be sentenced to a maximum of three years' imprisonment and a maximum fine of US$3,704. Patrons of prostitutes aged 16 or 17 are subjected to the same fine but no imprisonment. Pimps can be sentenced to life imprisonment and fined US$740,741.

Halfway houses provide rescued adolescent prostitutes with shelter, food, clothing, medical care, and counseling. These young women are

Drug Seizure and Persons Arrested for Drug Abuse

Item	1987	1988	1989	1990	1991	1992	1993	1994	1995	1996 (Jan.-April)
Narcotics (kg)*	5.57	4.14	4.66	36.68	154.52	90.82	814.18	526.99	105.58	21.72
Number of Cases	695	791	945	1,072	3,072	4,701	14,269	11,608	5,896	1,979
Number of People Charged	997	1,032	1,196	1,446	4,436	6,378	19,997	16,145	8,394	2,689
Age 12-17	5	3	27	44	156	214	614	523	258	72
Age 18-23	75	76	107	184	896	1,200	3,603	2,791	1,350	384
Amphetamines (kg)**-	-	-	414	1,298	886.94	963.55	615.24	899	79.56	
Number of Cases	-	-	-	2,798	16,099	28,878	31,972	21,276	18,126	8,072
Number of People Charged	-	-	-	4,400	24,310	40,741	43,998	28,721	25,214	11,064
Age 12-17	-	-	-	1,415	6,788	10,558	8,689	4,556	3,642	1,446
Age 18-23	-	-	-	1,526	7,916	11,954	11,780	6,988	6,531	2,833

Note: *Includes opium, poppy and seed, marijuana, morphine, cocaine, heroin, codeine, other derivatives and synthetic drugs.

**Since Oct. 9, 1990, amphetamine users and possessors have been indicted under the *Statutes for the Control of Narcotics*.

Source: National Police Administration, Ministry of the Interior

encouraged to go back to school or helped to seek a socially acceptable job. In Taipei City, teenage prostitutes are sent to the Occupation Training Center for Women at the Taipei Municipal Kuangtzu Po Ai Institution 台北市立廣慈博愛院. Its counterpart in Kaohsiung City and County is the 802 Military General Hospital 國軍802總醫院. And in Taiwan Province, teenage prostitutes are cared for by the Taiwan Provincial Yunlin Institute 台灣省立雲林教養院 and the Taiwan Provincial Jen Ai Vocational Training Center 台灣省立仁愛習藝中心. All in all, these public facilities can accommodate about 230 people. Their stay in these institutions ranges from 72 hours to one year, depending on the court decision.

Several halfway houses operated by private foundations such as the Good Shepherd Sisters 善牧基金會, a Catholic foundation, and the Garden of Hope Foundation 勵馨基金會. Their full capacity totals 75 people. In addition to this, they also accept teenage girls who are victims of incest and sexual abuse.

Women

Over the last decade, new definitions of women's roles have been formed as more Chinese women have received higher education, joined the work force, begun to compete with men, and become financially independent. Chinese women are resisting the traditional view that women are inferior to men and that, in male-female relationships, a woman should be submissive. Many women in Taiwan complain that they are unfairly burdened with both traditional and modern roles. It is, many women say, difficult to be simultaneously wage earners, good mothers, dutiful daughters-in-law, and dutiful wives.

At the end of 1995, there were 10.4 million women in the Taiwan area, compared to a male population of 11.0 million. On average, first-time

China Youth Corps

The China Youth Corps 中國青年反共救國團 (CYC) is a non-government organization aimed at guiding youth in their growth and development through various activities. Established in 1952, in addition to the counseling hotline, the CYC holds lectures and seminars to educate youth. Its most popular activities are the outdoor recreational programs during summer and winter vacations, designed for teenagers and young adults.

The organization also sponsors youth good will missions around the world, seeking to broaden young people's horizons. Since July, 1992, the CYC has organized youth cultural and education exchanges with the Chinese mainland. Through 1995, a total of 913 ROC youths had traveled to the mainland in 34 CYC groups, and 76 young mainlanders had come to visit the ROC.

Young Chinese who were born overseas and foreign youth are not excluded from CYC programs. During summer vacations, youth of Chinese descent can come to Taiwan to learn Chinese language, culture, and customs. In addition, each year groups of young foreigners are invited to Taiwan for cultural and academic exchanges with their Chinese counterparts.

These cross-Straits and intercultural exchanges are either partially or completely funded by government agencies, including the Ministry of Education 教育部, Overseas Chinese Affairs Commission 僑務委員會, Mainland Affairs Council 行政院大陸委員會, and Ministry of Foreign Affairs 外交部, among others.

brides were 28.2 years old that year, up from 25.8 in 1990. Most married women in the Taiwan area have their first child by age 34. Almost half of Taiwan's women are regular wage earners and help support their families financially.

For thousands of years, all Chinese women were expected to marry, and all married women in China had to give birth to and take care of

Rising Sun Project

Since July 1, 1991, a comprehensive youth guidance program—the Rising Sun Project 旭日方案 has been underway. Through this program, special task forces to help youth aged from 12 to 18 have been established in police departments around the island.

Activities within this program include informal visits to police departments, lectures and panel discussions on legal affairs and youth issues, hiking, camping, and mountain climbing. All teenagers, regardless of whether or not they have criminal records, are encouraged to attend. In this way, those who do have criminal records are able to interact with their more fortunate peers and receive correctional education in a healthy environment. Additionally, task force members visit delinquents in their homes, offering assistance to the teenagers as well as their guardians.

several children in addition to caring for their parents-in-law. At one time, most welfare agencies at the local level of government in Taiwan believed that women's welfare meant helping women meet these traditional obligations. According to this relatively conservative outlook, subsidies for the daycare, medical expenses, and education of children and elderly people supposedly reduced the burden on women. To the extent that women are still required to fulfill traditional roles, these welfare services do indeed benefit women. Nonetheless, the activism of feminist groups and recent media reports of domestic violence and rising divorce rates have challenged local authorities to change their parochial attitudes towards women.

Women's Educational Attainment

In ancient China, naivety was considered a feminine virtue. Consequently, few women were taught to read and write. Today, however, more and more women receive higher education. According to the Ministry of the Interior, at the end of 1995, some 42 percent of junior college graduates, 36 percent of university and college graduates, and 22 percent of graduate school graduates were women. Two decades earlier, the corresponding figures were 32, 24, and 15 percent, respectively. Clearly, women are enjoying better education opportunities, with the female portion of university/college and grad-school graduates having increased by half in 20 years.

Women's Service Networks

In the last 15 years, numerous women's organizations have arisen to help women cope with these problems, and to clarify liberalized roles for both men and women. Many local governments, under the supervision of the Ministry of the Interior, have organized regional coalitions of groups aiming to help women. These coalitions have generated public awareness about gender issues and provided medical, legal, psychological, educational, and vocational assistance to an ever growing number of women. Furthermore, they empower women by providing them with avenues for action and a collective voice. The most mature and successful women's welfare coalition is the Taipei Women's Service Network (see inset, next page).

In 1995, Taiwan Province boasted 65 comprehensive welfare centers offering counseling, vocational training, seminars, and other services to disadvantaged women. Halfway houses and shelters for women in need numbered 23 that year, up six from 1994. With a maximum capacity of 311 persons, they accommodated 191 in 1995, an increase of 118 over the previous year.

Female Employment Assistance

The *Employment Promotion Measures* 促進就業措施 initiated by the Employment and Vocational Training Administration of the Council of Labor Affairs 行政院勞工委員會職業訓練局 (EVTA) in 1985 target women, people of 45 and up, the disabled, aborigines, and families that are receiving welfare assistance. These measures involve promoting job equality between the sexes, providing women with vocational training, surveying the demand for part-time and freelance work to enlarge the women's employment market, and even offering daycare center for pre-school children, after-school classes for elemen-

tary students, and daycare for the elderly to alleviate the burden on women.

From July 1995 to April 1996, some 900 women graduated from Taiwan's 13 vocational training centers as full-time students, 2,000 as evening-class students. The government paid all school-related expenses for the full-time students and subsidized half the expenses for the evening-class students. During the same period, another 1,186 completed vocational programs organized by local county or city governments.

During 1995, the EVTA provided job-hunting assistance to 30,924 women, 2,399 people over 45, 1,406 handicapped, 615 aborigines and 46 persons from families that were receiving welfare assistance.

Divorce

Nothing illustrates the ongoing re-evaluation of women's roles in Taiwan better than the issue of divorce. A few decades ago, divorce was a relatively rare occurrence. During the 1980s, an increasing number of women in Taiwan started to earn their own paychecks. The experiences of women working outside the home have allowed them greater access to information and ideas about alternative lifestyles. Hence, their growing independence gives them more freedom to reject dysfunctional marriages. Data released by the Department of Population under the Ministry of the Interior 內政部戶政司 indicates that the divorce rate in the Taiwan area has more than quadrupled in the last 25 years while the marriage rate has only undergone a barely discernible increase. The divorce rate stood at 1.57 couples per 1,000 people in 1995, compared to 0.37 in 1970, and 0.76 in 1980. However, the marriage rate only showed a slight overall increase, having risen from 7.50 per 1,000 people in 1970 to 9.90 in 1980, and then fallen back to 7.54 by 1995. Thus, in 1995, divorced people accounted for 2.96 percent of the 15-and-over population, compared to 0.89 percent in 1970 and 1.07 percent in 1980.

In general, Taiwan society still demonstrates little sympathy for divorced women. The founder of the Warm Life Association for Women 晚晴婦

Taipei Women's Services Network

Legal Questions

The Taipei Citizen's Service Center 台北市政府聯合服務中心 725-6168

The Shihlin District Court 台灣士林地方法院 833-9697

Domestic Violence

Carnation Line 康乃馨專線 561-9595

Emergency Sanctuary

Suicide Prevention Center 生命線 505-9595

Emergency Relief

Department of Social Affairs, Taipei City Government 台北市政府社會局 759-7701

Rape

(Day) *Modern Women Foundation* 現代婦女基金會 391-7128

(Night) *Women's Police Squad* 台北市政府警察局女子警察隊 306-1444

Halfway Houses

The Garden of Hope Foundation 勵馨基金會 371-9583, 375-9595

Good Shepherd Sisters Social Welfare Services 善牧基金會 381-5402

Taipei Women's Rescue Foundation 婦女救援基金會 392-9595

Family Problems

Taipei Family Education Service Center 台北市社會教育館家庭教育服務中心 578-1885

Mackay Counseling Center 馬偕協談中心 571-8427

Psychological Problems

Huaming Counseling Center 華明心理輔導中心 382-1885

Peace Line of the *Mackay Counseling Center* 馬偕協談中心平安線 531-8595, 531-0505

Cosmic Light Media Center 財團法人基督教宇宙光輔導中心 362-7278, 363-2107

Unwed Mothers

Cathwel Service 財團法人天主教未婚媽媽之家 311-0223

Christian Salvation Service 財團法人台北市基督徒救世會社會福利事業基金會 729-0265

Child Abuse

Child Protection Hot Line of the Department of Social Affairs, Taipei City Government 台北市政府社會局兒童保護專線 704-8585

Children's Welfare League Foundation 財團法人中華民國兒童福利聯盟文教基金會 748-6006

Forced Labor

Taipei Women's Rescue Foundation 婦女救援基金會 392-9595

Job Counseling

Public Employment Service Center, Department of Labor Affairs, Taipei City Government 台北市政府勞工局國民就業輔導中心 591-4654

Vocational Training

Taipei Women's Development Center 台灣基督長老教會台北婦女展業中心 506-9835

Vocational Training Center, Department of Labor Affairs, Taipei City Government 台北市政府勞工局職業訓練中心 872-1940

Medical Issues

Medical Information & Service Association, ROC 中華民國醫療諮詢服務協會 314-1515

Divorcées and Widows

The Warm Life Association for Women 晚晴婦女協會 559-4740

Note: These telephone numbers are staffed by personnel who do not necessarily speak English.

女協會, an organization that helps divorced and widowed women and seeks to eliminate discrimination against divorcées while fighting for their equality in the eyes of the law, says that divorced women in Taiwan face more emotional problems than divorced men. Founded in Taipei in 1988, Warm Life now has branches in Taichung and Kaohsiung as well. The organization provides professional legal advice and psychological counseling, and operates telephone hotlines in Taipei, Taichung, and Kaohsiung that provide emergency counseling for women coping with dysfunctional marriages or divorce.

Women's attitudes with regard to marriage are changing much more quickly than may be apparent from currently available statistics. More and more women are resisting parental pressure to marry and have children early, seeing marriage and married life as risky, unnecessary, or simply not worth the trouble.

Rewriting the Law

Many women's groups have been lobbying lawmakers to change Book IV of the *Civil Code*, 民法 which concerns family matters. This section of the *Civil Code* went into effect in May 1931 and was only partially revised once in 1985. It covers divorce-related issues such as child custody, child support and alimony, and the division of property. The language of this section clearly favors men.

On September 6, 1996, several landmark revisions were made to Book IV by the Ministry of Justice 法務部. Article 1051, which automatically gave the father custody in the case of divorce by mutual consent, was struck from the books. Article 1055 was amended to stipulate that, when a court is ruling on a divorce, it must do so in the interest of any children involved, weigh all circumstances, and take into consideration all interview reports from social workers. Article 1089 was amended to give both parents equal priority with regard to parental rights and obligations to minor children, and to give the court—rather than the father—final say in resolving disputes. This revision was crucial to filling in the legal void left after the Council of

Grand Justices 大法官會議 ruled on September 23, 1994, that the original wording of Article 1089 giving fathers priority in the enforcement of parental rights violated the ROC Constitution.

Changes were also made with regard to property rights. Prior to the 1985 revision of the *Civil Code,* any property registered under a married woman's name belonged to her husband. The 1985 revision gave the wife full rights over property registered under her name, but these rights were extended only to women who married after the revision came into effect. The September 6, 1996, amendments extended this right retroactively to all married women, regardless of their date of marriage.

The Elderly

People who attain the grand age of 70 in Taiwan are apt to discover the advantages of filial piety, or reverence for one's parents, which has been the highest virtue in Chinese ethical relations since well before the time of Confucius. Chinese people today still feel a strong moral obligation to care for the elderly. The law in Taiwan reflects this moral compunction by mandating a broad range of services for anyone over the age of 70, from subsidized transportation and entertainment to free medical care and housing. Nevertheless, the government is not the primary source of support for most senior citizens: More than 60 percent of the 1.6 million people in Taiwan who are over the age of 65 are still personally cared for by their children in their own homes. However, this percentage is falling.

Welfare for the elderly is defined by the Ministry of the Interior as providing basic subsistence aid and health care to poor and helpless senior citizens. The government advocates that elderly people live with or near their children. In-home care is provided for senior citizens who live by themselves and have difficulties in performing everyday activities.

As the average life expectancy rises in Taiwan—to 77.74 and 71.85 years in 1995 for women and men, respectively—elderly people are making up a growing proportion of the population. In

December 1995, some 4.5 percent of the population was over 70 while 3.1 percent was between 65 and 70. By the year 2000, a full 8.5 percent of the total population is expected to be over 65. As the population grays, there will be proportionally fewer wage-earners to provide for the aged (see Chapter 2, People, and Chapter 15, Public Health). The Ministry of the Interior's proposed revisions to the *Welfare Law for the Elderly* 老人福利法 (promulgated in 1980) include a special exemption on real estate taxes for households with senior citizens.

Elderly Pensions

Elderly residents of Taipei City and County, Ilan County 宜蘭縣, Hsinchu County 新竹縣, Tainan County, Chiayi City 嘉義市, Kaohsiung County, and P'enghu County 澎湖縣 benefit from organized pension systems. Residents of these areas who are 65 years of age or older and do not receive other forms of pension or subsidy from the government are entitled to a pension ranging from US$111 to US$185 per month, depending on the county or city of residence. This welfare policy is budgeted separately by each county or city government, and is not universal throughout the Taiwan area.

Medical Services

Since March 1, 1995, senior citizens with low incomes have received free inpatient and outpatient medical assistance through the National Health Insurance program. The government also provides free in-home medical care for the indigent elderly. Nurses made over 150,000 such house calls in 1995. In addition, 45 geriatric nurseries, 17 medical institution-affiliated homes for the elderly, and 18 homes for retired servicemen have brought serenity and security to many seniors who do not have any family in Taiwan.

Elderly Daycare

Daycare for the elderly has become more important as younger family members go out for work. In May 1988, the Taipei City government inaugurated the Taiwan area's first daycare center for people over 65, the Neihu District Elderly Service Center 內湖老人服務中心. Now, this center and the Taipei Municipal Kuangtzu Po Ai Institution 台北市立廣慈博愛院 together can accommodate about 70 people per day. These centers conduct regular physical checkups and provide breakfast, lunch, and entertainment during working hours on weekdays and Saturdays. Five additional daycare centers are currently being planned in Taipei. Ideally, these will be located in every district, so that users will not need to travel far from home, and for the convenience of family members. Similar institutions are now operating throughout the Taiwan area. All told, elderly people paid nearly 190,000 visits to daycare centers in 1995.

Over 4,100 senior-citizen recreation centers and organizations such as the Evergreen Academy 長青學苑, Community Longevity 社區長壽俱樂部, and Pine Clubs 老人文康中心 serve senior citizens and provide activities such as folk dancing, Chinese "shadowboxing" 太極拳, folk music, opera, chess, and handicrafts. In 1995, nearly 67,000 people enrolled in classes provided by the 188 Evergreen Academies. Lung-shan Elderly Service Center 龍山老人服務中心, inaugurated in Taipei in June 1996, is the first service center for the elderly operated by the private-sector using government facilities. It is expected that future centers will follow this model.

Independent Housing

Although Taiwan's 62 old-age homes and nurseries accommodated over 7,800 elderly people in 1995, there is a desperate shortage of housing for elderly people who find it necessary to live independently of their family or who have no family. The private Kaohsiung County Senior Citizens' Apartments 崧鶴樓, which began operating in July 1995, has set a fine example for residential complexes catering exclusively to senior citizens. This 12-story building totals about 12,000 square meters, with rooms ranging in size from 21 to 34 square meters. Three stories (from the basement to the second floor) are for public use, and include a cafeteria, auditorium, library, fitness center, karaoke room, prayer room, two classrooms, and several other group activity rooms. This Kaohsiung County facility has a 350-person capacity. Similar institutions which together will accommodate about 500 people are under construction in Tainan City and Taipei County.

In Taipei City, two apartment buildings for the elderly, Yangming 陽明 and Churen 朱崙, are under construction. The two are expected to provide living quarters for about 200 people, and will include small single- and double-occupancy residential units, indoor recreational facilities, and plenty of outdoor space. Only people who are over 65, healthy, and able to handle daily chores qualify for residency. It is likely that these institutions will be operated by the private sector while the land and facilities remain publicly owned.

For elderly who require more medical care or assistance, there is an old people's nursing home serving 380 old people in Taipei's Wenshan District 文山區. Two other such facilities, one in Mucha District 木柵區 and one in Yangmingshan 陽明山, will join the Wenshan facility to serve an additional 1,200 elderly people.

The Taipei Municipal Kuangtzu Po Ai Institution provides comprehensive care for needy old people, women, and children. Benefits include free room and board, and even pocket money. At the end of June 1996, the institution was caring for 879 people, with a breakdown of 764 old people (including 34 who received monthly stipends of US$263 from the institution but lived outside), 43 women, and 72 children.

Disabled People

As of March 1996, about 408,000 people held Handicapped Certificates 殘障手冊 in the Taiwan area, up 30 percent since December 1994. Long-term observers of the social welfare movement in Taiwan note that advocates for the rights of disabled people are perhaps the best organized and most effective of all the special-interest groups competing for recognition and services. The ROC government spent about US$110 million on subsidies for disabled people in 1995, including more than US$65 million in living-expense subsidies.

The *Welfare Law for the Handicapped and Disabled* 殘障福利法 stipulates that welfare services must be provided for the autistic and for people with serious facial injuries or major organ malfunction. The law also states that all private enterprises with more than 100 employees must hire at least one disabled worker. In other words, any medium or large private enterprise must reserve one percent of its job positions for the disabled. Government offices, public schools, and public enterprises with 50 or more employees are held to a doubly stringent standard. Two percent of their employees must be disabled people. Thus, a police station with a staff of 150 ought to have at least three disabled employees.

In March 1996, the Department of Social Affairs under the Ministry of the Interior indicated that nearly 7,700 private or government employers in Taiwan are large enough to be subject to the provisions of the law and thus must hire a set number of disabled personnel. If each employer were to meet the quota exactly, nearly 29,000 disabled people would be employed. Such is not the case, however. Only about 22,000 disabled people had been hired as of March 1996, with 64 percent of employers having met or exceeded the minimum requirements, five percent more than had at the end of 1994.

Fortunately, the *Welfare Law for the Handicapped and Disabled* provides a set of punishments and inducements to encourage employer cooperation, and to fund services for the disabled. Employers who do not meet the quota must pay US$569 every month for each handicapped person they have not yet hired. For example, if a public school has 275 employees, it is legally required to hire at least five disabled employees. If only two are hired, the school must pay US$1,707 (US$569 x 3) per month for the three it failed to employ. The money is paid into a Special Account for Handicapped Welfare 殘障福利金專戶 set up and monitored by the Social Services Department 社會局 of the county or city where the employer is located. Employers who fail to pay the fine are prosecuted.

How is the money used? The Special Account for Handicapped Welfare set up by the Taipei City Government 台北市政府, for example, had a net balance of over US$312 million in March 1996. The money is used to make work places more accessible to disabled people, to pay the full salaries of disabled employees during their first three months of probationary employment, and to underwrite half the salary of each disabled employee who is hired after an employer has already met his quota.

Vocational Training

Seven consultation service centers around Taiwan handle telephone consultations, correspondence management, one-on-one sessions, and interviews for disabled people who wish to take classes, receive special medical care, or seek employment. The centers also host seminars, recreational activities, and social gatherings. Thirty-one public and private vocational training institutions for the disabled provide classes in practical skills to help disabled people lead independent lives. In 1995, over 1,500 individuals attended these classes, and an additional 1,400 received governmental assistance in finding jobs.

The first-ever civil service examination for disabled people took place in July 1996. The exam was open exclusively to disabled people aged between 18 and 55 with educational backgrounds from junior high school to graduate school. A total of 474 passed the exam and were admitted into the civil service.

Medical Care and Subsidies

Under the National Health Insurance program, people with severe or extremely severe disabilities pay no premium and receive free treatment for serious injuries. People whose disabilities are not so severe pay a discounted premium and a flat rate of US$2 for basic outpatient services. Prior to the implementation of the NHI program on March 1, 1995, subsidies for medical treatment and rehabilitation expenses were granted to disabled people on the basis of financial need. Disabled people received medical subsidies totaling US$39.5 million during 1995. Severely disabled people are eligible to receive long-term care at the 97 welfare institutions for the handicapped located across the island. In 1995, these institutions accommodated nearly 7,900 disabled people.

Education of the Disabled

Disabled people are integrated into regular educational institutions as much as possible. Many regular schools, from the elementary to the senior high and senior vocational level, offer special classes for the disabled. In addition, as of the 1995-96 school year, the Taiwan area boasted 17 government-established special education schools exclusively for handicapped students. (see Chapter 17, Education).

Indigenous Peoples

The welfare of the various indigenous peoples in the Taiwan area, who numbered nearly 370,000 at the end of 1995, is among the top priorities of the ROC social welfare system. Several new government organizations whose mission is to serve the aborigine population were created in 1996. On March 16, the Taipei City Government established its "Commission for Native Taiwanese Affairs" 原住民事務委員會. In May, the Kaohsiung City Government followed suit with a special task force on aboriginal affairs. On December 10 of the same year, a cabinet-level Council of Aboriginal Affairs under the Executive Yuan 行政院原住民委員會 was established. The Taiwan Provincial Government set up its Council of Aboriginal Affairs 臺灣省政府原住民事務委員會 in January 1997. As mandated by the *Additional Articles of the ROC Constitution* 中華民國憲法增修條文, the government actively seeks to protect the aborigines rights, and to assist and encourage them in many areas (see Chapter 2, People).

The government provides low-interest housing loans to aborigines. Under this program, aborigines can borrow a maximum of US$55,556 at an annual interest of 4.5 percent, repayable over a 20-year period. Aborigines are accorded special status when taking entrance exams for the high-school level and above. An extra 35 percent is added to the exam score of aborigines participating in the senior high school and senior vocational high school entrance examinations. And any aborigine who passes these tests and enters school is entitled to receive the same government subsidies as students in the ROC's normal universities. Aboriginal students who participate in the college and university entrance examinations enjoy a 25 percent discount on the standard passing grade. There are also scholarships for aborigines from low-income families. Tuition is waived for aborigines who take part in government-sponsored vocational training programs. They also receive monthly a US$73 food stipend and a US$222 living-expense stipend from the Taiwan Provincial Government. The Ministry of the Interior provides an additional US$148 monthly stipend to those who receive training for three months or more. A special civil-service examination for aborigines is administered biennially. Through the end of 1995, the exam had been held a total 17 times, with 1,446 aborigines passing.

Volunteer Services

The warm participation of the private sector plays an important role in the ROC social welfare scheme. At the end of 1995, there were over 37,000 volunteers working in the Taiwan area through both the public and private sector. On average, each volunteer provided 1.9 hours of service per week to the elderly, the handicapped, youth, children, women, and the community as a whole. In July 1995, the Ministry of the Interior initiated the Hsiang Ho Program 祥和計畫 to consolidate and strengthen volunteer work. In addition to recruiting volunteers through media campaigns, this program strives to balance the distribution of volunteer services so that those in need can receive proper care regardless of geographic location. Another purpose is to consolidate volunteer resources and provide volunteers with high-quality training and education.

Low-income Households

The ROC government provides several types of special subsidies and assistance to individuals and families having low incomes, including help in finding jobs, educational aid for children, stipends during traditional festivals, and child and maternal nutritional programs, as well as other cash and non-cash benefits. Most of the programs base eligibility on individual, household, or family income, and a few offer help on the basis of presumed need. To determine eligibility, each fiscal year a figure for "monthly minimum expenses" based on the consumer price index and variations in regional income distribution is assigned by the government. This figure differs from area to area: for example, for fiscal year 1997, in Taipei City the monthly minimum expenses is set at US$249, in Taiwan Province and Kaohsiung City it stands at US$222, and in Kinmen County 金門縣, US$174. Families whose average monthly income does not reach this amount are classified as low-income families. In 1995, only 114,000 people (48,500 households), or 0.5 percent of the population of Taiwan, were considered members of low-income families.

Starting in July 1993, the ROC government began providing a monthly subsidy to low-income elderly throughout the Taiwan area. The amount of this subsidy does not vary from locality to locality. All ROC citizens over the age of 65 whose average family income is less than or equal to 1.5 times the minimum monthly expenses are qualified to receive a monthly subsidy of US$222. Elderly people whose average family income is between 1.5 and 2.5 times the minimum expense are eligible for a monthly relief subsidy of US$111. Through June 1996, some 324,000 elderly people had benefited from this policy.

Some low-income families with children qualify for an additional monthly subsidy. Again, the standards vary depending on the locality. Children of families whose average monthly income does not exceed the minimum are entitled to a monthly subsidy. In Taiwan Province, the subsidy is US$59 per child, with each household being limited to collecting for a maximum of two children. In Kaohsiung City, each child qualifies for a monthly sum of US$67. Taipei City, with deeper pockets, is somewhat more generous: households with children below the age of two, and between the ages of 12 and 17, are eligible to collect US$166 per child. Children between the ages of 2 and 11 qualify a household for US$124 per month. In Taiwan Province, two-thirds of the cost of the subsidy program is borne by the central government, with the rest falling on the shoulders of the local government. A local government is allowed to pay more, but not less, than its allotted share.

FIRST COMMERCIAL BANK

重視自己及尊重他人之智慧財產權

IPPC

中華民國全國工業總會保護智慧財產權委員會
INTELLECTUAL PROPERTY PROTECTION COMMITTEE, R.O.C.

台北市復興南路一段390號12樓　　TEL：(02)7060223
12TH FL., 390, FU HSING S. RD., SEC. I, TAIPEI, TAIWAN, R.O.C.

20.
Labor

Above: Most of the now over 200,000 foreign workers in Taiwan are employed in the construction and manufacturing industries.

Right: Changing social values and an ongoing shortage of labor in many sectors have swelled the ranks of women in the labor force.

Previous page: The diligent and hard-working citizens of the ROC comprise one of the primary forces propelling Taiwan's economic development.

20 Labor

Taiwan's economic growth over the past 40 years has been powered by a well-educated and highly motivated work force. Over the years, the structural composition of labor has changed, but workers themselves have generally retained their traditional spirit of dedication and hard work. Today, Taiwan has a diversified and skilled work force of roughly 9.2 million people, with a comparatively low unemployment rate of less than 3 percent; approximately 6.26 million are paid workers, as opposed to those who are self-employed or have some other working status.

During 1995, as in previous years, the government has sought to maintain a productive and qualified work force. Legislative priorities have focused on the rights of workers, including workers' welfare, labor-management relations, safety and health, and appropriate quotas for foreign workers.

Labor Rights

Legal Framework

Legislative provisions for workers' welfare are prescribed in the ROC Constitution as a fundamental part of national policy. According to Article 153 of the Constitution, "[t]he State, in order to improve the livelihood of laborers and farmers and to improve their productive skill, shall enact laws and carry out policies for their protection." Under this constitutional provision, the legal framework accords all workers equal opportunity to work as well as guarantees their rights.

Labor Standards Law

The key labor law in the ROC, the 1984 *Labor Standards Law* 勞動基準法, defines such terms as worker, employer, wages, and contract. It delineates the rights and obligations of workers and employers, prescribes the minimum requirements for labor contracts, and has provisions on wages, work hours, leave, and the employment of women and children. The law protects against unreasonable work hours and forced labor, and grants workers the right to receive compensation for occupational injuries and layoffs, as well as a pension upon retirement.

The *Labor Standards Law* covers approximately 3.52 million workers in the Taiwan area, or close to 39 percent of the total work force. This group comprises workers in the eight broad categories of industry which are designated under the law: agriculture, forestry, fisheries, and animal husbandry; mining and quarrying; construction; manufacturing; public utilities; transportation, warehousing, and communication services; mass communications; and other occupations designated by the central government.

Beginning on May 1, 1997, some 140,000 workers in Taiwan's financial organizations, gas stations, and environmental pollution control industry will also be included under the *Labor Standards Law*, as stipulated in an administrative order issued by the Executive Yuan. The law was revised on December 6, 1996 to gradually expand coverage to the remaining 2.7 million employees (i.e. paid workers, as opposed to the self-employed) currently not covered by the law by the end of 1998 at the latest. Certain industries may be exempted from the *Labor Standards Law* should it prove difficult to apply, but the number of workers in such industries may not exceed one-fifth of the total number of employees not covered by the law.

Employment Services Act

The *Employment Services Act* 就業服務法, promulgated on May 8, 1992, guarantees equal job opportunities and access to employment services for all. It also calls for a balance of manpower supply and demand, efficient use of human resources, and the establishment of an employment information network. To protect workers' rights during times of economic slowdown, the act stipulates that the central government should encourage management, labor unions, and workers to negotiate on the possibility of work hour reductions, wage adjustments, and in-service training to avoid layoffs.

The *Employment Services Act* also regulates public and private employment service agencies. The act calls for the opening of new labor markets for the handicapped, aborigines, members of families on welfare, female heads of households, and potential workers between 45 and 65 years of

Council of Labor Affairs

The highest level of the labor administration in the ROC is the Council of Labor Affairs (CLA) of the Executive Yuan 行政院勞工委員會. The CLA serves as an advocate for labor opportunities, supervises labor-management relations, protects workers' rights and interests, and promotes positive working environments.

Under the direct purview of the CLA are specialized departments at the central government level which oversee specific aspects of labor affairs. They are the departments of Labor-Management Relations 勞資關係處, Labor Conditions 勞動條件處, Labor Welfare 勞工福利處, Labor Insurance 勞工保險處, Labor Safety and Health 勞工安全衛生處, Labor Inspection 勞工檢查處, Research and Planning 綜合規劃處, and Statistics 統計處, as well as an Appeals Committee 訴願委員會, a Data Information Center 資訊中心, the Employment and Vocational Training Administration 職業訓練局, the Institute of Occupational Safety and Health 勞工安全衛生研究所, the Labor Insurance Bureau 勞工保險局, and the Supervisory Commission of Labor Insurance 勞工保險監理委員會. The CLA also coordinates all the regional departments and bureaus of labor affairs at the provincial/municipal and county/city government levels.

age. Public agencies compile and analyze job market information such as wage fluctuations and manpower supply and demand, offer advice on the setting up of professional training programs, and recommend jobs or training for the unemployed. Private agencies also serve as intermediaries between job seekers and employers.

As of December 1995, employment discrimination evaluation committees 就業歧視評議委員會 have

ROC Labor Force

Unit: thousand

Year	Male	Female
1991	5,355	3,214
1992	5,460	3,304
1993	5,497	3,377
1994	5,595	3,485
1995	5,659	3,551

Labor Participation Rate

Unit: %

Year	Overall	Male	Female
1991	59.11	73.80	44.39
1992	59.34	73.78	44.83
1993	58.82	72.67	44.89
1994	58.96	72.44	45.40
1995	58.71	72.03	45.34

been established under the *Employment Services Act* in the cities of Taipei, Kaohsiung, Taichung, and Tainan, and the counties of Taoyuan 桃園, Miaoli 苗栗, Nant'ou 南投, and Kaohsiung. These committees, formed by government, labor, and management representatives, as well as scholars and experts, ensure equal employment opportunities and determine if any discriminatory actions have been taken by an employer against an employee.

The employment of alien workers is also regulated under the *Employment Services Act*. Foreign workers may be employed on the condition that they do not take away job opportunities from ROC citizens or adversely affect labor conditions, national economic development, or social stability. Nine broad categories of workers are permitted to work in Taiwan, including workers with specialized or technical expertise, foreign language teachers, and sports trainers and coaches. The act lays down rules on employment contracts and extension of contracts, change of employer, and labor insurance.

Recent Legal Developments

The labor welfare system has been modified by the revision of several labor-related laws. Revised drafts of the *Labor Union Law* 工會法, the *Collective Agreement Law* 團體協約法, and the *Settlement of Labor Disputes Law* 勞資爭議處理法 await legislative approval. A notable development has been the drafting of a work equality law designed to provide stronger protection for the rights of workers, especially women employees.

In July 1994, the government set up an Unemployment Assistance Program 失業輔助措施 to help workers adversely affected by recent economic changes. While discussion concerning the implementation of unemployment insurance continues, at present an unemployed worker may receive US$22.22 per day for 25 days a month for up to four months at a time.

Protecting Labor Rights
Labor Insurance

The *Labor Insurance Act* 勞工保險條例 was promulgated in 1958 to provide insurance coverage to workers in the private sector, including industrial workers, journalists, employees of nonprofit organizations, fishermen, persons receiving vocational training in institutes registered with the government, and members of unions. Teachers and employees working in government agencies who are not eligible for teachers' or civil servants' insurance are also covered under this law. When the labor insurance program was first launched in

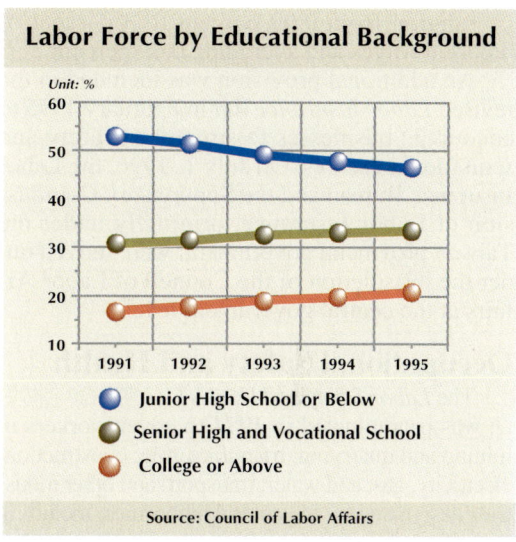

Labor Force by Educational Background

Unit: %

- ● Junior High School or Below
- ● Senior High and Vocational School
- ● College or Above

Source: Council of Labor Affairs

1950 under provincial regulations, there were 554 insured units and a total of 128,625 insured laborers in Taiwan. By the end of 1995, there were 386,206 insured units, and the number of workers covered had grown to 7,635,063.

Labor insurance coverage consists of two types: ordinary labor insurance with five kinds of benefits—maternity, injury and sickness, disability, old-age, and death; and occupational injury insurance with four kinds of benefits—injury and sickness, medical care, disability, and death. The *Labor Insurance Act* was partially revised in February 1995, transferring the medical care aspect of ordinary labor insurance to the National Health Insurance 全民健康保險 program in March of the same year (see section on Health Insurance in Chapter 15, Public Health).

Premium rates for ordinary labor insurance are 6.5 to 11 percent of the beneficiary's reported monthly salary, with the maximum monthly salary limited to US$1,344 for the purpose of premium calculation. The responsibility for premium payments are generally shared by employees, employers, and the government in the proportion 2:7:1. For occupational injury insurance, premiums are paid by employers. The rates differ among the 52 categories of businesses covered,

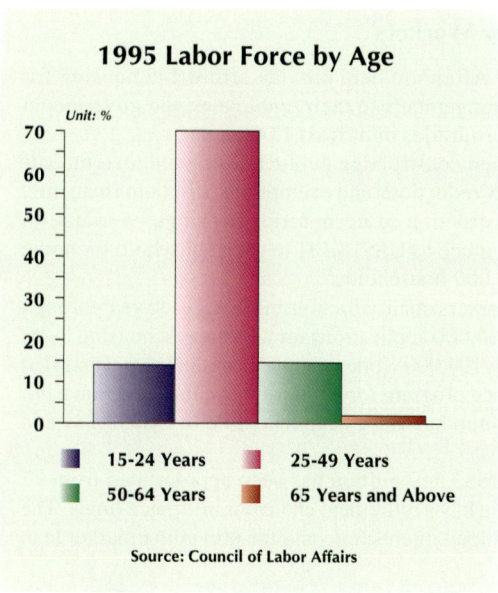

1995 Labor Force by Age

Unit: %

- ■ 15-24 Years
- ■ 25-49 Years
- ■ 50-64 Years
- ■ 65 Years and Above

Source: Council of Labor Affairs

ranging from 0.09 percent to 3 percent of reported wages and averaging 0.39 percent.

An additional provision was included in the revised *Labor Insurance Act* in February 1995 to encourage businesses to strengthen safety and sanitation measures. On July 1, 1996, the Labor Insurance Bureau and the Supervisory Commission of Labor Insurance, originally under the Taiwan provincial government, were moved under the jurisdiction of the Council of Labor Affairs at the central government level.

Occupational Safety and Health

The *Labor Safety and Health Law* 勞工安全衛生法 was promulgated in 1974 to cover workers in mining and quarrying; manufacturing; construction; electricity, gas, and water; transport; and other industries designated by the central authorities, including agriculture, forestry, fisheries, and animal husbandry; restaurants and hotels; machinery and equipment rental and leasing; mass media services; and repair services. Higher occupational safety standards to protect workers from exposure to toxic substances and hazardous working conditions were set in a 1991 revision of the law. Preventive measures must be

initiated and safety facilities installed in work places such as dockyards and fireworks factories. Women and employees under the age of 16 are prohibited from working in dangerous or harmful environments. By December 1995, the *Labor Safety and Health Law* covered 232,922 enterprises and 3.79 million laborers in the Taiwan area.

In 1995, the occupational accident rate in the ROC stood at 2.87 per 1,000 workers, with a mortality rate of 0.084 percent, down 0.125 percentage points from 1994. About 39.5 percent of all fatal occupational injuries were the result of motor vehicle accidents, and approximately 73 percent of serious disabilities were the result of human error.

To prevent occupational diseases, 496 hospitals islandwide are authorized by the government to offer annual medical checkups for workers. In 1995, some 84 percent of the 33,050 workers engaged in especially hazardous work received medical examinations. The Institute of Occupational Safety and Health was established in 1992 to conduct research on occupational injuries and diseases, ergonomics, safety in construction, mechanical and electrical facilities, and the analysis of hazardous substances.

Housing Loans for Workers

The rising cost of land has led the Council of Labor Affairs to help provide affordable housing for workers. To encourage enterprises to offer housing arrangements to their employees, the government provides low-interest loans for companies that build dormitories of at least 1,000 units.

Local governments in the last couple of years have been constructing public housing on government-owned land to alleviate the current housing shortage. Tax reductions and exemptions, discount financing, and subsidies are being offered to encourage the construction of dormitories for single workers. In addition, the CLA also provides low-interest loans of as much as US$18,181 to each household for home repairs. In 1995, the quota for home repair loans was 5,000 households.

The government is also helping a growing number of workers qualify for housing loans each year through labor insurance funds. In 1995, the CLA approved some 15,000 applications for low-interest housing loans of as much as US$54,545, to be repaid in 20 years. Nearly 104,000 workers applied for the loans. Qualified applicants had to have been enrolled in the labor insurance program for at least five years and to have not purchased a house within the last two years. The maximum has since been increased to US$58,181 at a 5.3 percent interest rate.

To finance this program, an aggregate bank loan of US$2,549 million has been appropriated from 27 financial institutions as well as partially raised through the labor retirement and labor insurance funds. The CLA subsidizes the difference between the 5.15 percent loan interest rate and the prevailing market loan rate of 8.575 percent.

Occupational Skill Testing

Occupational skill testing in the ROC serves as a guideline for determining the qualifications of workers. Examinees who pass are issued certificates designating the level of expertise attained. According to the *Vocational Training Act* 職業訓練法, laborers' skills are classified as A, B, or C level. Exams are offered by the Employment and Vocational Training Administration in 191 occupational categories. To date, a total of 727,954 examinees have passed these exams. In 1995, a total of 635 workers from 40 different occupations participated in the 26th National Vocational Training Competition 全國技能競賽.

To ensure that the skill testing system is in line with international standards and practices, the ROC has participated in the International Vocational Training Competition since 1970.

The ROC sent a team of 35 personnel to compete in Mechatronics and 33 other vocational trades in the 33rd International Vocational Training Competition held in Lyons, France, between September 5 and 19, 1995. Another team of 18 personnel competed in English Word Processing and 18 other occupational categories in the Fourth International Abilympics between September 1 and 5, 1995.

Labor Inspections

The *Labor Inspection Law* 勞動檢查法 was promulgated on February 3, 1993, to replace the *Factory Law* 工廠法. It empowers the Council of Labor Affairs and local governments to inspect labor conditions in the workplace and thereby safeguard the health and safety of workers. The scope of inspections carried out under the law covers labor health and safety, labor insurance, employee welfare funds, and the hiring of foreign workers. The approval of labor inspectors is required before workers are allowed to work at potentially dangerous sites. These include petroleum cracking plants; agrichemical, firework and gunpowder manufacturing factories; locations with containers holding gases under high pressure; construction sites; and sites where dangerous or harmful materials are manufactured or handled. In the event of a major occupational accident or disaster, the site is immediately inspected to determine the cause. Work at such sites may be completely or partially suspended should conditions be deemed too hazardous to workers.

A team of 212 inspectors oversees labor conditions at the 226,988 enterprises on the CLA's inspection list. Enterprises where hazardous working conditions are prevalent are a primary focus of inspections. Averaging three visits a day for each inspector, the team covered 5.8 percent of all enterprises in 1995. Over 16,000 visits were made in 1995 to workshops with high accident rates, such as firework factories, paint and varnish makers, construction sites, and worksites with high levels of noise and air pollution or where toxic or explosive substances were handled. The CLA is assisted by 21 authorized private and public inspection agencies, which have 657 qualified personnel trained to conduct thorough health and safety inspections. Violators of safety codes are fined between US$1,200 and US$6,000.

Labor Unions and Industrial Relations

Within the ROC's legal framework, three labor laws—the *Labor Union Law*, the *Collective Agreement Law*, and the *Settlement of Labor Disputes*

Average Monthly Income Per Industry in 1995

	US$
Mining and Quarrying	1,356
Manufacturing	1,202
Electricity, Gas, and Water	2,607
Construction	1,307
Commerce	1,225
Transport, Storage, & Communications	1,612
Finance, Insurance, and Real Estate	1,973
Business Services	1,627
Social and Personal Services	1,215

Source: Council of Labor Affairs

Vocational Training

Between 1981 and 1995, a total of 13 public vocational training institutes offered entry-level and advanced courses to more than 280,000 trainees. Another 250,000 trainees received vocational education through private commercial training schools.

Many local businesses now offer on-the-job training courses. Every year, approximately 230,000 workers receive on-the-job training conducted either by businesses or training institutes operating under government contracts. In 1995, the CLA assisted private enterprises in setting up a total of 41 vocational training centers which have completed training for nearly 1,280 job hunters as well as on-the-job training for more than 23,040 workers. In addition, the CLA held 175 courses to train supervisors and technical personnel for public and private institutions, and completed training for 23,878 workers in 1994. The CLA also offered vocational training to 5,215 foreign workers employed by investors based overseas.

The government offers start-up loans for vocational school graduates to establish their own businesses. A maximum loan of US$20,000 is available at a low interest rate for five years.

Law—protect the right of workers to organize labor unions, reach consensus on labor issues, protect their collective interests, and voice their grievances and opinions. Even though more than half of the six million paid employees in the Taiwan area belonged to a labor union in 1995, the number of industrial unions and craft guilds is on the decline as businesses transfer operations overseas. As of December 1995, a total of 1,218 industrial unions and 2,414 craft guilds had been formed to protect workers' interests. Under the CLA's efforts to strengthen labor-management relations, 10,458 enterprises had established work rules as of 1995, representing an increase of 7.09 percent over the previous year. However, only 1,005 enterprises had implemented stock option plans for their employees, a 15.33 percent decrease from 1994.

To better define labor relations, a revision of the *Collective Agreement Law* now awaiting legislative approval will designate labor unions as the sole labor representative in the signing of collective agreements. Such agreements will promote labor-management cooperation and cover labor conditions such as wages, work hours, layoffs, pensions, compensation for occupational injuries, and the handling of labor complaints and disputes. In 1995, however, the number of government and private enterprises that entered into collective agreements with employees dropped 3 percent from the previous year.

There were 2,271 labor disputes in 1995, a 10.19 percent increase over 1994. In terms of the 27,342 workers involved, however, the figure was down 11.19 percent from 1994. Only 1.8 percent of the 2,271 cases were left unresolved in 1995.

Elderly Workers and Pensions

According to the *Labor Standards Law* and the *Rules for the Allocation and Management of Workers' Retirement Fund* 勞工退休準備金提撥及管理辦法, a retiree is entitled to a maximum pension equal to 45 times his average wage in the six months prior to retirement. Each month, employers must pay between 2 to 15 percent of their employees' total monthly wage aggregate into the wage retirement fund. This fund is monitored by a supervisory committee made up of labor and management representatives.

The retirement fund allocation requirement was included in the 1984 *Labor Standards Law* to improve workers' welfare, but it has discouraged many enterprises covered by the law from hiring senior workers who might soon be eligible to

Overtime Pay

Overtime Worked	Pay
Less than 2 hours	1.33 x hourly wage or more
2-4 hours	1.67 x hourly wage or more
Emergencies	2 x hourly wage
Holidays	2 x hourly wage

Information and Service Centers

An islandwide network of 63 employee service centers offers career counseling, information on labor-management disputes, labor welfare, career planning, insurance, pensions, and labor education services to workers in the Taiwan area. Some 60,000 employees were served in 1994.

Every city and county government in Taiwan has established a regional Labor Education Promotion Team 勞工教育輔導小組 to offer career training courses. In 1995, these teams offered a total of 13,172 training programs to over 477,336 laborers.

A labor issues hotline for the Taiwan area [(02) 514-9241 or, toll free, (080) 211-459] averages between 500 and 600 calls per month. In addition, the *Labor Education Handbook* 勞工教育手冊, containing information on most of the ROC labor laws and the occupational rights of ROC workers, is available free of charge to all workers in the ROC.

collect large pensions. The service sector, which the law does not cover, has thus shown greater interest in employing these workers than other sectors, such as manufacturing. In July 1993, the CLA began offering subsidies to businesses that hired elderly workers (those over 60 years of age). Currently, the CLA provides a subsidy of US$74 per elderly worker per month, with a monthly quota of 1,800 elderly workers for fiscal 1997.

To ensure that workers receive due wages should their employers file for liquidation, the government has set up a Wage Arrears Repayment Fund 積欠工資墊償基金, to which employers are required to pay 0.05 percent of the reported wages for each employee. As of December 1995, nearly 88 percent of the 171,158 eligible firms in the Taiwan area were contributing to the fund and had set aside a total of US$88.4 million. However, the CLA found in January 1996 that some 20,000 enterprises with over 30 employees had ignored the regulation. These companies were formally notified that they would have to begin meeting their legal obligations.

Foreign Workers

Since the ROC liberalized its foreign labor policy in 1990 to remedy a labor shortage, over 200,000 foreign workers have been recruited to work in domestic industries. Nearly 70 percent of these workers are employed in the manufacturing industry, and 20 percent are working in construction. The majority come from Thailand—more than 184,000 in 1995. Approximately 11,600 foreign maids, mostly from the Philippines, are employed as domestic helpers in families with dependents under 12 or over 70 years of age. Another 15,200 foreign workers are legally employed in the nursing and caretaking sectors.

The employment of these foreign workers in nine broad occupational categories is provided for by the *Employment Services Act*. Foreign workers can apply for work visas of up to two years, and the visa may be extended for another year if the contract is renewed. Their diligence and readiness to work long hours have made foreign workers especially valuable to their employers. Indeed, many are prepared to work 12-hour days, which allows a daily rotation of three shifts to be reduced to two.

However, foreign workers have in some cases been viewed as a threat to local workers. Recent

Duration of Paid Leave

Unit: working days, unless otherwise noted

Annual
   7 (1-3 years)
   10 (3-5 years)
   14 (5-10 years)
   14 plus 1 additional day for every additional year over 10 years to a maximum of 30 days

Maternity (weeks)
   8 (childbirth)
   4 (miscarriage)

Funeral
   3-8 (length of leave depends on worker's relationship to the deceased)

Wedding
   7

Work Hours and Salaries

Year	Employees on Payroll (persons)	Average Monthly Earnings (US$)	Average Monthly Hours
Industrial Sector			
1991	2,856,143	941.56	200.1
1992	2,916,995	1,037.07	199.9
1993	2,936,313	1,173.74	199.9
1994	3,017,319	1,179	201.0
1995	2,968,967	1,237.74	200.2
Service Sector			
1991	1,998,933	1,076.78	192.1
1992	2,166,871	1,166	191.6
1993	2,298,235	1,252.89	191.5
1994	2,438,478	1,333.48	191.2
1995	2,635,695	1,397.67	188.0
Manufacturing Sector			
1991	2,399,645	906.26	201.9
1992	2,410,221	998.96	201.9
1993	2,397,135	1,067.74	201.9
1994	2,438,632	1,138.04	202.4
1995	2,399,659	1,201.52	201.5

Source: Council of Labor Affairs

disputes over the substitution of local workers by foreign laborers have focused attention on claims that foreign workers are no longer playing the supplementary role which had originally been envisioned. Meanwhile, employers argue that domestic workers have shown little interest in the kind of work in which foreign laborers are engaged. Thus, local businesses now offer foreign workers greater incentives, and as a result, their average monthly salary is fast approaching that of their local counterparts. Statistics show that after less than two years on the job, foreign workers already earn wages as high as 88 percent of the local standard. As of January 1996, foreign laborers on average collected a monthly salary of US$723, or 7.2 percent more than in the same period of the previous year.

To protect the rights of legal foreign workers and help them adjust to life in Taiwan, a consultation center was set up in Taipei in December 1995 to serve northern Taiwan, and another was established in Changhua 彰化 in January 1996 to serve the central part of the island. Plans for a third center in the south are under way. These centers offer foreign workers information on pertinent laws and regulations, provide psychological counseling, and mediate disputes. Hotlines have also been set up to offer guidance and other services.

Almost all enterprises provide programs and services for foreign employees. Nearly 97 percent of businesses employing foreign workers provide them with coverage under the government's labor insurance and private group insurance. Other programs and forms of assistance include recreational activities on weekends, cultural and recreation centers, counseling sessions, weekend religious activities, and Chinese language training.

Because of the slight slowdown in economic growth in recent years, the Council of Labor Affairs now allows foreign workers to apply for a change of employer in the event that a company shutdowns, suspends production, lays off employees, or automates production to save on labor costs. Foreign employees may also be transferred to other businesses or factories owned by the same employers, or may work for the new owners of a business in the event of a takeover.

Foreign workers in Taiwan also have the right to strike. To exercise this right, they must be working in either agriculture, forestry, fisheries, and animal husbandry; mining and quarrying; manufacturing; construction; water, electricity and gas; transportation, warehousing, and telecommunications; or mass communications. They must also belong to a local labor union. Domestic maids and teachers of foreign languages do not fall under these categories, but are instead protected by employment contracts drawn up in accordance with the ROC *Civil Code* 民法. Foreign maids may strike if they have joined a domestic services union; however, foreign teachers have no such union to join, and thus may not strike.

21.
The Arts

Above: The intricate carving on this door to T'ien-hou Temple 天后廟 on Peng-hu Island in the Pescadores can be found on nearly every beam, lintel, and altar surface of many Taiwan temples.

Right: Master puppeteer Lee Tien-lu 李天祿 teaches a new generation of Taiwan students the Southern Fukienese art of glove puppetry to pass on this fading tradition.

Previous page: Celebrating the past: Peking opera actors strike typical stage poses depicting Ts'ao-ts'ao 曹操 and Yang Hsiu 楊修, two famous historical figures in medieval Chinese fiction.

21 The Arts

The arts in the ROC are tremendously diverse: from gilded temple carvings to conceptual abstract sculpture; tradition-bound folk opera to avant-garde performance art; conservative Chinese ink painting to contemporary award-winning films; age-old aboriginal chanting to an experimental blend of Chinese and Western classical music; Peking opera to postmodern dance and everything in between.

Traditional and contemporary, Eastern and Western, local and international—artists in both visual and performing arts are exploring styles across several spectrums, combining elements from different periods and traditions. In fact, one characteristic that marks the art of Taiwan today is an increasingly sophisticated and successful blending of such seemingly opposite sensibilities.

Painting

For about 75 years, painting in Taiwan has followed its own unique path. At various times, artists have been heavily influenced by styles in mainland China, Japan, and the West, but still they have developed a distinct, indigenous tradition in art history. Only in recent years, however, has there been a widespread effort—by museums, scholars, and journalists—to evaluate the development of Taiwan art according to the particular social, political, and cultural milieu in which it has been nurtured.

Several major exhibitions at the Taipei Fine Arts Museum 台北市立美術館 have made an important contribution to this ongoing evaluation. In 1993, *The New Face of Taiwan Art: 1945-1993* 台灣美術新風貌 showcased the work of more than 100 artists according to their position in the main stylistic trends that have characterized Taiwan art since World War II. The *1996 Taipei Biennial: The Quest for Identity* 一九九六雙年展：台灣藝術主體性 was equally extensive, but focused on contemporary artists working under such themes as "Identity and Memories," "Environment and City Life," "Sexuality and Power," and "Visual Dialogue." Other comprehensive exhibitions have also been held in re-cent years at the Taiwan Museum of Art 台灣省立美術館 in Taichung and the Kaohsiung Museum of Art 高雄市立美術館, in addition to similar smaller-scale efforts at galleries and cultural centers around the island. One noteworthy effort in this regard was the *Chen Cheng-po Centennial Memorial Exhibition* 陳澄波百年紀念展, held in 1994 in Chen's hometown of Chiayi 嘉義 and later in Taipei; the show highlighted the works of one of the island's best-known art historical figures.

Creating A Unique Identity

The beginnings of a specifically Taiwan-oriented art began around the 1920s. Prior to this, there had been a limited tradition of Chinese literati painting during the 18th and 19th centuries. But the works produced, many of them conventional landscapes and flowers by scholars and government officials sent from the mainland, were mostly of amateur quality and had little influence on later artistic developments. The first artists of any note came out of the Japanese era, during a time when there were few if any cultural influences from mainland China affecting Taiwan. Painters such as Chen Cheng-po, Li Shih-chiao 李石樵, Li Mei-shu 李梅樹, and Yang San-lang 楊三郎 studied Western-style oil painting in Japan, mainly at the Tokyo Fine Arts Institute. They absorbed artistic techniques such as fixed perspective and a naturalistic rendering of light and shade. They were also strongly influenced by French Impressionism (as it had filtered through Japan), with its emphasis on small strokes of color used to capture immediate impressions and the natural qualities of reflected light.

These artists tended to paint outdoors, directly from life (an approach not found in traditional Chinese painting), and were eager to capture the immediate flavor and hues of the Taiwan landscape. Their subject matter often centered on common, daily scenes of the island's villages, farms, and rural areas.

Some of the artists who studied in Japan chose to paint in Japanese distemper 膠彩, or gouache, rather than oils. Among the best known of this

355

group are Lin Yu-shan 林玉山 and Chen Chin 陳進. Using subdued, opaque colors they created works that were more finely delineated and more subtly rendered than their Impressionist contemporaries, but that still evoked the spirit of Taiwan in their choice of subject matter. Lin's works, for example, included scenes of rural life, such as a farmer leading a water buffalo home from the fields. And Chen, one of Taiwan's best-known female artists, often depicted women in their home surroundings.

But it was the oil painters who had the most important influence on future artistic developments. Many of them became influential teachers and leading figures in artistic circles. They also dominated the two most important annual exhibitions of the time, the Taiwan Fine Arts Exhibition 台灣美術展覽會, first held in 1927, and the Taiyang Arts Show 臺陽展, which began in 1934. Through their influence at these exhibitions, the Taiwan impressionists ensured that Western-style painting would hold an important place in the future development of Taiwan art.

Their works also represented what came to be known as nativist 鄉土 art, which had a parallel development in literature. Characterized by a conscious desire to depict images that evoked Taiwan's unique identity, the nativist sensibility also proved to have a long-lasting influence. It would surface again in the 1970s, in both art and literature, and subsequently in music and film.

While many of the nativist impressionists were reaching their prime, an influx of traditional Chinese ink painters arrived with the ROC government in its move from the mainland. With the government eager to reintroduce Chinese culture to Taiwan, landscape artists such as Huang Chun-pi 黃君璧 and Fu Chuan-fu 傅狷夫 enjoyed official backing, and by the early 1950s their genre of painting had replaced Western styles at official art exhibitions and competitions and in school curriculums. Their works remained well within the traditional school of monochrome ink painting, characterized by standard subjects such as mountains, waterfalls, rocks, and bamboo, all painted in a set of strictly defined brush strokes,

and usually including classic poetic inscriptions written in beautiful, precise calligraphy.

The most important figure to emerge from the mainland emigre artists was Chang Dai-chien 張大千, who went far beyond the conventional precepts of Chinese painting. Before arriving in Taiwan, he had already made a significant contribution to the Chinese art world with his more than 200 detailed copies of the ancient Buddhist murals in China's Tunhuang Caves 敦煌石窟, which he painted in the early 1940s. Chang's mature paintings, which earned international recognition, were marked by his unique splash-ink technique. Using broad strokes and deliberate blotches of color—often deep greens and blues—he created powerful landscapes that were often monumental in size.

The Beginning of Abstract Art

By the late 1950s and early 1960s, many younger artists were beginning to feel disillusioned with traditional Chinese painting. Yet they also could not identify with the Japanese-trained impressionists, who by this time seemed out of date. Industrialization was transforming the island's agricultural society, and the influences of Western individualism were reshaping people's lives. These and other tumultuous social changes of the post-war era were begging for a new vehicle of expression. These younger artists, most of them also of mainland origin, were drawn to Western modernism, especially abstract art.

The rising young modernists were very outspoken in their criticism of the older traditionalists. They banded together in private art groups, the most prominent of which were the Eastern Art Group 東方畫會 and the Fifth Moon Group 五月畫會, both formed in the mid-1950s. The most influential among the pioneers of Taiwan abstract art was Li Chung-sheng 李仲生, who introduced the latest Western movements to many young artists at his private studio in Taipei. Once established, some of the more prominent artists of this generation sought to find a synthesis between modern abstraction and traditional painting. Liu Kuo-sung 劉國松 and Chuang Chê 莊喆, for example, sought to create a new, modern form of

Chinese landscape art. Liu is best-known for his ink series depicting large, carefully delineated spheres suggesting the moon or the sun, often in yellow or bright red. By contrast, Chuang used freer, abstract-expressionist strokes, splashes, and smears in black, gray, and brown ink to suggest the essence of a landscape scene. His works sometimes include descriptions in calligraphy that in places blur into the wash of the painting.

By the late 1960s, artists were working in a much greater variety of modernist styles as more Western movements filtered into Taiwan. American trends such as pop art, minimalism, and optical art all had their local followers. European trends such as surrealism and especially dada art also found avid supporters. Many modernist painters of the 1960s emigrated abroad to the United States and Europe in order to fully develop their Western-oriented art skills.

Localizing Painting

Artists in the late 1960s and 1970s began rejecting the idolization of Western-style art in search of something that was more in touch with their own environment and their own culture. A new nativist movement emerged, inspired also by Taiwan's growing diplomatic isolation, which made many artists—as well as writers, musicians, and dance choreographers—eager to establish an identity uniquely their own.

This new tendency found its expression among those who had been trained in Western-style oil painting as well as those with backgrounds in Chinese ink painting. A number of artists who had left Taiwan to find inspiration in America or Europe returned at this time. Among this group was Hsi Te-chin 席德進, who gave up his earlier devotion to abstraction and in 1966 began sketching and painting local scenery and architecture and exploring the island's folk art traditions. His turnaround had significant influence on younger artists of the time.

Another influential artist of this time was Wu Hao 吳昊, whose folk-like woodblock prints were often colorful and nostalgic renditions of the Taiwan countryside. At much the same time, Cheng Shan-hsi 鄭善禧 was giving a new direction to traditional ink painting. He focused on local landscape scenes rather than idealized memories of mainland scenery, and also left behind the refined brushstrokes of old in exchange for a more colorful and down-to-earth vitality. In the calligraphic inscriptions on his works, he replaced classical poetic lines with vernacular descriptions.

An important inspiration was also found in the work of "native" artists such as Ju Ming 朱銘 (see section on Sculpture) and Hung Tung 洪通. The latter had no training as a painter but possessed a rich imagination nurtured on Taiwanese folk traditions. His intriguing, childlike paintings, full of colorful patterns and simplistic figures and animals, became the talk of the art world, especially after the influential *Hsiung Shih Art Monthly* 雄獅美術 published a Hung Tung special issue in 1973.

Contemporary Trends

Admittedly, it is difficult to pinpoint trends in contemporary art, or to determine which artists' works will continue to have lasting importance. The artists that are mentioned in this section (and in the following sections on Sculpture, Installation, and Ceramics) represent only a handful of those who are currently active, and certainly others deserve to be included if space permitted. The choices are meant to show some of the tremendous variety in the local art world. The Hong Kong-based "*Asian Art News*" has called Taiwan's art scene "one of the most progressive in Asia."

The desire to express a "Taiwan consciousness" has certainly continued to be central to the works of many artists of the 1980s and '90s, although their approaches encompass a much greater variety of styles and subject matter than in the past. Their sense of local identity is also more likely to be marked by a greater sensitivity to social and political issues than the more nostalgic "nativist" genre. Some critics now discuss these artists not so much as searchers for a Taiwan consciousness but as processors of "Taiwan information" 台灣資訊, one of the many kinds of information surrounding them in the Information Age.

Taiwan consciousness was an important starting point for the influential 101 Art Group 一〇一現代藝術群, founded in 1982. These artists often expressed their sense of local identity with symbolic or metaphorical images. Wu Tien-chang 吳天章 and Yang Mao-lin 楊茂林, for example, crowded their canvases with primitive-looking images that often suggested the chaos that erupted in Taiwan's frequent, sometimes violent street protests of the time. Working often in monumental scale and with a harsh black and white palette, Wu has also done works commemorating the February 28 Incident 二二八事件 or commenting on other events and figures from Taiwan's past. By comparison, Yang's more recent *Made in Taiwan* 台灣製造 series often presents a quieter juxtaposition of things native to the island, such as sweet potatoes, sea shells, images of Taiwan's aboriginal peoples, or references to the 17th century Dutch occupation of Taiwan. His more subtle approach, however, still incorporates a discerning and critical view of Taiwan history and society.

Also emerging from the 101 Group was Lien Chien-hsing 連建興, whose works could be called "magic realism." In one series of Lien's paintings, deserted and decaying industrial landscapes are inhabited by alienated wild animals. Although the disturbing world he creates is an imaginary one, it is one unmistakably drawn from images of Taiwan, such as the old mining sites in Lien's native Keelung.

Other artists have given a more satirical bent to their use of Taiwan information, such as Huang Chin-ho 黃進河, who exhibited at the 1995 Venice Biennale. His gaudy, pop art-like paintings are filled with images of tacky, materialistic excess, industrial pollution, and sensual pleasure-seeking. The more abstract works of Lee Min-chung 李民中, overflowing with bright, contrasting colors and cartoonish organic shapes, suggest the sensory-overloaded imagery of video games or MTV commercials. By contrast, the works of Lien Te-cheng 連德誠, also a participant in the 1995 Venice Biennale, juxtapose traditional imagery, including Chinese characters, with elements of contemporary abstraction.

Still other artists have been classified as working through more direct response, using colors, materials, and techniques that reflect their environment, yet in an intuitive rather than intellectual way. These include abstract as well as more realistic painters, and a wide variety of styles. The works of Huang Ming-chang 黃銘昌, for example, are meticulous, photo-realistic paintings of expansive rice fields or ocean views that offer a poetic absorption of the rural landscape. Ni Tsai-chin 倪再沁, on the other hand, builds up dark, brooding landscapes and figures with layers of ink cross-hatching. Of a very different sensibility is someone like Chien Fu-chuan 簡福�, whose "paintings" are thick formations of burned plastic, wood scraps, cardboard, wire, and other discards that meld into frightening yet powerful human-like configurations. In his work *Big Disaster* 大浩劫, a group of these framed configurations line the floor and walls of a dim hallway like a postmodern catacomb.

Chinese ink painting has also continued to have a solid standing in Taiwan. Many artists, such as Chiang Chao-shen 江兆申, the late deputy director of the National Palace Museum 國立故宮博物院, remain fairly well-grounded in the traditional style, although many incorporate subtle innovations. Chiang's landscapes, for example, are characterized by a stronger use of large white spaces. Others have experimented more boldly, often using a much wider and freer range of brushstrokes than is allowed in orthodox Chinese painting. Yu Cheng-yao 余承堯, who only began painting after he retired from a long military career, ignores the traditional brushstroke lexicon and instead works over his mountains and trees with closely knit, interwoven strokes that create a richly textured surface. A much younger artist, Peng Kang-lung 彭康隆, has also brought a whole new sense of texture to ink painting. Ignoring the traditional importance of white space to balance out a landscape, Peng often fills his entire paper with a myriad balance of textures that express more of a personal emotional intensity than the harmonies of nature essential to conventional Chinese painting.

Other painters have departed from tradition not only in their brushstrokes, but in their subject matter. In Lo Ching's 羅青 *Palm Tree Boulevard* 棕櫚大道, for example, the artist replaces the standard pine or willow with palm trees and mountains, or waterfalls with an asphalt road. And in his inscriptions, he replaces traditional metaphors with modern-day references. Lo and other ink painters have also embraced the exploration of a Taiwan consciousness, drawing much of their inspiration from a local reality rather than distant memories of mainland China. The ink paintings of Yu Peng 于彭, who also works in a variety of other media, reflect a modern, urban existence in their fragmented images and illogical use of space. The subjects chosen are often linked to tradition—such as lotus flowers, cranes, unusual rock formations, and small human figures within a large natural setting—but they are placed in what seems to be an indiscriminate arrangement. Often, the overall composition is crowded with images, but each is isolated, with the white of the paper meandering between.

Museums and the Art Market
Art Museums

Taiwan's best-known museum is, of course, the National Palace Museum in Taipei, a repository for traditional art from mainland China. In 1933, the numerous treasures in the museum's collection started traveling from Peking to Taiwan in a harrowing 12,000-kilometer journey that took more than 16 years, evading both the Japanese army and the Chinese communists. The Taipei museum itself finally opened in 1965, and today is recognized for having one of the world's best collections of Chinese art, from ancient oracle bones to bronze urns to scroll paintings to snuff bottles, and more. The museum's current collection numbers some 640,000 items, a collection so big that only about 1 percent can be accommodated for display at any one time while the rest is kept in storage.

In 1996, the Palace Museum has greatly enhanced its international image with an unprecedented US tour of 452 of its finest works of art.

The exhibition, "Splendors of Imperial China," was slated to run from March 1996 through April 1997, with stops at the Metropolitan Museum of Art in New York, the Art Institute of Chicago, the Asian Art Museum of San Francisco, and the National Gallery of Art in Washington, D.C. Curators and scholars in the United States hailed the exhibition as a once-in-a-lifetime experience that could very well give new impetus to the study of Chinese art in the US, just as a smaller-scale 1961 exhibition inspired many of today's Chinese art scholars.

Before its departure, however, the exhibition stirred up controversy in Taiwan, with art lovers as well as politicians protesting that some of the works chosen were too delicate to withstand the tour. There were also concerns that Peking might try to claim the treasures once they were in the United States. Several of the initial sponsors, who happened to be companies also doing business in mainland China, backed out for fear of upsetting Peking. In the end, the Palace Museum and the Met assured legal protection of the exhibition items; they also agreed to bar 23 works from the tour, and limit exhibition hours for 19 others.

The National Museum of History 國立歷史博物館, also located in Taipei, is known for its impressive collection of ancient bronzes, pottery, and ceramic burial figurines. It has been prominent in showing the works of important ink painters such as Chang Dai-chien and for its international ceramics exhibition, which has been an important stimulus for Taiwan's growing ceramic art scene.

The Taipei Fine Arts Museum, opened in 1983, has been a major catalyst for the development of modern art, showcasing many local artists as well as hosting important foreign exhibitions, including a 1993 showing of Rodin sculptures. It also hosts annual and biennial competitions, as well as invitational exhibitions. Modern art museums have also been established in Taichung, and most recently in Kaohsiung. The Kaohsiung Museum of Art, which opened in 1993, is billed as the largest fine arts museum in Asia.

The island's first private museum showing Chinese art is the Chang Foundation Museum 鴻

禧美術館, set up in 1991. Although relatively small, with about 16,000 square feet of exhibition space, it has an impressive collection that features traditional painting, exquisite porcelain and other ceramics.

Galleries

The gallery scene in Taiwan has grown tremendously in the past 15 to 20 years from a single enterprise, the Lungmen Gallery 龍門畫廊 in 1975, to about 150 galleries today. The Lungmen has retained its prominence among the other newer galleries and shows works by artists from Taiwan as well as overseas. The Hanart Gallery 漢雅軒, which has a home gallery in Hong Kong, has also been important in promoting Taiwan's younger generation of artists.

Among the scores of other galleries, some that stand out include the Galerie Elegance 愛力根畫廊, the Eslite Gallery 誠品畫廊, the Taiwan Gallery 台灣畫廊 and Home Gallery 家畫廊 which focus on contemporary art, and the Caves Art Center 敦煌藝術中心 and Pristine Harmony Art Center 清韵藝術中心 which focus on Chinese ink paintings by both traditional and not-so-traditional artists. IT Park 伊通公園, on the other hand, is an alternative gallery for artists looking for a non-commercial environment. It has provided a much-needed venue for installation and performance artists.

Several galleries in central and southern Taiwan are also beginning to establish themselves in the art market. Some of the best known include Gallery Pierre 臻品藝術中心, East Gallery 東之畫廊, and Modern Art Gallery 現代藝術空間 in Taichung; New Phase Art Space 新生態藝術環境 in Tainan; the Up Gallery 阿普畫廊 and Duchamp Gallery 杜象藝術中心 in Kaohsiung; and Venus Gallery 維納斯藝廊 in Hualien 花蓮.

The boom in art galleries around the island has been partly due to the great increase in art collecting in the 1980s, which in turn has been driven by a boom in the stock and real estate markets. Taiwan collectors have also become involved in the art markets in Hong Kong and New York, prompting such high-profile auction houses as Sotheby's and Christie's to provide previews of their Hong Kong and New York auctions in Taiwan to attract buyers. This eventually led both houses to hold auctions right in Taiwan beginning in the early 1990s, with varying success. They have focused primarily on traditional Chinese painting and works by Taiwan's Japanese-trained impressionists such as Chen Cheng-po, whose 1931 painting *Sunset at Tamsui* 黃昏淡水 (see section on Painting) sold for US$0.38 million in 1993, a record-breaking price for a Chinese painting sold by Sotheby's.

Another major development has been the annual Taipei Art Fair 台北國際藝術博覽會, begun in 1992, which serves to promote the local art market both regionally and internationally. Organized by the ROC Art Galleries Association 中華民國畫廊協會, the 1995 fair included 60 galleries, including Pace Wildenstein of New York and other major names from Chicago, London, Zurich, and Tokyo.

Sculpture

Sculpture in Taiwan has progressed along much the same lines as painting. Traditionally, however, the Chinese never canonized sculpture as a fine art form. It was recognized only as a decorative or religious medium often done by anonymous craftsmen. As a result, there is no strong formal tradition of sculpture brought from mainland China as in painting. Before the 1920s, temple and folk sculpture (see section on Folk Arts) were the only sculptural forms thriving in Taiwan. It was not until the 1970s that sculpture became widely accepted as a fine-art genre, although there were a handful of artists before then who had made some impression on the art world.

Taiwan's first fine-art sculptor was Huang Tu-shui 黃土水, born in 1906. Like many painters of his generation, he studied Western-style techniques at the Tokyo Fine Arts Institute. And like the first generation of nativist painters, he applied what he had learned to depict the rural life he knew. His most celebrated works are of water buffaloes, an animal that symbolizes the heart of the Taiwan countryside. Marked by realism and rational composition, these works are gracefully rendered in low relief as well as in the round, using media ranging from plaster to bronze. After Huang, there were still very few professional sculptors, the most renowned being Chen Hsia-yu 陳夏雨. Chen was also trained in Japan and returned to Taiwan after World War II to create realistic portraits and figures, often of women in pensive poses.

The tide of Western-oriented abstraction that swept the local art world in the 1960s produced the first Taiwan sculptor to gain world attention. Yuyu Yang (also known as Yang Ying-feng 楊英風) is most famous for his stainless steel sculptures, which often convert traditional Chinese symbols like the phoenix and dragon into fluid abstract forms. His works are sometimes monumental in size and have been erected in cities around the world. His *East West Gate* 東西門 (1973) stands on Wall Street in Manhattan, and the 23-foot *Advent of the Phoenix* 鳳凰來儀 (1970) can be found in Osaka. In 1996, Yang held a major retrospective of his work in England, at the invitation of the Royal Society of British Sculptors.

The back-to-roots movement of the 1970s (see section on Painting) gave rise to Ju Ming, who was initially trained as a folk sculptor, then went on to study with Yuyu Yang. He was initially admired for his rustic, simple figures carved from wood, including the monumental *Tai Chi Series* 太極系列. Although many of these were highly abstract, they had an earthy crudeness that set them apart from Western-inspired abstract art and aligned them with a more local, rural tradition. In recent years, he has explored a variety of materials, including painted bronze and rolled stainless steel sheets, creating abstracted figures of athletes, ballerinas, and people in everyday poses. Like Yuyu Yang, Ju has also exhibited worldwide, in Hong Kong, England, New York, and elsewhere.

Although sculpture still does not have nearly as many proponents as painting, there are a number of other recognized artists working in this medium. Some are working in a figurative mode,

such as Shih Chen-hsiung 石振雄, a winner of the 1996 Taipei Annual Arts Competition 台北市第二十三屆美展, whose carved wooden figures represent deep emotional states. But many other sculptors working today tend toward a more conceptual, abstract aesthetic. The sculptor Hsiao Yi 蕭一, for example, has carved a monumental wooden foot and called it *The Way of Virtue and Justice* 大道. Artist Tsao Ya 曹牙 contrasts the stability of nature with the quasi-stability of the man-made world in his work *Spiritual Landscape* 意念山水, consisting of a large immovable rock surrounded by a thick stainless steel frame. The works of Ken Tsai 蔡根, display a lyrical mindset, assembling playful, even musical, formations out of wooden furniture legs, string, and other common items.

Installation and Performance Art

Just as in the West, sculpture in Taiwan has evolved into the avant-garde forms of installation and performance art. Such artists started making an appearance in the 1980s, and like many painters of the time, their creations are often tinged by social or political comments with a local orientation. The performance artist Lee Ming-sheng 李銘盛, who in 1993 became the first Taiwan artist to appear at the prestigious Venice Biennale, often reflects on the changing and deteriorating natural environment. He is best-known for his 1983 *Purification of the Spiritual Land* 精神的純化, in which he walked barefoot from village to village in Taiwan planting seeds.

A 1995 Venice Biennale exhibitor, Wu Ma-li 吳瑪悧, offers installation works with a social bent. Wu's Venice work, *Library* 圖書館, consisted of bookcases filled with both Eastern and Western literary classics, each of them shredded and encased in Plexiglass covers. A recent installation by Chen Chien-pei 陳建北 called *Basic Human Dignity* 戰爭？人類的基本尊嚴, combined Buddhist images such as white paper lotuses with a painting of Taiwan's February 28 monument. In comparison, Chen Shun-chu 陳順築 uses a more personal frame of reference, but one with broad inferences, in his installations using family photographs. Sometimes the photos are displayed in old wooden boxes along with miscellaneous mementos, or lined up in intriguing formations, as in *Conference, Family Parade* 集會・家庭遊行, which consists of more than 700 framed black-and-white portraits standing in rows that fill a large hallway.

Large-scale installations, sometimes known as environmental sculpture, have been the focus recently of the annual outdoor art exhibitions sponsored by the Taipei County Cultural Center 台北縣立文化中心. In 1995, nine groups joined the exhibition, many of them making huge fabric banners and balloons that were displayed along the Tamsui River 淡水河. One group hung large white fabric strips from a bridge into the river to emphasize the unnatural colors that the polluted water has taken on; another group flew huge colorful Tibetan-like religious banners as a blessing for the river.

Video installation is another form that is beginning to attract adherents in Taiwan. One example is Yuan Kuang-ming 袁廣鳴, who has shown such works as *The Cage* 鳥籠, a video that switches from close-ups of a caged bird to views of the city seen through cage-like bicycle spokes, and *Fish on Dish* 盤中魚, in which a videotaped goldfish seems to come charmingly to life when projected on a white ceramic bowl.

Ceramics

Less than two decades ago, ceramics as a contemporary art form akin to painting and sculpture was barely recognized in Taiwan. The field was largely confined to functional works and industrial production. The only long-time ceramic tradition that involved artistic considerations was Cochin ware, a folk craft originally from Kwangtung, brought to Taiwan in the 19th century. At that time, Cochin ware consisted mainly of decorations for the walls and roof ridges of temples, including human figures, animals, birds, and flowers in bright, glossy colors. Today, there are only a handful of craftspeople who still possess the traditional Cochin skills, most of whom are in the central-island city of

Chiayi. Among them is Liu Ming-wu 劉銘侮, who creates colorful, sometimes flamboyant statues of historical and religious figures.

Taiwan is also known for its high-quality reproduction ceramics, an industry that got its start in the late 1940s. Several talented figures, such as Lin Te-wen 林德文 and Tsai Hsiao-fang 蔡曉芳, became known for their skill at imitating ancient porcelain. Today, there are a number of kilns in the north-central city of Miaoli 苗栗 and in Yingke 鶯歌鎮, a small town southwest of Taipei, that are known worldwide for their reproductions of Ming and Ch'ing ceramics.

In the early 1950s, several ceramists—primarily Lin Pao-chia 林葆家, Wu Jang-nung 吳讓農, and Wang Hsiu-kung 王修功—made the first efforts to develop ceramics as a contemporary art form. These men began their careers by working in ceramics factories, helping to revive the industry after its decline during the Japanese occupation. But eventually they broke away to pursue their own creative ideas and to establish teaching studios. Although they remained within the traditional framework of functional ceramics—making vases, bowls, and pots—their works represented a creative venture into unusual shapes and experimental glaze effects. Wu, for example, is known for pouring and splashing thick glazes onto his vessels and firing them at very high temperatures, creating highly textured surfaces covered with cracks, bubbles, and drips.

It was not until the late 1960s, however, that creative ceramists began to gain widespread recognition, thanks in large part to exhibitions at the National Museum of History, which continues to play a central role in promoting the art form. In 1968, the museum held the island's first major solo ceramics show, featuring Wu Jang-nung. In the following decade, ceramic exhibitions at private galleries also gradually became more common. A key figure during this era was Chiu Huan-tang 邱煥堂, who studied ceramics in Hawaii and returned to introduce to Taiwan contemporary ideas from abroad. The ceramist Sun Chao 孫超 also started to gain renown during this time for his crystalline glazes 結晶釉. After a career in the Conservation Division of the National Palace Museum 國立故宮博物院科技室, Sun began applying his experiments there with ancient glazing techniques to his own work. In recent years, he has moved from making decorative crystal patterns on vases and bowls to large, flat glaze "paintings" that combine the sensibility of Chinese ink landscapes with abstract expressionism. Another seminal figure of this generation was Yang Yuan-tai 楊元太, the first to take ceramics completely into the realm of modern sculpture. His works are often large organic forms in natural sand or earth colors that appear as if they have been worn through by wind and waves.

After 1981, ceramic art quickly came into its own, boosted by the 1983 opening of the Taipei Fine Arts Museum, which included ceramics in its opening show. In the next few years, the museum sponsored several ceramics competitions as well as the island's first international exhibition of contemporary ceramics. In 1986, the National Museum of History held its first biennial ceramic show, which continues to play a key role in promoting ceramic art. Numerous art galleries have also begun to hold smaller-scale shows, and the number of artists working in ceramics has increased manyfold. The Chinese Ceramics Association was formed in 1992, and the following year held the first ceramist festival, which featured indoor and outdoor exhibitions, demonstrations, and lectures by prominent ceramic artists.

As with other artistic fields, ceramics today has taken on a wide variety of expressions, many of them highly personalized. While some ceramists continue to focus on the more traditional vessel forms and skilled glazing techniques, others might just as well be called sculptors or even installation artists who happen to use ceramics as their central medium. Even vessel-oriented ceramists often bring a highly individual touch to their works, as is the case with Hsu Chung-lin 徐崇林, who uses titles to give a new dimension to his vases and plates. For example, one of his vases with a thick pock-marked glaze is called

Beehive With Deteriorating Worms 蜂窩蟲蛀. Other ceramists such as Chen Cheng-hsun 陳政勳 (Andres Chen) draw inspiration from natural forms and colors to create earthy abstract works. Chen often incorporates natural elements, including wood, metal, stone, leaf imprints, and even water in simple geometric formations. The artist Francis Shao 邵婷如 represents a tendency to create modern-day allegories with a surrealistic touch, using for example repeated images of faces, small figures, or even TV sets, often set atop tall, thin poles. Still other ceramic artists offer more direct social comments in their work. Margaret Shiu Tan 蕭麗虹, for example, uses small, loosely formed figures in a variety of settings to suggest the modern oppressions of the human soul. She might sandwich her figures between two thick boards, or engage them in a desperate struggle to climb a ladder leading to nowhere. Another social critic is Marvin Fang (Fanchiang Ming-tao 范姜明道), who uses the color gold as a central motif—for example, hoarded masses of golden teapots, or golden feces-like shapes atop white pedestals—to represent the excesses of materialism, money-worship, and hypocrisy in today's society.

Seal Carving

Carving name chops, or Chinese seals, with names or other calligraphic inscriptions was once a necessary skill to master for any well-rounded literati artist. It followed right along with painting and calligraphy. Today, although machine-carved name chops are still commonly used for many business transactions, only a handful of artists specialize in hand-engraving name chops. Among them are Wang Pei-yueh 王北岳, who teaches seal carving at the art department of National Taiwan Normal University. Among the younger generation of chopmakers is Huang Ming-hsiu 黃明修, who was recognized in the 1994 Provincial Art Contest for his work. Name chops are made of ivory, jade, or soft precious stones such as yellow *t'ien huang* 田黃. The body of the chop may be a plain rectangle or it may be sculpted into a lion, dragon, or other symbolic image. Besides their use in business transactions, name chops are also stamped on traditional paintings and calligraphy, both to identify the artist and to add an authoritative air and a pleasing final touch.

Folk Arts
Preserving Folk Arts

While handicrafts like paper cutting, knotting, and dough sculpting are still fairly common in Taiwan, many other apprentice-oriented folk arts are barely surviving. It is simply too hard to compete against cheaper machine-made goods or to attract young people to undertake the long training that is often necessary to become an expert woodcarver, lanternmaker, or other type of craftsperson—jobs that promise only modest financial rewards. And traditional performing arts such as puppetry, dragon and lion dances, folk dance, folk opera, and traditional acrobatics have had an even tougher time competing with TV, movies, and karaoke (see sections on Puppetry, Dance, and Opera).

Still, many folk arts have benefited from a revival of interest in the past five to ten years, with government, scholars, artists, and private individuals joining in preservation and promotion efforts. One of the first steps in government support came in 1980, when the Ministry of Education 教育部 sponsored a survey of the island's folk arts. The results found 70 types of crafts and 56 types of traditional performing arts still being practiced, with some 4,000 artists involved. The next year, the Council for Cultural Affairs 行政院文化建設委員會 (CCA) was set up with the responsibility of giving equal weight to fine arts and folk arts. It has sponsored a number of folk arts festivals, publications, and other projects.

The *Cultural Heritage Preservation Law*, passed in 1982, gave even more substance to the government's commitment to preserve and promote folk arts. It paved the way for such programs as the Folk Art Heritage Award 民族藝術薪傳獎, set up in 1985 to honor outstanding folk art masters, and the prestigious prize of the Folk Arts Master 重要民族藝術藝師, established in 1989. The latter has provided leading woodcarvers, puppeteers, traditional musicians, and other craftspeople and performers with a monthly stipend and helps recruit and subsidize apprentices and training programs for these masters to pass on their skills. Other government efforts have included project to videotape and transcribe dialogues of traditional puppet plays.

One of the most extensive efforts to preserve and promote the folk arts and to bring them back into the community has been the CCA's National Festival of Culture and Arts 中華民國全國文藝季. In recent years, the annual festival has focused primarily on traditional arts, working in conjunction with private organizations and county cultural centers to organize folk art exhibitions and performances around the island. Festival events have showcased everything from paper umbrellas and lanterns, to Hakka yodeling songs, drum dances and carnival skits. Such activities as temple preservation seminars, tea-picking festivals, and folk operas have also been on the festival agenda.

Private organizations such as the Chinese Folk Art Foundation 中華民俗藝術基金會 have also been instrumental in promoting traditional crafts and performing arts. Besides its many local activities, the foundation promotes Taiwan folk arts overseas. In September 1996, for example, it sponsored a two-day outdoor festival of exhibitions, demonstrations, and performances in New York.

Other private efforts include the Taiwan Folk Art Museum 台灣民俗北投文物館 in Peitou 北投, near Taipei, which houses an extensive collection of folk arts as well as Chinese clothing and embroidery. The Tso Yang Workshop 左羊工作坊 in Lukang 鹿港 is another group that focuses on trying to increase public appreciation of the island's traditional art forms. The town of Lukang is itself an important folk arts center, as is Sanyi 三義, about 90 minutes south of Taipei, which features scores of shops specializing in traditional woodcarving, mostly of Buddha and other traditional figures.

Temple Arts

One of the most important roles in carrying on folk art traditions must be assigned to Taiwan's large community of temples—a fact that government and private groups recognize by organizing many of their folk art activities in connection with temples. Not only have temples been a traditional venue for many folk art displays and performances, particularly lantern-making competitions, puppet shows, and folk operas, but some of the buildings themselves are a virtual repository of some of the most important of the island's folk crafts. Examples of traditional stone-carving, colorful ceramic figurines (known as *chien-nien* 剪黏), and embroidered banners of legendary scenes are just some of the many arts that can be viewed at a well-preserved temple.

The most predominant form of temple craftsmanship, however, is woodcarving. From the entranceway to the back altar, nearly every beam, lintel, and other wooden support structure is covered with elaborate carvings of legendary figures and stories from history, literature, and folklore. Also common are symbolic animals, including birds, flowers, and dragons and other mythical creatures. The subject matter chosen is often not directly related to the religious function of the temple, but tends to promote traditional ethical values such as loyalty, chastity, filial piety, and patriotism.

Like most traditional crafts, exquisite hand-carvings are in danger of being replaced by simpler, machine-tooled decorations. Woodcarving, as well as other temple crafts, have gotten a boost, however, through several temple reconstruction projects. One of the most significant has been the 200-year-old Tsushih Temple 祖師廟 in Sanhsia 三峽, which has been undergoing extensive renovation for some 50 years and has employed some of the island's top craftspeople.

Among those who have worked on the Tsushih Temple is 94-year-old Huang Kwei-li 黃龜理, who has been named a national Folk Arts Master. In more than 75 years as a woodcarver, he has created thousands of carvings for more than 80 temples around the island, with many of his works depicting complex battle scenes taken from history or literature. Like most temple woodcarvers, Huang has been heavily influenced by the Taiwanese opera performances that were traditionally performed at temples as part of religious festivities. This shows in the scenes depicted as well as the dramatic poses of the figures.

Another well-known woodcarver is Lee Sung-lin 李松林, also in his nineties and known for his temple figurines. His works can be seen at the Tsushih Temple and the Tienhou Temple 天后宮 in Lukang, among others. Among the younger generation of carvers is 46-year-old Chen Cheng-hsiung 陳正雄, who has worked on the Tsushih reconstruction for more than a decade. Chen has studied under Huang Kwei-li at a special Folk Arts Master program at the National Taiwan College of Arts 國立台灣藝術學院; he specializes in a certain type of hornless dragon as well as figures and decorative patterns.

Woodblock Printing

An additional folk art that has benefited from renewed interest is woodblock printing 木板畫, used to make colorful Chinese New Year hangings. Traditional woodcut prints in Taiwan are of a simple, rural style brought over by early immigrants from Fukien Province in mainland China. Common images are the God of Wealth 財神, the Kitchen God 灶神, and door gods 門神—who often appear in the form of elaborately dressed and fierce-looking generals. These images are usually printed on red or orange paper in prominent black outlines filled in with several colors.

Among the handful of woodcut artists left is Pan Yuan-shih 潘元石, who has been a key figure in passing on the art to children as well as university students and teachers. Exhibitions and annual competitions sponsored by the Council for Cultural Affairs are also helping to keep the art of New Year printmaking alive. These events promote both traditional and modern methods—including lithography, silkscreening, and etching—as well as a wider variety of subject matter.

Puppetry

Up until the 1960s—before television had arrived in Taiwan—puppet shows were one of the primary forms of entertainment. Nearly any festive occasion, whether a wedding, holiday, or temple festival, called for a puppet performance. Numerous troupes were active throughout the island, and in the early days they often traveled from village to village by foot, carrying their stage, musical instruments, and trunks full of puppets on poles over their shoulders.

The styles of puppetry common in Taiwan—glove puppets 布袋戲, shadow puppets 皮影戲, and marionettes 傀儡—were brought here by immigrants from southeastern China in the early 19th century. Although the forms have evolved into distinct local styles and have also adopted modern innovations, they still retain many of the original characteristics, especially in their similarities to Chinese opera. As in opera, a puppet's costume and facial "makeup" indicate the type of character portrayed. Specific roles such as the young scholar, the refined woman, or the fierce general are also drawn from opera.

In glove puppetry, the stage is covered with intricate carvings that are painted gold, resembling the entrance to a traditional Chinese temple. The elaborate setting is ideal for offsetting the finely embroidered costumes, exquisite headdresses, and delicately carved faces of the puppets, which stand nearly a foot high. Shadow puppets, one to two feet high, are expertly cut out of leather, then engraved, dyed, and painted in bright colors. Audiences see the colorful profile forms, which can move at several joints, through a white screen lit from behind. Marionette puppets, about two feet high and manipulated by 11 to 14 strings, are usually presented in front of a simple backdrop. As in Chinese opera, many of the stories used in puppet shows are adapted from classical literature or ancient legends. Some popular examples are *The Tale of the White Serpent* 白蛇傳 and the *Journey to the West* 西遊記.

Traditional puppet performances, also like opera, are always accompanied by live music. The instruments used include the two-stringed *hu-chin* 胡琴, the trumpet-like *sona* 嗩吶, and drums, gongs, and cymbals. The musicians also sing parts of the story from backstage, often using classical Chinese, while the puppeteers usually present the dialogue in the local Taiwanese dialect.

Master Puppeteers

In the hands of several masters, puppetry in Taiwan developed along its own lines into a regional style distinct from puppetry in mainland China. This is especially true of glove puppetry. However, among the 200-some puppet troupes still active around the island, only a handful continue to work primarily in the traditional regional style. One of the most popular is Lee Tien-lu 李天祿, whose life has been immortalized in Hou Hsiao-hsien's 侯孝賢 award-winning film *The Puppetmaster* 戲夢人生 (see section on Film). Lee, who is now recognized as a national Folk Arts Master, first became famous in the 1950s and '60s for his serial dramas based on kungfu novels. Lee is especially popular for his innovative martial arts sequences, acrobatic stunts, and use of modern slang mixed with classical Chinese. Along with his two sons, Lee has also helped to set up two children's puppet troupes, the Wei Wan Jan 微宛然 and the Cheau Wan Jan 巧宛然, both of which have been highly praised. In addition, Lee's own troupe, I Wan Jan 亦宛然, has performed throughout Asia and in the United States and Europe, winning awards at puppetry festivals in New York and France.

Another key figure in glove puppetry is Hsu Wang 許王, whose Hsiao Hsi Yuan 小西園 has also toured extensively abroad, including trips to mainland China, Japan, Canada, and the United States. Hsu also keeps up a busy local schedule, often performing about twice a month. The Chinese Folk Art Foundation also frequently invites Hsu to perform at temples and other venues around the island.

One more acknowledged master is Huang Hai-tai 黃海岱, whose melodramatic tales of ancient swordsmen full of action-filled battle scenes were highlighted by elegant and highly literary dialogue. Huang's son, Huang Chun-hsiung 黃俊雄, was at the forefront of a trend that started in the 1960s to modernize puppet theater and adapt it to television. Using his father's chivalry repertoire, he added popular music and fantastic lighting and other visual effects to create *chin-kuang* 金光 or gold light puppetry. The Huang family now runs its own cable TV channel, devoted exclusively to puppet shows. Many other puppeteers have followed Huang's lead, so that since 1993, nearly all of the island's troupes are of the *chin-kuang* variety, which has proved to be highly popular among TV audiences. Unfortunately, many of these modern troupes put more emphasis on special effects than on the basic singing and movement skills that are the essence of traditional puppetry.

The less common forms of shadow and marionette puppetry have had a much harder time surviving than glove puppetry. Among the more prominent representatives of shadow puppetry that still perform are the family of Chang Te-cheng 張德成. Chang, who died in 1996, was named a national Folk Art Master. Chang's son, Chang Fu-gwo 張榑國, represents the sixth generation to carry on the family puppet troupe. Also of note is shadow puppeteer Hsu Fu-neng 許福能, whose group Fo Hsing Ko 復興閣皮影劇團 has earned two Folk Art Heritage Awards. The troupe has also toured abroad, to Asia, Europe and North America; and Hsu has been highly active in efforts to pass on his art, regularly giving lessons and demonstrations to students across the island.

Aboriginal Arts

While Chinese culture is dominant on Taiwan, the island is also enriched by the cultures of nine aboriginal peoples—the Atayal 泰雅族, Saisiyat 賽夏族, Ami 阿美族, Bunun 布農族, Tsou 鄒族, Rukai 魯凱族, Puyuma 卑南族, Paiwan 排灣族, and Yami 雅美族—whose ancestors arrived here perhaps 15,000 years ago. Arts such as woodcarving, weaving, and basketry, as well as ceremonial dances and songs have long played a central role in aboriginal life, with each people developing its distinct artistic style.

Although the rich culture of the aborigines is threatened by modernization and the emigration of many younger tribal members to urban areas, recent years have seen a growing interest in preserving and developing the aboriginal arts. Tribal members themselves have been involved in a number of projects, such as recording their songs and dances, as have researchers and individuals in the Chinese community. A major contribution was made, for example, by businessman Safe C.F. Lin 林清富, who in 1994 established the Shung Ye Museum of Formosan Aborigines 順益台灣原住民博物館 (see following section), the first of its kind in Taiwan. The government is also making efforts to promote tribal culture. In the last few years, the CCA's annual National Festival of Culture and Arts has included performances, exhibitions and seminars on aboriginal arts.

Recent years have also seen a demand on the part of aborigines for greater recognition for their artistic contributions. The most famous case has been one surrounding the use of excerpts by Ami singers in the theme song of the 1996 Olympics. The excerpts, sung by tribal elder Guo Ying-nan 郭英男 (Ami name, Livfon) and his wife Guo Hsiu-chu 郭秀珠, were first recorded in 1988 by a cultural organization in France during a tour of aboriginal performers. Rights to the recording were bought in 1992 by the German music producer Enigma, who incorporated it into the song "Return to Innocence," which became an international hit before it was chosen as the Olympic theme song. The Ami singers were given no credit or copyright protection for their part of the song. Through their Taiwan recording company Magic Stone Co. Ltd. 魔岩唱片公司, the couple are seeking recognition if not compensation for their talents. If nothing else, Livfon has said he wants recognition for the Ami tribe's singing tradition.

The Shung Ye Museum

The Shung Ye Museum of Formosan Aborigines was opened in 1994 across the street from the National Palace Museum. Housing a private collection, the four-floor museum is the first to be dedicated solely to Taiwan's tribal cultures. In addition to its displays of artifacts, costumes, musical instruments, household utensils, and weapons, the museum also provides extensive information on aboriginal history, lifestyles, social relationships, and religious beliefs and customs. The design of the museum itself is a tribute to aboriginal culture. The "A" shaped building is reminiscent of the houses found among many tribal peoples in the Pacific region, and the surrounding area is paved with the kind of slate often used by Taiwan's Paiwan tribe for building. The front features a central granite pillar, carved with aboriginal totem-like images, and a wooden fence made of relief carvings by different Taiwan tribes.

The museum has also helped to promote research of Taiwan's indigenous peoples, including grants to the Academia Sinica and to writers and filmmakers involved in recording aboriginal culture. It has also funded research projects at the University of California, Berkeley, and the University of Tokyo. In addition, the museum has provided money for university scholarships for aboriginal students.

In another project, the museum has invited tribal peoples to organize their own activities on the museum grounds. Programs have been presented, for example, by the Puyuma and Tsou tribes to show the unique qualities of their individual tribes, including hunting ceremonies, religious rituals, dance performances, and even meals of traditional tribal food.

The collections at the Shung Ye Museum, the Taiwan Provincial Museum 台灣省立博物館, the museum of Academia Sinica's Institute of Ethnology 中央研究院民族學研究所博物館, and the National Museum of Natural Science 國立自然科學博物館 in Taichung provide good introductions into the artistic traditions of the various peoples. In general, the art of Taiwan's aborigines has strong similarities in both form and design with other Pacific cultures, such as in Micronesia and the South Pacific islands. This is evident in the emphasis on two-dimensional, geometric, decorative effects as well as the close connection with nature, and also in specific motifs

such as recurrent squatting figures and snake designs. Still, each of the island's indigenous peoples has developed an art of unique characteristics.

Art Traditions

The richest artistic traditions are found among the Paiwan, Rukai, and Atayal peoples. The Paiwan and Rukai, which may have once been a single people, are known especially for their woodcarvings. The homes of important members of the people, for example, are embellished with relief carvings of simplified human figures, zigzag or triangular patterns, and the all-important hundred-pace snake with its menacing diamond-shaped head. The snake is particularly prominent in Paiwan and Rukai art, being revered as the incarnation of the tribal ancestors. It appears on totems, carved shields, wooden boxes used in religious ceremonies, clothing, and numerous other artifacts. It appears both elongated and curled up, with a pattern of diamonds running the length of its body. The Rukai are also known for their free-standing wooden sculptures, often of spear-carrying warriors.

Woodcarving skills are also highly developed among the Yami, who live primarily on Orchid Island, off the southern coast of Taiwan. The Yami are best known for their sturdy hand-built canoes, which can carry ten or more people and are made without nails or glue. They are decorated in delicately carved relief designs that feature a concentric sun-like motif and stylized human figures accented with spiral formations. The canoes are then painted white, red, and black, before undergoing an elaborate launching ceremony.

Another art form central to aboriginal culture is weaving, which is especially well-developed among the Atayal. Using simple back-strap looms, Atayal women create rectilinear patterns of squares, diamonds, and triangles, using mostly red, blue, black, and white. Some designs also incorporate strings of thin shell beads or rows of small bronze bells. Paiwan and Rukai textiles are distinguished by the same motifs found in their woodcarving, particularly snakes, human figures, and diamond patterns, all of which are often added to the woven material with cross-stitch embroidery or stitched-down glass beads.

The aboriginal peoples also have unique architectural traditions. Some of the best places to view these traditions are at the Formosan Aboriginal Cultural Village 九族文化村, a privately run facility close to Sun Moon Lake 日月潭 in central Taiwan, and the Taiwan Aboriginal Culture Park 台灣山地文化園區, set up by the provincial government in the south-island county of P'ingtung. While these two places are commercialized and touristy, they do have sections featuring carefully reproduced traditional homes of the different aboriginal peoples. Among the most interesting are Rukai houses, traditionally made of stacked slate, and Yami houses, which are situated partly underground as protection against typhoons.

Music and Dance

No discussion of aboriginal culture would be complete without including dance and music—perhaps the richest legacy of Taiwan's tribal peoples. Their communal dances, performed at regular ceremonies and rituals, consist mostly of simple but harmonious walking and stamping movements, often performed in unison and accompanied by melodic polyphonic choruses. The sound of small bells or other metal ornaments attached to the dancers' colorful costumes or to ankle bracelets complete the celebratory atmosphere.

Aboriginal dance rituals usually go on for several days and are performed in connection with specific customs or legends. The *Ilisin* spring festival of the Ami, for example, involves the annual rite of passage of the members of various age groups. The three-day *Pastáai* ceremony of the Saisiat (the Ceremony of the Dwarfs 矮人祭), held every other year in the tenth lunar month, is performed to appease a legendary race of dwarfs who are believed to have taught the Saisiat people how to farm. The Yami perform rituals every year to mark the launching of new boats and to celebrate the season of the flying fish, one of their staple foods. The latter ritual includes an impressive

"hair dance," in which the women swing their long hair back and forth through the air.

Even more than dance, aboriginal music is intimately connected to nearly every aspect of tribal life, from daily chores to religious rites, and has been studied by ethnomusicologists and other scholars from around the world. The songs have been divided into four groups, according to theme: harvests, daily work, love, and tribal legends.

Each indigenous people has a distinct singing style and song structure. The Paiwan, for example, sing extemporaneous lyrics accompanied by fixed melodies, while Puyuma songs feature rhymed couplets and an irregular rhythm. In both ethnic groups, choruses are led by a single person, often a tribal elder. The Bunun and Tsou peoples, both of central Taiwan, are known for their skillful harmonizing. In Bunun choruses, the singers slowly work their way up the scale to its highest note, whereas Tsou choruses are known for their solemn and calming music.

The musical instruments used by the aborigines also fall into four categories: drums, simple stringed instruments, woodwind instruments such as flutes, drums, and other percussion instruments such as rattles and wooden mortars and pestles. One interesting example is a kind of Jew's harp used by the Atayal, which consists of a piece of bamboo with one or more small metal strips that are played by moving a thread back and forth with the mouth. And the Paiwan are known for a double-piped flute that is played with the nose.

A number of efforts have been made in recent years to preserve and pass on tribal dance and music, and also to introduce it to general audiences. Many of the peoples have been involved in re-enacting their dance and song rituals on stage. The National Institute of the Arts 國立藝術學院, working in conjunction with the Institute of Ethnology at Academia Sinica, has also recorded dances of several tribes in Labanotation (an internationally recognized way of depicting dance movements on paper) and has reconstructed these for staged performances. Some private groups, including the Cloud Gate Dance Theater Foundation 財團法人雲門舞集文

教基金會, have also produced high-quality cassette and CD recordings of authentic aboriginal singing.

One of the most important developments was the creation of the Formosa Aboriginal Dance Troupe 原舞者 in April 1991. The troupe is made up of young aborigines from several different tribes who work directly with elder tribe members to learn the dances and songs of a particular ritual, often doing their fieldwork in conjunction with qualified ethnologists. Their performances have featured songs and dances of the Puyuma, Ami, Tsou, and Saisiat tribes, and the troupe has been praised by both scholars and dance critics for their skillful and authentic presentations. The troupe has also undertaken several overseas tours, including performances in New York and, in 1996, in France, Spain and Hungary.

Music

Taiwan has a very active music scene, in both the traditional Chinese and classical Western modes—and sometimes a combination of the two. The great variety of music that can be heard here has been highlighted by such events as "100 Years of Taiwanese Music" 台灣音樂一百年, a major festival and conference held in 1995. Performances included Taiwanese folk songs, Fukien and Hakka music, as well as contemporary compositions by some of Taiwan's leading composers (see section below on Composers). Other big music events, such as the 1994 Asian Composers League Conference and Festival 亞洲作曲家聯盟大會暨音樂節, held in Taipei, and more recently, the 1996 Taipei International Music Festival 台北國際樂展, also tend to encompass a wide range of music, traditional and contemporary, Chinese and Western.

Traditional Chinese Music

The four main professional groups performing primarily Chinese music are the Taipei Municipal Chinese Classical Orchestra (TMCCO) 台北市立國樂團, which has toured extensively abroad, the National Experimental Chinese Orchestra 國立台灣藝術學院實驗國樂團, the Kaohsiung Experimental Chinese Orchestra 高雄市實驗國樂團, and the Chinese Orchestra of the Broadcasting Corporation of China 中國廣播公司國樂團. In addition, about ten smaller ensembles perform regularly around the island. One of the more prominent is the Ensemble Orientalia of Taipei 台北民族樂團, which has performed in the United States and Australia. The ensemble is also involved in fieldwork, including researching and transcribing traditional music from throughout Taiwan.

While the musicians in these groups play mostly traditional Chinese instruments, they sometimes perform Western compositions or Chinese works that incorporate Western-style rhythms or harmonies. The TMCCO, for example, has performed such well-known classical works as Ludwig van Beethoven's Symphony No. 5 in c minor and Franz Schubert's Symphony No. 8 in b minor ("Unfinished") on Chinese instruments. And the National Experimental Chinese Orchestra has presented works by Aaron Copeland and Randall Thompson in conjunction with a Western-style chorus.

At times, Chinese musicians have also teamed up with Western orchestras or ensembles. On one such memorable occasion in 1991, bamboo flutist Chen Chung-sheng 陳中申 and *erhu* 二胡 (a double-stringed instrument) player Wen Chin-lung 溫金龍 accompanied the London Mozart Players on their tour of Taiwan. The performance prompted a controversy among musicians and critics over whether such an approach is appropriate or even aesthetically pleasing. Nevertheless, similar experiments continue to take place. The famous *Butterfly Lovers Concerto* 梁祝協奏曲, for example, which was originally written as a violin concerto, is sometimes accompanied by erhu. Often, however, such productions depend on the availability of compositions written specifically for East-West instrument combinations. One such work is the *Bamboo Flute Concerto* 梆笛協奏曲, composed by Ma Shui-lung 馬水龍 for a Western orchestra and bamboo flute. The work was last performed in May 1995 at the 100 Years of Taiwanese

Music Festival with Chen Chung-sheng accompanying the Egret Orchestra 白鷺鷥管弦樂團.

Increased cultural contacts with mainland China have also brought new ideas to Chinese music in Taiwan. Since the late 1980s, a number of groups from the mainland (represented by Western-style and traditional music) have performed here, including major orchestras such as the Shanghai National Music Orchestra and the China Central Ensemble of National Music, as well as smaller ensembles such as the Shanghai Quartet and the Shanghai Chinese Traditional Folk Music Ensemble. In other exchanges, well-known mainland soloists have been invited to perform with local groups. Some important guest artists from the mainland in 1996 were Chinese flutist Yu Xunfa 俞遜發, and erhu performer Xiao Baiyong 蕭白鏞.

Cross-Straits exchange has also included performers from Taiwan visiting the mainland, although these are mainly Western-style musicians, such as the Ju Percussion Group 朱宗慶打擊樂團 (see section on Western Classical Music below), the Taiwan String Quartet 台灣弦樂四重奏, and smaller groups such as the husband-wife piano duo of Lina Yeh 葉綠娜 and Rolf-Peter Wille.

Pei-Kuan and Nan-Kuan

While many traditional Chinese musicians are drawing on Western influences, others have shown a renewed interest in preserving the traditional quality of several types of ancient music—including *pei-kuan* 北管, a fast-tempo music that was once commonly played as an accompaniment at operas and traditional puppet shows, and *nan-kuan* 南管, which has a more delicate and soothing sound. The interest in *nan-kuan* music has been especially prominent. This musical form is thought to have flourished in southern China during the T'ang dynasty, and first appeared in Taiwan during the 16th century. A major performer of *nan-kuan* music today is the Han Tang Classical Musical Institute 漢唐樂府, founded in 1983 by Chen Mei-o 陳美娥, which has performed in the United States, Europe and

Asia, and has released a number of CDs. The group later set up the Liyuan Dance Studio 梨園舞坊, which draws its inspiration from "The Musical Theater of the Pear Orchard" 梨園戲, a form that also flourished during the 8th century A.D. and was brought to Taiwan in the 18th century. The two often perform together at Han Tang's own theater in Taipei, which offers a small, traditional teahouse-like setting.

Other main figures in passing on the tradition of *nan-kuan* music have been singer Wu Su-ching 吳素慶 and musician Lee Hsiang-shih 李祥石, who has been honored with the prestigious Folk Arts Master Award (see section on Folk Arts). Wu and Lee were both invited to teach in a special Nan-kuan Performance Program set up in 1988 at the National Institute of the Arts. The Changhua County Cultural Center 彰化縣立文化中心 has also maintained a Nan-kuan and Pei-kuan Center 南北管音樂劇曲館 since 1990.

Western Classical Music

While traditional Chinese music—whether it adopts foreign influences or maintains its original flavor—has an important position in Taiwan, Western classical music still predominates. In fact, many more musicians are trained in Western music than in Chinese music. And young classical musicians from Taiwan, along with their counterparts elsewhere in Asia, have been making a strong mark in international music circles in recent years. Violinists Lin Chao-liang 林昭亮, Hu Nai-yuan 胡乃元, and Edith Chen 陳毓襄 are just three of the many Taiwan-born musicians who have gone to top schools abroad, won prestigious competitions, and become prominent on the international concert circuit. Another prominent figure is conductor Lu Shao-chia 呂紹嘉, a graduate of the Vienna Conservatory and now the opera conductor for the Komische Oper Berlin. While these young talents often go on to successful careers abroad, many more are now returning to Taiwan, both as visiting musicians and regular members of orchestras and chamber groups. Taiwan's main Western-style orchestras are the National Symphony Orchestra 國家音樂廳交響

樂團, now under conductor by Chang Ta-sheng 張大勝, and the Taipei City Symphony Orchestra 台北市立交響樂團, conducted by Chen Chiu-sheng 陳秋盛. Both groups have frequent opportunities to work with visiting musicians and conductors from abroad, and the Taipei City Symphony Orchestra has toured overseas. Outside of Taipei are the Taiwan Symphony Orchestra 台灣省立交響樂團, based in Taichung, and the semi-professional Kaohsiung City Symphony Orchestra 高雄市實驗交響樂團.

The largest privately run orchestra is the Taipei Sinfonietta and Philharmonic Orchestra 台北愛樂室內及管弦樂團, founded in 1985 by conductor Henry Mazer. With some of the island's most talented musicians among its members, the group has toured the United States, Canada, and Europe.

Smaller established groups include the Contemporary Chamber Orchestra Taipei 台北人室內樂團, under music director Lee Chun-fung 李春峰, the Taipei Concerto Soloists 台北獨奏家室內樂團, and the Taiwan String Quartet, led by Hwang Wei-ming 黃維明. The 34-member Taipei Flute Ensemble 台北長笛室內樂團, conducted by Niu Hsiao-hua 牛效華, is one of the largest flute groups in the world. The ensemble has performed in Europe and the US, and in 1993 became one of the first chamber groups from Taiwan to perform in mainland China. One of the most active and popular ensembles is the Yeh Shu-han Brass Quintet 葉樹涵銅管五重奏, led by trumpeter Yeh Shu-han, which performs classical music as well as jazz.

Perhaps the busiest ensemble on the island is the Ju Percussion Group, directed by Ju Tsung-ching 朱宗慶. The group performs more than 100 times every year, at performance halls as well as at schools and outdoor venues, and holds many educational demonstrations for teachers and the general public. The group's music is often a hybrid of Western and Chinese, and its instruments range from traditional drums, gongs, and xylophones to empty beer bottles, sawed-off steel pipes, and even bursting balloons—anything that can make a noise.

The affiliated Ju Percussion Foundation 財團法人打擊樂文教基金會 oversees a research center for traditional Chinese percussion music and runs educational centers for children around the island. In 1996, the foundation organized the second International Percussion Convention, which included performances by seven top percussion groups from around the world, as well as presentations of Taiwan's own percussion tradition, including lion dance drum music, aboriginal percussion music, and drum-and-gong compositions from *pei-kuan* opera and Peking opera.

Choral Music and Western Opera

Choral music is also now an established tradition in Taiwan, evidenced by the 1996 Taipei International Choral Festival 台北國際合唱節. Along with groups from around the world, the festival featured the Taipei Philharmonic Chorus 台北愛樂合唱團, one of the island's top choral groups. Founded in 1972 and conducted by Dirk DuHei 杜黑, the chorus has performed extensively in the US, Europe and Asia, including mainland China. Other groups that have toured abroad include the Taipei Artists Chorus 台北藝術家合唱團, known for its acappella arrangements of Taiwanese folk songs, and the ROC National Experimental Chorus 實驗合唱團, which sings folk songs as well as Western oratorios.

Thanks to such groups as the Taipei Opera Theater 台北歌劇劇場, under Tseng Tao-hsiung 曾道雄, and the Taiwan Metropolitan Opera 首都歌劇團, directed by internationally known tenor William Wu 吳文修, Western opera has also established a foothold in Taiwan. The Taipei Opera Theater has performed such works as Gounod's *Faust*, Mozart's *Magic Flute*, and Verdi's *Rigoletto*. The Taiwan Metropolitan Opera has presented Puccini's *Madame Butterfly*, Leoncavallo's *Cavalleria Rusticana*, and Mascagni's *I Pagliacci*, as well as *The Great Wall* 萬里長城, a Western-style opera sung in Chinese and telling a Chinese story. Another active opera promoter has been the Taipei City Symphony Orchestra, which in 1995 presented

Verdi's *Aida*, and in January 1997 Wagner's *The Flying Dutchman*, both featuring international casts.

Composers

Three times, Taiwan has played host to the annual conference and festival of the highly regarded Asian Composers' League (ACL), most recently in 1994. The event itself, which includes performances of dozens of works by composers throughout Asia, is evidence of the prominent role that Taiwan has established for itself in contemporary musical composition. Hsu Chang-hui 許常惠, considered by many to be the father of local composers, was one of the founders of the ACL in 1973. Hsu, who studied in France, founded the Music Creative Group 製樂小集, which in the 1960s played an important role in promoting the development of local music composition. He also introduced to local music circles new, experimental developments from the West, such as Arnold Schoenberg's serialism. In addition, Hsu has also been involved for many years in extensive research of Taiwan folk music.

Other composers with strong reputations, locally as well as regionally and internationally, include Ma Shui-long, whose works have been performed in Europe, the United States, South Africa, and Southeast Asia, and Pan Huang-lung 潘皇龍, who has introduced some avant-garde ideas for composition to local audiences. Also of renown are composers Tseng Hsing-kuei 曾興魁, whose works have been played at music festivals in Europe and Asia, and Chang Hao 張昊.

Many local organizations and performing groups have made extensive efforts to promote Taiwan composers. In 1996, for example, the Council for Cultural Affairs and the Chiang Kai-shek National Concert Hall 國家音樂廳 sponsored the Taipei Composition Competition 台北作曲比賽, which featured an international jury and offered exposure to some of Taiwan's younger composers. In addition, the major orchestras, including the Municipal Classical Chinese Orchestra 省立國樂團, and ensembles such as the Taiwan String Quartet, Taipei Concerto Soloists, the Taipei Percussion Group 台北打擊樂團, and the Ju Percussion Group, all regularly include new compositions by local composers in their programs. Also important in this regard are dance companies, such as the Cloud Gate Dance Theater (see Dance section below), which over the years has commissioned 13 local musicians to write 27 compositions for its dance performances. Taiwan composers also enjoy the support of the ROC Composers Association 亞洲作曲家聯盟中華民國總會, set up in 1989 in affiliation with the ACL. Besides organizing the ACL conference and festival, the association sponsors annual concerts featuring new local works.

Chinese Music Theater

Chinese music theater is one of Taiwan's premier art forms. Although performances are not as frequent as they once were, they can still be seen on a weekly basis at opera schools, community theaters and temples, and on television, as well as in major seasonal productions at the National Theater 國家戲劇院 and other top venues. While the form includes many regional styles, the most common in Taiwan are Peking opera, which first reached maturity in the Ch'ing dynasty, and Taiwanese opera (see section on Taiwanese Opera below), which was influenced by operatic forms of southern China. Most regional forms of Chinese music theater are sung in the dialect of their region of origin, hence Taiwanese opera is performed by speaking and singing in Southern Fukienese. Peking opera is an exception, however. Dialogue is in the Peking dialect, but declamatory recitatives and arias are recited or sung in an artificial stage dialect that combines phonetic features of various parts of the Chinese mainland from which it was synthesized in the 18th century.

Peking Opera

Although traditionally performed on an empty or nearly empty stage, Peking opera is a colorful and often lively form of drama. Plots are adapted from enduring tales in Chinese history and classical literature where the theatricality of a particular point in the narrative can be successfully exploited on stage. The demands of theatrical spectacle ensure the inclusion of at least one exciting battle scene or acrobatic display per performance. Plot development reflects traditional Chinese Confucian moral values, such as loyalty, filial piety, and patriotism, although human foibles are also well represented. All characters in a given play are developed within the confines of traditional character roles, with each actor specializing in a specific type of character, such as the *hsiao-sheng* 小生, a handsome and scholarly young man, the *wu-tan* 武旦, a beautiful female warrior, or the *chou* 丑, a clown-like figure who brings comic relief. Each role is marked by a specific range of gestures and a codified style of makeup. Singing is highly stylized, with some characters requiring a high-pitched falsetto (since traditionally, only men appeared on stage, even in female roles). The live musical accompaniment is closely integrated with the action, with the conductor regulating the pace of performance and cueing actors through his control of the basic percussive beat. Traditional string and wind instruments accompany the singing, while percussion comments on virtually all stage movements, marks stage entrances and exits, and serves to bring additional excitement to fighting and acrobatic scenes through percussive commentary.

Taiwan's major Peking opera troupes are the National Kuo Kuang Chinese Opera Company 國光劇團 and the National Fu-Hsing Chinese Opera Theater 復興劇團. The former, which is funded by the Ministry of Education, was established in 1995 following the shutdown of three major military-sponsored opera troupes; performers from those groups merged into the new one. The Kuo Kuang maintains a highly traditional repertoire. Although most of the company's productions are long-established opera scripts, its most recent, in October 1996, featured a new script, which was based on a scenario originally written by opera great Mei Lan-fang 梅蘭芳.

The Fu-Hsing company is affiliated with the National Fu-Hsing Dramatic Arts Academy 國立復興劇藝實驗學校, the island's main training

school for Chinese opera. The company is known for being more adventuresome in its productions, which tend to be new scripts that often combine traditional and modern ideas. Its 1996 fall production, *When Chang O Meets Armstrong* 當嫦娥碰上阿姆斯壯, was billed as a Peking opera for children. Another 1996 production, *The Story of Ah-Q* 阿Q正傳, was based on an early 20th century novel by mainland writer Lu Hsun 魯迅. Rather than the traditional statesman or general, its protagonist is a tragi-comic, common-man character whom Lu used to reflect some less-appealing qualities that he saw in the Chinese character. *Ah-Q* also incorporates elements of Chinese comic drama such as modern-day slang, as well as elements of Taiwanese opera and Taiwanese folk songs. It was also one of Fu-Hsing's several cross-Straits collaborations, featuring a mainland librettist and composer.

Like Fu-Hsing, other opera groups have also tried to modernize the form. Some experts see this trend as a natural development, pointing out that Peking opera has always adopted elements of other forms. Others view the need for modernization as a backlash against a long-time government-supported emphasis on preserving traditional opera, at the expense of letting it develop naturally and grow along with society. For others, it is simply a natural reaction to the decline in audience interest. People today, especially the younger generation, often find the style of traditional opera outmoded and the moralistic stories irrelevant to contemporary life. Productions such as *Ah-Q* tend to attract younger audience members, many of whom do not regularly attend more traditional operas. In any case, such productions usually stir up controversy between old and new schools of thought.

One of the first to begin experimenting, although on a more modest scale, was Kuo Hsiao-chuang 郭小莊, who founded the Ya-yin Ensemble 雅音小集 in 1979. Kuo attracted many younger audience members by bringing a stronger visual dimension to her productions, adding more props, dramatic lighting effects, and revolving platforms to the nearly bare, evenly lit stage of traditional opera. The troupe has not been active in the last several years (although Kuo does continue to perform on occasion in mainland China), but during its heyday it won wide acclaim both in Taiwan and abroad—and also sparked controversy among some old-time opera fans.

Another important innovator has been the Contemporary Legend Theater 當代傳奇劇場, founded by opera actor Wu Hsing-kuo 吳興國 in 1984. The internationally acclaimed group is best known for its Peking opera adaptations of Western classics such as Shakespeare's *Macbeth* and Euripides' *Medea*. These adaptations incorporate elements of Western drama, including dramatic stage and costume designs, and greater psychological character development than is generally found in traditional Chinese opera. Using tragic stories that raise moral questions rather than provide conventional answers, is also a distinct departure from tradition. An even further departure was the group's most recent production, an adaptation of the Aeschylean dramatic trilogy, *Oresteia* 奧瑞斯提亞, made in collaboration with avant-garde American theater director Richard Schechner. Among other things, it incorporated postmodern theater tricks, for example by including a modern-day TV variety show hostess as the judge in the final scene. Some experts refuse to even classify this production as Peking opera, calling it instead simply modern Chinese theater.

Taiwanese Opera

Taiwanese opera 歌仔戲, the only traditional Chinese theatrical art form believed to have originated in Taiwan, was once performed on nearly any auspicious occasion, including weddings, birthdays, and temple festivals. By tradition, the form is said to have its roots in short songs originating in Ilan County 宜蘭縣 which, purportedly influenced by the narrative music of Taiwan's aboriginal peoples, evolved into a powerful musical form. These "Ilan folk songs" are distinguished by an orchestra consisting of the *san-hsien* 三絃, a three-stringed Chinese banjo;

the *pipa* 琵琶, a four-stringed vertical lute; the *tung-hsiao* 洞簫, a vertical flute; the *sona*, a trumpet-belled, double-reeded horn; and, various percussion instruments, including gongs and drums. However, various regional Chinese music theater forms clearly had an influence on Taiwanese opera, particularly the *pei-kuan* and *nan-kuan* music theater brought to Taiwan by early immigrants from southern China. This is evident in its colorful makeup and costumes, stage props, and stylized gestures. Taiwanese opera was a full-fledged musical genre by the 1930s.

The role of Ilan in the development of Taiwanese opera continues to be important today. Several major troupes are based there, including one sponsored by the Ilan County Cultural Center, which also houses a Taiwanese opera museum. Today, there are nearly 200 troupes performing around the island, but only a handful of professional calibre. The best-known is the highly popular Ming Hwa Yuan Theater Troupe 明華園歌劇團, established in 1929. Like other Taiwanese opera troupes, Ming Hwa Yuan started out playing only on outdoor stages, often set up in front of temples, but today it also performs at prestigious venues such as the National Theater. The troupe has also toured overseas, performing in Paris as well as mainland China.

The Ming Hwa Yuan's productions are evidence that Taiwanese opera is continuing to evolve and absorb new influences today. It combines the form's traditional folk theater heritage with concepts and techniques of modern cinema and theater, particularly in lighting and scenery. Other important companies include the Ho Lo Taiwanese Opera Troupe 河洛歌仔戲團, which recently performed in Brazil, the Han Yang Troupe 漢陽歌劇團, one of the most active troupes, and the Lan Yang Troupe 蘭陽戲劇團, which appeared in New York in 1996. Based at the Taipei County Cultural Center 台北縣立文化中心, Lan Yang plays a similar role as Fu-Hsing does in Peking opera, often featuring its own new productions. One of its recent operas was a collaboration with a Fukien opera company from mainland China.

Another important name in Taiwanese opera is Yang Li-hua 楊麗花, the genre's most celebrated actress. With a career spanning some 30 years, she continues to periodically present her own productions. Like many Taiwanese opera actresses, Yang is known for playing male roles. Although the form was originally dominated by male performers, today most of the major characters are played by women. Throughout her career, Yang has played only male roles, as in her 1995 production, *Lu Wen-lung* 雙槍陸文龍.

Television performances of Taiwanese opera have also played an important role in the form's development since the 1960s. Although many TV troupes have resorted to a soap opera mentality, complete with electronic music and pop songs, the Yeh Ching Taiwanese Opera Troupe 葉青歌仔戲團 is one that has worked to keep the basic traditional form intact. Actress Yeh Ching has developed an islandwide following through her TV performances and has won numerous prizes. Another major TV opera company is the Huang Hsiang-lien Troupe 黃香蓮歌仔戲團.

Other Regional Opera Forms

Besides Peking and Taiwanese opera, several other regional forms can also be found in Taiwan. The Kuo Kuang company 國光劇團豫劇隊, for example, has a section for Honan opera 河南梆子, which is sung in a natural voice rather than the falsetto common to Peking opera. Taiwan audiences have also been introduced to Hakka opera, which incorporates traditional tea-farming folk songs, through the Rom-shing Hakka Teapicker Opera Troupe 榮興客家採茶劇團. Rom-shing, which won a Folk Art Heritage Award in 1992, is firmly devoted to preserving the traditional form of Hakka opera. In keeping with tradition, the majority of its productions are presented outdoors, although it also performs at major venues such as the National Theater.

Another winner of the Heritage Award is the Hsin Mei Yuan Troupe 新美園劇團, the only professional *pei-kuan* opera group on the island. *Pei-kuan*, one of the oldest forms of Chinese music theater, is known for its loud gong-and-drum ac-companiment. The Lan Yang Troupe also includes *pei-kuan* performances in its repertoire.

Another form that is regaining attention is Kun opera 崑曲, which preserves late Ch'ing dynasty musical scores and singing techniques from the longest extant tradition of Chinese music theater that dates back potentially to the late 12th or early 13th centuries. Kun opera features more delicate and more complex music and singing, and more poetic language, than the later forms of Chinese music theater generally performed today. Written texts for at least the arias of Kun operas exist in various editions from the late 12th century onward, unlike the generally oral tradition of transmitting regional operatic forms such as Peking opera. Although there are currently only two amateur groups performing Kun opera in Taiwan, a major project is under way to establish a professional troupe. Under the sponsorship of the Kuo Kuang opera school and the private Chinese Folk Arts Foundation 中華民俗藝術基金會, 20 students were chosen in November last year for a three-year training program; the group will train under a series of Kun masters from the Chinese mainland.

Spoken Drama

Taiwan today boasts a dynamic theater scene, including numerous groups experimenting with both Western and Chinese drama traditions, as well as regular visits by international theater companies. The variety is especially surprising considering that spoken drama is a relatively new art form in Chinese culture. It arrived in Taiwan only in 1949, along with the Nationalist exodus from mainland China. This early drama was itself a relatively recent transplant into Chinese culture, brought to the mainland at the turn of the century by students returning from studies in the West. Before this, Chinese theater existed only in sung or operatic genres (see section on Chinese Music Theater). The only exception might be *hsiang-sheng* 相聲, a Vaudeville-like comic dialogue that can be traced back to the late Ch'ing dynasty. The first Western-style spoken drama in Taiwan was based on the realistic styles of 19th and early 20th century playwrights such as Ibsen, Chekhov, and Eugene O'Neill. The only plays produced, however, were dull and didactic performances by government-sponsored troupes that attracted little attention.

The beginnings of the dynamic theater scene of today began in the 1960s, with what is known as the Little Theater Movement 小劇場運動. Thanks to the enthusiasm and talent of several new dramatists, including Li Man-kuei 李曼瑰 and Yao Yi-wei 姚一葦, the repertoire of locally written plays expanded and took a more creative direction. Li alone wrote more than 50 plays, including full-length dramas, one-act works, and children's performances. These have been compiled in a volume entitled *Collection of Chinese Plays* 中華戲劇集.

The first professional stage play produced by an independent (rather than government-sponsored) troupe was Yao Yi-wei's *Red Nose* 紅鼻子, which became a classic among local plays, and was later staged in Peking and Japan as well. The 1970 debut of *Red Nose* helped to usher in the prolific era of the 1970s, when private mini-theaters proliferated and directors began experimenting more freely with staging techniques and imaginative interpretations of both local and Western plays.

Early Innovators

Among other things, the Lan-ling Drama Workshop 蘭陵劇坊, founded in 1977 by Wu Ching-chi 吳靜吉, was the first theater group to recast a Chinese opera in modern colloquial language. This involved a very experimental approach that emphasized strong physical movement and the importance of body language. Lan-ling's groundbreaking 1977 production *Ho-chu's New Match* 荷珠新配, adapted from a well-known Peking opera story, was a contemporary social satire on the new bourgeoisie. This play paved the way for a new theatrical genre in Taiwan, with future theater groups staging contemporary adaptations of other Peking operas. Other Lan-ling productions were even more avant-garde, such as its 1986 adaptation of the ancient Chinese poetry

anthology, *Nine Songs* 九歌, which dispensed with both plot and dialogue, in favor of improvisation, rhythmic movements, chanting, and other elements of ritualism. Although Lan-ling is no longer active, it continues to have an influence on theater in Taiwan. During its heyday, hundreds of students underwent the company's unique training program, and some of the major figures in theater today were at one time connected with Lan-ling.

Another pioneer in the theater world was the New Aspect Art Center 新象藝術中心, established in 1978. Although New Aspect never maintained an actual theater group (it has since developed into an arts agency, bringing a wide variety of performing arts to Taiwan from abroad), it has produced a number of major plays and presented some new dramatic forms to the local theater world. In 1982, it introduced a new multimedia approach associated with epic theater in the landmark production of *Wandering in the Garden and Waking From a Dream* 遊園驚夢. Taiwan's first homegrown musical, *The Chess King* 棋王, was also a New Aspect production. Staged in 1987, it was based on a well-known contemporary novel about a chess prodigy in Taiwan who is manipulated by unscrupulous entrepreneurs in an increasingly corrupt and materialistic society. In more recent years, New Aspect has brought translated versions of classic Western plays to the Taiwan stage, including Oscar Wilde's *The Importance of Being Earnest* 不可兒戲.

The Performance Workshop

The early efforts of Lan-ling and New Aspect helped set the stage for the mid-1980s, which saw the establishment of several leading theater companies that are still active today. Most prominent is the Performance Workshop 表演工作坊, set up in 1984 by Stan Lai 賴聲川, who introduced collective improvisational theater to Taiwan. For many of his productions, Lai first comes up with a basic outline for the play. Working with a strong group of actors, including the well-known Lee Li-chun 李立群, Lai allows everyone to contribute their own ideas, and through a collaborative process, the final script comes to fruition. Lai's ideas about collective theatre have been heavily influenced by Shireen Strooker's Amsterdam Werkteater.

The group's first production to attract more than just a student audience was *The Night We Became Hsiang-sheng Comedians* 那一夜我們說相聲. The play marked the first time that the highly stylized *hsiang-sheng* was expanded into a full-length play. The play was originally meant as a sort of eulogy for this dying dramatic form—and a symbol of the erosion of traditions in Taiwan's increasingly modern society. But its tremendous box-office success was actually seen by many as a revival of the form.

Performance Workshop's other productions have also offered reflections on modern Taiwan society. For example, *The Island and the Other Shore* 回頭是彼岸 (1989) and *Look Who's Cross-talking Tonight* 這一夜誰來說相聲 both grapple with the island's complex and controversial relationship with mainland China. In the 1994 play *Red Sky* 紅色的天空, the troupe revealed the experiences of Taiwan's elderly population. The Performance Workshop has also staged Chinese versions of well-known Western plays, sometimes changing the setting and background to Taiwan, sometimes remaining more faithful to the original. The company's 1996 production was an adaptation of Tony Kushner's *Angels in America*, a play about AIDS among the gay community in New York. Other adaptations include Alan Ayckbourn's *Absurd Person Singular*, Neil Simon's *Last of the Red Hot Lovers*, and Italian playwright Dario Fo's *Accidental Death of an Anarchist*. Two other major Performance Workshop productions, Arthur Miller's *Death of a Salesman* and *Equus*, featured the talents of guest director Daniel Yang, a producing director of the Colorado Shakespeare Festival who has been making a mark on Taiwan theater for some years. In addition, Performance Workshop director Stan Lai has ventured into filmmaking, with one of his movies based on his play *The Peach Blossom Land* 暗戀桃花源 (see section on Film, The Second New Wave).

Like the Performance Workshop, the Pin-Fong Acting Troupe 屏風表演班, set up in 1986, has become widely popular among local audiences.

Directed by Li Kuo-hsiu 李國修, who formerly worked with the Lan-ling as well as the Performance Workshop, the troupe presents mainly comedies, often of a slapstick nature. But underneath the pranks and wisecracks are satirical comments on Taiwan society. Li has often been called a "Chinese Woody Allen." His play *Shamlet* 莎姆雷特 tells the story of a group of actors trying to stage a Chinese version of *Hamlet*. While their misdirected efforts are full of pitiful mistakes, culminating in the collapse of the stage backdrop, these are underscored by references to the imitative excesses of modern Taiwan. Another successful Pin-Fong production was the play, *Wanted: Marriage Partner* 徵婚啟事, which looks at love and romance in the alienating urban surroundings of Taipei. Based on a real-life experience, the play relates the story of a woman who takes out a want ad for a spouse and receives responses from 21 very different men—with all 21 roles played by Li Kuo-hsiu. Pin-Fong's most recent production, in 1996, was *Peking Opera: The Revolution* 京劇啟示錄, which featured opera actors and pop singers.

A number of other, smaller companies are also playing an increasingly important role in Taiwan's theater world. These groups offer a range of styles, from fairly traditional to highly experimental. One up-and-coming group is the Godot Theater Company 果陀劇場, set up in 1988. Often using a combination of theater, music and dance, the company has staged Taiwan-oriented adaptations of such works as *Our Town* and Shakespeare's *The Taming of the Shrew*. The Godot's 1996 production was a martial arts drama called *Chiao Feng, the End of Destiny* 天龍八部之喬峰, adapted from a Chinese swashbuckler novel written by Chin Yung 金庸 about a beggar king.

Along very different lines, the Critical Point Theater Phenomenon 臨界點劇象錄 often tackles more controversial subjects, such as political dissidence or homosexuality. The group's style is also unconventional. They might, for example, use illogical dialogue to create a certain atmosphere, or mix Mandarin, Taiwanese and English, or draw on the language used in advertisements. A strong emphasis on movement and well-defined body language also sets the group apart. In 1996, Critical Point was one of the groups invited to take part in the Taiwan Arts Festival sponsored by the Ludwig Forum in Aachen, Germany (see Dance). The company, however, also encountered tragedy in 1996 with the death of its director, Tien Chi-yuan 田啟元.

Another unusual group is the U Theater 優劇場, founded by Liu Ching-min 劉靜敏 and dedicated to creating a form of contemporary theater that expresses a unique Taiwanese identity. To absorb the traditions of the culture, the actors and actresses take part in a strict physical training program that includes martial arts, and have also worked with a variety of folk artists, such as Taiwanese opera performers and traditional drummers. Drawing on these influences, their productions have included dramas as well as energetic drum performances.

Recent years has also seen a rise in theater companies based in central and southern Taiwan. These include the Hwa Teng Troupe 華燈劇團 in Tainan, the Taitung Theater Troupe 台東劇團, and the Nan Feng Theater Troupe 南風劇團 of Kaohsiung. The latter has also been active in efforts to improve the overall arts environment in Kaohsiung; in 1996, the troupe set up a theater and arts center and has been sponsoring professional training workshops for performing artists.

While contemporary theater is at the fore, recent years have also witnessed the resurgence in Taiwan of traditional Chinese stage dialogue, often referred to as *hsiang-sheng*, although in fact this is only one of many styles of this distinct art form. Stage dialogue is often comic and is performed in a rhythmic style, often accompanied by clappers, and includes stories, poems, songs, jokes, tongue twisters, word play, and bantering between partners. Vaudeville-like acts are sometimes part of the show as well. Subject matter is often a mixture of references to traditional stories and contemporary events. The current-day references tend to help keep this theatrical form up-to-date, despite its traditional grounding. In addition, some performers are updating it by using modern-day words and idioms, by combining the Mandarin and Taiwanese dialects, as is often done in common local speech, or by wearing street clothes rather than formal Chinese gowns. One group that stands out in the genre is the Taipei Musical Theater Troupe 台北曲藝團, founded in 1993, which performs a variety of different types of spoken dialogue. The group also offers productions for children.

Dance

The dance world in Taiwan today is surprisingly diverse, considering it really got its start only in the late 1960s. However, there are some early pioneers that should be mentioned, especially in modern dance. Tsai Jui-yueh 蔡瑞月 and Lee Tsai-o 李彩娥, having studied European-influenced modern dance in Japan, began giving performances in the 1940s. But soon after, when the Nationalists moved to Taiwan in 1949, modern dance began to take a back seat in favor of Chinese folk dance, which the government encouraged as a means for promoting traditional Chinese culture on the island.

In the 1960s, local dancers and audiences began to get a taste of new styles, thanks to tours by American companies such as Alvin Ailey and Paul Taylor. Modern dance again began to come to the forefront.

Mother of Modern Dance

One of the first to introduce modern dance to Taiwan was Liu Feng-hsueh 劉鳳學, whom many today consider the matriarch of the dance world. Using dancers from her own studio, established in 1967, and from her students in the physical education department at National Taiwan Normal University, Liu began presenting showings of modern choreography. In 1976, she formed the Neo-Classic Dance Company 新古典舞團, which continues to perform today. Her choreographic style is heavily influenced by Rudolf Laban, whose famous system of dance notation she studied in Germany in the

1970s. As a result, many of her works, such as *Nilpotent Group* 冪零群 (1977) and the full-length *Carmina Burana* (1993), appear very mathematical, with an emphasis on structural concepts of space and group formation. Her kinetic vocabulary draws frequently on the movements of Chinese opera and martial arts, but developed into modern movement phrases through Laban concepts of space, time, and direction.

Besides her modern choreography, Liu has also recreated a number of ancient Chinese dances, drawing on historical texts and scholarly research. *The Emperor Destroys the Formations* 皇帝破陣樂, for example, is a seventh century court dance that she recreated in conjunction with Dr. Laurence Picken of Cambridge University and Dr. Noee Nickson, who reconstructed the music. Her own expertise in this field is backed up by studies at London University's Laban Centre, where in 1987 she became the first person in Taiwan to hold a Ph.D. in dance. She has also used her research to create new works, such as the modernistic *Figurines* 俑之一 (1992), inspired by Han dynasty stone engravings of acrobats.

The Cloud Gate Dance Theater

At the same time that Liu was beginning to make her mark in the early 1970s, Lin Hwai-min 林懷民 was forming the Cloud Gate Dance Theater 雲門舞集, which would go on to become Taiwan's premier dance company, gaining a devoted local audience as well as an international reputation in numerous overseas tours. After studying under Martha Graham, Lin returned to Taiwan in 1973 and began using modern techniques along with Chinese opera movement. His early works had strong Chinese themes, as in *The Tale of the White Serpent*, an updated version of a classic story.

Similar to the nativist artists and writers (see section on Painting, and Chapter 24, Literature) of the 1970s, Lin was eager to express a local identity. Cloud Gate's signature work, *Legacy* 薪傳 (1978), told the dramatic story of the first Chinese pioneers to arrive in Taiwan. *Crossing the Black Water* 渡海, one segment of *Legacy* that has been performed on its own numerous

times, is a spellbinding portrayal of the pioneers crossing the Taiwan Straits, with a huge billowing white sheet acting as the treacherous water. Later works dealt with more contemporary concerns. *The Rite of Spring* 春之祭 (1983), for example, took a harrowing look at the plight of urban existence. The 1984 *Dreamscape* 夢土, and its recent November 1995 reproduction, explored the Chinese conflict between modern life and traditional culture. And *My Nostalgia, My Songs* 鄉愁 (1986) recaptures the harsh conditions of postwar life on the island in the 1950s.

In recent years, Lin has begin to combine more universal inspirations into his choreography. The 90-minute *Nine Songs* 九歌 (1993), which was re-staged at New York's Kennedy Center in 1995, draws on the work of ancient Chinese poet Ch'ü Yüan 屈原 and his many references to gods and goddesses, as well as traits found in Indian and Javanese dance and Chinese opera movement. References can also be found to historical tragedies, such as executions by the Japanese and Chinese governments in Taiwan, and the events at Tienanmen Square. The set for the dance—a backdrop of a giant lotus painting and in the front of the stage an actual water-filled lotus pond—was created by renowned New York stage designer Ming Cho Lee 李名覺 to re-emphasize the work's general theme of death and rebirth. Lin's 1995 dance *Songs of the Wanderers* 流浪者之歌 took a more spiritual approach by combining the image of a meditating Chinese monk with images drawn from the religious practices of Hindu ascetics, Tibetan Buddhists, and Japanese Zen practitioners, along with the music of Islamic-influenced Georgian folk songs. Cloud Gate also periodically presents works by young choreographers from Taiwan, as in its 1996 fall season, as well as by other established figures. One frequent Cloud Gate collaborator is Hong Kong choreographer Helen Lai 黎海寧, who has been represented in several of the companies recent seasons. Another memorable performance in 1996 featured two interpretations of Igor Stravinsky's *Rites of Spring*, one by Helen Lai and one by Lin Hwai-min.

Diverse Dance Styles

Since the 1980s, a number of smaller dance companies have started up, many of them founded by former Cloud Gate members. Among the most prominent is Lin Hsiu-wei's 林秀偉 Taigu Tales Dance Theater 太古踏舞團, known for its meditative dances based on Asian philosophical thought. With an emphasis on poetic expression and soul-searching, her works are stirring and cathartic, often with a primitive quality akin to the modern Japanese dance form Butoh. Another former Cloud Gate dancer is Liu Shao-lu 劉紹爐, who also studied with Liu Feng-hsueh early in his career and started his own group, the Taipei Dance Circle 光環舞集, seven years ago. Liu's best known work, *Olympics* 奧林匹克, is based on an innovative technique in which dancers with oiled bodies spin and slide on an oiled floor to create a surprisingly poetic display of motion. Other choreographers with a meditative or ritualistic style of dance include Tao Fu-lan 陶馥蘭 and Lin Li-chen 林麗珍. Tao's earlier works took a very different approach, fusing theater and dance, and inspired by the German choreographer Pina Bausch; she also explored some of the traditional theatrical forms of Taiwan, developing modern dances based, for example, on the *pei-kuan* folk opera. Recently, however, Tao has begun to focus on a more tranquil movement derived from an inner body awareness found through meditation and yoga, as in her 1994 piece *Body Phases* 體相四色 and 1996 *Temple of the Heart* 心齋. Lin Li-chen is a long-time dancer who returned to the stage in 1995 with the full-length production *Legend* 醮, based on Taiwanese temple rituals.

Working in a very different style is the Dance Forum Taipei 舞蹈空間, founded in 1989 by Ping Heng 平珩. Under artistic director Sunny Pang 彭錦耀, originally from Hong Kong, the group presents a wide mixture of styles, but is best known for works that combine a postmodern sensibility with a Chinese or Asian frame of reference. Pang's *Cadaverous Capers* 白虎嶺, for example, retells a chapter from the famous Chinese story *Journey to the West* 西遊記, but with hilarious cartoon-like images and outlandish costumes. The Dance Forum's 1996 production was a re-staging of Pang's *Kwaidan/Emaki*, 怪談／繪卷 inspired by Japanese ghost stories. Another unusual company is Peggy Wu's 吳佩倩 Jazz Ensemble 舞極舞蹈團, which merges jazz and Chinese dance movement, as in the company's 1996 production of *The Tale of the White Serpent*.

Although ballet has held a less prominent position in Taiwan's dance world, there are several schools and small companies that perform. One of the better known is the Taipei Chamber Ballet 台北室內芭蕾舞團, which presents annual summer concerts choreographed by Yu Neng-sheng 余能盛, also a dancer with the Osnabruck Ballet in Germany. Periodically, independent ballet productions are also presented by such organizations as the Chinese Dance Association 中華民國舞蹈協會, which in 1995 organized a full-length performance of Adolphe Adam's *Giselle* with an all-Chinese cast.

Many of Taiwan's smaller dance companies are gaining a reputation among international audiences, giving performances at venues around Asia and in Europe and the United States. Taigu Tales Dance Theater, for example, has performed several times in France and elsewhere in Europe, and the Dance Forum has performed in New York and elsewhere. And in 1996 in Aachen, Germany, the annual festival of the Ludwig Forum featured a Taiwan Arts Festival. Included in the programs were Taigu Tales, the Taipei Dance Circle, and the Taipei Crossover Dance Company 台北越界舞團. The latter was founded in 1994 by a group of well-known Cloud Gate veterans, Lo Man-fei 羅曼菲, Cheng Shu-chi 鄭淑姬, Wu Shu-chun 吳素君 and Yeh Tai-chu 葉台竹, all of whom teach at the dance department of the National Institute of the Arts.

Folk Dance

While modern performances are the mainstay of the dance world, folk dance has also developed a professional base in Tsai Li-hua's

蔡麗華 Taipei Folk Dance Troupe 台北民族舞團.
Founded in 1988, the group aims to preserve
ethnic dances from mainland China as well as
Taiwan, and also to create new dances based on
folk dance techniques. The troupe has performed
in a number of folk dance festivals abroad,
bringing home numerous awards. The troupe's
1996 production was a dance-drama based on a
Chinese fairy tale, "The Peacock Princess" 孔雀
公主, and incorporating folk dances from Yunnan
Province. The Taipei Folk Dance Troupe also
performed in September 1996 on the plaza opposite the United Nations building in New York
as part of a special Taiwan culture festival.
Several children's folk dance troupes have also
disseminated Chinese culture abroad. The best-
known internationally is the Lan Yang Dancers
天主教蘭陽舞蹈團, which was established in 1966
by Catholic missionary Gian Carlo Michelini
and has performed in more than 20 countries.
(See also, the Formosa Aboriginal Dance Troupe
in the section on Aboriginal Arts.)

Cinema

One of the most talked-about developments
in the international film world in recent years has
been the surge in award-winning works by Asian
directors and producers—and much of the conversation has centered around Taiwan.

Since the late 1980s, Taiwan films have se-
cured a regular place in film festivals and award
ceremonies around the world. The honors have
included the prestigious Golden Lion for best film
awarded by the Venice International Film Festival
to *City of Sadness* 悲情城市 (1989) by Hou Hsiao-
hsien, and *Vive l'Amour* 愛情萬歲 (1994) by Tsai
Ming-liang 蔡明亮; the Golden Bear awarded by
the Berlin International Film Festival to *The Wedding Banquet* 囍宴 (1993) by Ang Lee 李安; the
Jury Prize awarded by the Cannes Festival to Hou
Hsiao-hsien's *The Puppetmaster* (1993); and a
nomination of *The Wedding Banquet* for best
foreign film at the 1994 Academy Awards. A
number of other films have also won awards or
have been featured in special showings at various
international festivals.

Taiwan cinema continued to make a mark in
1996, with a particularly impressive showing at
the Asia-Pacific Film Festival: a best director's
award to Hou Hsiao-hsien for *Good Men, Good
Women* 好男好女, best screenplay to Lee Khan 李
崗 and Sylvia Chang 張艾嘉 for *Tonight, Nobody
Goes Home* 今天不回家, and a special juror's
award for *Ah Chung* 忠仔, directed by Chang Tso-
chi 張作驥.

It is only in the last dozen years, however, that
Taiwan cinema has come into its own. Although
during the late 1960s and early 1970s the island's
film industry was one of the strongest in Asia, the
scene was dominated by syrupy romances, grade-B
kungfu movies, and moralistic or propaganda-ori-
ented dramas. The public and the media were growing tired of the limited variety of domestically produced films. People were also being exposed to
high-quality foreign movies through film festivals
held by the National Film Archives 電影資料館
(originally the Motion Picture Library 電影圖書館),
set up in 1977, and through the surging availability of movies on videotape. Opportunities for
scholarships and awards for young filmmakers
and scriptwriters through the Motion Picture Development Fund 中華民國電影事業發展基金, established in 1975, also helped create a better
environment for quality cinema. Another plus
was the Golden Horse Awards 金馬獎, Taiwan's
version of the Oscars. Although established in
1962, the awards first started to attract attention in
1980, and since then have become a prestigious
affair in the Taiwan film world.

New Wave Cinema

The real breakthrough for Taiwan cinema came
in 1982 with *In Our Time* 光陰的故事, a four-part
film produced by the Central Motion Picture Corporation 中央電影公司 that featured four talented
young directors (Edward Yang 楊德昌, Tao Te-
chen 陶德辰, Ko I-cheng 柯一正, and Chang Yi 張
毅). The film won over audiences by replacing
melodrama and escapism with a realistic look at
life in Taiwan.

This new approach paved the way for what
came to be known as the New Cinema, or New

Wave Cinema, which has been compared stylistically to the Italian neo-realism. Initially inspired by Taiwan's nativist literature of the 1960s and 1970s (see also Chapter 24, Literature), New Wave directors such as Hou Hsiao-hsien, Edward Yang, and Wang Tung 王童 created a cinema with a unique Taiwanese flavor by focusing on realistic and sympathetic portrayals of both rural and urban life.

Many New Cinema films were actually based on famous nativist novels. This was in fact the continuation of an established tradition of adapting literary works to the screen. From 1965 to 1983, for example, a total of 50 films were adapted from the romance novels of Chiung Yao 瓊瑤. But the New Wave directors were interested not only in the stories of the nativist novels, but also in their realistic, down-to-earth style and spirit. They wanted to give a genuine local flavor to their films. And like the nativist writers, they took a critical look at some of the central issues facing Taiwan society—the struggle against poverty, the conflicts with political authority, the growing pains of urbanization and industrialization.

One of the first films in this mode was *The Sandwich Man* 兒子的大玩偶 (1983), a three-part movie by directors Hou Hsiao-hsien, Tseng Chuang-hsiang 曾壯祥, and Wan Jen 萬仁. It was adapted from short stories by the famous writer Huang Chun-ming 黃春明 that deal with the struggles of working class people in 1960s Taiwan.

As evident in *The Sandwich Man*, the New Cinema directors took a highly introspective approach in examining the effects of the tremendous political, social, and economic changes that Taiwan had experienced in the past 50 or more years. Their works thus offer a fascinating chronicle of the island's social transformation in modern times. For example, Wang Tung's *The Strawman* 稻草人 (1987) and *Hill of No Return* 無言的山丘 (1992) portray the tragic, work-burdened lives of rural Taiwanese during the Japanese occupation. Wang's latest work was *The Red Persimmon* 紅柿子 (1996), the story of a mainland family that escapes to Taiwan in 1949. Hou Hsiao-hsien's *The City of Sadness* takes place in the following era, focusing on the con-

flicts between the local Taiwanese and the newly arrived Nationalist government that came to a climax in the February 28 Incident of 1945 (for historical details, see section concerning the ROC on Taiwan in Chapter 4, History). Another of Hou's film *A Time to Live and a Time to Die* 童年往事 (1985) examines life in rural Taiwan in the 1950s and 1960s, and his more recent *Good Men, Good Women* covers political developments from the end of World War II to the present day. In contrast, the works of Edward Yang, such as *Taipei Story* 青梅竹馬 (1985), *The Terrorizers* 恐怖份子 (1986) and *Confucian Confusion* 獨立時代 (1994), reflect the clash of traditional values and modern materialism among young urbanites of the 1980s and '90s.

Second New Wave

While New Wave films have continued to win critical acclaim, the initial enthusiasm of local audiences began to wear off in the late 1980s. For one thing, the genre had now given rise to a slew of lesser-quality imitations. And many viewers, it seems, grew tired of the seriousness of New Wave subject matter and became more drawn to the escapist, action-packed entertainment of commercial-oriented Hong Kong films, which began to dominate the market. Local directors found it increasingly difficult to secure financing for auteur films that were not big box-office draws.

Nevertheless, during the lean years of the late '80s and early '90s, a number of talented new filmmakers started to create a "Second New Wave" for Taiwan cinema, one which is still going strong today. Compared with the older generation, these new directors are offering up a much greater variety, in both content and style, although they still appear strongly committed to portraying a uniquely Taiwan perspective. They also tend to reject the nostalgic, historical approach of older filmmakers, being drawn instead toward the pain and absurdities of contemporary life.

One of the major figures of the Second New Wave is Tsai Ming-liang, whose films *Rebels of the Neon God* 青少年哪吒 (1992) and the 1994 Venice winner *Vive l'Amour* take an existentialist approach to the plight of urban teenagers and young adults who are on the margins of today's affluent society. The latter also won praise for its unique style of filmmaking; it includes no music or soundtrack, only the background noises of the city, and a minimum of dialogue, relying instead on the power of simple but ambiguous images.

Second New Wave director Stan Lai (also a key figure in Taiwan's stage theater; see section on The Performance Workshop) has also brought an experimental as well as light-hearted touch to his films. *The Peach Blossom Land* (1992), which won prizes at the Tokyo and Berlin film festivals, is an adaptation of one of Lai's stage productions; the tragi-comic story revolves around two groups of actors who take turns rehearsing two very different plays on the same stage. His 1994 film *The Red Lotus Society* 飛俠阿達 juxtaposes a fantastic story—about a young man who is determined to fly like the martial arts masters of ancient China—against the realistic setting of modern-day Taipei.

The films of Ang Lee, another Second New Wave director, take a more realistic approach, yet still deal with current-day concerns. For example, *Pushing Hands* 推手 (1991), *The Wedding Banquet* and *Eat Drink Man Woman* 飲食男女 (1994) look at the generational and cultural conflicts confronting modern Chinese families.

Other new names have also begun to make an impression on Taiwan's film world in the last few years. Among them are Wu Nien-chen 吳念真, who already had a solid reputation as one of the island's top screenwriters before making his debut as a director. His 1994 *A Borrowed Life* 多桑 was awarded best film at the Turin International Film Festival, and *Buddha Bless America* 太平天國 (1996) was shown at the Venice Festival. Another new director, Chen Yu-hsun 陳玉勳, was awarded the Blue Leopard Prize at Switzerland's Locarno Film Festival for *Tropical Fish* 熱帶魚 (1995). Hsu Hsiao-ming 徐小明, Wan Jen, Steve Wang 王獻箎 and Lin Cheng-sheng 林正盛 are also among the latest generation of Taiwan directors whose works have been shown at prestigious film festivals around the world.

Cross-Straits Collaboration

As with many areas, the film world has been affected by the ROC government's relaxation on contacts with mainland China in recent years. Some of the first contacts were at international film festivals in the mid-1980s. And in 1991, the ROC allowed actors from Taiwan to attend the Golden Rooster awards in Peking, and mainland directors Chen Kaige 陳凱歌 and Peng Xiao Liang 彭小蓮 to attend the Golden Horse awards in Taipei. Soon after, actors and directors from both sides were regularly exchanging visits, and Taiwan directors were beginning to shoot footage, or even entire films, in the mainland—something that was once forbidden. The most recent examples are Wang Shau-di's 王小棣 *Accidental Legend* 飛天 (1996), shot in China, and Hou Hsiao-hsien's *Good Men, Good Women*, which includes several mainland scenes.

There was still some initial delay, however, in full government acceptance of the new cooperative film environment. One of the first films to be shot in the mainland, Yeh Hung-wei's 葉鴻偉 *Five Girls and a Rope* 五個女子和一根繩子 (1991), was banned from release in Taiwan for more than a year. The reason given was that it had violated regulations by including a mainland actress in its cast. Such rules were eventually relaxed, so that today half of a film's cast can be mainland actors and actresses.

But perhaps the most significant cross-Straits development in the cinema has been the surge in Taiwan financing of mainland films. Mainland director Chen Kaige's *Farewell to My Concubine* 霸王別姬, which won the Golden Palm at Cannes in 1994 and was nominated (along with *The Wedding Banquet*) for an Academy Award, was financed by Taiwan actress-turned-producer Hsu Feng 徐楓. Hsu also backed Chen's 1996 production, *Temperance Moon* 風月.

ERA International 年代影視 is another Taiwan company that has supported mainland directors. ERA collaborations include two highly successful films by Zhang Yimou 張藝謀: *Raise the Red Lantern* 大紅燈籠高高掛, which won the 1992 Silver Lion Award in Venice and an Academy Award nomination, and *To Live* 活著, winner of the Jury Grand Prize at Cannes in 1994. More recent Taiwan-backed mainland films include Huang Jianxin's 黃建新 *Wooden Man's Bride* 驗身 (1995) and Wu Xiniu's 吳子牛 *Don't Cry Nanking* 南京一九三七 (1995), both produced by Taiwan's Long Shong International 龍祥影視.

Animation and Documentaries

Taiwan has also started to make a name for itself in animation and documentary filmmaking. In animation, one of the key figures is Jay Shih 石 昌杰, whose works *Taipei, Taipei* 台北、台北 (1993) and *Post Human* 後人類 (1995) have been shown extensively at international film festivals. The latter is a science fiction animation with a post-apocalyptic theme. Among the island's top documentary makers is Lee Daw-ming 李道明, who has won awards both locally and internationally. His first work, *Beyond the Killing Fields* 殺戮 戰場的邊緣, filmed at refugee camps on the Thai-Cambodia border, was named Best Short Film at the 1986 Asia-Pacific Film Festival and Best Documentary at Taiwan's Golden Horse Awards. Other award-winning works by Lee include *Songs of Pastáai* 矮人祭之歌, on one of Taiwan's indigenous tribes, and *Voice of the People* 人民的聲 音, on local environmental issues.

Further Reading (in Chinese unless otherwise noted):

The Art of Classical Chinese Flower Arrangement (in English). The Women's Garden and Art Club of the Republic of China, ed. Taipei: Council for Cultural Affairs, Executive Yuan, 1986.

Chang Shao-tsai 張少載. *Chinese Architecture* (Chung-kuo te chien-chu yi-shu 中國的建築藝術). Taipei: Grand East Enterprise, 1979.

Ch'en Ch'i-lu 陳奇祿. *Woodcarving of the Paiwan Tribe of Taiwan* (Pai-wan-tsu mu-tiao wen-wu-chan 排灣族木雕文 物展). Taipei: Council of Chinese Culture Renaissance, 1992.

Chen Lydia 陳夏生. *Chinese Knotting* (in English). Taipei: Echo Publishing Co., Ltd., 1982.

Ch'iu K'un-liang 邱坤良. *Music in Traditional Chinese Opera* (Chung-kuo te ch'uan-t'ung hsi-ch'ü yin-yüeh 中國的 傳統戲曲音樂). Taipei: Yuan Liu Publishing Co., 1981.

Contemporary Ceramics from the Republic of China (Chung-hua min-kuo tang-tai t'ao-tz'u-chan 中華民國當代陶瓷展; Chinese-English bilingual). Taipei: Council for Cultural Affairs, Executive Yuan, 1988.

Contemporary Sculpture Exhibition: ROC, 1991 (Yi-chiu-chiu-yi chung-hua min-kuo tang-tai tiao-su-chan 一九九 一中華民國當代雕塑展; Chinese-English bilingual). Taipei: Taipei Fine Arts Museum, 1991.

Chuang Po-ho 莊伯和. *Chinese Sculpture* (Chung-kuo te tiao-k'e yi-shu 中國的雕刻藝術). Taipei: Council for Cultural Affairs, Executive Yuan, 1988.

Current Concerns: Humanistic Focus in Modern Taiwan Clay (Tang-hsia-kuan-chu: T'ai-wan-t'ao te jen-wen hsin-ching 當下關注：台灣陶旳人文新境; Chinese-English bilingual). Taipei: Taipei Find Arts Museum, 1995.

The Development of Modern Art in Taiwan (T'ai-wan ti-ch'ü hsien-tai mei-shu te fa-chan 台灣地區現代美術的發展). Taipei: Taipei Fine Arts Museum, 1990.

A Guide to the Taiwan Folk Arts Museum (T'ai-wan min-chien yi-shu hsin-shang 台灣民間藝術欣賞; Chinese-English bilingual). Taipei: Taiwan Folk Arts Museum, 1989.

International Conference, China: Modernity and Art (Chung-kuo hsien-tai mei-shu kuo-chi hsüeh-shu yen-t'ao-hui lun-wen-chi 中國現代美術國際學術研討會論文集; Chinese-English bilingual). Taipei: Taipei Fine Arts Museum, 1991.

International Print Exhibition: 1983 ROC (Chung-hua min-kuo kuo-chi pan-hua-chan 中華民國國際版畫展). Taipei: Council for Cultural Affairs, Executive Yuan, 1983.

Ju Ming Sculptures (Chu-ming tiao-k'e 朱銘雕刻; Chinese-English bilingual). Singapore: Ministry of Community Development, 1986.

Juan Ch'ang-jui 阮昌銳. *The Sculptural Art of Taiwan's Aborigines* (T'ai-wan shan-pao tiao-k'e yi-shu 臺灣山胞 雕刻藝術). Nant'ou: Department of Education, Taiwan Provincial Government, 1991.

Lai, T.C. *Chinese Seals* (in English). Seattle: University of Washington Press, 1976.

Lin Hsing-yüeh 林惺嶽. *The Vicissitudes of Taiwanese Art Over 40 Years* (T'ai-wan mei-shu feng-yün ssu-shih nien 台灣美術風雲四十年). Taipei: The Independence Evening Post, 1991.

Liu Liang-yu 劉良佑. *Chinese Handicrafts* (Chung-kuo ch'i-wu yi-shu 中國器物藝術). Taipei: Hsiung Shih Art Books Company, 1972.

Local Folk Arts (Hsiang-t'u te min-tsu yi-shu 鄉土的民族藝術). Taipei: Council for Cultural Affairs, Executive Yuan, 1988.

The Origins and Development of Chinese Calligraphy (Chung-hua shu-fa yüan-liu 中華書法源流). Yunlin: Association for the Promotion of the Welfare of the Hearing and Speaking Impaired in Taiwan Province, 1972.

An Overview of the Chinese Film Industry (in English). Taipei: Kwang Hwa Publishing Company, 1991.

So Yü-ming 索予明. *The Best of Classical Chinese Handicrafts* (Ku-tien kung-yi ching-hua 古典工藝精華). Taipei: Council for Cultural Affairs, Executive Yuan, 1984.

Sung Lung-fei 宋龍飛. *The Exquisite Art of Chinese Porcelain* (Ching-ya chüeh-lun chung-kuo tz'u-ch'i 精雅絕倫中國瓷 器). Taipei: Council for Cultural Affairs, Executive Yuan, 1988.

Taipei Biennial: The Quest for Identity (Yi-chiu-chiu-liu shuang-nien-chan: t'ai-wan yi-shu chu-t'i-hsing 一九九六雙年展：台灣藝術主體性; Chinese-English bilingual). Taipei: Taipei Fine Arts Museum, 1996.

Talks on Dance and the Cloud Gate Dance Company (Yün-men wu-hua 雲門舞話). Taipei: Yuan Liu Publishing Co., 1976.

Teng Sui-ning 鄧綏寧. *Chinese Drama* (Chung-kuo te hsi-chü 中國的戲劇). Nant'ou: Department of Information, Taiwan Provincial Government, 1969.

Tu Yun-chih 杜雲之. *Chinese Cinema* (Chung-kuo te tien-ying 中國的電影). Taipei: Crown Publishing Co., 1978.

"Yu Peng and the Postwar Generation of Chinese Painters in Taiwan," *Yu Peng a Contemporary Chinese Painter* (in English). Towson, Maryland: Asian Arts Center, Towson State University, 1991.

Yuyu Yang in Stainless Steel (Yang Ying-feng pu-hsiu-kang tiao-su 楊英風不鏽鋼雕塑; Chinese-English bilingual). Singapore: The Ministry of Information and the Arts, 1991.

100 Years of Taiwanese Music: 1895–1995 (T'ai-wan yin-yüeh yi-pai-nien 台灣音樂一百年). Taipei: The Egret Cultural and Educational Foundation, 1995.

At the Hotel Royal Chihpen
Even Breathing Is a Multiple Enjoyment

● Golf Training Course

Taking deep breaths as you can to breathe the fragrance of the forest, the sunlight shower and the hot springs.

With the natural resources of the local area, including hot springs, primitive natural environment and aboriginal culture, the Hotel Royal Chihpen uses its unique surroundings and the indoor leisure facilities to affirm itself as Taitung's sole International Grade Tourist Hotel.

● Archery Site

Its 182 rooms are full of aboriginal round rattan designs, presenting a combination of modern and traditional styles. Inside the hotel there is a swimming pool and tennis courts. In times within the beautiful natural environment you can still enjoy modern leisure pursuits.

In the peaceful, pollution-free leisure paradise away from the concrete jungle, just breathing provides you multiple enjoyments.

● Spa Complex

● Tennis Courts

● Open-air Spa Bath

● Aboriginal Camp

● Children's Playground

知本 老爺大酒店 溫泉
hotel royal chihpen spa

23, Lane 113, Long Chuien Rd., Wen Chuien Village, Peinan Hsiang, Taitung Hsien, Taiwan, R.O.C. TEL:(089)510666 FAX:(089)510678

22.
Tourism

Above: Confucius' birthday—a national holiday in Taiwan—is commemorated with a solemn yet elaborate dawn ceremony at Taipei's Confucius Temple.

Right: The Taipei International Food Festival is a feast for the eyes as well as the stomach.

Previous page: The dragon dance is an inseparable part of Chinese New Year celebrations.

22 Tourism

Exotic culture, breathtaking scenery, priceless art, the entire range of Chinese cuisine, and hospitable people make the Republic of China an excellent destination for tourists. Travelers to the ROC can enjoy themselves in comfort with fast and convenient transportation, excellent hotels, and clean restaurants. Unfortunately, many visitors to Taiwan never go far beyond the main city of Taipei, and thereby deprive themselves of some rich Chinese cultural experiences and the island's own scenic wonders.

Northern Taiwan: Where Ancient and Modern Coexist

The ROC's "economic miracle" has put a modern face on Taipei and its people, but Taipei is still Chinese at heart. Its underlying current of traditional lifestyles and culture is fascinating for travelers. For those who know where to look, the city is alive with beauty and culture.

Taipei's National Palace Museum 國立故宮博物院 houses the world's largest collection of Chinese art treasures, which spans over five millennia of Chinese culture. Much of the immense collection of jade, porcelain, paintings, and bronzes is regularly rotated, making each visit unique. The museum has regular guided tours in several foreign languages, including English and French. English-language tours are given daily at 10:00 A.M. and 3:00 P.M., and self-guided tape tours in English and Japanese are also available.

The Chiang Kai-shek Memorial Hall 中正紀念堂 in Taipei is the island's most impressive monument to the late president. The memorial hall's massive marble edifice dominates beautiful gardens, graceful pavilions, and placid ponds. A Ming-style arch at the main entrance is flanked by two classical-style buildings: the National Theater 國家戲劇院 and the National Concert Hall 國家音樂廳.

Many temples of various sizes are scattered throughout Taipei. The Lungshan Temple 龍山寺 is the city's oldest and most famous, and it is one of Taiwan's finest examples of temple architecture. The striking ornamentation alone merits a visit. Stone columns, alive with historical figures dancing on the backs of intricately carved dragons, support a roof which is similarly adorned with more of the cavorting figures.

The World of Yesterday 昨日世界 offers visitors a glimpse of Chinese history and culture with displays of mythology, ancient toys and games, traditional handicrafts, and folk culture. Chinese opera and live demonstrations of crafts and folk arts are presented on Sundays and holidays. The World of Yesterday is located across from the Taipei Fine Arts Museum 台北市立美術館 on Chung Shan North Road.

The Lin Family Garden 林本源園邸 is Taiwan's best example of classical Chinese-style landscaping and architecture. It calls to mind a small, serene village from an earlier time. The garden contains exquisite pavilions, towers, cottages, bridges, artificial mountains, and placid pools, and offers views of distant mountains.

Directly north of Taipei is Yangmingshan National Park 陽明山國家公園, where visitors can find pristine waterfalls, volcanic craters, picturesque lakes, steaming hot springs, and in the springtime, cherry and azalea blossoms. Well-maintained walkways and trails lead to the park's main scenic spots, where there are picnic and recreation areas.

Other areas of northern Taiwan beyond the borders of Taipei City are rich in countryside beauty. The natural rock formations at Yehliu 野柳 "wild willows," on the north coast west of Keelung 基隆, are an example; weather, erosion, and other natural forces have etched the rocks into a variety of shapes.

The coastline east of Keelung, set aside as the Northeast Coast National Scenic Area 東北角海岸風景特定區, is one of the loveliest regions on the island. A drive through this scenic area offers vistas of enchanting beauty.

A notable feature of this area is the magnificent sandstone promontory that rises from the sea

General Information for Visitors to the Taiwan Area

Climate

Taiwan's climate is subtropical, with an average annual temperature of 21.7°C (71.2°F) in the north and 24.1°C (75.7°F) in the south. Summers, which last from May through September, are usually hot and humid with daytime temperatures from 27°C to 35°C (in the 80s and 90s Fahrenheit). Winters, from December through February, are short and mild. Snow falls only on the island's higher mountains.

Currency

The Republic of China's unit of currency is the New Taiwan Dollar (NT$). The exchange rate, around NT$27.5 to US$1 in mid-1996, has fluctuated greatly in recent years. Foreign currencies can be exchanged at government-designated banks, hotels, and shops. Receipts are given when currency is exchanged, and travelers wishing to exchange unused NT dollars before departure must present these receipts. Foreign traveler's checks can be cashed at hotels or at the local branches of the issuing banks.

Time Differential

All territories under ROC government control, including Taiwan, the Pescadore (P'enghu) Islands, Quemoy (Kinmen), Matsu, Orchid Island, and Green Island, are under one time standard, which is UTC +8 hours. The ROC observes the same time standard all year, i.e., there is no daylight savings time during the summer months. Thus, Taiwan's relative time differential with a given part of the world usually increases by an hour in the spring and correspondingly decreases by an hour in the fall.

Language

The national language of the ROC is Mandarin Chinese. Many people can speak some English (the most widely studied foreign language), but most taxi drivers do not.

---

at Lungtung 龍洞. Farther down the coast, pure white sand and azure waters make the Fulung Seaside Park 福隆海濱公園 one of Taiwan's best beaches. A system of wooden pavilions and walkways lends an intensely Chinese character to the Yenliao Seaside Park 鹽寮海濱公園, which boasts the island's finest seashore leisure facilities. The scenic area also has a Ch'ing dynasty footpath. Sailing, surfing, camping, and fishing equipment can be rented in places.

Taiwan's largest camping area opened toward the end of 1991 in the most beautiful part of the Northeast Coast National Scenic Area. Lungmen Riverside Camping Resort 龍門露營渡假基地, a short distance from Yenliao and Fulung, provides sightseeing, water sports, camping, and bicycling.

An old fort, fresh seafood, and beautiful sunsets make the quaint seaside town of Tamsui 淡水 a popular day trip from Taipei. Old-fashioned shops along the main road give visitors a feel for the town's history. Two colleges and a hospital built in the late 1800s by Western mis-

sionaries remain to this day. Fort San Domingo, which came to be known by the name "Red-haired Barbarian Fort" 紅毛城 once it came into Dutch possession, was built by the Spanish in 1629, occupied by the Dutch in 1642, leased to the British in 1867, and bombarded by the French in 1884.

Tamsui has many fine seafood restaurants with large selections of fresh delicacies on display. Some of the restaurants are built along the Tamsui River to provide diners a riverside view of Tamsui's spectacular sunset.

Wulai 烏來, just south of Taipei, is an aborigine enclave where visitors can witness the traditional dances and ceremonies of Taiwan's Atayal tribe or savor the sight of a powerful waterfall cascading through lush vegetation.

An hour south of Taipei, you can take a one-stop tour of China's Great Wall, Peking's Forbidden City, and the Temple of Heaven. The place is Window on China 小人國, which captures in miniature 130 of the best-known

General Information for Visitors to the Taiwan Area (continued)

Credit Cards & Traveler's Checks

Major credit cards (including American Express, Carte Blanche, MasterCard, Diners Club, and Visa) are accepted, and traveler's checks may be cashed at international hotels, tourist-oriented restaurants, souvenir shops, and most department stores.

Tipping

The standard tip is NT$50 per piece of luggage at airports. A 10 percent service charge is automatically added to room rates and meals at hotels and most restaurants. All other tipping is optional.

Business Hours

Most of the island's people work a five-and-a-half-day week. Banks are open from 9 A.M. to 3:30 P.M. Monday through Friday and from 9 A.M. to noon on Saturdays. Most commercial firms are open from 9 A.M. to 5:30 P.M. Monday through Friday and from 9 to noon on Saturdays. Department stores are open daily from either 10:30 or 11 A.M. to 9:30 P.M., and most other stores are open daily from 9 or 10 A.M. to 9 or 10 P.M. Government offices are open from 8:30 A.M. to 12:30 P.M. and 1:30 to 5:30 P.M. Monday through Friday, and from 8:30 A.M. to 12:30 P.M. on Saturdays.

Electricity & Water

Electrical power used throughout Taiwan is 110 volts AC, 60 cycles. Drinking water served at hotels and restaurants is distilled or boiled.

Vaccinations

Vaccinations are not normally required for entry into Taiwan.

structures in both Taiwan and the Chinese mainland. A recently added section features famous buildings from all over the world. The careful attention to detail includes thousands of living trees and shrubs which were carefully shaped and grown to the correct sizes to complement the various buildings. Window on China also has a classical Chinese garden, restaurants, snack bars, a tea house, amusement park, and souvenir shops.

Buddhist temples, shrines, and monasteries, evoking the flavor of ancient China, are perched on the cool, verdant hills of Lion's Head Mountain 獅頭山, about halfway between Taipei and Taichung.

A short trip through the lush countryside southwest of Taipei brings you to a small town that produces hand-painted replicas of elegant Ming (1368-1644) and Ch'ing (1644-1911) vases. Yingke 鶯歌 is Taiwan's pottery center, and the narrow streets are lined with shops selling an endless variety of ceramics, from simple earthenware tea sets to delicate statues. Some of the factories allow tours where visitors can watch potters working the clay and artists painting vases. One factory that welcomes individual visitors without prior arrangement and provides English-speaking guides is the China Art Ceramic Co. 市拿陶藝有限公司 in Yingke 鶯歌鎮. The information desk at the Yingke Town Hall can help arrange tours of other factories as well.

For tourists who enjoy shopping and munching on savory Taiwanese snacks, night markets are a good choice. The markets offer fun, bargains, and a lot of local color, and generally sell a variety of traditional products, casual clothes, fruit, snacks, and novelty items.

Night markets with the best bargains on food, fashions, and curios in the Taipei area include the Shihlin 士林 night market, north of the Grand Hotel; the Kungkuan 公館 night market, near National Taiwan University; the Shihta 師大 night market, on Shih Ta Road off Hoping East Road; Hua Hsi Street 華西街, also known as Snake Alley; Tung Hua Street 通化街, near the World Trade Center; Jaoho 饒

河 night market, in the Sungshan district; and Chingkuang 晴光 market, off Chung Shan North Road.

Central Taiwan: Enchanting Cascades and Snowy Peaks

The central region of Taiwan displays the full range of the island's beauty: mountain lakes and shining seas, roaring rivers and steaming hot springs, lofty snow-capped peaks and lush tropical valleys, emerald forests and craggy ravines.

Taichung is the major city in this region and is one of Taiwan's main business centers. Taichung's location, quality hotels, and convenient transportation make it a favorite starting point for trips to many of the island's tourist sites.

Encore Garden 亞哥花園, a masterpiece of landscape gardening, is located just ten kilometers northeast of Taichung. In addition to a tremendous variety of flowering plants, the garden also has snack bars, a children's playground, hiking trails, and camping and barbecue sites. In the evenings, a fountain lit by multicolored lights pulses in time to music.

A statue of a Buddha sits on Pakua Hill 八卦山 overlooking the small city of Changhua 彰化, southwest of Taichung. Inside the hollow statue dioramas illustrate Buddhist teachings, and visitors can view the surrounding area through the statue's eyes. Near Changhua is the brand-new Taiwan Folk Village 臺灣民俗村, which displays buildings from the past 300 years, offers demonstra-

Visa Information

Tourist visas for the Republic of China can be obtained from the ROC Ministry of Foreign Affairs and ROC embassies, consulates, and designated representative offices in foreign countries (see Appendix IV, Directory of ROC Representatives Abroad).

Foreign nationals may obtain a visitor visa if they hold a foreign passport or travel document valid for more than six months and wish to stay less than six months in the Republic of China for the purpose of business, sightseeing, family visits, study or training, visits by invitation (with letter of invitation), transit, technical assistance, medical treatment, and other legitimate activities.

Visa requirements include one completed application form, incoming and outgoing travel tickets (or a letter of confirmation from a travel agency), three photos, documents verifying the purpose of the visit (except for transit or sightseeing), and a letter of guarantee (in some cases).

Those holding a tourist visa may stay in the ROC for two weeks to 60 days and, unless restricted to two weeks, may apply for a maximum of two extensions of 60 days each, for a total of six months. The visa may be single- or multiple-entry and valid for up to one year (or up to five years for citizens of those countries that have signed reciprocal agreements with the ROC) for stays of up to six months. Holders of a tourist visa are not permitted to assume employment in the ROC.

Participants in major international meetings, and VIP visitors invited by the ROC government, may be issued visas upon arrival if their names are on an approved list.

Citizens of 15 countries, including the United States, Japan, Sweden, Spain, Portugal, Austria, France, Germany, the United Kingdom, the Netherlands, Belgium, Luxembourg, Canada, Australia, and New Zealand, may enter the ROC visa-free for stays of up to 14 days so long as their passports are valid for at least six months from the date of entry and they possess onward or return tickets with confirmed seats.

Complete information on ROC visas can be obtained from:

Bureau of Consular Affairs
Ministry of Foreign Affairs
3F, 2-2 Chinan Rd., Sec. 1
Taipei, Taiwan, ROC
Phone: 886-2-343-2888

tions of traditional handicrafts, and runs a series of folk art performances. Just past Changhua is the quaint old town of Lukang 鹿港 "deer harbor," one of Taiwan's most important historical and cultural towns, noted for its impressive Matsu and Lungshan temples as well as for the annual four-day Lukang Folk Arts Festival, which begins three days before the Dragon Boat Festival.

The Central Cross-island Highway 中橫公路, Asia's most beautiful mountain road, winds its way from just outside of Taichung over the Central Mountain Range and through Taroko National Park 太魯閣國家公園 to the island's east coast. This route offers broad vistas across cloud-filled valleys, mist-shrouded peaks, starry skies, beautiful sunrises, delightful forest walks, rushing mountain streams, and hot springs.

Southeast of Taichung lie some of the region's most popular scenic spots. Emerald waters and jade mountains, temples, hiking, boating, and a picturesque pagoda make Sun Moon Lake 日月潭 Taiwan's premier honeymoon resort. At the nearby Formosan Aboriginal Culture Village 九族文化村 , groups from Taiwan's nine aboriginal tribes perform traditional songs and dances with ancient musical instruments and use traditional tools to make handicrafts and other items. Exceptional beauty and serenity make the Hsitou Forest Recreation Area 台大溪頭實驗林場, south of Sun Moon Lake, a favorite getaway for honeymooners, hikers, and campers.

Nearby Mount Ali (Alishan) 阿里山 is well known for its view of the sunrise over a sea of clouds; blue peaks rise from a fleecy gray ocean which is gradually painted vivid colors by the sunrise as the clouds dissipate. Visitors can reach Mount Ali from the city of Chiayi by rail or bus, but the scenery along the 72-kilometer railway from Chiayi is worth the three-hour trip.

Some 15 kilometers away from Mount Ali is Mount Jade (Yüshan) 玉山, which at 3,952 meters is Northeast Asia's highest peak. Yüshan National Park 玉山國家公園, which is dominated by Mount Jade's massive slopes, is Taiwan's largest national park. Mount Jade's towering main peak can be reached from Mount Ali or via an ancient trail known as the Pat'ung Pass Road 八通關古道.

Southern Taiwan: Bucolic Scenes from the Past

Southern Taiwan is a study in contrasts. Bustling modern cities with all the latest amenities are surrounded by the pastoral panorama of old Taiwan.

Tainan, the island's oldest and fourth largest city, has the unhurried atmosphere of a small country town. It is filled with reminders of the city's past: gates, memorial arches, remnants of forts, and temples that date back three centuries or more.

Tainan's more than 200 temples provide some of the best remaining examples of traditional Chinese architecture in Taiwan. They range from the serene Confucius Temple 孔廟, built in 1666, to the elaborate new Temple of the Goddess of the Sea 聖母廟 at Luerhmen 鹿耳門, a complex built by some of Taiwan's finest artisans.

Tainan's other major historical sites include Fort Zeelandia 安平古堡 and Fort Provintia 赤崁樓, both originally built during the Dutch occupation in the 1600s, and the "new" Eternal Fortress 億載金城, built by the Chinese in 1876.

Due south of Tainan is the vibrant city of Kaohsiung, Taiwan's second largest city, foremost industrial center, and largest international port. Kaohsiung offers excellent shopping, dining, and night life, and is close to many notable tourist attractions. The hillside temples, pavilions, shaded terraces, and city view make Mount Longevity 壽山 worth a stop. Ch'eng Ch'ing Lake 澄清湖, just north of Kaohsiung, features a stately pagoda, islands, pavilions, tree-lined pathways, and a variety of recreational facilities. Both the graceful Spring and Autumn Pavilions 春秋閣 and the nearby Dragon and Tiger Pagodas 龍虎塔 stand in the placid waters of Lotus Lake 蓮池潭. Beside the lake are temples dedicated to Confucius and the God of War.

About an hour's drive northeast of Kaohsiung, the island's tallest image of a Buddha gazes at the surrounding rice paddies in the

Pertinent Customs Regulations for Inbound Passengers

Each person may bring into the ROC, duty-free, one liter of alcoholic beverages, 25 cigars, 200 cigarettes, or one pound of other tobacco products.

A written declaration is required when bringing dutiable articles into the ROC. Duty is charged on gold in excess of 62.5 grams in weight. No more than NT$40,000 in cash may be brought into the country by each passenger. Undeclared New Taiwan currency in excess of this amount will be confiscated. Incoming passengers who want to bring in more than NT$40,000 in cash should apply, prior to entry, for a permit from the Ministry of Finance. Any amount of foreign currency may be brought in, but must be declared.

There are severe penalties for the importation, use, possession, or sale of the following prohibited articles:
• Counterfeit currency or forging equipment;
• Gambling apparatus or foreign lottery tickets;
• Obscene or indecent materials;
• Firearms or weapons of any kind (including air guns) and ammunition;
• Controlled substances (drugs or narcotics) of a non-prescription and non-medical nature (including marijuana);
• Toy guns;
• Articles infringing on the patents, designs, trademarks, or copyrights of another person;
• Contraband articles as specified by other laws, e.g., fruit, animals, and pets.
Pursuant to the provisions of Paragraph 2 of Article 87 of the *Copyright Law*:
• Importation of any audio-visual work for archival purposes by an organization operated for scholarly, educational, or religious purposes and not for private gain shall be limited to one copy.
• Importation of any work other than an audio-visual work for library lending or archival purposes by an organization operated for scholarly, educational, or religious purposes and not for private gain shall be limited to no more than five copies.
• Importation of any work for the importer's private use and not for distribution shall be limited to one copy of a work at any one time.
• Importation of any work forming part of the personal baggage of any person arriving from outside the territory shall be limited to one copy of a work at any one time.

Source: Ministry of the Interior

countryside. The huge 120-meter gilt statue is surrounded by 480 life-size gold-colored Buddha images near the entrance to the Light of Buddha Mountain 佛光山, home to one of Taiwan's largest temple complexes and the island's center of Buddhist scholarship.

The southernmost point of Taiwan, about two hours from Kaohsiung, forms a crescent known as the Hengch'un "eternal spring" Peninsula 恆春半島. Kenting National Park 墾丁國家公園 encompasses much of the peninsula and offers spectacular shorelines with interesting coral and rock formations. Kenting also has some of Taiwan's best beaches, with clean white sand, seashells, and all kinds of water sports. Pleasant wooded paths wind through a large botanical garden which contains a variety of exotic plant life. Visitors can wander through unusual dryland coral formations or rest at pavilions and enjoy the view by the sea. Facilities include an international-class resort hotel and a variety of more economical lodgings for travelers on a budget.

Moon World 月世界 is an area of banana and jujube orchards, bamboo groves and fish ponds. It is named for its lunar landscape of sharp-peaked clay hills with steep, deeply eroded slopes and sawtooth ridges. One of the most interesting sites here is the unpredictable "mud volcano," a small crater filled with thin, cold mud through which gas bubbles occasionally rise to the surface. A deep rumble gives a warning just before the gas bursts through and whips the mud into a bubbling gray mass that spills out of the crater.

The Pescadore (P'enghu) Archipelago 澎湖群島 consist of 64 separate islands situated in the Taiwan Straits roughly midway between Taiwan and the Chinese mainland. Fishing is the major source of income in the Pescadores, and a meal of fresh seafood is a must for visitors. The islands offer a wide variety of sightseeing opportunities, with ancient temples, picturesque farms, windswept fishing villages, friendly people, fine beaches, and rugged coastlines. Fishing, swimming, snorkeling, scuba diving, wind surfing, and boating are the major recreational activities in the archipelago. The government established the P'enghu National Scenic Area 澎湖風景特定區 here in July 1995.

Eastern Taiwan: Unspoiled Natural Beauty

Eastern Taiwan has some of the island's most beautiful and accessible attractions, notably the Taroko Gorge and the East Coast National Scenic Area 東部海岸風景特定區.

Taroko Gorge, a spectacular marble-walled cleft that runs for 19 kilometers through the mountains near the east coast, is the premier feature of Taroko National Park. At the head of the gorge is the picturesque village of Tienhsiang 天祥, known for its suspension bridge and pagoda.

Located at the eastern end of the Central Cross-island Highway, the small city of Hualien 花蓮 is renowned for producing the best marble products on the island. The vast marble deposits in the area are sculpted into an amazing range of products such as animal figures, chess sets, wine and coffee sets, bookends, ash trays, kitchen utensils, and furniture.

Hualien is also popular for performances of song and dance by the island's aborigines. Nearly 80,000 aborigines reside in the area, most from the Ami tribe 阿美族. The annual Ami harvest festivals are elaborate spectacles of color, costume, and native music and dance. The festivals are held at more than 20 villages in Hualien and Taitung counties on various days in July and August. Traditional tribal dances are performed regularly at the Ami Culture Village 阿美文化村, about a 15-minute drive from Hualien.

Along most of its length, the coastal road from Hualien to Taitung in the south runs through the East Coast National Scenic Area, an isolated, unspoiled region where development is strictly controlled to preserve the area's natural beauty. The coastal highway's attractions include picturesque temples inside mountain caves, venerable banyan trees, coral reefs, fantastic rock formations, and deserted beaches that stretch for miles.

Just south of Taitung is the Chihpen Hot Springs 知本溫泉 resort, which offers several interesting sites for tourists. First is the Chihpen Hot Spring itself, which is open to the public. Nearby hotels provide more-private bathing. A short distance from the hotels, a path leads to the beautiful White Jade Waterfall 白玉瀑布. On a lane off the main road from Chihpen to Inner Hot Spring 內溫泉 is Chingchueh Temple 清覺寺, which boasts two large Buddha images: a bronze one from Thailand and a jade one from Burma. Inner Hot Spring, two kilometers down the main road from Chihpen Hot Spring, boasts newer hotels and a mineral water swimming pool. A suspension bridge leads to the Chihpen Forest Recreation Area 知本森林遊樂區, perched on a mountainside covered with bamboo groves and dense forests. The recreation area offers a riverside picnic spot, campground, bonfire area, flower garden, and footpath to a waterfall. Near the top is a huge banyan tree with long gnarled roots that half surround a restful pavilion.

Green Island 綠島, off the Pacific coast of Taiwan, is now part of the East Coast National Scenic Area. The island is known for its saltwater hot spring (said to be one of only three in the world), fantastic coral formations, and spectacular coastal scenery. The reefs, waters, and beaches around the island are great for fishing, swimming, scuba diving, and collecting seashells.

Just south of Green Island lies Orchid Island 蘭嶼, a small islet which takes its name from the wild orchids that grow in the hills. The Yami, Taiwan's smallest and most isolated aboriginal tribe, call it home. They do some farming but live mainly by fishing. The tribe's richly decorated wooden boats are built entirely by hand and joined together by wooden pegs (for more about the Yami, see Chapter 2, People).

Chinese Festivals

The Chinese lunar calendar is crowded with traditional festivals, most of which are observed with great pomp and ceremony in the Taiwan area. These festivals offer visitors fascinating insights into 5,000 years of Chinese culture (see Appendix VII, National and Popular Holidays).

The first major festival of the year is Chinese New Year, often called Lunar New Year 春節, the most important of annual festivals, followed by the Lantern Festival 元宵節 on the first full moon of the lunar calendar (usually during the month of February on the solar calendar). Next on the calendar is the birthday of Matsu, Goddess of the Sea, celebrated with elaborate rites at Matsu temples throughout Taiwan; tourists should visit Peikang 北港 "north harbor" to see the annual pilgrimage and elaborate celebrations. Boat races during the Dragon Boat Festival 端午節 commemorate an attempt to rescue a drowning poet-statesman. The Ghost Festival 中元節, when the gates of Hell open and spirits have a vacation in the land of the living, is marked by temple ceremonies, feasts for wandering ghosts,

Customs Regulations for Outbound Passengers

Except in the following cases, completion of the Outbound Passenger's Declaration Form is optional. Outbound passengers must declare to Customs in writing when:
• Carrying foreign currencies, New Taiwan Dollar notes, or gold or silver ornaments in excess of the designated amounts (see below);
• Carrying gold and/or silver ornaments and, when leaving the country within six months of arrival, the unused portion of foreign currencies in excess of the designated amounts (see below) which were declared to Customs on entry;
• Carrying commercial samples and/or dutiable items (cameras, tape recorders, calculators, etc.) which will be brought back duty-free in the future;
• Carrying computer information storage media, including magnetic tapes, magnetic disks, diskettes, punched cards, and punched tapes.

Passengers who do not make a declaration to Customs and are found, on their departure from the ROC, to be carrying gold, silver, New Taiwan Dollar notes, and/or foreign currencies in excess of the designated limits, shall have the excess amount confiscated. They may also be subject to punishment under the law.

The designated limits on gold and/or silver ornaments and currency which a passenger is allowed to carry on departure from the ROC are as follows: Up to 62.5 grams (or two market taels) of gold ornaments or coins; up to 625 grams (or 20 market taels) of silver ornaments or coins; up to US$5,000 in notes or the equivalent in foreign currencies; and up to NT$40,000 in notes and 20 coins (of the types in circulation) of New Taiwan Dollar specie.

Articles that may not be taken out of the country include unauthorized reprints or copies of books, records, and videotapes; genuine Chinese antiques, ancient coins, and paintings; and items prohibited from entry, such as firearms, drugs, counterfeit currency, and contraband.

For further Customs information, contact:

Directorate General of Customs
85 Hsin Sheng S. Rd., Sec. 1, Taipei
Phone: 886-2-772-2392

Visitor Information Sources

• *The Tourism Bureau, Ministry of Transportation and Communications (MOTC)*
  9th Fl., 280 Chung Hsiao E. Rd., Sec. 4, Taipei
  Phone: 886-2-349-1635
  Internet Address: http://www. tbroc. gov. tw/
• *Taiwan Visitors Association*
  5th Fl., 9 Min Chuan E. Rd., Sec. 2, Taipei
  Phone: 886-2-594-3261
• *The Tourist Information Hot Line*
  Phone: 886-2-717-3737
  The Tourism Bureau's Tourist Information Hot Line provides a wide range of assistance and information
in Chinese and English (and other languages as needed) to callers from anywhere in the ROC or the world.
The hot line operates every day of the year from 8 A.M. to 8 P.M., local time (UTC +8 hours).

• *Travel Information Service Centers*
  The Tourism Bureau's Travel Information Service Centers provide information to inbound and outbound
tourists. The Tourism Bureau operates service centers at Chiang Kai-shek International Airport in Taoyuan,
Sungshan Domestic Airport in Taipei, and these other locations:

Taichung:
4th Fl., 216 Min Chuan Rd.
Phone: 886-4-227-0421

Tainan:
10th Fl., 243 Min Chuan Rd., Sec.1
Phone: 886-6-226-5681

Kaohsiung:
5th Fl.-1, 235 Chung Cheng 4th Rd.
Phone: 886-7-281-1513

and other activities. The Mid-Autumn or Moon Festival 中秋節 celebrates the harvest moon and is passed by gazing at the moon and eating rich pastries known as "moon cakes" 月餅. Confucius' Birthday, also celebrated as Teachers' Day 教師節, is marked with an ancient dawn ceremony of dances, costumes, music, and other rites.

The last major festival of the year is Double Tenth National Day 雙十節, which commemorates the anniversary of the October 10, 1911, revolution which led to the overthrow of the Ch'ing dynasty and the founding of the Republic of China. It is marked with huge parades in front of Taipei's Presidential Office building, displays of martial arts, folk dances, and other cultural activities.

Cuisine

Because of China's widely diverse geography, each region has developed its own distinctive cuisine. During the major waves of immigration from the mainland to Taiwan in the last century, and especially following World War II, those diverse cuisines found their way to the island. At Taipei's top Chinese restaurants visitors can savor the true taste of Chinese cuisine.

Representative of western Chinese food is Szechwan cuisine 川菜, which along with its cousin, Hunan cuisine 湘菜, favors liberal use of garlic, scallions, and chilies. Szechwan food is distinguished by its hot peppery taste, while Hunan food is richer, either spicy and hot or sweet and sour. Chicken, pork, river fish, and shellfish are all popular items.

Shanghai cuisine 江浙菜 is the best known branch of the eastern Chinese style, and because of the city's proximity to the ocean, major lakes, and rivers, this culinary style is renowned for superb seafood. For the most part, Shanghai dishes are lightly spiced and relatively oily, and sauces tend to be rich and slightly sweet.

Basically mild Peking cuisine 北平菜 was developed in the area of the imperial palace and uses wheat rather than rice as a basic staple. Noodles, steamed breads, and various "buns," or "dumplings," are the distinguishing features of this cuisine.

Cantonese food 粵菜 tends to be more colorful and less spicy. It is usually stir-fried to preserve both texture and flavor. Cantonese food is probably the best known Chinese cuisine in the West, and a noon meal of dim sum 點心, featuring snack-sized servings, is a great way to pick and choose a large variety of items yet not feel overly full.

Taiwanese cooking 臺菜 is an interesting branch of the eastern Chinese style: light, simple, easy to prepare, and often liberally spiced with ginger. Like its Shanghai cousin, Taiwanese cuisine features excellent seafood.

ROC Tourism in 1995

After a five-year decline, visitor arrivals experienced a 14.97 percent upturn in 1994. This growth continued into 1995, although at a slower pace. Arrivals for the year rose 9.62 percent, bringing the total to 2.33 million. Tourism officials are expecting this slowdown in the rate of growth to continue, with an increase of 5 percent at most in 1996.

Tourism sources say that the most important factor behind the increase is the visa-free entry program that was implemented at the beginning of 1994. This program initially covered citizens of 12 countries and allowed stays of up to five days. In 1995 three more countries were added to the list, and the length of stay was increased to 14 days. Another factor in the growth of arrivals was an increase in the Tourism Bureau's budget for international promotion. For fiscal 1996, the government gave the bureau an addi-

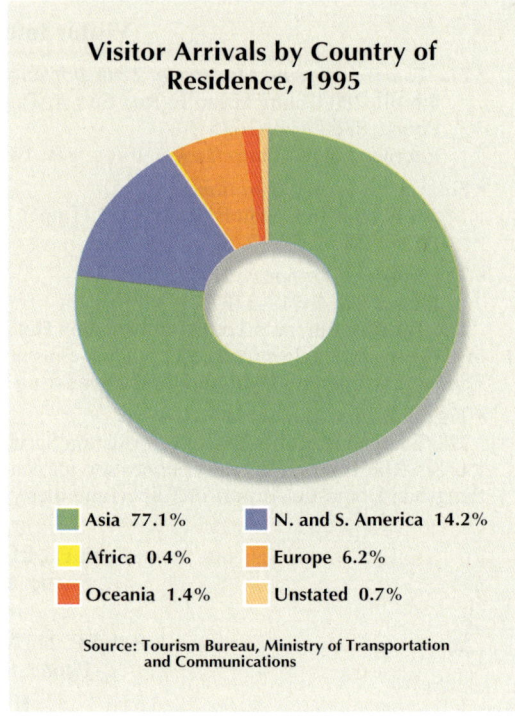

Visitor Arrivals by Country of Residence, 1995

Asia 77.1%   N. and S. America 14.2%
Africa 0.4%   Europe 6.2%
Oceania 1.4%   Unstated 0.7%

Source: Tourism Bureau, Ministry of Transportation and Communications

tional US$2 million for this purpose, bringing the total international promotion budget to a still-low US$5.5 million. About 20 percent of the additional funding has been absorbed by higher postage costs.

The bureau is striving to make the most of its financial resources by going onto the Internet. It has also increased allocations to overseas branch offices, demanding more effective work and setting up a review system to monitor performance. In addition, the Seoul branch office, which had been closed for years following the rupture in diplomatic ties with South Korea, was reopened in 1995. A branch office in Hong Kong, the bureau's tenth, was opened in June 1996.

Surprisingly, the highest growth rates in 1995 were recorded for arrivals from countries not on the visa-free list. This was due largely to the introduction of large numbers of foreign workers into Taiwan, which contributed to increases in arrivals of 12.23 percent from Malaysia, 18.19 percent from Indonesia, 26.57 percent from the Philippines, and 27.57 percent from Thailand.

Arrivals from Japan grew at a healthy rate of nearly 11 percent. This performance is especially significant in view of Japan's importance as Taiwan's main source of tourists. In 1995, Japanese swelled the arrivals total by 914,325. The growth in visitors from Europe, by contrast, fell to a below-average 7.15 percent. Austrian visitors were responsible for the greatest European increase, up 20.41 percent, but total arrivals from that country were only 4,289.

The US remained by far the largest market in the Americas, accounting for more than 290,000 of Taiwan's visitor arrivals in 1995. However, in terms of growth, this figure represents a low 1.19 percent. The number of Canadian visitors grew by 9.67 percent to 27,496. Australia and New Zealand are new and still relatively small markets, but arrivals from these two countries increased by high rates of 12.11 percent and 14.49 percent, respectively.

The growth in arrivals continued through the first four months of 1996, though at a much reduced rate of just under 3 percent. This brought the four-month total to 742,414. Asian markets as a whole grew 4.04 percent during the period, largely because of a 14.00 percent increase from Japan. Arrivals from the Americas, dragged down by a 3.50 percent drop in the number from the US, declined 2.87 percent. The European market grew by a respectable 5.30 percent, while the number of visitors from Australia and New Zealand grew by over 5 percent. Arrivals from Africa plummeted by 20.62 percent, but fortunately for Taiwan's tourism figures, the numbers from that continent were too small to have much of an impact on overall performance.

Outbound travel by ROC nationals had been growing at double-digit rates for years, pushing the total number of departures to over 5 million annually, or the equivalent of roughly one-fourth of the entire population. With such a large base, it was inevitable that the growth rate would slow down, and in 1994 it plummeted to just 1.93

percent. However, in 1995 the figure rebounded to 9.36 percent, bringing the total number of overseas trips taken by Taiwan residents to 5,188,658. In the first four months of 1996, the growth rate dropped again, to 2.47 percent. The number of outbound travelers for the period was 1,770,933.

Precisely where all the outbound travelers go is something of a mystery, since travelers going abroad are no longer required to fill out departure forms stating their destination. When compiling destination figures, authorities therefore must rely on the first landing point of the flights on which passengers depart, which is not necessarily accurate. It is clear, however, that the vast majority go to nearby destinations in Asia, especially Hong Kong (from where most travelers from Taiwan continue on to destinations in mainland China) and Japan.

The United States is the third-largest overseas destination, and the number of travelers to that

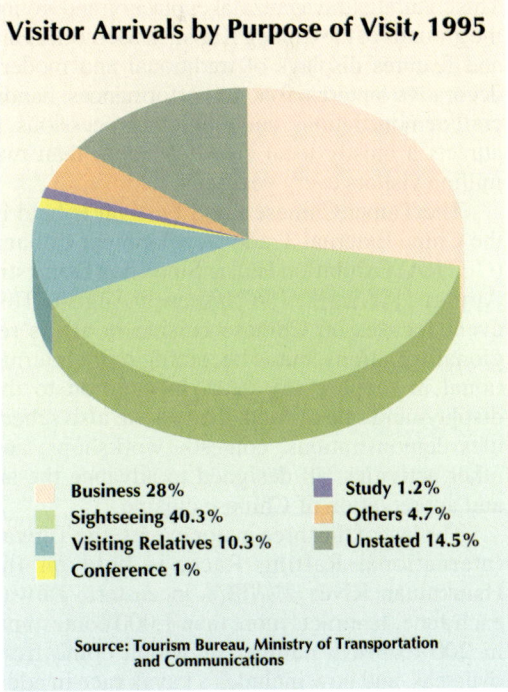

Visitor Arrivals by Purpose of Visit, 1995

Business 28%
Sightseeing 40.3%
Visiting Relatives 10.3%
Conference 1%
Study 1.2%
Others 4.7%
Unstated 14.5%

Source: Tourism Bureau, Ministry of Transportation and Communications

country grew by a rapid 15.2 percent in 1995. The number of outbound trips to Canada was also up by a strong 10.68 percent in the same year. Travel to Europe grew at a phenomenal pace of more than 104 percent in 1995, partly because of new direct flight routes between the ROC and that continent. Travel to Australia and New Zealand is burgeoning, but departures to Africa dropped by almost 7 percent in 1995.

Among its other promotional activities, the Tourism Bureau strives to bring in more foreign tourists while also providing local residents with a greater diversity of cultural and recreational activities. The bureau sponsors three major events each year: the Taipei Lantern Festival 台北燈會, the Taipei Chinese Food Festival 台北美食節, and the Taiwan International Rafting Race 國際泛舟比賽.

The Taipei Lantern Festival is held around the time of the traditional Chinese Lantern Festival, which falls two weeks after Chinese New Year on the first full moon of the year (usually in February). This cultural extravaganza takes place on and around the grounds of the Chiang Kai-shek Memorial Hall and features displays of traditional and modern decorative lanterns, folk art performances, handicraft demonstrations, and religious processions. It attracts a mostly local crowd of more than two million visitors every year.

The Taipei Chinese Food Festival is held in the China External Trade Development Council (CETRA) Exhibition Hall at Sungshan Domestic Airport 外貿協會松山展覽館 each August. This event focuses on Chinese cuisine in all its regional variations, but is becoming more international in scope every year. In addition to the displays and sale of food, the festival also schedules demonstrations, contests, workshops, and other activities, all designed to advance the art and appreciation of Chinese cuisine.

The last of the three major events, the Taiwan International Rafting Race, is held on the Hsiukuluan River 秀姑巒溪 in eastern Taiwan each June. It attracts more than 1,000 contestants in 200 teams, a number of which come from overseas, and now includes a kayak race in addi-

tion to the rafting competition. Another major event, the Taipei International Travel Fair 台北國際旅展, has become one of the largest and most important shows of its kind in Asia. It is held every two years and attracts dense crowds of local residents as well as large numbers of foreign delegates, most of whom want to develop Taiwan's huge outbound travel market. The next fair will be held in late 1997.

New Attractions

To keep tourists coming in ever-greater numbers and to provide a wider range of recreational choices, the Tourism Bureau is promoting a number of other attractions and activities. A series of mountain-climbing brochures has been published, one of which focuses on the 3,952-meter Mount Jade, the highest peak in Northeast Asia. Other new brochures cover different walking tours of Taipei and the quaintly scenic Chichi 集集 railway line in Chiayi County. A new booklet covers scuba diving, and another focuses on bird watching. A brochure now being prepared will describe Chiufen 九份, an old gold-mining town not far from Taipei. Mountain biking is another activity which the Tourism Bureau wants to develop in Taiwan.

Among the bureau's other efforts are the development and management of national scenic areas. The bureau itself plans and manages these areas and builds infrastructural facilities such as parking lots, pavilions, beach amenities, hiking trails, toilets, marinas, and food and beverage outlets. The private sector is then encouraged to invest in hotels, restaurants, and recreational facilities.

There are currently three national scenic areas, one on the northeast coast, one on the east coast, and one in the Pescadore (P'enghu) Islands. A preparatory office has been established for a fourth national scenic area at Tap'eng Bay 大鵬灣 in southwestern Taiwan, and a fifth is being considered for the valley that runs from Hualien to Taitung on the eastern part of the island.

Another new attraction is the Guinness World of Records Museum in Taichung. In addition to the unique architecture of the buildings, this new museum is said to be the largest of its kind in the world.

The fortress island of Quemoy 金門, situated less than two kilometers off the coast of the Chinese mainland, was opened to tourism in 1992. Besides its historical military interest (the failure of fierce attacks on this island discouraged communist forces from trying to invade Taiwan in the late 1940s and 1950s), Quemoy is also a fascinating repository of traditional Chinese architecture and culture.

In addition to pure tourism, growing numbers of foreign visitors come to Taiwan for international meetings and conventions, and the island's top hotels provide a wide range of meeting facilities and services. The premier convention venue, the Taipei International Convention Center 台北國際會議中心, opened in 1991 and is praised as one of the best such facilities in the world. The TICC is managed by CETRA, which is also in charge of the Taipei World Trade Center Exhibition Hall next door.

Accommodations

Three new hotels opened for business in 1995: the 148-room Howard Prince in Taichung, the 322-room Linden in Kaohsiung, and the 436-room Grand Hi-Lai, also in Kaohsiung. At the end of April 1996, Taiwan had a total of 79 registered tourist-class hotels with a total of 19,905 rooms, and at least 13 more properties with 3,402 rooms are scheduled to open by the end of the century. The year of 1996 alone should see the opening of the 239-room Howard Plaza in Kaohsiung, the 85-room King One Resort in Kaohsiung County, and the 225-room Grand Formosa Taroko in Hualien County. In Taipei, the existing Imperial Hotel is undergoing renovation in preparation for joining the Inter-Continental chain in 1997.

Hotels in Taiwan used to be rated by a plum blossom system analogous to the star system used internationally. The Tourism Bureau has long wanted to revise this system to portray the true class of the island's hotels more clearly, but numerous hotels resisted this change, fearing their certain downgrading, and the plum blossom system was therefore abandoned. Tourist hotels in Taiwan today are officially classified in just two categories, tourist class and international tourist class. In addition to the rated hotels, there are numerous unrated ones, some of which are quite luxurious and expensive. Others are inexpensive hostels and youth activity centers which vary widely in price, facilities, and services.

In addition to the usual guest rooms, shopping arcades, swimming and health facilities, entertainment systems, and business centers, Taiwan's hotels also offer fine dining. While most of the best Chinese restaurants on the island are independent establishments, some are also found inside international-class hotels. In the case of Western cuisine, top hotels frequently offer the best quality.

Transportation

Surface travel in the ROC is extremely convenient and reasonably priced. Express buses link all cities, towns, and scenic spots, and it is now possible to travel around the island of Taiwan entirely by train. Rental cars are widely available, although the major international car rental agencies have not yet succeeded in setting up their own fleet operations in the local market. To rent a car in Taiwan requires an international or ROC driver's license plus a major credit card or, frequently, a sizable deposit. Visitors who are reluctant to drive themselves, as most are given the island's ill-marked roads and chaotic traffic, can hire cars with drivers.

Major urban areas have comprehensive and convenient public bus services. Taxis are abundant, but few drivers speak any non-Chinese language. The first line of the island's premier mass rapid transit system recently began operating in Taipei, and additional systems are planned for other large cities as well. As for air travel, there are also over 50 international and domestic airlines now serving the ROC (for additional information see Chapter 14, Transportation).

SYM

往世界的頂端前進
RUN TO THE TOP

43年研發經驗和技術，
超過五百萬台銷售實績，以及通過ISO 9001國際標準，
三陽機車行銷網遍及亞洲、中南美洲、歐洲、非洲及大洋洲，
現在以"SYM"做為行銷世界統一形象。
SYM統合3S(完整的銷售、完善的服務、完備的零件)主張，
發展出"完全銷售服務"新策略。

43 years of experience and technology
in research and development,
Over 5,000,000 motorcycles and scooters sold,
And awarded the international recognition-ISO 9001
Quality Assurance Certificate.

Sanyang's sales network extends to all over Asia,
South & Central America, Europe, Africa, and Oceania.

Now, to unify international brand image,
Sanyang launches "SYM" as the new worldwide trademark.

SYM integrates the 3S principles, comprehensive sales,
satisfying service, and sufficient spare parts,
and gives you the best satisfaction with its complete sales and service.

"Most Innovative New Product for '97"

Giant's Compact Road Bikes

TCR 2   MCR 1

Frame Geometry

- Smaller frames - standard 46cm on all carbon fiber bikes
- Lighter weight, quicker handling, stiffer for better acceleration
- Blazing aerodynamics

Customized Fit

- Seat posts come in 7 sizes
- Adjustable stems come in 3 sizes

Leading Innovation

- Designed by Mike Burrows
- Manufactured by Giant

⊘GIANT

23.
Sports and
Recreation

Above: Taiwan's many miles of seashore, such as Fulung Seaside Park 福隆海濱公園 in the north of the island, provide ample opportunities for outdoor water recreation.

Right: Venues like the Roxy provide Taipei nightgoers with a Western-style coffeehouse atmosphere to supplement the choice of pubs, discos, bowling alleys and *karaoke* parlors.

Previous page: Birdwatchers lined up in Kenting National Park 墾丁國家公園 to enjoy a sightly sample of the wide variety of migratory birds that annually sojourn to Taiwan's forests and shores.

23 Sports and Recreation

The six-day work week and predilection of ROC citizens to put in long work hours may be the hallmark of the Taiwan "economic miracle," but as the standard of living on Taiwan continues to rise, citizens increasingly seek a more balanced lifestyle of sports and recreational activities that will provide a suitable physical and spiritual counterpoise to the frenetic pace of national development and raising national competitiveness. Healthy habits of proper exercise acquired early in life by students, and plentiful and well-appointed recreational facilities readily accessible to old and young alike have become more and more prominent goals in educational reform proposals and government plans. The growing value placed on exercise and leisure is also apparent at the individual consumer level. According to the Directorate-General of Budget, Accounting and Statistics 行政院主計處 (DGBAS), spending on sports and recreation by ROC citizens has increased by an average of 10 percent each year over the last decade. This chapter seeks to provide a reasonably balanced answer by introducing the sports programs and recreational options available to the public. First, though, it describes the sports and recreation infrastructure in the Taiwan area and details major government programs to bring sports to all the people.

Sports Facilities

In densely populated Taiwan, it takes time, money, and determination to participate in a sport. Just finding a place to play tennis or go jogging is often a major undertaking. The government, therefore, places a high priority on providing sports facilities. The Taiwan area has 45 major public stadiums with artificial tracks at various locations. Each county and major city in Taiwan has school playgrounds and a network of baseball parks.

Under the Ministry of Education's "sports for all people" 全民運動campaign begun in 1979, a total of 52 public recreation centers have been built around the island, each with a track, swimming pool, gymnasium, and tennis courts. An additional 4,000 elementary, 2,000 junior high, 400 senior high schools, and 130 colleges open their facilities to the public for a few hours each day.

Other facilities available to serious athletes in Taiwan include first-class living and training facilities at the Tsoying National Sports Training Center 左營運動訓練中心 and the Northern National Sports Training Center 北部運動訓練中心. In 1995, the two training centers put 735 athletes through a rigorous one- to two-month training to prepare for international competitions overseas. Taiwan has one stadium for soccer in Taipei, Chungshan Soccer Stadium 中山足球場, and two major competition arenas for track and field, Taipei Municipal Stadium 台北市立體育館 and Kaohsiung Municipal Stadium 高雄市立體育館. The island's largest competition-level indoor facility for basketball burned down in 1988, but was replaced by a much improved facility constructed at the National College of Physical Education and Sports 國立體育學院 in Linkou 林口, a suburb of Taipei.

Baseball fans are eagerly awaiting the construction of a domed stadium in Taipei. It is to be built on the site of the current Taipei City Baseball Stadium 臺北市立棒球場 and finished by the year 2001. A smaller indoor stadium will also be built in Tienmu 天母 on the outskirts of Taipei. This 16-hectare sports stadium, which will include a baseball stadium, swimming pools, and tennis courts, is expected to cost the Taipei city government almost US$1 billion for land acquisition alone.

Sports in the Schools

Physical education is a required subject in every elementary school, secondary school, college and university. However, in reality, physical education instruction programs in schools have traditionally been kept to a minimum in order to allow students more time to prepare for the all-important high school and college entrance exams. In practice, junior and senior high school students are only required to take two hours of P. E. class per week. Although they can also choose athletics for their two hours of weekly electives,

Hierarchy of ROC Government Units in Charge of Sports

Sports are subsumed under the government-run educational system. The government budget for sports is inextricably linked with the budget for education, and government educational units at each level of government are responsible for overseeing sports and sports-related activities in their jurisdictions.

The Ministry of Education 教育部 (MOE), the highest government agency in charge of education affairs, is likewise the highest government agency concerned with sports and recreation. The MOE has established a Committee for National Physical Education 國民體育委員會, which is responsible for policymaking, and a Department of Physical Education 體育司, which is responsible for testing, implementing and offering guidance on physical education-related policies.

Taiwan Province has a Department of Education 教育廳, and the special municipalities of Taipei and Kaohsiung also call their corresponding agencies departments of education 教育局. Bureaus of education under county and city governments have physical education and health care sections. Rural townships, townships, cities, and districts all have officials in charge of local sports activities.

In addition to government units, the Republic of China also has private physical education organizations which accept governmental guidance and promote various kinds of sporting events; physical education funds set up by sports enthusiasts to promote physical education; large enterprises which sponsor company teams for competition; and service groups such as the China Youth Corps, Lions Clubs, Rotary Clubs, and the Kiwanis, which commonly hold sports-related events.

most students use this time to study. In order to alter this situation, it has been suggested that physical fitness be included in the entrance evaluations to senior highs and colleges.

The regular P.E. courses cover physical hygiene and sports physiology, and are also designed to cultivate skills in a wide variety of sports including tennis, track and field, baseball and the martial arts. In practice, although the limited time available does not allow many students to become proficient at any particular sport, they do, however, get a good introduction to a variety of sports skills and games.

The government has had more success with programs that focus on physical health. It is currently reviewing the physical education curriculum and revising physical education textbooks. As part of the push to promote student health, the government has also drafted the Five-year Plan to Develop and Improve School Lunches 發展與改進學校午餐五年計畫, and established a student health checkup system. Currently, only 64 percent of the elementary schools around the island supply pupils with lunch.

Baseball is the most popular extracurricular activity. Little League baseball is now offered to both boys and girls in about 47 percent of elemen-tary and junior high schools, 16 percent of high schools, and a small fraction of colleges. Basketball is also popular. In 1995, nearly 60 percent of junior high schools and 50 percent of high schools had a basketball program. Other extracurricular sports range from softball, volleyball, table tennis, and badminton to judo, taekwondo, and kendo. Most schools have their own dance clubs, marching bands, drill teams, and ping-pong clubs.

Sports After Graduation

After graduating from high school, athletes have relatively little chance to continue their sporting careers. Most dedicated athletes have to choose between taking exams or training. Since 1992, the best players have been able to attend one of the nine colleges specializing in sports. Other universities and colleges can also recruit outstanding athletes according to individual need. In practice, this option remains limited since athletes are only admitted if they happen to meet the needs of the school's sports teams. Most athletes still end up majoring in physical education at one of the sports colleges.

Many in Taiwan believe that creating more options for athletes would make individual competitors happier and would also speed the development of Taiwan's college sports by spreading the best athletes throughout the school system. The result would be a more equal development of sports and a more competitive field for athletes.

In June 1996, a total of 229 students graduated from the National College of Physical Education and Sports 國立體育學院. For the majority of them, like most athletes nearing college graduation, the end of school meant the end of their athletic careers.

Amateur Sports in the ROC
The ROC Sports Federation

The Republic of China Sports Federation 中華民國體育運動總會 is the primary body in charge of amateur sports in the ROC. The federation is under the jurisdiction of and receives funding from the Ministry of Education's Department of Physical Education.

The primary functions of the Sports Federation are to provide its member sports associations with technical and administrative assistance, to raise their sports standards and administrative efficiency, to increase participation in international competitions, and to train good athletes. The following 54 sports are represented by national sports associations that belong to the federation: aikido, airsports, alpine sports, archery, badminton, baseball, basketball, billiards, bodybuilding, bowling, boxing, canoeing and kayaking, crossbow, cycling, dancing sports, equestrian, fencing, folk sports, football (soccer), gateball, golf, gymnastics, handball, hockey, judo, karate, kendo, korfball, kuoshu, luge and bobsledding, pentathlon and biathlon, powerlifting, roller skating, rowing, rugby, shooting, skating, skiing, softball, soft tennis, swimming, table tennis, taekwondo, tai chi chuan 太極拳, tchoukball, tennis, tug-of-war, volleyball, water skiing, track and field, weightlifting, wrestling, and yachting. Sports associations serving the armed forces and universities, district sporting associations (Taiwan Province, Taipei, Kaohsiung, and Quemoy 金門), and associations of athletic trainers and the disabled are also members of the federation.

The Sports Federation operates the Tsoying National Sports Training Center and the Northern National Sports Training Center to train national team members preparing for international competition. These centers provide accommodations, coaching, training facilities, and pocket money for athletes. The federation is planning a sports center on Mount Ali in central Taiwan to provide athletes with high-altitude training.

The Sports Federation also has been engaged in sports science research aimed at furthering athletic performance and prevention and care of injuries. A key component of this work was the

New Steps for Developing Athletic Talent

To discover and start training potentially outstanding athletes at an early age, the government has set up athletic aptitude classes in elementary and high schools throughout Taiwan. National sports foundations are responsible for selecting and training young people with superior athletic talent for participation in large-scale international competitions such as the Olympics and the Asian games. The ROC government rewards successful athletes with the Chungcheng Physical Education Award 中正體育獎章 or the Kuokuang Physical Education Award 國光體育獎章, and provides these athletes with educational or vocational guidance. In fiscal 1996, some US$4.64 million was awarded to local athletes through these prestigious awards.

Increased funding from the Ministry of Education for school athletic teams made it possible to maintain 570 primary school baseball teams in 1996. The ministry's plan also includes selecting various primary and junior high schools to specialize in a specific sport. For example, the Keelung Girls' High School 基隆女中 is building its taekwondo team while Taipei's Yucheng Elementary School 玉成國小 is expanding its swimming program. The ministry hopes to foster cooperation between these selected schools and the various national sports associations. In 1991, the MOE and the ROC Amateur Archery Association 中華民國射箭協會 began developing an archery program at Minglien Elementary School 明廉國小 in Hualien 花蓮.

establishment of a sports medicine research center at Veterans General Hospital 榮民總醫院 in Taipei, the largest hospital in Taiwan. There is also a center for sports medicine at the Navy General Hospital 海軍總醫院 in Kaohsiung for athletes in southern Taiwan. The federation also participates in international sports exchanges and has signed official sports exchange agreements with Hungary, South Korea, Germany, Peru, Guatemala, Paraguay, Argentina, Italy, Costa Rica, Nicaragua, and Uruguay.

International Competition

Since the 1984 Olympics, the Republic of China has competed in international competitions under the banner of "Chinese Taipei." Today, ROC athletes compete all over the world. In 1995 alone, 498 ROC teams with 3,839 athletes participated in international tournaments and competitions. Chinese Taipei teams attend an average of 46 international championships a year. In order to prepare for these championships, each national association holds its own championships to choose the best athletes.

1996 Summer Olympic Games

The Chinese Taipei team at the 1996 Atlanta Olympics consisted of 72 athletes competing in 13 sports: track and field, swimming, table tennis, tennis, weightlifting, shooting, judo, cycling, boxing, badminton, archery, and softball. Chen Ching 陳靜 won a silver medal in woman's table tennis, Taiwan's fifth-ever Olympic medal. At the 1960 Rome Olympics, Yang Chuankwang 楊傳廣 was awarded a silver medal in the decathlon. At the 1968 Mexico Olympics, Chi Cheng 紀政 gained a bronze medal in the women's 100m hurdle. At the 1984 Los Angeles Olympics, Tsai Wen-i 蔡溫義 won a bronze medal in weightlifting. The ROC team defeated Japan to win a silver medal in baseball at the 1992 Barcelona Olympics.

Other International Championships

Besides the Olympic and Asian Games, Chinese Taipei teams compete in a number of

Chinese Taipei Olympic Committee

Officially recognized by the International Olympic Committee, the Chinese Taipei Olympic Committee 中華奧林匹克委員會 (CTOC) is the sole sports organization with exclusive powers to organize and field representative delegations from the ROC at the Olympic Games, the Asian Games, and other international sports competitions recognized by the International Olympic Committee.

The mission of the Chinese Taipei Olympic Committee is to promote the Olympic Movement in the Republic of China in accordance with the Olympic Charter. CTOC members are approved by the CTOC Executive Board upon recommendation of the CTOC president. Currently, there are 59 members, the majority of whom are presidents of national sports associations.

The CTOC works hand-in-hand with the International Olympic Committee, the Olympic Council of Asia, the Association of National Olympic Committees, the General Association of International Sports Federations, and the Asian, Pacific and Oceania Sports Assembly. It also maintains close relations with other national Olympic committees worldwide.

international championships every year. At the 1995 World University Games in Fukuoka, Japan, the Chinese Taipei team won one gold, one silver, and one bronze. Tennis player Wang Shiting 王思婷 was the team's biggest winner, taking home three medals in mixed doubles, women's doubles, and the women's singles. In the inaugural Pacific Rim Games in Cali, Colombia in July 1995, the Chinese Taipei team, consisting of 70 athletes, including a 22-member baseball team, won 11 gold, 16 silver, and 14 bronze medals.

While the Chinese Taipei baseball team followed up its silver medal at the 1992 Barcelona Olympic Games with a disappointing fourth-place finish in the 1995 Asian Championships, the Fuhsing 復興 team from Kaohsiung City won the 1996 Little League World Series. It was the 17th championship in 21 attempts for a ROC team at Williamsport, Pennsylvania. Also in 1996, the Chinese Taipei team won the World Big League championship for the fourth consecutive year.

The Chinese Taipei basketball teams have also had success. The men's and women's teams both placed fourth at the 1995 Asian Championships. At the 1995 Asian Championships in Jakarta, the Chinese Taipei track and field team earned three medals with Hsu Pei-ching 徐佩菁 winning a gold medal in the 400m hurdles. In the inaugural World University Archery Championship held in France in March, 1996, the ROC team garnered three golds, one silver, and two bronzes.

Finally, the ROC has achieved marked successes in bowling. At the 1996 Asian Championships in Seoul, the ROC team won two golds, one silver, and one bronze. Tsai Jung-kun 蔡榮坤 and Liu Yung-lung 劉泳隆 won the gold medal in men's twins. Tseng Su-fen 曾素芬, Chou Miao-ling 周妙玲, and Hsu Su-chiu 徐素秋 won the women's trio gold medal. At the Pre-Olympic World Bowling Championship, held in July 1996 at Atlanta, Tseng Su-fen

Promotion of Sports in the Schools

Since the late 1980s, the Ministry of Education has taken several significant steps toward promoting sports in the schools. The ministry launched a US$740 million *National Physical Education Development Medium-Range Plan* 國家體育建設中程計畫 from1989 to 1993 that calls for the construction of 100 athletic facilities at schools islandwide and 36 basic recreation centers and parks in various counties and cities. To date, 100 stadiums have been constructed at elementary and secondary schools.

In an effort to establish an integrated system for the training of athletes, the government set up the National Taitung Experimental Senior High School of Physical Education 國立台東體育實驗高級中學 in 1995. To better guide and reward highly-gifted athletes, government education units revised the *Regulations for the Counseling and Academic Advancement of Athletically Gifted Secondary School Students* 中等學校運動成績優良學生升學輔導辦法.

won the bronze medal, beating 11 athletes representing different continents. In the same competition, Yang Cheng-ming 楊振明 ranked seventh in the men's singles.

World Sports Events in the ROC

The ROC hosts a growing number of international competitions in Taiwan, furthering international exchange and providing top-notch competition for Taiwan sports fans. First held in Taiwan in 1977, the annual R. William Jones Cup men's and women's basketball tournaments feature national teams from all over the world. In 1996, teams from the ROC, the United States, Canada, South Korea, North Korea, Australia, Japan, Russia, Thailand, Slovakia, Saudi Arabia, and the Philippines competed for the title in this tournament. It is one of the ROC's most popular sporting events, with the finals drawing thousands of fans to seven domed stadiums islandwide.

The 15th Asian Rugby Football Union Tournament was held in Taipei in November 1996, with eight Asian nations competing in the games. The second Taipei International Rugby Football Sevens was held on October 14 and 15, 1995, during which 24 countries participated. The ROC hosts an annual track and field competition called the Chinese Taipei CKS Cup and International Friendship Athletic Meet. Athletes from 13 Asian countries participated in the meet held at a first-class facility in Taoyuan in 1995. World-class international women's volleyball also comes to Taiwan. The Taipei leg of the US$2 million 1996 World Volleyball Grand Prix tour was held in September with national teams from Brazil, Japan, South Korea, and Cuba participating. The 1996 Worldwide Intercollegiate Rowing Invitational Regatta was held in Tungshan River, Ilan 宜蘭冬山河. Ten universities, including Britain's Oxford and Cambridge, as well as America's Yale and Harvard, participated.

The Taiwan Women's Tennis Open, a stop on the Women's Tennis Association (WTA) tour, is held every September in Taipei. In 1996, three rounds of the China Open Circuit were held in Taipei during March, June, and July. Tennis

Training Facilities

The facilities at the three sports colleges and at university sports departments vary widely. At the National Taiwan College of Physical Education 國立台灣體育學院 and the Taipei Physical Education College 台北市立體育學院, much of the equipment is older. In contrast, the nine-year-old National College of Physical Education and Sports is equipped with international-class training facilities. Located on a 66-hectare site near the northern town of Linkou, this school is considered Taiwan's best sports institution. Students can earn undergraduate degrees in health, physical education, or sports technique, and graduate degrees in physical education or sports science. Entrance into the undergraduate health program is by written examination, but applicants must also be top athletes for admission to the physical education and sports science programs.

players from Japan, Korea, and America participated in this competition with a total prize of US$60 thousand. The ROC's Weng Tzu-ting 翁子婷 won the women's singles. In table tennis, the National Chain Store World All-Stars in June 1995 featured the top players from the ROC, mainland China, Croatia, Sweden, and South Korea, and was broadcast across Asia on ESPN. Taiwan also hosted the Asian Women All-Stars Table Tennis tournament in November 1995 with the world's two top ranked players from mainland China defending their titles.

Taiwan Area Games

The largest annual amateur sports competition in the ROC is the Taiwan Area Games held annually in October. The games are held on a rotating basis either in Taipei City, Kaohsiung City, or a city or county of Taiwan Province. The 1996 games were held in P'ingtung City 屏東市, while the 1995 games were held in Kaohsiung City. In 1995, city and county sports associations and two teams from the US and the Philippines sent 10,571 athletes to compete in 39 sports.

Kuoshu

The development of traditional Chinese sports is vital to the preservation of Chinese culture. Kuoshu 國術 or "Chinese martial arts" is a collective name for more than 20 different styles of martial arts, including the better known tai chi chuan. Kuoshu is a recognized sport in the Asian Games. Reflective of the commitment to kuoshu, the Chinese Taipei Kuoshu Federation receives funding directly from the Ministry of Education, and the ROC is the headquarters of the International Chinese Kuoshu Federation. In July 1996, the Chinese Taipei Kuoshu Federation was invited by its American subsidiary to attend the 1996 United States Chinese Kuoshu Invitational Tournament. The tournament was held in Baltimore with 16 countries in attendance. The ROC hosted the 8th World Kuoshu Cup in November 1996 with athletes from 50 nations competing.

Training Amateur Athletes

Compared with some neighboring countries, the ROC has not achieved a high level of excellence in international sport competition. For example, the ROC has never won an Olympic gold medal. A key reason, as in many countries, is a lack of funding. While the Ministry of Education gives large cash rewards to some champions (e.g., each member of the silver medal-winning 1992 Olympic baseball team earned US$190,000), government funding for most national sports associations only covers costs and training for selected international competitions. Meager funding is allocated to train athletes; thus, they cannot reach international competitive levels or have a realistic chance at winning medals. Thus, there is little money available for the coaching, facilities, and support necessary for developing and training elite athletes.

A lack of facilities in Taiwan which meet international standards is another problem. The two facilities operated by the Sports Federation are only available for short-term use, forcing many athletes to share crowded ill-equipped facilities with the general public. To help overcome this problem, the Sports Federation began a program to train 470 athletes age ten to 20 who have been recommended by national sports associations. Under the program, athletes are trained at short-term camps during winter and summer vacation in order to identify elite talent.

Aboriginal Athletes

Without doubt the most famous athlete in ROC history is Yang Chuan-kwang. Yang, of the Ami indigenous tribe, won the silver medal in the decathlon at the 1960 Rome Olympics. Recognizing his achievement and that of the Ami team from Taitung County 台東縣 which won the ROC's first World Little League Baseball championship, the ROC Sports Federation organizes special programs to help cultivate aboriginal athletes. One of these programs, supported by the Chinese Taipei Amateur Baseball Association 中華民國棒球協會, is the Pacific League 太平洋聯盟, which started in 1993. With the participation of aboriginal professional baseball players, the Pacific League organizes baseball games and clinics for children in Ilan, Hualien 花蓮, and Taitung counties.

Coaching

One of the biggest obstacles facing local athletes is the lack of a comprehensive professional coaching system. Coaching school athletes has only recently become full-time work. In 1989, the MOE established a full-time school-coach training system wherein recruits receive three months of training before being assigned full-time coaching positions at a school, sports association, or at the Tsoying National Sports Training Center. Since coaches still receive lower salaries and have less job security than teachers, most prefer teaching positions instead. Consequently, most school teams are coached on a volunteer basis by teachers who enjoy sports. Many national associations choose to hire coaches on a part-time or contractual basis. These coaches hold short-term contracts and go back to their positions as P.E. teachers or coaches of professional teams after a particular event is over.

Most national associations and their athletes, however, cannot afford coaching. Therefore, athletes must rely on coaches willing to volunteer their time. In order to help alleviate the shortage of coaches, the ROC Sports Federation has invited distinguished coaches and athletic trainers to Taiwan from South Korea, Hungary, the Chinese mainland, and the United States to provide instruction in swimming, weightlifting, archery, basketball, and soccer.

Sports for Disabled People

The Chinese Taipei Sports Association for the Disabled 中華民國殘障體育運動協會 assists with athletic training and sponsors many competitions for disabled athletes. The association is a member of the International Paralympic Committee and other international sports federations for the disabled.

In July 1995, the ROC sent teams to the International Stoke Mandeville Wheelchair Games held in the UK and brought home four gold, two silver, and four bronze medals. Table tennis player Chou Chang-sheng 周長生 alone garnered three golds, setting a record in the 42-year history of the Games. The ROC sent 14 athletes to compete in the 1996 Atlanta Olympics for the Disabled. Lee Ching-chung 李青忠, who is blind, won a golden medal in judo. Hsu Chih-pin 許志彬 won a bronze medal in table tennis. And Chou Chang-sheng won bronze in wheelchair table tennis. This was a great improvement by the ROC team over its performance at the 1992 Barcelona Olympics for the Disabled, in which only three ROC athletes attended and only one bronze medal in judo was won. The association sponsors the Taiwan Area Games for the Disabled, which were first held in 1994 at Kaohsiung. The second games were held in Keelung in May 1996. Each time, more than 1,200 athletes competed in track and field, swimming, basketball, badminton, table tennis, judo, and weightlifting.

Special Olympics

The ROC is a member country of the Special Olympics International. The Chinese Taipei Spe-

ROC Track and Field National Records

Men's Events

Sports	Record	Units	Athlete	Date
100M	10.37	sec	Cheng Hsin-fu 鄭新福	6/28/86
200M	20.93	sec	Tao Wu-hsun 陶武訓	10/16/94
400M	46.94	sec	Wang Jung-hua 王榮華	5/12/77
800M	1:47.24	min/sec	Wang Jung-hua 王榮華	5/3/80
1,500M	3:46.4	min/sec	Huang Wen-chen 黃文成	6/11/83
5,000M	14:04.0	min/sec	Chang Chin-chuan 張金全	6/13/75
10,000M	29:12.10	min/sec	Hsu Chi-sheng 許續勝	11/28/93
110M hurdle	13.90	sec	Wu Ching-chin 吳清錦	11/5/83
400M hurdle	51.09	sec	Lin Cheng-chih 林正智	11/8/83
3,000M steeplechase	8:43.61	min/sec	Huang Wen-chen 黃文成	9/18/82
400M relay	39.27	sec	Lai Cheng-chuan 賴正全 Cheng Hsin-fu 鄭新福 Lin Chin-hsiung 林金雄 Hsieh Chung-tse 謝宗澤	10/3/90
1,600M relay	3:09.64	min/sec	Lin Kuang-liang 林光亮 Lin Tsai-tien 林再添 Hsu Juo-ta 徐若達 Lee Hsun-jung 李訓榮	7/31/87
high jump	2.22	meters	Liu Chin-chiang 劉金鎗	10/29/82
long jump	8.34	meters	Nai Hui-fang 乃慧芳	5/14/93
polevault	5.30	meters	Lee Fu-en 李福恩	10/29/90
triple jump	16.65	meters	Nai Hui-fang 乃慧芳	11/17/89
shot put	18.02	meters	Lu Ching-i 呂景義	4/29/94
discus	53.68	meters	Lin Chung-cheng 林宗正	8/10/85
hammer	63.34	meters	Hou Tang-sheng 侯堂盛	5/9/87
javelin	72.92	meters	Lin I-shun 林義順	3/17/90
decathlon	8,009	pts	Yang Chuan-kwang 楊傳廣	4/27-4/28/63
marathon	2:14.35	hr/min/sec	Hsu Chi-sheng 許續勝	2/5/95

cial Olympics 中華民國智障者體育運動協會 publishes newsletters, sponsors coaching workshops, and initiates local, area, and national games for people with mental handicaps. At the 1993 Fifth Winter Special Olympics in Salzburg, Austria, the Chinese Taipei team collected seven gold, three silver, and six bronze medals. In July 1995, the Chinese Taipei team sent 24 athletes to the Ninth Summer International Special Olympics at Yale University in Connecticut, USA. The team came home with 16 gold, ten silver, and 15 bronze medals. This total was a large increase over the ten won two years earlier.

Professional Sports
Professional Golf

Professional golf continues to boom in Taiwan, attracting more tournaments and international stars. The 1996 ROC PGA tour had thirteen tournaments, with a total purse of nearly US$2 million. In addition, the Ching-Fong Open 慶豐公開賽 was held in Taiwan in 1995 and 1996. The Sunrise Country Club 揚

ROC Track and Field National Records (continued)
Women's Events

Sports	Record	Units	Athlete	Date
100M	11.22	sec	Chi Cheng 紀政	7/18/70
200M	22.56	sec	Wang Huei-chen 王惠珍	10/30/92
400M	52.74	sec	Chi Cheng 紀政	7/29/70
800M	2:06.71	min/sec	Lai Li-chiao 賴利嬌	7/15/84
1,500M	4:22.80	min/sec	Lee Chiu-hsia 李秋霞	5/17/75
3,000M	9:37.68	min/sec	Lee Su-mei 李素梅	6/24/79
5,000M	17:30.68	min/sec	Lin Shu-huei 林淑惠	10/28/95
10,000M	36:29.75	min/sec	Su Tzu-ning 蘇子寧	10/22/93
100M hurdle	12.93	sec	Chi Cheng 紀政	7/12/70
400M hurdle	55.75	sec	Hsu Pei-ching 徐佩菁	10/14/94
400M relay	44.58	sec	Gao Yu-juan 高玉娟	10/16/94
			Hsu Pei-ching 徐佩菁	
			Chen Shu-chen 陳淑珍	
			Wang Huei-chen 王惠珍	
1,600M relay	3:39.88	min/sec	Hsu Ai-lin 徐愛齡	9/29/85
			Shen Shu-feng 沈淑鳳	
			Cheng Fei-ju 鄭妃汝	
			Lai Li-chiao 賴利嬌	
high jump	1.86	meters	Su Chiung-Yueh 蘇瓊月	4/23/89
triple jump	12.59	meters	Wang Kuo-hui 王國慧	5/25/96
long jump	6.43	meters	Wang Shu-hua 王淑華	7/23/91
shot put	14.88	meters	Tsai Mei-ling 蔡美玲	5/14/94
discus	48.48	meters	Fang En-hua 方恩華	10/3/93
javelin	55.02	meters	Fang En-hua 方恩華	4/25/95
heptathlon	5,786	pts	Ma Chun-ping 馬君萍	10/11/94
marathon	2:49.19	hr/min/sec	Su Tzu-ning 蘇子寧	11/12/92

昇高爾夫球場 in Yangmei 楊梅, Taoyuan County 桃園縣, is the permanent site for the Asian Masters 富豪亞洲名人賽. The 1996 Martell Skins Golf Classic also brought big names to Taiwan, including 1996 US Open champion Steve Jones and British Open champion Tom Watson.

Professional Baseball

If the ROC could be said to have a national sport, it certainly must be baseball. Taiwan fans pack local stadiums each season to watch the six teams in the Chinese Professional Baseball League 中華職棒聯盟: the Brother Elephants 兄弟象, Weichuan Dragons 味全龍, President Lions 統一獅, Mercury Tigers 三商虎, Sinon Bulls 興農牛, and China Times Eagles 時報鷹. Each team plays a 100-game regular season between March (February in 1997) and October. Fans islandwide can see the action, with games in Taipei, Hsinchu 新竹, Taichung, Tainan, Kaohsiung, and Pingtung. In 1996, a new 15,000-seat stadium in Chiayi 嘉義, the league's largest, was added to the schedule.

The CPBL has produced its own heroes, including Lions pitcher Kuo Chien-hsing 郭建興, who finished the 1995 season with a 20-7 record. The league has also recruited many foreign players. George Hinshaw from Panama started his baseball career in Taiwan when the CPBL was established in 1990.

Baseball fans are anticipating the formation of another professional league: Taiwan Major League Professional Baseball 臺灣大聯盟. The league will have four teams: Gida 太陽隊, Agan 金剛隊, Luka 勇士隊, and Fala 雷公隊, all with team names taken from aboriginal languages. Their debut in the 1997 pro-baseball season promises even fiercer competition and wider popularity as reflected in the record US$57.7 million bid to broadcast games for the 1997-99 seasons.

Professional Basketball

Professional basketball made its debut on November 12, 1994 with the inception of the Chinese Basketball Alliance 中華職業籃球股份有限公司. The initial season saw four teams battle for the title, the Tera Mars 泰瑞戰神, Hungkuo Elephants 宏國象, Yulon Dinos 裕隆恐龍, and Luckipar 幸福豹. Yulon emerged with the championship. The 72-regular game season proved successful with attendance by over 220,000 persons, predominately teenagers captivated by the idol-like quality of many players. For the 1995-96 season, two more teams, the Hungfu Rams 宏福公牛 and Chunghsin Tigers 中興虎, were added to the CBA; and the number of regular games was increased to 150. Games were held in 12 cities and counties islandwide, drawing about 275,000 people.

Recreation

Taipei appears exciting enough to a first-time visitor, but it is not exactly leisure-friendly. Major thoroughfares are jammed with traffic, and the sidewalks are crammed with people and parked motorcycles. There are few places to go to ride a bike, jog, or even just take a stroll without having to weave through a maze of clutter. Taipei, like the island's other urban centers, has a distinctive recreational style that has developed in response to rapid urbanization. The biggest single shift is that recreation has become increasingly constrained by diminishing physical space and lim-

ited free time. Except for a handful of private companies, all businesses require employees to work at least a half-day on Saturdays. This leaves little spare time for leisure activities.

Another factor that reduces leisure time in the urban centers is traffic. In metropolitan Taipei, rush-hour traffic frequently triples normal commuting time. It can be even worse on holidays and weekends; during Chinese New Year, a one-hour drive to a neighboring town can easily extend to three or four hours. Thus, although Taiwan boasts six national parks, accounting for 8.5 percent of the island's land mass, many people don't dare try to reach them. The result is that many people stick close to home.

According to a September 1995 DGBAS survey regarding the leisure activities of 15,316 interviewees over the age of 15, about 61.3 percent watched TV or videos from eight to nine o'clock every evening. High-school and elementary students spend a daily average of 51 minutes watching TV. The explosion in cable TV channels in recent years is quite likely to increase the amount of time people spend in front of "the tube."

A growing class of people who have money to spend but demand convenient places to spend it, has fueled a boom in indoor, easy-to-reach, urban activities. Thus, no matter where a person lives or works, there are nearby restaurants, video game parlors, discos, KTVs (see below), and clothing boutiques down the street next door, or even downstairs. To attract patrons who work long hours, most leisure spots are open late into the night. Bookstores and clothing boutiques are commonly crowded with browsers until 10 P.M. on week nights, and night markets (streets where outdoor vendors set up shop in the evenings) are packed with people of all ages until long after midnight.

Eating out and treating friends and family to a bite to eat are probably the most popular entertainments islandwide. Consequently, most neighborhoods have a wide range of restaurants. The Taipei City Department of Public Health 台北市政府衛生局 estimates that Taipei alone has between 5,000 and 6,000 restaurants.

KTV

KTV or Karaoke television is the ideal indoor entertainment of choice for thousands of people in Taiwan. It may be the fantasy element, the chance to be with friends, or the fact that there simply aren't many other leisure activities available—no one can say quite why, but KTV has become an islandwide craze.

Karaoke, a term coined by the Japanese, is a combination of *kara*, which means "none" in Japanese, and a modification of *orche*, the initial letters of the word "orchestra," which the Japanese pronounce as "okay." Literally, the term means "an orchestra without instruments." In fact, it is a microphone hooked up to a tape or videocassette player. As a singer croons into the mike, the sound is mixed with the taped music. No matter how hoarse or off-key one's voice might be, it will emerge from the speaker sounding professional.

Karaoke (minus the video) first showed up in local coffee shops and restaurants in 1976 as an import from Japan. Soon karaoke had swept the island, becoming immensely popular in both urban and rural areas. A second boom started in 1988, when the government cracked down on pirated videotapes. Many of the island's numerous MTV parlors, which rent videos for customers to watch in private rooms, were forced to stop showing pirated movies. To stay in business, many MTVs added karaoke equipment and switched a letter on the signboard to become KTVs. And so, a new trend was born.

Today, there are 740 registered KTVs in Taipei, and more than 1,500 around the island. Many are poshly decorated with private rooms in a variety of sizes, large-screen TVs, and comfortable sofas. Patrons pick songs from a catalogue, then use a keyboard to enter the identification number for each song into a computerized system. Choices are available in Taiwanese, Mandarin, Cantonese, and English.

KTV patrons include people of all ages and occupations, from teenagers to retirees, housewives to business people. Even high-ranking government officials have been known to pick up a microphone and belt out a few songs.

Prices vary according to the atmosphere, the equipment, and the service. At Cash Box 錢櫃 KTV, the island's largest KTV operator, hourly rates range from US$13 for a five-person room to US$29 for a 20-person room. An average visit for a mid-sized group lasts three to four hours. Each person must also pay a minimum of US$4 for food or drinks.

Outdoor Recreation

"Adventure sports" such as surfing, scuba diving, and sailboarding, although still on a small scale in Taiwan, are gaining popularity around the island as a result of interest generated by classes, rental shops, and clubs. Even gutsier activities such as paragliding and bungee jumping are attracting brave souls not scared off by the danger or expense. Since the island's first bungee jumping group set up operations in November 1991, thousands of people have paid a US$80 fee for the thrill of hurling themselves off a bridge while hooked to an elastic cord. A variety of fishing activities have also gain popularity since the *Recreational Fishing Regulatory Measures* 休閒漁業管理辦法 took effect in 1993. Sea parks and aquariums have been set up around the island.

In 1993, the National Taiwan College of Physical Education 國立台灣體育專科學校, located in Taichung, set up the first and only Department of Recreational Sports in Taiwan. It is aimed at training specialists in recreational sports coaching, planning, management, and promotion. Students choose from a variety of courses, including diving, bowling, skiing, surfing, and yachting. They also work in local recreational businesses. Private associations have also been formed to conduct research on leisured-related topics and to promote outdoor recreation through seminars, lectures, and group activities. In 1988, the Outdoor Recreation Association of the ROC 中華民國戶外遊憩學會 was founded. It has sponsored hiking lectures by botanists, geologists, or other nature specialists, allowing participants to learn as they picnic or hike.

Organized recreational activities are offered all year round by groups like the China Youth Corps 中國青年反共救國團. On weekends and holidays and during summer and winter vacations, the corps offers young people diverse outdoor activities like parachuting, rafting, skiing, and mountaineering. Each year it also organizes mock military exercises, back country hiking and camping, talent camps, and safari-style adventures for teenagers and young adults. For those who prefer indoor activities, the corps arranges arts and craft courses, such as guitar workshops, knitting courses, and painting classes. There are also self-improvement programs, including management courses, vocational workshops, and psychological counseling.

The China Youth Corps holds activities throughout the Taiwan area—in major cities, the countryside, and even on the off-shore island of P'enghu 澎湖. The corps has altogether 23 youth activity centers and hostels, complete with recreational, educational, and camping facilities. The Taipei International Youth Activity Center 臺北國際青年活動中心 previously provided services and programs especially for young foreigners traveling or studying in the Taipei area. Starting in 1995, this function has been taken over by the Chientan Overseas Youth Activity Center 劍潭海外青年活動中心.

For those who are able to get away from the city for a whole afternoon, golf is yet another tremendously popular form of recreation in Taiwan, and many international-standard courses dot the island. While the price of membership in one of the more prestigious golf clubs on Taiwan can be very high, people still flock to the greens on the weekends. The basic cost for playing 18 holes, not including rentals, caddie fees, and gratuities, ranges from US$50 to US$100.

Ultimately, however, the Chinese city park provides the best idea of how Chinese people seek exercise and relaxation. If one strolls through any park in Taipei early in the morning, one will witness people dancing folk dances, practicing kung fu, playing Chinese chess, doing aerobics, jogging, stretching, singing and even taking their birds "for a walk." After spending fifteen minutes in this peaceful microcosm, one gains a better understanding of the traditional Chinese concept of health through harmony.

For a change of atmosphere, many people retire to one of the numerous traditional teahouses or "tea art" shops all over Taiwan. Chinese teahouses are an unusual blend of contemplative serenity and buzzing activities. A casual afternoon at a teahouse will bring one to the heart of grassroots social, artistic, intellectual, and political activities brewing in Taiwan. A number of such teahouses have been local trend setters for arts and culture, hosting art exhibitions, ceramic displays, antique shows, and teapot collections.

Many of these teahouses, set in elegant cultured gardens, are ideal hideaways where tea drinkers can sample a wide selection of first-class teas. Tea drinking in Taiwan is akin to the high art of wine tasting in the west, and tea drinkers gladly pay between US$40 and US$80 for a half kilogram of good tea. On weekends, mountainside tea-art shops and restaurants offering open-air tea drinking, dining, and scenic views have become favorite destinations for Taipei residents. Perhaps the most notable of these are the teahouses in the Mucha 木柵 district of Taipei.

TAIWAN DELUXE CLASS

The Ambassador Hotels in Taipei and Kaohsiung finest have been completely redecorated and refurnished to offer the rooms and facilities for today's busy traveler. Both Ambassadors are more luxurious and elegant than ever, with every detail designed with you in mind. At each Ambassador, Health club gives you a place to work out at your own convenience. At the same time, our 24-hour Meeting Room and Business Center are available any time youneed to conduct business. Comfort, convenience and service, – the Ambassador Hotel does it all for you!

國賓大飯店
AMBASSADOR

The Ambassador Hotel *Taipei* Represented by SRS STEIGENBERGER RESERVATION SERVICE
中華民國台灣省台北市中山北路二段63號 TEL：(886)2-551-1111 FAX：(886)2-561-7883
The Ambassador Hotel *Kaohsiung* UTELL INTERNATIONAL
E-Mail:tebs@ambh.com.tw
中華民國台灣省高雄市民生二路202號 TEL：(886)7-211-5211 FAX：(886)7-281-1115
The Ambassador Hotel *Japan Sales Office*
日本東京事務所所長：郭啓炫 〒105東京都港区虎／門1丁目17番1号 第5森ビル10階
TEL：03(3504)2917 FAX：03(3504)2919
http://ambh.com.tw

Previous page: Flowers have always been a ready source of inspiration for Chinese poets.

Below: Publishing houses have recently put considerable amounts of money and effort into developing quality books for children.

24 Literature

The beginnings of Chinese literature go back thousands of years. The earliest pieces in the *Book of Songs* 詩經, which was required reading for any educated person in the Republic of China today, date to the 12th century B.C. It is this rich literary heritage that stretches unbroken from the *Book of Songs* to the literary, historical, and philosophical works of the present day—and not religion—that has provided the main source of spiritual comfort and intellectual sustenance to the majority of educated Chinese through the ages. This tradition has also shaped the relationship that the Chinese people share with both traditional and contemporary literature.

Literature in China has never been simply a source of aesthetic pleasure, a way to express pent-up emotions, or a channel to indulge in flights of fancy. It has, rather, from its inception served as a guide to everyday living and been a voice of social conscience, filling man's existence with meaning and leading him along life's path. Literature has also questioned the state of society, reflected on the trends of history, and attempted to right social wrongs. As a result, literature has always held a leading position in the cultural and intellectual life of the Chinese people, and its value and character cannot be defined or evaluated by its aesthetic characteristics alone.

Definition and Scope of Chinese Literature

Although some scholars have in recent times attempted to redefine the scope and tradition of Chinese literature with such Western literary concepts as "imaginativeness" or lyricism, these concepts clearly do not mesh with the historical facts of the Chinese literary tradition. Throughout Chinese history, "literature" has referred to any piece of writing, or even a particularly felicitous verbal expression, that relates to human nature and discusses human life and society. Thus, all linguistic discourse involving human response between an "addresser" and "addressee," excepting topics of a purely technical nature, may be viewed as potential "literature."

In China, the main distinction has not been between which writing is literature and which is not, but rather within literature itself, between poetry, which is allied with music and stresses melody and form, and prose, which stresses the recording of language and events. The former has its source in the *Book of Songs*, and the latter, in the *Book of History* 書經 (or 尚書).

Earliest Literary Traditions

A number of scholars influenced by Western literary concepts believe that writings in the *Book of History* tradition should be classified as history rather than literature. Furthermore, private accounts, as opposed to government archives, have since the time of Confucius been classified as expositions of thought. They relegated official archives to the realm of history, and private writings to that of philosophy, leaving only works belonging to the *Book of Songs* tradition to literature. And because the *Book of Songs* is an anthology of poetry, Chinese literature came to be regarded as a basically lyrical tradition.

The prevalence of this way of thinking has led some scholars to insist that China has no epic tradition, no fiction until the seventh century A.D., and no drama until the 13th century. They ignore the fact that public and private writings "recording words and events" have been produced in China without interruption since the *Book of History*, and that they have always enjoyed the status of fine literature. They often disregard the narrative tradition comprised by the numerous fables that appeared in histories after the *Book of History* and in philosophical works such as the *Chuang Tzu* 莊子, the *Mencius* 孟子, the *Han Fei Tzu* 韓非子, the *Spring and Autumn Annals of Mr. Lü* 呂氏春秋, and the *Lieh Tzu* 列子, all written after the fourth century B.C., along with the myths from earlier ages that were preserved in these and similar works.

The earliest fiction in China—be it in the form of a continuation of mythical narrative or an imitation of official history called *yeh-shih* 野史 ("unofficial history")—was created in the spirit of the fable. The narrative tradition—

comprising history, myth, fable, and fiction—balanced and supplemented the lyrical tradition of poetry produced subsequent to the *Book of Songs*.

"Recording words," the other expressed feature of the *Book of History*, in turn influenced philosophical works and essay-type prose 散文. Philosophical works produced since the sixth century B.C., like the *Analects* of Confucius 論語, are basically collections of quotations or records of a master's sayings, inseparable in content and style from the personalities, speech habits, and biographical experiences of the masters themselves. This style of writing, which fuses reason and emotion served as a model for the essay in later ages. The essay thus became the most important genre in Chinese literature, and *san-wen* (prose) even became a synonym for literature itself, while poetry was considered merely a specialized branch of literature.

In contrast to the personalism of the essay, Chinese poetry gradually departed from the spoken language and came to stress formalistic rules. Poetry thus became relatively objective and impersonal and, while still lyrical in nature, it was often more symbolic and constructive in nature than prose.

The Literary-Vernacular Split

Related to the division of Chinese literature into the traditions of the *Book of Songs* and the *Book of History* is the fact that the spoken and written Chinese language are actually two independent representational systems. Chinese writing, having evolved from pictographs, is an ideographic script that expresses meaning directly through the forms of the characters themselves. The Chinese system stands in contrast to the phonetic alphabets and syllabaries of Japan, Korea, and the West, which express meaning through phonetic representation. As a result, Chinese writing constitutes a notational system that is partially independent of the phonemic nature of the Chinese spoken language; and the relative independence of this notational system has had a major effect on Chinese literature.

One example of this effect can be seen in the *Book of Songs* tradition, which during the several centuries of its evolution gradually broke away from music in pursuit of its own metrical form. The combination of an independent writing system with the Chinese spoken language—which in early times was mainly monosyllabic—produced neat lines of four, five, or seven characters, and sometimes three or six. Tonal theory evolved in the fifth and sixth centuries, based on a new apprehension that Middle Chinese syllables had tonal or pitch distinctions that affected meaning. Thus "even" 平 and "deflected" 仄 tones were matched and contrasted, and words of parallel or antithetical meaning were aligned. Literary forms almost completely divorced from the spoken language developed, such as parallel prose 駢文 and regulated verse 律詩. This formalistic beauty, which derived from a neat matching of written characters, became an important aesthetic characteristic of traditional Chinese poetry.

Poetry often broke away from the speaking subject, and became a structural object in itself, objectivizing and collectivizing the lyrical self. This paved the way for the subsequent fusion of emotion 情 and scene 景 that resulted in a progression from an aesthetic "expression of self" 言志 to a "spiritual resonance" 神韻 over the first to eighth centuries.

Following territorial expansion and the establishment of a unified empire encompassing a large number of local dialects, the maintenance of the *Book of History* tradition depended increasingly on scholars and officials learning a form of written communication called *ku-wen* 古文 (classical prose). In early antiquity, the classical prose style may have reflected the contemporary spoken language, but it eventually evolved into a purely literary style that allowed the literary language to experience no major syntactic changes for 2,000 years.

Around the fifth century A.D., the spoken language began to gradually evolve from being mainly monosyllabic in nature toward bisyllabicity or polysyllabicity, as the Old Chinese consonant clusters were gradually lost and originally distinct vowels merged. The unchanging stability of the literary language, or *wen-yen* 文言, thus led to a gradual split with the vernacular language, or *pai-hua* 白話.

The simultaneous development toward balance and parallelism in belletristic writing further widened the gulf between the written language of the literati and the oral literature of the common people. Oral literature is by its very nature not easily preserved. But the tradition in China of writing down ballads and salon ditties to popular tunes of the time, combined with the growth of cities after the 10th century and a flourishing entertainment industry, led to the spread—through writing and printing—of the *tz'u* 詞 (lyric), music drama, and fiction. These were all popular oral literary genres that originated with storytellers and performing artists.

The vernacular literature of the common people, consisting for the most part of fiction and drama, developed parallel to the literature of the scholars, which was composed mainly of poetry and essays written in classical Chinese. Literature written in the classical language received official sanction by becoming the testing material for the examination system, while vernacular literature owed its increasing popularity mainly to growth in the popular entertainment industry.

An Outline of Traditional Chinese Literature

Traditional Chinese literature can be divided into four periods: early antiquity, from the 12th century B.C. to 206 B.C.; middle antiquity, from 206 B.C. to 618 A.D.; late antiquity, from 618 to 1279; and the pre-modern era, from 1279 to 1911.

Early Antiquity

The literature of early antiquity includes the classics preserved from the Chou 周 dynasty and organized by Confucian scholars; the works of philosophers from the Spring and Autumn 春秋 period and the Warring States 戰國 period; the *Songs of the South* 楚辭; and the early myths, which were compiled from various sources. Together these works laid the spiritual foundation of Chinese literature and culture. The *Book of Songs* from northern China and the *Songs of the South* represent the fundamental dichotomy of Chinese poetry: realism and lyricism versus romanticism and imagination.

The early myths are scattered among a number of works, chiefly the *Chuang Tzu*, the *Mountain and Sea Classic* 山海經 and the poem "Heavenly Questions" 天問 in the *Songs of the South*. The concept behind creation myths such as those of Pan Ku 盤古 and the goddess Nü Wa 女媧 that "the myriad things arise from the same source" had a profound influence on the intimate identification of the Chinese people with nature and on their pursuit of harmony, both of mankind and the universe as a whole. More importantly, this concept established in Chinese poetry the method of indirect metaphor 起興 and the fusion of emotion and scene.

The myths of Kun 鯀 and Yü 禹 controlling floodwaters and Hou I 后羿 shooting the nine suns illustrate the awakening of human consciousness and mankind's awareness of the need to control nature for his own purposes. Invention myths, such as Fu Hsi 伏羲 drawing the eight trigrams, reflect an awareness of the origins of civilization. Although the narratives are incomplete, the early myths had a fundamental influence on the way the Chinese people view the universe, mankind, nature, and civilization.

A total of 305 poems are preserved in the *Book of Songs*. They describe all aspects of social life, and include hymns from ancestral temples, sagas of nation-building, political satires and encomia, and simple love songs. The book is divided into three groups of *sung* 頌 (hymns), two of *ya* 雅 (odes), and 15 of *kuo-feng* 國風 (songs). The hymns were apparently composed to accompany ceremonial dances at ancestral temples in praise of Heaven and the virtuous achievements of former rulers, and in hope of continued blessings. The *ta-ya* 大雅 (greater odes) are generally classified as odes of the royal court, many of which laud the founding of the Chou dynasty. The *hsiao-ya* 小雅 (lesser odes) are thought to have been performed at feasts and banquets, and many contain political messages criticizing society and the life of the nobility. The songs are folk songs from various nation-states around the empire, expressing love between man and woman and the life experiences of the common people. The *Book of Songs* can thus be viewed as a composite portrait of the life of the people.

The richly imaginative *Songs of the South* contains poems from the southern kingdom of Ch'u 楚. The anthology includes religious pieces which reflect a worship of nature far different from the worship of ancestors and the theoretical God posited in the *Book of Songs*. Poems in the *Songs of the South* were written by Ch'ü Yüan 屈原 and other writers influenced by him.

Ch'ü Yüan was China's first major poet. He secularized the originally religious songs of Ch'u, producing a complete vision of human life that encompasses myth, history, nature, society, and politics. In his masterpieces, "Encountering Sorrow" 離騷 and "Nine Chapters" 九章, he repeatedly examines the ideals of human existence and the crises and degeneration to which they are subject.

From the *Book of History* tradition of recording the words of the early kings developed both the narratives of the historians and the speculative works of the philosophers. The most important works of history are the *Spring and Autumn Annals of Mr. Lü*, the *Tso Commentary* 左傳, and the *Conversations from the States* 國語. Corresponding to the recording of words in the *Book of History* is the recording of deeds in the *Spring and Autumn Annals*. This work records in concise language—often only a single sentence—major historical events in chronological order. It uses the method of "according praise or censure in a single word" to make penetrating ethical judgments about the events it relates. The *Kung-yang Commentary* 公羊傳, the *Ku-liang Commentary* 穀梁傳, and the *Tso Commentary* explicate the ethical appraisals of the *Spring and Autumn Annals* with commentary. The first two stress moral and ethical judgments, while the *Tso Commentary* supplements the *Spring and Autumn Annals* with detailed narratives. It is with the *Tso Commentary* and the *Conversations from the States*

that narrative literature in China became fully mature, fusing the twin traditions of recording words and recording deeds. These works used the techniques of recording deeds and rendering ethical appraisals from the *Spring and Autumn Annals* as models for their treatment of narrative and subject matter. They also applied the technique of recording words from the *Book of History* in creating dialogs that illumined the psychology and motivations of characters to thereby depict and morally judge historical events.

Thinkers of the ancient era prior to the third century B.C. not only made major contributions to the development of Chinese thought, but also had a lasting effect on Chinese aesthetics and literature. The effect of the Confucian thinkers is reflected in an emphasis on ethical, social, and political concerns. Taoist influence can be seen in a striving for transcendental, universal meaning, and in an awareness of an eternal, metaphysical significance of life beyond history and society, achieved through an appreciation and description of one's natural surroundings.

The works of these ancient philosophers, through their method of illustrating morals through fables, established narrative models for characterization and plot development, which was a break with the recording of words and deeds of outstanding historical figures in historical narrative. The various styles that evolved along these lines subsequently influenced the development of Chinese prose. The *Analects* of Confucius and the *Classic of The Way and Its Power* 道德經 of Lao Tzu made terseness and profundity the foremost criteria of prose style. The *Mo Tzu* 墨子 advanced the methods of logical exposition, while the *Chuang Tzu* established the model of an exuberantly imaginative composite form that defied classification. The *Mencius* made full use of the expressive powers of the spoken language in forging an eloquent verbal style. Hsun Tzu 荀子, in addition to being the first writer of Chinese *fu* 賦 (prose-poems), made full use of the isolating character of the Chinese writing system to develop a regulated aesthetic of parallelism and antithesis. All these works became sources and models for later literature, both spoken and written.

Middle Antiquity

The major political development of middle antiquity was the conclusion of the feudal system of the Chou dynasty and the establishment of a stable, unified empire under the Han. In the area of philosophical thought, the effect of this development was the triumph of Confucianism; in literature, it was the independence of literature from philosophy, and a striving for formal aesthetics and emotional experience. Its first literary product was the prose-poem, and the *Songs of the South*.

The prose-poem is a literary form that is recited rather than sung. Tied less to musical form than poetry, the prose-poem combined visual and aural elements in its attention to formal rules and to euphony. Because it developed in response to the preferences and patronage of the emperor, its earliest subjects were invariably praise and glorification of the splendor of the imperial palace, the capital, parks, and hunting grounds. Out of this arose a tradition of exhaustive description, often accompanied by the coining of new Chinese characters, which catered specifically to the ruler's consciousness of possessing the empire, the world, the universe, and everything in it. Works of this type which were presented to the emperor are called *ta-fu* 大賦 (greater prose-poems).

As writers came to realize that a consciousness of totality must be connected with a sense of individuality to have value and meaning, they began to experience anxiety over individual existence. Thus, "the scholar born out of his time" became a basic theme of the *hsiao-fu* 小賦 (lesser prose-poem). Chia I 賈誼 and Szu-ma Hsiang-ju 司馬相如 in the second century B.C., and Chang Heng 張衡 and Wang Tsan 王粲 in the second century A.D., were the most important writers of prose-poems, but the prose-poem continued to develop right up until the end of the 19th century.

Shih 詩, or poetry of lines of equal length, was still identified with song when the *Yüeh-fu* 樂府 (Music Bureau) was established during the reign of Emperor Wu Ti 武帝 (140-86 B.C.) in the Han 漢 dynasty. The amalgams of song and poetry produced then were generally referred to as *Yüeh-fu shih* (Music Bureau ballads). Often originating among the common people, these pieces were rich in narrative content and filled with laments over social issues, especially the gap between rich and poor, the posting of soldiers to distant regions, the plight of widows and orphans, and the vicissitudes of life and time. Poems that reflected social realities and contained a sharp consciousness of moral crisis continued to be created under the name of *yüeh-fu* in later times. Although they were no longer set to music, they preserved the external form of early *yüeh-fu*, with its lines of unequal length.

Another literary development during the nearly 400 years of the Han dynasty era was the appearance of poems written in neat five or seven-character lines that was unbound to music. The inspiration for replacing the harmonic effects of music with a strictly regulated form may have come from the prose-poem. Poetry consisting of lines of five or seven characters later became the universally acknowledged fundamental poetic form. The rules for matching and balancing characters in parallel constructions became increasingly refined, and ultimately resulted in the regulated verse of the seventh century onward. Middle antiquity can be considered the period of formalization of Chinese literary aesthetics. From the third century onward, the method of writing prose-poems was extended to the writing of essays, culminating in the blossoming of parallel prose in the sixth century.

The five-character line 五言詩 form of poetry emerged after the period of the lesser prose-poem. Anxiety over life and death became a basic theme for this new poetic form as well. Representative examples are found in the *Nineteen Ancient Poems* 古詩十九首 collection of the first century, the most important work in this genre of the time. Finding consolation in Taoist thinking to dispel the cares of existence, poets gradually turned to the subject of fields, gardens, hills, and streams, discovering and reveling in the natural beauty of landscapes. The most important poets of this period were Ts'ao Chih 曹植, Juan Chi 阮籍, T'ao Ch'ien 陶潛, and Hsieh Ling-yün 謝靈運.

Middle antiquity was also a fruitful period for the narrative tradition. First and foremost of works in this genre was Szu-ma Chien's 司馬遷 *Records of the Grand Historian* 史記. The *Records*, written during the first century B.C., was the first comprehensive work to recount China's ancient and recent history. It also established a model for historical writing centered around biography. Szu-ma Chien shifted the focus from unity of plot evident in the *Tso Commentary* and the *Conversations from the States* to a unity of character. Official Chinese historians after him all adopted the biography as the chief form of their works. Subjects chosen for his biographies included not only great figures of history but also individuals he considered noteworthy because of their special talents or personalities, such as jesters and assassins. His writing helped pave the way for the *ch'uan-ch'i* 傳奇 (classical tales) of the eighth and ninth centuries.

Pan Ku's 班固 *History of the Former Han Dynasty* 漢書 was the first history devoted to a single dynasty. Pan Ku's work, together with Fan Yeh's 范曄 *History of the Later Han Dynasty* 後漢書, Chen Shou's 陳壽 *Records of the Three Kingdoms* 三國志, and the *Records of the Grand Historian*, are traditionally considered the pillars of Chinese historical writing.

Although its narrative roots can be traced back to the *Chuang Tzu*, *Hsun Tzu*, and *Tso Commentary*, Chinese fiction is often said to have begun its development under the influence of the romantic and supernatural adventures related in the biographies of diviners and imperial concubines in the *Records of the Grand Historian*. This genre consisting of depictions of courtly affairs and supernatural occurrences was referred to as *chih-kuai* 志怪 ("recording the strange") fiction. Among the earlier examples of this sort of fiction were the *Private Life of Lady Swallow* 飛燕外傳 and the *Intimate Biography of Han Emperor Wu* 漢武內傳 of the 4th century.

Late Antiquity

A milestone in the development of Chinese society was the establishment of the bureaucratic examination system in the 7th century. This system produced a new class of officials who played a leading role in society both politically and culturally. The literature of late antiquity was the activity and expression of this new class. Unlike the old aristocracy, the members of the new class owed their entrance to officialdom to success in the examinations. They had to form factions to avoid isolation, and when policies changed or power alliances shifted, they had to worry about demotion or exile. The effect of this situation was twofold. On the one hand, the new officials felt a strong sense of self-awareness as individuals, and did not identify solely with the family; on the other, they traveled widely throughout the country, whether in exile or in official service. As a result, the literature of late antiquity is characterized by a high degree of mobility, autobiography, and sense of regionalism.

During the seventh through ninth centuries, examination candidates were tested in poetry, which led to the widespread development of that genre, whereas during the 10th through 12th centuries, they were tested in essays on public policy, which led to a flourishing of the literary language. The seventh century saw the refinement of regulated verse, in response to the needs of the examination system. Its most popular themes were closely tied to the efforts of the new class to advance as officials, and its basic spirit was emotional experience 感遇. The course of an official career might include a posting to the frontier headquarters of a commander, or temporary retirement to the countryside to cultivate one's reputation in hopes of being recruited for a higher office, or a trip to the capital to court powerful patrons and establish one's name as a scholar. Such experiences were brought out in particular in poems with border, forest, and banquet themes. Seventh through ninth century poems generally strived for a consciousness of human existence through descriptions of natural beauty:

Slender grass, a light breeze, on the river bank...
Stars loom over the broad plain's sweep;
The moon swells in the Great River's flow.

New Members of the Executive Yuan

On Thursday, May 15, 1997, the following Executive Yuan officials were appointed to their new posts:

Mr. Chao Shou-po
Minister of State*

Mr. Chi Su
Minister of State

Ms. Yeh Chin-fong
Minister of the Interior

Mr. Peng Tso-kwei
Chairman of the Council of Agriculture

Mr. Hsu Chieh-kwei
Chairman of the Council of Labor Affairs

Mr. David Tawei Lee
Director-General of the Government Information Office

*   In addition to his new position as Minister of State, Mr. Chao Shou-po serves concurrently as Secretary-General of the Executive Yuan.

Fame—how will my writings ever win me that?
Career—old age and sickness prompt me to retire.

細草微風岸
星垂平野闊
月湧大江流
名豈文章著
官應老病休

(from "Lü-yeh shu-huai" 旅夜書懷 ["Traveling at Night, Writing My Feelings"] by Tu Fu 杜甫)

Wang Wei 王維, Li Pai 李白, Tu Fu, Pai Chü-i 白居易, Han Yü 韓愈, and Li Shang-yin 李商隱 are the most important poets of the T'ang 唐 dynasty (which spanned the seventh through ninth centuries) and are major figures in the history of Chinese poetry.

The Sung 宋 dynasty poets of the 11th and 12th centuries introduced philosophy into poetry, and discourse and reasoning became important characteristics of their works. To the technique of conveying emotion through scenic description, they added the poetic metaphor:

Human life, everywhere,
what is it like?
It might be compared to a flying goose
stepping in the snow;
It leaves behind a random patch
of claw prints in the slush;
And after it's flown away, who can tell
whether east or west?

人生到處知何似
應似飛鴻踏雪泥
泥上偶然留指爪
鴻飛那復計東西

(from "Ho Tzu-yu Min-ch'ih Huai-chiu" 和子由澠池懷舊 ["Matching Tzu-yu's Poem Recalling the Past at Minchih"] by Su Shih 蘇軾)

They also added comic touches:

The road was long, we were beat,
and the lame mule wheezed.

路長人困蹇驢嘶

(from the same Su Shih poem)

T'ang and Sung poetry became the twin paradigms of Chinese poetry in later ages. Ou-yang Hsiu 歐陽修, Wang An-shih 王安石, Su Shih (Su Tung-po 蘇東坡), Huang T'ing-chien 黃庭堅, and Lu Yu 陸游 are the major representatives of Sung poetry.

The medieval era of the seventh through ninth centuries was a time of cultural fusion. Not only was there a melding of the contrasting cultures of earlier dynasties from the fourth through sixth centuries when China was politically divided, but the administration of the western regions and re-opening of the Silk Road led to the absorption and popularity of music and dance from Central Asia.

The lyric 詞, a poem originally set to music and with lines of unequal length, became the dominant poetic genre. Poems (i.e. *shih*) of the literati had by this time moved toward strict regulation (both in formal "neatness" and in tonal contraposition) due to the examination system, and had become increasingly alienated from the spoken language. The art of the lyric, on the other hand, was cultivated at banquets and entertainment activities among merchants and the common people.

The lyric genre began to attract the attention of the literati during the ninth and 10th centuries, and by the 11th century, had become the second most important poetic genre among literati. Due to the differing lengths of its lines and its origins among the common people, it preserved to a considerable degree characteristics of the spoken language. Because it was popular at performances and banquets attended by both men and women, its basic themes were love and feminine emotions. And even though poets later turned to this genre to express their thoughts about life, human experience, the nation, and history, it never fully broke away from its mild and gracious original character, and its minute observations of women's quarters, courtyards, and seasonal changes. The following example is typical of this style:

Free and easy flying blossoms
light as a dream;
Limitless the thread-like rain,

slender as sorrow.
The jeweled curtain loosely hangs
from tiny silver hooks.

自在飛花輕似夢
無邊絲雨細如愁
寶簾閒掛小銀鉤

("Huan-hsi sha" 浣溪沙 [To the tune of/"Sand of the Washing Stream"] by Ch'in Kuan 秦觀)

For poets of the Sung dynasty, the poem came to express the rational and public aspect of the writer's spirit, and the lyric, his emotional and private side. The most important lyricists were Wen T'ing-yün 溫庭筠, Wei Chuang 韋莊, Feng Yen-szu 馮延巳, Li Yü 李煜, Liu Yung 柳永, Su Shih, Chou Pang-yen 周邦彥, Hsin Ch'i-chi 辛棄疾, and Chiang K'uei 姜夔.

Another major literary development of late antiquity was the revival of the classical literary language, or *ku-wen*. *P'ien-wen*, or parallel prose, had been criticized as being beautiful in form but shallow in substance ever since the late sixth century. The reform of prose writing, however, had to await the mid-eighth century, when Han Yü and Liu Tsung-yüan 柳宗元 began to promote the classical literary language. Their models were the *Mencius* and the *Records of the Grand Historian*. They ultimately succeeded in developing a new, more comprehensive style of writing that reflected the life of people outside the class of officials and returned to the tenets of Confucian thought as a main theme.

This type of writing emphasized narration and argument, which became autobiographical and lyrical vehicles of expression by lending prominence to the writer as a subjective entity. The classical literary language achieved unprecedented success during the 11th century and became the main form of prose writing in China thereafter. Major writers in this genre during the Sung dynasty were Ou-yang Hsiu, Wang An-shih, Su Hsün 蘇洵, Su Shih, Su Ch'e 蘇轍, and Tseng Kung 曾鞏.

The career ups and downs experienced by the new class of officials inspired a narrative form that conveyed change. The form gradually encompassed social realities and human life, but was at the same time influenced by the *chih-kuai* (reportage) genre of fiction of the 4th century onward, and the *Records of the Grand Historian* tradition that emphasized outstanding individuals. By the 8th century, this type of fiction was called the *ch'uan-ch'i* (classical tale). These stories often added elements of the mysterious and fantastic to everyday occurrences.

Such tales might feature an overnight lodging turning into a dragon's palace; a fiancee revealing herself to be a fox spirit, an ant princess, or a dragon king's daughter; or some other extraordinary individual who changes the fate of the protagonist. The classical tale was typically based in reality but interwoven with fantasy and descriptions of a mysterious, imaginary world. Representative classical tales include the *Chen-chung Chi* 枕中記 by Shen Chi-chi 沈既濟, the *Nan-k'o T'ai-shou Chuan* 南柯太守傳 by Li Kung-tso 李公佐, and *Ying-ying Chuan* 鶯鶯傳 by Yüan Chen 元稹, and *Ch'ang-hen Ko-chuan* 長恨歌傳 by Ch'en Hung 陳鴻.

The Pre-Modern Era

The Mongolian invasion represented the end not only of the Sung dynasty, but also of the cultural patterns of late antiquity, which centered on a class of officials selected through the examination system. The imperial examinations were halted for some 80 years during the Great Mongol Empire, known in China as the Yuan 元 dynasty, and the social status of the Confucianists plummeted. Commerce and world-class cities, on the other hand, thrived in this age. This led to the growth of the entertainment industry and an unprecedented flourishing of vernacular literature aimed at the petty bourgeoisie. A vernacular narrative genre called *pien-wen* 變文 ("changed writing"), which was partly recited and partly sung, arose from the reciting of Buddhist sermons in temples from the 7th century onward. At the start of the 12th century, a form of *chantefable* involving a medley of tunes called the *chu-kung-tiao* 諸宮調 ("all keys and modes") was created. It was designed to be sung and narrated, and so was structurally organized around suites of poetic songs sung to popular tunes of the age. A work of oral storytelling, it was part of a professional storytelling tradition that seems to have developed by the 9th century, and was already highly popular in Pienliang and other cities during the 11th and 12th centuries. The most complete surviving example of this genre is available in English translation under the title *Master Tung's Romance of the Western Chamber* 西廂記諸宮調.

The musical influence on plot structure inherited from the *chantefable*, combined with the verbal repartee of the *yüan-pen* 院本 genre of dramatic skits of the 11th century, formed the basis for the earliest known form of completely developed music drama in China, the *Yüan tsa-chü* 元雜劇, or Yuan Music Drama of the 13th century. Less than 170 complete examples of this genre have survived, with plots ranging from melodrama and crime to comedy and spiritual redemption. Among these theatrical works are intensely melodramatic works, such as Kuan Han-ch'ing's 關漢卿 *Injustice to Tou O* 竇娥冤, Pai P'u's 白樸 *Rain on the T'ung Tree* 梧桐雨, Ma Chih-yüan's 馬志遠 *Autumn in the Han Palace* 漢宮秋, and Chi Chün-hsiang's 紀君祥 *Orphan of Chao* 趙氏孤兒. Most of the musical comedies were social satires, such as fantasies about scholars climbing the bureaucratic ladder, often through love and at the expense of merchants. One of the most influential romantic music comedies from the 14th centuries was the *Romance of the Western Chamber* 西廂記, traditionally attributed to Wang Shih-fu 王實甫, which had an enormous impact on the plot structure of later music drama and fiction with its popularization of the *chia-jen ts'ai-tzu* 佳人才子 ("Beauty-Scholar") motif.

The literary heart and soul of all three of these theatrical forms, the *chantefable*, *yüan-pen*, and Yuan Music Drama, was a new kind of poetry called the *ch'ü* (ditty) based on a new song form that appeared in the north of China during the 12th and 13th centuries. The lyrics of the ditty also became an independent poetic form in their own right, originally sung to the tune of the ditty

in a manner like the *lieder* settings of 18th and 19th century German poetry by Franz Schubert and other contemporary Viennese composers. The major difference was that these composers created music to match an already existing poetic text, while the 12th and 13th century Chinese ditty poets created text to match an already existing ditty melody. By the 14th century, the original northern ditty melodies were gradually lost, yet ditty lyrics were still successfully set to what succeeding generations preserved as their original tune matrix, and new music from southern China was ultimately created to again allow musical performance.

A special characteristic of the ditty was that filler words could be freely added outside the fixed metrical pattern for euphonic effect. The metrical pattern itself was flexible within certain musically proscribed limits. This freedom gave the ditty a strikingly colloquial nature. Furthermore, several or even a score of ditties in the same mode could be combined into a ditty sequence 套數. This enabled it to be freely extended to a length that surpassed the scope of ordinary poetry, and endowed it with a special vividness:

I'm a ring-a-dang-ding brass pea
that won't steam tender
won't cook soft
won't pound flat
and won't fry pop!
You brothers in vice,
who told you to go poking
her can't-be-hacked-through
can't-be-chopped-down
can't-be-worried-loose
can't-be-thrown-off
oh-so-slow thousand-loop brocade slipknot?

我是個蒸不爛煮不熟
搥不扁炒不爆
響璫璫一粒銅豌豆
恁（您）子弟每（們）
誰教你鑽入他
鋤不斷砍不下
解不開頓不脫

慢騰騰千層錦套頭

(Pu-fu-lao 不伏老 ["Not Bowing to Old Age"] by Kuan Han-ch'ing)

Verbal effects like these were possible only in ditties. As the above two verses show, ditty writers in either music dramas or independent verses often flirted with the comic and risqué, although nostalgic and angry ditties were also written. In addition to the Yuan playwrights who frequently wrote ditties outside the context of music dramas, major ditty poets included Chang Yang-hao 張養浩 and Ch'iao Chi 喬吉.

Earlier kinds of poetry, the *Shih* and lyric, were part of the fabric of vernacular fiction in its earliest manifestation, prompt books 底本 or *hua-pen* 話本. These seem to have arisen, either directly or indirectly, through imitation from the oral storytelling tradition whose roots extended back to the 11th or 12th centuries during the Sung dynasty. All three kinds of poetry played an integral role in short, medium, and full-length vernacular fiction until the 19th century. The vernacular fiction genre flourished in the 14th through 16th centuries of the Ming 明 dynasty, thanks to the expansion of commercial printing.

The most outstanding extant examples of short story collections from this period are Feng Meng-lung's 馮夢龍 *Three Collections of Words [to Awaken the World]* 三言 and Ling Meng-ch'u's 凌濛初 *Two Collections of Striking the Table [in Amazement]* 二拍. There are four great works of extended fiction, major editions of which date from the 15th and 16th centuries of the Ming: *The Romance of the Three Kingdoms* 三國演義; *Water Margin*, also translated as *All Men are Brothers* 水滸傳; *Journey to the West* 西遊記, also translated as *Monkey*; and *Golden Lotus* 金瓶梅.

Unlike earlier 9th through 12th century classical literary tales written in the literary language about scholars, courtesans, semi-mythical characters, fox-spirits, and ghosts, the vernacular short story generally featured characters in an urban, middle-class setting. Money, marriage, social and business ethics, and the vagaries of fortune often constituted the principal plot concern. Of the four great works of extended fiction, *The Romance of the Three Kingdoms, Water Margin,* and *Journey to the West* were all products of a long and gradual process of revision and embellishment by storytellers and editors over the centuries leading up to the Ming dynasty, so they can be considered collective national creations, even if their later Ming versions primarily reflect a single literary mind. This process of collective revision could even be said of *Golden Lotus*, which circulated in manuscript form among various Ming literati prior to appearing in several different editions. In their Ming manifestations, all four great works of extended fiction reflect a growing sense of literary irony in their retelling of the traditional story plot. This may be an expression of growing literati dissatisfaction with the moral and political climate of the Ming court and society.

The Ming also witnessed the flourishing of a new kind of literati music drama called *ch'uan-ch'i* 傳奇 (Grand Music Drama), the same Chinese name as the literary tales of the 8th century onward, but otherwise a completely separate literary genre. Unlike Yuan Music Drama, which continued to be written during the Ming, albeit in increasingly modified form, Grand Music Drama evolved from an early popular form of music drama in southern China known as *nan-hsi* 南戲 (Southern Music Drama) into a highly sophisticated theatrical genre that came to rival the prevailing Yuan Music Drama in literary quality. Grand Music Drama plots were more complex and expansive than the neat, highly structured Yuan Music Drama which organized acts around suites of ditties in the same key or mode. Instead of being dominated by musical considerations, the structure of Grand Music Drama plots often became bipolar, with two major strands of plot development interwoven through the length of the play. The dominant plot strand was almost always a variation on the "Beauty-Scholar" theme so prevalent in both drama and fiction throughout the Ming. Various actors on the stage could sing roles at the same time, unlike the northern Yuan

Music Drama which restricted the singing role to a single star throughout the drama.

The most influential early example of Grand Music Drama was *The Lute* 琵琶記 by Kao Ming 高明, which has even appeared in a highly modified version on the Broadway stage as *The Lute Song*. By its more extensive use of imagery and poetic diction than ever before, the 14th century Ming original set a new standard for the Southern Music Drama tradition, lifting it beyond the ken of casual theatergoers. As a result, Grand Music Drama after *The Lute* gradually evolved a new, highly complex musical tradition which took its name and some of its characteristics from the music of K'un-shan 崑山. *K'un-ch'ü* 崑曲 (K'un Music Drama), as Grand Music Drama had then come to be called, reached its peak of popularity during the 16th century when T'ang Hsien-tsu 湯顯祖 wrote his cycle of four dream plays, including *The Peony Pavilion* 牡丹亭. Although a famous scene from *The Peony Pavilion* is often performed today as one of the few remaining examples of K'un Music Drama, T'ang Hsien-tzu was in fact less concerned for musical effect than for achieving highly theatrical effects through the lyrical intensity and figural density in his poetic imagery.

The fall of the Ming dynasty and the ultimate consolidation of political power under the Manchus in the 17th century are reflected in the plot of the most famous 17th century K'un Music Drama, *Peach Blossom Fan* 桃花扇 by K'ung Shang-jen 孔尚任. The *Peach Blossom Fan* also bears witness to the increasing distance between the musical and literary dimensions of K'un Music Drama which culminated in the virtual demise of the form by the 18th century. But a century earlier, the genre reached the climax of its literary development in Hung Sheng's 洪昇 *Palace of Eternal Sorrow* 長生殿. Appropriately, it took as its plot kernel a well-known narrative poem by the 9th century poet Pai Chü-i titled, "Song of Eternal Sorrow" 長恨歌 depicting the story of the eighth century Emperor Hsüan-tsung 唐玄宗 and the loss of his favorite imperial consort, Yang Kuei-fei 楊貴妃. While echoing the era of medieval Chinese poetry when vernacular fiction and drama may have first taken form, the *Palace of Eternal Sorrow* also invoked the "Beauty-Scholar" theme, which usually resulted in the union of male and female principal leads by the final scene, in a more poignant, ironic way. Thus, 17th and 18th century K'un Music Drama achieved a literary richness beyond that of its predecessors, but in its greatest works, also conveyed a sense of despair and irrevocable loss indicative of the age.

This same mixture of literary qualities can be found in increasing intensity among the majority of 17th through 19th century works of extended fiction, such as Wu Ching-tzu's 吳敬梓 *The Scholars* 儒林外史, Li Ju-chen's 李汝珍 *Flowers in the Mirror* 鏡花緣, and Ts'ao Hsüeh-ch'in's 曹雪芹 *Dream of the Red Chamber* 紅樓夢 or as it is alternatively known, *The Story of the Stone* 石頭記. The extended fiction of the 19th and early 20th centuries generally displayed a growing sense of despair at the moral lethargy of contemporary society. Among them were Wu Yen-jen's 吳趼人 *Strange Events Witnessed in the Past Twenty Years* 二十年目睹之怪現狀, Li Po-yüan's 李伯元 *Bureaucracy Exposed* 官場現形記, and Liu O's 劉鶚 *The Travels of Lao Ts'an* 老殘遊記.

Although fiction became increasingly popular from the 13th century onward, this was mainly as leisure reading among the literati and merchant class. After the Mongols were driven out in the 14th century and Han Chinese rule re-established, efforts were made to return to the views and values of two earlier great periods of Han Chinese rule, the Han and T'ang dynasties. The formalistic eight-legged essay 八股文 (so named because it was divided into eight parts) also got its start at this time. The eight-legged essay was the form adopted for the explication of the Confucian classics, which formed the basis for a reinstatement of the examination system. Thus, the eight-legged essay and imitations of the classical literary language of the earlier eras of Chinese cultural greatness became the major written genres of the time. There were no further breakthroughs in literary writing, except for a style of artistically heightened descriptions of everyday life experiences, called *hsiao-p'in* 小品 ("little sketches"), which emerged in the 15th and 16th centuries.

Fiction in the form of jottings 筆記, written in the literary language, also regained popularity at this time. The most important fiction collections in this genre were P'u Sung-ling's 蒲松齡 *Strange Stories from a Chinese Studio* 聊齋誌異 and Chi Hsiao-lan's 紀曉嵐 *Jottings from the Thatched Hall of Close Observations* 閱微草堂筆記. Although vernacular literature developed greatly during the 14th through 19th centuries, literature written in the classical literary language by scholars still constituted the cultural mainstream, given that literacy was still primarily their specialized province. This situation remained essentially unchanged up until the emergence of the New Literature Movement.

Modern Chinese Literature
The New Literature Movement

After attempts by the Western powers, Japan, and Russia to carve up or annex China in the late 19th and early 20th century, several professors at National Peking University initiated the New Culture Movement with the founding of the monthly magazine *Hsin Ch'ing-nien* 新青年 *(La Jeunesse; New Youth)*. *New Youth* criticized traditional culture and welcomed the arrival of "Mr. Democracy" and "Mr. Science" from the West.

The new literature was to herald social reform. Hu Shih 胡適 raised the curtain for the literary revolution with his 1917 essay, "A Modest Proposal for the Reform of Literature." In another essay, "On a Constructive Literary Revolution," Ch'en Tu-hsiu 陳獨秀, Ch'ien Hsüant'ung 錢玄同, and Hu Shih advocated "...a literature in the national language, and a national language of literary quality." He hoped that a nation with more than 2,000 different dialects could adopt a unified "national language" 國語, and that the written literary language of the scholarly class be discarded in favor of this national

language, the ordinary speech of everyday, as the basis for writing (see Chapter 3, Language). In his *History of Vernacular Literature*, Hu Shih reevaluated the Chinese literary tradition, and attempted to raise the vernacular literature of the people from its previous position as a sub-branch of literature to the mainstream. His goal was for vernacular literature to replace the classical literature of the scholars, which he pronounced "dead writing."

The early period of new literature was fraught with contradiction: individual freedom was encouraged so as to oppose traditional society, but was at the same time to be abandoned in the name of social justice, social concern, and the building of modern organizations. Rejecting the traditional culture and literature of the scholars, the reformers insisted that vernacular literature was the only living literature. Yet because vernacular literature grew out of the professional storytelling tradition, they also viewed it as backward and primitive. And, except for a few great works rich in cultural criticism, they adopted a largely negative attitude towards the vernacular tradition because it had originated as popular entertainment.

Chou Tso-jen 周作人 and the others faced the dilemma of advocating a vernacular literature while being unable to identify with either the form or content of traditional Chinese vernacular literature. To solve this dilemma, Hu Shih, Ch'en Tu-hsiu, and others proposed using the genres, forms, and spiritual consciousness of Western literature as models for imitation. Translation became a required intermediary in the creation of the new literature. The first translators had no scruples about remolding the Chinese language along European lines, and the foreign flavor of their writing became one of its major characteristics. Thus, a deliberate "horizontal transfer" of literature was advocated as part of the movement to modernize China. Actual literary works of the time, however, were not simply imitations of foreign models. Lu Hsun's 魯迅 story, *Diary of a Madman* 狂人日記, for example, was obviously influenced by Gogol, but the thrust of its contents—its denunciation of the overly severe and demanding ethics of traditional culture—was an expression of a uniquely Chinese situation. Its style approached that of the fables of Chuang Tzu, Lieh Tzu, Han Yü, and Liu Tsung-yüan.

The New Literature: Early Period

The new literature experimented with different genres and drew on varied sources, and as a result was eclectic and multifaceted in nature. Works such as Lu Hsun's novella, *The True Story of Ah Q* 阿Q正傳 and Lao She's 老舍 novel *Rickshaw Boy* 駱駝祥子 are told in a satirical tone filled with sorrow and pity. They seem to recall stories of the early vernacular short story tradition that describe the fickle fate of the lower classes, in contrast to the entertainment-oriented themes of the "Beauty-Scholar," itinerant swordsman, or detective-officials fictional works popular in the 17th and 18th centuries. These early works of modern fiction were also influenced to a certain degree by left-wing Western thinking and by the tradition of the Confucian scholars of pleading to the emperor on behalf of the people.

The neat five and seven-syllable lines of traditional poetry were replaced in this period by the cadences of spoken Chinese, modeled after the line patterns of Western poems. Even more notable was the discord that resulted from the introduction of intellectual argumentation and search for meaning and freedom into the traditional themes of love and natural scenery. Whether through ardent passion or cold critique, these poems signaled an end to gentleness and ingenuousness, to the fusion of emotion and scenery, and to the original harmony of man and nature. They announced the beginning of an aesthetics of bitterness and anguish.

Prose writers such as Lin Yü-t'ang 林語堂 and Liang Shih-ch'iu 梁實秋, who were intimately acquainted with the Western tradition, wrote informal essays in the style of Montaigne and Lamb. Excepting for their use of the colloquial language, they generally followed the classical prose style of the 9th through 12th centuries, mixing reason with emotion, and musing on minor events of daily life. Chu Tzu-ch'ing 朱自清, Hsia Mien-tsun 夏丏尊, Feng Tzu-k'ai 豐子愷, and Hsü Chih-mo 徐志摩 were all masters of this genre of writing.

The impassioned critiques of Liang Ch'i-ch'ao 梁啟超, the cogent lucidity of Hu Shih, and the caustic wit of Lu Hsun were often expressed in "wars of the pen." Standing in contrast to this high level of social involvement were writers such as Chou Tso-jen and Lin Yü-t'ang, who rediscovered the informal essays of the 16th and 17th centuries. They advocated an easygoing humor and the *savoir-vivre* of sipping bitter herb tea and copying old books; but were at the same time conversant with Freud and D.H. Lawrence. Although both types of essays were written in the colloquial language, their spirit was still rooted in the old culture of the scholar. The writers themselves, however, were not government officials but college professors, publishing house editors, journalists, and high school teachers.

Leftism in the New Literature

Owing to continued internal turbulence and constant power struggles among the warlords, a number of writers (mainly members of the Creation Society 創造社 literary group) followed up the literary revolution with a call for a "revolutionary literature," advocating that literature should serve the revolution. The Chinese Communist Party (CCP) set up the League of Leftist Writers 左聯. By the eve of the War of Resistance against Japan, the CCP had, through the power of organized party struggle, effectively stifled creativity and freedom of expression in many writers. Following the Japanese invasion, literature became totally subservient to the war effort, and the vigor and diversity of the early period of modern literature drew to a halt.

In the process of fanning the flames of patriotism and nationalistic fervor during the War of Resistance, a higher reassessment was made of traditional Chinese culture and literature. Many writers began adopting methods from folk drama and storytelling in their propaganda campaigns, presaging the literature of workers, peasants, and soldiers later espoused by the Chinese communists. Immediately following the Japanese surrender, China was plunged into all-out civil war. After the Chinese mainland fell into Chinese communist hands, socialist realism and Mao Tsetung's talks on art and literature at Yenan set the narrow confines within which writers on the mainland could operate. At the same time, the withdrawal of the ROC government to Taiwan turned a new page in modern Chinese literature.

The New Literature: The Later Period

To accurately catalogue the enormous array of literary works written every year since 1949 throughout the entire Chinese nation would be a herculean task. The difficulty presented by the sheer magnitude of such works is compounded by the fact that at present the Chinese mainland is not under the administrative control of the ROC government, and the power of literature to expose and criticize social and political ills is still greatly dreaded by Chinese communist authorities, resulting in the suppression of a large number of literary works over the years. Hence, data regarding these works and their writers is either incomplete or unreliable. Therefore, to assure accuracy and authoritativeness, this chapter will primarily focus on literature written in areas currently under ROC government control.

Early Taiwanese Literature

Aboriginal Traditions

Originally, the aboriginal peoples settled on the island of Taiwan thousands of years ago, and have since developed their distinctive oral narratives, languages, customs, and cultures. For centuries, aboriginies on Taiwan have been marginalized in the expression of Taiwanese culture. As each tribe has its own language and customs, the inter-tribal communication or coordination is weak. Only until recently was some progress made for such inter-tribal purposes, and the major event that drew different tribes together was the 1985 Wu Feng Incident 吳鳳事件, in which the statue of Wu Feng, a fictional deity invented by the Han-Chinese to domesticate the "barbaric" aborigines, was crushed. Quite a few

aboriginal intellectuals joined their people in the demonstration, urging the government to drop the ethnocentric Wu Feng mythology in the primary school textbooks and to pay more attention to the crisis the aboriginal population was facing.

Since 1980, aboriginal intellectuals have tried to reinvent their own past by going back to articulating and reexpressing the oral traditions. A large body of oral narratives about creation myths and tribal heroes have been transcribed and circulated in the form of parallel texts in which the original aboriginal languages are spelled out in romanization, accompanied by Chinese translation. The texts are not only intended for Chinese-speaking audiences, but are also primarily used as textbooks for the younger generations in the aboriginal population. For many aboriginal intellectuals, such texts literally constitute the last utopian hope for their traditions to be transmitted in the struggle of culture survival, fully aware of the brutal fact that even their children are resisting the use of native tongue; as a result, the indigenous languages and literatures are on the verge of disappearance.

Chinese Immigrant Literature

Between 1612 and 1844, quite a few Chinese intellectuals visited or stayed in Taiwan, most notably the Ming poet Shen Kuang-wen 沈光文, who was forced to land on the island by a typhoon in 1662 and afterwards played an important role in forming a Taiwanese Poets Society under the name of *tung-yin* 東吟. Like Koxinga 鄭成功, who came with his soldiers and conquered the island in 1661, Shen was a royal subject to the Ming emperors, even though China had then been taken over by the Ch'ing. His poems were mostly composed in regulated verse, expressing his patriotic feelings and nostalgia for the empire well lost. Shen was thus instrumental in planting the seeds of classical Chinese literature on the island. Students were trained to familiarize themselves with the grand Chinese literary tradition. The lyric subjects were often on exotic landscapes or the poet's own inscapes of consciousness that had little to do with social reality in Taiwan. As a consequence, in more than two hundred years, there were only a few memorable pieces composed of prose narrative—*Chu-lo-hsien chih* 諸羅縣志 by Ch'en Meng-lin 陳夢林 (1716 as year of arrival in Taiwan) or *Hsiao-liu-chiu man-chih* 小琉球漫誌 by Chu Shih-chieh 朱士玠 who stayed from June 1763 until August 1764), for example—by high officials who happened to be in Taiwan for a brief period.

Several Taiwanese local poets began to make their names known during the mid-19th century, among them Ts'ai T'ing-lan 蔡廷蘭 (1811-1870), Ch'en Chao 陳肇, Huang Ching 黃敬, Cheng Yung-hsi 鄭用錫 (1787-1858), and Lin Tsan-mei 林占梅 (1816-1865). They were literati and cultural elites writing in the mode of classical Chinese lyrics; as these intellectuals played important roles in Taiwan's history, their infleunce on local culture remains strong. In response to the colonial world of late Ch'ing period and in reaction to their precursors, Taiwanese poets of the next two decades became more devoted to everyday subjects and often committed to expressing nationalist sentiment. T'ang Ching-sung 唐景崧 and Ch'iu Feng-chia 丘逢甲 were two prominent officials and poets who got deeply involved in establishing the Democratic Taiwan Nation 台灣民主國 on May 25, 1895, upon hearing the news that the Ch'ing court had ceded Taiwan to Japan. Other major poets of this generation, such as Ch'en Wei-ying 陳維英 and Wang K'ai-t'ai 王凱泰 were equally interested in describing ordinary people and popular culture. In many ways, they opened paths toward a more dynamic and democratic era of literary production, the period of Taiwanese literature under Japanese rule (1895-1945).

Early Colonial Literature

On April 7, 1895, in the Treaty of Shimonoseki which put an end to the first Sino-Japanese War, Japan compelled the Ch'ing empire to cede Taiwan and the nearby Pescadores. Subsequently, the Japanese army landed on Taiwan on May 29, 1895, but met fierce resistance from the Taiwanese, who had proclaimed independence. The Taiwan Republic established by a group of cultural elites and local people lasted only ten days; however, the Taiwanese fought the Japanese troops for four months before surrendering Tainan city in October 1895. Sporadic guerrilla resistance to the colonizer continued for some 20 years. The casualties on both sides were quite heavy; more than 10,000 Taiwanese died. As a result, the Japanese gradually modified their co-optation policies to seek the acquiescence of the Taiwanese elites and began to introduce modern technology and social reforms, instead of resorting to military or political forces.

Between 1895 and 1913, a minor group of national elites and largely poets in the classical Chinese tradition returned to China, thinking that they could not survive colonialism. The remaining local elites tried, on the other hand, to preserve their cultural heritage, retain ties with other provinces, and develop their distinctive arts of improvisation in the midst of colonial banality and brutality. Hung Ch'i-sheng 洪棄生 was probably the most famous writer of the period. He refused to cut off his queue, withdrew from public life, and wrote in classical Chinese, to make the point that he was identifying himself with the Ch'ing. In his poetical and prose works, Hung constantly referred to the society and culture of Taiwan of the time to reveal his patriotism and nationalism. However, the most important literary event in the first 20 years under Japanese occupation was the establishment of a Li Poetry Society 櫟社, of which the key members included Lien Ya-t'ang 連雅堂, Lin Ch'ih-hsien 林痴仙, Lin Hsien-t'ang 林獻堂, and many others. The society was responsible for publishing an influential journal on poetry and poetics, *T'aiwan Wen-i Chiu-chih* 台灣文藝舊誌; it was also instrumental in supporting nationalist movements. Lien's monumental work on Taiwan's history, *A Comprehensive History of Taiwan* 台灣通史, remains a classic in the field.

In 1911, Liang Ch'i-ch'ao 梁啟超 visited Taiwan and brought with him ideas of Western enlightenment and new experimental literature. Even though Taiwanese writers of the time were versed in the classical Chinese tradition, they were forced to confront the colonial reality and to get interested in more realistic modes of literary expression. This made a shift toward modern literature inevitable.

Taiwanese New Literature
The Colonial Context

Whereas most literature in Taiwan prior to 1920 was written in the style of the classical Chinese tradition, a new strand of modern Taiwanese literature emerged in the early 1920s in a process commonly referred to as the Taiwanese New Literature movement 台灣新文學運動. Compared with its mainland counterpart, Taiwanese New Literature displayed two distinctive features that seem to universally characterize colonial cultural products, its multi-linguisticity and its overriding political import. In addition to Chinese-language works, many of the literary products of this movement—especially in the later stage—were written in Japanese. There was also a viable Taiwanese Language movement 台灣話運動 in the early 1930s, advocating the use of a new written language based on spoken Taiwanese, which is a version of the southern Fukienese dialect used by the majority of population in Taiwan. From the beginning, Taiwanese New Literature was an integral part of a new phase of sociopolitical resistance by the Taiwanese people to the Japanese colonial rule. In the 1920s, the Taiwanese intelligentsia, revolving around the Taiwanese Cultural Association 台灣文化協會 (1921-1931), launched a large-scale cultural reform program with various sorts of political agendas, in lieu of the futile and often brutally suppressed armed revolts in the first two decades of the Japanese period. Key figures of the early stage of the movement, such as Lai He 賴和 (1894-1943), frequently regarded as the "father of Taiwanese New Literature," Ch'en Hsu-ku 陳虛谷 (1896-1965), and Ts'ai Ch'iu-t'ung 蔡秋桐 (b. 1900), were also active members of the Cultural Association, participating in its well-known islandwide mass education lecture tours. Not surprisingly, nationalistic sentiments were expressed through their literary works. Even after 1931, when a harsh crackdown by the colonial government put an end to the lively resistance activities of the previous decade, the New Literature nourished by the sociopolitical movements of the twenties continued to grow among the increasingly bilingual intellectual class of Taiwan. The legacy of resistance to colonialism, too, persisted, in either overt or covert forms, till the very end of the Japanese period.

However, the broadly defined political nature of the Taiwanese New Literature refers not only to explicit criticism of the colonizers, in works by such undaunted anti-imperialist fighters as Lai He and Yang K'ui 楊逵 (1906-1985), but also to the cultural hybridity in later works of the Taiwanese New Literature movement written in the colonizer's language, which was by definition a political product and carries with it imprints of an unjust power relationship. Whereas the first generation of Taiwanese New Literature writers, most of whom were born after the Japanese takeover, still exhibited a characteristically Chinese cultural and artistic outlook, there was a notable shift in the second generation of Taiwanese New Literature writers. As a matter of fact, the overall increase in the degree of hybridity in Taiwanese culture in the second half of the Japanese period may be explained by changes in the colonizer's governing policies.

Beginning in 1918-1919, the Japanese adopted an effective assimilation policy 內地延長主義, (which would translate as "the principle of treating Taiwan as an extension of Japan proper"), which shifted from high-handed police control and differential treatment of the Taiwanese to more enlightened civil governing, emphasis on education, and cultivation of a more congenial relationship between Japanese and Taiwanese. As the new colonial condition steadily took shape and Japanese language education became more effectively implemented, a greater number of students in the colony went to study in Japan. Those among them who enrolled in college literary departments and had contact with famous Japanese writers later played influential roles in the literary scene of Taiwan. An even more drastic change was that, during the last phase of the

Japanese period (1937-1945), as Japan declared war with China, the colonial government mobilized huge amounts of social resources to enforce an intensified Japanization program 皇民化運動, (literally, "the movement of converting Taiwanese into loyal subjects of the Japanese Emperor"), which included a ban on Chinese-language publications.

The hybrid nature of this colonial literature reflects Taiwan's colonial past and its relatively unusual experience as a Japanese colony. A state of Han 漢 settlers since the 17th century and a province of the Manchurian-governed China since 1885, in the early part of the 20th century Taiwan was incorporated by Japan into a different geopolitical and economic system, and as a result went through the initial stages of modernization via its East Asian colonizer, which had itself recently modernized after the Western model. The kind of society produced in Taiwan by this process was inevitably of a hybrid nature, with modern and traditional institutions of different ethnic origins coexisting side by side. Taiwan occupied a strategic position in Japan's imperialist project, serving as a base for Japan's further advancement into South China and Southeast Asia. For this reason, it is said to have received relatively benign treatment from the Japanese (as compared to Japan's other colonies, such as Korea), considerably mitigating the hostility between colonizer and colonized. The colonial condition in Taiwan is thus a product of the extremely intricate political and cultural negotiations between the colonial government and the local elite, articulated by progressive intellectuals who often served as spokesmen for the elite. Fine Taiwanese writers of the later period, such as Chang Wen-huan 張文環 (1909-1978), Lü Ho-jo 呂赫若 (1914-1950), Yang K'ui, and Lung Ying-tsung 龍瑛宗 (b. 1911), achieved their distinctive art under the influence of Western artistic trends through Japanese literary institutions.

Taiwanese New Literature Movement

As stated earlier, the Taiwanese New Literature movement began as part of a larger cultural reform movement during the 1920s. A brief introduction of this cultural movement, sometimes called the Taiwanese New Culture movement 台灣新文化運動, may be in order. The first events of this movement took place in 1920, when some Taiwanese expatriates in Tokyo organized the New People Association 新民會, followed by a student-based Taiwanese Youth Association 台灣青年會. The two organizations published a journal called *Taiwanese Youth* 台灣青年 to propagate progressive ideas and voice opinions about the current state of affairs in Taiwan. The zeal for cultural reform soon spread to the island itself and was carried on by the Taiwanese Cultural Association. There were significant parallels between the Taiwanese New Culture movement and the Chinese mainland's May Fourth movement 五四運動. First of all, intellectuals in both societies, faced with the imperative to modernize, identified the cultural sediments of Neo-Confucian moralism and the feudalist social order as reactionary forces obstructing progress. Inspired by democratic ideas of modern Western society, both groups had come to associate the "old" with the conservative mentality of the gentry class and the "new" with ways of the "modern citizen"— and sought to transform the masses through popular education and cultural enlightenment 文化啟蒙. The idea of social Darwinism, which equated rejuvenation of national culture with survival of the people, adds to the urgency of the task of cultural reform as a means of national self-preservation. Secondly, the new intellectuals of both societies were influenced by the dynamics of progressive discourses on national emancipation and socialist revolution in the years following the First World War. Such currents of thought created an imaginary alliance among the "weak and oppressed" nations in the world and provided a powerful rationale for nationalistic resistance by victims of imperialist aggression, as obviously the Chinese mainland and Taiwan both were. Thus, a patriotic discourse combining and constantly negotiating the two components of socio-cultural modernization (cultural enlightenment) and anti-imperialism (national salvation, anti-colonialism) was developed in the 1920s and shared by the new intellectuals on both the Chinese mainland and Taiwan.

Although in the first two issues of *Taiwanese Youth* there were already articles on language reform and the need for rejuvenating contemporary Taiwanese literature, it was not until the heated New Versus Old Literary Debate 新舊文學論戰, which began with Chang Wo-chün's 張我軍 attack on traditional poets in 1924 and lasted till 1926, that the Taiwanese New Literature movement was formally launched. During the debate, new literary concepts—mainly those centering around the advantage of adopting the vernacular as a new literary medium and the social functions of literature in a modern age—were introduced, criticized, and defended. Traditional poets were castigated for using literature to incur social gains and political favor, their literary style criticized as hackneyed and insincere. Advocates of new literature, on the other hand, were branded as shallow and ignorant charlatans, their literary views ungrounded in solid learning. As in the case of many literary debates in modern times, the heated antagonism between opposite camps precluded meaningful exchange of ideas; yet, there was very little theoretically sound defense on aesthetic grounds. Rather, the debate performed an important ritualistic function: after the debate, traditional literary activities were increasingly confined to poetry clubs that continued to thrive but with limited social reach, while New Literature was legitimized as a powerful social institution. Through this institution, the new intellectuals denounced their Chinese cultural heritage—partly by taking traditional men of letters and their world views as scapegoats—and endorsed a vision of "modern civilization." The denouncement and the vision constituted the major content of works of Taiwanese New Literature for at least a decade.

If the two New Culture movements on the Chinese mainland and Taiwan were analogous but separate, the relationship between the Chinese and Taiwanese New Literature movements, as consti-

tuting parts of the former, was actually much closer. At the initial stage, terms of literary reform in Taiwanese New Literature movement virtually mirrored those of its slightly earlier Chinese counterpart (1917-1925). When Chang Wo-chün wrote the polemical essays that triggered the Old Versus New Literary Debate, he was a student of the Peking Normal University. During the debate, the major tenets for the May Fourth literary revolution, such as Hu Shih's 胡適 "Principle of Eight Don'ts" 八不主義 from his "Preliminary Suggestions for Literary Reform" 文學改良芻議 were introduced with slight modifications. Even the harsh style of the way Chang Wo-chün castigated the traditional poets is immediately reminiscent of the radical Chinese reformist Ch'en Tu-hsiu 陳獨秀. Furthermore, throughout the decade of the 1920s, creative works by Chinese New Literature writers, such as Lu Hsun 魯迅, Hu Shih, Kuo Mo-jo 郭沫若, Ping Hsin 冰心, Wang Lu-yen 王魯彥, and Ling Shu-hua 凌淑華, were reprinted in Taiwanese journals and undoubtedly served as models for literary practice.

However, within a decade, this dependent relationship began to change. Apparently, during this time the deepening of Japanese colonization had begun to structurally transform Taiwan society and steered it further away from the cultural orbit of the Chinese mainland. Consciousness of this new reality among the Taiwanese intellectuals manifested itself in two consecutive literary debates in 1931-32, the Nativist Literature Debate 鄉土文學論戰 and the Taiwanese Language Debate 台灣語文論戰, which represented a turning point in the Taiwanese New Literature movement.

The Nativist Literature Debate testified to the prominent leftist presence in Taiwan's literary circles. The literary program proposed by its chief advocate Huang Shih-hui 黃石輝—suggesting that writers target their creative works at the working-class mass—was clearly modeled upon the leftist concept of proletarian literature. And the split of the Taiwanese Cultural Association in 1927 was primarily a result of disagreement in resistance strategies between the nationalist right wing and the socialist left wing. After the split, the association was controlled by the left-wing members, led by Lien Wen-ch'ing 連溫卿 and Wang Min-ch'uan 王敏川. The more moderate members formed the Taiwanese People's Party 台灣民眾黨 and continued to fight for greater constitutional rights for the Taiwanese people. Yet, the political climate in the colony was so disillusioning that even the Taiwanese People's Party later displayed a leftward leaning tendency and was forced to dissolve by the colonial government in 1931.

Initially, the Taiwanese New Culture movement focused on cultural enlightenment to address the society's internal needs to modernize, and the main targets of its attack were old Chinese customs and lingering social ills of feudalism. As Taiwan proceeded along the course of modernization, however, the worldwide economic depression in the late 1920s made typical social problems of a capitalist society, such as unemployment and class exploitation, even more manifest, which contributed to the thriving of socialist ideology in Taiwan, and, subsequently, the rise of hard-core nativism.

Primarily concerned with internal social problems and conflicts between classes, leftist intellectuals called for a Taiwan-centered view in literary creation. Aside from a class-oriented literary view, Huang Shih-hui also was known for forcefully arguing that Taiwanese writers should write in their own language and about things on their own homeland. Termed by historians as following the direction of "self-improvement based on one province (Taiwan)" 一島改良主義, advocates of the Nativist Literature clearly envisioned a "Taiwanese consciousness" as something to be distinguished from the more inclusive "Chinese consciousness," or the ethnic consciousness of the Han race 漢民族意識.

This Taiwanese consciousness was precisely the core spirit of Kuo Ch'iu-sheng's 郭秋生 campaign for Taiwanese language in the following year. The Taiwanese Language Debate, with the literary journal *Nan-yin* 南音 as its major forum, revealed the anxieties and ambivalent feelings of a colonized people in their attempts to develop a national language. As an effort to assert the Taiwanese subjectivity, the movement also, even just by implication, functions to sever the Taiwanese intellectuals' emotional ties with China. First and foremost, the movement called attention to the fact that early advocates of the Taiwanese New Literature had followed the Chinese model of the May Fourth movement too closely. They had thus unwittingly mistaken the latter's problematics and strategies for their own, without giving proper attention to the objective circumstances of Taiwan.

To facilitate popular education in a country of an extremely high illiteracy rate, advocates of the May Fourth movement proposed to replace the difficult, obsolete classical Chinese language with modern Chinese vernacular as the official written language. The basic theoretical assumption was that since there would be a close correspondence between the spoken and written versions of modern Chinese, as reflected in the famous slogan "我手寫我心" (My hand writes down whatever my mouth utters), the efforts required to become literate in Chinese would be greatly lessened. In reality, however, a standard Chinese vernacular was yet to be popularized within the country; people from different regions still predominantly used dialects for daily communication; and some Chinese dialects are even mutually unintelligible (see section, Dialects, Chapter 3, Language). There was, to be sure, a considerable disparity between the standard Chinese vernacular and the southern Fukienese dialect used by the majority of Taiwanese. Moreover, as Taiwan had already been politically separated from China for over two decades, its people had much fewer channels for learning the standard Chinese vernacular through public institutions such as an education system, publications, or a state bureaucracy.

Nevertheless, early advocates of the Taiwanese New Literature movement still favored the adoption of Chinese vernacular as the medium for Taiwanese New Literature. The fact that this position was uncontested at the time shows that by then the ethnic-cultural identity of Taiwanese intellectuals was still predominantly Chinese. One popular argument they espoused was that since most of the Taiwanese gentry class members were still tutored in the written language of classical Chinese in their childhood, minimal additional efforts would enable them to use the Chinese vernacular as a literary medium. The advantage of this was that it would facilitate the circulation of Taiwanese literary works in the larger Chinese community, since obviously Chinese recognition was still regarded as a significant symbolic capital by Taiwanese intellectuals. In practice, however, despite the goodwill on the part of most Taiwanese New Literature writers, the disadvantages are by no means negligible. It is said that Lai He had to write his works in classical Chinese first, then translate it into the Chinese vernacular, and finally revise it with the more life-like Taiwanese colloquialisms. Yang Shou-yü 楊守愚 (1905 1959), a writer well-versed in the Chinese vernacular because of special personal background, had to regularly rewrite the works submitted for publication when he served as the editor for the literary section of the *Taiwanese People's Newspaper* 台灣民報. Such a cumbersome and laborious process works against the fundamental principle of realistic literary writing, which explains why the kind of reevaluation offered by the Taiwanese Language Movement was well-received even by Lai He, a writer with ostensible Chinese consciousness.

Without political enforcement, however, the goals of the Taiwanese Language Movement were very difficult to materialize. The fact that many of the words in the Taiwanese spoken language are not believed to have corresponding Chinese characters made the development of a new writing system an enormous project beyond the reach of private groups. It is said that Lai He, after extensively using the Taiwanese language in writing his short story "A Letter of Criticism from a Comrade" 一個同志的批信 (1935), was so frustrated with the experiment that he completely stopped writing fiction in the New Literature style. The colonial government, not surprisingly, only tried to hinder such a nationalistically motivated project as an obstacle to the implementation of Japanese as the official language in Taiwan. The Taiwanese Language Debate thus reveals a typical dilemma facing colonized people: as the effort to develop a new national language based on the native tongue was seen by the Japanese colonial rulers as mainly a linguistic strategy of resistance and a means to assert one's own subjectivity, it was not likely to gain the political support required for its success. Despite the failure, however, the Taiwanese Language Movement must be regarded as a significant turning point in the Taiwanese New Literature movement. Since 1931 there was a marked decline in the number of works by Chinese New Literature writers reprinted in Taiwanese journals. From this point on, the development of Taiwanese New Literature began to consciously depart from the Chinese model, embarking on a path of its own.

Maturation and Growth

The crackdown of leftist organizations and the general suppression of sociopolitical movements in 1931 ironically heralded a period of maturation and growth for Taiwanese New Literature, which lasted for over a decade. Various literary organizations were formed and new literary journals mushroomed. Having passed its initial, experimental stage, the evolution of the new literary form, particularly in the technical respect, made impressive progress during this period. Whereas the first generation of Taiwanese New Literature writers continued to be productive, a group of young talents also joined the rank. There was, however, a notable gap between the two generations of Taiwanese New Literature writers in all such respects as cultural outlook, aesthetic preference, and vocational orientation. This apparent disjuncture in the relatively brief history of Taiwanese New Literature is particularly noteworthy, as it points to a rapidly changing cultural landscape in the second half of Taiwan's Japanese colonial period.

It has been argued that, by the time when the New Literature movement began, despite the fact that Taiwan had already been colonized by the Japanese for more than two decades, the cultural identity of Taiwanese intellectuals was still predominantly Chinese. Members of an ordinary Taiwanese gentry family were still sufficiently exposed to the Chinese cultural tradition, as children were still sent to private tutorial classes, or *shufang* 書房, to study classical Chinese. Most of the first generation of Taiwanese New Literature writers, being members of the traditional gentry class, were well-versed in classical Chinese and competent in traditional Chinese poetry writing, a practice to which some of them reverted after Chinese publications were banned in 1937. The fact that there were no substantial changes in the ethnic content of cultural production and reproduction in the society is attributable to the special kind of colonial policies that were applied to Taiwan during the first two decades of the Japanese colonial period: Acknowledging that the colony had a separate history of its own, the Japanese were primarily concerned with maintaining social stability, rather than culturally assimilating the Taiwanese people. The cultural upbringing and community imagination of Taiwanese writers whose formative years fell into the first half of the colonial period were therefore not fundamentally transformed by the colonial rule, even though most of them also received formal education in Japanese and were equipped with modern knowledge. Lai He, for example, went to the modern-style medical school and knew the Japanese language well, but he never used it in his creative writing. More important, as evidenced both by his writing and the role he played in the literary community, he was in many ways an exemplary traditional Chinese intellectual.

Significantly influenced by the Chinese May Fourth movement and its reformist ideology, the historical role played by this generation of Taiwanese writers was primarily that of new intellectuals in a pre-modern society struggling to break away from the past and to usher in progressive social visions. The past, however, was still very much with them. It can be easily demonstrated that, compared to their younger followers, this generation of Taiwanese writers carried over a considerable cultural legacy from the Chinese tradition in their New Literature-style works. Many of their works criticized the "spiritual disease" of the Taiwanese society directly reflecting the Neo-Confucian moralist world view. The formal dimension of literary works by writers of this generation also displays a characteristically transitional character. The omniscient narrative point of view and episodic plot structure were obvious traits inherited from Chinese vernacular fiction. Since the modern short story, the novel, and the free verse were essentially forms imported from the West, this generation of Taiwanese writers' assimilation of Western literary techniques and artistic conceptions was largely superficial.

The situation, however, was very different with writers born at later dates (Yang K'ui was born in 1906; Weng Nao 翁鬧, 1908; Chang Wen-huan, 1909; Lung Ying-tsung 龍瑛宗, 1911; and Lü Ho-jo, 1914). In their formative years, the colonial cultural institutions were increasingly consolidated, and there was consequently a marked decrease in the value of Chinese learning as cultural capital. Generally speaking, unlike their immediate predecessors, therefore, the generation of Taiwanese writers active in the 1930s and 1940s lacked a solid background in traditional Chinese learning and demonstrated a more characteristically hybrid cultural identity. (As Hsu Chün-ya 許俊雅 has pointed out, the use of Japanese in literary creation gradually increased since 1933, and, by the time around 1936 and 1937, there were actually very few works written in Chinese.) At the same time, whereas rapid social change was a norm in 20th-century non-Western countries, Japanese colonization generated an even more accelerated pace in Taiwan's course of modernization. The gap between the social visions of the two generations of writers was even more remarkable, as the younger writers were raised in a society at a considerably more advanced stage of modernization than their predecessors. Several critics have pointed out that Lai He seemed to be obsessed with the abusive power of laws and regulations enforced by the colonial government and its agents. These critics often justified Lai He's criticism with the fact that police control was notoriously harsh in Taiwan during the Japanese colonial period. Nevertheless, judging from many passages in Lai He's fiction in which he meditated on the demarcation line between justice and law from various philosophical points of view, one gets the impression that his ideals and framework of reference were still derived from a pre-modern, Confucianist world view. The fact that younger writers tended to present both the evil and the benign sides of the law indicates that these writers held a more realistic view of modern judicial system, in spite of discriminatory practices in the colonial context. Thus, in many ways the two generations of Taiwanese writers perceived the relationship between the individual and society quite differently.

Another significant factor is that the younger generation of writers were oriented to the literary profession in an entirely different manner from their predecessors. The 1930s saw the emergence of a new cohort of writers who had studied in Japan, a group that constituted the majority of second-generation Taiwanese New Literature writers. While in Japan, these aspiring young Taiwanese writers found themselves on the periphery of an entirely different system of cultural production, and many of them began to earnestly seek membership in the Japanese literary institutions. They enrolled in university literary classes, attended salons revolving around famous writers, and, above all, joined literary contests, which seemed to be an effective way of earning recognition from the "center," or mainstream Japanese literary circles (often referred to as *Chung-yang wen-t'an* 中央文壇). Yang K'ui, Lü Ho-jo, and Lung Ying-tsung were winners of literary prizes in the mid-1930s. As Japanese assimilation of the West surpassed that of Chinese in the same period, the Taiwanese writers' knowledge of Japanese seemed to have enabled them to have a closer grasp of Western artistic concepts, and, more important, of the kind of vocational vision that artists in a modern society often take for granted. As they came to perceive themselves as professional artists, with technical expertise and individualistic aesthetic vision, it is less conceivable that they would ever become such spiritual leaders as Lu Hsun or Lai He, whose status as major writers was derived from personal charisma and outstanding moral character as well as from literary talent.

Apparently, the younger writers enjoyed access to a wide range of literary models, mainly from the West, as evidenced by the remarkable diversity their works have shown in both artistic mode and ideological outlook. To give a few better known examples: Yang K'ui adhered to the more orthodox leftism and dedicated his literary works to humanitarian criticisms of class exploitation, imperialism, and general evils in a capitalist society. Chang Wen-huan's approach was more humanistic in a liberal vein. His interest in the mystic power of the individual's inner self, projected onto Nature, resulted in some beautifully written lyrical pieces. Lü Ho-jo successfully emulated naturalism, offering realistic portraits of Taiwan's degenerated gentry class through "typical characters." Lung Ying-tsung's works showed influences of Symbolism, delicately aesthetic, with visible touches of decadence.

It is perhaps ironic that, whereas early advocates of the Taiwanese New Literature movement insisted on using the Chinese vernacular to ensure a place in the Chinese literary world, two out of three Taiwanese stories first collected in anthologies published in China—"The Newspaper Man" 送報夫 by Yang K'ui, and "The Oxcart" 牛車 by Lü Ho-jo (the other story selected was the Chinese language "The Ill-fated" 薄命, by Yang Hua 楊華, 1900-1936)—were translated from Japanese. And significantly, too, the high reputation these two stories enjoyed was clearly derived from the fact that they had won prizes in literary contests sponsored by important Japanese magazines. Furthermore, Hu Feng 胡風, the editor of the Chinese collections in which these stories were found, *Mountain Spirit: Short Stories from Korea and Taiwan* 山靈：朝鮮台灣短篇小說集

and *Anthology of Stories from Weak and Small Nations in the World* 世界弱小民族小說選, was a renowned leftist literary theorist. The fact that Hu selected Yang and Lü's stories in recognition of their anti-imperialist spirit points to an extremely complex relationship between the Taiwanese authors and their Japanese colonizers, who were simultaneously oppressors and bestowers of cultural prestige. Such facts eloquently speak to the profoundly ambivalent cultural positions in which the second-generation Taiwanese New Literature writers found themselves in the 1930s.

End of an Era

After the Sino-Japanese War broke out in 1937, the colonial government in Taiwan started an intensive Japanization program, and banned the Chinese-language sections in newspapers and magazines. The impact of the harsh reality of war was not, however, fully felt until 1941, when Japan launched the Pacific War. The year of 1937, for example, still saw the publication of a literary magazine *Wind and Moon* 風月報 (the only Chinese-language magazine of this period), which featured popular types of literati writings, such as pulp romance, familiar essays, and occasional pieces of traditional scholarship, and enjoyed wide circulation. A literary organization consisting mainly of Japanese writers also published in 1940 an aesthetically-oriented journal *Literary Taiwan* 文藝台灣. With the onslaught of the Pacific War, however, the Japanese stepped up their war campaign efforts and began to actively mobilize people in the colony to make a contribution to the "Warfare of the Great East Asia" 大東亞戰爭. Between 1941 and 1942, *Literary Taiwan* chimed in with the colonial government's call for arms and published such stories as Chou Chin-po's 周金波 (b. 1920) "Volunteer Conscript" 志願兵 and other unabashedly propagandist poems and plays. Several well-known second-generation writers of Taiwanese New Literature, disapproving of both the political stance and artistic orientation of *Literary Taiwan*, formed their own literary organization

and began to publish *Taiwanese Literature* 台灣文學 in 1941. Before the two journals were forced to merge by the government under the new name *Taiwanese Literature and Art* 台灣文藝 in 1944, *Taiwanese Literature* published perhaps the most important works of second-generation Taiwanese New Literature writers: such as "Capon" 閹雞 and "Night Monkeys" 夜猿 by Chang Wen-huan; "Wealth, Offspring, and Longevity" 財子壽, "Peace for the Entire Family" 閤家平安, and "Guava" 石榴 by Lü Ho-jo; "A Village Without Doctors" 無醫村 by Yang K'ui; and "Rapid Torrents" 奔流 by Wang Ch'ang-hsiung 王昶雄 (b. 1916)

The contention between *Literary Taiwan* and *Taiwanese Literature* between 1941 and 1944 represented a significant turn of events, as second-generation Taiwanese New Literature writers began to directly confront oppressive relationships within the colonial structure. For these writers, who had been partially nourished by Japanese culture in their formative years and to which they held various degrees of allegiance, this experience must have been simultaneously disillusioning and educating. Above all, it became clear to them that artistic approaches were not ideologically innocent. One thing that the Taiwanese writers objected to was the Japan-centered, typically colonialist point of view of *Literary Taiwan* which treated Taiwan as an exotic "foreign" place to be romanticized for the connoisseurship of readers in Japan. To the Taiwanese writers, such a literary approach was obviously complicitous in the colonial government's effort to involve culture in the process of political domination by way of diverting people from socio-political concerns to purely aesthetic ones. Such realizations are undoubtedly behind the tactics used by writers of *Taiwanese Literature* in their endeavors to champion realism as opposed to the exquisite aestheticism and romanticism of *Literary Taiwan*. Aside from works directly informed by leftist ideology, such as those by Yang K'ui, it is said that some writers of the *Taiwanese Literature* group consciously shifted to more detailed depictions of local customs, rural life, and folk traditions of

Chinese/Taiwanese origin in order to register their resentment of the Japanization program.

The nationalistic orientation of *Taiwanese Literature*, however, failed to attract some of the ardent writers of an even younger generation, such as Yeh Shih-t'ao 葉石濤 (b. 1925) and Chou Chin-po, who published in *Literary Taiwan* and expressed either aestheticism or political loyalty to the colonizer. Yeh even wrote the controversial essay "Shit Realism" 糞寫實主義, which provoked heated response from colleagues of *Taiwanese Literature*. However, it was not until the next epoch that some of this younger generation of writers began to deeply reflect upon the complicated issues surrounding colonial subjectivity.

The unusually convoluted trajectory traveled by Taiwanese New Literature writers may also be illuminated by a brief examination of their intriguingly different attitudes toward the issue of modernity. The wholehearted embrace by many first-generation writers of modernity as an advanced stage of civilization was expressed in vacant terms, for essentially they never had any real experience of a truly modernized society. Most of the second generation, pressured by wartime literary policies, engaged in indirect resistance by means of asserting nativism, to the effect of notably decreasing their criticism of traditional, feudalist traits of the Taiwanese society. However, if some of them consciously denigrated modern urban civilization, symbolically represented by the Japanese metropolis, still others held exactly the opposite stance. In works of Ch'en Huo-ch'üan 陳火泉 (b. 1908) and the younger writer Chou Chin-po, who opted to side with progress, a prominent theme was the urgency to modernize in view of the obvious benefits that modernity could have brought to the Taiwanese people. As Japan is equated with civilization, they ardently supported Japanization, albeit not without doubts from time to time.

In artistic terms, the modern literary form of the Taiwanese New Literature significantly departed from the classical Chinese tradition, but its evolution was brought to an abrupt cessation at the end of the Second World War when Taiwan was returned to China. Several years later, the Nationalists, having lost the Chinese mainland to the communists in the civil war, relocated to Taiwan and started an entirely new era. The drastic changes such historical events brought to the society of Taiwan caused most of the Taiwanese New Literature writers to halt their creative activities. Many artistic potentials were therefore never allowed to develop to their fullest extent, and the movement ended before any genuinely masterful works of art could ever appear.

The legacy of the Taiwanese New Literature movement was suppressed in the postwar years, as the dominant culture was now constituted by the mainland Chinese tradition. But there were still significant works written and published, and the exploration of colonial subjectivity continued to be the dominant concern of works written by writers directly nourished by the Taiwanese New Literature of the Japanese colonial period, such as *The Orphan of Asia* 亞細亞孤兒 by Wu Cho-liu 吳濁流 (1900-1976), "The Oleander Flowers" 夾竹桃 by Chung Li-ho 鍾理和, *The Man Who Rolls On the Ground* 滾地郎 by Chang Wen-huan, and later works by Yeh Shih-t'ao. Despite their largely marginal position in the society's cultural production and reproduction, therefore, these writers played a crucial role in Taiwan's postwar literary history by offering alternative visions to the dominant culture, and their impact was increasingly felt in the Nativist 本土化 movement osf the last two decades.

Post-1949 Literature in Taiwan
Shifting Literary Trends

Taiwan's post-1949 era began when China's Nationalist government, led by Chiang Kai-shek, settled on the off-shore island-province of Taiwan after the mainland fell to the Chinese communists. The 40-year period under the rule of two presidents from the Chiang family was characterized by remarkable social, political, and cultural continuity and homogeneity. Drastic structural changes, however, have been occurring at all levels of the society since the mid-1980s, as direct consequences of the lifting of martial law, the recognition of an opposition party, the removal of the ban on founding newspapers, and the resumption of communication with mainland China at the civilian level. New intellectual and artistic currents have emerged, many with the explicit or implicit motive of reexamining existing orders. Nonetheless, it is undeniable that literary accomplishments of writers from the earlier post-1949 decades laid solid groundwork for Taiwan's vital and pluralistic cultural development in the 1990s.

With China split into two political entities with different sociopolitical systems since 1949, the tradition of Chinese New Literature 新文學 traveling along divergent paths in the two Chinese societies. Writers in post-1949 Taiwan have been selective in developing their literary heritage; whereas revolutionary literature and "critical realism" were suppressed, the more inoffensive, lyrical-sentimental strand enjoyed great popularity. From the anti-communist propaganda of the cold war decade of the 1950s, through the Modernist and the Nativist literary movements of the 1960s and 1970s, to the expression of today's pluralism and a burgeoning market-oriented mass culture, literary currents in post-1949 Taiwan have closely mirrored the country's larger sociopolitical transitions.

The Western-influenced Modernist literary movement of the sixties and the populist, Nativist literary movement of the 1970s may appropriately be regarded as "alternative" and "oppositional" cultural formations in Taiwan during this period. As the Modernists adopted literary concepts developed in Western capitalist society, they simultaneously longed for an ideological transformation, taking such bourgeois social values as individualism, liberalism, and rationalism as correctives for the oppressive social relations derived from a traditional system of values. The Nativist literary movement, in contrast, with its use of literature as a pretext to challenge the dominant sociopolitical order, may be properly considered as counterhegemonic. The movement was triggered by the nation's diplomatic setbacks in the international arena during the 1970s, and provided a forum for native Taiwanese intellectuals to vent their discontent with the socioeconomic problems that have accompanied the country's accelerated process of industrialization since the 1960s.

For different reasons, both movements dominated Taiwan's literary scene only for a relatively brief period of time. By the late 1970s and early 1980s, the influence of both the Modernists and the Nativists had sharply declined, and some of their inherent shortcomings had become obvious with the passage of time. As most of the Modernist writers advocated artistic autonomy and were politically disengaged, the subversive elements of their works were easily coopted by hegemonic cultural forces and their critical impact consequently diluted. The more radical subscription to aestheticism by certain writers, moreover, was deeply at odds with the predominantly lyrical sensibility of ordinary Chinese readers. Even though the essential dynamics of the Modernist movement were not entirely exhausted with the loss of popular favor, both critics and general readers received the movement's most mature output in the 1980s with a disheartening nonchalance. In the meantime, the militant political agenda of the Nativists both threatened and bored middle-class readers, who were largely satisfied with the status quo. The resistant activities of the more radical Nativists, moreover, were increasingly channeled into direct political involvement. The subsiding of these contending literary voices thus paved the way for the rise of a "serious" literature more popular in nature and a resurgence of the lyrical and sentimental strain in the 1980s. The younger generation of writers of this decade assimilated the technical sophistication of the Modernists and displayed a social awareness as a result of the Nativist influence. Their vocational visions, however, significantly departed from those of their mentors and were much more deeply conditioned by the market logic of Taiwan's increasingly commercialized cultural setting.

Fifties Mainland Émigré Literature

After Taiwan was returned to rule by a Chinese government in 1945, Mandarin Chinese replaced the Taiwanese dialect and Japanese as the official spoken language of the province. Creative activities of middle-aged native Taiwanese writers were then greatly hampered by this language barrier. Political fear is another factor that silenced native Taiwanese writers, as many Taiwanese intellectuals were persecuted during and after the February 28 Incident in 1947 (see pertinent section of Chapter 4, History). The literary scene in Taiwan during the 1950s was therefore virtually dominated by mainlander writers who followed the Nationalists to Taiwan around 1949. These émigré writers were frequently mobilized in the state-sponsored cultural programs and produced a literature that has often been characterized as anti-communist.

In addition to political propaganda, writers of the 1950s are frequently faulted for their amateurism, which is partly the product of a special institution in Taiwan, the *fu-k'an* 副刊, or literary supplement to newspapers. The *fu-k'an* undeniably has been the most significant sponsor of literary activities in contemporary Taiwan; nevertheless, with its large demand for works of immediate popular appeal, it at the same time fostered casual, light-weight writing and pandered to middlebrow literary tastes. As literary writing became less professional, the distinction between artistic and journalistic genres was often blurred.

Although the general climate in the 1950s was not conducive to production of serious art, works of considerable artistic merit by a number of writers deserve greater critical attention than usually given to them. Two broad categories of writings by these writers, traditionalist prose and realistic fiction, may be discussed as representative of literature in this decade.

Traditionalist prose

Contrary to the situation in the People's Republic of China, where gentry literature of China's feudal past was sometimes renounced for ideological reasons and where numerous political idioms designed to mobilize the masses were added to the vocabulary, the prose style in post-1949 Taiwan tended to be more literary, retaining

a great many more archaic expressions and allusions to classical literature. The proliferation of traditionalist prose 散文 in Taiwan during the 1950s, in the forms of familiar essay and the hybrid genre of essay-fiction, was apparently a continuation of an earlier trend on the mainland during and after the Sino-Japanese war. The decade's best-known essayists—Chang Hsiu-ya 張秀亞, Chung Mei-yin 鍾梅音, Hsu Chung-p'ei 徐鍾珮, Liang Hsuan 亮軒, and Ch'i-chün 琦君— were therefore all mainlander writers.

Realistic fiction

Having in their formative years been exposed to works of Lu Hsun, Mao Tun 茅盾, Pa Chin 巴金, and Lao She 老舍, mainland émigré writers active in the 1950s and 1960s by and large carried on the Chinese "realist" tradition—a somewhat atrophied version of 19th-century European realism—established during the May Fourth era and the thirties. For political reasons, however, they consciously or unconsciously modified those realistic conventions that might have been offensive to the dominant culture of post-1949 Taiwan: revolutionary and proletarian themes were taboo, and references to class consciousness were also to be avoided. Nevertheless, the nature of literary conventions is such that their suppression can never be as complete as it appears on the surface.

The 1960s saw the publication of several well-written, "anti-communist" realistic novels, such as *Rice-sprout Song* 秧歌, *The Whirlwind* 旋風, and *The Ti Village* 荻村傳. Although important in their own right, these stories were set exclusively in pre-Revolution China, and their authors either never resided in Taiwan (e.g., Eileen Chang 張愛玲), or were marginal to Taiwan's literary scene (e.g., Chiang Kui 姜貴 and Ch'en Hsi-ying 陳西瀅), thus diminishing their significance in Taiwan's post-1949 literary history. Far more relevant are such writers as Wang Lan 王藍, Meng Yao 孟瑤, P'an Jen-mu 潘人木, Lin Hai-yin 林海音, Nieh Hua-ling 聶華苓, P'eng Ko 彭歌, Chu Hsi-ning 朱西寧, Tuan Ts'ai-hua 段彩華, Ssu-ma Chung-yuan 司馬中

原, and Chung Chao-cheng 鍾肇政, writers who established their literary reputations around the mid-1950s and who have continued to play prominent roles in Taiwan's literary scene.

Although the fiction of these writers is also filled with nostalgic recollections of the mainland past, their works are nevertheless unique products of the contemporary cultural and political environment. Unmistakably, the emancipation ethos, a legacy of pre-1949 realist literature, has informed a number of their writings set in the past on subjects such as the oppression of women, the repressive nature of traditional Chinese family system, and the pathetic condition of working-class people and domestic servants. In addition, the realistic codes were rewritten and the critical messages mitigated or displaced: rightist political convictions and active support of the present government frequently caused these writers to domesticate the revolutionary spirit with counterdevices and to shift the thematic focus from the sociohistorical to the private domains. The rise of the young Modernists, with their liberalism and new aesthetic conceptions, challenged not only these older writers' artistic visions, but also the dominant culture's ideological control over creative writers. The changes brought forth by the Modernists in the artistic realm formed the basis for more radical cultural critiques found in later decades.

Modernist Literary Movement

The dominant culture in post-1949 Taiwan carries on many traditions established in China during the Republican era (1911-1949). The Modernist literary movement is an expression of the predilection by Chinese intellectuals of the time to emulate Western high culture. Ever since the end of the 19th century, shocked by the devastating effect of China's encounters with Western culture, modern Chinese intellectuals have attempted various kinds of cultural rejuvenation, the most potent formula for which consists in assimilation of Western cultural products. Taiwan's Modernist literary movement, as one of the latest in a series of such efforts, inevitably

displays some of its essential characteristics. Second, an important link can be perceived between this movement and the liberal strand of thought in China's pre-Revolution era, especially that of the Anglo-American wing of intellectuals. It is readily observable that ideas of important literary figures of post-1949 Taiwan, such as Liang Shih-ch'iu 梁實秋, former member of the Crescent Moon Society 新月社, Hsia Chi-an 夏濟安, mentor of a core group of Modernists, and Yen Yuan-shu 顏元叔, leading critic of the '60s who introduced New Criticism to Taiwan, are all fundamentally rooted in the Western liberal-humanist tradition. Yen Yuan-shu's proposition that "literature has the dual function of being the dramatization and criticism of life," in particular, closely echoes both Matthew Arnold and the Literary Studies Association's 文學研究社 famous tenet, "art for life's sake." Taiwan's Modernists particularly stressed the principle of artistic autonomy, among other liberal conceptions of literature, and, by and large, have more thoroughly adhered to this principle than their pre-1949 liberal predecessors.

From the point of view of literary history, however, the epoch-making significance of Taiwan's Modernist literary movement rests primarily in terms of its generation of new dynamics among contemporary writers and its redirecting of their artistic mode of expression.

New Thematic Conventions

In terms of theme and subject matter, writers of Taiwan's Modernist fiction endeavored to explore new spheres of human experience beyond the confines of traditional literature. In doing so, they continued the efforts of their early-20th century May Fourth Movement predecessors and even surpassed them in depth. To comprehend and analyze the complexity of human experience in the modern world, they generally favored rationalism, scientism, and serious, if at times immature, philosophical contemplations. We have thus witnessed the establishment of a set of thematic conventions that supposedly incorporate advanced knowledge of human behavior made available by the modern sciences. For example, apparently influenced by popular versions of Freudian psychoanalysis, young writers in the early stage of the Modernist literary movement were particularly fascinated with abnormal interpersonal relationships. Most of these writers such as Wang Wen-hsing 王文興, Pai Hsien-yung 白先勇, Ou-yang Tzu 歐陽子, Ch'en Jo-hsi 陳若曦, Shui Ching 水晶, Ch'en Ying-chen 陳映真, to name just a few—wrote stories featuring imaginary post-Freudian middle-class spiritual dilemmas, or have focused on scandalous revelations of some abnormal psychological traits. Most of such stories lack originality in thematic conception; yet, even the artistically less mature works by the young Modernists reveal serious attempts by individual authors to come to terms with troubling psychological obsessions. These young writers' sincerity and bold, honest self-analysis broke new ground in Taiwan's cultural context: such efforts have redefined boundaries of normality in human behavior and have thus presented challenges to conventional ethical prescriptions and the conservative middle-class mentality that have been the backbone of the dominant culture in post-1949 Taiwan.

Some truly radical cultural examinations are found in the movement's later, more mature stage. For example, with a common theme of father-son conflict, two of Taiwan's most significant modernist novels, Pai Hsien-yung's *Crystal Boys* 孽子 (1983) and Wang Wen-hsing's *Family Catastrophe* 家變 (1973), offered bitter protests against the traditional ethical norms that are crystallized in the Confucianist notions of loyalty 忠 and filial piety 孝, and thus called into question fundamental underpinnings of the superstructure of contemporary Taiwan society. Notably, in both works, the battle against the social retention of traditional values is waged with the aid of Western conceptual frames. *Family Catastrophe* features as its central theme the conflict of bourgeois individualism with the concept of filial piety in a financially strapped modern Chinese family. That the hero is portrayed as a fanatic rationalist shows the degree to which the author

is skeptical of the real efficacy of such an ideological transfer. *Crystal Boys* projects a more idealistic vision influenced by the countercultural movement of the 1960s in the United States, with its anarchic assertion of the emancipatory power of the Dionysian impulse, its celebration of youth and beauty in their ephemeral physical forms, and its romantic affirmation of the redeeming virtue of love. The author has further enriched the symbolic level of this book by infusing this vision with mythical themes from the Chinese classic *Dream of the Red Chamber* 紅樓夢. The underground homosexual community of New Park 新公園 in *Crystal Boys,* like residents of the Garden of the Grand Vision 大觀園 in the famous traditional novel, is ruled by the supreme order of sentimentality 情 and the heart 心, which can be both salvational and damning. This microcosm, however, is extremely vulnerable, as it is forever overshadowed by the law of the father—the dominant order of the patriarchal, Confucianist society outside the garden. The prominence of the father-quest motif in both *Family Catastrophe* and *Crystal Boys*—heroes in both novels are constantly searching for paternal surrogates—betrays their authors' anxiety over the general corruption of the terms governing human relationships in contemporary Taiwan society, terms that in history were solidly built on the patriarchal order.

Formal Innovations

Particularly eye-catching in the initial stage of the Modernist literary movement was the temporary surge of an avant-garde trend. One prominent feature of the self styled avant-garde writers of the 1960s was their infatuation with the intellectual current of existentialism. As Franz Kafka was introduced early in the movement, the use of obscure plots and bizarre language quickly became a fad, and the basic tenor of works by many young writers— Ch'i-teng Sheng 七等生, Ts'ung Su 叢甦, and Shih Shu-ch'ing 施叔青 among them—seemed to be dominated by nihilism, agonism, and an anxiety over the absurdity of existence.

The upsurge of aesthetic iconoclasm in the 1960s represented a significant moment in postwar Taiwan's literary history. The vigorous dynamics of newly introduced artistic conceptions associated with modernism called into question conventional forms and criteria of literary excellence. The more enduring efforts generated by this initial enthusiasm eventually ushered in a new era of modern Chinese literary history.

Most other Modernist fiction writers in Taiwan stayed within the general confines of realism, but they were no less experimental. Their conscious explorations of language and voice brought forth fundamental changes in rhetorical conventions of modern Chinese narrative. Since, as some scholars have observed, the attempts of earlier modern Chinese writers to offer realistic portraits of life were frequently hampered by the dominance of the subjective voice in the work's rhetorical structure, the Modernists tried to redress this deficiency by introducing a new "objective form." They strove to present an "impartial" picture of reality so that readers may be given the privilege of forming their own opinions and moral judgments. To be sure, these ideas are more reminiscent of the realists' concept of literary representation than the modernist view of literature as self-referential discursive practice. Throughout the 1960s, in fact, the majority of critical writings introducing Western literary concepts focused on basic technical rules and critical criteria that have long been naturalized and taken for granted in the West. Authoritative US-trained scholars and critics such as Yen Yuan-shu, Chu Li-min 朱立民, and Wai-lim Yip 葉維廉 systematically expounded the fundamentals of a whole set of Western literary codes, and their influence on creative writing and practical criticism in Taiwan was immeasurable. Such a phenomenon is actually not very difficult to understand, given that literary genres of the short story and the novel (in the strict sense) have been imported from the West only in this century.

It is also true, however, that the appropriation of foreign literary codes necessarily involves larger, more complicated networks of artistic and ideological systems. Given that the most noteworthy formal feature popularized by the Mod-

ernists is widened distance between author and text, their efforts may be seen as having continued the general trend in modern Chinese literary history away from the traditional expressive view toward the mimetic view of literature. With their denunciation of sentimentalism and express interest in the hidden complexities of the human psyche, personal emotions are no longer treated as the source or origin of literature, but rather as objects for detached observation.

It is arguable that, despite the fact that Taiwan's Modernist literary movement has taken place in a "postmodern" period from the standpoint of the West—in the 1960s and 1970s—and despite the fact that many newer artistic trends and techniques have been incorporated by the Modernist writers into their work, the dominant tendency of this movement nevertheless is closest to the early phase of Western modernism in the late 19th century and early 20th century. In other words, in the extremely compressed timetable of Taiwan's Modernist literary movement, one nevertheless discerns features such as the reversal of the conventional content-form hierarchy and the radical rejection of traditional writing techniques that can only be the result of a burgeoning skepticism about language and meaning. Most of the Modernists' explorations of language unmistakably reflect Western influences. However, more original experiments have also been made, which result from a new awareness of the unstable relationship between language and its referents, as well as of a reawakened sensitivity toward the ideographic nature of the Chinese language. These experiments, especially those found in Wang Wen-hsing's two novels *Family Catastrophe* and *Backed Against the Sea* 背海的人 (1981), and Li Yung-p'ing's latest story series *Chronicle of Chi-ling* 吉陵春秋 (1986), mark the apex of the development of modernist aestheticism in contemporary Chinese literature.

Nativist Literary Debate

In the late 1960s and early 1970s, as the Modernist fiction writers began to mature artistically, the resistance to modernism's dominance of Taiwan's literary scene also began. The precursor to a large-scale denunciation of the Modernist literary movement was the 1972 New Poetry debate 新詩論戰, which involved a number of academic critics and Modernist poets who discussed specific Western-influenced features in contemporary Taiwan poetry. The consensus reached in this debate seemed to be that, despite its other merits, the currently practiced New Poetry suffered from such unhealthy qualities as semantic obscurity, excessive use of foreign imagery and Europeanized syntax, and evasion of contemporary social reality. These features, furthermore, were considered symptomatic of the faulty style generally promoted in Taiwan's Modernist literary movement.

While it may not be unusual in literary history for critics and writers periodically to reexamine and revolt against the current dominant style, the New Poetry debate bore a special social implication in that it was closely tied to Taiwan intellectuals' growing consciousness of their endangered Chinese cultural identity. In what was later known as the "return to native roots" 回歸鄉土 trend around the turn of the 1970s, progressive intellectuals criticized the blind admiration and slavish imitation of Western cultural models, and exhorted their compatriots to show more respect for their indigenous cultural heritage, as well as greater concern for domestic social issues. Many liberal scholars, especially returnees from the United States, played important roles in igniting this new current, which at first revolved around several universities and intellectual magazines.

Shortly after the New Poetry debate, a group of critics began to renounce publicly the foreign-influenced Modernist work and to advocate a nativist, socially responsible literature. This trend reached its apex with the outbreak of a virulent Nativist Literature Debate in 1977 and 1978 and suddenly declined when, in 1979, several key figures of the Nativist camp exited from the literary scene and became directly involved in political protests. The tradition of Nativist literature as a creative genre—the main features of which are use of the Taiwanese dialect, depiction

of the plight of country folk or small-town dwellers caught up in economic difficulty, and resistance of the imperialist presence in Taiwan—can be traced back to the Nativist literary trend during the Japanese colonial period. While inheriting the dominant nationalist spirit from this earlier trend, the Nativist literature champions of the 1970s had their own political agenda as well.

Viewed retrospectively, the Nativist camp was the first oppositional formation at a critical juncture in Taiwan's post-1949 history. After two decades of political stability and steady economic growth, the country suffered a series of diplomatic setbacks at the turn of the decade—beginning with its expulsion from the United Nations in 1971, followed by Richard Nixon's visit to the Chinese mainland and the termination of the ROC's diplomatic relations with Japan in 1972—which caused not only international isolation, but also a confidence crisis among Taiwan intellectuals.

Unlike the majority of the country's liberal intellectuals who demanded democratization while supporting capitalist-style economic modernization, the Nativists believed that the socioeconomic system of Taiwan must be changed. They fiercely attacked the ROC government's economic dependence on Western countries (especially the United States), deplored the infiltration of "decadent" capitalist culture into the ordinary lives of Taiwan's people; expressed indignance on behalf of Taiwan's farmers and workers who paid a high economic price for the nation's urban expansion, and attempted to draw public attention to the adverse effects of the country's overall economic development.

The regionalist sentiment implied in the Nativist project immediately touched on an extremely sensitive issue, the "provincial heritage problem" 省籍問題. Tensions between native Taiwanese and mainlanders always existed, especially given the perceptions of an unbalanced distribution of political power at the time. As a consequence, even though some of the leading Nativist critics were socialists or nationalists rather than separatists promoting Taiwan Independence

(Ch'en Ying-chen, for example, has always been a staunch advocate of future reunification with China), the Nativist critical discourse as a whole could not but be part of the ongoing political strife.

It is therefore undeniable that literary nativism was used by a special group of people at a particular historical moment to challenge the existing sociopolitical order. However, it appears that ideological debates in modern Chinese society inevitably generate widespread polemics around literature, as evidenced by numerous such disputes in the May Fourth period, in the thirties, and during the entire communist reign on the mainland. The traditional Chinese pragmatic view of literature and the legacy of a gentry ideology, which assigns to intellectuals, especially writers, lofty social missions, have combined to make literary discourse a genuine political space. As a result, the attacks launched by the Nativists on the Modernist writers, whose literary ideology is a conspicuously apolitical one, have largely centered on the latter's default of their social responsibilities as members of the intelligentsia.

The home base for the anti-Modernist critics was the journal *Literary Quarterly* 文季, founded in 1966. With Yü T'ien-ts'ung 尉天聰 as the central mover, the journal's founding members included several writers already known for their Modernist work, such as Ch'en Ying-chen, Liu Ta-jen 劉大任, Shih Shu-ch'ing, and Ch'i-teng Sheng. The journal had, furthermore, discovered two important writers, Huang Ch'un-ming 黃春明 and Wang Chen-ho 王禎和, whose fiction significantly departed from the current Modernist fads and depicted rural life with unaffected realism. Although both writers refused to label their works as "Nativist," the literary reformers on the journal's editorial board were ready to use them as weapons in their fight against the Modernist hegemony.

In 1973, T'ang Wen-piao 唐文標, a visiting math professor closely associated with the *Literary Quarterly*, criticized the Modernists' elitist tendency and neglect of the masses. The straightforward accusations so startled the liberal critics that Yen Yuan-shu referred to this critical attack as the "T'ang Wen-piao Incident." However,

even more vehement militancy was to be seen when the Nativist critics chose individual writers as targets. Almost simultaneously with the T'ang Wen-piao Incident, the *Literary Quarterly* organized a series of seminars to examine the thematic implications of Ou-yang Tzu's fiction, and branded it "corrupt and immoral." By the mid-1970s, Taiwan's literary writers were already deeply split into opposing camps.

The literary climate in this decade became truly unpleasant with the increasing politicization of critical discourse. With the founding of a radical magazine *Summer Tide* 夏潮 in 1976 and its provocative use of such taboo terms as "proletarian literature" (literally, literature of workers, peasants, and soldiers) and "class consciousness," the deep-seated anti-communist sentiments of the liberals were incited. In the summer of 1977, the country's leading Modernist poet Yü Kuang-chung 余光中 wrote a short essay entitled "The Wolf Is Here" 狼來了 openly accusing the Nativists of being leftists. This fatal charge ignited highly emotional responses and retaliations from all sides, and polemical writings about literature and politics began to flood the country's newspapers and literary magazines. This so-called Nativist literary debate came to an end only in the middle of 1978 as a result of threatened government intervention.

Placed within a larger historical context, the Modernist-Nativist split is part of the continual struggle in modern Chinese history between liberal and radical intellectuals with different reform programs and different views of literature's social function. The new paradigm of ideological writing as established in the mid-1970s moved in a direction diametrically opposed to that of the introspective, humanist, and universalist approach of the Modernists and deliberately focused on the historical specificity of contemporary Taiwan society. In addition to later works by Huang Ch'un-ming on imperialism, such writers as Yang Ch'ing-ch'u 楊青矗 and Wang T'o 王拓 explored capitalist exploitation as it affected urban factory workers and fishermen. These literary efforts were also backed by some serious theoretical thinking, although most of the Nativist literary debate itself was virtually divorced from contemporary literary practice.

Wang T'o's 1977 essay, "It should be 'literature of the here and now,' not 'nativist literature'" 是現實主義文學，不是鄉土文學 stood out among numerous polemical writings precisely because of its accurate representation of the reality of recent literary practice. The main argument Wang proposes in this essay is that, instead of writing about rural regions and country people, Nativist literature is concerned with the "here and now" of Taiwan society, which embraces a wide range of social environments and people. Nativist literature thus should be defined as a literature rooted in the land of Taiwan, one that reflects the social reality and the material and psychological aspirations of its people. By using the term *hsien shih* 現實 (contemporary reality, the "here and now") rather than *hsieh shih* 寫實 (realism), and by enlarging the scope of Nativist literature to include all levels of social reality in Taiwan, Wang stressed high-priority Nativist issues. The essay, therefore, represented an important step in the Nativists' process of self-definition.

The critical evaluation of Nativist works produced in the 1970s, however, is in general not very positive. Although the change in thematic conventions since the seventies met the approval of most critics, excessive ideological concern is considered to have detracted from their literary achievement. Even though Huang Ch'un-ming is often regarded as such an exception, many have felt that his art, too, deteriorates in direct proportion to the increase in social commentary in his later works. However, just as Modernist literature continued to evolve after the rise of Nativist literature, the practice of Nativist literature did not come to an end even though the Nativist literary debate folded toward the end of the 1970s. In the continuing efforts made by such Nativist ideological writers as Ch'en Ying-chen, Sung Tse-lai 宋澤萊, Li Ch'iao 李喬, and Wu Chin-fa 吳錦發 in the 1980s, one can discern a sharp increase in formal consciousness as well as attempts to experiment with innovative techniques.

Eighties Pluralism

In a sense, the articulation of dissident views during the Nativist literary debate paved the way for more intense struggles toward democratization, which rapidly gained momentum in the early 1980s. Eventually, with the formation in 1987 of an opposition party, the Democratic Progressive Party, literature was largely relieved of its function as a pretext for political contestation. It became, however, even more inextricably involved in the country's booming mass media. Most notably, the two competing media giants, the *United Daily News* 聯合報 and *China Times* 中國時報 each claiming the loyalty of a group of writers, invested heavily in their literary pages for marketing purposes. The annual fiction contests they sponsored between the mid-1970s and mid-1980s gave creative writing a solid boost—an overwhelming majority of the writers of the baby-boom generation rose to literary prominence by winning one of these contests.

The Nativist theorists may have felt at once frustrated and vindicated in the 1980s, as the "spiritual corruption" of capitalist society, which they had predicted, appeared along with the ascendance of mammonism and a sharp rise in the crime rate. The overall cultural environment also became heavily consumer-oriented. Not without a touch of irony, even the Nativist literature itself was largely co-opted by the cultural establishment, especially between the late 1970s and early 1980s. Newspaper supplements and literary magazines were inundated by pseudo-Nativist works, which displayed Taiwanese local color but contained little ideological content.

As public fervor for both the Modernist and the Nativist causes subsided, the literary scene of the 1980s was largely dominated by the baby-boom generation, whose vocational visions were drastically different from those of their predecessors. Rather than treating creative writing as an intellectual project or a political quest, they were more concerned with popularity and with various problems affecting Taiwan's middle class urbanites, especially the new social affluence and the relaxation of moral standards. Some writers, such as

Huang Fan 黃凡 and Li Ang 李昂, with a cynical intellectual pose, offered critiques of materialism and the cultural impoverishment it caused; while others, such as Hsiao Sa 蕭颯 and Liao Hui-ying 廖輝英, with down-to-earth pragmatism, examined the new social factors that had changed ordinary people's way of life, showing particular interest in liberated sexual views and the problem of extra-marital relationships; and still others, such as Yuan Ch'iung-ch'iung 袁瓊瓊, Chu T'ien-wen 朱天文, and Su Wei-chen 蘇偉貞, falling back on the sentimental-lyrical tradition, focused their attention on subjective, private sentiment with a posture of complacency in regard to sociopolitical issues. Whether progressively or conservatively inclined, the new generation of writers seemed to share a common response to the emergence of new political situations. As knowledge about the Chinese on the other side of the Taiwan Straits suddenly became available, and with the public debate over the nature and pace of reunification with the Chinese mainland intensifying on a daily basis, many of the writers of the baby-boom generation tended to deliberately stress their unique cultural identity, rooted in the specific sociohistorical realities of Taiwan's post-1949 era.

Writers' approaches to literature in this decade were certainly pluralist. While writers of the Modernist generation published their more mature works during this decade, literary products of the younger generation were marked by a rich diversity— *chüan tsun* 眷村 (residential military community) literature, works about life in business corporations, political fiction (with a special sub-genre on the February 28 Incident), neo-Nativist literature, resistance literature, feminist works, and science fiction—a phenomenon that may be aptly characterized as the orchestration of a multitude of discordant "voices."

The broadly defined "return to native roots" trend carried over into the early 1980s beyond the Modernist-Nativist contention. After the Nativist literary debate, new interest in an indigenous literary heritage fostered a trend of cultural nostalgia. Several former Modernist writers made notable contributions to this trend. Shih Shu-

ch'ing and Li Ang, for example, consciously turned to folk traditions and native subject matter in their writing. Lin Huai-min 林懷民, a former Modernist writer who had studied under Martha Graham while in the US, founded the first Chinese modern dance troupe and produced the well-received "Cloud Gate Dance Series" 雲門舞集 and incorporated both classical Chinese and folk Taiwanese elements in his choreography (see section, Dance, in Chapter 21, The Arts). Their accomplishments set the tone for creative endeavors of the new decade, even while encouraging commercial exploitation of traditional and native cultural signs.

As the indigenous came to replace the foreign as the primary source of exotic imagination, and "Chinese/Taiwan cultural identity" came to occupy a prominent place in the public consciousness, "postmodernism" came into vogue after the mid-1980s and again raised issues about Western influences on contemporary Chinese literature. In a pattern closely resembling that by which such earlier Western literary trends as Romanticism, Realism, and Modernism were appropriated by Chinese writers, the postmodern mode of writing has become a new fad and its surface markers, such as double endings, juxtaposition of the factual and the fictional, and the technique of pastiche, among others, have appeared profusely in works by both greater and lesser writers. Such imitative literary products cannot but recall works written during the earliest phase of the Modernist literary movement and not surprisingly are considered to be of dubious value by some veteran Modernists.

Although the younger writers of the 1990s consciously subscribed to the more cynical, "postmodern" ideology—as evidenced by their emphasis on difference, tolerance of pluralistic co-existence of the incommensurable, and, above all, their appetite for the indeterminacy that is uncongenial to the Modernist temperament, there were also similarities between the two generations of writers: their intellectual disposition, their globalism, and the way they looked to the West—or Western-influenced literary traditions such as those of East Europe and Latin America—for literary models. As prescribed by "postmodern" ideology, however, the younger writers were more keenly aware of the self/other dichotomy and thus did not endorse universalism as the Modernists did.

Nineties Multiculturalism and Postidentity Politics

Taiwan has undergone an interpretive turn in terms of national identity and critical multiculturalism in the 1990s. Challenged by mainland China's ambivalent and often hostile policies toward Taiwan, President Lee Teng-hui has repeatedly proposed the nurturing of Taiwanese localism in the name of a common need for interdependence in order to assure communal survival 生命共同體 while promoting the cosmopolitan nationalism of "establishing a new cultural well-spring" 建立新中原 in pursuit of a peaceful and mutually rewarding reunification with China. As a result, Taiwanese literature of the '90s tend to use mixed genres and multilingual devices, drawing on a wide range of global/local cultural codes, idioms, and traditions, to express the fluid, albeit disoriented, structure of feelings.

Into the '90s, Chu T'ien-wen and Chang Ta-ch'un 張大春 are still prominent figures in the field of political fiction or nostalgic narrative on the dissolution of a certain culture within government housing compounds. Chang is reputed for his technique of intermixing literary and non-literary genres—history, dream text, diary, with news report, for example—and voices. Chu's *Notebooks from the Wasteland* 荒人手記 won the 1994 *China Times* best fiction award. Although the second-generation mainlanders as subjects of the novel reappear as if in a repetition compulsion, Chu's sensitivity to the ethnic tensions, rupture of tradition, and societal psychopathologies is nicely matched by her literary style and narrative coherence. As a writer appropriating all news and media events, Chang has gradually moved from writing cynical diaries and "factual fiction" based on the tragic death of a navy officer to producing public TV programs and increasingly becoming a media person. In between Chu and Chang stands a young talent Yang Chao 楊照, who has successfully blended romance with saga, collapsing the distinction between public and private, the personal and the social. Yang is currently a Harvard Ph.D candidate, cultural critic, political activist, and novelist. His multiple roles in contemporary Taiwanese public culture as well as his impressive talent in fusing personal and interpersonal histories are self-evident in one of his trilogies, *A Dark Alley on a Confusing Night* 暗巷迷夜.

In contrast to Li Ang, who has severely criticized the patriarchal system of domination, younger women writers emerging in the '90s, such as Lo Yi-chün 駱以軍 or Ch'eng Ying-shu 成英姝, are more playful in their treatment of sexual liasions in the (often gay or lesbian) bars, of object-choice "medial woman," of fantasies and frustrations of the so-called "neo neo-human breed" 新新人類 in relation to the new unsettling social milieu that has yet failed to take shape. Writers like Ch'eng are on the way to expressing postidentity politics, celebrating postmodern flexibility and unpredictability in the global cyberspace of easy accessibility. Their counterpart in the field of poetry is Lin Yao-te 林燿德, who employs the synecdoche of fax machine and computer terminal to describe the fluid human relations in a transnational capitalist society. Lin has been very active since the '80s in promoting postmodern poetry about urban culture and cityscapes, following poets like Lo Men 羅門, Lo Ch'ing 羅青, and others. These poets are far from the humanist tradition set up by Lo Fu 洛夫, Wai-lim Yip, Ya Hsien 亞弦, and later on revised by Chien Cheng-chen 簡政珍, Hsu hui-chih 許悔之, and Chiao T'ung 焦侗, with a phenomenological, psychoanalytical, or even poststructuralist twist.

To question Chinese nationalism, quite a few writers try to highlight several issues associated with the Taiwan Independence movement, minority discourse, political feminism, and environmental protection. Reportage, science fiction, and biography are the most popular modes of literary expression or ethnographic exploration of everyday political subjects among these writers. K'u Ling 苦苓 is a most celebrated political satirist who never fails to make fun of statesmen, as Yü Fu 魚夫 does in his political cartoons. A prolific poet writing on related subjects is Li Min-yung 李敏勇. However, it is in the mini theatre 小劇場 that serious political satires intermingle with comic reliefs. The stages for mini plays can take many forms; they can be in the theatre, on the street, in the city hall, or even in front of the Legislature 立法院. Some differing and milder versions of post-avant-garde theatre, on the other hand, are offered by playwrights like Stan Lai 賴聲川, Li Kuo-hsiu 李國修, and Chung Ming-te 鍾明德, who draw inspirations from a range of Chinese-Western drama—both ancient and modern (see Spoken Drama and Traditional Music Theater sections, Chapter 21, The Arts).

An important trend in the '90s has been to revive the local vernacular tradition. As localization processes take root, Taiwanese (southern Fukienese) or Hakka is often looked upon as a preferred linguistic medium for literary expression. In this regard, Chang Ch'un-huang 張春凰 has been hailed, since the publication of her pioneering prose work *Paths to Youth* 青春ê路途 in 1995, as the first prose writer in Taiwanese. From the perspective of a mother, the narrator attempts to introduce her son to the beauties of pronouncing everyday objects in Taiwanese. The work represents a crucial step toward rearticulating one's literary tradition and toward a more promising future in which linguistic nuances and cultural differences may be appreciated and cherished. After all, it is the diversity of languages and customs on the island that has enriched the literary expressions of the people of Taiwan.

Further Reading (in English unless otherwise indicated):

Birch, Cyril, ed. *Anthology of Chinese Literature*. New York: Grove Press, 1965.

——, tr. *Stories From a Ming Collection*. New York: Grove Press, 1958.

Brewitt-Taylor, C. H., tr. *Romance of the Three Kingdoms*. 2 vols. Rutland, Vt.: Charles E. Tuttle, 1959.

Chang Chien 張健, ed. *Chung-kuo wen-hsüeh p'i-p'ing lun-chi* 中國文學批評論集 (A Collection of Chinese Literary Criticism; in Chinese). Taipei: Heavenly Lotus Publishing Company, 1979.

Chen, Li-li, tr. *Master Dung's Western Romance, A Chantefable*. Cambridge: Cambridge University Press, 1976.

Ch'en Jo-hsi 陳若曦. *Spirit Calling: Tales about Taiwan*. Taipei: Heritage Press, 1962.

—— *The Execution of Mayor Yin* 尹縣長 *and Other Stories from the Great Cultural Revolution*. Bloomington: Indiana Univeristy Press, 1978.

——[Chen Ruoxi]. *The Old Man* 老人 *and Other Stories*. Renditions paperback. Hong Kong: Chinese University of Hong Kong, Research Centre for Translation, 1986.

Ch'en Ying-chen 陳映真. *Exiles at Home: Stories by Ch'en Ying-chen* 陳映真. Trans. Lucien Miller. Ann Arbor: University of Michigan, Center for Chinese Studies, 1986.

Chi Pang-yuan, ed. *An Anthology of Contemporary Chinese Literature*. Seattle: University of Washington Press, 1989.

Crump, J.I. *Chinese Theater in the Days of Kublai Khan*. Tucson: The University of Arizona Press, 1980.

Egerton, Clement, tr. *The Golden Lotus*. 4 vols. London: Routledge & Kegan Paul, 1972.

Chung-kuo ku-tien wen-hsüeh lun-ts'ung: ts'e-erh, wen-hsüeh p'i-p'ing yü hsi-chü chih pu 中國古典文學論叢：冊二，文學批評與戲劇之部 (Essays on Chinese Literature: Vol. 2, Literary Criticism and Drama; in Chinese). Taipei: Chung Wai Literary Monthly, 1976.

Chung-kuo ku-tien wen-hsüeh yen-chiu ts'ung-k'an: san-wen yü lun-p'ing chih pu 中國古典文學研究叢刊：散文與論評之部 (Essays on Classical Chinese Literature: Prose and Criticism; in Chinese). Taipei: Chu Liu Book Company, 1979.

Chung-kuo wen-hsüeh chiang-hua 中國文學講話 (On Chinese Literature; in Chinese). Taipei: Chu Liu Book Company, 1982. 6 vols.

Lo Lien-tien 羅聯添, ed. *Chung-kuo wen-hsüeh shih lun-wen hsüan-chi* 中國文學史論文選集 (Essays on the History of Chinese Literature; in Chinese). Taipei: Student Book Company, 1985. 5 vols.

Hawkes, David, and John Minford, trs. *The Story of the Stone*. Middlesex, Penguin, 1973-1982 5 vols.

Hsieh Wu-liang 謝無量. *Chung-kuo fu-nü wen-hsüeh shih* 中國婦女文學史 (History of Chinese Women's Literature; in Chinese). Taipei: Chung Hwa Book Company, 1973.

Hu Shih 胡適. *Pai-hua wen-hsüeh shih* 白話文學史 (A History of Chinese Vernacular Literature; in Chinese). Tainan: Tunghai Publishing Company, 1981.

Hu Yü-huan 胡毓寰. *Chung-kuo wen-hsüeh yüan-liu* 中國文學源流 (The Origins of Chinese Literature; in Chinese). Taipei: Commercial Press, 1967.

Hwa Yen 華嚴. *Lamp of Wisdom* 智慧的燈. Taipei: *Woman Magazine*, 1974.

Hwang Ch'un-ming 黃春明. *The Drowning of an Old Cat* 溺死一隻老貓 *and Other Stories*. Trans. Howard Goldblatt.

Bloomington: Indiana University Press, 1980.

K'e Ch'ing-ming 柯慶明, Lin Ming-te 林明德, ed. *Chung-kuo ku-tien wen-hsüeh yen-chiu ts'ung-k'an: hsiao-shuo chih-pu* 中國古典文學研究叢刊：小說之部 (Essays on Classical Chinese Literature: Novels; in Chinese). Taipei: Chu Liu Book Company, 1979.

K'ung Shang-jen. *The Peach Blossom Fan.* Trans. Chen Shih-hsiang and Harold Acton. Berkeley: University of California Press, 1976.

Kuo, Gloria Liang-hui 郭良蕙. *Taipei Women.* Hong Kong: New Enterprise Company, 1983.

Lau, Joseph S.M., ed. *Chinese Stories from Taiwan, 1960-1970.* New York: Columbia University Press, 1976.

Li Ang 李昂. *The Butcher's Wife* 殺夫: *A Novel by Li Ang.* Trans. Howard Goldblatt and Ellen Yeung. San Francisco: North Point Press, 1986.

Lin Hai-yin 林海音. *Green Seaweed and Salted Eggs* 綠藻與鹹蛋. Taipei: Heritage Press, 1963.

Lin Wen-keng 林文庚. *Chung-kuo wen-hsüeh fa-chan Shih* 中國文學發展史 (The Development of Chinese Literature; in Chinese). Taipei: Ching Liu Publishing Company, 1976.

Liu Chen-lu 劉振魯, ed. *Tang-ch'ien T'ai-wan so-chien ke-sheng hsi-ch'ü hsüan-chi* 當前台灣所見各省戲曲選集 (Selected Local Drama from Various Provinces Still Performed in Taiwan Today; in Chinese). Taichung: Taiwan Provincial Historical Commission, 1982. 2 vols.

Liu O 劉鶚. *The Travels of Lao Ts'an.* Trans. Harold Shadick. Ithaca: Cornell University Press, 1966.

Liu Wu-chi, ed. *An Introduction to Chinese Literature.* Bloomington: Indiana University Press, 1966.

——, ed. *Sunflower Splendor: Three Thousand Years of Chinese Poetry.* Bloomington: Indiana University Press, 1975.

Ma, Y.W. and Joseph S.M. Lau, eds. *Traditional Chinese Stories, Themes and Variations.* New York: Columbia University Press, 1978.

McNaughton, William, ed. *Chinese Literature: An Anthology from the Earliest Times to the Present.* Rutland: Charles E. Tuttle Company, 1974.

Mulligan, Jean, tr. *The Lute, Kao Ming's P'i-p'a chi.* New York: Columbia University Press, 1980.

Nieh, Hua-ling 聶華苓, ed. *Eight Stories by Chinese Women.* Taipei: Heritage Press, 1962.

——. *Mulberry and Peach* 桑青與桃紅: *Two Women of China.*

London: Women's Press, 1986, c1981.

Nienhauser, William H., ed. *The Indiana Companion to Traditional Chinese Literature.* Bloomington: Indiana University Press, 1986.

Pai Hsien-yung 白先勇. *Wandering in the Garden, Waking from a Dream* 遊園驚夢: *Tales of Taipei Characters.* Trans. Pai Hsien-yung and Patia Yasin. Ed. George Kao. Bloomington: Indiana University Press, 1982.

——. *Crystal Boys* 孽子: *A Novel by Pai Hsien-yung* 白先勇. Trans. Howard Goldblatt. San Francisco: Gay Sunshine Press, 1990.

P'eng Ko 彭歌. *Black Tears* 黑色的淚, *Stories of War Torn China.* Trans. Nancy Ing. Taipei: Chinese Materials Center Publications, 1986.

Shih Nai-an 施耐庵. *Outlaws of the Marsh.* Trans. Sidney Shapiro. Bloomington: Indiana University Press, 1981

Shih, Shu-ch'ing 施叔青. *The Barren Years* 那些不毛的日子 *and Other Short Stories and Plays.* Trans. John M. Mclellan. San Francisco: Chinese Materials Center, 1975.

Tang Xianzu, *The Peony Pavilion (Mudan Ting).* Trans. Cyril Birch. Bloomington: Indiana University Press, 1980.

Tseng Yung-i 曾永義. *Shuo hsi-ch'ü* 說戲曲 (On Drama; in Chinese). Taipei: Linking Publishing Company, 1976.

Yeh Ching-ping 葉慶炳. *Chung-kuo wen-hsüeh shih* 中國文學史 (The History of Chinese Literature; in Chinese). Taipei: Student Book Company, 1987. 2 vols.

Yip Wai-lim 葉維廉, ed. *Chung-kuo hsien-tai wen-hsüeh p'i-p'ing hsüan-chi* 中國現代文學批評選集 (An Anthology of Contemporary Chinese Literary Criticism; in Chinese). Taipei: Linking Publishing Company, 1976.

Wang Ch'iu-kuei 王秋桂, ed. *Chung-kuo wen-hsüeh lun-chu yi-ts'ung* 中國文學論著譯叢 (Essays on Chinese Literature; in Chinese). Taipei: Student Book Company, 1985.

Wang Shih-fu 王實甫. *The Romance of the Western Chamber.* Trans. S. I. Hsiung. New York: Columbia University Press, 1968.

Wang, Wen-hsing 王文興. *Family Catastrophe* 家變. Trans. Susan Dolling. Honolulu: University of Hawaii Press, 1995.

——. *Backed Against the Sea* 背海的人 Trans. Edward Gunn. Ithaca: Cornell East Asia Program, 1993.

Wu Ch'eng-en 吳承恩. *The Journey to the West* (Translated into English by Anthony C. Yu). 4 vols. Chicago: The University of Chicago Press, 1980.

25.
Religion

Above: Buddhist adherents, participating in an extended meditation program, practice at a ceremonial hall in Taipei.

Right: The Taipei Grand Mosque serves as the headquarters of the Chinese Muslim Association, which oversees the spiritual needs of the island's nearly 60,000 Muslims.

Previous page: Followers of Taoism, a folk religion which has its roots in the sixth-century B.C. writings of Chinese philosopher Lao Tzu, recite prayers at a temple ceremony.

25 Religion

Age-old religious customs, icons, and beliefs are evident at all levels of Taiwan's Chinese culture. Almost all adults in Taiwan, even those not formally subscribing to a religious belief or worshiping regularly at a particular temple, engage in religious practices stemming from one or a combination of traditional Chinese folk religions, Buddhism, or Taoism. It is very common in Taiwan to see homes and shops include a lighted shrine with incense burning to honor a deity, hero, or ancestor. Most families perform the filial duties of ancestral worship; and on important occasions, as when a son or daughter takes the university entrance examination, a visit to the temples is made to present petitions and solicit divine assistance. Most taxi drivers in Taiwan decorate their cars with charms, amulets, statuettes, and religious slogans for protection against accidents and harm. Yet strictly speaking, these people are not necessarily Buddhist, Taoist, officially affiliated with any certain temple, or registered with a religious organization.

The latest figures released by the Ministry of the Interior in December 1995 indicate that more than 11 million people—over half of the population—in the Taiwan area are religious believers (see chart, next page). Altogether, more than 16,000 temples and churches dot the island serving the spiritual needs of the 21.3 million people in the Taiwan area.

Polytheistic and syncretic, Chinese society is dominated by ancestor worship, religious Taoism, and Buddhism, but has never excluded the addition and development of other indigenous and foreign religions. Although each religion may appear to postulate an independent doctrine, some cannot be strictly differentiated. For example, the Taiwan folk deity Goddess of the Sea, Matsu 媽祖, and the Buddhist Goddess of Mercy, Kuanyin 觀音, may be worshiped in the same temple. This reveals the special character of the Chinese religious outlook, which can accommodate seemingly contradictory beliefs simultaneously.

Freedom of religion is a fundamental right of every citizen in the ROC: "The people shall have freedom of religious belief," states Article 13 of the ROC Constitution. People of all recognized religions can publicly proselytize, evangelize, and congregate as long as they do not violate ROC laws and regulations, public morals, and social systems. To be recognized, however, these groups must apply and register with the Department of Civil Affairs of the Ministry of the Interior 內政部民政司 after meeting stipulated requirements, including a minimum number of local believers, organizations, and churches. Currently, there are 12 religions recognized by the government: Buddhism, Taoism, Catholicism, Protestantism, Hsüan-yüan Chiao 軒轅教, Islam, Li-ism 理教, Tenrikyo 天理教, Baha'i faith, T'ien Dih Chiao 天帝教, T'ien Te Chiao 天德教, and I-kuan Tao 一貫道.

Religious groups have traditionally been the backbone of community services in Taiwan. As of December 1995, religious groups were operating 56 hospitals, 65 clinics, 65 homes for the elderly, 15 orphanages, and 17 nurseries in Taiwan. They have established some 470 kindergartens, 22 primary schools, 44 secondary schools, 23 colleges, and 11 universities. Charity donations by religious groups in 1995 totaled US$125.9 million, more than one-third of which comprised alms for the poor and contributions for victims of natural disasters.

Aside from sharing a common concern for the poor and disaster victims, religious organizations have also diversified into medical services, free health checkups, community projects, and visitations to homes and hospitals. The churches in Taiwan have also taken the lead in organizing cultural and recreational activities. Whereas the Protestant church has focused on promoting youth activities, Taoist organizations have channeled much of their efforts into preserving and staging traditional Chinese dramas, and Buddhist groups have offered a wide range of self-improvement seminars.

The important factor influencing religion in China is the extremely eclectic nature of the Chinese. The religions currently practiced in the Taiwan area described in the following sections are for the most part combinations of elements from sev-

Religious Population 1995

	Believers (thousands)	Percentage of Total Population
Buddhist	4,863	22.8
Taoist	3,852	18.1
I-Kuan Tao	942	4.4
Protestant & Catholic	726	3.4
Other	748	3.5
Total	11,131	52.3

eral religions. Even Chinese Taoism, while rooted in a traditional Chinese philosophy, has absorbed aspects of other non-Chinese dogmas. Unlike the Jewish and Christian religions of the West which require that believers adhere only to their particular doctrines, the Chinese have seldom felt it necessary to exclude aspects of other faiths from their personal or collective religious portfolios.

Taoism

Religious Taoism developed from a philosophic system based upon the writings of Lao Tzu 老子, who lived in the sixth century B.C. He and his disciples emphasized individual freedom, laissez-faire government, human spontaneity, and mystical experience. Taoist philosophy takes *The Classic of the Way and Its Power* 道德經 as its central text.

The themes of Taoism as a religion coalesced in the third century B.C., but Taoism did not become an organized religious movement until the second century A.D. The fundamental aim of Taoism as a religion (not as a philosophy) was the attainment of immortality. Accordingly, people who lived in harmony with nature were said to become "immortals" 仙. Lao Tzu, founder of the philosophy of Taoism, eventually was deified as a Taoist god at the head of a huge pantheon of "immortal" folk heroes. Famous generals and sages made up the rest of the pantheon once they ascended to immortal status. Taoist pursuit of everlasting life ultimately led to a search for immortality pills or potions. Medieval Taoist rituals to some extent mirrored alchemical research in Europe during the same period.

Taoism was adopted as the religion of the imperial court during the seventh through the ninth centuries, and Taoist mystical elements were codified. In the ensuing centuries, the Taoist religious community was increasingly fractionalized. Taoism became interlaced with elements of Confucianism, Buddhism, and folk religion. The particular forms of Taoist religion brought to Taiwan some 300 years ago (then regarded as an outlying frontier area) are considered typical of the fragmented Taoist traditions. The most distinctive feature of the present practice is the worship of one's forebears alongside Taoist deities.

During the period of Japanese occupation (1895-1945), the Japanese colonial government implemented a policy of suppressing Taoism in Taiwan, because it was associated with Chinese patriotism. Many religious images in Taoist temples were burned, and various repressive measures were directed against Taoist followers.

After Taiwan's retrocession to China in 1945, Taoist temples that had been registered as Buddhist under pressure from the Japanese colonial government returned to the Taoist fold. Taoist priests from the Chinese mainland, including Chang En-p'u 張恩溥, a 63rd generation Taoist priest of the Cheng I 正一 sect of Lung Hu Mountain 龍虎山, began moving to Taiwan in increasing numbers. In 1950, Chang En-p'u established a Taoist fellowship in Taiwan, assuming the position of director. This was the beginning of organized Taoism in Taiwan.

In the past, much emphasis was put on constructing luxurious temples and holding frequent, lavish festivals. Today, adherents and priests pay more attention to preaching through the mass media. Some Taoist leaders have turned to the strategy of using temple associations to unite the various "generic" temples under the umbrella of a common main deity, while at the same time trying to win over temple diviners from small local or home temples 神壇 and offering them guidance.

Taoist groups in Taiwan engage in extensive exchanges with their overseas counterparts. In May 1995, a group of Taoist priests from Taiwan participated in a statue dedication ceremony at the P'eng Lai Temple 蓬萊閣 in Toronto, Canada. ROC Taoist groups also took part in cultural and academic activities in the mainland province of Fukien in July and August 1995. Groups from the Chinese mainland and Japan have also come to Taiwan for cultural and academic activities in recent years.

As of 1995, about 8,300 Taoist temples and 32,000 Taoist clergy were meeting the spiritual needs of some 3.85 million Taoist faithful living in Taiwan. Two Taoist seminaries, one each in Taipei and Kaohsiung, were providing instruction in Taoist doctrines and rites. There were also one college, 53 kindergartens, one retirement home, one hospital, 18 clinics, nine libraries, six publishing houses, and 154 publications serving the needs of Taoist faithful.

Buddhism

Buddhism is a pan-Asian religion which originated in India and was brought to China sometime before the sixth century. The Buddha was an Indian prince named Siddhartha Gautama who renounced his royal family and luxurious lifestyle to search for religious understanding and release from the human condition. It is said that he achieved enlightenment through self-denial and meditation, and thereafter, instructed his followers on the nature of dharma, the true way. The Buddha preached a doctrine envisioned in the "Four Noble Truths": life is fundamentally difficult and disappointing; suffering is the result of one's desires; to stop disappointment one must control one's desires; and the way to stop desire is through right views, intention, speech, conduct, livelihood, effort, mindfulness, and concentration.

Buddhism spread south to Ceylon, Cambodia, and Laos to become Theravada or Hinayana (Little Vehicle 小乘) and north to China, Korea, and Japan, where it developed into Mahayana (Great Vehicle 大乘). Hinayana is concerned more with individual salvation through contemplation and self-purification, while Mahayana teaches compassion and universal salvation.

Mahayana adherents believe in powerful godlike bodhisattvas, enlightened individuals who are capable of saving all sentient beings and transporting them to a state of release (nirvana) from the human condition. Bodhisattvas possess the natural disposition to attain enlightenment and become Buddhas, a potential which is inherent in all men. Mahayana adherents also believe in a cycle of lives which continues until one attains nirvana and becomes a Buddha.

Several Mahayana concepts, such as a life of suffering, many powerful godlike figures, and possible transcendence to a higher state of being, meshed well with similar ideas in Taoism and folk religion already widely accepted in China. As a result, Mahayana Buddhism became the most popular form of Buddhism in China, and indeed, in all of Northeast Asia.

Although Buddhism originated in India, since its introduction to China almost two millennia ago it has undergone thorough Sinification. In terms of thought system, canons, and ceremonies, the Buddhism practiced in China today is distinctly Chinese, and few Chinese people consider it a foreign religion.

Buddhism was introduced into Taiwan in the late 16th century. By the time Ming loyalist Koxinga 國姓爺 escaped to Taiwan and drove out the Dutch, Buddhist monks were already coming to Taiwan with official sanction. Buddhist temples were built with the support of Koxinga and his followers. By the 17th century, several Buddhist temples had been erected by officials, the gentry, and local people; however, Buddhist missionary work at the time seems to have been limited in scope. Some Buddhist temples were used as temples of folk religion by the people, and thus received popular support.

Japanese Buddhism was introduced into Taiwan during the period of Japanese occupation at the turn of the 20th century. Eight Buddhist sects, namely, the Tendai 天台, the Shingon 真元, the Pure Land 淨土, the Soto 曹洞宗, the Rinzai 臨濟宗, the Shin 真, the Nichiren 日蓮, the Hokke 法華, and the Agon 阿含, came to Taiwan to proselytize. Buddhist sects already established in Taiwan responded to the incursion by accommodating the newcomers. By 1925, a large number of Japanese monks were in leading positions in Taiwan's established Buddhist temples. Buddhism in Taiwan gradually took on a Japanese cast, particularly in the areas of moral and disciplinary codes and education.

During the Japanese occupation, Buddhist groups in Taiwan separated into the northern, central, and southern schools. The monk Shan-hui 善慧 founded the Yüeh-mei Mountain 月眉山 school of Keelung 基隆 (the northern school), and the monk Chüeh-li 覺力 established the Fa-yün Szu 法雲寺 school of Miaoli 苗栗 (the central school) and the K'ai-yüan Szu 開元寺 school of Tainan (the southern school). Most Buddhist temples of this era belonged to one of these three schools. Towards the end of the Japanese occupation, many monks actively engaged in proselytizing activities and established Buddhist organizations. In 1947, Master Chang-chia 章嘉 established the Buddhist Association of the ROC 中國佛教會 in Nanking. Large numbers of Chinese monks followed the Chinese Nationalist government to Taiwan and established the Taiwan provincial chapter of the Buddhist Association of the ROC. Monks from the Chinese mainland headed the association at first, and temples throughout the island became association members.

Post-war Buddhism in Taiwan has witnessed the re-establishment of the Chinese Mahayana tradition, renewed stress on moral and disciplinary codes and the ceremony of ordination 傳戒大典, emphasis on Buddhist education and the establishment of Buddhist institutes, and active proselytization. As of 1995, Buddhists in the ROC had registered almost 4,000 temples, 24 seminaries, two universities, two colleges, eight high schools, 70 kindergartens, ten nurseries, five orphanages, 50 retirement homes, seven hospitals, three clinics and 48 publishing houses. There were also more than 9,000 Buddhist clergy serving some 4.9 million Buddhists in Taiwan.

Since the 1950s, the Buddhist Association of the ROC has held ordination ceremonies for Buddhist monks, nuns, and lay people. Temples recognized by the association hold an annual third-level ordination ceremony 三壇大戒, with monks and nuns receiving one month of strict training before ordination. A total of about 10,000 monks and nuns have been ordained in this ceremony at various temples and monasteries over the past four decades.

Since 1980, Tantric Buddhism, an esoteric sect which developed between the second and fourth centuries A.D. in India, has become increasingly popular in Taiwan. In recent years, exiled Tibetan monks of the Tantric sect have come to Taiwan, rapidly attracting a large following and thereby exercising a significant effect on Taiwan's religious culture.

Education

The road traveled by Buddhist education has not been a smooth one. Its beginning in post-retrocession Taiwan dates from the invitation by the Buddhist Master Miao-kuo 妙果 of the Yüan-kuang Temple 圓光寺 in Chungli 中壢 to the Buddhist Master Tz'u-hang 慈航 from the Chinese mainland to establish a Buddhist institute in Taiwan. Master Tz'u-hang later founded a Maitreya monastery in Hsichih 汐止, Taipei County; Master Yin-shun 印順 assumed the directorship of a Buddhist institute in Hsinchu 新竹, and subsequently over 50 Buddhist institutes were founded islandwide. Many of these institutes functioned intermittently; only a portion of them were able to maintain unbroken operations. One explanation for this is that Buddhist and other religious institutes are not officially recognized by the Ministry of Education. Another is that many Buddhist figures founded independent educational institutes instead of uniting to establish one large institute. The Buddhist-sponsored Tzu Chi Junior College of Nursing 慈濟護理專科學校 opened its gates in 1989, and Huafan College of Humanities and Technology 華梵人文科技學院 followed the next year. Tzu Chi Medical College 慈濟醫學院 began enrolling students in 1994. Another Buddhist institution of higher learning, the College of Humanities and Sociology of Fokuang University 佛光大學人文社會學院, is presently under construction in Ilan 宜蘭. And the Nanhua Management College of Fokuang University 佛光大學南華管理學院, located in Chiayi 嘉義, began enrolling students in October 1996. Dharma Drum College 法鼓人文社會學院 and Shuan Tsang College of Humanities and Social Sciences 玄奘大學人文社會學院 are currently under construction.

Trends

Buddhists are becoming more missionary in outlook. Over the past few years, television proselytizing has gained popularity, and lectures on Buddhism have begun to draw large crowds. Some of the leading figures in Buddhism have even expanded their missions to North America: The famous Master Hsing-yün 星雲 directed the construction of the Hsi-lai Temple 西來寺, completed in 1988, in Los Angeles. He also directed the construction of Nan-T'ien Temple 南天寺 (registered under the International Buddhist Association of Australia, Inc.) in Sydney, Australia, completed in 1995 and reputed to be the largest Buddhist temple in the southern hemisphere.

In addition to the chanting of mantras and sutras—the more traditional form of worshiping—meditation is gaining a foothold among believers. Buddhists have established centers to offer courses on meditation to the public. The practice is also becoming popular among politicians and businessmen as a means of relieving tension.

Intellectuals have been drawn to Buddhism from the beginning, for both academic and religious reasons. Some have become renowned monks and nuns. By stressing "Buddhism for this world," Buddhist leaders have also managed to attract people outside of academia who have contributed significant amounts of financial and spiritual support to Buddhist organizations.

Confucianism

Confucianism is a philosophy with a religious function. It is named after Confucius, whose discourses on ethical behavior have been passed down, generation to generation, to become the definitive marker of things Chinese. It embraces some elements of traditional Chinese religion such as a reverence toward heaven and the worship of ancestors. Moreover, it concerns the cultivation of an ethical life in order to establish harmonious relationships with other individuals and with society. It does not assert the existence of a deity. Most Chinese do not identify Confucianism as a religion; rather they view it as a philosophy. They regard Confucian temples more as halls to honor Confucius than places of worship. Visitors may witness an elaborate ceremony to honor Confucius at Taipei's Confucian Temple 孔廟 every year on his birthday, September 28, which is also Teachers' Day in the ROC.

Folk Religion

The majority of Taiwan's people believe in Chinese folk religion, a faith whose theology, rituals, and officiants are widely diffused into other secular and social institutions. Taiwan's difficult pioneer environment of the past two centuries created a strong need for religion, and folk religion was the choice of virtually all Chinese immigrants to the island. They brought from the mainland images of gods and traditional religious beliefs. While transplanting their religion, however, they adapted it functionally to their new society, sometimes even creating new gods and rituals to meet their needs for security and survival. The resulting "holy smorgasbord" is called folk religion for the sake of convenience.

Like Taoism, folk religion has a broad pantheon of gods and goddesses. Relations between gods and people, and between gods and gods, are of paramount importance. Like Buddhism, folk religion offers salvation, or at least temporary aid for true believers. Although folk religion has been significantly influenced by Buddhism and Taoism, it is neither Buddhist nor Taoist. People associated with Taoism often place folk religion in the same category as Taoism; however, they concede that folk religion includes a number of gods that Taoism does not recognize.

In folk religion, the supreme deity is the God of Heaven 天公, who is recognized as a personification of justice. Below this supreme deity are hundreds of lesser gods. Almost every neighborhood in Taiwan has a temple of the Earth God 土地公, and families make offerings to the House God 地基主 when they move into a house.

One of the most popular deities is Matsu 媽祖, also patron goddess of fishermen. Worshipers celebrated the 1,000th anniversary of her ascent to heaven in 1987 with a round-the-island parade of her image. Her birthday is celebrated with great pomp as worshipers carry her image in a procession through cities around Taiwan. The brave warrior Kuan Yü 關羽 of the Period of the Three Kingdoms 三國時代; the general Koxinga, who drove the Dutch colonists from Taiwan in the 17th century; and the renowned healer Hua T'uo 華陀, who lived sometime between the first and third century A.D., all have faithful followings in Taiwan.

Taiwan's Wang Yeh 王爺 are believed to be celestial emissaries sent by the heavens to ensure the safety of mankind by driving away evil spirits and preventing and eradicating epidemics. There are said to be 360 Wang Yeh in Taiwan, but the religious practices surrounding each of these celestial lords differ from locality to locality and change with the times. The Wang Yeh are often worshiped in groups of three or five.

While the Wang Yeh are worshiped mainly by those originally from Fukien Province, the San Shan Kuo-wang 三山國王, literally, the Three Kings of the Mountains, are revered by Chinese of Hakka descent (an ethnic and linguistic subset of Han Chinese culture). Legendary stories surrounding the two groups of deities are similar, the only difference being that the San Shan Kuo-wang originated from the worship of mountains. With the outward spread of Hakka Chinese from the Hsinchu and Miaoli areas throughout Taiwan, the three gods have been separated and are often worshiped individually instead of as a group.

Meanwhile, traditional magical calculations, such as geomancy 風水 and physiognomy 看相, are not only still in fashion, they are also changing with the times. Forecasts based on magical calculations are made to strike it rich in the stock market.

I-kuan Tao

The Chinese words I-kuan Tao 一貫道 can be roughly translated as the Religion of One Unity. The name belies I-kuan Tao's nature as a religious doctrine that draws upon both traditional Chinese teachings and each of the world's major religions. I-kuan Tao is a modern, syncretic faith, and the third most popular religion in Taiwan.

According to I-kuan Tao adherents, this religion attempts to identify common principles underlying Taoism, Buddhism, Christianity, Islam, Judaism, and Hinduism. I-kuan Tao faithful believe that by uncovering a single set of universal truths, the "increasing chaos" of modern times can be defeated and the world can live in peaceful harmony. They believe in a God beyond all other gods, called Ming-ming Shang-ti 明明上帝 (the God of Clarity).

I-kuan Tao evolved from the Hsien-t'ien Tao 先天道 founded by Huang Te-hui 黃德輝 of the Ch'ing Dynasty (during the Shun-chih period, which lasted from 1644-1661 A.D.) Huang Te-hui combined the three main belief systems of China with the belief in the *Wu-Sheng Lao-Mu* 無生老母 ("Lifeless Old Mother") deity to form the Hsien-t'ien Tao.

As a religion, I-kuan Tao was highly accessible to Chinese. One reason for its rapid spread throughout China over the years was that, although I-kuan Tao claimed to be a universal religion, its basic writings, forms of religious observance, and moral precepts were all couched in traditional Chinese terms. By drawing heavily on Confucian, Buddhist, Taoist, and folk religious terminology, I-kuan Tao was readily understandable in traditional Chinese religious terms, but was less appealing to non-Chinese.

To some extent, this still holds true today. While I-kuan Tao boasts large numbers of faithful in Australia, Canada, the United States, South Africa, France, Italy, and elsewhere, it is widely embraced only by the overseas Chinese communities in these countries, and only limited fragments of I-kuan Tao scripture have been translated into non-Chinese languages.

I-kuan Tao adherents more or less follow the rituals of Confucianism and engage in ancestor worship. Services are usually held at family shrines and are aimed at both cultivating personal character and regulating family relations—two key concepts in Chinese culture. By 1995, there were 87 large or medium-sized I-kuan Tao temples in Taiwan with some 75,000 temple priests serving approximately 942,000 I-kuan Tao believers. By increasing the number of I-kuan Tao temples, faithful believe they are bringing the Buddhist "Western Paradise" to earth and creating a world of brotherhood and universal love as envisioned by Confucian teachings.

The goodness of personal sublimation and the grace of a life of service are key tenets in the I-kuan Tao moral scheme, and adherents devote a great deal of resources to social work. In Taiwan, there are four I-kuan Tao seminaries, 34 kindergartens, four retirement homes, 21 hospitals, nine clinics, 30 publishing houses, and 32 publications. This service ethic is closely related to the order's tradition that each believer should "give his heart to the universe and contribute his life to humanity."

In the 40-some years since I-kuan Tao was brought to Taiwan, it has established many cultural and educational units which have trained an average of 10,000 I-kuan Tao devotees each year. Over half of the vegetarian restaurants around the island are run by I-kuan Tao adherents, who are required to follow a strict vegetarian diet.

Proselytism of I-kuan Tao has not always been such an open matter. Indeed, I-kuan Tao teachings incorporate a tradition of secrecy inherited from the various clandestine religious sects which have thrived during periods of chaos in Chinese history.

In their day-to-day lives, I-kuan Tao followers strive to uphold the precepts of not killing, stealing, committing adultery, lying, or drinking alcohol, while putting into practice the I-kuan Tao ideals of benevolence, righteousness, courtesy, wisdom, and faith.

Other Independent Religions

There are several other independent religions in Taiwan that generally fall into one of the following four categories: religions brought to Taiwan from the Chinese mainland; religions brought in from foreign countries; new religions developed from existing ones; and new religions created in Taiwan.

Included in the first category are Chai Chiao 齋教, Hsia Chiao 夏教 (Chai Chiao and Hsia Chiao are not recognized by the ROC government as religions), Li-ism, and T'ien Te Chiao. Chai Chiao entered Taiwan during the 17th century, and is divided into three major schools: Lung Hua 龍華, Chin Ch'uang 金幢, and Hsien T'ien 先天 (a precursor of I-kuan Tao). It is a modified form of Buddhism combined with elements of Confucianism, Taoism, and folk beliefs. Chai Chiao adherents worship the Buddha and the goddess Kuanyin. As vegetarians who neither shave their heads nor don the monk's robes, they worship in the home, thus giving Chai Chiao the common title "Lay Buddhism." During the Japanese occupation of Taiwan, the group joined the Soto sect of Buddhism to escape Japanese suppression, and the religion greatly declined as a result.

Hsia Chiao was founded by Lin Chao-en 林兆恩 in the 16th century, and was brought to Taiwan during the Japanese occupation. When praying, adherents burn four incense sticks—instead of the usual folk practice of burning three—to venerate Confucius, Lao Tzu, the Buddha, and the founder of the religion. Hsia Chiao has three temples and several hundred followers.

Li-ism (doctrine of order) was founded by Yang Lai-ju 楊來如 in the 17th century. Its creed stresses traditional Chinese morals and ethics, such as the loyalty and filial piety of Confucianism, the world salvation and forgiveness of Buddhism, and the natural way and inaction of Taoism. It is, in fact, the synthesis of Confucianism, Buddhism, and

Taoism given a new dimension by the worship of Kuanyin. Though Li-ists worship Kuanyin, they do not reject deities of other religions. They believe the providence may be revealed in the form of other deities and prophets. Li-ists abide by the great law of Li-ism called *Fa Pao Tieh Wen* 法寶牒文 (precious and official decrees), written by Yang.

Some Li-ist clergy came to Taiwan from the Chinese mainland in 1949. The Association of Li-ism 中華理教總會 was officially re-established in Taiwan in 1950, with headquarters in Taipei. Today, Li-ism has spread to Korea, the United States, Hong Kong, Japan, and the Philippines. In 1952, Sheng-li College 聖理書院 was established for Li-ists to study the classics. Today, there are over 600 Li-ist clergy in 125 temples islandwide serving about 140,000 adherents. There are also three Li-ist seminaries, two kindergartens, eight institutes for Li-ist proselytization, three clinics, and one publishing house. Adherents enthusiastically provide the needy with relief in winter, free medication, and scholarships.

T'ien Te Chiao was founded in 1923 in China by a young shaman, Hsiao Chang-ming 蕭昌明, now known to his followers as the "celestial worthy." T'ien Te Chiao is a synthesis of the two major religio-philosophical traditions of China—Confucianism and Taoism—and three world religions—Buddhism, Christianity, and Islam. Adherents are required to strictly follow 20 principles: loyalty, forbearance, honesty, openness, virtue, uprightness, righteousness, faith, endurance, fairness, universal love, filial piety, benevolence, kindness, consciousness, moral integrity, frugality, truth, courtesy, and harmony. T'ien Te Chiao adherents also practice various methods of self-cultivation, health preservation, and psychic healing. They are trained to tap acupuncture points to cure ailments. Believers learn to meditate under the guidance of their masters in order to search for their original being, which is free and untainted from worldly ties and yearnings.

Since T'ien Te Chiao was introduced into Taiwan in 1953, worship and medical service centers have been set up throughout Taiwan. T'ien Te Chiao was finally officially recognized by the government in 1989. By 1995, there were three T'ien Te Chiao temples and 24 masters for its more than 290,000 believers in Taiwan. Members must be over 20 years old. There were also 15 institutes for T'ien Te Chiao proselytization, two T'ien Te Chiao libraries, one publishing house, and two publications.

Religions from Abroad

Foreign religious groups in Taiwan include Baha'i, Judaism, and Tenrikyo, (Islam and the various sects of Christianity are discussed separately later in this chapter).

The first Taiwan convert to the Baha'i faith was an overseas student in the United States in 1949. An Iranian husband-wife team came from mainland China in 1954 to do pioneer work, and established Taiwan's first Baha'i center in Tainan. There are currently about 15,000 Baha'i followers who gather in 46 Baha'i meeting places and centers around the country. Four foreign missionaries and one publishing house help serve the faithful in Taiwan. The local Baha'i headquarters, the National Spiritual Assembly of the Baha'is of Taiwan 財團法人巴哈伊教台灣總靈體會, is located in Taipei.

Baha'i communities all over the world target urgent social issues in each region. In Taiwan, the local Baha'i assemblies have singled out environmental protection as their main area of social concern. Since 1990, the Baha'i community has launched joint projects with government organizations to promote environmental education amongst kindergarten and elementary schoolteachers around the country. Baha'i teams visit schools all over Taiwan, organizing simulation games designed to teach basic environmental principles. The Baha'i community has also produced about 30 radio programs on environmental issues and published a book on environmental education in collaboration with the Homemakers' Union and Foundation 主婦聯盟環保基金會.

Jews from Persia and other areas began to settle in China about 1,000 years ago during the T'ang dynasty. Thriving communities developed in many large cities, but particularly in Kaifeng, which became the center of Chinese Jewish life. Due to gradual assimilation, however, these communities had virtually disappeared by the middle of the 19th century. During the 20th century, China again received an influx of Jews, this time refugees from persecution in Europe—first from Russia and later from eastern European countries taken over by the Nazis. The largest groups of Jews settled in Harbin in Manchuria and in Shanghai. But after World War II and the communist threat in China, most of this population moved to the West.

Today the small Taiwan Jewish community of about 40 families consists of expatriates (mainly Americans, but also Israelis and Europeans) who are either long-term Taipei residents or assigned here on tours of duty by multinational corporations, academic institutions, or international organizations. The community is affiliated with the Asia-Pacific Jewish Association based in Australia. Activities include religious observances, a Sunday school program in Bible and religious instruction for children, holiday celebrations, and cultural events. Most activities are held in a community center maintained in the Tienmu 天母 district of Taipei.

Tenrikyo was founded in Japan in 1838 by a farming woman, Miki Nakayama. The religion was first introduced into Taiwan during the period of Japanese occupation. The doctrine of Tenrikyo stresses respect for ancestors, filial piety, self-cultivation, and service to mankind, and thus resembles traditional Chinese ethics and the concept of universal brotherhood. The religion was therefore readily accepted in Taiwan, continued to develop, and was formally recognized by the Ministry of the Interior in 1973. As of 1995, there were 140 Tenrikyo temples and 420 clergymen serving 20,000 believers in Taiwan. There were also 18 foreign clergymen, 15 institutes for Tenrikyo proselytization, one clinic, one publishing house, and two publications.

New Extensions

There is also a large group of new religions in Taiwan that have developed on the basis of previously existing ones. The main representatives of this group are Confucian Spirit Religion 儒宗神教 and T'ien Dih Chiao 天帝教. Both religions practice spiritual and psychic healing.

Instead of temples or churches, the Confucian Spirit Religion has "phoenix halls" 鳳廳 in which "phoenix writing" is created by means of "spirit writing." The central deity at these phoenix halls is the Jade Emperor 玉皇大帝. Other deities vary from hall to hall, and include such figures as the warrior Kuan Yü 關羽 and prime minister K'ung Ming 孔明 of the Period of the Three Kingdoms. Although not all phoenix halls belong to the same organization, they remain in frequent contact and sometimes work together.

T'ien Dih Chiao was founded by Li Yü-chieh 李玉階 in the mid-1980s after he split with T'ien Te Chiao. The emphasis of its doctrine is placed on cultivation of one's moral self, and it has "20 True Words" 二十字真言 that serve as "required daily homework" for its believers. Believers in T'ien Dih Chiao are especially concerned about nuclear war. Since its founding, T'ien Dih Chiao has established 51 temples with 200 clergymen, that are concentrated mainly in Taipei, Taichung, Tainan, P'ingtung 屏東, and Hualien 花蓮. It currently claims a following of 185,000 believers in Taiwan. They have five foreign clergymen, two seminaries, one kindergarten, two institutes for proselytization, one library, and two publishing houses. Temples have also been opened overseas in Los Angeles and San Francisco, USA.

Religions Founded in Taiwan

Few religions fall into the fourth category of new religions founded in Taiwan. A typical example is Hsüan-yüan Chiao 軒轅教, which was formally founded in Taiwan in 1957 by 82-year-old legislator Wang Han-sheng 王寒生. Hsüan-yüan Chiao attempts to raise people's sense of nationalism, and to organize and unite the religious thought of China over the ages, including Confucianism, Taoism, and Mohism. Its main creed is respect for heaven and ancestors. Hsüan-yüan Chiao is named after the ancient legendary founder of the Chinese nation, whose name was Hsüan-yüan.

The religion was inspired by Wang's grief over the loss of the Chinese mainland to the Chinese communists. Wang attributed the loss primarily to the absence of national spirit, which could only be restored by a renewal of Chinese culture. Hsüan-yüan Chiao is an attempt to revive national spirit through an unnamed religion which dates from Hsüan-yüan to the Western Han dynasty. The religion inherits orthodox Chinese traditions from Hsüan-yüan to Dr. Sun Yat-sen. Adherents abide by the principles set forth in the Hsüan-yüan Chiao scriptures, the *Huang Ti Ching* 黃帝經.

Hsüan-yüan Chiao affirms the existence of a creator who can be identified as the "Tao" or Way. Hsüan-yüan Chiao holds that man can become divine through self-cultivation and enlightenment in the Tao. The highest state attainable in the new religion is "the union of heaven and man" where "the self is denied and yet is omnipresent." This progress can only be accomplished through self-purification, cultivation of illustrious virtues and helping others to achieve salvation.

As of 1995, Hsüan-yüan Chiao had 18 temples and 109 clergy serving 136,000 adherents, one seminary, one retirement home, one clinic, one publishing house, and three institutes for proselytization.

Christianity

Christianity came to Taiwan with the Dutch in 1624. They were just two years ahead of their Spanish competitors for converts. The first person to win souls in Taiwan was Georgius Candidius of the Reformed Church of Holland. Six P'ing-p'u 平埔 aborigine communities near modern day Tainan were the center of his mission activities. (The P'ing-p'u tribe was later assimilated by Han settlers.) Robert Bunius continued Candidius' mission work in southern Taiwan, where he lived for 14 years. By the year 1643, over 6,000 aborigines had converted to Christianity. Mass conversions were typical of his evangelistic style.

In 1626, a Spaniard, Father Martinez, in the company of Spanish troops, brought with him four Dominican missionaries from the Philippines to the Keelung 基隆 and Tamsui 淡水 areas to do mission work. The Spanish army occupied a portion of northern Taiwan, and ruled there for 16 years. Missionaries actively spread Roman Catholicism in this period, during which they won approximately 4,000 aborigines over to their faith.

In 1642, the Dutch forces occupying southern Taiwan pushed north to rout the Spaniards, arresting them and driving them out of Taiwan. It is not known what became of the Roman Catholic converts, since no trace of them is to be found. All that remains from this period of Roman Catholic missionary activity are a few historical records. By the time the Chinese general Koxinga 國姓爺 drove the Dutch off the island, this scantily documented page in the history of Christianity in Taiwan had more or less come to an end. By the year 1714, when the Roman Catholic Jesuits came to Taiwan for map-making, they found a few descendants of these early Christians who had still preserved some remnants of their forebears' beliefs. In 1859, the Spanish Dominican Father Fernando Sainz and Father Angel Bofurull arrived in Kaohsiung from the Philippines via Amoy, and founded the first Roman Catholic church in Kaohsiung, the Holy Rosary Church 玫瑰聖母堂. Father Sainz later conducted mission work in the Kaohsiung, Tainan, and P'ingtung areas. In 1861, he founded the Immaculate Conception Church in what today is Wanchin Village 萬金村 in Wanluan 萬巒. This is the oldest extant Roman Catholic church in Taiwan.

In 1860, the British missionaries Reverend Carstairs Douglas and Reverend H.L. Mackenzie came to Tamsui and Mengchia 艋舺, now called Wanhua 萬華, in Taipei to preach the gospel. In 1864, Dr. James L. Maxwell was officially sent to Taiwan by the English Presbyterian Mission to preach Christianity. With Tainan as his base, he concentrated his efforts in southern Taiwan. In 1872, the Canadian Presbyterian Church dispatched George L. Mackay to northern Taiwan to do mission work, choosing Tamsui as his center.

Prior to the Japanese occupation of Taiwan in 1895, there were 97 Protestant churches, 4,854 believers, about 90 mission workers, and 13 foreign missionaries in Taiwan. During the period of Japanese occupation, the colonial government exercised control over churches, and had them absorb Japanese Christian groups. The Japanese also strictly forbade Christian mission work among the aborigines. After the Japanese left in 1945, Taiwan had about 238 Protestant churches and 60,000 believers.

During the period of Japanese occupation, Roman Catholicism experienced a relatively slow development. Some theorize that this was due to suppression by the Japanese colonial government; however, there is no concrete evidence to support this. By 1945, there were only about 10,000 Roman Catholics (some records report 8,000), 52 churches or missions, and 20 missionaries in Taiwan.

Christianity in Taiwan developed in a new direction after the mainland fell to communism and the central government relocated to Taiwan in 1949. Churches of numerous denominations flocked to Taiwan, and the number of Christian denominations active in Taiwan went from just three in 1945 to approximately 40 in 1955.

Taiwan's Protestant churches experienced rapid growth between 1950 and 1964, but after the mid-1960s, they entered a phase of sluggish and even negative growth. By 1979, believers totaled only 360,000. This flock had expanded to approximately 422,000 by 1995, with nearly 2,700 protestant churches, 2,500 ministers, and 1,100 foreign missionaries in Taiwan that year.

In 1995, there were at least 57 known Protestant denominations in Taiwan. According to the Churches Union of the Republic of China 中華民國基督教會協會, the largest denominations in Taiwan are the Presbyterian Church, with 217,000 members, 1,100 clergy, and 1,200 congregations; the Chinese Baptist Convention, with 19,000 members, about 230 clergymen, and 190 congregations; the Taiwan Lutheran Church, with 6,000 members, 60 clergymen, and 42 congregations; the Methodist Church in the Republic of China, with 2,200 members, 26 clergymen, and 23 congregations; and the Episcopal Church, with 2,000 members, 14 clergy, and 17 congregations.

Although some other churches may have greater numbers of believers, such as the True Jesus Church (46,323 members and 223 congregations) and the Church of Jesus Christ of Latter Day Saints (22,500 members and 52 congregations), for various reasons they are not members of the Churches Union of the Republic of China. Other Christian churches not having CUROC membership include the Taiwan Mission of Seventh-Day Adventists, the Jehovah's Witnesses, the Unification Church, the Mandarin Church 國語禮拜堂 and the Ling Leung Church 靈糧堂.

Roman Catholicism made a remarkable comeback in Taiwan after retrocession. In 1948, the number of believers stood at 13,000. When the central government moved to Taiwan in 1949, multitudes of Roman Catholic clergy and believers followed, infusing Roman Catholicism in Taiwan with new strength and vigor. The number of converts grew rapidly in the 1953-1963 period, going from 27,000 to 300,000. The number of practicing Roman Catholics was highest in 1969, when the total reached nearly 306,000, and seven dioceses were formed: the Taipei archdiocese, and the Hsinchu 新竹, Taichung, Chiayi 嘉義, Tainan, Kaohsiung, and Hualien 花蓮 dioceses. Since then, the Roman Catholic church of Taiwan has faced a period of stagnancy. As of 1995, there were some 800 Catholic churches, 2,800 clergymen, and 700 foreign missionaries in Taiwan serving almost 304,000 believers.

While mainstream Protestant churches and the Roman Catholic Church have enjoyed a head start in their evangelical work, independent churches are also growing consistently by emphasizing fundamentalist theology, flexible administration, and self-supporting financial power. Popular independent churches include the True Jesus Church, the Mandarin Church, and the Ling Leung Church.

The first missionaries from the Church of Jesus Christ of Latter Day Saints, also known as the

Mormon Church, arrived in Taiwan in 1956. By 1963, the book of Mormon had been translated from English into Chinese by Hu Wei-I 胡唯一 and a branch of the Mormon Church had been established locally. Since then, the Mormon gospel has been spread to even the most remote reaches of Taiwan. Today the Mormon church has a local membership of more than 22,000 members.

Some 360 full-time Mormon missionaries, including 70 locals, work in Taiwan, proselytizing and performing community service. In most areas, the foreign missionaries also offer free English conversation classes to the public. There are also a handful of full-time church workers who administer to the needs of the members of Taiwan. Although assisted by a steady rotation of foreign missionaries, all Mormon churches in Taiwan are headed by local Chinese leaders.

The Jehovah's Witnesses came to Taiwan in 1950 and registered with the Ministry of the Interior in 1964. As of June 1996, they had 48 congregations around the island, with 50 foreign missionaries and more than 3,000 faithful engaging in volunteer Bible education work in Taiwan.

The Unification Church, registered as the Holy Spirit Association for the Unification of World Christianity 財團法人「世界基督教統一神靈協會」came to Taiwan in 1971. By June 1996, it had 32 congregations and more than 40,000 believers in the Taiwan area. On August 25, 1995, the church founder, Reverend Sun Myung Moon of Korea, and his wife, Mrs. Hak Ja Han Moon, led over 8,000 couples in Taiwan in a group wedding ceremony via satellite.

Christian missions have, along with their evangelical intent, contributed to Taiwan's education and social work as well. The success of the Roman Catholic missions is seen in the establishment, as of 1995, of three universities, seven seminaries, 15 colleges, 27 high schools, ten elementary schools, 103 institutes for spreading the gospel, 271 kindergartens, 39 libraries, 23 centers for the retarded, 17 clinics, 15 hospitals, seven publishing houses, five handicapped welfare institutions, four retirement homes, four orphanages, three sanitariums, and seven nursing homes in Taiwan. The Protestants boast 38 seminaries, six universities, ten colleges, nine high schools, 12 elementary schools, 43 kindergartens, six orphanages, five retirement homes, two handicapped welfare institutes, 12 hospitals, 14 clinics, one library, and 99 publishing houses producing 60 publications.

Various international Christian organizations have established branches in Taiwan and they, along with local groups which have sprung up, provide a network of welfare and social services to various target groups in the society. World Vision of Taiwan has been instrumental in aboriginal welfare and child welfare; Campus Crusade and Navigators are active on college campuses; the Garden of Hope runs halfway houses for teenage prostitutes; Mackay Counseling Center offers family and psychological counseling services; and Cathwel Service and Christian Salvation Service provide assistance for unwed mothers.

Islam

The troops that Koxinga led to Taiwan in the mid-17th century included a number of Muslims. Some of them made Taiwan their permanent home, leaving historical traces which are still visible in Lukang 鹿港 and Tamsui, among other places. By the time of Taiwan's retrocession to China, however, most of the descendants of these early Mohammedan soldiers no longer embraced Islam; at best, some Islamic burial traditions were still observed.

Approximately 20,000 Muslims accompanied the central government to Taiwan in 1949; most were soldiers, civil servants, or food service workers. Two Muslim organizations re-established themselves in Taiwan to preach Islamic doctrines and build mosques: the Chinese Muslim Association 中國回教協會 and the Chinese Muslim Youth League 中國回教青年會.

Differences in everyday habits and customs, such as food and drink, and religious ceremonies and activities led to diminished contact between Muslims and Han Chinese in Taiwan during the 1950s. Believers in Islam depended to a large extent on a liaison network that regularly met in a house on Lishui Street 麗水街 in Taipei. By the 1960s, realizing that return to the mainland would not likely be possible in the immediate future, Muslims in Taiwan began to engage in relatively permanent occupations. Although there was still a considerable degree of interdependence in the Islamic community, Muslims began, primarily out of professional need, to have increasingly frequent contact with Han Chinese.

Limited by a non-Muslim environment, Muslims in Taiwan today struggle to observe orthodox Islamic practices. Only a few Muslim women have adopted the traditional veil; and a handful of halal butchers and restaurants prepare meat according to the strict Islamic food observances. The busy urban lifestyle in the cities poses many constraints: For example, it is virtually impossible to keep the Islamic Sabbath which falls on Fridays, or to faithfully perform the salat, a set of daily prayers repeated five times a day. Besides, all prayers are conducted in Arabic which means that every adherent must master the language in spite of cultural and linguistic constraints.

Despite the restraints imposed by a non-Muslim environment, three new Arabian-style mosques, constructed in Kaohsiung, Taichung, and Lungkang 龍崗 have recently joined Taipei's two mosques in meeting the needs of Muslim faithful. These new facilities cost a total of US$2.7 million, half of which was funded by overseas donations, predominantly from the Middle East. As of 1995, Taiwan was also home to a Muslim population of approximately 52,000, along with 30 Muslim priests, three Islamic libraries, and two publishing houses.

Further Reading (in Chinese unless otherwise noted):

Cheng, Chih-ming 鄭志明. *T'ai-wan te tsung-chiao yü mi-mi chiao-p'ai* 台灣的宗教與秘密教派 (Religions and Clandestine Religious Sects of Taiwan). Taipei: Tai-uain Publishing Co., 1991.

Chiang, I-cheng 姜義鎮, comp. *T'ai-wan te min-chien hsin-yang* 台灣的民間信仰 (Folk Beliefs of Taiwan), 3rd ed. Taipei: Woolin Publishing Co., Ltd., 1990.

Ch'ien-lung Chü-shih 潛龍居士. *Chung-kuo min-chien chu-shen chuan* 中國民間諸神傳 (Stories of the Folk Gods of China). Taipei: Chuan Yuan Publishing Co., 1992.

Chü, Hai-yuan 瞿海源. *T'ai-wan ti-ch'ü Min-chung te tsung-chiao hsin-yang yü tsung-chiao t'ai-tu* 台灣地區民眾的宗教信仰與宗教態度 ("Religious Beliefs and Religious Attitudes of People in the Taiwan Area"). *Pien-ch'ien-chung te t'ai-wan she-hui* 變遷中的台灣社會 (Taiwan Society in Transition) ed. by Yang, Kuo-shu 楊國樞 and Chü, Hai-yuan. Taipei: Institute of Ethnology, Academia Sinica, 1987.

Fang, Li-t'ien 方立天. *Chung-kuo fo-chiao yü ch'uan-t'ung wen-hua* 中國佛教與傳統文化 (Traditional Culture and Chinese Buddhism). Taipei: Laureate Book Co., Ltd., 1990.

I-kuan Tao chien-chieh 一貫道 簡介 (Introduction to I-kuan Tao). Tainan: Tien Jiuh Book Store, 1988.

Nan, Huai-chin 南懷瑾. *Tao-chiao mi-tsung yü tung-fang shen-mi-hsüeh* 道教密宗與東方神祕學 (Tantric Religions of Taoism and Oriental Mystic Study). Vols. I & II, 7th ed. Taipei: Lao Ku Cultural Foundation Inc., 1990.

P'ing, Ch'uan-chang 平川彰 (Hsü, Ming-yin 許明銀, tr.) *Fo-chiao yen-chiu ju-men* 佛教研究入門 (An Introduction to the Study of Buddhism). Taipei: Dharma-tatha, 1990.

Religions in the Republic of China (in English). 4th ed. Taipei: Kwang Hwa Publishing Co., 1991.

Tsung-chiao chien-chieh 宗教簡介 (Introduction to Religion). Taipei: Ministry of the Interior, 1991.

Yao, Li-hsiang 姚麗香. *T'ai-wan te tz'u-szu yü tsung-chiao* 台灣的祠祀與宗教 (Worship and Religion in Taiwan). 2nd ed. Taipei: Taiwan Publishing Co., 1990.

Yang, Sen-fu 楊森富. *Chung-kuo chi-tu-chiao shih* 中國基督教史 (The History of Christianity in China). Taipei: The Commercial Press Ltd., 1991.

中國輸出入銀行
The Export-Import Bank
of the Republic of China
A SPECIALIZED BANK
THAT OFFERS

Medium-And Long-Term Loan For Purchase of Machinery, Equipment And Turnkey Plants From The ROC

Our low-interest loans with repayment periods of up to seven years make it easy for overseas buyers to procure machinery, equipment and turnkey plants from the ROC.

Head Office	8th Fl., 3 Nan Hai Road, Taipei, Taiwan, R.O.C.
	Tel: (02) 321-0511 Fax: (02) 394-0630 Tlx: (02) 26044
Kaohsiung Branch	8th Fl., 74, Chung Cheng 2nd Road, Kaohsiung, R.O.C.
	Tel: (07) 224-1921 Fax: (07) 224-1928
Taichung Branch	5th Fl., 1-18, Sec. 2, Tai Chung Kan Road, Taichung, R.O.C.
	Tel: (04) 322-5756 Fax: (04) 322-5755
Representative Office in Jakarta	Wisma Dharmala Sakti 11th Fl., Jl Jendral Sudirman No. 32 Jarkarta Indonesia
	Tel: 6221-5704320, 5701136 Fax: 6221-5704321
Representative Office in Mexico	Edificio Omega, Campos Eliseos 345-PISO 4, Col. Chapultepec Polanco, 11560 Mexico, D.F.
	Tel: 525-2021741, 2021962 Fax: 525-5405802
Representative Office in Budapest	7th Floor, Karoly Korut 11, 1075 Budapest, Hungary Tel: 361-2697893, 361-2697894 Fax: 361-2697895

Who's Who
in the ROC

Who's Who in the ROC
Abbreviations Used

AARRO	Afro-Asian Rural Reconstruction Organization	*c.*	child; children
Acad.	Academy; Academic; Academia	CA	California
Acct.	Accountant; Accounting	CAC	Central Advisory Committee
Add.	Address	Calif.	California
Adm.	Admiral	Can.	Canada; Canadian
Admin.	Administration; Administrative; Administrator	CAPD	See COA
		Capt.	Captain
Adv.	Advisor; Advisory	CBC	Central Bank of China
AEAR	See TECROJ	CC	Central Committee
AEC	Atomic Energy Council, Executive Yuan	CCA	Council for Cultural Affairs, Executive Yuan (Known as Council for Cultural Planning and Development, Executive Yuan, CCPD, before July 16, 1995)
Aff.	Affairs		
Affi.	Affiliation		
Agr.	Agriculture; Agricultural		
Alt.	Alternate	CCoun.	City Council
Am.	America(n)	CCNAA	Coordination Council of North American Affairs (Known as TECO/TECRO after Oct. 10, 1994)
Amb.	Ambassador		
APACL	See APLFD		
APLFD	Asian Pacific League for Freedom and Democracy (Known as Asian Pacific Anti-Communist League, APACL, before April 1, 1991)	CCPD	Council for Cultural Planning and Development, Executive Yuan (See CCA)
		CDN	Central Daily News
		Cent.	Center; Central
		CEC	Central Executive Committee
APPU	Asian-Pacific Parliamentarians' Union	CEIC	Central Election Commission, Executive Yuan
Apt.	Apartment		
Ass.	Assembly	CEPD	Council for Economic Planning and Development, Executive Yuan
Assc.	Associate(d)		
Assn.	Association(s)	Cert.	Certificate(s)
Asst.	Assistant(s)	CETRA	China External Trade Development Council
b.	born		
B.	Bachelor	CFC	Central Finance Committee
BA	Bachelor of Arts	CG	Commanding General
BBA	Bachelor of Business Administration	CGSC	Command and General Staff College
BCC	Broadcasting Corporation of China	Ch.	Chinese; China
BCE	Bachelor of Civil Engineering	Chem.	Chemistry; Chemical
BCiS	Bachelor of Civil Science	Chmn.	Chairman
BCoS	Bachelor of Commercial Science	CIECD	Council for International Economic Cooperation and Development
Bd.	Board		
BD	Bachelor of Divinity	C-in-C	Commander-in-Chief
BEE	Bachelor of Electrical Engineering	CITC	Committee of International Technical Cooperation, Executive Yuan
BFA	Bachelor of Fine Arts		
BJ	Bachelor of Journalism	Cmd.	Command
Bk.	Bank(s); Book(s)	Cmdg.	Commanding
Bldg.	Building	Cmdr.	Commander
B.Lit.	Bachelor of Literature; Bachelor of Letters	Cmdt.	Commandant
Bn.	Battalion	Cml.	Commercial
BPS (BPs)	Bachelor of Political Science (or Politics)	CNA	Central News Agency
Br.	Branch	CNRRA	Chinese National Relief and Rehabilitation Administration
Brig.	Brigade; Brigadier		
BS	Bachelor of Science	Co.	Company
BSA	Bachelor of Science in Agronomy	COA	Council of Agriculture, Executive Yuan (Known as Council for Agricultural Planning and Development, Executive Yuan, CAPD, before Sept. 20, 1984; Also known as Joint Commission on Rural Reconstruction, JCRR, before March 16, 1979)
BSE	Bachelor of Science in Education		
BSEE	Bachelor of Science in Electrical Engineering		
B.Th.	Bachelor of Theology		
Bu.	Bureau		

481

CoCoun.	County Council	Dr.	Doctor
Col.	Colonel	Dr.PH	Doctor of Public Health or Public Hygiene
COLA	Council of Labor Affairs, Executive Yuan	D.Sc.	Doctor of Science
Coll.	College	DSEE	Doctor of Science in Electrical Engineering
Com.	Commerce; Commission	E.	East
Comm(s).	Communication(s)	Ea.	Eastern
Comr.	Commissioner	ECAFE	Economic Commission for Asia and the Far East
concur.	concurrently		
Conf.	Conference(s)	Econ.	Economic(al); Economy; Economics
Cong.	Congress	Ed.	Editor; Editorial
Consl.	Consulate; Consular	Ed.B.	Bachelor of Education
Const.	Constitutional; Constitution; Constituency	Ed.D.	Doctor of Education
Corp.	Corporation(s); Corporate	Ed.M.	Master of Education
Corr.	Correspondent; Corresponding	educ.	education(al)
Coun.	Council; Councilor	EE	Electrical Engineer (Engineering)
Counsl.	Counselor	Elec.	Electric; Electrical
CPA	Central Personnel Administration, Executive Yuan	Elect.	Electronic(al); Electronics
		Emb.	Embassy
CPC	Central Planning Committee	Eng.	England; English
CRC	Central Reform Committee	Engr.	Engineer; Engineering
CRRA	Chinese Refugees Relief Association (Known as Free China Relief Association, FCRA, before Aug. 16, 1991)	Ent.	Enterprise(s)
		EPA	Environmental Protection Administration, Executive Yuan
C/S	Chief-of-Staff	EPC	Economic Planning Council
CSC	Central Standing Committee	Exam.	Examination
CSF	Combined Service Forces	Exec.	Executive
CTC	Central Trust of China	FAO	United Nations Food and Agriculture Organization
CTS	Chinese Television System		
Cttee.	Committee	FCRA	See CRRA
CTV	China Television Company	Fed.	Federation
Cul.	Culture; Cultural	Fel.	Fellow; Fellowship(s)
CUSA	Council for United States Aid	FETC	Foreign Exchange and Trade Commission
CWAAL	Chinese Women's Anti-Aggression League	FETCC	Foreign Exchange and Trade Control Commission
d.	daughter(s)		
DCS	Doctor of Commercial Science	Fl.	Floor
DD	Doctor of Divinity	For.	Foreign
DE	Doctor of Engineering	Found.	Foundation
DGBAS	Directorate General of Budget, Accounting & Statistics, Executive Yuan	GA	General Assembly
		Gen.	General
Def.	Defense	Geog.	Geographic; Geography
Del.	Delegate; Delegation	Geol.	Geology; Geological
Dem.	Democrat(ic); Democracy	GHQ	General Headquarters
Dep.	Deputy	GIO	Government Information Office, Executive Yuan
Dept.	Department; Departmental		
Dev.	Development(al); Developing	Gov.	Governor
Dip.	Diplomat(ic); Diplomacy	Govt.	Government
Dir.	Director(s)	Grad.	Graduate; Graduated
Dist.	District	Hist.	History; Historical
Disting.	Distinguished	Hon.	Honour; Honorable; Honorary
Div.	Division	Hosp.	Hospital
D.Lit.	Doctor of Literature; Doctor of Letters	Hqs.	Headquarters
DMS	Doctor of Medical Science	ICOM	International Council of Museums
DOH	Department of Health, Executive Yuan	Ind.	Industrial; Industry
DPP	Democratic Progressive Party	Info.	Information
DPS (DPs)	Doctor of Political Science (or Politics)	Ins.	Insurance

Insp.	Inspector	MOC	See MOTC
Inst.	Institute; Institution(al)	MOE	Ministry of Education, Executive Yuan
Instr.	Instructor	MOEA	Ministry of Economic Affairs, Executive Yuan
Int.	Interior		
Intl.	International	MOF	Ministry of Finance, Executive Yuan
JCRR	See COA	MOFA	Ministry of Foreign Affairs, Executive Yuan
J.D.	Doctor of Jurisprudence		
Jour.	Journalism; Journalist; Journal(s)	MOI	Ministry of the Interior, Executive Yuan
Jr.	Junior	MOJ	Ministry of Justice, Executive Yuan
Jud.	Judicial; Judiciary	MOTC	Ministry of Transportation and
KMT	Kuomintang		Communications, Executive Yuan (Known
Lab.	Laboratory		as Ministry of Communications, Executive
Lang.	Language(s)		Yuan, MOC, before July 31, 1991)
Lectr.	Lecturer	MPA	Master of Public Administration
Legis.	Legislative; Legislator	MPH	Master of Public Health
Lib.	Library; Librarian; Liberal	MPS (MPs)	Master of Political Science (or Politics)
Lit.	Literature; Literary	MS	Master of Science
LHD	Doctor of Humanities	MSEE	Master of Science in Electrical Engineering
LL.B.	Bachelor of Laws	MTAC	Mongolian and Tibetan Affairs
LL.D.	Doctor of Laws		Commission, Executive Yuan
LL.M.	Master of Laws	M.Th.	Master of Theology
Lt.	Lieutenant	Mun.	Municipal; Municipality
Ltd.	Limited	N.	North
m.	married	NA	National Assembly
M.	Master	Nat.	National(s)
MA	Master of Arts	NCHU	National Chung Hsing University
MAC	Mainland Affairs Council, Executive Yuan	NCKU	National Cheng Kung University
Mach.	Machine(ry)	NCTU	National Chiao Tung University
Mag.	Magazine	NCU	National Chengchi University
Magis.	Magistrate	NMC	National Military Council
Maj.	Major	No.	Number
M.Arch.	Master in Architecture	NP	New Party
Math.	Mathematics; Mathematical	Nr.	Northern
MB	Bachelor of Medicine	NSC	National Security Council
MBA	Master of Business Administration	NScC	National Science Council, Executive Yuan
MCE	Master of Civil Engineering	NTHU	National Tsing Hua University
MCL	Master of Comparative Law	NTNU	National Taiwan Normal University
MD	Doctor of Medicine	NTU	National Taiwan University
Mech.	Mechanical; Mechanics; Mechanism	NUC	National Unification Council,
Med.	Medical; Medicine		Office of the President
MEE	Master of Electrical Engineering	NYC	National Youth Commission,
Mem.	Member		Executive Yuan
Metro.	Metropolitan	OCAC	Overseas Chinese Affairs Commission,
Mfg.	Manufacturing		Executive Yuan
Mfr.	Manufacture	Off.	Office; Officer(s)
Mgr.	Manager	Op.	Operation(s)
Mil.	Military	Org.	Organization
Min.	Minister; Ministry	Outsdg.	Outstanding
MIT	Massachusetts Institute of Technology, USA	Ovs.	Overseas
		PA	Public Administration
ML	Master of Laws	PCRM	Planning Commission for the Recovery of
M.Lit.	Master of Literature; Master of Letters		Mainland China (was withdrawn in 1991)
MND	Ministry of National Defense, Executive Yuan	PDAF	Provincial Department of Agriculture and Forestry
Mng.	Managing; Management	Penn.	Pennsylvania

Pers.	Personnel
Ph.D.	Doctor of Philosophy
Phys.	Physical; Physician; Physics
Pol.	Political; Politics
PPRC	Political Party Review Commmittee, Ministry of the Interior (PPRC was under the auspices of the Executive Yuan before Sept. 1, 1992)
Pres.	President
Prin.	Principal
Prof.	Professor; Profession(al)
Prog.	Program
Prov.	Province; Provincial
Pub.	Publisher; Publishing
Publ.	Publication(s)
Recon.	Reconstruction; Reconnaissance
Rd.	Road
RDEC	Research, Development and Evaluation Commission, Executive Yuan
Regln.	Regulation(s)
Regt.	Regiment
Rel.	Relation(s)
Rep.	Representative
Repub.	Republic(an)
Res.	Research; Researched
Resr.	Reseacher
Rev.	Revolution; Revolutionary
Rm.	Room
ROC	Republic of China
ROCAF	ROC Air Force
ROCN	ROC Navy
Rwy.	Railway
S.	South
s.	son(s)
Sc.	Science(s); Scientific
Sch.	School
Sec.	Secretary; Security; Securities
Sect.	Section
SEF	Straits Exchange Foundation
Sess.	Session(s)
S.J.D.	Doctor of Juridical Science
So.	Southern
Soc.	Society; Social
Sp.	Special; Specialist
Spkr.	Speaker
Sr.	Senior
St.	Saint; Street
STAG	Science & Technology Advisory Group, Executive Yuan
Sup.	Supervisor(y); Supervision
Supt.	Superintendent
TCG	Taipei City Government
Tchr(s).	Teacher(s)
Tech.	Technical; Technician; Technology

TECO	Taipei Economic & Cultural Office
TECRO	Taipei Economic & Cultural Representative Office (Known as Coordination Council of North American Affairs, CCNAA, before Oct. 10, 1994)
TECROJ	Taipei Economic and Culture Representative Office in Japan (Known as Tokyo Office, Association of East Asian Relation, AEAR, before May 30, 1992)
Telecom.	Telecommunications
Tng.	Training
TPA	Taiwan Provincial Assembly
TPG	Taiwan Provincial Government
Trans.	Transportation; Transport
Transl.	Translated; Translation
TTV	Taiwan Television Enterprise Ltd.
TV	Television
Twn.	Taiwanese; Taiwan, Republic of China
UC-Berkly.	University of California—Berkeley, USA
UCLA	University of California at Los Angeles, USA
USAEC	United States Atomic Energy Commission
U.	University(-ies)
UN	United Nations
UNESCO	United Nations Educational, Scientific and Cultural Organization
UNICEF	United Nations International Children's Emergency Fund
UNIRO	United Nations International Refugee Organization
UNGA	United Nations General Assembly
UNRRA	United Nations Relief and Rehabilitation Administration
USA	United States of America
USSR	Union of the Soviet Socialist Republics
V.	Vice
VAC	Veterans Affairs Commission, Executive Yuan (Known as Vocational Assistance Commission for Retired Servicemen, Executive Yuan, VACRS, before January 1, 1997)
VACRS	See VAC
Voc.	Vocational
Vol.	Volume(s)
W.	West
WACL	See WLFD
We.	Western
WLFD	World League for Freedom and Democracy (Known as World Anti-Communist League, WACL, before April 1, 1991)
WHA	World Health Assembly
WHO	World Health Organization
YMCA	Young Men's Christian Association
YWCA	Young Women's Christian Association

Who's Who in the ROC I

Sample I

[1] LEE, YUAN-TSEH 李遠哲
[2] Pres., Acad. Sinica 94-, Mem. 80-; Nat. Policy Adv. to the Pres. 91-; **[3]** *b.* Twn. Nov. 29, '36; **[4]** *m.* Wu, Bernice; **[5]** 2 *s.,* 1 *d.;* **[6]** *educ.* BS, NTU; MS, NTHU; Ph.D., UC-Berkly., Postdoctoral Fel. 65-67; **[7]** Res. Fel., Harvard U. 67-78; Asst. Prof., U. of Chicago 68-71, Assc. Prof. 71-72, Prof. 73-74; Mem., Nat. Acad. of Scs., USA; Prof. of Chem., UC-Berkly. 74-92, U. Prof. of Chem., UC-Berkly. 92-94; Nobel Prize in Chem. 86; Nat. Medal of Sc., White House, USA 86; Peter Debye Award, ACS 86; Faraday Medal 92. **[8]** *Publ.:* 280 papers; **[9]** *Add.* Acad. Sinica, Nankang, Taipei.

Item

[1]	Name		
[2]	Occupation	**[6]**	Education
[3]	Vital statistics	**[7]**	Experience
[4]	Marriage	**[8]**	Publication
[5]	Number of sons and daughters / or children	**[9]**	Address

AI, SHIH-HSUN
(See NGAI, SHIH-HSUN 艾世勛)

AU, HO-NIEN 歐豪年
Artist; Prof., Ch. Cul. U. 70-, Chmn., Dept. of Fine Arts 83-; *b.* Kwangtung Aug. 6, '35; *m.* Chu, Moo-lan; *educ.* Ph.D., Ch. Acad.; Art exhibitions held by Nat. Museum of Hist. 68, 74, 78, 81, & 84; US Cul. Cent., Hong Kong 68; Nara Museum, Japan 76; San Jose Museum of Art, USA 76; Tokyo Cent. Museum of Art, Japan 77, 78, & 82; San Diego Museum of Art, USA 79; Spink Gallery, UK 84; Art Gallery of Greater Victoria, Can. 85; Fung Ping Shan Museum, U. of Hong Kong 87; Museum Cernuschi, Paris 90; Rijksmuseum Voor Volkenkunde, Leiden, Netherlands 90; Museum für Volkerkunde, Wien 90; Taipei City Arts Museum 90; Bersee-Museum, Bremen 91; Bomand Museum, Lelle, Germany 91. *Works:* 10 selections of works of art published by Nat. Museum of Hist. 78; Ni Cen Sha Co., Japan 82; Mitsukoshi Gallery, Japan 83; Art Bk. Co., ROC 84; Art Gallery of Greater Victoria 85; Fung Ping Shan Museum 87; GIO 89; Museum Cernuschi 90; Rijksmuseum Voor Volkenkunde 90; Pacific Cul. Found., ROC 91; *Add.* 9th Fl., 133 Sung Ping Rd., Hsinyi, Taipei.

BAI, HSIU-HSIUNG 白秀雄
Dep. Mayor, Taipei City 94-; *b.* Twn. Sept. 27, '41; *m.* Han, Chu-teh; 1 *s.,* 2 *d.; educ.* LL.B. & LL.M., NCU; Assc. Prof., Dept. of Sociology, NCU & Prof., Dept. So. Work, Tunghai U. 71-81; Adv., Kaohsiung City Govt. 79-81, Dir., Bu. of Soc. Aff. 81-86; Dir., Bu. of Soc. Aff., TCG 86-93; Dir., Soc. Aff., MOI 93-94. *Publ.: Soc. Welfare in ROC* 80; *Soc. Work* 92; *Soc. Welfare Admin.* 93; *Add.* 1 Shih Fu Rd., Taipei.

CHAI, CHOK-YUNG 蔡作雍
Mem. & Sr. Investigator, Inst. of Biomed. Sc., Acad. Sinica 82-; *b.* Canton Feb. 17, '28; *m.* Shih, J.Y.; 2 *s.,* 1 *d.; educ.* MD, Nat. Def. Med. Cent. (NDMC) 53; Ph.D., Columbia U. 66; Assc. Prof., NDMC 62-67; Visiting

Assc. Prof., Columbia U. 68; Prof. & Chmn., Biophys. Dept., NDMC 68-75, Dean of Faculty 72-75, Dir. 75-82. *Publ.:* Over 140 papers on physiology & pharmacology in nat. & intl. sc. jour.; *Add.* 16 Alley 5, Lane 24, Ting Chou Rd., Sect. 3, Taipei.

CHAI, TZUNG-CHUAN
(See CHIA, CHUNG-CHUAN 翟宗泉)

CHAN, HOU-SHENG 詹火生
V. Chmn., COLA 95-; Prof., NTU 88-; *b.* Feb. 10, '49; *m.* Ying Chan; *educ.* BA, NTU 71; Sp. Diploma, Oxford U. 76; MS, Econ., Wales U. 78, Ph.D. 84; Visiting Assc. Prof., NTU 84-86, Assc. Prof., 86-88, Prof. 88-; Dir. & Prof., Grad. Inst. of Soc. Welfare, NCU 89-90; Prof. & Chmn., Dept. & Grad. Inst. of Sociology, NTU 90-93. *Publ.:* "Soc. Welfare in Twn." in *Soc. Welfare in Asia* 84; *Theories on Soc. Welfare* 88; *Soc. Change & Soc. Welfare* 92; "Aging in Twn." in *Aging in E. & S.E. Asia* 92; *Add.* COLA, 15th Fl., 132 Ming Sheng E. Rd., Sect. 3, Taipei.

CHAN, HSIEN-CHING 詹憲卿
Rep., TECO, Philippines 95-; *b.* Twn. Oct. 17, '39; *m.* Chan, Jenny; 1 *s.; educ.* LL.B., NCU 62; Staff, MOFA 64-67; 3rd & 2nd Sec., Emb. in Brazil 67-74; Sect. Chief, Protocol Dept., MOFA 74-77; 1st Sec., Emb. in S. Korea 77-81; Dep. Dir., Dept. of Cent. & S. Am. Aff., MOFA 81-83; Consul-Gen. in Cape Town 83-89; Dir., Dept. of Pers., MOFA 89-91, Dir., Dept. of Consl. Aff. 91-92; Dir.-Gen., CCNAA, San Francisco 92-94; Rep., TECO, Brazil 94-95; *Add.* P.O. Box 1097, Makati Cent. Post Off., 1250 Makati, Metro Manila, Philippines.

CHAN, I-CHANG
(See CHAN, YIH-CHANG 詹益彰)

CHAN, SUNNEY I. 陳長謙
Mem., Acad. Sinica 88-, Exec. Off., Chem. 89-94; Hoag Prof., Biophys. Chem., Calif. Inst. of Tech. 92-; *b.* Ch. Oct. 5, '36; *m.* Tam, Irene Yuk-hing; 1 *s.; educ.* BS, UC-Berkly. 57, Ph.D. 60; Grad. Teaching Asst., UC-Berkly. 57-58; Nat. Sc. Found. Postdoctoral Fel., Harvard U. 60-61; Asst. Prof., U. of Calif., Riverside 61-63; Asst. Prof., Calif. Inst. of Tech. 63-64, Assc. Prof. 64-68, Prof., Chem., Phys., & Biophys. Chem. 68-92; Acting Exec.

Off., Chem. 77-78; Exec. Off., Chem. 78-80; Visiting Prof., Stanford U. 81; Chmn. of the Faculty, Calif. Inst. of Tech. 87-89; Wilson T.S. Wang Int. Disting. Prof., Ch. U. of Hong Kong 93. *Publ.:* 260 sc. papers on chem., phys., & biochem.; *Add.* 327 Camino del Sol, S. Pasadena, CA 91030, USA.

CHAN, TE-HO
(See JAN, DE-HO 詹德和)

CHAN, WING-TSIT 陳榮捷
Mem., Acad. Sinica; Adjunct Prof., Ch. Thought, Columbia U. 65-; *b.* Kwangtung Aug. 18, '01; *m.* Lei, Wai-hing L.; 3 *c.; educ.* BA, Lingnan U. 24; Ph.D., Harvard U. 29; Dean of Faculty, Lingnan U. 29-37; Prof., Ch. Philosophy, U. of Hawaii 37-42, Dartmouth Coll. 42-66, & Chatham Coll. 66-82; *Add.* 228 Sharon Drive, Pittsburgh, PA 15221, USA.

CHAN, YIH-CHANG 詹益彰
Dir., 1st Bu. Off. of the Pres. 96-; *b.* Twn. Jan. 1 '39; *m.* Chan Chien, Kuei-chia; 1 *s.,* 1 *d.; educ.* LL.B., NTU 61; Grad. Study, Meiji U. 71; Dep. Dir., Dept. of Labor Aff., MOI 81-85; Dir., Dept. of Population Admin., MOI 85-88; Gen. Sec., MOI 88-91; Dep. Sec.-Gen., CEIC 91-92; Gen. Sec., MOI 92-93; Counsl., Control Yuan 93-96; *Add.* 122 Chungking S. Rd., Sect. 1, Taipei.

CHANG, AN-PING
(See CHANG, NELSON AN-PING 張安平)

CHANG, C.P. 張昌邦
Pol. V. Min. of MOEA 96-; Adjunct Prof., Fu Jen Catholic U. 71-; *b.* Twn. Nov. 13, '46; *m.* Huang, Chuan-chuan; 1 *s.,* 1 *d.; educ.* LL.B., Fu Jen Catholic U. 68; LL.M., NCU 71; Visiting Scholar, Harvard Law Sch. 86; Sect. Chief, Laws & Reglns. Cttee., Exec. Yuan 73-76; Sr. Sp., Secretariat, MOF 77, Exec. Sec., Laws & Reglns. Cttee., 77-82, V. Chmn., Sec. & Exchange Com. (SEC) 82-88, & Chmn., SEC 88-93; V. Min. of Finance 93-95. Dep. Sec.-Gen., Exec. Yuan 95-96. *Publ.: Thesis on Tax Collection & Assessment Law; A Res. on Burden of Proof in Criminal Procedure; Add.* 15 Foochow St., Taipei.

CHANG, C.Y. 張慶衍
Amb. to the Honduras 96-; *b.* Chekiang Feb. 28, '34; *m.* King, Theresa; 1 *d.; educ.* LL.B., Soochow U.; Grad.

Sch., Law Cent., Georgetown U.; V. Consul, Honolulu 65-68; Sect. Chief, MOFA 69-71; Counsl., Emb. in USA 71-78; Div. Dir., CCNAA, Washington, D.C. 79-83; Sec.-Gen., CCNAA 84-88; Dir.-Gen., CCNAA, Chicago 88-89; Dir.-Gen., CCNAA, Los Angeles 89-94; Amb. to the Bahamas 94-96; *Add.* Apartado Postal 3433, Tegucigalpa, D.C., Honduras, C.A.

CHANG, CHANG-PANG
(See CHANG, C.P. 張昌邦)

CHANG, CHE-CHEN
(See CHANG, CHE-SHEN 張哲琛)

CHANG, CHE-SHEN 張哲琛
Dep. Sec.-Gen., Exec. Yuan 96-; *b.* Shanghai May 14, '45; *m.* Wong, Deh-hwa; 2 *s.,* 1 *d.; educ.* B., NTU 70; M., Cent. Michigan U. 75; Sp., MOF 76-77; Asst. Dir., DGBAS 77-79, Sect. Chief 79-85, Dep. Dir., 1st Bu. 87-90, Dir. 90-92; Dir.-Gen. of Depts., DGBAS 92-96. *Publ.: Improvement of the Compilation of the ROC Govt. Budget; An Assessment of the ROC Govt. Budget Structure & Decision-making; Add.* 1 Chung Hsiao E. Rd., Sect. 1, Taipei.

CHANG, CHI-CHUNG 張啟仲
Nat. Policy Adv. to the Pres.; Pres., ROC Cooperative Union, ROC Credit Cooperative Union, & Taichung Bus Co.; Chmn., Twn. Regional Dev. Inst., & 7th Credit Cooperative, Taichung; *b.* Twn. May 10, '16; *m.* Lee, Chiu-rong; 2 *s.,* 4 *d.; educ.* Grad., Japan Med. U. 42; Pres., Chi Jen Hosp. 48-64; Spkr., Taichung CCoun. 55-58; Mayor, Taichung City 64-67; Mem., Legis. Yuan 73-81; Chmn., Prov. Bus Fed. Twn. 78-84; Gov., Dist. 300, Lions Club Intl. 79-80; Adv., Exec. Yuan 81-90; *Add.* Rm. 710, 150 Chi Lin Rd., Taipei.

CHANG, CHI-JEN
(See CHANG, CHRISTOPH CHI-JEN 張己任)

CHANG, CHIA-CHU
(See CHANG, CHIA-JUCH 張家祝)

CHANG, CHIA-HSIANG 張家驤
Pres., CTS 92-; Chmn., ROC TV Acad. of Arts & Scs. 94-; *b.* Shantung Aug. 15, '28; *m.* Chang, Mei-tze; 2 *s.,* 1 *d.; educ.* BJ, Fu Hsing Kang Coll.; Dir., City Desk, *Youth Daily News* 64-69, Ed.-in-Chief 69-74; Pres., Mil. News Agency 74-78; Pres., *Youth Daily News* 78-85; Pres., *Twn. Daily News* 85-92; *Add.* 100 Kuang Fu S. Rd., Taipei.

CHANG, CHIA-JUCH 張家祝
V. Min. of Trans. & Comms., 95-; *b.* Twn. June 25, '50; *m.* Chen, Eugenia; 1 *s.,* 1 *d.; educ.* BS, Civil Engr., NCKU 73; MS, Civil Engr., Calif. State U., San Jose, 76; Ph.D., Purdue U. 79; Asst. Prof., Dept. of Civil Engr., Marquette U., USA 79-81; Assc. Prof., Inst. of Traffic & Trans., NCTU 81-82, Prof. & Dir. 82-87; Dir.-Gen., Inst. of Trans., MOTC 87-95. *Publ.:* More than 90 papers on trans. in prof. jour.; *Add.* 2 Changsha St., Sect. 1, Taipei.

CHANG, CHIEH-CHIEN 張捷遷
Mem., Acad. Sinica 64-, & New York Acad. of Sc.; Prof. Emeritus, Catholic U. of Am.; *b.* Peking July 21, '13; *m.* Chang, Than-chie; 3 *c.; educ.* BS, N.E. U. 32; MS, Calif. Tech. 41, Ph.D. 50; Guggenheim Fel. 52-53; Instr., NTHU 34-40; Assc. Prof., Johns Hopkins U. 47-52; Res. Prof., U. of Maryland 52-54; Prof., U. of Minnesota 54-62; Chmn. & Prof., Catholic U. of Am. 62-77. *Publ: Real Fluid Mech.; Ed. Process of Plasma Space Sc. System*; & more than 100 sc. papers; *Add.* 2122 Galewood Place., Silver Spring, MD 20903, USA.

CHANG, CHIEN-CHUN
(See CHANG, PAUL C.C. 張堅浚)

CHANG, CHING-YEN
(See CHANG, C.Y. 張慶衍)

CHANG, CHING-YU
(See CHANG, KING-YUH 張京育)

CHANG, CHRISTOPH CHI-JEN 張己任
Prof., Music Dept., Soochow U. 84-, Chmn. 90-, Dir., Grad. Sch. of Music 93-; *b.* May 4, '45; *m.* Kuo, Su-tseng; 2 *d.; educ.* B., Sociology, Tunghai U. 63-67; Grad. Study, Grad. Sch. of Music, W. Texas State U. 69-70; Prof. Diploma in Orchestral Conducting with Distinction, Mannes Coll. of Music, NYC 70-73; Grad. Study, Ph.D. Prog. in Music, City U. of New York 78-81; Ph.D., Music & Music Educ., Columbia U. 81-83;

Asst. Conductor, Mannes Opera Workshop 73-75; Music Dir. & Conductor, Young Artists' Chamber Orchestra, New York 73-75; Prin. Conductor, Twn. Prov. Symphony Orchestra 75-77; Lectr., Music Dept., Tunghai U. 75-78; Conductor & Ed., "Symphony Project," Grad. Cent., City U. of New York 78-83; Conductor, Soochow U. Orchestra 84; Conductor in residence, "List-Glenn Inst. Summer Festival", Los Angeles 88. *Publ.: Alexsander Tcherepnin & His Influence on Modern Ch. Music* 83; *A Hist. of We. Musical Style* 83; *Music, Man & Ideas* 85; *On Music* 86; *Musical Questions* 90; *Musical Anecdotes* 91; *On Latin Requiem* 95; *Add.* 9th Fl., 351 Chang Chun Rd., Taipei.

CHANG, CHUAN-CHIUNG 張傳炯
Mem., Acad. Sinica 76-; Prof., Pharmacology, NTU 65-; *b.* Twn. Oct. 23, '28; *m.* Chen, Wang-shyu; 1 *s.*, 2 *d.; educ.* BS, NTU 50; Ph.D., Tokyo U. 65; Assc. Prof., NTU 60-65; Fel., NIH Res. 62-64. *Publ.:* More than 100 original articles on the discovery of ß-Bungarotoxin & synaptic transmission of the nervous system; *Add.* 3rd Fl., 3 Lane 60, Chou Shan Rd., Taipei.

CHANG, CHUN-YEN 張俊彥
Dir., Nat. Nano Device Lab., NScC 90-; Dir. Microelectronics & Info. Systems Res. Cent., NCTU 96-; *b.* Twn. Oct. 12 '37; *m.* Lee, Shun-mei; 3 *s.; educ.* BS, NCKU 60; MS, NCTU 62; Ph.D., NCTU 70; Chair Prof., NCTU 69-; Visiting Prof., U. of Florida 87; Visiting Prof., Stuttgart U. 89; Dean, Coll. of Engr., NCTU 90-94; Dean, Coll. of EE & Computer Sc., NCTU 94-95; *Add.* 1001-1 Ta Hsueh Rd., Hsinchu.

CHANG, CHUNG-CHIEN 張鍾潛
Chmn., Twn. Power Co. 89-; Mem., CC, KMT 93-; *b.* Shanghai July 23, '46; *m.* Yao, Chien; 2 *d.; educ.* BS, Ind. Engr., Chung Cheng Inst. of Tech. 70; MS, Mng. Sc. & Engr., Worcester Polytechnic Inst. 74; Ph.D., Business Admin., U. of Colorado 79; Dir., Dept. of Mng. Info. Systems, RDEC 81-83, Dir., Dept. of Overall Planning 83; Head, Grad. Sch. of Resources Mng., Nat. Def. Mng. Inst. 83-84; Counsl., MOEA 84-85; Exec. Dir., Com. of Nat. Corp., MOEA 85-87; Chmn., Twn. Metal Mining Corp. 87; V. Chmn. & Exec. Dir., Com. of Nat. Corp., MOEA 87-89; Chmn., Twn. Aluminum Corp. 88;

Admin. V. Min. of Econ. Aff. 89; *Add.* 242 Roosevelt Rd., Sect. 3, Taipei.

CHANG, CHUNG-MOU
(See CHANG, MORRIS 張忠謀)

CHANG, DAVID H.C. 張希哲
Nat. Policy Adv. to the Pres.; Prof., NCU; Hon. Chmn., Sino-Indonesia Assn., Sino-Ryukyuan Cul. & Econ. Assn., Amateur Roller Skating Assn., Ovs. Ch. Assn., & Friends of Hong Kong & Macau Assn.; *b.* Kwangtung Oct. 14, '18; *m.* Liu, Hui-shao; 2 *s.*, 5 *d.; educ.* LL.B., NCU; Nat. War Coll.; Postgrad. Study, U. of Washington; Hon. DPS, Konkuk U. 81; Mng. Ed., *Chungshan Daily News* 41-44; Pub., *Canton Daily News* 46-49; Mem., Canton Mun. Coun. 45-48; Adv., Kwangtung Prov. Govt. 48-49; Dir., 1st Dept., Min. of Info., KMT 49-50; Dir., Dept. of Gen. Aff., MOE 50-51; Mem., Legis. Yuan 50-91; Prof., NCU 58-62; Mem., CPC, KMT 62-72; Pres., Fengchia Coll. of Engr. & Business 63-73; Mem., CC, KMT. *Publ.: Planned Govt. & Planned Econ.; Election System in US; Cong. & Pol. Parties in Various Countries; Const. Tendency of Post-War Countries; Ovs. Ch. Policy & Work of the Ch. Communists; The Ideal & Practice of Higher Educ.; The KMT Party of Ch. & Party Pol.; Add.* 10 Lane 70, Min Tsu St., Peitou, Taipei.

CHANG, DING-CHONG 張鼎鍾
Comr., Exam. Yuan 90-; Prof., NCU 90-; *b.* Nanking Feb. 4, '34; *m.* Fung, John; 1 *s.*, 2 *d.; educ.* BA, NTU 55; M., Lib. Sc., Marywood Coll. 59; Ph.D., Indiana U. 83; Dep. Dir., Lib., Ch. U. of Hong Kong 66-67; Assc. Prof., NTU 69-74; Assc. Prof., NTNU 74-80, Dir., Lib. 77-80, & Prof. 80-84; Visiting Prof., U. of Illinois 84-87; Exec. Dir., Wang Inst. of Grad. Studies, USA 85-87; Visiting Prof., NTU 88-90. *Publ.: Lib. & Info.* 79; *On Lib. & Info. Sc.* 82; *Guide to Info. Sc.* 84; *The Evolving Soc. Mission of the Nat. Cent. Lib. in Ch. 1928-1966* 84; *A Primer of Lib. Automation* 87; *Reflections on Civil Service & Lib./Info. Sc.* 96; *Add.* P.O. Box 2-53, Mucha, Taipei.

CHANG, DOMINIC T.H. 章德惠
Rep., TECO, Spain 92-; *b.* Anhwei Aug. 15, '29; *m.* Chang, Isabel; 1 *s.*, 2 *d.; educ.* LL.B., NTU 51; ROCAF

Interpreter 51-55; Staff Asst., MOFA 55-58; Rep. to Colombia 80-85; Dir., Dept. of Treaty & Legal Aff., MOFA 86-87, Chief Sec. 87-89; Amb. to the Kingdom of Swaziland 89-92; *Add.* Apartado 36016, 28080 Madrid, Spain.

CHANG, FENG-HSU
(See CHANG, FENG-SHU 張豐緒)

CHANG, FENG-SHU 張豐緒
Mem., CC, KMT 93-; Chmn., Finance Cttee., Olympic Coun. of Asia 91-; Chmn., Sponsorship & Funding Com., Asia Pacific & Oceania Sports Assn. 91-; Pres., Ch. Taipei Olympic Cttee. 87-; Hon. Pres., Soc. for Wildlife & Nature 93-; Chmn., Adv. Bd., Traffic Taipei 92-; *b.* Twn. Aug. 5, '28; *m.* Chen, Chiu-charn; 1 *s.; educ.* BA, NTU 52; MA, U. of New Mexico 56; Hon. DPS, Kyung Hee U., S. Korea 73; Sp., MOFA 56-59; Mem., TPA 60-64; Magis., Pingtung County 64-72; Mayor, Taipei City 72-76; Min. of the Int. 76-78; Min. of State 78-90; Nat. Policy Adv. to the Pres. 90-96; Bd. Dir., SEF 90-92; Pres., Mongolian & Tibetan Found. 92-93; Pres., ROC Sports Fed. 87-92; Pres., Soc. for Wildlife & Nature 82-93; *Add.* 20 Chu Lun St., Taipei.

CHANG, HSI-CHE
(See CHANG, DAVID H.C. 張希哲)

CHANG, HSIAO-YEN 章孝嚴
Min. of For. Aff. & concur. Min. of State 96-; Mem., CC & CSC, KMT 93-; *b.* Kiangsi May 2, '41; *m.* Chang Huang, Helen; 3 *c.; educ.* BA, Soochow U.; MS, Georgetown U.; 3rd & 2nd Sec., Emb. in USA 74-78; Sect. Chief, Dept. of N. Am. Aff., MOFA 78, Dep. Dir. 80-81; Sec.-Gen., CCNAA 81-82; Dir., Dept. of N. Am. Aff., MOFA 82-86; Admin. V. Min. of For. Aff. 86-90; Dir.-Gen., Dept. of Ovs. Aff., CC, KMT 90; Pol. V. Min. of For. Aff. 90-93; Min., OCAC 93-96. *Publ.: Damansky Island Incident; Add.* 2 Kaitakelan Boulevard, Taipei.

CHANG, HSIAO-YUEH
(See CHANG, KATHERINE S.Y. 張小月)

CHANG, HUNG-TSAO 張鴻藻
Rep., TECO, Finland 94-; *b.* Kiangsu Sept. 12, '32; *m.* Hsieh, I-fang; 3 *s.; educ.* Mil. Acad.; Desk Off., MOFA 67-70; 3rd & 2nd Sec., Emb. in Malawi 70-76; Sect. Chief & Dep. Dir., MOFA 77-80; 1st Sec. & Counsl., Emb. in the Repub. of Korea 80-90; Dir., Dept. of Gen. Aff., MOFA 90-94. *Publ.: An Anthology of Poetry; Add.* TECO, World Trade Center, P.O. Box 800, FIN-00101 Helsinki, Finland.

CHANG, JAMES WEN-CHUNG 張文中
Dep. Sec.-Gen., NSC 96-; *b.* Szechwan Dec. 24, '35; *m.* Chang, Chin-ning; 2 *d.; educ.* LL.B., NTU 58; 3rd Sec., Emb. in Senegal 64-65; 3rd & 2nd Sec., Emb. in the Togolese Repub. 65-68; Sect. Chief & Dep. Dir., Dept. of African Aff., MOFA 68-73; Consul, Consl. Gen. in New York City 73-76; 1st Sec., Emb. in USA 76-78; Dir., Service Div., CCNAA, Washington, D.C. 79-83; Counsl., Emb. in S. Africa 83-84; Dir., Dept. of Consl. Aff., MOFA 84-88; Dir.-Gen., CCNAA, Seattle 88-90, & Boston 90-93; Dep. Rep., CCNAA 93-94; Dep. Rep., TECRO 94-96; *Add.* 122 Chungking S. Rd., Sect. 1, Taipei.

CHANG, JEFFREY P. 張伯毅
Mem., Acad. Sinica; Prof. Emeritus, U. of Texas Med. Br., Galveston 87-; *b.* Hunan Oct. 10, '17; *m.* Tang, Sulaine; 3 *s.,* 2 *d.; educ.* BS, Nat. Cent. U.; MS & Ph.D., U. of Illinois; Res. Assc., U. of Kansas Med. Sch. 52-55; Asst. Prof., Assc. Prof., & Prof., U. of Texas, Houston 55-72; Prof., U. of Texas Med. Br., Galveston 72-87; Invented fresh frozen sectioning technique for pathologic diagnosis; Dev. open-top cryostat; Invented sect. freeze substitution, monolayer flat embedding, mitochondia staining technics; Established Chang hepatoma cell lines; Proposed tublin-cilia formation hypothesis. *Publ.:* Over 150 sc. papers; *Add.* 1103 Sprague Lane., Austin, TX 78746, USA; 6th Fl.-1, 236 Chung Hsiao E. Rd., Sect. 3, Taipei.

CHANG, JEN-SHU
(See CHEN, RENEE REN-SHU 張仁淑)

CHANG, JEN-TANG
(See CHANG, THOMAS J.T. 張仁堂)

CHANG, JUNG-WEI 張榮味
Pres., Yunlin CoCoun. 90-; Prov. Rep., Construction Assn. 88-; Chmn., Chianglungchung Construction Co.

87-; *b.* Twn. July 10, '46; *m.* Wang, Yueh-hsia; 1 *s.*, 2 *d.; educ.* Studying in Nat. Chia-Yi Inst. of Agr. Sch.; Apprentice, Sanyuan Lumber Yard 62-64; Homei Store 64-76; *Add.* 2 Ho Ping St., Tuku, Yunlin County.

CHANG, KATHARINE S.Y. 張小月
Dir.-Gen., TECO, Seattle 95-; *b.* Twn. Feb. 12, '53; *m.* Ho, Jei-fu; *educ.* B., NCU 75; M., Long Island U. 85; Desk Off., Dept. of Intl. Org., MOFA 76-80; Sec., CCNAA, New York 80-89; Sect. Chief, Dept of N. Am. Aff., MOFA 89-91, 2nd Dep. Dir. 92-93, Dep. Dir. 93-94; *Add.* 2001 6th Avenue., Suite 2410, Seattle, WA 98121, USA.

CHANG, KING-YUH 張京育
Chmn., MAC 96-; *b.* Hunan Apr. 27, '37; *m.* Yu, Grace Yu-dih; 2 *s.; educ.* LL.B., NTU 58; LL.M., NCU 61; MCL, Columbia U. 64, Ph.D. 71; Hon. LL.D., Sung Kyun Kwan U., S. Korea 90; Lectr., Hofstra U. 68-69; Asst. Prof., We. Illinois U. 72; Assc. Prof., NCU 72-75, Dir., Dept. of Dip. 74-77, Dean, Grad. Sch. of Intl. Law & Dip. 75-77, Prof. 75-89; Visiting Fel., Johns Hopkins U. 76-77; Dep. Dir., Inst. of Intl. Rel., NCU 77-81, Dir. 81-84; Disting. Visiting Scholar, Inst. of E. Asian Studies, UC-Berkly. 83; Dir.-Gen., GIO 84-87; Dir., Inst. of Intl. Rel., NCU 87-90; Pres., NCU 89-94; Min. of State 94-96. *Publ.: Intl. Rel. & Intl. Pol.; Looking at the World from Taipei; A Framework for Ch.'s Unification; Add.* 15th Fl., 2-2 Chi Nan Rd., Sect. 1, Taipei.

CHANG, KUANG-CHENG
(See CHANG, SAMUEL K.C. 張光正)

CHANG, KUN 張琨
Mem., Acad. Sinica; Prof., Oriental Lang., U. of Calif.; *b.* Honan Nov. 17, '17; *m.* Shefts, Betty; *educ.* BA, NTHU 38; Ph.D., Linguistics, Yale U. 55; Asst. Prof., Assc. Prof., & Prof., U. of Washington, Seattle 51-63. *Publ.: A Comparative Study of the Kathinavastu; A Manual of Spoken Tibetan; The Proto. Ch. Final System & the Chieh-yun; Spoken Tibetan Texts; Add.* Dept. of Oriental Lang., UC-Berkly., CA 94708, USA.

CHANG, KUO-CHENG 張國政
Acting Dir.-Gen., Civil Aeronautics Admin., MOTC 96-; *b.* Chekiang May 14 '43; *m.* Pan, An-na; 2 *s.*, 1 *d.;*

educ. Air Force Acad. 66; Armed Forces U. 75; War Coll., Armed Forces U. 82; Squadron Cmdr. 79-80; Squadron Cmdr. 84-85; Armed Forces Attaché, Pretoria, Repub. of S. Africa 85-89; Wing Cmdr. 92-94; Chief Exec. of WSAMO, GHQ, Air Force 94; *Add.* 340 Tun Hua N. Rd., Taipei.

CHANG, KWANG-CHIH 張光直
Mem., Acad. Sinica, Adjunct Res. Fel., Inst. of Hist. & Philology; John E. Hudson Prof., Archaeology, Harvard U. 84-; *b.* Peiping Apr. 15, '31; *m.* Li, Hwei; 1 *s.*, 1 *d.; educ.* BA, NTU 54; Ph.D., Harvard U. 60; Lectr., Harvard U. 60-61; Instr., Yale U. 61-63, Asst. Prof. 63-66, Assc. Prof. 66-69, Prof. 69-77, Chmn., Dept. of Anthropology 70-73; Chmn., Coun. on E. Asian Studies 75-77, 86-89; Prof., Anthropology, Harvard U. 77-84, Chmn., Dept. of Anthropology 81-84. *Publ.: The Archaeology of Ancient Ch.; Art, Myth & Ritual;* & about 150 articles & 40 bk. reviews; *Add.* Peabody Museum, Harvard U., Cambridge, MA 02138, USA.

CHANG, LEROY L. 張立綱
Mem., Acad. Sinica 94-; Dean of Sc. & Prof. of Phys., Hong Kong U. of Sc. & Tech. 93-; *b.* Kirin Jan. 20, '36; *m.* Chang, Helen H.; 1 *s.*, 1 *d.; educ.* BS, NTU 57; MS, U. of S. Carolina 61; Ph.D., Stanford U. 63; Staff Mem., IBM Watson Res. Cent. 63-68; Assc. Prof., MIT 68-69; Res. Mgr., IBM Watson Res. Cent. 69-92. *Publ.: Molecular Beam Epitaxy & Heterostructures* 85; *Synthetic Modulated Structures* 85; *Resonant Tunneling in Semiconductors: Phys. & Application* 91; *Add.* Hong Kong U. of Sc. & Tech., Clear Water Bay, Kowloon, Hong Kong.

CHANG, LI-KANG
(See CHANG, LEROY L. 張立綱)

CHANG, LIANG-JEN 張良任
Dep. Sec.-Gen., SEF 96-; *b.* Anhwei Aug. 21 '46; *m.* Chen, Alice; 1 *s.*, 1 *d.; educ.* BA, Dip., NCU 68; MA, Grad. Sch. of E. Asian Studies, NCU 71; MA, Harvard U. 84; Ed., TTV 73-75; Dir., Div. of Info. & Protocol, GIO 86-88 & Dept. of Compilation & Transl. 88-91; Dir., Dept. of Info. & Liaison, MAC 91-93, Dept. of Cul. & Educ. Aff. 93-96 & Dept. of Hong Kong & Macau Aff. 96; *Add.* 17th Fl., 156 Min Sheng E. Rd., Sect. 3, Taipei.

CHANG, LIN-SHENG 張臨生
Dep. Dir., Nat. Palace Museum 91-; *b.* Shantung July 3, '46; *m.* Mei, Kuang; 1 *s.; educ.* BA, NTU 68; MA, Ch. Cul. U. 72; Grad. Studies, Harvard U. 72-74; Asst. Curator, Nat. Palace Museum 74-76, Assc. Curator 76-79, Sr. Res. Fel. 79-82, Curator, Dept. of Antiquities 83-91. *Publ.:* "Yun Shou-p'ing, a Great Ch'ing Dynasty Artist," *Nat. Palace Museum Quarterly (NPMQ)* 75; "The Dating of the We. Chou Bronze '90 Meng Kuei' & a Transl. of Its Inscription," *NPMQ* 77; "Chien Ware: A Suggestion for a Revised Dating in the Light of Our Knowledge of the Tea Drinking Contests of the Nr. Sung Period," *NPMQ* 78; "On the Function of Ho and Yi Bronze Vessel-types as Ceremonial Water Vessels," *NPMQ* 82; & numerous other articles; *Add.* Nat. Palace Museum, Waishuanghsi, Shihlin, Taipei.

CHANG, MORRIS 張忠謀
Chmn., Twn. Semiconductor Mfg. Co. Ltd. 86-; Chmn., Wyse Tech. Inc. 90-; Chmn., Vanguard Intl. Semiconductor Corp. 94-; *b.* Chekiang July 10, '31; 1 *d.; educ.* BS, Mech. Engr., MIT 52, MS 53; DSEE, Stanford U. 64; Sr. Engr., Sylvania Elec. Products 55-58; Mng. Position, Texas Instrument Inc. 58-69; Corp. V. Pres., Integrated Circuits 67-72; Corp. Group V. Pres. & Sr. V. Pres., Worldwide Semiconductor Business 72-83; Pres., Gen. Instrument Corp. 84-85; Pres. & Chmn., Ind. Tech. Res. Inst. 85-94; *Add.* Rm. 1803, 18th Fl., 333 Keelung Rd., Sect. 1, Taipei.

CHANG, NELSON AN-PING 張安平
Pres., Chia Hsin Cement Corp.; V. Chmn., Ch. Mng. Systems Corp.; Exec. Dir., Ch. Nat. Assn. of Ind. & Com. 90-; *b.* Twn. June 8, '52; *m.* Koo, Huai-ju; 2 *d.; educ.* BA, Princeton U.; MBA, New York U.; V. Pres., Chia Hsin Cement Corp. 78-88; Sup., Ch. Trust Co. 85-89; Pres., Ch. Mng. Systems Corp. 81-89; Pres. & Chief Exec. Off., Ch. Sec. Co. 88-89; Bd. Chmn., Channel Intl. Corp. 89-90; *Add.* 96 Chung Shan N. Rd., Sect. 2, Taipei.

CHANG, PAO-SHU 張寶樹
Sr. Adv. to the Pres.; Mem., CAC, KMT 81-; *b.* Hopei Dec. 30, '11; *m.* Lan, Chi-min; 2 *s.,* 1 *d.; educ.* Tokyo Imperial U.; Ph.D., Tokyo U.; Mem., Legis. Yuan 47-79; Prof., NTU 49-66; Dir., 5th Sect., Dir., 1st Sect., Sec.-Gen., Policy Coordination Cttee., & Sec.-Gen., CC,

KMT 68-79. *Publ.: A Study of Ch. Fisheries Recon.; Ch. Fisheries; A Study of the Law of the Sea; Construction of People's Livelihood & Org. of Farmers-Fishermen in Cent. & N. Europe & Japan; Advice & Expectations of the Japanese; US Gen. Election & Pol. Party System; Add.* 18th Fl., 43 Hsin Yi Rd., Sect. 3, Taipei.

CHANG, PAUL C.C. 張堅浚
Chmn., Leadwell CNC Mach. Mfg. Corp. 80-; *b.* Twn. Sept. 5, '48; *m.* Chang, Wendy; 1 *s.,* 2 *d.; educ.* BS, Mech. Engr., NCKU 70, M. 80; Ph.D. Candidate in Engr., So. Methodist U.; Pres., Lian Feng Mach. Co. 72-78; Pres., Yang Iron Works Co. 79-79; *Add.* 5 Gong 10th Rd., Taichung Ind. Park, Taichung.

CHANG, PETER 昌彼得
Dep. Dir., Nat. Palace Museum 84-; *b.* Hupei Jan. 24, '21; *m.* Fan, Ching-ju; 1 *c.; educ.* BA, Nat. Cent. U.; Ed. & Head, Sp. Collections Dept., Nat. Cent. Lib. 45-70; Curator, Dept. of Bk. & Documents, Nat. Palace Museum 68-83. *Publ.: Comments on Bk. by Chin-an; A Study of Shuo Fu; Descriptive Bibliography to Woodblock Editions* (2 Vol.); *Add.* 7th Fl., 5-3 Alley 12, Lane 190, Chung Shan N. Rd., Sect. 7, Taipei.

CHANG, PI-TE
(See CHANG, PETER 昌彼得)

CHANG, PO-I
(See CHANG, JEFFREY P. 張伯毅)

CHANG, PO-LONG 章博隆
Nat. Policy Adv. to the Pres. 96-; *b.* Twn. Nov. 10 '25; *m.* Chang Chen, Chin-lin; 3 *d.; educ.* Prov. Taitung Agr. Sch.; LL.B. Kinki U; Coun., Taitung CoCoun. 50-60; Mem., Twn. Prov. Ass. 60-77; Comr., Twn. Prov. Coun. 78-81. *Add.* 171 Chuan Kuan Rd., Taitung.

CHANG, PO-LUNG
(See CHANG, PO-LONG 章博隆)

CHANG, PO-YA 張博雅
Dir.-Gen., DOH 90-; *b.* Twn. Oct. 5, '42; *m.* Chi, Tsan-nan; 1 *s.,* 1 *d.; educ.* MD, Kaohsiung Med. Coll. 68; MPH, Inst. of Public Health, NTU 70; MPH, Johns Hopkins U. 74; Ph.D., Kyorin U. 94; Prof. & Dir., Dept.

of Public Health, Kaohsiung Med. Coll. 80-83; Mayor, Chiayi City 83-89; Mem., Legis. Yuan 90. *Publ.: Study of Occupational Lead Poisoning in S. Twn., ROC* 87; *Add.* 14th Fl., 100 Ai Kuo E. Rd., Taipei.

CHANG, RENEE REN-SHU 張仁淑
Pres., Ch. Women Judges Assn., Twn., ROC 94-; Dir., Intl. Women Judges Assn. 92; Bd. Mem., Hwa Hsia Cul. & Educ. Found. 92-; Justice of Supreme Court 79-; *b.* Shanghai Aug. 3, '22; *m.* Chen, Chen-kai; 1 *s.,* 1 *d.; educ.* LL.B., Fu Tan U. 46; M. in Comparative Law, Law Sch., So. Methodist U., USA 79; Judge in Taipei & Taichung Dist. Courts; Judge in Taichung Br., Twn. High Court & Twn. High Court Hqs.; *Add.* Surpreme Court, 6 Changsha St., Sect. 1, Taipei.

CHANG, SAMUEL K.C. 張光正
Pres., Chung Yuan Christian U. 91-; *b.* Chungking Feb. 8, '46; *m.* Chang Kuo, Datong; 2 *d.; educ.* BS, Meteorology, NTU 68; MS, State U. of New York, Albany 72, Ph.D., Atmospheric Sc. 77, MBA 79; System Analyst, New York State Ass. Off. of Mng. & Budget 79-80; Chmn. & concur. Dir., Dept. of Business Admin., Chung Yuan Christian U. 81-84; Visiting Scholar, Sch. of Business, UC-Berkly. 84-85; Dean, Coll. of Business, Chung Yuan Christian U. 85-91. *Publ.:* "Am. & Ch. Mgr. in US Co. in Twn.: A Comparison," *Calif. Mng. Review* 85; "Managerial Attitude & Leadership Power in US Co. in Twn., ROC," *Intl. Jour. of Comparative Sociology* 87; *Add.* Chung Yuan Christian U., Chungli, Taoyuan County.

CHANG, SHIH-CHENG 張士丞
Rep. to Papua New Guinea 92-; *b.* Fukien Aug. 8, '25; *m.* Chang, Ai-chu Y.; 2 *s.; educ.* LL.M., NCU; Ph.D., U. of Santo Tomas, Philippines; 3rd. & 2nd Sec., Emb. in the Philippines 62-68; 2nd Sec., Emb. in Peru 68-70; Dep. Dir., Info. Dept., MOFA 71-73; Consul, Consl. Gen. in New York, USA 73-78; Consul, Consl. in Pusan, S. Korea 78-81; Counsl. & Consul-Gen., Emb. in S. Korea 81-83; Dir., Dept. of Consul Aff., MOFA 83-84; Chief Sec., MOFA 84-87; Dir.-Gen., CCNAA, Off. in Houston 87-90; Amb. to Solomon Islands & to Nauru Repub. 90-92. *Publ.: The Am. For. Policy Toward Ch. 53-56; The Legal & Pol. Status of Twn.; Add.* P.O. Box 334, Port Moresby (NCD), Papua New Guinea.

CHANG, SHU-CHI 張書杞
Amb. to Belize 92-; *b.* Twn. Oct. 1, '33; *m.* Chang Lee, Siu-siang; 3 *s.; educ.* LL.B., NTU 57; MA, Dip., NCU 61; 3rd. & 2nd Sec., Emb. in Belgium 63-68; 1st Sec., Emb. in the Holy See 71-75; Dep. Dir., Dept. of African Aff., MOFA 75, Dep. Dir., Dept. of Treaty 76-79; Counsl., Emb. in Ivory Coast 79-81; Dep. Dir., Dept. of Intl., MOFA 82-84; Rep., Trade Mission in Mauritius 84-88; V. Chmn., Laws & Reglns. Cttee., MOFA 89-92. *Publ.: The Renunciation of the Anglo-Japanese Alliance & the Conclusion of a Treaty by UK, USA, France & Japan; A Study of the Termination of the Mutual Def. Treaty Between the ROC & the USA; An Analytical Study of the Application of the Principle of Reciprocity Between the Countries of Different Soc. Systems or Between the Countries of Different Dev. Levels; Add.* P.O. Box 1020, Belize City, Belize.

CHANG, TAO-MIN
(See CHANG, TAO-MING 張導民)

CHANG, TAO-MING 張導民
Nat. Policy Adv. to the Pres. 88-; *b.* Hupei Jan. 1, '08; *m.* Tsai, Shiao-i; 4 *s.,* 4 *d.; educ.* Grad., Chung Hua U., Wuchang; London U.; Dir., Kwangtung Tax Bu., MOF 39-41; Comr. of Finance, Kwangtung Prov. Govt. 41-45; Chief, Land Tax Dept., Min. of Food 46-49; Adv., CBC 50-57; Dep. Dir.-Gen., DGBAS 57-63, Dir.-Gen. 63-68; Auditor-Gen., Nat. Audit Off., Control Yuan 69-87; Standing Mem., Const. Res. Coun., NA; *Add.* 24 Lane 62, Hsin Sheng N. Rd., Sect. 3, Taipei.

CHANG, TE-HUI
(See CHANG, DOMINIC T.H. 章德惠)

CHANG, TE-MING
(See CHANG, TEH-MING 張德銘)

CHANG, TE-TZU 張德慈
Sp. Consultant, CITC 94-; *b.* Shanghai Apr. 3 '27; *m.* Hwa, Szu-mei; 2 *s.; educ.* BSA, U. of Nanking 49; MS, Cornell U. 54; Ph.D., U. of Minnesota 59; Jr. Sp., JCRR 49-52; Sr. Sp., JCRR 59-61; Geneticist/Prin. Scientist, Intl. Rice Res. Inst. (in Philippines) 61-91. *Publ.:* More than 250 tech. papers dealing with plant genetic, conservation of plant germ plasm evolution & improvement of

rice, appearing in jour., bk., proceedings, encyclopedia pub. in the US, UK, Netherlands & other sources; *Add.* 2nd Fl., 2 Alley 13, Lane 131, Sha Lun Rd., Tamsui, Taipei County.

CHANG, TEH-MING 張德銘
Mem., Control Yuan 93-; Tchr. 90-; *b.* Twn. Nov. 1, '38; *m.* Chang Yeh, Li-tzu; 2 *s.,* 1 *d.; educ.* LL.B., NTU; Attorney-at-Law; Mem., Legis. Yuan 75-77, & Taipei CCoun. 85-89; *Add.* Control Yuan, 2 Chung Hsiao E. Rd., Sect. 1, Taipei.

CHANG, THOMAS J.T. 張仁堂
Dir., 2nd Dept., Exec. Yuan 94-; *b.* Honan Aug. 15, '33; *m.* Chien, Grace Yin-fen; 1 *s.,* 1 *d.; educ.* BA, NTU 57; Ph.D., Nat. Ankara U., Turkey 64; Sp., MOFA 70-71, Sect. Chief, Dept. of W. Asian Aff. 71; 1st Sec., Emb. in Vietnam 74-75, & Emb. in Tonga 75-82; Dep. Dir., Off. of Pers., MOFA 82-86; Dir., Travel Documents Div., Far E. Trade Off. in Bangkok 86-89; Rep., Twn. Trade Off. in Nicosia, Cyprus 89-91; Rep., Cml. Off. of the ROC to the State of Kuwait 91-94; *Add.* 1 Chung Hsiao E. Rd., Sect. 1, Taipei.

CHANG, TIEN-CHIN
(See CHANG, TIEN-JIN 張天津)

CHANG, TIEN-JIN 張天津
Pres., Nat. Taipei Inst. of Tech. 94-; Chmn., Soc. of Mfg. Engr., Taipei Chapter 94-, & Ch. Taipei U. Sports Fed. Table Tennis Cttee. 94-; *b.* Twn. Apr. 13, '40; *m.* Chang, Tu Kuei-hui; 5 *d.; educ.* BS, Ind. Educ., NTNU 65; Ph.D., Ind. Educ., Penn. State U. 74; Pres., Tower Inst. of Tech. 74-78; Assc. Prof., NTNU 78-79, NTU & NTHU 77-79; Pres., Twn. Prov. Hai-san Sr. Ind. Voc. Sch. 79-80; Pres., Nat. Yunlin Inst. of Tech. 80-89; Pres., Nat. Taipei Inst. of Tech. 89-94. *Publ.: Admin. & Sup. in Voc. Tech. Educ.; Tool Design; Mech. Drawing; Mach. Mfg.; Heat Treatment; Jigs & Fixtures; Metal Working; Add.* 1 Chung Hsiao E. Rd., Sect. 3, Taipei.

CHENG, TING-CHUNG
(See CHANG, DING-CHONG 張鼎鍾)

CHANG, TZU-CHIANG
(See CHANG, TZU-CHYANG 張自強)

CHANG, TZU-CHYANG 張自強
Dir.-Gen., Tourism Bu., MOTC 91-; *b.* Chekiang Mar. 14, '48; *m.* Lin, Mei-yun; 1 *s.,* 1 *d.; educ.* LL.B., NCHU 70, LL.M. 75; MBA, Cent. State U., Oklahoma 81; Ph.D., NCU 88; Counsl., MOTC 91; *Add.* 9th Fl., 290 Chung Hsiao E. Rd., Sect. 4, Taipei.

CHANG, WEN-CHUNG
(See CHANG, JAMES WEN-CHUNG 張文中)

CHANG, WEN-HSIEN
(See CHANG, WEN-SHIANN 張文獻)

CHANG, WEN-HSIUNG
(See CHANG, WEN-SHION 張文雄)

CHANG, WEN-SHIANN 張文獻
Nat. Policy Adv. to the Pres. 96-; *b.* Twn. Jan. 28 '34; *m.* Chang Hu, Ching-yueh; 1 *s.,* 3 *d.; educ.* LL.B. NTU 56; Mem., TPA 63-68; Mem., Legis. Yuan 73-81; Mem., Control Yuan 81-93; *Add.* 10th Fl., 237 Fu Hsing S. Rd., Sect. 1, Taipei.

CHANG, WEN-SHION 張文雄
Pres., Nat. Yunlin Inst. of Tech. 91-; *b.* Taipei June 10, '38; *m.* Chang Liu, Michelle M.H.; 3 *d.; educ.* BS, Chung Yuan Christian U. 61; MS, Waseda U. 65, DE 69; Acting Chmn., Union Ind. Res. Inst., MOEA 69-72; Dean of Acad. Aff., Nat. Kaohsiung Normal U. 72-78; Pres., Nat. Kaohsiung Inst. of Tech. 78-84, & Nat. Taipei Inst. of Tech. 84-89; Dir., Preparatory Off., Nat. Yunlin Inst. of Tech. 89-91. *Publ.: A Study of the Org. & Function of Tech. Sch.* 88; *A Study of the Curricula in Tech. Coll.* 91; & over 60 publ. on bio-tech. & engr. educ.; *Add.* 123 U. Rd., Sect. 3, Touliu, Yunlin County.

CHANG, WEN-YING 張文英
Mayor, Chiayi City 89-; Pediatric Sp.; *b.* Twn. Feb. 3, '38; *m.* Lai, Chung-shuan; 2 *s.,* 1 *d.; educ.* Grad., Kaohsiung Med. Coll. 62; Res., U. of Massachusetts; Assc. Prof., Chungshan Med. Coll. 73-75; Assc. Prof., Ch. Med. Coll. 75-76; Lectr., Twn. Prov. Public Health Inst. 77; Dir., Pediatric Dept., Prov. Taipei Hosp. 81-82; Dir., Kuting Dist. Health Cent., Taipei 82-89; Mem., NA 87-93. *Publ.: Clinical Observation of Early Congenital Syphilis; Acute Lymphoplastic Leukemia in Twins; Survey &*

Study of Mothers with More Than 3 C. in Taipei; Survey & Study of the Public Understanding & Use of Public Health Cent.; Survey of the Current State of Pharmacies in Taipei & Improvement of Their Mng.; Add. 1 Min Sheng N. Rd., Chiayi.

CHANG, YAO-KO 張耀科
Pres., Yih Fong Chem. Corp. 92-; Chmn., Twn. Agrochem. Ind. Assn. 94-; Pres., Twn. San Lee Chem. Ind. Co. Ltd. 95-; *b.* Twn. Nov. 22, '27; *m.* Chang, Lai-may; 2 *s.,* 2 *d.; educ.* Grad., Nat. Taichung Tchrs. Coll.; Gen. Mgr., Twn. San Lee Chem. Ind. Co. Ltd. 68-95; Sup., Twn. Agrochem. Ind. Assc. 70-72, Dir. 72-75, Exec. Dir. 75-81, Dir. 81-84, Exec. Dir. 84-87, Dir. 87-90; *Add.* 39 An Hsi W. Rd., Ta Chu Li, Changhua.

CHANG, YU-FA 張玉法
Mem., Acad. Sinica & concur. Res. Fel., Inst. of Modern Hist. 75-; Prof., Inst. of Hist., NTNU 75-95, & NCU 78-95; *b.* Shantung Dec. 28, '36; *m.* Li, Chung-wen; 1 *s.,* 1 *d.; educ.* BA, Dept. of Hist. & Geog., NTNU 59; MA, Jour., NCU 64; MA, Hist., Columbia U. 70; Assc. Res. Fel., Inst. of Modern Hist., Acad. Sinica 71-75, Assc. Dir. 82-85, Dir. 85-91. *Publ.: Const. Parties in Late Ch'ing Ch.* 71; *Rev. Parties in Late Ch'ing Ch.* 75; *The Modernization of Ch.: The Case of Shantung Prov. (1860-1916)* 82; *Pol. Parties in the Early ROC* 85; *Ind. Hist. of Modern Ch. (1860-1916)* 92; *Collected Papers on the 1911 Rev. of Ch.* 93; *Add.* Inst. of Modern Hist., Acad. Sinica, 128 Yen Chiu Yuan Rd., Sect. 2, Taipei.

CHANG, YU-SHENG 張豫生
Pres., Pacific Cul. Found. 87-; Mem., CC, KMT 93-; *b.* Fukien Feb. 4, '29; *m.* Yang, Shi-jy; 2 *s.,* 1 *d.; educ.* LL.B., NTU 53; MA, Dip. & Intl. Law, NCU 59; MA, St. John's U. 66; Chief Exec. Off., Fed. of Free Ch. Youth for Anti-communism 51-52; Assc. Prof., Tamkang U. 67-74; Sec. & Dep. Chief, CC, KMT 68-78, Dir.-Gen., Dept. of Youth Aff., CC 78-84; Dep. Dir.-Gen., Ch. Youth Corps 84-87; Assc. Prof., NTU 78-92; *Add.* 38 Chungking S. Rd., Sect. 3, Taipei.

CHANG, YUNG-PING 張永平
Chmn., Chia Hsin Cement Corp. 89-, Tong Yong Chia Hsin Intl. Corp. 90-, & Lattice Corp. 92-; Dir., Twn. Cement Corp. 91-; *b.* Chekiang July 18, '46; *m.* Chang,

Chieh-ju; 1 *s.; educ.* B., Architecture, Ch. Cul. U.; MBA, New York U.; V. Pres., Chia Hsin Cement Corp. 82-86, Pres. 86-89; *Add.* 96 Chung Shan N. Rd., Sect. 2, Taipei.

CHAO, BEI-TSE 趙佩之
Mem., Acad. Sinica, & US Nat. Acad. of Engr.; Fel., Am. Soc. of Mech. Engrs., Am. Assn. for the Advancement of Sc., & Am. Soc. for Engr. Educ.; Consultant to Ind. & Govt. Agencies 50-; *b.* Kiangsu Dec. 18, '18; *m.* Kiang, May; 2 *c.; educ.* BEE, NCTU 39; Ph.D. (Boxer Indemnity Scholar), Victoria U., UK 47; Asst. Engr., Tool & Gauge Div., Cent. Mach. Works, Kunming 39-41, Assc. Engr. 41-43, Mgr. 43-45; Res. Asst., U. of Illinois, Urbana 48-50, Asst. Prof., Dept. of Mech. Engr. 51-53, Assc. Prof. 53-55, Prof. 55-87, Head, Thermal Sc. Div. 71-75, Head, Dept. of Mech. & Ind. Engr. 75-87; Assc. Mem., U. of Illinois (Cent. for Advanced Study) 63-64; Russell S. Springer Prof., UC-Berkly. 73; Mem., Reviewing Staff Zentralblatt für Mathematik, Berlin 70-82; Mem., US Engr. Educ. Del. to Mainland Ch. 78; Mem., Adv. Screening Cttee. in Engr., Fulbright-Hays Awards Prog. 79-81, Chmn. 80 & 81; Mem., Cttee. for US Army Basic Sc. Res., NRC 80-83; Prince Disting. Lectr., Arizona State U. 84; Mem., Bd. of Dir., Aircraft Gear Corp, Rockford, Illinois 89-94. *Publ.: Advanced Heat Transfer;* & numerous articles on mech. engr. in prof. jour.; *Add.* 101 W. Windsor Rd., Apt. 6103, Urbana, IL 61801-6697, USA.

CHAO, CHANG-PING 趙昌平
Mem., Control Yuan 93-; *b.* Twn. Feb. 1, '40; *m.* Chien, Yu-yun; 2 *s.,* 1 *d.; educ.* Grad., Taipei Mun. Tchrs. Coll. 59; Passed Sp. Exam. for Jud. Pers.; Grad., Judges & Prosecutors Tng. Cent. 73; Sup., Prosecutors' Off., Taipei Dist. Court 83-84; Prosecutor, Twn. High Court 84-86; Chief Prosecutor, Kinmen Dist. Court 86-89, Taitung Dist. Court 89-91, & Ilan Dist. Court 91-93; Chmn., Presidium, NA 86-92; Mem., APPU 84; Convener, 1st Cttee., Const. Res. Cttee. 81-89; *Add.* Control Yuan, 2 Chung Hsiao E. Rd., Sect. 1, Taipei.

CHAO, CHIH-YUAN 趙知遠
V. Min. of Nat. Def. 94-; *b.* Hupei May 19, '27; *m.* Chao, Chih-kuei; 2 *s.; educ.* BS, Ch. Air Force Acad. 48; Aviation Safety Prog., USA 59; Air Cmd. & Staff Coll. 62; War Coll., Armed Forces U. 73; Sect. Chief, Op. Sect.,

Off. of Dep. Chief of Staff (DCS), Hqs., ROCAF 75-76, Dep. Wing Cmdr., 427th Air Combat Wing 76-78, Wing Cmdr., 443rd Air Combat Wing 78-79; Asst. Dep. Chief of Gen. Staff (DCGS), Off. of DCGS/Ops., MND 79-80; DCS, Off. of DCS/Ops., Hqs., ROCAF 80-82; DCGS, Off. of DCGS/Intelligence, MND 82-86; Dep. C-in-C, Hqs., ROCAF 86-87; Dep. Chief of Gen. Staff, Off. of Gen. Staff, MND 87-94; *Add.* 8th Fl., 1 Lane 31, Wo Lung St., Taipei.

CHAO, CHING-CHUAN
(See CHAO, HELEN C.J. 趙鏡涓)

CHAO, HELEN C.J. 趙鏡涓
Dir.-Gen., Public Radio System 91-; *b.* Hunan May 28, '41; *m.* Tang, Pan-pan; 1 *s.*, 1 *d.; educ.* BJ, Fu Hsing Kang Coll. 64; Public Aff. Reporter, Public Radio System 66-76, News Dir. 76-84, Prog. Dir. 84-87, Dep. Dir.-Gen. 87-91; *Add.* 17 Kuang Chou St., Taipei.

CHAO, JUNG-YAO
(See CHOW, LOUIS R. 趙榮耀)

CHAO, LI-YUN
(See CHAO, NANCY LI-YUN 趙麗雲)

CHAO, LOUIS R. 趙榮耀
Mem., Control Yuan 93-; *b.* Twn. Aug. 17, '43; *m.* Chao Hu, Sally; 1 *s.*, 1 *d.; educ.* BEE, NTU 65; Ph.D., Duke U. 71; Dir., Computer Sc. Dept., Tamkang U. 71-73, Dean, Engr. Coll. 73-78, Dean of Acad. Aff. 78-84, V. Pres. 84-89, Pres. 89-93. *Publ.: Introduction to Computers; Numerical Analysis; Advanced Numerical Analysis; Add.* 2 Chung Hsiao E. Rd., Sect. 1, Taipei.

CHAO, NANCY LI-YUN 趙麗雲
Dir., Nat. Inst. for Compilation & Transl. 92-; Mem., CC, KMT 93-; Mem., Bd. of Gov., Intl. Coun. for Health, Phys. Educ., Recreation, Sport & Dance (ICHPERSD) 82-; *b.* Twn. Aug. 8, '52; *m.* Chien, Feng-wen; 1 *d.; educ.* Ed.B., NTNU 75, Ed.M. 77; Ed.D., Columbia U. 87; Lectr., Fu Jen Catholic U. 77-84; Staff, Sp., & Sect. Chief, Dept. of Phys. Educ. & Sports, MOE 78-85, Sr. Sp., Dep. Dir., & Dir. 85-89; Assc. Prof., Nat. Coll. of Phys. Educ. & Sports 87-89; Assc. Prof., NTNU 88-91. *Publ.: A Descriptive Study of Teaching: Pupil Motor*

Engagement Time in Phys. Educ. Classes in Taipei City 87; *Sports for All Movement in the ROC* 91; *Add.* 247 Chou Shan Rd., Taipei.

CHAO, PEI-CHIH
(See CHAO, BEI-TSE 趙佩之)

CHAO, SHOU-PO 趙守博
Sec.-Gen., Exec. Yuan 94-; Mem., CC, KMT 93-; *b.* Twn. Mar. 1, '41; *m.* Lu, Miao-shen; 2 *s.*, 1 *d.; educ.* LL.B., Cent. Police Coll.; MCL & S.J.D., U. of Illinois; Prof., Law, Cent. Police Coll. 72-76; Dir., Dept. of Sch. Youth Service, Ch. Youth Corps 75-76; Comr., Dept. of Info., TPG 76-79, Comr. 79-81; Mem., Bd. of Intl. Assn. for Community Dev. 81; Dep. Dir.-Gen., Dept. of Cul. Aff., CC, KMT 79-83; Comr., Dept. of Soc. Aff., TPG 81-87; Dir.-Gen., Dept. of Soc. Aff., CC, KMT 87-89; Chmn., COLA 89-94, Pres., Nat. Water Life Saving Assn., ROC, 95-; Pres., the Coun. of Soc. Welfare, ROC 95. *Publ.: Getting Involved; A Comparative Study of the Choice of Law in Domestic Rel.; Law & Innovation; Soc. Policy, Family Welfare & Community Dev.; Soc. Problems & Soc. Welfare; Labor Policy & Labor Problems; Add.* 1 Chung Hsiao E. Rd., Sect. 1, Taipei.

CHAO, SHU-TE
(See CHAO, SHWU-DER 趙淑德)

CHAO, SHWU-DER 趙淑德
Mem., Exam. Yuan 96-; *b.* Peiping Aug. 22, '41; *m.* Chang, Ming-wen; 2 *s.*, 1 *d.; educ.* BA, NCHU; Prof., NCHU 83-; Head, Dev. of Land Econ. & Admin., NCHU 87-92; Dir., Cent. for Land Econ. & Admin. Res. 92-96; Pres., the Ch. Inst. of Land Appraisal 91-93; Pres., Real Estate Res. & Dev. Assn. of Ch. 94-96; Pres., *Jour. of Modern Land Admin. Assc.* 87-96. *Publ.: Hist. of Ch. Land System; Study of Twn. Urban Readjustment; From Rural Land Usage to See Twn. Population Problem; The Practices of Housing Purchase; How to Ensure Mortage Debt; Add.* 1 Shih Yuan Rd., Wenshan, Taipei.

CHAO, TZE-CHI 趙自齊
Sr. Adv. to the Pres. 92-; Comr., NUC 90-; Pres., WLFD 91-, & WLFD/APLFD, ROC Chapter 89-; *b.* Jehol Jan. 1, '15; *m.* Cheng, Li-zrin; 3 *s.*, 2 *d.; educ.* Nat. Nankai U.; Mil. Acad.; Sun Yat-sen Inst. on Policy Res. & Dev.;

Nat. War Coll.; Hon. Ph.D., Kyung Hee U., S. Korea 79;
Mem., Legis. Yuan 48-91; Mem., Jehol Prov. Cttee.,
KMT 55-56; Chmn., San-Min Chu-I Youth Corps in
Jehol Prov. 56-59; Comr., Jehol Prov. Govt. 58-60;
Chmn., Taichung City Cttee., KMT 55-64; Mem., KMT
Caucus, Legis. Yuan 68-70; Mem., CAC, KMT 74-80
& 94; Mem., CC, KMT 74-94; Dep. Sec.-Gen., Policy
Coordination Cttee., CC, KMT 70, Sec.-Gen., CC 70-
88, Dir.-Gen., Dept. of Org. Aff., CC 78; Prof., Ch. Cul.
U. 76-77; Lectr., Nat. War Coll. 82-84; Chmn., Lung
Kong World Fed. 88-92; Mem., CSC, KMT 84 & 88-
94. *Publ.: The Refugee's Mng. of Recovery of the Main-
land; US, Don't Wander Again; 6 Hours in E. Berlin;
Add.* 3rd Fl., 333 Tun Hua S. Rd., Sect. 2, Taipei.

CHAO, TZU-CHI
(See CHAO, TZE-CHI 趙自齊)

CHAO, WAN-FU 趙萬富
Strategy Adv. to the Pres. 91-; *b.* Yunnan Mar. 11, '28;
m. Chao Yang, Pi-yu; 3 *d.; educ.* 21st Class, Ch. Mil.
Acad. 47; Sr. Class, Army Coll. 58; Army CGSC 64;
War Coll., Armed Forces U. 79; Platoon Leader, Battery
Cmdr., Bn. Cmdr., Regt. Cmdr., Brig. Cmdr., & Div. C/
S 47-71; Cmdr., 19th Div., ROC Army (Maj. Gen.) 74-
77; C/S, Army Tng. Combat Dev. Cmd. 77-79; Cmdr.,
32nd Army Corps (Lt. Gen.) 80-81; Cmdr., Matsu Def.
Dept. 81-84; Cmdr., 10th Army Corps Cmd. 84-85;
Cmdr., Kinmen Def. Dept. (Gen.) 85-87; Dep. C-in-C,
Hqs., ROC Army 88-91; *Add.* 5th Fl., 3 Lane 31, Wo
Lung St., Taipei.

CHAO, YANG-CHING 趙揚清
Chmn., Fair Trade Com., Exec. Yuan 96-; *b.* Kiangsu
Dec. 14, '49; *educ.* BC, Tamkang Coll. 72; LL.M. NCU
75; Sect. Chief, Taxation & Tariff Com. MOF 82-85; Sr.
Sp./Dir., Dept. of Nat. Treasury, MOF 85-90; Coun.,
MOF 90-91; Dep. Exec. Sec., Dev. Fund, Exec. Yuan
90-91; Dep. Dir.-Gen., Dept. of Nat. Treasury, MOF 91-
95, Dir.-Gen. 95-96; *Add.* 150 Tun Hua N. Rd., Taipei.

CHAO, YU 趙域
V. Chmn., VAC 95-; *b.* Shantung, Oct. 7, '30; *m.* Hsueh,
Hsueh-ho; 3 *d.; educ.* Ch. Mil. Acad. 48; US Army Engr.
Sch. 64; Army CGSC, ROC 68; War Coll., Armed
Forces U. 75; Br. Chief, DCS/Logistics, GHQ, ROC

Army 76-77; Cmdr., Engr. Cmd., 10th Field Army 77-
79; Dep. Chief of Engr., GHQ, ROC Army 79-82; Asst.
Dep. Chief of the Gen. Staff/Logistics, MND 82-86; Dir.,
Min.'s Off., MND 86-89, Dir., Bu. of Gen. Aff. 89-90;
Dep. Sec.-Gen., VAC 91-93, Sec.-Gen. 93-95; *Add.* 222
Chung Hsiao E. Rd., Sect. 5, Taipei.

CHEN, ARTHUR YU 陳豫
Chmn., Public Construction Com., Exec. Yuan 95-; V.
Chmn., RDEC 91-; Exec. Sec., Public Construction Sup.
Bd., Exec. Yuan 91-; *b.* Chekiang Mar. 27, '27; *m.* Chen,
Lily T.; 1 *s.,* 2 *d.; educ.* BEE, NCTU 48; Advanced
Mng. Prog., Grad. Sch. of Business, Harvard U. 77; Plan-
ning Engr., Project Engr., & Dir., Engr. Dept., Shihmen
Dev. Com. 53-66; Dep. Gen. Mgr. & Mgr., Guam &
Thailand Br., Pan Asia Corp. 66-73; Gen. Mgr., Saudi
Arabia Br. Off., Ret-Ser Engr. Agency 73-82, V. Pres. &
Gen. Mgr. 82-84, V. Pres. & concur. Dir. of Ovs. Dept.
84-86, Pres. 87-91; *Add.* 9th Fl., 4 Chung Hsiao W. Rd.,
Sect. 1, Taipei.

CHEN, CHAI
(See CHEN, JAI 陳霽)

CHEN, CHANG-CHIEN
(See CHAN, SUNNEY I. 陳長謙)

CHEN, CHANG-WEN
(See CHEN, CHARNG-VEN 陳長文)

CHEN, CHAO-KUANG 陳朝光
Prof., NCKU 76-; *b.* Fukien Oct. 17, '34; *m.* Chen Chang,
Liang; 1 *s.,* 1 *d.; educ.* B. Sc., NCKU 58; M. Sc., NCKU
64; M. Sc., Georgia Inst. of Tech. 70; Ph.D., U. of
Liverpool 87; Mech. Engr., CPC 60-66; Instr., NCKU
66-71; Assc. Prof., NCKU 71-76; Head, Inst. of Mech.
Engr., NCKU 90-93. *Publ.:* More than 200 mech. engr.
papers; *Add.* Dept. of Mech. Engr., NCKU, Tainan.

CHEN, CHARNG-VEN 陳長文
V. Pres., Red Cross Soc. of the ROC 88-; Sr. Partner,
Lee & Li, Attorneys-at-Law 72-; Mem., Taipei, Hsinchu
& Kaohsiung Bar Assn.; Adv., Exec. Yuan 88-; Legal
Consultant, CBC 88-, & MOFA; Gen. Counsl., MND;
Mem., Cttee. on Review & Drafting of Socioecon. Laws,

CEPD; Gov., Cml. Arbitration Assn. of the ROC; Adv., Ch. Aviation Dev. Found.; Hon. Pres., Harvard Club of the ROC 87-; Adjunct Prof., Law, NCU, & Soochow U. 72-; *b.* Ch. Oct. 25, '44; *m.* Chen, Suzy K.W.; 1 *s.,* 1 *d.; educ.* LL.B., NTU; LL.M., U. of British Columbia, Can.; S.J.D., Harvard Law Sch.; Mem., Am. Bar Assn.; Coun. Mem., Asian Patent Attorneys Assn. *Publ.: Public Intl. Law; World Unfair Competition Law;* & numerous textbk. & articles; *Add.* 7th Fl., 201 Tun Hua N. Rd., Taipei.

CHEN, CHE-CHIA 陳啟家
Pub. & concur. Dir., *Great News Daily* 94; *b.* Shanghai Jan. 6, '35; *m.* Chen, Pi-chih; 1 *s.,* 2 *d.; educ.* LL.B., NCU 59; Reporter, *Twn. Shin Sheng Daily News* 60-71, City Ed. 71-78; Dep. Ed.-in-Chief, *Min Sheng Pao* 78-84, Ed.-in-Chief 84-90, Dep. Dir. 90; Pub., *Great News Daily* 90-94; *Add.* 216 Chen Teh Rd., Sect. 3, Taipei.

CHEN, CHEN-TUNG
(See CHEN, CHEN-TUNG ARTHUR 陳鎮東)

CHEN, CHEN-TUNG ARTHUR 陳鎮東
Dir., Marine Sc. Res. Cent., Nat. Sun Yat-Sen U. 89-, Prof., Inst. of Marine Geol. 85-; Scientist, STAG 88-; Chmn., Intl. Geosphere Biosphere Prog. ROC Cttee. 91-; *b.* Twn. Apr. 22, '49; *m.* Chen, Joanne Hwa; 2 *d.; educ.* BS, Chem. Engr., NTU 70; MS, Chem. Oceanography, U. of Miami 74, Ph.D., Chem. Oceanography 77; Asst. Prof., Oregon State U. 77-81; Faculty Res. Participant, Oak Ridge Nat. Lab., USA 80; Assc. Prof., Oregon State U. 81-84; Visiting Prof., Inst. of Marine Biology, Nat. Sun Yat-Sen U. 84-85, Prof. & Dir., Inst. of Marine Geol. 85-89, Prof. & Dean, Coll. of Marine Sc. 89-92. *Publ.:* Over 400 papers & tech. reports; *Add.* Inst. of Marine Geol., Nat. Sun Yat-Sen U., Kaohsiung.

CHEN, CHENG-HSIUNG
(See CHEN, DAVID T.H. 陳澄雄)

CHEN, CHI-NAN 陳計男
Grand Justice, Jud. Yuan 94-; Adjunct Prof., Soochow U. 87-, & NCU 88-; *b.* Twn. Oct. 28, '37; *m.* Ko, Ching-chih; 2 *s.,* 1 *d.; educ.* LL.B., NTU 60; Justice, Supreme Court 79-86; Div. Chief Justice, Admin. Court 86-94.

Publ.: Law of Bankruptcy; Law of Civil Procedure I & II; A Study of the Law of Procedure I & II; Add. 4th Fl.-2, 2 Lane 163, Yen Ping S. Rd., Taipei.

CHEN, CHI-NAN 陳其南
V. Chmn., CCA 94-; *b.* Twn. Oct. 29, '47; *m.* Chang, Chiu-pao; 1 *d.; educ.* B., NTNU 70; M., NTU 75; M., Yale U. 78, Ph.D., Yale U. 84; Assc. Res. Fel., Inst. of Ethnology, Acad. Sinica 78-85; Visiting Prof., Dept. of Anthropology, U. of Virginia 89; Lectr. & Assc. Dir., Off. of Intl. Studies Progs., CUHK 85-91, Sr. Lectr. & Chmn., Dept. of Anthropology, CUHK 91-93; Visiting Prof., Dept. of Sociology, Doshisha U., Kyoto 93; Mem., Educ. Reform Cttee., Exec. Yuan 94-; Res. Fellow, Inst. of Twn. History, Acad. Sinica 95-. *Publ.: Twn. at a Turning Point: Nat. Identity, Legal State & Agrarian Policies* 88; *Family & Soc.: Basic Concepts in the Soc. Studies of Twn. & Ch.* 90; *The Idea of Civil State & Pol. Dev. in Twn.* 92; *Add.* 3rd Fl., 102 Ai Kuo E. Rd., Taipei.

CHEN, CHIEN-CHIH 陳健治
Spkr., Taipei CCoun. 89-, Mem. 69-; Mem., CC & CSC, KMT 93-; *b.* Twn. Jan. 25, '44; *m.* Tsai, Lee-chu; 1 *s.,* 1 *d.; educ.* BA, NCU 67; MA, N.E. Missouri State U. 85; Dep. Spkr., Taipei CCoun. 81-89; *Add.* 18 Lane 61, Nei Hu Rd., Sect. 1, Taipei.

CHEN, CHIEN-CHUNG 陳建中
Sr. Adv. to the Pres.; *b.* Shensi Oct. 12, '13; *m.* Chen Fan, Ching-jun; 2 *s.,* 4 *d; educ.* BA, Shanghai U.; Ph.D., Tankuk U., S. Korea; Mem., 1st NA; Sec.-Gen., NA; *Add.* 9th Fl., 237-1 Fu Hsing S. Rd., Sect. 1, Taipei.

CHEN, CHIEN-JEN 程建人
Pol. V. Min., MOFA 96-; *b.* Chungking Aug. 11, '39; *m.* Chen Ho, Yolanda; 1 *s.,* 1 *d.; educ.* LL.B., NCU 60, Grad. Sch. of Intl. Rel. 62; LL.B., U. of Cambridge 65; Res. Fel., U. of Madrid 66; Sp., Info. Dept., MOFA 67-69, Sect. Chief 69-71; Adjunct Lectr., Intl. Law, NCU 68-71; 3rd Sec., Emb. in USA 71-74, 2nd Sec. 74-76, & 1st Sec. 76-79; Dir., Public Aff., CCNAA, Washington, D.C. 79-80; Dir., Dept. of N. Am. Aff., MOFA 80-82; Adjunct Lectr., Intl. Rel., NCU 80-82; Adv., CCNAA, Washington, D.C. 82, Dep. Rep. 82-89; Admin. V. Min. of For. Aff. 89-93; Alt. Mem., CC, KMT 88-93; Convener, For. Aff. Cttee., 1st, 2nd & 4th Sess., Legis. Yuan

93-96; Dir.-Gen., Dept. of Ovs. Aff., CC, KMT 93-96; *Add.* 2 Kaitakelan Boulevard., Taipei.

CHEN, CHIEN-NIEN 陳建年
Magis., Taitung County 93-; *b.* Twn. Oct. 10, '47; *m.* Huang, Yu-hsia; 1 *s.,* 2 *d.; educ.* B., Pharmacology, Kaohsiung Med. Coll. 72; Mem., Taitung CoCoun. 82-86; Charter Mem., Naruwan Jaycees 83-84; Mem., TPA 86-93; Mem., Twn. Prov. Cttee., KMT 87-93; Dep. Dir., Taitung Cttee., Ch. Youth Corps 90-94; Dir., Taitung Off., VAC 93-94; *Add.* 36 Alley 360, Chuan Kuang Rd., Taitung.

CHEN, CHIEN-WU 陳千武
Poet; Hon. Dir., Bd. of Trustees, Soc. of C.'s Lit. 94-; *b.* Twn. May 1, '22; *m.* Hsu, Yu-lan; 2 *s.,* 1 *d.;* Dir., Taichung Mun. Cul. Cent. 76-82, Curator, Wen Ying Hall 82-87; Dir., Bd. of Trustees, Soc. of C.'s Lit. 90-93. *Publ.: Thick Woods; Twn. Contemporary Poetry; Spring in Fengyuan;* etc.; *Add.* 16 Lane 307, San Min Rd., Sect. 3, Taichung.

CHEN, CHIN-JANG
(See CHEN, CHING-JANG 陳金讓)

CHEN, CHIN-LI
(See CHERN, JINN-LIH 陳進利)

CHEN, CHING-JANG 陳金讓
Min. of Exam., Exam. Yuan & Mem., NA 96-; Mem., CSC, KMT 93-; *b.* Twn. Feb. 1, '35; *m.* Chen Pai, May-yun; 1 *s.,* 4 *d.; educ.* LL.B., Soochow U. 58; Spkr., Yungho Rep. Conf. 64-72; Mem., NA 73-87; Dep. Dir.-Gen., Dept. of Org. Aff., CC, KMT 79-84, Chmn., Taipei Mun. Cttee. 84-88, V. Chmn., Policy Coordination Cttee., CC 88-90, Dir., Secretariat 90, & Dir.-Gen., Dept. of Org. Aff., CC 90-92; Sec.-Gen. & Mem., NA 92-96; *Add.* Min. of Exam., 1 Shih Yuan Rd., Taipei.

CHEN, CHIU-SEN 陳秋盛
Music Dir., Taipei City Symphony Orchestra; *b.* Twn. July 9, '42; 2 *d.; educ.* Grad., Tamkang U.; Staat Hochschule für Musik und Darstellung, München; Prof., Nat. Twn. Acad. of Arts 72-77; Conductor, Twn. Symphony Orchestra 77-79; *Add.* 7th Fl., 25 Pa Te Rd., Sect. 3, Taipei.

CHEN, CHIU-SHENG
(See CHEN, CHIU-SEN 陳秋盛)

CHEN, CHIUNG-LING 陳瓊玲
Dir.-Gen., Directorate Gen. of Posts, MOTC 96-; *b.* Twn. Dec. 1, '34; 3 *s.,* 2 *d.; educ.* BA, NTNU; Chief, Acct. Div., Taipei Post Off. 70-77; Chief, Acct. Div., Twn. Post Admin. 77-79; Dep. Dir., Acct. Dept., Directorate Gen. of Posts 79-85; Dir., Data Processing Cent., Directorate Gen. of Postal Remittances & Savings Bk. 85-88; Dir., Secretariat of Planning & Evaluation Cttee., Directorate Gen. of Posts 88-89, Dir., Acct. Dept. 89-90; Regional Postmaster Gen., Twn. Cent. Region Head Off. 90-92; Dep. Dir., Directorate Gen. of Postal Remittances & Savings Bk. 92-96; Dep. Dir., Directorate Gen. of Posts 96-96; *Add.* 55 Chin Shan S. Rd., Sect. 2, Taipei.

CHEN, CHO-MIN
(See CHEN, J.M. 陳倬民)

CHEN, CHUAN 陳川
Sec.-Gen., NA 96-, Dep. Sec.-Gen., KMT Caucus 85-, Mem. 81-; Mem., CC, KMT 93-; *b.* Twn. June 29, '34; *m.* Chen Tsai, Ray-in; 2 *s.,* 2 *d.; educ.* LL.B., Land Admin. Dept., NCHU 59; Staff, Land Admin. Bu. 57-61; Dir., Wufeng Dist. Land Admin. Off. 61-70; Sect. Chief, Taoyuan Land Admin. Dept. 70-82; Dep. Dir., Secretariat, NA 82-85; Dep. Sec.-Gen., NA 90-96; *Add.* 9th Fl.-9, 107 Chung Hua Rd., Taoyuan.

CHEN, CHUN-KUAN 陳重光
Chmn., Yakult Co. Ltd., & Glory Navigation Co. Ltd.; Mem., NA 92-; Adv., CC, KMT; *b.* Twn. Dec. 10, '13; 1 *s.,* 2 *d.; educ.* Grad., Cheng Cheng High Sch.; Mem., TPA 60-68, & Taipei CCoun. 69-73; Chmn., Twn. Paper Ind. Assn. 67-73; Chmn., TTV 91-95; Pres., Kuan Hwa Pulp Co. Ltd., & Twn. Tarpaulin Co. Ltd. *Publ.: 8 Years in the TPA; Twn.'s Paper Ind.; Add.* 3rd Fl., 261 Sungkiang Rd., Taipei.

CHEN, CHUNG-HUA 陳重華
Comr., Chiang Kai-shek Memorial Hall 95-; *b.* Fukien May 15, '35; *m.* Chen, Guey-shiang; 1 *s.,* 1 *d.; educ.* BSE, NTNU 59; Dep. Dir., Employment & Voc. Tng. Admin., MOI 87-94; Coun., COLA 95. *Publ.:*

Heaven, Earth, Human Beings 82; *Add.* 21 Chung Shan S. Rd., Taipei.

CHEN, CHUNG-KUANG
(See CHEN, CHUN-KUAN 陳重光)

CHEN, CHUNG-SHENG 陳聰勝
V. Chmn., NYC 94-; *b.* Twn. Jan. 21, '44; *m.* Wu, Yin-hwa; 2 *s.; educ.* BPS, NTU 66; MPS, NCU 70, Ph.D. 78; Sect. Chief, Exec. Yuan 78, Counsl. 78-81; Counsl., MOI 82-83; Dir., Dept. of Soc. Aff., MOI 84; Dep. Dir.-Gen., Employment & Voc. Tng. Admin., MOI 84-87; Dir.-Gen., Employment & Voc. Tng. Admin., COLA 87-94. *Publ.: A Study of the Org. of Twn.'s Farm Assc.* 79; *Voc. Tng., License System, & Employment Services of Service Ind. in Germany, Switzerland & Austria* 85; *Reform & Dev. of Voc. Tng. in Korea & Japan* 87; *Voc. Tng. & Employment Assistance in the ROC; A New Milestone in Dev. Voc. Tng. to Meet the Changing Times* 93; *Add.* 14th Fl., 5 Hsuchow Rd., Taipei.

CHEN, DAVID T.H. 陳澄雄
Exec. Dir., Twn. Musical Cul. Educ. Found. 92-; Music Dir., Twn. Symphony Orchestra 91-; *b.* Twn. Aug. 26, '41; *m.* Wu, Margaret Kuei-mei; 2 *s.; educ.* Grad., Nat. Twn. Acad. of Arts; Music Dept., Nat. Akademie Mozarteum, Salzburg; 1st Flutist, Twn. Symphony Orchestra 63-65; Assc. Prof., Nat. Twn. Acad. of Arts 68-77; Music Dir., Taipei Mun. Tchrs. Coll. 79-83, & Taipei Mun. Ch. Orchestra 83-91; Pres., ROC Band Assn. 88-92. *Publ.:* Theses & articles on music; *Add.* 3rd Fl., 7-5 Lane 22, Hsin Sheng S. Rd., Sect. 3, Taipei.

CHEN, DING-SHINN 陳定信
Mem., Acad. Sinica 92-; Prof., Coll. of Med., NTU 83-; Dir., Hepatitis Res. Cent., NTU Hosp. 88-; *b.* Taipei July 6, '43; *m.* Hsu, Hsu-mei; 1 *s.,* 1 *d.; educ.* MD, Coll. of Med., NTU 68; Lectr., Dept. of Internal Med., Coll. of Med., NTU 75-78, Assc. Prof. 78-83, Dir., Grad. Inst. of Clinical Med. 85-91. *Publ.:* More than 300 sc. papers published in intl. jour. & ed. of 2 bk.; *Add.* Hepatitis Res. Cent., NTU, 7 Chung Shan S. Rd., Taipei.

CHEN ENG-RIN 陳瑩霖
Dep. Dir.-Gen., DOH 93-; *b.* Twn. Aug. 9, '34; *m.* Chen Ko, Chun-chin; 2 *s.,* 1 *d.; educ.* MD, Kaohsiung Med. Coll. 60; M., London Sch. of Hygiene & Tropical Med. 69; DMS, Nat. Chiba U., Japan 73; Teaching Asst., Kaohsiung Med. Coll. 61-66; Res. Fel., Nat. Inst. of Health, USA 68-69; Assc. Prof., Kaohsiung Med. Coll. 69-72, Prof. & Dir., Dept. of Parasitology 72-91, Dir., Dept. of Public Health 73-74, Dir., Grad. Inst. of Med. 86-88, Dean of Studies 83-91; Sp. Gen., DOH 91-93. *Publ.: Recent Studies on Endemic Ascariasis in Twn.* & 90 other papers; *Add.* 14th Fl., 100 Ai Kuo E. Rd., Taipei.

CHEN, FEI-LUNG 陳飛龍
Chmn., Namchow Group 82-; *b.* HK Oct. 2, '37; *m.* Chen Huang, Shiao-chuan; 2 *s.,* 1 *d.; educ.* MPA, U. of San Francisco 83; Pres., Namchow Chem. Ind. Co., Ltd. 68-74; Chmn. 74. *Publ.: Labor Disputes in Twn. & Japan; Add.* 100 Yen Ping N. Rd., Sect. 4, Taipei.

CHEN, HAN 陳涵
State Public Prosecutor-Gen., Public Prosecutors' Off., Supreme Court 92-; *b.* Kwangtung May 6, '27; *m.* Wu, Tsai-hsiu; 3 *s.,* 1 *d.; educ.* LL.B., NCU 52; Chief Judge, Kinmen Dist. Court 72-74; Presiding Judge, Tainan Br., Twn. High Court 75-76; Chief Public Prosecutor, Public Prosecutors' Off., Chiayi Dist. Court 78-79; Dir., Dept. of Prosecution Aff., MOJ 79-82; Chief Public Prosecutor, Public Prosecutors' Off., Kaohsiung Dist. Court 82; Chief Public Prosecutor, Public Prosecutors' Off., Taipei Dist. Court 82-85; Admin. V. Min. of Justice 85-86; Public Prosecutor-Gen., Public Prosecutors' Off., Twn. High Court 86-92. *Publ.: Oughtopia; Add.* 130 Chungking S. Rd., Sect. 1, Taipei.

CHEN, HSI-FAN
(See CHEN, STEPHEN S.F. 陳錫蕃)

CHEN, HSIN-KUANG
(See CHEN, STARK 陳信光)

CHEN, HSING-LING 陳燊齡
Strategy Adv. to the Pres. 91-; *b.* Peiping Aug. 9, '24; *m.* Tang, Chiao-chung; 2 *s.,* 4 *d.; educ.* Ch. Air Force Acad.; Pilot Tng. Sch., Luke Field, USA; War Coll., Armed Forces U.; Group Cmdr., 3rd Tactical Fighter Group, ROCAF 64-66, Wing Cmdr. 72-74; Asst. to DCGS/Planning, MND 77; Dep. C/S for Op., Hqs., ROCAF 77-79; CG, Combat Air Cmd., ROCAF 79-80; Dir., Pol. War-

fare Dept., Hqs., ROCAF 80-82; Dep. C-in-C, ROCAF 82-83; V. Chief of the Gen. Staff, MND 83-86; C-in-C, ROCAF 86-89; Chief of the Gen. Staff, MND 89-91; *Add.* 5 Lane 118, Jen Ai Rd., Sect. 3, Taipei.

CHEN, HSING-SHEN
(See CHERN, SHIING-SHEN 陳省身)

CHEN, HSUEH-PING 陳雪屏
Sr. Adv. to the Pres. 90-; Mem., CAC, KMT; *b.* Kiangsu Nov. 1, '01; *m.* Lin, Min; 2 *s.*, 1 *d.; educ.* BA, Nat. Peking U. 26; MA, Columbia U. 27; Prof., Nat. Peking U. 32-47; Min., KMT Youth Bd. 47-48; Acting Min. of Educ. 48; Comr., Dept. of Educ., TPG 49-53; Min. of Exam., Exam. Yuan 57-58; Sec.-Gen., Exec. Yuan 58-63; Min. of State 63-72; Nat. Policy Adv. to the Pres. 72-90; V. Bd. Chmn., Nat. Palace Museum 83-91. *Publ.: Psychology of Rumor; 20th Century Psychology; Psychology & Life; Add.* 13 Lane 22, Hsin Sheng S. Rd., Sect. 3, Taipei.

CHEN, I-YANG
(See CHEN, YIH-YOUNG 陳義揚)

CHEN, JAI 陳霽
Pub. & Dir., *Youth Daily News* 89-; *b.* Anhwei Dec. 25, '42; *m.* Cheng, Wan-li; 2 *s.; educ.* Fu Hsing Kang Coll. 66; News Off., Mil. News Agency, Mil. Police Hqs. 71-73; Ed.-in-Chief, New Ch. Pub. Agency 85-87, Dir. 88-89; *Add.* 3 Hsin Yi Rd., Sect. 1, Taipei.

CHEN, JUNG-CHIEH
(See CHAN, WING-TSIT 陳榮捷)

CHEN, J.M. 陳倬民
Pres., Nat. Changhua U. of Educ. 92-; Mem., CC, KMT 93-; *b.* Hunan Aug. 23, '44; *m.* Chen Su, Linda; 2 *s.*, 1 *d.; educ.* B., Mech. Engr., NTU 68; MS, Tulane U. 71, DE 74; Assc. Prof., Tamkang U. 74-76; Assc. Prof., NTHU 76-79, Prof. 79-80; Chmn., NCTU 80-81 & 83-85; Dean & Prof., Coll. of Engr., Nat. Cent. U. 81-83; Counsl. & concur. Dir., Dept. of Tech. & Voc. Educ., MOE 85-86, Counsl. & concur. Dir., Dept. of Higher Educ. 86-87; Comr., Dept. of Educ., TPG 87-92. *Publ.: Renovative, Practical & Creative New Era of Educ.; Love & Educ.; Everlasting Spring: A Utopia of Educ.;*

Trouble-Free Educ. Admin.; On Educ.: A Casual Way; Add. Nat. Changhua U. of Educ., Paisha Village, Changhua.

CHEN, JUI-HUNG 陳瑞宏
Pres., Pao An Fire Equipment Co., Ltd. 79-; *b.* Twn. July 22, '47; *m.* Chao, Hsiu-hsing; 1 *s.*, 1 *d.; educ.* Grad. Inst. of Mng. Sc., Tamkang U.; *Add.* 281 Chung Hua 2nd Rd., Kaohsiung.

CHEN, KANG-CHIN 陳庚金
Dir.-Gen., CPA 93-; Mem., CC, KMT 93-; *b.* Twn. Feb. 2, '39; *m.* Chen Liu, Jin-feng; 1 *s.*, 2 *d.; educ.* BPS, NCU 65, MPA 69; Sect. Chief, RDEC 69-76; Dir., Dept. of Soc. Aff., CC, KMT 77-80; Magis., Taichung County 81-89; Admin. V. Min. of Exam., Exam. Yuan 90, Pol. V. Min. of Exam. 90-93. *Publ.: Current System for the Appointment of Govt. Employees; Mng. in Theory & Practice; Applied Behavioral Sc. on Mng.; Human Rel. & Mng.; Add.* 109 Huai Ning St., Taipei.

CHEN, KEN-TE 陳根德
Spkr., Taoyuan CoCoun. 95-, Mem. 94-; Mng. Dir., Twn. Regional Assc. of Gen. Contractors 95-; *b.* Twn. Jan. 18, '56; 2 *s.*, 2 *d.; educ.* Grad., Twn. Prov. Taoyuan Agr. & Tech. Prof. Sch. 74; Pres., Chien Tao Construction Co. Ltd. 86-95; Dir., Twn. Regional Assc. of Gen. Contractors 91-94, Chief, Taoyuan Off. 91-94; *Add.* 18-46 Lin 6, Tahai Village, Tayuan Hsiang, Taoyuan County.

CHEN, KENG-CHIN
(See CHEN, KANG-CHIN 陳庚金)

CHEN, KUANG-YU
(See CHEN, KWANG-YU 陳光宇)

CHEN, KUEI-HUA 陳桂華
Nat. Policy Adv. to the Pres. 95-; *b.* Kwangtung July 19, '18; *m.* Yi, Kuei-chen; 1 *s.*, 1 *d.; educ.* 11th Class, Mil. Acad.; 18th Class, Army Coll.; 1st Sp. Class, CGSC, USA; 1st Class, Pragmatism Inst.; Div. Cmdr., 8th Reserved Div. & 32nd Div., ROC Army; C/S, 2nd ROC Army Corps; Dean, Pragmatism Inst.; V. C/S, GHQ, ROC Army; Dir.-Gen., Pers. Admin., MND 66-68, Dept. Chief, Gen. Staff for Pers. 68-72; Dir.-Gen., CPA 72-84; Min. of Pers., Exam. Yuan 84-94. *Publ.: A Study of*

Hitler's Unsuccessful Aggression on Russia; Add. 1 Shih Yuan Rd., Taipei.

CHEN, KUEI-MIAO 陳癸淼
Convener, NP 95-; Convener, Educ. Cttee., 88th Sess., Legis. Yuan; *b.* Twn. July 1, '34; *m.* Lu, Shu-mei; *2 s.,* 1 *d.; educ.* BA, NTNU; Tchr., Lectr., Assc. Prof. & Prof., NCHU; Part-time Prof., Tunghai U. & Providence U.; Chmn., Taichung City Cttee., KMT; Exec. Off., Twn. Prov. Cttee., KMT; Comr., TPG; Interim Mayor, Tainan City; Dir., Nat. Museum of Hist. *Publ.: Interpretations of Kung-sun Lung-tzu; Contemporary Studies of Ming-chia & Mohist Debates; Study of Renowned Pre-Chin Works;* etc.; *Add.* 1 Tsingtao E. Rd., Taipei.

CHEN, KWANG-YU 陳光宇
Mem., Control Yuan 93-; *b.* Shanghai Jan. 22, '32; *m.* Ou-Yang, Chin; 1 *s.,* 1 *d.; educ.* LL.B., NTU 54; Prosecutor, Taipei Dist. Court 57-64, Judge 64-67; Presiding Judge, Hsinchu Dist. Court 67-68; Judge, Taichung Br., Twn. High Court 68-70, Judge, Twn. High Court 70-73; Presiding Judge 73-76; Judge, Twn. High Court 70-73; Justice, Supreme Court 76-82, Public Prosecutor 82-87, Chief Public Prosecutor 87-93. *Publ.: A Study on the Modernization of Ch. Criminal Procedural Law Since 1902; Add.* 2 Chung Hsiao E. Rd., Sect. 1, Taipei.

CHEN, LIH J. 陳力俊
Prof., Dept. of Material Sc. & Engr., NTHU 79-; Pres., Ch. Soc. for Materials Sc. 91-; Ed., *Materials Chem. & Phys.* 92-; *b.* Chekiang Aug. 13, '46; *m.* Wu, Hsiang; 2 *s.; educ.* Ph.D., Phys., UC-Berkly. 74; BS, Phys., NTU 68; Chmn. & Dir., Dept. of Materials Sc. Cent. 84-85. *Publ.:* 200 referred papers in intl. jour.; 200 papers in conf. proceedings; 30 bk., monographs & others; *Add.* Dept. of Materials Sc., NTHU, Hsinchu.

CHEN, MASON MEI-SHENG 陳梅生
Pres., Ch. Med. Coll. 87-; *b.* Chekiang May 6, '23; *educ.* Ed.B., Nat. Sun Yat-Sen U.; Ed.M. & Ed.D., U. of Tennessee; Tchr. & Prin. 48-60; Sect. Chief, Dept. of Educ. 61-68; Expert, UNESCO 68-69; Dir., Twn. Prov. Inst. for Elementary Sch. Tchrs.' Inservice Educ. 70-76; Dir., Dept. of Higher Educ., MOE 76-79; Dir., Dept. of Educ., Kaohsiung City Govt. 79-82; Admin. V. Min. of Educ. 82-87; Prof., Grad. Inst. of Educ., NTNU 83-89. *Publ.:*

On Elementary Educ.; A Comparison Study of Math. Educ. in the US & ROC; Add. Ch. Med. Coll., 91 Hsueh Shih Rd., Taichung.

CHEN, MEI
(See CHENG, MEI 陳邁)

CHEN, MEI-SHENG
(See CHEN, MASON MEI-SHENG 陳梅生)

CHEN, MENG-LING 陳孟鈴
Mem., Control Yuan 93-; *b.* Twn. May 1, '34; *m.* Liou, Sin-chuan; 1 *s.,* 1 *d.; educ.* BA, Eng. Lit., Tamkang U. 58; Tchr., Dean, & Prin. 58-73; Magis., Taichung County 73-81; Comr., TPG 81-84, Comr., Dept. of Civil Aff. 84-87; V. Chmn., Twn. Prov. Cttee., KMT 87-90; Admin. V. Min. of the Int. 90; Pol. V. Min. of the Int. 90-93. *Publ.: Standard Eng. Grammar* (4 Vol.); *Res. of Soc. Worker System of Twn. Prov.; Add.* 2 Chung Hsiao E. Rd., Sect. 1, Taipei.

CHEN, MU-TSAI 陳木在
Admin. V. Min. of Finance 95-; *b.* Twn. Dec. 18, '45; *m.* Wang, Yu-mei; *educ.* BA, Tunghai U. 68; MA, NTU 72; Sect. Chief, Dept. of Monetary Aff., MOF 76-78, Asst. Dir. 78-80; Dir. & Sr. V. Pres., City Bk. of Taipei 80-84; Dep. Dir.-Gen., Dept. of Monetary Aff., MOF 84-89, Dir.-Gen. 89-91, Dir.-Gen., Bu. of Monetary Aff. 91-95. *Publ.: US Tax System Reform—Also of ROC's Tax System* 73; *Essays on Twn. Finance & Price Level* 73; *Money & Finance During Econ. Fluctuation* 77; *Twn's Financial Dev. & Strategies After the Retrocession* 78; *Issue of High Denominated Paper Money & Improving Combination of NT Dollar Denomination* 83; *Gen. Overview of ROC's Econ. Dev. Strategies* (2 Vol.) 87; *Add.* 2 Ai Kuo W. Rd., Taipei.

CHEN, PAN 陳槃
Mem., Acad. Sinica; *b.* Kwangtung Feb. 2, '06; *m.* Tseng, Chu-yin; 4 *s.,* 1 *d.; educ.* BA, Nat. Sun Yat-Sen U.; Res. Asst. 31-40; Assc. Res. Fel., Inst. of Hist. & Philology, Acad. Sinica 40-46; Prof., NTU 55-59. *Publ.: Additional Commentary on "Shi-chi" in Shi-chia; Remarks on Some Works of the Occult Sc. of Prognostics of Ancient Ch.; A Review of Treatises on Ancient Ch. Hist.; Add.* Acad. Sinica, Nankang, Taipei.

CHEN, PAO-CHUAN 陳寶川

Nat. Policy Adv. to the Pres. 90-; Adv., CBC 87-; Standing Sup., Const. Soc., ROC; Standing Sup., Constitutionality Soc., ROC; Chmn., Unity & Self-Reliance Assn., ROC; *b.* Twn. Mar. 22, '17; 2 *s.,* 2 *d.; educ.* Grad., Nat. Taipei Inst. of Tech. 37; Grad., Dept. of Law, N.E. U. 41; 2-year Res., Kyoto Imperial U.; Assc. Prof., Twn. Prov. Coll. of Laws & Com. 45-47; Assc. Prof., NTU 46-50; Mgr. & Sect. Chief, Planning & Inspecting Sect., Chang Hwa Cml. Bk. 50-53; Gen. Mgr. & Dir., Medium Business Bk. of Taipei 53-64; Chmn., Kuohua Life Ins. Co. 64-71; Mem., NA 69-91; Chmn., Medium Business Bk. of Twn. 71-77, Chang Hwa Cml. Bk. 77-83, & First Cml. Bk. 83-87. *Publ.: Res. of Entrepreneurialization of Govt. Bk.; Implementation of the Const. & Twn. Econ.; A Study of the Promotion of Twn. as the Trade & Monetary Cent. in the Far E.; Add.* 34 Lane 279, Fu Hsing S. Rd., Sect. 1, Taipei.

CHEN, PO-CHANG 陳伯璋

Pres., Nat. Hualien Tchrs. Coll. 93-; *b.* Twn. Dec. 20, '48; *m.* Lu, Meei Quay; 1 *s.; educ.* Ed.B., NTNU 72, ED.M. 77, Ph.D. 84; Asst. Resr., NTNU 75-77, Instr. 77-85, Assc. Prof. 85-91; Postdoctor, London U. 85-86; Prof. & Dir. of Extension, NTNU 91-93. *Publ.: Secondary Educ.* 82; *Hidden Curriculum Res.* 85; *Curriculum Res. & Educ. Innovation* 87; *Ideology & Educ.* 88; *Neil & Summerhill Sch.* 89; *Open Educ.* 91; *Res. on Educ. Issues* 87; *New Trend of Educ. Res.—Quantitative Method* 89; *Add.* 123 Hua Hsi, Hualien.

CHEN, ROBERTO MING-TEH 陳明德

Dir.-Gen., TECO in Miami 96-; *b.* Taipei Nov. 1, '51; *m.* Ramos, Manuela; 2 *s,; educ.* BA, NCU 73; MA 77, Ph.D. 80, U. Complutense de Madrid ; 3rd, 2nd, 1st Sec., Emb. in Uruguay 82-86; Sect. Chief, 2nd Dep. Dir.-Gen., Dep. Dir.-Gen., Cent. & S. Am. Aff., MOFA 86-92; Rep. to Uruguay 92-94; Dep. Dir.-Gen., Cent. & S. Am. Aff., MOFA 94-96. *Publ.: Econ. Aspects of British Foreign Policy Toward the Spanish Civil War; Add.* 2333 Ponce de Leon Boulevard, Suite 610, Coral Gables, FL 33134, USA.

CHEN, RONG-JYE 陳榮傑

Dep. Rep., TECRO, USA 95-; *b.* Twn. Sept. 19, '43; *m.* Chen Chang, Yueh-ho; 2 *d.; educ.* BA, NTU 67; LL.M., So. Methodist U., USA 73; Juris Dr. 79; Sp., Dept. of Treaty & Legal Aff., MOFA; 3rd Sec., Emb. in Saudi Arabia; Sect. Chief & Dep. Dir., Dept. of Treaty & Legal Aff., MOFA; Counsl., Emb. in S. Africa; Rep., Observer's Mission of the ROC in Namibia; Adjunct Prof. of Law, Soochow U. & Cent. Police Coll.; Dep. Sec.-Gen. & Sec.-Gen., SEF; Adv., MAC; Pres., *Independence Evening Post & Independence Morning Post;* Counsl., MOFA. *Publ.: The Theory & Practice of Extradition* 86; *The For. Sovereign Immunities Act of 1976 & Its Application to Cml. Transactions Involving For. States; Co-ed., Ch. Yearbk. of Intl. Law & Aff.; Add.* 4201 Wisconsin Avenue, NW, Washington, DC 20016, USA.

CHEN, SHEN-LING
(See CHEN, HSING-LING 陳燊齡)

CHEN, SHOU-SHAN 陳守山

Nat. Policy Adv. to the Pres. 91-; *b.* Twn. Feb. 20, '21; *m.* Chen Huang, Shu-nu; 1 *s.,* 5 *d.; educ.* 16th Class, Mil. Acad. 40; 6th Class, Army CGSC 55; 13th Regular Class, Armed Forces Joint Staff Coll. 65; 11th Class, Nat. War Coll. of Res. 70; Gen. Off. Course, War Coll., Armed Forces U. 72; Cmdt., Fu Hsing Kang Coll. 73-75; Exec. Off., Pol. Warfare Dept., MND 75-76; CG, Army Tng. & Combat Dev. Com. 78-79; CG, 8th Field Army 79-81; Dep. C-in-C, ROC Army 81; C-in-C, Twn. Garrison GHQ, & concur. CG, Twn. Corps Area Cmd. 81-89; V. Min. of Nat. Def. 89-91. *Publ.: Prospects & Retrospect of the Build-up of the ROC Armed Forces in the Past 60 Years; A Study of the Dev. of E. Twn.; Add.* P.O. Box 90001, Taipei.

CHEN, SHOU-AN
(See CHEN, SHOW-AN 陳壽安)

CHEN, SHOW-AN 陳壽安

Prof., Dept. of Chem. Engr., NTHU; *b.* Fukien Apr. 8, '40; *m.* Chen Pi, Chuan-chih; 2 *d.; educ.* Sr. Chemist, UniRoyal Inc. 69-70; Res. Scientist, W.R. Grace & Co. 70-73; Assc. Prof., Dept. of Chem. Engr., NTHU 73-74. *Publ.: A Note on the Thermodynamics of Surface Tension of Binary Solution; Polymerization; Emulsion Polymerization: Theory of Particle Size Distribution in Copolymerization System; Oriented Surface & Fibrillar Morphologies of Electrochemically Polymerized Polypyrrole at Wylene/Water Interface; Add.* 100-12 Chien Chung Rd., Hsinchu.

CHEN, SHUI-BIAN 陳水扁
Mayor, Taipei City 94-; Mem., CSC, DPP; *b.* Twn. Feb. 18, '51; *m.* Wu, Shu-chen; 1 *s.,* 1 *d.; educ.* LL.B., NTU 74; Head, Formosa Intl. Marine & Cml. Law Off. 76-89; Mem., Taipei CCoun. 81-85; Mem., CSC, DPP 87-89; Mem., Legis. Yuan 89-94, Exec. Off., DPP Caucus 90-93, Convener, Nat. Def. Cttee. 92-94, Convener, Organic Laws Cttee. 93, Mem., Jud. Cttee. 94; Chmn., Formosa Found. 90-94; V. Pres., Taipei N. Gate Rotary Club 93. *Publ.: Series on Justice* (4 Vol.); *Conflict, Compromise & Progress; Nat. Def. Black Box & White Paper; Through the Line Between Life & Death; Add.* 1 Shih Fu Rd., Taipei.

CHEN, SHUI-PIAN
(See CHEN, SHUI-BIAN 陳水扁)

CHEN, STARK 陳信光
Pres., Fortune Battery Corp. 89-; *b.* Twn. June 27, '54; *m.* Liao, Fortune; 1 *s.,* 1 *d.; educ.* BEE, Mingshin Inst. of Tech. & Com. 73; Elec. Engr., Tatung Co. Ltd. 75-88; *Add.* 8th Fl., 815 Chung Hsiao E. Rd., Sect. 5, Taipei.

CHEN, STEPHEN S.F. 陳錫蕃
Dep. Sec.-Gen. to the Pres. 96-; *b.* Nanking Feb. 11, '34; *m.* Chen, Rosa Te; 2 *s.,* 1 *d.; educ.* BA & MA, U. of Santo Tomas, Manila; Passed the For. Service Exam. 60; Served in Emb. in the Philippines 53-60; Sp. Asst., MOFA 60-63; 2nd & 1st Sec., Emb. in Brazil 63-69; Chief, 2nd Sect., Dept. of Latin Am. Aff., MOFA 69-71; Counsl., Emb. in Argentina 71-72; Chargé d'affaires, Emb. in Bolivia 72-73; Consul-Gen., Atlanta 73-79; Dir., CCNAA, Atlanta 79-80; Dir., CCNAA, Chicago 80-82; Consul-Gen. attached to the Secretariat, MOFA 82-84, Dir., Dept. of Treaty & Legal Aff. 84-86, Dir., Dept. of Intl. Org. 86-88.; Dir.-Gen., CCNAA, Los Angeles 88-89, Dep. Rep., CCNAA, Washington, D.C. 89-93; Admin. V. Min. of MOFA 93-96. *Publ.: A Critical Study of Sino-Filipino Rel.; Add.* 122 Chungking S. Rd. Sect. 1, Taipei.

CHEN, STEVEN Y. 陳堯
Bd. Chmn., Chunghwa Telecom. Co., Ltd. 96-; Mem., CC, KMT 93-; Pres., Ch. Inst. of Elec. Engr. 95-; *b.* Twn.

Mar. 7, '34; *m.* Chou, Tsai-hsing; 3 *s.; educ.* B., NCKU 59; M., NCU 66; Studied, Am. U. 72; Dir., Pers. Dept., Directorate Gen. of Telecom. 68-74, Dep. Insp.-Gen. 74-75, Exec. Sec., Res. & Planning Cttee. 75-81, Dir., Traffic Dept. 81-82, Insp.-Gen. 82-85, V. Chmn., Res. & Planning Cttee. 85-87; Mng. Dir., Cent. Twn. Telecom. Admin. 87-89; Dep. Dir.-Gen., Directorate Gen. of Telecom.; Dir.-Gen., Directorate Gen. of Telecom., MOTC 93-96. *Publ.: The Application of Behavior Sc. on Business Mng.; Add.* 31 Ai Kuo E. Rd., Taipei.

CHEN, TAN-SUN 陳唐山
Magis., Tainan County 93-; Adv., Cent. for Twn. Intl. Rel. 88-; *b.* Twn. Sept. 16, '36; *m.* Lin, June; 3 *s.; educ.* BS, NTU 59; Ph.D., Purdue U. 72; Pres., Twn. Assn. of Am. 78-79, Fed. of Twn. Assn. 79-83, Formosan Assn. for Public Aff. 84-86, & Twn. Found. 87-91; Mem., Legis. Yuan 93. *Publ.: Returning to the Motherland—Twn.; Add.* 36 Min Chih Rd., Hsinying, Tainan County.

CHEN, TANG-SHAN
(See CHEN, TAN-SUN 陳唐山)

CHEN, TIEN-MAO 陳田錨
Spkr., Kaohsiung CCoun. 81-; Mem., CC & CSC, KMT 93-; Pres., Our Cml. Bk. 92-; V. Pres., Twn. Cement Corp. 94-; Pres., Shin-Kao Gas Co. Ltd. 83-; *b.* Twn. Apr. 16, '28; *m.* Huang, Shu-hui; 2 *s.,* 1 *d.; educ.* Grad., Kinki U., Japan; Mem., Kaohsiung CCoun. 58-73, Dep. Spkr. 64-68, Spkr. 68-73; Bd. Mem., Twn. Cement Corp. 82-85 & 89-91, Standing Bd. Mem. 91-94; *Add.* 12th Fl., 58 Chung Cheng 2nd Rd., Kaohsiung.

CHEN, TING-AN 陳聽安
Comr., Exam. Yuan 96-; Prof., NCU 72-; Consultant, CEPD 78; *b.* Kiangsu Oct. 8, '33; *m.* Sy, Chung-ao; 2 *s.; educ.* BA, NCHU 61; Res., Friburg U., Germany; Dr. in Econ., Münster U. 69; Dir., Grad. Sch. of Public Finance, NCU 73-81, Dean, Sch. of Law & Com. 81-84, Dir., Grad. Sch. of Econ. 85-87; Chmn., Tax Reform Com. 87-89; Visiting Prof., Cambridge U. & Harvard U. 89-90 & 90-91. *Publ.: The Relationship Between Population & Tax Policies* 76; *Fiscal Reform & Econ. Dev.* 81; *A Study on European Single*

Mart 91; *New Trend of Econ. Regulation Toward the 21st Century* 95; *Add.* Exam. Yuan, 1 Shih Yuan Rd., Wenshan, Taipei.

CHEN, TING-CHONG 陳廷寵
Personal C/S to the Pres. 93-; *b.* Kiangsu Sept. 4, '31; *m.* Chan, Chia-tai; *2 s., 1 d.; educ.* 24th Class, Ch. Mil. Acad. 53; Army CGSC, Germany 66; War Coll., Armed Forces U. 76; Platoon Leader; Battery Cmdr.; Bn. Cmdr.; Divisional Artillery Cmdr.; Div. Cmdr.; Corps Cmdr.; Cmdr., Field Army; Dep. C-in-C, ROC Army; Dep. Dir., Pol. Warfare Dept., MND; C-in-C, ROC Army 91-93; *Add.* Off. of the Pres., Taipei.

CHEN, TING-CHUNG
(See CHEN, TING-CHONG 陳廷寵)

CHEN, TING-HSIN
(See CHEN, DING-SHINN 陳定信)

CHEN, TING-HUEI 陳庭輝
Chmn., Yangming Marine Trans. Corp. 95-; Chmn., Ch. Merchants Steam Navigation Co. Ltd. 91-; Chmn., Ch. Shipowner's Assn. of Taipei 95-; *b.* Twn. Dec. 10, '36; *m.* Chen Chiu, Mei-yu; 1 *s.,* 1 *d.; educ.* B., Business Mng., NCKU 60; Mgr., Ch. Merchants Steam Navigation Co. Ltd. 78-81; V. Pres., Yangming Marine Trans. Corp. 81-88, Pres. 88-95; Sec.-Gen., Assn. of Shipping Services 84-95; *Add.* 5th Fl., 53 Huai Ning St., Taipei.

CHEN, TING-HUI
(See CHEN, TING-HUEI 陳庭輝)

CHEN, TSO-CHEN 陳佐鎮
Dir.-Gen., Nat. Bu. of Standards (NBS), MOEA 94-; *b.* Twn. Aug. 1, '42; *m.* Chang, Kuo-ying; 2 *s.; educ.* LL.B., NCHU 75; Chief, Trademarks Div., NBS, MOEA 78-80; Dep. Dir. & Dir., Trademarks Dept., NBS, MOEA 82-84 & 84-88; Dir., Patents Dept., NBS, MOEA 88; Dep. Dir.-Gen., NBS, MOEA 88-94. *Publ.:* Various publ. concerning IPR protection in Twn.; *Add.* 19th Fl., 185 Hsin Hai Rd., Sect. 2, Taipei.

CHEN, WEI-CHAO
(See CHEN, WEI-JAO 陳維昭)

CHEN, WEI-JAO 陳維昭
Pres., NTU 93-; Prof., Surgery & Public Health, NTU 83-; *b.* Twn. Nov. 15, '39; *m.* Tang, Shiang-yang; 1 *s.,* 1 *d.; educ.* MD, NTU 65; DMS, Tohoku U. Japan 73; MPH, Johns Hopkins U. 89; Resident, NTU Hosp. 66-69, Chief Resident 69-70, Visiting Staff 70-72; Lectr., Coll. of Med., NTU 75-79, Assc. Prof. 79-83; Visiting Res. Assc. Prof., U. of Cincinnati 81-82; Dep. Dir., NTU Hosp. 87-91; Dean, Coll. of Med., NTU 91-93. *Publ.: Ah-jen, Ah-i & I—A Story about the Separation of Siamese Twins;* & more than 100 sc. publ.; *Add.* 5th Fl., 15 Hsin Yi Rd., Sect. 2, Taipei.

CHEN, WEN-HWA 陳文華
Prof., Coll. of Engr., NTHU 92-; Ed.-in-Chief, *Ch. Jour. of Mech.* 86-, & *Proceedings of NScC, Series B, ROC* 94-; *b.* Twn. Aug. 15, '48; *m.* Chang, Hsiao-chen; 2 *s.; educ.* BS, Engr., NCKU 71; Ph.D., Georgia Inst. of Tech. 77; Prof. & Head, Dept. of Power Mech. Engr., NTHU 81-88, Chmn., Cttee. of Res. & Dev. 88-92. *Publ.:* Over 100 res. papers in mech.-related areas; *Add.* Coll. of Engr., NTHU.

CHEN, WU-FU 陳五福
Nat. Policy Adv. to the Pres. 96-; Pres., Mu Kuang Rehabilitation Cent. for the Blind 59-; *b.* Twn. Dec. 20, '18; *m.* Chen, Len-len; 2 *s.,* 3 *d.; educ.* MD, NTU 43; DMS, Fukushima Med. U. 66; Dir., Wu Fu Eye Clinic 45-93; *Add.* 108 Chung Cheng Rd., Lotung, Ilan County.

CHEN, WU-HSIUNG 陳武雄
(See CHEN, CHIEN-WU 陳千武)

CHEN, YAO
(See CHEN, STEVEN Y. 陳堯)

CHEN, YIH-YOUNG 陳義揚
Pres., Nat. Open U. 91-; *b.* Chekiang Sept. 15, '43; *m.* Cheng, Jui-shan; 2 *s.; educ.* BEE, NCKU 65; MEE, NCTU 68, & Washington U. 70; Ph.D., EE, Tulane U. 74; Assc. Prof., Coll. of Engr., NCTU 74-77, Prof. 77-83; Dept. Dir., NYC 78-82; Dir., Bu. of Intl. Cul. & Educ. Rel. 82-83; V. Pres., St. John's U. 83-84; Dean of Student Aff., NCTU 85-87, Dean of Acad. Aff. 87-91. *Publ.: Automation of Pathology Labs.* 74; *Add.* 172 Chung Cheng Rd., Luchou, Taipei County.

CHEN, YING-LIN
(See CHEN, ENG-RIN 陳瑩霖)

CHEN, YING-WEN 陳膺文
(See CHEN, LI 陳黎)

CHEN, YU
(See CHEN, ARTHUR YU 陳豫)

CHEN, YU-CHU 陳毓駒
Rep., Taipei Rep. Off. in Denmark 94-; *b.* Hupei Aug. 17, '32; *m.* Yang, Chiu-ping; 3 *s.,* 1 *d.; educ.* BPS, NTU; 3rd Sec., Emb. in S. Korea 61-62; 2nd Sec. & Consul, Emb. in the Philippines 65-67; Consul, Consl. Gen. in Los Angeles 67-74; Sect. Chief, Dept. of N. Am. Aff., MOFA 74-77, Dep. Dir. 77-80; Dep. Dir.-Gen., CCNAA, Los Angeles 80-82; Dir.-Gen., CCNAA, Seattle 82-85, CCNAA, Houston 85-87; Dir., Dept. of Info. & Cul. Aff., & Spokesman, MOFA 87-90; Rep., Taipei Rep. Off. in Singapore 90-94; *Add.* Amaliegade 3, 2, 1256 Copenhagen K, Denmark.

CHEN, YUNG-CHIEH
(See CHEN, RONG-JYE 陳榮傑)

CHENG, CHIA-LIN 成嘉玲
Pres., World Coll. of Jour. & Comms. 91-; *b.* Tientsin Sept. 17, '37; *m.* Chow, Liang-yen; 1 *s.,* 1 *d.; educ.* B., Econ., NTU 61; Ph.D., Agr. Econ., U. of Hawaii 68; Asst. Prof., NCHU 68-69; Head, Dept. of Econ., Soochow U. 77, Dir. 78-79, Dean, Sch. of Business 83-90. *Publ.: A Comparative Study of Employment & Income of Public & Private U. Grad.—An Analysis of the Utility of Govt. Investment in Public & Private U.; Add.* 1 Lane 17, Mu Cha Rd., Taipei.

CHENG, CHIEN-JEN
(See CHEN, CHIEN-JEN 程建人)

CHENG, FENG-SHIH 鄭逢時
Dir.-Gen., Dept. of Intra- & Inter-Party Rel., CC, KMT 93-; Mem., Legis. Yuan 93-; *b.* Twn. Dec. 27, '41; *m.* Wang, Lin-hui; 1 *s.; educ.* Grad., Supplementary Open Jr. Coll. for PA, NCU; MPA, Tunghai U.; Mem., Taipei CoCoun. 68-73; Mem., NA 73-79; Mem., TPA 81-93; Dep. Dir., Twn. Prov. Cttee., KMT 89-93; *Add.* 158 Chung Shan Rd., Sect. 1, Panchiao, Taipei County.

CHENG, LIANG-HSIUNG 程良雄
Dir., Twn. Prov. Lib. at Taichung 91-; *b.* Twn. Aug. 23, '37; *m.* Lin, Shu-tzu; 2 *s.; educ.* B., Agr. Educ., NCHU 60; Ed.M., NCU 76; Dir., Pao Shan Middle Sch., Hsinchu 80-81; Dir., Dept. of Educ., Hsinchu County Govt. 81-82; Dir., Dept. of Educ., Hsinchu City Govt. 82-84, Sec.-Gen. 84-86; Sr. Sp. & concur. Dir., Secretariat, Dept. of Educ., TPG 86-91. *Publ.: A Study of Campus Planning & Mng. of Secondary Sch. in Taipei; Add.* 291-3 Ching Wu Rd., Taichung.

CHENG, MEI 陳邁
Prin. Architect, Fei & Cheng Assc. 73-; Bd. Chmn., Cosmos Inc. 90-; Exec. Dir., Taipei Architects Assn., & Architectural Inst. of the ROC 91-; *b.* Shanghai May 1, '30; *m.* Su, Cecilia; 2 *d.; educ.* B., Architectural Engr., NCKU 62; Res., Swiss Federal Inst., Switzerland 65; M., Architecture, MIT 70; Architect, W. Niehus Architects & Assc., Switzerland 65-68; Architect, Verner Johnson Architects & Assc., USA 70-71; Chmn. & Assc. Prof., Dept. of Architecture, Tunghai U. 71-75; Assc. Prof., Chung Yuan Christian U. 75-79; Assc. Prof., Nat. Twn. Inst. of Tech. 79-83; Standing Sup., Architectural Inst. of the ROC 79-83 & 85-87; Standing Dir., Nat. Architects Alliance of the ROC 80-84; *Add.* 36-3 Lane 260, Kuang Fu S. Rd., Taipei.

CHENG, SHU-MIN
(See CHENG, SU-MING 鄭淑敏)

CHENG, SHUI-CHIH 鄭水枝
V. Pres., Control Yuan 93-; *b.* Twn. Apr. 10, '26; 7 *s.; educ.* Taipei Mun. Tchrs. Coll.; Sun Yat-sen Inst. on Policy Res. & Dev.; Dir., Jr. High Sch., & Prin., Elementary Sch. 46-54; Sec., MOI 54-60; Township Mayor 60-64; Mem., CoCoun. 64-70, & Legis. Yuan 70-78; Comr., TPG 78-81, Comr., Dept. of Recon. 81-84; Pol. V. Min. of the Int. 84-87; Chmn., COLA 87-89; Dep. Sec.-Gen., CC, KMT 89-90; Nat. Policy Adv. to the Pres. 89-93; Chmn., Cent. Motion Picture Corp. 90-93; *Add.* 110 Chi Chih St., Shulin, Taipei County.

CHENG, SU-MING 鄭淑敏
Chmn. of the Bd., CTV 96-; *b.* Taipei Apr. 7, '46; *m.* Wei, Duan; *educ.* BA, NCKU 68; M., Mass Comms., Université Catholique de Louvain, Belgium 72; Studied at Yale U. 77; Ed. & Screener, CTS 72-75; Producer,

CTS 75-79; Pub. & Ed.-in-Chief, *Ch. Times Mag.*; Dep. Dir., Dept. of Compilation & Transl., GIO 83-84; Dep. Mgr., CTS 84-88; Exec. V. Pres., CTS Cul. Ent. 88-91; Mgr., CTS 91-94; Chmn., CCA 94-96, Nat. Endowment for Cul. & Arts 94-96. *Publ.:* Numerous articles & bk.; *Add.* CTV, 120 Chung Yang Rd., Nankang, Taipei.

CHENG, TIEN-SHOU 鄭天授
Dir.-Gen., TECO in Boston 96-; *b.* Fukien July 11, '46; *m.* Tung, Wen-wen; 2 *s.; educ.* BA, NCU 68; MA, NTU 73; MS, Georgetown U. 83; Counsl., Chargé d'Affaires, Emb. in the Commonwealth of Dominica 84-88; Dir., FETO, Bangkok 88-89; Dep. Dir., Off. of the Pers., MOFA 89-90; Dir., CCNAA in Washington, D.C. 90-93; Dir.-Gen., TECO in Toronto 93-96; *Add.* 99 Summer St., Suite 801, Boston, MA 02110, USA.

CHENG, TIEN-TSO
(See TSONG, TIEN T. 鄭天佐)

CHENG, TING-WANG
(See CHENG, TING-WONG 鄭丁旺)

CHENG, TING-WONG 鄭丁旺
Pres., NCCU 94-; *b.* Twn. Feb. 15, '42; *m.* Cheng Chen, Yueh-hua; 3 *d.; educ.* BA, NCCU 64, MA 68; MA, U. of Missouri-Columbia 70, Ph.D. 74; Asst. Prof., Indiana U. 74-75; Assc. Prof., Prof., Dept. Chair, Grad. Prog. Chair, NCCU 75-84; Prof. & Dean, Coll. of Com., NCCU 85-91; Prof. & Provost, NCU 92-94. *Publ.: Current Value Acct.* 79; *Intermediate Acct.* 93; *Introductory Acct.* 94; *Advanced Acct.* 94; *Add.* 64 Chih Nan Rd., Sect. 2, Wenshan, Taipei.

CHENG, WEN-HUA
(See TZEN, WEN-HUA 鄭文華)

CHENG, WEN-TUNG 鄭文銅
Spkr., Nantou CoCoun. 94-; Bd. Chmn., Puli Farmers' Assn. 93-; *b.* Twn. June 19, '48; *m.* Wang, Meng-hua; 2 *s.; educ.* Ling Tung Coll.; *Add.* 663 Chung Hsing Rd., Nantou.

CHENG YEN 證嚴
Dharma M.; Pres., Buddhist Compassion Relief Tzu Chi Assn.; Chmn., Tzu Chi Found., Tzu Chi Gen. Hosp., Tzu Chi Jr. Coll. of Nursing, & Tzu Chi Coll. of Med.; *b.* Twn. May 14, '37; *educ.* Tien Long Buddhist Acad.; Hon. Dr., Sociology, Ch. U. of Hong Kong 93. *Publ.: Still Thoughts* (2 Vol.); *3 Essentials of Pure Genesis; Treasury Hunt; Lectures on 37 Principles of Enlightenment; Still Thoughts, Wisdom, & Love; On Sutra of 8 Great Ways of Enlightenment; A Mind of Equanimity; 20 Difficulties of Humanity; After Breakfast Talks; Tzu Chi Lamp of Heart; Kindness & Compassion; Sympathetic Joy & Total Dedication; The Pure & Clean Wisdom; Dharma M. Cheng Yen's Lotus of Pure Heart; Morning Dialogues of Still Thoughts; Return to the Hometown of My Mind; Joyful & Even-Minded; Tzu Chi Lotus of Heart; Wisdom of Life; Words for Tzu Chi World; Spring of Wisdom Words; Bodhisattva in Our Life; Joy of Giving; The Clear Mind; Ease of Mind; Add.* 21 Kanglo Village, Hsincheng, Hualien County.

CHENG, YUNG-CHI 鄭永齊
Mem., Acad. Sinica 94-; Prog. Dir., Dev. Therapeutical Chemotherapy, Yale Comprehensive Cancer Cent. 90-, Prof. of Pharmacology & Internal Med. 89-; Henry Bronson Prof. of Pharmacology, Sch. of Med., Yale U. 89-; *b.* England Dec. 29, '44; *m.* Cheng, Elaine H.C.; 2 *s.; educ.* BS, Tunghai U. 66; Ph.D., Brown U.; Postdoctoral Res. Staff in Pharmacology with Dr. W.H. Prusoff, Yale U. 72-73; Res. Assc., Dept. of Pharmacology, Sch. of Med., Yale U. 73-74; Asst. Prof., Dept. of Pharmacology, State U. of New York 74-77, Assc. Prof. 77-79, Sr. Cancer Res. Scientist, Roswell Park Memorial Inst. 74-76; Am. Leukemia Soc. Scholar 76-81; Cancer Res. Scientist, Dept. of Experimental Therapeutics, Roswell Park Memorial Inst. 77-79; Head, Drug Dev. Prog., Lineberg Cancer Res. Cent., USA 79-89; Prof., Dept. of Pharmacology & Med., U. of N. Carolina 79-89; Sp. Chair, Inst. of Biomedical Sc., Acad. Sinica 87. *Publ.:* Over 200 articles on related fields; *Add.* 961 Baldwin Rd., Woodbridge, CT, USA.

CHERN, JINN-LIH 陳進利
Mem., Control Yuan 93-; *b.* Twn. Sept. 7, '42; *m.* Wang, Jung; 1 *s.,* 2 *d.; educ.* B., Agr., NCHU 66; M., Agr., Kyushu U., Japan 73, Ph.D. 78; Assc. Prof., Dept. of Biology, Nat. Chang Hua U. of Educ. 78-81, Dir. 80-86, Prof. 82-93; Visiting Prof., U. of Wisconsin 86-87; Bd. Chmn., Assn. for the Promotion of Aborigines' Welfare

88-93; Adv., CC, KMT 89-93; Visiting Prof., Grad. Sch. of Agr., Kyushu U. 90-91. *Publ.: Phylogenetic Studies on Sect. Sativa by Use of Electrophoretic Patterns; Electrophoretic Estimation of Progenitor of the C Genome Species Constituting Tetraploid-Punctata (BBCC); RFLP Analysis of Introgressed Segment in a Near Isogenic Line of Rice for the Bacterial Blight Resistance Gene Xa-10; Add.* 2 Chung Hsiao E. Rd., Sect. 1, Taipei.

CHERN, SHIING-SHEN 陳省身

Mem., Acad. Sinica; Emeritus Math. Educator; Prof. Emeritus, U. of Calif. 79-; Dir. Emeritus, Math. Sc. Res. Inst. 84-; Fel., Third World Acad. of Sc.; Mem., NAS, Am. Math. Soc., Am. Acad. of Arts & Sc., New York Acad. of Sc., Am. Philosophical Soc., Indian Math. Soc., Brazilian Acad. of Sc., Royal Soc. of London, Acad. Peloritana, London Math. Soc., Acad. des Sc. of Paris, Acad. der Lincei of Rome; *b.* Chekiang Oct. 26, '11; *m.* Chern, Shih-ning; 1 *s.,* 1 *d.; educ.* BS, Nankai U. 30; MS, NTHU, Peiping 34; D.Sc., U. of Hamburg 36, Hon. D.Sc. 72; Hon. D.Sc., U. of Chicago 69, & State U. of New York-Stony Brook 85; LL.D. Honoris Causa, Ch. U. of Hong Kong 69; Hon. Dr. Math., Eidgenossische Technische Hochschule, Switzerland 82; Hon. D.Sc., U. of Notre Dame, USA 94; Prof., Math., NTHU, Peiping 37-43; Mem., Inst. for Advanced Study, Princeton U. 43-45; Acting Dir., Inst. of Math., Acad. Sinica 46-48; Prof., Math., U. of Chicago 49-60, & UC-Berkly. 60-79; Dir., Math. Sc. Res. Inst. 81-84; Dir., Inst. of Math., Tientsin; *Add.* 8336 Kent Ct., El Cerrito, CA 94530, USA.

CHIA, CHUNG-CHUAN 翟宗泉

Mem., Control Yuan 93-; *b.* Anhwei July 6, '31; *m.* Tan, Li-yu; 2 *s.,* 1 *d.; educ.* LL.B., NTU 54; Pres., Kinmen Dist. Court 67-69, & Hualien Dist. Court 69-73; Chief Procurator, Public Prosecutors' Off., Changhua, & Tainan dist. courts 73-82; Chief Procurator, Public Prosecutors' Off., Kaohsiung Dist. Court 82-85, & Tainan Br., Twn. High Court 85-89; Admin. V. Min. of Justice 89-93. *Publ.:* About 20 articles on legal theories & practices of the freedom of speech, ass., & demonstrations in the US & UK; *Add.* 2 Chung Hsiao E. Rd., Sect. 1, Taipei.

CHIA, YU-HUEI
(See JEA, YU-HUEI 賈玉輝)

CHIANG, CHIA-HSING 蔣家興

V. Chmn., RDEC 94-; *b.* Twn. July 15, '39; *m.* Lee, Chiou-yueh; 1 *s.; educ.* Nat. Taipei Inst. of Tech. 60; MS, Materials Engr., N. Carolina State U. 73, Ph.D. 77; Assc. Prof. & Head, Mech. Engr. Dept., Tamkang U. 78-81; Sr. Staff Engr., CEPD 81-84; Dir., Ovs. Ch. Scholars & Students Service Cent., NYC 84-87, Acting Chmn. 87-94. *Publ.: Compressive Behavior of Angle-Wound Fiber Composites; Influence of Graphite on Young's Modulus of Cast Iron;* etc.; *Add.* 11th Fl., 4 Chung Hsiao W. Rd., Sect. 1, Taipei.

CHIANG, CHUNG-LING 蔣仲苓

Min. of Nat. Def., & concur. Min. of State 94-; Mem., CC, KMT 93-; *b.* Chekiang Sept. 21, '22; *m.* Wu, Su; 4 *s.,* 1 *d.; educ.* 16th Class, Mil. Acad. 40; 6th Class, Army CGSC 55; Gen. Off. Course, War Coll., Armed Forces U. 76; 26th Infantry Div. Cmdr. 68-72; 9th Corps Cmdr. 73-75; 6th Field Army Cmdr. 77-79; CG, Kinmen Def. Cmd. 79-81; C-in-C, ROC Army 81-88; Exec. V. Chief of the Gen. Staff, MND 88-89; Personal C/S to the Pres. 89-92; Nat. Policy Adv. to the Pres. 92-94; *Add.* 122 Chungking S. Rd., Sect. 1, Taipei.

CHIANG, FENG-CHI
(See JIANG, FENG-CHYI 江奉琪)

CHIANG, HAO 姜豪

Admin. V. Min. of Justice 93-; *b.* Kiangsu Dec. 24, '32; *m.* Chiang, Soun-san; 1 *s.,* 2 *d.; educ.* LL.B., NTU; Judge, Taichung Dist. Court 69-73, & Taipei Dist. Court 73-79; Presiding Judge, Kaohsiung Dist. Court 79-80, & Taipei Dist. Court 80-84; Judge, Twn. High Court 84-85, Procurator, Public Prosecutors' Off. 85; Counsl., MOJ 85, Sec.-Gen. 85-91; Procurator, Public Prosecutor Gen.'s Off., Supreme Court 90-91; Chief Procurator, Public Prosecutors' Off., Keelung Dist. Court 91-93. *Publ.: Res. on the Law Governing the Disposition of Juvenile Delinquents; Disposition of Financial Cases; Add.* 130 Chungking S. Rd., Sect. 1, Taipei.

CHIANG, KAI-SHEK, MADAME
(See SOONG, MAYLING 宋美齡)

CHIANG, KUAN-FENG 蔣冠峰

Dir.-Gen., 3rd Bu., Off. of the Pres. 94-; *b.* Chekiang Sept. 27, '38; *m.* Lee, Lin-chun; 1 *d.; educ.* Ch. Army

Acad. 63; Army Coll., Armed Forces U. 73, War Coll. 87; Artillery Cmdr., 193rd Div., ROC Army 78-80; C/S, 292nd Div., ROC Army 80-83; Sect. Chief, Planning Bu., Army GHQ 83-85; Artillery Cmdr., 6th Army Corps 85-88; Dep. Chief Aide-de-Camp, Off. of the Pres. 88-91; Dep. Dir.-Gen., 3rd Bu., Off. of the Pres.; *Add.* 2nd Fl., 17 Lane 17, Kuang Fu S. Rd., Taipei.

CHIANG, NANCY ZI 蔣徐乃錦
Pres., Nat. YWCA of the ROC 91-; Chmn., Chronicle Sec. Investment Trust Co. Ltd. 93-; Bd. Mem., World Vision of Twn. 89-, Kingvic Investment Co. Ltd. 88-, & Chinesisch-Deutscher Kultur- und Wirtschaftsverband 88-; Mem., Exec. Cttee., World YWCA 87-; Bd. Mem., Taipei Intl. Community Cul. Found., & Chmn., Prog. Cttee. 84-; Exec. Dir., Raw Materials Ltd. 78-; *b.* Shanghai Mar. 24, '38; *m.* Chiang, Alan Hsiao-wen (deceased); 1 *d.; educ.* BA, NTU; MS, U. of So. Calif.; Lectr., Ch. Cul. U. 63-64; 1st V. Pres., Intl. Women's Club 64-65 & 66-67, & Taipei YWCA 69-70 & 73-75; Exec. Sec., Intl. Aff. Off., CTC, & Producer 73-80; Chief Ed., *Bi-monthly Update* 74-76; Chmn., L'Escargot Co. Ltd. 77-82; Chmn., Europa Haus Co. Ltd. 78-87; 1st V. Pres., Nat. YWCA of the ROC 78-87; Adv., Admin., & Planning Coun., Nat. Theater & Nat. Concert Hall 83-86; V. Chmn., Kingvic Intl. Dev. & Investment Co. Ltd. 88-92; *Add.* 6th Fl., 7 Tsingtao W. Rd., Taipei.

CHIANG, PEN-CHI 蔣本基
Prof., Grad. Inst. of Environmental Engr., NTU 87-; Adv., Ind. Pollution Prevention Service Corps, MOEA; Convener, Environmental Engr. Sect., Engr. Div., NScC; Mem., Cttee. of Environmental Quality, EPA 92-; *b.* Hunan Nov. 29, '50; *m.* Chiang, Hsiu-laing; 3 *s.; educ.* BCE, NTU 72, MCE 76; MS, Environmental Engr., U. of Cincinnati 78; Ph.D., Environmental Engr., Purdue U. 82; Lectr., Nat. Cent. U. 76-77; Assc. Resr., Grad. Sch. of Civil/Environmental Engr., Purdue U. 82-83; Visiting Assc. Prof., Grad. Inst. of Environmental Engr., NTU 83-84, Assc. Prof. 84-87. *Publ.:* 17 articles published in prof. jour.; 25 papers presented at intl. conf.; *Add.* 18-3 Alley 3, Lane 56, Min Sheng E. Rd., Sect. 4, Taipei.

CHIANG, PENG-CHIEN 江鵬堅
Mem., Control Yuan 96-; *b.* Taipei, Apr. 25, '40; *m.* Peng, Fong-mei; 1 *s.,* 2 *d.; educ.* LL.B., NTU 62, Stud-

ies in the Grad. Sch. of Law 63-64; Attorney-at-Law 65; Sec.-Gen., Ch. Comparative Law Soc. 76-77; Mem., Legis. Yuan 84-87; Founding Pres., Twn. Assn. of Human Rights 84-86, & DPP 86-87; Sr. Fel., Cent. of Dev. Policy (in D.C.) 88; Sec.-Gen., DPP 92-93. *Publ: Recall Soc. Justice* 82; *Pamphlet of Human Rights* 82; *Viva Human Rights* 83; *Vote Vs. Bullets* 87; *Add.* 2 Chunghsiao E. Rd., Sect. 1, Taipei.

CHIANG, PIN-KUNG 江丙坤
Chmn., CEPD 96-; Mem., CC, KMT 93-; *b.* Twn. Dec. 16, '32; *m.* Chen, Mei-huey; 3 *c.; educ.* Ph.D., Agr. Econ., Tokyo U. 62-71; Asst. Cml. Attaché, Emb. in Japan 67-74; Cml. Attaché, Consl. Gen. in Johnnesburg 74-79; Econ. Counsl., Emb. in S. Africa 79-81; Dep. Dir.-Gen., Bd. of For. Trade (BOFT), MOEA 82-83; Sec.-Gen., CETRA 83-88; Dir.-Gen., BOFT 88-89; Admin. V. Min., MOEA 89-90; Pol. V. Min., MOEA 90-93; Min. of MOEA 93-96. *Publ.: Study of Twn. Land-tax Reform; Add.* 9th Fl., 87 Nanking E. Rd., Sect. 2, Taipei.

CHIANG, PING-KUN
(See CHIANG, PIN-KUNG 江丙坤)

CHIANG, WEI-PING
(See KIANG, WEBSTER WEI-PING 江偉平)

CHIANG, YEN-SHIH
(See TSIANG, YIEN-SI 蔣彥士)

CHIANG HSU, NAI-CHIN
(See CHIANG, NANCY ZI 蔣徐乃錦)

CHIAO, HSIUNG-PING
(See CHIAO, HSIUNG-PING PEGGY 焦雄屏)

CHIAO, HSIUNG-PING PEGGY 焦雄屏
Dir., Twn. Film Cent. 95-; Assc. Prof., Nat. Inst. of the Arts 87-; Adjunct Assc. Prof., NCU 88-; *b.* Twn. Aug. 8, '53; *educ.* BA, NCU 75; MA, Radio-TV-Film, U. of Texas, Austin 81; Film Dept., UCLA 85-86; Screenplay, *Actress* 92; Adjunct Prof., Ch. Cul. U. 81-86, Fu Jen Catholic U. 85-86, Nat. Twn. Acad. of the Arts 82-83; Coordinator, *Ch. Times* Film Award 88-95; Mng. Dir., Nat. Film Year 93-94. *Publ.: Twn. New Cinema* 88;

Hong Kong Cinema 75-86 87; *Reading Mainstream Cinema* 90; *Anthropology of Film Writings* 91; *Authors & Genre: A Study of Twn. & Hong Kong Cinema* 91; *Hou Hsiao-hsien* 93; *Musicals* 93; *The Five Years That Changed Twn. Film History: A Study of Kuo Lien Studio* 93; *Add.* 11 Lane 86, Tung An St., Taipei.

CHIAO, JEN-HO 焦仁和
V. Chmn. & concur. Sec.-Gen., SEF 93-; Mem., CC, KMT 93-; Prof., Law, Ch. Cul. U. 74-; *b.* Chekiang Nov. 11, '48; *m.* Tang, Hai-chu; 1 *s.*, 2 *d.; educ.* LL.B., Ch. Cul. U. 70; MCL, So. Methodist U. 72; J.D., Ohio Nr. U. 74; Res., London Sch. of Econ. & Pol. Sc. 79; Dean of Student Aff., Ch. Cul. U. 75-78, Dean of Studies 79-80; Dir., Secretariat, Yang Ming Inst. 80-82, Dir., Guidance Sect. 82-83; Counsl., Off. of the Pres. 84-85, Dep. Dir., 1st Bu. 85-88, Dir., Confidential Aff. & concur. Press Sec. 88-93; V. Chmn., MAC 93. *Publ.: A Comparative Study on Products Liability; A New Approach on the Study of Private Intl. Law; Add.* 17th Fl., 156 Min Sheng E. Rd., Sect. 3, Taipei.

CHIEN, EUGENE Y.H. 簡又新
Rep., Taipei Rep. Off. in the UK 93-; Mem., CC, KMT 88-; *b.* Twn. Feb. 4, '46; *m.* Wang, Kuei-jung; 2 *s.*, 1 *d.; educ.* BS, Mech. Engr., NTU 68; MS, Aeronautics & Astronautics, New York U. 71, Ph.D. 73; Prof. & Chmn., Dept. of Aeronautical Engr., Tamkang U. 76-78, Prof. & Dean, Coll. of Engr. 78-84; Mem., Legis. Yuan 84-87; Admin., EPA 87-91; Min. of Trans. & Comms. 91-93; *Add.* 50 Grosvenor Gardens, London SW1W OEB, UK.

CHIEN, FREDRICK FU 錢復
Spkr., NA 96-; Mem., CSC, KMT 88-; Mem., CC, KMT 76-; *b.* Peiping Feb. 17, '35; *m.* Chien Tien, Julie; 1 *s.*, 1 *d.; educ.* BA, NTU 56; MA, Yale U. 59, Ph.D. 62; Hon. LL.D., Sung Kyun Kwan U., S. Korea; 10th Class, Nat. War Coll.; Sec. to the Premier, Exec. Yuan 62-63; Visiting Assc. Prof., NCU 62-64; Sp. & Sect. Chief, Dept. of N. Am. Aff., MOFA 64-67, Dep. Dir. 67-69, Dir. 69-72; Visiting Prof., NTU 70-72; Dir.-Gen., GIO 72-75; Admin. V. Min. of For. Aff. 75-79; Pol. V. Min. of For. Aff. 79-82; Rep., CCNAA, Washington, D.C. 83-88; Chmn., CEPD & concur. Min. of State 88-90; Min., MOFA 90-96. *Publ.: The Opening of*

Korea: A Study of Ch. Dip. 1876-1885; Speaking as a Friend; More Views of a Friend; Faith & Resilience: The ROC Forges Ahead; Add. 53 Chung Hua Rd., Sect. 1, Taipei.

CHIEN, FU
(See CHIEN, FREDRICK FU 錢復)

CHIEN, GEORGE L.T. 錢龍韜
Bd. Chmn., Hu-Chiang High Sch. 93-; Exec. Dir., Ch. Latin-Am. Cul. & Econ. Assc.; Coun., KMT 93-; *b.* Chekiang Sept. 9, '22; 3 *s.*, 1 *d.; educ.* BA, U. of Shanghai; Rep. & Comr., Shansi Prov. Govt. 45-47; Econ. Sp., MND 47-48; Dep. Mgr., Kaohsiung Br., Bk. of Twn. 49-50, Dep. Mgr., Treasury Dept. 50-57, & Mgr. 58-61; Dir., Twn. Navigation Co. 58-61; Gen. Mgr., Treasury Dept., CBC 61-82; Adv., Bk. of Twn. 62-63; Bd. Mem., City Bk. of Taipei 70-83; Chmn., Chung Kuo Ins. 82-89; Chmn., Ch. Bills Finance Corp. 89-93; Chmn. of the Bd., Bills Finance Assc. of Taipei 92-93; Exec. Dir., Taipei Bills Finance Assc. 93-96; Adv., Ovs. Ch. Bk. 93-96; *Add.* 9th Fl.-3, 43 Hsin Yi Rd., Sect. 3, Taipei.

CHIEN, HAN-SHENG
(See CHIEN, HANSEN 簡漢生)

CHIEN, HANSEN 簡漢生
Dep. Sec.-Gen., CC, KMT 96-; Mem., CC, KMT 88-; Adv., OCAC; *b.* Hanko Oct. 12, '46; *m.* Chien Lai, Elza; 2 *d.; educ.* BS, NTU 68; MS, Purdue U. 71, Ph.D. 75; Lectr., Purdue U. 71-75; Prof., U. of Sao Paulo, Brazil 75-85; Hon. Rep. to Brazil, CETRA 82-84; Mem., Legis. Yuan 83-89, & Convener, For. & Ovs. Ch. Aff. Cttee.; Dep. Dir.-Gen., Dept. of Ovs. Aff., CC, KMT 89-90; Prof., Ch. Cul. U. 88-90; Chmn., Taipei Mun. Cttee., KMT 90-94; Dir.-Gen., Dept. of Cul. Aff., CC, KMT 94-96; Mem., NA 92-96. *Publ.:* Many essays on meteorology & pol. aff.; *Add.* 11 Chung Shan Rd., Taipei.

CHIEN, HSU
(See CHIEN, SHU 錢煦)

CHIEN, LUNG-TAO
(See CHIEN, GEORGE L.T. 錢龍韜)

CHIEN, MING-CHING 簡明景
Bd. Chmn., TTV 95-; Mem., CC & CSC, KMT 93-; *b.*
Twn. Mar. 2, '35; *m.* Lan, Miao-cheng; 1 *s.,* 2 *d.; educ.*
LL.B., NTU 59; High Sch. Tchr., Pingtung City; Sec.-
Gen., Pingtung Farmers' Assn.; Chmn., Kaohsiung Fruit
Marketing Cooperative; Gen. Mgr., Twn. Prov. Fruit
Marketing Cooperative; Spkr., TPA 89-94, Mem. 81-
94; *Add.* TPA, Wufeng, Taichung County.

CHIEN, SHU 錢煦
Chmn., Adv. Cttee., Inst. of Biomed. Sc., Acad. Sinica,
Mem. 76-; Chmn., Adv. Cttee., Nat. Health Res. Inst.
93-; Founding Fel., Am. Inst. of Med. & Biological Engr.
92-; Mem., Inst. of Med., USA 94-; Prof., Bioengr. &
Med., & Dir., Inst. for Biomed. Engr., U. of Calif., San
Diego 88-; Chair, Dept. of Bioengr. 94-; *b.* Peiping June
23, '31; *m.* Chien Hu, Kuang-chung; 2 *d.; educ.* MB,
NTU 53; Ph.D., Columbia U. 57; Instr., Physiology,
Columbia U. 56-58, Asst. Prof. 58-64, Assc. Prof. 64-
69, Prof. 69-88, Dir., Div. of Circulatory Physiology 74-
88; Dir., Inst. of Biomed. Sc., Acad. Sinica 87-88; Pres.,
Am. Physiological Soc. 90-91; Pres., Fed. of Am. Soc.
for Experimental Biology 92-93. *Publ.:* 8 bk. & over 300
original sc. papers; *Add.* 9445 La Jolla Farms Rd., La
Jolla, CA 92037-1128, USA.

CHIEN, YU-HSIN
(See CHIEN, EUGENE Y.H. 簡又新)

CHIEN, YUEH-WEI
(See KAN, YUET-WAI 簡悅威)

CHIN, HSIAO-YI 秦孝儀
Dir., Nat. Palace Museum 83-; *b.* Hunan Feb. 11, '21; *m.*
Hsu, Hai-ping; 3 *s.,* 1 *d.; educ.* Grad., Law Dept., Shang-
hai Law Coll.; Hon. Dr., Humane Letters, Oklahoma City
U.; Exec. Sec. to Pres. Chiang Kai-shek 50-75; Dep. Sec.-
Gen., CC, KMT 61-75, & Mem., CC, KMT 63-93; Prof.,
San Min Chu I Inst., NTU 74-88; Chmn., Party Hist.
Com., CC, KMT 76-91; Pres., Ch. Hist. Assn. 84-91;
Pres., Ch. Assn. of Museums 90-95. *Publ.: Basic
Courses in Dr. Sun Yat-sen's Thought; The Spring of
Advancing Virtue; Pres. Chiang Kai-shek's Thorough
Understanding & Forthright Application of Dr. Sun Yat-
sen's Thought; Add.* 7 Lane 138, Chih Shan Rd., Sect. 1,
Waishuanghsi, Shihlin, Taipei.

CHIN, KAI-HSIN
(See CHIN, LUKE K. 金開鑫)

CHIN, LUKE K. 金開鑫
Dir.-Gen., Com. of Evaluation & Discipline, CC, KMT
94-; Adjunct Prof., Tamkang U. 65-; *b.* Hupei, Sept. 17,
'34; *m.* Kung, Hsiang-li; 1 *s.,* 1 *d.; educ.* BA, Tamkang
U. 61; MA., Bristol U., UK 65; Ph.D., New York U. 79;
Res. Fel., Inst. of Intl. Rel., NCU 66-80; Dean of Acad.
Aff., Sun Yat-sen Inst. on Policy Res. & Dev. 80-88,
Dep. Dir.-Gen., Com. of Evaluation & Discipline, CC
89-90; Dep. Dir.-Gen., Sun Yat-sen Inst. on Policy Res.
& Dev. 90-94. *Publ.: The Dramatic Function of the Su-
pernatural in Shakespeare's Plays; The Pol. of Drama
Reform in Communist Ch.; Add.* 4th Fl., 5 Alley 61, Lane
208, Jui An St., Taipei.

CHIN, SHU-CHI
(See KING, CHARLES SHU-CHI 金樹基)

CHIN, WEI-CHUN
(See JIN, WEI-TSUN 金惟純)

CHIN, YAO-CHI
(See KING, AMBROSE Y.C. 金耀基)

CHIOU, I-JEN 邱義仁
Dep. Sec.-Gen., CC, DDP; *b.* Twn. May 9, '39; *m.*
Chiang, Mei-ling; 1 *s.; educ.* MPS, U. of Chicago; *Add.*
33 Lane 5, Hu Tung St., Hsichih, Taipei County.

CHIOU, JIN-SONG 邱金松
Pres., Nat. Coll. of Phys. Educ. & Sports 90-, Prof. 87-;
b. Twn. Dec. 5, '39; *m.* Liao, Kuei-mei; 3 *d.; educ.*
Ed.M., Tokyo U. of Educ.; Ph.D., Chukyo U., Japan;
Tchr., Prov. Twn. Pingtung Tchrs. Coll.-affiliated El-
ementary Sch. 58-59, & Pingtung County Houchuang
Elementary Sch. 59-60; Instr., World Coll. of Jour. 64-
65, & Prov. Chingmei Girls' High Sch. 65; Lectr., Assc.
Prof., & Prof., NTNU 66-87. *Publ.: Theory & Methods
in Sociology in Phys. Educ.; Current Thoughts in Phys.
Educ. & Sports* (2 Vol.); *Handbk. of Sch. Phys. Educ.
Mng. & Its Evaluation; Dev. of Twn.'s Public Recre-
ational Activities; Add.* 250 Wen Hua 1st Rd., Kueishan,
Taoyuan County.

CHIOU, JONG-NAN 邱榮男
Amb. to Haiti 96-; *b.* Twn. Oct. 6, '39; *m.* Chiou, Jacqueline; 1 *s.,* 1 *d.; educ.* LL.B., NTU 62; Dep. Dir., Dept. of European Aff., MOFA 77-79; Rep. to Switzerland 79-85; Dir., Dept. of European Aff., MOFA 85-90; Rep., Taipei Rep. Off. in France, Paris 90-96; *Add.* P.O. Box 655 Port-au-Prince, Haiti.

CHIOU, LIAN-GONG 邱聯恭
Nat. Policy Adv. to the Pres. 96-; Prof. of Law, NTU 83-; Mem., Cttee. for Proposed Amendments to the Code of Civil Procedure at the Judicature 83-; *b.* Twn. Apr. 10, '38; *m.* Lin, Ya-ying; 1 *s.,* 1 *d.; educ.* LL.B., NTU 61; ML, U. of Tokyo 73; Ph.D., U. of Tokyo 81; Judge of the Tainan Dist. Court 65-66; Judge of the Taipei Dist. Court 66-70; Mem., Cttee. for Proposed Amendments to the Code of Notary Public Law 89-95. *Publ.: The Role of Lawyer in Modern Soc.; Der Zweck des Zivilprozesses; Über die Prozesshindernde Einrede des Schiedsvertrages; Über Funktionen der Verfahrensgarantie im Zivilprozess; Add.* 3rd Fl., 10 Lane 92, Shih Ta Rd., Taipei.,

CHIOU, LIEN-HUI 邱連輝
Nat. Policy Adv. to the Pres. 96-; *b.* Twn. Oct. 15. '32; *m.* Chiou Hsieh, Kan-mei; 1 *s.,* 3 *d.; educ.* LL.B., NCHU 58; Tchr. of Secondary Sch., 58-59; Mayor, Linlo Township 59-68; Coun., Pingtung CoCoun. 68-73; Coun., Twn. Prov. Coun. 73-81; Magis., Pingtung County 81-85; Adv. of Twn. Prov. Govt. & Chief of Twn. Appeal Cttee. 85-91; Mem., Legis. Yuan 86-96; *Add.* 150 Cheng Kung Rd., Linlo, Pingtung County.

CHIU, CHENG-HSIUNG
(See CHIU, PAUL CHENG-HSIUNG 邱正雄)

CHIU, CHENG-TUNG
(See YAU, SHING-TUNG 丘成桐)

CHIU, CHEYNE J.Y. 邱進益
Min. of Personnel, Exam. Yuan 96-; Nat. Policy Adv. to the Pres. 93-; Mem., CC, KMT 93-; *b.* Kiangsu Nov. 19, '36; *m.* Cheng, Jean; 2 *s.; educ.* LL.B., NCU 60; Grad. Studies, NCU 61-64, Vienna U. 65-66, & Bonn U. 74-76; Staff Mem., MOFA 62, Sect. Chief, Dept. of European Aff. 72-74, Dep. Dir. 79-81; Chargé d'Affaires,

Emb. in Malta 70-72; Rep. to Sweden 81-83; Dir., Protocol Dept., MOFA 83-85, Spokesman 85-87; Amb. to Swaziland 87-88; Dep. Sec.-Gen. to the Pres. 88-93; Spokesman, Off. of the Pres. 90-93; Convener, Res. Cttee., & Exec. Sec., Secretariat, NUC 90-93; V. Chmn. & concur. Sec.-Gen., SEF 93; Rep., Taipei Rep. Off. in Singapore 94-96; *Add.* 1 Shih Yuan Rd., Wenshan, Taipei.

CHIU, CHIN-I
(See CHIU, CHEYNE J.Y. 邱進益)

CHIU, CHIN-SUNG
(See CHIOU, JIN-SONG 邱金松)

CHIU, CHUANG-HUAN 邱創煥
Acting V. Chmn., KMT 96-; Sr. Adv. to the Pres. 96-; Mem., CSC, KMT 79-, Mem., CC 76-; *b.* Twn. July 25, '25; *m.* Pai, Ling-yu; 2 *s.,* 2 *d.; educ.* MPS, NCU; Dir., 3rd Dept., Min. of Pers., Exam. Yuan 65-67; Dep. Dir., 5th Sect., CC, KMT 67-69; Comr., Dept. of Soc. Aff., TPG 69-72; Dir.-Gen., Dept. of Soc. Aff., CC, KMT 72-78; Min. of State 76-78; Dep. Sec.-Gen., CC, KMT 78; Min. of the Int. 78-81; Chmn., CEIC 78-81; V. Premier 81-84; Gov., TPG 84-90; Sr. Adv. to the Pres. 90-93; Pres., Exam. Yuan 93-96. *Publ.: Thought Regarding Soc. Welfare in the Three Principles of the People; A Summary of Ch. Soc. Welfare System; Soc. Welfare & People's Livelihood; A Treatise of Civil Service System; Add.* 122 Chungking S. Rd., Sect. 1, Taipei.

CHIU, HUNGDAH 丘宏達
Prof., Sch. of Law, U. of Maryland; Chief Ed., *Ch. Yearbk. of Intl. Law & Aff.;* Mem., NUC; Pres., Ch. Soc. of Intl. Law 93-; *b.* Fukien Mar. 23, '36; *m.* Hsieh, Yuan-yuan; 1 *s.; educ.* LL.B., NTU; MA, Long Island U. 62; LL.M., Harvard U. 62, S.J.D. 65; Assc. Prof., NTU 65-66; Res. Assc., Law Sch., Harvard U. 66-70 & 72-74; Prof., NCU & NTU 70-72; Assc. Prof., U. of Maryland 74-77; Observer, Intl. Law Assn. to the 3rd UN Conf. on the Law of the Sea 76-82; Pres., Assn. of Ch. Soc. Scientists in N. Am. 84-86; Pres., Am. Assn. for Ch. Studies 85-87; Min. of State 93-94; Bd. Dir., SEF 93-95; Sp. envoy to the 20th anniversary of the independence of Grenada 94. *Publ.: The Capacity of Intl. Org. to Conclude Treaties; Ch. & the Question of Twn.; Documents*

& Analysis; Ch. & the Twn. Issue; Ch.: 70 Years After the 1911 Hsinhai Rev.; Criminal Justice in Post-Mao Ch.; The Future of Hong Kong, Toward 1997 & Beyond; Survey of Recent Dev. in Ch. (Mainland & Twn.) 85-86; The US Const. & Constitutionism in Ch.; The Draft Basic Law of Hong Kong: Analysis & Documents; Intl. Law of the Sea: Cases, Documents & Readings; Modern Intl. Law (Ch.)*;* Reference documents on modern Intl. Law (Ch.); etc.; *Add.* 500 W. Baltimore St., Baltimore, Maryland 21201, USA.

CHIU, HUNG-TA
(See CHIU, HUNGDAH 丘宏達)

CHIU, HWA-YEN 邱華演
Pres. & Gen. Mgr., Flower Queen Enterprise Co., Ltd. 74-; Leading Mng. Dir., Bd. of Trustees, Twn. Printing Ind. Assn. 92-; *b.* Twn. Mar. 19, '39; *m.* Chen, Shiou-chen; 1 *s.,* 2 *d.; educ.* B., Econ., Soochow U.; Asst. Mgr., Chung Hua Wire & Cable Co.; Mgr., Ting Hou Enterprise; Mgr., Ch. Reebar Co.; *Add.* 1 Lane 483, Hsin Hsu Rd., Hsinchuang, Taipei County.

CHIU, I-JEN
(See CHIOU, I-JEN 邱義仁)

CHIU, JUNG-NAN
(See CHIOU, JONG-NAN 邱榮男)

CHIU, LIEN-HUI
(See CHIOU, LIEN-HUI 邱連輝)

CHIU, LIEN-KUNG
(See CHIOU, LIAN-GONG 邱聯恭)

CHIU, MAO-YING
(See TJIU, MAU-YING 邱茂英)

CHIU, PAUL CHENG-HSIUNG 邱正雄
Min. of Finance 96-; *b.* Twn. Feb. 19, '42; *m.* Chang, Mei-pao; 2 *s.; educ.* BA, NTU 64; MA & Ph.D., Ohio State U. 71-78; Eisenhower Fel. 88; Assc. Prof., NTU 73-75; Dep. Gen. Mgr., Banking Dept., CBC 75-76, & For. Exchange Dept. 76-81, Gen. Mgr., Banking Dept. 81-88; Pres., Hua Nan Cml. Bk. 88.; Dep. Gov., CBC 88-96. *Publ.: Optimal Open Market Strategy: A Gener-*

alized Kareken-Muench-Wallance Model in Econ. Essays 73; Optimal Monetary Policy Indicator—An Application of Kalman Filter to the St. Louis Equation & the Minnie Equation of the US Econ. in Econ. Essays 78; The 2-Stage Decision Rule for the Conduct of Monetary Policy 78; Performance of Financial Inst. in Twn. in Conf. on Experiences Lessons of Econ. Dev. in Twn. 81; "Money & Financial Markets: The Domestic Perspective," in Twn.: From Developing to Mature Econ. 92; "Prices, Money & Monetary Policy Implementation under Financial Liberalization: the Case of Twn." in Financial Opening: Policy Issues & Experiences in Dev. Countries 93; Add. 2 Ai Kuo W. Rd., Taipei.

CHIU, YING-NAN 丘應楠
Mem., Acad. Sinica; Prof., Catholic U. of Am.; Fel., Am. Phys. Soc. 86-; *b.* Canton Nov. 25, '33; *m.* Chiu Chow, Lue-yung; 2 *c.; educ.* NTU 50-52; BS, Berea Coll. 55; MS, Yale U. 56, Ph.D. 60; Res. Fel., Columbia U. 60-62; Res. Assc., U. of Chicago 62-64; Asst. Prof., Catholic U. of Am. 64-66, Assc. Prof. 66-70, Prof. & Chmn., Dept. of Chem. 70-80; Sloan Fel. 69-71. *Publ.:* 103 res. articles in referred jour.; *Add.* Dept. of Chem., Catholic U. of Am., Washington, D.C. 20064, USA.

CHO, ALFRED Y. 卓以和
Mem., Acad. Sinica; Dir., Semiconductor Res., Bell Labs., Lucent Tech., USA; Bd. Mem., Instruments SA Inc., USA 84-; Adjunct Prof., Dept. of EE, U. of Illinois 87-; *b.* Peking July 10, '37; *m.* Willoughby, Mona Lee; 1 *s.,* 3 *d.; educ.* BSEE 60; MSEE 61; Ph.D., U. of Illinois 68; Mem., Tech. Staff, Materials Sc. Res. Dept., AT&T Bell Labs. 68-84, Head, Elect. & Photonic Res. Dept. 84-87, Dir., Materials Processing Res. 87-90. *Publ.:* Over 400 publ. & 48 patents; *Add.* Bell Labs., Lucent Technologies, 700 Mountain Avenue, Murray Hill, NJ 07974, USA.

CHO, CHUAN-CHEN
(See JWO, JACKSON 卓傳陣)

CHO, I-HE
(See CHO, ALFRED Y. 卓以和)

CHO, YUNG-TSAI
(See CHUO, ERIC Y.T. 卓永財)

CHOU, CHANG-HUNG 周昌弘
Mem., Acad. Sinica 94-; Fel., Third World Acad. of Sc. 93-; Exec. Cttee. Mem. & Chmn., Nat. Cttee., IUBS, SCOPE 88-; Prof., NTU 76-; Adjunct Prof., NTNU 76-; *b.* Twn. Sept. 5, '42; *m.* Chou Yang, Liang-hui; 1 *s.,* 1 *d.; educ.* BS, Botany, NTU 65, MS, Botany 68; Ph.D., Plant Ecology, U. of Calif., Santa Barbara 71; Res. Asst., U. of Calif., Santa Barbara 68-71; Postdoctoral Fel., U. of Toronto 71-72; Assc. Prof., Acad. Sinica 72-76; Prof., Res. Fel., & Dir., Inst. of Botany 89-96; Dir., Life Sc. Res. Promotion Cent., NScC 89-96. *Publ.: Plant Ecology;* Over 180 allelopathic res. papers, 10 monographs, & more than 10 review articles; *Add.* Inst. of Botany, Acad. Sinica, Taipei.

CHOU, CHU-YUAN
(See CHOW, PETER CHI-YUAN 周鉅原)

CHOU, CHUNG-NAN
(See CHOW, CHUNG-NAN 周仲南)

CHOU, HUNG-TAO
(See CHOW, HONG-TAO 周宏濤)

CHOU, KUO-JUI
(See CHOU, LOUIS KUO-RUEY 周國瑞)

CHOU, LIEN-HUA
(See CHOW, LIEN-HWA 周聯華)

CHOU, LOUIS KUO-RUEY 周國瑞
Amb. to Guinea Bissau 95-; *b.* Sept. 25, '42; *m.* Chou Peng, Helen; 1 *s.,* 2 *d.; educ.* BA, NTU 66; MPS, NTU 70; Sec. Chief, Pers. Off., MOFA 82-85; Dep. Dir., Pers. Off., MOFA 85-89; Consul-Gen., Consl. in Capetown 89-92; Dir.-Gen., TECO in Sao Paulo 92-95; *Add.* P.O. Box 66, Bissau, Guinea Bissau, W. Africa.

CHOU, SHIH-PIN 周世斌
Bd. Chmn., CTS 95-; Mem., CC & CSC, KMT 93-; *b.* Szechwan Sept. 6, '30; *m.* Chou Hwang, Sheue-er; 1 *s.,* 1 *d.; educ.* Ch. Army Acad. 53; CGSC, Führungsakademie, Bundeswehr, W. Germany 67; War Coll., Armed Forces U. 79; Div. Cmdr. 75-77; Cmdt., Chung-cheng Armed Forces Preparatory Sch. 77-81; Corps Cmdr. 81-83; Cmdt., Cent. Police Coll. 83-87; Dep. C-in-C, Twn. Gar-

rison GHQ 87-90; Sec.-Gen., VAC 90-91, V. Chmn. 91-93, Chmn. 93-94; *Add.* 100 Kuang Fu S. Rd., Taipei.

CHOU, YUAN-SHEN
(See CHOW, YUAN-SHIH 周元燊)

CHOW, CHUNG-NAN 周仲南
Strategy Adv. to the Pres. 92-; *b.* Kiangsu Sept. 14, '32; *m.* Lin, Ming-hsiu; 4 *d.; educ.* 26th Class, Ch. Army Acad. 55; Hawk Missile Off. Course, US Air Def. Sch. 63; Army CGSC, Armed Forces U., Class 1971, War Coll., Class 1973; 3rd Class, Sun Yat-sen Inst. on Policy Res. & Dev.; Platoon Leader, Army Air Def. Missile Bn. 60-61, Co. Cmdr. 65-67; Bn. Cmdr. Artillery, Army Infantry Div. 71-72; Cmdr., 601st Field Artillery Group, 2nd Army Corps 73-75; Cmdr., 605th Army Air Def. Group 75-78; Cmdr., 284th Army Infantry Div. 78-79; Chief Aide-de-camp to late Pres. Chiang Ching-kuo 79-85; Provost Marshal Gen., MP Cmd. 85-89; C-in-C, Twn. Garrison GHQ, & CG, Twn. Corps Area Cmd. 89-92; *Add.* Off. of the Pres., Taipei.

CHOW, GREGORY CHI-CHONG 鄒至莊
Mem., Acad. Sinica, & Am. Philosophical Soc.; Prof. of Econ. & Class of 1913 Prof. of Pol. Econ., Princeton U. 70-, Dir., Econometric Res. Prog.; *b.* Canton Dec. 25, '29; *m.* Chen, Paula K.; 2 *s.,* 1 *d.; educ.* BA, Cornell U.; MA & Ph.D., U. of Chicago; Hon. Dr., Zhongshan U.; LL.D., Lingan Coll.; Asst. Prof., MIT 55-59; Assc. Prof., Cornell U. 59-62; Res. Staff, IBM Res. Cent. 62-70; Visiting Prof., Cornell U. 64-65, Harvard U. 67, & Rutgers U. 69; Adjunct Prof., Columbia U. 65-70. *Publ.: Demand for Automobiles in the US; Analysis & Control of Dynamic Econ. Systems; Econ. Analysis by Control Methods; Econometrics; The Ch. Econ.; Understanding Ch.'s Econ.; Dynamic Econ.; Add.* Dept. of Econ., Princeton U., Princeton, NJ 08544, USA.

CHOW, YUAN-SHIH 周元燊
Mem., Acad. Sinica; Prof., Statistics, Columbia U. 68-; *b.* Hupei Sept. 1, '24; *m.* Chang, Yi; 5 *c.; educ.* BS, Nat. Chekiang U. 49; MA, U. of Illinois 55, Ph.D. 58; Asst., NTU 49-54; Res. Assc., U. of Illinois 58-59; IBM Res. Mathematician 59-62; Dir., Inst. of Math., Acad. Sinica 70-77; Assc. Prof. & Prof., Purdue U. 62-68; Fel., Inst of Math. Statistics; Mem., Intl. Statistical Inst. *Publ.*

Optimal Stopping; Probability Theory; Add. 144 Washington Avenue, Dobbs Ferry, NY 10522, USA.

CHU, CHI-YING
(See CHU, JAMES C.Y. 祝基瀅)

CHU, CHIEN-HUNG 褚劍鴻
Nat. Policy Adv. to the Pres. 93-; Prof., Fu Jen Catholic U. 70-; Pres., Ch. Soc. of Law 89-; *b.* Kiangsu May 10, '19; *educ.* LL.B., Nat. Futan U.; Chief Prosecutor, Keelung Dist. Court 59-63, & Chiayi Dist. Court 63-64; Pres., Yunlin Dist. Court 64-68, & Changhua Dist. Court 68-70; Chief Prosecutor, Taipei Dist. Court 70-72, Pres. 72-78; Chief Prosecutor, Twn. High Court 78-79, Pres. 79-87; Prof., Ch. Cul. U. 71-85; Chief Justice, Supreme Court 87-93; Convener, Cttee. for Jud. Officials' Tng. 90-93. *Publ.: Gen. Part of Criminal Code; Sp. Part of Criminal Code; Code of Criminal Procedures; Criminal Procedure Practices & Sp. Topics; Essays on Criminal Law; Add.* 6 Changsha St., Sect. 1, Taipei.

CHU, CHIEN-I
(See CHU, C.Y. 朱建一)

CHU, CHING-WU
(See CHU, PAUL CHING-WU 朱經武)

CHU, FU-SUNG 朱撫松
Nat. Policy Adv. to the Pres. 79-; *b.* Hupei Jan. 5, '15; *m.* Hsu, Chung-pei; *educ.* BA, Shanghai U.; Acting Dir., ?K Off., Min. of Info., KMT 46-47; Dir., Dept. of Intl. ?o. Service, GIO 48-49; Counsl., TPG 49-50; Sr. Sec. ?ounsl., Exec. Yuan 50-54; Adv., Off. of Govt. ?esman 50-54; Dir., Info. Dept., MOFA 52-56; ?. & Min., Emb. in USA 56-60; Min., Emb. in Can. ? Min. of For. Aff. 62-65; Amb. to Spain 65-71; ?razil 71-74; Amb. to S. Korea 75-79; Min. of ?9-87; *Add.* 262 Kuang Fu S. Rd., Taipei.

?IA WAN-CHING 朱婉清
?r., 6th Dept., Exec. Yuan 93-; Lectr., ?-; Chmn., Ch. Women Writers' Assn. ?. 9, '50; *m.* Ho, Marvin Ching-hsien; 1 ?Ch. Lit., NCHU 73; MA, St. John's ?tudied at City U. of New York 81; ?CPD 81-87; Lectr., Pol. Warfare

Coll. 81-88; Insp., OCAC 87-88; Sr. Sp., Dept. of Info. & Cul. Aff., MOFA 88-90; Coun., Adv., & Dir., Taipei Off., TPG 90-93. *Publ.: The Age of TV Simulcasting; Cross-section of So. USA—A Potpourri; The Lowest of the Low* (transl.); *Selection of Gloria Chu's Lit. Works; Selection of Contemporary Ch. Authoresses* (ed.); *Add.* 1 Chung Hsiao E. Rd., Sect. 1, Taipei.

CHU, JAMES C.Y. 祝基瀅
Min., OCAC 96-; Mem., CC, KMT 93-; *b.* Fukien Apr. 3, '35; *m.* Lin, Ruth; 2 *d.; educ.* LL.B., NTU 57; MA, Jour., NCU 60; MA & Ph.D., Jour., So. Illinois U. 70; Sect. Chief, GIO; Reporter, *Daily Repub.,* Marion, Illinois 67-68; Asst. Prof., Assc. Prof., Chmn., Comm. & Info. Res. Dept., & Dir. of Res. Cent., Calif. State U., Chico 70-88; Visiting Res. Prof., NCU 84-86; Dep. Dir.-Gen., Dept. of Cul. Aff., CC, KMT 89, Dir.-Gen. 89-94; Dep. Sec.-Gen., CC, KMT 94-96. *Publ.: Mass Comm.* 73; *Pol. Comm.* 83; *Comm. Dev. & Modern Soc.* 85; *Comm., Soc. & Tech.* 86; *Meditation of Modern Men* 86; *2-Way Traffic* 89; *Add.* 16 Fl., 5 Hsuchow Rd., Taipei.

CHU, JU-CHIN 朱汝瑾
Mem., Acad. Sinica 64-; Bd. Chmn. & Pres., Tech. Res. Inc., Irvine, CA 72-; *b.* Kiangsu Dec. 14, '19; *m.* Lee, Ching-chen; 3 *s.; educ.* BS, NTHU 40; D.Sc., MIT 45; Sr. Chem. Engr., Shell Chem. Corp. 46; Asst. Prof., Chem. Engr., U. of Washington 46-49; Assc. Prof., Polytechnic Inst. of Brooklyn 49-54, Prof. 54-66; Tech. Dir., Chem. Construction Corp. 56-57; Consultant, US Govt. & over 60 major chem., petroleum, propulsion, & nuclear firms in US, Britain, W. Germany, Italy, Netherlands, & Japan 48-66; Tech. Adv., Strategic Missiles Div., N. Am. Rockwell Corp., Orange, Calif. 69-70; Prof., Virginia Polytechnic Inst. & State U. 67-72. *Publ.: Distillation; Fluidixation; Weapon Systems; Environmental Pollution Control; Propulsion; Nuclear Tech.; Mass Transfer; Drying; Extraction; Engr. Thermodynamic & Kinetics; Reactor Design; Radiation Effect; Space Vehicle System & Subsystem Optimization; Cyogenics & Ind. Newly Processed Products Utilization of Agr. Products;* etc.; *Add.* 21 Yorktown, Irvine, CA 92720, USA.

CHU, MING
(See JU, MING 朱銘)

CHU, PAUL CHING-WU 朱經武
Mem., Acad. Sinica 88-, Nat. Acad. of Sc. 89-, Am. Acad. of Arts & Sc. 89-, & Third World Acad. of Sc. 90-; Dir., Texas Cent. for Superconductivity at the U. of Houston 87-; T.L.L. Temple Chair of Sc., U. of Houston 87-; Prof. of Phys., U. of Houston 79-; Mem., Intl. Adv. Cttee., HK Baptist Coll. 95-; Mem., Sc. Adv. Bd., Cent. for Nanoscale Sc. & Tech. (Rice U.) 95-; Mem., Adv. Bd., Intl. Inst. for Condensed Matter Phys., U. of Brasilia 93-; Mem., Bd. of Dir., Coun. on Superconductivity for Am. Competitiveness 89-; *b.* Hunan Dec. 2, '41; *m.* Chern, May P.; 2 *c.; educ.* BS, NCKU 58-62; MS, Fordham U.63-65; Ph.D., U. of Calif., San Diego 65-68; Mem., Tech. Staff, Bell Labs., USA 68-70; Assc. Prof., Phys., Cleveland State U. 70-73, Prof. 75-79; Solid State Prog. Dir., Nat. Sc. Found. 86-87; Dir., Space Vacuum Epitaxy Cent., NASA/U. of Houston 86-88; Nat. Medal of Sc.; Comstock Award; Intl. Prize for New Mats., Medal of Sc. Merit, Phys. & Math. Sc. Award; NASA Achievement Award; Texas Instruments Founders' Prize; Leroy Randle Grumman Medal; Sigma Xi Res. Excellence Award. *Publ.:* 360 sc. papers; *Add.* Texas Cent. for Superconductivity, U. of Houston, Houston Sc. Center, Houston, TX 77204-5932, USA.

CHU, SHAO-HWA 瞿韶華
Nat. Policy Adv. to the Pres. 95-; *b.* Hopei Dec. 4, '14; *m.* Sun, Shao-kang; 1 *s.,* 1 *d.; educ.* LL.B., Chaoyang U.; Dep. Sec.-Gen., Exec. Yuan 58-73; Sec.-Gen., TPG 73-78; Sec.-Gen., Exec. Yuan 78-84; Min. of Exam., Exam. Yuan 84-90; Pres., Acad. Historica 90-95; *Add.* 122 Chungking S. Rd., Sect. 1, Taipei.

CHU, SHIH-LIEH 朱士烈
Nat. Policy Adv. to the Pres. 92-; *b.* Liaoning July 23, '15; *m.* Wu, Yu-lien; 2 *s.,* 2 *d.; educ.* LL.B., Nat. Wuhan U.; Justice, Revision Trial, Hupei & Szechwan Prov. 41-49; Justice & Admin. Chief Off., dist. courts in Twn. 49-70; Chief, Prison Dept., Min. of Legal Aff. 70-74; Public Prosecutor, Supreme Court 74-77; Lawyer 77-80 & 87-89; Chief Sec., KMT Caucas, NA 79-84 & 89-90; Dep. Sec.-Gen., Policy Coordination Cttee., CC, KMT 84-87; Sec.-Gen., NA 90-92; *Add.* 3rd Fl., 1 Lane 75, Yung Kang St., Taipei.

CHU, STEVEN 朱棣文
Mem., Acad. Sinica 94-; Prof., Phys., & Applied Phys., Stanford U. 87-, Theodore & Frances Geballe Prof. 90-; Mem., Nat. Acad. of Sc.; Fel., Am. Acad. of Arts & Sc.; *b.* USA Feb. 28, '48; 2 *s.; educ.* BS, Math., U. of Rochester 70, BS, Phys. 70; Ph.D., Phys., UC-Berkly. 76, Postdoctoral Res. Fel. 76-78; Mem., Tech. Staff, Electromagnetic Phenomena Res. Bell Labs., Murray Hill 78-83; Head, Quantum Elect. Res. Dept., AT&T Bell Labs., Holmel 83-87; Morris Loeb Lectr., Harvard U. 88; Sp. Visitor to JILA 89; Visiting Prof., Coll. de France 90; Chair, Phys. Dept., Stanford U. 90-93; *Add.* Dept. of Phys., Stanford U., Stanford, CA 94305-4060, USA.

CHU, TI-WEN
(See CHU, STEVEN 朱棣文)

CHU, WAN-CHING
(See CHU, GLORIA WAN-CHING 朱婉清)

CHU, YEN 朱炎
Writer; Prof., For. Lang., NTU 71-; Res. Fel., Inst. of European & Am. Studies, Acad. Sinica; Pres., Ki Ko Cul. & Educ. Found.; *b.* Shantung June 6, '36; *m.* Chu Hsu, Li-ching; 1 *s.,* 1 *d.; educ.* BA, For. Lang., NTU 60; Ph.D., La Universidad de Madrid 65; Assc. Prof., For. Lang., NTU 65-71; Dir., Inst. of Am. Studies, Acad. Sinica 77-83; Dean, Coll. of Arts, NTU 84-90; V. Chmn., NScC 92-93; Pres., British & Am. Lit. Assn., ROC 92-93. *Publ.: La Dramática Shakespeariana en Ch.; Love in the Morning; Collection of Criticisms of Am. Lit.; Bitter Growth; Sour Plum;* 10 essays on lit. & soc.; etc.; *Add.* 21 Alley 5, Lane 30, Chou Shan Rd., Taipei.

CHUA, NAM-HAI 蔡南海
Mem., Acad. Sinica 88-; Andrew W. Mellon Prof. 88-; Prof. & Head, Lab. of Plant Molecular Biology, Rockefeller U. 81-; Fel., Royal Soc. 88-; Assc. Fel., Third World Acad. of Sc. 88-; *b.* Ch. Apr. 8, '44; *m.* Suat-Choo (Pearl); 2 *d.; educ.* BS, U. of Singapore 65; MS, Harvard U. 67, Ph.D. 69; Lectr., Biochem. Dept., U. of Singapore Med. Sch. 69-71; Res. Assc., Cell Biology Dept., Rockefeller U. 71-73, Asst. Prof. 73-77, Assc. Prof. 77-81; Hon. Mem., Japan Biochem. Soc. 92. *Publ.:* 220 sc.

papers; *Add.* Lab. of Plant Molecular Biology, Rockefeller U., 1230 York Avenue, New York, NY 10021-6399, USA.

CHUAN, HAN-SHENG 全漢昇
Mem. & Res. Fel., Acad. Sinica 84-; Dir., New Asia Inst. of Advanced Ch. Studies 83-; *b.* Kwangtung Nov. 19, '13; *m.* Hwang, Hui-fang; 2 *s.; educ.* BA, Nat. Peking U. 35; Res. Fel., Harvard U. 44-45 & 62-63; Visiting Scholar, Columbia U. 45-47; Visiting Scholar, U. of Chicago 61-62; Prof., Econ. Dept., NTU 49-65, Dir. 52-57; Dir.-Gen., Acad. Sinica 58-61; Sr. Lectr. & Reader, New Asia Coll., Ch. U. of Hong Kong 65-77, Pres. 75-77. *Publ.: Collected Essays on Ch. Econ. Hist.; Studies on the Econ. Hist. of Ch.; Add.* B2 Edward Mansion, 230 Prince Edward Rd., Kowloon, Hong Kong.

CHUANG, HENG-TAI 莊亨岱
Nat. Policy Adv. to the Pres. 93-; Consultant, Exec. Yuan 93-; Mem., CC, KMT 93-; *b.* Fukien Oct. 7, '26; *m.* Chou, Ming-lih; 3 *s.,* 3 *d.; educ.* 17th Class, Cent. Police Coll., & 1st Class, Advanced Course I for Sr. Police Off.; Comr., Ilan Police Bu. 75-78; Comr., Taoyuan Police Bu. 78-82; Comr., Rwy. Police Bu. 82-85, 1st Peace Preservation Corps 85-87, & Bu. of Criminal Investigation 87-90; Dir.-Gen., Nat. Police Admin., MOI 90-93; Chmn., Po Hsin Multimedia Inc. 94-96; *Add.* 78 Ta Hu Shan Chuang St., Neihu, Taipei.

CHUANG, HUAI-I
(See JUANG, HWAI-I 莊懷義)

CHUANG, K. CASEY 莊國欽
Chmn., Far E. Mach. Co. Ltd. 87-, Logitech Inc., & Cimtek Inc.; *b.* Twn. Oct. 13, '35; *m.* Cho, S.H.; 2 *s.,* 1 *d.; educ.* BS, NCKU; Ph.D., MIT 65; Consultant Engr., IBM, USA 65-68; Plan Engr., Bendix Co., USA 68-72; Gen. Mgr., Far E. Mach. Co. Ltd. 72-87; Exec. Dir., Ch. Nat. Fed. of Ind.; Chmn., Twn. Assn. of Mach. Ind.; Mem., Legis. Yuan 90-92; *Add.* 14th Fl., 101 Fu Hsing N. Rd., Taipei.

CHUANG, KUO-CHIN
(See CHUANG, K. CASEY 莊國欽)

CHUANG, MING-CHE
(See TSUANG, MING T. 莊明哲)

CHUANG, MING-YAO 莊銘耀
Rep., TECRO in Japan 96-; *b.* Twn. Nov. 16, '29; *m.* Sheu, Shiow-ing; 2 *s.,* 2 *d.; educ.* Ch. Naval Acad., Class 1952; Naval Staff Coll., Class 1967; War Coll., Class 1973; Capt., Landing Ship Tank, Destroyer Escort, & Destroyer 63-75; Cmdr., Recruit Tng. Cent., ROCN 75-76; Dir., Service Bu., ROCN 76-79; Cmdr., 142 Fleet Squadron; Asst. Dep. Chief of the Gen. Staff for Intelligence, MND 80-83; Dir., Pers. Dept., ROCN 83-84; Cmdr., Fleet Tng. Cmd. 84-86; C/S, GHQ, ROCN 86-89, Dep. C-in-C 89-91; V. Min. of Nat. Def. 91-92; C-in-C, ROCN 92-94; Strategy Adv. to the Pres. 94-95; Nat. Policy Adv. to the Pres. 95-96; *Add.* 20-2, 5-Chome Shirokanedai, Minato-Ku, Tokyo 108 Japan.

CHUANG, YI-CHOU 莊逸洲
Nat. Policy Adv. to the Pres. 96-; *b.* Kaohsiung Oct. 20, '49; *m.* Chang, Chiao-mei; 1 *s.,* 4 *d.; educ.* MHA, Hosp. Adm., Ch. Med. Coll.; Asst. Mgr., Formosa Chem. & Fibre Corp.; Mgr., Chang-Gung Hosp.; Sp. Asst., Chang-Gung Hosp.; *Add.* 199 Tun Hua N. Rd., Taipei.

CHUNG, CHAO-CHENG
(See CHUNG, CHAU-CHENG 鍾肇政)

CHUNG, CHAU-CHENG 鍾肇政
Novelist; *b.* Twn. Jan. 20, '25; *m.* Chung Chang, Chiu-mei; 2 *s.,* 3 *d.; educ.* Attended at Dept. of Ch. Lit., NTU; Instr., Dept. of Japanese, Soochow U. 74-77; Chief, *Twn. Lit. Mag.* 76-82; Ed.-in-Chief, *Commons Daily* 78-80. *Publ.: Troubled River: A Triology; Twn. Hist.: A Triology; Expecting the Spring Wind;* etc.; *Add.* 53 Lung Hua Rd., Lungtan, Taoyuan County.

CHUNG, CHEN-HUNG 鍾振宏
Rep., TECO, Tel-Aviv 93-; *b.* Twn. July 11, '29; *m.* Huang, Chin-lien; 1 *s.,* 1 *d.; educ.* BA, Twn. Normal Coll.; MA, Meiji U.; Am. U.; Press Counsl., Emb. in Japan 71-72; Adv. & concur. Dir. of Press, Tokyo Off., AEAR 73-80; Dir., Dept. of Info., TPG 80-85; Counsl., GIO 85; Adv. & concur. Dir. of Press, Tokyo Off., AEAR 85-87; Dep. Dir.-Gen., GIO 87-89; Dep. Rep.,

TECO, Japan 89-93; *Add.* 91 Nordau St., Herzliya B, 46591, Israel.

CHUNG, DAVID J.C. 鍾榮吉

Dep. Sec.-Gen., CC, KMT 95-; *b.* Twn. Jan. 27, '43; *m.* Liu, Yu-yuan; 1 *s.,* 1 *d.; educ.* BJ, NCU 65; Grad., E.-W. Cent., Inst. of Cul. & Comm.; Grad., 15th Class, Sun Yat-sen Inst. on Policy Res. & Dev.; Eisenhower Fel. 92; Reporter, Assc. Ed., & City Ed.,*United Daily News* 66-80; Mem., Legis. Yuan 80-86; Sec.-Gen., Unity & Self-Reliance Assn. 84-87; Dep. Dir.-Gen., Dept. of Ovs. Aff., CC, KMT 86-89; Mem., Control Yuan 87-93; Dir.-Gen., Dept. of Soc. Aff., CC, KMT 89-94, Chmn., Twn. Prov. Cttee. 94-95; *Add.* 53 Jen Ai Rd., Sect. 3, Taipei.

CHUNG, JUNG-CHI

(See CHUNG, DAVID J.C. 鍾榮吉)

CHUNG, MING-DER 鍾明德

Artistic Dir., Environmental Theatre 425, 89; Assc. Prof., Nat. Inst. of Arts 92; Rep., Asian Cul. Coun., Taipei 94; *b.* Twn. Apr. 1, '53; *m.* Lu, Hui-ping; 1 *s.; educ.* BA, NTU 75; MA, New York U. 84, Ph.D. 92; Lectr., Nat. Inst. of Arts 86-91; Film/Theatre Critic, *World Jour., USA* 84-86; Dir., Twn. Film Studio 81-82. *Publ.: Inside the Noises of Postmodernism* 89; *The Little Theatre Movement of Twn.* 93; *Mending the Sky: The Bread and Puppet Theatre in Twn.* 94; *Modern Theatre: From Realism to Postmodernism* 95; *Add.* 9A, 303 Chung Hsiao E. Rd., Sect. 4, Taipei.

CHUNG, MING-TE

(See CHUNG, MING-DER 鍾明德)

CHUO, ERIC Y.T. 卓永財

Chmn. & Chief Exec. Off., Hiwin Techs. Corp. (Twn.) 88-, & Hiwin Techs. Corp., USA 92-; Geschäftsführer, Hiwin Tech. GmbH, Germany 93-; Mem., Ind. Dev. Adv. Cttee., MOEA 93-; *b.* Twn. Nov. 20, '42; *m.* Chuo Hsu, Huei-chien; 1 *s.,* 2 *d.; educ.* BBA, Tamkang U. 70; MPA, U. of San Francisco 81; Passed Sr. Civil Service Exam. in Financial & Banking Aff. 69; V. Pres. & concur. Exec. Sec., Chiao Tung Bk. 68-84. *Publ.: Corp. For. Exchange* (5th Edition); *Add.* 5th Fl., 23 Chang An E. Rd., Sect. 1, Taipei.

DEN, CHI-FU 鄧啟福

Pres., NCTU 92-; *b.* Hupei Nov. 29, '31; *m.* Den, Irene; 1 *s.,* 1 *d.; educ.* BSEE, NTU 56; MS, Inst. of Elect., NCTU 60; MSEE & DSEE, U. of Michigan 66; Assc. Resr., Radiation Lab., U. of Michigan 66-67; Mem., Tech. Staff, AT&T Bell Labs. 67-75; Dir. & Prof., Dept. of Comm. Engr., NCTU 75-78, Dean, Coll. of Engr. 78-84; Dir., Engr. & Applied Sc. Div., NScC 84-87, V. Chmn. 87-90; Dean of Acad. Aff., NCTU 91-92; *Add.* NCTU, 1001 Ta Hsueh Rd., Hsinchu.

DING, MOU-SHIH 丁懋時

Sec.-Gen., NSC 94-; Mem., CC, KMT 93-; *b.* Yunnan Oct. 10, '25; *m.* Shih, Mei-chang; 1 *s.,* 1 *d.; educ.* Paris U.; Reporter, CNA 56-58; Consultant, MOFA 58-60, Sect. Chief, Dept. of W. Asian Aff. 60-62; 1st Sec., Ch. Mission to the European Off. of the UN 62; Chargé d'Affaires, Emb. in Rwanda 62-64; Amb. to Rwanda 64-67; Amb. to Zaire 67-71; Alt. Rep., ROC Del. to the 24th & 25th Sess. of UNGA 69-70; Dir., Dept. of African Aff., MOFA 72-74; Govt. Spokesman & Dir.-Gen., GIO 75-79; Dir., Dept. of Cul. Aff., CC, KMT 77-79; Admin. V. Min. of For. Aff. 79; Amb. to S. Korea 79-82; Pol. V. Min. of For. Aff. 82-87; MOFA 87-88; Rep., CCNAA, Washington, D.C.; *Add.* 122 Chungking S. Rd., Sect. 1, Taipei.

DING, MOW-SUNG 丁懋松

Consultant on British & US laws, Ding & Ding Law Off.; *b.* Yunnan Feb. 25, '38; 1 *s.,* 1 *d.; educ.* LL.B., Tokyo U. 59; LL.M., Yale Law Sch. 65; Barrister-at-Law, Inner Temple, UK 67; Attorney-at-Law, New York State 73, & Calif. State 74; Asst. Prof., Nanyang U., Singapore 69-71; Attorney-at-Law, Winthrop, Stimson, Putnam & Roberts, New York 68-69 & 71-74, & Graham & James, San Francisco 75; Partner, Kirkwood, Kaplan, Russin & Vecchi, Washington 76-78; *Add.* Ding & Ding Law Off., 10th Fl., 563 Chung Hsiao E. Rd., Sect. 4, Taipei.

DUNN, KAN C. 鄧權昌

Amb. to Liberia 89-; *b.* Kwangtung '25; *m.* Dunn, Tina L.; 3 *s.; educ.* NCU; Ch. Naval Acad.; US Naval Tng. Sch.; Sec. to the C-in-C, ROCN 50-52; Sec. to the Personal C/S to the Pres. 52-54; Sp. Asst., Off. of the Chief of the Gen. Staff, MND 54-55; Asst., MOFA 55-58; V.

Consul, Davao City, Philippines 58-59, & San Francisco 59-64; Consul, Los Angeles 64-67, & New York 67-70; Consul-Gen., Chicago 70-72; Dep. Dir., Dept. of Consular Aff., MOFA 72-73; Consul-Gen., Houston 73-77; Dir., Dept. of Gen. Aff., MOFA 77; Consul-Gen., New York 77-79; Dir.-Gen., CCNAA, New York 79-86; V. Chmn., Res. & Planning Bd., MOFA 86-88; Rep., Trade Mission of the ROC in Liberia 88-89; *Add.* P.O. Box 5970, 101 Pan Africa Plaza, Monrovia, Liberia.

FAN, CHEN-TZUNG 范振宗
Magis., Hsinchu County 89-; *b.* Twn. Nov. 20, '42; *m.* Chang, Hui-mei; 1 *s.,* 2 *d.; educ.* B., Nat. Twn. Ocean U. 73; Mem., Hsinchu CoCoun. 76-86, Dep. Spkr. 82-86; Mem., NA 87-90; *Add.* 10 Kuang Ming 6 Rd., Chupei, Hsinchu County.

FAN, CHI
(See FAN, KY 樊畿)

FAN, HSU-YUN 范緒筠
Mem., Acad. Sinica 59-; Prof. Emeritus, Purdue U. 48-; *b.* Shanghai July 15, '12; *m.* Bien, Li-nien; 2 *s.,* 2 *d.; educ.* BS, Harbin Polytechnic 32; D.Sc., MIT 37; Prof., NTHU 37-48; *Add.* Dept. of Phys., Purdue U., W. Lafayette, IN 47907, USA.

FAN, KY 樊畿
Mem., Acad. Sinica 64-; Prof. Emeritus, U. of Calif., Santa Barbara 85-; Hon. Prof., Peking U. & Peking Normal U. 89-; Mem., Ed. Bd., *Linear Algebra & Its Application* 68-; *Topological Methods in Nonlinear Analysis* 93-; *Set-valued Analysis* 93-; *b.* Chekiang Sept. 19, '14; *m.* Yen, Yu-fen; *educ.* BS, Peking U. 36; Docteur äs Sc. Math., U. of Paris 41; Docteur Honoris Causa, U. Paris IX Dauphine 90; Charge de Recherches, Cent. Nat. de la Recherche Scientifique, France 42-45; Mem., Inst. for Advanced Study, Princeton 45-47; Asst. Prof., U. of Notre Dame 47-49, Assc. Prof. 49-52, Prof. 52-60; Prof., Wayne State U. 60-61; Prof., Northwe. U. 61-65; Prof., Dept. of Math., U. of Calif., Santa Barbara 65-85, Chmn. 68-69; Dir., Inst. of Math., Acad. Sinica 78-84; Visiting Prof., U. of Texas, Austin 65, U. Hamburg 72, U. Paris IX Dauphine 81, U. Perugia, Italy 85 & 87; Mem., Ed. Bd., J*our. of Math. Analysis & Applications* 60-92, & *Linear & Multilinear Algebra* 73-92.

Publ.: Over 120 res. papers in various intl. math. jour.; *Add.* 1402 Santa Teresita Drive, Santa Barbara, CA 93105, USA.

FANG, CHIN-HAI 方金海
Spkr., Tainan CCoun. 94-; *b.* Twn. June 15, '55; *m.* Li, Hong-ying; 1 *s.,* 3 *d.; educ.* Grad., Nan-tai Coll.; Gen. Mgr., Bao-min Co. Ltd.; *Add.* 3 Chung Cheng Rd., Tainan.

FANG, CHIN-YEN 房金炎
Rep., TECO in Can. 96-; *b.* Twn. Nov. 11, '31; *m.* Hsu, Hui-ying; 2 *d.; educ.* BA, NTU 54; MA, Am. U. 67, Ph.D. 77; Staff Asst., Info. Dept., MOFA 56-58; Attaché & 3rd Sec., Emb. in USA 58-65; 2nd Sec., Emb. in the Philippines 66; Sect. Chief & Dep. Dir., Dept. of Intl. Org., MOFA 66-71; Adv., Del. to 24th UNGA 69; Alt. Rep., Del. to UNIDO Sp. Conf. 71; Amb. to Nicaragua 72-76; Sr. Sec., MOFA 77, Counsl. 78-81; Assc. Prof., Soochow U. & NCU 79-81; V. Chmn., Res. & Pol. Planning Bd., MOFA 80-81; Rep. in UK 82-90; Admin. V. Min., MOFA 90-93; Pol. V. Min., MOFA 93-96; *Add.* Suite 1960, 45 O'Connor St., Ottawa, Ont., K1P 1A4 Can.

FANG, HSI-CHING 方錫經
Pres., Shih Chien Coll. 93-; Adjunct Prof., Taipei Med. Coll. 93-; Chmn., Assn. of Private U. & Coll. in ROC 95-; *b.* Twn. Jan. 20, '31; *m.* Wu, Su-shyu; 2 *s.,* 1 *d.; educ.* BS, NTNU 57; Grad., Inst. of Nuclear Sc., NTHU 62; Ph.D. Candidate, Radiation Biophys. Atomic Disease Inst., Nat. Nagasaki U. 70, Ph.D., Sch. of Med. 94; Res., Nat. Grad. Inst. of Radiology Sc. 69; Instr., Taipei Med. Coll. 61-64, Lectr. 64-68, Assc. Prof. 68-74, Prof. 74-76, Prof. & concur. Dean of Gen. Aff. 76-78, Prof. & concur. Dean of Studies 78-83, Prof. & concur. Dean of Student Aff. 83-93; Pres. (acting), Taipei Med. Coll. 83-84; Resr., Nat. Cancer Cent. Hospital, Japan 70-71; Resr., Nat. Inst. of Radiology Sc., Japan 70-71. *Publ.: Comparison of Synchronous DNA Synthesis Between Colony Forming and Random Population of L-Strain Mouse Cells; Whole Body Counter; Counting Statistics on Radioisotope; Properties of ThO² at the Time of Animal Experiment; Biological Effects of Cells to Radiation Measurements of a.β Rays Activity in Mice Organs; Add.* 3 Alley 62, Ta Chih St., Taipei.

FANG, HUAI-SHIH
(See FANG, HWAI-SZE 方懷時)

FANG, HWAI-SZE 方懷時
Mem., Acad. Sinica 78-; Prof. Emeritus, NTU 86-; *b.* Chekiang Nov. 7, '14; *m.* Loh, Kun-cheng; 1 *s.,* 1 *d.; educ.* Chekiang Prov. Med. Coll. 37; MD, Nagoya U. 52; Res. Fel., W. Virginia U. & Ohio State U. 52-53, Columbia U. 60-61; Asst. & Instr., Nat. Kweiyang Med. Coll. 38-41; Assc. Prof., Nat. Kiangsu Med. Coll. 43-47; Assc. Prof., NTU 47-50, Prof. 50-85, Dean of Student Aff., Coll. of Med. 72-78; Nat. Res. Chair, Nat. Coun. on Sc. Dev. 66-68; Visiting Prof., Columbia U. 68-69; Sr. Lectr., Tng. Unit of Aviation Safety & Mng., Coll. of Engr., NTU 73-86. *Publ.: Aviation Physiology; Altitude Convulsion; Explosive Decompression; Hypoxia & Gastrointestinal Motility;* etc.; *Add.* Inst. of Physiology, Coll. of Med., NTU, 1 Jen Ai Rd., Sect. 1, Taipei.

FANG, JUNG-CHUEH
(See FANG, RONG-JYUE 方榮爵)

FANG, RONG-JYUE 方榮爵
Pres., Nat. Taitung Tchrs. Coll. 94-; *b.* Twn. Aug. 26, '51; *m.* Hwang, Hsu-wuen; 1 *s.,* 1 *d.; educ.* B.Ed., Nat. Kaohsiung Tchrs. Coll. 74; M.Ed., NTNU 79; MS, Ea. Illinois State U. 80; Ph.D., Penn. State U. 84; Teaching Asst., Nat. Kaohsiung Tchrs. Coll. 74-75; Tchr., Elect., Hsilo Voc. High Sch. 77-78; Teaching Asst., Ea. Illinois U. 78-80; Res. Asst., Penn. State U. 80-84; Assc. Prof., Nat. Kaohsiung Tchrs. Coll. 84-89, Dir., Computation Cent. 85-87; Prof., Nat. Kaohsiung Normal U. 89, Chmn., Dept. of Tech. Educ. 92-94. *Publ.:* 40 papers published in prof. jour.; 13 theses presented in acad. seminars; *Add.* 684 Chung Hua Rd., Sect. 1, Taitung.

FENG, YUAN-CHEN
(See FUNG, YUAN-CHENG 馮元楨)

FU, MEI-HUA
(See FUH, MEI-HWA 傅美華)

FU, SHEN-LI 傅勝利
Pres., Kaohsiung Polytechnic Inst. 90-; *b.* Shantung Aug. 1, '45; *m.* Chang, Show-chung; 1 *s.,* 1 *d.; educ.* BS, NCKU 69, MS 72, Ph.D. 77; Assc. Prof., NCKU 77-82,

Prof. 82-90, Dean of Student Aff. 87-89; Visiting Scholar, UCLA 80-81; Dir., Engr. & Tech. Promotion Cent., NScC 89-90. *Publ.:* Author & co-author of 100 acad. papers about elect. material sc. & microelect.; *Add.* 1 Hsueh Cheng Rd., Sect. 1, Tashu, Kaohsiung County.

FU, SHENG-LI
(See FU, SHEN-LI 傅勝利)

FUH, MEI-HWA 傅美華
Mem., Control Yuan 93-; *b.* Kiangsi Apr. 25, '28; *m.* Ping, Shu-fang; 1 *d.; educ.* Grad., Kiangsi Prov. Chang Hsu High Sch. 46; Studied in the Advanced Class, Admin. Sch. 60; Passed Sr. Civil Service Exam. 52; Passed Sp. Exam. B 65; Recorder, Statistics Off., Iwu Dist. Court, Chekiang 47-48; Statistics Off., Sec., Sect. Chief of Statistics, Sect. Chief of Admin., ROCN Hqs. 48-64; Recorder & Statistics Off., Twn. High Court 64-66; Insp., Sect. Chief, & Sup., DGBAS 66-67; Chief Acct., MOE 77-80; Acct. Off. & concur. Dir., 1st Bu., DGBAS 80-88, Dep. Dir.-Gen. 88-93; *Add.* 2 Chung Hsiao E. Rd., Sect. 1, Taipei.

FUNG, YUAN-CHENG 馮元楨
Mem., Acad. Sinica 66-; Prof. Emeritus 90-; Chmn., World Cttee. for Biomech. 90-; Mem., US Nat. Acad. of Engr. 79-, Inst. of Med., US Nat. Acad. of Sc. 90-; Fel., Am. Inst. of Med. & Biological Engr. 92-; *b.* Kiangsu Sept. 15, '19; *educ.* BS, Nat. Cent. U. 41, MS 43; Ph.D., Calif. Inst. of Tech. 48; Asst. Prof., Calif. Inst. of Tech. 51-55, Assc. Prof. 55-59, Prof. 59-66; Consultant, Boeing Aircraft Co. 58-62, Douglas Aircraft 60, Aerospace Corp. 62, N. Am. Aviation 63; Prof., U. of Calif., San Diego 66; Mem., Am. Heart Assn. 67; V. Pres., Intl. Soc. of Biorheology 74-83; Chmn., US Nat. Cttee. for Biomech. 80; Pres., Soc. of Biomed. Engr. 82-83; Pres., Am. Acad. of Mech. 83. *Publ.: Theory of Aeroelasticity; Found. of Solid Mech.; 1st Course in Continuum Mech.; Biomech.-Mech. Properties of Living Tissues; Biodynamics-Circulation; Biomech.: Motion, Flow, Stress & Growth;* numerous tech. papers in prof. jour.; *Add.* 2660 Greentree Lane, La Jolla, CA 92037, USA.

HAN, KUANG-WEI 韓光渭
Mem., Acad. Sinica 90-; Chair Prof., Yuan-Ze Inst. of Tech. 95; Dep. Dir., System Dev. Cent., Chung Shan

Inst. of Sc. & Tech. 82-; Adjunct Prof., NTU 92-; *b.* Shantung Jan. 29, '30; *m.* Han, Mei-lei; 3 *d.; educ.* BS, Ch. Naval Coll. of Tech. 55; Ph.D., US Naval Postgrad. Sch. 61; Hon. Ph.D., NCTU 95; Rear Adm.; Assc. Prof., Ch. Naval Coll. of Tech. & NCTU 62-64; Visiting Res. Assc., UC-Berkly. 64-65; Scientist, Chung Shan Inst. of Sc. & Tech. 55-94; Adjunct Prof., NCTU 62-92; Adjunct Prof., NTU 92-94; *Add.* 135 Far E. Rd., Neili, Chungli, Taoyuan County.

HAN, SHAO-HUA
(See HAN, SHOU-HWA 韓韶華)

HAN, SHOU-HWA 韓韶華
Prof. & Dir., Cent. for Immunology, Nat. Yang Ming U. 96-; *b.* Kiangsu Jan. 19, '30; *m.* Wei, Yun-tse; 2 *s.,* 1 *d.; educ.* MD, Nat. Def. Med. Cent. 55; Ph.D., U. of Washington 66; Investigator, Dept. of Med. Res., Veterans Gen. Hosp., Taipei 66-79, Dir. 79-90; Assc. Prof. of Immunology, Nat. Def. Med. Cent. 66-70, Prof. 70-90; Pres., Ch. Microbiology Soc. 77-79; Pres., Ch. Immunology Soc. 78-80; Ed.-in-Chief, *Ch. Med. Jour.* 79-81; Dean, Grad. Studies, Nat. Def. Med. Cent. 82-88. Pres., Nat. Yang Ming U. 90-96. *Publ.:* 172 referred papers; *Add.* 155 Li Nung St., Sect. 2, Shihpai, Taipei.

HAO, YEN-PING 郝延平
Mem., Acad. Sinica 96-; Prof., U. of Tennessee 72-; Lindsay Young Prof., Hist., U. of Tennessee 84-; *b.* Nanking Dec. 22, '34; *m.* Hao T., Pin-han; 2 *s.; educ.* BA, NTU 58; Ph.D., Harvard U. 66; Asst. Prof., U. of Tennessee 65-68, Assc. Prof. 68-72. *Publ.: The Comprador in 19th-Century Ch.* 70; *The Cml. Rev. in 19th-Century Ch.* 86; *Add.* 1101 McClung Tower, Knoxville, Tennessee 37996-0411, USA.

HER, TYH-HUEI 何智輝
Magis., Miaoli County 93-; *b.* Twn. Apr. 17, '50; *m.* Wang, Suh-yun; 1 *d.; educ.* Grad., NTIT; Coun. & V. Spkr., Miaoli CoCoun. 86-90; Mem., Legis. Yuan 90-93; *Add.* 89 Fu Tung Rd., Miaoli.

HO, CHIEN 何潛
Mem., Acad. Sinica; Prof., Dept. of Biological Sc. & Dir., Pittsburgh NMR Cent. for Biomed. Res., Carnegie Mellon U. 86-, Alumni Prof. of Biological Sc. 85-; *b.* Shanghai Oct. 23, '34; *m.* Tseng, Nancy; 2 *d.; educ.* BS, Williams Coll., USA 57; Ph.D., Yale U. 61; Res. Chemist, Linde Co., Union Carbide Tonowanda 60-61; Res. Assc., MIT 61-64; Asst. Prof., U. of Pittsburgh 64-67, Assc. Prof. 67-70, Prof. 70-79; Prof. & Head, Dept. of Biological Sc., Carnegie Mellon U. 79-86. *Publ.:* Over 190 articles in sc. jour.; *Add.* 2034 Garrick Drive, Pittsburgh, PA 15235, USA.

HO, CHIH HUI
(See HER, TYH-HUEI 何智輝)

HO, FRED FWU-TYAN 何福田
Pres., Nat. Pingtung Tchrs. Coll. 90-; *b.* Kaohsiung Nov. 9, '42; *m.* Ho Feng, Rong-jean; 1 *s.,* 3 *d.; educ.* Studied at Ball State U., Muncie, Indiana 80-81; Ph.D., NCU 82; Hon. D.Lit., Trinity Coll., Hartford, Connecticut 95; Sec., Bu. of Educ., TCG 69-74; Dir. & Assc. Prof., Taipei Mun. Tchrs. Coll. for Women 74-77; Prof., Dir. & Chmn., Tamkang U. 81-85; Dean of Acad. Aff., Nat. Kaohsiung Tchrs. Coll. 85-89; Dean, Coll. of Educ., & concur. Curator, Lib., Nat. Changhua U. of Educ. 89-90. *Publ.: Parenthood & Teachership* 79; *A Study of Elementary & Secondary Schs.: Tchrs.' In-Service Educ. in Twn.* 82; *Face Our Educ.* 91; *"Knowing" & "Doing" for the Benefit of Nat. Educ.* 95; *Add.* 1 Lin Sen Rd., Pingtung.

HO, FU-TIEN
(See HO, FRED FWU-TYAN 何福田)

HO, I-WU
(See HO, IRWINE W. 何宜武)

HO, ING-KANG 何英剛
Chmn. & Prof., Dept. of Pharmacology & Toxicology, U. of Mississippi Med. Cent. 82-; Dir., Grad. Prog., U. of Mississippi Med. Cent. 82-; *b.* Twn. May 7, '39; *m.* Ho, Patricia; 1 *s.,* 2 *d.; educ.* BS, NTU 62; Ph.D., UC-San Francisco 68; Instr., Baylor Coll. of Med. 68-70; Asst. Res. Pharmacologist, UC-San Francisco 70-73; Asst. Prof., UC-San Francisco 73-75; Assc. Prof., U. of Mississippi Med. Cent. 75-78; Prof., U. of Mississippi Med. Cent. 78-82. *Publ.:* 270 res. papers; *Add.* 2500 N. State St., Jackson, Mississippi 39216-4505, USA.

HO, IRWINE W. 何宜武

Sr. Adv. to the Pres.; *b.* Fukien Dec. 10, '13; *m.* Wang, Hsiu-chiao; 2 *s.*, 1 *d.; educ.* BA, Chaoyang U.; Resr., U. of Washington; Chief Sec., Dept. of Finance, TPG 45-46; Comr. & Mem., OCAC 49-61, V. Chmn. 62-72; Comr., Fukien Prov. Govt. 49-86; Sec.-Gen., NA 80-90; Mem., CSC, KMT; Chmn., Cul. & Charity Found. of United World Ch. Cml. Bk.; Prof., Ch. Cul. U.; Chmn., Feng Chia U. *Publ.: Res. on Econ. of Ovs. Ch.; Add.* 22 Lane 63, Ta Hu Villa St., Neihu, Taipei.

HO, MAN-TE
(See HO, MONTO 何曼德)

HO, MONTO 何曼德

Mem., Acad. Sinica; Prof. of Med., Microbiology & Pathology, & concur. Dir., Dept. of Infectious Diseases & Microbiology, Grad. Sch. of Public Health, U. of Pittsburgh; Mem., Assn. of Am. Phys.; Mem., Am. Soc. of Clinical Investigation; *b.* Hunan Mar. 28, '27; *m.* Tsu, Carol; 2 *c.; educ.* B., Harvard Coll., USA 49; MD, Harvard Med. Sch. 54; Fulbright Sr. Scholar 67-68; Max-Planck Inst. for Virology 67-68; Josiah Macy Sr. Scholar 78-79; John Curtin Sch. of Med. Res., Canberra. *Publ.: Ho, M. Cytomegalovirus: Biology & Infection; Add.* Crabtree Hall A-427, U. of Pittsburgh, Pittsburgh, PA 15261, USA.

HO, PENG-YOKE 何丙郁

Mem., Acad. Sinica 88-; Emeritus Prof., Griffith U., Australia; Dir., Needham Res. Inst., Cambridge, Eng.; Prof. & Res. Assc., U. of London; *b.* Ch. Apr. 4, '26; *m.* Ho Fung, Mei-yiu; 1 *s.*, 4 *d.; educ.* BS, U. of Malaya 50, MS 51, Ph.D. 59; Prof., Ch. Studies, U. of Malaya 64-73; Visiting Prof., Yale U. 65; D.Sc., U. of Singapore 69; Fel., Inst. of Phys., London 71; Asian Fel., Australian Nat. U. 72; Fel., Leverhulme; Visiting Prof., Keio U. 75; Fel., Australian Acad. of Humanities 76; Prof., U. of Hong Kong 81-87; Visiting Prof., NTHU 91; Hon. D.Lit., Edinburgh, UK 95. *Publ.: The Astronomical Chapters of the Chin Shu; Li, Qi & Shu: An Introduction to Ch. Sc.; Add.* Needham Res. Inst., 8 Sylvester Rd., Cambridge, CB3 9AF, UK.

HO, PING-TI 何炳棣

Mem., Acad. Sinica 55-; Fel., Am. Acad. of Arts & Sc. 79-; *b.* Tientsin Sept. 1, '17; *m.* Shao, Ching-lo; 2 *s.;*

educ. BA, NTHU 38; Ph.D., Columbia U. 52; Hon. LL.D., Ch. U. of Hong Kong 75; Hon. LHD, Lawrence U., USA 78; Hon. LHD, Dennison U., USA 88; Instr., NTHU 39-45; Asst. Prof. & Prof., U. of British Columbia 48-63; Pres., Assn. for Asian Studies 75-76; James Westhall Thompson Prof. of Hist., U. of Chicago 63-87; Visiting Disting. Prof., U. of Calif., Irvine 87-90. *Publ.: Studies on the Population of Ch., 1368-1953* 59; *The Ladder of Success in Imperial Ch., 1368-1911* 62; *The Cradle of the E. 5000-1000 B.C.* 75; etc.; *Add.* 5471 Sierra Verde Rd., Irvine, CA 92612, USA.

HO, PING-YU
(See HO, PENG-YOKE 何丙郁)

HO, SHOU-SHAN
(See HO, SHOW-SHEN 何壽山)

HO, SHOW-SHEN 何壽山

Chmn., Yuen-Foong-Yu Paper Mfg. Co. Ltd. 89-, Hsin-Yi Ent. Co. Ltd., Hsin-Yi Recreation Ent. Co. Ltd. 89-, Shin-Foong Chem. Ind. Co. Ltd. 79-, Twn. Hopax Inds. Co. Ltd. 74-, & Intl. Lonkon Ent. Co. Ltd.; Standing Sup., Ch. United Trust & Investment Corp.; *b.* Twn. June 6, '29; *m.* Ho Tsai, Hue-shine; 1 *s.*, 3 *d.; educ.* MS, Chem. Engr., U. of Washington, Seattle 59; Mill Mgr., Yuen-Foong-Yu Paper Mfg. Co. Ltd. 59-61, Pres. 61-83, V. Bd. Chmn. 68-73; Sup., Intl. Cml. Bk. of Ch. 75-81; Mng. Dir., Taitung Ent. Corp. 68-92; Bd. Mem., Chung-Hwa Pulp Corp. 77-89, Mng. Dir. 89-92; Bd. Mem., Ch. Color Printing Co. Inc. 80-92; Bd. Mem., P.T. Indah Kiat Pulp & Paper Corp., Indonesia 77-92; *Add.* 51 Chungking S. Rd., Sect. 2, Taipei.

HO, YING-KANG
(See HO, ING-KANG 何英剛)

HONG, DAVID C.S. 洪敏雄

Rep., TECO in Australia 96-; *b.* Twn. Feb. 25, '38; *m.* Chang, Linda Kwei-siu; 1 *s.*, 3 *d.; educ.* Grad. Study, Cape Town U.; B. of Law, Dept. of Dip., NCU; Staff Mem., Dept. of Am. Aff., MOFA 60-64; 3rd Sec., Emb. in Sierra Leone 64-68; 2nd Sec., Emb. in Malawi 68-71; Sect. Chief, Dept. of African Aff., MOFA 71-73; Dep. Dir., Dept. of African Aff., MOFA 73-75;

Consul-Gen., Cape Town, RSA 75-83; Min., Emb. in RSA 83-88; Dir., Dept. of Consl. Aff., MOFA 88-90; Amb. to Belize 90-92; Dir.-Gen., Bu. of Consl. Aff., MOFA 92-96; *Add.* Unit 8, Tourism House, 40 Blackall St., Barton, ACT 2600 Australia.

HONG, YUH-CHIN 洪玉欽
Dep. Dir.-Gen., CC, KMT 95-; V. Pres., ROC-USA Inter-Parliamentary Amity Assn. 95-; Mem., Legis. Yuan 81-; *b.* Twn. July 11, '43; *m.* Shen, Mei-chu; *educ.* LL.B., Soochow U. 67; LL.M., Ch. Cul. U., LL.D. 79; V. Chmn., Policy Coordination Cttee., CC, KMT 88-89, Dir., Dept. of Intra- & Inter-Party Rel. 92-93, Dir., Legis. Inter-Party Coordination Cttee. 92-93, Sup., Cent. Policy Cttee. 93-94; *Add.* Rm. 515, 1 Ching Tao E. Rd., Taipei.

HOU, CHIA-CHU 侯家駒
Prof., Intl. Econ., Soochow U. 74-; *b.* Anhwei Aug. 6, '28; *m.* Shen, Tsui-ying; 3 *s.; educ.* MS, NCHU; MA, Agr. Econ., U. of New Eng.; Assc. Prof., Coll. of Ch. Cul. 66-67; Assc. Prof., Soochow U. 67-72; Visiting Fel., Yale U. 73. *Publ.: Introduction to Factor Prices; Marginal Analysis & Average Analysis; Hist. of Ch. Econ. Thought; Add.* 5th Fl., 101-1 Hsin Tien Rd., Hsintien, Taipei County.

HOU, HSIAO-HSIEN 侯孝賢
Film Dir.; *b.* Kwangtung '47; *educ.* Grad., Film Dept., Nat. Twn. Acad. of Arts 72; Script Sup.; Screenplay Writer; Winner, Sp. Jury Award, Asia-Pacific Film Festival & Award for Best Film, Rotterdam Film Festival for *The Time to Live & the Time to Die* 85; Award for Best Dir.; Award for Best Photography & Award for Best Music, Nantes Festival for *Dust in the Wind* 86; Sp. Jury Award, Durin Intl. Festival for d. of the Nile 87; Golden Lion of Venice Award, Venice Intl. Film Festival for *City of Sadness* 90; Jury Prize, Cannes Intl. Film Festival for *The Puppetmaster* 93; officially selected for Cannes Intl. Film Festival for *Good Men, Good Women* 95; *Goodbye S., Goodbye* 96. *Films: Cute Girl* 80; *Green, Green Grass of Home* 82; *The Sandwich Man* 83; *The Boys from Feng-kuei* 83; *A Summer at Grandpa's* 84; Exec. Producer for films *Raised the Red Lanterns & Dust of Angel; Add.* 2nd Fl., 5 Lane 23 Wan Ning St., Wenshan, Taipei.

HSIA, HAN-MIN 夏漢民
Nat. Policy Adv. to the Pres. 96-; *b.* Fukien May 3, '32; *m.* Wang, Show-mee; 2 *s.,* 1 *d.; educ.* BS, Marine Engr., Ch. Naval Acad. 54; MS, Mech. Engr., NCKU 62; Ph.D., Mech. Engr., U. of Oklahoma 65; Prof. & Chmn., Dept. of Engr. Sc., NCKU 67-71; Pres., Prov. Kaohsiung Inst. of Tech. 72-77; Dir., Dept. of Voc. & Tech. Educ., MOE 77-79; Admin. V. Min. of Educ. 79-80; Pres., NCKU 80-88; Pres., Ch. Inst. of Engr. 88-89; Chmn., NScC 88-93; Min. of State 93-96. *Publ.:* Over 40 publ. in the fields of heat transfer, voc. & tech. educ.; *Add.* 3rd Fl., 13-2 Lane 97, Hsin Sheng S. Rd., Sect. 1, Taipei.

HSIA, TIEN 夏甸
Rep., TECO, Austria 96-; *b.* Hopei Feb. 8, '29; *m.* Hsia Wang, Hsi-ming; 2 *s.,* 1 *d.; educ.* Grad., Ch. Naval Acad. 50, Class A, Fire Control in US Navy 57, Cmd. Coll., US Naval War Coll. 72, & War Coll., Armed Forces U. 73; Cmdg. Off., RCS Yung-tai (PCE 41) 63, RCS Tai-ho (DE 23) 68, RCS Nan-yang (DD17) 70; Chief, Bu. Planning, GHQ, ROCN 75, Cmdr., Destroyer Squadron 77; Cmdt., Naval Cmd. & Staff Coll., Armed Forces U. 79; Dep. Chief of the Gen. Staff, Planning (J-5), MND 82, Dep. Chief of the Gen. Staff 87; Rep., Taipei Representative Off. in the Netherlands 92-96; *Add.* Stubenring, 4/III/18, A-1010, Vienna, Austria.

HSIANG, WU-CHUNG 項武忠
Mem., Acad. Sinica; Prof. of Math., Princeton U.; *b.* Chekiang June 12, '35; *m.* Hsiang, Pei-ying; 2 *s.; educ.* BS, NTU 57; Ph.D., Princeton U.; *Add.* Dept. of Math., Princeton U., Washington Rd., Princeton, NJ 68544, USA.

HSIAO, CHENG 蕭政
Mem., Acad. Sinica 96-; Prof. of Econ., U. of So. Calif. 85-; Ed., *Jour. of Econometrics* 91-; *b.* Chungking June 27, '43; *m.* Hsiao, Amy; 2 *s.,* 2 *d.; educ.* BA, NTU 65; B., Philosphy, Oxford U. 68; MS., Stanford U. 70; Ph.D., Stanford U. 72; Bd. Mem., Ch. Res. Inst. for Land Econ. 80-; Asst. Prof., UC-Berkly. 72-77; Prof. of Econ., U. of Toronto 77-85; Visiting Prof., Princeton U. 80-81; Consultant, Bell Lab. 81-82. *Publ.: Analysis of Panel Data* 86; *Econometric Models, Techniques & Applications* 96; *Add.* Dept. of Econ., USC, Los Angeles, CA 90089 USA.

HSIAO, CHIN 蕭勤

Painter, Sculptor & Printmaker; Prof., Accademia di Belle Arti di Brera, Milan, Italy 85; *b.* Shanghai Jan. 30, '35; *educ.* Fine Arts Faculty, Taipei Prov. Normal Coll. 54; Tchr., Taipei Chingmei Elementary Sch. 54-56; Visiting Artist, Southampton Coll., Long Island U. 69; Prof., Istituto Europeo, Milan 71-72; Visting Prof., Louisiana State U. 72; Accademia di Belle Arti, Urbino, Italy 83-84, Accademia Albertina di belle Arti, Turin 84-85, Prof., Accademia di Belle Arti di Brera, Milan 85. *Publ.: Prints by Hsiao Chin,* Milan 63; *Oh! Che Vertigine,* Milan 66; *Un Processo di Penetrazione,* Milan 72; *Serigrafie di Hsiao Chin,* Jesi-Italy 76; *Ch'an (Sergrafie di Hsiao Chin),* Milan 77; *Hsiao Chin (Prints),* Macerata 77; *Hsiao Chin's Retrospective,* Twn. Museum of Art, Taichung 92; *Hsiao Chin: The Odyssey 53-94,* Taipei Fine Arts Museum 95; *Add.* Via G. Modina, 3520129 Milano, Italy.

HSIAO, DENG-PIAO 蕭登標

Spkr., Chiayi CoCoun. 94-; Bd. Chmn., Chimei Jen-ai Home 94-; Chmn., Chiayi County Mil. Conscripts Assn. 94-; Bd. Chmn., Chiayi County Athletics Assn. 89-; *b.* Twn. Feb. 24, '57; 1 *s.;* Dep. Spkr., Chiayi CoCoun. 90-94; Owner, Yungfu Furniture, & Haiwangtzu Restaurant; *Add.* 226 Chung Shan Rd., Sect. 1, Taitzu, Chiayi County.

HSIAO, HSIN-HUANG

(See HSIAO, HSIN-HUANG MICHAEL 蕭新煌)

HSIAO, HSIN-HUANG MICHAEL 蕭新煌

Nat. Policy Adv. to the Pres. 96-; Res. Fel., Inst. of Sociology, Acad. Sinica 95-; Prof., Dept. of Sociology, NTU 84-; *b.* Taipei Dec. 26, '48; *m.* Hsiao Lee, Yu-Hsiang; 2 *s.; educ.* BA, NTU 71; MA, State U. of NY-Buffalo 76; Ph.D., State U. of NY-Buffalo 79; Assc. Res. Fel. & Res. Fel., Inst. of Ethnology, Acad. Sinica 79-83 & 83-95; Assc. Prof., NTU 80-84. *Publ.: In Search of an E. Asian Dev. Model; Twn.: A Newly Industralized State; Twn. 2000; Discovery of the Middle Classes in E. Asia; Dev. & Underdev.; Middle Classes in Changing Twn. Soc.; Dev. & Exchange of Sociology in Twn., Hong Kong & Ch.; Add.* 3rd Fl., 55 Lane 70, Yen Chiou Yuan Rd., Sect. 2, Taipei.

HSIAO, TENG-PIAO

(See HSIAO, DENG-PIAO 蕭登標)

HSIAO, TENG-TZANG 蕭天讚

Bd. Chmn., *CNA* 96-; *b.* Twn. Aug. 25, '34; *m.* Hsu, Ling-miao; 2 *s.,* 3 *d.; educ.* LL.B., NTU; Tchr., Twn. Prov. Chiayi High Sch. 60-61; Judge, Dist. Courts 63-70; Chief, Dept. of Trainees' Aff., Judges & Prosecutors Tng. Inst. 67-68; Judge, Twn. High Court 70-73; Mem., Legis. Yuan 73-86; Dep. Dir.-Gen., Dept. of Org. Aff., CC, KMT 79, Dir.-Gen., Dept. of Soc. Aff. 79-84, Dep. Sec.-Gen., Policy Coordination Cttee. 84-86; Min. of State 86-88; Min. of Justice 88-89; Nat. Policy Adv. to the Pres. 89-96; *Add.* 209 Sungkiang Rd., Taipei.

HSIAO, TENG-WANG 蕭登旺

Spkr., Chiayi CCoun. 90-; *b.* Twn. Dec. 1, '47; *m.* Lin, Jui-man; 2 *s.,* 1 *d.; educ.* Grad., Sr. High Sch.; Dir., Chimei Jen-ai Home; Chmn., Chiayi Dog Rearing Assn.; Hon. Chmn. of Bd., Chiayi Chamber of Com.; Pres., Weiming Construction Corp.; *Add.* 80 Jen Ai Rd., Chiayi.

HSIAO, TIEN-TSAN

(See HSIAO, TENG-TZANG 蕭天讚)

HSIEH, CHIN-CHU

(See SHIEH, CHIN-CHU 謝金菊)

HSIEH, HSIN-LIANG

(See SHIEH, SHINN-LIANG 謝信良)

HSIEH, KUN-SHAN

(See HSIEH, KUN-SHUN 謝崑山)

HSIEH, KUN-SHUN 謝崑山

Mem., Control Yuan; *b.* Twn. Oct. 18, '34; *m.* Chen, Jun-hui; 2 *s.,* 1 *d.; educ.* Grad., Twn. Prov. Normal Coll.; LL.B., Tungyang U., Japan; MPA, San Francisco; Tchr., Elementary Sch. 54-67; Mem., Tainan CoCoun. 68-72; Mem., TPA 73-80; *Add.* 2 Chung Hsiao E. Rd., Sect. 1, Taipei.

HSIEH, LUNG-SHENG

(See SHIEH, LUNG-SHENG 謝隆盛)

HSIEH, MENG-HSIUNG

(See SHIEH, MUNG-SHIUNG 謝孟雄)

HSIEH, SEN-CHUNG
(See SHIEH, SAMUEL C. 謝森中)

HSIEH, SHEN-FU 謝生富
Chmn., Twn. Mach. Mfg. Corp. 96-; *b.* Twn. Oct. 7. '39; *m.* Huang, Li-yu; 2 *s.,* 1 *d.; educ.* Taichung Normal Coll. 58; LL.B., Toyou U. 84; MA, Meiji U. 86, LL.D. 89; Tchr., Elementary & Jr. High Schs. 58-65; Agent, Investigation Bu., MOJ 65-70; Staff Mem., TPG 67-69; Judge, Dist. Courts 70-81; Mem. & Convener, Legis. Yuan 81-87; Instr., Fu Hsing Kang Coll. 86; Counsl., Exec. Yuan 87; Comr., Laws & Reglns. Cttee. 87; Chief, Cong. Contact Team 90-91; V. Chmn., MAC 91-92; Sec.-Gen., Legis. Yuan 92-96. *Publ.: Claim for Damages Due to Breach of Contract; Principles of Publ. in Immunity from Liabilities for Committing Libel & Slander; To Be Responsible to Hist.; Add.* 3 Tai Chi Rd., Hsiaokang, Kaohsiung.

HSIEH, SHEN-SAN 謝深山
Chmn., COLA 94-; *b.* Twn. Feb. 3, '39; *m.* Chien, Shu-neu; 2 *s.,* 1 *d.; educ.* Hualien Ind. Voc. Sr. High Sch.; Dep. Sec.-Gen., CC, KMT 91-94, Mem., CSC 88-94; Mem., Legis. Yuan 73-94; Pres., Ch. Fed. of Labor 88-94; V. Pres., Ch. Taipei Baseball Assn. 84-92; Mem., Standing Cttee., Ch. Fed. of Railway Worker's Union 82-85; Mem., Standing Cttee., Twn. Railway Worker's Union 71-85; *Add.* 15th Fl., 132 Min Sheng E. Rd., Taipei.

HSIEH, SHENG-FU
(See HSIEH, SHEN-FU 謝生富)

HSIEH, THOMAS TONG-LIANG 謝棟樑
Amb. to Solomon Islands 96-; Overseer, Ch. Intl. Law Assn. 94-; Adv., Intl. Etiquette Assn. 90-; *b.* Twn. Oct. 6, '39; *m.* Hsieh, Martha; 2 *d.; educ.* BA, Dept. of Dip., NCU 62; Customs Off., Inspectorate Gen. of Customs, MOF 63-67; 3rd Sec., Emb. to Botswana 70-74; Dep. Dir., Dept. of Protocol, MOFA 87-91, Dir., Dept. of Treaty & Legal Aff. 91-96. *Publ.: Intl. Preventive Measures Against Hijack; Add.* P.O. Box 586, Honiara, Solomon Islands.

HSIEH, TUNG-LIANG
(See HSIEH, THOMAS TONG-LIANG 謝棟樑)

HSIEH, TUNG-MIN
(See SHIEH, TUNG-MIN 謝東閔)

HSIN, WEN-PING 辛文炳
Nat. Policy Adv. to the Pres. 96-; Bd. Chmn., Nan Tai Inst. of Tech. 89-; *b.* Twn. Feb. 1, '12; *m.* Hsin, Wong-mei; 3 *s.,* 2 *d.; educ.* LL.B., Meiji U. 34; Spkr., Tainan CCoun. 50-60; Mayor, Tainan City 60-64; Mem., TPA 64-73; Mem., Legis. Yuan 73-80; Pres., Nan Tai Coll. 69-89; *Add.* 1 Nan Tai St., Yung Kang City, Tainan County.

HSU, CHANG-HUI
(See HSU, TSANG-HOUEI 許常惠)

HSU, CHI-MING
(See HSU, STEVE CHI-MING 徐啟明)

HSU, CHIA-TUNG
(See SHEA, JIA-DONG 許嘉棟)

HSU, CHIEH-KUEI
(See HSU, CHIEH-KWEI 許介圭)

HSU, CHIEH-KWEI 許介圭
Admin. V. Min. of Trans. & Comms. 96-; Mem., CC, KMT 93-; *b.* Twn. Nov. 5, '32; *m.* Lin, Chieh-fang; 2 *s.,* 2 *d.; educ.* B., NCHU; Dir., Secretariat, Planning & Evaluation Cttee., Twn. Postal Admin. 71-78; Dep. Dir., Engr. Dept., Directorate Gen. of Posts 78-79, Dir., Postal Tng. Inst. 78-80, Dir., Engr. Dept. 80-83, Sec.-Gen. 83-85; Dep. Dir.-Gen., Directorate Gen. of Postal Remittances & Savings Bk. 85-87, Dir.-Gen. 87-92; Dep. Dir.-Gen., Directorate Gen. of Posts 87-92; Dir.-Gen., Directorate Gen. of Posts, MOTC 92-96; *Add.* 2 Changsha St. Sect. 1, Taipei.

HSU, CHIEH-LIN 許介鱗
Nat. Policy Adv. to the Pres. 96-; Prof. Dept. of Pol. Sc., NTU 75-; Chief Dir., Japanese Res. Cent., NTU 93-; *b.* Twn. Sept. 1, '35; *m.* Fujii, Shizue; 3 *d.; educ.* BPS, NTU 61; DPS, Nat. Tokyo U. 69; Assc. Prof., Dept. of Pol. Sc., NTU 70-75. *Publ.: Studies on Watergate Aff.* 74; *The Rise & Fall of the Nixon Admin.* 75; *On Japanese Pol.* 77; *From the Ch. View: On Modern Japan* 77; *The Outline of the Hist. of the Great Britain* 81; *Evidence! the Wushe Aff.!* 85; *On Modern Japan* 87; *The Order & Ethics of*

Pol. of Pol. Parties 89; *Who Understands Japan* 89; *The Hist. of Contemporary Japan* 91; *The Pol. Process of Japan after WWII* 91; *The Asian Pacific Strategy of the ROC* (with C.J. Shiau & W.C. Li) 91; *Econ. Cooperation in the Asian Pacific Area & the Asian Pacific of USA* (with C.J. Shiau & W.C. Li) 94; *The Hist. of Twn. After WWII* 96; *Add.* Rm. 337, 30 Hsin Hai Rd., Sect. 3, Taipei.

HSU, CHIEH-SU 徐皆蘇
Mem., Acad. Sinica 90-, & Nat. Acad. of Engr., USA 88-; Prof., Dept. of Mech. Engr., UC-Berkly. 64-; *b.* Kiangsu May 27, '22; *m.* Tse, Helen Yung-feng; 1 *s.,* 1 *d.; educ.* Grad., Nat. Inst. of Tech. 45; MS, Mech. Engr., Stanford U. 48, Ph.D. 50; Engr., Shanghai Naval Dockyard & Engr. Works 46-47; Res. Asst., Stanford U. 48-51; Tech. & Project Engr., IBM Corp. 51-55; Assc. Prof., U. of Toledo 55-58; Assc. Prof., UC-Berkly. 58-64; John Simon Guggenheim Fel. 64-65; Miller Res. Prof., UC-Berkly. 73-74. *Publ.: Cell-to-Cell Mapping: A Method of Global Analysis for Nonlinear Systems* 87; 106 sc. & tech. res. papers; *Add.* Dept. of Mech. Engr., UC-Berkly., CA 94720, USA.

HSU, CHIH-WEI
(See HSU, STEPHAN 許智偉)

HSU, CHING-HUA
(See HSU, KENNETH J. 許靖華)

HSU, CHO-YUN 許倬雲
Mem., Acad. Sinica 80-; U. Prof. of Hist. & Sociology, U. of Pittsburgh 82-; Weilun Prof. of Hist., Ch. U. of Hong Kong 93-97; John Burns Prof. of Hist., U. of Hawaii 95-; *b.* Amoy (native of Kiangsu) July 10, '30; *m.* Sun, Man-li; 1 *s.; educ.* BA & MA, NTU; Ph.D., U. of Chicago; Assc. Prof. & Prof., NTU 62-70; Asst. Fel., Assc. Fel. & Fel. 60-71; Mem., Phi Beta Kappa. *Publ.: Ancient Ch. in Transition; Han Agr. & Hist. of W. Chou Civilization;* etc.; *Add.* 5742 5th Avenue, Unit 103, Pittsburgh, PA 15232, USA.

HSU, DOUGLAS TONG 徐旭東
Chmn., Twn. Textile Fed. 95-; Hon. Pres., Intl. Textile Manufacturers Fed. 94-; Chmn., Far Ea. Textile Ltd. 91-; Chmn., Asia Cement Corp. 93-; Chmn., Far Ea. Dept. Stores Ltd. 88-; Chmn., Oriental Union Chem.

Corp. 94-; Chmn., U-Ming Marine Trans. Corp. 95-; V. Chmn., Far Ea. Intl. Bk. 92-; V. Chmn., Intl. Business Cttee., the Metropolitan Museum of Art in NY; Trustee, U. of Notre Dame; Mem. of IBM Greater Ch. Adv. Bd.; Dir., Prudential/Asia Pacific Fund; Intl. Dir., The Asia Soc.; Consul-Gen., Consl. of the Rep. of Malawi & Ivory Coast in Taipei; *b.* Shanghai Aug. 24, '42; *m.* Morris, Mary Dustin; 1 *s.,* 2 *d.; educ.* BA & MA, U. of Notre Dame; Postgrad., Columbia U.; *Add.* 38th Fl., 207 Tun Hua S. Rd., Sect. 2, Taipei.

HSU, FRANCIS L.K. 許烺光
Mem., Acad. Sinica; Author; Lectr., Consultant & Prof. Emeritus of Anthropology, Northwe. U.; *b.* Liaoning Oct. 28, '09; *m.* Tung, Vera Y.N.; 2 *d.; educ.* BA, Shanghai U. 33; Ph.D., U. of London 40; Lectr., Columbia U. 44-45; Asst. Prof., Cornell U. 45-47; Prof., Anthropology, Northwe. U. 47-78, Chmn., Dept. of Anthropology 57-75; Prof. & Dir., Cent. for Cul. Studies in Educ., U. of San Francisco 78-82; Pres., Am. Anthropological Assn. 78-79. *Publ.:* 16 bk. & over 110 articles; *Add.* 61 Milland Drive, Mill Valley, CA 94941, USA.

HSU, HENG
(See HSU, HENRY HENG 徐亨)

HSU, HENRY HENG 徐亨
Nat. Policy Adv. to the Pres. 87-; Mem., CAC, KMT 88-; Pres., Red Cross Soc. of the ROC 88-; Hon. Mem., Intl. Olympic Cttee. 88-; Pub., *Twn. Daily News* 94-, Chmn. 78-; Chmn., Taipei Fortuna Hotel 82-, & Universal Fortuna Investment Inc.; Corporate Gen. Partner, Fortuna Ents., L.P.; Owner, Los Angeles Airport Hilton & Towers 92-; *b.* Kwangtung Dec. 6, '12; *m.* Yue, Amy So-hing; 1 *s.,* 2 *d.; educ.* Whampoa Naval Coll. 32; LL.B., Nat. Ch. U., Shanghai 35; US Naval Tng. Cent., Cmdg. Off. Class, Miami 46; Hon. LL.D., Kyung Hee U., S. Korea 75; Hon. Dr. of Humanics, Springfield Coll., Massachusetts 95; Cmdg. Off., "Yung Ning," ROCN 45-46, Capt. 47; Rear Adm. (Retired), ROCN 78; Chmn., Fortuna Athletic Assn., Hong Kong 53; Governing Dir., Intl. Finance Corp. Ltd., Hong Kong 54; Pres., Amateur Swimming Assn., ROC 54-65; Mng. Dir., Burlington Investment Co. Ltd., Hong Kong 60; Hon. Pres., Volleyball Assn., Hong Kong 60-69; Pres., Ch. Swimming Assn., Hong Kong 60, Hon. Pres. 61-69;

Mng. Dir., Walton Investment Co. Ltd., Hong Kong 62; Pres., Sea Dragon Skin Diving Club, Hong Kong 63, Hon. Pres. 64; Hon. Pres., Hong Kong Amateur Basketball Assn. 65-69; V. Pres., Amateur Swimming Fed. of Asia 66-72; Mem., Intl. Olympic Cttee. 70-87; Mem., Legis. Yuan 72-86; Mem., CC, KMT 83-88; *Add.* Fortuna Hotel, 122 Chung Shan N. Rd., Sect. 2, Taipei.

HSU, HSIAO-PO
(See HSU, PAUL S.P. 徐小波)

HSU, HSIEN-HSIU
(See SHU, HSIEN-SIU 徐賢修)

HSU, HSIN-CHIH 許新枝
Mem., Control Yuan 93-; *b.* Twn. Oct. 25, '28; *m.* Su, Shu-ai; 2 *s.,* 2 *d.; educ.* BA, NCHU; LL.B., Soochow U.; MPS, Ch. Cul. U.; Ph.D., Hosei U., Japan; Magis., Taoyuan County 68-72; Comr., Dept. of Civil Aff., TPG 72-75; V. Chmn., RDEC 75-77; Mem., TPA 77-81; Pol. V. Min. of the Int. 81-84. *Publ.: Admin. Sc. & Admin. Problems; The Org. of the Local Admin. Inst. in Twn.; Add.* 2 Chung Hsiao E. Rd., Sect. 1, Taipei.

HSU, HSIN-LIANG 許信良
Chmn., DPP 96-; *b.* Twn. May 27, '41; *m.* Chung, Pi-hsia; 2 *s.,* 2 *d.; educ.* BPS, NCU 63, M. 67; M., U. of Edinburgh 69; Mem., TPA 73-77; Magis., Taoyuan County 77-79; Dir., *Formosa Mag. of Twn. Dem. Movement* 79; Dir., *Formosa Weekly of Twn. Dem. Movement* 80. *Publ.: The Sound of Wind & Rain* 77; *To Rest in Benevolence Without Regret* 88; *Add.* 12th Fl., 22 Chung Cheng Rd., Sect. 2, Tienmu, Taipei.

HSU, HSU-TONG
(See HSU, DOUGLAS TONG 徐旭東)

HSU, HUEI-HUEI 許慧慧
Bd. Chmn., Berlin Co. Ltd. 91-; Dir., Shu Te Girls Home Econ. & Com. Voc. High Sch. 66-; Dir., YWCA Kaohsiung 92-; *b.* Twn. Nov. 7, '38; *m.* Chen, Wen-yuan; 2 *s.; educ.* BS., Bluffton Coll. 63; Tchr., Prov. Kaohsiung Sr. High Sch. 64-75; Exec. Sec., Berlin Co. Ltd. 76-79, Admin. Mgr. 79-81; Dir., 82-91; *Add.* 43 Ta Yeh S. Rd., Lin Hai Ind. Zone, Kaohsiung.

HSU, HUI-YU
(See SHI, HWEI-YOW 許惠祐)

HSU, I-HSIUNG
(See HSU, YI-HSUNG 徐義雄)

HSU, I-YUN
(See HSU, YIH-YUN 許翼雲)

HSU, KE-SHENG
(See SHEU, KE-SHENG 許柯生)

HSU, KENNETH J. 許靖華
Mem., Acad. Sinica 90-; Prof., E.T.H., Zurich 67-; For. Assc., US Nat. Acad. of Sc. & Third World Acad. of Sc.; *b.* Nanking June 28, '29; *m.* Eugster, Christine; 3 *s.,* 1 *d.; educ.* BS, Nat. Cent. U. 48; MA, Ohio State U. 50; Ph.D., UCLA 53; Dr. Sc. Nat., H.C.S., Nanjing U.; Shell Dev. Co., Texas 54-63; Assc. Prof., State U. of New York, Binghamton 63-64; Assc. Prof., U. of Calif., Riverside 64-67. *Publ.: Ein Schiff Revolutionist die Wissenschaft; Mediterranean was a Desert; The Great Dying; Geol. of Switzerland;* Author or Ed. of over 10 bk. & 300 sc. articles; *Add.* E.T.H., Zurich, Switzerland.

HSU, KUEI-LIN 許桂霖
Mem., Exam. Yuan 96-; *b.* Twn. May 4, '34; *m.* Ho, Ing-jau; 2 *s.,* 1 *d.; educ.* B., PA., NCHU 55; Chief Sec., Kaohsiung City Govt. 78-79, Dir., Dept. of Civil Aff. 79-87; Dir., Dept. of Civil Aff., MOI 87-89; Sec.-Gen., CEIC 89-96; *Add.* 1 Shih Yuan Rd., Wenshan, Taipei.

HSU, KUN-NAN 許坤南
Architect, K. Hsu Architect & Assc. 76-; Sec.-Gen., Architectural Inst. of the ROC 87-; Mem., City Planning Com., Taipei City 92-; *b.* Taipei Apr. 7, '32; *m.* Tong, Show-in; 2 *s.,* 1 *d.; educ.* BS, Architectural Engr., NCKU 56; Pres., Twn. Prov. Architects Assn. 80-84; Pres., Nat. Union of Architects Assn., ROC 84-89; *Add.* 11th Fl., 445 Jen Ai Rd., Sect. 4, Taipei.

HSU, LANG-KUANG
(See HSU, FRANCIS L.K. 許烺光)

HSU, LI-CHIH
(See TSUI, LAP-CHEE 徐立之)

HSU, LI-TE
(See HSU, LI-TEH 徐立德)

HSU, LI-TEH 徐立德
V. Premier, ROC 93-; Mem., CSC, KMT 93-; *b.* Honan
Aug. 6, '31; *m.* Liu, Ching-sheng; 2 *s.; educ.* LL.M.,
NCU; MPA, Harvard U. 86; Admin. V. Min. of Finance
76-78; Comr., Dept. of Finance, TPG 78-81; Min. of
Finance 81-84; Min. of Econ. Aff. 84-85; Chmn., Lien
Ho Jr. Coll. of Tech. 86-88; Chmn., CFC, KMT 88-93,
Dep. Sec.-Gen. 90-93; Chmn, CEPD 94-96. *Publ.: Theory
of Modern Financial Policy; Theory of Modern Econ.
Policy; Equity & Efficiency; Add.* 1 Chung Hsiao E. Rd.,
Sect. 1, Taipei.

HSU, LU 徐璐
Gen. Mgr., Voice of Taipei Broadcasting Co. 95-; *b.*
Twn. Mar. 23, '58; *educ.* BA, Tamkang U.; Visiting
Scholar, Columbia U.; Pub., *Mother Earth* 81-83; Exec.
Dir., *The Eighties* 83-86; Gen. Mgr., *The Jour.* 86-87;
Chief Ed., *The Independent Evening News* 87-92; *Add.*
10th Fl.-B, 15-1 Hangchow S. Rd., Sect. 1, Taipei.

HSU, PAUL S.P. 徐小波
Sr. Partner, Lee & Li, Attorneys-at-Law 69-; Prof. of
Law, NTU 69-; *b.* Hong Kong Mar. 25, '39; 1 *s.; educ.*
LL.B., NTU 62; MA, Fletcher Sch. of Law & Dip., Tufts
U., USA 65; LL.M., Law Sch., New York U. 69; Mem.,
Asia Soc.'s Corp. Coun.; Bd. Mem., Pacific Basin Econ.
Coun. Ch. Mem. Cttee. in Taipei; Exec. Dir., ROC-USA
Econ. Coun.; Mem., Ch. Taipei Pacific Econ. Coopera-
tion Cttee.; Chmn., ROC-New Zealand Business Coun.;
Chmn., Epoch Found. *Publ.: Recent Govt. Policy & In-
centive Measure Regarding For. Investment in ROC; A
Study of Capital Market Dev. in the ROC From A Legal
Perspective; Twn., Hong Kong, & Ch.: the Ch. Produc-
tivity Triangle; A Study of the Legal Guide Issues Relating
to Joint Venture Ent.; Licensing of Tech. in Twn.; Licensing in the ROC; Add.* 7th Fl., 201 Tun Hua N. Rd., Taipei.

HSU, PENG-HSIANG
(See HSU, PENG-SIANG 許鵬翔)

HSU, PENG-SIANG 許鵬翔
Dir.-Gen., Bu. of Commodity Inspection & Quarantine,
MOEA; *b.* Twn. Aug. 1, '31; *m.* Shih, Shu-hui; 4 *s.*, 1 *d.;*
educ. BS, Chem., NTU 54; Jr. Sp., Twn. Ind. Res. Inst.
55-59; Sp., Twn. Prov. Inspection Bu. 59-67; Sp., Bu.
of Commodity Inspection & Quarantine, MOEA 71-
82, Sect. Chief 76-79, Dep. Dir., Inspection Dept. 80-
82, Dir., Hsinchu Br. 82-84, Dir., Inspection Dept. 84-
89, Dep. Dir.-Gen. 89-93; *Add.* 4 Chi Nan Rd., Sect.
1, Taipei.

HSU, SHENG-FA
(See HSUI, SHENG-FA 許勝發)

HSU, SHENG-HSIUNG 許勝雄
Chmn., Kinpo Elect. Inc. 92-, Compal Elect. Inc. 94-,
First Twn. Venture Capital Inc. 90-, Twn. Asia Space
Cable Inc. 94-; Exec. Dir., Baotek Ind. Materials Ltd.
92-, & Twn. Elec. & Elect. Mfr.'s Assn. 89-; Bd. Mem.,
Norm Pacific Automation Corp. 90-, Sinoca Ent. Co.
Ltd. 94-, Elec. & Elect. Products & Dev. Assn. of ROC
85-, & Importers & Exporter Assn. of Taipei 91-; *b.* Twn.
Sept. 30, '43; *m.* Tsai, Li-chu; 1 *s.*, 2 *d.; educ.* BA, NTNU
74; *Add.* 10th Fl., 99 Nanking E. Rd., Sect. 5, Taipei.

HSU, SHUI-TE
(See HSU, SHUI-TEH 許水德)

HSU, SHUI-TEH 許水德
Pres., Exam. Yuan 96-; Mem., CSC, KMT 88-; *b.* Twn.
Aug. 1, '31; *m.* Yang, Shu-hua; 2 *s.; educ.* Ed.B., NTNU;
Ed.M., NCU; Grad. Sch., Tokyo U.; Assc. Prof.; Adjunct
Prof.; Dir., Bu. of Educ., Kaohsiung City Govt. 70-73,
Chief Sec. 73-75; Comr., Dept. of Soc. Aff., TPG 75-79;
Dir.-Gen., Dept. of Soc. Aff., CC, KMT 79; Sec.-Gen.,
Kaohsiung City Govt. 79-82; Mayor, Kaohsiung City
82-85; Mayor, Taipei City 85-88; Min. of the Int. 88-91;
Rep., TECROJ 91-93; Sec.-Gen., CC, KMT 93-96.
*Publ.: The Childhood Educ. of Emile; Psychology;
Introduction to Psychology; Essay on Modern Educ.; A
Study of High Sch. Curriculum in Japan; My Compli-
ments—Recollections of Those Days Serving as
Kaohsiung Mayor; A Thousand Sunrises & Midnights;
My Scoopwheel Philosophy; A Study of Welfare Admin.
for the Aged; Add.* 1 Shih Yuan Rd., Wenshan, Taipei.

HSU, STEPHAN 許智偉
Rep., Taipei Econ. & Trade Off. in Thailand 94-; Mem.,
CC, KMT 88-; *b.* Shanghai Dec. 27, '31; *m.* Yen, Tsui-

nien; 1 *s.,* 2 *d.; educ.* LL.B., NCHU 60; Ph.D., U. of Münster 69; Tchr. & Dir., Taipei Mun. Chengkung Sr. High Sch. 52-62; Assc. Prof., Grad. Sch. of Educ., NCU 69-72; Pres., Twn. Prov. Coll. of Educ. 71-74; Comr., Dept. of Educ., TPG 72-75, Comr. 72-78; Sup., Cooperative Bk. of Twn. 78-84; Prof. & Dean, Grad. Sch. of European Studies, Tamkang U. 78-84; Dir., Free Ch. Info. Off., Copenhagen 84-91, Rep., TECO 91-94. *Publ.: Normal Educ. in Germany* 68; *Voc. Educ. in Germany* 72; *Dev. of Educ. in Twn.* 81; *Heaven & People* 83; *Ovs. Ch. in Nordic Countries* 89; etc.; *Add.* 10th Fl., Kian Gwan Bldg., 140 Wireless Rd., Bangkok 10330, Thailand.

HSU, STEVE CHI-MING 徐啟明
Amb. to Grenada, St. Vincent, Commonwealth of Dominica, St. Lucia, & St. Christopher & Nevis 94-; *b.* Hupei Nov. 6, '27; *m.* Mo, Hsu-hsia; 2 *s.,* 2 *d.; educ.* BA, NTU 53; Ed., Eng. Dept., CNA 66-68, Corr. in E. Africa 69-71; Corr. in USA, *Ch. Times* 71-74; Press Attaché, Emb. in USA 74-79; Dep. Dir., Secretariat, CCNAA, Washington, D.C. 80-84, Dir. 85-90; V. Chmn., Res. & Planning Bd., MOFA 90-92; Rep., TECO, Oslo 92-94. *Publ.: The Prof. Jour.* (transl.); *Add.* P.O. Box 36, Emb. of the ROC, St. George's, Grenada, W. Indies.

HSU, SUNG-JEN 徐頌仁
Head, Music Dept., Nat. Inst. of the Arts 93-, & Prof. 82-; *b.* Twn. Sept. 1, '41; *m.* Huang, Ju-in; 2 *s.; educ.* BA, Philosophy, NTU 66; Diploma, Staatliche Hochschule für Musik, Köln 74; Opera House, Karlsruhe 74-75, Opera House, Dortmund, Germany 75-76; Conductor, Taipei City Symphony Orchestra 76-82; *Musical Works:* Piano Works, Songs, Sonata for Violin & Piano, Concerto Capriccioso for Orchestra, Concerto for Piano & Orchestra, Piano Trio. *Publ.: Music Esthetics, Instrumentation, Performing Practice; Add.* 1st Fl., 11-3 Lane 38, Tien Yu St., Taipei.

HSU, TSAI-EN 許再恩
Spkr., Taipei CoCoun. 90-; Chmn., Yungfeng Secs. Co. 90-; Adv., Ocean World; *b.* Taipei June 3, '42; *m.* Chang, Mei-ching; 1 *s.,* 2 *d.; educ.* Grad., Nat. Taipei Coll. of Business; Chmn., Fu-hua Co. Ltd., & Fu-teh Co. Ltd.; Head & Corr., Hsintien Bu., *Twn. Daily News;* Dir. & Mgr., Changfeng Construction Co. Ltd.; Dir., Hsintien

Lions Club Intl.; Dep. Dir., Soc. of Contemporary Forum; *Add.* 116 Wen Hua Rd., Sect. 2, Panchiao, Taipei County.

HSU, TSAI-LI 許財利
Spkr., Keelung CCoun. 90-, Mem. 82-; Leader, Keelung Voluntary Fire Service 90-; *b.* Twn. Nov. 5, '47; *m.* Chien, Hsiu-chin; 2 *s.,* 1 *d.; educ.* Sun Yat-sen Inst. on Policy Res. & Dev. 92; Studying at Nat. Open U.; Mem., Urban Planning Cttee., Keelung 90-94; Chmn., Keelung CCoun. Mem. Assn. 91-94; *Add.* 5 Shou Shan Rd., Keelung.

HSU, TSANG-HOUEI 許常惠
Nat. Policy Adv. to the Pres. 96-; Dir., Grad. Inst. of Music, NTNU 91-, Prof. 80-; Pres., Soc. for Music Educ. 93-, & Ch. Soc. for Ethnomusicology 90-; *b.* Twn. Sept. 6, '29; *m.* Lee, Chu-huei; 3 *s.; educ.* BA, Music, NTNU; MA, Institut de Musicologue, U. of Paris. *Publ.: A Study of Debussy; Essays on Folk Music* (3 Vol.); *Colorful Music of Twn.; An Introduction to Ch. Ethnomusicology; Hist. of Music in Twn.* Compositions: *Legend of the White Snake; C. of Lion Mountain; Spring for All; Ch. Festival Overture;* etc.; *Add.* 7th Fl., 6 Lane 122, Jen Ai Rd., Sect. 4, Taipei.

HSU, WEN-CHIH
(See HSU, WEN-TSU 許文志)

HSU, WEN-LUNG
(See SHI, W.L. 許文龍)

HSU, WEN-PIN
(See HSU, WEN-BING 許文彬)

HSU, WEN-TSU 許文志
Dir., Dept. of Org., CC, KMT 96-; *b.* Twn. Sept. 30, '36; *m.* Lin, Su-chen; 2 *s.,* 2 *d.; educ.* LL.B., Ch. Cul. U. 68; LL.B., Meiji U. 71; Magis., Yunlin County 81-89; Comr., Dept. of Recon., TPG 90-94; Sec.-Gen., TPG 94-96; *Add.* 53 Jen Ai Rd., Sect. 3, Taipei.

HSU, YI-HSUNG 徐義雄
Pres., Sunrace Roots Enterprise Co. Ltd. 72-; *b.* Twn. Aug. 18, '41; *m.* Lin, Patty; 1 *s.,* 1 *d.; educ.* B., NCHU 67; Sales Mgr., Ta Ming Ind. 65-72; *Add.* 9 Lane 130, Kuang Fu Rd., Sect. 1, Sanchung, Taipei County.

HSU, YU-PU 許毓圃
Dep. Dir.-Gen., CPA 90-; *b.* Kwangtung Dec. 27, '34; 2 *s.*, 1 *d.; educ.* Grad., Supplementary Open Jr. Coll. for PA, NCU 80, Grad. Prog., PA of Civil Servants 89; Staff, Dept. of Pers., Taichung City Govt. 60-64; Staff, Dept. of Finance, TPG 64-67; Sp. & Sect. Chief, CPA 67-72; Dir., Pers. Off., Dept. of Health 72-77; Sr. Sp. & Dep. Dir., CPA 77-81; Dep. Dir., Dept. of Pers., TCG 81-83; Counsl., Dir., & Chief Sec., CPA 83-90; *Add.* 109 Huai Ning St., Taipei.

HSU, YUAN-TUNG
(See SHEU, YUAN-DONG 許遠東)

HSU, YUAN-YIH 許源浴
Prof., Dept. of Elec. Engr., NTU 87-; *b.* Twn. June 19, '55; *m.* Yang, Mu-jang; 1 *s.; educ.* B.Sc., NTU 77; M.Sc., NTU 80; Ph.D., NTU 83; Instr., U. of Calgary, Can. 82-83; Visiting Scholar, UC-Berkly. 88-89; Instr., NTU 80-84; Assc. Prof. 84-87; V. Chair, Dept. of EE 92-94. *Publ.:* Over 97 intl. jour. papers & 50 reports & papers; *Add.* Dept. of E.E., NTU, 1 Roosevelt, Sect. 4, Taipei.

HSU, YUAN-YU
(See HSU, YUAN-YIH 許源浴)

HSUEH, CHI
(See SCHIVE, CHI 薛琦)

HSUEH, JEN-YANG 薛人仰
Nat. Policy Adv. to the Pres. 92-; Sec.-Gen., Asian-Pacific Cul. Cent., APPU 88-; *b.* Fukien Nov. 15, '13; *m.* Chow, Shu-yuan; 1 *s.*, 2 *d.; educ.* Ed.B., Nat. Cent. U. 34; Nat. War Coll. 59; Hon. LL.D., Dankook U., S. Korea 74; Magis., Tainan County 48-51; Sec.-Gen., TPA 51-60; Mem., NA 53-91; V. Min. of the Int. 60-62; Chmn., Twn. Prov. Cttee., KMT 62-68, Dep. Sec.-Gen., CC 68-76; Prof., Ch. Cul. U. 68-76; Amb. to Nicaragua 76-79; Amb. to Guatemala 79-81; Min. of State & Adjunct Chmn., MTAC 81-84. *Publ.: Hist. of Educ. System of Ch.; An Eyewitness of the Turmoil in Nicaragua; Add.* 3 Lane 10, Foochow St., Taipei.

HSUEH, YUEH 薛岳
Strategy Adv. to the Pres.; *b.* Kwangtung Dec. 17, 1896; *m.* Tan, Hsin-shen; 3 *s.*, 5 *d.; educ.* Paoting Mil. Acad.; CG, 1st Div. 26-30; CG, 5th Army Corps. 34-36; Dep.

Pacification C-in-C of Yunnan & Kweichow Area & Gov. of Kweichow 36-37; C-in-C, 3rd War Area 37-38; C-in-C, 9th War Area & Gov. of Hunan 39-45; CG, Pacification Cmd., Hsuchow Area; Presidential Chief Aide-de-camp 46-48; Mem., NA 47-91, Mem., Presidium; Gov. of Kwangtung & CG, Hainan Def. Cmd. 49-50; Strategy Adv. to the Pres. 51-66; Min. of State; Chmn., PCRM. *Publ.: Introduction on the Tactics, Changsha Def. Op. Pol. Aff. in Hunan Prov.; Memoir of the War with Ch. Communists; Memoir of the War Against Japan; Pacification Op. in Hsuchow Area; Add.* 8th Fl., 33 Pin Ting Rd., Tamshui, Taipei County.

HSUI, SHENG-FA 許勝發
Nat. Policy Adv. to the Pres. 95-; V. Chmn., SEF 93-; Mem., NA 92-; Chmn., Prince Motors Group Corp., Cosmos Bk. 91-, & Ch. Chamber of Com. & Ind. 93-; Hon. Chmn., Ch. Fed. of Ind. 94-; *b.* Taipei Jan. 24, '25; *m.* Cheng, Wen-wen; 1 *s.*, 2 *d.; educ.* LL.B., NTU; Hon. Dr. of Business Admin., Santa Tomas U., Philippines 92; Chmn., Taipei County Ind. Assn. 75-81; Mem., Legis. Yuan 81-91, Dep. Sec.-Gen., KMT Caucus 84-86; Chmn., Twn. Prov. Ind. Assn. 81-87; Dep. Sec.-Gen., Policy Coordination Cttee., CC, KMT 86-88, Mem., CSC 88-93; *Add.* 50 Sungkiang Rd., Taipei.

HU, CHEN-CHUN 胡振春
Spkr., Miaoli CoCoun. 90-; Dir., KPT Ind. Ltd.; Chmn., Miaoli Dist., Red Cross Soc. of the ROC; Gen. Mgr., Liangshen Garment Co. Ltd. 76-; *b.* Twn. Sept. 13, '44; *m.* Hu Wang, Shi; 1 *s.*, 1 *d.; educ.* Prov. Sanhua Sr. High Sch.; Chmn., Nanchuang Rural Coun. 86-90, Tacheng Sr. High Sch. Parents Assn. 88-90; *Add.* 275 Tzu Chiang Rd., Toufen, Miaoli County.

HU, CHI-JU
(See HWU, REUBEN JIH-RU 胡紀如)

HU, CHIH-CHIANG
(See HU, JASON C. 胡志強)

HU, CHIN-PIAO
(See HU, CHING-PIAO 胡錦標)

HU, CHING-PIAO 胡錦標
Chmn., AEC 96-; Prof., Dept. of Mech. Engr., NTU 79-; *b.* Taipei July 1, '43; *m.* Huang, Su-yuan; 2 *s.*, 2 *d.;*

educ. Ph.D., U. of Illinois 74; Assc. Prof., Civil Engr. Dept., NTU 74-76; Res. Visiting Prof., Cornell U. 77-78; Dep. Dir. & Dir., Tjingling Ind. Res. Inst. 80-89; Dir., Engr. & Applied Sc. Div., NScC 89-90.; V. Chmn., NScC 90-96. *Publ.:* 4 bk. & over 70 acad. papers; *Add.* 1st Fl.-2, 10 Lane 57 Chung Hsing St., Taipei.

HU, CHUN-HUNG
(See HU, CHUNG-HONG 胡俊弘)

HU, CHUNG-HONG 胡俊弘
Pres., Taipei Med. Coll. 90-; Clinical Prof., Stanford U. 91-; *b.* Taipei Jan. 1, '42; *m.* Hu, Mimi; 2 *s.; educ.* MD, Taipei Med. Coll. 66; Instr., Mayo Med. Sch. 74-75; Asst. Prof., Case We. Reserve U., USA 75-79; Dir., Dermato-pathology, U. Hosp. of Cleveland 77-79; Asst. Prof. & Assc. Prof., Stanford U. 79-90; Chief, Dermatology, Palo Alto Veterans Admin. Med. Cent. 79-85; Dir., Dermatology Clinic, Stanford U. Med. Cent. 85-90; Visiting Prof., U. of Geneva 90. *Publ.:* 42 papers, 16 abstracts, & 6 chapters; *Add.* 250 Wu Hsing St., Taipei.

HU, FU 胡佛
Prof., Dept. of Pol. Sc., NTU; *b.* Kiangsu May 14, '32; *m.* Hu Han, Hsia-ying; 4 *c.; educ.* LL.B., NTU 55; MPS, Emory U. 60; Visiting Scholar, Yale U. 69-70; Res. Fel., NScC 73-74; Visiting Scholar, U. of Chicago & Columbia U. 87-88. *Publ.: The Structure of Pol. Cul.; Issue Orientations of the Voter; Behavior of Pol. Participation of the People on Twn.; The Structural Variation & Recon. of Our Const. System; Add.* 16 Lane 61, Ta Hu Villa St., Neihu, Taipei.

HU, JASON C. 胡志強
Rep., TECRO in the US 96-; Mem., CC, KMT 93-; *b.* Kirin May 15, '48; *m.* Shaw, Shirley; 1 *s.,* 1 *d.; educ.* LL.B., Dept. of Dip., NCU 70; M. of Soc. Sc., Dept. of Pol., U. of Southampton 78; D.Phil., Oxford U. 84; Res. Fel., St. Anthony's Coll., Oxford U. 85; Assc. Prof., Sun Yat-sen Inst. for Interdisciplinary Studies, Nat. Sun Yat-Sen U. 86-90; Dep. Dir., First Bu., Off. of the Pres. 91; Chief, Conf. Dept., NUC 90-91; Dir.-Gen., GIO & Govt. Spokesman 91-96. *Publ.: "On the Role of PLA in Post-Mao Ch. Pol.," Ch. Pol. After Mao* 77; *Add.* 4201 Wisconsin Avenue, N.W., Washington, D.C. 20016, USA.

HU, KAI-CHEN 胡開誠
Mem., Control Yuan 93-; *b.* Kiangsu Dec. 28, '25; *m.* Tsou, Shi-ming; 1 *s.,* 2 *d.; educ.* LL.B., Nat. Chinan U.; Judge-Advocate 50-61; Head, Off. of Law, Nat. Gen. Mobilization Cttee. 67-72; Sec., Exec. Yuan 72-73, Chmn., Laws & Reglns. Cttee. & Com. of Admin. Reappeals 73-87, Adv. 87-89; Adjunct Prof., NTU 62-92; Dep. Sec.-Gen., Exec. Yuan 89-93. *Publ.: Comment on the Code of Criminal Procedure; The Essentials of Civil Law; Family;* etc.; *Add.* 15 Alley 2, Lane 97, Min Sheng E. Rd., Sect. 4, Taipei.

HU, KAI-CHENG
(See HU, KAI-CHEN 胡開誠)

HU, SHIH-CHEN
(See HU, SZE-TSEN 胡世楨)

HU, SZE-TSEN 胡世楨
Mem., Acad. Sinica; Prof. of Math., UCLA 60-; *b.* Chekiang Oct. 9, '14; *m.* Wang, Shia-zong; 1 *s.,* 1 *d.; educ.* BS, Nat. Cent. U. 38; Ph.D. & D.Sc., U. of Manchester; Assc. Res. Fel., Acad. Sinica 47-48; Mem., Inst. for Advanced Study, Princeton U. 50-52; Assc. Prof., Tulane U. 52-55; Prof., U. of Georgia 55-56; Prof., Wayne State U. 56-60. *Publ.: Homotopy Theory; Introduction to Contemporary Math.; Elements of Gen. Topology; Elements of Modern Algebra; Threshold Logic; Homology Theory; Math. Theory of Switching Circuit & Automata; Differentiable Manifolds; Calculus; Linear Algebra with Differential Equation;* etc.; *Add.* 1076 Tellem Drive, Pacific Palisades, CA 90272, USA.

HUA, CHIA-CHIH 華加志
Chmn., Aboriginal Aff. Com., Exec. Yuan 96-; *b.* Twn. Apr. 2, '36; *m.* Lee, Yan-mey; 1 *s.,* 2 *d.; educ.* BS, Educ., NTNU; High Sch. Tchr.; Mem., TPA; Comr., TPG; Chmn., Cul. Assn. of Twn. Indigenous People; Pub., *Sanhai Cul. Mag.; Add.* 3rd Fl., 6 Chung Hsiao W. Rd. Sect. 1, Taipei.

HUAN, TONG-SHONG 黃東熊
Pres., NCHU 94-, Prof., Grad. Sch. of Law 83-; *b.* Twn. Nov. 11, '32; *m.* Lin, Chieng; 1 *s.,* 1 *d.; educ.* LL.B., NCHU 61; LL.M., Tokyo U. 66, LL.D. 73; Visiting Assc. Prof., NCU 76-78, Assc. Prof. 78-80, Prof. 80-82; Prof., Fu Jen Catholic U. 82-83; Dir., Grad. Sch. of Law,

NCHU 88-93, Dean, Coll. of Law & Com. 93-94. *Publ.: Outlines of Evidence* 80; *Treatises on Criminal Procedure* 81; *Criminal Procedure* 85; *Comparative Studies on the Systems of Prosecution in Several Countries* 86; *"Acad. Freedom" & "U. Autonomy" in Japan* 92; *Add.* 250 Kuo Kuang Rd., Taichung.

HUANG, ALICE S. 黃詩厚
Mem., Acad. Sinica 90-; Dean for Sc. & Prof. of Biology, New York U. 91-; Sc. Adv., Inst. of Molecular & Cell Biology, Nat. U. of Singapore 84-; Trustee, Found. for Microbiology, New York 86-, Chair 93-; Trustee, Johns Hopkins U. 92-; *b.* Kiangsi Mar. 22, '39; *m.* Baltimore, David; 1 *c.; educ.* BA, Johns Hopkins U. 61, MA, Microbiology 63, Ph.D. 66; Hon. MA, Harvard U. 80; Hon. D.Sc., Wheaton Coll., USA 82; Hon. D.Sc., Mt. Holyoke Coll., USA 87; Hon. D.Sc., Med. Coll. of Penn. 91; Postdoctoral Fel., Salk Inst. for Biological Studies, San Diego 67; Postdoctoral Fel., Dept. of Biology, MIT 68-69, Res. Assc. 69-70; Lectr., Acad. Sinica 70; Asst. Prof., Microbiology & Molecular Genetics, Harvard Med. Sch. 71-73, Assc. Prof. 73-78, Prof. 79-91; Prof., Microbiology in Health Sc. & Tech., Harvard-MIT Prog. 79-91; Dir., Lab. of Infectious Diseases, C.'s Hosp., Boston 79-89; Trustee, U. of Massachusetts 88-92. *Publ.:* Over 100 papers on vesicular stomatitis virus; *Add.* 6 Washington Square N., New York, NY 10003, USA.

HUANG, CHAO-HENG 黃肇珩
Mem., Control Yuan 93-; Assc. Prof., NTNU, Fu Jen Catholic U., & Ch. Cul. U. 69-; *b.* Fukien Jan. 26, '31; *m.* Ma, Chi-shen; 1 *s.,* 1 *d.; educ.* Ed.B., NTNU 59; Reporter, Dep. Dir., & Dir., Domestic News Dept., CNA 60-81; Private Sec. to Dr. Lin Yutang in the editing of Dr. Lin Yutang's *Ch.-Eng. Dictionary of Modern Usage* 65-71; Chief Ed., *Rambler Monthly* 67-75; Dep. Dir., Dir., & Pub., *Ch. Daily News* 81-86; Gen. Mgr., Cheng Chung Bk. Co. 86-93; Dir. & Ed.-in-Chief, *Water of Life* 91-93. *Publ.: Hubbub of Human Habitation* 72; *Asian & Pacific Way of Life Series: Ch.* 75; *Talk from the Wise; A Great Modern Ch. Maestro—the Biography of Tsai Yuan-pei; Women & Jour. in Twn.; Add.* 2 Chung Hsiao E. Rd., Sect. 1, Taipei.

HUANG, CHEN-KUAI 黃振塊
Spkr., Kaohsiung CoCoun. 95-, Mem. 90-; Pres., Chiang Sheng Yacht Co. Ltd. 87-; Pres., Chiao Hung Construc-

tion Co. Ltd. 89-; *b.* Twn. Aug. 1, '37; *m.* 2 *s.,* 1 *d.; educ.* Grad. from Fengshan Jr. High Sch.; Gen. Mgr., Yu Cheng Industry Co. Ltd. 74-76; V. Chmn., Feng Shan City Citizen Rep. Coun. 82-86, Chmn. 86-90; Coun., Kaohsiung CoCoun. 90-94; Dep. Spkr., Kaohsiung CoCoun. 94-95; *Add.* 74 Lung Cheng Rd., Fengshan, Kaohsiung County.

HUANG, CHEN-TAI
(See HWANG, JENN-TAI 黃鎮台)

HUANG, CHEN-YEH 黃鎮岳
Mem., Control Yuan 93-; *b.* Twn. Jan. 26, '35; *m.* Hung, Mai-yeh; 2 *s.,* 2 *d.; educ.* LL.B., Soochow U. 58; High Sch. Tchr. 61-63; Mem., Yunlin CoCoun. 64-73; Mem., TPA 73-93, Dep. Spkr. 81-93; *Add.* 2 Chung Hsiao E. Rd., Sect. 1, Taipei.

HUANG, CHEN-YUEH
(See HUANG, CHEN-YEH 黃鎮岳)

HUANG, CHENG-KU
(See HWANG, CHEN-KU 黃正鵠)

HUANG, CHI
(See HWANG, CHYI 黃奇)

HUANG, CHIA-MING 黃嘉明
Chmn., Twn. Prov. Certified Public Accts. (CPA) Assn. 92-; Comr., Com. for the Discipline of CPA 93-; Dir., Acct. Res. & Dev. Found. 93-; CPA, Chia-ming CPA 73-; *b.* Kaohsiung May 26, '40; *m.* Chiang, Chin-feng; 1 *s.,* 2 *d.; educ.* B., Com., NCHU 69; Pers. Mng., Twn. Power Corp. 61-65; Accts. Mng., MOEA 65-73; Sup., Taipei City CPA Assn. 80-83; Dir. & Mng. Dir., Twn. Prov. CPA Assn. 83-92; Dir., Nat. Fed. of CPA Assns. (NFCPA) of ROC 89-92; NFCPA-Rep., Twn. Prov. & Taipei City CPA Assn. 86-92; Chief Comr., Com. for the Discipline of Twn. Prov. CPA Assn. 89-92; *Add.* 9th Fl.-1, 1 Nan Hai Rd., Taipei.

HUANG, CHIEN-CHU 黃建築
Spkr., Penghu CoCoun. 90-, Mem. 82-; Pres., Shengkuo Hotel 77-; *b.* Twn. Mar. 2, '41; *m.* Hsu, Hsui-ying; 1 *s.,* 5 *d.; educ.* Grad., Fengshan Jr. Coll.; *Add.* Penghu CoCoun., Penghu.

HUANG, CHIH-HSIANG
(See HUANG, JACK C. 黃致祥)

HUANG, CHING-FENG
(See HWANG, CHING-FONG 黃鏡峰)

HUANG, CHIU-CHIN 黃秋琴
Gold Medalist, '95 World Taekwondo Championships; *b.* Twn. Oct. 17, '78; *educ.* Studying at Nat. Ovs. Ch. High Sch.; Champion, 7th Intl. Taekwondo Game, Stuttgart 92; Twn. Area High Sch. Athletic Meet, Taekwondo 93 & Chung Cheng Cup Taekwondo Championship 93; Winner, 2nd Prize, Open Dutch (Taekwondo) 95 & Women's Taekwondo Competition, Twn. Area Athletic Meet 94; Winner, Taipei Chung Cheng Cup Intl. Jr. Taekwondo Championship 95; Winner, Taekwondo, Twn. Area High Sch. Athletic Meet, Taekwondo 95; *Add.* 14 Alley 2, Lane 326, Ta Hu Rd., Yingko, Taipei County.

HUANG, CHUN-YING
(See HUANG, JUNYING 黃俊英)

HUANG, FU-SHUN 黃富順
Pres., Nat. Chiayi Tchr. Coll. 96-; Sec.-Gen., Ch. Adult Educ. Assn. (Taipei) 90-; *b.* Twn. Jun. 25, '44; *m.* Liau, Iue-li; *2 d.; educ.* Ph.D., NTNU; Assc. Prof., Dept. of Soc. Educ., NTNU 85-88, Prof., 89-95; Dir., Adult & Continuing Educ., Nat. Chung Cheng U. 93-96. *Publ.: Motivation of Adult Learning; Comparative Adult Educ.; Adult Dev. & Learning; Adult Dev.; Aging & Health; Ch. Adult Educ. Dictionary; Add.* 85 Wenlung Village, Minhsiung, Chiayi County.

HUANG, HSIEN-JUNG
(See HUANG, HSIEN-YUNG 黃顯榮)

HUANG, HSIEN-YUNG 黃顯榮
C-in-C, ROCAF 95-; *b.* Twn. Aug. 9, '35; *m.* Tzeng, Fang-ching; *2 s.; educ.* Grad., Ch. Air Force Acad. 58; Squadron Off. Course 59, Regular Course 76, Air Cmd. & Staff Coll.; War Coll., Armed Forces U. 85; Fighter Pilot, Element Leader, & Squadron Cmdr. 58-74; Dir., Pol. Warfare Dept., 828th Wing ROCAF 82-84, Wing Cmdr. 86-88, Dep. Chief of Staff for Op. 88-90, V. CG, Combat Air Cmd. 90-91, Insp. Gen. 92, CG 92-94, Dep. C-in-C 94-95; *Add.* P.O. Box 90251-1, Taipei.

HUANG, HSIN-CHIANG
(See HUANG, HSING-CHIANG 黃幸強)

HUANG, HSIN-CHIEH 黃信介
Sr. Adv. to the Pres. 96-; Mem., Legis. Yuan 93-; *b.* Taipei Aug. 20, '17; *m.* Chang, Yueh-ching; *2 s., 3 d.; educ.* BPA, NCHU; Mem., Taipei CCoun.; Mem., Legis. Yuan 69-80; Pub., *Twn. Pol. Review* 75, & *Formosa Mag. of Twn. Dem. Movement* 79; Adv., DPP 87-88, Chmn. 88-91; Mem., NA 92-93; *Add.* 23 Lane 137, Chungking N. Rd., Sect. 3, Taipei.

HUANG, HSIN-PI 黃新壁
Rep., TECO, Malaysia 91-; *b.* Twn. Mar. 26, '33; *m.* Chang, Ming-tze; *educ.* LL.B., NTU 56; Grad. Sch., NCU 58-61; Sec., Emb. in Japan 61-66; Sec. to Min., MOFA 66-69, Dep. Dir.-Gen., Off. of Records & Compilation 69-71; Consul Gen., Fukuoka, Japan 71-72; Chief, Osaka Off., AEAR 73-75; Dep. Dir., Dept. of E. Asian & Pacific Aff., MOFA 75-78; Counsl., Emb. in Korea 78-85, Min. 85-88; Chief Sec., MOFA 89-90, Dir.-Gen., Dept. of Info. & Cul. Aff. & concur. Spokesman 90-91; *Add.* Lot 901, 9th Fl., Amoda Bldg., 22 Jalan Imbi, 55100 Kuala Lumpur, Malaysia.

HUANG, HSING-CHIANG 黃幸強
Rep., TECO, Athens 94-; Strategy Adv. to the Pres. 93-; *b.* Hunan June 19, '31; *m.* Lee, Miao-mei; *1 s.; educ.* Ch. Mil. Acad. 49; Advanced Course, Infantry Sch. 61; CGSC 71; War Coll., Armed Forces U. 80; Co. Cmdr. 54; Bn. Cmdr. 64; Infantry Brig. Cmdr. 71; Infantry Div. Cmdr. 77; Corps Cmdr. 81; CG, Penghu Def. Cmd. 82; Supt., Mil. Acad. 83; CG, Field Army 85; CG, Kinmen Def. Cmd. 87; C-in-C, ROC Army 88-91; Dep. Chief of the Gen. Staff (Exec.), MND 91-93; *Add.* 57 Marathonodromon Avenue., 154 52 Psychico, Athens, Greece.

HUANG, HSING-KUO 黃興國
Sec.-Gen., CETRA 93-; Pres., Far E. Trade Service, Inc. 93-; Pres., Taipei World Trade Cent. Co. Ltd. 93-; *b.* Taipei Sept. 15, '29; *m.* Lu, Chun-shueh; *1 s.; educ.* LL.B., NTU 52; Translator & ed., MND 55-71; *Add.* 333 Keelung Rd., Sect. 1, Taipei.

HUANG, HUAN-CHI 黃煥吉
Spkr., Hsinchu CCoun. 94-; *b.* Twn. Mar. 19, '40; *m.* Wen, Yueh-mei; *3 s., 1 d.; educ.* Grad., Chutung Jr. High

Sch.; Mem., Dep. Chmn., & Chmn., Chutung Rep. Conf.; *Add.* 48 Lane 664, Chang Chun Rd., Chutung, Hsinchu County.

HUANG, JACK C. 黃致祥
Pub. & concur. Dir., *Ch. Post* 93-; Exec. Dir., Nancy Yu Huang Found. 92-; Lectr., Dept. of Mass Comm., Ch. Cul. U. 94-; *b.* Taipei Mar. 7, '49; *m.* Chao, Yu; 1 *s.; educ.* BA, Ch. Lit., Soochow U. 71; MA, Jour., So. Illinois U. 76; MS, Telecomms. Mng., Golden Gate U., USA 86; Reporter & Ovs. Corr., *Ch. Post* 69-73, Dep. Dir. 76-83, Dir. 90-93; Lectr., Ch. Cul. U. 73-74; Business Broker, Vendorhurst 86-87. *Publ.: A Study of a Day's Newspaper* 71; *Add.* 8 Fu Shun St., Taipei.

HUANG, JUN-YING 黃俊英
Dep. Mayor, Kaohsiung City 95-; *b.* Twn. Dec. 31, '41; *m.* Liao, Mei-chin; 2 *s.,* 1 *d.; educ.* BA, NTU 64; MBA, NCU 68 & Michigan State U. 70; Ph.D., U. of Iowa 74; Prof., NCU 74-80; V. Chmn., RDEC 81-86; Dean, Coll. of Mng., Nat. Sun Yat-sen U. 87-89, Dean of Acad. Aff. 89-94. *Publ.: Marketing Res.; Multivariate Data Analysis; Business Mng.; Business Res. Methods; Business & Soc.; Add.* 2 Ssu Wei 3rd Rd., Kaohsiung.

HUANG, KUANG-NAN 黃光男
Dir., Nat. Museum of Hist. 95-; Prof., Grad. Sch. of Fine Arts, Nat. Inst. of the Arts 95-; *b.* Kaohsiung Feb. 15, '44; *m.* Kuo, Chiu-yen; 2 *s.; educ.* BA, Ch., Nat. Kaohsiung Normal Coll. 81; MA, Fine Arts, NTNU 84; Ph.D., Ch. Lang. & Lit., Nat. Kaohsiung Normal U. 93; Lectr., Nat. Pingtung Normal Coll. 77-86; Assc. Prof., Fine Arts Dept., Nat. Twn. Acad. of Arts 87-93; Assc. Prof., Grad. Sch. of Fine Arts, NTNU 88-93; Dir., Taipei Fine Arts Museum 86-95. *Publ.: Painting Album of Kuang-Nan Huang* (4 Vol.); *Appreciation & Instruction of the Ch. Painting; A Study on the Style of the Flower & Bird Painting of Sung Dynasty; Aesthetics & Recognition; Museum Admin.; Temperature of Aesthetics; The Aesthetic Dynamism in Ch. Art & Lit.; Add.* 49 Nan Hai Rd., Taipei.

HUANG, KUN-HUEI 黃昆輝
Sec.-Gen., Off. of the Pres. 96-; Mem., CSC, KMT 93-; *b.* Twn. Nov. 8, '36; *m.* Lin, Mann; 1 *s.,* 3 *d.; educ.* Ed.B., Twn. Prov. Normal U. 64, Ed.M. 67; Ed.D., U. of

Nr. Colorado 71; Elementary & Jr. High Sch. Tchr. 55-65; Teaching Asst., Dept. of Educ., Twn. Prov. Normal U. 65-67; Instr., Dept. of Educ., NTNU 67-71, Assc. Prof., Prof., & Dir., Grad. Inst. of Educ. 71-78, Dir., Dept. of Educ. 76-78; Comr., TPG 78-79; Dir., Bu. of Educ., TCG 79-81; Comr., Dept. of Educ., TPG 81-83; Dep. Dir.-Gen., Dept. of Cul. Aff., CC, KMT; V. Chmn., NYC 84-87; Dir.-Gen., Dept. of Youth Aff., CC, KMT 87-88; Chmn., MAC 91-94; Min. of State 88-91; Min. of the Int. 94-96. *Publ.: Analysis of Investment in Educ.; Educ. Admin. & Educ. Issues; Theory & Practice of Educ. Admin.: Theory & Res.; Add.* 122 Chungking S. Rd., Sect. 1, Taipei.

HUANG, KUN-HUI
(See HUANG, KUN-HUEI 黃昆輝)

HUANG, LIEN-HUA 黃璉華
Pres., Sigma Theta Tau Intl. 95-; Assc. Prof., NTU 89-; Dir., Dept. of Dietetics, NTUH 94-; Standing Dir., Nurses' Assn. ROC 94-; *b.* Twn. Jan. 28, '53; *m.* Lee, Tiee-min; 1 *s.,* 1 *d.; educ.* BS, NTU 74; MS, U. of Colorado 84, Ph.D. 88; Asst. Instr., NTU 74-81, Instr., 81-89. *Publ.:* Over 60 papers; *Add:* 1 Jen Ai Rd., Sect. 1, Taipei.

HUANG, LIN-HSIANG
(See HUANG, LIN-SHYANG 黃麟翔)

HUANG, LIN-SHYANG 黃麟翔
Chmn., Kaohsiung City Cttee., KMT 96-; *b.* Twn. Dec. 20, '41; *m.* Lee, Yu-mei; 2 *s.,* 1 *d.; educ.* Cert. for Extension Grad. Prog in Soc. Sc., Nat. Sun Yat-sen U.; Sec., Dept. of Public Housing, Kaohsiung City Govt. 79-80, Chief Sec., Dept. of Public Housing 80-83, Dir., Off. of Motor Vehicle Inspection 83-86, Counsl. 86, Dir., Bu. of Recon. 86-91, Dir., Bu. of Civil Aff. 91-95; Sec.-Gen., Kaohsiung City Govt. 95-96; *Add.* 463 Chien Kuo 1st Rd., Kaohsiung.

HUANG, MAO-HSIUNG
(See HUANG, THEODORE M.H. 黃茂雄)

HUANG, NAN-TU 黃南圖
Chmn., Wei Chuan Foods Corp., Twn. 95-, Concord System Mng. Corp., Twn. 95-, Concord System Corp., Twn. 95-; *b.* Taipei Oct. 16, '46; *m.* Lin, Lee-Hwa; 1 *s.,*

1 *d.; educ.* MBA, U. of S. Calif.; Exec. V. Pres., Wei Chuan Foods Corp., USA 72-80; Pres., Concord Trust Corp., USA 77-80; *Add.* 125 Sungkiang Rd., Taipei.

HUANG, PANG-CHOU 黃邦洲
Pres., Scientrade Ent. Co. Ltd. 83-; *b.* Twn. July 10, '56; *m.* Chuang, Pei-fang; 2 *s.; educ.* BEE, NCKU; *Add.* 3rd Fl., 123 Pa Te Rd., Sect. 4, Taipei.

HUANG, PIEN-CHIEN 黃秉乾
Mem., Inst. of Molecular Biology, Acad. Sinica; Prof., Biomed., NTHU 93-, Dean, Coll. of Life Sc. 93-; Prof., Johns Hopkins U. 65-; *b.* Shanghai July 13, '31; *m.* Chow, Ru-chih; 1 *s.*, 1 *d.; educ.* BS, NTU 52; MS, Virginia Polytechnic Inst. 56; Ph.D., Ohio State U.; Fel., Calif. Inst. of Tech. 60-65; Asst. Prof. & Assc. Prof., Johns Hopkins U.; Visiting Prof., Cambridge U. 72. *Publ.:* Over 100 res. articles; *Add.* NTHU, Hsinchu.

HUANG, PING-CHIEN
(See HUANG, PIEN-CHIEN 黃秉乾)

HUANG, SHI H. 黃世惠
Chmn., Nan Yang Ind. Co. Ltd., San Yang Ind. Co. Ltd., Chinfon Global Corp., & Chinfon Bk.; *b.* Taipei May 7, '26; *m.* Huang, Janet; 1 *s.*, 2 *d.; educ.* MD, NTU & Washington U.; Resident & Fel. in Neurosurgery, Washington U., Barnes Hosp. 53-59; V. Supt., Yodogawa Christian Hosp., Japan 59-74; Prof. of Neurosurgery, Washington U. 75-80; *Add.* 14th Fl., 180 Chung Hsiao E. Rd., Sect. 4, Taipei.

HUANG, SHIH-CHENG 黃石城
Nat. Policy Adv. to the Pres. 96-; Sec.-Gen., Nat. Cul. Assn. 91-; Chmn., CElC 94-; Pres., World Ch. Writer's Assn. 93-; *b.* Twn. Aug. 27, '35; *m.* Chen, Chau-o; 2 *s.*, 1 *d.; educ.* LL.B., Soochow U.; Lawyer 66-81; Magis., Changhua County 81-89; Del., Nat. Aff. Conf. 90; Min. of State 90-96; *Add.* 15th Fl.-3, 43 Hsin Yi Rd., Sect. 3, Taipei.

HUANG, SHIH-HOU
(See HUANG, ALICE S. 黃詩厚)

HUANG, SHIH-HUI
(See HUANG, SHI H. 黃世惠)

HUANG, SHOU-KAO
(See HUANG, SHOU-KAU 黃守高)

HUANG, SHOU-KAU 黃守高
Admin. V. Min. of the Int. 95-; *b.* Taipei July 10, '38; *m.* Lin, Chiung-chen; 2 *s.*, 1 *d.; educ.* LL.B., NTU 60, LL.M. 64; Chief Sec., Min. of Pers. 75-77; Counsl., Jud. Yuan 77-78; Chief Sec., MOTC 78-82; Chief Sec., MOJ 82-85, Dir. Dept. 85-87; Chmn., Cttee. of Legal Aff. & Appeals, Exec. Yuan 87-95. *Publ.: The Comparative Res. of Modern Admin. Penalty; The Soc. Mission of Modern Admin. Law; Add.* 5 Hsuchow Rd., Taipei.

HUANG, TA-CHOU 黃大洲
Chmn., RDEC 96-; Mem., CSC, KMT 93-; *b.* Twn. Feb. 7, '36; *m.* Lin, Wen-ying; 2 *d.; educ.* BS, Agr. Econ., NTU 60, MS, 62; MS, Rural Sociology, Cornell U. 66, Ph.D., Rural Dev. 71; Instr., NTU 66-68, Assc. Prof. 71-76; Sr. Res. Fel., E.-W. Cent., Hawaii 76 & 77; Prof., NTU 76; Counsl., CEPD 77; Adv., TCG 79-81; Exec. Sec., RDEC 79-81; Dep. Sec.-Gen., TPG 81-84; Dean of Business Aff., NTU 84-87; Sec.-Gen., TCG 87-90; Fel., Eisenhower Exchange Fel. 89; Acting Mayor, Taipei City 90; Mayor, Taipei City 90-94; Coun. Mem., CEPD 94-96. *Publ.:* 37 articles & bk.; *Add.* 7th Fl., 99-1 Ningpo W. St., Taipei.

HUANG, THEODORE M.H. 黃茂雄
Chmn., ROC & Australia Business Coun., TECO Elec. & Mach. Co. Ltd., Taian Elec. Co. Ltd.; V. Chmn., Coordinate Coun. on Sino-Japanese Business Aff.; *b.* Twn. June 19, '39; *m.* Lynn, H.H.; 2 *s.*, 1 *d.; educ.* BA, Econ., Keio U., Japan 62; MBA, Wharton Sch., U. of Penn. 64; Chmn., Twn. Chapter of Young Pres. Org., Elec. & Elect. Products Dev. Assn.; Pres., Taian Elec. Co. Ltd.; *Add.* 156-2 Sungkiang Rd., Taipei.

HUANG, TING-CHIA 黃定加
Acting Pres., NCKU 95-; Prof., Dept. of Chem. Engr., NCKU 68-; *b.* Twn. June 1, '32; *m.* Huang Wan, Juei-chin; 2 *s.*, 2 *d.; educ.* BS, NCKU 55; Dr. Engr., U. of Tokyo 79; IAEA Res. Fel., Japan Atomic Energy Res. Inst., Tokai-mura, Ibaraki-ken 62; Res. Assc., Dept. of Chem. Engr., U. of Houston 69-70; Chmn. & Dir., Dept. of Chem. Engr., NCKU 81-87; Consultant, MOE 88-94. *Publ.: Experimental Phys. Chem.* 63; *Chem. Engr. Ther-*

modynamics 71; *Phys. Chem.* 78; *Experiments in Phys. Chem.* 83; Over 160 articles to prof. jour., proceedings & symposiums; *Add.* Dept. of Chem. Engr., NCKU, Tainan.

HUANG, TSU-YAO 黃祖耀

Curator, Kaohsiung City Lib.; *b.* Twn. July 1, '48; *m.* Wu, Chin-lien; 1 *s.*, 1 *d.; educ.* Educ. Media (Lib. Sc.), Tamkang U.; M., Ch. Lit., Nat. Cent. U., S. Korea; Sect. Chief, Chiang Kai-shek Cul. Cent., Kaohsiung City 85-86; Sec., Dept. of Soc. Aff., Kaohsiung City Govt. 86-87; Dir., Kaohsiung Voc. Tng. Cent.; *Add.* 80 Min Sheng 2nd Rd., Kaohsiung.

HUANG, TSUN-CHIU
(See HWANG, TZUEN-CHIOU 黃尊秋)

HUANG, TUNG-HSIUNG
(See HUAN, TONG-SHONG 黃東熊)

HUANG WEN-SUNG 黃文松
Pres., Tycoons Group Ent. Co. Ltd. 80-; *b.* Twn. Feb. 26, '55; *m.* Lu, Yen-chuan; 1 *s.; educ.* Grad., Voc. High Sch. 75; *Add.* 79-1 Shin Li St., Kangshan, Kaohsiung County.

HUANG, YAO-YU 黃耀羽
Dir.-Gen., Dept. of Mainland Aff., CC, KMT 93-; *b.* Canton Jan. 25, '31; *m.* Chen, Pao-yun; 1 *s.*, 1 *d.; educ.* Ch. Army Mil. Acad. 52; Ch. Army CGSC 69; War Coll., Armed Forces U. 72; Prof., War Coll., Armed Forces U. 73-75; Armored Brig. Cmdr. 78-82; Infantry Div. Cmdr. 82-84; Cmdr., Armor Tng. Cmd. & Cmdt., Armor Sch. 84-85; Supt., Ch. Mil. Acad. 85-87; Dep. Dir., Nat. Sec. Bu. 87-93; *Add.* 5th Fl., 53 Jen Ai Rd., Sect. 3, Taipei.

HUANG, YEN-CHAO 黃演鈔
Rep., Taipei Rep. Off. in Belgium 94-; *b.* Twn. Oct. 31, '34; *m.* Lin, Mei-hui; 3 *c.; educ.* LL.B., NTU; Staff, MOFA 61-64; 3rd Sec., Emb. in Italy 64-66; 2nd & 1st Sec., Ch. Mission to the European Off. of the UN 66-73; Dir., Off. in Switzerland, MOEA 75-83, Dir., Investment & Trade Service Off. in USA 83-86, Dir.-Gen., Bu. of Commodity Inspection & Quarantine 86-93; Dir.-Gen., Bd. of For. Trade, MOEA 93-94. *Publ.: Res. on the European Common Market; Questions on the Euro Dollar; Econ. Growth & Soc. Justice; Add.* Av. des Arts, 41, 1040 Brussels, Belgium.

HUANG, YUNG-HOU 黃永厚
Dep. Min. of Nat. Def. 93-; *b.* Kwangtung July 16, '37; *m.* Wang, Shi-lin; 1 *d.; educ.* Ch. Air Force Acad. 58; Air Force Cmd. & Staff Coll., Armed Forces U. 74; Corr. Course, Ind. Coll. of the Armed Forces, USA 78; War Coll., Armed Forces U. 83; Wing Cmdr. 86-87; Cmdr., Flying Squadron Tng. Cent. 87-88; Dep. Cmdt. & Instr.-Gen., Air Force Cmd. & Staff Coll., Armed Forces U. 90-91; Dep. Cmdr., Kinmen Def. Cmd. 91-93; *Add.* 6th Fl., 12-1 Lane 185, Chien Kang Rd., Taipei.

HUANG, YUNG-WU 黃永武
Prof., Dept. of Lang. Educ., Taipei Mun. Tchrs. Coll. 88-; *b.* Chekiang Feb. 9, '36; *m.* Hsu, Hua-mei; 2 *s.*, 1 *d.; educ.* BA, Ch., Soochow U. 62; MA, Ch., NTNU 64; Ph.D. 71; Prof. & Chmn., Dept. of Ch. Lang., & Dir., Inst. of Ch. Lang., Nat. Kaohsiung Normal U. 71-77; Prof. & Dean, Coll. of Lib. Arts, NCHU 77-83; Visiting Prof., Dept. of E. Asian Lang., Cornell U. 83-84; Prof., Dept. of Ch. Lang., NCHU 84-85; Prof. & Dean, Coll. of Lib. Arts, NCKU 85-88. *Publ.: Poetic Heart* 71; *Ch. Poetry* (4 Vol.) 75-79; *Patriotic Wall of Poetry* 81; *Tunhuang Treasury* (140 Vol.) 81-85; *Poetry & Beauty* 84; *Boat of Pearls* 85; *Study & Appreciation of Poetry* 87; *Walking in the Forest of Poetry* 89; *Fragrant Valley of Poetry* 92; *Ai Lu Essays* (4 Vol.) 92; *Add.* 2nd Fl., 17-1 Alley 18, Ho Ping E. Rd., Sect. 2, Taipei.

HUANG CHOU, JU-CHI
(See HUANG CHOW, RU-CHIH 黃周汝吉)

HUANG CHOW, RU-CHIH 黃周汝吉
Mem., Acad. Sinica; Prof., Johns Hopkins U.; *b.* Nanking Apr. 2, '32; *m.* Huang, Pien-chien; 1 *s.*, 1 *d.; educ.* BS, NTU; Ph.D., Ohio State U.; Fel., Calif. Inst. of Tech. 50-55; *Add.* 4604 Kerneway, Baltimore, MD 21212, USA.

HUNG, CHIEN-CHAO 洪健昭
Rep., Ufficio Economico e Culturale di Taipei, Rome 93-; *b.* Twn. Feb. 15, '32; *m.* Lu, Li-ying; 1 *d.; educ.* BA, NTU 54; MA, So. Illinois U. 65; Ph.D., Georgetown U. 81; M. Checker, Army GHQ 58-60; Chief Press Ed., USIS, Taipei 60-64; Assc. Prof., NCU 66-73; Mng. Dir., *Ch. Post* 65-70; Chief, Eng. Dept., CNA 71-74, Bu. Chief, Middle E. 74-77, Chief Corr., Washington, D.C. 77-80, Bu. Chief, Houston 80-83, Tokyo 83-87, & W.

Europe 87-89; Pres., CNA 90-93. *Publ.: Twn. Today; Formosa Under the Cheng; Add.* Via Sardegna 50, II P. Int. 12, 00187 Rome, Italy.

HUNG, MIN-HSIUNG
(See HONG, DAVID C.S. 洪敏雄)

HUNG, TE-HSUAN
(See HUNG, TEH-SHUAN 洪德旋)

HUNG, TEH-SHUAN 洪德旋
Chmn., Twn. Prov. Cttee., KMT 96-; *b.* Twn. July 10, '45; *m.* Huang, Feng-mei; *2 s., 1 d.; educ.* BPS, NTU 63, MA 72; Studied at Maryland U.; Sect. Chief, Legis. Yuan 77-79; Counsl. & concur. Chief, Compilation Off., Exam. Yuan 79-84; Counsl. & concur. Exec. Sec., MOC 84-87; Dir., Dept. of Publ. Aff., GIO 87-90; Counsl. & concur. Dir., 3rd Dept., Exec. Yuan 90-91; Dir., Dept. of Soc. Aff., TPG 91-93; V. Chmn., VAC 93-95; Dir.-Gen., Dept. of Soc. Aff., KMT 95-96. *Publ.: On Laws & Pol.; Investigation Power for the US Cong.; Prevention of & Legislation on the Hijacking of Airplanes; A Study of the Legislation & Soc. Aid for the Disabled; An Index of the US Welfare Admin.; Add.* 445 San Min Rd., Sect. 3, Taichung.

HUNG, WEN-HSIANG 洪文湘
Comr., Exam. Yuan 90-; Prof., Dept. of Acct., NTU 78-; *b.* Anhwei Nov. 12, '40; *m.* Cheng, Hsueh-ying; *educ.* BBA, NTU 63; MBA, U. of Houston 67; Instr., NTU 70-73, Assc. Prof. 73-78, Chmn., Dept. of Business Admin. 75-79, Chmn., Grad. Sch. of Business Admin. 75-79. *Publ.: Goodwill; Issue of Price Levels; CPA Exam. of ROC; Add.* 1 Shih Yuan Rd., Wenshan, Taipei.

HUNG, YU-CHIN
(See HONG, YUH-CHIN 洪玉欽)

HWAN FU 桓夫
(See CHEN, CHIEN-WU 陳千武)

HWANG, CHANG-CHIEN 黃彰健
Mem., Acad. Sinica 82-, Corr. Res. Fel., Inst. of Hist. & Philology 89-; *b.* Hunan Feb. 2, '19; *m.* Peng, Wei-tzu; *3 d.; educ.* BA, Nat. Cent. U.; Asst., Inst. of Hist. & Philology, Acad. Sinica 44-48, Asst. Res. Fel. 48-55,

Assc. Res. Fel. 55-61, Res. Fel. 61-89; Nat. Res. Chair Prof., NScC 65-69. *Publ.: Studies on the Hist. of the 1898 Reform; On the Hist. of the Ming & Ch'ing Dynasties; The Authentic Memorials by K'ang Yu-wei in 1898; New Light on the Controversies Between the New-text Sch. & the Old-text Sch.; Add.* 1st Fl., 51 Lane 70, Yen Chiu Yuan Rd., Sect. 2, Taipei.

HWANG, CHYI 黃奇
Prof. & Chmn., Dept. of Chem. Engr., Nat. Chung Cheng U. 93-; *b.* Fukien May 18, '52; *m.* Lin, Ya-jung; *2 s.; educ.* BS, NCKU 76, MS 78; Ph.D. 81; Instr., NCKU 78-81, Assc. Prof., 81-87, Prof. 87-93. *Publ.:* More than 140 acad. jour. papers; *Add.* 160 San Hsing Village, Minhsiung, Chiayi County.

HWANG, CHEN-KU 黃正鵠
Pres., Nat. Kaohsiung Normal U. 92-; *b.* Chekiang Dec. 20, '37; *m.* Hu, Chyi-fang; *1 s., 1 d.; educ.* Ed.B., NTNU; Ed.M., NCU; Ed.D., U. of Nr. Colorado 82; Dir., Lib., Nat. Kaohsiung Tchrs.' Coll. 69-75, Dir., Counseling Cent. 76-77, Dir. of Student Aff. 77-80, Head, Secretariat 82-84, Dean of Student Aff. 84-87; Dir., Grad. Inst. of Educ., Nat. Kaohsiung Normal U. 87-88, Dean of Studies 88-92. *Publ.: Basic Theory on Mental Analysis 67; Infant-Parent Relationship 73; A Survey of Disabled Students in Twn., ROC to Assess the Need of Rehabilitation Services 81; Res. on Prof. Tng. & Occupational Guidance for the Mentally Retarded in Kaohsiung City 90; &* numerous articles in prof. jour.; *Add.* 116 Ho Ping 1st Rd., Kaohsiung.

HWANG, CHING-FONG 黃鏡峰
V. Chmn., VAC 95-; Mem., NA 92-; *b.* Twn. Sept. 5, '30; *m.* Hsu, Chiung-ying; *2 s., 3 d.; educ.* Prov. Taitung Sr. High Sch.; Passed Sr. Civil Service Exam.; Passed Sp. Civil Service Exam. A; Completed 1st-term Courses on Nat. Dev., Sun Yat-sen Inst. on Policy Res. & Dev.; Sec., Taitung County Govt. 64; Mgr., Credit Corp., Taitung County 64-68; Magis., Taitung County (2 terms); Chmn., Ch. Youth Corps Cttee., Taitung County 68-76; Dir., Twn. Prov. Food Bu., TPG 84, Comr., Dept. of Recon. 84-87, Comr. 87-89; Acting Mayor, Taichung City 89; Chmn., Kaoshiung Mun. Cttee., KMT 89-93; Dir.-Gen., Secretariat, CC, KMT 93-95; *Add.* 222 Chung Hsiao E. Rd., Sect. 5, Taipei.

HWANG, JENN-TAI 黃鎮台
Pres., Feng Chia U. 95-; Adjunct Prof., Chem. Dept., NTHU 91-; Bd. Mem., Ch. Chem. Soc. 91-; *b.* Twn. Oct. 17, '48; *m.* Sun, Lucy; 1 *s.,* 1 *d.; educ.* BS, NTU 70; Ph.D., Columbia U. 77; Postdoctoral Res., Princeton U. & U. of Chicago 78-79; Assc. Prof. & Prof., NTHU 79-89; Dir. of Admin. & Planning, Tzu-chiang Res. Inst. 85-86; Dir., Div. of Natural Scs., NScC 86-89; Dir., Dept. of Higher Educ., MOE 89-90; Dir., Soc. of Explosives & Propellants, ROC 86-90; Chmn., Ch. Chem. Soc. 89-91; V. Chmn., RDEC 91-94; V. Min.of Educ. 94-95. *Publ.:* Over 20 phys. & chem. res. papers published in local & intl. jour.; *Add.* 100 Wen Hua Rd., Taichung.

HWANG, TZUEN-CHIOU 黃尊秋
Sr. Adv. to the Pres. 93-; *b.* Twn. Dec. 5, '23; *m.* Yuan, Tsui-lan; 3 *s.,* 2 *d.; educ.* Cent. Police Coll.; Judge & Chief, Hsinchu, Kaohsiung, & Taipei Dist. Courts 56-65; Judge, Tainan High Court 65-67; Chief Prosecutor, Penghu & Taitung Dist. Courts 67-71; Chief Judge, Tainan High Court 71-73; Mem., Control Yuan 73-81, V. Pres. 81-87, Pres. 87-93; *Add.* 5th Fl., 71 Shih Ta Rd., Taipei.

HWANG, YUEH-CHIN 黃越欽
Mem., Control Yuan 93-; *b.* Twn. May 30, '41; *m.* Wang, Shu-wan; 2 *s.,* 1 *d.; educ.* LL.B., NCU 65; LL.D., U. of Vienna 70; Assc. Prof., NCU 70-79, Prof. 79-93; Visiting Prof., Grad. Sch. of Law, U. of Zurich 86-87. *Publ.: Theses on Private Laws; Labor Laws; Add.* 2 Chung Hsiao E. Rd., Sect. 1, Taipei.

HWU, REUBEN JIH-RU 胡紀如
Prof. of Chem., NTHU 90-; Res. Fel., Acad. Sinica 90-; Assc. Mem., IUPAC Com. on Nomenclature of Organic Chem. 89-; Res. Consultant, State U. of New York 87-; *b.* Taipei Apr. 17, '54; *m.* Leu, Alice Show-mei; 2 *d.; educ.* BS, NTU 76; Ph.D., Stanford U. 82; Asst. Prof. of Chem., Johns Hopkins U. 82-88, Assc. Prof. 88-91; Alfred P. Sloan Fel., USA 86-90; Pres., Ch. Am. Chem. Soc. 91-93. *Publ.:* 57 sc. papers published in intl. jour.; *Add.* Dept. of Chem., NTHU, Hsinchu.

I, CHIA-HSUN
(See YIH, CHIA-SHUN 易家訓)

I, CHING-CHIU
(See YEE, CHIN-CHIU 易勁秋)

JAN, DE-HO 詹德和
Dir.-Gen., Directorate Gen. of Customs, MOF 91-; *b.* Twn. Oct. 19, '34; *m.* Huang, Jui-ling; 2 *s.,* 1 *d.; educ.* BA, Econ., NTU; MPA, U. of So. Calif.; Clerk & Asst., Taipei Customs 60-72, Acting Dep. Comr. 73-74; Acting Dep. Comr., Keelung Customs 74-78, Dep. Comr. 78; Admin. Dep. Comr., Taipei Customs 78-79, Acting Admin. Comr. 79, Comr., Secretariat 79-82; Comr., Taichung Customs 83-84; Comr., Kaohsiung Customs 84-87; Dep. Insp.-Gen., Inspectorate Gen. of Customs 87-90, Insp.-Gen. 90-91. *Publ.: Quality Customer Service of ROC Customs Service—A Case Study Based on Contemporary US Mng. Concept; Add.* 85 Hsin Sheng S. Rd., Sect. 1, Taipei.

JAO, CHI-MING
(See RAU, CHYI-MING 饒奇明)

JAO, YIN-CHI
(See YAO, ENG-CHI 饒穎奇)

JEA, YU-HUEI 賈玉輝
Dir.-Gen., Directorate Gen. of Telecom. 96-; *b.* Chekiang Jun. 1, '43; *m.* Chang, Kang; 2 *s.,* 2 *d.; educ.* BS, NTU 66; MS, NTU 70; MS, U. of Texas 76, Ph.D. 77; Dir., Computer Time-Sharing Cent., Twn. Telecom. Admin. 72-79; Dean & Chmn., Computer Sc. Dept., Telecom. Tng. Inst. 79-81; Dep. Mng. Dir., Data Comm. Inst. 81-84, Mng. Dir. 84-94; Dir.-Gen., Dept. of Posts & Telecom., MOTC 94-96. *Publ.:* More than 50 papers; *Add.* 16 Chi Nan Rd., Sect. 2, Taipei.

JEN, CHIH-KUNG 任之恭
Mem., Acad. Sinica; *b.* Shansi Oct. 2, '06; *m.* Tao, Pao-cheng; 4 *d.; educ.* BS, Tsinghua Coll. 26; BS, MIT 28; MS, U. of Penn. 29; Ph.D., Harvard U. 31; Instr., Harvard U. 31-33; Prof. of Phys., U. of Shantung 33-34; Prof., Phys. & EE, NTHU 34-37, & Nat. S.W. Assc. U.; Head, Radio Res. Inst., NTHU 38-45; Lectr., Harvard U. 45-50; Physicist & Assc. Dir., Res. Cent., Applied Phys. Lab., Johns Hopkins U. 50-76; *Add.* 10203 Lariston Lane, Silver Spring, MD 20903, USA.

JIANG, FENG-CHYI 江奉琪
Pres., CTV 96-; *b.* Twn. June 8, '44; *m.* Shen, Yen-ching; 1 *s.,* 1 *d.; educ.* BPA, Tamkang U. 72; Sr. Sp., Cul. Off.,

MOE 71-73; Sr. Sp., Sect. Chief, & Asst. Dir., GIO 73-84; Dep. Dir., Dept. of Info., Kaohsiung City Govt. 84-85; Sec.-Gen., Dept. of Cul. Aff., CC, KMT 85-88; Dept. Dir., MOI 88-90; Pres., Cent. Motion Picture Corp. 90-95; Chmn., Motion Picture & Drama Assn. 91-95; Dir.-Gen., Secretariat, CC, KMT 95-96; *Add.* 120 Chung Yang Rd., Nankang, Taipei.

JIN, WEI-TSUN 金惟純
Chmn., Shang Chou Co. Ltd 87-; V. Chmn., The Business Dev. Found. of Ch. Straits 93-; *b.* Twn. Jan. 16, '52; *m.* Kao, Hsiao-chin; 1 *d.; educ.* BA, NCU 74; Grad. Sch., NCU 80; Grad. Sch., New York U. 86; Columnist, *Ch. Times* 79; Writer, *Ch. Times*-US edition 84; Ed., *Commonwealth* 86; *Add.* 5th Fl., 62 Tun Hua N. Rd., Taipei.

JOEI, BERNARD T.K. 芮正皋
Sr. Adv., MOFA 86-, Mem., Res. & Planning Bd. 94-; Sr. Adv. for UN Aff., TECO, New York 93-; Prof., Intl. Law, Ch. Cul. U. 93-; Chmn., Sino-Vietnam Ind. & Comm. Assn. 87-; Gen. Counsl., Chen & Lin Attorneys-at-Law 94-; Mem., Nat. Columnist Assn. 93-; Ed. Writer & Columnist, *Ch. Post, CDN, & Independent Evening Post*; Bd. Mem., Taipei European Schs. Found. 94-; *b.* Chekiang Aug. 14, '19; *m.* Liu, Yumei; 3 *s.; educ.* LL.B., Aurora U., Shanghai; Grad., Inst. of Pol. Sc., Paris 51; Dr. of Intl. Law, U. of Paris 50; Proficiency of Eng. Cert., Cambridge U. 71; Prof. & Dir., Grad. Inst. of European Studies, Tamkang U. 84-92, Dir., Cent. for Regional Studies 84-90; Amb. to Mali 60; Amb. to Upper Volta 61-68; Amb. to Gambia 65-68; Amb. to Côte d'Ivore 68-83; Alt. Rep. to regular sess. of UNGA 65-71. *Publ.:* *"Pragmatic Dip. in the ROC—Hist. & Prospects," Quiet Revolutions on Twn., ROC;* 100 articles on intl. pol., UN Aff., Twn.'s pragmatic dip., & domestic pol. published in jour. & newspapers; *Add.* Suite 6-G, 56 Tun Hua S. Rd., Sect. 2, Taipei.

JU, MING 朱銘
Sculptor; Prof.; *b.* Twn. Jan. 20, '38; *m.* Chen, Fu-may; 2 *s.,* 2 *d.; educ.* Studied traditional wood carving with Lee Chin-chuan 53; Studied with sculptor Yang Yu-yu; Exhibitions: Nat. Hist. Museum 77; Cent. Gallery, Tokyo 78; Hong Kong Art Cent. 80; Max Huchinson Gallery, New York 81; Nat. Museum, Singapore 86; Hong Kong 87; S. Bk. Cent., London 91; Museum of

Contemporary Art, Dunkirk, Paris 91; Yorkshire Sculpture Park, W. Yorkshire 92; Intl. Contemporary Art Fair, Yokohama 92; *Add.* 28 Lane 460, Chih Shan Rd., Sect. 2, Taipei.

JUAN, KANG-MENG 阮剛猛
Magis., Changhua County 93-; *b.* Twn. Jan. 5, '51; *m.* Huang, Li-hua; 1 *s.,* 2 *d.; educ.* Grad., Prov. Taichung Tchrs. Coll.; Tchr., Changhua County Tachia Elementary Sch. 72-80; Reserve Judge, Tainan Dist. Court 80-81; Reserve Judge, Taichung Dist. Court 81-82, Judge 82-87, Judge & concur. Presiding Judge 89, Justice & concur. Presiding Judge 89-92, Presiding Judge 92-93; Judge, Shihlin Br., Taipei Dist. Court 87-89; *Add.* 416 Chung Shan Rd., Sect. 2, Changhua.

JUAN, TA-NIEN
(See YUAN, DANIEL TA-NIEN 阮大年)

JUAN, VEI-CHOW 阮維周
Mem., Acad. Sinica, & Coun. of Acad. Sinica; Prof. Emeritus, NTU 81-; *b.* Anhwei May 23, '12; *m.* Sun, Yolanda; 1 *s.,* 1 *d.; educ.* BS, Peking U. 35; Ph.D., U. of Chicago; Prof., Nat. Peking U. 47-49; Prof., NTU 50, Chmn., Dept. of Geol. 52-62, Dean, Coll. of Sc. 54-62; Dir.-Gen., Acad. Sinica 62-64.; Hon. Prof., Peking U. 92; Hon. Prof., Ch. U. of Geoscience 92; Hon. Res., Ch. Geoscience Acad. 92. *Publ.: The Earth's Tectonosphere; Diatomaceous Earth* 37; *Mineral Resources of Ch.* 46; *13 Lectures on Geol.* 52; *Educ. & Res. in Geol.* 60; *Lunar Exploration* 74; *Tectonic Evolution of Twn.* 75; *Thermal-Tectonic Evolution of E. Ch. Sea* 86; *Evolution of Ecologite* 90; & 13 lectures on Geol.; *Add.* 2nd Fl., 1 Lane 16, Wenchow St., Taipei.

JUAN, WEI-CHOU
(See JUAN, VEI-CHOW 阮維周)

JUANG, HWAI-I 莊懷義
Dir., Sun Yat-sen Inst. on Policy Res. & Dev. 94-; Mem., CC, KMT 93-; *b.* Twn. June 14, '35; *m.* Juang, Chen-fen; 1 *s.,* 1 *d.; educ.* Ed.B., NTNU; Ed.D., Columbia U.; Counsl., Dept. of Labor & Ind., New Jersey State Govt. 73-79; Dep. Dir.-Gen., Dept. of Ovs. Aff., CC, KMT 79-85, Dep. Dir.-Gen., Dept. of Cul. Aff. 85-86; Pres., Nat. Open U. 86-88; Dir.-Gen., Dept. of Youth Aff., CC, KMT 88-91; Bd. Chmn., *CDN* 91-94. *Publ.: Res. on*

Educ. Problems; A Cost-Benefit Analysis of Educ.: Theory & Practice; Problems & Guidance of Youth & Adolescents; Envisioning the 21st Century; Introduction to Educ; Add. 290 Mu Cha Rd., Sect. 1, Taipei.

JWO, JACKSON 卓傳陣
Chmn., Kaohsiung CPA Assn. 94-; Sup., Nat. Federal of CPA Assn. 94-; CPA & Partner, Moore Stephens Twn. CPAs & Co. 91-; *b.* Twn. May 18, '56; *m.* Chen, Yuchueh; 2 *s.; educ.* B., Acct., NCU 78, M. 82; Dir., Kaohsiung CPA Assn. 88-91; Mng. Dir., Kaohsiung CPA Assn. 91-94; CPA & Partner, Sanders CPAs & Co. 83-91. *Publ.: The Res. of Application & Its Predicting Function About Financial Ratios; Add.* 2nd Fl.-1, 91 Chung Shan 2nd Rd., Kaohsiung.

KAN, YUET-WAI 簡悅威
Mem., Acad. Sinica 88-; Prof., Dept. of Med. & Lab. Med., U. of Calif., San Francisco 77-, Louis K. Diamond Prof. 83-; Investigator, Howard Hughes Med. Inst. 76-; *b.* Ch. June 11, '36; *m.* Kan, Alvera; 2 *d.; educ.* MD, U. of Hong Kong 58, D.Sc. 80; Asst. Prof., Pediatrics, Harvard Med. Sch. 70-72; Assc. Prof., Dept. of Med., U. of Calif., San Francisco 72-77. *Publ.:* Over 200 papers in sc. jour.; *Add.* U. 426, U. of Calif., San Francisco, CA 94143-0724, USA.

KANG, NING-HSIANG 康寧祥
Chmn., For. Aff. Cttee., Control Yuan 95-, Convener, Nat. Def. Cttee. & Mem. 93-; Mem., NA 91-; Mem., NUC 90-; V. Pres., Inst. of Intl. Aff. 91-; *b.* Taipei Nov. 16, '38; *m.* Chen, Li-jung; 1 *s.,* 1 *d.; educ.* BPA, NCHU; Visiting Scholar, E. Asian Inst., Columbia U. 85; Mem., Taipei CCoun. 69-72; Founder, *Twn. Pol. Review* 75, *The Eighties, The Asians, & The Current* 79-86; Mem., CSC, DPP 86-88; Mem., Legis. Yuan 72-90; Pub., *Capital Morning Post* 89-90; Chmn., Presidium & Mem., Preparatory Cttee., Nat. Aff. Conf. 90. *Publ.: 3 Years in Parliament; 6 Years in Parliament; Problems of Const. Dem.; Crisis & Hope; Gas Station Serviceman, Ch. Petroleum Corp.; Add.* 2 Chung Hsiao E. Rd., Sect. 1, Taipei.

KAO, CHARLES H.C. 高希均
Founder & Pres., *Commonwealth Mag., Global Views Monthly,* & Commonwealth Pub. Co.; Prof., Dept. of Econ., U. of Wisconsin, River Falls; Dir., Cent. for Pacific Rim Studies; *b.* Nanking Apr. 16, '36; *m.* Kao, Anne; 2 *c.; educ.* BS, NCHU; Ph.D., Michigan State U. 64; Adv., CIECD 69-70; Chmn., Dept. of Econ., U. of Wisconsin, River Falls 71-80; Yuan-Tung Prof., Grad. Sch. of Business Admin., NTU 77-79; Visiting Prof., NTNU 82; Dir., Cent. for Quality of Life Studies, Ming-Teh Found. 80-85. *Publ.: The Brain Drain; A Case Study of Ch.; The Role of the Agr. Sector in Twn.'s Econ. Dev.; The World of Econ.; Add.* 7th Fl., 87 Sungkiang Rd., Taipei.

KAO, CHARLES K. 高錕
Mem., Acad. Sinica; V. Chancellor (Pres.), Ch. U. of Hong Kong 87-; *b.* Shanghai Nov. 4, '33; *m.* Wong, May-wan; 1 *s.,* 1 *d.; educ.* BSC, U. of London 57, Ph.D. 65; Engr., Standard Telephones & Cables Ltd., UK 57-60; Res. Scientist/Res. Engr., Standards Telecomms. Lab. Ltd., UK 60-70; Prof. & Chmn., Elect. Dept., Ch. U. of Hong Kong 70-74; Chief Scientist, Electro Optical Products Div., ITT, USA 74-81, V. Pres. & Dir. of Engr. 81-83; Exec. Scientists & Dir., Res., ITT Advanced Tech. Cent., USA 83-87; Adjunct Prof. & Fel., Trumbull Coll., Yale U. 86. *Publ.:* 5 bk. on fiber optics & high tech.; Over 100 papers on fiber optics; *Add.* V. Chancellor's Off., Ch. U. of Hong Kong, Shatin, N.T., Hong Kong.

KAO, CHIN-YEN 高清愿
Mem., CSC, KMT 94-; V. Chmn., Pres. Ents. Corp. 89-; Chief Exec. Off., Pres. Group 89-; Chmn., Pres. Chain Store Corp. 86-, Ton Yi Ind. Corp. 79-, & Ztong Yee Ind. Co. Ltd. 77-; *b.* Twn. May 24, '29; *m.* Kao, Lai-kwan; 1 *d.; educ.* Grad., Tainan County Tienchow Elementary Sch. 37; Hon. Ph.D., Lincoln U. 83; Sales Mgr., Tainan Fabric Corp. 57-67; Pres., Pres. Ents. Corp. 67-89; *Add.* 301 Chung Cheng Rd., Yungkang, Tainan County.

KAO, CHING-YUN
(See LIAU, MARIETTA 高青雲)

KAO, CHING-YUAN
(See KAO, CHIN-YEN 高清愿)

KAO, CHUNG-HSIN 高忠信
Chmn., ROC Taoist Assn. 86-; Chmn., ROC Religious Followers Assn. 94-; Mem., NA 92-; Bd. Chmn., Chihnan Bus Trans. Co. 71-; *b.* Taipei May 19, '33; *m.* Kao, Liao-chiu; 3 *s.,* 1 *d.; educ.* Dongkuk U., S.

Korea; Mem., Legis. Yuan 84-87; *Add.* 115 Wan Shou Rd., Wenshan, Taipei.

KAO, HSI-CHUN
(See KAO, CHARLES H.C. 高希均)

KAO, KOONG-LIAN 高孔廉
V. Chmn., MAC 91-; Prof., Grad. Sch. of Business Admin., NCU; *b.* Fukien Nov. 9, '44; *m.* Kao L., Halina H.C.; 2 *s.; educ.* MBA, NCU 69; Ph.D., Louisiana State U. 75; Prof. & Chmn., Dept. of Business Admin., Soochow U. 76-81; Dept. Dir., RDEC 81-83, V. Chmn. 83-91. *Publ.: Theories & Applications of Finite Markov Chains; Op. Res.: A Quantitative Approach to Decision-Making; Planning & Control Systems; Add.* 15th Fl., 2-2 Chi Nan Rd., Sect. 1, Taipei.

KAO, KUEI-YUAN 高魁元
Strategy Adv. to the Pres.; *b.* Shantung Mar. 26, '07; *m.* Teng, Yu-chin; *educ.* Mil. Acad.; Armed Forces Staff Coll.; CGSC, US; CG, 295th Brig. 38-39; CG, 99th, 118th & 88th Divs., ROC Army 40-48; CG, 18th, 96th, & 45th Corps 49-53; Dir., Pol. Warfare Dept., Army GHQ 55-57; Dep. C-in-C, ROC Army 57-58; CG, Reserve & Replacement Tng. Cmd. 58; CG, 2nd Field Army 59-60; Dir., Gen. Pol. Warfare Dept., MND 61-65; C-in-C, ROC Army 65-67; Chief of the Gen. Staff, MND 67-70; Personal C/S to the Pres. 70-73; Min. of Nat. Def. 73-81. *Publ.: Mil. Theories & Mags.; Add.* 10 Lane 124, Pei Yi Rd., Sect. 1, Hsintien, Taipei County.

KAO, KUN
(See KAO, CHARLES K. 高錕)

KAO, KUNG-LIEN
(See KAO, KOONG-LIAN 高孔廉)

KAO, YING-MAO
(See KAU, YING-MAO 高英茂)

KAO, YU-MIN
(SEE KAU, YUH-MIN 高育民)

KAU, YING-MAO 高英茂
Prof. of Pol. Sc. & Dir., E. Asian Sec. Project, Brown U. 68-; Ed., *Ch. Law & Govt. Quarterly* 73-; Pres., Assn. of Ch. Soc. Sc. in N. Am. 86-, & 21st Century Found. 88-; *b.* Twn. Aug. 31, '34; *m.* Huang, Anna; 2 *s.,* 1 *d.; educ.* BA, NTU 56; MA, Cornell U. 60, Ph.D. 68. *Publ.: Critical Issues Facing Twn.'s Current Reform; The Writings of Mao Zedong; Ch.'s Unification & Communist-Nationalist Negotiation; The Twn. Experience; Mao Zedong Text; The Future of Twn.;* & 4 bk.; *Add.* 9th Fl., 380 Keelung Rd., Sect. 1, Taipei.

KAU, YUH-MIN 高育民
Pres., Nat. Bar Assn. 95-; Pres., Inst. for Tng. Attorney at Law 95-; Pres., Twn. Law Off. 93-; *b.* Twn. Jan. 9, '33; *m.* Kau-Wang, Hai-ching; 2 *s.,* 4 *d.; educ.* LL.B., NTU 57; Standing Dir., Taipei Bar Assn.; Standing Insp., Taipei Bar Assn.; Standing Dir., Nat. Bar Assn. of the ROC; Standing Dir., Prof. Com. of the ROC; *Add.* 5th Fl., 130 Chungking S. Rd., Sect. 1, Taipei.

KIANG, WEBSTER WEI-PING 江偉平
V. Chmn., RDEC 96-; *b.* Kiangsu July 10, '46; *m.* Kiang, Caroline 1 *s.,* 2 *d.; educ.* BS, NTU 68; MBA, N.W. U. 79; MS, Washington U. 72, D.Sc. 74; Staff Res. Engr., Amoco Chem. Corp. 78-81; Res. Assc., Quantum USI Div. 81-93; Mem., Legis. Yuan 93-96; *Add.* 11th Fl., 4 Chung Hsiao W. Rd., Sect. 1, Taipei.

KING, AMBROSE Y.C. 金耀基
Mem., Acad. Sinica 94-; Pro-V. Chancellor, Ch. U. of Hong Kong 89-, Prof., Sociology 83-; *b.* Ch. Feb. 14, '35; *m.* Tao, Yuan-jan; 4 *s.; educ.* BA, NTU 57; MPS, NCU 59; Ph.D., U. of Pittsburg 70; Instr., NCU 65-67; Assc. Ed., *Twn. Cml. Press* 65-70; Ed.-in-Chief, *Ea. Miscellany* 67-70; Lectr., Sociology, New Asia Coll., Ch. U. of Hong Kong 70-74, Head, Dept. of Sociology 72-75, Chmn. & Dir. of Studies in Sociology 76-89, Head, New Asia Coll. 77-85. *Publ.: Hist. Dev. of Ch. Dem. Thought; From Tradition to Modernity: An Analysis of Ch. Soc. & Its Change; Ecology of Public Admin.; Modernization of Ch. & Intellectuals; Idea of the U.; Predicament & Dev. of Dem. in Ch.; Pol. of the 3 Ch. Soc.; Salient Issues of Ch. Soc. & Cul.; Add.* Dept. of Sociology, Ch. U. of Hong Kong, Shatin, N.T., Hong Kong.

KING, CHARLES SHU-CHI 金樹基
Rep., Taipei Wirtschafts-und Kulturbüro, Bonn; *b.* Chekiang Nov. 11, '36; *m.* Yang, Wan-yu; 1 *s.,* 2 *d.; educ.*

BA, Econ., NTU; 2nd Sec., Emb. in Thailand 68-69; 1st Sec., Emb. in Japan 69-72; Sect. Chief, Dept. of N. Am. Aff., MOFA 73-74, Dep. Dir. 74-77, Acting Dir., Dept. of Info. 77-78, Dir. 78-80; Dir.-Gen., CCNAA, Los Angeles 80-83; Amb. to Costa Rica 83-85; Admin. V. Min. of For. Aff. 85-89; Pol. V. Min. of For. Aff. 89-90; Extraordinary & Plenipotentiary Amb. to S. Korea 90-92; *Add.* Villichgasse 17, IV, OG, 53177 Bonn, Germany.

KO, FEI-LE
(See KOH, FEI-LO 柯飛樂)

KO, I-TSAI
(See KO, YIH-TSAIR 葛義才)

KO, MIN-MOU 柯明謀
Mem., Control Yuan 87-; *b.* Twn. Sept. 23, '38; *m.* Hung, Yueh-mei; 1 *s.,* 3 *d.; educ.* BCE, NCKU 62; Mem., TPA 73-85; Adv., TPG 86-87; *Add.* 187 Chang Shou St., Changhua.

KO, MING-MOU
(See KO, MIN-MOU 柯明謀)

KO, SHOU-JEN
(See KUH, ERNEST SHIU-JEN 葛守仁)

KO, TSE-TUNG 柯澤東
Exec. Dir., ROC Dist., Kiwanis Intl. 92-; Prof. of Law, NTU 81-, Chmn., Dept. of Law 93-, Dean, Sch. of Law 94-; Arbitrator, Cml. Arbitration Assn. of the ROC 93-, Mem. 89-; Mem., Gen. Chamber of Com. of the ROC 90-; Bd. Mem., Twn. Fire & Marine Ins. Co. Ltd. 80-; Chair, Inst. for Judges' Tng. 88-; *b.* Twn. Aug. 23, '37; *m.* Ko, Grace M.H.; 1 *s.; educ.* LL.B., NTU 61; MPS, U. of Minnesota 66; LL.D., U. of Paris 75; Charter Pres., Kiwanis Club of Keelung 78-79; Mem., CCPD 90-91; Gov., ROC Dist. Kiwanis Intl. 91-92. *Publ.: Intl. Trade Law; Maritime Law; Environmental Law* (2 Vol.); *Add.* 1-8th Fl., 90 Fu Hsing S. Rd., Sect. 1, Taipei.

KO, WEI-SHIN 葛維新
V. Min., OCAC 96-; *b.* Anhwei Sept. 9, '40; *m.* Wu. Jin-shiang; 1 *s.,* 2 *d.; educ.* LL.B., NCU 64; BBA, We. Illinois U. 72, MA 74; Sr. Sp., Nat. Youth Com. 75-78; Superintendent, Twn. Prov. Cttee., KMT 78-79; Sr. Sp.,

Dep. Dir. & Dir., Ch. Youth Corps 79-90; Dep. Dir.-Gen., Dept. of Ovs. Aff., KMT 90-96. *Publ.: Org. Change of the Ch. Communist Party During Cul. Rev.; Add.* 16th Fl., 5 Hsu Chou Rd., Taipei.

KO, YIH-TSAIR 葛義才
Pres., Supreme Court, Jud. Yuan 96-; Chmn., Public Notorization Assn. of ROC 94-; *b.* Chekiang Jan. 9, '28; *m.* Chen, Miao-yun; 4 *d.; educ.* LL.B., NTU 55; Sp. Exam. on Judge 56; Dir., 1st Dept., Jud. Yuan 80-83; Pres., Taoyuan Dist. Court 83-86, & Taichung Dist. Court 86-87; Dep. Sec.-Gen., Jud. Yuan 87-89; Pres., Tainan Br., Twn. High Court 89-90, & Taichung Br. 90; Pres., Twn. High Court 90-93; Sec.-Gen., Jud. Yuan 93-94; Chmn., Cttee. on the Discipline of Public Functionaries 93-96. *Publ.: Legal Theory on Non-Lawsuit; Add.* 6 Changsha St., Sect. 1, Taipei.

KOH, FEI-LO 柯飛樂
Pres., Export-Import Bk. of the ROC 89-; *b.* Twn. Sept. 4, '31; *m.* Lee, Shie; 1 *s.,* 1 *d.; educ.* LL.B., NTU 54; Sup. & Gen. Mgr., Res. & Investigation Dept., First Cml. Bk. 75-84, Exec. V. Pres. 84-89; *Add.* 8th Fl., 3 Nan Hai Rd., Taipei.

KOH, WEI-HSIN
(See KO, WEI-SHIN 葛維新)

KOO, ANTHONY YING-CHANG 顧應昌
Mem., Acad. Sinica 68-; Prof. of Econ., Michigan State U.; *b.* Shanghai Nov. 22, '18; *m.* Wei, Delia Zung-fung; 3 *d.; educ.* BA, St. John's U. 40; MS, U. of Illinois 41; MA & Ph.D., Harvard U. 46; Asst. Prof., Assc. Prof. & Prof., Michigan State U.; Prof., U. of Michigan; Adjunct Prof., Florida State U. 90. *Publ.: Environmental Repercussions on Trade & Investment; Land Market Distortions & Tenure Reform;* Ed. & Author, *Lib. Econ. Order* (2 Vol.) 93; *Add.* 4554 Sequoia Trail, Okemos, MI 48864, USA; (winter) 1008 Mimosa Drive, Tallahassee, FL 32312, USA.

KOO, CHEN-FU 辜振甫
Sr. Adv. to the Pres. 91-; Chmn., SEF 91-; Mem., CSC, KMT; Chmn., Twn. Cement Corp., & Twn. Polypropylene Co.; Hon. Chmn., Ch. Nat. Assn. of Ind. & Com., Chinatrust Cml. Bk., & Ch. Nat. Fed. of Ind.; Hon. Pres.,

Confed. of Asian Chambers of Com. & Ind.; *b.* Twn. Jan. 6, '17; *m.* Yen, Cho-yun; 2 *s.,* 3 *d.; educ.* LL.B., Taihoku (Taipei) Imperial U.; Hon. Ph.D., U. of Penn.; Hon. Ph.D., Econ., Korea U.; Hon. Ph.D., U. of Victoria, Can.; Chmn., Twn. Stock Exchange 62-64; Founder, Twn. Econ. Res. Inst.; Convener, Econ. Reform Cttee. Exec. Yuan 85; Nat. Policy Adv. to the Pres. 88-91; Intl. Pres., Pacific Basin Econ. Coun. 90-92; Rep. of Pres. Lee Teng-hui to APEC Leaders Econ. Meeting, Osaka 95 & Subic 96. *Publ.: Collected Essays & Speeches of Koo Chen-fu; Add.* 1 Lane 25, Shuang Cheng St., Taipei.

KOO, CHENG-CHEU 顧正秋
Adv., Nat. Fu-hsing Dramatic Arts Acad.; Mem., Prog. Cttee., Nat. Theater & Concert Hall; *b.* Shanghai Sept. 3, '30; *m.* Jen, Hsien-chun (deceased); 1 *s.,* 1 *d.; educ.* Grad., Shanghai Opera Acad. 46; Performed with Tan Fu-ying in Shanghai Queen's Theater 46; Performed with Lee Tsungi in Shanghai Golden Theater 46; Founder & Dir., Koo Troupe 47-53; *Performances: The 4th M. Visits His Mother* 91, & *The Unicorn Bag* 93. *Works: Treasurable Art Pieces in Video: The Treasure Bag; The Story of Wang Chiang; The Romance of Susan; The Legend of the White Snake; Wong Bao-chuen; The Green Sparkling Sword; The Red Mark on the Palm; The Lantern of the Precious Lotus; The Meander of River Fin; The Phoenix Back to the Nest; The 4th M. Visits His Mother; The Unicorn Bag; Add.* 21th Fl., 169 Jen Ai. Rd., Sect. 4, Taipei.

KOO, JEFFREY L.S. 辜濂松
Chmn. & Chief Exec. Off., Chinatrust Cml. Bk. 92-; Chmn., Ch. Nat. Assn. of Ind. & Com., ROC-USA Econ. Coun., Ch. Taipei Pacific Econ. Cooperation Cttee., Twn. Inst. of Econ. Res., & Taipei Intl. Community Cul. Found.; Nat. Policy Adv. to the Pres.; Chmn. & Chief Exec. Off., Ch. Trust. Bk., New York & Calif., Chinatrust (Philippines) Com. Bk.; Hon. Pres., Confed. of Asia-Pacific Chambers of Com. & Ind.; Mem., Bd. of Trustees, Eisenhower Exchange Fel. Inc., USA; Chmn., Asia-Pacific Bd., Visa Intl.; *b.* Twn. Sept. 8, '33; *m.* Koo, Mitzi; 3 *s.,* 1 *d.; educ.* BA, Soochow U.; MBA, New York U.; Hon. Ph.D., Business Mng., De La Salle U., Philippines; Chmn., Ch. Trust Co. 88-92; *Add.* 3 Sung Shou Rd., Taipei.

KU, CHEN-FU
(See KOO, CHEN-FU 辜振甫)

KU, CHENG-CHIU
(See KOO, CHENG-CHEU 顧正秋)

KU, CHUNG-LIEN NELSON 顧崇廉
C-in-C, ROCN 94-; *b.* Shanghai June 6, '31; *m.* Kao, Shiun-yung; 1 *s.,* 1 *d.; educ.* Ch. Naval Acad. 54; Naval Cmd. & Staff Coll., Armed Forces U. 66; US Naval War Coll. 77; Cmdg. Off., Guided Missile Destroyer 75; Mil. Sr. Aide to the State Pres. 78; Cmdr., 1st Destroyer Squadron 84; Chief, Bu. of Planning, GHQ, ROCN 85; Supt., Naval Acad. 86; Cmdr., Fleet Cmd. 88; Dep. C-in-C, ROCN 90; Dep. Chief of the Gen. Staff, MND 92; V. Min. of Nat. Def. 93; *Add.* P.O. Box 90151, Taipei.

KU, FU-CHANG 顧富章
Rep. to Brazil 95-; *b.* Kiangsu July 29, '35; *m.* Heh, Esther Ming-lin; 1 *d.; educ.* LL.B., Fu Hsing Kang Coll.; Studied at Grad. Sch. of Pol. Sc. & Admin., Lovanium U.; Asst., Fu Hsing Kang Coll. 57-59; Asst. Resr., Inst. of Intl. Rel., NCU 61-64; Official, MOFA 64-67; 3rd, 2nd, & 1st Sec., Emb. in Abidjan, Kinshasa, & Ouagadougou 67-72; Sect. Chief, MOFA 72-75; Counsl., Emb. to the Holy See 75-81; Dep. Dir., Dept. of European Aff., MOFA 81-85; Rep. to Switzerland 85-91; Amb. to Guinea-Bissau 91-95. *Publ.: The Analysis of the Org. of the Communist Party of the Soviet Union; The Const. of the Repub. of Zaire; Add.* EECT-SEPN, W3/Norte, Quadra 513, Bloco D, n 30, Edificio Imperador, 1 andar, sala 121 a 1, 70760-545, Brasilia DF, Brazil.

KU, LIEN-SUNG
(See KOO, JEFFREY L.S. 辜濂松)

KU, YING-CHANG
(See KOO, ANTHONY YING-CHANG 顧應昌)

KU, YU-HSIU 顧毓琇
Mem., Acad. Sinica 59-; Prof. Emeritus, EE & System Engr., U. of Penn. 72-; Consultant, Gen. Elec. Co., Univac, & RCA; Personal Mem., GA, Intl. Union of Theoretical & Applied Mech. 46-; *b.* Kiangsu Dec. 24, '02; *educ.* BS, MS, & Sc.D., MIT 25-28; MA, Hon. LL.D., U. of Penn. 72; Prof. & Dir., EE Dept., Nat.

Chekiang U. 29-30; Dean, Coll. of Engr., Nat. Cent. U. 31-32; Prof. & Dir., EE Dept., NTHU, Dean, Coll. of Engr. 32-37; V. Min. of Educ. 38-44; Pres., Nat. Cent. U. 44-45; Educ. Comr., Shanghai 45-47; Pres., NCU 47-49; Visiting Prof., MIT 50-52; Prof., U. of Penn. 52-71; Fel., AIEE 45, IRE 61, Inst. of Elec. & Elect. Engrs., IEE; Mem., US Nat. Cttee. on Theoretical & Applied Mech. *Publ.: Analysis & Control of Nonlinear Systems* 58; *Elec. Energy Conversion* 59; *Transient Circuit Analysis* 61; *Analysis & Control of Linear Systems* 62; *Collected Sc. Papers* 72; *Woodcutter's Song* 63; *Pine Wind* 64; *Ch. Collected Works* (12 Vol.) 61; *Lotus Song* 66; *Lofty Mountains* 68; *The Liang River* 70; *The Hui Spring* 71; *The Si Mountain* 72; *The Great Lake* 73; *300 Recent Poems* 76; *Hist. of Chan (Zen) Masters* 76; *Hist. of Japanese Zen Masters* 77; *Hist. of Zen* 79; *The Long Life* 81; *One Family—Two Worlds* 82; *Poems After Chin Kuan* 83; *Poems After Tao Chien* 84; *303 Poems After Tang Poets* 86; *Flying Clouds & Flowing Water* 87; *Poems After Wu Wen-ying* 89; *Selected Plays* 90; *Eyebrows* 92; *Sc. Papers* 92; *Old Age* 93; *Clear Water & Beautiful Flowers* 94; *Banana Hut Poems* 95; *Add.* 1420 Locust St. (22G), Philadelphia, PA 19102, USA.

KUAN, CHUNG
(See KUAN, JOHN C. 關中)

KUAN, JOHN C. 關中
V. Pres., Exam. Yuan 96-; Chmn., Dem. Found. 90-, & Asia & World Inst. 90-; Assc. Prof., NCU; *b.* Tientsin June 9, '40; *m.* Kuan, Grace C.; 1 *s.,* 1 *d.; educ.* BA, NCU; Ph.D., Fletcher Sch. of Law & Dip., Tufts U.; Hon. LL.D., Indianapolis U. 91; Dir., Asia & World Inst. 77-83; Dep. Dir.-Gen., Dept. of Youth Aff., CC, KMT 77-79, Dep. Sec.-Gen., CPC 79-81, Chmn., Taipei Mun. Cttee. 81-84, Chmn., Twn. Prov. Cttee. 84-87; Chmn., NYC 87; Dir.-Gen., Dept. of Org. Aff., CC, KMT 87-89, Dep. Sec.-Gen. 89-90; Chmn., BCC 90-93; Mem., Legis. Yuan 93-94; Mem., CSC, KMT 93-94; Visiting Prof., Stanford U., U. of Virginia, & Ohio State U.; Min. of Civil Service 94-96. *Publ.: A Review of US-ROC Rel. 49-78; Notes on Communist Ch.'s For. Policy; The KMT-CCP Wartime Negotiation 37-45; The Modernization of the KMT: Observations & Expectation; Democratization of Twn. & the Future of Ch. Unification; On Parliamentary Reform; Essays on Issues of Public Policy; Add.* 2nd Fl., 88 Tun Hua S. Rd., Sect. 1, Taipei.

KUH, ERNEST SHIU-JEN 葛守仁
Mem., Acad. Sinica 74-; Prof., EE, UC-Berkly.; *b.* Peiping Oct. 2, '28; *m.* Chow, Bettine; 2 *s.; educ.* NCTU, Shanghai 45-47; BS, U. of Michigan 49; MS, MIT 50; Ph.D., Stanford U. 52; Tech. Staff, Bell Labs. 52-56; Chmn., Dept. of EECS, UC-Berkly. 68-72, Dean, Coll. of Engr. 73-80; Mem., Nat. Acad. of Engr., USA. *Publ.:* 4 bk.; *Add.* Dept. of EECS, UC-Berkly., CA 94720, USA.

KUNG, CHENG-TING
(See KUNG, SAINTING 龔政定)

KUNG, SAINTING 龔政定
Amb. to Burkina Faso 94-; *b.* Prague Aug. 5, '34; *m.* Lee, Theresa; 2 *s.; educ.* BA, NTU 58; LL.M., NCU 63; 3rd Sec., Emb. in Upper Volta 63-65; 3rd & 2nd Sec., Emb. in Rwanda 66-68; Sect. Chief, Dept. of African Aff., MOFA 68-72; 1st Sec., Emb. in Togo 72; 1st Sec., Emb. in Zaire 72-73; 1st Sec., Emb. in Ivory Coast 73-76; Dir., Service d'Info., Assn. pour la Promotion des Echanges Com. et Touristiques, France 76-80, Rep. 80-90; Dir., Dept. of European Aff., MOFA 90-94; *Add.* 01 B.P. 5563, Ouagadougou 01, Burkina Faso.

KUNG, TE-CHENG
(See KUNG, TEH-CHENG 孔德成)

KUNG, TEH-CHENG 孔德成
Sr. Adv. to the Pres.; 77th lineal descendant of Confucius; Sacrificial Official to Confucius; Prof., NTU & Fu Jen Catholic U.; *b.* Shantung Feb. 23, '20; *m.* Sun, Chi-fang; 4 *c.; educ.* Hon. Res. Fel., Grad. Sch., Yale U.; The Holy Duke (20-35); Mem., Const. NA 46-48; Mem., Nat. Law-Making Cttee. 47-48; Mem., NA 48-91; Pres., Exam. Yuan 84-93. *Publ.: Commentary on I-Li Ching Chuan; Commentary on the Formalities of Tso-Chuan; Supplement to the Lit. on Metal Instruments of the Hsia, Shang, Chou, Ch'in, & Han Dynasties; Sundry Notes & Comments on the Lit. on Metal Instruments; A Correlative Interpretation of the Various Texts of & Notes on The Ritual; An Interpretation of the Bk. of Rites; On the Rites & Customs in the Annals of Spring & Autumn Interpreted by Tso Chiu-ming; A Supplement to the List of the Characters on Bronze Bells & Tripods in Pre-Han & Han Dynasties* (2205 *B.C.*- *A.D.*220); *Notes on the Hieroglyphic Inscriptions on Bronze Bells & Tripods;*

Confucius, His Life, Thought, & Influence: A Collection of Speeches During a European Tour 84; Add. 4th Fl., 119 Chung Yang Rd., Hsintien, Taipei County.

KUO, ALEX T.T. 郭聰田
Chmn. & Pres., Twn. Hopax Chem. Co. 75-; *b.* Twn. May 16, '46; *m.* Kuo, Winifred Y.; 2 *d.; educ.* BSCE, NTU 68; Ph.D., Chem. Engr., U. of Missouri 74; Assc. Prof., Chem. Engr., Nat. Cent. U. 75-77; Dir., Res. Cent., Yuen Foong Yu Mfg. Co. 81-87; *Add.* 94-2 Feng Jen Rd., Fengshan, Kaohsiung County.

KUO, CHE 郭哲
Nat. Policy Adv. to the Pres. 90-; Mem., NA 92-; Pres., Churches Union of the ROC; V. Pres., World Interfaith Friendship Assn., & Ch. Refugees Relief Assn.; *b.* Shensi Dec. 15, '19; *m.* Whai, Li-tan; 1 *s.,* 1 *d.; educ.* Grad., Dept. of Ind. Mng., Soochow U.; Sun Yat-sen Inst. on Policy Res. & Dev.; Nat. Def. Res. Cent.; Mem., Design & Evaluation Cttee., CSC, KMT 68-69, Dep. Dir., 1st Sect., CC 69-72, V. Chmn., Twn. Prov. Cttee. 72-78, Dep. Dir.-Gen., Dept. of Org. Aff., CC 78-79, Chmn., Kaohsiung Mun. Cttee. 79-81, Dep. Sec.-Gen., CPC 81-84, Dir.-Gen., Dept. of Soc. Aff., CC 84-85, Dep. Sec.-Gen., CC 85-87; Chmn., BCC 87-90. *Publ.: Res. on Party Aff.; Soc. Construction & Soc. Problems; Tchrs.' Soc. Responsibility; Nat. Prospects & Goals; Add.* 11 Alley 17, Lane 96, Ho Ping E. Rd., Sect. 3, Taipei.

KUO, CHENG-CHAO
(See KUO, CHENG-CHAU 郭正昭)

KUO, CHENG-CHAU 郭正昭
Pub., *Independent Evening Post & Independent Morning Post* 94-; *b.* Twn. Feb. 24, '37; *m.* Wang, Fu-mei; 2 *s.; educ.* LL.B., NTU 62; Sr. V. Pres., City Bk. of Taipei 82-87, Exec. V. Pres. 87-88; Bd. Mem. & Pres., Cent. Deposit Ins. Corp. 88-90; Bd. Mem. & Pres., Taishin Intl. Bk. 92-93; *Add.* 11th Fl., 48 Chung Yang N. Rd., Sect. 1, Peitou, Taipei.

KUO, HSIAO-LAN 郭曉嵐
Mem., Acad. Sinica 88-; Prof. Emeritus, Meteorology, U. of Chicago 85-; *b.* Hopei Jan. 7, '15; *m.* Yen, Hsia-mei; 2 *s.,* 1 *d.; educ.* BS, NTHU 37; MA, Nat. Chekiang U. 42; Ph.D., U. of Chicago 48; Res. Assc., Acad. Sinica 37-45;

Res. Assc., Sr. Sp., & Dir. of Hurricane Project, MIT 49-54 & 55-61; Prof., U. of Chicago 62-85. *Publ.: Dynamics of the Atmosphere;* over 120 papers on atmospheric dynamics & theorems of weather & climate; *Add.* 5501 S. Kimbark Avenue, Chicago, IL 60637, USA.

KUO, JU-LIN 郭汝霖
Nat. Policy Adv. to the Pres.; *b.* Anhwei Dec. 10, '20; *m.* Kuo Chen, Ming-shien; 1 *s.; educ.* Ch. Mil. Acad. 40; Ch. Air Force Acad. 43; Regular & Res. Course, Air CGSC; Gen. Grade Off. Course, War Coll., Armed Forces U. 79; Tactical Fighter Cmdr. & Wing Cmdr. 61-64 & 69-71; Supt., Air Force Acad. 75-77; C-in-C, ROCAF 81-86; V. Chief of the Gen. Staff (Exec.), MND 86-88; Personal C/S to the Pres.; Pol. Adv. to the Pres.; *Add.* 122 Chungking S. Rd., Sect. 1, Taipei.

KUO, KANG 國剛
Extraordinary & Plenipotentiary Amb. to the Dominican Repub. 90-; *b.* Shantung May 9, '27; *m.* Tsao, Ai-yen; 1 *s.,* 1 *d.; educ.* BA, Sociology, NCHU 60; 3rd & 2nd Sec., Emb. in Argentina 60-66; Sect. Chief & Dep. Dir., Dept. of Treaty & Legal Aff., MOFA 66-71; Counsl., Del. in UN 71-72; Counsl., Emb. in Colombia 72-75; Chargé d'Affaires, Emb. in Bolivia 75-76; Dir., 2nd Dept., Exec. Yuan 76-77; Rep., ROC's Cml. Off. in Ecuador 77-87; Dir., Treaty Dept., MOFA 87-88, Dir., Dept. of Cent. & S. Am. Aff. 88-90; *Add.* Edificio Palic-Primer 1 Piso, Avenue Abraham Lincoln, Esq. José, Amado Soler, Santo Domingo, Republica Dominicana.

KUO, SHIRLEY W.Y. 郭婉容
Min. of State 93-; Mem., CSC, KMT; *b.* Twn. Jan. 25, '30; *m.* Nieh, Wen-ya; 3 *d.; educ.* BA, NTU; MS, MIT; Dr. in Econ., Kobe U.; Lectr. & Assc. Prof., NTU; Prof., NTU 66-89; Fulbright-Hays Exchange Prof., MIT 71-72; V. Chmn., EPC, Exec. Yuan 73-77; V. Chmn., CEPD 77-79; Dep. Gov., CBC 79-88; Min. of Finance 88-90; Chmn., CEPD 90-93. *Publ.: The Twn. Econ. in Transition;* Co-author, *Growth with Equity: The Twn. Case;* Co-author, *The Twn. Success Story: Rapid Growth with Improved Distribution in the ROC '52-'79; Macroecon.; Microecon.; Add.* 11th Fl.-1, 289 Tun Hua S. Rd., Sect. 1, Taipei.

KUO, SZU-FEN
(See KUO, TZU-FEN 郭嗣汾)

KUO, TSONG-TEH 郭宗德
Mem., Acad. Sinica 74-, Res. Fel., Inst. of Botany 68-; Prof., Dept. of Botany, NTU 77-; *b.* Twn. Feb. 27, '33; *m.* Chuang, Tzu-hua; 1 *s.*; 1 *d.*; *educ.* BS, Twn. Prov. Taichung Coll. of Agr. 57; MS, NTU 60; Ph.D., U. of Calif., Davis 65; Res. Fel., Biology Div., Calif. Inst. of Tech. 70-71; Dir., Inst. of Botany, Acad. Sinica 71-77; Visiting Prof., Dept. of Biochem. & Biophys. Sc., Sch. of Hygiene & Public Health, Johns Hopkins U. 77; Dir., Biology Res. Cent., NScC 71-84; Acting Dir., Inst. of Molecular Biology, Acad. Sinica 94-95. *Publ.: Recent Dev. of Genetic Engr. Techniques; Loss of Sigma Factor of RNA Polymerase of Xanthomonas campestris pv. oryzae During Phage XP 10 Infection* 86; *Add.* 128 Yen Chiu Yuan Rd., Sect. 2, Nankang, Taipei.

KUO, TSUNG-CHIN 郭宗清
Pres., ROC Sports Fed. 94-; Strategy Adv. to the Pres.; *b.* Taipei Apr. 7, '27; *m.* Ho, Ya-chen; 1 *s.*, 1 *d.*; *educ.* Grad., Ch. Naval Acad. 50; Studied at Sr. Off. Course, US Mil. Intelligence Sch.; Grad., Staff Coll., ROCN; Studied at Gen. Grade Course of War Coll., Ch. Armed Forces U.; Asst. Naval Attaché, Emb. in Egypt 53; Naval Attaché, Emb. in Japan 69; Cmdg. Off., Oil Tanker, Destroyer Escort, Destroyer; Cmdg. Off., Service Squadron, ROCN; Asst. C/S for Intelligence, MND 77; Dep. Cmdr., ROC Naval Fleet Cmd. 80; Cmdg. Off., 1st Naval Dist., ROCN; Dep. Min. For Navy, MND; V. Min. of Nat. Def. 87; Dir., Combined Op. & Tng. Cmd., MND 89; Amb. to Paraguay 90; *Add.* 20 Chu Lun St., Taipei.

KUO, TSUNG-TIEN
(See KUO, ALEX T.T. 郭聰田)

KUO, TZU-FEN 郭嗣汾
Adv., Lit. Adv. Cttee., CCA 92-; Exec. Dir., Ch. Writers & Artists Assn. 91-; Pub., Kiang Shan Pub. Co. 84-; *b.* Szechwan Oct. 26, '19; *m.* Tang, Kuo-hua; 3 *s.*, 1 *d.*; *educ.* Grad., Cent. Mil. Acad. 39; Sun Yat-sen Inst. on Policy Res. & Dev. 59; Platoon Leader, Co. & Bn. Cmdr. 40-44; Sect. Chief, Rehabilitation & Relief Admin., Exec. Yuan 46-48; Sect. Chief & Mil. Instr., Ch. Naval Acad. 48-50; Ed., ROCN Press 51-58; Sect. Chief, Dept. of Info., TPG 59-67; Chief Sec., Twn. Film Studio 68-77; Pub., Chin Hsiu Pub. Co. 80-84; Pres., Ch. Writers & Artists Assn. 91-92. *Publ.: A Romance in Tapa Ridge; A Tale of a Town in Peril; A Sea Battle at Dawn; Fall in Cumberland; Tragedy at a Cliff; Flower Alley; The Cloud & the Mud; Over the Spring Streams; Songs of Waves; Battles on the Yellow Sands;* & over 50 other bk.; *Add.* 7th Fl., 65 Lane 233, Tun Hua S. Rd., Sect. 1, Taipei.

KUO, TZUNG-CHING
(See KUO, TSUNG-CHIN 郭宗清)

KUO, TZUNG-TE
(See KUO, TSONG-TEH 郭宗德)

KUO, WAN-JUNG
(See KUO, SHIRLEY W.Y. 郭婉容)

KUO, WEI-FAN 郭為藩
Rep., TECO, the Netherlands 96-; *b.* Twn. Sept. 3, '37; *m.* Lin, Mei-ho; 1 *s.*, 1 *d.*; *educ.* BA & Ed.M., NTNU; Ph.D., U. of Paris; Assc. Prof., NTNU 67-70, Prof. 70-72 & 77-78; Admin. V. Min. of Educ. 72-77; Pres., Ch. Sp. Educ. Assn. 73-75 & 79-81; Dir., NTNU 78, Pres. 78-84; Pres., Ch. Educ. Soc. 84-86; Min. of State 84-88; Chmn., CCPD 88-93; Min. of Educ. 93-96. *Publ.: Educ. of Exceptional C. & Youth: Psychology of Self-Concept; Concepts of Educ.; Humanistic Educator in Tech. Age; Reflections on Educ. Reform; Add.* 6th Fl., 25 Lane 2, Ching Tien St., Taipei.

KUO, YANN-SHENG 郭晏生
Spkr., Taichung CCoun. 94-, Mem. 74-; Bd. Chmn., Yunchung Comms. Co.; Hon. Chmn., Taichung Orchids Assn.; Chmn., Taichung Mil. Conscripts Assn.; *b.* Twn. Feb. 20, '44; *m.* Chen, Mei-yu; 3 *s.*, 2 *d.*; *educ.* Grad., Kaiming Sr. Voc. Sch.; 2-year Course at Tokyo U.; Dep. Spkr. 86-94; Chmn., ROC Alliance of Hon. Probation Officers Assns., & Taichung Hon. Probation Officers Assn.; Chmn., Taichung N.W. Dist., Lions Club Intl.; Chief Exec. Off., Taichung Br., Jaycees Intl.; *Add.* 195 Tai Yuan Rd., Sect. 2, Taichung.

KUO, YEN-SHENG
(See KUO, YANN-SHENG 郭晏生)

KUO, YUN 果芸
V. Chmn. & Pres., Inst. for Info. Ind. 91-; *b.* Hopei Oct. 10, '25; *m.* Hu, Shirley; 1 *s.*, 2 *d.*; *educ.* Grad., Air Force

Inst. for Tech. & Def. Ind. Coll., USA; Dir., Air Force Logistic Control Cent. 70-76; Dir., Def. Mng. Cent. 76-81; Dep. Cmdr., Army Logistic 81-83; Pres., Def. Mng. Coll. 83-84; Pres., Inst. for Info. Ind. 82-84; Chief of Mil. Mission in USA 84-91; Strategy Adv. to the Pres. 91-93; Adv. to the Premier 91-93; *Add.* 11th Fl., 106 Ho Ping E. Rd., Sect. 2, Taipei.

KUO, YUNG-CHAO
(See KUO, YUNG-CHAU 國永超)

KUO, YUNG-CHAU 國永超
Dep. Auditor-Gen., Nat. Audit Off., Control Yuan 91-; *b.* Shantung Mar. 19, '31; *m.* Yee, Yi-huey; 1 *d.; educ.* BBA, Feng Chia U. 73; Asst. Auditor, Nat. Audit Off., Control Yuan 63-73, Auditor & concur. Acting Sect. Chief 73-81, Auditor & concur. Br. Chief 81-86, Sr. Auditor 86-87, Sr. Auditor & concur. Dir., 5th Bu. 87-91; *Add.* 1 Hangchow N. Rd., Taipei.

LAI, CHING-CHEN
(See LAI, KINGSON 賴經臣)

LAI, IN-JAW 賴英照
V. Gov. & Comr., Dept. of Finance, TPG 96-; *b.* Twn. Aug. 24, '46; *educ.* S.J.D., Harvard U. 81; Chmn., Grad. Sch. of Laws, NCHU 82-84; Dir.-Gen., Customs Dept., MOF 84-89; Admin. V. Min. of Finance 89; Pol. V. Min. of Finance 89-93; Comr., Dept. of Finance, TPG 93-96. *Publ.: Annotations of the ROC Sec. Exchange Law* (4 Vol.); *Essays on the Corp. Law; Add.* Chunghsing Village, Nantou County.

LAI, KINGSON 賴經臣
Pres., Twn. Group, Asian Patent Attorneys Assn., ROC Chapter 94-, Coun., Japan Chapter 88-; Adv., Twn. Sporting Goods Manufacturers Assn. 83-; Lectr., Tamkang U. 83-; Pres., Union Patent Service Cent. 74-; *b.* Feb. 1, '45; *m.* Linda Lai-su; 1 *s.; educ.* BS, Tunghai U. 66; MS, U. of Utah 70; Lectr., Tunghai U. 71-73; *Add.* 7th Fl., 125 Nanking E. Rd., Taipei.

LAI, MICHAEL M.C. 賴明詔
Mem., Acad. Sinica 92-; Prof. of Microbiology, U. of So. Calif. 83-; Investigator, Howard Hughes Med. Inst. 90-; *b.* Twn. Sept. 8, '42; *m.* Wung, Cathy Hwei-ying; 2 *d.; educ.* MD, NTU 68; Ph.D., UC-Berkly. 73; Asst. Prof.,

U. of So. Calif. 73-78, Assc. Prof. 78-83; Visiting Prof., Inst. of Molecular Biology, Acad. Sinica 88; Pres., Soc. of Ch. Bioscientists in Am. 91-92; Chmn., RNA Virus Div., Am. Soc. for Microbiology 92-93. *Publ.:* 198 articles published in *Sc., Nature, Proceedings of Nat. Acad. of Sc., EMBO Jour., Jour. of Virology, Virology;* etc.; *Add.* 1215 Wabash St., Pasadena, CA 91103, USA.

LAI, MING-CHAO
(See LAI, MICHAEL M.C. 賴明詔)

LAI, SHENG-CHUAN
(See LAI, STAN 賴聲川)

LAI, STAN 賴聲川
Playwright, Dir. & Filmmaker 84-; Artistic Dir., Perform-ance Workshop Theater 84-; Prof., Grad. Sch. of Theater, Nat. Inst. of the Arts 92-; *b.* Washington, D.C. Oct. 25, '54; *m.* Ding, Nai-chu; 2 *d.; educ.* BA, Fu Jen Catholic U. 76; Ph.D., Dramatic Art, UC-Berkly. 83; Assc. Prof., Theater Dept., Nat. Inst. of the Arts 83-92, Chmn. 87-92, Dir., Grad. Sch. of Theater 90-92; The Nat. Award for Lit. & Arts, Nat. Endowment for Cul. & Arts, ROC 88; Award for the 10 Outsdg. Youths, ROC 89; Silver Award, Young Cinema Competition, Tokyo Intl. Film Festival 92; Golden Horse Award 92; Caligari Award, Berlin Intl. Film Festival 93; Best Dir., Best Film, FIPRESCI Award, Singapore Intl. Film Festival 93. *Plays: We All Grew Up This Way* 84; *Plucking Stars* 84; *The Passers-by* 84; *The Other Evening, We Performed Xiangsheng* 85; *Bach Variations* 85; *Secret Love for the Peach Blossom Spring* 86; *Pastorale* 86; *Circle Story* 87; *The Island & the Other Shore* 89; *Look Who's Cross-talking Tonight* 89; *Strange Tales from Twn.* 91; *Opera: Journey to the W.* 87; *Films: The Peach Blossom Land* 92; *The Red Lotus Soc.* 94; *Add.* 3rd Fl., 153 Kang Ning St., Hsichih, Taipei County.

LAI, TZE-LEUNG 黎子良
Mem., Acad. Sinica 94-, Adv. Cttee., Inst. of Statistical Sc. 90-; Prof. of Statistics, Stanford U. 87-; External Assessor, Dept. of Statistics, Ch. U. of Hong Kong 91-; *b.* Hong Kong June 28, '45; *m.* Letitia Chow; 2 *s.; educ.* BA, U. of Hong Kong 67; MA, Columbia U. 70, Ph.D. 71; Asst. Prof., Dept. of Math. Statistics, Columbia U. 71-74, Assc. Prof. 74-77, Prof. 77-87; External Examiner, Dept. of Maths., Nat. U. of Singapore 89-93. *Publ.:*

Over 150 articles & papers; *Statistics: Inference & Decisions; Add.* Dept. of Statistics, Stanford U., Stanford, CA 94305-4065, USA.

LAI, YING-CHAO
(See LAI, IN-JAW 賴英照)

LAI, YUAN-HO 賴源河
Mem., Exam. Yuan 96-; V. Chmn., Fair Trade Com., Exec. Yuan 95-; Adjunct Prof., Laws Dept., NCU 95-; *b.* Twn. Dec. 20, '38; *m.* Kang, Su-i; 3 *d.; educ.* LL.B., NTU 62; LL.M., Penn. State U.; LL.M. & LL.D., Kobe U., Japan 72 & 76; Prof. of Laws, NCU 82-95, Dean, Sch. of Laws, & concur. Dir. & Head, Laws Dept. 93-94; Mem., Cttee. of Laws & Regln. *Publ.: Concise Practical Cml. Laws; On Fair Trade Laws; Intelligence Properties under Trade Protection; Sec. Mng. Regln.; Study on Co. Laws; Add.* 150 Tun Hua N. Rd., Taipei.

LAN, CHIH-MIN 藍智民
Rep., TECO in Mexico 94-; *b.* Fukien Aug. 27, '39; *m.* Hung, Chiu-fang; 1 *s.,* 1 *d.; educ.* BA, Tunghai U. 61, U. of Chile 66; Sp., Sect. Chief & Dep. Dir.-Gen., Dept. of Cent. & S. Am. Aff., MOFA 67-70, 77-80 & 80-82; 3rd & 2nd Sec., Emb. in Uruguay 70-77; Dep. Dir.-Gen., TECO in Spain 82-83; Counsl., Emb. in Paraguay 83-84; Rep., TECO in Chile 85-90; Dir.-Gen., Dept. of Cent. & S. Am. Aff. 90-94; *Add.* Paseo de la Reforma 905, Lomas de Chapultepec, CP11000, D.F., Mexico.

LAO, KAN 勞榦
Mem., Acad. Sinica 58-; Prof. Emeritus, UCLA 74-; *b.* Shensi Jan. 13, '07; *m.* Chou, Yen-pu; 3 *s.,* 1 *d.; educ.* BA, Nat. Peking U.; Res., Acad. Sinica & Harvard U. 32-62 & 53-55; Lectr., Nat. Peking U. 36-37; Prof., Nat. Cent. U. 46-48; Prof., NTU 49-61; Prof., UCLA 62-74. *Publ.: Studies in Wooden Ships of the Han Dynasty from Edzin Gol; Hist. of the Han Dynasty; Hist. of the Six Dynasties; An Anthology of the Articles in Acad. Works; Cheng-lu Shih-kao, A Collection of Poems; A New Explanation of the Han & Chin Wooden Ships; On the Problems of Cul. & Hist. in Ancient Ch.; Add.* 777 Valley Blvd., Alhambra, CA 91801, USA.

LAU, LAWRENCE J. 劉遵義
Mem., Acad. Sinica; Kwoh-ting Li Prof. of Econ. Dev.; Prof. of Econ. & Co-Dir., Asia/Pacific Res. Cent., Stanford U.; Bd. Mem., Chiang Ching-kuo Found. for Intl. Scholarly Exchange; Mem., Gov.'s Coun. Econ. Policy Adv., CA 93-; *b.* Kweichow Dec. 12, '44; *m.* Jablonski, Tamara; 1 *s.; educ.* BS, Stanford U. 64; MA & Ph.D., UC-Berkly. 66-69; Acting Asst. Prof. of Econ., Stanford U. 66-67, Asst. Prof. 67-73, Assc. Prof. 73-76. *Publ.: Farmer Educ. & Farm Efficiency; Models of Dev.—A Comparative Study of Econ. Growth in S. Korea & Twn.;* & over 120 articles & papers; *Add.* Dept. of Econ., Stanford U., Stanford, CA 94305-6072, USA.

LEE, AN
(See LEE, ANG 李安)

LEE, ANG 李安
Film Dir. 91-; *b.* Twn. Oct. 23, '54; *m.* Lin, Jane Huey-chai; 2 *s.; educ.* Diploma, Nat. Twn. Acad. of Arts 76; BFA, U. of Illinois 80; M. of Fine Arts, New York U. 84. *Films: Pushing Hands; Wedding Banquet; Eat Drink Man Woman; Sense & Sensibility; The Ice Storm; Add.* 2nd Fl., 526 W. 25th Street, New York, NY 10001, USA.

LEE, CHEN-YUAN 李鎮源
Mem., Acad. Sinica 70-; Prof. Emeritus, Pharmacological Inst., NTU 86-; Counsl., Acad. Sinica 69-96; Hon. Mem., Am. Soc. Pharmacology & Experimental Therapeutics 77-; Hon. Mem., Japanese Pharmacol Soc. 87-; Pres., Ch. Toxicol Soc. 87-; *b.* Twn. '15; *m.* Lee, Shu-yue; 1 *s.,* 4 *d.; educ.* MD, Faculty of Med., Taihoku Imperial U.; Dr. Med. Sc., Taihoku Imperial U.; Res. Fel., U. of Penn. 52-53, & U. of Oxford 58-59; Asst. Prof., Faculty of Med., Taihoku Imperial U. 44-45; Assc. Prof., Coll. of Med., NTU 45-49, Prof. 49-86, Dean 72-78; Pres., Ch. Pharmacol Soc. 81-88; Pres., Intl. Soc. Toxinology 85-88; Pres., Ch. Toxicol Soc. 87-93. *Publ.: Snake Venom* (ed.) 79; *Discovered Bungarotoxins* 63; & over 150 original papers; *Add.* 2 Lane 32, Shao Hsing S. St., Taipei.

LEE, CHENG-TAO
(See LEE, TSUNG-DAO 李政道)

LEE, CHIA-TUNG 李家同
Pres., Providence U. 94-; *b.* Shanghai Jan. 5, '39; *m.* Hwlang, R.B.; 1 *d.; educ.* BSEE, NTU 61; MSEE, UC-Berkly. 63, DSEE & Dr. of Computer Sc. 67; Chmn.,

Grad. Inst. of Applied Math., NTHU 75-77, Chmn., Grad. Inst. of Computer & Decision Sc. 77-81, Chmn., Dept. of EE 81-82, Dean of Engr. 82-87; Dean of Acad. Aff., NTHU 87-93; IEEE Fel. *Publ.: Symbolic Logic & Mech. Theorem Proving; Add.* Providence U., Shalu Chen, Taichung County.

LEE CHIAO 李喬
Writer 82-; Ed.-in-Chief, *Twn. Lit.* 94-; *b.* Twn. June 15, '34; *m.* Lee Hsiao, Yin-chiao; 1 *s.,* 3 *d.; educ.* Hsinchu Normal Sch. 54; Tchr., Elementary & High Schs., Agr. & Voc. Schs. 54-82; Ed.-in-Chief, *Twn. Lit.* 83-84. *Publ.: Informer; Cold Night Trilogy; Love Without Regret; The Dark Side of Twn.* (ed.); *Dilemma & Transition of Twn. Movements* (ed.); etc.; *Add.* 261-10, Yu Chuan, 10 Lin, Yu Chuan Village, Kung Kuan, Miaoli.

LEE, CHIEN-HSING
(See LEE, CHIEN-SING 李建興)

LEE, CHIEN-SING 李建興
Admin. V. Min. of Educ. 92-; *b.* Twn. Apr. 22, '41; *m.* Wang, Shou-tzu; 1 *s.,* 1 *d.; educ.* Ed.M. & Ed.D., NTNU; Ed.M., U. of Wisconsin; Prof. & concur. Dir., Dept. of Soc. Educ., NTNU 78-86; Dir., Dept. of Secondary Educ., MOE 86-89, Sec.-Gen. 90-91. *Publ.: A New Approach to Secondary Educ.; Soc. Educ. & Nat. Dev.; A Hist. of Ch. Soc. Educ. Dev.; Educ. & Life; A Study on Secondary Educ.; Soc. Change & the Dev. of Educ.; Concepts on Educ. Admin.; Add.* 5 Chung Shan S. Rd., Taipei.

LEE, CHIN-LUNG
(See LEE, JIN-LONG 李金龍)

LEE, CHING-PING 李慶平
Dep. Sec.-Gen., SEF 92-; *b.* Canton July 14, '46; *m.* Wu, Delhi; 1 *s.,* 1 *d.; educ.* LL.B., Dip. Dept., NCU 69, LL.M. 73; Fel., Prog. for Sr. Mgrs. in the Govt., John F. Kennedy Sch. of Govt., Harvard U.; Dir., Cul. Div., TECRO, USA 86-92; *Add.* 17th Fl., 156 Min Sheng E. Rd., Sect. 3, Taipei.

LEE, CHUNG-HSIEN 李忠憲
Spkr., Taitung CoCoun. 90-, Mem. 73-; *b.* Twn. July 20, '43; *m.* Lin, Mei-chun; 1 *s.,* 1 *d.; educ.* Studied at Twn. Prov. Yulee High Sch.; Grad., Environmental Study Prog., U. of Illinois; Dep. Spkr., Taitung CoCoun. 86-90; *Add.* 416 Keng Sheng Rd., Taitung.

LEE, CHUNG-TAO
(See LEE, ROBERT CHUNG-TAO 李崇道)

LEE, DAVID TAWEI 李大維
Dep. Dir.-Gen., GIO 96-; Assc. in Res., Fairbank Cent., Harvard U. 93-; *b.* Twn. Oct. 15, '49; *m.* Chih, Lin; 1 *s.,* 1 *d.; educ.* BPS, NTU 73; MA & Ph.D., For. Aff., U. of Virginia 82; Mng. Ed., *Asia & the World Forum* 76-77; Staff Consultant, TECRO, USA 82-88; Prin. Asst. to the Min. of For. Aff. 88-89; Adjunct Assc. Prof., Intl. Pol., Grad. Sch., NTNU 88-93; Dep. Dir., Dept. of Intl. Info. Service, GIO 89-90; Dep. Dir., Dept. of N. Am. Aff., MOFA 90-93; Dir.-Gen, TECO, Boston 93-96; Dir., Dept. of N. Am. Aff., MOFA 96. *Publ.: Legis. Process of the Twn. Rel. Act* 89; *Cong. Vs. Pres.: A Case Study of the Twn. Rel. Act;* & many articles on Sino-Am. Rel. & Am. Nat. Inst.; *Add.* 2 Tientsin St., Taipei

LEE, EDWARD Y.T. 李義燦
Counsl. & Dir., 4th Dept., Exec. Yuan 90-; *b.* Hopei Jan. 5, '35; *m.* Chi, Hui-ju; 3 *s.; educ.* B., Econ., NTU 59; Sr. Acct., Twn. Sugar Corp. 61-67; Auditor, Sr. Sp., Controller, Dep. Dir. & Dir., CEPD 68-90; *Add.* 2nd Fl., 32 Alley 16, Lane 199, Tun Hua N. Rd., Taipei.

LEE, HARRY H.K. 李厚高
Chmn., MTAC & concur. Min. of State 94-; *b.* Hupei Oct. 21, '26; *m.* Lee Yu, Shian-chung; 3 *s.,* 1 *d.; educ.* LL.B., NCHU; Resr., Grad. Sch., Am. U.; Dir., Dept. of Taxation, TPG 74-75, Dir.-Gen., Tax. Admin. 75-76, Dep. Comr., Dept. of Finance 76-81, Comr. 81-93, Sec.-Gen. 87-93; Sec.-Gen., Exec. Yuan 93-94. *Publ.: Finance; Intl. Trade & For. Exchange; The Tax System of the US; Add.* 4th Fl., 5 Hsuchow Rd., Taipei.

LEE, HOU-KAO
(See LEE, HARRY H.K. 李厚高)

LEE, HUAN 李煥
Sr. Adv. to the Pres. 90-; Mem., CSC, KMT 88-; *b.* Hankow Sept. 24, '17; *m.* Pan, Hsiang-ning; 2 *s.,* 2 *d.; educ.* LL.B., NCU 44; Ed.M., Columbia U. 56; Hon. Ph.D., Dankuk U., S. Korea 78; Hon. LL.D., Sung Kyun

Kwan U., S. Korea 81; Dir., *Shenyang Daily News* 46-48; Sec.-Gen., Dep. Dir., & Dir., Ch. Youth Corps 52-77; Prof., NCU 62-79; Chmn., NYC 67-72; Chmn., Twn. Prov. Cttee., KMT 68-72, Dir.-Gen., Dept. of Org. Aff., CC 72-78, Dir., Sun Yat-sen Inst. on Policy Res. & Dev. 76-78; Prof., NTNU 78-79; Pres., Nat. Sun Yat-sen U. 79-84; Min. of Educ. 84-87; Sec.-Gen., CC, KMT 87-89; Premier 89-90. *Publ.: Guidance of Youth; Dr. Sun Yat-sen & Youth: Essays on Educ.; Pres. Chiang Kai-shek & Youth; Add.* 23 Lane 44, Ssu Wei Rd., Taipei.

LEE, HUANG-KUEI 李皇葵
Pres. & concur. Gen. Mgr., Summit Computer Tech. Co. 88-; Founder & Convener, Multimedia CD-ROM Title Alliance, ROC 94-; Bd. Mem., Computer Assn., Taipei County 94-; Bd. Mem., Software & Hardware Assn., ROC 94-; *b.* Twn. Aug. 29, '58; *m.* Wang, Shu-chin; 1 *s.; educ.* BBA, NTU 80; Mgr., Info. Cent. & Sales Dept., Hitach Elect. Co. 85-88. *Publ.: Acct. Principles; Basic Acct.; Twn. CD-ROM Dev.; The Op. of Software Resources in Ch. Mainland; Add.* 6th Fl.-1, 492-19 Wan Shou Rd., Sect. 1, Kweishan, Taoyuan County.

LEE, I-TSAN
(See LEE, EDWARD Y.T. 李義燦)

LEE, JIN-LONG 李金龍
Dep. Auditor-Gen., Nat. Audit Off., Control Yuan 94-; *b.* Twn. July 16, '42; *m.* Tsai, Ho; 1 *s.,* 2 *d.; educ.* B., Com., Tamkang U.; Sect. Chief, Nat. Audit Off. 74-78, Dir., Hualien County Audit Off. 78-80, Pingtung County Audit Off. 83-85, Taipei County Audit Off. 86-86, Taipei Mun. Audit Dept. 87-88, Comr., 2nd Bu. & 5th Bu. 90-91 & 91-94; *Add.* 1 Hangchow N. Rd., Taipei.

LEE, JO-I 李若一
Admin. V. Min. of Pers., Exam. Yuan 94-; *b.* Twn. Oct. 25, '42; *m.* Wu, Mei-chin; 1 *s.,* 2 *d.; educ.* Prov. Tainan Normal Sch. 61; LL.B., Ch. Cul. U. 68, MPS 71; Sect. Chief, CPA 74-76, Dir., Pers. Dept. 76-78, Sr. Sp. 78-81, Dep. Dir. 81-83; Dep. Dir., Pers. Dept., TPG 83-84; Exec. Sec., CPA 84, Dir. 84-89; Dir., Pers. Dept., TCG 89-94; *Add.* Min. of Pers., 1 Shih Yuan Rd., Wenshan, Taipei.

LEE, JUI-PIAO
(See LEE, SHUI-PIAO 李瑞標)

LEE, KAO-CHAO 李高朝
V. Chmn., CEPD 95-; *b.* Twn. May 17, '38 ; *m.* Liang, Chiu-mei; 2 *s.,* 1 *d.; educ.* MS, Agr. Econ., NTU 64; M. of Econ., Vanderbilt U., USA 73; Sp., Econ. Planning Coun., Exec. Yuan 69-74, Sr. Sp. 74-83; Dep. Dir., Econ. Res. Dept., CEPD 83-84, Dir. 84-95. *Publ.: On the Leakage of Repercussion Effects* 70; *Short- & Mid-Term Resources Utilization Model of Twn.* 80; *The Impact of Changes in Energy Supply & Prices on Twn. Econ.* 81; *Add.* 12th Fl., 87 Nanking E. Rd., Sect. 2, Taipei.

LEE, KUANG-HSIUNG
(See LEE, KWANG-SHIANG 李光雄)

LEE, KWANG-SHIANG 李光雄
Comr., Exam. Yuan 96-; *b.* Twn. Aug. 1, '45; *m.* Lu, Ai-jane; 1 *s.; educ.* BA, Pol., NTU 67, MPs 71 ; M.Lit. in Soc. Psychology, U. of Glasgow, UK 74; Dir., Pers. Off., Exam. Yuan 74-80, Sr. Compiler 80-82; Sr. Sec. to the V. Premier 82-84; Dep. Dir., Pers. Dept., TPG 84-87; Dir. 87-93; Dep. Dir.-Gen., CPA 93-94; Pol. V. Min. of Educ. 94-96. *Publ.: The Legis. Process of US Cong.: A Case Study of the Civil Rights Act* 64; *A Comparative Study of the Attitudes of Scottish & Twn. Students; The Exam. & Pers. Systems of the ROC Since 1912; Add.* 1 Shih Yuan Rd., Wenshan, Taipei.

LEE, KUO-HSIUNG 李國雄
Mem., Acad. Sinica 96-; Kenan Prof., Medicinal Chem., U. of N. Carolina at Chapel Hill 92-; *b.* Twn. Jan. 4, '40; *m.* Chen, Lan-Huei; 1 *s,* 1 *d.; educ.* Ph.D., U. of Minnesota 68; Postdoctoral, UCLA 68-70; Asst. Prof., U. of N. Carolina 70-74, Assc. Prof. 74-77, Prof. 77-91, Dir. 83-; Adjunct Prof., Kaohsiung Med. Coll. 77-; Elected Fel., Acad. of Pharmaceutical Sc. 78; Fel., Am. Assn. of Pharmaceutical Sc. 86; Fel., Am. Assn. for Advancement of Sc. 94; *Add.* Sch. of Pharmacy, CB# 7360, Beard Hall, U. of N. Carolina, Chapel Hill, NC 27599-7360, USA.

LEE, LIN-SHAN 李琳山
Dir., Inst. of Info. Sc., Acad. Sinica 91-; Prof., Dept. of EE & Dept. of Computer Sc. & Info. Engr., NTU 82-; *b.* Twn. Sept. 23, '52; *m.* Mei, Chia-ling; 1 *c.; educ.* BSEE, NTU 74; MS & Ph.D., Stanford U. 75 & 77; Tech. Consultant , Edutel Comms. & Dev. Inc., USA 77-79; Assc. Prof., Dept. of EE, NYU 79-82, Dir., Dept. of

Computer Sc. & Info. Engr. 82-87. *Publ.:* About 170 tech. papers (45 on intl. jour. & 75 in intl. conf.); *Add.* 3rd Fl., 7 Lane 58, Wen Chou St., Taipei.

LEE, MING-LIANG 李明亮
Dean, Tzu Chi Coll. of Med. 94-; *b.* Twn. June 26, '36; *m.* Liau, Ya-hwei; 3 *d.; educ.* MD, NTU 62; Ph.D., Molecular Biology & Biochem., U. of Miami 69; Helen Hay Whitney Fel., U. of Cambridge 71; Pediatric Residency, Med. Cent., Duke's U. 65-69; Visiting Prof., NTU 71-73; Asst. Prof., Sch. of Med., U. of Miami 73-76; Chief Fel., Johns Hopkins Hosp. 76-80; Dir. of Med. Genetics & Prof. in Pediatrics, U. of Med. & Dentistry of New Jersey 76-92; *Add.* 16 Hsin Sheng S. Rd., Hualien.

LEE, NENG-CHI 李能棋
(See LEE CHIAO 李喬)

LEE, PEN-JEN 李本仁
Admin. V. Min. of the Int. 92-; *b.* Hunan Feb. 10, '37; *m.* Lin, Hui-mei; 1 *s.,* 1 *d.; educ.* B., Soochow U. 60; Dep. Sec.-Gen., TCG 88-91; Sec.-Gen., MOI 91-92; *Add.* 9th Fl., 5 Hsuchow Rd., Taipei.

LEE, ROBERT CHUNG-TAO 李崇道
Nat. Policy Adv. to the Pres. 90-; Consultant, COA 81-; *b.* Shanghai Oct. 2, '23; *m.* Chi, Winnie Tung; 2 *d.; educ.* Grad., Nat. Kwangsi U.; Ph.D., Cornell U.; LL.D., Jeonbug U.; Chief Vaccine Rm., Twn. Prov. Veterinary Serum Inst. 47-50; Sr. Sp., JCRR 50-60; Chief, Animal Ind. Div. 62-70, Sec.-Gen. 70-73 & 77-81; Chmn., CAPD 79-81; Pres., NCHU 81-84; Comr., Exam. Yuan 84-90; V. Pres., Acad. Sinica 91-93. *Publ.: Reports on Hog Cholera Prog. & Vaccine; Micromorphology of Hog Cholera Virus Inflected Cells Grown in Vitro; An Atlas of Gen. Pathology, Veterinary Pathology;* etc.; *Add.* 37 Nan Hai Rd., Taipei.

LEE, SHEN-I 李伸一
Mem., Control Yuan 93-; *b.* Twn. Aug. 14, '42; *educ.* LL.B., NTU; LL.D., Ch. Cul. U.; Passed the Sr. Civil Service Exam. for Lawyers; Passed the Sr. Civil Service Exam. for Pers. Admin.; Lawyer 73; Bd. Chmn., ROC Consumers' Found.; Pres., Shihlin Br., Rotary Club; Mem., Fair Trade Com. *Publ.: Laws on Consumers' Life; Consumers' Protection Org. & Legis. in the Philosophy of Soc. Well-being; Commentary upon Consumer Protection Law; Add.* 2 Chung Hsiao E. Rd., Sect. 1, Taipei.

LEE, SHU-JOU 李樹久
Cmn., Ch. Petroleum Corp. 96-; *b.* Kiangsu Nov. 8, '36; *m.* Lu, Chien-hsia; 1 *s.,* 1 *d.; educ.* BS, Chem., NTU 61; MS, Chem., U. of Tennessee 65, Dr. of Chem. 69; Assc. Prof. & Prof., Chem. Dept., NTU 70-81, Dir. 71-74; Dep. Dir., Preparatory Off., Tung-lien Co. 74-76; Sr. Adv., Tateh Petrochemical Co. 77-79; Adv., CEPD 79-80, Dir., Sectoral Planning Dept. 80-90; Admin. V. Min. of Econ. Aff. 90-96; *Add.* 15 Foochow St., Taipei.

LEE, SHUI-PIAO 李瑞標
Pub. & Pres., *The Commons Daily* 50; Gen. Mgr., Hsin-lung Gas Co. 72; ROC Newspaper Business Assn. 92-; Pres., Nanchen Gas Co. 93-; *b.* Twn. June 10, '17; *m.* Lee Chang, Kuei-hsiang; 2 *s.,* 3 *d.; educ.* Ph.D., Kinki U.; Ph.D., Woodbury U., USA; Gen. Mgr., *Taipei Public Daily* 49; Gen. Counsl., Corr. Union of Keelung 51-69; Mem., Keelung CCoun. 65; Gen. Counsl., Twn. Newspaper Business Assn. 71-72, Chmn. 72-75; Bd. Mem., Gas Assn., ROC 94; Chmn., Kaohsiung Newspaper Business Assn. 81-95; Chmn., Worldwide Lee Clansmen; *Add.* 180 Min Chuan 2nd Rd., Kaohsiung.

LEE, SI-CHEN 李嗣涔
Prof., NTU 86-; *b.* Twn. Aug. 13, '52; *m.* Cheng, May-ling; 1 *s.,* 1 *d.; educ.* BE, NTU 74; MS, Stanford U. 77, Ph. D., 81; Resr., Energy Conversion Devices Inc. 80-82; Assc. Prof., NTU 82-86, Chmn., 89-92; Counsl., MOTC 93-94. *Publ.: Phys. of Semiconductor Devices;* over 200 jour. and conf. papers; *Add.* 5th Fl., 5 Alley 1, Lane 40, Chou Shan Rd., Taipei.

LEE, TA-WEI
(See LEE, DAVID TAWEI 李大維)

LEE, TE-WU 李德武
Dir., 7th Dept., Exec. Yuan 93-; *b.* Honan Oct. 11, '36; *m.* Tong, Gwo-guey; 2 *s.,* 2 *d.; educ.* LL.B., Soochow U. 60; Sect. Chief & Sr. Sp., NYC 66-81; Dir., MOTC 81-87, Counsl. 87-93; *Add.* 1 Chung Hsiao E. Rd., Sect. 1, Taipei.

LEE, TENG-HUI 李登輝
Pres., ROC 88-; Chmn., KMT 88-; *b.* Twn. Jan. 15, '23; *m.* Tseng, Wen-fui; 2 *d.; educ.* Kyoto Imperial U. 45; BS,

NTU 48; MA, Iowa State U. 53; Ph.D., Cornell U. 68; Asst. Prof., NTU 48-55, Assc. Prof. 56-58; Res. Fel., Twn. Cooperative Bk. 55-57; Sp., JCRR 57-61, Sr. Sp. & Consultant 61-70; Chief, Rural Econ. Div., JCRR 70-72; Prof., NCU 58-78; Min. of State 72-78; Mayor, Taipei City 78-81; Gov., TPG 81-84; V. Pres., ROC 84-88. *Publ.: Agr. Dev. & Its Contributions to Econ. Growth in Twn.; An Analytical Review of Agr. Dev. in Twn.; Intersectoral Capital Flows in the Econ. Dev. of Twn.; Initial Conditions of Agr. & Dev. Policy; Process & Pattern of Growth in Agr. Production of Twn.; Agr. Diversification & Dev.; On the Problems of Agr. Price Policy & Price Level; Add.* c/o Off. of the Pres., Taipei.

LEE, TIEN-LU 李天祿
Dir., I Wan Ran Traditional Chang Chung Hsi Puppet Troupe 45-; *b.* Twn. Dec. 2, '10; *m.* Chen, Cha; 2 *s.*, 2 *d.; educ.* Private tuition; Prin. Puppeteer 45-78; Instr., Syau Wan Ran Troupe, Chung Wan Ran Puppetry Troupe, Wei Wan Ran C.'s Traditional Puppetry Troupe, & Chau Wan Ran Troupe; Performance Distinction Award, USA 75; Artistic Distinction Award, USA 84; Nat. Heritage Award, CCA 85; Prize of the Important Artists of the Nation, CCA 89; Prize of Artistic Accomplishment of the Whole Life, USA 91; Cul. Award CCA; *Performances in:* France 77, 80, 81, 83, 88 & 90; 5th Annual Hong Kong Arts Festival, Hong Kong Cul. Cent. 77; Seoul, S. Korea 84; Eda & Yokohama 85; Arkansas, New York & Chicago 85; Italy 88; World Puppetry Festival 88; Netherlands & Morocco 90; *Add.* 5th Fl.-2, 18 Alley 16, Lane 167, Tung Ho E. St., Sect. 1, Taipei.

LEE, TSUNG-DAO 李政道
Mem., Acad. Sinica 57-; Enrico Fermi Prof. of Phys., Columbia U. 64-, U. Prof. 84-; *b.* Shanghai Nov. 25, '26; *m.* Chin, Jeannette; 1 *s.*, 1 *d.; educ.* Nat. Chekiang U. 43-44; Nat. S.We. Assc. U. 45-46; Ph.D., U. of Chicago 50; D.Sc., Princeton U. 58; LL.D., Ch. U. of Hong Kong 69; D.Sc., City Coll., CUNY 78; Dip. di Perfezionamento in Phys., Scuola Normale Superiore, Pisa, Italy 82; D.Sc., Bard Coll. & Peking U. 84 & 85; Res. Assc., Astronomy, U. of Chicago 50; Res. Assc. & Lectr. of Phys., U. of Calif. 50-51; Mem., Inst. of Advanced Study, Princeton U. 51-53; Asst. Prof., Phys., Columbia U. 53-55, Assc. Prof. 55-56, Prof. 56-60, Adjunct Prof. 60-62; Loeb

Lectr., Harvard U. 57 & 64; Guggenheim Fel. 66; Mem., Am. Acad. of Arts & Sc., Am. Philosophical Soc., Acad. Nazionaledej Lincei, Rome; *Add.* Dept. of Phys., Columbia U., New York, NY 10027, USA.

LEE, TZUNG-RU 李宗儒
Amb. to Gambia 95-; *b.* Hunan Dec. 21, '45; *m.* Chen, Chia-chun; 1 *s.*, 3 *d.; educ.* LL.B., Dip., NCU 66; LL.M., Pol. Sc., NTU 69; Staff Mem., Dept. of Intl. Org., MOFA 69-72; 3rd Sec., Emb. in Gambia 72-75; Consul., Consl. Gen. in Johannesburg, S. Africa 75-77; Chief, Dept. of European Aff., MOFA 77-81; Dir., Public Aff. Div., Free Ch. Cent. in London, UK 81-88; Dep. Dir., Dept. of Intl. Org., MOFA 88-91; Rep., Taipei Econ. & Cul. Off. in Australia 91-94; Dir., Dept. of European Aff., MOFA 94-95. *Publ.: US Open Door Policy & Ch.; Add.* P.O. Box 916, Banjul, Gambia, W. Africa.

LEE, WEN-HUA
(See LEE, WEN-HWA 李文華)

LEE, WEN-HWA 李文華
Mem., Acad. Sinica 94-; Dir., Cent. for Molecular Med., Inst. of Biotech., U. of Texas Health Sc. Cent., San Antonio, Chair, Grad. Prog. of Molecular Med., Prof., Dept. of Cellular & Structural Biology & Dept. of Pathology 91-; *b.* Twn. June 1, '50; *m.* Lee, Eva; 1 *s.*, 1 *d.; educ.* BS, Biology, NTNU 72; MS, Biochem., NTU 77; Ph.D., Molecular Biology, UC-Berkly. 81. *Publ.:* Co-author of "Human Retinoblastoma Susceptibility Gene: Cloning, Identification & Sequence," *Sc.* (235; 1987), "The Retinoblastoma Gene Product Regulates Progression Through the G1 Phase of the Cell Cycle," *Cell* (67; 1991); "Mice Deficient for RB Are Nonviable & Show Defects in Neurogenesis & Hematopoiesis," *Nature* (359; 1992); *Add.* 15355 Lambda Drive, San Antonio, Texas 78245-3207, USA.

LEE, YING-MING 李英明
Chmn., Ch. Shipbuilding Corp. 94-; *b.* Peking Dec. 25, '34; *m.* Feng, Shu-chuan; 1 *s.*, 1 *d.; educ.* Ch. Naval Acad. 59; Naval Inst. Sch. 62; War Coll., CGSC 84; Mng. Dir., 2nd & 4th Naval Shipyards, ROCN 85-88, Logistics Off. 88-90, Dep. C/S, Navy GHQ 90-94, Cmdr., Navy Logistics Cmd. 93-94; *Add.* 3 Chung Kang Rd., Hsiaokang, Kaohsiung.

LEE, YUAN-CHUAN 李遠川
Mem., Acad. Sinica 94-; Prof., Johns Hopkins U. 65-; *b.* Twn. Mar. 30, '32; *m.* Reiko Takasaka; 1 *s.; educ.* Ph.D., Biochem., U. of Iowa. *Publ.:* Over 200 articles in prof. jour.; *Add.* Johns Hopkins U., 3400 N. Charles St., Baltimore, MD 21218, USA.

LEE, YUAN-CHE
(See LEE, YUAN-TSEH 李遠哲)

LEE, YUAN-TSEH 李遠哲
Pres., Acad. Sinica 94-, Mem. 80-; Nat. Policy Adv. to the Pres. 91-; *b.* Twn. Nov. 29, '36; *m.* Wu, Bernice; 2 *s.,* 1 *d.; educ.* BS, NTU; MS, NTHU; Ph.D., UC-Berkly., Postdoctoral Fel. 65-67; Res. Fel., Harvard U. 67-78; Asst. Prof., U. of Chicago 68-71, Assc. Prof. 71-72, Prof. 73-74; Mem., Nat. Acad. of Sc., USA; Prof. of Chem., UC-Berkly. 74-92, U. Prof. of Chem. 92-94; Nobel Prize in Chem. 86; Nat. Medal of Sc., White House, USA 86; Peter Debye Award, ACS 86; Faraday Medal 92. *Publ.:* 280 papers; *Add.* Acad. Sinica, Nankang, Taipei.

LEE, YUNG-SAN 李庸三
Chmn., Farmers Bk. of Ch.; Prof., NTU 73-; Consultant, CEPD 94-; *b.* Twn. Dec. 7, '38; *m.* Tzeng, S.C.; 3 *d.; educ.* BA, NTU 61; MA, U. of Wisconsin 68, Ph.D. 70; Asst., Inst. of Econ., Acad. Sinica 62-66, Asst. Res. Fel. 66-70, Assc. Res. Fel. 70-73, Res. Fel. 73-90, Dep. Dir. 85-87, Dir. 88-90; Assc. Prof., NTU 70-73; Visiting Scholar, Harvard U. 76-77; Dir., Econ. Res. Dept., CBC 77-85; Sup., City Bk. of Taipei 78-90; Consultant, CEPD 88-91; Pres., Chiao Tung Bk. 90-94. *Publ.: Expectation in the Consumption Function: Permanent Income Hypothesis Revisited* 70; *Econometric Methods* 73; *Analysis of Changes in Prices in Twn.* 74; *Comparative Analysis of Interest Receipts & Payments by Major Econ. Sectors in Twn. 1965-85* 87; *Add.* 85 Nanking E. Rd., Sect. 2, Taipei

LEU, HSI-MU
(See LEU, HSI-MUH 呂溪木)

LEU, HSI-MUH 呂溪木
Pres., NTNU 93-, Prof. 77; Bd. Mem., Ch. Math. Soc. 62-; *b.* Twn. Nov. 6, '40; *m.* Leu Tseng, Yue-mei; 3 *d.; educ.* BS in Math., NTNU 63; Ph.D. in Math., Washington State U. 72; Bd. Chmn., Ch. Sc. Educ. Soc. 80-91; Rep., Intl. Cong. of Math. Educ. 75-93; Teaching Asst.

& Tchr. 63-68; Asst. Prof., Washington State U. 72-73; Visiting Assc. Prof., NTNU 73-75, Assc. Prof. & concur. Chmn. 75-78; Dir., Sc. Div., NScC 85-87; Dir., Sc. Div., TECO, Los Angeles 87-90; Dean of Acad. Aff., NTNU 90-93. *Publ.: Morita Contexts & Rings of Quotients* 72; "On Semi-Simple Rings of Quotients" & "Rings of Quotients of R & eRe.," *Ch. Jour. of Math.* 74 & 76; "Idempotent Kernel Factors & Quotient Rings," *Bulletin of Inst. of Math., Acad. Sinica* 77; etc.; *Add.* NTNU, 162 Ho Ping E. Rd., Sect. 1, Taipei.

LI, CHIA-WEI 李家維
Prof., NTHU 90-; *b.* Hopei Sept. 17, '53; *m.* Hwu, Tieh-lan; 2 *s.; educ.* Ph. D., UC, San Diego 79-83; Resr., Marine Biology 83-85; Assc. Prof., NTHU 85-87, Dir. 87-90, Gen.-Sec. 90-92; Dep. Dir., Nat. Museum of Natural Sc. 92-95, Dir. 95-96. *Publ.: Magnetoreception in Honeybees Sc.* 94; *Add.* 101 Kuang Fu Rd., Sect. 2., Hsinchu.

LI, CHEN-YING
(See LY, GABRIEL CHEN-YING 李振英)

LI, CHIEN-CHUNG
(See LI, JOHN C. 李建中)

LI, CHING-CHUN 李景均
Mem., Acad. Sinica; Prof. of Biometry & Human Genetics, U. of Pittsburgh; *b.* Tientsin Oct. 27, '12; *m.* Lem, Clara; 1 *s.,* 1 *d.; educ.* BS, U. of Nanking; Ph.D., Cornell U.; Prof. of Agronomy, U. of Nanking 43-46; Chmn., Dept. of Agronomy, Nat. Peking U. 46-50; Pres., Am. Soc. of Human Genetics 60. *Publ.: Population Genetics; No. from Experiments; Human Genetics; Introduction to Experimental Statistics; Path Analysis; Analysis of Unbalanced Data; Add.* 1360 Terrace Drive, Pittsburgh, PA 15228-1637, USA.

LI, CHUNG-KUEI
(See LI, TCHONG-KOEI 李鍾桂)

LI, HUI-LIN 李惠林
Mem., Acad. Sinica; Prof. Emeritus, U. of Penn.; *b.* Kiangsu July 15, '11; *m.* Hsu, Chih-ying; 2 *d.; educ.* BS, Soochow U.; MS, Yenching U.; Ph.D., Harvard U.; Instr., Soochow U. 32-40; Tech. Asst., Arnold Arboretum 41-42; Res. Assc., Acad. of Natural Sc. of Philadel-

phia 42-46; Head & Prof., Dept. of Botany, NTU 47-50; Prof. of Botany, U. of Penn. 63-79; Dir., Morris Arboretum 70-75. *Publ.: Woody Flora of Twn.; Add.* 201 W. Evergreen Avenue, Philadelphia, PA 19118, USA.

LI, I-YUAN
(See LI, YIH-YUAN 李亦園)

LI, JOHN CHIEN-CHUNG 李建中
V. Chmn., Public Construction Com., Exec. Yuan 95-; Prof., Nat. Cent. U. 95-; *b.* Shanghai Nov. 21, '47; *m.* Shen, Hsiao-ling; 1 *s.,* 1 *d.; educ.* BS., NCKU 71; MS., Michigan State U. 75, Ph. D. 79; Asst. Prof., Dept. of Civil Engr., Wayne State U. 79-80; Assc. Prof., Dept. of Civil Engr., Nat. Cent. U., 80-95; Dir., Off. of Planning & Res., Ret-Ser Engr. Agency 85-88; Chmn., Civil Engr. Dept., Nat. Cent. U. 88-91, Dir., Dep. Exec. Sec., PCSB, Exec. Yuan 91-95. *Publ.:* Over 100 tech. papers; *Add.* 9th Fl., 4 Chung Hsiao W. Rd., Sect. 1, Taipei.

LI, KUO-TING
(See LI, KWOH-TING 李國鼎)

LI, KWOH-TING 李國鼎
Sr. Adv. to the Pres.; Mem., NSC & CAC, KMT; Hon. Bd. Chmn., Chiang Ching-kuo Found. for Intl. Scholarly Exchange 95-; *b.* Nanking Jan. 28, '10; *m.* Sung, Pearl; 1 *s.; educ.* BS, Nat. Cent. U., Nanking; Cambridge U., UK; Hon. Ph.D., Econ., Sung Kyun Kwan U., S. Korea 78; D.Sc., Nat. Cent. U. 83 & U. of Maryland 89; Ph.D., Engr., NCTU 89; Ph.D., Chung Yuan Christian U. 90; LL.D., Boston U. 90; Hon. Fel., Emmanuel Coll., Cambridge U. 91; LL.D., Ch. U. of Hong Kong 91; Hon. D.Lit., New York State U. at Stony Brook 95; Pres. & Prof., Nat. Wuhan U. 37-40; Twn. Shipbuilding Corp. 48-53; Mem., Ind. Dev. Com., Econ. Stabilization Bd. 53-58; Sec.-Gen., CUSA 58-63; V. Chmn., CIECD 63-73; Min. of Econ. Aff. 65-69; Min. of Finance 69-76; Gov., Intl. Bk. for Recon. & Dev., Intl. Dev. Assn. 69-76; Min. of State 76-88; Bd. Chmn., Chiang Ching-kuo Found. for Intl. Scholarly Exchange 89-95. *Publ.: Symposium on Nuclear Phys.; British Ind.; Japanese Shipbuilding Ind.; The Econ. Transformation of Twn.; The Growth of Private Ind. in Free Ch.; The Experience of Dynamic Econ. Growth on Twn.; The Evolution of Policy Behind Twn.' Dev. Success; Vision & Devotion* 87; *Witnessing Econ. &*

Soc. Dev. on Twn., ROC; Experience & Belief 91; etc.; *Add.* 3 Lane 2, Tai An St., Taipei.

LI, LIEN-CHUN
(See LI, RIEN-CHUN 李連春)

LI, RIEN-CHUN 李連春
Nat. Policy Adv. to the Pres. 76-; *b.* Twn. Jan. 10, '04; *m.* Wang, Pao-yu; 2 *s.,* 2 *d.; educ.* Grad., Cml. Sch., Kobe, Japan; Comr. & concur. Dir., Food Bu., TPG, & Bd. Chmn., Cooperative Bk. of Twn. 46-70; Min. of State 70-76; *Add.* 8 Hsi Ning S. Rd., Taipei.

LI, TCHONG-KOEI 李鍾桂
Dep. Sec.-Gen., CC, KMT 93-, Mem., CSC 93-, & Mem., CC 69-; Pres., Ch. Youth Corps 87-, & Cul. Promotion Assn. 82-; Prof., NCU & NTU 65-; Res. Fel., Inst. of Intl. Rel., NCU 69-; *b.* Kiangsu July 7, '38; *m.* Shih, Chi-yang; *educ.* BA, NCU; LL.D., U. of Paris; Chmn., Dept. of Dip., NCU 70-72; Dir., Bu. of Intl. Cul. & Educ. Rel., MOE 72-77; Pres., Pacific Cul. Found. 77-87; Dep. Dir.-Gen., Dept. of Youth Aff., CC, KMT 79-87; Dir.-Gen., Dept. of Women's Aff. 88-93. *Publ.: The Evolution of the Anglo-French Dip. Rel. Between the 2 World Wars; A Study of the European Problems; World Aff. in the Past & Future; Sino-Am. Rel. & Our Nation's Prospect; Nat. Sec. & Human Rights; Add.* 219 Sungkiang Rd., Taipei.

LI, TING-I
(See LI, TINGYE 厲鼎毅)

LI, TINGYE 厲鼎毅
Mem., Acad. Sinica 94-; Head, Lightwave Systems Res. Dept., AT&T Bell Labs. 67-; *b.* Nanking July 7, '31; *m.* Wu, Edith Hsiu-hwei; 2 *d.; educ.* BSEE, U. of Witwatersrand, S. Africa 53; MSEE, Northwestern U. 55, Ph.D. 58; Hon. Engr. Dr., NCTU 91; Mem. of Tech. Staff, AT&T Bell Labs. 57-67; Mem., Nat. Acad. of Engr. 80. *Publ.:* Over 90 papers in the areas of antennas, microwaves, lasers, optical comms.; 15 patents in the above areas; 2 bk. on lightwave comms.; *Add.* 11 Sheraton Lane, Rumson, NJ 07760, USA.

LI, TZU-LIANG
(See LAI, TZE-LEUNG 黎子良)

LI, YIH-YUAN 李亦園
Mem., Acad. Sinica; Pres., Chiang Ching-kuo Found. for Intl. Scholarly Exchange 95-; Prof. of Anthropology, NTHU; *b.* Fukien Aug. 20, '31; *m.* Liu, Shih-shun; 3 *c.; educ.* BA, NTU; MA, Anthropology, Harvard U.; Prof., NTU 63-84; Assc. Dir., Inst. of Ethnology, Acad. Sinica 69-71, Dir. 71-77; Fulbright Visiting Prof., U. of Pittsburgh, USA 80-81; Dean, Coll. of Humanities & Soc. Sc., NTHU 84-90; Fel., Royal Anthropological Soc. *Publ.: Belief & Cul.; Cul. & Behavior; Anthropology & Modern Soc.; Soc. & Cul. of the Twn. Aborigines; The Nat. Character of the Ch.; The Images of Cul.;* etc.; *Add.* 4 Alley 3, Lane 4, Yen Chiu Yuan Rd., Sect. 2, Nankang, Taipei.

LI, YU-HSI
(See NI, YUE-SI 黎玉璽)

LI, YUAN-TSU
(See LI, YUAN-ZU 李元簇)

LI, YUAN-ZU 李元簇
Sr. Adv. to the Pres. 96-; V. Chmn., KMT 93-; *b.* Hunan Sept. 24, '23; *m.* Hsu, Man-yung; 2 *s.; educ.* LL.B., NCU; LL.D., Bonn U.; Hon. DPS, Sung Kyun Kwan U., S. Korea; Hon. LL.D., Hanyang U., S. Korea; Dir., Legal Dept., MND 69-72; Chmn., Legal Com., Exec. Yuan 72-73; Dean, Grad. Sch. of Law, NCU 70-73, Pres. NCU 73-77; Min. of Educ. 77-78; Dir.-Gen., Ch. Youth Corps 77-78; Min. of Justice 78-84; Nat. Policy Adv. to the Pres. 84-89; Sec.-Gen. to the Pres. 88-90; V. Pres., ROC 90-96. *Publ.: Inwieweit Sind Die Auslaendischen Strafrechte im Inlande Anwendbar?; Add.* c/o Off. of the Pres., Taipei.

LI, YUN-HAN 李雲漢
Dir., Party Hist. Com., CC, KMT 91-; Adjunct Prof., NCU 71-; *b.* Shantung Apr. 22, '27; *m.* Han, Jung-chen; 1 *d.; educ.* M., NCU 56, & St. Johns U., USA 69; Mem., Preparatory Cttee., Party Hist. Com., CC, KMT 57-68, Ed. 69-77; Ed. & Chief Sec., Acad. Historica 77-79; Dep. Dir., Party Hist. Com., CC, KMT 79-91. *Publ.: Contemporary Ch. Hist.; The Spirit of KMT's Hist.; The Lukouchiao Incident; The Life of Yu, Yu-jen; Sung, Cheyuan & the July 7th Incident; A Complete Hist. of the KMT;* etc.; *Add.* 7th Fl., 53 Jen Ai Rd., Sect. 3, Taipei.

LIANG, CHENG-CHIN
(See LIANG, PATRICK C.J. 梁成金)

LIANG, PATRICK C.J. 梁成金
Dep. Gov., CBC 95-; *b.* Twn. Mar. 16, '39; *m.* Liang, Nancy; 1 *s.,* 1 *d.; educ.* BBA & MBA, NCU; Gen. Mgr., Banking Dept., CBC, & Cent. Deposit Ins. Corp.; V. Chmn., CEPD 92-95; *Add.* CBC, 2 Roosevelt Rd., Sect. 1, Taipei.

LIANG, SHANG-YUNG 梁尚勇
Mem., Control Yuan 93-; *b.* Shansi Sept. 20, '30; *m.* Liang Kung, Yu-ling; 1 *s.,* 2 *d.; educ.* Ed.B., NTNU 52; Ed.M., NCU 57; MA, N.E. Missouri U. 60; Ed.D., U. of Missouri 63; Chmn. & Prof., Dept. of Educ., NCU 69-72; Admin. V. Min. of Educ. 72-75; Comr., Dept. of Educ., TPG 75-78; Prof., Grad. Sch. of Educ., NCU 78-81; Dean of Acad. Aff. & Prof. of Educ., NTNU 82-84, Pres. 84-93. *Publ.: Educ. of Exceptional C.; Org. & Admin. of the Am. Higher Learning Inst.; Trends & Issues in Educ.; Add.* 2 Chung Hsiao E. Rd., Sect. 1, Taipei.

LIANG, TUNG-TSAI
(See WAY, E. LEONG 梁棟材)

LIAO, CHENG-CHING 廖正井
Sec.-Gen., TCG 94-; *b.* Twn. Jan. 8, '45; *m.* Yang, Chi-chin; 1 *d.; educ.* BA, Dept. of Public Finance, Feng Chia U. 73; MA, Public Finance, NCU 76; Passed the Civil Service Sp. Exam. A 86; Staff Mem., CBC 73-74; Auditor & Sp., MOF 74-77; Sect. Chief & Sp., Twn. Tobacco & Wine Monopoly Bu. 77-83; Sect. Chief, MOI 84-86; Adjunct Assc. Prof., Ming Chuan Coll. & Feng Chia U. 84; Sr. Off., MOI 86-87, Counsl. 87-88; Counsl., TCG 88-90, Dir., Finance Bu. 90-94; Acting Chmn., Taipei Bank 94; *Add.* 1 Shih Fu Rd., Taipei.

LIAO, CHENG-HAO 廖正豪
Min. of Justice 96-; *b.* Twn. Mar. 30, '46; *m.* Liao Lin, Li-chen; 5 *d.; educ.* LL.B., NTU 68, LL.M. 73, LL.D. 91; Studied at Tokyo U. 78-79; Visiting Scholar, Stanford U. 92; Chief Sec., Dept. of Land, TPG 79-81; Counsl., Laws & Regln. Cttee., Exec. Yuan 81-84; Adv. & concur. Dir. of the Gov.'s Off., TPG 84-85; Chmn., Cttee. on Admin. Regln., Petition & Appeals Com., TPG 85-86; Dir., 1st Dept., Exec. Yuan 86-88; Dep. Dir.-Gen., GIO 88-92; Adv., Exec. Yuan 92-93; Dep. Sec.-Gen., Exec. Yuan 93-95; Dir.-Gen., Investigation Bu., Min. of Justice 95-

96. *Publ.: Studies on Libel Charge; An Analysis of the Draft of Japanese Criminal Code Amendment in 1972; A Study of Criminal Negligence* (doctoral disseration); *Add.* 130 Chungking S. Rd., Sect. 1, Taipei.

LIAO, CHUAN-YU
(See, LIAO, CHUAN-YUH 廖泉裕)

LIAO, CHUAN-YUH 廖泉裕
Magis., Yunlin County 90-; *b.* Twn. Dec. 24, '38; *m.* Liao Hsu, Heng-tzu; 1 *s.,* 3 *d.; educ.* BS, Pingtung Coll. of Agr.; MA, New Calif. U.; Tchr. 73-78; Mem., TPA 78-90; *Add.* 1 Fu Hsing Rd., Huwei, Yunlin County.

LIAO, CHUN-MU 廖俊穆
Artist; Sr. Admin. Sec., CCA 88-; Adjudicator, Twn. Prov. Fine Art Exhibition 83-; Adjudicator, ROC Fine Art Exhibition 89-; Adjudicator, Cul. & Art Award, MOE 93-; *b.* Twn. Jan. 8, '39; *m.* Chang, Hsiu-tai; 1 *s.,* 1 *d.; educ.* Inst. of Admin. Mng., NCU 83; Counsl., RDEC 70-77; Sect. Chief, Nat. Audit Off., Control Yuan 77-84, Sr. Sp. 84-85; Dir., CCA, Exec. Yuan 86-88. *Publ.: Collected Paintings & Calligraphy by Liao Chun-mu; Collected Paintings by Liao Chun-mu; Collected Prize-winning Ch. Ink Paintings by Liao Chun-mu; Add.* 10th Fl., 22 Sungkiang Rd., Taipei.

LIAO, FENG-TE 廖風德
Dir., Secretariat, KMT 96-; *b.* Twn. Apr. 17, '51; *m.* Kuo, Fan-mei; 1 *s.,* 1 *d.; educ.* BA, Tamkang U. 72, MA 76; Ph.D., NCU 91; Assc. Prof., World Coll. of Jour. & Comms. 76-78; Assn. Prof., NCU 78-82, Assc. Prof. 82-89; Dep. Dir., Dept. of Cul. Aff. 89-95; V. Chmn., Twn. Prov. Cttee., KMT 95-96; *Add.* 53 Jen Ai Rd., Sect. 3, Taipei.

LIAO, HSIU-PING
(See LIAO, SHIOU-PING 廖修平)

LIAO, HUEY-MING 廖慧明
Prin., H.M. Liao & Assc. 76-; Adjunct Prof., NCKU 79-; *b.* Taipei Mar. 8, '34; *m.* Liao, Shun-hsiang; 2 *d.; educ.* Grad., Nat. Taipei Inst. of Tech. 55; BS, Architecture, Tokyo U. 59, M.Arch. 61, D.Sc. 65; Postdoctoral Fel., U. of Texas 65-66; Structural Engr., Ammann & Whitney, New York 66-67; Asst. Resr., UC-Berkly. 67-68; Struc-tural Engr., T.Y. Lin Intl., San Francisco. *Publ.: Seismic Design of Highrise Bldg. in Twn.* 94; *Add.* 4th Fl., 116 Huai Ning St., Taipei.

LIAO, HUI-MING
(See LIAO, HUEY-MING 廖慧明)

LIAO, HUI-YING 廖輝英
Writer 88-; *b.* Twn. Apr. 2, '48; *m.* Yang, Po-nan; 1 *s.,* 1 *d.; educ.* BA, NTU 70; Ed., *Women's World Mag.* 74-76; Kai-mei Housing Co., 76-78; Auo-mei Advertising Co. 78-80; Lun Lin Bldg. Co. 80-82. *Publ.: Blind Spot; Migratory Birds in the City; The Shadow of the Moon; Add.* 3rd Fl., 19 Lane 63, Tun Hua S. Rd., Sect. 2, Taipei.

LIAO, I-CHIU 廖一久
Mem., Acad. Sinica 92-; Dir.-Gen., Twn. Fisheries Res. Inst. 87; Prof., Zoology, NTU 74; Fel., 3rd World Acad. of Sc. 92-; *b.* Ch. Nov. 4, '36; *m.* Chao, Nai-hsien; 2 *s.; educ.* BS, Zoology, NTU 60; M. of Agr., U. of Tokyo 64, Ph.D. 68; Res. Fel., Rockefeller Found. Prog. 68-69; Assc. Prof., Dept. of Zoology & Inst. of Oceanology, NTU 68-74; Dir., Tungkang Marine Lab., Twn. Fisheries Res. Inst. 71-87; Tech. Adv., Milkfish Project, US Agency for Intl. Dev. 82-86; Bd. Mem., Asian Fisheries Soc. 84-92; Chmn., Asian Chapter 85. *Publ.: Generation Cycle of Grey Mullet, Mugil Cephalus in Captivity;* & 260 papers; *Add.* 199 Ho I Rd., Keelung.

LIAO, JUNG-CHI 廖榮祺
Nat. Policy Adv. to the Pres. 93-; Pres., Changsheng Clinic; Mem., TPA 77-; *b.* Twn. Sept. 17, '21; *m.* Liao Fu, Hung-yeh; 1 *s.,* 5 *d.; educ.* Sun Yat-sen Inst. on Policy Res. & Dev.; Adv., Exec. Yuan; *Add.* 498 Cheng Kung Rd., Taichung.

LIAO, LIAO-I
(See LIAO, LIOU-YI 廖了以)

LIAO, LIOU-YI 廖了以
Magis., Taichung County 89-; *b.* Twn. Oct. 29, '47; *m.* Liao Wen, Mei-li; 3 *d.; educ.* BS, Business, Feng Chia U. 71; MS, PA, San Francisco U.; Staff, Hua Nan Cml. Bk. 72-77; Chmn., Fu Chuan Ltd. 77-80; Mgr., Fei Chien Trade Ltd. 80-82; Mayor, Fengyuan City 82-89; *Add.* 71 Hsi An St., Fengyuan, Taichung County.

LIAO, SHIOU-PING 廖修平
Visiting Prof., ROC Nat. Inst. of Arts 94-; Mem., Soc. of Am. Graphic Artists; Adjudicator, Intl. Biennial Prints Exhibition of Twn. & Nat. Twn. Fine Arts Exhibition; *b.* Twn. Sept. 2, '36; *m.* Wu, Shur-jen; 2 *c.; educ.* BA, NTNU 59; MA, Tokyo U. of Educ. 64; Res. at L'Eecole des Beau-Arts, Paris 65-68; Continued Printmaking Work at Pratt Graphics Cent., New York; Assc. Prof., NTNU; Adjunct Prof., Coll. of Ch. Cul. & Nat. Twn. Acad. of Arts 73-76; Lectured at Ch. U. of Hong Kong 74, Japan Aichi Art U. 78, & Tsukuba U.; Adjunct Prof. of Art, Ston Hall U. 79-92; *Exhibitions:* Taipei Fine Arts Museum 89; Tainan Museum of Art 92. *Publ.: The Art of Printmaking; Appreciation of Modern Printmaking; Printmaking Techniques; Add.* 160 Jen Ai Rd., Sect. 3, Taipei.

LIAO, SHU-TSUNG
(See LIAO, SHUTSUNG 廖述宗)

LIAO, SHUTSUNG 廖述宗
Mem., Acad. Sinica 94-; Prof., Dept. of Biochem. & Molecular Biology, Ben May Inst., U. of Chicago, Cttee. on Dev. Biology, Cttee. on Cancer Biology, Cancer Res. Cent. 72-; Mem., N. Am. Twn. Prof. Assn. (NATPA) 80-; *b.* Twn. Jan. 1, '31; *m.* Kuo, Shuching; 4 *d.; educ.* BS & MS, NTU 53 & 56; Ph.D., U. of Chicago 61; Asst. Prof., U. of Chicago 64-69, Assc. Prof. 69-71; Pres., NATPA 80-81. *Publ.:* Over 200 articles in prof. jour. in the fields of molecular action of steroid hormones, androgen & other nuclear receptors, gene mutations in hereditary abnormalities, carcinogenesis & chemotherapy of cancers; *Add.* MC 6027, U. of Chicago, 5841 S. Maryland Avenue, MC 6027, Chicago IL 60637, USA.

LIAU, MARIETTA 高青雲
Dir.-Gen., TECO in Atlanta 96-; *b.*Taipei Feb. 16, '49; *m.* Liau, Hermann; 1 *s.,* 1 *d.; educ.* BA, Fu Jen Catholic U.; Tourism Bu., MOTC 72-78; Staff, MOFA 78-82; Sp. Asst., CCNAA, Off. in USA 82-89; Sect. Chief, MOFA 89-92; Dir.-Gen., TECO in Hamburg, Germany 92-96; *Add.* Suite 1290, 1349 W. Peachtree St., Atlanta, GA 30309, USA.

LIEN, CHAN 連戰
V. Pres. & concur. Premier, ROC 96-; V. Chmn., KMT 93-; *b.* Twn. Aug. 27, '36; *m.* Fang, Yui; 2 *s.,* 2 *d.; educ.* BPS, NTU 57; MA, Intl. Law & Dip., U. of Chicago 61, DPS 65; Asst. Prof., Dept. of Pol. Sc., U. of Wisconsin 65-66 & U. of Connecticut 67-68; Visiting Prof., Dept. of Pol. Sc., NTU 68-69, Prof. & Chmn., Dept. of Pol. Sc. & concur. Dir., Grad. Inst. of Pol. Sc. 69-75; Amb. to El Salvador 75-76; Dir.-Gen., Dept. of Youth Aff., CC, KMT 76-78, Dep. Sec.-Gen. 78; Chmn., NYC 78-81; Min. of Comms. 81-87; Mem., CSC, KMT 84-93; V. Premier, ROC 87-88; Min. of For. Aff. 88-90; Gov., TPG 90-93; Premier, ROC 93-96. *Publ.: The Found. of Dem.; Twn. in Ch.'s External Rel.; The We. Pol. Thought; Add.* Exec. Yuan, 1 Chung Hsiao E. Rd., Sect. 1, Taipei.

LIN, BIH-JAW 林碧炤
Dep. Sec.-Gen., NSC 94-; *b.* Twn. Jan. 20, '49; *m.* Lin, Lien; 2 *s.; educ.* LL.B., NCU 70; MA, U. of Manchester, UK 74; Ph.D., U. of Wales, UK 81; Asst. Resr., Inst. of Intl. Rel. (IIR), NCU 77-80, Assc. Resr. & Sect. Chief of Intl. Cooperation 81-84; Assc. Prof. & Dean, Grad. Sch. of Law & Dip., NCU 84-87, Prof. & Dean 88-90, Dir., IIR 90-94. *Publ.: Intl. Rel. & For. Policy; Add.* 122 Chungking S. Rd., Sect. 1, Taipei.

LIN, CHEN-KUO 林振國
Min. of State 96-; Mem., CC, KMT 88-; *b.* Fukien Dec. 9, '37; *m.* Lin, Judia Chi; 2 *d.; educ.* BA, Econ., NTU 60; Studied in Econ. Dept., Oklahoma State U. 66-67, & Harvard U. 73-74; Dir., Dept. of Finance, TCG 84-87; Comr., TPG Coun. & concur. Comr., Dept. of Finance, TPG 87-93; Min. of Finance & concur Min. of State 93-96; *Add.* 1 Chung Hsiao E. Rd., Sect. 1, Taipei.

LIN, CHENG-CHIH
(See LIN, HELEN CHEN-CHI 林澄枝)

LIN, CHI-CHENG
(See LIN, KI-TSENG 林基正)

LIN, CHIH-CHIA
(See LIN, JIH-JIA 林志嘉)

LIN, CHIN-CHANG
(See LIN, CHING-CHANG 林錦章)

LIN, CHIN-SHENG 林金生
Sr. Adv. to the Pres. 93-; *b.* Twn. Aug. 4, '16; *m.* Cheng, Pien-pien; 4 *s.,* 1 *d.; educ.* BA, Law Coll., Tokyo

Imperial U.; Magis., Chiayi County 51-54; Chmn., Yunlin County Cttee., KMT 54-57; Magis., Yunlin County 57-64; Dir., Cheng Ching Lake Ind. Water Works 64-67; Comr., TPG 66-70; Sec.-Gen., Twn. Prov. Cttee., KMT 67-78, Chmn., Taipei Mun. Cttee. 69-70, Dep. Sec.-Gen., CC 70-72; Min. of the Int. 72-76; Min. of Comms. 76-81; Min. of State 81-84; Mem., CSC, KMT 76-87; V. Pres., Exam. Yuan 84-93; *Add.* 40 Lane 286, Chien Kuo S. Rd., Sect. 1, Taipei.

LIN, CHING-CHANG 林錦章
Bd. Chmn. & concur. Gen. Mgr., Good Will Instrument Co. 75-; *b.* Twn. Jan. 11, '45; *m.* Chang, Hsiu-mei; 1 *s.,* 2 *d.; educ.* Grad., Nat. Taipei Inst. of Tech.; *Add.* 4th Fl., 4 Lane 235, Pao Chiao Rd., Hsintien, Taipei County.

LIN, CHING-CHIANG
(See LIN, CHING-JIANG 林清江)

LIN, CHING-JIANG 林清江
Mem., the Exam. Yuan 96-; *b.* Twn. Dec. 2, '40; *m.* Liang, Lee-yun; 2 *s.,* 1 *d.; educ.* Ph.D., U. of Liverpool, UK; Assc. Prof. & Prof., NTNU 68-72; Dir., Dept. of Higher Educ., MOE 72-75; Admin. V. Min. of Educ. 75-76; Dir.-Gen., Dept. of Ovs. Aff., CC, KMT 76-78; Prof., Dean of Grad. Inst. of Educ. & Dean of Student Aff., NTNU 78-81; Pres., Nat. Kaohsiung Tchrs. Coll. 81-83; Comr., Dept. of Educ., TPG 83-87; Admin. V. Min. of Educ. 87-89; Pres., Nat. Chung Cheng U. 89-96. *Publ.: The Sociology of Educ.; British Educ.; Primary Sch. & the Family; New Perspectives on the Sociology of Educ.; Cul. Dev. & Educ. Innovation; Educ. in the ROC; The Future Orientation of Educ.; The Growth of Nat. Chung Cheng U.; Educ. Ideas & Educ. Dev.; Add.* Nat. Chung Cheng U., Minghsiung, Chiayi County.

LIN, CHIOU-SHAN 林秋山
Mem., Control Yuan 93-; Prof., Ch. Cul. U. 65-; *b.* Twn. Jan. 28, '36; *m.* Lin Liao, Pi-ring; 2 *d.; educ.* LL.B., NCU 59; MA, Kyung Hee U., Korea 63, Ph.D. 73; Asst. Dir., GIO 66-67; Sr. Sp., Dept. of Cul. Aff., MOE 67-73; Mem., NA 87-93. *Publ.: Biography of Pres. Park Chong-hee* 77; *Dev. of the Korean Press System of Self-restraint* 68; *New Discourse of Korean Hist.* (transl.); *System of the Korean Const.* (transl.); *Modern Hist. of Korea* (transl.); *Add.* 4 Lane 7, Chih Yu Rd., Shihlin, Taipei.

LIN, CHIU-SHAN
(See LIN, CHIOU-SHAN 林秋山)

LIN, CHONG-PIN 林中斌
V. Chmn., MAC 96-; Adjunct Prof., Govt. Dept., Georgetown U. 88-; *b.* Yunnan May 7, '42; *educ.* BA, Geol., NTU 65; MA, Geol., Bowling Green State U., USA 69; MBA, UCLA 75; Ph.D., Govt., Georgetown U. 86; 2nd Lt., ROC Army 65-66; Sr. Geologist/Financial Analyst, Johns-Manville Corp. 76-78; Res. Asst. to US Amb. Jeane Kirkpatrick 86-87; Sun Yat-sen Prof. of Ch. Studies, Georgetown U. 90-92.; Resident Scholar & Assc. Dir., Asian Studies Prog., Am. Ent. Inst., USA 87-95; Prof., Nat. Sun Yat-sen U. 95-96. *Publ.: Ch.'s Nuclear Weapons Strategy: Tradition Within Evolution* 88; Guest Ed., "Ch.'s 1989 Upheaval," *World Aff.* (Winter 89-90); Ed., "Dem. in Twn.," *World Aff.* (Fall/Winter 92); "Limits to Professionalism: The Extramilitary Roles of the PLA in Modernization," *Sec. Studies* (Summer 92); "The Role of the PLA in the Process of Reunification: Exploring the Possibilities," *PLA Year Bk.* 93; "The Coming Ch. Earthquake," *Intl. Econ.* (May/June 92); "Beijing & Taipei," *Ch. Quarterly* (Dec. 93); "Red Fist: Ch.'s Army in Transition," *Intl. Def. Review* (Feb. 95); *Add.* 17th Fl., 4 Chung Hsiao W. Rd., Sec., Taipei, Taiwan.

LIN, CHRIS J.F. 林日峰
Pres., *Excellence Mag.* 84-; *b.* Twn. Nov. 19, '49; *m.* Tsao, Vickie; 1 *s.,* 3 *d.; educ.* MA, NCU 73; Adv., SEC, MOF 83-89; Adv., MOTC 90-91; Pres., Excellent Business Consulting & Dev. Inc. 83-95; Pres., Asian Inst. of Mng. Alumni 93-96; *Add.* 17 Lane 3, Chien Kuo N. Rd., Sect. 2, Taipei.

LIN, CHUAN-HSENG 林詮勝
Sr. Partner, Connect Law Off. 90-; Chief Exec., Pre-job Orientation of Attorneys of the ROC 95-; Comr., Attorney Discipline Cttee. 96-; *b.* Twn. Aug. 20, '47; *m.* Chang, Mei-ying; 2 *s.,* 2 *d.; educ.* BA, the World Coll. of Jour. 71; MA, Ch. Cul. U. 95; Judge, Kaohsiung Dist. Court 81-86; Public Prosecutor, Prosecutors' Off. of Taipei Dist. Court 86-87; Chief Public Prosecutor, Prosecutors' Off., Hualien, Changhua & Keelung Dist. Courts 88-90. *Publ.: A Study on PRC Enterprise: Twn. Businessmen's Strategy in Investment; A Study of PRC Investment; Add.* 11th Fl.-4, 17 Cheng Te Rd., Sect. 1, Taipei.

LIN, CHUAN-SHENG
(See LIN, CHUAN-HSENG 林詮勝)

LIN, CHUNG
(See LIN, FRANK C. 林鍾)

LIN, CHUNG-HSIUNG
(See LIN, JONG-CHONG 林鐘雄)

LIN, CHUNG-PIN
(See LIN, CHONG-PIN 林中斌)

LIN, CHUNG-SEN
(See LIN, JOIN-SANE 林中森)

LIN, FENG-CHENG
(See LIN, FONG-CHENG 林豐正)

LIN, FONG-CHENG 林豐正
Min. of the Int. 96-; *b.* Twn. Mar. 20, '40; *m.* Hwang, Hsieu; 1 *s.,* 2 *d.; educ.* LL.B., NCHU 63; Chief Exec., Taoyuan County Cttee., Ch. Youth Corps 73; Dir., Dept. of Civil Aff., Taipei County Govt. 73-74, & Dept. of Soc. Aff. 74-76; Chief Sec., Taipei County Govt. 76-78, Dir., Dept. of Soc. Aff. 78-80; Chmn., Tainan County Cttee., KMT 80-81; Magis., Taipei County 81-89; Comr., Dept. of Civil Aff., TPG 90-92; Chmn., Twn. Prov. Cttee., KMT 92-93; Sec.-Gen., TPG 93-94; Pol. Lt. Gov., TPG 94-96; *Add.* 9th Fl., 5 Hsuchow Rd., Taipei.

LIN, FRANK C. 林鍾
Rep., TECO in New Zealand 94-; *b.* Fukien Jan. 8, '35; *m.* Lin Tai, Hong-hwa; 1 *s.,* 2 *d.; educ.* BPS, NTU 55; 1st Sec., Emb. in the Dominican Repub. 75-77; Consul, Consl. at Bananguilla in Colombia 77-80; Dep. Exec. Sec.-Gen., Com. of Intl. Tech. Cooperation, MOFA 80-81, Dep. Dir., Dept. of E. Asian & Pacific Aff., 81-83; Consul-Gen., Emb. at Seoul 83-86, Min. 88-91; Min., Emb. at Riyadh 86-88; Dir., Dept. of Pers. & Govt. Ethics, MOFA 91-94; *Add.* 21st Fl., 105 The Terrace, Wellington, New Zealand.

LIN, HELEN CHEN-CHI 林澄枝
Chmn., CCA 96-; *b.* Twn. Feb. 17, '39; *m.* Shieh, Mung-shiung; 4 *d.; educ.* M., U. of Columbia; Hon. Ph.D., Pacific Coll., Hawaii; Pres., Shih Chien Coll.; Dep. Dir.-Gen., Dept. of Women's Aff., KMT 93-96; *Add.* 60 Hsin Sheng S. Rd., Sect. 2, Taipei.

LIN, HSI-HU
(See LIN, SHYI-HWU 林錫湖)

LIN, HSIANG-NENG
(See LIN, SHIANG-NUNG 林享能)

LIN, HUAI-MIN
(See LIN, HWAI-MIN 林懷民)

LIN, HWAI-MIN 林懷民
Dancer; Choreographer; Writer; Founder & Artistic Dir., Cloud Gate Dance Found. 73-; *b.* Twn. Feb. 19, '47; *educ.* BJ, NCU 68; M. of Fine Arts, U. of Iowa 72; Resident Artist, Dance Dept., UCLA & Am. Dance Festival 78; Fulbright Scholar, Performance Study, New York U.; Producer, Taipei Festival of Intl. Dance Acad. 86; Founding Chmn. & Assc. Prof., Dance Dept., Nat. Inst. of the Arts 83-88. *Publ.: Cicada* 69; *On Dance* 81; *Passing by Brushing the Shoulders* 85; *Add.* B1, 64 Tun Hua N. Rd., Taipei.

LIN, I-FU
(See LIN, YI-FU 林義夫)

LIN, I-SHOU 林義守
Chmn., Kaohsiung Polytech. Inst. 86-, Yieh Hsing Ent. Co. 78-, Yieh Loong Ent. Co. 83-, Yieh Phui Ent. Co. 86-, Yieh United Steel Co. 88-, Yieh Mau Corp. 88-, & Lien Kang Heavy Ind. Co. 89-; *b.* Twn. Nov. 4, '41; *m.* Tsai, Yueh-o; 4 *s.,* 1 *d.; educ.* Ming Te High Sch.; *Add.* 297 Yu Liao Rd., Chiaotou, Kaohsiung County.

LIN, JESSE 林瑞章
Pres., Twn. Fu Hsing Ind. Co. 84-; *b.* Twn. Jun. 9, '53; *m.* Chang, Betty; 2 *s.; educ.* Soochow U. 77; Sales Mgr., Twn. Fu Hsing Ind. Co.; *Add.* 55-10 Pin Chou Rd., Kangshan, Kaohsiung.

LIN, JIH-FENG
(See LIN, CHRIS. J.F. 林日峰)

LIN, JIH-JIA 林志嘉
Dir.-Gen., Dept. of Policy Res., KMT 94-; Mem., Legis. Yuan 89-; Bd. Chmn., C.'s Welfare League, Ching-chuan

Found. for C.'s Safety; *b.* Twn. Mar. 31, '58; *m.* Chen, Chin-man; 2 *s.,* 1 *d.; educ.* BS, Chem., Fu Jen Catholic U. 81; MS, Chem., Tennessee State U. 87; Convener, Home & Border Aff. Cttee. & Organic Laws Cttee., Exec. Yuan; Pres., Welfare Soc., Legis. Yuan 93-94; Mem., Cent. Policy Coordination Cttee., KMT; Dir., KMT Legis. Aff. 94; *Add.* 2nd Fl., 16 Hangchow S. Rd., Sect. 1 Taipei.

LIN, JOIN-SANE 林中森
Dep. Mayor, Kaohsiung City Govt. 94-; *b.* Twn. Dec. 17, '44; *m.* Chu, Sheue-ying; 1 *s.,* 1 *d.; educ.* LL.D., NCU 76; Sp., MOI 74-77; Chief, Dept. of Land Aff., TCG 77-81, Sp. 81-83, Sr. Sp. 83; Dep. Dir., Dept. of Land Aff., Kaohsiung City Govt. 83-84, Dir. 85-90, Sec.-Gen. 90-94. *Publ.: Study of the Compensation for Expropriation; Study of the Land Value Issues in Taipei; Study of Twn.'s Idle Farm Land; The Econ. Model for Urban Land's Utilization; A Study on the Impact of Urban Land Consolidation on Urban Utilization—An Empirical Analysis of Kaohsiung Sp. Mun.; Add.* 7-1 Kai Shuen 2nd Rd., Kaohsiung.

LIN, JONG-SHONG 林鐘雄
Chmn., E. Sun Bk. 92-; *b.* Twn. Mar. 24, '38; *m.* Lee, Hui-mei; 1 *s.,* 1 *d.; educ.* BA, NTU 60, MA 64; Sp., CIECD 64-71; Assc. Prof., Econ. Dept. NCU 71-76, Prof. 76-81; Prof., Finance Dept. NTU 81-92. *Publ.: Money & Banking* 69; *Study of Quantity Theory of Money* 67; *Econ.* 84; *Hist. of Econ. Thought* 86; *Econ. Hist. of Europe* 87; *Post-War Econ. Dev. of Twn.* 89; *Essays on Econ. Hist. of Twn.* 95; *Add.* 77 Wu Chang St., Sect. 1, Taipei.

LIN, JUI-CHANG
(See LIN, JESSE 林瑞章)

LIN, JUI-HSIUNG
(See LIN, RUEY-SHIUNG 林瑞雄)

LIN, JUNG-HSING 林榮星
Spkr., Ilan CoCoun. 94-; *b.* Twn. June 29, '40; *m.* Lin Fan, Shu-jung; 4 *s.,* 2 *d.; educ.* Grad., Ilan County Toucheng High Sch.; Bd. Chmn., Lita Minerals 75-86; Mem., Ilan CoCoun. 82-94, Dep. Spkr. 86-94; Gen. Mgr., Tung-i Iron & Steel Co. Ltd. 87-94; Bd. Chmn.,

Mei-chou Concrete Ind. Co. Ltd. 92-94; *Add.* 98 Wei Shui Rd., Ilan.

LIN, JUNG-SAN
(See LING, RONG-SAN 林榮三)

LIN, JUNG-YAO
(See LIN, JUNG-YAW 林榮耀)

LIN, JUNG-YAW 林榮耀
Mem., Acad. Sinica 96-; Prof., NTU 72-; *b.* Taipei Twn. May 27, '34; 2 *s.,* 2 *d.; educ.* BS, NTU 57; MS, NTU 60; Ph.D., UC-Berkly. 67; Instr., NTU 60-67, Assc. Prof. 67-72; *Publ.:* 111 papers; *Add.* 1 Jen Ai Rd., Sect. 1, Taipei.

LIN, KAI-FAN 林鎧藩
Chmn., CFC, KMT 93-; *b.* Fukien Jan. 21, '23; *m.* Tseng, Yu-chin; 1 *s.,* 3 *d.; educ.* B., NCU 48; Sect. Chief & Sr. Sp., Dept. of Budget, Acct. & Statistics, TPG 48-67, Dir. 74-83; Chief Sec., Dept. of Budget, Acct. & Statistics, TCG 67-69, Dir. 71-74; Insp., DGBAS 69-71, Dep. Dir.-Gen. 83-86; Pres., Cent. Deposit Ins. Corp. 86-92; Pres., Twn. Telecom. Network Service Co. 92-93; *Add.* 9th Fl., 6 Chung Hsiao W. Rd., Sect. 1, Taipei.

LIN, KI-TSENG 林基正
Amb. to Nicaragua 91-; *b.* Twn. June 5, '36; *m.* Yin, Su-mey; 2 *s.,* 1 *d.; educ.* LL.B., NTU 59; Sp. Asst., Taipei Post Off. 58-61; Sec., Info. Dept., MOFA 61-64; 3rd Sec., Emb. in Dominican Repub. 64-66; Sect. Chief, 2nd & 1st Sect., Treaty Dept., MOFA 66-71; Sec., Ch. Del. to UN Conf. of Treaties, Vienna, Austria 69; Mem., Ch. Del. for Negotiation on Bilateral Treaties 67-71; 1st Sec., Emb. in Spain 71-74, & Emb. in Portugal 74-77; Dep. Dir., Dept. of Cent. & S. Am. Aff., MOFA 77-80; Sr. Adv., Oficina Cml. del Lejano Oriente, Bogota, Colombia 80-81; Dir., Oficina Cml. de Twn., ROC in Caracas, Venezuela 81-90; Dir., Dept. of Consl. Aff., MOFA 90-91; *Add.* Emb. of the ROC, P.O. Box 4653, Managua 5, Nicaragua.

LIN, KU-FANG 林谷芳
Freelancer & Scholar on Ch. Music; Convener, Wanyueh Ensemble 91-; *b.* Twn. May 8, '50; *m.* Chou, Chin-hsia; 2 *s.; educ.* Grad., Dept. of Anthropology, NTU; *Performances:* 21 performances including *Tea & Music: A Dialogue; A Meeting of Music with Painting & Calligra-*

phy; P'i-P'a Art of the Putung Sch. Publ.: *This Land, This People-A Listeners' Guide to Traditional Ch. Music; The Story of P'i-P'a; An Aesthetic Predicament: The Influence of Symphonic Music on Traditional Ch. Music;* over 100 articles on arts & cul.; *Add.* 30 Alley 36, Lane 369, Yuan Tung Rd., Chungho, Taipei County.

LIN, KUO-HSIEN 林國賢
Grand Justice, Jud. Yuan 94-; Prof. of Laws, NCHU, & Dr. Sun Yat-sen Inst., Ch. Cul. U.; *b.* Twn. Feb. 6, '36; *m.* Lu, Hsueh-hua; 3 *s.,* 1 *d.; educ.* LL.B., NTU 60; LL.M., Ch. Cul. U. 71, J.S.D. 81; Justice, Supreme Court 82-84; Comr., Criminal Dept., Jud. Yuan 85-90; Pres., Shihlin Br., Taipei Dist. Court 90-93; Prof., Dept. of Law, NCHU 93-94; Prof., Ch. Cul. U. 92-94; Dep. Sec.-Gen., Jud. Yuan 93-94; Lectr., Judges & Prosecutors Tng. Inst.; Mem., Sr.- & Jr.-Grade Civil Service Exam. Bd., Min. of Exam., Exam. Yuan. *Publ.: The Five-power Const. & the Current Const.; The Self-Appeal System of Criminal Procedure; Add.* 124 Chungking S. Rd., Sect. 1, Taipei.

LIN, LIANG 林良
Writer, Prose & C.'s Lit.; Pub., *Mandarin Daily News* 93-; *b.* Fukien Oct. 10, '24; *m.* Jeng, Shiou-jy; 3 *d.; educ.* Sp. Course, Ch. Lang., NTNU 52; BA, Eng. Lang. & Lit., Tamkang U. 70; Ed., *Mandarin Daily News* 48-63, Chief Ed., Pub. Dept. 64-71, Mgr. 72-93. *Publ.: Little Sun; The Art of Simple Lang.; 16 Letters from My Father;* & over 160 bk. for c.; *Add.* 19 Lane 15, Chungking S. Rd., Sect. 3, Taipei.

LIN, ME-LIN 林敏霖
Spkr., Taichung CoCoun. 90-, Mem. 82-; *b.* Twn. Mar. 10, '49; *m.* Hwang, Yueh-shiang; 2 *s.,* 1 *d.; educ.* BS, Tamkang U. 72; *Add.* 545 Chung Cheng Rd., Fengyuan, Taichung County.

LIN, MENG-KUEI 林孟貴
Mem., Control Yuan 93-; *b.* Twn. Oct. 30, '43; *educ.* MPA, San Francisco State U.; *Add.* Control Yuan, 2 Chung Hsiao E. Rd., Taipei.

LIN, MIN-LIN
(See LIN, ME-LIN 林敏霖)

LIN, MING-TE
(See LIN, MING-TEH 林明德)

LIN, MING-TEH 林明德
Pres., Admin. Court, MOJ 95-; *b.* Taipei Nov. 18, '31; *m.* Lin Chien, Tuang-li; 2 *s.,* 3 *d.; educ.* LL.B., NTU; Prosecutor, Judge, Chief Judge, Dist. Courts & High Courts 56-71, Chief Prosecutor, Yunlin Dist. Court & Keelung Dist. Court 71-72 & 72-78, Mem., Cttee. on Discipline of Public Functionaries 79-80; Dep. Sec.-Gen., Jud. Yuan 89-90; Pres., Twn. Taipei Dist. Court 90-93, Pres., Taichung Br., Twn. High Court 93-95. *Publ.: A Review of Court Decisions on ROC's Current Jud. Practice Relevant to Mainland Residents; A Report on Japan's Appellant Criminal Procedures & the Precise Procedural Rule System; Add.* Admin. Court, 1 Lane 126, Chungking E. Rd., Sect. 1, Taipei.

LIN, PANG-CHUNG
(See LIN, VINCENT P.C. 林邦充)

LIN, PI-CHAO
(See LIN, BIH-JAW 林碧炤)

LIN, SHENG-HSIEN 林聖賢
Mem., Acad. Sinica 84-, Dir. & Sp. Disting. Res. Fel., Inst. of Atomic & Molecular Sc. 93-; Prof., Arizona State U. 72-; Hon. Prof., Nanking U. 88-; Adjunct Prof., Shantung U. 90-; Prof., Dept. of Chem., NTU 94-; *b.* Twn. Sept. 17, '37; *m.* Lin Pi, Hsiu-ping; 2 *s.; educ.* BS & MS, NTU; Ph.D., U. of Utah; Postdoctoral Fel., Columbia U. 64-65; Asst. Prof., Arizona State U. 65-68, Assc. Prof. 68-72, Prof. 72-95, Adjunct Prof. 95-96, Regent's Prof. 88-96, Alfred P. Sloan Fel. 67-71; John Simon Guggenheim Fel. 71-73; Visiting Prof., Cambridge U. 72-73, Tech. U. of Munich 79-80 & 87, & Louis Pasteur U. 86. *Publ.:* 16 bk. & 352 papers; *Add.* 1915E Calle De Caballos, Tempe, AZ 85284, USA.

LIN, SHIANG-NUNG 林享能
V. Chmn., COA 89-; Chmn., Cttee. of Intl. Tech. Cooperation; Chmn., Ovs. Fisheries Dev. Coun., ROC; Chmn., Twn. Meat Dev. Found.; *b.* Twn. Dec. 20, '36; *m.* Huang, Kuei-mei; 1 *s.,* 2 *d.; educ.* LL.B., NCU 60; MA, Ch. Cul. U. 65; Sect. Chief, MOFA 72-75, Dep. Dir., Dept. of Cent. & S. Am. Aff. 75; Dir., Cml. Off. of Twn. in Venezuela 75-81, & Cml. Off. of Taipei in Chile 81-84; Coordinator to Parliament, MOFA 88-89. *Publ.: Peaceful Strategy of J.F. Kennedy; Analysis of CBI Initiative;*

Legal Basis of the High Seas Driftnet Fishing in the N. Pacific Ocean Between CCNAA & AIT; Wildlife Conservation on Twn.; Add. 37 Nan Hai Rd., Taipei.

LIN, SHOU-HUI 林壽惠
Pres., Nat. Taipei Coll. of Nursing 94-; Standing Mem., Nurses' Assn. of ROC, & Nat. Union Nurses' Assn., ROC; *b.* Twn. June 1, '44; *educ.* Grad., Twn. Prov. Jr. Coll. of Nursing 65; BS, Nursing Sc., Syracuse U., New York 77; MS, Nursing Sc., Boston U. 80; D.Sc., Nursing Sc., Rush U., Chicago 91; Dean of Studies, Nat. Taipei Coll. of Nursing 82-87, Pres. 90-94; Dean, Nat. Taipei Coll. of Nursing Hosp. 90-91. *Publ.:* "Home Health Care & Soc. Support for Stroke Patients," *Jour. of Twn. Med. Assn.* (92: S177-83) 93; "New Role in Nursing—A Brief of Freestanding Home Health Care," *Further Med. Educ.* (Vol. 3, no. 3) 93; *Add.* 365 Ming Te Rd., Peitou, Taipei.

LIN, SHU 林樹
Pres., Chung-hua Polytech. Inst. 94-; *b.* Twn. Oct. 9, '41; *m.* Juang, Yu-mei; 1 *s.,* 3 *d.; educ.* Ed.B., NTNU 68; Curator, Lib. of NCTU 72-88, Prof. 80-92; Dir., Secretariat, Nat. Open U. 88-89. *Publ.: A Study on Basic Ch. Characters for Computer Use; A Comprehensive Dictionary for Ch. Index; Add.* Chung-hua Polytech. Inst., 30 Tung Hsiang, Hsinchu.

LIN, SHU-HUNG
(See LIN, SUHON 林書鴻)

LIN, SHUI-CHI
(See LIN, SUI-CHI 林水吉)

LIN, SHUI-MU 林水木
Mayor, Keelung City 89-; *b.* Twn. Oct. 12, '37; *m.* Hsu, Shao-pin; 2 *s.; educ.* Grad., NTNU 61; Tchr., Keelung 3rd Jr. High Sch. 61-65, Prov. Keelung Girls' High Sch. 65-71, & Taipei Mun. Chinhua Girls' High Sch. 71-72; Tchr., Prov. Keelung Girls' High Sch. 72-76, Dean of Gen. Aff. 76-80; Mem., TPA 81-89; *Add.* 1 Yi 1st Rd., Keelung.

LIN, SHYI-HWU 林錫湖
Pol. V. Min. of Justice 89-; Prof., Tng. Inst. for Jud. Pers. 73-; *b.* Twn. Feb. 26, '26; *m.* Lin, Bi-hua; 2 *s.,* 2 *d.; educ.* Cent. Police Coll.; Judges' Tng. Inst.; Sun Yat-sen Inst.

on Policy Res. & Dev.; Passed the Sr. Civil Service Exam. for Ordinary Admin.; Prosecutor, Judge & Div. Chief, Taipei Dist. Court 58-65; Judge, Twn. High Court 66-75; Chief Prosecutor, Yunlin Dist. Court & Keelung Dist. Court 76-81, & Hualien Br. Court, Twn. High Court 82-86; Admin. V. Min. of Justice 87-89. *Publ.: How to Write Indictments & Judgments: Introduction to Civil Jud. Precedent of Japan; Add.* 130 Chungking S. Rd., Sect. 1, Taipei.

LIN, SUHON 林書鴻
Pres., Chang Chun Petrochemical Co. 64-; Exec. Mng. Dir., Chang Chun Plastics Co. 57-; Chmn., Dairen Chem. Corp. 79-; *b.* Twn. Aug. 1, '28 ; *m.* Lin Wong, Li-Ching; 1 *s.,* 3 *d.; educ.* Grad., Taipei High Sch. of Tech.; *Add.* 7th Fl., 301 Sungkiang Rd., Taipei.

LIN, SUI-CHI 林水吉
Rep., TECO in Vietnam; *b.* Twn. Mar. 21, '38; *m.* Lin, Su-man; 2 *s.,* 1 *d.; educ.* LL.B., NCU 60, LL.M., Dip. 64; 3rd & 2nd Sec., Emb. in Vietnam 65-70; 1st Sec., Emb. in S. Korea 71-72; Div. Dir., Dept. of E. Asian & Pacific Aff., MOFA 73-75; Consul, Consl. in Pago Pago, Am. Samoa 75-78; Dep. Dir., Dept. of Info., MOFA 79-81; Adv., TECRO, USA 82; Dir.-Gen., TECO, Boston 83-90; Dir., Dept. of E. Asian & Pacific Aff., MOFA 90-92; *Add.* 2D Vanphuc, Hanoi, Vietnam.

LIN, TA-HSIUNG 林達雄
Dep. Admin., EPA 93-; *b.* Twn. Oct. 23, '44; *m.* Lu, Hsiu-chen; 2 *s.; educ.* BS, Dept. of Water Conservation, NCHU; Div. Chief, Bu. of Environmental Protection, DOH 82-85, Dep. Dir. 85-87; Dir., Water Quality Protection Bu., EPA 87-89, Air Quality Protective Planning Bu. 89-92, Performation Evaluation & Dispute Settlement Bu. 92-93; *Add.* 100 Ai Kuo E. Rd., Taipei.

LIN, TING-SHENG 林挺生
Sr. Adv. to the Pres. 91-; Chmn., Presidium, CAC, KMT; Prof. & Pres., Tatung Inst. of Tech.; Chmn., Tatung Co.; Mem., Intl. Adv. Bd., Am. U., Washington, D.C.; Gov., Asian Inst. of Mng., Manila; Bd. Mem., Assc. Harvard Business Sch., USA; Mem., Faculty Exchange Promotion Cttee. Between Tatung Inst. of Tech. & UK Glasgow U.; *b.* Twn. Nov. 15, '19; *educ.* BS, Chem., NTU 42; Hon. D.Sc., Chungang U., S. Korea 73; Hon. LL.D.,

Pepperdine U., USA 78; Hon. Dr. of Engr., Inha U., S. Korea 78; Hon. D.Sc., U. of Glasgow, UK 91; Legis.; Mng. Dir., Ch. Nat. Fed. of Ind.; Chmn., Twn. Assn. of Mach. Ind., Twn. Elec. Appliance Manufacturers' Assn., & Taipei Mun. Cttee. of Ch. Youth Anti-Communists & Nat. Salvation Corp.; Mem., CSC, & Chmn., Taipei Mun. Cttee., KMT; Chmn., Chung-hsin Elec. & Mach. Mfg. Corp.; Pres., Ch. Chem. Soc. 62, & Ch. Inst. of Engrs. 67; Spkr., Taipei CCoun. 69-81; Mem., ROC Del. to the UN 71; Chmn., Ch. Nat. Fed. of Ind. 75-81; Leader, Econ. Goodwill Mission of the ROC for Celebrating the Bicentennial of the Founding of the USA 76; *Add.* 22 Chung Shan N. Rd., Sect. 3, Taipei.

LIN, TONG 林棟
Nat. Policy Adv. to the Pres. 91-; Mem., CElC 92-; Pres., Tasco Chem. Corp.; Mem., CAC, KMT; Prof., Fu Jen Catholic U.; *b.* Kiangsu July 2, '13; *m.* Liu, Kwei-cheng; 4 *d.; educ.* LL.B., Nanking U.; MA, U. of Michigan; LL.D., U. of Plano, USA; Grad., Nat. War Coll.; Prof., Nat. Cent. U. 39-41; Comr., Kiangsu Prov. Govt. 42-45; Sec., Exec. Yuan 46-48; Mem., Legis. Yuan 49-91; Prof., NTNU 58-80; Adv., Ch. Del. to the 13th UNGA 62-63; Chmn., Policy Coordination Cttee., CC, KMT 89-91. *Publ.: A Study of the Ch. Const.; Add.* 3-5 Lane 21, Li Shui St., Taipei.

LIN, TSAI-MEI 林彩梅
Pres., Ch. Cul. U. 93-, Prof., Intl. Business Mng. 86-; *b.* Twn. Nov. 12, '36; *educ.* Dr. of Business Admin., Kinki U.; Dir., Dept. of Ind. Mng., Intl. Trade, Cooperative Econ., Mng. Sc., Tamkang U. 77-86; Pres., Assn. of Intl. Business Studies 85-89; Chmn., Grad. Sch. of Business Admin., Ch. Cul. U. 86-87, 90, Dean of Acad. Aff. 88-93, Dean of Business Coll. 86-93, Acting Pres. 93. *Publ.:* 4 bk. & 44 articles; *Add.* 55 Hua Kang Rd., Yangmingshan, Taipei.

LIN, TSUN-HSIEN 林尊賢
Rep., Taipei Mission in Korea 94-; *b.* Twn. July 20, '30; *m.* Lin, Lucy Hsiu-chu; 2 *s.,* 1 *d.; educ.* BA, NTU 53; MA, NCU 55; 2nd Sec., Emb. in Australia 59-64; 1st Sec., Emb. in Japan 66-72; Dep. Dir., Protocol Dept., MOFA 72-75; Rep., Trade Mission to Fiji 75-80; Dir., Dept. of E. Asian & Pacific Aff., MOFA 80-83; Dir., TECO, Atlanta 83-89; Dep. Rep., TECRO, USA 89-92;

Amb. to Grenada, Dominica, St. Lucia, St. Kitts & Nevis, & St. Vincent & Grenadines 92-93; *Add.* Taipei Mission in Korea, 6th Fl., Kwanghwamoon Bldg., 211 Sejong-Ro Chongro-Ku, Seoul, Korea 110-050.

LIN, TUNG
(See LIN, TONG 林棟)

LIN, TUNG-YEN 林同棪
Mem., Acad. Sinica, & Nat. Acad. of Engr., Washington, D.C.; Bd. Chmn., Lin Tung Yen Ch. Consulting Engr. 53-; *b.* Fukien Nov. 14, '11; *m.* Kao, Margaret Shun-chun; 1 *s.,* 1 *d.; educ.* BS, Tangshan Coll. & NCTU; MS, UC-Berkly.; LL.D., Ch. U. of Hong Kong & Golden Gate U., San Francisco; NCTU; Tongji U., Shanghai; Hon. Bd. Chmn., T.Y. Lin Intl. Consulting Engr. 53-92; Prof. of Civil Engr., U. of Calif., Chmn., Div. of Structural Engr., Dir., Structural Engr. Lab., U. of Calif. 46-76. *Publ.: Design of Prestressed Concrete Structures; Design of Steel Structure, Structural Concepts & Systems; Add.* 315 Bay St., San Francisco, CA 94133, USA.

LIN, VINCENT P.C. 林邦充
Pres., Chang Jung U. 93-; *b.* Twn. Jan. 9, '41; *m.* Wu, Ching-tu; 2 *s.,* 1 *d.; educ.* BA, NTU 63, MA, Econ. 68; Ph.D. in Agr. Econ., Tokyo Agr. U. 81; Prof. & Chmn., Dept. of Intl. Trade, Fu Jen Catholic U. 79-86. *Publ.: For. Exchange; Add.* 100 Chang Jung Rd., Tatan Tsun, Kueijen Hsiang, Tainan County.

LIN, WEN-JUI 林文睿
Dir., Twn. Br., Nat. Cent. Lib. 92-; *b.* Twn. May 24, '49; *m.* Liu, Mei-feng; 3 *s.; educ.* LL.B., NCHU 82; M., NTU 89; Sect. Chief, MOE 84-87; Sect. Chief, CPA 87-92, Sr. Sp. 92. *Publ. The Study of U. Lib.' Personnel System in Twn. Area; Add.* 1 Hsin Sheng S. Rd., Sect. 1, Taipei.

LIN, WEN-LI 林文禮
Strategy Adv. to the Pres. 92-; Dir.-Gen., Aero Ind. Dev. Cent. 93-; Mem., CC, KMT 94-; *b.* Szechwan Aug. 5, '30; *m.* Wu, Shun-lan; 2 *s.,* 2 *d.; educ.* Ch. Air Force Preparatory Sch. 48; Ch. Air Force Acad. 51; Cmd. & Staff Coll., Air Force U., US Air Force, USA 66; War Coll., Armed Forces U. 79; C-in-C, ROCAF 89-92; Personal C/S to the Pres. 92-93; *Add.* P.O. Box 90008-10, Taichung.

LIN, WEN-SHAN 林文山
Counsl. & Dir., 3rd Dept., Exec. Yuan 93-; *b.* Twn. Aug. 6, '46; *m.* Hung, Tsui-pin; 2 *s.; educ.* MPA, NCU 73; Staff Mem., Exec. Yuan 82-88, Admin. Sec. 88-93. *Publ.: Planning-Programming-Budgeting System; Add.* 5th Fl., 1 Lane 218, Po Ai Rd., Taipei.

LIN, YI-FU 林義夫
Dir.-Gen., Bd. of For. Trade, MOFA 95-; *b.* Taipei Nov. 15, '42; *m.* Lin, Mei-shiow; 3 *d.; educ.* BA, NCU; Asst. Cml. Attaché, Emb. in the Philippines 73-75; Cml. Attaché, Econ. Div., Taipei Econ. & Trade Off. in Thailand 75-82; Sect. Chief, 3rd Dept., Bd. of For. Trade 82-83, Dep. Dir & Dir., 2nd Dept. 83-85 & 86-88; Dir., Far E. Trade Service Inc., Toronto 88-90; Dep. Dir-Gen., Bd. of For. Trade 90-95; *Add.* 1 Hu Kou St., Taipei.

LIN, YU-SAN 林玉山
Prof. of Arts, NTNU; *b.* Twn. Apr. 1, '07; *m.* Lin Huang, Hui; 2 *s.,* 5 *d.; educ.* Kawabata Painting Sch., Tokyo; Painting Exhibition 70, 86 & 91. *Publ.: Painting Collections of Lin Yu-san* (4 Vol.); *Add.* 5 Alley 1, Lane 199, Chin Hua St., Taipei.

LIN, YU-SHAN
(See LIN, YU-SAN 林玉山)

LIN, YU-SHENG 林毓生
Mem., Acad. Sinica 94-, Adjunct Fel., Inst. of Hist. & Philology 83-; Prof., Dept. of Hist., U. of Wisconsin-Madison 81-; Hon. Prof., Ch. Cul. Coll. (Peking) & Inst. of Ch. Cul. (Shanghai) 88-; *b.* Shenyang Aug. 7, '34; *m.* Lin Sung, Tsu-gein; 1 *s.,* 1 *d.; educ.* BA, Hist. Dept., NTU 58; Ph.D., U. of Chicago 70; Postdoctoral Studies, E. Asian Cent., Harvard U. 69-70; Lectr., Yale U. 62; Visiting Asst. Prof., Hist. Dept., U. of Viriginia 66-67; Acting Asst. Prof., U. of Oregon 68; Asst. Prof., Dept. of Hist. & Dept. of E. Asian Lang. & Lit., U. of Wisconsin-Madison 70-75, Assc. Prof. 75-81; Sr. Resr. Fellow, Inst. of E. Asian Philosophy, Singapore 88-90. *Publ.: The Crisis of Ch. Consciousness: Radical Anti-Traditionalism in the May Fourth Era* 79; *Thought & Personalities* 83; *Pol. Order & Pluralistic Soc.* 89; Over 21 articles; *Add.* Dept. of Hist., 3211 Humanities Bldg., U. of Wisconsin-Madison, Madison, WI 53706, USA.

LIN, YUAN-LANG 林源朗
Magis., Nantou County; *b.* Twn. Dec. 28, '40; *m.* Wang, Fu-mei; 1 *s.,* 2 *d.; educ.* Twn. Prov. Taichung Tchrs. Coll. 62-64; Tchr., Toushe Elementary Sch., Nantou 59-62, Tungyuan Elementary Sch., Taipei 64-68; Mandarin Promoter, Dept. of Educ., Nantou County Govt. 68-80; Mem., NA 81-87, & Legis. Yuan 87-89; *Add.* 30 San Ho 1st Rd., Nantou.

LIN, YUN-SHAN 林雲山
Pres. & Prof., Tamkang U. 92-; *b.* Twn. Sept. 25, '29; *m.* Lin, Pao-erl; 1 *s.,* 2 *d.; educ.* BS, Chem., NTU 52; Ph.D., U. of Massachusetts 68; Asst. Engr., Union Ind. Res. Inst. 53-59; Lectr., Tamkang Coll. of Arts & Sc. 59-61, Assc. Prof. 61-63; Res. Assc., State U. of New York 68-70; Prof. & concur. Dean, Coll. of Sc. & Engr., Tamkang Coll. of Arts & Sc. 70-74, Dean of Acad. Aff. 74-78, V. Pres. 78-92. *Publ.:* 21 res. papers on Chem.; *Add.* 151 Ying Chuan Rd., Tamsui, Taipei County.

LIN, YUNG-HSI
(See LIN, YUNG-SHI 林永喜)

LIN, YUNG-MOU 林永謀
Grand Justice, Jud. Yuan 94-; *b.* Twn. Nov. 2, '38; *m.* Wang, Shu-hui; 2 *s.,* 1 *d.; educ.* LL.B., NTU 61; Judge, Chiayi Dist. Court 63-65, & Pingtung Dist. Court 71-73; Prosecutor, Taichung Dist. Court 65-71; Judge, Taichung Br., Twn. High Court 73-78, & Twn. High Court 78-91; Justice, Supreme Court 91-94. *Publ.:* 30 articles on criminal law; *Add.* Jud. Yuan, 124 Chungking S. Rd., Sect. 1, Taipei.

LIN, YUNG-SHI 林永喜
Pres., Taipei Mun. Tchrs. Coll. 95-; *b.* Taipei Dec. 17, '38; *m.* Lin Tsay, M.C.; 4 *d.; educ.* Ed.B., NTNU 69; Ed.M., U. of the Philippines 72; Ed.D., U. of S. Dakota 90; Resr., UNESCO 71-72; Assc. Prof., Taipei Mun. Tchrs. Coll. for Women 76-83 & concur. Dean of Students Aff. 76-78; Prof., Taipei Mun. Tchrs. Jr. Coll. 83-87; Visiting Prof., U. of Chicago 84; Prof., Taipei Mun. Tchrs. Coll. 87-95, Head, Dept. of Elementary Educ. 92-94. *Publ.: Essays on Curricula* 71; *A Comparative Studies on the Educ. Philosphies of Confucius, Mencius, & Hsun-Tzu* 76; *A Study of Idealistic Educ. Thought* 79; *An Introduction of the Three Sch. of Educ.*

Philospohy 84; *An Introduction of Tchrs. Educ.* 85; *Essays on Sc. Educ. & Curricula for Elementary Sch.* 89; & other 46 articles; *Add.* 1 Ai Kuo W. Rd., Taipei.

LING, RONG-SAN 林榮三

Nat. Policy Adv. to the Pres. 93-; *b.* Twn. May 27, '39; *m.* Ling Chang, Su-o; 4 *c.; educ.* Grad., Kai Nan Com. & Tech. High Sch.; Pres., Lang Bong Bldg. Ltd. 65-80; Mem., Legis. Yuan 75-79, & Control Yuan 80-91; V. Pres., Control Yuan 92-93; *Add.* 18th Fl., 109 Min Sheng E. Rd., Sect. 3, Taipei.

LING, SONG-LONG 凌嵩郎

Pres., Nat. Twn. Coll. of Arts 84-; Mem., Adv. Bd., MOE 91-; Pres., Arts Educ. Soc., ROC 92; *b.* Kiangsu Dec. 19, '32; *m.* Yu, Yuan-chun; 2 *s.,* 1 *d.; educ.* BA, NTNU 57; Lectr., Asst. Prof., & Prof., Nat. Twn. Acad. of Arts, Dean & Dean of Studies, Evening Coll.; Adjunct Prof., NTNU & Ch. Cul. U., 64-88 & 65-84. *Publ.: An Introduction to Arts; Ch. Arts Dev. Hist.; The Evolution of Ch. Ceramics; Arts Appreciation; The Expression of Ch. Arts; Han's Painting; The Current Art Educ. in the ROC; Add.* 59 Ta Kuan Rd., Panchiao, Taipei County.

LING, SUNG-LANG

(See LING, SONG-LONG 凌嵩郎)

LIOU, CHING-TIEN 劉清田

Pres., Nat. Twn. Inst. of Tech. 90-; *b.* Twn. Mar. 13, '44; *m.* Lin, Liang-ching; *educ.* BS, NCKU 66; MS, Purdue U. 71, Ph.D. 72; Postdoctoral Resr., Purdue U. 72-73; Prof. & Chmn., NCTU 73-78; Prof., Chmn., & Dean of Acad. Aff., Nat. Twn. Inst. of Tech. 78-90; Chief Sec., MOE 87-90. *Publ.:* 138 papers & 51 bk. & tech. reports; *Add.* 43 Keelung Rd., Sect. 4, Taipei.

LIU, CHAN-AO

(See LIU, CHAN-NAO 劉占鰲)

LIU, CHAN-NAO 劉占鰲

Mem., Acad. Sinica; Prof., Med. Sch., U. of Penn.; *b.* Hopei Mar. 17, '10; *m.* Chao, Chung-yu; 1 *s.,* 1 *d.; educ.* BS, Nat. Peking Normal U.; Ph.D., U. of Penn. *Publ.:* Papers on the regeneration & sprouting of the cent. nervous system following injury; *Add.* 109 Grasmere Rd., Bala Cynwyd, PA 19004, USA.

LIU, CHAO-HAN 劉兆漢

Pres., Nat. Cent. U. 90-; Pres., Sc. Cttee. on Solar-Terrestrial Phys., Intl. Coun. of Sc. Union (ICSU) 94-; *b.* Hunan Jan. 3, '39; *m.* Liu Mong, Tsuei-chu; 1 *s.,* 1 *d.; educ.* Ph.D., Brown U., USA 65; Res. Assc., U. of Illinois 65-66, Asst. Prof. 66-70, Assc. Prof. 70-74, Prof. 74-90; Visiting Scientist, Max Plank Inst. for Aeronomy, Germany 74 & 77; Chair Prof., Dept. of EE, NTU 81, & Nat. Cent. U. 89-90; Sc. Sec., Sc. Coun. on Solar-terrestrial Phys. 81-94. *Publ.: A Model for Spaced Antenna Observational Mode for MST Radars; Spatial Interferometer Measurements with the Chungli VHF Radars; Add.* Nat. Cent. U., Chungli, Taoyuan County.

LIU, CHAO-HSUAN

(See LIU, CHAO-SHIUAN 劉兆玄)

LIU, CHAO-SHIUAN 劉兆玄

Chmn., NSC 96-; Prof., NTHU 75-; *b.* Hunan May 10, '43; *m.* Chien, Ming-sai; 3 *c.; educ.* BS, NTU; Ph.D., U. of Toronto; Assc. Prof., NTHU 71-75; Dir., Div. of Planning & Evaluation, NScC 79-82; Dean, Coll. of Sc., NTHU 82-84; V. Chmn., NScC 84-87; Pres., NTHU 87-93; Min. of Trans. & Comms., & concur. Min. of State 93-96. *Publ.: Jour. Am. Chem. Soc.,* 108, 3231 (1986); & 50 papers on inorganic & organometallic chem.; *Add.* 106 Ho Ping E. Rd., Sect. 2, Taipei.

LIU, CHEN 劉真

Nat. Policy Adv. to the Pres. 91-; Pres., Dr. Sun Yat-sen Cul. Found. 91-; V. Pres., Nat. Cult. Ass. 95-; Dir., Steering Cttee. of Humanistic & Soc. Sc. Educ., MOE 87-; Dir., Dictionary Compilation Cttee., Nat. Inst. for Compilation & Transl. 91-; Pres., Inst. of Ch. Lang. & Lit. 81-; Chmn., Presidium, CAC, KMT 93-; *b.* Anhwei Oct. 17, '13; *m.* Shih, Yu-ching; 2 *s.,* 1 *d.; educ.* Grad., Anhwei U.; Studied at Tokyo Normal Coll. & U. of Penn.; Prof., Nat. Hopei Normal Coll. 41-44; Mem., Legis. Yuan 48-53; Pres., Twn. Prov. Normal U. 49-51 & NTNU 55-57; Comr., Dept. of Educ., TPG 57-63; Dir., Grad. Sch. of Educ., NCU 63-73; Mem., Nat. Dev. Planning Group & concur. Dir., Cul. Group, NSC 57-91; Standing Mem., Coun. of Acad. Review & Evaluation, MOE 61-89. *Publ.: Educ. Admin.; Res. on European & Am. Educ.; Religion & Educ.; The Future of Ch. Cul.; Educ. & Dedication;* etc.; *Add.* 11 Foochow St., Taipei.

LIU, CHIN-PIAO
(See LIU, KING 劉金標)

LIU, CHING-TIEN
(See LIOU, CHING-TIEN 劉清田)

LIU, EDMUND Y. 劉瑛
Rep., Cml. Off. of the ROC (Twn.), Amman, Jordon 94-; *b.* Dec. 28, '29; *m.* Hu, Marianne; 1 *s.,* 1 *d.; educ.* BA, NTU 53; MA, U. of S. Africa 68; Staff Mem., MOFA 57-60; 3rd Sec., Emb. in Mauritania 61-62; V. Consul & Consul, Consl. Gen., Johannesburg, S. Africa 63-68; Sect. Chief, MOFA 69-71; 1st Sec., Emb. in Botswana 72-74; Dep. Dir., Dept. of W. Asian Aff., MOFA 74-76; Counsl., Emb. in S. Africa & Nicaragua 77-78; Counsl. & Chargé d'Affairs, Emb. in Honduras 79; Rep., Far E. Cml. Off., Amman, Jordan 80-85; Dir., Dept. of W. Asian Aff., MOFA 86-89; Rep., Taipei Econ. & Trade Off., Thailand 90-94. *Publ.: A Study of Ch. Classic Novels* (Co-author); *A Study of Short Stories of Tang Dynasty; Add.* Cml. Off. of the ROC, P.O. Box 2023, Jabal Amman 11181, Jordan.

LIU, EN-TI
(See LIU, ENTI 劉恩第)

LIU, ENTI 劉恩第
Amb. to Kingdom of Swaziland 92-; *b.* Liaoning June 3, '27; *m.* Chang, Linda; 2 *s.; educ.* BA, NTU 52; Inst. of Intl. Rel., U. of George Washington, D.C. 61; 3rd Sec., Emb. in USA 58-62; Sp., MOFA 63-66; 1st Sec., Emb. in Spain 66-71; Sect. Chief, MOFA 72-74; Consul in Guam, USA 75-79; Dep. Dept. Dir., MOFA 79-80; Acting Dir., Chamber of Com., Indonesia 81; Dir.-Gen., TECO, Houston 82-85; Dept. Dir., MOFA 85-89; Dir.-Gen., TECO, San Francisco 89-92; *Add.* Emb. of the ROC, P.O. Box 56, Mbabane, Swaziland.

LIU, FENG-HSUEH
(See LIU, FENG-SHUEH 劉鳳學)

LIU, FENG-SHUEH 劉鳳學
Artistic Dir., Neo-Classic Dance Co. 76-; *b.* Nunkiang June 19, '25; *m.* Chi, Pei-lin; *educ.* Ed.B., Nat. Changpai Tchrs. Coll. 49; Ph.D., Laban Cent. for Movement & Dance, U. of Goldsmith's Coll., London, UK 87; Studied

at Tokyo U. of Educ. 66-67, & Volkwang Hochschule, Essen, Germany 71-72; Teaching Asst., Nat. Changpai Tchrs. Coll. 49-50; Twn. Prov. Taichung Tchrs. Coll. 50-53; Lectr., Assc. Prof. & Prof., NTNU 54-85; Prof. & Dir., Dance Dept., Nat. Twn. Acad. of Arts 85-88; Dir., Mng. & Planning Coun., Nat. Theater & Concert Hall 88-90; *Dance Works: Nilpotent;* other 106 pieces. *Publ.: Educ. Dance; Introduction of Dance; Study of Ethic Dance-Mankind Dance; Add.* 2nd Fl., 25 Alley 4, Lane 118, Ho Ping E. Rd., Sect. 2, Taipei.

LIU, HO-CHIEN 劉和謙
Chief of the Gen. Staff, MND 92-; *b.* Anhwei Sept. 28, '26; *m.* Liu Ku, Wei-ping; 2 *c.; educ.* Ch. Naval Acad. 47; Naval CGSC 58; Armed Forces U. 72; Amphibious Warfare Course, USN 53, P.G. Sch. 61, Naval War Coll. 69; Shipbuilding Duties & Staff Assignments 47-70; Dep. Cmdr., Destroyer & Patrol Squadron, Cmdr., Service Squadron, Chief, Bu. of Op., & Dep. C/S, ROCN Hqs. 70-75; Dep. Chief, Gen. Staff for Planning, MND 75-78; Cmdr., Fleet Cmd., ROCN 78-80, Dep. C-in-C 80-83, C-in-C 83-88; Dir., Joint Op. Tng. Dept., MND 88-89; Strategy Adv. to the Pres. 89-92; *Add.* P.O. Box 90011, Taipei.

LIU, HSIANG-CHUAN 劉湘川
Pres., Nat. Taichung Tchrs. Coll. 94-; *b.* Szechwan Apr. 6, '41; *m.* Pan, Fei; 1 *s.,* 1 *d.; educ.* BS, Math., NTNU 66; MS, Experimental Statistics, NTU 82, D.Sc. 87; Tchr., Taichung Tchrs. Coll. 66-70, Taichung 1st High Sch. 70-73; Lectr., Assc. Prof., Prof., Prov. Tchrs. Jr. Coll. of Taichung 73-94; Prof., Dept. of Math. & Sc., Nat. Taichung Tchrs. Coll. 87-94, Chmn. 87-90, Acting Dean of Acad. Aff. 90-91, Dean 91-93, Dean & concur. Acting Pres. 93-94. *Publ.: Optical Feasible High Degree Polynomial STEIN-RULE Estimators for Gaussian Linear Models; A Study on Ridge Regression Analysis & Selecting of Variables; A Study on Magic Squares; Add.* 140 Min Sheng Rd., Taichung.

LIU, HSIANG-PU 劉祥璞
Amb. to the Cent. African Repub. 94-; *b.* Shantung June 6, '41; *m.* Wen, Ruoh-guey; 1 *s.,* 1 *d.; educ.* BPS, NTU65; MA, Ch. Cul. U. 67; Staff Mem., Dept. of E. Asia & Pacific Aff., MOFA 72-75; 3rd, 2nd, & 1st Sec., Sun Yat-sen Cul. Cent. in Beligium 75-82; Sect. Chief,

Dept. of European Aff., MOFA 82-86, Sr. Sp. 84-86, Dep. Dir. 86-88; Dir., Taipei Trade Cent. in Norway 88-90; Rep., Sp. Del. of the ROC to the Repub. of Madagascar; *Add.* B.P. 1058, Bangui, Republique Centrafricaine.

LIU, HSIEN-TA
(See LIU, SHAN-DA 劉顯達)

LIU, HSIN-SUN 劉興善
Comr., Exam. Yuan 96-; Prof., NCU 78-; *b.* Twn. May 6, '49; *m.* Liu Wong, May; 2 *d.; educ.* LL.B. NTU 71; M.C.L., U. of Virgina 75, S.J.D. 77; Mem., Legis. Yuan 84-93; *Add.* 3rd Fl., 9 Alley 32, Chia Hsin St., Wenshan, Taipei.

LIU, HSING-SHAN
(See LIU, HSIN-SUN 劉興善)

LIU, KING 劉金標
Chmn., Giant Mfg. Co. 72-; Giant Sales Co. 81-; Standing Bd. Mem., Twn. Trans. Vehicle Manufacturers' Assn. 84-; Chmn., Twn. Bicycle Exporters' Assn. 92-; *b.* Twn. July 2, '34; *m.* Liu Wang, Liu-hsia; 1 *s.,* 3 *d.; educ.* Grad., Taichung Jr. Coll. of Ind.; *Add.* 19 Shun Fan Rd., Tachia, Taichung County.

LIU, KUANG-CHING
(See LIU, KWANG-CHING 劉廣京)

LIU, KWANG-CHING 劉廣京
Mem., Acad. Sinica 76-; Prof. of Hist., U. of Calif., Davis 65-; Visiting Chair Prof., NTU 94-95; *b.* Peking Nov. 14, '21; *m.* Warren, Edith; 1 *s.,* 1 *d.; educ.* BA, Harvard U. 45, MA 47, Ph.D. 55; Teaching Fel., Regional Studies, Harvard U. 47-48; Ch. Translator, UN Secretariat 48-56; Res. Fel. in Ch. Econ. Studies, Harvard U. 55-57, Instr. in Hist. 57-60, Res. Fel. in E. Asian Studies 60-62; Visiting Assc. Prof. of Hist., Yale U. 62-63; Assc. Prof. of Hist., U. of Calif., Davis 63-65; Visiting Prof. of Hist., Harvard U. 68-69; Visiting Chair Prof. NTU 93. *Publ.: Orthodoxy in Late Imperial Ch.* 90; *Statecraft & the Rise of Ent.* 90; *Am. & Ch.: A Hist. Essay & a Bibliography* 63; *Anglo-Am. Steamship Rivalry in Ch., 1862-1874* 62; Co-ed., *The Cambridge Hist. of Ch.* (Vol. 11, Late Ch'ing, 1800-1911) 80; *Add.* Dept. of Hist., U. of Calif., Davis, CA 95616, USA.

LIU, PING-WEI 劉炳偉
Spkr., TPA 94-; Mem., CSC, KMT 95-; *b.* Twn. Nov. 30, '52; *m.* Hsieh, Wen-jou; 1 *s.,* 2 *d.; educ.* Grad., Hsingwu Jr. Coll. of Com.; Chmn., Panchiao CCoun.; Mem., TPA 81-91; Dep. Spkr., TPA 91-94; *Add.* 734 Chung Cheng Rd., Wufeng Hsiang, Taichung County.

LIU, S-LAIN 劉思量
Pres., Nat. Inst. of the Arts 94-, Prof. 90-; *b.* Yunnan Oct. 1, '47; *m.* Sun, Chang-cherng; 1 *s.; educ.* Ed.B., NCU 71, Ed.M. 73; Ph.D., Educ. Psychology, U. of Wisconsin-Madison 81; MA, Fine Arts Dept., We. Michigan U. 82; Lectr., Fu Jen Catholic U. 75-78; Asst. Prof., Nat. Inst. of the Arts 83-90, Dir., Extracurricular Activities Div. 82-83, Dir., Dept. of Fine Arts 83-88, Dean of Students Aff. 90-93. *Publ.: Identification of Gifted & Talented Students in Visual & Performing Arts* 86; *Art Psychology* 89; *Add.* 1 Hsueh Yuan Rd., Peitou, Taipei.

LIU, SAI-YUN
(See LIU, RENEE SAI-YUN 劉塞雲)

LIU, SHAN-DA 劉顯達
Pres., Nat. Pingtung Polytechnic Inst. 93-; *b.* Twn. Oct. 10, '47; *m.* Chen, Hsiang-yin; 2 *s.; educ.* BS, Dept. of Plant Pathology, NCHU 70, MS 73; Ph.D., Plant Pathology, Colorado State U. 79; Assc. Prof. & Sec., Nat. Pingtung Inst. of Agr. 79-84, Prof. 83-93, Dean of Acad. Aff. 83-85, Head., Dept. of Plant Protection 84-90, Dir., Tech. Cooperation Dept. 91-93; Chmn., The Ch. Plant Pathology Soc. 94-96. *Publ.:* "Integrated Control of Chrysanthemum Stem Rot," *Plant Protection Bulletin* (Co-author) 90, "Biolological Control of Adzuki-bean Root Rot Diseases Caused by Rhizoctonia solani" 91; & over 40 res. papers; *Add.* 1 Hseuh Fu Rd., Neipu, Pingtung County.

LIU, SHUEI-SHEN 劉水深
Pres., Da Yeh Inst. of Tech. 90-; *b.* Twn. Feb. 15, '42; *m.* Huang, Hsiu-mei; 1 *s.,* 2 *d.; educ.* BS, NCKU 67; MBA, NCU 70; Ph.D., N.We. U., USA 75; Lectr., NCU 70-71, Assc. Prof. 74-79, Prof. 79-89, Dean 79-86; Dean, NCKU 89-90. *Publ.: Op. Mng.—A Systematic Approach; Product Mng.; Add.* 112 Shan Chiao Rd., Tatsun Hsiang, Changhua County.

LIU, SHUI-SHEN
(See LIU, SHUEI-SHEN 劉水深)

LIU, SUNG-FAN
(See LIU, SUNG-PAN 劉松藩)

LIU, SUNG-PAN 劉松藩
Pres., Legis. Yuan 92-; Mem., CSC, KMT 93-; Hon. Chmn., ROC-German Inter-Parliamentary Amity Assn. 92-, & ROC-Japan Inter-Parliamentary Amity Assn. 91-; Chmn., ROC-USA Inter-Parliamentary Amity Assn. 88-; *b.* Twn. Dec. 3, '31; *m.* Liu Tsai, Yun-chin; 2 *s.,* 1 *d.; educ.* Twn. Prov. Taichung Inst. of Com.; Grad., Kinki U.; Convener, Econ. Cttee., Legis. Yuan 74, 77, 81, 83 & 86; Chmn., Ch. Martial Arts Fed. of ROC 77-81 & Taichung Harbor Dev. Com. 80-90; Dep. Sec.-Gen., Policy Coordination Cttee., CC, KMT 88-89, Dir.-Gen., Secretariat 89-90; V. Pres., Legis. Yuan 90-92; *Add.* 1 Chung Shan S. Rd., Taipei.

LIU, SZU-LIANG
(See LIU, S-LAIN 劉思量)

LIU, TA-JEN 劉達人
Chmn., CCNAA 94-; *b.* Shanghai Dec. 24, '19; *m.* Liu, Eve Y.F.; 2 *s.; educ.* BA, Nat. Cent. U.; MA, New York U.; Ph.D., Santo Tomas U., Philippines; Counsl., Emb. in Italy 66-67; Counsl. & Consul-Gen., Emb. in the Philippines 67-69; Dir., Dept. of Gen. Aff., MOFA 69-72; Amb. to Lesotho 72-80; Dir., Inf. Dept., MOFA 80-83; Dir.-Gen., TECO, Los Angeles 83-88; Rep., TECO in the Philippines 88-92, & TECO in Greece 92-94. *Publ.: Australia & Ch.; Ryukyu Islands; A Hist. of Sino-Am. Official Rel., 1840-1990; Add.* CCNAA, 133 Po Ai Rd., Taipei.

LIU, TAI-PING 劉太平
Mem., Acad. Sinica; Prof., Math., Stanford U. 90-; *b.* Twn. Nov. 18, '45; *m.* Liu, Leslie Y.; 2 *s.; educ.* BS, NTU 68; MS, Oregon State U. 70; Ph.D., U. of Michigan 73; Asst. Prof., U. of Maryland 73-78, Prof. 78-88; Prof., New York U. 88-90. *Publ.:* Math. papers on shock wave theory; *Add.* Dept. of Math., Stanford U., Stanford, CA 94305, USA.

LIU, TAI-YING 劉泰英
Chmn. & CEO, Ch., Dev. Corp. 94-; Chmn., Business Mng. Cttee., KMT 94-; Pres., Twn. Res. Inst. 94-;

Consultant, CEPD & MOEA; *b.* Twn. May 14, '36; *m.* Liu Yen, Anna; 2 *s.; educ.* BA, NTU 55-59; MA, U. of Rochester, New York 65-67; Ph.D., Cornell U. 67-71; Sp., CEPD 62-65; Dir., 3rd Div., Tax Reform Com. 68-70; Dep. Dir.-Gen., Dept. of Customs, MOF 72-76; Dean of Business Sch., Tamkang U. 80-83; Sec.-Gen., Ch. Mem. Cttee. of PBEC in Taipei 84-91; Sec.-Gen. & Mem., Ind. Dev. Adv. Coun., MOEA 85-93; Dep. Dir., Twn. Inst. of Econ. Res. 76-82, Dir 82-89, Pres. 89-93. *Publ.: Econ. Problems Should Be Solved by Econ. Measures; Principles of Econ.; Trade Relationship Between Twn., ROC & Japan—An Interregional Input-Output Analysis; Add.* 15th Fl., 125 Nanking E. Rd., Sect. 5, Taipei.

LIU, TIEH-CHENG 劉鐵錚
Grand Justice, Jud. Yuan; *b.* Chungking Sept. 8, '38; *m.* Chiu, Helen S.I.; 1 *s.,* 1 *d.; educ.* LL.B., NCU; MCL, So. Methodist U., USA; J.D., U. of Utah; Assc. Prof., NCU 71-74, Prof. 74-85, Head, Dept. of Law 77-83, Dean, Grad. Sch. of Law 81-85. *Publ.: Selected Essays on the Conflict of Laws; Add.* 124 Chungking S. Rd., Sect. 1, Taipei.

LIU, TSUI-JUNG 劉翠溶
Res. Fel., Acad. Sinica 79-; Prof., NTU 80-; *b.* Twn. Dec. 5, '41; *educ.* BA, NTU 63, MA 66; MA, Harvard U. 70, Ph.D., 74; Assc. Res. Fel., Acad. Sinica 74-78; Postdoctoral Fel., U. of Penn. 76-77; Part-time Prof., NTNU 79-80; Fulbright Fel., Prof. in Georgetown U. 84; Visiting Prof., UCLA 89. *Publ.:* 48 papers; *Add.* Inst. of Econ., Acad. Sinica, Taipei.

LIU, TSUN-I
(See LAU, LAWRENCE J. 劉遵義)

LIU, VICTOR W. 劉維琪
Pres., Nat. Sun Yat-sen U. 96-; *b.* Ch. Nov. 17, '52; *m.* Fang, Grace F.; 1 *s.,* 1 *d.; educ.* BBA, NCKU 74; MBA, N.We. U. 78, Ph.D. 82; Assc. Prof., Prof., Dept. Head, & Dir., Nat. Sun Yat-sen U. 82-90, Dean of Mng. Sch. 90-91; Dir., Dept. of Higher Educ., MOE 91-92; Pres., Cent. Investment Holding Co. Ltd. 93-96. *Public Utility Pricing with Asymmetric Info.; The Determination of the Dev. Priority of Sc. & Tech.; Case Studies in Financial Mng.; Add.* Nat. Sun Yat-sen U., 70 Lien Hai Rd., Kaohsiung.

LIU, WAN-HANG
(See LIU, WANN-HONG 劉萬航)

LIU, WANN-HONG 劉萬航
V. Chmn., CCA 85-; *b.* Chungking June 1, '39; *m.* Liu
Tung, Chia-li; 3 *c.; educ.* BA, NCHU; M. of Fine Arts,
So. Illinois U.; Assc. Res. Fel., Nat. Palace Museum 71-
75, Res. Fel. 75-81, Res. Fel. & Curator of Conservation
Dept. 81-85. *Publ.: Res. on the Mfr. of Bronze Art
Objects (Casting Tech.); A Study on the Ind. Mfr. of
Jewelry; Casting Reproductions of Ch. Bronze Vessels
by the Lost-Wax Process; A Study of Mfr. of Nonferrous
Metal Art Objects by Forging & Raising Method; Add.*
102 Ai-Kuo E. Rd., Taipei.

LIU, WEI-CHI
(See LIU, VICTOR W. 劉維琪)

LIU, YING
(See LIU, EDMUND Y. 劉瑛)

LIU, YUAN-CHUN
(See LIU, YUAN-TSUN 劉源俊)

LIU, YUAN-TSUN 劉源俊
Pre., Soochow U. 96-; Bd. Chmn., Assn. for Skill Dev.
of the Handicapped 93-; Bd. Chmn., Sc. Monthly Soc.
95-; *b.* Kunming Feb. 5, '45; *m.* Fwu, B.L.; 1 *s.,* 1 *d.;
educ.*BS, NTU 66; Ph.D. in Phys., Columbia U. 72;
Assc. Prof., Phys. Dept., Soochow U. 72-96, Dept. Head
74-83, Dean, Sch. of Sc. 77-83, Dean of Acad. Aff. 83-
87; V. Pres., Coll. Entrance Exam. Cent. 90-93. *Publ.:*
Effective Energy Forumlation for the Random Impurity
System, *Annals of Phys.* 73; *Collected Articles on Educ.;
Collected Articles on Sc.; Add.* Pres.'s Off., Soochow U.,
Shihlin, Taipei.

LO, BENJAMIN J.Y. 羅致遠
Dir.-Gen., TECO in San Francisco 94-; *b.* Hupei Mar. 23,
'40; *m.* Lo Wang, Yun-tsun; 1 *s.,* 1 *d.; educ.* BA, Dip.,
NCU, MA, Intl. Law & Dip.; MA, Intl. Rel., U. of Santo
Tomas, Philippines; Staff Mem., Dept. of Intl. Org.,
MOFA 64-66; 3rd Sec. & 2nd Sec., Emb. in the Philip-
pines 66-70 & 70; Dir., ROC Off. in Hong Kong 70-74;
Dir. Attaché, Dept. of Inf. & Cul. Aff., MOFA 74-76,
Sect. Chief 76-78; Dir., Secretariat, Taipei Econ. &

Trade Off. in Thailand 78-88; Dep. Rep., Taipei Econ. &
Trade Off. in Indonesia 88-91; Dir., Dept. of W. Asian
Aff., MOFA 91-94; *Add.* Suite 501, 555 Montgomery
St., San Francisco, CA 94111, USA.

LO, CHENG-TIEN 羅成典
Dep. Sec.-Gen., Legis. Yuan 92-; *b.* Twn. Nov. 4, '40; *m.*
Lo Lu, Shu; 2 *s.,* 3 *d.; educ.* LL.B., NCU 65, LL.M. 69;
Sp., Organic Laws Cttee., Legis. Yuan 70-87, Sec. 75-
90, Chief Sec., Secretariat 90-92. *Publ.: Res. on Urban
Population of Twn. & the Utilization of Urban Land;
Tech. on Legislation; The Standard Laws for Cent.
Regln.; Add.* 1st Fl., 11 Alley 19, Lane 160, Min Chuan
E. Rd., Sect. 3, Taipei.

LO, CHI-TANG
(See LO, JAMES C.T. 羅際棠)

LO, CHIH-YUAN
(See LO, BENJAMIN J.Y. 羅致遠)

LO, HAO
(See LOH, HORACE H. 羅浩)

LO, I-CHIANG
(See LO, YIH-CHIANG 羅益強)

LO, JAMES C.T. 羅際棠
Chmn., Bk. of Twn. 95-; *b.* Twn. Apr. 20, '30; *m.* Cheng,
Kin-lan; 3 *d.; educ.* BA, Econ., NTU; Studied at Wash-
ington State U.; Clerk & Sect. Chief, Hua Nan Cml. Bk.
54-67, Asst. V. Pres. 67-71, V. Pres. 71-73, Sr. V. Pres.
& Gen. Mgr. 73-80, Exec. V. Pres. 80-85; Pres., Taipei
City Bk. 85-88 & Hua Nan Cml. Bk. 88-91; Chmn., Twn.
Cooperative Bk. 91-94; Chmn., Hua Nan Cml. Bk. 94-
95; *Add.* 120 Chungking S. Rd., Sect. 1, Taipei.

LO, KOON-TSAN 羅坤燦
Acting Sec.-Gen., Ass. of E. Asian Rel. 96-; *b.* Twn. Apr.
11, '50; *m.* Wu, Chia-hwe; 1 *s.,* 1 *d.; educ.* MA, Meiji U.;
Sect. Chief, MOFA 92-94, Sr. Sp. 95; Dep. Sec.-Gen.,
Assn. of E. Asian Rel. 95; *Add.* 4th Fl., Yu-ming Man-
sion, 7 Roosevelt Rd., Sect. 1, Taipei.

LO, KUN-TSAN
(See LO, KOON-TSAN 羅坤燦)

LO, LOON 羅龍
Rep., Rep. Off. in Moscow for the Taipei-Moscow Econ. & Cul. Coordination Com. 93-; *b.* Kiangsu July 14, '28; *m.* Lo, Jane Shu-chen; 1 *s.*, 1 *d.; educ.* BA, NTU 52; LL.M., Grad. Sch. of Dip., NCU 56; Mem., Treaty Dept., MOFA 56-59, Asst. to the Admin. V. Min. of For. Aff. 59-60; 3rd, 2nd & 1st Sec., Permanent Mission of the ROC to the UN 60-71; Counsl., Emb. in the Philippines 72-75; Dep. Dir., Dept. of European Aff. & Protocol Dept., MOFA 75-77; Dir., Trade Mission of the ROC to Bahrain 77-80; Min. & concur. Counsl., Emb. in Saudi Arabia 80-81; Dir., Inst. of Ch. Cul., Vienna, Austria 81-86; Dep. Rep., TECRO, USA 86-89; Rep., Inst. of Ch. Cul., Austria 89-93; *Add.* 24/2 Tverskaya St., Korpus 1, Gate 4, 3rd Fl., Moscow 103050, Russian Federation.

LO, LUNG
(See LO, LOON 羅龍)

LO, MING-YUAN 羅明元
Rep., Trade Mission of the ROC in Nigeria 91-; *b.* Shanghai Feb. 5, '22; *m.* Wang, Chien-chih; *educ.* BA, Malaysian U. 49; Sp. & Sect. Chief, MOFA 43-53; Consul, Consl. Gen., Johannesburg, S. Africa 53-55; Consul, Consl. in Dili, Timor 57-59; Rep. in Hong Kong 59-64; Tech. Counsl., UN Mission 64-66; Consul-Gen., Consl. Gen., Johannesburg 66-71; Amb. to Swaziland 68-73; Consul-Gen. in Los Angeles 73-74; *Add.* P.O. Box 80035, Victoria Island, Lagos, Nigeria.

LO, PEN-LI 羅本立
Chief of the Gen. Staff, MND 95-; Gen., ROC Army; *b.* Anhwei Feb. 11, '27; *m.* Lo Chang, Tzu-hsia; 2 *s.*, 1 *d.; educ.* 49th Class, Mil. Acad.; Advanced Class, Infantry Sch. 59; Army CGSC 64; War Coll., Armed Forces U. 79; Div. Cmdr. 74-77; Corps Cmdr. 79-80; Dean, Army CGSC, Armed Forces U. 80-83; Field Army Cmdr. 83-86; Pres., Armed Forces U. 87-89; C-in-C, CSF 89-93; V. Chief of the Gen. Staff & Exec. Off., MND 93-95. *Add.* P.O. Box 90011, Taipei.

LO, TUNG-BIN 羅銅壁
Mem., Acad. Sinica 86-, V. Pres. 93-; Pres., Coll. Entrance Exam. Cent. 93-; *b.* Twn. Feb. 15, '27; *m.* Lo Wu, Su-shia; 3 *s.; educ.* BS, NTU; D.Sc., Tohoku Imprial U.; Assc. Fel., UC-Berkly. 59-61; Visiting Prof., U. of

Calif., San Francisco 68-69; Dir., Grad. Inst. of Biochem. Sc., NTU 72-78, & Inst. of Biological Chem., Acad. Sinica 72-80; Dean, Coll. of Sc., NTU 78-84, Dean of Acad. Aff. 84-90; Prof. of Biochemistry, NTU 64-95. *Publ.:* 110 sc. papers on snake venom & pituitary hormone; *Add.* 1 Roosevelt Rd., Sect. 4, Taipei.

LO, TUNG-PI
(See LO, TUNG-BIN 羅銅壁)

LO, WEN-FU 羅文富
Mem., Control Yuan 87-; *b.* Twn. Sept. 1, '28; *m.* Lo, Cheng-shen; 2 *s.*, 3 *d.; educ.* 21st Class, Police Acad.; Bd. Chmn., Hui-hung Trans. Co. & Tien-mou Amusement Co.; Mem., Taipei CCoun.; *Add.* 20 Lane 44, Yang Te Avenue, Sect. 3, Taipei.

LO, YIH-CHIANG 羅益強
Pres. & CEO, Philips (Twn.) & Philips Components A.P. B.V. 88- & 91-; *b.* Chekiang Aug. 27, '39; *m.* Liu, Hsiao-ru; 1 *s.*, 2 *d.; educ.* BS, Phys., NCKU 63; Studied in Exec. Mng. Course at Harvard U.'s Business Sch. 85; IC Engr., Philips Elect. Bldg. Elements Ind. (Twn.) Ltd.—IC 69-72, Factory Mgr. 72-78, Gen. Mgr. 78-85; Exec. V. Pres., Philips Twn. 85-88; *Add.* 30th Fl., 66 Chung Hsiao W. Rd., Sect. 1, Taipei.

LOH, HORACE H. 羅浩
Mem., Acad. Sinica 86-; Frederick & Alice Stark Prof. & Chmn., Dept. of Pharmacology, U. of Minnesota; Prof., Med. Cent., U. of Calif.; *b.* Kwangtung May 28, '37; *m.* Loh, Dana; 1 *s.*, 1 *d.; educ.* BS, NTU 58; Ph.D., U. of Iowa 65. *Publ.:* About 350 res. papers on pharmacology; *Add.* Dept. of Pharmacology, 3-249 Millard, U. of Minnesota, 435 Delaware St., S.E., Minneapolis, MN 55455, USA.

LOH, I-CHENG 陸以正
Amb. to S. Africa 90-; *b.* Kiangsu Aug. 29, '24; *m.* Yeh, Jane; 2 *s.*, 1 *d.; educ.* BA, NCU; MS, Columbia U.; With UN Forces in S. Korea 51-53; City Ed., *Ch. News* 53-54; Asst. Mng. Ed., *Ch. Daily News* 55-56; Dir., Intl. Info. Service Dept., GIO 56-63; Min. & Counsl. for Info., Emb. in USA & concur. Dir., Ch. Info. Service, New York 63-78; Pres. & Dir., Inst. of Ch. Cul., Vienna,

Austria 79-81; Amb. to Guatemala 81-90; *Add.* Emb. of the ROC, 1147 Schoeman St., Hatfield, Pretoria 0083, Repub. of S. Africa.

LOH, JEN-KONG 陸潤康
Chmn. & Chief Exec. Off., Dah An Cml. Bk. 91-; Chmn., Rule of Law Dev. Found. 94-; Mem., CC, KMT 93-; *b.* Kiangsu June 19, '27; *m.* Loh Lin, De-yun; 2 *s.; educ.* LL.B., Soochow U. 56; MCL, So. Methodist U., USA 59; Comr., Nat. Tax Admin. of Taipei, MOF 74-78, Dir.-Gen., Dept. of Customs 78-80; Pres., CTC 80-81; Pol. V. Min. of Finance 81-84; Min. of Finance 84-85; Mng. Dir., CBC 84-85; Mem., CEPD 84-85; Mng. Partner, Alliance Intl. Law Off. 87-91. *Publ.: The Const. of the USA* (in Ch.); *Credit & Sec. in the ROC* 74 (in Eng.); *Add.* 3rd Fl., 117 Min Sheng E. Rd., Sect. 3, Taipei.

LU, ALEXANDER YA-LI 呂亞力
Prof., Pol. Sc., NTU 77-; Mem., Cent. Election Com.; *b.* Chekiang Sept. 18, '35; *m.* Tso, Ding-wen Cindy; 2 *s.; educ.* BA, NTU 57; MA, Indiana U. 63, Ph.D. 71; Asst. Prof., Pol. Sc., Berry Coll., Georgia 67-71; Assc. Prof., NTU 71-76; Prof. & Dir., Inst. of Pol. Sc., Nat. Sun Yat-sen U. 93-95. *Publ.: An Introduction to Pol. Sc.; Pol. Sc. Methodology; Pol. Dev. & Dem.; Pol. Opposition in Twn.; The Future Dem. Dev. in the ROC; Pol. Modernization in the ROC; Pol. Dev. in the ROC; Pol. Dev. in the ROC; Add.* 2nd Fl., 11 Lane 60, Chou Shan Rd., Taipei.

LU, ANNETTE HSIU-LIEN 呂秀蓮
Magis., Taoyuan County 97-; Initiator, Cttee. for Twn.'s Participation in the UN 91-; *b.* Twn. June 7, '44; *educ.* LL.B., NTU 67; MA, U. of Illinois 71; LL.M., Harvard U. 77; Sect. Chief, Exec. Yuan 71-74; Mem., Legis. Yuan; Sr. Adv. to the Pres. 96-97; *Add.* 4th Fl.-1, 178 Ho Ping E. Rd., Sect. 1, Taipei.

LU, CHIN-KUEI 呂金貴
Sec.-Gen., Nat. Bar Assn. of the ROC 94-; *b.* Twn. Nov. 10, '35; *m.* You, Shiao-chin; 2 *s., educ.* LL.B., Martial Law Sch. 62; Martial Prosecutor, MND 62-67, Sup. 67-74; Attorney-at-Law 74-96; *Add.* 5th Fl., 11 Changsha St., Sect. 2, Taipei.

LU, HSIU-LIEN
(See LU, ANNETTEE HSIU-LIEN 呂秀蓮)

LU, I-CHENG
(See LOH, I-CHENG 陸以正)

LU, JUN-KANG
(See LOH, JEN-KONG 陸潤康)

LU, LIEN-SHENG 盧聯生
Founder, Horwath & Co., CPAs 83-; Chmn., Taipei CPA Assn.; *b.* Jan. 10, '49; *m.* Chen, Chun-yin; 3 *s.; educ.* BA, Fu Jen Catholic U. 76; MA, Soochow U. 78; Staff, Chiao Tung Bank 72-79; Staff, MOF 79-83; Certified Acct., Horwath & Co. 83-96; Instr., Fu Jen Catholic U. 78-96. *Publ.: Financial Statement Analysis; Add.* 7th Fl., 111 Chung Shan N. Rd., Sect. 2, Taipei.

LU, PAO-SUN 陸寶蓀
Rep., Taipei Econ. & Trade Off. in Indonesia 92-; *b.* Chekiang Dec. 8, '27; *m.* Lu Tsai, Shu-kun; 3 *s.; educ.* BS, Ch. Naval Coll. of Tech. 52; MS, N.We. U., USA 65, Ph.D. 69; Dep. Dir., Elect. Res. Div., Chung Shan Inst. of Sc. & Tech. 68-75, Dir., Planning Dept. 75-78, Dir., Elect. Res. Div. 78-84; Pres., Chung Cheng Inst. of Tech. 84-87; Rep., TECO in the Netherlands 88-92. *Publ.: Microwave Cavity Technique of Measuring High Conductivity Semi-Conductors; Cryogenical Diagnostics of Solid-State Plasma in Semiconducting Compounds; Add.* Wisma Dharmala Sakti, 7th Fl., J1. Jend. Sudirman No. 32, Jakarta 10220, Indonesia.

LU, PING-YEN 魯炳炎
Rep., Taipei Mission in Sweden 95-; *b.* Chekiang Jan. 21, '33; *m.* Helen S.C. Yin; 2 *d.; educ.* BA, Econ., NTU 59; Jr. staff, Coun. for US Aid 62-63; Sp., Coun. for Intl. Econ. Cooperation & Dev., Exec. Yuan 63-69; Sec., Trade Mission in Singapore, MOFA 69-77 & Ch. Investment & Trade Off. in USA at N.Y. 77-80; Dep. Dir. & Dir., Bd. of For. Trade, MOEA 69-71; Dep. Rep., Trade Mission in Singapore 82-86; Econ. Counsl., Emb. in Saudi Arabia 86-92; Dir., Dept. of Econ. & Trade Aff., MOEA 92-94; *Add.* Wenner-Gren Centre, Sveavagen 166, 18 tr, S-11346 Stockholm, Sweden.

LU, SHAO-CHIA 呂紹嘉
Chief Conductor, Komische Opera, Berlin 95-; *b.* Twn. Feb. 7, '60; *m.* Tu, Wen-chu; *educ.* B., Psychology, NTU 83; Studied at Indiana U. 85; M. in Conducting,

Hochschüle für Musik U. Darstellende Kunst 91; Assc. Conductor, Taipei Symphony Orchestra 86-87; Diploma di Merito, Acad. Musicale Chigiana in Siena, Italy 88; 1st Prize of "Concours Intl. de Jeunesse Chef d' Orchestre" in Besanáon, France 88; Würdigungspreis, Austrian Govt. 91; 1st Prize, "Concorso Internationale per Direttori d'Orchestra 'Antonio Pedrotti'" in Trento, Italy; 1st Prize, Kondrashin Intl. Conductor's Competition in Amster-dam, Holland 94; *Add.* Unter den Linden 39, D-10117, Berlin, Germany.

LU, YA-LI
(See LU, ALEXANDER YA-LI 呂亞力)

LU, YU-WEN 呂有文
V. Pres., Jud. Yuan 93-; *b.* Szechwan Dec., 11, '26; *m.* Wu, Yun-yi; 1 *s.,* 3 *d.; educ.* LL.B., Chaoyang U. 48; Judge, Kaohsiung Dist. Court 51-57; Presiding Judge, Tainan Br., Tainan High Court 57-63, & Taichung Br., Twn. High Court 63-65; Pres., Kinmen Dist. Court 65-67, & Taichung Dist. Court 67-70; Presiding Judge, Twn. High Court 70-73; Pres., Hsiamen Br., Fukien High Court 73-75, & Hualien Br., Twn. High Court 75-79; Chief Prosecutor, Taichung Br., Twn. High Court 79-80; Dir., 2nd Dept., Jud. Yuan 80-82, Dep. Sec.-Gen. 82-87; Pol. V. Min. of Justice 87-89; Min. of Justice 89-93. *Publ.: The Sp. Provisions of Criminal Law; Add.* 124 Chungking S. Rd., Sect. 1, Taipei.

LY, GABRIEL CHEN-YING 李振英
Pres., Fu Jen Catholic U. 92-, Prof. of Philosophy 63-; *b.* Tientsin Oct. 14, '29; *educ.* MA & M.Th., Urban U., Rome 52 & 56, Ph.D., Sacred Heart U., Milan 61; Sec.-Gen., Tainan Diocese 61-63; Prin., Tekuang Girls' High Sch. 63-67; Dir., Window Press, Tainan 67-70; Sec.-Gen., Ch. Catholic Bishops Conf. 75-78; Prof. of Philosophy, NCU 77-78; Dir., Cent. of Ch. Catholic Hist., Fu Jen Catholic U. 73-81, Chief Sec. 78-85, Dean of Acad. Aff. 85-88, Dir., Cross-Cul. Cent. 89-92. *Publ.: The Spiritual World of Eyodor Dostoevski; Basic Philosophy; Philosophical Res. of the Cosmos; Man & God* (4 Vol.); *Add.* 510 Chung Cheng Rd., Hsinchuang, Taipei County.

MA, AN-LAN 馬安瀾
Nat. Policy Adv. to the Pres.; *b.* Liaoning Apr. 27, '16; *m.* Wu, Fu-yin; 2 *s.,* 1 *d.; educ.* 10th Class, Mil. Acad.; 18th Class, Army War Coll.; 1st Class, Joint Op. Sch.; Sp., 1st Class, CGSC, US Army; 8th Class, Armed Forces Staff Coll.; Cmdr., 10th Infantry Div., ROC Army 56-59; Cmdr., 2nd Corps, & Dep. CG, Kinmen Def. Cmd. 60-65; Cmdr., 2nd Field Army, ROC Army 65-69; CG, Kinmen Def. Cmd. 69-72; Dep. C-in-C, ROC Army 72-75, C-in-C 75-78; Exec. V. Chief of the Gen. Staff, MND 78-81; Personal C/S to the Pres.; *Add.* c/o Off. of the Pres., Taipei.

MA, CHANG-SHENG 馬長生
Gen. Mgr., Twn. Broadcasting Co. Ltd. 78-; Pres., Nat. Joint Assn. of Private Radio Stations of the ROC 92-; *b.* Anhwei Jan. 21, '50; *m.* Kao, Yu; 2 *s.,* 1 *d.; educ.* BS in Agr., NCHU 71; MS, U. of Wisconsin 77; *Add.* 11th Fl., 17 Chungking S. Rd., Sect. 3, Taipei.

MA, CHI-CHUANG 馬紀壯
Sr. Adv. to the Pres. 90-; Chmn., AEAR 91-; *b.* Hopei Oct. 14, '12; *m.* Li, Liang-pi; 2 *d.; educ.* Ch. Naval Acad.; Studied in USA; Nat. War Coll.; Served successively as Squadron Cmdr., C/S, ROCN, C-in-C 52-54; Asst. CG, MND 54-55; V. Min. of Nat. Def. 55-59; C-in-C, CSF 59; Exec. V. Chief of the Gen. Staff, MND 59-65; V. Min. of Nat. Def. 65-72; Dep. Chmn., Nat. Gen. Mobilization Cttee., NSC 67-72; Amb. to Thailand 72-75; Chmn., Ch. Steel Corp. 75-78; Sec.-Gen., Exec. Yuan 78; Sec.-Gen. to the Pres. 78-84; Min. of State 84-86; Rep., Tokyo, Off., AEAR 86-90; *Add.* 2 Lane 1, Tai An St., Taipei.

MA, LI-SUI 馬履綏
Rep. in Papua New Guinea 96-; *b.* Shansi Jan. 25, '33; *m.* Chan, Sio-tim; 1 *s.; educ.* Ch. Naval Acad. 58; Amphibious Warfare Sch., USMC 66; Cmd. & Staff Coll., USMC 70; Armed Forces Ind. U., USA 73; War Coll., Armed Forces U. 77; Res. Inst. of Mil. Sc., Armed Forces U. 84; Dep. C/S, ROCN 83-84; Dir., 5th Div., MND; C/S, HQ, ROC Marine Corps 85-86, Asst. Cmdt. 88-92; Dep. C-in-C, Twn. Guard Cmd. & Armed Forces Reserve Cmd., MND 92-93; Dep. Dir.-Gen., Nat. Sec. Bu. 93-96; *Add.* P.O. Box 334, Port Moresby, Papua New Guinea.

MA, SHU-LI
(See MAH, SOO-LAY 馬樹禮)

MA, SHUI-LONG 馬水龍
Prof., Dept. of Music, Nat. Inst. of the Arts 95-; Composer; Chmn., ROC Nat. Cttee., Asian Composers' League; Chmn., ROC Composers' Assn.; Mem., Sc. & Tech. Adv. Off., MOE, Mem., Coun. of Acad. Reviewal & Evaluation; Mem., Bd. of Trustees of the Nat. Fund for Lit. & Art; Music Mem. & Trustee, CCA, USA 88-; *b.* Twn. July 17, '39; 2 *s.; educ.* Grad., Music Dept., Nat. Twn. Acad. of the Arts 64; Diploma, Regensburg Kirchenmusik Hochschule 75; Scholar, Fulbright Found., Columbia U., & U. of Penn. 86-87; Prof., Dept. of Music, Soochow U. 75-81; Prof. & Chmn., Music Dept., Nat. Twn. Acad. of the Arts 81-82; Prof. & Chmn., Dept. of Music, Nat. Inst. of the Arts 82-87, Dean of Acad. Aff. 87-91; Sec.-Gen., Asian Composers' League 84-86; Pres., Nat. Inst. of the Arts 91-94; Scholar & Resr., CCPD Found., USA 94-95. *Publ.: Counterpoint Theory; 12-Tone Composition Study; From the Ballet Liao T'ien-Ting to a Discussion of the Creation of Dance Music;* & over 40 works of orchestra, chamber, vocal, solo; etc.; *Add.* 5th Fl., 11 Lane 20, Ta Chih St., Taipei.

MA, SHUI-LUNG
(See MA, SHUI-LONG 馬水龍)

MA, SUN 馬遜
Pres., Huafan Coll. of Humanities & Tech. 95-; *b.* Hunan June 7, '47; *educ.* BS, NTU 70; Diplom Chemiker, RWTH Aachen, Germany 77, Dr. 80; Asst., RWTH, Aachen 77-80; Assc. Prof., NCKU 80-86, Prof. 86-95; Dir., Tainan Regional Inst. Cent. 88-93. *Publ.:* 50 papers; *Add.* 1 Hua Fan Rd., Shihting Hsiang, Taipei County.

MA, YING-CHIU
(See MA, YING-JEOU 馬英九)

MA, YING-JEOU 馬英九
Min. of State 96-; Assc. Prof. of Law, NCU; Mem., CC, KMT 93-; *b.* Hunan July 13, '50; *m.* Chou, Christine Mei-ching; 2 *d.; educ.* LL.B., NTU 72; LL.M., New York U. 76; S.J.D., Harvard U. Law Sch. 81; Consultant, Law Off., First Nat. Bk. of Boston, USA 80-81; Assc., Cole & Deitz Law Off., New York 81; Res. Consultant, U. of Maryland Law Sch. 81; Dep. Dir., 1st Bu., Off. of the Pres. 81-88; Dep. Sec.-Gen., CC, KMT 84-88; Sr. Sec., Off. of the Pres. 88; Chmn., RDEC 88-91; V.

Chmn., MAC 91-93, Mem. 88; Min. of Justice, & concur. Min. of State 93-96. *Publ.: Legal Problems of Seabed Boundary Delimitation in the E. Ch. Sea; Two Maj. Legal Issues Relating to the Intl. Status of the ROC; Taipei-Beijing Rel. & E. Asian Stability: Implications for Europe; Add.* 1 Chungsiao E. Rd., Sect. 1, Taipei.

MAH, SOO-LAY 馬樹禮
Sr. Adv. to the Pres. 90-; Chmn., Presidium of CAC, KMT 88-, & Ch. Reunification Alliance 88-; *b.* Kiangsu Aug. 3, '09; *m.* Wu, Wei-lin; *educ.* Meiji U. 30; BS, U. of Santo Tomas, Philippines 38; Hon. LL.D., Meiji U. 82; Hon. LHD, U. of Santo Tomas 88; Ed., *Minkuo Daily News,* Singapore 31-33, & *New Ch. Herald,* Manila 36-38; Ed.-in-Chief & Dir., *Front Daily News,* Anhwei-Kiangsu-Fukien-Shanghai 38-49; Mem., Legis. Yuan 48-89; Dir. & Ed.-in-Chief, *Ch. Cml. Daily News,* Jakarta 53-59; Adv. to Ch. Mission to 24th, 25th, & 26th UNGA 69-71; Chief, 3rd Dep., CC, KMT 62-72, Mem. 63-88; Prof., Nat. War Coll. 65-70; Rep., Tokyo Off., AEAR 72-85; Bd. Chmn., BCC 72-85; Sec.-Gen., CC, KMT 85-87, Convener, Sup. Panel for Mainland Op. 88-89; Chmn., CTV 87-90, & AEAR 90-91. *Publ.: Hist. of Indonesia's Independence; Indonesia in Turmoil; Dasar 2 Anti Komunis by Pres. Chiang Kai-shek* (Indonesian Transl.); *Add.* 11th Fl., 7 Lane 26, Yat Sen Rd., Taipei.

MAI, CHAO-CHENG 麥朝成
Mem., Acad. Sinica 94-; Res. Fel., Sun Yat-sen Inst., Acad. Sinica 79-; Prof., NTU 79; *b.* Twn. Feb. 26, '43; *m.* Lin, Su-chen; 1 *s.; educ.* BA, NTU 66, MA 70; MA, U. of Rochester 73; Ph.D., Texas A&M U., 76; Assc. Prof., NCU 76-79; Assc. Prof., NTU 77-80; Prof., NCU 79-81; Visiting Scholar, Harvard U. 81-82; Dir., Sun Yat-sen Inst., Acad. Sinica 87-93; Fulbright Visiting Scholar & Visiting Prof. of Alabama State U. 90-91. *Publ.* 107 papers; *Add.* 3rd Fl., 22 Alley 4, Lane 61, Yen Chiu Yuan Rd., Sect. 2, Nankang, Taipei.

MAI, CHUN-FU 麥春福
Sr. Adv. to the Pres. 96-; *b.* Twn. Feb. 9, '24; *m.* Lu, Su-o; 2 *s.,* 5 *d.; educ.* BA, Kinki U., Japan; V. Spkr., 7th, 8th, 9th Taipei CoCoun.; Chmn., Tamsui First Credit Cooperative Bk. 54-80; Chmn., the Credit Cooperative Bk. Union of the ROC 85-90; Comr., TPG 90-94; Sr. Adv. to the Premier 94-96; *Add.* 70 Po Ai St., Tamsui, Taipei County.

MAO, CHI-KUO 毛治國
Admin. V. Min. of Trans. & Comms. 93-; Cttee. Mem., Nat. Info. Infrastructure Project, Exec. Yuan 94-, & Nat. Space Prog. Steering Cttee. 93-; Comr., Regional Planning Com., MOI, & Investment Com. & Energy Com., MOEA 93-; Bd. Mem., Yangming Marine Trans. Corp. 93-; *b.* Chekiang Oct. 4, '48; *m.* Chien, Yin-yin; 1 *s.*, 1 *d.; educ.* BCE, NCKU 71; MS, Systems Engr., Asian Inst. of Tech., Bangkok 75; Ph.D., Trans. Mng., MIT 82; Engr., Ch. Engr. Consultants Inc. 73-74; Engr. & Div. Dir., Trans. Planning Bd., MOTC 76-78; Res. Asst., Cent. of Trans. Studies, MIT 78-82; Assc. Prof., Trans. & Mng. Dept., NCTU 82-84, Prof. & Dept. Head, Mng. Sc. Dept. 84-87; Chief Sec., MOTC 87-88, Dir.-Gen., Tourism Bu. 89-91, & Provisional Engr. Off. of High Speed Rail 91-93; Bd. Mem., Chung Kuo Property Ins. Corp. 93-94; Cttee. Mem., Task Force on the Liberalization of Service Ind., Econ. Planning & Evaluation Coun., Exec. Yuan 94-95. *Publ.:* 101 theses, reports, critiques, & essays; *Add.* Rm. 403, 2 Changsha St., Sect. 1, Taipei.

MAO, CHIH-KUO
(See MAO, CHI-KUO 毛治國)

MAO, HO-KWANG 毛河光
Mem., Acad. Sinica; Geophysicist, Geophysical Lab., Carnegie Inst. of Washington (CIW) 72-; Mem., Nat. Acad. of Sc., USA; For. Mem., Ch. Acad. of Sc., PRC; *b.* Shanghai June 18, '41; *m.* Mao Liu, Agnes; 3 *c.; educ.* BS, NTU 63; MS & D.Sc., U. of Rochester, New York 66 & 68; Assc. Resr., U. of Rochester 67-68; Postdoctoral Fel. & Assc. Resr., Geophysical Lab., CIW 68-70 & 70-72. *Publ.:* 380 papers on high pressure, phys., chem., & geol. in jour. & symposia; *Add.* 11322 Edenderry Drive, Fair Fox, VA 22030, USA.

MAO, KAO-WEN 毛高文
Amb. to Costa Rica 96-; Mem., CC, KMT 93-; *b.* Chekiang Feb. 9, '36; *m.* King, May-ling; 1 *d.; educ.* BS, NTU; MS, UC-Berkly.; Ph.D., Carnegie-Mellon U., USA; Res. Engr., Electrochemical Dept., Gen. Motors Res. Labs., USA 64-65; Project Engr., Chem. Engr. Dept., Carnegie-Mellon U. 65-69; Sr. Res. Engr., Electrochemical Dept., Gen. Motors Res. Labs. 69-74; Prof. & Dir., Inst. of Ind. Chem., NTHU 72-73, Prof. & Dean, Coll. of Engr. 74-78; Ed.-in-Chief, *Jour. of the Ch. Inst.*

of Engr. 78-82; Pres., Ch. Inst. of Ind. Engr. 81, Nat. Twn. Inst. of Tech. 78-81, & NTHU 81-87; Min. of Educ. 87-93; V. Pres., Exam. Yuan 93-96. *Publ.:* More than 20 papers on chem. engr. & electrochemical; *Add.* Apartado 907-1000, San Jose, Costa Rica.

MEI, CHIANG-CHUNG 梅強中
Mem., Acad. Sinica 94-; E.K. Turner Prof., Civil & Environmental Engr., MIT 93-; *b.* Ch. Apr. 4, '35; *m.* Kao, Caroline; 1 *d.; educ.* BE, NTU 55; ME, Stanford U. 57; DE, MIT 63; Postdoctoral Res., Calif. Inst. of Tech. 63-65, Asst. Prof. 65-68, Assc. Prof. 68-74, Prof. 74-93; Mem., U.S. Nat. Acad. of Engr. 86. *Publ.:* "Applied Dynamics of Ocean Surface Waves," *World Sc.; Math. Analysis in Engr.; Add.* Rm. 48-413, Ralph M. Parsons Lab., Dept. of Civil Engr., MIT, Cambridge, MA 02139, USA.

MEI, TSU-LIN 梅祖麟
Mem., Acad. Sinica 94-, Hu Shih Prof. of Ch. Lit. & Philology, Cornell U. 94-; *b.* Peking Feb. 14, '33; *m.* Yip, Teresa; 1 *s.*, 2 *d.; educ.* BA, Oberlien Coll. 54; MA, Harvard U. 55; Ph.D., Yale U. 62; Instr., Philosophy, Yale U. 62-64; Asst. Prof., Ch., Harvard U. 64-69, Assc. Prof. 69-71; Assoc. Prof., Ch. Lit., Cornell U. 71-79, Prof. 79-94, Chmn., Dept. of Asian Studies 72-77, Dir., Ch.-Japan Prog. 77-80. *Publ.:* Over 50 articles in *Harvard Jour. of Asian Studies, Bulletin of the Inst. of Hist. & Philology* & other jour.; *Add.* Dept. of Asian Studies, Rockefeller Hall, Cornell U., Ithaca, NY 14853, USA.

MING, CHEN-HUA
(See MING, CHUN-HWA 明鎮華)

MING, CHUN-HWA 明鎮華
V. Min., OCAC 90-; *b.* Kwangtung Sept. 27, '24; *m.* Ming Chen, Li-wen; 1 *s.*, 1 *d.; educ.* LL.B., Kwangtung U.; Sec.-Gen., Ovs. Ch. Assn.; Dep. Dir.-Gen., Dept. of Ovs. Aff., KMT; *Add.* 16th Fl., 5 Hsuchow St., Taipei.

MOU, TZUNG-TSAN
(See MU, PAUL TZUNG-TSANN 牟宗燦)

MU, PAUL TZUNG-TSANN 牟宗燦
Pres., Nat. Dong Hwa U. 94-; *b.* Shantung Oct. 13, '39; *m.* Mu, Corrina H.; 1 *s.*, 1 *d.; educ.* BA, Econ., NTU 60; MS, Econ., U. of Nevada 65; Ph.D., Econ., U. of Calif.,

Davis 70; Asst. Prof., Econ., Calif. State U., Los Angeles 69-72, Prof. 77-91, Assc. V. Pres., Acad. Aff. 86-88; Visiting Prof., Nat. Sun Yat-sen U. 80-81; Mem., Legis. Yuan 86-91; Dir., Preparatory Off., Nat. Dong Hwa U. 91-94. *Publ.:* "The False Promise of Protectionism," *Business Forum* 86; "Tax Reform & Policy Implication in Twn.," *We. Econ. Assn.* 89; *Income Taxes, Econ. Growth, & Quality-of-Life Mng.* 95; *Add.* Nat. Dong Hwa U., 1 Ta Hsueh Rd., Sect. 2, Chihhsueh Village, Shoufeng, Hualien.

NGAI, SHIH-HSUN 艾世勛
Mem., Acad. Sinica; Prof. Emeritus, Coll. of Phys. & Surgeons, Columbia U.; *b.* Hupei Sept. 15, '20; *m.* Wang, Hsueh-hwa; 1 *s.,* 2 *d.; educ.* MD, Sch. of Med., Nat. Cent. U. *Publ.:* Res. publ., monographs, chapters in monographs & reference bk.; etc.; *Add.* 281 Edgewood Avenue, Teaneck, NJ 07666, USA.

NI, TE-MING
(See YEE, TEH-MING 倪德明)

NI, TUAN-CHIU 倪摶九
Nat. Policy Adv. to the Pres. 91-; Dep. Sec.-Gen., Grand Alliance for Ch.'s Unification under the Three Principles of the People 82-; Adv., World Freedom & Dem. League 68-; *b.* Shantung Aug. 7, '16; *m.* Chou, Shang-hsien; 4 *s.,* 1 *d.; educ.* LL.B., NCU 46; Resr., Inst. of Rev. Implementation 50, Workshop on Joint War Aff. Op. by the Party, Govt. & Armed Force 54, & Workshop on Pol. War Aff. 67; Sec. & Sect. Chief, MTAC 46-48; Sec. & Dir., Legis. Yuan 48-67; Mem., Nat. Dev. Planning Group, NSC 67-73; Adv. & Dep. Sec.-Gen., Const. Res. Cttee., NA 73-91. *Publ.: Gen. Ho Yin-chin's Hist. Chronicle; Biography of Gen. Ho Yin-chin; Conceptual Theory on Accomplice; Florescent Stream Anthology; Add.* 9th Fl., 306 Shih Tung Rd., Shihlin, Taipei.

NI, WEN-YA
(See NIEH, WEN-YA 倪文亞)

NI, YUE-SI 黎玉璽
Strategy Adv. to the Pres. 78-; *b.* Szechwan May 28, '14; *m.* Ha, Chun-chi; 1 *s.; educ.* Ch. Naval Acad.; Mil. Staff Coll.; Naval Tng. at Miami; Nat. Def. Coll.; Cmdg. Off., PCE 46-47; Chief, Op. Dept., GHQ, Navy 47-48; Cmdg.

Off., DE-21 48-49; Cmdr., 2nd Squadron 49-50; C/S, GHQ, ROCN 50-52, Dep. C-in-C & concur. Fleet Cmdr. 52-59, C-in-C 59-65; V. Chief of the Gen. Staff, MND 65, Chief of the Gen. Staff 65-67; Personal C/S to the Pres. 67-70; Amb. to Turkey 70-71; Personal C/S to the Pres. 73-78; Pres., ROC Amateur Athletic Fed. 73-82. *Publ.: On Adm. Lord Nelson* (transl.); *Add.* 62 Chin Shan S. Rd., Sect. 1, Taipei.

NIEH, WEN-YA 倪文亞
Sr. Adv. to the Pres. 89-; Chmn., CAC, KMT 93-; *b.* Chekiang Mar. 2, '05; *m.* Kuo, Shirley W.Y.; 2 *s.,* 3 *d.; educ.* MA, Columbia U.; Hon. LL.D., Hanyang U., S. Korea; Mem., Const. NA; Min. of Youth; Chmn., Twn. Prov. Cttee., KMT; Mem., CC, KMT 41; Prof. & Head, Dept. of Educ., Great Ch. U., & Nat. Ch. U.; Chmn., APPU Coun.; V. Pres. & Pres., Legis. Yuan 61-72 & 72-89; Mem., CSC, KMT 47-93; *Add.* Apt. 1, 11th Fl., 289 Tun Hua S. Rd., Sect. 1, Taipei.

OU, CHIN-DER 歐晉德
Chmn., Public Construction Com., Exec. Yuan 96-; *b.* Fukien Nov. 19, '44; *m.* Huang, Mai-chi; 2 *s.; educ.* BCE, NCKU 66, MCE, 68; Ph.D., Case We. Reserve U. 72, Res. Asst., Case We. Reserve U. 69-73; Assc. Engr., Ch. Engr. Consultants Inc. 73-76; Sr. Engr. & Mgr., Moh & Assc. Inc. 76-79; V. Pres. & Resident Mgr., Moh & Assc. Private Ltd., Singapore 79-82; Sr. V. Pres., Moh & Assc. Intl. 82-87; Chief Engr., Ret-Ser Engr. Agency 87-89; Dir., Taipei-Ilan Expressway Project Off. 89-90; Dir.-Gen., Twn. Area Nat. Expressway Engr. Bu., MOTC 90-95. *Publ.:* 73 Geotech. related publ. in intl. & domestic jour.; *Add.* 9th Fl., 4 Chung Hsiao W. Rd., Sect. 1, Taipei.

OU, CHIN-TE
(See OU, CHIN-DER 歐晉德)

OU, FRANCISCO H.L. 歐鴻鍊
Admin. V. Min. of For. Aff. 96-; *b.* Twn. Jan. 5, '40; *m.* Liu, Chih-yuan; 2 *s.,* 2 *d.; educ.* LL.B., Dept. of Dip., NCU 62; 3rd & 2nd Sec., Emb. in Lima 67-71; Sect. Chief, Dept. of Cent. & S. Am. Aff., MOFA 71-73, Dep. Dir. 73-75; Dir., Ch. Com. Off., Chile 75-81, & Dept. of Cent. & S. Am. Aff., MOFA 81-84; Amb. to Nicaragua 84-85; Rep., Ch. Cml. Off. in Argentine 86-90; Amb. to Guatemala 90-96; *Add.* 2 Kaitakelan Boulevard, Taipei.

OU, HAO-NIEN
(See AU, HO-NIEN 歐豪年)

OU, HUNG-LIEN
(See OU, FRANCISCO H.L. 歐鴻鍊)

OU, YU-CHAN 歐育誠
Dep. Dir.-Gen., CPA 94-; *b.* Twn. Nov. 26, '39 *m.* Wu, Shu-nu; 1 *s.,* 1 *d.; educ.* LL.B., Ch. Cul. U. 74; Studied at the Grad. Sch. of Senshu U., Japan 80; Sp., CPA 70-71, Sect. Chief 71-77, Comr. 77-79, Dep. Dir. 79-84, Dir. 84-90, Chief Sec. 90-94. *Publ.: Problems & Mng. of Small & Medium-Sized Ent.; The Japanese Pers. System of Civil Servants; Add.* 109 Huai Ning St., Taipei.

OU, YUNG-SHENG 歐用生
Pres., Nat. Taipei Tchrs. Coll. 95-, Prof. 80-; *b.* Twn. Aug. 27, '43; *m.* Chuang, Hsiu-chin; 1 *s.,* 1 *d.; educ.* Grad. Twn. Prov. Tainan Tchrs. Sch. 62; Ed.B., NTNU 69; Ed.M., U. of Tokyo 79; Ed.D., NTNU 88; Tchr., Elementary Sch. 62-65, Secondary Sch. 69-71; Teaching Asst. 71-72; Instr. 79-80; Assc. Prof. 80-84; Dean of Acad. Aff., Jr. Tchrs. Coll. & Tchrs. Coll. 84-86 & 87-91; Dir., Sp. Educ. Cent. 86-87; Dir., Twn. Prov. Inst. for Elementary Sch. Tchrs. Educ. 91-93. *Publ.: Methodologies in Curriculum Res.; Qualitative Res.; Educ. Innovation in an Open Soc.; Tchrs.' In-Service Educ. & Prof. Dev.; Tchrs.' Prof. Growth & Learning; Add.* 134 Ho Ping E. Rd., Sect. 2, Taipei.

OU-YANG, CHAO-HO 歐陽兆和
Mem., Acad. Sinica 84-; Prof. Emeritus, NTU 89-; Mem. Emeritus, Sc. Coun., MOE 91-; *b.* Twn. May 27, '19; *m.* Hong, Shiu-hong; 1 *s.,* 3 *d.; educ.* MD, Taihoku Imperial U.; MD, Kyoto U.; Teaching Asst., NTU 47-53, Instr. 53-56, Assc. Prof. 56-61, Prof. 61-89; Chmn., Dept. of Pharmacology, Pharmacological Inst., NTU 72-78; Mem., Sc. Coun., MOE 88-91. *Publ.:* About 70 papers concerning snake venoms, blood coagulation & platelet aggregation; *Add.* 54 Alley 2, Lane 65, Chung Shan N. Rd., Sect. 2, Taipei.

OUYANG, JUI-HSIUNG 歐陽瑞雄
Dir.-Gen., TECO, Los Angeles 94-; *b.* Twn. Nov. 23, '40; *m.* Tang, Pee-yin; 2 *s.; educ.* BA, NCU; MA, NTU; Staff Mem., MOFA 68-70; Sec., Trade Mission of the ROC to Singapore 70-79; Dir., Dept. of For. Aff., TPG

79-81; Dept. Dir., Protocol Dept., MOFA 82-83; Dept. Dir.-Gen., TECO, Los Angeles 84-86; Dir.-Gen., TECO, Kanasa City, Missouri 86-90; Dir.-Gen., TECO Houston, Texas 90-91; Spokesman of MOFA & Dir., Info. & Cul. Dept. 91-94. *Publ.: Studies on ASEAN; Add.* 3731 Wilshire Boulevard, Suite 700, Los Angeles, CA 90010, USA.

PAI, PEI-YING 白培英
Chmn., Intl. Cml. Bk. of ROC 93-; *b.* Hopei Mar. 30, '40; *m.* Lin, Lily Z.L.; 1 *s.; educ.* LL.B., Soochow U. 57; Intl. Tax Prog., Harvard Law Sch. 72; Dir., Tax Admin., Nantou, Changhua, & Tainan 62-69; Div. Chief & Dep. Dir.-Gen., Taxation Dept., MOF 69-80; Dir., 4th Div., Exec. Yuan 80-82; Chmn., Sec. & Exchange Com., MOF 82-84; V. Min. of Finance 84-86; Chmn., Import-Export Bk. of ROC 86-92, & Intl. Cml. Bk. of ROC 92; Min. of Finance 92-93; *Add.* 100 Kirin Rd., Taipei.

PAN, CHEN-CHEW 潘振球
Pres., Acad. Historica 95-; *b.* Kiangsu June 2, '18; *m.* Chu, Chu-i; 3 *s.,* 1 *d.; educ.* Nat. Tchr.'s Coll.; Postgraduate Studies, NCU; Nat. War Coll.; LL.D., Konkuk U., S. Korea; Dean of Trainees, Kiangsu Prov. Civil Service Tng. Cent. 46-48; Prin., Youth Middle Sch., Hangchow 48-49, Twn. Prov. Taichung 2nd Middle Sch. 49-50, & Twn. Prov. Taipei Chengkung Middle Sch. 50-56; Dir., Twn. Prov. Tng. Corps 56-64; Prof., Inst. of Ch. Cul. 62-63; Comr., Dept. of Educ., TPG 64-72; Chmn., NYC 72-78, & Twn. Prov. Cttee., KMT 78-79; Dir.-Gen., Ch. Youth Corps 79-87; Dir., Org. Aff. Dept., CC, KMT 87-88; Nat. Policy Adv. to the Pres. 88-95. *Publ.: The Educ. Thought of Mencius; Add.* 5th Fl.-3, 43 Hsin Yi Rd., Sect. 3, Taipei.

PAN, CHEN-CHIU
(See PAN, CHEN-CHEW 潘振球)

PAN, HUANG-LUNG
(See PAN, HWANG-LONG 潘皇龍)

PAN, HWANG-LONG 潘皇龍
Composer; Music Educator; Prof., Nat. Inst. of the Arts 91-; Del., Intl. Rostrum of Composers (IRC)/UNESCO 91-; Jury, Music Adv. Cttee., Nat. Theater & Nat. Concert Hall 90-; Mem., Adv. Cttee. Nat. Cul. Cent.; *b.* Twn. Sept. 9, '45; *m.* Lin, Yu-ching; 2 *s.; educ.* BA, NTNU 71; Diploma, Musikhochschule und Musikakademie in

Zurich 76; Staatliche Hochschule für Musik und Theater in Hanover, Germany 76-78; Hochschule der Künste Berlin 78-80; Assc. Prof., Nat. Inst. of the Arts 82-91; Mem., Music Cttee., CCA 87-91; Pres., Ch.-Taipei Sect., Intl. Soc. for Contemporary Music 89-93; Seoul Philharmonic Orchestra 93. *Publ.: Modern Music's Focus; Let's Appreciate Modern Music; Add.* 7th Fl., 230 Ta An Rd., Sect. 1, Taipei.

PAO, I-HSING
(See PAO, YIH-HSING 鮑亦興)

PAO, TE-MING
(See PAO, TEH-MING 包德明)

PAO, TEH-MING 包德明
Nat. Policy Adv. to the Pres. 96-; Founder & Pres., Ming Chuan Coll. 90-; V. Chmn., People to People Intl., USA 92-; Chmn., Found. for Intl. Educ. & Mng. Sc. 88-, & Asian Women Football Confederation 85-; V. Pres., People to People Assn., ROC 79-; Chmn., Adv. Cttee., Intl. Assn. of U. Pres., NGO UN; V. Chmn., UN/IAUP Com. on Arms Control Educ.; *b.* Szechwan July 22, '13; *m.* Lee, Ying-chao; 3 *s.,* 1 *d.; educ.* LL.B., Nat. Peking U. 35; Ph.D., Wesleyen Women's Coll., USA 80; Mem., Const. NA 46-49; Asst. Mgr., CTC 56-68; Chmn., Adv. Cttee., Intl. Assn. of U. Pres., NGO, UN 89-93; *Add.* 250 Chung Shan N. Rd., Sect. 5, Taipei.

PAO, YIH-HSING 鮑亦興
Mem., Acad. Sinica 86-; Mem., US Nat. Acad. of Engr. 85-; Prof., Inst. of Applied Mech., NTU 89-; Joseph C. Ford Prof. of Theoretical & Applied Mech., Cornell U. 84; Mem., US Nat. Acad. of Engr.; *b.* Nanking Jan. 19, '30; *m.* Shih, Amelia K.T.; 3 *c.; educ.* BCE, NTU 52; MS, Rensselaer Polytech. Inst. 55; Ph.D., Columbia U. 59; Hon. Dr., NCTU 95; Asst. Prof., Cornell U. 58, Prof. 68, Chmn., Dept. of Theoretical & Applied Mech. 74-80; Dir., Inst. of Applied Mech., NTU 84-86, 89-94. *Publ.: Diffraction of Elastic Waves & Dynamics Stress Concentration* (with C.C. Mow) 72; & more than 100 papers published in sc. & engr. jour.; *Add.* 26-5 Lane 60, Chou Shan Rd., Taipei.

PENG, HUAI-NAN
(See PERNG, FAI-NAN 彭淮南)

PENG KO 彭歌
(See YAO, PENG 姚朋)

PENG, MENG-CHI 彭孟緝
Strategy Adv. to the Pres.; *b.* Hupei Aug. 17, '08; *m.* Cheng, Big-yun; 5 *s.,* 1 *d.; educ.* Nat. Sun Yat-sen U.; Mil. Acad.; Japanese Artillery Sch.; Armed Forces Joint Staff Coll.; Chief Instr., Artillery Sch. 31; Br. Cmdr., 1st 18 Artillery Brig. 32; Cmdr., 10th Artillery Regt. 35; CG, 1st Artillery Brig. 43; Artillery Cmdr., GHQ, Army 45; CG, Kaohsiung Fort Cmd. 46; Cmdr., Twn. Garrison GHQ 47; Dep. Cmdr., Twn. Peace Preservation Hqs. 49-54; V. Chief of the Gen. Staff, MND 54, Acting Chief of the Gen. Staff 54-55, Chief of the Gen. Staff 55-57; C-in-C, ROC Army 57-59; Chief of the Gen. Staff, MND 59-65; Personal C/S to the Pres. 65-66; Amb. to Thailand 66-69; Amb. to Japan 69-72; *Add.* 120 Jen Ai Rd., Sect. 3, Taipei.

PENG, MING-TSUNG 彭明聰
Mem., Acad. Sinica 78-; Prof. Emeritus, NTU 88-; Bd. Chmn., Childhood Burn Found. of the ROC 95-; Bd. Mem., Ch. C.'s Found., Twn. & Kaohsiung Med. Coll.; *b.* Twn. Nov. 28, '17; *m.* Yuan, Sen-chin; 3 *s.,* 1 *d.; educ.* MD & Ph.D., Taihoku Imperial U.; Prof. of Physiology, Coll. of Med., NTU 48-88, Dean of Acad. Aff. 61-72, Chmn., Dept. of Physiology 72-78, Dean, Coll. of Med. 78-83; Dir., McKay Sch. of Nursing 88-93; Res. Fel., Coll. of Phys. & Surgeons, Columbia U. 56-57, & Neuroendocrinology Group, Oxford U., UK 63-64; Guest Resr., NIH, USA 89. *Publ.:* "Changes in Hormone Uptake & Receptors in the Hypothalamus During Aging," in *Neuroendocrinology of Aging* (J. Meites, ed.); "Rejuvenation of Sexual Behavior of Aging Rats with Neurotransmitters," Vol. *Interdisciplinary Topics in Gerontology* Vol. 24 (A.V. Everitt, J.R. Walton); *Add.* 4th Fl.-B, 1 Lane 91, Jen Ai Rd., Sect. 2, Taipei.

PENG WANG, CHIA-KANG
(See WHANG-PENG, JACQUELINE 彭汪嘉康)

PERNG, FAI-NAN 彭淮南
Bd. Chmn., CTC 95-; *b.* Twn. Jan. 2, '39; *m.* Lai, Yang-chu; 2 *s.; educ.* BA, Econ., NCHU 62; MS, Econ., U. of Minnesota 71; Dir., Econ. Res. Dept., CBC 86-89, Gen. Mgr., For. Exchange Dept. 89-94, Dep. Gov. 94-95.

Publ.: Applicable Methods to the Liberalization of For. Exchange Control; Money Supply & For. Exchange; Balance of Payment & For. Exchange; Add. 49 Wu Chang St., Sect. 1, Taipei.

PIAN CHAO, RULAN 卞趙如蘭

Mem., Acad. Sinica 90-; Prof. Emeritus, Dept. of E. Asian Lang. & Civilizations, & Dept. of Music, Harvard U. 92-; Hon. Prof., Cent. Ch. U. of Tech., Wuhan 90-; Hon. Res. Fel., Shanghai Conservatory of Music 91-; Hon. Prof., Cent. S. U. of Tech., Changsha 91-; Hon. Prof., S.W. Chiaotung U. Chengtu 94; Hon. Permanent Pres. of the Conf. on Ch. Oral & Performing Lit. 95; *b.* USA Apr. 20, '22; *m.* Pian, Theodore Hsueh-huang; 1 *d.; educ.* BA & MA, We. Music Hist. & Theory, Radcliffe Coll., Ph.D., Musicology & Far Ea. Lang.; Teaching Asst., Harvard U. 47-58, Instr. 59-61, Lectr. 61-74; Visiting Prof., Ch. U. of Hong Kong 75, 78-79, 82, & 94, NTHU 90, & Nat. Cent. U. 92; Faculty Mem., Cttee. on Degrees in Folklore & Mythology, Harvard U. 76; Full Prof., Dept. of Music, Harvard 74-92. *Publ.: A Syllabus For The Mandarin Primer; Sung Dynasty Musical Sources & Their Interpretation; Complete Musical Works of Yuen Ren Chao; Found. Work in Pronunciation of Mandarin Ch.;* & 30 articles; *Add.* 14 Brattle Circle, Cambridge, MA 02138, USA.

PIEN CHAO, JU-LAN

(See PIAN CHAO, RULAN 卞趙如蘭)

RAU, CHYI-MING 饒奇明

Admin. V. Min. of Exam., Exam. Yuan 94-; *b.* Twn. Mar. 10, '38; *m.* Chiu, Min-Chen; 2 *s.,* 2d.; *educ.* B., Lit., NTNU 61; Studied in Pittsburgh State U. 85; Grad., Grad. Sch. of Law, Civil Servants' Cent., NCU 91; Elementary & Secondary Sch. Tchr. 56-66; Dir., Dept. of Gen. Aff., Min. of Exam. 87-89 & Dept. of Sp. Exam. 89-93, Chief Sec. 93-94; *Add.* 1 Shih Yuan Rd., Wenshan, Taipei.

SCHIVE, CHI 薛琦

V. Chmn., CEPO 93-; Adjunct Prof. of Econ., NTU 88-; *b.* Chungking June 28, '47; *m.* Ho, Jane Bih-yih; 2 *s.; educ.* BA, Econ., NTU 69, MA, Econ. 72; MA, Econ., Case We. Reserve U., USA 74, Ph.D., Econ. 78; Prof., NTU 83-85; Prof. & Dir., Grad. Inst. of Ind. Econ., Nat.

Cent. U. 85-88, Dean, Coll. of Mng. 85-87; Consultant Mem., CEPD 88-93; Visiting Prof., Free U., Berlin 90; Dir., Dept. of Econ., NTU 90-93. *Publ.: For. Factor: The Multinational Corp.'s Contribution to the Econ. Modernization of the ROC; Twn.'s Econ. Role in E. Asia;* articles pub. in prof. jour.; *Add.* 9th Fl., 87 Nanking E. Rd., Sect. 2, Taipei.

SHAN, KUO-HSI 單國璽

Bishop, Kaohsiung Diocese 91-; Pres., Ch. Catholic Bishops Conf. 87-; Mem., Cent. Cttee., Fed. of Asian Bishops Conf. 87-, Mem., Pol. Coun. for Soc. Comms. 90-; *b.* Hopei Dec. 2, '23; *educ.* MA, Berchmans Coll. 51; M.Th., Bellarmino Theological Coll. 56; Ph.D., Gregorian U., Rome 61; Rector, Jesuit Manresa Seminary 64-70; Pres., Rector & Prin., St. Ignatius High Sch. 70-76; Pres., Kuangchi Prog. Service 76-80; Bishop, Hualien Diocese 80-91; Bd. Chmn., Fu Jen Catholic U. 91-94; Pres., FABC Com. for Soc. Comm. 82-90. *Publ.: Dedication & Leadership; How to be a Leader; Add.* 125 Szu Wei 3rd Rd., Kaohsiung.

SHAW, YU-MING 邵玉銘

Dir., Inst. of Intl. Rel., NCU 94-, Prof., Grad. Inst. of Intl. Law & Dip. 91-; Res. Fel., NUC 95-; Bd. Mem., Cul. Found. of the United Daily News Group 92-; *b.* Harbin Nov. 3, '38; *m.* Lu, Shiow-jyu; 1 *s.,* 1 *d.; educ.* LL.B., NCU 61; MA, Fletcher Sch. of Law & Dip., Tufts U., USA 67; Ph.D., U. of Chicago 75; Hon. Dr., Franklin Coll., USA 91; Asst. Prof. of Hist., Newberry Coll., S. Carolina 67-68 & 72-73; Res. Assc., Cent. for Far Ea. Studies, U. of Chicago 76-77; Visiting Sp., Acad. Sinica 79-81; Reviewer, Panelist & Evaluator, Nat. Endowment for the Humanities, USA 79-82; Assc. Prof., Dept. of Hist., U. of Notre Dame, Indiana 73-81, Tenured Assc. Prof. 81-82; Dir., Asia & World Inst. 83-84; Dean, Grad. Inst. of Intl. Law & Dip., NCU 84, Dir., Inst. of Intl. Rel. 84-87; Dir.-Gen., GIO & Govt. Spokesman 87-91; Adjunct Prof., Grad. Inst. of Intl. Law & Dip., NCU 83-91; Thornton D. Hooper Fel. in Intl. Aff., For. Policy Res. Inst., USA 92-93. *Publ.: Ch. & Christianity; Problems in 20th Century Ch. Christianity; 20th Century Sino-Am. Rel.; From the Open Door Policy to the US Dip. Rupture with the ROC; Hist. & Pol. in Modern Ch.; Discourses on Nat. Issues by Ch. Intellectuals; Intl. Pol. & Ch.'s Future; Beyond the Econ. Miracle: Reflections on the Dev. Experience of the ROC on Twn.; Lit., Pol., & Intellectuals; Amidst Great Change: Reflections of a Public Servant; An Am. Missionary in Ch.: John Leighton Stuart & Ch.-Am. Rel.; Add.* 64 Wan Shou Rd., Wenshan, Taipei.

SHEA, JIA-DONG 許嘉棟

Dep. Gov., CBC 96-; Res. Fel., Inst.of Econ., Acad. Sinica 82-; Bd. Dir., Chung-hua Inst. for Econ. Res. 93-; *b.* Twn. Oct. 9, '48; *m.* Kuo, Ruey-huey; 2 *s.,* 1 *d.; educ.* BA, NTU 70, MA 74; Ph.D., Stanford U. 78; Prof., NTU 83-96; Dir., Acad. Sinica 91-96; V. Pres., Ch. Econ. Assn. 95-96. *Publ.: Ch. Taipei: The Origins of the Econ. "Miracle"* (ed. Dessus, Sebastien, Jia-dong Shea, & Mau-shan Shi) (1995); *Add.* 2 Roosevelt Rd., Sect. 1, Taipei.

SHEN, CHANG-HUAN 沈昌煥

Sr. Adv. to the Pres. 88-; *b.* Kiangsu Oct. 16, '13; *m.* Shen, Helen L.; 1 *s.; educ.* BA, Kwanghua U. 33; MA, U. of Michigan 37; Hon. LL.D., Yonsei U., Seoul; Prof., Nat. Sun Yat-Sen U., Kwangtung 37-40; Counsl. to CG of Ch. Expeditionary Forces 43-44; Personal Sec. to Pres. Chiang Kai-shek 45-48; Dir., Protocol Dept., MOFA 48; Dir.-Gen., GIO 49; V. Min. of Info., KMT 50; Adv., Exec. Yuan 50-53; Mem., CRC, KMT 50-52, Chief, 4th Sect., CC 50-53; Govt. Spokesman 50-53; Mem., CC, KMT 52; Pol. V. Min. of For. Aff. 53-59; Sp. Rep. of Pres. Chiang Kai-shek & Head of Ch. Goodwill Mission to Latin Am. Countries 57; Amb. to Spain 59-60; Head, Del. to the 4th Asian For. Min. Conf., Manila 61; Chief Del. to UNGA 61 & 64; Sp. Envoy to Coronation of Pope Paul VI 63; Official visits to 17 countries in Africa 63, & to Australia, New Zealand, & Japan 65; Min. of For. Aff. 60-66; Amb. to the Holy See 66-69; Amb. to Thailand 69-72; Leader, Del. to the 7th Min. Meeting, ASPAC 72; Min. of For. Aff. 72-79; Sec.-Gen., NSC 79-84; Sp. Envoy to attend the Presidential Inauguration in Honduras 82; Sec.-Gen. to the Pres. 84-88; *Add.* 11th Fl., 8 Lane 180, Kuang Fu S. Rd., Taipei.

SHEN, CHUN-SHAN 沈君山

Pres., NTHU 94-; Mem., Coun. on Educ. Reform 94-; Coun. Mem., Acad. Sinica 89-; *b.* Nanking Aug. 29, '32; *m.* Tsen, Li-hua; 1 *s.; educ.* MS, Phys., NTU 56; Ph.D., Phys., U. of Maryland 61; Res. Assc., Princeton U. 61-

62; Res. Assc., Inst. for Space Studies, NASA 62-64; Asst. Prof., Purdue U. 64-67, Assc. Prof. 67-71; Prof., NTHU 71-94, Dean, Coll. of Sc. 73-79 & 84-87; Min. of State 88-89; Comr., CEIC 89-95; Standing Mem., Preparatory Cttee. for Ch. Public TV 91-95; Res. Fel., NUC 91-95; *Add.* 101 Kuang Fu Rd., Sect. 2, Hsinchu.

SHEN, HSUEH-YUNG 申學庸

Mem., CAC, KMT 93-; Prof., Dept. of Music, Ch. Cul. U. & Nat. Twn. Acad. of Arts; Hon. Dir., Asia Opera Co. 86-; Bd. Dir., Nat. Music Coun. of Ch. 88-; Mem., Preparatory Cttee. for Ch. Public TV 91-; *b.* Szechwan Oct. 5, '29; *m.* Quo, James C.; 1 *s.,* 1 *d.; educ.* Grad., Szechwan Prov. Acad. of Arts; Isabella Rosati Musicale, Italy; Tokyo U. of Arts; Aspen Festival & Music Sch., USA; Chmn., Music Dept., Nat. Twn. Acad. of Arts 57-63, & Ch. Cul. U. 63-69; Dir., 3rd Dept., CCPD 81-84, Mem. 88-93, Chmn. 93-94; *Add.* 6th Fl., 28-5 Lane 200, Kuang Fu S. Rd., Taipei.

SHEN, SHAN-FU 沈申甫

Mem., Acad. Sinica, & Nat. Acad. of Engr., USA; Corresponding Mem., Intl. Acad. of Astronautics; John Edson Sweet Prof. Emeritus of Engr., Cornell U. 92-; *b.* Shanghai Aug. 31, '21; *m.* Tung, Ming-ming; 1 *s.,* 1 *d.; educ.* BS, Aeronautical Engr., Nat. Cent. U. 41; D.Sc., Aeronautical Engr., MIT 49; Res. Asst., Ch. Air Force Inst. of Aeronautical Res. 41-45; Res. Assc., Dept. of Math., MIT 48-50; Asst. Prof. & Prof., Dept. of Aeronautical Engr., U. of Maryland 50-61; Prof., Grad. Sch. of Aeronautical Engr., Cornell U. 61-78, John Edson Sweet Prof. of Engr. 78-92; *Add.* Sibley Sch. of Mech. & Aerospace Engr., Cornell U., Upson & Grumman Halls, Ithaca, NY 14853-7501, USA.

SHEN, SHEN-FU

(See SHEN, SHAN-FU 沈申甫)

SHEN, TIAN-FUH 沈添富

Prof. & Dean, NTU 95-; *b.* Twn. June 9, '41; *m.* Tsai, Wenli; 1 *s.,* 1 *d.; educ.* BA, NTU 64; MS, U. of Alberta, Can. 68; Ph.D., U. of Wisconsin 72; Res. Assc., Albert Einstein Coll. 72-74; Assc. Prof., NTU 74-79, Prof. 79-87, Dept. Chmn. 87-93. *Publ.:* About 50 papers 72-95; *Add.* 2nd Fl., 9 Lane 60, Chou Shan Rd., Taipei.

SHEN, Y.R. 沈元壞
Mem., Acad. Sinica 96-; Prof., Phys. Dept., UC-Berkly. 64-; *b.* Shanghai Mar. 25, '35; *m.* Shen T., Hsiao-lin; 1 *s.*, 2 *d.; educ.* BS, NTU 56; MS, Stanford U. 59; Ph.D., Harvard U. 63, Postdoctoral Resr. 63-64; Asst. Prof., UC-Berkly. 64-67, Assc. Prof. 67-70, Prof. 70; Visiting Prof., U. de Paris 73; Visiting Sr. Scholar, Max-Plank-Inst. in Quantenoftik, W. Germany 84 & 88; Visiting Prof., Tech. U. of Wien, Austria 91. *Publ.: The Principles of Nonlinear Optics;* & more than 300 papers in periodicals & mags.; *Add.* Phys. Dept., UC-Berkly., Berkeley, CA 94720, USA.

SHEN, YUAN-JANG
(See SHEN, Y.R. 沈元壞)

SHEU, KE-SHENG 許柯生
Admin. V. Min. of Econ. Aff. 93-; *b.* Kiangsi Apr. 15, '33; *m.* Chang, Chung-ching; *educ.* BA, NTU 57; MA, U. of Hawaii 68; Dir., 1st & 4th Dept., Bd. of For. Trade (BOFT), MOEA 69-74; Trade Rep. in London & Brussels 75-87; Dir., Econ. Div., CCNAA, Washington, D.C. 87-89; Dir.-Gen., BOFT 89-93; *Add.* 15 Foochow St., Taipei.

SHEU, YUAN-DONG 許遠東
Gov., CBC 95-; Chmn., Bankers Assn. of the ROC 89-, & Coordination Coun. on Sino-Japanese Business Aff. 91-; *b.* Twn. May 22, '27; *m.* Huang, Men-mei; 1 *s.*, 2 *d.; educ.* BA, NTU 52; Exec. V. Pres., Cooperative Bk. of Twn. 74-79; Pres., Land Bk. of Twn. 79-80, & First Cml. Bk. 80-82; Dir., Dept. of Monetary Aff., MOF 82-84; Chmn., Land Bk. of Twn. 84-90; Chmn., Bk. of Twn. 90-95; Bd. Mem., CBC 90-95. *Publ.: Cooperative Finance in Twn.; The Role of Agr. Credit Inst. in Twn.; The Innovation of Financial Admin. in the ROC; Add.* 120 Chungking S. Rd., Sect. 1, Taipei.

SHI, HWEI-YOW 許惠祐
V. Chmn., SEF 96-; *b.* Twn. Nov. 2, '52; *m.* Chang, Chong-wen; 1 *s.*, 1 *d.; educ.* LL.B., NCU 75, LL.M. 80, LL.D. 87; Judge, Tainan Dist. Court 81-84, Shihlin Br., Taipei Dist. Court 84-90, & Taipei Dist. Court 90-91; Dep. Sec.-Gen., SEF 93-96. *Publ.: A Study on Travel Contracts; The Use of Computers in Trials; Add.* 16th Fl., 2-2 Chi Nan Rd., Sect. 1, Taipei.

SHI, W.L. 許文龍
Chmn., Chi Mei Corp. 59-; *b.* Twn. Feb. 25, '28; *m.* Liao, Hsiu-lan; 1 *s.*, 2 *d.; educ.* Tainan Voc. High Sch. 48; Exec. Dir., Chi Lin Plastics Co. Ltd. 65-74; Founder & Exec. Dir., Poly Chem. Co. Ltd. 68-85, & Jen Te Ind. Co. Ltd. 68-90; *Add.* 59-1 Sanchia Village, Jente, Tainan County.

SHIEH, CHIN-CHU 謝金菊
Dir., Taipei Mun. Lib. 91-; *b.* Twn. Aug. 16, '44; *m.* Chang, Hsin-ching; 1 *s.*, 1 *d.; educ.* BA, Dept. of Adult & Continuing Educ., NTNU 68; Passed Sr. Civil Service Exam. 68; Promotion Exam. 83; Mng. Staff, Acad. Sinica 67-74; Sp. Asst., Secretariat, NA 74-83; Sr. Sp. Asst., TPG 83-91; *Add.* 125 Chien Kuo S. Rd., Sect. 2, Taipei.

SHIEH, LUNG-SHENG 謝隆盛
V. Spkr., NA 96-; Mem., CC, KMT 93-; *b.* Twn. Apr. 24, '41; *m.* Wu, Hsueh-hui; 1 *s.*, 3 *d.; educ.* B., Tatung Inst. of Tech.; 19th Class, Sun Yat-sen Inst. on Policy Res. & Dev.; Mem., Taipei CoCoun.; Bd. Chmn., Szehai Inst. of Tech. & Com.; Mem., Disciplinary Cttee., KMT Caucus, NA; Dep. Dir.-Gen., Dept. of Org. Aff., CC, KMT; Chmn., Presidium, NA; Dir.-Gen., Dept. of Party-Govt. Coordination, NA, & Party Whip, KMT Caucus; *Add.* 6 Alley 7, Lane 763, Chung Shan N. Rd., Sect. 6, Taipei.

SHIEH, MUNG-SHIUNG 謝孟雄
Mem., Control Yuan 93-; Adjunct Assc. Prof., Taipei Med. Coll. 83-; Pres., Ch. Community Dev. Coun. 77-; *b.* Kwangtung Oct. 12, '34; *m.* Lin, Cheng-chih; 4 *d.; educ.* MD, Kaohsiung Med. Coll. 60; Studied at Grad. Sch. of Med., U. of Penn. 66; Assc. Prof. & Dept. Head, Shih Chien Coll. 69-72, Pres. 72-78; Pres., Taipei Med. Coll. 78-83, Shih Chien Coll. 83-93, Ch. Nutrition Soc. 74-83, & Ch. Home Econ. Assn. 87-91; Mem., Bd. of Exam., Min. of Exam., Exam. Yuan 81-93. *Publ: A Res. on Abnormal Bleeding in the Uterus; Diseases of Middle-Aged Women & Their Prevention; An Overall Res. on the Population Plan—An Ecological Approach; Marriage & Health; Pregnancy & Nursing; The Sunshine of Shih Chien; Soc. Work & Med. Care; Add.* 2 Chung Hsiao E. Rd., Sect. 1, Taipei.

SHIEH, SAMUEL C. 謝森中
Nat. Policy Adv. to the Pres. 94-; Adv., CBC 94-; Chmn., Exec. Bd., Chinatrust Cml. Bk. 94-; *b.* Kwangtung Nov.

13, '19; *m.* Shieh, Alice Yen-hee; 2 *s.,* 2 *d.; educ.* BA, Nat. Cent. U. 43, MA 45; Ph.D., U. of Minnesota 57; Hon. LL.D., U. of the Philippines 93; Prof., NTU 50-60; Sr. Sp., Chief Economist, & Sec.-Gen., JCRR 51-65; Dir., Projects Dept., Asian Dev. Bk. 67-81; V. Chmn., CEPD 81-83; Chmn., Chiao Tung Bk. 83-89; Gov., CBC 89-94. *Publ.: The Rice & Sugarcane Competition in Cent. Twn.: The Application of Linear Programming Technique to Crop Competition Study; Linear Programming as a Modern Technique in Ind. Mng. & Econ. Res.; An Analytical Review of Agr. Dev. in Twn.—An Input-Output & Productivity Approach; Environmental, Technological, & Inst. Factors in the Growth of Rice Production: Philippines, Thailand, & Twn.; Gov. Samuel C. Shieh's Selected Addresses & Messages* (4 Vol.); *Add.* 2 Roosevelt Rd., Sect. 1, Taipei.

SHIEH, SHINN-LIANG 謝信良
Dir.-Gen., Cent. Weather Bu. 94-; *b.* Twn. Jan. 1, '44; *m.* Tseng, Li-hua; 1 *s.,* 1 *d.; educ.* BS, Meteorology, NTU 68; MS, Atmospheric Sc., U. of Washington 75; Forecaster, Twn. Prov. Weather Bu. 69-70; Chief, Forecast Sect., Cent. Weather Bu. 71-73, Dep. Dir. 76-81, Dir. 82-89; Sec.-Gen., Cent. Weather Bu. 90-91, Dep. Dir.-Gen. 91-94; *Add.* 64 Kung Yuan Rd., Taipei.

SHIEH, TUNG-MIN 謝東閔
Sr. Adv. to the Pres. 85-; *b.* Twn. Jan. 25, '07; *m.* Pan, Ying-ching (deceased); 4 *s.,* 1 *d.; educ.* Grad., Nat. Sun Yat-sen U.; Magis., Kaohsiung County; Dep. Dir., Dept. of Civil Aff., V. Comr. of Educ., Comr., & Sec.-Gen., TPG; Pres., Twn. Prov. Tchrs. Coll.; Chmn., Cooperative Bk. of Twn.; Bd. Chmn., Hsin Sheng Daily News Co. Ltd.; Pres., Shih Chien Coll.; Dep. Dir., Ch. Youth Corps; Spkr., TPA; Gov., TPG 72-78; V. Pres., ROC 78-84; Mem., CSC, KMT. *Publ.: Econ. Geog.; Japanese Grammar Readings; Add.* 410 Pei An Rd., Taipei.

SHIH, CHANG-JU 石璋如
Mem. & Res. Fel., Acad. Sinica 49-; *b.* Honan Oct. 4, '05; *m.* Yuan, Shin; 1 *s.,* 1 *d; educ.* BA, Honan U.; Assc., Acad. Sinica 34-49, Assc. Res. Fel. 40-49. *Publ.: Yin-Hsu Architectural Remains; Hsiao-T'un, Architectural Remains; Hsiao-T'un, Burials of the Nr. Sect.; Hsiao-T'un, Burials of the Middle Sect.; Hsiao-T'un, Burials of the S. Sect.; Hsiao-T'un, Burials Above & Underneath the B-area Founds.; Hsiao-T'un, Burials at the C-area; Hsiao-T'un, Pit Provenience of the Oracle Bones; Hsiao-T'un, Pit Provenience of the Oracle Bones Illustrations; Hsiao-T'un, Pit Provenience of the Oracle Bones II; Ta-Ma-Lin; Hou-Chia-Chuang IX; Add.* Inst. of Hist. & Philology, Acad. Sinica, Nankang, Taipei.

SHIH, CHEN-JUNG
(See SHIH, STAN 施振榮)

SHIH, CHENG-JEN
(See SHIH, ROBERT C.J. 石承仁)

SHIH, CHI-PING 石齊平
Dep. Sec.-Gen., SEF 91-; Adjunct. Assc. Prof., Tunghai U. & Soochow U. 79-; Ed. Writer, *Cml. Times & CDN* 86-; *b.* Chekiang Aug. 15, '46; *m.* Chung, Chao-chun; 1 *s.,* 1 *d.; educ.* LL.B., NTU 68, MS, Econ. 71; Res., Trans. Planning Bd., MOTC 71-72; Trainee System Engr., IBM Twn. Corp. 72-73; Assc. Instr., Ngee Ann Tech. Coll., Singapore 73-75; Instr., Dept. of Econ., Tunghai U. 75-78; Exec. Sec., Laws & Regln. Cttee., & concur. Sp. & Adv., CEPD 78-91. *Publ.: Application & Theory of Current Individual Econ.; Policy & Theory of Current Macroeconomy; What are the Problems?—My Observation & Exam. on Twn.'s Dramatically Changing Econ. Situation; The Road to Econ. Modernization;* etc.; *Add.* 17th Fl., 156 Min Sheng E. Rd., Sect. 3, Taipei.

SHIH, CHI-YANG 施啟揚
Pres., Jud. Yuan 94-; *b.* Twn. May 5, '35; *m.* Li, Jeanne Tchong-koei; *educ.* LL.B., NTU 58, LL.M. 62; LL.D., Heidelberg U., W. Germany 67; Assc. Prof., Dept. of Law, NTU 67-71, Adjunct Prof. 71-87; Res. Asst., Inst. of Intl. Rel., NCU 67-69, Res. Fel. 69-71; Dep. Dir., 5th Dept., CC, KMT 69-72, & Dept. of Youth Aff. 72-76; Pol. V. Min. of Educ. 76-80; Pol. V. Min. of Justice 80-84; Min. of Justice 84-88; V. Premier 88-93; Sec.-Gen., NSC 93-94; Mem., CC & CSC, KMT 84-94. *Publ.: The W. German Federal Const. Court; Add.* 124 Chungking S. Rd., Sect. 1, Taipei.

SHIH, CHIA-MING 施嘉明
Comr., Exam. Yuan 90-; *b.* Twn. Mar. 10, '33; *m.* Wang, Fang-shue; 3 *d.; educ.* LL.B., TPLCC 59; LL.M., NCU 62; Dep. Dir., Dept. of Recon., TPG 77-78, & Dept. of

Civil Aff. 78-79; Counsl. & Dept. Dir., Exec. Yuan 79-86; Admin. V. Min. of Exam. 86-89, Pol. V. Min. of Exam. 90. *Publ.: Local Coun. of Japan; An Outline of Japanese Hist.; Add.* 3rd Fl., 1 Alley 15, Lane 31, Shao Hsing N. St., Taipei.

SHIH, CHIH-MING 施治明
Mayor, Tainan City 89-; *b.* Twn. Oct. 28, '52; *m.* Wu, Li-ching; 2 *s.,* 2 *d.; educ.* Tamsui Coll. of Tech. & Com. 75; Studied at Ch. Cul. U. & NCKU 81-82; Mem., Tainan CCoun. 71-75, & TPA 75-78; *Add.* 1 Chung Cheng Rd., Tainan.

SHIH, CHIN-TAI
(See SHIH, CHINTAY 史欽泰)

SHIH, CHINTAY 史欽泰
Pres., Ind. Tech. Res. Inst. 94-; *b.* Twn. Oct. 15, '46; *m.* Chen, Fung-yong; 1 *d.; educ.* BSEE, NTU 68; DSEE, Princeton U. 75; MS, Mng., Stanford U. 85; Engr. Mgr., Plant Mgr., & Dep. Gen. Dir., Elect. Res. & Service Org. 76-84, V. Pres. & Gen. Dir. 84-89; Exec. V. Pres., Ind. Tech. Res. Inst. 89-94; *Add.* 195 Chung Hsin Rd., Sect. 4, Chutung, Hsinchu.

SHIH, GASPER 石滋宜
Pres., Ch. Productivity Cent.; Dir., Asian Productivity Org., ROC; *b.* Twn. Jan. 28, '37; *m.* Su, Ming-tsu; 1 *s.,* 1 *d.; educ.* Ph.D., Tokyo U.; Dep. Plant Mgr., Dunham-Bush, Can. 73-84; Mgr., Advanced Mfg. Engr., Gen. Elec., Can. 77-82; Mem., CAD/CAM Tech. Advancement Coun., Can. Fed. Govt. 80-82; Chmn., Aluminum Alloy Welding Tech. Cttee., Can. Standard Assn. 83-85; Mng. Dir., Factory Automation Task Force, MOEA 72-74; *Add.* 2nd Fl., 79 Hsin Tai 5th Rd., Sect. 1, Hsichih, Taipei County.

SHIH HSIN TAO 釋心道
Dharma M.; Abbot, Ling Chiu Shan Wu-sheng Monastery 83-; Chmn., Ling Chiu Shan Prajna Cul. Found. 89-; Chmn., World Religions Museum Dev. Found., Charitable Org. & Found. for Soc. Welfare; *b.* Yunnan Aug. 8, '48. *Publ.: The Quality of Mercy* (Ch. & Eng. editions); *The Refreshing Taste of Dharma; Window onto Wisdom; The Path to Spirituality; The Tip for a Happy Zen Life; Mystery of the Mind; Day & Night; Life & Death; Add.* 10th Fl., 92 Nanking E. Rd., Sect. 5, Taipei.

SHIH, MING-FA 施明發
Dir., Twn. Museum 94-; *b.* Twn. Feb. 3, '47; *m.* Wang, Andrea; 2 *s.; educ.* BA, NTNU 69, MA 74, Ed.D. Candidate; Non-degree Study, Ohio State U. 89; Counsl., Taichung Br., Ch. Youth Corp 73-74, Chief of Soc. Work 74-77, Gen. Sec., Changhua Br. 77-82; Dir., Educ. Bu., Miaoli County Govt. 82-85; Dir., Gen. Aff. Off., Dept. of Educ., TPG 85, Sect. Chief 85-90; Prin., Twn. Prov. Panchiao Sr. High Sch. 90-95. *Publ.: Confucian Thoughts on Character Bldg.; Voc. Educ. at the Crossroads—the Case of Twn.; Add.* 48 Hsuchow Rd., Taipei.

SHIH, MING-TE
(See SHIH, MING-TEH 施明德)

SHIH, MING-TEH 施明德
Former Chmn., DPP 93-96; Mem., Legis. Yuan 93-; Convener, Cttee. for Rebuilding New Twn. 92-; *b.* Kaohsiung Jan. 15, '41; 2 *d.; educ.* B., Artillery Sch. 61; Jailed 68-77; Reporter, *Twn. Times* 78; Sec.-Gen., Tangwai (outside the then KMT Party) Cent. Backing Cttee. for the 1978 Elections 78; Gen. Mgr., *Formosa Mag.* Twn. Dem. Movement 79; Jailed 80-90; Chmn., Twn. Assn. for Human Rights 90-91; Res., Pol. Dept. & Human Resources Cent., San Diego State U. 91; Mem., CC, DPP 91-93; Convener, DPP Caucus, Legis. Yuan 93. *Publ.: Spring in the Prison; Shih Ming-teh's Pol. Will;* etc.; *Add.* Rm. 601, 10 Tsingtao E. Rd., Taipei.

SHIH, ROBERT C.J. 石承仁
Amb. to Malawi 90-; *b.* Chekiang Dec. 18, '27; *m.* Cheng, Anna Chi; 3 *s.; educ.* LL.B., NTU 53; 3rd Sec., Emb. in Liberia 59-61, & Emb. in Senegal 61-64; 2nd Sec., Emb. in Zaire 64-66; Sec. to the V. Min. of For. Aff. 66-69; Dep. Dir., Dept. of Consl. Aff., MOFA 69-71; Consul, Consl. in Melbourne 71, & Consl. in Perth 71-73; Dir., Far E. Trade Service, Lebanon Off. 73-76; Consul-Gen., Consl. in Kansas City, Missouri 76-79; Sr. Asst. to the Min. of For. Aff. 79-81; Min., Emb. in S. Korea 81-85; Dep. Rep., Far E. Trade Mission, Thailand 85-87; Dir., Dept. of E. Asian & Pacific Aff., MOFA 87-90; *Add.* Emb. of the ROC, P.O. Box 30221, Lilongwe 3, Malawi.

SHIH, STAN 施振榮
Nat. Policy Adv. to the Pres. 96-; Chmn. & Chief Exec. Off., The Acer Group; *b.* Twn. Dec. 18, '44; *m.* Yeh,

Carolyn; *2 s., 1 d.; educ.* MSEE, NCTU; Unitron Ind. Corp. 71-72; Qualitron Ind. Corp. 72-76. *Publ.:* Over 100 articles on mng., marketing, res. & dev., & ent. cul.; *Add.* 6th Fl., 156 Min Sheng E. Rd., Sect. 3, Taipei.

SHIH, TSUI-FENG 施翠峰

Prof., Grad. Sch. of Art, Ch. Cul. U. 92-; Visiting Prof., Takasaki Art Cent. Coll., Japan 89-; Chmn., Twn. Watercolor Assn. 71-, & Ch.-Japan Artist Assn. 88-; Judge, Nat. Fine Art Exhibition 71-; *b.* Twn. Dec. 9, '25; *m.* Lee, Chin-shiang; *2 s., 3 d.; educ.* BA, NTNU 50; Ph.D., We. Pacific U. 95; Chmn., Craft Dept., Nat. Twn. Acad. of Arts 64-70; Chmn., Fine Arts Dept., Ch. Cul. U. 70-76. *Publ.: Current Thoughts on Modern Art* 61; *Twn. Folklore* 66; *The Twn. Folk Art* 79; *The Admiration of Ch. Ancient Bronze Mirrors* 80; *Add.* 5th Fl., 45 Feng Tan Pai Lu Community, Kuantu, Tamsui, Taipei County.

SHIH, TZU-I

(See SHIH, GASPER 石滋宜)

SHIH, WEN-SEN

(See SZE, VINCENT 施文森)

SHU, SHIEN-SIU 徐賢修

Mem., Acad. Sinica 78-; *b.* Chekiang Sept. 12, '12; *m.* Hsia, Irene; *2 s., 2 d.; educ.* BS, NTHU 35; Ph.D., Brown U. 47; Hon. Ph.D., Purdue U. 93; Lectr., NTHU 35-43; Mem., Inst. for Advanced Study, Princeton U. 47-48; Res. Assc., MIT 48; Asst. & Assc. Prof. of Math., Illinois Inst. of Tech. 48-55; Prof. of Engr. Sc., Purdue U. 55-63; Prof., Illinois Inst. of Tech. 63-68; Prof. of Aeronautic, Astronautic & Engr. Sc., Purdue U. 68-70; Consultant, Cook Elec. Lab., RCA, Gen. Elec., Boeing Airplane Co., Mid-W. Applied Sc. Corp., & Argonne Nat. Lab.; Pres., NTHU 70-75; Chmn., NScC 73-81; Bd. Chmn., Ind. Tech. Res. Inst. 78-89. *Publ.: Fourier Transformer; Group Theory; Non-Linear Differential Equation: Aerodynamics; Add.* 110 Colony Rd., W. Lafayette, IN 47906-1209, USA.

SHU, WEN-BING 許文彬

Nat. Policy Adv. to the Pres. 96-; Mem., Cttee. for Nat. Health Ins. Dispute Review, DOH 95-; Sup., Nat. Lawyers Assn. of the ROC 93-; Mem., Twn. Lawyers Disciplinary Cttee. 96-; *b.* Twn. Nov. 3, '48; *m.* Liu, Yuen-

ying; *1 s., 3 d.; educ.* LL.B., NTU 70; Prosecutor, Kaohsiung County Court 72-76; *Add.* 3rd Fl., 25 Jen Ai Rd., Sect. 2, Taipei.

SOONG, CHANG-CHIH 宋長志

Strategy Adv. to the Pres. 91-; Mem., CC & CSC, KMT 93-; *b.* Liaoning June 10, '16; *m.* Fang, Cheng-ying; *3 s., 1 d.; educ.* Ch. Naval Acad. 37; Royal Naval Coll., Greenwich, UK; 4th Class, Nat. War Coll.; 1st Class, Armed Forces U.; Hon. Ph.D., Konkuk U., S. Korea 82; Hon. LL.D., Southea. U., USA 85; Cmdg. Off. on Bd. Various Combat Ships & Rating Tng. Sch. 49-52; Cmdr., Landing Ship Squadron 54-55; Supt., Ch. Naval Acad. 55-62; Cmdt., 1st Naval Dist. 62-65; C/S, ROCN GHQ 65-67, Dep. C-in-C 67-70, C-in-C 70-76; Chief of the Gen. Staff, MND 76-81; Min. of Nat. Def. 81-86; Strategy Adv. to the Pres. 86-87; Amb. to Panama 87-91; *Add.* 538 Pei An Rd., Taipei.

SOONG, JAMES C.Y. 宋楚瑜

Gov., Twn. Prov. 93-; Res. Fel., Inst. of Intl. Rel., NCU 74-; Mem., CC, KMT 81-, & CSC 88-; *b.* Hunan Mar. 16, '42; *m.* Chen, Viola; *1 s., 1 d.; educ.* LL.B., NCU 64; MA, UC-Berkly. 67; M.A.L.S., Catholic U. of Am. 71; Ph.D., Georgetown U. 74; Hon. Ph.D., Catholic U. 95; Hon. Ph.D., U. of S. Australia 95; Sec., Exec. Yuan 74-77; Assc. Prof., NTU 75-78, & NTNU 75-80; Dep. Dir.-Gen., GIO 77-79, Dir.-Gen. & Govt. Spokesman 79-84; Personal Sec. to the Pres. 78-81 & 84-89; Dir.-Gen., Dept. of Cul. Aff., CC, KMT 84-87; Mng. Dir., CTV 84-93, & TTV 84-93; Dep. Sec.-Gen., CC, KMT 87-89, Sec.-Gen. 89-93. *Publ.: A Manual for Acad. Writers; How to Write Acad. Papers; Pol. & Public Opinion in the USA; Keep Free Ch. Free; Add.* 1 Sheng Fu Rd., Chung Hsing New Village, Nantou County.

SOONG, MAYLING 宋美齡

(Madame Chiang, Kai-shek)

Pres. & Founder, Nat. Women's League of the ROC; Chmn., Bd. of Trustees, Fu Jen Catholic U.; Bd. Chmn. & Founder, Hua Hsing C.'s Home, Hua Hsing High School, & Chen Hsing Rehabilitation Med. Cent.; Dir.-Gen., Women's Assn., KMT; Hon. Pres., Taipei Intl. Women's Club, Nurses' Assn. of Ch., Girl Scouts Assn. of Ch., & Ch. Women's Relief Assn. of New York; Hon.

Chmn., Am. Bu. for Med. Aid to Ch.; Mem., Bd. of Govs., Nat. Palace Museum, Catherine Lorillard Wolfe Art Club, & Tau Zeta Episilon; Hon. Mem., Phi Beta Kappa, Eta Chapter, Phi Delta Gamma, & New York Zoological Soc.; *b.* Kwangtung Feb. 12, 1898; *m.* Chiang, Kai-shek; *educ.* LHD, Bryant Coll., Providence, Rhode Island; Hobart & William Smith Coll., Geneva, New York; John B. Stetson U., Deland, Florida; Nebraska Wesleyan U., Lincoln, Nebraska; Piedmont Coll., Demorest, Georgia; LL.D., Goucher Coll., Baltimore, Maryland; Hahnemann Med. Coll., Philadelphia; Loyola U., Los Angeles; Russell Sage Coll., Troy, New York; Rutgers U., New Brunswick, New Jersey; U. of Hawaii; U. of Michigan, Ann Arbor; Wellesley Coll., Wellesley, Massachusetts; Wesleyan Coll., Macon, Georgia; LL.D. Honoris Causa, Boston U. Sesquicentennial; 1st Ch. Woman Appointed Mem., Child Labor Com.; inaugurated Moral Endeavor Assn.; established Schs. in Nanking for C. of Rev. Martyrs; Mem., Legis. Yuan; 1st Sec.-Gen. & Mem., Ch. Com. on Aeronautical Aff.; Dir.-Gen., New Life Movement; Chmn., Women's Adv. Coun.; frequently made inspection tours with the Pres. to all areas of free Ch.; Chmn. & Founder, Nat. Assn. for Refugee C., Nat. Ch. Women's Assn. for War Relief; Hon. Pres., Cttee. for Promotion of Welfare of the Blind; Hon. Chmn., British United Aid to Ch. Fund, Soc. for the Friends of the Wounded; Can. Red Cross Ch. Cttee.; Bd. Mem., India Famine Relief Cttee.; Patroness, Intl. Red Cross Com.; Life Mem., San Francisco Press Club & Assn. of Countrywomen of the World; Hon. Mem., Bill of Rights Commemorative Soc. & Filipino Guerrillas of Bataan Assn.; Chmn., CAC, KMT. *Publ.: Madame Chiang Kai-shek Messages in War & Peace 30-40; Sian: A Coup d'Etat 37; Ch. in Peace & War 39; Ch. Shall Rise Again 40; This is our Ch. 40; We Ch. Women 42; Am. Tour Speeches 42-43; Madame Chiang Kai-shek, Selected Speeches 58-59, 65-66; 10 Eventful Years, Encyclopedia Britannica 46; Albums of Reproductions of Paintings 52, 62; The Sure Victory 55: Speech Delivered to the Am. U. Club, Taipei 55; Speech Delivered at Shriners' Annual Ceremonial Banquet 57; Religious Writings 63; Opening Add. to the Int. Symposium on Ch. Painting 70; Album of Orchid Paintings 71; Album of Bamboo Paintings 72; Anti-Practiced Moral Cowardice & Anti-Marginal Thinking 72; Album of Landscape Paintings 73; Album of Floral Paintings 74; 3*

Unobscured Vistas-Tout Court 74; Gems of Truth Versus Brummagems 74; We Do Beschrei It 75; Maj. Gen. Claire Lee Chennault in Memoriam 75; Conversations with Mikhail Borodin 76; Messages to the Graduating Classes of Fu Jen Catholic U. 77-89; Christian Businessmen's Cttee. Intl. 3rd Asian CBMCI Convention 78; In Commemoration of the 50th Anniversary of Fu Jen Catholic U. 79; Madame Chiang Reminds Liao Cheng-chih of Communist Atrocities 82; Pledge of Resurgam 86; Sursum Corda 86; And Shall It Be See Ye To It? 86; An Introduction to Gen. Albert C. Wedemeyer's Book "On War & Peace" 87; Madame Chiang Kai-shek's Comments on Gen. Albert C. Wedemeyer's Bk. "On War & Peace" 87; Add. to the 13th Nat. Cong. of the KMT of Ch. 88; Boston U. Convocation Add. 89; A Salute to D-Day (June 6, 1944) on Pres. Eisenhower's Birthday Centenary 90; 50th Anniversary of AVG in Ch. 91; Message to Am. Volunteer Group in Ch. 91.

SU, CHEN-PING 蘇振平
Auditor-Gen., Nat. Audit Off., Control Yuan 89-; *b.* Twn. Oct. 28, '27; *m.* Huang, Su-mei; 2 *s.*, 1 *d.; educ.* Grad., NTU; Resr., Syracuse U.; Auditor, Sect. Chief, & Dir., Nat. Audit Off., Control Yuan 53-78, Dep. Auditor-Gen. 78-89; *Add.* 1 Hangchow N. Rd., Taipei.

SU, CHI 蘇起
Dir.-Gen., GIO 96-; Prof., Dept. of Dip., NCU 90-; *b.* Twn. Oct. 1, '49; *m.* Chen, Grace; 1 *s.*, 1 *d.; educ.* BA, Dip., NCU 71; MA, Johns Hopkins U. 75; MPS, Columbia U. 80, DPS 84; Assc. Prof., Dept. of Dip., NCU 84-90, Sec., Off. of the Pres. 89-90; Dep. Dir., Dept. of Mainland Aff., CC, KMT 92-93; Sec.-Gen., Ch. Pol. Sc. Assn. 90-91; Dep. Dir., Inst. of Intl. Rel., NCU 90-93; Mem., RDEC 90-94; V. Chmn., MAC 93-96. *Publ.: The Normalization of Sino-Soviet Rel.;* more than 20 papers & commentaries; *Add.* 2 Tientsin St., Taipei.

SU, CHING-SHEN 蘇青森
V. Chmn., AEC 95-; *b.* Kwangtung Oct. 10, '30; *m.* Lee, Kuei-chen; 1 *s.*, 2 *d.; educ.* BS, Naval Coll. of Tech. 54; MS, NTHU 63; Ph.D., Renselaer Polytechnic Inst. 66; Sr. Res. Assc., Marshall Space Flight Cent. 73-74; Dir., NScC 76-86; Assc. Prof. & Prof., NTHU 67-95, Dean 88-95. *Publ.: Vacuum Tech.* 78; & 100 papers; *Add.* 67 Lane 144, Keelung Rd., Sect. 4, Taipei.

SU, CHUN-HSIUNG
(See SU, J.H. 蘇俊雄)

SU, GERTRUDE 蘇玉珍
Pub., *Twn. Shin Sheng Daily News* 93-; Pres., Ch. Chapter, World Assn. of Women Jour. & Writers 94-; *b*. Indonesia Dec. 21, '32; 1 *d.; educ*. BA, NTU 54; Studied at Grad. Sch. of Jour., So. Illinois U. 58; Reporter, *CDN* 54-69; Corr. in Indonesia, CNA 69-78; Dep. Chief Ed., *CDN* 78-89; Dep. Dir., *Hong Kong Times* 89-93. *Publ.: The World of a Woman Reporter; Add*. 4th Fl.-2, 90 Tun Hua S. Rd., Sect. 1, Taipei.

SU, J.H. 蘇俊雄
Grand Justice, Jud. Yuan 94-; *b*. Twn. Aug. 12, '35; *m*. Su, Millie; 1 *s*., 1 *d.; educ*. LL.B., NTU 58, LL.M. 62; LL.D., Universität Freiburg, Germany 66; Asst., Inst. for Intl. Criminal Law, Freiburg, W. Germany 62-67; Res. Fel., U. of Köln 67-70; Assc. Prof., NTU 70-74, Prof. 74-94; Sr. Fel., Cul. Learning Inst., E.-W. Cent., U. of Hawaii 75-76; Mem., TPA 77-81; Comr., TPG 84-90; Mem., NA 91-94. *Publ.: Theory of Contract & Its Applications; Regierung und Verwaltung der Volkspublik Ch.; Theses on Const. Law; Method of Case-Study on Criminal Law; Theory on Rule of Law; German Party Law; Add*. 10th Fl., 54 Sungkiang Rd., Taipei.

SU, MING-TE
(See SUE, ALEXANDER 粟明德)

SU, YAN-KUIN 蘇炎坤
Prof., NCKU 83-, Dir.-Gen., Off. of Res. & Dev. 95-; Adjunct Prof., New York State U. 91-; Dir., ROC Vacuum Sc. Soc. 94-; *b*. Twn. Aug. 23, '48; *m*. Wang, Shiu-chi; 1 *s*., 2 *d.; educ*. BA, NCKU 71, MA 73, Ph.D. 79; Chmn., Dept. of Elec. Engr., NCKU 90-94, Assc. Dean 93-95; Visiting Prof., Stuttgart U., Germany 93-93. *Publ.:* 170 papers published in intl. jour. & conf.; *Add*. 36 Lane 201, Tung Ning Rd., Tainan.

SU, YANN-HUEI 蘇燕輝
Chmn., Ho Yu Investment Co. 81-, Kuo Zui Motors Ltd. 88-, Kuo Tu Motors Co. Ltd. 88-, & Ho Tai Motor Co. Ltd. 92-; V. Chmn., Fung Yong Co. Ltd. 86-; Dir., Wei Chuan Foods Corp. 69-; *b*. Twn. Nov. 1, '27; *m*. Wang, Ching-yun; 1 *s*., 3 *d.; educ*. Changhua Tech. Sch. 43;

Gen. Mgr., Ho Tai Motor Co. Ltd. 59-77, V. Chmn. 78-92; Chmn., Ch. Gravure Ind. Inc. 67-87, & Ho Tai Dev. Co. Ltd. 71-77; V. Chmn., Kuo Zui Motors Ltd. 84-88; *Add*. 14th Fl., 121 Sungkiang Rd., Taipei.

SU, YEN-HUI
(See SU, YANN-HUEI 蘇燕輝)

SU, YEN-KUN
(See SU, YAN-KUIN 蘇炎坤)

SU, YEONG-CHIN 蘇永欽
V. Chmn., Fair Trade Com. 96-; Prof., NCU 88-; *b*. Twn. Mar. 28, '51; *m*. Peng, Feng-jie; 1 *s*., 1 *d.; educ*. LL.B., NTU 72; Ph.D., U. of München 81; Assc. Prof., NCU 81-88; Mem., NA 92-96; Dean, NCU 95-96. *Publ.: Marching onto Const. Rule; A Challenge from the Econ. Law; Theory & Practice Under the Control of Const.; Add*. 4th Fl., 17 Lane 43, Mu Hsin Rd., Sect. 2, Wenshan, Taipei.

SU, YU-CHEN
(See SU, GERTRUDE 蘇玉珍)

SU, YUNG-CHIN
(See SU, YEONG-CHIN 蘇永欽)

SUE, ALEXANDER 粟明德
Bd. Chmn., Twn. Hardware Assn. 95-; Bd. Mem., Twn. Steel & Iron Ind. Assn. 94-; Pres., Hsin Kuang Steel Co. Ltd., Ching Shun Hardware Co. Ltd., & Ching Tung Co. Ltd. 85-; *b*. Taipei May 7, '53; *m*. Liu, Ling-wan; 1 *s*., 2 *d.; educ*. Advanced Class for Mgr., Cent. for Public & Business Admin. Educ., NCU; Pres., Ching Lai Hardware Co. Ltd.; Bd. Mem., Taipei County Hardware Assn. 92-95; *Add*. 17th Fl., 97 Chung Hsin Rd., Sect. 4, Sanchung, Taipei County.

SUN, CHIH-PING
(See SUN, TSE-PING 孫治平)

SUN, CHIN-SHU
(See SUN, CHIN-SU 孫金樹)

SUN, CHIN-SU 孫金樹
Pres., Kaohsiung Assn. of Certified Public Acct. (CPA) 91-; CPA, Chien Hsing Union & Co. 72-; *b*. Twn. Apr. 20, '43; *m*. Chen, Li-yu; 2 *s.; educ*. B., NCKU 72; Sup.,

Twn. Assns. of CPA 77-79; Standing Bd. Mem., Kaohsiung Assn. of CPA 79-91; Dir., Nat. Fed. of CPA Assn. of the ROC 88-91; *Add.* 12th Fl., 21 Lin Sen 2nd Rd., Kaohsiung.

SUN, I-HSUAN
(See SUN, I-SHUAN 孫義宣)

SUN, I-SHUAN 孫義宣
Chmn., Banking Inst. of the ROC; Exec. Dir., Bd. of Govs., CBC; Bd. Mem., Intl. Cml. Bk. of Ch.; *b.* Chekiang June 26, '20; *m.* Wang, Jeanne; 1 *s.,* 3 *d.; educ.* BS, Econ., St. John's U., Shanghai 42; Ph.D., Econ., U. of Wisconsin 53; Alt. Exec. Dir., Intl. Monetary Fund, Washington, D.C. 60-65; Dep. Gov., CBC, & concur. Gen. Mgr., For. Exchange Dept. 66-71; Pres., CTC 71-77 & Chiao Tung Bk. 77-80; Chmn., Bankers Assn. of the ROC 79-89, Export-Import Bk. of the ROC 80-86, & Bk. of Twn. 86-90. *Publ.: Salt Taxation in Ch.; Trade Policies & Econ. Dev. in Twn.; Add.* 4th Fl., 3 Nan Hai Rd., Taipei.

SUN, JACK T. 孫道存
Pres. & Dir., Pacific Elec. Wire & Cable Co. Ltd 86-; Chmn., Twn. Aerospace Corp. 94-; Exec. Dir., Walsin Lihwa Corp. 72-; V. Chmn., Pacific Construction Co. Ltd. 92-; Chmn., Coun. for Ind. & Com. Dev. 94-; Chmn., Twn. Electric Wire & Cable Ind. Assn. 90, & Twn. Aerospace Ind. Assn. 94-; Dir., Ch. Nat. Fed. of Ind. 91-; *b.* Taipei Aug. 27, '49; 2 *s.,* 3 *d.; educ.* Grad., Tamkang U.; *Add.* 4th Fl., 285 Chung Hsiao E. Rd., Sect. 4, Taipei.

SUN, JU-LING 孫如陵
Writer; *b.* Kweichow July 10, '17; *m.* Tsou, Shih-chin & Hsu, Ling-chia; 4 *s.,* 1 *d.; educ.* BJ, NCU 42; Asst. Ed., *CDN,* Chungking 42-44; Pres. & concur. V. Ed., *Hsi Chien Daily News,* Kweichow 44-46; Asst., Dept. of Jour., NCU 47; Dep. Dir., *CDN,* Nanking; Chief Ed., *CDN,* & *Mil. Weekly* 47-53; Mem., NA 53-92; Sec.-Gen., Coun. for Ch. Cul. Renaissance 79-93. *Publ.: A Res. on Newspapers; Writing & Contribution; A Match; One Hundred Essays; Two Hundred Essays; Add.* 68 Chung Yang 2nd Rd., Hsintien, Taipei County.

SUN, MING-HSIEN
(See SUN, PAUL MING-HSIEN 孫明賢)

SUN, PAUL MING-HSIEN 孫明賢
Nat. Policy Adv. to the Pres. 96-; Mem., CC, KMT 93-; *b.* Twn. June 8, '37; *m.* Shen, Chia-huei; 1 *s.,* 2 *d.; educ.* BS, NTU 60; MS, U. of Minnesota 66; Ph.D., Purdue U. 71; Hon. Ph.D., Purdue U. 96; Tchr., Tainan Mun. Nanning Jr. High Sch. 61-62; Tech., Tainan Dist. Agr. Improvement Station 62-67; Asst. Sp., Sr. Sp., & Chief of Plant, Ind. Div., JCRR 67-79; Adjunct Assc. Prof., NCHU 72; Adjunct Assc. Prof. & Prof., NTU 73-80; Sr. Sp. & concur. Chief of Planet, Ind. Div., COA 79-80; Dep. & Acting Dir.-Gen., Asian Vegetable Res. & Dev. Cent. 80-88; Comr., TPG 81-82, & Dept. of Agr. & Forestry 88-92; Chmn., COA 92-96; *Add.* 37 Nan Hai Rd., Taipei.

SUN, SEN-YEN 孫森焱
Grand Justice, Jud. Yuan 94-; *b.* Twn. Nov. 6, '33; *m.* Huang, Lu-hsing; 1 *s.,* 2 *d.; educ.* BS, NTU 56; Prosecutor, Dist. Court 61-62, Judge 62-70; Judge, Twn. High Court 70-79; Judge, Supreme Court 79-90, & concur. Presiding Judge 90-94. *Publ.: On Civil Law;* & several essays on laws & regln.; *Add.* 4th Fl.-3, 56 Ho Ping W. Rd., Sect. 1, Taipei.

SUN, TAO-TSUN
(See SUN, JACK T. 孫道存)

SUN, TSE-PING 孫治平
Nat. Policy Adv. to the Pres.; Mem., Com. of the Grand Alliance for Ch.'s Reunification Under the Three Principles of the People; V. Chmn., TTV; *b.* USA; *m.* Chang, May; 1 *s.; educ.* BA, UC-Berkly. 39; MA, New York U. 40; *Add.* Rm. A, 4th Fl., 261 Nanking E. Rd., Sect. 3, Taipei.

SUN, YUN-HSUAN
(See SUN, YUN-SUAN 孫運璿)

SUN, YUN-SUAN 孫運璿
Sr. Adv. to the Pres. 84-; *b.* Shantung Nov. 11, '13; *m.* Yu, Hui-hsuan; 2 *s.,* 2 *d.; educ.* BEE, Harbin Polytechnical Inst. 34; Engr. Tng. in Tennessee Valley Authority 43-45; Hon. Ph.D., Asian Inst. of Tech., Thailand 86; Engr., Nat. Resources Com. 37-40; Supt., Tienshui Elec. Power Plant 40-43; Head Engr., Elec. & Mech. Dept., Twn. Power Co. 46-50, Chief Engr. 50-53, V. Pres. & concur. Chief Engr. 53-62, Pres. 62-64; Chief Exec. Off. & Gen. Mgr., Electricity Corp. of Nigeria 64-

67; Min. of Comms. 67-69; Min. of Econ. Aff. 69-78; Premier 78-84; *Add.* 7th Fl., 106 Ho Ping E. Rd., Sect. 2, Taipei.

SUNG, CHANG-CHIH
(See SOONG, CHANG-CHIH 宋長志)

SUNG, CHU-YU
(See SOONG, JAMES C.Y. 宋楚瑜)

SUNG, JUEI-LOW 宋瑞樓
Mem., Acad. Sinica 82-, Intl. Soc. for the Study of the Liver 67-, & Ed. Bd., *Jour. of Gastroenterology & Hepatology* 86-; Chmn., Hepatitis Control Cttee., DOH 83-; Prof. Emeritus, Coll. of Med., NTU 87-; Dir., Sun Yat-sen Cancer Cent., Koo Found. 90-; Hon. Pres., Digestive Endoscopy Soc. of Twn. 92-; Soc. of Internal Med., ROC 93-, & Gastroenterology Soc. of Twn., ROC 94-; *b.* Twn. Aug. 6, '17; *m.* Wu, Fang-ing; 1 *s.,* 3 *d.; educ.* MB, Taihoku Imperial U.; MD, Kyushu U.; Prof., Dept. of Internal Med., NTU 55-87, Chmn., Dept. of Clinical Pathology 55-58, Dir., Sch. of Med. Tech. 56-58, Chmn., Dept. of Internal Med. 71-77, & Inst. of Clinical Med. 78-83; Dir., Clinical Res. Cent., NTU Hosp. 82-89; Pres., Gastroenterological Soc. of the ROC 71-91; Rep. of the ROC, Chapter of the Intl. Soc. for Diseases of the Esophagus 81-85; Pres., Formosan Med. Assn. for the Study of the Liver 90-91; V. Pres., World Org. of Digestive Endoscopy 90-94. *Publ.: Lab. Exam. of Hepato-Biliary Disease; Hepatitis B Virus Infection & Its Sequelae in Twn.; Control of Hepatitis B in Twn.; Hepatocellular Carcinoma: Early Detection & Treatment; Prevention of Hepatocellular Carcinoma; Add.* 17th Fl., 63 Jen Ai Rd., Sect. 2, Taipei.

SUNG, JUI-LOU
(See SUNG, JUEI-LOW 宋瑞樓)

SUNG, MEI-LING
(See SOONG, MAYLING 宋美齡)

SZE, VINCENT 施文森
Grand Justice, Jud. Yuan 94-; *b.* Chekiang Mar. 11, '33; *m.* Sze, Celestina; 2 *s.; educ.* LL.B., NTU 58; MS, Oregon U. 62; Jur.D., Willamette U., USA 65; Visiting Scholar, Harvard U. 70; Assc. Prof. of Law, NCU 67-

70, Prof. 71-94, Chmn., Dept. of Law 69-72, Dean, Grad. Sch. of Ins. 85-92, Chmn., Dept. of Ins. 90-92. *Publ.: Law of Negotiable Instruments; Law of Ins.; Essays on Ins. Law; Analytical Study of Ins. Cases; Add.* P.O. Box 1-191, Taipei.

TAI, JUI-MING
(See TAI, RAYMOND R.M. 戴瑞明)

TAI, RAYMOND R.M. 戴瑞明
Amb. Extraordinary & Plenipotentiary of the ROC to the Holy See 96-; Mem., CC, KMT 93-; *b.* Chekiang July 21, '34; *m.* Lu, Teresa H.N.; 1 *d.; educ.* BA, For. Lang. & Lit., NTU 65; MA, Am. Studies, U. of Hawaii 68; Sch. of Intl. Aff., Columbia U. 68; Georgetown Leadership Seminar, Sch. of For. Aff., Georgetown U. 84; Sp., Dept. of N. Am. Aff., MOFA 68-70; Instr., Dept. of For. Lang. & Lit., NTU 69-71; 3rd Sec., Del. to the UN 71; 3rd Sec., Emb. in the USA 72-75, 2nd Sec. 75; Adv., Del. to Intl. Telecom. Satellite Org. 72-75; Dir., Dept. of Ovs. Prog., GIO 75-79, Sec.-Gen. 79-80, Dep. Dir.-Gen. 80-87; Prof., Dept. of Jour., Ch. Cul. U. 86-87; Dir.-Gen., Dept. of Cul. Aff., CC, KMT 87-89; Sec. to the Pres. 89-90; Adv. & V. Chmn., Res. & Planning Bd., MOFA 90; Rep., Taipei Rep. Off. in the UK 90-93; Dep. Sec.-Gen., Off. of the Pres. 93-96; Spokesman, Off. of the Pres. 93-96; Res. Fel. & Convener, Res. Cttee., NUC 93-96, Exec. Sec., Secretariat 93-96. *Publ.: A Study of Am. Public Opinions & Ch. Policy* 76; *Ovs. Images of the ROC* 82; *Add.* The Emb. of the ROC to the Holy See, Presso la Santa Sede, Piazza Delle Muse 7, 00197 Roma, Italia.

TAN, CHIEN-KUO
(See TARN, JIANN-QUO 譚建國)

TANG, CHEN-CHU
(See TANG, HENRY C. 唐振楚)

TANG, FEI 唐飛
C-in-C, ROCAF 92-; *b.* Kiangsu Mar. 15, '32; *m.* Chang, Ming-tsan; 1 *s.,* 2 *d.; educ.* Grad., Air Force Preparatory Sch. 51; Ch. Air Force Acad. 52; Air Force Squadron Off. 61; ROCAF CGSC 71; War Coll., Armed Forces U. 79; Pilot 53-60; Op. Off. 60-61; Flight Leader 61-65; Squadron Cmdr. 68-70; Assc. Air Attaché, Emb. in the USA 72-75; Wing Chief, Op. Sect., 3rd Wing, ROCAF 75-76; Group Cmdr. 76-78; Armed Forces Attaché, Emb.

in S. Africa 79-82; Wing Cmdr. 83-84; Dep. C/S, Directorate, MND 84-85; Supt., Ch. Air Force Acad. 85-86; Dir., Dept. of Pol. Warfare 86-89; Op. Cmdr. 89; Dep. C-in-C, ROCAF 89-91; Dir., Dept. of Inspection, MND 91-92; *Add.* ROCAF GHQ, Jen Ai Rd., Sect. 3, Taipei.

TANG, P.P. 唐盼盼
Pres., *CDN*; Hon. Pres., Ch. Prof. Baseball Org.; *b.* Hunan Apr. 3, '42; *m.* Chao, Helen; 1 *s.,* 1 *d.; educ.* BJ, Pol. Warfare Coll. 64; MA, Jour., So. Illinois U. 73; Chief Ed., *CDN* 76-77, Dep. Ed.-in-Chief 77-79; Dir., Dept. of Media Res., GIO 79-82; Dir., News & Ovs. Prog., BCC 80-83, V. Pres. 83-86; Pres., CNA 92-93; *Add.* 260 Pa Te Rd., Sect. 2, Taipei.

TANG, PAN-PAN
(See TANG, P.P. 唐盼盼)

TANG, YAO-MING
(See TANG, YIAU-MIN 湯曜明)

TANG, YIAU-MIN 湯曜明
C-in-C, ROC Army 96-; *b.* Twn. Nov. 29, '38; *m.;* Liu, Hsiu; 2 *s.,* 1 *s.; educ.* BS, Ch. Mil. Acad. 62; Dip., Cmd. & Staff Coll., Armed Forces U. 74, Dip., War Coll. 87; Div. Cmdr., ROC Army 84-86, Corps Cmdr. 88-90, Dep. Field Army Cmdr. 90-93, Field Army Cmdr. 93-95, Dep. C-in-C 95-96; *Add.* P.O. Box 90601, Lungtan, Taoyuan County.

TAO, CHIN-SHENG
(See TAO, JING-SHEN 陶晉生)

TAO, JING-SHEN 陶晉生
Mem., Acad. Sinica 90-; Prof., E. Asian Studies, U. of Arizona; *b.* Hupei '33; *m.* Pao, Chia-lin; 3 *d.; educ.* BA & MA, NTU; Ph.D., Indiana U. 67; Res. Fel., Acad. Sinica 73; Prof., U. of Arizona 76, Chmn., Dept. of Oriental Studies 87-88; Chair Prof., Ch. U. of Hong Kong 88-90. *Publ.: The Jurchen in 12th-Century Ch.; Two Sons of Heaven; Add.* Dept. of E. Asian Studies, U. of Arizona, Tucson, AZ 85721, USA.

TAO, PAI-CHUAN 陶百川
Nat. Policy Adv. to the Pres. 77-; Mem., NUC 90-; *b.* Chekiang Jan. 19, '03; *m.* Chang, Shu-chun; 4 *s.,* 1 *d.; educ.* LL.B., Shanghai Law Coll.; Res. Fel., Harvard U.; Mem., Nat. Pol. Coun.; Mng. Dir., *CDN*; Mem., Control

Yuan. *Publ.: Searching for Truth in the USSR; The Three Principles of the People & Communism; The Cold War & Ch.'s Situation; Comparative Parliamentary Control of Admin.; The Complete Works of Tao Pai-chuan* (33 Vol.); etc.; *Add.* 57 6th St., Cent. Villa, Hsintien, Taipei County.

TARN, JIANN-QUO 譚建國
Prof., Dept. of Civil Engr., NCKU 79-; Ed.-in-Chief, *Jour. of the Ch. Inst. of Civil & Hydraulic Engr.* 94-; *b.* Ch. July 25, '46; *m.* Yang, Lih-Jean; 3 *d.; educ.* BCE, NCKU 68, MCE 71; Ph.D., Civil Engr., Duke U. 76; Assc. Prof., NCKU 76-79, Chmn. & Dean, Coll. of Engr. 85-91. *Publ.:* More than 50 papers; *Add.* Dept. of Civil Engr., NCKU, Tainan.

TENG, CHANG-LI
(See TENG, LEE CHANG-LI 鄧昌黎)

TENG, CHARLES S.S. 鄧申生
Dep. Rep., TERCO in the USA 96-; *b.* Shanghai Oct. 17, '40; 2 *s.; educ.* BA, NCU 64; Dip. Trainee, Australian Nat. U. 72; Asst. Ed., CNA 67-70; Staff, Dept. of N. Am. Aff., MOFA 72-74; V. Consul, Consl. in Portland, USA 74-76; 3rd Sec., Emb. in the USA 76-79; Sr. Asst., CCNAA, Washington, D.C. 79-82; Dep. Dir., Dept. of N. Am. Aff., MOFA & concur. Sect. Chief, 1st Sect. 82-86; Dep. Dir.-Gen., CCNAA, New York 86-89; Dir., Secretariat Div., CCNAA, Washington, D.C. 89-93; Rep., TECO, Austria 93-96; *Add.* Praterstrasse 31/15 OG, A-1020 Vienna, Austria.

TENG, CHI-FU
(See DEN, CHI-FU 鄧啟福)

TENG, CHUAN-CHANG
(See DUNN, KAN C. 鄧權昌)

TENG, LEE CHANG-LI 鄧昌黎
Mem., Acad. Sinica; Fel., Am. Phys. Soc.; Adjunct Prof. of Phys., U. of Wisconsin 91-; Dir., Accelerator Phys. & Diagnostics, Advanced Photon Source Project, Argonne Nat. Lab. 89-; Bd. Chmn., Synchrotron Radiation Res. Cent. 83-; *b.* Peking Sept. 5, '26; *m.* Huang, Nancy Laishen; 1 *s.; educ.* BS, Peking Fu Jen Catholic U. 46; MS, U. of Chicago 48, Ph.D. 51; Lectr., U. of Minnesota 51-52, Asst. Prof. 52-53; Asst. Prof., U. of Wichita 53-54, Assc. Prof. 54-55; Asst. Physicist, Argonne Nat. Lab.

55-56, Assc. Physicist 56-61, Sr. Physicist 61-67; Visiting Prof., NTHU 59; Head of Theoretical Group, Particle Accelerator Div., Argonne Nat. Lab. 56-62, Div. Dir. 62-67; Professorial Lectr., U. of Chicago 63-69; Dir., US-Korea "Sister Lab." Arrangements (AEC-AID Prog.) 64-67 & US-Ch. "Sister Lab." Arrangements (AEC-AID Prog.) 64-70; Head, Accelerator Theory Sect., Fermi Nat. Accelerator Lab. 67-72, Assc. Dir., Accelerator Div. 72-76, Head, Advanced Projects Dept., Accelerator Phys. Dept. 80-87, Lab. Dir.'s Off. for Sp. Projects 87-89; Chmn., US Nat. Accelerator Conf. 77; Dir., Synchrotron Radiation Res. Cent. Project Off. 83-85; Argonne Fel. 85-87. *Publ.:* About 400 tech. papers on high energy phys. & particle accelerator phys.; *Add.* 400 E. 8th St., Hinsdale, IL 60521, USA.

TENG, PEI-YIN
(See TENG, P.Y. 鄧備殷)

TENG, P.Y. 鄧備殷
Rep., Taipei Econ. & Cul. Cent. in New Delhi 95-; *b.* Ch. Jan. 9, '43; *m.* Gi, Yann-erl; 1 *s.,* 1 *d.; educ.* BA, NCU 65, MA, 69; Jr. Clerk, MOFA 72-73; Sec., Dir., & Rep., Chung Hwa Travel Service, Hong Kong 73-90; Dep. Dir., Bu. of Consular Aff., MOFA 91-92, Dir., Dept. of E. Asian & Pacific Aff. 92-95; *Add.* Taipei Econ. & Cul. Cent., 3A Palam Marg, Vasant Vihar, New Delhi-110057, India.

TENG, SHEN-SHENG
(See TENG, CHARLES S.S. 鄧申生)

TENG, TA-LIANG 鄧大量
Mem., Acad. Sinica 90-; Prof. of Geophysics, U. of So. Calif. 76-; *b.* Kwangsi July 3, '37; *m.* Lee, Evelyn May; 1 *s.,* 1 *d.; educ.* BS, Geol., NTU 59; Ph.D., Geophysics & Applied Math., Calif. Inst. of Tech. 66; Asst. Prof., U. of So. Calif. 67-70, Assc. Prof. 70-76. *Publ.:* About 100 sc. publs.; *Add.* 1474 Rose Villa St., Pasadena, CA 91106, USA.

TIAO, CHIN-HUAN
(See TIAO, GEORGE C. 刁錦寰)

TIAO, GEORGE C. 刁錦寰
Mem., Acad. Sinica 76-; W. Allen Wallis Prof. of Statistics, Grad. Sch. of Business, U. of Chicago 82-; *b.* Lon-

don Nov. 8, '33; *m.* Chu, Pao-hsing; 4 *c.; educ.* BS, Econ., NTU 55; MBA, New York U. 58; Ph.D., U. of Wisconsin 62; Asst. Prof., U. of Wisconsin 62-65, Assc. Prof. 66-68, Prof. 68-81, Chmn., Dept. of Statistics 73-75; Visiting Chair Prof., NTU 75-76; Visiting Ford Found. Prof. of Statistics 80-81; Bascom Prof. of Statistics & Business, U. of Wisconsin 81-82. *Publ.: Bayesian Inference in Statistical Analysis; Directions in Time Series; The Collected Works of G.E.P. Box;* & 100 articles; *Add.* U. of Chicago, Grad. Sch. of Business, 1101 E. 58th St., Chicago, IL 60637, USA.

TIEN, CHANG-LIN 田長霖
Mem., Acad. Sinica 88-; Chancellor, Faculty Mem., & A. Martin Berlin Chair Prof. of Mech. Engr., UC-Berkly. 90-; *b.* Hupei July 24, '35; *m.* Liu, Di-hwa; 3 *c.; educ.* BS, NTU 55; MS, Mech. Engr., U. of Louisville 57; MA & Ph.D., Princeton U. 59; Faculty Mem., UC-Berkly. 59-88, Prof. of Mech. Engr. 68-88, Chmn., Thermal Systems Div. 69-71, & Dept. of Mech. Engr. 74-81, V. Chancellor-Res. 83-85; Consultant & Bd. Mem. of numerous ind., govt., & educ. org. 83-85; A. Martin Berlin Chair Prof. of Mech. Engr., UC-Berkly. 87-88; Exec. V. Chancellor, U. of Calif., Irvine 88-90. *Publ.:* 1 bk., 11 ed. Vol., 25 review & monograph articles, & over 280 refereed res. papers in heat transfer, thermal radiation, & other related energy & environmental subjects; *Add.* Off. of the Chancellor, UC-Berkly., Berkly., CA 94720, USA.

TIEN, PAO-TAI 田寶岱
Sec.-Gen., APLFD 91-; *b.* Peking Sept. 28, '16; *m.* Tien, Stella I.; 2 *s.,* 1 *d.; educ.* B., U. of Peking 39; Studied at U. of Chicago 47; V. Consul, Consl. in Chicago 43-47, Consul 47-49; Consul-Gen., AEAR in Yokohama 49-51; 1st Sec. & Counsl., Emb. in the Philippines 51-56; Dep. Dir., Dept. of E. Asian & Pacific Aff., MOFA 56-60; Consul-Gen., Consl. in Sydney 60-63; Charge d'Affaires, Emb. in the Philippines 63-64, Min. 64-67; Dir., Dept. of E. Asian & Pacific Aff., MOFA 67-69, & Dept. of W. Asian Aff. 69-70; Amb. to Saudi Arabia 70-75; *Add.* 2nd Fl., 261 Tun Hua S. Rd., Sect. 1, Taipei.

TIEN, PING-KENG
(See TIEN, PING-KING 田炳耕)

TIEN, PING-KING 田炳耕
Mem., Acad. Sinica; Fel. Emeritus, Photonics Res. Lab., AT&T Bell Labs; Mem., Nat. Acad. of Sc., Nat. Acad.

of Engr., USA, & Third World Acad. of Sc.; *b.* Chekiang Aug. 2, '19; *m.* Tien, Nancy N.Y.; 2 *d.; educ.* BEE, Nat. Cent. U. 42; MEE, Stanford U. 48, DSEE 51; Mem., Tech. Staff, AT&T Bell Labs 52-61, Head, Dept. of Electron Phys. 61-74, Dept. of Microelectronics 74-83, & Dept. of High Speed Elect. Res. 83-90. *Publ.:* More than 50 articles in microwave tech. & electron dynamics, parametric amplifier, acoustic & acousto-elec. effect, wave phenomena, superconductivity, optics & lasers, integrated optics, high speed elect.; *Add.* AT&T Bell Labs, Rm. 4F 307, Holmdel, NJ 07733, USA.

TIEN, WEI-HSIN 田維新
Comr., Exam. Yuan 90-; *b.* Shensi Aug. 16, '34; *m.* Lin, Su-o; 2 *s.; educ.* Ph.D., Michigan State U.; Asst., NTNU 64-66, Instr. 66-72, Assc. Prof. 72-78; Prof., Nat. Cent. U. 78-87, Prof. & Dept. Chmn. 79-85, Prof. & Coll. Dean 82-86; Res. Fel., Acad. Sinica 87-90. *Publ.: Mailer's Search for a Hero; A Study of Faulkner's Trilogy; Ideological Encounters; Add.* 3rd Fl., 5 Lane 377, Chung Cheng Rd., Hsintien, Taipei County.

TING, CHAO-CHUNG
(See TING, SAMUEL CHAO-CHUNG 丁肇中)

TING, CHIH-FA 丁之發
C-in-C, Combined Service Forces 96-; *b.* Anhwei Nov. 25, '35; *m.* Chao, Ju-yu; 1 *s.,* 1 *d.; educ.* BS, Ch. Mil. Acad. 59; Dip., CGSC 70, Dip., War Coll. 80; Dip., Sun Yat-sen Inst. on Policy Res. & Dev. 86; Cmdr., Matsu Def. Cmd. 86-88; Cmdr., Army Logistics Cmd. 88-90; Admin. V. Min. of Nat. Def. 90-92; Dep. C-in-C, ROC Army 92-94; Gen. Dir., Inspection Dept., MND 94-96; *Add.* P.O. Box 90481, Nankang, Taipei.

TING, CHUNG-MING
(See TING, HADJ DAWOOD C.M. 定中明)

TING, HADJ DAWOOD C.M. 定中明
Mem., Constituent Coun., World Muslim League RABITA 82-; Imam, Taipei Grand Mosque 72-; Adv., MOFA 81-; *b.* Hunan June 3, '13; *m.* Geng, Ching-lien; 1 *s.,* 3 *d.; educ.* BC, Nat. Al-azhar U., Cairo 38; Sect. Chief, MOFA 51-54; Counsl., Emb. in Lebanon 58-60; Chargé d'Affaire, in Mauritania 60-64; Min., Emb. in Libya, & concur. Dir., Off. in Beida 68-70; *Add.* 2nd Fl., 8 Alley 1, Lane 56, Min Sheng E. Rd., Sect. 4, Taipei.

TING, MAO-SHIH
(See DING, MOU-SHIH 丁懋時)

TING, MAO-SUNG
(See DING, MOW-SUNG 丁懋松)

TING, PANG-HSIN 丁邦新
Mem., Acad. Sinica; Prof. of Ch. Linguistics, UC-Berkly.; *b.* Kiangsu Oct. 15, '36; *m.* Chen, Chi; 3 *c.; educ.* BA & MA, Ch. Linguistics, NTU; Ph.D., Asian Lang. & Lit., U. of Washington; Assc. Res. Fel., Acad. Sinica 70-75; Assc. Prof., NTU 72-75, Prof. 75-89; Chmn., Linguistics Sect., Inst. of Hist. & Philology, Acad. Sinica 73-81, Assc. Dir. 81-85, Dir. 85-89. *Publ.: The Origin of Twn. Lang.; Ch. Phonology of the Wei-Chin Period; The Tan Chou Ts'un-Hua Dialect; Add.* Dept. of E. Asian Lang., UC-Berkly., Berkeley, CA 94720, USA.

TING, SAMUEL CHAO-CHUNG 丁肇中
Mem., Acad. Sinica 75-; Prof. of Phys., MIT 69-; Prof., Thomas Dudey Cabot Inst. 77-; *b.* Ch. Jan. 27, '36; *m.* Marks, Susan Carol; 1 *s.,* 2 *d.; educ.* BS, U. of Michigan 59, MS 60, Ph.D. 62, Hon. D.Sc. 78, Hon S.C.D. 78; Hon. S.C.D., Ch. U. of Hong Kong 87; Hon. S.C.S.U., Bologna 88; Fel., European Org. Nuclear Res., Geneva 63; Instr. of Phys., Columbia U. 64, Asst. Prof. 65-67; Group Leader, Deutsches Elektronen-Synchrotron, Hamburg, W. Germany 66; Assc. Prof., Phys., MIT 67-68; Prog. Cons. Div., Particles & Fields Am. Phys. Soc. 70; Fel., Am. Acad. Arts & Sc. 75; Mem., Pakistani Acad. Sc.; Assc. Ed., *Nuclear Phys. Bulletin* 70; Ed. Bd., *Nuclear Instruments & Methods; Add.* CERN, Geneva 23, Switzerland; Dept. of Phys., MIT, 51 Vassar St., Cambridge, MA 02139, USA.

TING, SHOU-CHUNG 丁守中
Dir.-Gen., Dept. of Youth Aff., CC, KMT 96-; Chmn., Bridge Across the Straits Found. 89-; Assc. Prof., Inst. of Pol. Sc., NTU 85-; *b.* Chekiang Sept. 1, '54; *m.* Wen, Tzu-ling; 2 *s.; educ.* BPS, NTU 76; MS, Intl. Pol., The Fletcher Sch. of Law & Dip., Tufts U. 82, Ph.D., 85; Chief Ed., *Free Ch. Monthly*, Boston 81-84; Assc. Resr., Inst. of Intl. Rel., NCU 85-92; Mem., Legis. Yuan 90-96, Convener, Nat. Def. Cttee., 88th Sess. *Publ.: The Dilemma of Disintegration—Nationalist Ch.'s Policy Towards Japan,* 1931-1937; *The Theory*

& *Practice of Crisis Mng.; Add.* 6th Fl., 61 Tien Mu W. Rd., Taipei.

TJIU, MAU-YING 邱茂英
Chmn., COA 96-; *b.* Kaohsiung Jan. 6, '36; *m.* Chern, Shiow-jyi; 1 *s.; educ.* BS, NCHU; Ph.D., U. of Goettingen, W. Germany; Assc. Prof., NCHU 68-72; Sr. Sp., JCRR 72-76; Dir., Dept. of Food & Salt Admin., MOF 76-81, & 5th Dept., Exec. Yuan 81-82; Dir.-Gen., Bu. of Agr., MOEA 82-84; V. Chmn., COA 84-92; Comr., Dept. of Agr. & Forestry, TPG 92-96. *Publ.: Strategy of Rice Production, Marketing & Price in Twn.; Add.* 37 Nan Hai Rd., Taipei.

TO, TE-JUNG
(See TUO, DER-RONG 脫德榮)

TONG, C.H. 董炳熙
Chmn., Ability Ent. Co. Ltd.; *b.* Kaohsiung Jan. 27, '36; *m.* Tokiko, Nishio; 2 *d.; educ.* Grad., Waseda U.; *Add.* 147 Fu Hsing N. Rd., Taipei.

TONG, SHEN-NAN 童勝男
Mayor, Hsinchu City 89-; *b.* Twn. Feb. 10, '44; *m.* Chiang, Wen-chiao; 2 *s.; educ.* Ph.D., Polymer Inst., U. of Akron, USA 82; Dep. Dir., Union Ind. Res. Lab., Ind. Tech. Res. Inst. 73-82; Visiting Scientist, Case We. Reserve U., USA 78; V. Pres., Ch. Carbon Fiber Ind. Corp. 83-85; Dep. Dir.-Gen., Union Chem. Lab., Ind. Tech. Res. Inst. 85-89. *Publ.:* 21 patents & 80 articles; *Add.* 9 Lane 182, Lin Sen Rd., Hsinchu.

TOU, CHOU-SENG 杜筑生
Amb. to Senegal 96-; *b.* Kweichow Mar. 30, '42; *m.* Chiu, Maria Da-rouin; 2 *s.; educ.* LL.B., NTU; Docteur en droit, U. of Paris; Fel., Cent. for Intl. Aff., Harvard U. 88-89; Adjunct Assc. Prof., Soochow U. 76-79; Sect. Chief, MOFA 77-81; Dep. Dir.-Gen., Taipei Econ. & Cul. Off., Belgium 81-85; Sr. Sp., Dept. of European Aff., MOFA 85-86, Dep. Dir., Dept. of Treaty & Legal Aff. 86-89; Dir.-Gen., TECO, Greece 89-91; Dir.-Gen., CCNAA, Off. in Chicago 91-93; Dir.-Gen., Dept. of Protocol, MOFA 93-94, Dir.-Gen., Dept. of N. Am. Aff. 94-96; Adjunct Prof., Tamkang U. *Publ.: La Personalite Juridique Internationale d'Organes Subsidiaires des Nation-unies* 75; *The External Rel. of the European Communities* 87; *The Impact of the Single European Act on the Rel. Between the EC & E. Asia* 89; *Add.* 30 Avenue Nelson Mandela, B.P. 4164, Dakar, Senegal.

TOU, JULIUS T. 竇祖烈
Mem., Acad. Sinica; Grad. Res. Prof.; Dir., Cent. for Info. Res.; *b.* Shanghai Aug. 15, '26; *m.* Lisa; 3 *s.,* 1 *d.; educ.* BS, NCTU; MS, Harvard U.; Ph.D., Yale U.; Project Engr., Philco Corp. 52-54; Asst. Prof., U. of Penn. 54-57; Assc. Prof., Purdue U. 57-61; Prof., Northwe. U., USA 61-64; Dir., Battelle Inst. 64-67; Adjunct Prof., Ohio State U. 64-67. *Publ.: Digital Control Systems* 59; *Optimum Control Systems* 63; *Modern Control Theory* 64; *Computer & Info. Sc. I & II,* 63 & 66; *Software Engr.* 69; *Info. Systems* 72; *Pattern Recognition Principles* 74; *Computer-based Automation* 82; *Highly Redundant Sensing in Robotic Systems* 89; *Add.* Cent. for Info. Res., Coll. of Engr., U. of Florida, 314 CSE Bldg., Gainesville, FL 32611, USA.

TOU, TSU-LIE
(See TOU, JULIUS T. 竇祖烈)

TSAI, BIH-HWANG 蔡璧煌
Mem., Legis. Yuan 96-; Dir.-Gen., Dept. of Cul. Aff., CC, KMT 96-; Prof., NTNU 85-; *b.* Twn. Sept. 29, '45; *m.* Lee, Mei-li; 2 *s.; educ.* B.Ed., NTNU 72; MA, NCU 77; Ph.D., Stanford U. 85; Sect. Chief., Dept. of Educ., TPG 71-72; Instr., Tung Nan Jr. Coll. of Tech. 78-79; Dep. Sec.-Gen., Nat. Educ. Assn. *Publ.: Sch. & Students' Pol. Socialization; Classroom Climate & Pol. Socialization; Add.* 7 Lin Sen N. Rd., Taipei.

TSAI, CHANG-CHI
(See TSAI, CHOUN-CHI 蔡長啟)

TSAI, CHAO-SHENG 蔡朝生
Pres., Fang Sheng Intl. Corp. 85-; *b.* Twn. Oct. 9, '48; *m.* Lai, Hsiu-chu; 2 *s.,* 2 *d.; educ.* Grad., Kangshan Jr. High Sch. 65; Worked for Hsin Yi Screw Co. Ltd. 66-67, He Feng Factory 70-79; *Add.* 2-1 Lane 29, Min Chuan Rd., San Chieh Village, Luchu, Kaohsiung County.

TSAI, CHAO-YANG
(See TSAY, JAW-YANG 蔡兆陽)

TSAI, CHENG-WEN 蔡政文
Min. of State 96-; Prof., Pol. Sc., NTU 78-; Mem., RDEC 88-; Mem., CEC 95-; *b.* Taipei May 23, '40; *m.* Pien,

Yun-li; 2 *s.; educ.* BA, NTU 58-62; Licensie en Sc. Politiques et Sociales, U. Catholique de Louvain, Belgium 64-67; Ph.D., Katholike U., Belgium 67-73; Chmn., Dept. & Grad. Inst. of Pol. Sc., NTU 85-91; Dep. Dir.-Gen., Dept. of Org., CC, KMT 91-92; *Add.* 1 Chung Hsiao E. Rd., Sect. 1, Taipei.

TSAI, CHIA-CHE
(See TSAY, GREGORY J. 蔡嘉哲)

TSAI, CHING-CHU 蔡慶祝
Mem., Control Yuan 93-; *b.* Philippines Apr. 27, '40; *m.* Velez, Rosalina A.; 2 *s.*, 1 *d.; educ.* LL.B., NCU 63; Prin., Lety Ch. High Sch., Philippines 65-67; Mem., Legis. Yuan 84-87; *Add.* 2 Chung Hsiao E. Rd., Sect. 1, Taipei.

TSAI, CHING-YEN
(See TSAY, CHING-YEN 蔡清彥)

TSAI, CHOUN-CHI 蔡長啟
Pres., Nat. Twn. Coll. of Phys. Educ. 91-; *b.* Twn. May 19, '30; *educ.* BA, Normal U. 55; Advanced Study, Nat. Tokyo U. 66-67; Tchr., Prov. Changhua High Sch. 55-62, Tchr. & Chief of Phys. Educ. 62-64, Tchr. & Dean of Student Aff. 64-66; Tchr. 66-69; Lectr., Prov. Twn. Coll. of Phys. Educ. 69-72, Assc. Prof. 72-75; Dep. Dir. & Dir., Dept. of Phys. Educ., MOE 74-86; Prof., Nat. Twn. Coll. of Phys. Educ. 75-96. *Publ.: Sports Bldgs. & Equipment; Sports Admin.; Curriculum Standards of the Dept. of Phys. Educ., the Dept. of Recreational Sports & the Dept. of Dance, Nat. Twn. Coll. of Phys. Educ. & Taipei Phys. Educ. Coll.; Add.* 5th Fl., 28-1 Lane 91, Wei Tao St., Taichung.

TSAI, CHUNG-PO 蔡仲伯
Pres., Rotary Club in the ROC 94-; Bd. Chmn., Yuan Shun Construction Co. Ltd. 68-; *b.* Twn. Feb. 22, '27; *m.* Li, King-fan; 3 *s.*, 3 *d.; educ.* NTU 47; 21st Class, Cent. Police Coll. 49; Exec. Sec.-Gen., Assn. of Ch. Martial Arts of Taipei City 71-83; Gov., Dist. 348, Rotary Intl. 89-90; *Add.* 8th Fl., 20 Lane 53, Chung Shan N. Rd., Sect. 1, Taipei.

TSAI, JUEI-HSIUNG 蔡瑞熊
Pres., Kaohsiung Med. Coll. (KMC) 91-, Prof. of Internal Med. 73-; Phys. in Internal Med., Chung Ho Memorial Hosp. attached to KMC 70-; *b.* Twn. Dec. 26, '35;

m. Chang, Fown-tzu; 2 *d.; educ.* MD, KMC 60; DMS, Tokyo U. 69; Res. Fel., Pharmacology Div., Nat. Inst. of Radiological Sc., Japan 69; Visiting Fel., Cellular & Molecular Res. Lab., Cardiac Unit, Massachusetts Gen. Hosp., Med. Sch., Harvard U. 90-91; Resident, KMC Hosp. 61-64; Assc. Prof. of Internal Med., KMC 69-73; Dean of Student Aff. 72-73; Dir., Dept. of Internal Med., Chung Ho Memorial Hosp. 73-80 & 83-87, Dir., Dept. of Nuclear Med. 80-84; Visiting Prof. of Med., U. of Arkansas for Med. Sc. 82; V. Supt., Chung Ho Memorial Hosp. 85-90. *Publ.:* 123 original acad. reports & 367 abstract articles; *Add.* 100 Shih Chuan 1st Rd., Kaohsiung.

TSAI, JUI-HSIUNG
(See TSAI, JUEI-HSIUNG 蔡瑞熊)

TSAI, M.H. 蔡茂興
Bd. Chmn., Chang Hwa Cml. Bk. 95-; *b.* Twn. Nov. 9, '39; *m.* Chang, Ming-chao; 2 *s.; educ.* B., Cooperative Econ., NCHU 62; Clerk, Twn. Cooperative Bk. 63-70; Sect. Chief, Monetary Aff. Dept., MOF 70-75; Div. Chief, Dept. of Finance, TPG 75-78; Exec. V. Pres., Twn. Dev. & Trust Corp. 78-80; Pres., Twn. Life Ins. Co. Ltd. 80-87, Medium Business Bk. of Twn. 87-91, Hua Nan Cml. Bk. 91-94, & Bk. of Twn. 94-95. *Publ.: Preferential Tariff & Dev. Countries; Tax Problems of Cooperative Org. in Various Nations; Add.* 57 Chung Shan N. Rd., Sect. 2, Taipei.

TSAI, MAO-HSING
(See TSAI, M.H. 蔡茂興)

TSAI, NAN-HAI
(See CHUA, NAM-HAI 蔡南海)

TSAI, PI-HUANG
(See TSAI, BIH-HWANG 蔡璧煌)

TSAI, TSO-YUNG
(See CHAI, CHOK-YUNG 蔡作雍)

TSAI, WAN-TSAI 蔡萬才
Chmn., Fubon Group; Adv., Exec. Yuan & CC, KMT; Bd. Chmn., Assn. of Friends of Police, ROC; *b.* Taipei Aug. 5, '29; *m.* Yang, Shiang-shun; 2 *s.*, 2 *d.; educ.* LL.B., NTU; Mem. & Convener, Legis. Yuan; Chmn.,

ROC Amateur Athletic Fed., & Taipei Chamber of Com.; *Add.* 237 Chien Kuo S. Rd., Sect. 1, Taipei.

TSAI, WEN-CHING
(See TSAI, WEN-JING 蔡文景)

TSAI, WEN-JING 蔡文景
Spkr., Hualien CoCoun. 94-, Mem. 82-; *b.* Twn. June 8, '46; 1 *s.,* 3 *d.; educ.* Grad., Sr. High Sch.; Dep. Spkr., Hualien CoCoun. 90-94; *Add.* 23 Fu Chien Rd., Hualien.

TSAI, WEN-PIN 蔡文斌
Comr., Exam. Yuan 96-; Mem., NA 96-; Nat. Pres., ROC Jr. Chamber 87-; Convener, DPP caucus, NA 93-; *b.* Twn. Mar. 29, '53; *m.* Chen, Mei-hui; 1 *s.* 1 *d.; educ.* BA, NTU 75; Lawyer 77-96; Chmn., Presidium, NA 93-94. *Publ.: Practice Rule of Meeting; See You Tomorrow, Mr. Pres.; Add.* 1 Shih Yuan Rd., Wenshan, Taipei.

TSAN, KENNETH B.K. 曾文謙
Chmn., Hua Nan Cml. Bk. 95-; Chmn., Bankers Assn. of Twn., ROC 92-; *b.* Taipei Jan. 22, '28; *m.* Tseng Lin, Ying-Hwa; 3 *s.,* 1 *d.; educ.* B., Com., NTU 48; Exec. V. Pres., Bk. of Twn. 78-85; Pres., First Cml. Bk. 85-92; Chmn., Twn. Business Bk. 92-95; *Add.* 38 Chungking S. Rd., Sect. 1, Taipei.

TSAO, AN-PANG
(See TSO, PAUL O.P. 曹安邦)

TSAO, HSING-CHENG
(See TSAO, ROBERT H.C. 曹興誠)

TSAO, ROBERT H.C. 曹興誠
Chmn., United Microelectronics Corp. (UMC) 91-, Unipac Microelectronics Corp. 89-, World Wiser Elect. Inc. 89-; V. Chmn., TECO Info. System Co. Ltd. 95-; Standing Bd. Mem., Ch. Nat. Fed. of Ind. (CNFI); *b.* Shantung Feb. 24, '47; *educ.* BS, NTU 69; MS, NCTU 72; Dep. Dir., Elect. Res. Service Org. 79-81; V. Pres., UMC 80, & Pres. 81-91; Chmn., Assn. of Allied Ind. in Sc.-Based Ind. Park 87-93; Chmn., Intellectual Property Protection Cttee., CNFI 91-94; *Add.* 13 Chuang Hsin 1st Rd., Sc.-Based Ind. Park, Hsinchu.

TSAY, CHING-YEN 蔡清彥
V. Chmn., NSC, Exec. Yuan 96-; Adjunct Prof., NTU; *b.* Twn. Sept. 29, '44; *m.* Wu, Su-hwa; 1 *s.,* 1 *d.; educ.*

BS, NTU 67; Ph.D., U. of Utah 72; Postdoctoral Fel., Nat. Cent. for Atmospheric Res., USA 72-73; Res. Fel., Harvard U. 73-74; Assc. Prof., NTU 74-78, Prof., 78-89, Chmn., Dept. of Atmospheric Sc. 82-88; Dir.-Gen., Cent. Weather Bu., MOTC 89-94; Dir.-Gen., Civil Aeronautics Admin., MOTC 95-96. *Publ.:* More than 50 papers in domestic & intl. jour.; *Add.* 19th Fl., 106 Ho Ping E. Rd., Sect. 2, Taipei.

TSAY, GREGORY J. 蔡嘉哲
Pres., Chung Shan Med. & Dental Coll. 95-, Chmn., Rheumatology & Immunology Div. 86-, Prof., 90-; *b.* Kaohsiung May 15, '50; *m.* Huang, Elise; 3 *s.; educ.* MD, Tokyo Med. Coll. 73, Ph.D. 92; Dean, Chung Shan Med. & Dental Coll. 89-94, Dean of Student Aff. 94-95; *Add.* 113 Ta Ching St., Sect. 2, Taichung.

TSAY, JAW-YANG 蔡兆陽
Min. of Trans. & Comms. 96-; *b.* Twn. Jan. 2, '41; *m.* Wei, Shu-hui; 1 *s.; educ.* BE, NCKU 63; Studied, Hygienic Engr., Calif. State U. 73; Resr., MIT 93; Sect. Chief, TPG 74-76; Acting Dir., TCG 76-78; Dep. Dir.-Gen., Construction Dept., TPG 79-81, Dir.-Gen., 81-88; Dir.-Gen., MOI 88-91; Admin. V. Min. of Trans. & Comms. 94-96; *Add.* 2 Chang Sha St., Sect. 1, Taipei.

TSENG, CHI-CHUN 曾濟群
Dir., Nat. Cent. Lib. 92-; Prof., NCU; *b.* Kwangtung Sept. 9, '37; *educ.* LL.D., NCU; Prof., NCU 76-86; Dir., Nat. Inst. for Compilation & Transl. 86-92. *Publ.: Study of Legis. Proposal in Ch.; A Study of the Standing Cttee. of the Legis. Yuan; A Study of People's Petitions to the Legis. Yuan; Add.* 23 Lane 13, Yung Kang St., Taipei.

TSENG, CHIH-LANG
(See TZENG, OVID J.L. 曾志朗)

TSENG, HUA-SUNG 曾華松
Grand Justice, Jud. Yuan 94-; *b.* Twn. June 7, '36; *m.* Liang, Shu-yun; 2 *s.,* 1 *d.; educ.* Grad., Law Dept., Twn. Prov. Law & Com. Coll. 59; Attorney 61; Judge, Dist. Court 63-64, Prosecutor 64-71; Judge, Dist. Court 71-73, Twn. High Court 73-79, & Admin. Court 79-85; Divisional Chief Justice, Admin. Court 85-94. *Publ.: Admin. Litigation on Taxation; Admin. Litigation on Trademark Law; Admin. Court's Judgments on*

Remeasurement of Land Chart; Comparative Study of ROC & PRC Admin. Trial; Add. 3rd Fl., 4 Lane 48, Chaochow St., Taipei.

TSENG, IKE 曾鼎煌
Bd. Chmn., Merida Ind. Co. Ltd. 72-; Exec. Dir., Long Bon Construction Co. Ltd. 88-, & Chief Construction Corp. 89-; Bd. Mem., United Epitaxy Co. Ltd. 93-; *b.* Twn. Dec. 14, '32; *m.* Lin, Hsiu-feng; 1 *s.,* 1 *d.; educ.* High Sch. Grad.; V. Pres., Far E. Mach. Co. Ltd. 52-57; Bd. Chmn., Far Great Plastic Ind. Co. Ltd. 57-72; Pres., Merida Ind. Co. Ltd. 72-74; *Add.* 116 Mei Kang Rd., Mei Kang Village, Tatsun, Changhua County.

TSENG, TANG-KUANG 曾騰光
Pres., Chaoyang Inst. of Tech. 94-; *b.* Twn. Mar. 9, '38; *m.* Chen, Hsiu-ling; 1 *s.; educ.* BA, Sociology, Tunghai U. 67; Ed.B., Oklahoma City U. 87; Ed.D., Drake U., USA 91; Sect. Chief, Soc. Youth Services, Tainan City Cttee., Ch. Youth Corps 69-71, Sup., Chiayi County Cttee. 71-74, V. Sect. Chief, Soc. Youth Services, Taipei Hqs. 75-78, Dir. 78-91; Adjunct Lectr., Ch. Cul. U. 88-89; Adjunct Assc. Prof., NCU 91-92; Assc. Prof. & concur. Dean of Student Aff., Tunghai U. 92-94. *Publ.: A Study of the Effect of a Counseling Tng. Prog. on Job Satisfaction of Volunteer Counsl.; A Study of the Perception of Characteristics of Voluntary Work & Willingness to Participate in Voluntary Work Among Coll. Students; A Study of the Sup. & Mng. of Volunteers; Add.* 168 Chi Feng E. Rd., Wufeng, Taichung County.

TSENG, TENG-KUANG
(See TSENG, TANG-KUANG 曾騰光)

TSENG, TING-HUANG
(See TSENG, IKE 曾鼎煌)

TSENG, WEN-CHIEN
(See TSAN, KENNETH B.K. 曾文謙)

TSENG, YEN-YI 曾元一
Pres., Ret-Ser Engr. Agency (RSEA) 91-; Mem., CC, KMT 93-; *b.* Ch. June 9, '41; *m.* Liao, Shu-mei; 1 *s.,* 1 *d.; educ.* MSE, NTU 63; BSCE, System Engr., Asian Inst. of Tech., Thailand 73; Prog. for Mng. Dev., Harvard

U. 83; Asst., Tamkang U. 64-66; Engr., Vinnel Corp. 66-73; Engr. Prog. Mgr., Gen. Mgr., V. Pres., & Chief Engr., RSEA 73-91; *Add.* 12th Fl., 207 Sungkiang Rd., Taipei.

TSENG, YUAN-I
(See TSENG, YEN-YI 曾元一)

TSIANG, YIEN-SI 蔣彥士
Sr. Adv. to the Pres. 89-; Adv., COA 79-; Mem., CC & CSC, KMT 93-; Chmn., Rural Dev. Found. 95-; *b.* Chekiang Feb. 27, '15; *m.* Cheng, May-ying; *educ.* BS, U. of Nanking 36; MS, U. of Minnesota 40, Ph.D. 42; Instr., U. of Minnesota 42-45; Exec. Sec., Off. of Rep. of Ch. Min. of Agr. & Forestry, Washington, D.C. 45-46; Chief, Dept. of Sp. Crops, Nat. Agr. Res. Bu. 46-48; Sec.-Gen., JCRR 48-61; Pres., Agr. Assn. of Ch. 61-63; Comr., JCRR 61-79; Sec.-Gen., Exec. Yuan 67-72; Min. of Educ. 72-77; Sec.-Gen., Off. of the Pres. 78; Min. of For. Aff. 78-79; Sec.-Gen., CC, KMT 79-85; Nat. Policy Adv. to the Pres. 85-89; Sec.-Gen., Off. of the Pres. 90-94; V. Chmn., Cttee. on Sc. Dev., NScC 67-91; Counsl., Acad. Sinica 63-96; *Add.* 122 Chungking S. Rd., Sect. 1, Taipei.

TSO, PAUL O.P. 曹安邦
Mem., Acad. Sinica 72-, & European Acad. of Arts, Sc. & Humanities 80-; Prof. of Biophysics, Dept. of Biochemistry, Sch. of Hygiene & Public Health, Johns Hopkins U.; *b.* Hong Kong July 17, '29; *m.* Wong, Muriel M.Y.; 1 *s.,* 2 *d.; educ.* BS, Lingnan U. 49; MS, Michigan State U. 51; Ph.D., Calif. Inst. of Tech. 55; Res. Fel., Biology Div., Calif. Inst. of Tech. 55-61, Sr. Res. Fel. 61-62; Co-organizer (with Prof. James Bonner) of the 1st World Conf. on Histone Biology & Chem. 63; Assc. Prof., Biophysical Chem., Dept. of Radiological Sc., Johns Hopkins U. 62-67, Prof. 67-73; 1st Dir., Inst. of Molecular Biology (IMB), & concur. Chmn., IMB Adv. Cttee., Acad. Sinica 82-94; Co-organizer (with Dr. J. Dipaolo) of World Symposium on Model Studies in Chem. Carcinogenesis 72; Organizer of Intl. Symposium on Molecular Biology of Mannalian Genetic Apparatus 75; Co-organizer (with Prof. B. Pullman & Dr. E.L. Schneider) of Jerusalem Symposium on Carcino-Genesis-Fundam. Mech. & Environmental Effects 80; Organizer, Symposium on Establishment of a Bioassay Sys-

tem for Risk Assessment in Energy Tech. 82; Organizer, 4th Gen. Meeting of European Expert Cttee. on Biophysics, UNESCO 82; Co-organizer (with Prof. C. Nicolini), 4th Course of Intl. Sch. Pure & Applied Biostructure, NATO Adv. Study Inst. 83; Co-organizer (with Prof. B. Pullman & Dr. E.L. Schneider), Jerusalem Symposium on Interrelation Among Differentiation, Cancer, & Aging 85; Organizer, Intl. Conf. on Nucleic Acid Med. Applications, Mexico 93. *Publ.:* Over 350 sc. papers, 13 bk., & 40 reviews; *Add.* Johns Hopkins U., Dept. of Biochemistry, Rm. 3102, 615 N. Wolfe St., Baltimore, MD 21205, USA.

TSONG, TIEN T. 鄭天佐
Res. Fel. & concur. Dir., Inst. of Phys., Acad. Sinica 92-, Mem. 93-; *b.* Twn. Sept. 6, '34; *m.* Tsong, Miaw F.; 3 *d.; educ.* BS, Phys., NTNU 60; MS, Phys., Penn. State U. 64, Ph.D. 66; Postdoctoral Resr., Phys. Dept., Penn. State U. 67-69, Asst. Prof. 69-71, Assc. Prof. 71-75, Prof. 75-90, Disting. Prof. 90-93. *Publ.: Field Ion Microscopy, Principles & Applications; Field Ion Microscopy, Field Ionization & Field Evaporation; Atom-Probe Field Ion Microscopy;* & over 200 articles; *Add.* Inst. of Phys., Acad. Sinica, Taipei.

TSOU, CHIEN 鄒堅
Nat. Policy Adv. to the Pres. 90-; *b.* Fukien Aug. 16, '21; *m.* Pei, Linda Hsiang-yuen; 2 *s.,* 2 *d.; educ.* Ch. Naval Acad.; Royal Naval Coll., Greenwich, UK; Royal Naval Submarine Sch., UK; War Coll., Armed Forces U.; Capt., Destroyer-14 59-60; Aide-de-Camp to the Pres. 60-64; Cmdg. Off., Naval Post Grad. Sch. 64-65; Naval Attaché, Emb. in the USA 65-69; Cmdr., Destroyer Squadron 69-71, Surface Force 62, & Task Force 71-72; Chief Aide-de-Camp to the Pres. 72-75; Dep. C-in-C, ROCN 75-76, C-in-C 76-83; Dep. Chief of the Gen. Staff, MND 83-86; Amb. to S. Korea 86-90; *Add.* c/o Off. of the Pres., Taipei.

TSOU, CHIH-CHUANG
(See CHOW, GREGORY CHI-CHONG 鄒至莊)

TSUANG, MING T. 莊明哲
Mem., Acad. Sinica 96-; Stanley Cobb Prof. & Dir., Harvard 93-, Prof. 85-; *b.* Twn. Nov. 16, '31; *m.* Tsuang, Snow H.; 1 *s.* 2 *d.; educ.* MD, Coll. of Med., NTU 57; Ph.D., Psychiatry, U. of London 65, D.Sc., Psychiatric

Epidemiology & Genetics, Dept. of Sc. 81; Prof., U. of Iowa 75-82; Prof. & V. Chmn., Brown U. 82-85. *Publ.:* 243 reviews papers, 61 chapters, & 14 bk.; *Add.* Supt.'s Off., Mass. Mental Health Cent., 74 Fenwood Rd., Boston, MA 02115, USA.

TSUI, LAP-CHEE 徐立之
Mem., Acad. Sinica; Fel., Royal Soc. of Can. & Royal Soc. of London; Geneticist-in-Chief, Hosp. for Sick C., Toronto 88-; Sellers Chair in Cystic Fibrosis 89-; U. Prof., U. of Toronto 94-; *b.* Shanghai Dec. 21, '50; *m.* Tsui, Lan-fong; 2 *s.; educ.* B.Sc., Ch. U. of Hong Kong 72, M., Philosphy 74; Ph.D., U. of Pittsburgh 79; Resr., Biology Div., Oak Ridge Nat. Lab. 79-80, & Dept. of Genetics, Hosp. Sick C. 83. *Publ.:* Over 150 sc. papers in peer-reviewed jour. & over 45 review articles on human genetics, cystic fibrosis, chromosome 7 mapping & lens dev.; *Add.* Dept. of Genetics, Hosp. Sick C., Toronto, Ontario M5G 1X8, Can.

TU, CHI-KWANG 屠繼光
Amb. of the ROC in Kingdom of Tonga 96-; *b.* Chekiang Apr. 20, '32; *m.* Tu Tsen, Huey-Hsien; 1 *s.; educ.* LL.B., NCU 58; LL.M., Sydney U., Australia 86; Sr. Off., MOFA 64-66; 3rd Sec., Emb. in Australia 66-70, 2nd Sec., 70-73; Sect. Chief, MOFA 73-76; Consul, Consl. Gen. in New York 76-85; Sr. Sp. & Sect. Chief, MOFA 85-86, Dep. Dir. 86-89; Rep., Taipei Econ. & Cul. Off., New Zealand 89-94; Dir., MOFA 94-96; *Add.* P.O. Box 842, Nuku'alofa, Kingdom of Tonga.

TU, CHIN-JUNG 杜金榮
Dir., Gen. Pol. Warfare Dept., MNT 94-; *b.* Chekiang Nov. 21, '32; *m.* Chen, Yu-hui; 2 *s.; educ.* BA, Mil. Acad. 57; Dip., War Coll., Armed Forces 75; Div. Cmdr., Dep. Army Cmdr., Admin. V. Min. of Def., Dir.-Gen., Inspection Dept., Dep. Chief of the Gen. Staff, MND; *Add.* P.O. Box 90012, Taipei.

TU, HSIU-HSIUNG 涂秀雄
Dep. Rep., TECROJ 93-; *b.* Twn. Sept. 1, '30; *m.* Lin, Shu-jong; 1 *s.,* 2 *d.; educ.* BA, NTU 53; 2nd Sec., Emb. in Japan 72; Dir., Dept. of Sec., AEAR 78-80, Dir., Visa Dept., Tokyo Off. 81-82, & Osaka Off. 83-88; Dir., Dept. of Gen. Aff., MOFA 89-90; Sec.-Gen., AEAR 90-93; *Add.* 20-2, 5-Chome, Shirokanedai, Minato-ku, Tokyo 108, Japan.

TU, KUO-WEI 屠國威
Sculptor 75-; Academico, Accademia Delle Muse, Firenze, Italy 88-; *b.* Taipei Mar. 12, '47; *m.* Lin, Hui-chen; 1 *d.; educ.* Grad., Nat. Twn. Acad. of Arts 70; Diploma di Licenza, Accademia di Belle Arti-Roma 75; Resident Artist in Acad., Nat. Twn. Acad. of Arts 89-90. *Works: The Wave of 4 Seasons* (exhibited at Campo Del Sole, Trassimeno Lake, Italy) 88; *Surveying* (Kaohsiung Fine Arts Museum) 91; *The Monument of 2·28* (Kaohsiung) 93; *Position* (Twn. Fine Arts Museum) 95; *Add.* 3-2 Lane 9, Li Shui St., Taipei.

TU, SHAN-LIANG 杜善良
Counsl. & Dir., 1st Dept., Exec. Yuan 95-; *b.* Kaohsiung Aug. 28, '40; *m.* Chang, Kuei-ying; 2 *s.,* 1 *d.; educ.* LL.B., NCU 65, MPA 69; Sect. Chief, RDEC 72-78, Sr. Resr. & concur. Sect. Chief 76-78; Sr. Sp., CEPD 78-81, Dep. Dir. 81-87, Dir. 87-95. *Publ.: Evaluation of Econ. Dev. Plans; Problems of Public Construction Projects & Countermeasures; Add.* 3rd Fl., 11 Alley 39, Lane 308, Ho Ping E. Rd., Sect. 3, Taipei.

TUNG, CHIUNG-HSI
(See TONG, C.H. 董炯熙)

TUNG, HSIANG-FEI 董翔飛
Grand Justice, Jud. Yuan 94-; Adjunct Prof., NCHU 94-; *b.* Kiangsu July 21, '33; *m.* Shen, Jung; 2 *s.,* 1 *d.; educ.* LL.B., NCHU 58; LL.M., NCU 69; Visiting Scholar, Calif. State U., Sonoma 86; Dep. Dir., Dept. of Civil Aff., MOI 69-79; Dep. Sec.-Gen., CEIC 72-78; Assc. Prof., NCHU 79-83, Prof. 83-95, Chmn., Dept. of PA 80-93, Sec.-Gen. 93-94; Mem., NA 92-94; Adjunct Prof., NCU, NTNU, Tunghai U. & Soochow U. *Publ.: A Theory of Local Self-Govt.; The Const. & Govt. of the ROC; Add.* 9th Fl.-3, 226 Fu Hsing N. Rd., Taipei.

TUNG, SHENG-NAN
(See TONG, SHEN-NAN 童勝男)

TZEN, WEN-HUA 鄭文華
Admin. V. Min., MOFA 96-; *b.* Twn. May 30, '36; *m.* Chang, Mei-yu; 2 *d.; educ.* BA, NTU 58; MA, U. of Hawaii 63; Staff Mem., MOFA 63-66; V. Consul, Consl., Cebu 66-68; Sect. Chief, Dept. of African Aff., MOFA 68-73; 1st Sec., Emb. in Swaziland 73-78; Rep. to New Zealand 78-84; Dep. Dir., Dept. of African Aff., MOFA 84-86, Dir., Dept. of E. Asian & Pacific Aff. 86-87; Rep., Taipei Econ. & Trade Off. in Indonesia 87-91; Dep. Rep., CCNAA, Off. in Washington, D.C. 91-94; Dep. Sec.-Gen., NSC 94-96; *Add.* 2 Kaitakelan Boulevard, Taipei.

TZENG, OVID J.L. 曾志朗
Mem., Acad. Sinica 94-; Dean, the Coll. of So. Sc., NCKU 92-, Dir., Cognitive Sc. Cent. 90-; Visiting Scientist, Salk Inst. for Biological Sc., La Jolla 83-; *b.* Twn. Sept., 8, '44; *m.* Hung, Daisy Lan; 1 *s.; educ.* BA, NCU 66, MA 69; Ph.D., Penn. State U. 73; Visiting Assc. Prof., UC-Berkly. 78-79; Visiting Assc. Prof., the Haskins Lab., Yale U. 80-81; Visiting Prof., TNU 84-85; Prof., U. of Calif. at Riverside 80-94. *Publ.:* Co-author of "Cross-Linguistic Studies of Aphasia: A Ch. Perspective," *Handbook of Ch. Psychology;* "The Classifier Problem in Ch. Aphasia," *Brain & Lang.;* "Lateralization of Reading: Neurolinguistic Studies on Writing Systems," *Oxford Intl. Encyclopedia of Linguistics; Add.* 160 Sanhsing Village, Minghsiung Hsiang, Chiayi County.

WANG, C.C. 王正中
Mem., Acad. Sinica 92-; Prof., U. of Calif., San Francisco 81-; *b.* Peking Feb. 10, '36; *m.* Lee, Alice; 1 *s.,* 1 *d.; educ.* B.Sc., NTU 58; Ph.D., Biochemistry, UC-Berkly. 66; Postdoctoral Fel., Columbia U. 66-67, Princeton U. 67-69; Sr. Investigator, Merck & Co. Inc. 69-81; Dir., Inst. of Molecular Biology, Acad. Sinica 91-94. *Publ.:* 125 peer-reviewed papers, 40 bk. chapters, 114 abstracts, & 6 patents; *Add.* 22 Miraloma Drive, San Francisco, CA 94127, USA.

WANG, CHANG-CHING 王章清
V. Chmn., SEF 93-; Chmn., CETRA 88-; *b.* Hupei Sept. 22, '20; *m.* Lin, Hsueh-chen; 1 *s.,* 1 *d.; educ.* BCE, NCTU; MS, Environmental Engr., Johns Hopkins U. 66; Sr. Engr. & concur. Div. Chief, Dept. of Comms., TPG 49-58, Dir., Twn. Public Works Bu. 58-69; Dir., Dept. of Public Works, TCG 67-69; Pol. V. Min. of Comms. 69-77; V. Chmn., CEPD 77-84; Sec.-Gen., Exec. Yuan 84-88; *Add.* 7th Fl., 333 Keelung Rd., Sect. 1, Taipei.

WANG, CHAO-MING
(See WANG, CHOU-MING 王昭明)

WANG, CHENG-CHUNG
(See WANG, C.C. 王正中)

WANG, CHIA-YI 土甲乙
Exec. Dir., Judges' Assn., ROC; *b.* Twn. Oct. 29, '26; *m.* Lin. Tung-hsin; 2 *s.,* 2 *d.; educ.* Juges & Prosecutors Tng. Inst.; Hon. LL.D., New Coll. of Calif. 85; Judge, Dist. Court & Twn. High Court 56-65; Chief Prosecutor, Dist. Court 65-67; Presiding Judge, Twn. High Court 67-72; Justice & concur. Chief, Supreme Court 72-76; Pol. V. Min. of Justice 76-80; Pres. Admin. Court 80-87; Sec.-Gen., Jud. Yuan 87-93; Chief Justice, Supreme Court 93-96. *Publ.: Revised Civil Procedure; A Study of Civil Procedure; Add.* 10 Alley 1, Lane 24, Jen Ai Rd., Sect. 3, Taipei.

WANG, CHIH-KANG 王志剛
Min., MOE 96-; Prof., Sch. of Business, NTU 78-; *b.* Hopei Sept. 7, '42; *m.* Sung, Ye-li; 1 *s.,* 1 *d.; educ.* Ph.D., Texas A&M U.; Lectr., Coll. of Com., Texas A&M U. 77-78; Dir., Dept. of Intl. Trade, NTU 85-87; Exec. Sec., Investment Com., MOEA 88-89, Dir., Dept. of Com. 89-90; Admin. V. Min. of Econ. Aff. 90-92; Chmn., Fair Trade Com., Exec. Yuan 92-96. *Publ.: Theory of Marketing; Introduction to Business Admin.; Marketing;* etc.; *Add.* 12th Fl., 150 Tun Hua N. Rd., Taipei.

WANG, CHIN-FENG 王慶豐
Magis., Hualien County 93-; *b.* Twn. May 7, '33; *m.* Huang, Yi-yi; 2 *s.,* 2 *d.; educ.* Grad., Hualien Sr. High Sch.; Studied in Japan & USA; Mem., Hualien CoCoun. 61-86, Spkr. 71-86; Bd. Chmn., Medium Business Bk. of Twn. 86-90; Mem., TPA 90-93; *Add.* 17 Fu Chien Rd., Hualien.

WANG, CHIN-PING
(See WANG, JIN-PYNG 王金平)

WANG, CHING-FENG
(See WANG, CHIN-FENG 王慶豐)

WANG, CHING-HSU 汪敬煦
Strategy Adv. to the Pres. 88-; Bd. Chmn., Ch. Aviation Dev. Found. 88-; *b.* Peking May 30, '18; *m.* Ho, Shao-yao; 3 *d.; educ.* Studied at Nankai U. 38; Grad., Ch. Mil. Acad. 38, & US CGSC 48; Armed Forces U. 70; Cmdr., Army Platoon, Co., Battalion, Regiment, & Div. 38-51; Mil. Attaché to Iran 52-55; Cmdr., 81st & 17th Infantry Div. 58-60; Cmdt., Army Engr. Sch., & Chief, Army Engr. 60-67; Dep. Chief of Gen. Staff, Logistics & Op., MND 70-73; Cmdr., Army Logistics, Mil. Pol. Forces 73-75; Dir., Intelligence Bu., MND, C-in-C, Garrision Cmd., & Dir., Nat. Sec. Bu. 75-85; Personal Chief of Staff to the Pres. 85-88; *Add.* 2nd Fl., 131 Nanking E. Rd., Sect. 3, Taipei.

WANG, CHO
(See WANG, JAMES C. 王偉)

WANG, CHOU-MING 王昭明
Nat. Policy Adv. to the Pres. 96; *b.* Fukien Aug. 5, '20; *m.* Hu, Ping-hsin; 1 *d.; educ.* LL.B., Soochow U.; Nat. Def. Res. Inst.; Sec.-Gen., MOEA 65-69, & MOF 69-72; Dir., Dept. of Finance, TCG 72-75, & Dept. of Customs Admin., MOF 75-78; Admin. V. Min. of Finance 78-81; Pol. V. Min. of Econ. Aff. 81-84; V. Chmn., CEPD 84-88; Chmn., Twn. Power Co. 88-89; Sec.-Gen., Exec. Yuan 89-93; Min. of State 90-96; *Add.* 1 Chung Hsiao E. Rd., Sect. 1, Taipei.

WANG, CHUANG-WEI 王壯為
Calligrapher; Mem., Exec. Cttee., Ch. Calligraphy Assn. & Ch. Painting Assn.; Adv. to the Nat. Palace Museum; Prof., Ch. Cul. U. & NTNU; *b.* Hopei Jan. 22, '09; *m.* Chang, Ming-sui; 1 *s.; educ.* Peiping Chaoyang U.; Res. Fel. & Prof. 49-79. *Publ.: Collection of Calligraphy;* & 4 bk. on calligraphy; *Add.* 46 Lane 96, Hsing Lung Rd., Sect. 2, Taipei.

WANG, CORAL L.S. 王力行
Pub. & Ed.-in-Chief, *Global Views Monthly* 86-; Pub. & Ed.-in-Chief, *Commonwealth* 82-; *b.* Chungking Oct. 16, '45; *m.* Chang, Tsuan-sheng; 2 *s.; educ.* BA, NCU 67; Mng. Ed., the *Women Mag.* 72-78; Dir., *Ch. Times,* Hong Kong Off. 78-80; Dep. Ed.-in-Chief, *Ch. Times Mag.* 80-81; Dep. Ed.-in-Chief, *Commonwealth* 81-86. *Publ.: Meeting the Influential; With A Clear Conscience; Dedication: In Search of View; Add.* 7th Fl., 87 Sungkiang Rd., Taipei.

WANG, FEI
(See WANG, STEVEN F. 王飛)

WANG, HO-HSIUNG 王和雄
Grand Justice, Jud. Yuan 94-; *b.* Twn. Sept. 2, '41; *m.* Lin, Yueh-ling; 1 *s.,* 2 *d.; educ.* LL.D., NCU 92; Judge, Taipei Dist. Court 71-80, Prosecutor 80-81; Prosecutor, Twn. High Court 81-82, Kinmen Dist. Court 82-83, Twn.

High Court 83-87, & Supreme Court 87-88; Adv., MOJ 88-89; Prosecutor, Kinmen Br., Fukien High Court 90-93; Sec.-Gen., MOJ 93-94. *Publ.:* 30 articles on the sc. of law; *Add.* 124 Chungking S. Rd., Sect. 1, Taipei.

WANG, HSIAO-LAN
(See WANG, SHAW-LAN 王效蘭)

WANG, HSIU-HSIUNG 王秀雄
Prof., Tunghai U. 95-; Adjunct Prof., NTNU 95-; *b.* Twn. Mar. 5, '31; *m.* Lin, Pao-hsiu; 1 *s.,* 1 *d.; educ.* BA, NTNU 59; M. of Art Educ., Nat. Tokyo U. of Educ. 66; Instr., NTNU 66-70, Assc. Prof. 70-73, Prof. 73-95, Head, Dept. of Fine Arts & Dean, Grad. Inst. of Fine Arts 84-87. *Publ.: Art & Educ.* 90; *Psychology of the Fine Arts* 90; *A Discussion of the Hist. Dev. of Twn.'s Fine Arts* 95; *Add.* 4th Fl., 14 Alley 54, Lane 118, Ho Ping E. Rd., Taipei.

WANG, JAMES C. 王倬
Mem., Acad. Sinica; Mallinckrodt Prof. in Biochemistry & Molecular Biology, Harvard U. 88-; Mem., US Nat. Acad. of Sc. 86-; Fel., Am. Acad. of Arts & Sc. 84-; Mem., Ed. Bd., *Quarterly Reviews of Biophysics* 88-; *b.* Ch. Nov. 18, '36; *educ.* BS, NTU 59; MA, U. of S. Dakota 61; Ph.D., U. of Missouri 64; Asst. Instr., NTU 59-60; Res. Fel., Calif. Inst. of Tech. 64-66; Asst. Prof., Assc. Prof., & Prof. of Chem., UC-Berkly. 66-77; Mem., NIH Biophysics & Biophysical Chem. Study Sect. 72-76; Mem., Ed. Bd., *Jour. of Molecular Biology* 75-78; Prof. of Biochemistry & Molecular Biology, Harvard U. 77-88; Mem., Nat. Sc. Found. Adv. Cttee. for Physiology, Cellular & Molecular Biology 80-82; Mem., Ed. Cttee., *Annual Review of Biochemistry* 80-85, & Ed. Bd., *Nuclei Acids Res.* 81-85; Chmn., Dept. of Biochemistry & Molecular Biology, Harvard U. 83-85; Dir., Inst. of Molecular Biology, Acad. Sinica 86-87; Mem., NIH Molecular Biology Study Sect. 87-90, Chmn. 90-91; *Add.* Fairchild Bldg., 7 Divinity Avenue, Cambridge, MA 02138, USA.

WANG, JEN-HUNG
(See WANG, PETER JEN-HUONG 王仁宏)

WANG, JIN-PYNG 王金平
V. Pres., Legis. Yuan 93-, Mem. 75-; *b.* Twn. Mar. 17, '41; *m.* Chen, Tsai-lien; 1 *s.,* 2 *d.; educ.* BS, NTNU 65;

Convener, Finance Cttee., Legis. Yuan; Dep. Chmn., Policy Cttee., CSC, KMT, Chmn., Finance Cttee.; Dir., Dept. of Part-Govt. Coordination of the Legis. Yuan, & concur. Sec.-Gen., KMT Caucus; Mem., CSC, KMT; Pres., Sino-Japanese Interparliamentary Amity Assn.; *Add.* 1 Chung Shan S. Rd., Taipei.

WANG, JUI-HSIN 王瑞馼
Mem., Acad. Sinica; Einstein Prof. of Sc., State U. of New York, Buffalo 72-; *b.* Peking '21; *m.* Yang, Yen-chan; 2 *d.; educ.* BS, Nat. S.W. Assc. U. 45; Ph.D., Washington U. 49; Postdoctoral Fel., Washington U. 49-51; Res. Fel., Yale U. 51-53; Instr., Dept. of Chem., Yale U. 53-55, Asst. Prof. 55-58, Assc. Prof. 58-60, Prof. 60-62; Eugene Higgins Prof. of Chem. 62-64; Eugene Higgins Prof. of Chem. & Molecular Biophysics 64-72; Guggenheim Fel., Cambridge U. 60-61, & Yale U. 71-72; Mem., Am. Chem. Soc., Chem. Soc. (London), Am. Soc. of Biochemistry, Biophysics Soc., Am. Phys. Soc, Materials Res. Soc., Am. Soc. of Photobiology, & Electrochemistry Soc.; Sigma Xi; Fel., AAAS, Am. Inst. of Chem., & Am. Acad. of Arts & Sc. *Publ.:* Numerous articles pub. in prof. jour. & chapters in several monographs; *Add.* NSM Complex, State U. of New York at Buffalo, Buffalo, NY 14260-3000, USA.

WANG, KANG-PEI 王亢沛
Pres., Tunghai U. 95-; *b.* Fukien Dec. 10, '38; *m.* Wang Chen, Chi-hsiang; 1 *s.,* 1 *d.; educ.* BS, Tunghai U. 59; Ph.D., Temple U. 68; Prof., NTU 70-95; Pres., Ch. Phys. Soc. 77-78, Pres. 81-82 & 84-85; Visiting Prof., Cornell U. 85-86; Chmn., Dept. of Phys., NTU 91-93. *Publ.:* 34 papers; *Add.* 181 Taichung Harbor Rd., Sect. 3, Taichung.

WANG, KUANG-TSAN
(See WANG, KUNG-TSUNG 王光燦)

WANG, KUN 汪錕
Nat. Policy Adv. to the Pres. 96-; Chmn., Joint Credit Info. Cent. 96-; Mem., CC, KMT 93-; *b.* Kansu Jan. 9, '23; *m.* Lu, Ming-che; 1 *s.,* 2 *d.; educ.* LL.B., Econ., NCU 48; Res. Fel., Michigan State U. 59; Nat. War Coll. 70; Sun Yat-sen Inst. on Policy Res. & Dev. 77; Statistician, Bu. of Statistics, Min. of Budget, Acct. & Statistics 48-50; Insp., Bu. of Budget, DGBAS 50-57, Sect. Chief, 1st

Bu. 57-64, Sec. & Sr. Sp. 64-70, Dir. 70-78, Dep. Dir.-Gen. 78-90; Bd. Chmn., Intl. Trade Bldg. Corp., Taipei World Trade Cent. 90-93; Dir.-Gen., DGBAS 93-96; *Add.* 10th Fl., 2 Chungking E. Rd., Sect. 1, Taipei.

WANG, KUNG-TSUNG 王光燦
Distinguished Res. Fel., Inst. of Biochemistry, Acad. Sinica 72-; Prof., Dept. of Chem., NTU 68-; *b.* Twn. Oct. 19, '29; *m.* Yang, Mei-nien; 3 *s.,* 1 *d.; educ.* BS, Chem., NTU 52; D.Sc., Tohoku U., Japan 62; Teaching Asst., Dept. of Chem., NTU 54-58, Instr. 58-64; Assc. Res. Fel., Dept. of Chem., Stanford U. 62-64; Assc. Prof., Dept. of Chem., NTU 64-68; Visiting Scientist, Hormone Res. Lab., U. of Calif., San Francisco 69-71; Res. Fel. & Dir., Inst. of Biochemistry, Acad. Sinica 80-86. *Publ.:* 207 papers; *Add.* 7 Lane 58, Wenchow St., Taipei.

WANG, LI-HSING
(See WANG, CORAL L.S. 王力行)

WANG LIU, SHIAW 王劉笑
Pres., Wang-jih Aquatic Corp. 90-; *b.* Twn. Mar. 12, '41; *m.* Wang, Maw-sheng; 2 *s.,* 1 *d.; educ.* Studied, Chiatso Elementary Sch.; Pres., Yeong-Cherng Bakery 70-90; *Add.* 97 Chung Shan Rd., Chaochou, Pingtung County.

WANG, MAN-CHAO
(See WANG, MANN-TCHAO 王曼肇)

WANG, MANN-TCHAO 王曼肇
V. Chmn., AEC 93-; *b.* Ch. June 6, '47; *m.* Wu, Mei-luen; 1 *s.,* 1 *d.; educ.* BS, Phys., Tamkang U. 73; MS, Phys., Florida Inst. of Tech. 75; Ph.D., Phys., U. of Alabama 82; Asst. Prof., Judson Coll., USA 81-82, & U. of Alabama 82-84; Assc. Prof., Nat. Yang Ming Med. Coll. 85-90, & Nat. Def. Med. Cent. 86-90; Consultant, Veterans Gen. Hosp. 85-90; Dir., AEC 90-92; *Add.* 67 Lane 144, Keelung Rd., Sect. 4, Taipei.

WANG, MAO-LING
(See WANG, MAW-LING 王茂齡)

WANG, MAW-LING 王茂齡
Prof., Dept. of Chem. Engr., NTHU 79-; *b.* Twn. Aug. 21, '45; *m.* Lee, You-nan; 2 *s.; educ.* BS, NCKU 67, MS 69; Ph.D., Clarkson U., USA 74; Postdoctoral Res., Cornell U. 74-75; Assc. Prof., NTHU 76-79; Visiting

Scholar, UC-Berkly. 79-80; Chmn., Dept. of Chem. Engr., NTHU 85-88. *Publ.:* 160 articles in domestic & for. sc. jour.; *Add.* Dept. of Chem. Engr., NTHU, Hsinchu.

WANG, NENG-JANG 王能章
Dir.-Gen., Ovs. Aff. Dept., KMT 96-; *b.* Twn. Nov. 17, '43; *m.* Liu, Yu-mei; 1 *s.,* 2 *d.; educ.* LL.B., NCU 67; MA & Ph.D., U. of Madrid 73; Prof., Fu Jen Catholic U., Tunghai U., & Nat. Twn. Ocean U. 73-81; Adv., Ch. Youth Corps 75-76; Chmn., Keelung City Cttee., KMT 76-78, Twn. Prov. Cttee. 78-79, & Pingtung County Cttee. 79-81, Corr. in Latin Am. 81-86; Adv., A.S.P.E.C.T., & Pres., Ch. Cul. Cent., Paris 86-93; Comr., OCAC 91-93, V. Min. 93-96. *Publ.: Comparative Governmental Systems; The Policy & Admin. of Ovs. Ch. Aff.; Add.* 7th Fl., 53 Jen Ai Rd., Sect. 3, Taipei.

WANG, PETER JEN-HUONG 王仁宏
Nat. Policy Adv. to the Pres. 96-; Acting Pres. & concur. Sec.-Gen., Sino-German Cul. & Econ. Assn. 85-; Adv., MOEA & MOE 78-; *b.* Kaohsiung Aug. 10, '39; *m.* Du, Christine Min-shih; 3 *s.,* 1 *d.; educ.* LL.B., NTU 62; J.D., Heidelberg U. 70; Res. at Georgetown U. Law Cent. 77-78; Assc. Prof., Dept. of Law, NTU 70-75, Prof. 75-94; Visiting Scholar, Inst. for Intl. & For. Trade Law, Georgetown U. 77-78; Pres., Ch. Soc. of Comparative Law 79-80; Sup., CEIC 79-90; Visiting Prof., Law Dept. Vienna U. 84-85; Chmn., Dept. of Law, & concur. Dir., Grad. Inst. of Law, NTU 87-90; Comr., TPG 90-93; Dean of Gen. Aff., NTU 93-94; Chmn., RDEC 94-96; *Add.* 5th Fl., 180 Keelung Rd., Sect. 2, Taipei.

WANG, PI-LI
(See WANG, PI-LY 王必立)

WANG, PI-LY 王必立
Pub., *Econ. Daily News;* Chief Exec. Off., United Daily News Group; Pub., Ch. Econ. News Service, *United Evening News; b.* Szechwan May 2, '45; 1 *s.; educ.* Grad., Cml. Coll., Waseda U., Japan; Res. at Wright State U., Ohio; Japan & US Corr., *Econ. Daily News* 72-73, Asst. to Pub. 73-74, V. Pres. 74-77; *Add.* 555 Chung Hsiao E. Rd., Sect. 4, Taipei.

WANG, SAN-CHUNG 王三重
V. Chmn., COLA 94-; *b.* Twn. May 10, '39; *m.* Liang, Feng-yi; 3 *s.,* 1 *d.; educ.* LL.B., NTU 63; Pers. Off.,

Employment Service Dept., Bu. of Soc. Aff., TCG 70; Sp., Secretariat, TPG 70-74, Sect. Chief, Laws & Regln. Cttee. 74-79, Sec.-Gen. 79-85; Chmn., Laws & Rgln. Cttee., Kaohsiung City Govt. 85-87; V. Comr., Dept. of Soc. Aff., TPG 87-89, Dep. Sec.-Gen. 89-93; Chmn., Sup. Com. of Labor Ins. for Twn.-Fukien Area 93-94; *Add.* 15th Fl., 132 Min Sheng E. Rd., Sect. 3, Taipei.

WANG, SHAW-LAN 王效蘭
Pub., *Min Sheng Daily & United Daily News; b.* Chekiang July 7, '41; 1 *s.,* 1 *d.; educ.* Grad., World Coll. of Jour.; Universite de Fribourg, Institut de Langue Franáaise, Switzerland; Reporter, *United Daily News* 64-78; *Add.* 555 Chung Hsiao E. Rd., Sect. 4, Taipei.

WANG, SHENG 王昇
Nat. Policy Adv. to the Pres. 92-; Pres., Acad. Found. for the Promotion of Ch. Modernization; *b.* Kiangsi Oct. 28, '17; *m.* Hsiung, Hui-ying; 4 *s.,* 1 *d.; educ.* Grad., 16th Class, Ch. Mil. Acad.; 1st Class, Res. Dept., Cent. Pol. Cadre Coll.; 3rd Combined Combat Class, Rev. & Practice Res. Inst.; 4th Class, Inst. of Nat. Def. Res.; Hon. LL.D., Dankok U., S. Korea; Chief, Mil. Sect., Govt. of Kan Hsiang 41-45; Prefect of Students, Chia Hsing Youth High Sch., MND 45-46, Col. & Insp., Bu. of Preparatory Cadres 47-48, Cmdr., Pol. GP (Maj. Gen.) 49, Dep. Dir., Gen. Pol. Warfare Dept. (Maj. Gen.) 50-51; Maj. Asst. Cmdt., Pol. Staff Coll. 52-54; Cmdt., Pol. Staff Coll. (Maj. Gen.) 54-60; Exec. Dep. Dir., Gen. Pol. Warfare Dept., MND (Lt. Gen.) 60-74, Dir. (Gen.) 74-83; Amb. to Paraguay 83-91. *Publ.: The Theory & Practice of Enlightenment; The Theory & Practice of Pol. Warfare; Dr. Sun Yat-sen's Thoughts; A Study of San Min Chu I; A Tour of Am. Outlook on Vietnam; A Comparative Study of San Min Chu I & Other Isms; Leader & Nation; A Study of the Strategy Behind Russia's Invasion of Ch.; Life & Thoughts of Pres. Chiang Kai-shek; Duties of Intellectuals; Impressions of a Visit to the US; Add.* 5th Fl., 5 Lane 31, Wo Lung St., Taipei.

WANG, SHIH-CHUN 王世濬
Mem., Acad. Sinica; Prof., Coll. of Phys. & Surgeons, Columbia U.; *b.* Hopei Jan. 25, '10; *m.* Kwoh, Mamie H.W.; 2 *d.; educ.* BS, Yenching U. 31; MD, Nat. Peking U. 35; Ph.D., Northwe. U., USA 40; Asst. of Physiology, Peiping Union Med. Coll. 35-37; Fel., Ch. Med. Bd. 37-40; Instr., Northwe. U. 38-40; Instr., Asst. Prof.,

Assc. Prof., & Prof. of Physiology, Columbia U. 41-54; Prof. of Pharmacology 54-74; Gustavus A. Pfeiffer Prof. 74-78; Pfeiffer Prof. Emeritus; *Add.* 18 Kent Rd., Tenafly, NJ 07670, USA.

WANG, SHIH-YUAN
(See WANG, WILLIAM S.Y. 王士元)

WANG, SHU-MING 王叔銘
Strategy Adv. to the Pres.; *b.* Shantung Oct. 16, '07; *m.* Yu, Hsiang-yun; 1 *s.; educ.* Grad., Ch. Mil. Acad. 24; Kwangtung Mil. Aviation Sch. 25; Soviet Aviation Sch. 27; Soviet Advanced Fighter-Bombardment-Gunnery Sch. 28; Soviet Flying-Recon. Sch. 29; Ch. Cent. Aviation Sch. 32; Nat. Def. Coll. 54; Cmdr., 2nd Bomber Squadron, ROCAF 34; Dir., Cent. Aviation Sch., Loyang Br. 36; Cmdt., Airman Pilot Sch. 40; Cmdt., Ch. Air Force Acad., & concur. Cmdr., 5th Route Cmd. 41; Dir., US Air Force Voluntary Group, Com. on Aeronautical Aff. 42; Cmdr., 3rd Route Cmd., & concur. Cmdt., Air Force Cmd. & Staff Coll. 42; Dep. Dir., Com. on Aeronautical Aff. 45; Dep. CG & C/S, ROCAF 46, C-in-C 52; Chief of the Gen. Staff, MND 57-59; V. Chmn., Strategy Adv. Cttee. 59-62; Chief Del. to the UN Mil. Staff Cttee. 62-71; Amb. to Jordan 72-75; *Add.* 7th Fl., 7 Lane 31, Wo Lung St., Taipei.

WANG, STEVEN F. 王飛
Dir.-Gen., Oficina Economica y Cul. de Taipei en Chile 90-; *b.* Kirin July 7, '38; *m.* Ta, Mary; 2 *c.; educ.* LL.B., NCU; Princeton-in-Asia Fel., Woodrow Wilson Sch. of Public & Intl. Aff., Princeton U.; Chargé d'Affaires, Ch. Legation, Portugal 65-69; Dir., Cent. of Sun Yat-sen, Spain 73-77; Dir., Dept. of Intl. Aff., MOFA 78-82, & Dept. of European Aff. 82-85; Amb. to Swaziland 85-87; Pol. V. Min. of For. Aff. 87-89; Amb. to S. Africa 89-90; *Add.* Burgos 345, Las Condes, Santiago, Chile.

WANG, SUNG-MAO 王松茂
Exec. Sec., STAG 92-; Mem., Adv. Coun., RDEC; *b.* Twn. Nov. 3, '23; *m.* Hsu, Liu-yu; 2 *s.,* 1 *d.; educ.* BS, NTNU 51; Ph.D., Chem., Duquesne U., USA 65; Asst. to Instr., NTNU 51-61; Res. Assc., Duquesne U. 65-66; Assc. Prof. & Prof., NTHU 66-82, Dir., Inst. of Chem. 66-76, Dean of Acad. Aff. 76-82; Dir. of Planning Div. & V. Chmn., NScC 82-84; Prof., NTHU 84-87; V. Chmn., NScC 87-92. *Publ.:* 50 papers on chem., includ-

ing NMR Studies of Metal Complexation, Solvent Extraction Chem., Hemocyanin & Model Compounds in Jour. Am. Chem. Soc., Nuclear & Inorganic Chem., Inorganic Chem. Acta; etc.; *Add.* 4th Fl., 7 Alley 20, Lane 96, Ho Ping E. Rd., Sect. 2, Taipei.

WANG, TO-NIEN 王多年
Nat. Policy Adv. to the Pres.; *b.* Antung Oct. 20, '13; 1 *s.,* 1 *d.; educ.* 10th Class, Ch. Mil. Acad.; 18th Class, Ch. Army U.; 2nd Class, Nat. Def. Coll.; US Army CGSC; Def. Cmdr., Kinmen 61-65; Dep. C-in-C, ROC Army 65-72; Dep. C/S, MND 72-75; C-in-C, CSF 75-78; Cmdt., Armed Forces U. 78-83; *Add.* 14 Alley 11, Lane 16, Wen Chang St., Taipei.

WANG, TSO-JUNG
(See WANG, TSO-YUNG 王作榮)

WANG, TSO-YUNG 王作榮
Pres., the Control Yuan 96-; *b.* Hupei Jan. 6, '19; *m.* Fang, Hsin-hsiang (deceased); 2 *s.,* 1 *d.; educ.* BA, Nat. Cent. U. 43; MA, U. of Washington 49, & Vanderbilt U., Nashville 58; Counsl. & Dir., Econ. Res. Cent., CUSA 59-63; Dir., 3rd Div., CIECD 63-65, Adv. 65-66; Chief, Ind. Studies Sect., ECAFE, UN 67-70; Prof. of Econ., NTU 53-88; Comr., Exam. Yuan 84-90; Ed.-Writer, *Ch. Times & Com. Times* 64-90; Min. of Exam. 90-96. *Publ.: Essays on Twn.'s Econ. Dev.; Essays on Twn.'s Econ. & Financial Problems; Twn.'s Econ. Miracle; Add.* 6th Fl., 22 Lane 116, Kuang Fu S. Rd., Taipei.

WANG, WILLIAM S.Y. 王士元
Mem., Acad. Sinica; Prof., Linguistics, Grad. Sch., UC-Berkly. 66-; *b.* Shanghai Aug. 14, '33; 2 *s.,* 2 *d.; educ.* Ph.D., U. of Michigan 60. *Publ.: Explorations in Lang.; Add.* 1142 Brown Avenue, Lafayette, CA 94549, USA.

WANG, YO-HUEI 王友輝
Dir., Playwright & Actor, Godot Theatre Co. 93-; Adjunct Lectr., Nat. Inst. of the Arts 93-; *b.* Taipei Sept. 19, '60; *educ.* BA, Dept. of Drama & Cinema, Ch. Cul. U. 82; M. of Fine Arts, Nat. Inst. of the Arts 93; Teaching Asst., Ch. Cul. U. 82-83; Dir. & Playwright, The Little House Theatre 82-84; Programmer & Mgr., Min-Shin TV & Cinema Co. 85-89; Programmer, Audio-Visual Div., Ch. Productivity Cent. 89-90; Dir. & Playwright, C. Theatre, Taichung City Cul. Cent. 90, & Tainan Hwa

Dan Theatre Group 93; Lectr., Hua Kang Arts Sch. 93-94. *Publ.: Autumn Elegy of the Cricket; Skyline I; The Baseball Dream of Youth; Skyline II; The Egret; Sketching; Add.* 11th Fl., 17 Lane 80, Tzu Chiang Rd., Tamsui, Taipei County.

WANG, YOU-THENG 王又曾
Mem., CC, KMT 93-, & CSC 94-; Chmn., Gen. Chamber of Com. of the ROC; V. Chmn., Ch. Business Coun. of the ICC in Taipei; Chmn., Ch. Bk.; Hon. Chmn., Ch. Rebar Co. Ltd., Chia Hsin Flour, Feed & Vegetable Oil Corp., Union Ins. Co. Ltd., & Omni Bk. N.A.; *b.* Hunan Mar. 5, '27; *m.* Ching, She-ying; 6 *s.,* 2 *d.; educ.* Hunan Prov. Coll. of Com.; Hon. Doctorate, St. John's U., USA; *Add.* 8th Fl., 219 Chung Hsiao E. Rd., Sect. 4, Taipei.

WANG, YU-CHEN
(See WANG, YU-CHENG 王玉珍)

WANG, YU-CHENG 王玉珍
Pub., *Twn. Times; b.* Twn. Oct. 26, '43; *m.* Wu, Li-yen; 4 *c.; educ.* Grad., World Coll. of Jour.; Pub., *Twn. Times* 82-87; Mem., Control Yuan; *Add.* 11th Fl., 210 Nanking E. Rd., Sect. 3, Taipei.

WANG, YU-HUI
(See WANG, YO-HUEI 王友輝)

WANG, YU-TSENG
(See WANG, YOU-THENG 王又曾)

WANG, YU-YUN 王玉雲
Nat. Policy Adv. to the Pres. 88-; Sr. Adv., Twn. Fertilizer Co. Ltd. 88-; *b.* Kaohsiung Mar. 22, '25; *m.* Lee, Su-mei; 4 *s.,* 4 *d.; educ.* Grad., Sauno Jr. Coll., Japan; Mem., Kaohsiung CCoun. 58-68, Dep. Spkr. 61-64, Spkr. 64-68; V. Chmn., Kaohsiung Mun. Cttee., KMT 68-73; Mayor, Kaohsiung City 73-81; Bd. Chmn., Twn. Fertilizer Co. Ltd., & concur. V. Chmn., Com. of Nat. Corp., MOEA 81-88; *Add.* 55 Chi Nan Rd., Sect. 2, Taipei.

WANG, YUNG-CHING 王永慶
Bd. Chmn., Formosa Plastics Corp., Nan Ya Plastics Corp., Formosa Chem. & Fibre Corp., & Cyma Plywood & Lumber Co. Ltd.; Chmn., Ming-chi Inst. of Tech.; *b.* Twn. Jan. 18, '17; *m.* Wang, Yueh-lan; 2 *s.,* 8 *d.; Add.* 201 Tun Hua N. Rd., Taipei.

WANG, YUNG-TSAI 王永在
Pres., Formosa Plastics Corp., & Formosa Chem. & Fibre Corp.; *b.* Twn. Jan. 8, '22; *m.* Wang, Pih-ruan; 2 *s.,* 5 *d.; Add.* 201 Tun Hua N. Rd., Taipei.

WAY, E. LEONG 梁棟材
Mem., Acad. Sinica 80-; Prof. Emeritus, U. of Calif., San Francisco 87-; *b.* Ch. July 10, '16; *m.* Li, Madeline; 1 *s.,* 1 *d.; educ.* BS, MS & Ph.D., UC-Berkly. & U. of Calif., San Francisco; Pharmaceutical Chemist, Merck & Co., USA 42-43; Instr., George Washington U. 43-46, Asst. Prof. 46-48; Asst. Prof., U. of Calif., San Francisco 49-52, Assc. Prof. 52-57, Prof. 57-87, V. Chmn. 57-67, Acting Chmn. 66-67, Chmn. 73-78; Tsumura Prof., Neuropsychopharmacology, Gunma U., Japan 89-90; Sr. Staff Fel., Nat. Inst. on Drug Abuse 90-91. *Publ.: New Concepts in Pain; Fundamentals of Drug Metabolism & Drug Disposition; The Biologic Disposition of Morphine & Its Surrogates; Endogenous & Exogenous Opiate Agonists & Antagonists;* sc. reviews & 400 original articles on drug metabolism, analgetics, dev. pharmacology, drug tolerance, dependence & Ch. materia medica; *Add.* Dept. of Pharmacology, U. of Calif., San Francisco, CA 94143-0450, USA.

WEI, CHIEN-KUANG
(See WEI, JAMES 韋潛光)

WEI, DUAN 韋端
Dir.-Gen., DGBAS 96-; Mem., Coun. on Educ. Reform 94-; *b.* Kwangsi Feb. 12, '49; *m.* Cheng, Su-ming; 2 *d.; educ.* BS, NTHU 71; MS, U. of S. Carolina 75, Ph.D. 77; Prof., Nat. Sun Yat-Sen U. 80-83; Dir., Dept. of Statistics, VAC 81-84; Dep. Dir., 3rd Bu., DGBAS 84-86, Dir. 86-92; Dir., Dept. of Budget, Acct. & Statistics, TCG 92-93; Dep. Dir.-Gen., DGBAS 93-96. *Publ.: Laws of Large No. of Tight Random Elements in Normed Linear Spaces; Nat. Sec., Nat. Def. & Econ. Dev.; Practical World Almanac; Practical Soc. Indicator; On the Structure of Public Expenditure; Add.* 1 Chung Hsiao E. Rd., Sect. 1, Taipei.

WEI, HAI-MING 魏海敏
Ch. Opera Actress 79-; Dir., Ch. Opera Assn. of the ROC 90-; Chmn., Taipei Ch. Opera Soc. 90-; *b.* Taipei Nov. 13, '57; *m.* Wong, Kwok-yue; 1 *s.,* 1 *d.; educ.* Grad., Hai-kuang Ch. Opera Sch. 78; Nat. Twn. Acad. of Arts 86; Performed in *The Kingdom of Desire* (a Ch. adoption of *Macbeth*), *War & Eternity* (a Ch. adoption of *Hamlet*) with the Contemporary Legend Theatre; *Add.* 3rd Fl., 203 Sung Jen Rd., Taipei.

WEI, HSIAO-MENG
(See WEI, SIMONE 魏小蒙)

WEI, JAMES 韋潛光
Mem., Acad. Sinica; Dean, Sch. of Engr. & Applied Sc., Princeton U. 91-; Pres., Am. Inst. of Chem. Engr. 88-; *b.* Shanghai Dec. 7, '30; *m.* Fang, Virginia; 4 *c.; educ.* NCTU, Shanghai; BS, Georgia Inst. of Tech. 52; D.Sc., MIT 55; Engr., Mobil Oil Co. 55-70; Prof., U. of Delaware 71-77; Prof. & Head, Dept. of Chem. Engr., MIT 78-91; V. Pres., Am. Inst. of Chem. Engr. 87-88. *Publ.: Structure of Chem. Process Ind.; Add.* 571 Lake Drive, Princeton, NJ 08540, USA; Engr. Quadrangle, Olden Avenue, Princeton, NJ 08540, USA.

WEI, MIN
(See WEI, HAI-MING 魏海敏)

WEI, SIMONE 魏小蒙
Chmn. & Pub., *Ch. News; b.* Peking Jan. 4, '35; 2 *d.; educ.* BFA, Pratt Inst., New York; Pres., Sim Co. Ltd. 77-79; Chmn., Artapala Survey Co. Ltd. 83, & Artapala Tour Ltd. 84; *Add.* 16th Fl., 127 Sung Te Rd., Taipei.

WEI, TUAN
(See WEI, DUAN 韋端)

WEI, YUNG 魏鏞
Mem., Legis. Yuan 92-, & CC, KMT 93-; Prof., NCTU 90-; Bd. Chmn. & Dir. of Policy Res. Inst., Vanguard Found. 91-; Mem., IISS, London 81-; *b.* Hupei May 5, '37; *m.* Sun, Serena Ning; 2 *d.; educ.* LL.B., NCU 59; MA, U. of Oregon 63, Ph.D. 67; Instr. & Asst. Prof., Dept. of Pol. Sc., U. of Nevada 66-68; Asst. Prof., Dept. of Pol. Sc., Memphis State U. 68-69; NSF Visiting Scholar, Survey Res. Cent., U. of Michigan 69; Assc. Prof. of Pol. Sc., Memphis State U. 69-74; Visiting Assc. Prof., NCU 70-71; Prof. of Pol. Sc., Memphis State U. 74-76; Nat. Fel., Hoover Inst., Stanford U. 74-75; Dep. Dir., Inst. of Intl. Rel., NCU 75-76; Visiting Scholar,

Brookings Inst. 77; Chmn., RDEC 76-88; Chancellor, Sun Yat-sen Inst. on Policy Res. & Dev. 88-90. *Publ.: The Nature & Methods of the Soc. Scs.; Twn.: A Modernizing Ch. Soc.; Pol. Dev. in the ROC on Twn.; Analysis & Projections; A Methodological Critique of Current Studies on Ch. Pol. Cul.; Policy Planning: Theories & Practice; Sc., Elite, & Modernization; Striving for a Future of Growth, Equality, & Sec.; Add.* 4th Fl., 15 Chi Nan Rd., Sect. 1, Taipei.

WEN, SHING-CHUN 溫興春
Nat. Policy Adv. to the Pres. 96-; Prin., Mei Ho Jr. Coll. of Nuring & Admin., Pingtung 90-; *b.* Twn. Nov. 16, '26; *m.* Wen Chung, Den-mei; 1 *s.; educ.* BE, NTNU 51; Dean & Acting Prin., Pingtung's Chung Cheng, Kaohsiung's Feng Hsi, & Pingtung's Ming Cheng & Chih Cheng Jr. High Schs. 66-70, 70-74, 75-82, & 82-84; Prin., Pingtung's Chaochow Sr. High Sch. 84-85; Prin., Yunlin's Pei Kang Agri. & Ind. Voc. High Sch. 85-87; Mem., Legis. Yuan 87-90; *Add.* 12 Shuiyuan Lane, Fengtien Li, Pingtung.

WENG, CHI-HUI
(See WONG, CHI-HUEY 翁啟惠)

WENG, CHIN-KO 翁進科
Chmn., Intl. Life Line Assn., ROC Chapter; *b.* Twn. Jan. 24, '31; *m.* Hsiao, Lan-hsiang; 2 *s.,* 3 *d.; educ.* Prov. Chiayi Ind. Voc. Sch. 49; Tech., Chiayi Plant, Ch. Petroleum Corp. 48-52, Foreman, Kaohsiung Refinery 52-57; Foreman, Kaohsiung Plant, Ch. Am. Petrochemical Co. Ltd. 78-92; *Add.* 23 Lane 29, Nan Tzu Chiu St., Nantzu, Kaohsiung.

WENG, YUEH-SHENG 翁岳生
Grand Justice, Jud. Yuan 72-; Prof., NTU 70-; *b.* Twn. July 1, '32; *m.* Chuan, Shu-chen; 3 *d.; educ.* LL.B., NTU; D.J., Heidelberg U., W. Germany; Assc. Prof., NTU 66-70; Comr., Legal Com., Exec. Yuan 71-72, & RDEC 72; Visiting Prof., Sch. of Law, U. of Washington 91. *Publ.: Die Stellung der Justiz im Verfassungsrecht der Republik Ch.; Admin. Law & Rule of Law; Admin. Law & Jud. in a State Under the Principle of the Rule of Law; Add.* 19 Alley 9, Lane 143, Chun Kung Rd., Taipei.

WHANG-PENG, JACQUELINE 彭汪嘉康
Mem., Acad. Sinica 84-, Adv. Cttee., Lab. of Biomedical Sc. 85-; Chief, Cytogenetic Oncology Sect., Med.

Br., NCI, NIH, Med. Off. & Sr. Staff 68-; Med. Dir., Public Health Service 76-; *b.* Kiangsu Sept. 19, '32; *m.* Peng, George Pih-hsi; 2 *s.,* 2 *d.; educ.* MD, Coll. of Med., NTU 56; Intern, Resident & Chief Resident in Surgery, New UK Hosp., Boston 57-60; Visiting Fel., Sc. in Med. Br., NCI 60-68; Resident in Med., George Washington U. Hosp., Washington, D.C. 79. *Publ.:* More than 200 articles; *Add.* 6812 Tilden Lane, Rockville, MD 20852, USA.

WONG, CHI-HUEY 翁啟惠
Mem., Acad. Sinica; Prof., Dept. of Chem., Scripps Res. Inst., USA 89-; Elected Fel., Am. Acad. of Arts & Sc. 96-; Head, Frontier Res. Prog. on Glycotechnology, Riken, Japan 91-; *b.* Twn. Aug. 3, '48; *m.* Wong, Yiengli; 1 *s.,* 1 *d.; educ.* BS, NTU 70, MS 77; Ph.D., MIT 82; Postdoctoral Fel., Harvard U. 83; Asst. Prof., Texas A&M U. 83-86, Assc. Prof. 86-87, Prof. 87-89. *Publ.:* Over 300 essays on bio-organic chem., enzyme chem., & biotechnology; *Add.* Scripps Res. Inst., La Jolla, CA 92037, USA.

WU, AH-MING 吳阿明
Pres. & Pub., *Liberty Times; b.* Twn. Jan. 22, '24; *m.* Lee, Yu-yeh; 2 *s.,* 1 *d.; educ.* Keelung Cml. Acad.; Mem., Taipei CCoun. 54-68; Bd. Chmn., Twn. Gen. Trade Union 63-72; Mem., Taipei Provisional CCoun. 68-70; *Add.* 11th Fl., 137 Nanking E. Rd., Sect. 2, Taipei.

WU, ANDREW J.S. 吳仁修
Amb. to Guatemala 96-; *b.* Twn. Apr. 2, '37; *m.* Chen, Fu-mei; 2 *s.; educ.* LL.B., NCU 60; MA, Pol. Sc., U. Pedro Henriquez Urena, Dominican Repub. 84; Sr. Mem., Protocol Dept., MOFA 63-66; 3rd & 2nd Sec., Emb. in Guatemala 66-71; 2nd & 1st Sec., Emb. in Venezuela 71-74; 1st. Sec., Emb. in Panama 74-76; Sect. Chief & Sr. Sp., MOFA 76-79; Counsl., Emb. in Dominican Repub. 79-87; Dep. Dir.-Gen., MOFA 87-90; Rep., Taipei Econ. & Cul. Off. in Venezuela. *Publ.: Const. Law of the ROC; Add.* Apartado Postal 1646, Guatemala City, Guatamala.

WU, CHARLES C.L. 吳中立
V. Chmn., CCA 97-; Adjunct Prof., Coll. of Public Health, NTU 88-; *b.* Hopei Feb. 25, '50; *m.* Chou, Yung-yung; 2 *s.; educ.* BA, Econ., NTU 71; MA, Econ., State

U. of New York (SUNY), Albany 80, Ph.D., Econ. 82; Passed Civil Service Sp. Exam. A 88; Teaching Asst., Dept. of Econ., NTU 73-74; Adjunct Instr., Inter-U. Prog. for Ch. Lang. Studies, Stanford Cent. in Taipei 73-74, Admin. Off. 74-76; Grad. Res. Asst., Dept. of Econ., SUNY, Albany 76-78, Grad. Teaching Asst. 78-81; Grad. Student Intern, Dept. of Soc. Services, New York 79; Adjunct Lectr., Dept. of Econ., SUNY, Albany 81-82; Adjunct Instr., Dept. of Business Admin. & Econ., N. Adams State Coll., Massachusetts 82; Adjunct Assc. Prof., Inst. of Business Admin., Chung Yuan Christian U. 83-87, & Inst. of Public Health, Coll. of Med., NTU 83-88; Adjunct Assc. Resr., Inst. of Intl. Rel., NCU 85; Assc. Resr., Inst. of Econ., Acad. Sinica 82-88, Resr. 88-89; Dir., Dept. of Domestic Info. Services, GIO 89-92 ; Dep. Dir.-Gen., GIO 92-97. *Publ.: An Econometric Analysis of the Demand for Higher Educ. in the US, 1947-1978; Demand for Health—Past & Present; &* many other articles; *Add.* CCA, 1st-4th Fl., 102 Ai Kuo E. RD., Taipei.

WU, CHEN-TSAI 吳俊才
Chmn., CTV 93-; Nat. Policy Adv. to the Pres. 87-; *b.* Hunan Dec. 25, '21; *m.* Chen, Chwen-hwa; 1 *s.,* 2 *d.; educ.* Cent. Inst. of Pol. Sc., NCU; Post-grad. Sch., New Delhi, India; Sch. of Econ. & Pol. Sc., U. of London; Hon. Dr., Sung Kyun Kwan U., S. Korea; Rep. to India, *CDN* 47-49, Dir., Hong Kong Edition 51; Dir., Inst. of Intl. Rel., NCU 64-72; Pres., 1st Sino-Am. Conf. on Mainland Ch., Taipei 70 & 71; Prof. & Dean, Grad. Sch. of E. Asian Studies, NCU 68-73; Prof., NTU, NTNU, & Nat. War Coll.; Chief Del. to 2nd Sino-Am. Conf. on Mainland Ch., San Francisco 72; Dir.-Gen., Dept. of Cul. Aff., CC, KMT 72-76; Amb. to El Salvador 77-78; Pres. & Pub., *CDN* 78-79; Pub., *Ch. Forum;* Chmn., Bd. of Trustees, Nat. Fund for Lit. & Arts; Dep. Sec.-Gen., CC, KMT 79-84, & concur. Dep. Dir., Sun Yat-sen Inst. on Policy Res. & Dev. 84-87. *Publ.: Modern Hist. of India; Hist. of S.E. Asia; Indian Independence & Sino-Indian Rel.: Kashmiri & Indo-Pakistani Strife; Mahatma Gandhi & Modern India; On Cul. & Nat. Policy; Add.* 4th Fl.-1, 35 Lane 151, Jen Ai Rd., Sect. 4, Taipei.

WU, CHENG-CHUAN 吳澄泉
Chmn., Twn. Fertilizer 95-; *b.* Taipei Dec. 3, '30; *m.* Yen, Chueh-feng; 1 *s.,* 1 *d.; educ.* BS, NTU; Exec. V. Pres.,

Twn. Fertilizer Co. 88-94; Pres., Al Jubail Fertilizer Co. 84-88; Pres., Twn. Fertilizer Co., Ltd. 94-95; *Add.* 7th Fl., 90 Nanking E. Rd., Sect. 2, Taipei.

WU, CHENG-WEN 吳成文
Mem., Acad. Sinica 84-; Pres. & Disting. Scientist, Nat. Health Res. Inst. 96-; Disting. Res. Fel., Inst. of Biomedical Sc., Acad. Sinica 92-; Fel., Am. Inst. of Chemists 86-; *b.* Taipei June 19, '38; *m.* Chen, Felicia Y.H.; 2 *s.,* 1 *d.; educ.* MD, NTU 64; Ph.D., Biochemistry, Case We. Reserve U., USA 69; Postdoctoral Assc., Cornell U. 69-71; Sp. Fel., Yale U. 71-72; Asst. to Full Prof., Albert Einstein Coll. of Med. 72-78; Visiting Prof., Pasteur Inst., France 79-80; Prof. of Pharmacological Sc., State U. of New York, Stony Brook 80-90; Sp. Med. Res. Chair, NScC 88-92; Dir., Inst. of Biomedical Sc. 88-95. *Publ.:* More than 150 articles in biology & med.; *Add.* 128 Yen Chiu Yuan Rd., Sect. 2, Taipei.

WU, CHIA-SHENG 吳家聲
Admin. V. Min., MOF 96-; *b.*Twn. Oct. 2, '48; *m.* Tseng, Yu-fang; 1 *s.,* 1 *d.; educ.* BE, Soochow U. 72; ME, NCU 74; Ph.D., U. of Utah 81; Resr., CEPD 81-83, Sr. Sp. 83-87; Dir., Dept. of Overall Planning, COLA 87-89, Sec.-Gen. 89-94; Dir.-Gen., Dept. of Customs, MOF 94-96. *Publ.:* More than 30 papers; *Add.* 2, Ai Kuo W. Rd., Taipei.

WU, CHIN-TSAN
(See WU, KING-CHAN 吳金贊)

WU, CHING
(See WU, JIN 吳京)

WU, CHING-TANG 吳慶堂
Rep., TECO, Poland 92-; *b.* Twn. May 5, '40; *m.* Chen, Elena H.T.; 1 *d.; educ.* LL.B., NCU 63; Studied at Grad. Sch. of Dip., NCU 65, & Grad. Sch. of Business Admin., Evansville U., USA 70; Ph.D., Lincoln U., USA 82; Asst., MOFA 64-67; 3rd Sec., Emb. in Dominican Repub. 67-70; Sp. & Sect. Chief, MOFA 71-73; 2nd Sec., Emb. in Paraguay 73-76; Dir., Dept. of For. Aff., TPG 76-79, & US Liason Cent. of the Gen. Chamber of Com. 79-82; Dir., Dept. of Gen. Aff., MOI 82-84, & concur. Dep. Sec.-Gen., CElC 82-84; Counsl., Exec. Yuan 84; Dep. Dir.-Gen., Bd. of For. Trade, MOEA 84-90, Dir.-Gen., Dept. of Com. 90-92. *Publ.: The Role of*

US Chamber of Com. in Am. Pol. & Business; Add. 4th Fl., 54 Koszykowa St., 00-675 Warsaw, Poland.

WU, CHUN-TSAI
(See WU, CHEN-TSAI 吳俊才)

WU, CHUNG-LI
(See WU, CHARLES C.L. 吳中立)

WU, DELON 吳德朗
Chancellor, Chang Gung Coll. of Med. & Tech. 84-; *b.* Twn. Sept. 17, '41; *m.* Hung, Iou-jih; 1 *s.; educ.* MD, NTU 66; Intern & Resident in Med., Cook County Hosp., Illinois 67-69; Resident in Med. & Fel. in Cardiology, U. of Illinois 69-73; Asst. & Assc. Prof., U. of Illinois 73-78; V. Supt., Chang Gung Memorial Hosp. 78-82; Prof., U. of So. Calif. 82-84. *Publ.:* More than 150 original sc. papers on cardiology; *Add.* 5 Fu Hsing St., Kueishan, Taoyuan County.

WU, DEN-YIH 吳敦義
Mayor, Kaohsiung City 90-; Mem., CC, KMT 88-, & CSC 93-; *b.* Twn. Jan. 30, '48; *m.* Tsai, Lihng-yir; 3 *s.,* 1 *d.; educ.* BA, NTU 70; Ed.-Writer & Jour., *Ch. Times* 71-73; Mem., Taipei CCoun. 73-81; Magis., Nantou County 81-89; Chmn., Taipei Mun. Cttee., KMT 89-90. *Publ.: The Voice Beneath the Grassroots; Add.* 7 Kai Hsuan 2nd Rd., Kaohsiung.

WU, GENG 吳庚
Grand Justice, Jud. Yuan; Prof. of Law & Pol. Sc., NTU; *b.* Hainan Jan. 28, '40; *m.* Liu, S.L.; 1 *s.,* 1 *d.; educ.* LL.B. & MPS, NTU; DPS & Public Law, U. of Vienna; Prosecutor, Dist. Courts 68-73; Assc. Prof., NTU 77-81, Chmn., Dept. & Grad. Sch. of Pol. Sc. 84-85; Mem., Laws & Regln. Cttee., Exec. Yuan 79-85. *Publ.: Die Staatslehre des Han Fei; Pol. Neo-Romanticism; On Governmental Contacts; Admin. Law: Theory & Practice; Add.* 5th Fl., 101 Chaochow St., Taipei.

WU, HUA-PENG 吳化鵬
Nat. Policy Adv. to the Pres. 93-; *b.* Mongolia Nov. 21, '25; *educ.* LL.B., NCU; LL.M., U. of Oregon; Res. Fel., U. of Washington; 12th Class, Rev. & Implementation Res. Inst.; Rep., Mongolian Off. to the Nat. Govt. 46; Comr., MTAC 47-86; Mem., NA 47-89, Planning Bd.,

MOC 52, Planning Bd., Exec. Yuan 53-58, & CC, KMT 53-59; Educ. Sp., MOE 61-67; Mem., Const. Res. Coun. 68; Cul. Attaché & Counsl., Emb. in the USA 68-75; Rep., MTAC in Europe & USA 83-86; Chmn., MTAC 86-93; Adv., CAC, KMT 62-93; Chmn., Mongolian & Tibetan Found.; *Add.* 4th Fl., 3 Lane 8, Ching Tien St., Taipei.

WU, JEN-HSIU
(See WU, ANDREW J.S. 吳仁修)

WU, JIANN-KUO 吳建國
Acting Pres., Nat. Twn. Ocean U., 96-, Dean of Acad. Aff. 93-; *b.* Taipei, July 15, '50; *m.* Wu Kuo, Li-hwa; 1 *s.,* 2 *d.; educ.* Grad., Taipei Inst. of Tech. 71; MS, S. Dakota Sch. of Mines 81; Ph.D., U. of Nebraska 84; Engr., Sup., Twn. Metal & Mining Corp. 73-80; Assc. Prof. & Prof., Tatung Inst. of Tech. 85-89; Convener, preparatory cttee. of the Materials Eng. Inst., Nat. Twn. Ocean U. 92-93. *Publ.:* Over 150 jour. & conf. papers in materials Sc. & electrochemistry; *Add.* Nat. Twn. Ocean U., Keelung, Taiwan.

WU, JIN 吳京
Min. of Educ. 96-; Mem., Acad. Sinica 86-; Prof. of Hydraulic & Ocean Engr., NCKU 94-; Mem., Nat. Acad. of Engr. 95-; Pres., Ch. Soc. of Marine Sc. & Tech. 95-; Ocean Sc. Educator, Off. of Naval Res., USA 91-; Prof., H. Fletcher Brown Chair, U. of Delaware 80-; Dir., Air-Sea Interaction Lab., USA 79-; Adv., Tainan Hydraulics Lab., NCKU 77-; *b.* Nanking Apr. 9, '34; *m.* Chang, Tze-chen; 3 *s.; educ.* BS, Civil Engr., NCKU 56; MS, Mech. & Hydraulics, U. of Iowa 61, Ph.D. 64; Civil Engr., ROCN Hqs. 56-58; Tchr., Prov. Taitung Sr. High Sch. 58-59; Res. Asst., Inst. of Hydraulic Res., U. of Iowa 59-60, Res. Assc. 60-63; Head, Fluid Motions Div. 66-72, & Div. of Geophysical Fluid Dynamics 72-74; Visiting Lectr., Von Karman Inst. for Fluid Dynamics, Belgium 70; Coordinator, Phys. Oceanography Prog., Grad. Coll. of Marine Studies, U. of Delaware 74-75 & 79-80; Assc. Prof., Marine Studies & Civil Engr., U. of Delaware 74-75, Prof. 75-80; Expert-Consultant, Naval Res. Lab., USA 80; Hon. Res. Consultant, NScC 83; Visiting Prof., U. of Calif. 85; Mem., Hydrodynamics Adv. Com., Dept. of Def., USA 85; Nat. Invitation Chair, Inst. of Ocean-ography, NTU 86, & Coll. of Engr., NCKU 87; Adv.

Cttee. Mem., Res. Inst. for Applied Mech., NTU 88; Mem.-Consultant, Intl. Adv. Panel, Nat. Acad. of Sc. 88; Pres., NCKU 94-96. *Publ.:* 200 papers in intl. jour.; *Add.* MOE, 5 Chung Shan S. Rd., Taipei.

WU, JUI
(See WU, RAY 吳瑞)

WU, JUNG-I
(See WU, RONG-I 吳榮義)

WU, JUNG-MING
(See WU, RONG-MING 吳容明)

WU, KENG
(See WU, GENG 吳庚)

WU, KING-CHAN 吳金贊
Gov., Fukien Prov. 86-; Mem., CC, KMT 93-; *b.* Fukien Dec. 8, '36; *m.* Tang, Ching-ming; 4 *c.; educ.* Ph.D., Agr., Ch. Cul. U. 80; Dir., Forestry Aff. Off., Kinmen 64-71; Mem., Legis. Yuan 71-85. *Publ.: What Am I Doing in Legis. Yuan; Devoting to My Native Place for 14 Years; Add.* 2 Lane 228, Pei Hsin Rd., Sect. 2, Hsintien, Taipei County.

WU, MING-YEN 吳明彥
Amb. to Commonwealth of the Bahamas; *b.* Twn. Oct. 3, '39; *m.* Wu Lin, Mei-shiue; 3 *d.; educ.* LL.B., NCU 62 & 63-65; 2nd Sec., ROC Emb. in New Zealand 67-73; Sect. Chief, MOFA 73-75; Div. Chief, ROC Rep. Off. in Thailand 75-78; 1st Sec., Dept. of Consl. Aff., MOFA 84-87; Rep. of ROC in Sweden; *Add.* P.O. Box N-8325, Nassau, Bahamas.

WU, POH-HSIUNG 吳伯雄
Sec.-Gen., KMT, 96-; Mem., CC, KMT 76-, & CSC 86-; *b.* Twn. June 19, '39; *m.* Dai, Mei-yu; 2 *s.,* 1 *d.; educ.* BS, NCKU 62; Sun Yat-sen Inst. on Policy Res. & Dev.; 2nd Class, Construction Policy Res., Nat. Construction Inst.; Tchr., Twn. Prov. Chungli Cml. High Sch. 63-65; Mem., TPA 68-72; Assc. Prof., Nan Ya Jr. Coll. of Tech. 71-73; Magis., Taoyuan County 73-76; Dir., Inst. of Ind. Tng. for Workmen, & Friends of Labor Assn., & concur. Dir.-Gen., Twn. Tobacco & Wine Monopoly Bu. 76-80; Chmn., ROC Amateur Boxing Assn. 81-82; Dir.-

Gen., Secretariat, CC, KMT 82-84; Min. of the Int. 84-88; Chmn., CEC, KMT; Mayor, Taipei City 88-90; Min. of State 90-91 & 94; Min. of the Int., Mem. & Chmn. of the CElC, & Mem. of the PPRC 91-94; Sec.-Gen., Off. of the Pres. 94-96; *Add.* 122 Chungking S. Rd., Sect. 1, Taipei.

WU, RAY 吳瑞
Mem., Acad. Sinica; Prof., Sect. of Biochemistry, Molecular & Cell Biology, Cornell U. 66-; *b.* Peking Aug. 14, '28; *m.* Chan, Christina; 1 *s.,* 1 *d.; educ.* BS, U. of Alabama 50; Ph.D., U. of Penn. 55; Asst. Instr., Biochemistry Dept., U. of Penn. 51-55; Postdoctoral Fel., Dept. of Biochemistry, Public Health Res. Inst., New York 55-57, Asst. 57-58, Assc. 58-61, Assc. Mem. 61-66; Sr. Visiting Investigator, Stanford U. 65-66; Sr. Visiting Scholar, MRC Lab. of Molecular Biology, Cambridge, UK 71; Assc. Prof., Cornell U. 66-72; Visiting Assc. Prof., MIT 72; Chmn., Sect. of Biochemistry, Molecular & Cell Biology, Cornell U. 76-78. *Publ.:* Over 280 res. papers & 9 ed. bk.; *Add.* 111 Christopher Circle, Ithaca, NY 14850, USA.

WU, RONG-I 吳榮義
Sec. Gen., Control Yuan 96-; Dir.-Gen., Ch. Taipei Pacific Econ. Cooperation Cttee. 93-; Sec.-Gen., Ind. Dev. Adv. Coun., MOEA 93-; Prof., Inst. of Econ., NCHU 84-; Mem., Com. on Nat. Income Statistics, DGBAS 80-, & Adv. Cttee., CEPD 77-; *b.* Twn. Dec. 15, '39; *m.* Lin, Hui-mei; 1 *s.,* 1 *d.; educ.* BS, Econ., NTU 62, MS 66; MS, Econ., U. Catholique de Louvain, Belgium 70, D.Sc. 71; Assc. Prof., Prof., Acting Chmn. & Chmn., Dept. of Econ., NCHU 75-79, Prof. & Dir., Inst. of Econ. 79-84; Sr. Res. Fel. & Dir., Div. I, Twn. Inst. of Econ. Res. 85-92, V. Pres. 91-92; Dep. Dir.-Gen., Pacific Econ. Cooperation Cttee., Ch. Taipei 91-92; Dir.-Gen., Ch. Mem. Cttee., Pacific Basin Econ. Coun. 91-92; Comr., Fair Trade Com., Exec. Yuan 92-93; Pres., Twn. Inst. of Econ. Res. 93-96. *Publ.: The Strategy of Econ. Dev.: A Case Study of Twn.; Some Aspects of Export Trade & Econ. Dev. in Post-War Twn.;* & many articles published in prof. jour.; *Add.* 7th Fl., 16-8 Te Wei St., Taipei.

WU, RONG-MING 吳容明
Lt. Gov., Twn. Prov. 94-; *b.* Twn. Dec. 23, '43; *m.* Hsu, Fang-liang; 2 *s.,* 1 *d.; educ.* LL.B., NCHU 67, LL.M. 70;

Ph.D., NCU 90; Tech., Ind. Dev. Bu., MOEA 70-78; Chief Sec., Dept. of Land Admin., TCG 78-80, Sec.-Gen. 80-84, Dep. Dir. 84-86; Dep. Dir., Land Dept., TPG 86-88; Dep. Sec.-Gen., TPG 88-89, Dir., Land Dept. 89-93; Instr., Ch. Cul. U. 85-89; Assc. Prof., NCHU 90-91; Sec.-Gen., Exam. Yuan 93-94. *Publ.: A Study of the Result Analysis of Urban Land Readjustment & Its Evaluation Model; A Study of the Dev. of Slope Land in Twn.; A Comparative Study of Urban Land Readjustment & Zone Expropriation; Add.* 1 Sheng Fu Rd., Chung Hsing New Village, Nantou County.

WU, ROY Y.Y. 烏元彥
Dir.-Gen., TECO, Chicago 94-; *b.* Yunnan Feb. 8, '43; 1 *s.*, 1 *d.; educ.* BA, Tunghai U. 65; MA, U. of Penn. 68; Sec. to the Min. of For. Aff. 72-74; V. Consul, Consl.-Gen. in Los Angeles 74-77; 2nd Sec., Emb. in the USA 77-80; Eng. Interpreter to Former V. Pres. Shieh Tung-min 80-82; Sect. Chief, Dept. of N. Am. Aff., MOFA 80-82; Dep. Sec.-Gen., CCNAA 82-84; Dep. Dir.-Gen., CCNAA, Boston 84-89; Sec.-Gen., CCNAA 89-91; Dir.-Gen., CCNAA, Honolulu 91-93, & Chicago 93-94; *Add.* 57th Fl., 180 N. Stetson Avenue, Chicago, IL 60601, USA.

WU, SHOEI-YUN 吳水雲
Mem., Control Yuan 92-; *b.* Twn. May 10, '30; *m.* Chang, Chuen-hoei; 3 *s.; educ.* Ed.B., NTNU 53; Prin., Ming Yi Elementary Sch. 57-66, & Mei Lun Jr. High Sch. 66-73; Mem., 5th TPA 73-77; Magis., Hualien County 77-85; Dep. Dir.-Gen., Dept. of Cul. Aff., CC, KMT 86-88; Dir., Educ. Aff., Sun Yat-sen Inst. on Policy Res. & Dev. 88-90; Dir.-Gen., Secretariat, CC, KMT 90-92; *Add.* 2 Chung Hsiao E. Rd., Sect. 1, Taipei.

WU, SHUI-YUN
(See WU, SHOEI-YUN 吳水雲)

WU, TA-CHUN
(See WU, TAI-TSUN 吳大峻)

WU, TA-YOU 吳大猷
Mem., Acad. Sinica; Fel., Royal Soc., Can.; Chmn., Ch. Found. for the Promotion of Educ. & Cul.; *b.* Canton Sept. 29, '07; *m.* Yuan, Kuan-shih; 1 *s.; educ.* BS, Nankai U. 29; MA, U. of Michigan 32, Ph.D. 33; Instr., Nankai U. 29-31; Prof., Nat. Peking U. 34-46; Visiting Prof., U.

of Michigan 47, & New York U. 48-49; Res. Assc., Columbia U. 47-49; Prin. Res. Off. & Head, Theoretical Phys. Sect., Nat. Res. Coun. of Can. 49-63; Mem., Inst. for Advanced Study, Princeton U. 58-59; Visiting Prof., U. of Lausanne, Switzerland 60-61; Prof., Polytechnique Inst. of Brooklyn, USA 63-65, & State U. of New York, Buffalo 65-78. *Publ.: Vibrational Spectra & Structure of Polyatomic Molecules; Quantum Theory of Scattering; The Kinetic Equations of Gases & Plasmas; Quantum Mech.;* etc.; *Add.* Acad. Sinica, Nankang, Taipei.

WU, TAI-CHENG 吳泰成
Mem., Control Yuan 96-; *b.* Twn. Nov. 28, '45; 2 *s.; educ.* LL.B., NCHU 69; LL.M., NCU 79; Staff, Sp., Sect. Chief, & Authorized Rank Insp., Certified Public Acct. 71-83; Sec.-Gen., Pers. Dept., TCG 83-85; Dir., Off. of Res. & Control, Min. of Pers. 85-87, & Laws & Regln. Cttee. 87-90; Sec.-Gen., Min. of Civil Service, Exam. Yuan 90-93, Admin. V. Min. of Civil Service 93-94; Pol. V. Min. of Civil Service, Exam. Yuan 94-96. *Publ.: A Study of the Position Classification System in the ROC; Add.* 1 Shih Yuan Rd., Taipei.

WU, TAI-TSUN 吳大峻
Mem., Acad. Sinica; Prof., Harvard U.; *b.* Shanghai Dec. 1, '33; *m.* Yu, Sau-lan; *educ.* BS, U. of Minnesota 53; MS, Harvard U. 54, Ph.D. 56; Putnam Scholar 53; Jr. Fel., Soc. of Fel., Harvard U. 56-59, Asst. Prof. 59-63, Assc. Prof. 63-66; Mem., Inst. for Advanced Study, Princeton U. 58-59, 60-61, & 62-63; Visiting Prof., Rockefeller U., USA 66-67; Sc. Assc., Deutsches Elektronen-Synchrotron, Hamburg, W. Germany 70-71 & 82-83; Kramers Prof., U. Utrecht, Netherlands 77-78; Sc. Assc., CERN, Geneva, Switzerland 77-78. *Publ.: Scattering & Diffraction of Waves* (with Ronald W.P. King); *The Two-Dimensional Ising Model* (with Barry M. McCoy); *Antennas in Matter: Fundamentals, Theory, & Applications* (with Ronald W.P. King, Glenn S. Smith, & Margaret Owens); *Expanding Protons: Scattering at High Energies* (with Hung Cheng); *The Ubiquitous Photon: Helicity Method for QED & QCD* (with Raymond Gastmans); *Lateral Electromagnetic Waves: Theory & Applications to Comms., Geophysical Exploration, & Remote Sensing* (with Ronald W.P. King & Margaret Owens); *Add.* 35 Robinson St., Cambridge, MA 02138, USA.

WU, TE-LANG
(See WU, DELON 吳德朗)

WU, THEODORE YAO-TSU 吳耀祖
Mem., Acad. Sinica 84-; Prof. of Engr. Sc., Calif. Inst. of Tech. 61-; Mem., Nat. Acad. of Engr., USA 82-; *b.* Kiangsu Mar. 20, '24; *m.* Shih, Chin-hua; 1 *s.,* 1 *d.; educ.* BS, Chiao Tung U., Shanghai 46; MS, Iowa State Coll. 48; Ph.D., Calif. Inst. of Tech. 52; Res. Fel., Asst. Prof. & Assc. Prof., Calif. Inst. of Tech. 52-61. *Publ.:* Over 100 res. articles in prof. jour.; *Add.* Calif. Inst. of Tech., Pasadena, CA 91125, USA.

WU, TIEH-HSIUNG 吳鐵雄
Pres., Nat. Tainan Tchrs. Coll. 92-; *b.* Twn. Sept. 28, '39; *m.* Tsai, Lily; 2 *s.; educ.* Grad., Twn. Prov. Tainan Jr. Tchrs. Coll. 58; BA, NTNU 66; MA, U. of Rochester, USA 72; Ph.D., State U. of New York, Buffalo 79; Teaching Asst., Dept. of Psychology, Chung Yuan Christian Coll. of Sc. & Engr.; Res. Assc., Dept. of Behavioral Sc., State U. of New York, Buffalo 77-79; Assc. Prof., Dept. of Educ., Nat. Kaohsiung Tchrs. Coll. 79-80; Dir., Computing Cent., NTNU 80-83, Prof., Dept. of Educ. Psychology 83-85, Dir. & Prof., Dept. of Info. & Computer Educ. 85-91, Prof. 91-92. *Publ.: CAI in Twn.: State & Problems; A Long-Term Effect for Promoting Computer Educ. in the ROC; Add.* 33 Shu Lin St., Sect. 2, Tainan.

WU, TORNG-CHUANG 吳同權
V. Chmn., COA 92-; *b.* Mar. 7, '36; *m.* Tsai, Mei-yueh; 1 *s.,* 1 *d.; educ.* BS, Twn. Prov. Coll. of Agr. 57; MS, U. of Minnesota 63; Ph.D., U. of Calif., Davis 79; Asst., Twn. Sugar Corp. 59; Jr. Sp., Water Conservancy Bu., TPG 59-61, Sp., Dept. of Agr. & Forestry 64-68; Sr. Sp., JCRR 68-79; Div. Chief & Dep. Dir., CAPD 79-84, Dir. 84-90; Sec.-Gen., COA 90-92. *Publ.: Food Demand in Twn.; Add.* 3rd Fl., 19 Alley 1, Lane 5, Jen Ai Rd., Sect. 3, Taipei.

WU, TUN-I
(See WU, DEN-YIH 吳敦義)

WU, TUNG-CHUAN
(See WU, TORNG-CHUANG 吳同權)

WU, TSUNG-YI 吳聰義
Silver Medal, the 38th World Archery Championship 96; Student, Inst. of Sport Coaching Sc., Dept. of Phys. Educ. Ch. Cul. U. 96-; *b.* Twn. Oct. 25, '72; *educ.* Hualien's Jui Mei Elementary Sch., Jui Hui Jr. High Sch.; Prov. Hualien Sr. Voc. Sch. 91; BS, Ch. Cul. U. 96; *Add.* 268 Changhua Rd., Juisui Hsiang, Hualien County.

WU, TZU-DAN 吳子丹
Dir.-Gen., TECO, New York 94-; *b.* Ch. July 28, '37; *m.* Ma, L.M.; 2 *s.; educ.* LL.B., NCU 59, LL.M. 65; Staff, MOFA 63-66; 3rd & 2nd Sec., Emb. in Japan 66-71; Sect. Chief & Exec. Asst. to Min. of For. Aff. 71-76; Counsl., Emb. in S. Africa 76-78; Dep. Consul-Gen., Consl.-Gen. in New York 78-79; Dep. Dir.-Gen., CCNAA, New York 79-85, Dir.-Gen., Kansas City 85-86, & Chicago 86-88; Dir., Dept. of Intl. Orgs., MOFA 88-93; Dir.-Gen., CCNAA, New York 93-94. *Publ.: The Legal Status of Outer Space; Add.* 47th Fl., 885 2nd Avenue, New York, NY 10017, USA.

WU, TZU-TAN
(See WU, TZU-DAN 吳子丹)

WU, YAO-TSU
(See WU, THEODORE YAO-TSU 吳耀祖)

WU, YEN-HUAN 吳延環
Nat. Policy Adv. to the Pres. 91-; Pres., Ch. Mainland Aff. Res. Cent. 88-, & ROC Columnists Assn. 71-; Ed., CNA 66-; *b.* Hopei Mar. 7, '09; *m.* Chang, Tao-kun; 1 *s.,* 4 *d.; educ.* BA, NCU 35; Comr., Hopei Prov. Govt. 36-37; Mem., Hopei Prov. Cttee., KMT 38-44; Prin., Chieh Shou Jr. High Sch., Hopei Prov. 45-48; Mem., Legis. Yuan 48-90. *Publ.: A Study of the Analects of Confucius; Four Characters' Primer; 36 Stories of Filial Piety; 36 Stories of Brotherly Love; 36 Stories of Loyalty; 36 Stories of Trustworthiness; Add.* 247 Chou Shan Rd., Taipei.

WU, I-HSIUNG
(See WU, YI-SHIUNG 吳義雄)

WU, YI-SHIUNG 吳義雄
Dep. Admin., EPA 96-; *b.* Twn. Oct. 7, '42; *m.* Cheng, Mei-hsiang; 3 *s.; educ.* BA, Acct. Dept., NCKU 72; Studied on Civic Aff., PA Grad. Sch., NCU 91; Dep. Dir.,

Dept. of Environment Protection, TCG 76-79, Dep. Dir., Dept. of Soc. Aff. 79-80, Sec.-Gen. 83-83; Adv. to the Premier 94-96; *Add.* 41 Chung Hua Rd., Sect. 1, Taipei.

WU, YUAN-YEN
(See WU, ROY Y.Y. 烏元彥)

YANG, C.C. 楊振忠
Mem., Acad. Sinica 90-; Disting. Chair Prof., NTHU 94-; *b.* Taipei July 15, '27; *m.* Lin, Yeh-hsiang; 2 *s.,* 3 *d.; educ.* Med. Coll., NTU 50; DMS, Tokyo Ji-Kei U. 56; Res. Assc., U. of Wisconsin-Madison 61-62; Assc. Prof., Kaohsiung Med. Coll. 56-58, Prof. 58-73; Nat. Res. Chair Prof., NScC 64-67; Pres., Kaohsiung Med. Coll. 67-73; Dep. Dir., Ch. Youth Corps 73-78; Dir., Inst. of Molecular Biology, NTHU 73-85, Prof., Inst. of Life Sc. 73-94; Pres., Ch. Biochem. Soc. 79-81; Coun. Mem., Intl. Soc. on Toxinology 88-91. *Publ.:* More than 140 res. articles on biochem. & immunochem. of snake venom proteins published in intl. jour.; *Add.* 5th Fl., 61 W. Compound, NTHU, Hsinchu.

YANG, CHAO-HSIANG
(See YUNG, CHAUR-SHIN 楊朝祥)

YANG, CHEN-CHUNG
(See YANG, C.C. 楊振忠)

YANG, CHEN-NING 楊振寧
Mem., Acad. Sinica; Prof., State U. of New York, Stony Brook 66-; *b.* Anhwei Sept. 22, '22; *m.* Tu, Chih-li; 3 *c.; educ.* BS, Nat. Southwe. Assc. U. 42; Ph.D., U. of Chicago 48; Hon. D.Sc., Princeton U. 58, Brooklyn Polytech. Inst., USA 65, U. of Wroclaw, Poland 74, Gustavus Adolphus Coll. 75, U. of Maryland 79, & Durham U., USA 79; Instr., U. of Chicago 48-49; Mem., Inst. for Advanced Study, Princeton U. 49-55, Prof. 55-56; V. Prof., U. of Paris 57; *Add.* State U. of New York, Dept. of Phys., Stony Brook, NY 11790, USA.

YANG, CHIN-MU
(See YANG, JIN-MUH 楊金木)

YANG, CHUAN-KWANG 楊傳廣
Tng. Dir., ROC Amateur Athletic Fed.; *b.* Twn. July 10, '33; *m.* Jue, Daisy; 2 *c.; educ.* Grad., Dept. of Phys.

Educ., UCLA; Coach 64-77; Mem., Legis. Yuan 72-75; *Add.* P.O. Box 7855-39, Tsoying, Kaohsiung County.

YANG, CHUNG-TAO 楊忠道
Mem., Acad. Sinica; Emeritus Prof., U. of Penn. 91-; *b.* Chekiang May 4, '23; *m.* Kang, Agnes Ying-fong; 1 *s.,* 2 *d.; educ.* BS, Nat. Chekiang U. 46; Ph.D., Tulane U., USA 52; Asst., Nat. Chekiang U. 46-48, & Acad. Sinica 48-49; Asst. Mem., Acad. Sinica & concur. Lectr., NTU 49-50; Res. Assc., U. of Illinois 52-54; Mem., Inst. for Advanced Study, Princeton U. 54-56, Asst. Prof. 56-58, Assc. Prof. 58-61; Chmn., Dept. of Math., U. of Penn. 78-83, Prof. 61-91; Assc. Dir., Nankai Inst. of Math. 90-95. *Publ.:* More than 40 acad. articles published in various math. jour.; *Add.* 311 Hidden River Rd., Narberth, PA 19072, USA.

YANG, EDWARD 楊德昌
Filmmaker, Scriptwriter, & Dir. 81-; Gen. Partner, Atom Films & Theatre 89-; Teaching Assc., Nat. Inst. of the Arts; *b.* Shanghai Sept. 24, '47; *m.* Tsai, Chin; *educ.* BS, NCTU 69; MS, U. of Florida 72; Res. Asst., U. of Florida 71-72; Project Engr., U. of Washington 74-80; Consultant, Times Pub. Co. 89-91. *Publ.: Graphical Implementation of the Ch. Text; MK 69 Computer Generated Phanthom Target for Underwater Warfare Applications; Feature Films: In Our Time* 82; *That Day on the Beach* 83; *Taipei Story* 86; *The Terrorizer* 86; *A Brighter Summer Day* 91; *A Confucian Confusion* 94; *Add.* 121 Lane 350, Kuang Fu S. Rd., Taipei.

YANG, H.K. 楊西崑
Nat. Policy Adv. to the Pres. 89-; *b.* Kiangsu Jan. 28, '10; *m.* Leung, Anna; 2 *s.; educ.* Grad., Nat. Peking U.; Grad. Sch., Columbia U.; Ph.D. (Honoris Causa), U. of Pretoria 89; Instr., Nat. Peking U., & Southwe. Assc. U. 38-41; Tech. Counsel, Ch. Del. to the UN, & Alt. Rep. to the Trusteeship Coun., UN 48-59; Dir., Dept. of W. Asian Aff., MOFA 59-63; Mem., UN Visiting Mission to W. Africa Trust Territories 52 & 55, & Ch. Goodwill Mission to W. & E. Africa 60; Head, Ch. Econ. Mission to E. & Cent. Africa 61; Alt. Rep. of Ch. Del. to the 17th UNGA 62; Sp. Envoy at the independence ceremonies of Rwanda 62, Malawi 64, Botswana & Lesotho 66, Swaziland 68; Head, Ch. Goodwill Mission to Africa 63-73; Admin. V. Min. of For. Aff. & concur. Dir., Dept.

of African Aff., MOFA 63-66; Admin. V. Min. of For. Aff. 66-68; Rep. of Ch. Del. to the 20th through 26th UNGA 65-71; Sp. Rep. to negotiate with US govt. on Sino-Am. future relationship after the rupture of dip. rel. between the two countries 79; Pol. V. Min. of For. Aff. 68-79; Chmn., Sino-Africa Tech. Cooperation Cttee., & Intl. TCC 61-79; Amb. to S. Africa 79-89; Hon. Citizen of the City of Pretoria 89; Mem, CC, KMT; *Add.* 9th Fl., 263 Tun Hua S. Rd., Taipei.

YANG, HENRY T.Y. 楊祖佑
Mem., Acad. Sinica 92-; Chancellor, U. of Calif. at Santa Barbara 94-; Mem., US Nat. Acad. of Engr. 91-; *b.* Chungking Nov. 29, '40; *m.* Yang, Dilling; 2 *d.; educ.* BS, NTU 62; MS, W. Virginia U. 64; Ph.D., Cornell U. 68; Head, Sch. of Aeronautics & Astronautics, Purdue U. 79-84, Dean 84-94, Neil Armstrong Disting. Prof. 88-94. *Publ.:* One bk. & 150 jour. papers; *Add.* U. of Calif., Santa Barbara, CA 93106-2030, U.S.A.

YANG, HSI-KUN
(See YANG, H.K. 楊西崑)

YANG, HSIANG-FA
(See YANG, SHANG-FA 楊祥發)

YANG, HUEY-ING 楊慧英
Grand Justice, Jud. Yuan 94-; *b.* Twn. July 14, '34; *m.* Hsu, Hsiang-neng; 1 *s.,* 1 *d.; educ.* LL.B., NTU 57; Judge, Hsinchu Dist. Court 61-62, Taichung Dist. Court 62-64; Procurator & Judge, Taichung Dist. Court 64-71; Chief Judge, Taipei Dist. Court 71-72; Judge, Twn. High Court 72-79; Justice, Admin. Court 79-80; Judge, Supreme Court 90-92, Presiding Justice 92-94; *Add.* 4th Fl., 124 Chungking S. Rd., Sect. 1, Taipei.

YANG, HUI-YING
(See YANG, HUEY-ING 楊慧英)

YANG, JIN-MUH 楊金木
Spkr., Hsinchu CCoun. 96-, Mem. 82-; Standing Mem., Bd. of Trustees, Twn. Ch. Kungfu Assn. 72-, & ROC Ch. Kungfu Assn. 84-; Bd. Chmn., Hsinchu Ch. Kungfu Assn. 86-; *b.* Twn. Apr. 26, '36; *m.* Lin, Shiow-jen; 3 *s.,* 5 *d.; educ.* Grad., Sr. High Sch.; *Add.* 122 Chung Cheng Rd., Hsinchu.

YANG, KUO-SHIH 楊國賜
Admin. V. Min. of Educ. 95-; *b.* Twn. Sept. 26, '39; *m.* Yang Ho, Fu-mei; 2 *s.,* 1 *d.; educ.* Ed.D., NTNU 77; Res. at London U.; Prof., Dept. of Soc. Educ., NTNU 78-88, Dir. 85-88, Dean, Grad. Sch. of Soc. Educ. 84-88; Dir., Dept. of Soc. Educ., MOE 88-92, Sec.-Gen. 92-93, Dir., Dept. of Higher Educ. 93-95. *Publ.: The Ideas of Soc. Educ.; Progressivism & Educ. Philosophy; The Thought of Contemporary Educ.; Comparative Educ. Methodology; Modernization & Educ. Innovation; Add.* 5 Chung Shan S. Rd., Taipei.

YANG, KUO-SZU
(See YANG, KUO-SHIH 楊國賜)

YANG, NIEN-CHU C. 楊念祖
Mem., Acad. Sinica 82-; Gustavus F. & Ann M. Swift Disting. Service Prof., Dept. of Chem., U. of Chicago 92-; *b.* Shanghai May 1, '28; *m.* Hwang, Ding-djung; 2 *s.,* 1 *d.; educ.* BS, St. John's U. 48; Ph.D., U. of Chicago 52; Res. Assc., MIT 52-55; Res. Fel., Harvard U. 55-56; Asst. Prof., U. of Chicago 56-61, Assc. Prof. 61-63, Prof. 63-92. *Publ.:* Over 150 articles published in sc. jour.; *Add.* 5729 S. Blackstone Avenue, Chicago, IL 60637, USA.

YANG, NIEN-TSU
(See YANG, NIEN-CHU C. 楊念祖)

YANG, PAO-FA 楊寶發
Pol. V. Min. of the Int. 93-; Mem., CC, KMT 93-; *b.* Twn. Oct. 29, '30; *m.* Wu, Su-chu; 2 *s.,* 1 *d.; educ.* LL.B., NTU 53; Sect. Chief, Dept. of Civil Aff., TPG 54-61; Insp. & Sr. Sp., MOI 61-66; Chmn., Maoli County Cttee., KMT 66-70, & Nantou County Cttee. 70-72; Dir., Dept. of Civil Aff., TCG 72-77; Magis., Tainan County 77-85; Mng. Dir., Bk. of Land 87-90; Comr., TPG, & concur. Chmn., EPC 90-93. *Publ.: Outline Map of Twn. Prov.; Nat. Rev. & Twn.; Add.* 9th Fl., 5 Hsuchow Rd., Taipei.

YANG, SHANG-FA 楊祥發
Disting. Res. Fel. & Dir., Inst. of Botany, Acad. Sinica 95-, Mem. 92-; Nat. Acad. of Sc., USA 90-; Prof., U. of Calif., Davis 74- & Hong Kong U. of Sc. & Tech. 94-; Fel., Guggenheim Found. 82-; *b.* Twn. Nov. 10, '32; *m.* Yang, Eleanor; 2 *s.; educ.* BS, NTU 56, MS 58; Ph.D., Utah State U. 62; Postdoctoral Resr., U. of Calif., Davis

62-63, New York U. 63-64, & U. of Calif., San Diego 64-65; Visiting Prof., U. of Konstanz, Germany 74, NTU 83, & Cambridge U., UK 83. *Publ.:* More than 200 papers on plant biochem. & molecular biology; *Add.* Mann Lab., U. of Calif., Davis, CA 95616, USA; Inst. of Botany, Acad. Sinica, Nankang, Taipei.

YANG, SHIH-CHIEN 楊世緘
Min. of State 96-; *b.* Shanghai Oct. 5, '44; *educ.* BEE, NTU; MEE & Ph.D., Northwe. U., USA; Res. Engr., Chung Shan Inst. of Sc. & Tech. 73-78; Sr. Engr., Sectoral Planning Dept., CEPD 78-80, Dep. Dir. 80-83; Dir., Planning & Evaluation Div., NScC 83-84; Dep. Dir.-Gen., Sc.-based Ind. Park Admin. 84-86; Dir.-Gen., Ind. Dev. Bu., MOEA 86-92; Pol. V. Min. of Econ. Aff. 93-96; *Add.* 1 Chung Hsiao E. Rd., Sect. 1, Taipei.

YANG, TE-CHANG
(See YANG, EDWARD 楊德昌)

YANG, TING-YUN 楊亭雲
Chmn., VAC 94-; *b.* Hupei Dec. 27, '28; *m.* Fang, Chih-shun; 2 *s.,* 1 *d.; educ.* Pol. Warfare Coll. 55; War Coll., Armed Forces U. 79; Dean, Polwar Cadre Tng. Cent., MND 76-77; Dir., Pol. Warfare Dept., 10th Field, Army 77-79, Pol. Warfare Dept., Mil. Police Cmd. 79-81, & Pol. Warfare Dept., Twn. Garrison Cmd. 81-84; Dep. Dir.-Gen., Gen. Pol. Warfare Dept., MND 84-87; Dep. C-in-C, Twn. Garrison Cmd. 87-88; Dep. Dir.-Gen., Gen. Pol. Warfare Dept., MND 88-90, Dir.-Gen. 90-94; *Add.* 222 Chung Hsiao E. Rd., Sect. 5, Taipei.

YANG, TSU-YU
(See YANG, HERNY T.Y. 楊祖祐)

YANG, WEN-HSIN 楊文欣
Dep. Spkr., TPA 95-; *b.* Twn. July 17, '62; *m.* Liao, Hsiu-ling; 2 *s.,* 1 *d.; educ.* Tung Nan Jr. Coll. of Tech.; Mem., TPA 89-94; *Add.* 734 Chung Cheng Rd., Wufeng, Taichung County.

YANG, YING-FENG
(See YANG, YUYU 楊英風)

YANG, YUYU 楊英風
Sculptor; Founder, Yuyu Yang Lifescape Sculpture Museum 92-; *b.* Twn.'26; *educ.* Architecture Dept., Tokyo Art Sch.; Art Dept., Fu Jen Catholic U., Peking, NTNU, & Nat. Acad. of Art, Rome; Sculpture Philosopher earned hon. mention, 1st Intl. Youth Arts Festival, Paris 59; Print & Sculpture Exhibition, Nat. Hist. Museum 60; Designed giant reliefs for the Sun Moon Lake Tchrs.' Hostel, Taichung 61; Dispatched by the Catholic Church to meet Pope Paul VI in Rome to thank him for his support of reinstating Fu Jen Catholic U. 63; Mem., Medallion Sculpture Assn. of Italy 65; Designed Sculpture *Advent of the Phoenix,* Ch. Pavilion, Expo'70 Osaka 70; Stainless steel lifescape Sculpture *E. W. Gate,* in front of Orient Ovs. Bldg., Wall S. New York 73; Designed *Spring Again over the Good Earth,* Ch. Pavilion, Spokane World's Fair, USA 74; Organized the 1st Laser & Lifescape Exhibition, ROC 81; Designed *New Forever,* an Earth Day sculpture at the Chiang Kai-shek Memorial Hall, Taipei 90; Designed & made *Phoenix Scales the Heavens* for permanent display, Peking Olympic Sports Cent., Ch. 90; Stainless Steel Sculptures Exhibition, Nat. Museum of Singapore 91; *Add.* 6th Fl., 31 Chungking S. Rd., Sect. 2, Taipei.

YAO, ENG-CHI 饒穎奇
Exec. Sec., Policy Coordination Cttee., KMT 96-; Dir., Dept. of Party-Govt. Coordination of the Legis. Yuan, CC, KMT 93-; Dir., Coun. of Soc. Service, ROC Chapter 93-; Mem., Legis. Yuan 81-; Pres., Twn. Soc. Aff. Coun. 87-; *b.* Twn. Nov. 5, '34; *m.* Kao, Shu-tuan; 3 *d.; educ.* BA, NCHU 63; Sun Yat-sen Inst. on Policy Res. & Dev.; Sr. Sp., TCG; Instr., NCHU; Dep. Sec.-Gen., CC, KMT 92-93. *Publ.: Theory & Practice of Soc. Work; Welfare for the Elderly; Services for the Elderly; Hakka-One of the Main Ethnic Groups of the Han People; Add.* 1 Chung Shan S. Rd., Taipei.

YAO, KAO-CHIAO 姚高橋
Dir.-Gen., Nat. Police Admin., MOI 96-; *b.* Twn. Dec. 15, '38; *m.* Yao Lu, Ming-chu; 1 *s.* 2 *d.; educ.* BA, Cent. Police U. 63; Grad., Criminal Investigation Dept., Japanese Police Coll. 69; LL.M., Law Sch., Meiji U. 75; Dep. Chief, Keelung City 78-79; Cmdr., Police Battalion, Twn. Prov. Police Admin. 79-82; Chief, Yunlin County Police 82-84; Chief, Chiayi County & City Police Dept. 84-84; Chief, Taipei County Police Dept. 84-88; Chief, Kaohsiung City Police Dept. 88-92; Pres., Twn. Police Coll. 92-93; Dep. Dir.-Gen., Nat. Police Admin., MOI

93-95; Pres., Cent. Police U. 95-96; *Add.* 7 Chung Hsiao E. Rd., Sect. 1, Taipei.

YAO, I-WEI
(See YAO, YI-WEI 姚一葦)

YAO, PENG 姚朋
Novelist; *b.* Tientsin Jan. 8, '26; *m.* Yao Hsu, Shih-fen; 2 *s.; educ.* MS, U. of Illinois 64; Ed.-in-Chief & V. Pres., *Twn. Shin Sheng Daily News* 49-72; Chief Ed., Writer & V. Pres., *CDN* 72-81, Pres. & Pub. 81-87; Pres., Taipei Cent., PEN Intl. 79-86; Chmn., *Hong Kong Times* 87-91. *Publ.: Coming Back from Champagne; Father & D.; The Dream of Last Night; The Ivory Balls; Beyond the Horizon; Black Tears;* & more than 70 novels & transl. works.

YAO, YI-WEI 姚一葦
Prof., Dept. of Theatre, Nat. Inst. of the Arts 87-; *b.* Kiangsi Apr. 5, '22; *m.* Lee, Ing-chiang; 2 *s.,* 1 *d.; educ.* Grad., Nat. Amoy U. 46; Prof. & Dir. of Drama Sect., Grad. Sch. of the Arts, Ch. Cul. U. 65-82; Chmn., Dept. of Theatre & concur. Dean of Studies, Nat. Inst. of the Arts 82-87. *Publ.:* Bk.: *A Commentary on Aristotle's Poetics; The Secrets of Arts; Essays on Drama; Collected Essays of Yao Yi-wei; Aesthetic Categories; Appreciation & Criticism; Essays on Life; Theory of the Drama; Three Topics on the Aesthetic; Drama & Life* 95; *Art Criticism* 96; Scripts: *The People from Phoenix Town; Sun Fei-hu Kidnaps the Bride; The Goddess of Mercy Carved in Jade; The Man with Red Nose; The Crown Prince Shen Sheng; Suitcase; Dr. Fu Ching-chu; Let's Go Together; The Story of Tso Po-tao; The Visitor; The Romance of the Tree God; The Ma-wei Post House; Miss X; Let's Start Again; Add.* 13 Lane 1, Hsing Lung Rd., Sect. 4, Wenshan, Taipei.

YAU, SHING-TUNG 丘成桐
Mem., Acad. Sinica; Prof. of Math., Harvard U. 87-; *b.* Kwangtung Apr. 4, '49; *m.* Kuo, Yu-yun; 2 *s.; educ.* Ph.D., UC-Berkly. 71; Prof., Stanford U. 74-79, Inst. for Advanced Study, Princeton U. 79-84, & U. of Calif., San Diego 84-87; For. Mem., Ch. Acad. of Sc. 94; *Add.* Dept. of Math., Harvard U., Cambridge, MA 02138, USA.

YEE, CHIEN-CHIU 易勁秋
Nat. Policy Adv. to the Pres.; Mem., CAC, KMT; *b.* Szechwan Jan. 17, '18; *m.* Lin, Chih-jung; 2 *s.,* 1 *d.; educ.*

LL.B., NCU; Cent. Pol. Cadre Sch.; Nat. Def. Coll.; Dir., Pers. Admin. Bu., MND 59-66; Chief, Cadre Mng., CC, KMT 66-72, Chmn., Taipei Mun. Cttee. 72-79; Bd. Chmn., CTS 79-92; Mem., CC, KMT; Adv. to CTS; *Add.* 100 Kuang Fu S. Rd., Taipei; P.O. Box 20-15, Hsintien, Taipei County.

YEE, TEH-MING 倪德明
Chmn., En Ti Cml. Bk.; *b.* Shanghai Mar. 6, '22; *m.* Liu, Chao-hwa; 2 *s.,* 3 *d.; educ.* Fu Tan U. 44; U. of Illinois 56; Br. Mgr., Land Bk. 69; Exec. V. Pres., Taipei Bk. 69-73; Pres., Land Bk. 73-75 & United World Ch. Cml. Bk. 75-89; *Add.* 158 Min Sheng E. Rd., Sect. 3, Taipei.

YEH, ALBERT T.H. 葉天行
Former Dep. Dir.-Gen., GIO 91-96; Rep., Taipei Econ. & Cul. Off., Luxembourg 96-; *b.* Chekiang Jan. 10, '34; *m.* Sun, Pu-fei; 1 *d.; educ.* BS, Econ., NTU 56; M., Jour., NCU 58; Passed Sr. Civil Service Exam. 57, & Sp. Exam. A 68; Staff Mem., GIO 58-62; Asst. Press Sp., Emb. in Thailand 63-69; Sr. Sp., GIO 69-71; Liaison Off. in Mid-E. Area 71-76; Dir., Press Div., ROC Rep. Off. in Thailand 76-77; Dep. Dir., Intl. Info. Services Dept., GIO 77-79, Dir., Publ. Aff. Dept. 79-80, & Intl. Info. Services Dept. 80-84; Dep. Dir.-Gen. & concur. Dir. of Press Div., Taipei Wirtschafts-und Kulturbüro, Bonn 84-91. *Publ.:* "A Study of the Econ. News in Twn.'s Newspapers," *Jour. Semiannually,* Vol. 2, No. 4; *Add.* Taipei Econ. & Cul. Off., 50 Route d'Esch, Luxembourg-Ville, L-1470 Grand-Duche de Luxembourg.

YEH, CHANG-TUNG 葉昌桐
Strategy Adv. to the Pres. 94-; *b.* Fukien Aug. 2, '29; *m.* Chao, Jung; 1 *s.,* 2 *d.; educ.* Ch. Naval Acad. 49; US Naval Post Grad. Sch. 61; US Naval War Coll. 67; Destroyer Cmdr. 69-70; Dep. Dir., 3rd Bu., Off. of the Pres. 73-75; Cmdr., Destroyer Squadron 75-76; Dep. C/S, GHQ, ROCN 76-77; Dep. Chief of the Gen. Staff Planning, MND 77-82, V. Chief of the Gen. Staff 82-88; C-in-C, GHQ, ROCN 88-92; Pres., Armed Forces U. 92-94; *Add.* 3rd Fl., 3 Lane 31, Wo Lung St., Taipei.

YEH, CHIA-WU 葉家梧
Rep., TECRO, Saudi Arabia 91-; *b.* Nanking Dec. 1, '30; *m.* Lai, Sue-yun; 1 *d.; educ.* BA, NTU; Consul, Consl.-Gen. in Chicago 64-67; Sect. Chief, MOFA 67-70; 1st

Sec., Emb. in Saudi Arabia & Jordan 71-75; Dep. Dir., Dept. of W. Asian Aff., MOFA 76-80; Dir., Ch. Cml. Off. in Libya 80-85; Far E. Cml. Off., Amman, Jordan 85-89, & Dept. of W. Asian Aff., MOFA 89-91; *Add.* P.O. Box 94393, Riyadh 11693, Saudi Arabia.

YEH, CHIN-FENG
(See YEH, CHIN-FONG 葉金鳳)

YEH, CHIN-FONG 葉金鳳
Min. of State 96-; Mem., Standing Cttee., Twn. Prov. Br., Soc. for Strategic Studies, ROC 91-; Mem., CC, KMT 88-, & Evaluation & Discipline Cttee. 90-; *b.* Twn. June 22, '43; *m.* Lin, Yao-tong; *educ.* LL.B., NCHU 65; LL.D., La Salle U., USA 91; Judge & Presiding Judge, Taichung & Yunlin Dist. Courts 69-81; Prof., Providence U. 81-85; Mem, NA 81-93, Chmn., Presidium, NA 81-92; Judge, Taichung Br., Twn. High Court, & Supreme Court 81-86; Sr. Sp., Jud. Yuan 86-87; Justice, Supreme Court 87-88; Comr., Exam. Yuan; Sec. & Chmn., Taichung Br., Zonta Intl., Mem., Standing Bd., ROC Hqs.; Mem., Nat. Aff. Conf. 90; V. Chmn., MAC 92-96; Chmn., Zonta Intl. 91-95. *Publ.: Discussing the Rotation System of Judge & Dist. Attorney; A Study of Petition & Petition Laws; Reinforcing the Claim of Violent & Econ. Crime in Order to Maintain the Soc. Order; Implementation of Const. & the Soc. Status of the Women; Women & Pol. Dev.; A Discussion of Contemporary Const. Reform; Scrutinizing the Controversy of Revising & Drafting the Const.;* etc.; *Add.* Exec. Yuan, 1 Chung Hsiao E. Rd., Sect. 1, Taipei.

YEH, KUO-HSIN 葉國興
Chmn., Taipei Bk. 94- & Bankers Assn. of Taipei 92-; *b.* Taipei Feb. 1, '32; *m.* Tsang, Hsiu-mei; 1 *s.,* 2 *d.; educ.* LL.B., NTU 54; Exec. V. Pres., Hua Nan Cml. Bk. 75-81; Pres., Banking Inst. of the ROC 81-88; Chief Exec. Off., Financial Info. System Group, MOF 84-88; Chmn., Bankers Assn. of Twn. 88-92; Pres., Chang Hwa Cml. Bk. 88-94. *Publ.: Credit Mng.; Add.* 50 Chung Shan N. Rd., Sect. 2, Taipei.

YEH, KUO-HSING
(See YEH, KUO-HSIN 葉國興)

YEH, NENG-CHE 葉能哲
Pres., Tamsui Oxford Coll. 71-; *b.* Taipei Sept. 14, '34; *m.* Yeh Lin, Tzu-huei; 5 *s.,* 3 *d.; educ.* B., Tamkang Coll.

of Arts & Sc. 63; M., NTHU 65; Ph.D., Kyushu U. 69; M., Twn. Theological Coll.; Prof., Dept. of Math., Tamkang Coll. of Arts & Sc. 69-71, Dean, Grad. Sch. of Math. 70-71; Prof., Grad. Sch. of Math., NTHU 69-75. *Publ.:* 14 bk. & 8 theses on statistics & math.; *Add.* 32 Chen Li St., Tamsui, Taipei County.

YEH, SHIH-TAO 葉石濤
Writer; *b.* Twn. Nov. 1, '25; *m.* Chen, Yueh-te; 2 *s.; educ.* Grad., Tainan Normal Coll. 66; Tchr., Tainan City Li Jen Elementary Sch. 44-48, Tainan City Yung Fu Elementary Sch. 49-51, Chiayi Kuo Lu Elementary Sch. 55-57, Tainan County Wen Hsien Elementary Sch. 57-65, Ilan County Kuang Hsing Elementary Sch. 66-67, & Kaohsiung County Chia Wei Elementary Sch. 67-91. *Publ.: Essays of Native Twn. Writers; Toward Twn. Lit.; A Little Twn. Man "A Tao"; The Red Shoes; Girl Friend;* etc.; *Add.* 196 Sheng Li Rd., Tsoying, Kaohsiung County.

YEH, SHU 葉曙
Mem., Acad. Sinica; Part-time Prof., NTU 78-, Prof. Emeritus; *b.* Hupei Mar. 16, '08; *m.* Hsu, Siu-lien; 1 *s.,* 1 *d.; educ.* MB, Chiba Med. Coll., Japan 34, MD 38; Pathologist, Juntendo Hosp., Tokyo 39-43; Prof., Shanghai S.E. Med. Coll. 42-46, & NTU 46-78. *Publ.: Skin Cancer in Chronic Arsenicism; Cancer in Twn.; Add.* 4th Fl., 2 Lane 6 Tai An St., Taipei.

YEH, TIEN-HSING
(See YEH, ALBERT T.H. 葉天行)

YEN, BING-FAN 顏秉璠
Amb. to Repub. of El Salvador 96-; *b.* Kiangsu June 5, '35; *m.* Liu, Rosa Hsiao-mei; 1 *d.; educ.* BA, NTNU; Madrid C.U., Spain; 3rd Sec., Emb. in Italy & Spain 70 & 70-72; Sec., Sun Yat-sen Cent., Spain 72-77; Dir., Quayaquil Br., Ch. Cml. Off., Ecuador 77-82; Dep. Dir., Dept. of Cent. & S. America Aff., MOFA 82-84; Rep., Taipei Econ. & Cul. Off., Brazil; *Add.* Apartado Postal (06)956, San Salvador, El Salvador, C.A.

YEN, CHEN-HSING 閻振興
Sr. Adv. to the Pres. 94-; Prof. Emeritus, NTU 81-; Mem., Acad. Sinica 82-; *b.* Honan July 10, '12; *m.* Yen, Sou-lien; 2 *s.,* 1 *d.; educ.* BS, NTHU; MS & Ph.D., U. of Iowa; Engr., Yunnan-Burma Highway Bu. 41; Prof., Nat. Southwe. Assc. U. 41-46; Chief Engr., Yellow River

Engr. Bu. 46-47; Dean, Coll. of Engr., Honan U. 47-48; Dir., Engr. Dept., GHQ, Ch. Navy 48-49; Chief Engr., Kaohsiung Harbor Bu. 49-57; Dean, Coll. of Engr., NTU 53-55; Comr. of Educ., TPG 62-63; Pres., NCKU 57-65; Min. of Educ. 65-69; Pres., Ch. Inst. of Engr. 66-67; Chmn., NYC 66-70, & AEC 66-72; Pres., NTHU 69-70, Chung Shan Inst. of Sc. & Tech. 69-75, & NTU 70-81; Chmn., AEC 81-90; Nat. Policy Adv. to the Pres. 90-94. *Publ.: The Tractive Force on Pebbles by Flowing Water; Determination of the Best Proportion of Canal Bends; Soil Consolidation & Settlement; Soil Compaction & Its Application; Gap-Closure Work of Yellow River at Hue-Yuan-Kou; The Educ. Thought of Confucius; The Planning & Implementation of 9-year Free Educ.; Add.* 3 Lane 11, Ching Tien St., Taipei.

YEN, CHIN-LIEN 顏清連
Prof. of Civil Engr., NTU; *b.* Twn. Sept. 7, '37; *m.* Yen Lin, Agnes Feng; *2 d.; educ.* BS, NTU 60; MA, Queen's U., Can. 64; Ph.D., U. of Iowa 67; Asst. Prof. of Engr., U. of Puerto Rica, USA 66-67; Asst. Prof., Assc. Prof., & Prof., Howard U. 68-77; Prof. of Civil Engr., NTU 77-88; Chmn., Dept. of Civil Engr. 79-83; Sc. & Tech. Adv., MOE 85-87; Dean, Coll. of Engr., NTU 90-93; Miller Visiting Prof., U. of Illinois 94. *Publ.:* More than 70 papers & 40 tech. reports on hydraulics; *Add.* 16 Lane 18, Wenchow St., Taipei.

YEN, CHING-LIEN
(See YEN, CHIN-LIEN 顏清連)

YEN, CHING-CHANG 顏慶章
Pol. V. Min. of Finance 96-; *b.* Twn. Apr. 7, '48; *m.* Lo, Yueh-ching; *1 s., 1 d.; educ.* LL.B., NTU 70, LL.M. 74; MS, Comparative Law, U. of Michigan 81; Sec.-Gen., Medium Business Bk. of Twn. 78-79; Sr. Sp., MOF 81-83; Exec. Sec., Legal Com., MOF 83-85, & Taxation & Tariff Com. 85-92; Dep. Dir.-Gen., 1st Bu., Off. of the Pres. 92-93; Dir.-Gen. of 1st Bu. & Keeper of Nat. Seals, Off. of the Pres. 93-96; Fel., Eisenhower Exchange Fel. 95. *Publ.: The Anti-Dumping Act & Customs Policy; Legal Problems of Sino-Am. Trade Negotiations; Unveil "GATT": Order & Trend of World Trade; Laws & Regln. of Intl. Econ. Rel.; Add.* 2 Ai Kuo W. Rd., Taipei.

YEN, PING-FAN
(See YEN, BING-FANG 顏秉璠)

YIH, CHIA-SHUN 易家訓
Mem., Acad. Sinica, & US Nat. Acad. of Engr.; Stephen P. Timoshenko Disting. U. Prof., U. of Michigan 68-; Fel., Am. Phys. Soc.; Grad. Res. Prof., U. of Florida 87-; *b.* Kweichow July 25, '18; *m.* Yih, Shirley A.; *3 c.; educ.* BS, Nat. Cent. U. 42; MS, U. of Iowa 47, Ph.D. 48; Instr. of Math., U. of Wisconsin 48-49; Lectr. of Math., U. of British Columbia, Can. 49-50; Assc. Prof. of Civil Engr., Colorado State U. 50-51; Attaché de Recherche, U. de Nancy 51-52; Res. Engr. & Assc. Prof., U. of Iowa 52-56; Assc. Prof., U. of Michigan 56-58, Prof. 58-68; Sr. Postdoctoral Fel., US Nat. Sc. Found. 59-60; Guggenheim Fel. 64; Visiting Prof. (appointed by the French govt.), U. of Paris, & U. of Grenoble, France 70-71; Lectr., von Kármán Inst. of Aeronautics, Belgium 81; Ch. Acad. of Sc., Peking 81; Ed., Advances in Applied Mech. 70-82; Mem. of Ed. Bd., Advances in Applied Mech., Phys. of Fluids 69-72, Annual Review of Fluid Mech. 69-72, *SIAM Jour. of Applied Math.* 71-72, Advances in Mech., Acta Mechanica Sinica, Applied Math. & Mech. 72-89, & *Jour. of Hydrodynamics* 86-89; Chmn., Exec. Cttee., Fluid-Dynamics Div. of Am. Phys. Soc. 73-74; Henry Russel Lectr., U. of Michigan 74; Visiting Prof., U. of Karlsruhe, W. Germany 77-78; Alexander von Humboldt Sr. Scientist Award, W. Germany 77-78; Theodore von Kármán Medal, Am. Soc. of Civil Engr. 81; Fluid-Dynamics Prize, Am. Phys. Soc. 85; Otto Laporte Award, Am. Phys. Soc. 89; Ch. Acad. of Sc., Bejing 81; Intl. Cent. of Theoretical Phys., Trieste, Italy 94; NCKU 95. *Publ.: Dynamics of Nonhomogeneous Fluids, Fluid Mech., Stratified Flows;* & more than 120 articles on fluid mech.; *Add.* 2250 G. G. Brown, Ann Arbor, MI 48109-2125, USA.

YIN, CHANG-FU 殷章甫
Mem., Control Yuan 93-; Prof., Grad. Sch. of Land Econ., NCU 76-; Pres., Ch. Inst. of Land Econ. 92-; *b.* Twn. July 22, '29; *m.* Wu, Hsi-li; *1 s., 3 d.; educ.* BS, Twn. Prov. Agr. Coll. 52; MS, U. of Tokyo 67, Ph.D. 72; Assc. Prof., NCU 72-76, Dean, Grad. Sch. of Land Econ. 78-85; Mem., Regional Planning Cttee., MOI 81-93; Pres., Ch. Inst. of Land Econ. 91-95. *Publ.: Econ. Dev. & Land Utilization; Land Reform in Ch.; The Impact of Current Land Taxation on Land Utilization; Land Economics; Add.* 2 Chung Hsiao E. Rd., Sect. 1, Taipei.

YIN, YUN-PENG
(See YING, DIANE Y.P. 殷允芃)

YING, DIANE Y.P. 殷允芃
Pub. & Ed., *CommonWealth Mag.* 81-; Comr., Nat. Unification Coun. 90-; Comr., Nat. Cul. Assn.; *b.* Sian May 13, '41; *educ.* BA, Eng. Lit., NCKU; MS, Jour., U. of Iowa; Twn. Corr., *Asian Wall St. Jour.* 77-81, *New York Times* 77-79, & *United Press Intl.* 73-76; Staff Reporter, *Philadelphia Inquirer* 68-70; Lectr., NCU 70-87. *Publ.: The Brilliance of the Ch. & Others; The Rising Generation; The Decision-makers, People of the Pacific Century; Waiting for Heroes; One Who Lights the Lamp; Respect Heaven & Love People; Add.* 4th Fl., 87 Sungkiang Rd., Taipei.

YU, ALBERT 余建新
Pub., *Ch. Times* 85-; *b.* Taipei May 31, '52; *m.* Cheng, Sophia; 2 *c.; educ.* Grad., San Francisco U.; Chief, San Francisco Off., *Ch. Times* 77-78, Dep. Gen. Mgr. 78-82, Gen. Mgr., *Ch. Times* US Edition 82-84; *Add.* 132 Ta Li St., Taipei.

YU, ALICE 余範英
Pub., *Cml. Times; b.* Ch. July 11, '44; 2 *c.; educ.* BA, Waseda U.; MA, Stanford U.; Dep. Dir. & City Desk, *Ch. Times* 82-83; Pub., *Ch. Times Express; Add.* 132 Ta Li St., Taipei.

YU, CHEN S. 俞政
Chmn., Chiao Tung Bk. 94-; *b.* Kiangsu Feb. 10, '30; *m.* Yu Hu, Doris; 1 *d.; educ.* BS, U. of Wisconsin; Exec. V. Pres., Export-Import Bk. of ROC 79-80, & Chiao Tung Bk. 80; Dir., Dept. of Sec., CBC 80-81, Gen. Mgr., Dept. of For. Exchange 81-85; Dep. Gov., CBC 85-94; *Add.* 91 Heng Yang Rd., Taipei.

YU, CHENG
(See YU, CHEN S. 俞政)

YU, CHI-CHUNG 余紀忠
Bd. Chmn., *Ch. Times;* Hon. Pres., Ch. Taipei Basketball Assn.; *b.* Kiangsu July 19, '11; *m.* Tsai, Alice; 2 *s.,* 2 *d.; educ.* BA, Nat. Cent. U., Nanking; Grad. Study at Sch. of Econ., U. of London; Dir. of Info., C-in-C Hqs. in the N.E. Ch.; Prof., NTNU & NCHU; Mem., CAC, KMT; *Add.* 132 Ta Li St., Taipei.

YU, CHIEN-HSIN
(See YU, ALBERT 余建新)

YU, CHING 尤清
Magis., Taipei County 89-; *b.* Twn. Mar. 20, '42; *m.* Tsao, Tzu-chin; 2 *s.; educ.* LL.B., NCU; LL.D., Heidelberg U.; Part-time Assc. Prof., NCU; Mem., Control Yuan 80-86 & CC, DPP; Convener, DPP Caucus, Legis. Yuan 86-89; *Add.* 32 Fu Chung Rd., Panchiao, Taipei County.

YU, CHUAN-TAO 余傳韜
Chmn., Asia & Pacific Coun. for Sc. & Tech. 89-; *b.* Hupei June 27, '28; *m.* Chen, Shing; 1 *c.; educ.* MS, N. Carolina State U.; Ph.D., UC-Berkly.; Pres., Nat. Chiayi Inst. of Agr. 72-79; Chief, Dept. of Tech. & Voc. Educ., MOE 79-80; Admin. V. Min. of Educ. 80-82; Pres., Nat. Cent. U. 82-90; Comr., Exam. Yuan 90-96; *Add.* 8th Fl., 81 Chang An E. Rd., Sect. 2, Taipei.

YU, FAN-YING
(See YU, ALICE 余範英)

YU, HAO-CHANG
(See YU, HOA-CHANG 于豪章)

YU, HOA-CHANG 于豪章
Nat. Policy Adv. to the Pres.; *b.* Anhwei Apr. 22, '18; *m.* Kou, Yu; 4 *c.; educ.* 12th Class, Cent. Army Acad.; 18th Class, Ch. Mil. Acad.; CGSC, US Army; Cmdr., Marine Corps 64-68; V. Chief of the Gen. Staff, MND 68-69; C-in-C, GHQ, ROC Army 69-75; *Add.* 5-8 Alley 11, Lane 16, Wen Chang St., Taipei.

YU, HSI-KUN
(See YU, SHYI-KUN 游錫堃)

YU, HUI-CHUNG
(See YU, HUI-JUNG 于惠中)

YU, HUI-JUNG 于惠中
Comr., Exam. Yuan; Prof., NTU 74-; *b.* Shansi Jan. 22, '38; *m.* Peng, Yuan-chiao; 3 *c.; educ.* BSEE, NTU; MSEE, U. of Missouri; Visiting Scientist, IBM T.J. Watson Lab. 74-75; Visiting Scholar, UC-Berkly. 82-83. *Publ.: A Routing Tool; The Design & Implementation of a Mixed-level Logic Simulator; Add.* 4th Fl., 7 Lane 16, Wenchow St., Taipei.

YU, KUANG-HWA 余光華
Chmn., Twn. Salt Ind. Corp. 94-; *b.* Hupei May 20, '40; *m.* Lu, Li-kang; 1 *s.,* 2 *d.; educ.* BS, Mining & Metallurgy Engr., NCKU 64; V. Gen. Mgr., Twn. Aluminium Corp. 65-85; Dir., Prof. Tng. Cent., MOEA 85-89; Pres., Twn. Salt Works 89-94. *Publ.: Factor of the Influence on Electrolytic Pot-line; Application of Computer in Operating the Electrolytic Cell; Study on Saving Energy of Anode Block; Add.* 135 Nan Men Rd., Tainan.

YU, KUO-HWA 俞國華
Sr. Adv. to the Pres. 89-; Mem., CSC, KMT 79-; *b.* Chekiang Jan. 10, '14; *m.* Toong, Me-tsung; 2 *s.; educ.* NTHU 34; Grad. Sch., Harvard U. 44-46; London Sch. of Econ., UK 46-47; Hon. Doctorate of Com., St. John's U., USA 73; Sec. to the Pres., NMC 36-44; Alt. Exec. Dir., Intl. Bk. for Recon. & Dev. 47-50, & Intl. Monetary Fund 51-55; Pres., CTC 55-61; Mng. Dir., Ch. Dev. Corp. 59-67; Bd. Chmn., Bk. of Ch. 61-67, & Ch. Ins. Co. 61-67; Alt. Gov., Intl. Bk. for Recon. & Dev. 64-67; Min. of Finance 67-69; Gov., Intl. Bk. for Recon. & Dev. for the ROC 67-69, & CBC 69-84; Min. of State 69-84; Gov., Intl. Monetary Fund for the ROC 69-80, & Asian Dev. Bk. for the ROC 69-84; Chmn., CEPD 77-84; Premier 84-89; *Add.* c/o Off. of the Pres., Taipei.

YU, KWANG-CHUNG 余光中
Prof., Inst. of For. Lang. & Lit., Nat. Sun Yat-Sen U. 91-; *b.* Nanking Sept. 9, '28; *m.* Fan, Wo-chun; 4 *d.; educ.* BA, NTU; MA, Iowa State U. ; Lectr., NTNU 58-66; Assc. Prof., W. Michigan U. 65-66, & NTNU 66-70; Chmn., Dept. of W. Lang. & Lit., NCU 72-74; Prof., Ch. U. of Hong Kong 74-85; Dean, Coll. of Lib. Arts, Nat. Sun Yat-Sen U. 85-91; Sun Yat-sen Chair Prof.; Pres., Taipei Ch. Cent., PEN Intl.; Hon. Fel., Hong Kong Transl. Soc. *Publ.: White Jade Bitter Gourd; The Untrammeled Traveler; Assns. of the Lotus; Selected Poetry of Yu Kwang-chung; Memory is Where the Railway Reaches; Calling for Ferry; Dream & Geog.; The Night Watchman; From Hsü Hsia-ke to van Gogh; The Pomegranate;* Ch. Versions of Oscar Wilde's: *The Importance of Being Earnest; Lady Windermere's Fan; & An Ideal Husband; Add.* Nat. Sun Yat-Sen U., Kaohsiung.

YU, SHYI-KUN 游錫堃
Magis., Ilan County 89-; Chmn., Lanyang Cul. & Educ. Found. 90-; *b.* Twn. Apr. 25, '48; *m.* Yang, Pao-yu; 2 *s.;* *educ.* Grad., Chih Lee Coll. of Business 75; LL.B., Tunghai U. 85; Farmer 62-70; Mem., TPA 81-89; Sec.-Gen., Tangwai (outside the KMT Party) Cent. Backing Cttee. to the 1983 Elections; Founder, *Kavalan Jour.,* Pres. 86-88; Convener, Tangwai's Nat. Backing Cttee. to the 1986 Elections; Mem., CSC, DPP 87-90; Founder, Youngsun Cul. & Educ. Found. 90. *Publ.: The Resignation of Tangwai Assemblymen 85; The Rd. to Dem., The Love for Native Land* 89; *Add.* 23 Chiu Cheng S. Rd., Ilan.

YU, TSUNG-HSIEN
(See YU, TZONG-SHIAN 于宗先)

YU, TZONG-SHIAN 于宗先
Mem., Acad. Sinica 88-; Pres., Chunghua Inst. for Econ. Res. 90-; *b.* Shantung Sept. 10, '30; *m.* Chao, Hsiu-ying; 3 *d.; educ.* BS, Econ., NTU 56; MS, Jour., NCU 59; Ph.D., Econ., Indiana U. 66; Assc. Res. Fel., Inst. of Econ., Acad. Sinica 66-70, Res. Fel. 71-91, Dep. Dir. 72-76, Dir. 76-82; Assc. Prof. of Econ., NTU 66-70, Prof. 71-91; V. Pres., Chunghua Inst. for Econ. Res. 81-90; Pres., Ch. Econ. Assn. 86-88. *Publ.: Econ. Forecasting; The Contemporary For. Trade of the ROC; Breakthrough in Econ. Thinking; Response to Econ. Challenges; Complications of Econ. Dev.; Twn.'s Econ. in Transition;* & more than 120 articles on econ.; *Add.* 75 Chang Hsing St., Taipei.

YU, YING-SHIH 余英時
Mem., Acad. Sinica; Michael Henry Strater U. Prof., Princeton U.; *b.* Tientsin Jan. 22, '30; *m.* Chen, Monica Shu-ping; 2 *d.; educ.* BA, New Asia Coll., Ch. U. of Hong Kong 52; Ph.D., Harvard U. 62; Instr., Harvard U. 62; Asst. Prof., U. of Michigan 62-66; Assc. Prof. & Prof. of Ch. Hist., Harvard U. 66-77; Pres., New Asia Coll., & concur. Pro-V. Chancellor, Ch. U. of Hong Kong 73-75; Charles Seymour Prof. of Hist., Yale U. 77-87. *Publ.: Trade & Expansion in Han Ch.; Fang I-chih: His Last Years & His Death; Tai Chen & Chang Hsueh-cheng; A Study in Mid-Ch'ing Intellectual Hist.; Hist. Studies on the Ch. Intelligentsia; Add.* 4588 Prov. Line Rd., Princeton, NJ 08540, USA.

YUAN, CHIA-LIU
(See YUAN, LUKE CHIA-LIU 袁家騮)

YUAN, CHIEN-SHENG
(See YUAN, JASON C. 袁健生)

YUAN, CHIH-YEH
(See YUAN, IVAN CHIH-YEH 袁志業)

YUAN, I-CHIN 袁貽瑾
Mem., Acad. Sinica 48-; *b.* Hupei Oct. 30, 1899; *m.* Chen, Be-yuan; 2 *s.*, 1 *d.; educ.* MD, Med. Coll., Nat. Peking U.; Dr.PH & D.Sc., Johns Hopkins U.; Prof. of Public Health & Dept. Head, Med. Coll., Nat. Peking U.; Dir., Inst. of Epidemiology, & Nat. Inst. of Health; Dep. Min. of Health; Dep. Dir., Tuberculosis Res. Off., WHO; WHO Med. Dir. & concur. Chief Med. Adv. to UNICEF at the UN Hqs.; Visiting Prof. of Public Health, Coll. of Med., NTU; Visiting Scholar, E.-W. Cent., U. of Hawaii; Dir.-Gen., Acad. Sinica. *Publ.:* Articles on public health, including biostatistics, epidemiology, demography, tuberculosis, nutrition, family planning; etc.; *Add.* 2441 Webb Avenue, Apt. 15C, Bronx, New York, NY 10468, USA.

YUAN, IVAN CHIH-YEH 袁志業
Bd. Chmn. & CEO, Kiss 99.9 Broadcasting Co. Ltd. 95-; *b.* Taipei Nov. 16, '63; *m.* Liu, Leah Li-ya; 2 *d.; educ.* MBA, Calif. State Polytechnic U. at Pomona 91; Exec. Asst. to the Pres. & Sale Mgr., Fang-ming Broadcasting Co. Ltd 91-95; *Add.* 34th Fl.-2, 6 Min Chuan 2nd Rd., Chienchen, Kaohsiung.

YUAN, JASON C. 袁健生
Amb. to the Repub. of Panama 96-; *b.* Kweichow Feb. 1, '42; *m.* Yuan, Margaret; 1 *s.*, 1 *d.; educ.* B., Ch. Naval Acad. 63; MBA, Southea. U., Washington, D.C. 77; Aide to Chief of Gen. Staff, MND 71-74; Asst. Naval Attaché, Emb. in the USA 74-79 & Acting Naval Attaché 79-80; Sr. Staff, Public Aff. Div., CCNAA in the USA 79-80, Dep. Dir. 80-86, Dir. 86-91; Dir., Dept. of N. Am. Aff., MOFA 91-94; Rep., TECO, Can. 94-96; *Add.* Apartado 4285, Panama 5, Republica de Panama.

YUAN, LUKE CHIA-LIU 袁家騮
Mem., Acad. Sinica; Bd. Chmn., Synchrotron Radiation Res. Cent. 83-; Bd. Mem., Adelphi U. Energy Res. Cent.;

Hon. Prof., Ch. U. of Sc. & Tech., Hofeh, Anhwei Prov., Nankai U., Honan U., & Southwe. U.; Mem., New York Acad. Sc.; Hon. Mem., Honan Acad. of Sc.; Fel., Am. Phys. Soc.; Mem., Sigma Xi; *b.* Honan Apr. 5, '12; *m.* Wu, Chien-hsiung; 1 *s.; educ.* BS, Yenching U. 32, MS 34; Ph.D., Calif. Inst. of Tech. 40; Hon. Dr. of Sc., Nanking U.; Intl. House Fel., U. of Calif. 36-37; Grad. Asst., Calif. Inst. of Tech. 37-40, Res. Fel. 40-42; Res. Physicist, RCA Lab. 42-47; Res. Assc., Princeton U. 47-49; Assc. Physicist, Physicist, & Sr. Physicist, Brookhaven Nat. Lab. 49-78; Guggenheim Fel. 57; Visiting Prof., Centre d'Etudes Nucleaires de Saclay, France, & CERN, Geneva, Switzerland 72-73; Visiting Prof., Inst. for High Energy Phys., Serpukhov, USSR 79, & U. of Paris 82. *Publ.: Nature of Matter; Interaction of Particle Phys. Res. in Sc. & Tech.; Sc. Papers & Methods of Experimental Nuclear Phys.; Add.* 15 Claremont Avenue, New York, NY 10027, USA.

YUAN, SONG-SHI 袁頌西
Pres., Nat. Chi Nan U. 95-; *b.* Kiangsu Jan.23, '33; *m.* Wu, Wen-fan; 1 *s.* 1 *d.; educ.* MS in Pol. Sc., NTU 60, & Indiana U., USA 68; Dir., Dept. of Higher Educ., MOE 76-77, Head, Dept. of Pol. Sc., NTU & concur. Dir., Inst. of Pol. Sc. 81-84; Dean, Coll. of Law, NTU 84-88; Pol. V. Min. of Trans. & Comms. 88-91; Pol. V. Min. of Educ. 92-94; Convener, the Preparatory Off. of Nat. Chi Nan U. 94-95; *Add.* 1 U. Rd., Puli, Nantou County.

YUAN, SUNG-HSI
(See YUAN, SONG-SHI 袁頌西)

YUNG, CHAUR-SHIN 楊朝祥
Pol. V. Min. of Educ. 94-; *b.* Twn. Nov. 5, '47; *m.* Gou, Jen-huey; 1 *s.*, 1 *d.; educ.* BA, NTNU 70; MA, U. of Minnesota 75; Ph.D., Penn. State U. 78; Asst. Prof. of Voc. Tchr. Educ., U. of Arkansas 78-80; Assc. Prof. of Ind. Educ., NTNU 80-82, Prof. & Dept. Head of Ind. Arts Educ. 82-86; Dir.-Gen., Dept. of Tech. & Voc. Educ., MOE 86-89; Admin. V. Min. of Educ. 89-94. *Publ.: Career Guidance—Lifelong Process; Terminology of Voc. & Tech. Educ.; The Found. of Voc. Tech. Educ.; Job-seeking Skills; Add.* 5 Chung Shan S. Rd., Taipei.

Who's Who in the ROC II
Parliamentarian Profiles

Sample II

[1] **HU, JASON C.** 胡志強
[2] Rep., TECRO in the USA 96-; [3] *b.* May 15, '48; [4] *educ.* LL.B., Dept. of Dip., NCU 70; M. of Soc. Sc., Dept. of Pol., U. of Southampton 78; D.Phil., Oxford U. 84; [5] *Pol. Affi.* KMT; [6] *Const.* Taichung City; [7] Mem., CC, KMT; Dir.-Gen. & Govt. Spokesman, GIO 91-96; [8] *Add.* 4201 Wisconsin Avenue, NW, Washington, DC 20016, USA.

Item

[1] Name	[5] Political affiliation
[2] Occupation	[6] Constituency
[3] Vital statistics	[7] Political experience
[4] Education	[8] Address

Members of the Third National Assembly
(May 20, 1996—May 19, 2000)

CHANG, CHANG-HSIEN 張倉顯
Mem., NA; *b.* Oct. 24, '4; *educ.* Res., Georgetown U.; *Pol. Affi.* DPP; *Const.* Taipei County; *Add.* 57 Chung Hsin Rd., Sect. 3, Sanchung, Taipei County.

CHANG, CHAO-LUN 常照倫
Lawyer; *b.* Apr. 3, '59; *educ.* LL.M., NCU; *Pol. Affi.* NP; *Const.* Taichung City; *Add.* 11 Lane 470, Ying Tsai Rd., Taichung.

CHANG, CHEN-HSIANG
(See CHANG, MONTY C.H. 張禎祥)

CHANG, CHENG-CHI 張政治
Mem., NA; *b.* Aug. 22, '57; *educ.* M., Educ. Admin.; *Pol. Affi.* KMT; *Const.* Lowland Aborigines; *Add.* 19 Lane 22, Lin Yuan Rd., Chihnan Tsun, Shoufeng Hsiang, Hualien County.

CHANG, CHIEN-LUNG
(See CHANG, JIANN-LONG 張建隆)

CHANG, CHIN-HUA
(See CHANG, KING-HUA 張金華)

CHANG, CHUAN-TIEN 張川田
Mem., NA 92-; *b.* Aug. 15, '45; *educ.* BPS, Tunghai U. 73; *Pol. Affi.* DPP; *Const.* Nat.; Mem., CAC, DPP 90-92; *Add.* 60 Ta Wen Rd., Shihchao Tsun, Chiaohsi Hsiang, Ilan County.

CHANG, FU-MEI
(See CHEN CHANG, FU-MEI 張富美)

CHANG, FU-TANG
(See CHANG, HU-TANG 張馥堂)

CHANG, HSIAO-YEN
(See CHANG, JOHN HSIAO-YEN 章孝嚴)

CHANG, HSIU-CHEN 張秀珍
Mem., NA; *b.* Aug. 1, '51; *educ.* Grad., Ming Chuan Coll.; *Pol. Affi.* DPP; *Const.* Ovs. Nat.; *Add.* 15 Arthur Place, Montville, NJ 07045, USA.

CHANG, HU-TANG 張馥堂
Mem., NA 92-; *b.* Oct. 9, '38; *educ.* Res., U. of Hawaii; *Pol. Affi.* NP; *Const.* Nat.; Mayor, Panchiao City 82-90; *Add.* Rm. 1002, 2 Chung Shan N. Rd., Sect. 1, Taipei.

CHANG, HUI-YUAN 張輝元
Chmn., Irrigation Assn., Yunlin County 90-; *b.* Apr. 26, '38; *educ.* MBA, U. of Pacific 94; *Pol. Affi.* KMT; *Const.* Nat.; *Add.* 106-1 Jung Kuan, Mayuan Tsun, Tsutung Hsiang, Yunlin County.

CHANG, JIANN-LONG 張建隆
Mem., NA 92-; *b.* July 2, '54; *educ.* Grad., Chienhsin Jr. Coll. of Tech.; *Pol. Affi.* KMT; *Const.* Taoyuan County; *Add.* 50-1 Chung Cheng E. Rd., Tayuan Tsun, Tayuan Hsiang, Taoyuan County.

CHANG, JOHN HSIAO-YEN 章孝嚴
Min. of For. Aff.; *b.* May 2, '41; *educ.* MS, Georgetown U.; *Pol. Affi.* KMT; *Const.* Hsinchu County; Admin. V. Min. of For. Aff. 86-90; Pol. V. Min. of For. Aff. 90-93; Min., OCAC 93-96; *Add.* MOFA, 2 Kaitakelan Boulevard, Taipei.

CHANG, JUNG-HSIEN 張榮顯
Mem., NA; *b.* Mar. 1, '43; *educ.* Res., Nat. Sun Yat-Sen U.; *Pol. Affi.* KMT; *Const.* Kaohsiung City; *Add.* 818 Chien Kung Rd., Sanmin Dist., Kaohsiung.

CHANG, KENNY C. 張國慶
Assc. Prof., NTU; *b.* Aug. 23, '54; *educ.* Ph.D., Eng., U. of Rochester; *Pol. Affi.* DPP; *Const.* Nat.; Chmn., Twn. Environmental Protection Union (Taipei Chapter); *Add.* 1 Roosevelt Rd., Taipei.

CHANG, KING-HUA 張金華
Pres., Rotary Club; *b.* Feb. 26, '50; *educ.* Dip., Ch. Cul. U.; *Pol. Affi.* KMT; *Const.* Keelung City; *Add.* 72 Yi 1st Rd., Keelung.

CHANG, KUANG-HUEI 張光輝
Pres., Kate Ind. Corp.; *b.* Mar. 1, '45; *educ.* B., Engr., Chiba U., Japan 74; *Pol. Affi.* KMT; *Const.* Nat.; *Add.* 12 Ta Hua St., Taichung.

CHANG, KUANG-HUI
(See CHANG, KUANG-HUEI 張光輝)

CHANG, KUEN-LIN 張坤霖
Mem., NA; *b.* Mar. 10, '50; *educ.* Grad., Nat. Chiayi Inst. of Agr.; *Pol. Affi.* KMT; *Const.* Yunlin County; *Add.* 24 Mao Hsing Rd., Linmao Tsun, Linnei Hsiang, Yunlin County.

CHANG, KUO-CHING
(See CHANG, KENNY C. 張國慶)

CHANG, LING 張玲
Mem., NA; *b.* July 4, '53; *educ.* Studied, Grad. Sch., Ch. Cul. U.; *Pol. Affi.* KMT; *Const.* Taipei City; Mem., Taipei CCoun.; *Add.* 5th Fl., 8 Alley 10, Lane 4, Shih Yuan Rd., Wenshan, Taipei.

CHANG, LUNG-SHENG 張隆盛
Mem., CEPD 96-; *b.* Mar. 8, '40; *educ.* MPA, U. of Penn.; *Pol. Affi.* KMT; *Const.* Taichung County; Dir.-Gen., Construction & Planning Admin., MOI 81-88; Admin. V. Min. of the Int. 88-90; V. Chmn., CEPD 90-92; Admin., EPA 92-96; *Add.* Rm. 1210, 12th Fl., 87 Nanking E. Rd., Sect. 2, Taipei.

CHANG, MING-CHIH 張明致
Sec-Gen., Dept. of Org. Aff., CC, KMT 91-; *b.* Dec. 6, '47; *educ.* LL.M., Ch. Cul. U.; *Pol. Affi.* KMT; *Const.* Nat.; Dir., People Service Station, Lungshan, Shihlin, & Neihu Dist. 84-88; Sec.-Gen., Taipei Mun. Cttee., KMT 88-91; *Add.* 321 Mu Cha Rd., Sect. 1, Taipei.

CHANG, MONTY C.H. 張禎祥
Chmn., Presidium, NA 96-; *b.* Sept. 10, '52; *educ.* BA, Tamkang U.; Fel., Redstone Inst. of Tech., USA; *Pol. Affi.* DPP; *Const.* Taipei County; *Add.* 2nd Fl., 27 Hangchow S. Rd., Sect. 1, Taipei.

CHANG, SHENG-HUA 張勝華
Chmn., Changhua Construction Assc.; *b.* Jan. 6, '58; *educ.* Grad., Nat. Twn. Inst. of Tech.; *Pol. Affi.* KMT; *Const.* Changhua County; *Add.* 262 Ping Ho Rd., Sect. 1, Nanchen Tsun, Tienwei Hsiang, Changhua County.

CHANG, SONG-SUE 張松樹
Chmn., Chiachuan Construction Co. Ltd.; *b.* Feb. 11, '26; *educ.* Grad., Sr. High Sch.; *Pol. Affi.* KMT; *Const.* Chiayi County; Mem., Chiayi CoCoun. 82-90; Magis.,

Minhsiung Hsiang; *Add.* 33-2 Wen Hua Rd., Chungle Tsun, Minhsiung Hsiang, Chiayi County.

CHANG, SUNG-SU
(See CHANG, SONG-SUE 張松樹)

CHAO, LIN-LIN 趙玲玲
Dir. & Prof., Dr. Sun Yat-sen Inst., NTNU 90-; Mem., CC, KMT 93-; *b.* May 5, '45; *educ.* Ph.D. 73; *Pol. Affi.* KMT; *Const.* Nat.; *Add.* 162 Ho Ping E. Rd., Sect. 1, Taipei.

CHAO, LING-LING
(See CHAO, LIN-LIN 趙玲玲)

CHAO, NING 趙寧
Prof., NTNU; Mem., CC KMT; *b.* Sept. 10, '43; *educ.* Ph.D., U. of Wisconsin; *Pol. Affi.* KMT; *Const.* Nat.; *Add.* 7th Fl.-2, 88 Min Chuan E. Rd., Sect. 3, Taipei.

CHAO, SHU-YUAN 趙淑媛
Mem., NA; *b.* Feb. 27, '35; *educ.* Grad., Nat. Taichung Tchrs. Coll.; *Pol. Affi.* KMT; *Const.* Changhua County; *Add.* 542 Chung Shan Rd., Sect. 1, Changhua.

CHEN, CHAO-LUNG
(See CHEN, TSIAO-LONG 陳朝龍)

CHEN, CHARLES CHENG-KUNG 陳政寬
Bd. Dir., Tainan Business Bk.; *b.* Apr. 21, '43; *educ.* Hon. DCS, Oklahoma City U.; *Pol. Affi.* KMT; *Const.* Chiayi City; *Add.* 19 Chung Shan Rd., Chiayi.

CHEN, CHENG-KUAN
(See CHEN, CHARLES CHENG-KUNG 陳政寬)

CHEN, CHI-HUI 陳琪惠
Mem., NA; *b.* Aug. 25, '47; *educ.* MA, U. of Oklahoma; *Pol. Affi.* KMT; *Const.* Hsinchu County; *Add.* 343 Tung Feng Rd., Chutung, Hsinchu County.

CHEN, CHI-SAN 陳志三
Chmn., Taoyuan Ind. Assn.; *b.* Nov. 18, '44; *educ.* BA, U. of Hawaii; *Pol. Affi.* KMT; *Const.* Taoyuan County; *Add.* 10 Tung Yuan Rd., Chungli, Taoyuan County.

CHEN, CHI-YANG 陳淇陽
Mem., NA; *b.* July 17, '31; *educ.* Grad., Pingtung Agr. High Sch.; *Pol. Affi.* KMT; *Const.* Pingtung County; *Add.* 25-14 Chung Shan Rd., Taiping Tsun, Likang Hsiang, Pingtung County.

CHEN, CHIEN-MIN 陳建銘
Mem., NA; *b.* July 24, '61; *educ.* MBA, USA; *Pol. Affi.* KMT; *Const.* Taipei City; *Add.* 233 Yen Ping N. Rd., Sect. 6, Shihlin, Taipei.

CHEN, CHIH-KUAN 陳志寬
Pres., Hsinchang Elec. & Mach. Co.; *b.* May 2, '49; *educ.* Grad., Pingtung Com. & Ind. Sch.; *Pol. Affi.* KMT; *Const.* Pingtung County; Mem., Pingtung CoCoun.; *Add.* 104 Hsin Tsuo Rd., Hsinyuan Hsiang, Pingtung County.

CHEN, CHIH-NAN
(See CHEN, CHIH-NAAN 陳志男)

CHEN, CHIH-NAAN 陳志男
Chmn., Chunhan Construction Corp.; *b.* Feb. 1, '42; *Pol. Affi.* KMT; *Const.* Taipei County; *Add.* 111 Min Chi St., Yungho, Taipei County.

CHEN, CHIN-FA 陳進發
Mem., NA; *b.* Sept. 25, '48; *educ.* Grad., Taipei Phys. Educ. Coll.; *Pol. Affi.* DPP; *Const.* Tainan County; *Add.* 273 Hsin Yi St., Yungkang, Tainan County.

CHEN, CHIN-JANG
(See CHEN, CHING-JANG 陳金讓)

CHEN, CHIN-TE
(See CHEN, CHING-TE 陳金德)

CHEN, CHIN-TING 陳進丁
Chmn., Changhua Trans. Assn.; *b.* Sept. 26, '46; *educ.* Grad., Army Trans. Acad.; *Pol. Affi.* KMT; *Const.* Changhua County; *Add.* 30-32 Yen Cheng Lane, Tungshih, Lukang, Changhua County.

CHEN, CHING-JANG 陳金讓
Min. of Exam., Exam. Yuan 96-; Mem., CSC, KMT 93-; *b.* Feb. 1, '35; *educ.* LL.B., Soochow U. 58; *Pol. Affi.* KMT;

Const. Nat.; Dep. Dir.-Gen., Dept. of Org. Aff., CC, KMT 79-84, Chmn., Taipei Mun. Cttee. 84-88, V. Chmn., Policy Coordination Cttee., CC 88-90, Dir., Secretariat, CC 90, Dir.-Gen., Dept. of Org. Aff., CC 90-92; Sec.-Gen., NA 92-96; *Add.* Min. of Exam., 1 Shih Yuan Rd., Taipei.

CHEN, CHING-JEN 陳鏡仁
Mem., NA; *b.* July 7, '43; *educ.* Grad., Nat. Taipei Coll. of Business; *Pol. Affi.* KMT; *Const.* Nat.; Chmn., Chiayi Ind. Assn.; *Add.* 600 Chung Hsiao Rd., Chiayi.

CHEN, CHING-TE 陳金德
Mem., NA 92-; *b.* Sept. 26, '61; *educ.* MS, NTU; *Pol. Affi.* DPP; *Const.* Ilan County; Personal Sec., Ilan County Govt.; *Add.* 8-1 Shu Jen Rd., Lotung, Ilan County.

CHEN, CHUAN 陳川
Mem., NA; *b.* June 29, '34; *educ.* LL.B., Land Admin. Dept., NCHU 59; *Pol. Affi.* KMT; *Const.* Nat.; Dir., Wufeng Dist. Land Admin. Off. 61-70; Sect. Chief, Taoyuan Land Admin. Dept. 70-82; Dep. Dir., Secretariat, NA 82-85; Dep. Sec.-Gen., NA 90-96 & KMT Caucus 85; *Add.* 53 Chung Hua Rd., Sect. 1, Taipei.

CHEN, HAN-CHUN
(See CHEN, HENRY C. 陳漢春)

CHEN, HENG-SHENG 陳恆盛
Mem., NA 96-; *b.* Oct. 10, '29; *educ.* BA, NCHU; *Pol. Affi.* KMT; *Const.* Nat.; Mem., Control Yuan; *Add.* 5 Hsin Chien Lane, Taian Li, Pingtung.

CHEN, HENRY C. 陳漢春
Mem., NA 92-; *b.* Mar. 2, '33; *educ.* BS, NTU 57; *Pol. Affi.* KMT; *Const.* Nat.; *Add.* 7th Fl.-1, 103 An Ho Rd., Sect. 4, Taipei.

CHEN, HSIU-HUI
(See CHEN, SHIU-HUEI 陳秀惠)

CHEN, HSUEH-SHENG 陳雪生
Mem., NA; *b.* Jan. 1, '52; *educ.* Fengyuan Cml. High Sch.; *Pol. Affi.* KMT; *Const.* Lienchiang County, Fukien Prov.; *Add.* 5th Fl., 94 Mei Lun St., Shihlin, Taipei.

CHEN, I-SHEN
(See CHEN, YI-SHEN 陳儀深)

CHEN, I-WEN
(See CHEN, YI-WEN 陳亦文)

CHEN, I-YANG 陳義揚
Pres., Nat. Open U.; *b.* Sept. 15, '43; *educ.* Ph.D., Tulane U.; *Pol. Affi.* NP; *Const.* Nat.; *Add.* 172 Chung Cheng Rd., Luchou, Taipei County.

CHEN, JUI-LIN 陳瑞麟
Mem., NA; *b.* Mar. 22, '46; *educ.* BA, Tamkang U.; *Pol. Affi.* DPP; *Const.* Hualien County; Chief Exec., Hualien County Cttee., DPP; *Add.* 13 Chen Kuo St., Hualien County.

CHEN, JUN-WU 陳潤吾
Prof., San Jose State U.; *b.* May 9, '49; *educ.* Ph.D., U. of Santa Clara; *Pol. Affi.* KMT; *Const.* Ovs. Nat.; *Add.* 1198 Nikulina Court, San Jose, CA 95120, USA.

CHEN, MEI-TZU 陳美子
Tchr., Lukang High Sch. 64-; *b.* Feb. 22, '43; *educ.* BA, Providence U.; *Pol. Affi.* KMT; *Const.* Changhua County; *Add.* 24 Lane 95, Fu Hsing Rd., Lukang, Changhua County.

CHEN, MIN-CHI 陳明吉
Mem., NA 92-; Sec.-Gen., Nat. Tng. Inst. for Farmers' Org. 93-; *b.* Dec. 15, '41; *educ.* LL.B., NCU; MBA, Cent. U., Philippines; *Pol. Affi.* KMT; *Const.* Nat.; Gen. Mgr., Tungshan Hsiang Farmers' Assn. 75-92; *Add.* 33 Hsin Yi 2nd St., Lin 11, Yingchien Tsun, Hsiaying Hsiang, Tainan County.

CHEN, MING-CHI
(See CHEN, MIN-CHI 陳明吉)

CHEN, MING-JEN 陳明仁
Standing Sup., Twn. Prov. Farmer's Assn.; *b.* Feb. 20, '53; *educ.* Ph.D., Fu Jen Catholic U. 91; *Pol. Affi.* KMT; *Const.* Nat.; *Add.* 1 Lane 915, Min Tsu Rd., Chiayi.

CHEN, PI-FENG 陳碧峰
Mem., NA; *b.* Dec. 11, '44; *educ.* Grad., Nat. Taipei Coll. of Business; *Pol. Affi.* DPP; *Const.* Taipei City; *Add.* 133 Yen Ping N. Rd., Sect. 7, Taipei.

CHEN, SAN-SZU 陳三思
Mem., NA 92-; *b.* Apr. 25, '47; *educ.* Grad., Tatung Jr. Coll. of Comm.; *Pol. Affi.* DPP; *Const.* Kaohsiung County; Rep., 5th CC, DPP; *Add.* 47 Le Yuan St., Fengshan, Kaohsiung County.

CHEN, SHENG 陳盛
Sp., OCAC; *b.* Feb. 9, '62; *educ.* Ph.D., U. of New Orleans; *Pol. Affi.* NP; *Const.* Taoyuan County; *Add.* 5th Fl., 224 Yuan Hua Rd., Chungli, Taoyuan County.

CHEN, SHIU-HUEI 陳秀惠
Mem., NA 92-; V. Chmn., Women's Dev. Cttee., DPP 94-; *b.* Dec. 15, '51; *educ.* BA, NTNU 76; *Pol. Affi.* DPP; *Const.* Nat.; Chmn., Homemakers' Union & Found. 90-92; Exec., Women's Dev. Cttee., DPP 93-94; *Add.* 53 Chung Hua Rd., Sect. 1, Taipei.

CHEN, SHU-NUAN 陳淑暖
Mem., NA; *b.* Feb. 25, '54; *educ.* LL.B., Fu Jen Catholic U.; *Pol. Affi.* DPP; *Const.* Ilan County; Mem., Ilan CoCoun.; *Add.* 221 Chung Hua Rd., Lotung, Ilan County.

CHEN, TA-CHUN 陳大鈞
Mem., NA; *b.* Mar. 24, '63; *educ.* MPS, Ch. Cul. U.; *Pol. Affi.* DPP; *Const.* Taichung City; *Add.* 9th Fl., 107 Wu Chuan W. Rd., W. Dist., Taichung.

CHEN, TAO-MING
(See CHEN, TAW-MING 陳道明)

CHEN, TAW-MING 陳道明
Ophthalmologist, Tai Ming Eye Clinic; *b.* Nov. 21, '47; *educ.* MD, Taipei Med. Coll.; *Pol. Affi.* DPP; *Const.* Nat.; 92-8 Yen Ping St., Hualien.

CHEN, TSAN-HUNG 陳燦鴻
Mem., NA; *b.* Jan. 27, '58; *educ.* Studied, NCU; *Pol. Affi.* KMT; *Const.* Taipei City; *Add.* 7th Fl., 1 Lane 6, Cheng Kung Rd., Sect. 3, Taipei.

CHEN, TSIAO-LONG 陳朝龍
Chmn., Juifang Township Cttee., DPP; *b.* Oct. 1, '53; *educ.* BA, Nat. Taipei Inst. of Tech.; *Pol. Affi.* DPP; *Const.* Nat.; *Add.* 6th Fl., 10 Lane 130, Nan Kang Rd., Sect. 3, Taipei.

CHEN, TSUN-HSIUNG 陳村雄
Mem., NA 96-; *b.* Dec. 21, '40; *educ.* BA, NTNU; *Pol. Affi.* KMT; *Const.* Kaohsiung City; Mem., Kaohsiung CCoun. 81-94; *Add.* 5th Fl., 308 Pa Te 1st Rd., Hsinshing Dist., Kaohsiung.

CHEN, TZU-CHIN
(See CHEN, ZU-CHIN 陳子欽)

CHEN, TZU-MING 陳自明
Mem., NA; *b.* Nov. 28, '57; *educ.* M., Hofstra U., USA; *Pol. Affi.* NP; *Const.* Ovs. Nat.; *Add.* 450 Potrero Avenue, San Francisco, CA 94110, USA.

CHEN, TZUNG-JEN 陳宗仁
Mem., NA 92-; *b.* Oct. 2, '59; *educ.* BPS, Ch. Cul. U. 82; *Pol. Affi.* DPP; *Const.* Taoyuan County; Mem., Taoyuan CoCoun. 86-90; *Add.* 1061 Yung An Rd., Taoyuan.

CHEN, WAN-CHEN 陳婉真
Mem., NA; *b.* June 10, '50; *educ.* B., NTNU; *Pol. Affi.* DPP; *Const.* Taipei County; Mem., Legis. Yuan; *Add.* 2nd Fl., 260 Hsueh Fu Rd., Sect. 1, Tucheng, Taipei County.

CHEN, YAO-CHANG 陳耀昌
Prof., Sch. of Med., NTU; *b.* Feb. 9, '49; *educ.* MD, NTU; Fel., Rush-Presbyterian-St. Luke Med. Cent., Chicago; *Pol. Affi.* DPP; *Const.* Nat.; *Add.* Rm. 321, 7 Chung Shan S. Rd., Taipei.

CHEN, YI-SHEN 陳儀深
Assc. Prof., Soochow U.; *b.* Feb. 18, '54; *educ.* Ph.D., NCU; *Pol. Affi.* DPP; *Const.* Nat.; *Add.* 3rd Fl., 6 Lane 8, Yu Sheng St., Shihlin, Taipei.

CHEN, YI-WEN 陳亦文
Mem., NA 92-; *b.* Aug. 26, '49; *educ.* Grad., Sheng Te Christian Coll.; *Pol. Affi.* KMT; *Const.* Keelung City; Mem., Keelung CCoun.; Pres., Keelung Suicide Prevention Cent.; *Add.* 3rd Fl., 495-2 Hsiang Feng St., Keelung.

CHEN, YU-HUI 陳玉惠
Pres., Hua Lun Co. Ltd.; *b.* Apr. 5, '43; *educ.* Taichung Agr. High Sch.; *Pol. Affi.* DPP; *Const.* Taichung City; *Add.* 458 Wu Chuan W. Rd., Sect. 2, Nantun, Taichung.

CHEN, YUN-TUNG 陳運棟
Prin., Ta Cheng Sr. High Sch. 89-; *b.* Aug. 23, '33; *educ.* LL.M., Ch. Cul. U. 85; *Pol. Affi.* KMT; *Const.* Miaoli County; *Add.* 146 Ta Cheng St., Toufen, Miaoli County.

CHEN, ZU-CHIN 陳子欽
Mem., NA 92-; *b.* Mar. 10, '47; *educ.* BBA, U. of Texas; *Pol. Affi.* KMT; *Const.* Nat.; Pres., World Hakka Fed.; *Add.* 33 Tai An Rd., Meinung, Kaohsiung County.

CHEN CHANG, FU-MEI 張富美
Exec. Dir., Com. for Examining Petitions & Appeals, TCG 94-; Mem., NA 92-; *b.* Oct. 10, '38; *educ.* LL.M., Northwe. U. 61; Ph.D., Harvard U. 70; *Pol. Affi.* DPP; *Const.* Ovs. Nat.; Bd. Mem., Formosan Assn. for Public Aff., USA 87-91; Founding Pres., N. Am. Twn. Women's Assn. 88-89; Res. Fel., Hoover Inst., Stanford U. 78-94; Convener, DPP Caucus, NA 94-95; *Add.* Com. for Examining Petitions & Appeals, 1 Shih Fu Rd., Taipei.

CHENG, HSIN-CHU 鄭新助
Mem., NA; *b.* Feb. 21, '41; *educ.* Grad., Twn. Prov. Fengshan High Sch.; *Pol. Affi.* DPP; *Const.* Nat.; *Add.* 14 Fu Chien Rd., Fengshan, Kaohsiung County.

CHENG, KUEI-LAN 鄭貴蓮
Chmn., Hope Found. 94-; *b.* Dec. 25, '50; *educ.* BA, Soochow U.; *Pol. Affi.* DPP; *Const.* Kaohsiung County; Rep., 5th CC, DPP 92-94; Chmn., Assn. for Dem. Women in Chiaotou 93; *Add.* 110 Pai Shu Rd., Chiaotou Hsiang, Kaohsiung County.

CHENG, KUEI-LIEN
(See CHENG, KUEI-LAN 鄭貴蓮)

CHENG, LI-WEN 鄭麗文
Mem., NA; *b.* Nov. 12, '69; *educ.* LL.M., Temple U., USA; *Pol. Affi.* DPP; *Const.* Taipei City; Sec.-Gen., Twn. Human Rights Promotion Assn.; *Add.* 6th Fl., 9 Lane 188, Ho Chiang St., Taipei.

CHENG, MEI-LAN 鄭美蘭
Chmn., Twn. Fishery Assn.; *b.* Oct. 28, '57; *educ.* Grad., Ilan Cml. High Sch.; *Pol. Affi.* KMT; *Const.* Nat.; Mem., Ilan CoCoun.; *Add.* 5 Keng Hsin Rd., Toucheng, Ilan County.

CHI, HSIN 紀欣
Mem., NA; *b.* Dec. 28, '51; *educ.* LL.D., Guild Law Sch., USA; *Pol. Affi.* NP; *Const.* Taipei City; Attorney-at-Law; *Add.* 14th Fl.-1, 84 Fu Hsing S. Rd., Sect. 2, Taipei.

CHI TSAI, YUEH-HSIEN 紀蔡月仙
Standing Sup., Taichung County Cttee., KMT; *b.* July 20, '44; *educ.* Grad., Mingtai High Sch.; *Pol. Affi.* KMT; *Const.* Taichung County; *Add.* 7 Lane 177, Kung Yeh Rd., Chunghe Tsun, Lungtan Hsiang, Taichung County.

CHIANG, CHAO-I 江昭儀
Mem., NA; *b.* Aug. 2, '43; *educ.* M., Memphis State U.; *Pol. Affi.* DPP; *Const.* Ovs. Nat.; *Add.* DPP Nat. Budget Cent., Legis. Yuan, 1 Chung Shan S. Rd., Taipei.

CHIANG, CHI-YEN 江吉源
Mem., NA 96-; *b.* Mar. 23, '41; *educ.* Grad., Kaofeng Sr. Voc. High Sch.; *Pol. Affi.* KMT; *Const.* Kaohsiung County; Mem., Kaohsiung CoCoun.; *Add.* 85-8 Ching Wu Rd., Fengshan, Kaohsiung County.

CHIANG, CHI-YUAN
(See CHIANG, CHI-YEN 江吉源)

CHIANG, HUEI-CHEN 江惠貞
Mem., NA 92-; *b.* Jan. 28, '63; *educ.* BA, Fu Jen Catholic U.; *Pol. Affi.* KMT; *Const.* Taipei County; Mem., Taipei CoCoun.; *Add.* 16 Lane 37, Hsueh Fu Rd., Sect. 1, Tucheng, Taipei County.

CHIANG, HUI-CHEN
(See CHIANG, HUEI-CHEN 江惠貞)

CHIANG, JUI-TIEN 江瑞添
Mem., NA; *b.* Dec. 26, '61; *educ.* BA, NTU; *Pol. Affi.* DPP; *Const.* Taoyuan County; Chief Exec., Taoyuan County Cttee., DPP; *Add.* 160 Lin 2, Tsaolei Tsun, Kuanyin Hsiang, Taoyuan County.

CHIANG, SHUN-YU 江順裕
Mem., NA; *b.* Oct. 22, '56; *educ.* M., NTNU; *Pol. Affi.* KMT; *Const.* Hsinchu County; *Add.* 43 Lin 10, Hsiashan Tsun, Chiunglin Hsiang, Hsinchu County.

CHIANG, SU-HUI
(See CHIANG, SUSIE SU-HUI 江素惠)

CHIANG, SUSIE SU-HUI 江素惠
Dir., Kwang Hwa Info. & Cul. Cent., Hong Kong 92-; *b.* Feb. 7, '47; *educ.* LL.B., NCHU; *Pol. Affi.* NP; *Const.* Ovs. Nat.; *Add.* 40th Fl., One Pacific Place, 88 Queensway, Hong Kong.

CHIANG, WEN-JU 江文如
Mem., NA 96-; *b.* Dec. 15, '68; *educ.* Grad., Tamsui Oxford U. Coll.; *Pol. Affi.* Independent; *Const.* Taipei County; *Add.* 12 Lane 294, Pi Hua St., Sanchung, Taipei County.

CHIEN, FREDRICK F. 錢復
Spkr., NA; Mem., CSC, KMT 88-; *b.* Feb. 17, '35; *educ.* Ph.D., Yale U.; *Pol. Affi.* KMT; *Const.* Nat.; Rep., CCNAA, Washington, D.C. 83-88; Chmn., CEPD & concur. Min. of State; Min. of For. Aff. 90-96; *Add.* 53 Chung Hua Rd., Sect. 1, Taipei.

CHIEN, FU
(See CHIEN, FREDRICK F. 錢復)

CHIEN, SHU-HUI 簡淑慧
Mem., NA; *b.* Dec. 14, '65; *educ.* LL.B., Soochow U.; *Pol. Affi.* DPP; *Const.* Taipei County; *Add.* 1 Alley 5, Lane 177, Szu Yuan Rd., Hsinchuang, Taipei County.

CHIEN, TAI-LANG 簡太郎
Dir., Dept. of Population Admin., MOI; *b.* Feb. 15, '47; *educ.* BA, NCHU; *Pol. Affi.* KMT; *Const.* Pingtung County; Chief Sec., Bu. of Population Admin., Kaohsiung City Govt.; *Add.* 2nd Fl., 31 Pao An St., Hsintien, Taipei County.

CHIEN, TE-YUAN
(See CHIEN, TEH-YUAN 簡德源)

CHIEN, TEH-YUAN 簡德源
Gen. Mgr., Shulin Chen Farmers' Assn. 70-; *b.* Dec. 14, '34; *educ.* Grad., Taoyuan Agr. Voc. Sch. 51; *Pol. Affi.* KMT; *Const.* Taipei County; Sec., Taoyuan County Cttee., KMT 59-62; Dir., Wanli Hsiang People Service Station 62-64; *Add.* 77 Chen Chien St., Shulin, Taipei County.

CHIEN, TZU-HUI 簡慈慧
Tchr.; *b.* Jan. 18, '52; *educ.* BA, NCU; *Pol. Affi.* DPP; *Const.* Nantou County; *Add.* 46 Yu Ching St., Nantou.

CHIN, CHI-HUA
(See CHIN, JIH-HUA 秦繼華)

CHIN, JIH-HUA 秦繼華
Prof., NCTU; *b.* Feb. 9, '53; *educ.* Dr. of Engr., U. of Stuttgart, Germany; *Pol. Affi.* NP; *Const.* Hsinchu City; *Add.* 1st Fl., 48 Lane 42, Tung Kuang Rd., Hsinchu.

CHING, CHIH-JEN
(See GENE, CHIH-JEN 荆知仁)

CHING, HSI-YU
(See GING, CHI-YU 荆溪昱)

CHIU, AUSTIN I-PIN 邱奕彬
Chmn., Ch. Policy Cttee., DPP Caucus, NA 96-; *b.* Nov. 10, '50; *educ.* Orthodontist Sp. Prog., Sch. of Dentistry, New York U.; *Pol. Affi.* DPP; *Const.* Taoyuan County; *Add.* Rm. 403, 53 Chung Hua Rd., Sect. 1, Taipei.

CHIU, CHIA-CHIEN 邱家乾
Mem., NA; *b.* Sept. 10, '38; *educ.* Grad., Chengkung Ind. & Com. High Sch.; *Pol. Affi.* KMT; *Const.* Taoyuan County; *Add.* 267 Chieh Shou Rd., Tahsi, Taoyuan County.

CHIU, CHIEN-YUNG 邱建勇
Mem., NA; *b.* Nov. 9, '58; *educ.* M., NTU; *Pol. Affi.* NP; *Const.* Taoyuan County; *Add.* 9-1 Lane 23, Kuang Feng Rd., Pate, Taipei County.

CHIU, I-PIN
(See CHIU, AUSTIN I-PIN 邱奕彬)

CHIU, I-YING 邱議瑩
Mem., NA; *b.* June 1, '71; *educ.* Grad., Taoming High Sch.; *Pol. Affi.* DPP; *Const.* Pingtung County; *Add.* 271 Chung Cheng Rd., Pingtung.

CHIU, KUO-CHANG 邱國昌
Mem., NA; *b.* Nov. 21, '46; *educ.* LL.B., NCHU; *Pol. Affi.* DPP; *Const.* Taipei City; *Add.* 4th Fl., 4, Lane 49, Yi Li St., Peitou, Taipei.

CHIU, TAI-SAN 邱太三
Mem., NA; *b.* Aug. 30, '56; *educ.* LL.B., NTU; *Pol. Affi.* DPP; *Const.* Taichung County; Prosecutor; Lawyer; *Add.* 132 Kung Kuan Rd., Taichung.

CHO, CHENG-FANG 卓政防
Dir., Div. of Gen. Aff., EPA, Kaohsiung City Govt.; *b.*
June 15, '47; *educ.* BA, Nat. Kaohsiung Normal U.; *Pol.
Affi.* KMT; *Const.* Kaohsiung County; *Add.* Environ-
mental Protection Admin., Kaohsiung City Govt.

CHOU, HENG 周衡
Mem., NA; *b.* June 6, '58; *educ.* Grad., High Sch.; *Pol.
Affi.* DPP; *Const.* Taipei County; *Add.* 15 Ho Ping St.,
Taishan Hsiang, Taipei County.

CHOU, MIN-CHIN 周民進
Mem., NA; *b.* Sept. 1, '51; *educ.* Grad., High Sch.; *Pol.
Affi.* DPP; *Const.* Nat.; Exec. Mem., Taipei City Cttee.,
DPP; *Add.* 2nd Fl., 295-4 Ti Hua St., Sect. 2, Taipei.

CHOU, WEI-YU 周威佑
Mem., NA; *b.* Sept. 15, '62; *educ.* LL.B., NTU; *Pol. Affi.*
DPP; *Const.* Taipei City; *Add.* 4-1 Chung Hua Rd., Sect.
2, Taipei.

CHU, CHAO-HSIANG 曲兆祥
Mem., NA; *b.* Jan. 4, '56; *educ.* Ph.D., NCU; *Pol. Affi.*
NP; *Const.* Taipei City; *Add.* 602-1 Chung Hua Rd., Sect.
2, Taipei.

CHU, CHUN-HSIAO 朱俊曉
Mem., NA 92-; *b.* Mar. 20, '63; *educ.* B., Engr., Nihon
U., Japan 89; *Pol. Affi.* KMT; *Const.* Taipei County; *Add.*
85 Cheng I N. Rd., Sanchung, Taipei County.

CHU, HSIN-MIN 朱新民
Prof., Grad. Inst. of Dip., NCU; *b.* Apr. 27, '53; *educ.*
LL.D., Grad. Inst. of Pol. Sc., NCU; *Pol. Affi.* KMT;
Const. Nat.; *Add.* 2nd Fl., 6 Lane 20, An Ho Rd., Sect.
2, Taipei.

CHU, TUNG-SHU 朱銅樹
Mem., NA; *b.* June 12, '54; *educ.* Grad., Voc. Sr. High
Sch.; *Pol. Affi.* DPP; *Const.* Nat.; Mem., Kaohsiung
CoCoun.; *Add.* 243 Kuang Fu Rd., Sect. 2, Fengshan,
Kaohsiung County.

CHUANG, JUNG-CHANG 莊隆昌
Pres., Twn. Chamber of Com. 95-; V. Chmn., Taipei
County Br., Ch. Youth Corps 94-; *b.* June 23, '52; *educ.*

Grad., Supplementary Open Jr. Coll. for Public Admin.,
NCU; *Pol. Affi.* KMT; *Const.* Nat.; Dep. Dir., Dept. of
Party-Govt. Coordination of the NA, KMT 96; *Add.* 39
Chung Cheng Rd., Luchou, Taipei County.

CHUANG, LUNG-CHANG
(See CHUANG, JUNG-CHANG 莊隆昌)

CHUANG, SHENG-JUNG 莊勝榮
Lawyer; *b.* Jan. 20, '61; *educ.* LL.B., NTU; *Pol. Affi.*
DPP; *Const.* Taipei City; *Add.* 11th Fl., 1 Foochow
St., Taipei.

CHUNG, CHIA-PIN 鍾佳濱
Mem., NA; *b.* Feb. 23, '65; *educ.* B., NTU; *Pol. Affi.*
DPP; *Const.* Pingtung County; *Add.* 6 Chung Lin Rd.,
Linpien Hsiang, Pingtung County.

CHUNG, SHU-CHI 鍾淑姬
Sec.-Gen., Hsinchu City Pollution Prevention Assn.; *b.*
Apr. 24, '60; *educ.* BA, Nat. Cent. U.; *Pol. Affi.* DPP;
Const. Nat.; *Add.* 1 Lane 183, Kung Yuan Rd., Hsinchu.

FAN, YANG-KUNG 范楊恭
Mem., NA; *b.* Aug. 18, '42; *educ.* Grad., World Coll. of
Jour. & Comms.; *Pol. Affi.* KMT; *Const.* Hsinchu
County; *Add.* 3-20 Lin 13, Hohsing Tsun, Hukou Hsiang,
Hsinchu County.

FENG, HU-HSIANG
(See FUNG, HU-HSIANG 馮滬祥)

FENG, JU-CHENG 馮汝城
Mem., NA; *b.* June 19, '29; *educ.* M., Law & Pol. U.,
Japan; *Pol. Affi.* KMT; *Const.* Ovs. Nat.; *Add.* 9 Lane
79, Chien Kuo S. Rd., Sect. 2, Taipei.

FENG, PAO-CHENG 馮寶成
Mem., NA; *b.* June 27, '41; *educ.* Grad., Hsinchu Bible
Coll.; *Pol. Affi.* KMT; *Const.* Highland Aborigines;
Mem., Pingtung CoCoun.; *Add.* 13 Sanhe Tsun, Machia
Hsiang, Pingtung County.

FU, SHU-CHEN 傅淑真
Mem., NA; *b.* Oct. 8, '57; *educ.* BA, Nat. Kaohsiung
Normal U.; *Pol. Affi.* DPP; *Const.* Taichung County;

Add. 25 Lane 105, Chung Hsiao St., Fengyuan, Taichung County.

FUNG, HU-HSIANG 馮滬祥
Prof., Nat. Cent. U. 86-; Sec.-Gen., Alliance for Dem. Reform 94-; *b.* May 8, '48; *educ.* Ph.D., Boston U.; *Pol. Affi.* NP; *Const.* Nat.; Sec. to the Pres. 79-86; Adv., Exec. Yuan 91-92; *Add.* 12th Fl.-1, 66 Ai Kuo E. Rd., Taipei.

GENE, CHIH-JEN 荊知仁
Full Prof., NCU 66-92; *b.* July 25, '27; *educ.* MA, NCU 58; *Pol. Affi.* KMT; *Const.* Nat.; *Add.* 11th Fl., 36 Lane 65, Hsin Kuang Rd., Sect. 1, Taipei.

GING, CHI-YU 荊溪昱
Assc. Prof., Nat. Kaohsiung Normal U.; *b.* May 27, '52; *educ.* Ph.D., Virginia Polytechnic State Inst.; *Pol. Affi.* NP; *Const.* Kaohsiung City; *Add.* 22nd Fl.,-1, Bldg. E, 88-1 Min Tsu 1st Rd., Kaohsiung.

HO, CHEN-SHENG
(See HO, JENG-SHENG 何振盛)

HO, CHI-CHIEN
(See HO, LEO C. 何啟建)

HO, JENG-SHENG 何振盛
Dep. Sec.-Gen., NP; *b.* Jan. 26, '62; *educ.* LL.M., NCU; *Pol. Affi.* NP; *Const.* Nat.; Sec., TECO in Vietnam 92-95; *Add.* 4th Fl., 65 Kuang Fu S. Rd., Taipei.

HO, LEO C. 何啟建
Adv., KMT; *b.* Sept. 2, '40; *educ.* Ph.D., Wayne State U. 75; *Pol. Affi.* KMT; *Const.* Ovs. Nat.; Comr., OCAC; Pres., Grand Alliance, Michigan Chapter, USA; *Add.* 3810 Manchester Court, Bloomfield Hills, MI 48302, USA.

HO, MARK M.H. 何敏豪
Mem., NA; *b.* July 10, '58; *educ.* BA, NCHU; *Pol. Affi.* DPP; *Const.* Taichung City; *Add.* 75 Liao Yang 4th St., Peitun, Taichung.

HO, MIN-HAO
(See HO, MARK M.H. 何敏豪)

HOU, CHING-CHANG 侯慶昌
Mem., NA; *b.* Oct. 10, '53; *educ.* Grad., Taipei Phys. Educ. Coll.; *Pol. Affi.* DPP; *Const.* Chiayi County; *Add.* 22 Kuang Fu Rd., Putzu, Chiayi County.

HOU, SHUI-SHENG 侯水盛
Mem., NA; *b.* Jan. 10, '49; *educ.* B., Ch. Med. Coll.; *Pol. Affi.* DPP; *Const.* Tainan County; *Add.* 351-1 Chung Shan Rd., Shanhua, Tainan County.

HOU, TSAI-FENG 侯彩鳳
Mem., CC, KMT; *b.* Dec. 25, '52; *educ.* Grad., Chenghsiu Jr. Coll. of Tech. & Com.; *Pol. Affi.* KMT; *Const.* Nat.; *Add.* 228 Chien Hsing Rd., Sanmin, Kaohsiung.

HSIAO, CHIU-TE 蕭秋德
Mem., NA; *b.* Nov. 8, '52; *educ.* Ph.D., U. of Oklahoma; *Pol. Affi.* DPP; *Const.* Ovs. Nat.; *Add.* 14149 Arbolitos Drive, Poway, CA 92064, USA.

HSIAO, SHU-LI 蕭淑麗
Mem., NA; *b.* Mar. 1, '67; *educ.* Grad., Chiayi Jr. Coll. of Com.; *Pol. Affi.* KMT; *Const.* Chiayi County; *Add.* 1 Hsiang Ho 1st Rd., W. Sect., Putzu, Chiayi County.

HSIEH, CHING-WEN 謝清文
Mem., NA; *b.* Dec. 11, '42; *educ.* Grad., Nat. Taipei Inst. of Tech.; *Pol. Affi.* DPP; *Const.* Tainan County; *Add.* 22 Kung Yeh S. Rd., Kuantien Hsiang, Tainan County.

HSIEH, CHUNG-YU 謝仲瑜
Mem., NA; *b.* May 15, '67; *educ.* LL.M., Tunghai U.; *Pol. Affi.* NP; *Const.* Kaohsiung City; *Add.* 4th Fl., 3 Chung Hua Rd., Sect. 1, Kaohsiung.

HSIEH, DUNG-SUNG 謝東松
Pres., Talung Construction Co.; *b.* Mar. 20, '51; *educ.* Grad., Fengyuan Jr. High Sch.; *Pol. Affi.* KMT; *Const.* Changhua County; *Add.* 3 Lane 28, Nan An Rd., Nankuang Li, Erlin, Changhua County.

HSIEH, JUI-CHIH
(See HSIEH, ZUI-CHI 謝瑞智)

HSIEH, LUNG-SHENG
(See SHIEH, LUNG-SHENG 謝隆盛)

HSIEH, MING-CHANG 謝明璋
Mem., NA; *b.* Oct. 9, '58; *educ.* Studied, Nat. Open U.; *Pol. Affi.* DPP; *Const.* Penghu County; *Add.* 43 Yang Ming Rd., Makung, Penghu County.

HSIEH, MING-HUI 謝明輝
Mem., NA; *b.* Jan. 16, '59; *educ.* B., Cent. Police Coll.; *Pol. Affi.* NP; *Const.* Taipei County; *Add.* 11th Fl., 3 Lane 25, Yang Ming St., Panchiao, Taipei County.

HSIEH, TUNG-SUNG
(See HSIEH, DUNG-SUNG 謝東松)

HSIEH, ZUI-CHI 謝瑞智
Prof., NTNU 82-; *b.* Mar. 31, '35; *educ.* LL.M., U. of Waseda 68; LL.D., U. of Vienna 70; *Pol. Affi.* KMT; *Const.* Nat.; Avd., CC, KMT; V. Min. of Pers. 93-94; Sr. Adv., NSC 95-96; *Add.* 1st Fl., 1-3 Lane 16, Wenchow St., Taipei.

HSU, CHING-FU 許慶復
Mem., NA; *b.* Nov. 8, '45; *educ.* MA, NTU; *Pol. Affi.* KMT; *Const.* Nat.; Chmn., ROC Public Policy Soc.; *Add.* Dept. of Pol. Sc., NTU, 21 Hsuchow Rd., Taipei.

HSU, HSIANG-KUN
(See HSU, SHIANG-KUEEN 徐享崑)

HSU, HSIN-I 許信義
Mem., NA; *b.* Apr. 25, '50; *educ.* Grad., Wufeng Agr. High Sch.; *Pol. Affi.* KMT; *Const.* Nantou County; Mem., Nantou CoCoun.; *Add.* 24 Min Chuan St., Lungchuan Li, Nantou.

HSU, HUNG-CHIN 徐鴻進
Mem., NA; *b.* Aug. 1, '41; *educ.* MBA, Korea; *Pol. Affi.* KMT; *Const.* Taoyuan County; Chmn., Taoyuan Construction Investment Assn.; *Add.* 2nd Fl., 5 I Shou 8th St., Taoyuan.

HSU, I-SHENG 徐宜生
Mem., NA; *b.* Nov. 5, '63; *educ.* BA, NCU; MA, New Sch. for Soc. Res., USA; *Pol. Affi.* DPP; *Const.* Taichung County; *Add.* 352 Chung Hsing E. Rd., Taiping, Taichung County.

HSU, KUO-SHIH 徐國士
Mem., NA; *b.* June 26, '42; *educ.* Ph.D., Purdue U.; *Pol. Affi.* NP; *Const.* Hualien County; *Add.* 15-5 Lane 234, Chung Cheng Rd., Hualien.

HSU, LI-NUNG 許歷農
Mem., NA 96-; *b.* Mar. 4, '19; *educ.* Gen. Class, Armed Forces U.; *Pol. Affi.* NP; *Const.* Nat.; Cmdr., Kinmen Def. Cmd. Hqs. 81-83; Dir.-Gen., Gen. Pol. Warfare Dept., MND 83-87; Chmn., VAC 87-93; Nat. Policy Adv. to the Pres. 93-96; *Add.* 53 Chung Hua Rd., Sect. 1, Taipei.

HSU, LUNG-CHUN 許龍俊
Mem., NA; *b.* Oct. 2, '52; *educ.* Dr. of Dental Surgery, Chung Shan Med. & Dental Coll.; *Pol. Affi.* DPP; *Const.* Nat.; Exec. Dir., CC, DDP; Chmn., Yunlin County Cttee., DPP 94; *Add.* 75 Ching Ming 2nd St., Taichung.

HSU, PEI-HSIU 許丕修
Mem., NA; *b.* Nov. 11, '44; *educ.* Grad., Hsilo Agr. High Sch.; Studied, NCHU; *Pol. Affi.* KMT; *Const.* Yunlin County; Chmn., Mailiao Farmers Assn.; *Add.* 1 Chung Cheng Rd., Maifeng Tsun, Mailiao Hsiang, Yunlin County.

HSU, SHIANG-KUEEN 徐享崑
Dir.-Gen., Water Resources Dept., MOEA 93-; *b.* Apr. 23, '54; *educ.* Ph.D., NCKU; *Pol. Affi.* KMT; *Const.* Miaoli County; *Add.* 15 Foochow St., Taipei.

HSU, SHENG-FA
(See HSUI, SHENG-FA 許勝發)

HSU, SHOU-CHIH 徐守志
Mem., NA; *b.* Feb. 1, '48; *educ.* M., Penn. State U.; *Pol. Affi.* KMT; *Const.* Tainan City; Mem., Tainan CCoun.; *Add.* 35 Lane 197, Ta Tung Rd., Sect. 1, Tainan.

HSUI, SHENG-FA 許勝發
Mem., Steering & Policy Cttee., KMT 92-; *b.* Jan. 24, '25; *educ.* BS, Econ., NTU; Hon. Ph.D., Business Admin., St. Thomas U., Philippines; *Pol. Affi.* KMT; *Const.* Nat.; Mem., Legis. Yuan; Dep. Sec.-Gen., Policy Coordination Cttee., KMT 86-89, Standing Mem., CC 88-93; *Add.* 4th Fl., 50 Sungkiang Rd., Taipei.

HU, CHIH-CHIANG
(See HU, JASON C. 胡志強)

HU, JASON C. 胡志強
Rep., TECRO in the USA 96-; *b.* May 15, '48; *educ.* LL.B., Dept. of Dip., NCU 70; M. of Soc. Sc., Dept. of Pol., U. of Southampton 78; D.Phil., Oxford U. 84; *Pol. Affi.* KMT; *Const.* Taichung City; Mem., CC, KMT; Dir.-Gen. & Govt. Spokesman, GIO 91-96; *Add.* 4201 Wisconsin Avenue, NW, Washington, DC 20016, USA.

HU, WEI-KANG
(See HU, WENDELL K. 胡維剛)

HU, WENDELL K. 胡維剛
Attorney-at-Law; *b.* Nov. 18, '45; *educ.* Ph.D., U. of Oklahoma; *Pol. Affi.* DPP; *Const.* Ovs. Nat.; *Add.* Suite 300, 55 S. Raymond Avenue, Alhambra, CA 91801, USA.

HUANG, CHAO-KAI 黃昭凱
Mem., NA; *b.* Aug. 26, '42; *educ.* Grad., Nat. Inst. of the Arts; *Pol. Affi.* DPP; *Const.* Tainan City; Mem., CC, DPP, & CAC; *Add.* 4 Alley 101, Lane 148, Kai Yuan Rd., Tainan.

HUANG, CHE-LIANG 黃哲諒
Mem., NA; *b.* Apr. 15, '60; *educ.* Hon. Ph.D., Am. Commonwealth U.; *Pol. Affi.* KMT; *Const.* Pingtung County; *Add.* 53 Tsingtao St., Pingtung.

HUANG, CHE-SAN 黃哲三
Pres., Tai Ji Construction Co. Ltd.; V. Pres., Ch. Taipei Track & Field Assn. 87-; *b.* Sept. 16, '43; *educ.* Business Mgrs. Prog., Nat. Sun Yat-sen U.; *Pol. Affi.* KMT; *Const.* Kaohsiung City; Dist. Gov., Dist. 300 E, Lions Clubs Intl., 94-95; *Add.* 3rd Fl., 64 Tzu Chiang 1st Rd., Kaohsiung.

HUANG, CHIEN-TING 黃健庭
Mem., NA; *b.* Nov. 6, '59; *educ.* MBA, U. of Santa Clara; *Pol. Affi.* KMT; *Const.* Taitung County; *Add.* 136 An Ching St., Taitung.

HUANG, MIN-HUI 黃敏惠
Mem., NA; *b.* Jan. 20, '59; *educ.* BA, NTNU; *Pol. Affi.* KMT; *Const.* Chiayi City; *Add.* 79 Kuang Ning St., Ichan Li, W. Dist., Chiayi.

HUANG, MING-TSUNG 黃明聰
Mem., NA; *b.* Feb. 10, '50; *educ.* Grad., Wuling Sr. High Sch.; *Pol. Affi.* KMT; *Const.* Taipei County; Mem., Yingko Rep. Conf. 90-91; Chmn., Presidium, NA; *Add.* 2nd Fl., 628 Ying Tao Rd., Yingko, Taipei County.

HUANG, PENG-HSIAO 黃澎孝
Mem., NA; *b.* June 3, '53; *educ.* BPS, Pol. Warfare Acad.; *Pol. Affi.* KMT; *Const.* Taipei County; *Add.* 140 Min Yu St., Chungho, Taipei County.

HUANG, TE-CHIH 黃德治
Mem., NA; *b.* Mar. 26, '42; *educ.* Grad., Elementary Sch.; *Pol. Affi.* Independent; *Const.* Taichung County; *Add.* 67 Wen Chang St., Tachia, Taichung County.

HUANG, TE-HUNG 黃德鴻
Mem., NA; *b.* Jan. 26, '42; *educ.* Grad., Tai Pei Sr. High Sch.; *Pol. Affi.* KMT; *Const.* Yunlin County; Magis., Tungshih Hsiang, Yunlin County; *Add.* 24 Min Sheng Rd., Tungnan Tsun, Tungshih Hsiang, Yunlin County.

HUANG, TE-LUNG 黃德隆
Mem., NA; *b.* Mar. 2, '50; *educ.* Ph.D., Texas Tech U.; *Pol. Affi.* DPP; *Const.* Taoyuan County; *Add.* 32 Lin 4, Nanhsing Li, Tahsi, Taoyuan County.

HUANG, TZUNG-SHIH 黃宗詩
Mem., NA; *b.* Dec. 1, '48; *educ.* Grad., Chengkung Elementary Sch.; *Pol. Affi.* KMT; *Const.* Taoyuan County; Mem., Taoyuan CCoun.; *Add.* 580 Chung Cheng Rd., Taoyuan.

HUANG, WEI-CHE 黃偉哲
Mem., NA; *b.* Sept. 26, '63; *educ.* M., Yale U.; *Pol. Affi.* DPP; *Const.* Tainan County; *Add.* 6-2 Min Chih Rd., Hsinying, Tainan County.

HUANG, WEN-HO 黃文和
Mem., NA; *b.* Mar. 20, '49; *educ.* Cert., Intl. Trade, NCU; *Pol. Affi.* DPP; *Const.* Nat.; Rep., Tienchung Chen, Changhua County 78-87, Chmn., Arbitration Cttee. 81-87; V. Chmn., Twn. Farmers' Assn.; Dir., Changhua County Cttee., DPP 89-91; *Add.* 446 Tou Chung Rd., Sect. 1, Tienchung, Changhua County.

HUANG, WO-CHUNG
(See WONG, N.C. 黃握中)

HUANG, YUNG-HUANG 黃永煌
Chmn., Chiayi City Cttee., DPP 94-; *b.* Dec. 10, '56; *educ.* Grad., Nat. Chiayi Agr. Coll.; *Pol. Affi.* DPP; *Const.* Chiayi City; Prog. Dir., Chiayi Station, Voice of Twn.; *Add.* 21-1 Hsuan Hsin St., Chiayi.

HUNG, HSIU-CHU 洪秀菊
Mem., NA; *b.* Nov. 22, '49; *educ.* Ph.D., Columbia U.; *Pol. Affi.* KMT; *Const.* Tainan County; *Add.* 13th Fl.-8, 117 Chung Shan Rd., Hsinying, Tainan County.

HUNG, MAO-TSE 洪茂澤
Mem., NA; *b.* Mar. 9, '44; *educ.* B., Kaohsiung Med. Coll.; *Pol. Affi.* DPP; *Const.* Kaohsiung County; *Add.* 43 Hua Chung 1st Rd., Taliao Hsiang, Kaohsiung County.

HUNG, PING-LANG 洪平朗
Mem., NA; *b.* July 24, '55; *educ.* Grad., Voc. Sr. High Sch.; *Pol. Affi.* DPP; *Const.* Nat.; *Add.* 88 Ho Pei Rd., Lingya, Kaohsiung.

HUNG, SHUN-WU 洪順五
Mem., NA; *b.* Sept. 2, '44; *educ.* Ph.D., Iowa State U.; *Pol. Affi.* DPP; *Const.* Ovs. Nat.; *Add.* 7573 Hollanderry Place, Cupeytino, CA 95014, USA.

JAO, SHU-CHEN 饒淑貞
Mem., NA; *b.* May 21, '58; *educ.* B., NCU; *Pol. Affi.* KMT; *Const.* Kaohsiung County; *Add.* 82 Shu Jen Rd., Tungping Li, Chishan, Kaohsiung County.

KANG, KUO-FENG 康國鋒
Sup., 300-B Dist., ROC Lions Club; *b.* Oct. 6, '46; *educ.* B., Ottawa U., USA; *Pol. Affi.* KMT; *Const.* Taipei County; *Add.* 3 Alley 7, Lane 430, Chu Lin Rd., Linkou, Taipei County.

KANG, TAI-SHAN 康泰山
Mem., NA; *b.* Sept. 26, '36; *educ.* Ph.D., Syracuse U.; *Pol. Affi.* DPP; *Const.* Ovs. Nat.; *Add.* 26 Clive Hill Rd., Short Hills, NJ 07078, USA.

KANG, YAO-CHUNG 康耀忠
Mem., NA; *b.* Sept. 12, '60; *educ.* Grad., Taipei Civil Admin. Coll.; *Pol. Affi.* DPP; *Const.* Taipei City; *Add.* 142 Chu Kuang Rd., Taipei.

KAO, CHUNG-HSIN 高忠信
Pres., Chih Nan Bus Co.; *b.* May 19, '33; *educ.* B., Philosophy, Tung Kuo U., Korea; *Pol. Affi.* KMT; *Const.* Nat.; Mem., Legis. Yuan; Mem., CAC, & Standing Cttee., Wenshan Br., Taipei Mun. Cttee., KMT; *Add.* 155 Chiu Kang St., Taipei.

KAO, MENG-TING 高孟定
Dir., Inst. of Architecture & Urban Planning, Feng Chia U.; *b.* Oct. 20, '54; *educ.* Ph.D., NTU; *Pol. Affi.* Green Party; *Const.* Yunlin County; *Add.* 39 Jao Ping W. Rd., Chihtung Hsiang, Yunlin County.

KAO, PAO-HUA 高寶華
Mem., NA; *b.* Jan. 6, '61; *educ.* M., NTNU; *Pol. Affi.* NP; *Const.* Taipei County; Dep. Sec.-Gen., ROC Elec. Studies Soc.; *Add.* 13th Fl., 251-1 Yu Min Rd., Tucheng, Taipei County.

KE, SAN-CHI 柯三吉
Mem., NA; *b.* Dec. 1, '47; *educ.* Ph.D., U. of Hawaii; *Pol. Affi.* KMT; *Const.* Nat.; Dir., Elec. Studies Cent., NCHU; *Add.* 21 Hsuchow Rd., Taipei.

KUNG, HSING-SHENG 龔興生
Mem., NA; *b.* Nov. 11, '56; *educ.* Grad., Erlun Jr. High Sch.; *Pol. Affi.* KMT; *Const.* Yunlin County; *Add.* 116 Hsi Hsing S. Rd., Hankuang Li, Hsiluo, Yunlin County.

KUO, CHENG-CHUNG
(See KUO, JENG-CHUNG 郭正崇)

KUO, JENG-CHUNG 郭正崇
Group Leader, SEARLE; *b.* Feb. 21, '50; *educ.* Ph.D., Iowa State U.; *Pol. Affi.* KMT; *Const.* Ovs. Nat.; *Add.* 100 Chang Jung St., Chiayi.

KUO, SU-CHUN 郭素春
Gen. Mgr., Business Admin. Corp.; *b.* Dec. 11, '55; *educ.* MBA, NCHU; *Pol. Affi.* KMT; *Const.* Taipei County; *Add.* 8th Fl., 346 Chang Chun Rd., Taipei.

LAI, CHIEN-JUNG 賴健榮
Chief, Insp.'s Team, EPA; *b.* Jan. 22, '56; *educ.* Ph.D., NTU; *Pol. Affi.* KMT; *Const.* Pingtung County; *Add.* 5 Lane 640, Hsueh Jen Rd., Hehsing Tsun, Neipu Hsiang, Pingtung County.

LAI, CHING-LIN 賴勁麟
Dir.-Gen., Twn. Labor Movement Assn.; *b.* Jan. 27, '62; *educ.* BPS, NTU; *Pol. Affi.* DPP; *Const.* Taipei County; *Add.* 52 Ching An Rd., Chungho, Taipei County.

LAI, CHING-TE
(See LAI, WILLIAM C.D. 賴清德)

LAI, FU-HSING
(See LAI, FWU-HSING 賴福興)

LAI, FWU-HSING 賴福興
Rep. to Japan, Wufu Travel Agents; *b.* Sept. 5, '46; *educ.* Ph.D., Shen Shiu U., Japan; *Pol. Affi.* DPP; *Const.* Chiayi County; *Chmn.*, Ch. Students Assn. in Japan; *Add.* 15 Min Hsiang St., Shuishang Tsun, Shuishang Hsiang, Chiayi County.

LAI, I-SUNG 賴儀松
Mem., NA; *b.* July 2, '55; *educ.* Grad., High Sch.; *Pol. Affi.* DPP; *Const.* Changhua County; *Chmn.*, Changhua County Cttee., DPP; *Add.* 4 Alley 44, Lane 359, Yuan Shui Rd., Sect. 2, Yuanlin, Changhua County.

LAI, SHIH-PAO
(See LAI, SHYH-BAO 賴士葆)

LAI, SHYH-BAO 賴士葆
Prof., NCU 85-; *b.* June 20, '51; *educ.* Ph.D., U. of So. Calif.; *Pol. Affi.* NP; *Const.* Taipei City; *Add.* 4th Fl., 8 Alley 15, Lane 175, Ho Ping E. Rd., Sect. 2, Taipei.

LAI, TZUNG-HSIN 賴宗炘
Mem., NA; *b.* Sept. 13, '35; *educ.* Grad., Yuanlin High Sch.; *Pol. Affi.* KMT; *Const.* Changhua County; Mem., Changhua CoCoun.; *Add.* 2nd Fl., 70 Chung Shan Rd., Sect. 2, Yuanlin, Changhua County.

LAI, WILLIAM C.D. 賴清德
Physician, NCKU Hosp.; *b.* Oct. 6, '59; *educ.* MB, NCKU; *Pol. Affi.* DPP; *Const.* Tainan City; *Add.* 42 Ching Nien Rd., Tainan.

LAN, SHIH-TSUNG 藍世聰
Mem., NA; *b.* Sept. 16, '56; *educ.* B., Kaohsiung Med. Coll.; *Pol. Affi.* DPP; *Const.* Taipei City; *Add.* 47 Liang Chou St., Taipei.

LANG, YU-HSIEN
(See LONG, YU-HSIEN 郎裕憲)

LAW, I-TIEG 劉一德
Ed.-in-Chief, *Congressional Gen. Bi-weekly Report; b.* Apr. 15, '60; *educ.* BS, Pol., NTU; *Pol. Affi.* DPP; *Const.* Taipei City; Chief Ed. & Writer, *DPP News,* DPP 88-89; Asst. to Legis. 90-91; Sp., CC, DPP 91-92; *Add.* 19 Szu Wei Rd., Chinshan Hsiang, Taipei County.

LEE, ALEXANDER Y.T. 李榮堂
Pres., R-Flog Ent. Co.; *b.* Aug. 30, '50; *educ.* MBA, W. Coast U., USA; *Pol. Affi.* KMT; *Const.* Tainan County; *Add.* 83 Nan Wan St., Yungkang, Tainan County.

LEE, ANTHONY S. 李學英
Pres., Asia Pacific Group Co.; *b.* Oct. 15, '40; *educ.* MBA, Golden Gate U., USA; *Pol. Affi.* KMT; *Const.* Ovs. Nat.; Adv., CC, KMT; *Add.* 230 Stonecrest Drive, San Francisco, CA 94132, USA.

LEE, CHENG-CHIA 李成家
Mem., NA; *b.* Mar. 12, '48; *educ.* MBA, Kennedy U., USA; *Pol. Affi.* KMT; *Const.* Nat.; *Add.* 8th Fl., 181 Fu Hsing N. Rd., Taipei.

LEE, CHENG-CHONG 李正宗
Pres., Ch. Fed. of Labor; Mem., NUC; *b.* Oct. 10, '48; *educ.* Grad., World Coll. of Jour. & Comms. 77; *Pol. Affi.* KMT; *Const.* Nat.; *Add.* 11th Fl., Back Bldg., 201-18 Tun Hua N. Rd., Taipei.

LEE, CHENG-TZUNG
(See LEE, CHENG-CHONG 李正宗)

LEE, CHI-SHENG 李繼生
Magis., Hsiulin Hsiang, Hualien County; *b.* Sept. 18, '51; *educ.* Grad., Pol. Warfare Acad.; *Pol. Affi.* KMT; *Const.* Highland Aborigines; Mem., Hualien CoCoun.; *Add.* 62 Hsiu Lin Rd., Hsiulin Hsiang, Hualien County.

LEE, CHIN-HSIANG 利錦祥
Mem., NA; *b.* Dec. 29, '56; *educ.* Grad., Fengyuan High Sch.; *Pol. Affi.* DPP; *Const.* Nat.; *Add.* 21 San Min Rd., Fengyuan, Taichung County.

LEE, CHIN-I 李金億
Mem., NA; *b.* Sept. 30, '48; *educ.* Grad., Mingchi Inst. of Tech.; *Pol. Affi.* DPP; *Const.* Tainan City; *Add.* 11th Fl.-2, 132 Fu Wei St., Tainan.

LEE, CHING-TSEN 李清圳
Mem., NA; *b.* May 20, '48; *educ.* MBA, Am. Commonwealth U.; *Pol. Affi.* KMT; *Const.* Chiayi County; Mem., Chiayi CoCoun.; *Add.* 15 Lane 1, Shih Tung Rd., Putsu, Chiayi County.

LEE, CHING-YUAN 李慶元
City Ed., *Ch. Times Weekly; b.* Aug. 29, '58; *educ.* MA, NTNU; *Pol. Affi.* NP; *Const.* Taipei City; *Add.* 7 Alley 21, Lane 45, Chih Nan Rd., Sect. 2, Wenshan, Taipei.

LEE, CHU-FENG
(See LEE, JUH-FENG 李炷烽)

LEE, HSIEN-JEN
(See LEE, SHANGREN 李先仁)

LEE, HSIN 李新
Mem., NA; *b.* July 16, '53; *educ.* B., NCHU; *Pol. Affi.* NP; *Const.* Nat.; *Add.* 4th Fl., 434 Yen Shou St., Taipei.

LEE, HSUEH-YING
(See LEE, ANTHONY S. 李學英)

LEE, JUH-FENG 李炷烽
Tchr., Nat. Kinmen Agr. Sr. High Sch.; *b.* May 6, '53; *educ.* B., Educ., NTNU; *Pol. Affi.* NP; *Const.* Kinmen County; *Add.* 3rd Fl., 201 Chung Hsing Rd., Chincheng, Kinmen County.

LEE, JUNG-TANG
(See LEE, ALEXANDER Y.T. 李榮堂)

LEE, LESTER T.C. 李宗正
Mem., NA; *b.* Dec. 16, '34; *educ.* Ph.D., New York State U.; *Pol. Affi.* KMT; *Const.* Taipei City; Mem., Legis. Yuan 93-96; *Add.* 44 Alley 8, Lane 36, Min Sheng E. Rd., Sect. 5, Taipei.

LEE, MING-HSIEN 李明憲
Mem., NA; *b.* Oct. 26; '48; *educ.* Studied, Tunghai U.; *Pol. Affi.* DPP; *Const.* Taichung City; *Add.* 154-1 Kung Cheng Rd., W. Dist., Taichung.

LEE, PING-NAN 李炳南
Mem., NA; *b.* June 23, '56; *educ.* Ph.D., NCU; *Pol. Affi.* NP; *Const.* Nat.; *Add.* 1 Roosevelt Rd., Sect. 4, Taipei.

LEE, SHANGREN 李先仁
Mem., Draft of Nat. Standards, Nat. Bu. of Standards, MOEA 92-; *b.* Nov. 6, '63; *educ.* BS, Naval Architecture, NTU 86; MS, Ind. Engr., Stanford U. 90, & Statistics 92; *Pol. Affi.* KMT; *Const.* Taipei County; Instr., Ch. Cul. U. 94-; Chmn., KMT Const. Res. Cttee.; *Add.* 189 Fu Hsing Rd., Luchou, Taipei County.

LEE, TZUNG-CHENG
(See LEE, LESTER T.C. 李宗正)

LEE, WEN-HUNG 李文鴻
Mem., NA; *b.* Sept. 3, '45; *educ.* Grad., Mingtai High Sch.; *Pol. Affi.* KMT; *Const.* Taichung County; *Add.* 278 Ssu Te Rd., Wufeng Hsiang, Taichung County.

LI, HUNG-YU 李宏裕
Mem., NA 92-; *b.* Nov. 6, '54; *educ.* Grad., Nan Kai Jr. Coll. of Tech. 76; *Pol. Affi.* KMT; *Const.* Nantou County; *Add.* 7th-1, 9 Jen Ai Rd., Tsaotun, Nantou County.

LI, KUN-TSE 李昆澤
Mem., NA 96-; *b.* Apr. 29, '64; *educ.* BA, Fu Jen Catholic U. 93; *Pol. Affi.* DPP; *Const.* Kaohsiung City; Asst. to Legis. Shih Ming-teh & Chen Ting-nan; Asst. to Nat. Assemblyman Chen Chu; *Add.* 1011-1 Chiu Ju 4th Rd., Kaohsiung.

LI, SHIH-YI 李詩益
Mem., NA; *b.* July 12, '34; *educ.* Grad., Chungli Voc. High Sch.; *Pol. Affi.* KMT; *Const.* Nat.; Mem., TPA; Mem., Control Yuan; *Add.* 3 Jen Ai Rd., Tahsi, Taoyuan County.

LI, WEN-CHUNG 李文忠
Mem., NA; *b.* June 20, '58; *educ.* Studied, Pol. Sc., NTU; *Pol. Affi.* DPP; *Const.* Taipei County; Mem., Labor Educ. Cttee., Taipei County Govt.; *Add.* 37 Hai Shan Rd., Panchiao, Taipei County.

LIAO, FANG-CHOU 廖芳洲
Mem., NA; *b.* Oct. 21, '51; *educ.* B., Manila U.; *Pol. Affi.* KMT; *Const.* Ovs. Nat.; Mem., OCAC; *Add.* 32 Sineguelas St., Valle Verde 1 Pasig M., Manila, Philippines.

LIAO, JUNG-CHING 廖榮清
Alt. Mem., CC, KMT 93-; Convener, 1st Review Cttee., NA; *b.* Nov. 27, '57; *educ.* M., Pacific We. U., USA 94; *Pol. Affi.* KMT; *Const.* Taipei County; Dep. Sec.-Gen., KMT Caucus, NA 93-94; *Add.* 11 San Min Rd., Sect. 2, Panchiao, Taipei County.

LIAO, KUO-TUNG
(See LIAW, GWO-DONG 廖國棟)

LIAO, WAN-JU 廖婉汝
Prin., Pingtung Private Ming Der Sr. High Sch. 93-; *b.* Jan. 27, '60; *educ.* B., NTNU 83; *Pol. Affi.* KMT; *Const.* Pingtung County; *Add.* 202-1 Yung Kang St., Chaochou, Pingtung County.

LIAW, GWO-DONG 廖國棟
MD, Taitung Christian Hosp.; *b.* Jan. 8, '55; *educ.* B., Kaohsiung Med. Coll.; *Pol. Affi.* KMT; *Const.* Lowland Aborigines; *Add.* 369-4A Kai Feng St., Taitung.

LIN, A-JEN 林阿仁
Gen. Mgr., Farmers' Assn. of Wuku Hsiang 71-; *b.* Dec. 10, '42; *educ.* Grad., Twn. Prov. Sr. Ind. & Agr. Voc. Sch. 61; *Pol. Affi.* KMT; *Const.* Taipei County; *Add.* 13 Min I Rd., Sect. 1, Wuku Hsiang, Taipei County.

LIN, CHANG-JU 林嫦茹
Mem., NA; *b.* Mar. 30, '51; *educ.* Grad., Supplementary Jr. Coll. of Nat. Open U.; *Pol. Affi.* KMT; *Const.* Taichung County; Gen. Mgr., Farmers' Assn. of Tantzu Hsiang, Taichung County 81-87; *Add.* 278 Tan Hsing Rd., Sect. 1, Chuhsing Hsiang, Taichung County.

LIN, CHENG-CHIH
(See LIN, HELEN CHEN-CHI 林澄枝)

LIN, CHENG-KUO 林正國
Mem., NA; *b.* July 6, '40; *educ.* B., Kwa Kiu Coll. of Engr. & Com., Hong Kong; *Pol. Affi.* KMT; *Const.* Tainan City; Mem., Tainan CCoun.; *Add.* 759 Hai Chung St., Annan Dist., Tainan.

LIN, CHING-CHI 林慶麒
Mem., NA; *b.* Nov. 7, '36; *educ.* Grad., Taipei County Shuanghsi Jr. High Sch.; *Pol. Affi.* KMT; *Const.* Taipei County; Mem., Taipei CoCoun.; *Add.* 11 Chung Hua Rd., Shuanghsi Hsiang, Taipei County.

LIN, CHU-LEE 林居利
Mem., NA; *b.* Jan. 1, '44; *educ.* B., Tamkang U.; *Pol. Affi.* KMT; *Const.* Pingtung County; *Add.* 46 Lane 145, Jen Ai St., Tunghai Tsun, Fangliao Hsiang, Pingtung County.

LIN, CHUNG-MO 林重謨
Mem., NA; *b.* Apr. 2, '47; *educ.* BS, Chung Yuan Christian U.; *Pol. Affi.* DPP; *Const.* Taipei City; Sec.-Gen., Assn. of Public Calamity Prevention; *Add.* 18 Lane 74, Hu Lin St., Taipei.

LIN, CHUNG-SHAN 林忠山
Dir., Dept. of PA, Ch. Cul. U.; *b.* June 8, '56; *educ.* Ph.D., NYU; *Pol. Affi.* NP; *Const.* Taipei City; Sr. Sp., RDEC; *Add.* 4th Fl., 102 Min Sheng E. Rd., Sect. 5, Taipei.

LIN, HELEN CHENG-CHI 林澄枝
Chmn., CCA 96-; *b.* Feb. 17, '39; *educ.* Hon. Ph.D., Pacific Coll., Hawaii; *Pol. Affi.* KMT; *Const.* Nat.; Dir.-Gen., Dept. of Women's Aff., KMT 93-96; *Add.* 12th Fl., 60 Hsin Sheng S. Rd., Sect. 2, Taipei.

LIN, HUNG-CHIH 林鴻池
Mem., NA; *b.* Aug. 22, '55; *educ.* MPS, NCU 83; *Pol. Affi.* KMT; *Const.* Taipei County; Personal Sec. to the Magis., Taipei County Govt. 86-89; Personal Sec. to Comr., Dept. of Civil Aff., TPG 89-90; *Add.* 7th Fl.-1, 62 Chung Shan Rd., Sect. 2, Panchiao, Taipei County.

LIN, I-CHEN
(See LIN, YI-CHEN 林意楨)

LIN, I-LU
(See LIN, YI-LU 林益陸)

LIN, I-MIN
(See LIN, TOMMY YET-MIN 林逸民)

LIN, JEN-TE 林仁德
Mem., NA; *b.* Dec. 1, '39; *educ.* Grad., High Sch.; *Pol. Affi.* KMT; *Const.* Hualien County; Mem., Hualien CoCoun.; *Add.* 75 Kuo Min 9th St., Hualien.

LIN, JUNG-TE 林榮德
Pre., Sinyih Ceramic Co. Ltd.; *b.* Oct. 6, '59; *educ.* BBA, Pacific We. U., USA; *Pol. Affi.* KMT; *Const.* Miaoli County; *Add.* 200 Tapu Li, Chunan, Miaoli County.

LIN, KUANG-HSIEN
(See LIN, PAUL KUANG-HSIEN 林光顯)

LIN, MAO-JUNG 林懋榮
Mem., NA; *b.* Apr. 8, '46; *educ.* B., NCKU; *Pol. Affi.* DPP; *Const.* Kaohsiung County; Magis., Alien Hsiang; *Add.* 51 Lane 120, Min Chuan Rd., Alien Hsiang, Kaohsiung County.

LIN, MING-CHANG 林明昌
Mem., NA; *b.* Apr. 20, '49; *educ.* B., Feng Chia U.; *Pol. Affi.* KMT; *Const.* Ilan County; Mem., Ilan CoCoun.; *Add.* 102 Kang Le Rd., Ilan.

LIN, PAUL KUANG-HSIEN 林光顯
Prof., Statistics, U. of Michigan, Dearborn; *b.* Nov. 12, '46; *educ.* Ph.D., Wayne State U.; *Pol. Affi.* KMT; *Const.* Ovs. Nat.; Pres., Twn. Benevolent Assn. of Michigan; *Add.* 5159 Providence Drive, Bloomfield Hills, MI 48302, USA.

LIN, SHENG-LI
(See LIN, VICTOR S.L. 林勝利)

LIN, SHU-HUNG 林叔宏
Gen. Mgr., Yungchuen Construction Co. Ltd.; *b.* June 3, '63; *educ.* BBA, Tunghai U.; *Pol. Affi.* KMT; *Const.* Taichung County; *Add.* 242-6 Chih Shan Rd., Tali, Taichung County.

LIN, SHU-MEI 林束梅
Mem., NA; *b.* Dec. 23, '33; *educ.* Grad., Wuchieh Elementary Sch.; *Pol. Affi.* KMT; *Const.* Ilan County; *Add.* 236 Sheng Hu Rd., Suao, Ilan County.

LIN, SHU-SHAN 林樹山
Mem., NA; *b.* Dec. 1, '58; *educ.* B., Nat. Kaohsiung Normal U.; *Pol. Affi.* DPP; *Const.* Yunlin County; *Add.* 121 Wen Kang Tsun, Taihsi Hsiang, Yunlin County.

LIN, SUNG-SHAN 林嵩山
Mem., NA; *b.* Feb. 11, '49; *educ.* BA, NCU; *Pol. Affi.* KMT; *Const.* Hualien County; *Add.* 8th Fl.-5, 136 Kuang Fu St., Hualien.

LIN, TOMMY YET-MIN 林逸民
Pres., Wu-fu Eye Clinic; *b.* June 28, '43; *educ.* DMS, Kitasato U., Japan; *Pol. Affi.* DPP; *Const.* Nat.; *Add.* 108 Chung Cheng Rd., Lotung, Ilan County.

LIN, VICTOR S.L. 林勝利
Mem., NA; *b.* June 2, '47; *educ.* MA, Tunghai U.; *Pol. Affi.* DPP; *Const.* Changhua County; *Add.* 153 Hsing Hua St., Yuanlin, Changhua County.

LIN, YI-CHEN 林意楨
Assc. Prof., Tamkang U.; *b.* Dec. 4, '52; *educ.* Ph.D., Civil Engr., N. Carolina State U.; *Pol. Affi.* DPP; *Const.* Nat.; *Add.* 3rd Fl., 6-1 Lane 61, Tien Mu E. Rd., Taipei.

LIN, YI-LU 林益陸
Mem., NA; *b.* Dec. 8, '54; *educ.* BA, Econ., Fu Jen Catholic U.; *Pol. Affi.* KMT; *Const.* Highland Aborigines; *Add.* 4th Fl., 6-3 Lane 61, Tai Yuan Rd., Sect. 3, Taichung.

LIN, YU-SHENG 林育生
Dir., Pingtung Broadcasting Station; *b.* Oct. 28, '57; *educ.* B., NTU; *Pol. Affi.* DPP; *Const.* Pingtung County; Chmn., Pingtung County Cttee., DPP; *Add.* 22 Yung An Lane, Chienhsing Tsun, Neipu Hsiang, Pingtung County.

LIN, YUAN-YUAN 林淵源
Mem., NA; *b.* June 6, '25; *educ.* B., NCHU; *Pol. Affi.* KMT; *Const.* Nat.; Comr., Twn. Prov. Coun.; *Add.* 9 Fu Chien Rd., Fengshan, Kaohsiung County.

LIOU, GIN-SHOW 劉俊秀
Prof., NCTU; *b.* Aug. 24, '52; *educ.* Ph.D., UC-Berkly.; *Pol. Affi.* DPP; *Const.* Nat.; *Add.* Dept. of Civil Engr., NCTU, 1001 Ta Hsueh Rd., Hsinchu.

LIOU, JIING-YIH 劉景義
Mem., CAC, KMT 93-; Public Prosecutor-Gen., Public Prosecutor's Off., Twn. High Court 92-; *b.* Mar. 6, '26; *educ.* LL.B., Nat. Sun Yat-Sen U. 49; *Pol. Affi.* KMT; *Const.* Nat.; Mem., CC, KMT 88-93; *Add.* 2nd Fl., 124 Chungking S. Rd., Sect. 1, Taipei.

LIOU, MING-LONE 劉銘龍
Sec.-Gen., Enviromental Protection Found.; *b.* Feb. 23, '64; *educ.* M., NTU; *Pol. Affi.* NP; *Const.* Taipei County; Sec., EPA; *Add.* 3rd Fl., 316 Ching Ping Rd., Chungho, Taipei County.

LIU, CHAO-CHANG 劉櫂漳
Mem., NA; *b.* July 14, '49; *educ.* Grad., Nat. Taipei Inst. of Com.; *Pol. Affi.* KMT; *Const.* Taitung County; Mem., Taitung CoCoun.; *Add.* 252 Chung Shan Rd., Taitung.

LIU, CHEN-HSIANG 劉貞祥
Chmn., Kaohsiung City Cttee., DPP 94-; *b.* June 6, '45; *educ.* LL.B., NCU 72; *Pol. Affi.* DPP; *Const.* Kaohsiung City; *Add.* 42-1 Chen Nung Lane, Chienchen, Kaohsiung.

LIU, CHIA-CHI 劉家驥
Mem., NA; *b.* Apr. 15, '51; *educ.* Grad., Nat. Taichung Tchrs. Coll.; *Pol. Affi.* KMT; *Const.* Taichung City; Prosecutor; Judge; *Add.* 16 Tai Yuan S. 2nd Rd., Nr. Dist., Taichung.

LIU, CHING-I
(See LIOU, JIING-YIH 劉景義)

LIU, CHUN-HSIU
(See LIOU, GIN-SHOW 劉俊秀)

LIU, HSIEN-TUNG
(See LIU, SEN-TONG 劉憲同)

LIU, I-TE
(See LAW, I-TIEG 劉一德)

LIU, MENG-CHANG 劉孟昌
Chmn., Presidium, NA 93-, Dep. Dir.-Gen., KMT Caucus 94-; *b.* Dec. 6, '48; *educ.* BBA, Pacific We. U., USA 93; *Pol. Affi.* KMT; *Const.* Kaohsiung City; *Add.* 39 Kaifeng St., Hsinhsing, Kaohsiung.

LIU, MING-LUNG
(See LIOU, MING-LONE 劉銘龍)

LIU, SEN-TONG 劉憲同
Pres., Sym Wang Iron Steel Co. Ltd. & Airstar Ent. Co. Ltd.; Chmn., Presidium, NA; Mem., CC, KMT; *b.* Mar. 24, '52; *educ.* B., Feng Chia U.; MBA, Regis U., USA; *Pol. Affi.* KMT; *Const.* Kaohsiung City; *Add.* 15, Lane 229, Chien Kung Rd., Kaohsiung.

LIU, TE-CHEN 劉德成
Mem., CC, KMT 93-; Chmn., Ch. (Taipei) Packaging Assn. 94-; *b.* Jan. 25, '48; *educ.* Grad., Nat. Taipei Inst. of Tech. 70; B., U. of So. Calif. 89; *Pol. Affi.* KMT; *Const.* Taichung County; *Add.* Rm. 800, 8th Fl., 54 Min Sheng E. Rd., Sect. 4, Taipei.

LIU, TE-CHENG
(See LIU, TE-CHEN 劉德成)

LIU, TUNG-LUNG 劉東隆
Mem., NA; *b.* June 21, '53; *educ.* B., Fu Jen Catholic U.; *Pol. Affi.* KMT; *Const.* Taoyuan County; Chmn., MD-300, Group 18, Lions Club Intl.; *Add.* 1 Lung Yuan Rd., Lungtan Hsiang, Taoyuan County.

LIU, YU-YU
(See LIU, YUE-YAO 劉裕猷)

LIU, YUE-YAO 劉裕猷
Mem., NA; *b.* July 5, '31; *educ.* B., NTU; *Pol. Affi.* KMT; *Const.* Nat.; Magis., Nantou County 72-81; Comr., Dept. of Civil Aff., TPG 81-84, & Mem. 84-90; *Add.* 4th Fl., 20 Pa Te Rd., Sect. 3, Taipei.

LIU, YUNG-FU 劉永福
Mem., NA; *b.* Dec. 23, '45; *educ.* Studied, Nat. Taichung Inst. of Com.; *Pol. Affi.* KMT; *Const.* Changhua County; Mem., Changhua CoCoun.; *Add.* 277 San Min E. Rd., Yuanlin, Changhua County.

LO, I-TE
(See LOH, LLOYD E. 羅怡德)

LO CHUNG, CHEN-CHIH 羅鍾澄枝
Bd. Chmn., Miaoli County Br., Twn. Prov. Women's Assn. 90-; *b.* June 7, '41; *educ.* Grad., Prov. Miaoli Sr. Cml. Voc. Sch.; *Pol. Affi.* KMT; *Const.* Miaoli County; Chmn., Miaoli Ind. & Cml. Women's Assn. 86-90; Dir., Miaoli Chapter, Red Cross Soc., ROC 89-93; *Add.* 608 Chung Shan Rd., Miaoli.

LO CHUNG, CHENG-CHIH
(See LO CHUNG, CHEN-CHIH 羅鍾澄枝)

LOH, LLOYD E. 羅怡德
Prof., Fu Jen Catholic U.; *b.* Aug. 28, '59; *educ.* J.D., So. Methodist U.; *Pol. Affi.* NP; *Const.* Taipei City; *Add.* 3rd Fl., 22 Alley 12, Lane 325, Chien Kang Rd., Taipei.

LONG, YU-HSIEN 郎裕憲
Mem., NA 92-; *b.* Aug. 18, '26; *educ.* MA, NCU 62; *Pol. Affi.* KMT; *Const.* Nat.; Prof., NCU 62-92; *Add.* 3rd Fl., 1 Alley 13, Lane 299, Mu Hsin Rd., Sect. 2, Taipei.

LU, CHUN-HUNG 呂鈞鴻
Mem., NA; *b.* Mar. 8, '73; *educ.* Grad., Fuhsing Inst. of Tech.; *Pol. Affi.* KMT; *Const.* Taipei County; *Add.* 2nd Fl., 20 Chung Cheng Rd., Tamsui, Taipei County.

LU, HSUAN-TUNG 呂軒東
Mem., NA; *b.* Dec. 16, '63; *educ.* B., Nat. Sun Yat-Sen U.; *Pol. Affi.* KMT; *Const.* Taichung County; *Add.* 146 Hsin I St., Fengyuan, Taichung County.

LU, HSUEH-CHANG 呂學樟
Mem., NA; *b.* Nov. 5, '52; *educ.* Studied, NCTU; *Pol. Affi.* KMT; *Const.* Hsinchu County; *Add.* 43 Chung Hua Rd., Sect. 1, Hsinchu.

LU, I-HSUEN 盧憶萱
Mem., NA; *b.* May 24, '64; *educ.* M., Nat. Twn. Ocean U.; *Pol. Affi.* KMT; *Const.* Tainan County; *Add.* 30 Alley 18, Lane 44, Chung I St., Yungkang, Tainan County.

LU, KUO-HSIUNG 盧國雄
Mem., NA; *b.* Apr. 4, '39; *educ.* Grad., Nat. Taipei Tchrs. Coll.; *Pol. Affi.* DPP; *Const.* Taipei County; Magis., Tucheng Hsiang; *Add.* 2 Alley 3, Lane 27, Chung I Rd., Tucheng, Taipei County.

LU, WEN-FENG 盧文峰
Mem., NA; *b.* Nov. 17, '59; *educ.* Grad., Lite Cml. & Ind. Voc. Sch.; *Pol. Affi.* KMT; *Const.* Kaohsiung County; *Add.* 90 Kung Yuan W. Rd., Kangshan, Kaohsiung County.

LU, WEN-I 呂文義
Mem., NA; *b.* Jan. 4, '53; *educ.* Grad., Air Force Com. & Elect. Acad.; *Pol. Affi.* KMT; *Const.* Penghu County; *Add.* 48 Lane 77, Chung Hsiao Rd., Kuangming Dist., Makung, Penghu County.

LUNG, YING-TA 龍應達
Mem., NA; *b.* Dec. 1, '49; *educ.* B., Soochow U.; *Pol. Affi.* KMT; *Const.* Taoyuan County; Mem., Kueishan Hsiang Rep. Conf.; *Add.* 10 Hua Mei 2nd St., Kueishan Hsiang, Taoyuan County.

MA, CHANG-FENG 馬長風
Mem., NA; *b.* May 24, '69; *educ.* BA, Soochow U.; *Pol. Affi.* KMT; *Const.* Nantou County; *Add.* 36 Hsi Ning Rd., Puli, Nantou County.

NI, CHANG-I
(See NI, JOHN C.I. 黎昌意)

NI, JOHN C.I. 黎昌意
Dir.-Gen., Small & Medium Ent. Admin., MOEA; *b.* Dec. 17, '41; *educ.* MBA, Stanford U.; *Pol. Affi.* KMT; *Const.* Taipei County; Dir.-Gen., Chung Hwa Travel Service, Hong Kong; Dir.-Gen., Ind. Dev. & Investment Cent., MOEA; *Add.* 3rd Fl., 95 Roosevelt Rd., Sect. 2, Taipei.

NIEN, YUNG-HO 粘永和
Mem., NA; *b.* Sept. 6, '56; *educ.* B., NTNU; *Pol. Affi.* DPP; *Const.* Changhua County; *Add.* 160 Chung Shan Rd., Lukang, Changhua County.

PAN, HUAI-TZUNG
(See PAN, WYNN H.T. 潘懷宗)

PAN, WYNN H.T. 潘懷宗
Assc. Prof., Nat. Yang Ming U.; *b.* July 2, '61; *educ.* Ph.D., Emory U., USA; *Pol. Affi.* NP; *Const.* Taipei City; *Add.* 155 Li Nung St., Sect. 2, Shihpai, Taipei.

PENG, CHIN-PENG 彭錦鵬
Mem., NA; *b.* Sept. 25, '52; *educ.* Ph.D., U. of Georgia; *Pol. Affi.* KMT; *Const.* Nat.; Sec.-Gen., Ch. Soc. of Pol.; *Add.* 3 Alley 4, Lane 61, Yen Chiu Yuan Rd., Sect. 2, Taipei.

PENG, FANG-KU 彭芳谷
Mem., NA; *b.* June 20, '30; *educ.* B., Nat. Def. Med. Cent.; *Pol. Affi.* KMT; *Const.* Nat.; *Add.* 201 Shihpai Rd., Sect. 2, Taipei.

PENG, PAI-CHUNG 彭百崇
Mem., NA; *b.* June 28, '56; *educ.* Ph.D., Ch. Cul. U.; *Pol. Affi.* DPP; *Const.* Nat.; Sec.-Gen., ROC Labor Educ. Promotion Assn.; *Add.* 3rd Fl., 54 Chung Hsiao E. Rd., Sect. 2, Taipei.

SHEN, YIN-HO 沈銀和
Dir., Dept. of Admin. Litigation & Discipline, Jud. Yuan
95-; *b.* Mar. 8, '36; *educ.* J.D., U. of Munich; *Pol. Affi.*
KMT; *Const.* Taipei City; *Add.* 117 Chin Hua St., Taipei.

SHIH, CHUN-I 施純義
Mem., NA; *b.* Apr. 23, '44; *educ.* Grad., Cml. High Sch.;
Pol. Affi. NP; *Const.* Nat.; Dep. Sec.-Gen., NP; *Add.* 13th
Fl.-3, 1 Fu Hsing N. Rd., Taipei.

SHIH, YUAN-NA 石元娜
Dir., Broadcasting Corp. of Ch.; *b.* Dec. 21, '53; *educ.*
Grad., Chungkuang Girl's High Sch.; *Pol. Affi.* KMT;
Const. Nat.; *Add.* 53 Jen Ai Rd., Sect. 3, Taipei City.

SHIEH, LUNG-SHENG 謝隆盛
Dep. Spkr. 97-; *b.* Apr. 24, '41; *educ.* B., Tatung Inst. of
Tech.; 19th Class, Sun Yat-sen Inst. on Policy Res. &
Dev.; *Pol. Affi.* KMT; *Const.* Nat.; Mem., Taipei
CoCoun., & Disciplinary Cttee., KMT Caucus, NA; Dep.
Dir., Dept. of Org. Aff., CC, KMT; Chmn., Presidium,
NA; Dir.-Gen., Dept. of Party-Govt. Coordination of the
NA, KMT 91-96; *Add.* 5th Fl., 16 Hangchow S. Rd.,
Sect. 1, Taipei.

SU, CHIH-FEN 蘇治芬
Mem., NA; *b.* July 10, '53; *educ.* Grad., Nat. Taipei Coll.
of Business; *Pol. Affi.* DPP; *Const.* Nat.; *Add.* 3rd Fl.-7,
5 Tsingtao E. Rd., Taipei.

SU, MIN-NAN 蘇明南
Mem., NA 92-; *b.* Dec. 5, '54; *educ.* Nat. Twn. Coll. of
Phys. Educ. 76; *Pol. Affi.* DPP; *Const.* Nat.; Personal
Sec. to the Magis., Pingtung County 89-93; Exec. Mem.,
Pingtung County Cttee., DPP; *Add.* 7 Tienchuo Tsun,
Wantan Hsiang, Pingtung County.

SU, MING-NAN
(See SU, MIN-NAN 蘇明南)

SU, NAN-CHENG 蘇南成
Nat. Policy Adv. to the Pres. 90-; *b.* Jan. 14, '36; *educ.*
BS, NCKU 59; Hon. LL.D., Pepperdine U., USA 82;
Hon. DPS, De La Salle U., Philippines 90; *Pol. Affi.*
KMT; *Const.* Nat.; Mem., Tainan CCoun. 68-77; Mayor,
Tainan City 77-85, & Kaohsiung City 85-90; Mem.,
CSC, KMT 85-93; *Add.* 53 Chung Hua Rd., Sect. 1, Taipei.

SUN, ING-SHAN 孫英善
Mem., NA; *b.* Apr. 20, '34; *educ.* MBA, Calif. State U.,
Northridge; *Pol. Affi.* KMT; *Const.* Ovs. Nat.; Comr.,
OCAC; *Add.* 238 E., Mira Verde Drive, La Habra
Heights, CA 90631, USA.

SUN, YING-SHAN
(See SUN, ING-SHAN 孫英善)

TAI, JUNG-SHENG 戴榮聖
Mem., NA; *b.* Oct. 14, '64; *educ.* LL.B., NCHU; *Pol.
Affi.* DPP; *Const.* Kaohsiung City; *Add.* 142 Chi Hsien
3rd Rd., Kaohsiung.

TANG, A-KEN 湯阿根
Lawyer; *b.* Apr. 7, '36; *educ.* LL.B., Mil. Law Acad.;
Pol. Affi. NP; *Const.* Nat.; Mem., Kaohsiung CCoun.;
Add. 2nd Fl., 75 Min Sheng 2nd Rd., Kaohsiung.

TANG, HUO-SHEN 湯火聖
Mem., NA; *b.* Oct. 29, '56; *educ.* MBA, Regis U., USA;
Pol. Affi. DPP; *Const.* Nantou County; Chmn., Nantou
County Cttee., DPP; *Add.* 12nd Fl.-3, 14 Pi Shan Rd.,
Tsaotun, Nantou County.

TANG, HUO-SHENG
(See TANG, HUO-SHEN 湯火聖)

TANG, MEI-E 湯美娥
Mem., NA; *b.* Oct. 3, '54; *educ.* LL.B., NTU; *Pol. Affi.*
DPP; *Const.* Taoyuan County; Sp., MOI; *Add.* 12 Alley
1, Lane 527, Chung Cheng Rd., Lungtan Hsiang,
Taoyuan County.

TANG, MEI-O
(See TANG, MEI-E 湯美娥)

TANG, PI-O 唐碧娥
Mem., NA 92-; *b.* May 3, '49; *educ.* BA, Pol., Nat.
Utsunomiya U., Japan; *Pol. Affi.* DPP; *Const.* Tainan
City; Bd. Mem., Japan Br., Formosan Assn. for Public
Aff. 88-90; *Add.* 271-11 Chung Hsueh Rd., Tainan.

TANG, SHAO-CHENG 湯紹成
Assc. Res. Fel., Inst. of Intl. Rel.; *b.* Apr. 25, '55; *Pol.
Affi.* NP; *Const.* Taipei County; Ph.D., U. Bonn; *Add.*
3rd Fl., 12 Pei Hsin Rd., Sect. 2, Hsintien, Taipei County.

TANG, YUAN-LIANG 唐元亮
Assc. Prof., Nat. Pingtung Inst. of Com.; *b.* May 2, '64; *educ.* Ph.D., Penn. State U.; *Pol. Affi.* NP; *Const.* Taichung County; *Add.* 2 Alley 2, Lane 311, Chung Shan Rd., Sect. 2, Taiping Hsiang, Taichung County.

TENG, HUNG-CHI 鄧鴻吉
Mem., NA; *b.* Mar. 8, '64; *educ.* Grad., Chienkuo Tech. Acad.; *Pol. Affi.* KMT; *Const.* Taichung City; Pres., Mil. Reservist Assn.; *Add.* 20-5 Kiangsi Chuo Lane, Hsi Tun Rd., Sect. 3, Taichung.

TIEN, CHAO-JUNG 田昭容
Tchr., Tahua Jr. Coll. of Tech. & Com.; *b.* Feb. 2, '60; *educ.* B., Kaohsiung Med. Coll.; *Pol. Affi.* NP; *Const.* Hsinchu County; *Add.* 83 Kang Ning St., Chutung, Hsinchu County.

TING, YUNG-SUN 丁詠蓀
Mem., NA; *b.* Jan. 16, '59; *educ.* Grad., Ming Chuan Coll.; *Pol. Affi.* DPP; *Const.* Changhua County; *Add.* 300 Tao Chou Rd., Hemei, Changhua County.

TSAI, ALEX KING-YOUNG 蔡正元
Gen. Mgr., Chingfeng Semiconductor & Tech. Co.; *b.* Dec. 25, '53; *educ.* M., Harvard U.; Ph.D. candidate, Columbia U.; *Pol. Affi.* KMT; *Const.* Taipei City; *Add.* 12th Fl., 550 Chung Hsiao E. Rd., Sect. 4, Taipei.

TSAI, CHENG-YUAN
(See TSAI, ALEX KING-YOUNG 蔡正元)

TSAI, CHI-FANG 蔡啟芳
Chmn., Chu-Lo-Shan CATV System 92-; *b.* July 12, '54; *educ.* Shen Chou Sr. High Sch.; *Pol. Affi.* DPP; *Const.* Chiayi City; Urban Township Magis., Putai Chen, Chiayi County 90-94; Chmn., Chiayi County Cttee., DPP 90-92, & Chiayi City Cttee. 92-94; *Add.* 34 Hsuchow 6th St., Chiayi.

TSAI, CHIH-HONG 蔡志弘
Mem., NA; *b.* Dec. 12, '53; *educ.* M., So. Methodist U., USA; *Pol. Affi.* KMT; *Const.* Taipei City; Asso. Res. Fel., NSC; *Add.* 2nd Fl., 448 Jen Ai Rd., Sect. 4, Taipei.

TSAI, CHIH-HUNG
(See TSAI, CHIH-HONG 蔡志弘)

TSAI, CHUNG-CHI 蔡重吉
Mem., NA 92-; *b.* Oct. 9, '44; *educ.* Mil. Police Acad.; *Pol. Affi.* KMT; *Const.* Taipei City; Rep., 13th Nat. Cong., KMT; *Add.* 7-4 Lane 185, Nanking W. Rd., Taipei.

TSAI, HSIN-TE 蔡信德
Mem., NA; *b.* Jan. 3, '46; *educ.* BA, Eng., Fu Jen Catholic U.; *Pol. Affi.* DPP; *Const.* Kaohsiung City; Resr., Twn. Parliamentarians Off.; *Add.* 3-9 Chung Cheng Rd., Chunghsing Tsun, Taliao Hsiang, Kaohsiung County.

TSAI, JEN-CHIEN 蔡仁堅
Mem., Presidium, NA 92-; Dir., Dept. of Publicity, DPP; *b.* Oct. 27, '52; *educ.* B., Pharmacology, Taipei Med. Coll.; *Pol. Affi.* DPP; *Const.* Hsinchu City; Mem., Hsinchu CCoun.; *Add.* 143 Chung Shan Rd., Hsinchu.

TSAI, LIANG-LIANG 蔡亮亮
Mem., NA; *b.* Oct. 1, '49; *educ.* BA, NCU; *Pol. Affi.* KMT; *Const.* Ovs. Nat.; *Add.* 306-9B, Tun Hua S. Rd., Sect. 1, Taipei.

TSAI, LING-LAN 蔡鈴蘭
Gen. Mgr., 11th Credit Co-Operative Assn. of Taichung; *b.* May 13, '42; *educ.* Grad., Nat. Taichung Inst. of Com.; Hon. Ph.D., Union Calif. U.; *Pol. Affi.* KMT; *Const.* Nat.; *Add.* 316 Wen Hsin Rd., Sect. 1, Taichung.

TSAI, TING-PANG 蔡定邦
Pres., Fong Kuo Shipbldg. Co. Ltd.; *b.* Aug. 2, '43; *educ.* BS, NCHU; *Pol. Affi.* KMT; *Const.* Nat.; Chmn., Kaohsiung City Br., Fishermen's Assn.; *Add.* Room 221, 3 Yu Kang E. 2nd Rd., Chienchen, Kaohsiung.

TSAI, WEN-PIN 蔡文斌
Attorney-at-Law 77-; Convener, DPP Caucus, NA 93-; Chmn., Tainan City Cttee., DPP 94-; *b.* Mar. 29, '53; *educ.* LL.B., NTU 75; *Pol. Affi.* DPP; *Const.* Tainan City; *Add.* 39 Lane 289, Chin Hua Rd., Sect. 2, Tainan.

TSAI, YUNG-CHANG 蔡永常
Bd. Chmn., Yunlin Fisherman Assn.; *b.* Aug. 5, '50; *educ.* Grad., Shanghai Agr. Coll.; *Pol. Affi.* KMT; *Const.* Yunlin County; 51-5 I Min Rd., Peikang, Yunlin County.

TSAO, YUAN-CHANG 曹原彰
Exec. Off., NP; *b.* May 24, '48; *educ.* B., NTNU; *Pol. Affi.* NP; *Const.* Matsu; Jour.; *Add.* 8th Fl., 129 An Ping Rd., Chungho, Taipei County.

TSENG, HSIEN-CHI 曾憲棨
Mem., Presidium, NA 92-; *b.* July 28, '43; *educ.* BA, Fu Hsing Kang Coll.; MA, Comm. Sc., United Calif. U.; *Pol. Affi.* KMT; *Const.* Taipei City; Adv., Army Cmd. & Staff Coll., Armed Forces U. 68-70, & War Coll. 70-72; Dir., TV Cent., MND 81-85; *Add.* 3rd Fl., 133 Tao Hsiang Rd., Peitou, Taipei.

TSENG, PING-HUANG 曾炳煌
Gen. Mgr., Hsichih Chen Br., Farmers' Assn. 73-; *b.* Jan. 9, '46; *educ.* Tamsui Oxford Coll. 69; *Pol. Affi.* KMT; *Const.* Taipei County; *Add.* 207 Hsin Tai 5th Rd., Hsichih, Taipei County.

TSUNG, SHU-KUEI 叢樹貴
Mem., NA; *b.* Jan. 8, '59; *educ.* Grad., Kaohsiung Intl. Coll. of Com.; *Pol. Affi.* KMT; *Const.* Kaohsiung City; *Add.* 518 Tzu Mien New Village, Tsoying, Kaohsiung.

TU, CHEN-HUA
(See TU, JENN-HWA 杜震華)

TU, JENN-HWA 杜震華
Assc. Prof., NTU; *b.* Dec. 26, '54; *educ.* Ph.D., Johns Hopkins U.; *Pol. Affi.* NP; *Const.* Taipei County; *Add.* 9 Chuang Ching Rd., Chungho, Taipei County.

TZUNG, CHING-I 宗景宜
Mem., NA; *b.* Feb. 28, '52; *educ.* B., Ch. Cul. U.; *Pol. Affi.* NP; *Const.* Nat.; Pres., Hsinlu Cul. & Educ. Found.; *Add.* 1st Fl., 1 Alley 25, Lane 7, Ta Hsin St., Hsintien, Taipei County.

WANG, ANDREW MING-LONG 王明隆
Assc. Prof., NCKU; *b.* Apr. 20, '56; *educ.* Ph.D., City U. of New York; *Pol. Affi.* KMT; *Const.* Tainan City; *Add.* 9th Fl.-1, 99 Lin Sen Rd., Sect. 2, Tainan.

WANG, CHIH 王智
Mem., NA; *b.* Dec. 3, '20; *educ.* Studied, Asia U., Japan; *Pol. Affi.* KMT; *Const.* Ovs. Nat.; *Add.* 101 Bldg. A, Nuwaro City, Minamisenju, Arakawa Ku, Tokyo, Japan.

WANG, CHIH-PING 汪志冰
Mem., NA; *b.* Apr. 20, '57; *educ.* MA, Ea. Michigan U.; *Pol. Affi.* NP; *Const.* Taipei City; *Add.* 83 Hsing An St., Taipei.

WANG, CHING-SAN 王慶三
Mem., NA; *b.* Sept. 19, '40; *educ.* B., NCU; *Pol. Affi.* DPP; *Const.* Taipei County; Chief Exec., Taipei County Cttee., DPP; *Add.* 3rd Fl., 6 Min Tsu Rd., Hsintien, Taipei County.

WANG, FENG-MING 王逢明
Mem., NA; *b.* June 16, '57; *educ.* Studied, Kaohsiung Kaoyuan Jr. Coll.; *Pol. Affi.* KMT; *Const.* Kaohsiung County; *Add.* 11 Li Ta Rd., Luchu Hsiang, Kaohsiung County.

WANG, HSIU-YUAN 王琇媛
Mem., NA; *b.* Mar. 14, '59; *educ.* Grad., Nat. Taichung Inst. of Com.; *Pol. Affi.* KMT; *Const.* Yunlin County; *Add.* 82-1 Chen Nan Rd., Touliu, Yunlin County.

WANG, KAO-CHENG 王高成
Assc. Prof., Tamkang U.; *b.* Mar. 10. '61; *educ.* Ph.D., U. of Penn.; *Pol. Affi.* NP; *Const.* Taipei City; *Add.* 4th Fl., 19 Lane 177, Min Chuan Rd., Tamsui, Taipei County.

WANG, KUO-CHING 王國清
Mem., NA; *b.* Sept. 6, '44; *educ.* Grad., Asia Ind. & Business High Sch.; *Pol. Affi.* KMT; *Const.* Tainan City; Mem., Tainan CCoun.; Mem., Legis. Yuan; *Add.* 10 Lane 72, Fu Nung St., Sect. 1, E. Dist., Tainan.

WANG, LAN-FEN 王蘭芬
Lectr., Dept. of Acct., NCHU 88-; *b.* Oct. 19, '58; *educ.* MBA, NCU; *Pol. Affi.* KMT; *Const.* Chiayi County; *Add.* 185 Putzupu, Wanchiao Tsun, Chuchi Hsiang, Chiayi County.

WANG, MEI-YUEH 王美月
Mem., NA; *b.* Nov. 20, '54; *educ.* Studied, NCU; *Pol. Affi.* KMT; *Const.* Taipei County; *Add.* 260 Kuang Ming St., Hsintien, Taipei County.

WANG, MING-LUNG
(See WANG, ANDREW MING-LONG 王明隆)

WANG, MING-YU 王明玉
Mem., NA; *b.* May 18, '46; *educ.* B., NTU; *Pol. Affi.*
DPP; *Const.* Nat.; *Add.* 3rd Fl.-3, 7 Tsingtao E. Rd., Taipei.

WANG, MING-YUAN 王銘源
Mem., NA; *b.* Sept. 10, '66; *educ.* Grad., World Coll.
of Jour. & Comms.; *Pol. Affi.* DPP; *Const.* Taipei
City; Dir., Twn. Welfare State Off.; *Add.* 31 Fu Kuo
Rd., Taipei.

WANG, PEI-CHU 王培珠
Mem., NA; *b.* July 9, '56; *educ.* BA, Shih Chien Coll.;
Pol. Affi. NP; *Const.* Miaoli County; *Add.* 2nd Fl., 29 Fu
Chien Rd., Miaoli.

WANG, SHIH-HSIUNG 王世雄
Mem., NA; *b.* June 24, '61; *educ.* B., NCU; *Pol. Affi.*
KMT; *Const.* Nat.; Mem., Legis. Yuan; *Add.* 1st Fl., 4
Alley 5, Lane 346, Pa Te Rd., Sect. 4, Taipei.

WANG, TUNG-HUI 王東暉
Mem., NA; *b.* Feb. 23, '56; *educ.* Studied, U. of Calif.,
San Diego; *Pol. Affi.* DPP; *Const.* Keelung City; Mem.,
Keelung CCoun.; *Add.* 30 Nan Hsin St., Keelung.

WANG DAY, CHUEN-MAN 王戴春滿
Mgr., Dsen Chiou Chen Ent. Co.; *b.* July 3, '41; *educ.*
M., U. of San Francisco; *Pol. Affi.* KMT; *Const.*
Taichung County; Mem., Taichung CoCoun.; *Add.* 13
Lin Hai Rd., Tsaonan Li, Wuchi, Taichung County.

WANG TAI, CHUN-MAN
(See WANG DAY, CHUEN-MAN 王戴春滿)

WEN, HSI-CHIN 溫錫金
Mem., NA; *b.* Mar. 27, '64; *educ.* B., Nat. Cent. U.; *Pol.
Affi.* KMT; *Const.* Changhua County; *Add.* 2 Lane 81,
Yung Le St., Changhua.

WEN, MEI-KUEI 溫梅桂
Mem., NA; *b.* Jan. 10, '59; *educ.* M., Ea. Theology Inst.;
Pol. Affi. NP; *Const.* Nat.; *Add.* 149 Lane 58, Chung Shan
N. Rd., Sect. 3, Taipei.

WENG, HSING-WANG
(See WONG, HSING-WANG 翁興旺)

WONG, HSING-WANG 翁興旺
Pres., Chen-Huei Ind. Co. Ltd. 81-; *b.* Mar. 25, '48; *educ.*
MBA, NTU; *Pol. Affi.* KMT; *Const.* Tainan County; *Add.*
18 Lane 758, Chung Shan Rd., Jente, Tainan County.

WONG, N.C. 黃握中
Chmn., Hong Kong Cinema & Theatrical Assn.; *b.* Aug.
5, '35; *educ.* B.Lit., Far E. Coll., Hong Kong; *Pol. Affi.*
KMT; *Const.* Ovs. Nat.; *Add.* 3rd Fl., 118 Hou Kang St.,
Shihlin, Taipei.

WU, CHENG-CHUN 吳正群
Mem., NA; *b.* Jan. 12, '60; *educ.* B., Ch. Cul. U.; *Pol.
Affi.* NP; *Const.* Taoyuan County; *Add.* 5th Fl., 859 Ching
Kuo Rd., Taoyuan.

WU, CHI-MEI 吳綺美
Chmn., Changhua County Br., Women's Assn.; *b.* May
16, '34; *educ.* Changhua Girls' High Sch.; Studied, Nat.
Yunlin Inst. of Tech.; *Pol. Affi.* KMT; *Const.* Changhua
County; Mem., Changhua CoCoun.; Dir., Bo Ai Tng.
Cent. for the Handicapped, Changhua County; *Add.* 107
Kuang Fu Rd., Changhua.

WU, CHING-YU 吳靜瑜
Mem., NA; *b.* Feb. 23, '37; *educ.* Grad., Chungshan High
Sch.; *Pol. Affi.* KMT; *Const.* Kaohsiung City; *Add.* 4th
Fl., 288 Erh Sheng 1st Rd., Chiencheng, Kaohsiung.

WU, CHUN-AN 吳俊岸
Gen. Mgr., Hsinchu County Br., Fishermen's Assn.; *b.*
Oct. 11, '36; *educ.* Grad., Supplementary Open Jr. Coll.
for PA, NCU; *Pol. Affi.* KMT; *Const.* Hsinchu County;
Add. 106 Chih Fu Rd., Hsinfeng, Hsinchu County.

WU, CHUN-MING 吳俊明
Mem., NA; *b.* Mar. 20, '48; *educ.* Grad., World Coll. of
Jour. & Comms.; *Pol. Affi.* DPP; *Const.* Tainan County; *Add.*
132-1 Sunchiao Tsun, Kuanmiao Hsiang, Tainan County.

WU, ERIC T. 吳東昇
Dep. Dir.-Gen., Dept. of Ovs. Aff., KMT; Sec.-Gen.,
APPU, Asian-Pacific Cul. Cent.; *b.* July 14, '53; *educ.*
MBA, Harvard U. 80, LL.D. 90; *Pol. Affi.* KMT; *Const.*
Nat.; Convener, Judicial Cttee., Legis. Yuan; *Add.* Suite
B, 5th Fl., 44 Chung Shan N. Rd., Sect. 2, Taipei.

WU, FU-KUEI 吳富貴
Mem., NA; *b*. Dec. 30, '53; *educ*. B., NTNU; *Pol. Affi*. DPP; *Const*. Taichung County; *Add*. 303 Po Ai St., Fengyuan, Taichung County.

WU, HE-CHUNG 吳鶴中
Mem., NA; *b*. May 22, '61; *educ*. Grad., Lite Ind. & Cml. Voc. Sch.; *Pol. Affi*. KMT; *Const*. Kaohsiung County; Mem., Kangshan Rep. Conf.; *Add*. 25 Lane 11, Min Tsu Rd., Kangshan, Kaohsiung County.

WU, KUANG-HSUN 吳光訓
Mem., NA 92-; *b*. June 17, '50; *educ*. Yungtah Jr. Coll. of Tech. & Com.; *Pol. Affi*. KMT; *Const*. Kaohsiung County; *Add*. 21 Lane 122, Kwangchow 1st St., Kaohsiung.

WU, KUO-CHUNG 吳國重
Chmn., Nantou Import-Export Assn.; *b*. Feb. 11, '51; *educ*. MD, Taipei Med. Coll.; *Pol. Affi*. KMT; *Const*. Nantou County; *Add*. 272 Nan Kang 3rd Rd., Nantou.

WU, MAO-HSIUNG 吳茂雄
Mem., NA; *b*. July 7, '38; *educ*. LL.B., Soochow U.; *Pol. Affi*. KMT; *Const*. Taipei City; Dep. Sec.-Gen., Intl. Bar Assn. of the ROC; *Add*. 2nd Fl., 192 Chung Hua Rd., Sect. 1, Taipei.

WU, TSANG-HAI 吳滄海
Mem., NA; *b*. Apr. 21, '45; *educ*. LL.D., Ch. Cul. U.; *Pol. Affi*. NP; *Const*. Keelung City; *Add*. Rm. 901, 34 Chung Cheng Rd., Keelung.

WU, TUNG-SHENG
(See WU, ERIC T. 吳東昇)

WU, YING-CHIN 吳映卿
Mem., NA; *b*. Nov. 3, '53; *educ*. B., Fu Jen Catholic U.; *Pol. Affi*. KMT; *Const*. Tainan County; *Add*. 13th Fl., 114 Cheng Kung Rd., Tainan City.

WU, YUAN-SHAN 吳遠山
Mem., NA; *b*. Mar. 12, '63; *educ*. M., Ch. Cul. U.; *Pol. Affi*. NP; *Const*. Taipei County; *Add*. 19 Lane 2, Yu Shih Rd., Wuku Hsiang, Taipei County.

YANG, CHIN-HAI 楊金海
Mem., NA; *b*. July 11, '32; *educ*. Studied, U. of San Diego; *Pol. Affi*. DPP; *Const*. Kaohsiung County; Chmn.,

Kaohsiung County Cttee., DPP; *Add*. 39 Min Sheng Rd., Hsinhsing Li, Fengshan, Kaohsiung County.

YANG, CHING-SHENG 楊荊生
Mem., NA; *b*. July 15, '44; *educ*. Ph.D., NTNU; *Pol. Affi*. KMT; *Const*. Taitung County; *Add*. 46 Lin Tung St., Taitung.

YANG, JEN-HUANG 楊仁煌
Comr. & Chief Sec., MTAC; *b*. Sept. 1, '50; *educ*. Ph.D., NCU; *Pol. Affi*. KMT; *Const*. Lowland Aborigines; *Add*. 2 Chien Te St., Hualien.

YANG, JUNG-MING 楊榮明
Sup., Twn. Rice Ind. Assn.; *b*. Dec. 15, '44; *educ*. Grad., Tainan Hsinjung Business & Ind. Sch.; *Pol. Affi*. KMT; *Const*. Tainan County; Mem., Tainan CoCoun.; *Add*. 45 Wushantou, Hushan Tsun, Kuantien Hsiang, Tainan County.

YANG, MIN-HUA 楊敏華
Mem., NA; *b*. Mar. 2, '58; *educ*. LL.M., Nat. Twn. Ocean U.; *Pol. Affi*. NP; *Const*. Taichung City; Chief, Case Assignment Dept., Supreme Court; *Add*. 95 Lane 31, Yu Men Rd., Hsitun, Taichung.

YANG, SHIH-HSIUNG
(See YANG, THOMAS 楊世雄)

YANG, SU-YUAN
(See YANG, SUH-YUAN 楊肅元)

YANG, SUH-YUAN 楊肅元
Mem., NA 92-; *b*. Jan. 25, '39; *educ*. Tchrs. Sp. Prog., Kinmen Sr. High Sch.; *Pol. Affi*. KMT; *Const*. Kinmen County; Chmn., Assn. of Com., Kinmen 84-90; *Add*. 21-3 Min Tsu Rd., Chincheng, Kinmen County.

YANG, THOMAS 楊世雄
Prof., NCU; *b*. Feb. 3, '47; *educ*. Ph.D.; *Pol. Affi*. NP; *Const*. Nat.; *Add*. 16 Kuo Kuang Rd., Yungho, Taipei County.

YEH, YUN-HSU
(See YEH, YUN-HSUI 葉雲勗)

YEH, YUN-HSUI 葉雲勗
Mem., NA; *b*. Feb. 19, '36; *educ*. Grad., Chungli Agr. High Sch.; *Pol. Affi*. KMT; *Const*. Taoyuan County; *Add*. 8th Fl., 582 Chung Cheng Rd., Chungli, Taoyuan County.

YEN, MING-SHENG 顏明聖
Mem., NA 92-; *b.* Jan. 29, '36; *educ.* Nat. Tainan Tchrs. Coll.; *Pol. Affi.* DPP; *Const.* Kaohsiung City; *Add.* 253 Chiu Ju 2nd Rd., Sanmin, Kaohsiung.

YEN, YAO-HSING
(See YEN, YAO-SHING 顏耀星)

YEN, YAO-SHING 顏耀星
Lectr., Nanjung Jr. Coll. of Tech. & Com. 90-; *b.* Oct. 16, '58; *educ.* BA, Soochow U. 83; MBA, Wakayama U., Japan 90; *Pol. Affi.* KMT; *Const.* Tainan County; *Add.* 28 Min Chih Rd., Hsinying, Tainan County.

YING, CHIH-HUNG
(See YING, LEVI C. 營志宏)

YING, LEVI C. 營志宏
Attorney-at-Law, USA; *b.* July 4, '49; *educ.* J.D., Whittier Coll. Law Sch.; *Pol. Affi.* NP; *Const.* Ovs. Nat.; Pres., Friends of NP Assn., Los Angeles; *Add.* 1101 W. Valley Boulevard, #203, Alhambra, CA 91803, USA.

YU, SHU-CHIEH 于樹潔
Mem., NA; *b.* Nov. 2, '46; *educ.* LL.B., NTU; *Pol. Affi.* NP; *Const.* Kaohsiung City; Mem., Kaohsiung CCoun. 72-80; Mem., Legis. Yuan 80-83; *Add.* 2nd Fl., 24 Wen Heng 2nd Rd., Kaohsiung.

YU, TUNG-CHIN 余東錦
Mem., NA; *b.* Sept. 28, '52; *educ.* Grad., Shalu Ind. High Sch.; *Pol. Affi.* KMT; *Const.* Miaoli County; Mem., Miaoli CoCoun.; *Add.* 142 Shan Chiao Li, Yuanli, Miaoli County.

Members of the Third Legislative Yuan
(February 1, 1996—January 31, 1999)

CHANG, CHIN-CHENG
(See CHANG, MICHAEL C. 張晉城)

CHANG, CHUN-HSIUNG 張俊雄
Mem., Trans. & Comms. Cttee., Legis. Yuan 97-, Mem. 83-; *b.* Mar. 23, '38; *educ.* LL.B., NTU 60; Qualified lawyer; *Pol. Affi.* DPP; *Const.* Kaohsiung City; Mem., CC, DPP, Exec. Mem., CSC 87-89; Convener & Exec. Dir., DPP Caucus, Legis. Yuan; Convener, Jud. Cttee., Legis. Yuan 91, Home & Border Aff. Cttee. 92, Trans. & Comms. Cttee. 95; *Add.* Rm. 319, 1 Tsingtao E. Rd., Taipei.

CHANG, CHUN-HUNG 張俊宏
Mem., Nat. Def. Cttee., Legis. Yuan 97-; Mem., CSC, DPP 92-; *b.* May 17, '38; *educ.* BPS & MPS, NTU; *Pol. Affi.* DPP; *Const.* Taipei City; Mem., TPA 77-79; Jailed for Kaohsiung Incident 79-87; Sec.-Gen., DPP 88-91; Mem., NA 92; Mem., For. & Ovs. Ch. Aff. Cttee., Legis. Yuan 94; *Add.* 6th Fl., 16 Peiping E. Rd., Taipei.

CHANG, JEN-HSIANG 章仁香
Mem., Budget Cttee., Legis. Yuan 97-; *b.* June 27, '53; *educ.* MA, Ch. Cul. U.; Lectr., Ch. Cul. U.; *Pol. Affi.* KMT; *Const.* Lowland Aborigines; Mem., Home & Border Aff. Cttee., 1st Sess., Legis. Yuan 96; *Add.* Rm. 612, 10 Tsingtao E. Rd., Taipei.

CHANG, KUANG-CHIN 張光錦
Mem., Nat. Def. Cttee., 1st & 2nd Sess., Legis. Yuan 96-; *b.* Jan. 3, 36; *educ.* BA, Ch. Mil. Acad.; Air Def. & Missile Sch., USA; *Pol. Affi.* KMT; *Const.* Nat.; *Add.* Rm. 101, 1 Tsingtao E. Rd., Taipei.

CHANG, MICHAEL C. 張晉城
Mem., Econ. Cttee., 1st & 2nd Sess., Legis. Yuan 96-; *b.* Mar. 5, '49; *educ.* LL.B., NTU 71; LL.M., U. of London 78; *Pol. Affi.* Independent; *Const.* Taipei City; *Add.* Rm. 124, 1 Tsingtao E. Rd., Taipei.

CHANG, HSU-CHENG
(See CHANG, PARRIS H. 張旭成)

CHANG, PARRIS H. 張旭成
Mem., Nat. Def. Cttee., 1st Sess., Legis. Yuan 97-; Prof., Pol. Sc., Penn. State U. 70-; Dir., Twn. DPP Mission in the USA; Pres., Steering Cttee., Unrepresented Nations & Peoples Org. 93-; *b.* Dec. 30, '36; *educ.* MPS, U. of Washington 63; DPS, Columbia U. 69; *Pol. Affi.* DPP; *Const.* Ovs. Nat.; Convener, For. & Ovs. Ch. Aff. Cttee., Legis. Yuan 93, Mem., For. & Ovs. Ch. Aff. Cttee. 94; *Add.* Rm. 603, 10 Tsingtao E. Rd., Taipei.

CHANG, WEN-YI 張文儀
Convener, Finance Cttee., Legis. Yuan 94-; *b.* Nov. 15, '48; *educ.* Ching Shui Sr. High Sch.; *Pol. Affi.* KMT; *Const.* Taichung County; Mem., NA 92-93; Mem., 2nd Legis. Yuan; *Add.* Rm. 616, 10 Tsingtao E. Rd., Taipei.

CHAO, ERH-CHUNG 曹爾忠
Mem., Nat. Def. Cttee., 2nd Sess., Legis. Yuan 97-; *b.* Aug. 24, '54; *educ.* LL.M., Cent. Police Coll.; *Pol. Affi.* KMT; *Const.* Lienchiang County; Dir., Lienchiang County Police Station 90-91; Convener, Organic Laws Cttee., Legis. Yuan 94; *Add.* Rm. 417, 1 Tsingtao E. Rd., Taipei.

CHAO, YUNG-CHING
(See JAO, EUGENE YUNG-CHING 趙永清)

CHEN, CHAO-JUNG 陳朝容
Mem., Trans. & Comms. Cttee., 2nd Sess., Legis. Yuan 97-; *b.* Feb. 25, '56; *educ.* Grad., Nat. Taichung Inst. of Com. 90; *Pol. Affi.* KMT; *Const.* Changhua County; Mem., Changhua CoCoun. 86-93; Mem., Econ. Cttee., Legis. Yuan 96; *Add.* 6 Ping Ho 12th St., Changhua.

CHEN, CHI-MAI 陳其邁
Mem., Trans. & Comms. Cttee., 2nd Sess., Legis. Yuan; *b.* Dec. 23, '64; *educ.* MPH, NTU; *Pol. Affi.* DPP; *Const.* Kaohsiung City; *Add.* Rm. 303, 1 Tsingtao E. Rd., Taipei.

CHEN, CHIEH-JU 陳傑儒
Mem., Econ. Cttee., Legis. Yuan 94-; *b.* Nov. 25, '37; *educ.* BA, NCKU; *Pol. Affi.* KMT; *Const.* Taichung

County; Mem., 7th & 8th Taichung CoCoun.; Mem., Taichung County Cttee., & Twn. Prov. Cttee., KMT; Sec.-Gen., KMT Caucus, 2nd Legis. Yuan; *Add.* Rm. 615, 10 Tsingtao E. Rd., Taipei.

CHEN, CHIEN-MIN 陳健民
Mem., Organic Laws Cttee., 2nd Sess., Legis. Yuan 97-; *b.* Oct. 5, '42; *educ.* LL.B., NTU 64; LL.M., Ch. Cul. U. 72; *Pol. Affi.* KMT; *Const.* Nat.; Judge & Div. Chief Judge, Taipei Dist. Court; Judge, Twn. High Court; Pres., Kinmen Dist. Court 84-86, Hualien Dist. Court 86-90, Chiayi Dist. Court 90-91, & Tainan Dist. Court 91-92; Counsl. & Chief Sec., MOJ 92-93; Convener, Jud. Cttee., Legis. Yuan 94; *Add.* Rm. 107, 1 Tsingtao E. Rd., Taipei.

CHEN, CHIH-PIN 陳志彬
Mem., Finance Cttee., Legis. Yuan 93-; *b.* Apr. 1, '49; *educ.* BBA, NCHU; *Pol. Affi.* KMT; *Const.* Nantou County; Mem., Nantou CoCoun. 77-81, & TPA 85-89; Dep. Chmn., Nantou County Cttee., KMT 89-92; *Add.* Rm. 609, 1 Chung Shan S. Rd., Taipei.

CHEN, CHING-PAO 陳清寶
Mem., Budget Cttee., 2nd Sess., Legis. Yuan 97-; *b.* Dec. 9, '55; *educ.* BA, Nat. Twn. Ocean U.; *Pol. Affi.* KMT; *Const.* Kinmen County; Convener, Expenditure Inspection Cttee., Legis. Yuan, Disciplinary Cttee., Nat. Def. Cttee., Rules Cttee., Mem., Trans. & Comms. Cttee. 94; *Add.* Rm. 429, 1 Tsingtao E. Rd., Taipei.

CHEN, CHIUNG-TSAN
(See CHEN, JOHNSON C.T. 陳瓊讚)

CHEN, DING-NAN 陳定南
Mem., Home & Border Aff. Cttee., 2nd Sess., Legis. Yuan 97-; *b.* Sept. 29, '43; *educ.* LL.B., NTU; *Pol. Affi.* DPP; *Const.* Ilan County; 9th & 10th term Magis., Ilan County 81-89; Mem., Budget Cttee., Legis. Yuan 94; *Add.* Rm. 311, 1 Tsingtao E. Rd., Taipei.

CHEN, HAN-CHIANG 陳漢強
Mem., Budget Cttee., 1st & 2nd Sess., Legis. Yuan 96-; *b.* July 3, '37; *educ.* Ed.M., NCU; TPG 81-86; Dir., Dept. of Educ., TCG 86-91; Pres., Nat. Hsinchu Tchrs. Coll. 91-96; *Pol. Affi.* NP; *Const.* Taipei City; *Add.* 10 Tsingtao E. Rd., Taipei.

CHEN, HORNG-CHI 陳鴻基
Mem., Home & Border Aff. Cttee., Legis. Yuan 96-; *b.* Sept. 30, '49; *educ.* BA, Japan U.; MA, Notre Dame U., USA; *Pol. Affi.* KMT; *Const.* Taipei City; Mem., NA, KMT; Dep. Dir., Dept. of Party-Govt. Coordination of the Legis. Yuan, KMT; *Add.* 2nd Fl., 5-1 Chen Chan St., Taipei.

CHEN, HUNG-CHI
(See CHEN, HORNG-CHI 陳鴻基)

CHEN, HUNG-CHANG 陳宏昌
Mem., Home & Border Aff. Cttee., Legis. Yuan 94-; *b.* Mar. 2, '56; *educ.* M., Far Ea. U., Philippines; *Pol. Affi.* KMT; *Const.* Taipei County; Chmn., Taipei County Folk Athletics Cttee.; *Add.* Rm. 503, 1 Tsingtao E. Rd., Taipei.

CHEN, JOHNSON C.T. 陳瓊讚
Mem., Finance Cttee., Legis. Yuan, 96-; *b.* July 1, '41; *educ.* LL.B., NTU; *Pol. Affi.* KMT; *Const.* Tchr., Mem., NA; Taipei & Kaohsiung Dist. Court Prosecutor; Lawyer; *Add.* Rm. 213, 4 Tsingtao E. Rd., Taipei.

CHEN, KUANG-FU 陳光復
Mem., Educ. Cttee., Legis. Yuan 94-; *b.* Oct. 25, '55; *educ.* Grad., Hsi Hsin Theology Coll.; *Pol. Affi.* DPP; *Const.* Kaohsiung City; Mem., 2nd & 3rd Kaohsiung CCoun.; Mem., 2nd Legis. Yuan, Convener, Educ. Cttee.; Dep. Exec. Dir., DPP Caucus, Legis. Yuan; Mem., 1st, 2nd, & 3rd NA, DPP, Exec. Mem., 4th term CC; *Add.* Rm. 327, 1 Tsingtao E. Rd., Taipei.

CHEN, KUEI-MIAO 陳癸淼
Mem., For. & Ovs. Ch. Aff. Cttee., 2nd Sess., Legis. Yuan 97-; *b.* July 1, '34; *educ.* B., NTNU 57; *Pol. Affi.* NP; *Const.* Nat.; Chmn., Taichung City Cttee., KMT 78-80, Exec. Mem., Twn. Prov. Cttee. 80-83; Comr., TPA 83-86; Acting Mayor, Tainan City 86; Curator, Nat. Museum of Hist. 86-90; Mem., Nat. Def. Cttee., Legis. Yuan 94; *Add.* Rm. 407, 1 Tsingtao E. Rd., Taipei.

CHEN, TING-NAN
(See CHEN, DING-NAN 陳定南)

CHEN, WEN-HUI 陳文輝
Mem., Econ. Cttee., 2nd Sess., Legis. Yuan 97-; *b.* Sept. 26, '43; *educ.* Grad., Hsinming High Sch. *Pol. Affi.* DPP;

Const. Miaoli County; Mem., Miaoli CoCoun.; *Add.* Rm. 618, 1 Tsingtao E. Rd., Taipei.

CHEN, YI-HSIN 陳一新

Mem., Nat. Def. Cttee., 2nd Sess., Legis. Yuan 97-; *b.* Feb. 5, '50; *educ.* BA, Sch. of Arts & Sc., Columbia U., Ph.D., Dept. of Pol. Sc.; *Pol. Affi.* NP; *Const.* Nat.; Inst. of Intl. Rel., NCU 88-96; Dep. Sec.-Gen., APLFD 90-96; Convener, For. & Ovs. Ch. Aff. Cttee., Legis. Yuan 96; *Add.* Rm. 626, 10 Tsingtao E. Rd., Taipei.

CHEN, YONG-HSIN 陳永興

Mem., Educ. Cttee., 2nd Sess., Legis. Yuan 97-; *b.* Aug. 12, '50; *educ.* MPH, Berkeley U.; *Pol. Affi.* DPP; *Const.* Hualien County; Mem., CSC & DPP; Gen. Convener, DPP Caucus, NA; Pub., *Twn. Lit.*; Sec.-Gen., Twn. Union of Med.; Chmn., Twn. Human Rights Soc.; Founder, Voice of Hope Radio, Hualien; Convener, Educ. Cttee., Legis. Yuan 96; *Add.* Rm. 315, 10 Tsingtao E. Rd., Taipei.

CHEN, YUNG-HSING

(See CHEN, YONG-HSIN 陳永興)

CHENG, CHAO-MING 鄭朝明

Mem., Organic Laws Cttee., 2nd Sess., Legis. Yuan 97-; *b.* Mar. 9, '52; *educ.* MBA, Mercer U., USA; *Pol. Affi.* DPP; *Const.* Pingtung County; Exec. Dir., 1st term Pingtung Cttee., DPP; Mem., 10th term Pingtung CoCoun., Dep. Spkr., 11th term Pingtung CoCoun.; Mem., Budget Cttee., Legis. Yuan 96; *Add.* Rm. 326, 10 Tsingtao E. Rd., Taipei.

CHENG, FENG-SHIH 鄭逢時

Mem., Educ. Cttee., 2nd Sess., Legis. Yuan 97-; Dir.-Gen., Dept. of Intra- & Inter-Party Rel., CC, KMT 93-; *b.* Dec. 27, '41; *educ.* Grad., Supplementary Open Jr. Coll. for PA, NCU; MPA, Tunghai U.; *Pol. Affi.* KMT; *Const.* Taipei County; Mem., Taipei CoCoun. 68-73, NA 73-79, & TPA, 81-93; Dep. Dir., Twn. Prov. Cttee., KMT 89-93; Mem., Trans. & Comms. Cttee., Legis. Yuan 94; *Add.* 158 Chung Shan Rd., Sect. 1, Panchaio, Taipei County.

CHENG, LUNG-SHUI 鄭龍水

Mem., Educ. Cttee., Legis. Yuan 96-; *b.* Dec. 7, '59; *educ.* BA., Tamkang U.; *Pol. Affi.* NP; *Const.* Nat.;

Founder, Pub. & Ed.-in-Chief, *Echo; Add.* Rm. 643, 1 Tsingtao E. Rd., Taipei.

CHENG, PAO-CHING 鄭寶清

Mem., Trans. & Comms. Cttee., 2nd Sess., Legis. Yuan 97-; *b.* Jan. 10, '55; *educ.* MPA, NCHU; *Pol. Affi.* DPP; *Const.* Taoyuan County; Mem. & Convener, NA; Dir., Secretariat, CC, DPP; Chmn., DPP's Taoyuan County Cttee.; Pres., Soc. of DPP's Cttees. Chmn. Nationwide; Mem., Educ. Cttee., Legis. Yuan 96; *Add.* Rm. 302, 10 Tsingtao E. Rd., Taipei.

CHENG, YUNG-CHIN 鄭永金

Convener, Trans. & Comms. Cttee., Legis. Yuan 96-; *b.* Oct. 8, '49; *educ.* Grad., Tahua Ind. Coll.; *Pol. Affi.* KMT; *Const.* Hsinchu County; Dep. Spkr. & Spkr., Hsinchu CoCoun.; *Add.* Rm. 106, 10 Tsingtao E. Rd., Taipei.

CHIEN, CHIN-CHING 簡金卿

Mem., Econ. Cttee., 2nd Sess., Legis. Yuan 97-; *b.* Oct. 30, '28; *educ.* Grad., Law Sch., Kinki U., Japan; *Poli. Affi.* KMT; *Const.* Nat.; Mem., Nantou CoCoun. 58-61 & 77-89, Dep. Spkr. 82-89; Mem., Nantou CoCoun. 58-61, 77-80; Mem., TPA 89-92; Mem., CC, KMT 94; Mem., NUC, Off. of the Pres. 95; Mem., Educ. Cttee., 1st Sess., Legis. Yuan 96; *Add.* Rm. 122, 1 Tsingtao E. Rd., Taipei.

CHIEN, HSI-CHIEH 簡錫堦

Mem., Home & Border Aff. Cttee., 2nd Sess., Legis. Yuan 97-; *b.* Mar. 15, '47; *educ.* BA, Tamsui Oxford U. Coll.; *Pol. Affi.* DPP; *Const.* Nat.; Mem., CC, DPP 86-87; Sec.-Gen., Twn. Labor Front 90-95; Adv., Twn. Labor Union of Comms. Ind. & Twn. Labor Union of Petroleum Ind.; Convener, Jud. Cttee., Legis. Yuan 96; *Add.* 4th Fl.-8, 4 Tsingtao E. Rd., Taipei.

CHIEN, TA 錢達

Mem., For. & Ovs. Ch. Aff. Cttee., Legis. Yuan 96-; *b.* Jan. 11, '53; *educ.* MS, Texas U., USA; *Pol. Affi.* NP; *Const.* Ovs. Nat.; Chmn., 1st & 2nd term, Bd. of Trustees, Ch. Dem. Front; Exec. Mem., Ovs. Br. of Soc. for Regenerating Ch.; Exec. Dir., Soc. for Preserving Hist. Archives Concerning War Against Japanese Aggression; *Add.* Rm. 407, 10 Tsingtao E. Rd., Taipei.

CHIN TSEN, CHEN-LI 靳曾珍麗
Convener, Nat. Def. Cttee., Legis. Yuan 96-; *b.* Aug. 29, '33; *educ.* MPH, U. of Dubuque; *Pol. Affi.* KMT; *Const.* Nat.; *Add.* Rm. 413, 10 Tsingtao E. Rd., Taipei.

CHIU, CHUI-CHEN 邱垂貞
Convener, Econ. Cttee., Legis. Yuan 94-; *b.* Oct. 13, '51; *educ.* Grad., Ch. Jr. Coll. of Marine Tech.; *Pol. Affi.* DPP; *Const.* Taoyuan County; Jailed for Kaohsiung Incident 79-85; Chmn., Taoyuan County Cttee., DPP 88-91, Dir., Dept. of Soc. Movement 91-92; *Add.* Rm. 631, 10 Tsingtao E. Rd., Taipei.

CHOU, ANGELA 周荃
Mem., Home & Border Aff. Cttee., 2nd Sess., Legis. Yuan 97-; *b.* July 3, '56; *educ.* BA, Ch. Cul. U.; *Pol. Affi.* NP; *Const.* Taipei City; Reporter, CTC; Mem., 1st & 2nd Legis. Yuan, Convener, Nat. Def. Cttee. 94; *Add.* Rm. 219, 1 Tsingtao E. Rd., Taipei.

CHOU, CHUAN
(See CHOU, ANGELA 周荃)

CHOU, DAVID P.L. 周伯倫
Mem., Organic Laws Cttee., 2nd Sess., Legis. Yuan 97-; *b.* Nov. 13, '54; *educ.* LL.B., Soochow U. 82; *Pol. Affi.* DPP; *Const.* Taipei County; Exec. Mem., 1st, 2nd, 3rd, & 6th term, CC, DPP, Mem., CSC; Mem., 5th & 6th term, Taipei CCoun. 87-92; Exec. Dir., DPP Caucus, Taipei CCoun.; Mem., 2nd Legis. Yuan, Mem., Educ. Cttee. 94; Exec. Dir., DPP Caucus, 6th Sess., 2nd Legis. Yuan; *Add.* 4th Fl.-3, 4 Tsingtao E. Rd., Taipei.

CHOU, PO-LUN
(See CHOU, DAVID P.L. 周伯倫)

CHOU, YANG-SHAN 周陽山
Mem., Jud. Cttee., 2nd Sess., Legis. Yuan 97-; *b.* Aug. 24, '57; *educ.* Ph.D., Columbia U., USA; *Pol. Affi.* NP; *Const.* Taipei City; Sp. Review Writer; Prof., NTU; Mem., For. & Ovs. Ch. Aff. Cttee., Legis. Yuan 96; *Add.* Rm. 405, 1 Tsingtao E. Rd., Taipei.

CHU, FENG-CHIH
(See CHU, HELEN FONG-CHI 朱鳳芝)

CHU, HELEN FONG-CHI 朱鳳芝
Mem., Nat. Def. Cttee., 2nd Sess., Legis. Yuan 97-; *b.* June 27, '48; *educ.* BS, NCKU 74; MBA, Northrop U. 86; *Pol. Affi.* KMT; *Const.* Taoyuan County; Mem., Taoyuan CoCoun.; Convener, Nat. Def. Cttee., 3rd Sess., 2nd Legis. Yuan, Organic Laws Cttee., 4th Sess. 94; Dep. Dir.-Gen. & Dep. Sec.-in-Chief., Dept. of Part-Govt. Coordination of the Legis. Yuan, KMT; *Add.* Rm. 429, 1 Tsingtao E. Rd., Taipei.

CHU, HSING-YU 朱星羽
Mem., Finance Cttee., Legis. Yuan 94-, & CSC, DPP 92-; *b.* Dec. 22, '56; *educ.* Grad., Dept. of Ind. Mng., Chenghsiu Jr. Coll. of Tech. & Com.; *Pol. Affi.* DPP; *Const.* Kaohsiung City; Mem., Kaohsiung CCoun. 75-93; *Add.* Rm. 620, 10 Tsingtao E. Rd., Taipei.

CHU, HUI-LIANG 朱惠良
Mem., Educ. Cttee., Legis. Yuan 96-; *b.* Dec. 16, '50; *educ.* Ph.D., Princeton U., USA; *Pol. Affi.* NP; *Const.* Taipei City; Assc. Prof., NTU; *Add.* Rm. 408, 10 Tsingtao E. Rd., Taipei.

CHUAN, WEN-SHENG 全文盛
Mem., Home & Border Aff. Cttee., Legis. Yuan 96-; *b.* Nov. 23, '58; *educ.* Grad., Chung Shan Med. & Dental Coll.; *Pol. Affi.* KMT; *Const.* Highland Aborigines; Magis., 11th & 12th term, Hsinyi Rural Township, Nantou County; *Add.* Rm. 102, 10 Tsingtao E. Rd., Taipei.

CHU, KAO-CHENG
(See JU, GAU-JENG 朱高正)

CHUANG, CHIN-SHENG 莊金生
Mem., Legis. Yuan 93-, Finance Cttee., 2nd Sess. 97-; *b.* July 13, '41; *educ.* LL.B., NCHU 64; *Pol. Affi.* KMT; *Const.* Lowland Aborigines; High Sch. Tchr.; Magis., Kuangfu Rural Township, Hualien County 73; Mem., TPA 78-85; *Add.* Rm. 112, 1 Tsingtao E. Rd., Taipei.

CHUNG, LI-TE 鍾利德
Mem., Trans. & Comms. Cttee., Legis. Yuan 96-; *b.* June 15, '42; *educ.* BA, NCHU; *Pol. Affi.* KMT; *Const.* Hualien County; Bu. Chief, Civil Aff., Hualien County Govt., Dir., Planning Dept.; *Add.* Rm. 211, 10 Tsingtao E. Rd., Taipei.

FAN, HSUN-LU 范巽綠
Mem., Educ. Cttee., 2nd Sess., Legis. Yuan 97-; *b.* Oct. 3, '52; *educ.* MA, Tamkang U.; *Pol. Affi.* DPP; *Const.* Nat.; Dir., Secretariat, CC, DPP, Mem., CAC (1st through 3rd term); Convener, Educ. Cttee., Legis. Yuan 96; *Add.* Rm. 221, 10 Tsingtao E. Rd., Taipei.

FENG, TING-KUO 馮定國
Mem., Home & Border Aff. Cttee., 2nd Sess., Legis. Yuan 97-; *b.* Sept. 24, '50; *educ.* Ph.D., U. of Denver, USA; *Pol. Affi.* NP; *Const.* Taichung County; Mem., CC, KMT; Mem., 5th term, Taipei CCoun., Adv.; Mem., Presidium, NA; Mem., Budget Cttee., Legis. Yuan 96; *Add.* Rm. 428, 1 Tsingtao E. Rd., Taipei.

FU, KUEN-CHEN 傅崑成
Mem., Organic Laws Cttee., 2nd Sess., Legis. Yuan 97-; *b.* Nov. 4, '51; *educ.* LL.D., U. of Virginia; *Pol. Affi.* NP; *Const.* Taipei County; Bd. Mem. & Sec.-Gen., Ch. Intl. Law Soc.; *Ch. Times*'s Corr. in New York, Sp. Review Writer, Ed. & Translator; Mem., NA; Mem., For. & Ovs. Ch. Aff. Cttee., Legis. Yuan 96; *Add.* Rm. 625, 10 Tsingtao E. Rd., Taipei.

FU, KUN-CHENG
(See FU, KUEN-CHEN 傅崑成)

HAN, DANIEL K.Y. 韓國瑜
Mem., Nat. Def. Cttee., Legis. Yuan 96-; *b.* June 17, '57; *educ.* BA, Soochow U.; LL.M., NCU; *Pol. Affi.* KMT; *Const.* Taipei County; Writer, *Ch. Times;* Mem., Taipei CoCoun.; Mem., 2nd Legis. Yuan; *Add.* Rm. 103, 1 Tsingtao E. Rd., Taipei.

HAN, KUO-YU
(See HAN, DANIEL K.Y. 韓國瑜)

HAO, LUNG-PIN
(See HAU, LUN-PIN 郝龍斌)

HAU, LUN-PIN 郝龍斌
Mem., Budget Cttee., 2nd Sess., Legis. Yuan 97-; *b.* Aug. 22, '52; *educ.* Ph.D., U. of Massachusetts; *Pol. Affi.* NP; *Const.* Taipei City; Project Adv., ROC Red Cross; Convener, Educ. Cttee., Legis. Yuan 96; *Add.* Rm. 130, 10 Tsingtao E. Rd., Taipei.

HONG, CHI-CHANG 洪奇昌
Mem., For. & Ovs. Ch. Aff. Cttee., Legis. Yuan 89-; *b.* Aug. 23, '51; *educ.* MPH, NTU; M., Health Sc., U. of Toronto; *Pol. Affi.* DPP; *Const.* Nat.; Mem., NA 86-89; Convener, Econ. Cttee.; *Add.* Rm. 307, 1 Tsingtao E. Rd., Taipei.

HONG, YUH-CHIN 洪玉欽
Mem., For. & Ovs. Ch. Aff. Cttee., Legis. Yuan 96-; Sup., Cent. Policy Cttee., KMT 93-; *b.* July 11, '43; *educ.* LL.B., Soochow U. 67; LL.M., Ch. Cul. U., LL.D. 79; *Pol. Affi.* KMT; *Const.* Tainan County; Dep. Sec.-Gen., Cent. Policy Cttee., KMT 88-89; Dir.-Gen., Dept. of Intra- & Inter-Party Rel., CC, KMT & concur. Dept. of Party-Govt. Coordination of the Legis. Yuan 92-93, Mem., Cent. Policy Cttee. 93-94; Mem., Econ. Cttee., Legis. Yuan 94, For. & Ovs. Aff. Cttee. 95; Dep. Sec.-Gen., CC, KMT 94-96; *Add.* Rm. 515, 1 Tsingtao E. Rd., Taipei.

HSIAO, CHIN-LAN 蕭金蘭
Mem., Budget Cttee., 2nd Sess., Legis. Yuan 97-; *b.* Aug. 26, '48; *educ.* B., Dept. of Acct., NCU 70; *Pol. Affi.* KMT; *Const.* Kaohsiung County; Mem., CC, KMT, & Kaohsiung CoCoun. (2 terms); Convener, Budget Cttee., & Organic Laws Cttee., Legis. Yuan, Exec. Mem., KMT Caucus; Mem., Finance Cttee., Legis. Yuan 94; *Add.* Rm. 403, 1 Tsingtao E. Rd., Taipei.

HSIAO, YU-CHEN 蕭裕珍
Mem., Trans. & Comms. Cttee., 2nd Sess., Legis. Yuan 97-; *b.* Aug. 6, '56; *educ.* LL.B., NTU; *Pol. Affi.* DPP; *Const.* Taipei City; Exec. Mem., CC, DPP, Exec. Dir., Women's Dev. Cttee., Convener, 1st term CAC; Mem., For. & Ovs. Ch. Cttee., Legis. Yuan 96; *Add.* Rm. 331, 10 Tsingtao E. Rd., Taipei.

HSIEH, C.T. 謝啟大
Mem., Jud. Cttee., 2nd Sess., Legis. Cttee. 97-; *b.* Feb. 10, '49; *educ.* LL.M., NTU 84; *Pol. Affi.* NP; *Const.* Hsinchu City; Judge, Hualien Br., Twn. High Court, Hsinchu Dist. Court, & Ilan Dist. Court; Convener, Organic Laws Cttee., Legis. Yuan 96; *Add.* Rm. 216, 1 Tsingtao E. Rd., Taipei.

HSIEH, CHIN-CHUAN 謝錦川
Mem., Finance Cttee., 2nd Sess., Legis. Yuan 97-; *b.* Feb. 11, '44; *educ.* Grad., World Coll. of Jour. & Comms.;

Studied, Georgetown U.; *Pol. Affi.* DPP; *Const.* Tainan County; Mem., Tainan CoCoun.; Chmn., Tainan Cttee., DPP; Mem., Budget Cttee., Legis. Yuan 96; *Add.* Rm. 318, 10 Tsingtao E. Rd., Taipei.

HSIEH, CHIN-TZUNG 謝欽宗
Mem., Home & Border Aff. Cttee., Legis. Yuan 96-; *b.* May 20, '52; *educ.* BCE, Ch. Cul. U.; *Pol. Affi.* KMT; *Const.* Taipei; *Add.* Rm. 416, 10 Tsingtao E. Rd., Taipei.

HSIEH, CHI-TA
(See HSIEH, C.T. 謝啟大)

HSIEH, ROGER 謝聰敏
Mem., Organic Laws Cttee., 2nd Sess., Legis. Yuan 97-; *b.* May 2, '34; *educ.* LL.B., NTU 58; LL.M., NCU 62; *Pol. Affi.* DPP; *Const.* Nat.; Mem., Formosan Assn. for Public Aff. 81-89, V. Chmn.; Sec.-Gen., Twn. Dem. Org. Ovs. 86-88; Mem., Econ. Cttee., Legis. Yuan 94; *Add.* Rm. 205, 1 Tsingtao E. Rd., Taipei.

HSIEH, TSUNG-MIN
(See HSIEH, ROGER 謝聰敏)

HSU, CHENG-KUN
(See HSU, ROBERT 徐成焜)

HSU, CHUNG-HSIUNG
(See SHYU, JONG-SHYONG 徐中雄)

HSU, ROBERT 徐成焜
Mem., Econ. Cttee., 2nd Sess., Legis. Yuan 97-; *b.* Jan. 4, '47; *educ.* BPS, NTU; *Pol. Affi.* KMT; *Const.* Miaoli County; Convener, Econ. Cttee., 4th Sess., 2nd Legis. Yuan 94, Mem., 5th & 6th Sess.; Chmn., New Policy Assn., Legis. Yuan; Dep. Sec.-in-Chief, Dept. of Party-Govt. Coordination of the Legis. Yuan, KMT; *Add.* 16th Fl., 15-1 Hangchow S. Rd., Sect. 1, Taipei.

HSU, SHAO-PING 徐少萍
Mem., For. & Ovs. Ch. Cttee., Legis. Yuan 96-; *b.* May 16, '41; *educ.* LL.B., Soochow U.; *Pol. Affi.* KMT; *Const.* Keelung City; *Add.* Rm. 108, 10 Tsingtao E. Rd., Taipei.

HSU, SHU-PAO 許舒博
Mem., Econ. Cttee., 2nd Sess., Legis. Yuan 97-; *b.* July 10, '63; *educ.* BA, Luven U., Belgium; *Pol. Affi.* KMT;

Const. Yunlin County; Convener, Econ. Cttee., Legis. Yuan 96; *Add.* Rm. 423, 1 Tsingtao E. Rd., Taipei.

HSU, TAIN-TSAIR 許添財
Mem., Finance Cttee., 2nd Sess., Legis. Yuan 97-; Mem., World United Formosans for Independence 85-, & N. Am.'s Twn. Prof. Assn. 85-; *b.* Jan. 23, '51; *educ.* M., Econ., Ch. Cul. U. 76; *Pol. Affi.* Independent; *Const.* Tainan City; Convener, Budget Review Cttee., Legis. Yuan, Mem., Rules Cttee.; *Add.* Rm. 310, 1 Tsingtao E. Rd., Taipei.

HSU, TIEN-TSAI
(See HSU, TAIN-TSAIR 許添財)

HUANG, CHING-LIN 黃清林
Mem., For. & Ovs. Ch. Cttee., 2nd Sess., Legis. Yuan 97-; *b.* Feb. 15, '32; *educ.* MPS, Cent. U., Japan; *Pol. Affi.* KMT; *Const.* Ovs. Nat.; Chmn., Ovs. Ch. Students Assn. in Japan; Convener, For. & Ovs. Ch. Aff. Cttee., Legis. Yuan 96; *Add.* Rm. 509, 10 Tsingtao E. Rd., Taipei.

HUANG, CHU-WEN 黃主文
Mem., Jud. Cttee., Legis. Yuan 94-; Dep. Exec., Cent. Policy Cttee., KMT 94-; *b.* Aug. 20, '41; *educ.* LL.B., NTU 64; *Pol. Affi.* KMT; *Const.* Taoyuan County; Public Prosecutor 67-76; Attorney-at-Law 76-84; Dir., Policy Res. Cttee., KMT 93-94; *Add.* Rm. 421, 1 Tsingtao E. Rd., Taipei.

HUANG, ERH-HSUAN 黃爾璇
Mem., Nat. Def. Cttee., 2nd Sess., Legis. Yuan 97-; *b.* Mar. 5, '36; *educ.* MPA & DPS, NCU; *Pol. Affi.* DPP; *Const.* Nat.; Sec.-Gen., DPP 86-88; Mem., Econ. Cttee., Legis. Yuan 96; *Add.* Rm. 602, 10 Tsingtao E. Rd., Taipei.

HUANG, HSIU-MENG 黃秀孟
Mem., Econ. Cttee., 2nd Sess., Legis. Yuan 97-; *b.* Oct. 2, '44; *educ.* BA, NTNU; *Pol. Affi.* KMT; *Const.* Tainan County; Mem., TPA; Mem., Finance Cttee., Legis. Yuan 96; *Add.* Rm. 412, 10 Tsingtao E. Rd., Taipei.

HUANG, KUO-CHUNG 黃國鐘
Mem., Budget Cttee., Legis. Yuan 96-; *b.* Aug. 16, '54; *educ.* LL.M., Yale U.; *Pol. Affi.* NP; *Const.* Kaohsiung

City; Acting Chmn., Ch. Soc. Dem. Party; *Add.* Rm. 629, 10 Tsingtao E. Rd., Taipei.

HUANG, TIEN-FU 黃天福
Mem., Budget Cttee., 2nd Sess., Legis. Yuan 97-; *b.* Feb. 8, '38; *educ.* BPS, NTU; *Pol. Affi.* NP; *Const.* Taipei City; Mem., NA; Convener, Organic Laws Cttee., Legis. Yuan 96; *Add.* Rm. 225, 1 Tsingtao E. Rd., Taipei.

HUNG, CHAO-NAN 洪昭男
Mem., Organic Laws Cttee., 2nd Sess., Legis. Yuan 97-; Dep. Dir., Cent. Policy Cttee., KMT 94-; *b.* Aug. 24, '43; *educ.* BA, Soochow U.; MA, U. of Arkansas; *Pol. Affi.* KMT; *Const.* Taichung City; Consul, Consl.-Gen., San Francisco 68-80; Mem., Legis. Yuan; Dep. Dir.-Gen., Dept. of Ovs. Aff., CC, KMT 93-94; Mem., Trans. & Comms. Cttee., Legis. Yuan 94; *Add.* Rm. 212, 1 Tsingtao E. Rd., Taipei.

HUNG, CHI-CHANG
(See HONG, CHI-CHANG 洪奇昌)

HUNG, HSING-JUNG 洪性榮
Mem., Organic Laws Cttee., 2nd Sess., Legis. Yuan 97-; *b.* May 13, '40; *educ.* B., Nat. Changhua U. of Educ.; *Pol. Affi.* KMT; *Const.* Changhua County; Mem., Changhua CoCoun., & 7th & 8th TPA; Adv., TPG; Mem., Finance Cttee., Legis. Yuan 94; *Add.* Rm. 433, 1 Tsingtao E. Rd., Taipei.

HUNG, HSIU-CHU 洪秀柱
Mem., Educ. Cttee., Legis. Yuan 94-; Dep. Dir., Dept. of Youth Aff., CC, KMT 94-; *b.* Apr. 7, '48; *educ.* LL.B., Ch. Cul. U. 70; Ed.M., N.E. Missouri State U. 91; *Pol. Affi.* KMT; *Const.* Taipei County; Dir., Dept. of Women's Aff., Taipei County Cttee., KMT 80-86, Sup., Twn. Prov. Cttee. 86-90; Dep. Sec.-Gen., KMT Caucus, Legis. Yuan 93-94; Dep. Dir., Cent. Policy Cttee. of the Legis. Yuan, KMT 93-94; *Add.* Rm. 113, 1 Tsingtao E. Rd., Taipei.

HUNG, YU-CHIN
(See HONG, YUH-CHIN 洪玉欽)

HWANG, CHAO-SHUN 黃昭順
Mem., Jud. Cttee., 2nd Sess., Legis. Yuan 97-; *b.* Aug. 22, '53; *educ.* B., Pharmacology, Kaohsiung Med. Coll.;

Pol. Affi. KMT; *Const.* Kaohsiung City; Mem., Kaohsiung CCoun. 81-92; Mem., Trans. & Comms. Cttee., Legis. Yuan 94; *Add.* Rm. 422, 1 Tsingtao E. Rd., Taipei.

JAO, EUGENE YUNG-CHING 趙永清
Convener, Home & Border Aff. Cttee., Legis. Yuan 94-; *b.* Nov. 9, '57; *educ.* BPS, NCU; MPS, New York U.; *Pol. Affi.* KMT; *Const.* Taipei County; Founding Mem., New Policy Assn., Legis. Yuan; *Add.* Rm. 511, 2nd Fl., 3 Tsingtao E. Rd., Taipei.

JAO, YING-CHI
(See YAO, ENG-CHI 饒穎奇)

JU, GAU-JENG 朱高正
Mem., Organic Laws Cttee., 2nd Sess., Legis. Yuan 97-, Mem. 87-; *b.* Oct. 6, '54; *educ.* LL.B., NTU 77; Ph.D., U. of Bonn 85; *Pol. Affi.* NP; *Const.* Yunlin County; Bd. Chmn., Taipei County Br., DPP Public Policy Res. Cttee. 86-87; Founding Chmn., Ch. Soc. Dem. Party 91-94; *Add.* Rm. 111, 1 Chung Shan S. Rd., Taipei.

KAO, ALICE H.E. 高惠宇
Mem., For. & Ovs. Ch. Aff. Cttee. 97-; *b.* Jan. 21, '48; *educ.* BA, NTNU 70; MA, U. of Utah; *Pol. Affi.* NP; *Const.* Taipei City; Mem., Organic Laws Cttee., Legis. Yuan 96; *Add.* Rm. 409, 1 Tsingtao E. Rd., Taipei.

KAO, HUI-YU
(See KAO, ALICE H.E. 高惠宇)

KAO, YANG-SHEN 高揚昇
Mem., Econ. Cttee., Legis. Yuan 96-; *b.* July 11, '52; *educ.* BA, Fu Jen Catholic U.; *Pol. Affi.* KMT; *Const.* Highland Aborigines; *Add.* Rm. 621, 10 Tsingtao E. Rd., Taipei.

KAO, YU-JEN 高育仁
Mem., Finance Cttee., 2nd Sess., Legis. Yuan 97-; Chmn., UN Assn. of ROC 95-, Ch. Assn. for Human Rights 93-, & the 21st Century Found. 88-; *b.* Aug. 30, '34; *educ.* LL.B., NTU 56; Hon. LL.D., St. Johns U. 90; *Pol. Affi.* KMT; *Const.* Tainan County; Magis., Tainan County 73-76; Admin. V. Min. of the Int. 76-78; Dir., Secretariat, CC, KMT 78-79; Comr., Dept. of Civil Aff., TPG 79-81; Spkr., TPA 81-89; Chmn., Ch. C.'s Fund. 94; Mem., Trans. & Comms. Cttee., Legis. Yuan 94; *Add.* 10th Fl., 380 Keelung Rd., Sect. 1, Taipei.

KER, CHIEN-MING 柯建銘
Mem., Econ. Cttee., Legis. Yuan 94-; *b.* Sept. 8, '51; *educ.* Grad., Chung Shan Med. & Dental Coll.; *Pol. Affi.* DPP; *Const.* Hsinchu City; Convener, Arbitrary Cttee., Hsinchu City Br., DPP 86-93; Dep. Dir., DPP Caucus, Legis. Yuan 93-94; *Add.* Rm. 619, 10 Tsingtao E. Rd., Taipei.

KO, CHIEN-MING
(See KER, CHIEN-MING 柯建銘)

KO, YU-CHIN 葛雨琴
Mem., For. & Ovs. Ch. Aff. Cttee., Legis. Yuan 94-; *b.* June 21, '39; *educ.* LL.B., Soochow U. 62; *Pol. Affi.* KMT; *Const.* Nat.; Comr., COLA; Convener, Home & Border Aff. Cttee., & For. & Ovs. Ch. Aff. Cttee.; *Add.* Rm. 429, 1 Tsingtao E. Rd., Taipei.

KUO, CHENG-CHUAN 郭正權
Mem., Finance Cttee., Legis. Yuan 94-; *b.* Nov. 13, '53; *educ.* Grad., Cent. Police Coll.; *Pol. Affi.* KMT; *Const.* Taichung County; Chief, Wufeng Police Precinct Hqs., Taichung County Police Hqs.; Sup., Twn. Prov. Police Admin.; *Add.* Rm. 418, 1 Tsingtao E. Rd., Taipei.

KUO, CHIN-SHENG 郭金生
Mem., Budget Cttee., 2nd Sess., Legis. Yuan 97-; *b.* Feb. 23, '53; *educ.* Grad., Nat. Kaohsiung Inst. of Marine Tech. 89-91; *Pol. Affi.* KMT; *Const.* Kaohsiung City; Mem., Kaohsiung CCoun. 89-92; Convener, Finance Cttee., Legis. Yuan 94; *Add.* 8th Fl.-2, 71 Jen Ai Rd., Sect. 2, Taipei.

KUO, TING-TSAI 郭廷才
Mem., Finance Cttee., Legis. Yuan 94-; *b.* Sept. 28, '36; *educ.* Grad., Dept. of Business Mng., Calif. Multiversity U.; *Pol. Affi.* KMT; *Const.* Pingtung County; Magis., Tungkang Urban Township, Pingtung County 68-78; Mem., Pingtung CoCoun. 78-92, Spkr. 82-92; *Add.* Rm. 626, 10 Tsingtao E. Rd., Taipei.

LAI, LAI-KUN 賴來焜
Mem., Jud. Cttee., 2nd Sess., Legis. Yuan 97-; *b.* Jan. 25, '56; *educ.* LL.D. NCU; *Pol. Affi.* NP; *Const.* Taoyuan County; Mem., Taipei City Election Cttee.; Assc. Prof., Chung Yuan Christian U., Soochow U., Tunghai U., & World Coll. of Jour. & Comms.; Convener, Jud. Cttee., Legis. Yuan 96; *Add.* Rm. 128, 1 Tsingtao E. Rd., Taipei.

LEE, CHIN-YUNG
(See LEE, JOHN C.Y. 李進勇)

LEE, CHING-HUA 李慶華
Mem., Educ. Cttee., 2nd Sess., Legis. Yuan 97-; Convener, NP Caucus, Legis. Yuan; *b.* Dec. 3, '48; *educ.* Ph.D. in Hist., New York U. 84; *Pol. Affi.* NP; *Const.* Taipei City; Co-founder, NP; Convener, NP Caucus, Legis. Yuan; Mem., Nat. Def. Cttee., Legis. Yuan 94; *Add.* 2nd Fl.-1, 4 Tsingtao E. Rd., Taipei.

LEE, CHUN-I
(See LEE, CHUN-YEE 李俊毅)

LEE, CHUN-YEE 李俊毅
Mem., Home & Border Aff. Cttee., 2nd Sess., Legis. Yuan 97-; *b.* Mar. 20, '59; *educ.* MCE, NCU; *Pol. Affi.* DPP; *Const.* Tainan County; Sp., CEC, DPP, Exec. Dir., Tainan County Cttee. 92; Election campaigns mgr. for Chen Ting-nan, Chen Tang-shan, Peng Ming-min, & Hsieh Chang-ting; Mem., Organic Laws Cttee., Legis. Yuan 96; *Add.* Rm. 329, 1 Tsingtao E. Rd., Taipei.

LEE, HSIEN-JUNG
(See LEE, SEN-ZONG 李顯榮)

LEE, JOHN C.Y. 李進勇
Mem., Jud. Cttee., 2nd Sess., Legis. Yuan 97-; *b.* Aug. 1, '51; *educ.* LL.B., NCHU 75; LL.M., NTU 81; *Pol. Affi.* DPP; *Const.* Keelung City; Judge, Haulien, Ilan, Taichung Dist. Court; Dir.-Gen., Keelung City Cttee., DPP; Mem., Budget Cttee., Legis. Yuan 94; *Add.* Rm. 628, 10 Tsingtao E. Rd., Taipei.

LEE, SEN-ZONG 李顯榮
Mem., Trans. & Comms. Cttee., Legis. Yuan 94-; *b.* July 23, '47; *educ.* M., Public Engr., U. of San Francisco; *Pol. Affi.* KMT; *Const.* Taipei County; Mem., Taipei CoCoun. 81-89; Convener, Home & Border Aff. Cttee., Legis. Yuan 93-94, Trans. & Comms. Cttee. 94; *Add.* Rm. 213, 1 Tsingtao E. Rd., Taipei.

LEE, YEOU-CHI 李友吉
Mem., Home & Border Aff. Cttee., Legis. Yuan 94-; Standing Mem., Ch. Fed. of Labor 75-; *b.* Oct. 19, '39; *educ.* Grad., Nat. Twn. Acad. of Arts 71; *Pol. Affi.* KMT;

Const. Nat.; Mem., NA 73-81; Chmn., Twn. Prov. To-bacco & Wine Ind. Unions 72-76; *Add.* Rm. 501, 1 Tsingtao E. Rd., Taipei.

LEE, YING-YUAN 李應元
Mem., Home & Border Aff. Cttee., 2nd Sess., Legis. Yuan 97-; *b.* Mar. 16, '53; *educ.* Ph.D., U. of N. Carolina at Chapel Hill; *Pol. Affi.* DPP; *Const.* Taipei County; V. Chmn., Twn. Independence & Nation-Building Alliance; Convener, For. & Ovs. Ch. Aff. Cttee., Legis. Yuan 96; *Add.* Rm. 325, 10 Tsingtao E. Rd., Taipei.

LEE, YU-CHI
(See LEE, YEOU-CHI 李友吉)

LI, M.K. 李鳴皋
Mem., Nat. Def. Cttee., Legis. Yuan 94-; *b.* Nov. 22, '32; *educ.* Grad., Naval Cmd. & Staff Coll., Armed Forces U. 70, & Naval War Coll. 80; *Pol. Affi.* KMT; *Const.* Nat.; Fleet Cmdt.; Rear Adm.; V. Adm., Lo-gistic; C-in-C, Admiralty; *Add.* Rm. 206, 1 Tsingtao E. Rd., Taipei.

LI, MING-KAO
(See LI, M.K. 李鳴皋)

LI, PI-HSIEN 李必賢
Mem., Jud. Cttee., 2nd Sess., Legis. Yuan 97-; Chmn., Soc. for Wildlife & Nature of Kaohsiung, ROC; *b.* Nov. 26, '47; *educ.* LL.B., Osaka City U.; *Pol. Affi.* KMT; *Const.* Kaohsiung City; Mem., Finance Cttee., Legis. Yuan 94, Convener; *Add.* 7th Fl., 7 Tsingtao E. Rd., Taipei.

LI, WEN-LANG 李文郎
Mem., Educ. Cttee., 2nd Sess., Legis. Yuan 97-; Prof., Sociology, U. of Penn. 81-; *b.* Sept. 19, '38; *educ.* Ph.D., U. of Penn. 67; *Pol. Affi.* KMT; *Const.* Ovs. Nat.; Dir., Grad. Sch. of Sociology, U. of Penn. 84-88; Exec. Sec.; Am. Ch. Studies Assn.; Mem., For. & Ovs. Ch. Aff. Cttee., Legis. Yuan 96; *Add.* Rm. 627, 10 Tsingtao E. Rd., Taipei.

LIAO, HSUEH-KUANG 廖學廣
Mem., Home & Border Aff. Cttee., 2nd Sess., Legis. Yuan 97-; *b.* Jan. 23, '54; *educ.* MA, San Diego State U.; BA,

NTU; *Pol. Affi.* Independent; *Const.* Taipei County; Mem., 10th & 11th term, Taipei CoCoun.; Magis., 11th & 12th term, Hsichih Urban Township, Taipei County; *Add.* Rm. 429, 10 Tsingtao E. Rd., Taipei.

LIAO, FU-PEN
(See LIAO, HWU-PENG 廖福本)

LIAO, HWU-PENG 廖福本
Mem., Budget Cttee., Legis. Yuan 94-; *b.* June 1, '38; *educ.* B., NTU; M., Ch. Cul. U.; *Pol. Affi.* KMT; *Const.* Yunlin County; Chmn., Hualien County Cttee., KMT 77-79; Sect. Chief, Dept. of Civil Aff., TPG 79-81; Dep. Party Whip, KMT Caucus, Legis. Yuan; Dep. Dir.-Gen., Dept. of Ovs. Aff., CC, KMT; Dir.-Gen., Dept. of Party-Govt. Coordination of the Legis. Yuan, KMT 94; *Add.* 7th Fl.-7, 7 Tsingtao E. Rd., Taipei.

LIAO, TA-LIN
(See LIAU, T. LIN 廖大林)

LIAU, T. LIN 廖大林
Mem., Finance Cttee., 2nd Sess., Legis. Yuan 97-; *b.* Mar. 5, '36; *educ.* B., Econ., NTU; Ph.D., Statistics, Texas A & M U.; *Pol. Affi.* DPP; *Const.* Yunlin County; Twn. Human Rights Assn. (Washington, D.C.) 88-89; Mem., For. & Ovs. Ch. Aff. Cttee., Legis. Yuan 94; *Add.* Rm. 328, 1 Tsingtao E. Rd., Taipei.

LIN, CHE-FU 林哲夫
Mem., For. & Ovs Ch. Aff. Cttee., Legis. Yuan 96-; *b.* June 2, '32; *educ.* Grad., NTNU; Ph.D., Toronto U., Can.; *Pol. Affi.* DPP; *Const.* Ovs. Nat.; Chmn., Twn. In-dependence & Nation-Building Alliance, Can., Chmn., Cttee. of Human Rights; *Add.* Rm. 308 1 Tsingtao E. Rd., Taipei.

LIN, CHENG-TSE 林政則
Mem., Educ. Cttee., Legis. Yuan 96-; *b.* Feb. 5, '44; *educ.* MA, Nat. U., USA; *Pol. Affi.* KMT; *Const.* Hsinchu City; Mem. Hsinchu CCoun.; Mem., NA; *Add.* Rm. 427, 10 Tsingtao E. Rd., Taipei.

LIN, CHIEN-JUNG 林建榮
Mem., Trans. & Comms. Cttee., Legis. Yuan 96-; *b.* Jan. 18, '46; *educ.* MA., Educ., NTNU; Instr., NTNU; *Pol.*

Affi. KMT; *Const.* Ilan County; Mayor, 9th, 11th & 12th term, Ilan City; *Add.* Rm. 502, 10 Tsingtao E. Rd., Taipei.

LIN, CHIH-CHIA 林志嘉
Mem., Jud. Cttee., 2nd Sess., Legis. Yuan 97-; Sec.-Gen., KMT Caucus, Legis. Yuan 94-; Dir., Policy Res. Cttee., KMT 94-; *b.* Mar. 31, '58; *educ.* BS, Chem., Fu Jen Catholic U. 81; MS, Chem., Tennesse State U. 87; *Pol. Affi.* KMT; *Const.* Taipei County; Convener, Home & Border Aff. Cttee., Legis. Yuan 91-92, Dep. Dir., KMT Caucus 92-93; Mem., Home & Border Aff. Cttee., Legis. Yuan 94; *Add.* Rm. 230, 1 Tsingtao E. Rd., Taipei.

LIN, CHO-SHUI 林濁水
Mem., Organic Laws Cttee., 2nd Sess., Legis. Yuan 97-; *b.* Mar. 25, '47; *educ.* B., NCU; *Pol. Affi.* DPP; *Const.* Taipei City; Mem., CAC, DPP; Convener, Organic Laws Cttee., Legis. Yuan 94; Chief Ed. Writer, *New Tide Mag. & Dem. Progressive Jour.; Add.* Rm. 632, 10 Tsingtao E. Rd., Taipei.

LIN, CHUNG-CHENG 林忠正
Convener, Budget Cttee., Legis. Yuan 96-; *b.* Jan. 9, '54; *educ.* BA, Econ., Tunghai U.; MA, NTU; Ph.D. in Econ., U. of Hawaii, Expertise diploma in demography; Sp. Asst. to the Chmn., DPP, Exec.-Dir., So. of Ch. Aff.; *Pol. Affi.* DPP; *Const.* Nat.; Dep. Sec.-Gen., CEC, DPP; *Add.* Rm. 328, 1 Tsingtao E. Rd., Taipei.

LIN, FENG-SHI 林豐喜
Mem., Organic Laws Cttee., 2nd Sess., Legis. Yuan 97-; *b.* Dec. 12, '50; *educ.* Fu-chun Elementary Sch., Taichung County; *Pol. Affi.* DPP; *Const.* Taichung County; Chmn., Twn. Farmers Alliance; Exec. Mem., CC, DPP; Mem., Taichung CoCoun.; Mem., Budget Cttee., Legis. Yuan 96; *Add.* Rm. 229, 10 Tsingtao E. Rd., Taipei.

LIN, HONG-CHUNG 林宏宗
Mem., Home & Border Aff. Cttee., Legis. Yuan 96-; *b.* Oct. 26, '41; *educ.* Grad., Kaohsiung Ind. High Sch.; *Pol. Affi.* Independent; *Const.* Kaohsiung City; *Add.* Rm. 411, 10 Tsingtao E. Rd., Taipei.

LIN, HSI-SHAN 林錫山
Mem., Econ. Cttee., 2nd Sess., Legis. Yuan 97-; *b.* Mar. 17, '62; *educ.* Grad., Dept. of Civil Engr., Nan Ya Jr.

Coll. of Tech.; *Pol. Affi.* KMT; *Const.* Changhua County; Exec. Mem., Dept. of Party-Govt. Coordination of the Legis. Yuan, KMT; Dep. Sec.-Gen., KMT Caucus, Legis. Yuan; Mem., Organic Laws Cttee., Legis. Yuan 94; *Add.* Rm. 231, 1 Tsingtao E. Rd., Taipei.

LIN, JUI-CHING 林瑞卿
Mem., Nat. Def. Cttee., 2nd Sess., Legis. Yuan 97-; *b.* Jan. 26, '54; *educ.* Chung Hsing Sr. High Sch.; *Pol. Affi.* DPP; *Const.* Nat.; Chmn., Yunlin County Cttee., DPP, Exec. Mem., CC; Mem., Finance Cttee., Legis. Yuan 94; *Add.* Rm. 607, 10 Tsingtao E. Rd., Taipei.

LIN, KUANG-HUA
(See LIN, KWANG-HUA 林光華)

LIN, KUO-LUNG 林國龍
Mem., Econ. Cttee., 2nd Sess., Legis. Yuan 97-; *b.* Dec. 8, '44; *educ.* Grad., Nat. Tatung Tchrs. Coll. 64, & Nat. Pingtung Tchrs. Coll. 77; *Pol. Affi.* KMT; *Const.* Pingtung County; Magis., Linpien Rural Township, Pingtung County 78-81; Mem., Pingtung CoCoun. 82-85, & TPA 86-89; Convener, Econ. Cttee., Legis. Yuan 94; *Add.* Rm. 510, 1 Tsingtao E. Rd., Taipei.

LIN, KWANG-HUA 林光華
Mem., Jud. Cttee., Legis. Yuan 94-; *b.* Oct. 25, '45; *educ.* Grad., NTNU; *Pol. Affi.* DPP; *Const.* Hsinchu County; Founding Mem., DPP, Mem., CAC; Convener, Trans. & Comms. Cttee., Legis. Yuan; *Add.* Rm. 506, 1 Tsingtao E. Rd., Taipei.

LIN, MING-I 林明義
Mem., Budget Cttee., Legis. Yuan 94-; *b.* June 1, '54; *educ.* Grad., Chianan Sr. Voc. Sch. for Home Econ. & Cml. 80; *Pol. Affi.* KMT; *Const.* Yunlin County; Mem., Yunlin CoCoun. 85-92; *Add.* Rm. 123, 1 Tsingtao E. Rd., Taipei.

LIN, PING-KUN 林炳坤
Mem., Trans. & Comms. Cttee., Legis. Yuan 96-; *b.* Aug. 15, '48; *educ.* BA, NTU; *Pol. Affi.* KMT; *Const.* Penghu County; Chmn., Police's Friends Assn.; *Add.* Rm. 109, 10 Tsingtao E. Rd., Taipei.

LIN, WEN-LAN 林文郎
Mem., Finance Cttee., 2nd Sess., Legis. Yuan 97-; *b.* Mar. 12, '45; *educ.* Grad., Taipei Cml. High Sch.; *Pol.*

Affi. DPP; *Const.*, Nat.; Mem., Taipei CCoun.; Mem., For. & Ovs. Ch. Aff. Cttee., Legis. Yuan 96; *Add.* Rm. 317, 10 Tsingtao E. Rd., Taipei.

LIN, YAO-HSING 林耀興
Mem., Home & Border Aff. Cttee., Legis. Yuan 96-; *b.* Oct. 17, '59; *educ.* Ph.D., Nat. Ssiga Med. U., Japan; *Pol. Affi.* KMT; *Const.* Taichung County; *Add.* Rm. 622, 10 Tsingtao E. Rd., Taipei.

LIN, YEN-SAN 林源山
Mem., Econ. Cttee., Legis. Yuan 94-, & Dept. of Party-Govt. Coordination of the Legis. Yuan, KMT 93-; *b.* Dec. 2, '40; *educ.* BBA, U. of Lincoln, San Francisco; *Pol. Affi.* KMT; *Const.* Kaohsiung County; Mem., TPA 81-93; Adv., TPG 85-89; Mem., Kaohsiung CoCoun. 88-92; *Add.* 7th Fl.-1, 10 Hangchow S. Rd., Sect. 1, Taipei.

LIN, YUAN-SHAN
(See LIN, YEN-SAN 林源山)

LIN, YU-FANG 林郁方
Mem., Nat, Def. Cttee., 2nd Sess., Legis. Yuan 97-; *b.* Mar. 15, '51; *educ.* Ph.D., Intl. Aff., U. of Virginia; *Pol. Affi.* NP; *Const.* Nat.; Mem., Jud. Cttee., Legis. Yuan 96; *Add.* Rm. 615, 10 Tsingtao E. Rd., Taipei.

LIN YU, LIN-YA 林余玲雅
Mem., Econ. Cttee., Legis. Yuan 94-; *b.* June 29, '50; *educ.* BA, Hist. Dept., NCU; *Pol. Affi.* DPP; *Const.* Nat.; Mem., TPA 82-93, & CEC, DPP 92-94; Convener, Educ. Cttee., Legis. Yuan 93-94; *Add.* Rm. 228, 1 Tsingtao E. Rd., Taipei.

LIU, CHIN-HSING 劉進興
Mem., Educ. Cttee., 2nd Sess., Legis. Yuan 97-; *b.* Aug. 30, '49; *educ.* Ph.D., Washington U., St. Louis, USA; *Pol. Affi.* DPP; *Const.* Nat.; Bd. Mem., Labor Educ. Cttee., Taipei City; Dir., Res. Dept., Twn. Labor Front, 93-95; Mem., Jud. Cttee., Legis. Yuan 96; *Add.* Rm. 633, 10 Tsingtao E. Rd., Taipei.

LIU, K.C. 劉國昭
Mem., Budget Cttee., 2nd Sess., Legis. Yuan 97-; *b.* Mar. 19, '42; *educ.* B., Econ., Tunghai U.; MBA, Meiji U.; *Pol. Affi.* KMT; *Const.* Nat.; Mem., Econ. Cttee., Legis. Yuan 94; *Add.* Rm. 207, 1 Tsingtao E. Rd., Taipei.

LIU, KUANG-HUA 劉光華
Mem., Organic Laws Cttee., Legis. Yuan 94-; Dep. Dir., Policy Res. Cttee., KMT 93-; *b.* Sept. 19, '43; *educ.* LL.D., NCU 81; *Pol. Affi.* KMT; *Const.* Nat.; Convener, Jud. Cttee., Legis. Yuan; *Add.* Rm. 121, 1 Tsingtao E. Rd., Taipei.

LIU, KUO-CHAO
(See LIU, K.C. 劉國昭)

LIU, SHENG-LIANG 劉盛良
Mem., Budget Cttee., 2nd Sess., Legis. Yuan 97-; *b.* Mar. 18, '39; *educ.* BCoS, Tatung Inst. of Tech.; *Pol. Affi.* KMT; *Const.* Taipei County; Mem., Taipei CoCoun.; Chmn., Veterans Assn., Taipei County; Convener, Nat. Def. Cttee., Legis. Yuan 96; *Add.* Rm. 425, 10 Tsingtao E. Taipei.

LIU, SUNG-FAN
(See LIU, SUNG-PAN 劉松藩)

LIU, SUNG-PAN 劉松藩
Pres., Legis. Yuan 92-; Mem., CSC, KMT 93-; Mem., For. & Ovs. Ch. Aff. Cttee., 2nd Sess., Legis. Yuan 97-; *b.* Dec. 3, '31; *educ.* Grad., Twn. Prov. Taichung Inst. of Com., & Kinki U., Japan; *Pol. Affi.* KMT; *Const.* Taichung County; Dep. Sec.-Gen., Policy Coordination Cttee., KMT 88-89, Dir., Secretariat, CC 89-90; V. Pres., Legis. Yuan 90-92; *Add.* Legis. Yuan, 1 Chung Shan S. Rd., Taipei.

LO, FU-CHU 羅福助
Convener, Jud. Cttee., 2nd Sess., Legis. Yuan 97-; *b.* July 2, '43; *Pol. Affi.* Independent; *Const.* Taipei County; Mem., Trans. & Comms. Cttee., Legis. Yuan 96; *Add.* Rm. 639, 10 Tsingtao E. Rd., Taipei.

LO, CHUAN-CHIN
(See LO, HERMAN 羅傳進)

LO, HERMAN 羅傳進
Convener, Educ. Cttee., Legis. Yuan 94-; *b.* Sept. 12, '39; *educ.* B., Botany, NCHU 64; *Pol. Affi.* KMT; *Const.* Nat.; Mem., NA; Convener, Budget Cttee., Finance Cttee., & Econ. Cttee., Legis. Yuan, Chief Sec., KMT Caucus; *Add.* Rm. 415, 1 Tsingtao E. Rd., Taipei.

LU, HSIU-YI 盧修一
Mem., Organic Laws, 2nd Sess., Legis. Yuan 97-; *b.* May 22, '41; *educ.* MPS, Ch. Cul. U.; DPS, U. de Paris; *Pol. Affi.* DPP; *Const.* Taipei County; Dir., Dept. of Pol. Sc., & Dept. of Admin. Mng., Ch. Cul. U. 75; Jailed 83-86; Dir., Dept. of For. Aff., DPP 88; Mem., Home & Border Aff. Cttee., Legis. Yuan 94; *Add.* Rm. 313, 1 Tsingtao E. Rd., Taipei.

PAN, TINA WEI-KANG 潘維剛
Mem., Trans. & Comms. Cttee., 2nd Sess., Legis. Yuan 97-; Pres., Modern Women Found.; *b.* Mar. 31, '57; *educ.* Grad., Dept. of Acct. & Statistics, Ming Chuan Coll. 89; Diploma, Grad. Sch. of PA, NCU 91; *Pol. Affi.* KMT; *Const.* Taipei City; Mem., Taipei CCoun. 81-93, & CC, KMT 88-94; Mem., Organic Laws Cttee., Legis. Yuan 94; *Add.* Rm. 420, 1 Tsingtao E. Rd., Taipei.

PAN, WEI-KANG
(See PAN, TINA WEI-KANG 潘維剛)

PANG, PAI-HSIEN 彭百顯
Convener, Finance Cttee., Legis. Yuan 96-; *b.* June 14, '49; *educ.* M., Econ. Dept., Ch. Cul. U. 76; *Pol. Affi.* DPP; *Const.* Nantou County; Convener, Finance Cttee., Legis. Yuan 90-93, Convener, Econ. Cttee. Legis. Yuan 93; Sec.-Gen., DPP Caucus, Legis. Yuan; Mem., CEC, DPP 94-96; Chmn., Justice Alliance DPP 95; *Add.* Rm. 316, 1 Tsingtao E. Rd., Taipei.

PAYEN-TALU 巴燕達魯
Mem., Budget Cttee., Legis. Yuan 96-; *b.* Dec. 16, '51; *educ.* Grad., jr. high sch. *Pol. Affi.* DPP; *Const.* Nat.; *Add.* Rm. 612, 10 Tsingtao E. Rd., Taipei.

PENG, PAI-HSIEN
(See PANG, PAI-HSIEN 彭百顯)

PENG, SHAO-CHIN 彭紹瑾
Mem., Home & Border Aff. Cttee., 2nd Sess., Legis. Yuan 97-; *b.* Feb. 28, '57; *educ.* LL.D., Munich U., Germany; *Pol. Affi.* DPP; *Const.* Taoyuan County; Lawyer; Mem., Jud. Cttee., Legis. Yuan 96; *Add.* Rm. 306, 1 Tsingtao E. Rd., Taipei.

SHEN, CHIH-HUI 沈智慧
Mem., Budget Cttee., 2nd Sess., Legis. Yuan 97-; *b.* Sept. 16, '57; *educ.* BJ, Ch. Cul. U. 81; *Pol. Affi.* KMT; *Const.* Taichung City; Convener, Trans. & Comms. Cttee., Legis. Yuan 94; *Add.* Rm. 429, 5th Fl.-9, 4 Tsingtao E. Rd., Taipei.

SHEN, FU-HSIUNG 沈富雄
Convener, Organic Laws Cttee., Legis. Yuan 96-; Exec. Mem., Assn. for Plebiscite in Twn., & Twn. Found. for Intl. Rel.; *b.* Aug. 23, '39; *educ.* MD, NTU 65; Ph.D., San Francisco Med. Cent. U. 69; Postdoctoral Fel., U. of Washington 72; *Pol. Affi.* DPP; *Const.* Taipei City; Mem., CC, Formosan Assn. for Public Aff., Washington, D.C. 82; *Add.* 4th Fl.-3, 5 Tsingtao E. Rd., Taipei.

SHIH, MING-TEH 施明德
Mem., Nat. Def. Cttee., 2nd Sess., Legis. Yuan 97-; Chmn., DPP 94-; *b.* Jan. 15, '41; *educ.* Army Artillery Coll. 61; *Pol. Affi.* DPP; *Const.* Tainan City; Jailed 62-77, & 80-90; Pres., Twn. Human Rights Promotion Assn. 90-91; Guest Prof., Dept. of Pol. Sc., San Diego State U. 91; Mem., CSC, DPP 91-93; Convener, DPP Caucus, Legis. Yuan 93, Mem., For. & Ovs. Ch. Aff. Cttee. 94; *Add.* Rm. 601, 1 Tsingtao E. Rd., Taipei.

SHIH, TAI-SHENG 施台生
Mem., Nat. Def. Cttee., 2nd Sess., Legis. Yuan 97-; Mem., CC, KMT 93-; *b.* Oct. 24, '46; *educ.* Grad., 11th Class, Ch. Mil. Acad., Kunshan Inst. of Tech. & Com., & Ch. Med. Coll.; *Pol. Affi.* KMT; *Const.* Tainan City; Mem., Tainan CCoun. 90-92, & Tainan Br., Evaluation & Discipline Cttee., KMT; Dep. Sec.-Gen., KMT Caucus, Legis. Yuan 93-94, Mem., Finance Cttee. 94; *Add.* Rm. 640, 10 Tsingtao E. Rd., Taipei.

SHYU, JONG-SHYONG 徐中雄
Mem., Home & Border Aff. Cttee., Legis. Yuan 94-; *b.* Oct. 17, '57; *educ.* BPS, Soochow U. 81; M., U. of Nr. Colorado 84, Ph.D. 87; *Pol. Affi.* KMT; *Const.* Taichung County; Convener, Home & Border Aff. Cttee., 2nd Sess., Legis. Yuan; Asst. Resr., Tng. Inst. for High Sch. Tchrs., TPG, Sp., Dept. of Soc. Aff.; *Add.* Rm. 217, 1 Tsingtao E. Rd., Taipei.

SIEW, VINCENT C. 蕭萬長
Mem., Nat. Def. Cttee., 2nd Sess., Legis. Yuan 97-; *b.* Jan, 3, '39; *educ.* MA, NCU; *Pol. Affi.* KMT; *Const.* Chiayi City; Chmn., MAC 94-95; Min. of State; Mem., CC & CSC, KMT 93-; Mem., Econ. Cttee., Legis. Yuan 96; *Add.* Rm. 623, 10 Tsingtao E. Rd., Taipei.

SU, CHIA-CHUAN
(See SU, JIA-QUAN 蘇嘉全)

SU, HUAN-CHIH
(See SU, HUAN-DJI 蘇煥智)

SU, HUAN-DJI 蘇煥智
Mem., Econ. Cttee., 2nd Sess., Legis. Yuan 97-; *b.* July 20, '56; *educ.* LL.B., NTU; LL.M., Fu Jen Catholic U.; *Pol. Affi.* DPP; *Const.* Tainan County; V. Pres., Twn. Assn. for Human Rights; Convener, Jud. Cttee., Legis. Yuan 94; *Add.* Rm. 401, 1 Tsingtao E. Rd., Taipei.

SU, JIA-QUAN 蘇嘉全
Mem., Organic Laws Cttee., 2nd Sess., Legis. Yuan 97-; Chmn., Pingtung Br., Assn. for Plebiscite in Twn.; *b.* Oct. 22, '56; *educ.* B., Nat. Twn. Ocean U.; *Pol. Affi.* DPP; *Const.* Pingtung County; Mem., NA 86-92; Mem., Home & Border Aff. Cttee., Legis. Yuan 94; *Add.* Rm. 332, 1 Tsingtao E. Rd., Taipei.

SU, TSENG-CHANG 蘇貞昌
Mem., Home & Border Aff. Cttee., 2nd Sess., Legis. Yuan 97-; *b.* Jul. 28, '47; *educ.* LL.B. NTU; *Pol. Affi.* DPP; *Const.* Taipei County; Sec.-Gen., CEC, DPP; Magis. Pingtung County; Mem., Educ. Cttee., Legis. Yuan 96; *Add.* Rm. 608, 10 Tsingtao E. Rd., Taipei.

TING, SHOU-CHUNG 丁守中
Mem., Educ. Cttee., 2nd Sess., Legis. Yuan 97-; Dir.-Gen., Dept. of Youth Aff., KMT 95-; *b.* Sept. 1, '54; *educ.* BS, NTU 76; M., Fletcher Sch. of Law & Dip., Harvard U. 82, Ph.D., Intl. Pol. 85; *Pol. Affi.* KMT; *Const.* Taipei City; Dep. Dir., Asia & World Inst. 85-87; Convener, Nat. Def. Cttee., Legis. Yuan 91-92; Chmn. Bridge Across the Straits Found. 91-96; Mem., Nat. Def. Cttee., Legis. Yuan 94; *Add.* Rm. 209, 1 Tsingtao E. Rd., Taipei.

TSAI, BIH-HWANG 蔡璧煌
Mem., Educ. Cttee., Legis. Yuan 96; *b.* Sept. 29, '45; *educ.* Ph.D., Stanford U.,USA; *Pol. Affi.* KMT; *Const.* Nat.; Dep. Dir., Dept. of Cul. Aff., CC, KMT; *Add.* Rm. 419, 10 Tsingtao E. Rd., Taipei.

TSAI, CHENG-YANG 蔡正揚
Me., Trans. & Comms. Cttee., 2nd Sess., Legis. Yuan 97-; *b.* May 39, '57; *educ.* DE, MIT, USA; Post Dr. Resr., Kennedy Admin. Inst., Harvard U.; *Pol. Affi.* NP; *Const.* Taipei County; Dir., Admin. of Ind. & Mining Inspection, TCG; Mem., Organic Laws Cttee., Legis. Yuan 96; *Add.* Rm. 406, 10 Tsingtao E. Rd., Taipei.

TSAI, CHUNG-HAN
(See TSAY, CHUNG-HAN 蔡中涵)

TSAI, HUANG-LANG 蔡煌瑯
Mem., Trans. & Comms. Cttee., 2nd Sess., Legis. Yuan 97-; *b.* July 5, '60; *educ.* PA Class, NCU; *Pol. Affi.* DPP; *Const.* Nantou County; Mem., Nantou CoCoun.; Dir., DPP Nantou County; Mem., Educ. Cttee., Legis. Yuan 96; *Add.* Rm. 221, 10 Tsingtao E. Rd., Taipei.

TSAI, KUEI-TSUNG
(See WALIS-PELIN 蔡貴聰)

TSAI, MICHAEL M. 蔡明憲
Mem., Jud. Cttee., Legis. Yuan 96-; *b.* Aug. 9, '41; *educ.* MBA, U. of Wisconsin 72; J.D., Calif. We. Sch. of Law 89; *Pol. Affi.* DPP; *Const.* Taichung City; Mem. NA; DPP Caucus 96-97; Attorney-at-Law; *Add.* Rm. 305, 1 Tsingtao E. Rd., Taipei.

TSAI, MING-HSIEN
(See TSAI, MICHAEL M. 蔡明憲)

TSAI, SHIH-YUAN 蔡式淵
Mem., Organic Laws Cttee., 2nd Sess., Legis. Yuan 97-; *b.* Jan. 1, '49; *educ.* Ph.D., Psychology, Am. U. 79; *Pol. Affi.* DPP; *Const.* Chiayi County; Mem. NA 86-92; Dep. Sec.-Gen., DPP 88-90; Mem., Econ. Cttee., Legis. Yuan 94; *Add.* Rm. 222, 1 Tsingtao E. Rd., Taipei.

TSAO, ERH-CHUNG
(See CHAO, ERH-CHUNG 曹爾忠)

TSAY, CHUNG-HAN 蔡中涵
Mem., Trans. & Comms. Cttee., 2nd Sess., Legis. Yuan 97-; *b*. Sept. 25, '43; *educ*. Ph.D., Sociology, Tokyo U.; *Pol. Affi*. KMT; *Const*. Lowland Aborigines; Mem., Budget Cttee., Legis. Yuan 94; *Add*. Rm. 505, 1 Tsingtao E. Rd., Taipei.

TSENG, ALLEN 曾振農
Mem., Jud. Cttee., Legis. Yuan 94-; Dep. Dir.-Gen., Dept. of Party-Govt. Coordination of the Legis. Yuan, KMT 93-; *b*. Feb. 25, '51; *educ*. Grad., Shen Chou Supplementary Sr. High Sch.; *Pol. Affi*. KMT; *Const*. Chiayi County; *Add*. 3rd Fl.-1, 12 Lin Sen S. Rd., Taipei.

TSENG, CHEN-NUNG
(See TSENG, ALLEN 曾振農)

TSENG, YUNG-CHUAN 曾永權
Mem., Organic Laws Cttee., 2nd Sess., Legis. Yuan 97-; *b*. Nov. 1, '47; *educ*. M., Ind. Mng., Northrop U.; *Pol. Affi*. KMT; *Const*. Pingtung County; Mem. NA; Dep. Sec.-Gen., Ch. Taipei Olympic Cttee.; Adv., Directorate-Gen. of Customs, MOF; Mem., Trans. & Comms. Cttee., Legis. Yuan 94; *Add*. Rm. 325, 1 Tsingtao E. Rd., Taipei.

TU, CHENG-JUNG 杜振榮
Mem., Econ. Cttee., 2nd Sess., Legis. Yuan 97-; *b*. Nov. 25, '43; *educ*. BCoS, Tamkang U.; *Pol. Affi*. KMT; *Const*. Nat.; Mem., NA; Mem., Trans. & Comms. Cttee., Legis. Yuan 96; *Add*. Rm. 507, 1 Tsingtao E. Rd., Taipei.

WALIS-PELIN 蔡貴聰
Mem., Budget Cttee., 2nd Sess., Legis. Yuan 97-; *b*. Aug. 8, '52; *educ*. B.Th., Fu Jen Catholic U., BA, Philosophy 75; *Pol. Affi*. Independent; *Const*. Highland Aborigines; Mem., Nantou CoCoun. 86-90; Mem., Educ. Cttee., Legis. Yuan 94; *Add*. Rm. 425, 1 Tsingtao E. Rd., Taipei.

WANG, CHIH-HSIUNG 王志雄
Mem., Trans. & Comms. Cttee., Legis. Yuan 96-; *b*. June 24, '52; *educ*. MBA, U. of So. Calif.; *Pol. Affi*. KMT; *Const*. Kaohsiung City; Dep. Dir., Policy Coordination Cttee., KMT; *Add*. Rm. 513, 1 Tsingtao E. Rd., Taipei.

WANG, CHIN-PING
(See WANG, JIN-PYNG 王金平)

WANG, HSIEN-MING 王顯明
Mem., Nat. Def. Cttee., Legis. Yuan 94-; *b*. June 25, '41; *educ*. Grad., Nat. Twn. Coll. of Phys. Educ.; Studied, 45th Class, Sun Yat-sen Inst. on Policy Res. & Dev., & 34th Res. Course; *Pol. Affi*. KMT; *Const*. Changhua County; Mem., 6th to 8th TPA, & 8th Changhua CoCoun.; *Add*. Rm. 613, 10 Tsingtao E. Rd., Taipei.

WANG, HSUEH-FUNG 王雪峰
Mem., Finance Cttee., 2nd Sess., Legis. Yuan 97-; *b*. Aug. 26, '64; *educ*. LL.M., Cornell U. USA; *Pol. Affi*. DPP; *Const*. Taipei City; Acting Dir., Dept. of So. Movement, CC, DPP; Mem., NA; Mem., Jud. Cttee., Legis. Yuan 96; *Add*. Rm. 630, 10 Tsingtao E. Rd., Taipei.

WANG, JIN-PYNG 王金平
V. Pres., Legis. Yuan 93-; Mem., Organic Laws Cttee., 2nd Sess., Legis. Yuan 97-; *b*. Mar. 17, '41; *educ*. BS, NTNU 65; *Pol. Affi*. KMT; *Const*. Kaohsiung County; Mem., CSC, KMT; Dir.-Gen., Dept. of Party-Govt. Co-ordination of the Legis. Yuan, CC, KMT, & concur. Sec.-Gen., KMT Caucus, Legis. Yuan; *Add*. Off. of the V. Pres., Legis. Yuan, 1 Chung Shan S. Rd., Taipei.

WANG, LING-LIN 王令麟
Mem., Finance Cttee., Legis. Yuan 96-; *b*. Feb. 23, '55; *educ*. Grad., Tamsui Oxford U. Coll.; *Pol. Affi*. KMT; *Const*. Nat.; Chmn., Taipei Chamber of Com.; Chmn., ROC Business Arbitary Assn.; *Add*. 20th Fl., 15-1 Hangchow S. Rd., Sect. 1, Taipei.

WANG, SHU-YUN 王素筠
Mem., Jud. Cttee., 2nd Sess., Legis. Yuan 97-; *b*. Feb. 19, '53; *educ*. Grad., Pingtung Girl's High Sch.; *Pol. Affi*. KMT; *Const*. Miaoli County; Mem., Pingtung CoCoun.; Legis. & Convener, Econ. Cttee., Legis. Yuan 96; *Add*. Rm. 426, 1 Tsingtao E. Rd., Taipei.

WANG, TEIN-GING 王天競
Mem., Nat. Def. Cttee., Legis. Yuan 94-, & CC, KMT 93-; *b*. July 23, '47; *educ*. B., Ch. Cul. U.; M., Roosevelt U.; *Pol. Affi*. KMT; *Const*. Kaohsiung City; Convener, Nat. Def. Cttee. 92-94, & Jud. Cttee., 88th

Sess., Legis. Yuan; Bd. of Trustees, Assn. of Free Ch. in the USA; Sec.-Gen., Kaohsiung Mun. Cttee., KMT, & Dept. of Ovs. Aff.; *Add.* Rm. 116, 1 Tsingtao E. Rd., Taipei.

WANG, TIEN-CHING
(See WANG, TEIN-GING 王天競)

WANG, TO 王拓
Mem., Educ. Cttee., Legis. Yuan 96-; *b.* Jan. 9, '44; *educ.* MA, NCU; *Pol. Affi.* DPP; *Const.* Nat.; Dir., Dept. of Org., CEC, DPP; Mem., NA; *Add.* Rm. 223, 1 Tsingtao E. Rd., Taipei.

WENG, CHIN-CHU
(See WONG, CHIN-CHU 翁金珠)

WENG, CHUNG-CHUN
(See WONG, CHUNG-CHUN 翁重鈞)

WONG, CHIN-CHU 翁金珠
Mem., Organic Laws Cttee., 2nd Sess., Legis. Yuan 97-; *b.* Jan. 31, '47; *educ.* B., NTNU 77; *Pol. Affi.* DPP; *Const.* Changhua County; Chmn., Extraordinary Presidium, NA 87-93, & New Tide Movement 93-94; Convener., Educ. Cttee., Legis. Yuan 94; *Add.* Rm. 635, 10 Tsingtao E. Rd., Taipei.

WONG, CHUNG-CHUN 翁重鈞
Convener, Trans. & Comms. Cttee., Legis. Yuan 96-; *b.* May 31, '55; *educ.* BA, Ch. Cul. U. 77; *Pol. Affi.* KMT; *Const.* Chiayi County; Mem., CoCoun. 82-89; *Add.* Rm. 230, 1 Tsingtao E. Rd., Taipei.

WU, HUI-TSU 吳惠祖
Mem., For. & Ovs. Ch. Aff. Cttee., Legis. Yuan 96-; *b.* June 4, '51; *educ.* BA, Chuhai Coll., Hong Kong; *Pol. Affi.* KMT; *Const.* Ovs. Nat.; V. Chmn., 123 Dem. Alliance; *Add.* Rm. 301, 1 Tsingtao E. Rd., Taipei.

WU, LUKE KO-CHING 吳克清
Mem., Econ. Cttee., 2nd Sess., Legis. Yuan 97-; *b.* Apr. 29, '54; *educ.* BA, Tamkang U.; *Pol. Affi.* KMT; *Const.* Taoyuan County; Mem., NA; Mem., Home & Border Aff. Cttee., Legis. Yuan 96; *Add.* Rm. 233, 1 Tsingtao E. Rd., Taipei.

YANG, CHI-HSIUNG 楊吉雄
Mem., Budget Cttee., 2nd Sess., Legis. Yuan 97-; Mem., CC, KMT 93-; *b.* July 8, '43; *educ.* Grad., Sr. High Sch.; *Pol. Affi.* KMT; *Const.* Nat.; Mem., Presidium, NA 86-91; Convener, Budget Cttee., Legis. Yuan 94; *Add.* Rm. 126, 1 Tsingtao E. Rd., Taipei.

YAO, ENG-CHI 饒穎奇
Mem., For. & Ovs. Ch. Aff. Cttee., 2nd Sess., Legis. Yuan 97-; Exec. Sec., Policy Coordination Cttee., KMT; *b.* Nov. 5, '34; *educ.* B., NCHU 63; *Pol. Affi.* KMT; *Const.* Taitung County; Sec.-Gen., KMT Caucus, Legis. Yuan, Mem., Organic Laws Cttee. 94; *Add.* Rm. 105, 1 Tsingtao E. Rd., Taipei.

YAO, LI-MING 姚立明
Mem., For. & Ovs. Ch. Aff. Cttee., 2nd Sess., Legis. Yuan 97-; *b.* Jan. 15, '52; *educ.* LL.D., Bellevue U., Germany; *Pol. Affi.* NP; *Const.* Kaohsiung County; Mem., Jud. Cttee., Legis. Yuan 96; *Add.* Rm. 617, 1 Tsingtao E. Rd., Taipei.

YAO, YING-CHI
(See YAO, ENG-CHI 饒穎奇)

YEH, CHU-LAN 葉菊蘭
Mem., Nat. Def. Cttee., 2nd Sess., Legis. Yuan 97-; *b.* Feb. 13, '49; *educ.* LL.B., Fu Jen Catholic U.; *Pol. Affi.* DPP; *Const.* Nat.; Tchr., Yuming Sr. Voc. Sch. of Ind. & Home Econ.; Dir., United Advertising Co.; Bd. Chmn., Cheng Nan-jung Memorial Fund; Mem., Home & Border Aff. Cttee., Legis. Yuan 94; *Add.* Rm. 312, 1 Tsingtao E. Rd., Taipei.

YEN, CHIN-FU 顏錦福
Mem., Nat. Def. Cttee., 2nd Sess., Legis. Yuan 97-; *b.* Mar. 2, '37; *educ.* BS, NTNU; *Pol. Affi.* DPP; *Const.* Taipei City; Mem., 5th & 6th Taipei CCoun.; Chmn., Taipei Cttee., DPP, Mem., CSC; Mem., Trans. & Comms. Cttee., Legis. Yuan 94; *Add.* Rm. 625, 1 Tsingtao E. Rd., Taipei.

YIU, HUAI-YIN 游淮銀
Mem., Finance Cttee., 2nd Sess., Legis. Yuan 97-; Dep. Sec.-Gen., KMT Caucus, Legis. Yuan 93-; *b.* Apr. 26, '42; *educ.* MBA, U. of San Francisco 83; Hon. LL.D.,

St. Jones U. 94; *Pol. Affi.* KMT; *Const.* Changhua County; Mem., Budget Cttee., Legis. Yuan 94; *Add.* 4th Fl., 18 Chang An E. Rd., Sect. 1, Taipei.

YOK, MU-MING 郁慕明
Mem., Nat. Def. Cttee., 2nd Sess., Legis. Yuan 97-; *b.* July 19, '40; *educ.* BS, Dept. of Pharmacy, Nat. Def. Med. Cent. 63, M., Dept. of Biomorphics 69; *Pol. Affi.* NP; *Const.* Taipei City; Prof., Anatomy 79; Mem., Taipei CCoun. 82-90; Convener, Nat. Def. Cttee., Legis. Yuan 94; *Add.* Rm. 129, 1 Tsingtao E. Rd., Taipei.

YU, HONG 尤宏
Mem., Home & Border Aff. Cttee., Legis. Yuan 94-; *b.* July 21, '50; *educ.* LL.B., Ch. Cul. U. 75; Res., Human Resource Dev. Cent., San Diego State U.; *Pol. Affi.* DPP;

Const. Kaohsiung County; Pres., Kaohsiung Br., Twn. Farmers' Rights Assn. 88-89; Chmn., Found. of the Pol. Oppressed, Kaohsiung & Pingtung Br.; *Add.* Rm. 330, 1 Tsingtao E. Rd., Taipei.

YU, HUAI-YIN
(See YIU, HUAI-YIN 游淮銀)

YU, HUNG
(See YU, HONG 尤宏)

YU, LING-YA
(See LIN YU, LIN-YA 林余玲雅)

YU, MU-MING
(See YOK, MU-MING 郁慕明)

Appendix

Appendix I
Chronology: January 1911 - June 1996

1911

Oct. 10 — A revolt against the Manchu (Ch'ing) dynasty erupts in Wuch'ang and is followed by revolutionary activities throughout China.

1912

Jan. 1 — The Republic of China is founded, with Dr. Sun Yat-sen as the first provisional president.

28 — A provisional senate is established in Nanking.

Feb. 12 — Henry Pu Yi abdicates as emperor, ending the rule of the Manchu dynasty.

13 — Dr. Sun tenders his resignation to the provisional senate.

15 — Yuan Shih-kai is elected provisional president by the provisional senate.

Mar. 11 — A provisional constitution is promulgated.

Apr. 2 — The provisional senate resolves to move the seat of the government to Peking.

Aug. 25 — The Tung-meng Hui (Society of the Common Cause) is reorganized as the Kuomintang (Nationalist Party).

1913

Apr. 6 — The provisional senate is dissolved.

8 — The Republic's first congress is organized.

May 2 — The United States recognizes the Republic of China.

July 12 — Li Lieh-chun of the Kuomintang starts the second revolution against Yuan's dictatorial rule.

Oct. 6 — Yuan forces the congress to elect him president.

10 — Yuan formally assumes the presidency.

1914

May 1 — Yuan annuls the provisional constitution.

June 23 — The Kuomintang is reorganized as the Chung-hua Ke-ming Tang (Chinese Revolutionary Party) in Tokyo. Dr. Sun is elected director-general.

Aug. 6 — Yuan declares China's neutrality in World War I.

1915

Jan. 18 — Japan presents the notorious 21 Demands to the Peking government.

May 15 — Yuan signs the *"Sino-Japanese Agreement"* (the 21 Demands).

Dec. 12 — Yuan proclaims himself emperor.

25 — Tsai O, Tang Chi-yao, and Li Lieh-chun revolt against Yuan in Yunnan Province.

1916

June 6 — Yuan dies, and the republican form of government is restored.

7 — Li Yuan-hung becomes president of the Peking government.

1917

July 12 — An attempted coup d'état by Chang Hsun to restore the Manchu dynasty fails.

Aug. 14 — The Peking government declares war on Germany and Austro-Hungary.

25 — Dr. Sun forms a military government in Canton.

Sept. 1 — The congress elects Dr. Sun Yat-sen as grand marshal of the Army and Navy of the Chinese Military Government.

1918

Sept. 4 — The "Militarists' Parliament" in the north elects Hsu Shih-chang president.

Nov. 23 — The Ministry of Education adopts the National Phonetic Symbols.

1919

Apr. 30 — The Paris Peace Conference allows Japan to take over Germany's prewar rights in Shantung Province.

May   4 — More than 3,000 students demonstrate in Peking against the Paris Peace Conference decision.

June   28 — China refuses to sign the *Versailles Treaty* on grounds that German rights in Shantung were given to Japan.

Oct.   10 — The Chung-hua Ke-ming Tang (Chinese Revolutionary Party) is reorganized as the Chung-kuo Kuo-min Tang (abbreviated as Kuomintang, or Nationalist Party).

1920

June   29 — China joins the League of Nations.

1921

May   5 — Dr. Sun Yat-sen assumes the presidency of the newly formed southern government in Canton.

1922

Feb.   4 — China signs an agreement with Japan in Washington to settle the Shantung dispute.

June   2 — Hsu Shih-chang resigns as president of the Peking government.

11 — Li Yuan-hung resumes the presidency in Peking.

16 — Chen Chiung-ming revolts against Dr. Sun.

Aug.   15 — Dr. Sun issues a manifesto urging the unification of China by peaceful means.

1923

Jan.   26 — Dr. Sun and Adolf Joffe, representative of the Soviet Communist Party, issue a joint statement declaring that neither the communist social order nor the Soviet system is suitable for China.

1924

Jan.   20 — The first National Congress of the Kuomintang in Canton adopts a policy of cooperation with the Soviet Union and the Chinese Communist Party.

May   3 — Chiang Kai-shek is appointed superintendent of the Whampoa Military Academy.

Nov.   10 — Dr. Sun, in a manifesto, calls for the early convocation of a national people's convention and the abolition of unequal treaties.

24 — Tuan Chi-jui becomes provisional chief executive in Peking.

1925

Mar.   12 — Dr. Sun dies in Peking at the age of 59.

July   1 — The national government is established in Canton.

Nov.   3 — The Kuomintang proposes disciplinary measures to restrict communist activities.

1926

Apr.   9 — Tuan Chi-jui resigns as provisional chief executive.

June   5 — Chiang Kai-shek becomes commander-in-chief of the National Revolutionary Forces.

27 — Chiang Kai-shek launches the Northern Expedition from Canton.

1927

Apr.   12 — The Kuomintang starts a "purification" movement by expelling communist members.

18 — The national government is established in Nanking by the Kuomintang.

Aug.   1 — The Chinese communists stage the Nanch'ang Uprising against the national government.

13 — Commander-in-chief of the National Revolutionary Forces, Chiang Kai-shek, resigns in order to unify the Nanking and Hankow factions of the Kuomintang.

1928

May   3 — Japanese troops attack the Northern Expeditionary Forces in Tsinan, touching off the May 3 (Tsinan) Incident.

June   4 — Chang Tso-lin is killed on a train by a

bomb explosion. His son, Chang Hsueh-liang, succeeds him as ruler of Manchuria.

Oct.   29 — Peking is renamed Peiping.

Oct.   8 — Chiang Kai-shek is elected chairman of the national government of the Republic of China.

Dec.   5 — The Legislative Yuan is formally established.

        29 — Chang Hsueh-liang pledges allegiance to the national government, which leads to the unification of China.

1929

May   20 — Japanese troops withdraw from Tsinan.

July   23 — The national government severs diplomatic relations with the Soviet Union.

Dec.   30 — The Ministry of Foreign Affairs proclaims the nullification of consular jurisdiction in China to rid China of foreign privileges.

1930

Jan.   6 — The Examination Yuan is formally established.

July   13 — Rebels set up a government in Peking under the leadership of Wang Ching-wei.

1931

Feb.   16 — The Control Yuan is formally established.

May   5 — The National People's Convention is held in Nanking under the chairmanship of Chiang Kai-shek.

June   1 — The Provisional Constitution for the Period of Political Tutelage is promulgated.

July   4 — Korean immigrants occupy Wanpaoshan in Kirin Province at the instigation of Japanese militarists.

Sept.   18 — Japanese troops occupy Shenyang (Mukden) in a surprise attack. Important cities in Liaoning and Kirin provinces fall to the Japanese.

Oct.   24 — The Council of the League of Nations adopts a resolution urging Japan to withdraw its troops from Northeast China by November 16.

        26 — Japan turns down the League's resolution.

        27 — Nanking and Canton representatives meet in Shanghai for peace negotiations.

Nov.   18 — Ma Chan-shan puts up a stiff fight against the Japanese in Heilungkiang.

Dec.   15 — Chiang Kai-shek retires in the interest of party unity.

        28 — The national government is reorganized, with Lin Sen as chairman.

1932

Jan.   3 — The Chinese communists set up a Soviet regime in Kan Hsien in Kiangsi.

        8 — US Secretary of State Henry Stimson declares that the United States will not recognize any treaty that violates the Open Door Policy.

        28 — Japanese naval forces attack Shanghai. The 19th Army Corps puts up stiff resistance.

Feb.   6 — The National Military Council is established.

        19 — The United States refuses to recognize Japanese puppet state of "Manchukuo" (State of Manchuria).

Mar.   14 — The League of Nations' Lytton Commission arrives in China to investigate the Shenyang (Mukden) Incident.

        18 — Chiang Kai-shek becomes chairman of the National Military Council.

May   5 — China and Japan sign an armistice in Shanghai.

June   28 — Chiang Kai-shek arrives in Hankow from Lushan to direct the campaign against the Chinese communists.

Dec.   12 — China resumes diplomatic relations with the Soviet Union.

1933

Feb.   14 — The League of Nations refuses to recognize "Manchukuo."

Apr.   18 — Fighting spreads in North China. Several strategic passes along the Great Wall fall to the Japanese.

May   31 — The *Sino-Japanese Tangku Armistice Agreement* is signed, ending hostilities in North China.

Nov. 20 — Leaders of the 19th Army Corps form a "People's government" in Fukien.

1934

Feb. 19 — Chiang Kai-shek launches the "New Life Movement" in Nanch'ang.

Mar. 1 — Henry Pu Yi is enthroned as "Emperor of Manchukuo" in Ch'angch'un by the Japanese militarists.

Oct. 10 — The main forces of the Chinese communist troops flee their bases in Kiangsi to the northwest, launching the "Long March."

21 — Government troops capture Juichin, the communist capital in Kiangsi.

1935

Oct. 2 — Chiang Kai-shek is appointed commander-in-chief of the Northwestern Communist-Suppression Army and Chang Hsueh-liang, deputy commander-in-chief, with headquarters in Sian.

Nov. 4 — The national government proclaims the nationalization of all silver, making notes issued by the Central Bank of China and the Bank of Communications legal tender.

1936

May 5 — The government promulgates the May 5 Draft Constitution.

Dec. 12 — Chang Hsueh-liang's troops mutiny in Sian and hold Chiang Kai-shek and other ranking government officials hostage.

22 — Madame Chiang, accompanied by W.H. Donald and T.V. Soong (Sung Tzu-wen), fly to Sian.

25 — Chang Hsueh-liang accompanies Generalissimo Chiang Kai-shek and Madame Chiang to Loyang, en route to Nanking.

1937

July 7 — Japanese troops near Lukouchiao (Marco Polo Bridge), southwest of Peking, attack Wanping city at night, formally starting the war between China and Japan.

17 — In a speech at Kuling, Chiang Kai-shek lays down four conditions for settlement of the Lukouchiao Incident.

Aug 21 — China and the Soviet Union sign a non-aggression treaty in Nanking.

Sept. 28 — The League of Nations adopts a resolution denouncing Japan's aggression in China.

Oct. 6 — The US State Department condemns Japan's invasion of China.

7 — The League of Nations adopts a resolution pledging moral support for China.

30 — The national government decides to move the capital from Nanking to Chungking.

Nov. 3 — China presents her case at The Nine-Power Conference in Brussels.

Dec. 13 — Japanese troops occupy Nanking. During the following two months, the aggressors rape and kill some 300,000 defenseless Chinese.

1938

Mar. 28 — The Ministry of Foreign Affairs issues a statement denouncing the "Reform Government of China," a puppet regime set up by the Japanese in Nanking.

Apr. 1 — The Emergency National Congress of the Kuomintang in Wuch'ang elects Chiang Kai-shek as its director-general and decides to organize a People's Political Council and a San-min-chu-i Youth Corps.

July 6 — The first session of the People's Political Council opens in Hankow and adopts a program of armed resistance and national reconstruction.

7 — Chinese troops win a victory in T'ai-erhchuang.

9 — The San-min-chu-i Youth Corps is established with Chiang Kai-shek as head.

Oct. 25 — Chinese troops evacuate Wuch'ang and Hankow.

Dec. 22 — The Japanese prime minister, Prince Konoye, lays down three points as guiding principles for the settlement of the Sino-Japanese conflict and the establishment of the "New Order in East Asia."

26 — Chiang Kai-shek reiterates China's determination to carry on the war of resistance against Japan and charges that Konoye's statement clearly reveals Japan's intention to conquer China.

1939

Jan.   28 — The fifth plenary session of the Fifth Central Committee of the Kuomintang decides to create a Supreme National Defense Council with Chiang Kai-shek as chairman.

Nov.   20 — Chairman Chiang Kai-shek is appointed to the concurrent post of president of the Executive Yuan.

1940

Mar.   29 — Wang Ching-wei establishes a puppet regime in Nanking which is recognized by Japan on November 19.

30 — The Ministry of Foreign Affairs declares the Nanking puppet organization illegal.

Sept.   6 — Chungking is proclaimed provisional capital of China.

1941

Jan.   4 — The Communist New Fourth Army revolts against the national government.

14 — The revolt of the New Fourth Communist Army is suppressed.

Apr.   14 — Condemning the *Soviet-Japanese Neutrality Pact*, Foreign Minister Wang Chung-hui declares that Outer Mongolia and the northeastern provinces are Chinese territory and that the Soviet-Japanese statement is not binding on China.

17 — US President Roosevelt approves the first military aid program of US$45 million for China.

Sept. 30 — Chinese troops win the second battle of Ch'angsha.

Dec.   9 — China formally declares war on Japan.

1942

Jan.   2 — Chinese Expeditionary Forces enter Burma.

— Generalissimo Chiang assumes office as supreme commander of the China Theater of War.

15 — Chinese troops win the third battle of Changsha.

Mar.   4 — General Joseph Stilwell arrives in Chungking to assume duties as chief of staff of the China Theater of War and also to take command of all American armed forces in China, Burma, and India.

Apr.   19 — Chinese Expeditionary Forces capture Yenangyuang, rescuing more than 7,000 British and Burmese troops from Japanese encirclement.

June   2 — Foreign Minister T.V. Soong and US Secretary of State Cordell Hull sign the *Sino-American Lend-Lease Agreement* in Washington.

Oct.   10 — The US and UK governments announce their intention to relinquish extraterritoriality and related rights in China.

1943

Jan.   11 — China signs the new *Sino-American Treaty* in Washington and the new *Sino-British Treaty* in Chungking.

Oct.   10 — Chiang Kai-shek is sworn in as chairman of the national government.

Nov.   23 — Chiang Kai-shek, US President Franklin D. Roosevelt, and UK Prime Minister Winston Churchill confer in Cairo.

Dec.   3 — The Joint Declaration of the Cairo Conference is issued simultaneously in Chungking, Washington, and London.

1944

June   16 — Chinese Expeditionary Forces capture Kaimaing in northern Burma.

18 — US Vice President Henry Wallace visits China.

25 — Chinese Expeditionary Forces capture Magaung in northern Burma.

Sept. 29 — The Chinese-American-British phase of the Dumbarton Oaks Conference begins.

Oct.   9 — China, the US, the UK, and the USSR

promulgate the draft for the *Charter of the United Nations.*

29 — US General Albert C. Wedemeyer is appointed chief of staff of the China Theater of War.

1945

Feb.   4 — The US, UK, and the USSR hold a conference in Yalta. A secret agreement, among other conclusions, is reached on Feb. 11 by the three that the USSR shall enter the war against Japan on condition that its former rights (in China) plundered by Japan in 1904 shall be restored.

Mar.   5 — China, the US, the UK, and the USSR issue joint invitations to the United Nations Conference in San Francisco on April 25.

June   26 — Representatives of 50 nations, including China, sign the UN Charter in San Francisco.

July   26 — Chiang Kai-shek, US President Truman, and UK Prime Minister Churchill issue a joint ultimatum, calling for Japan's unconditional surrender.

Aug.   9 — Soviet troops enter Manchuria.

11 — The Chinese communist headquarters in Yenan order communist troops to launch an all-out revolt against the government.

14 — Japan surrenders.

— The *Sino-Soviet Treaty of Friendship and Alliance* is signed in Moscow.

— Chiang Kai-shek invites Mao Tse-tung to come to Chungking for a conference.

15 — The Legislative Yuan unanimously approves the *Charter of the United Nations.*

23 — Soviet troops occupy Manchuria.

Sept.   2 — Japan's surrender is signed on the USS Missouri, with General Hsu Yung-chang signing for China.

9 — General Ho Ying-chin receives the formal surrender of Japanese forces in China from General Okamura in Nanking.

Oct.   25 — Taiwan is formally retroceded to China after 50 years of Japanese occupation.

Dec.   20 — Soviet troops move an estimated US$2 billion worth of machinery from Manchuria to the Soviet Union.

22 — General George C. Marshall arrives in Chungking as US President Truman's special envoy.

28 — The Big Three Foreign Ministers' Conference in Moscow announces agreements on a commission and allied council for Japan, the ultimate establishment of a free Korea, and the withdrawal of Soviet and US troops from China.

1946

Jan.   7 — Government and communist representatives hold their first truce meeting with General Marshall as mediator.

10 — The government issues a cease-fire order.

— The Political Consultative Conference opens.

13 — The UN Security Council is created, with China as one of the five permanent members.

Feb.   11 — US Secretary of State James Byrnes makes public the *Yalta Secret Agreement.*

20 — The Ministry of Foreign Affairs declares the *Yalta Secret Agreement* not binding on China.

22 — More than 20,000 students demonstrate against the *Yalta Secret Agreement* and call for the Soviet Union to withdraw its forces from China.

Mar.   5 — The Ministry of Foreign Affairs announces that China has rejected the Soviet claim to all Japanese military enterprises in Manchuria.

13 — Government forces enter Mukden following the evacuation of Soviet troops.

Apr.   17 — Communist troops enter Ch'angch'un.

26 — Communist troops take over Harbin and Tsitsihar as the Soviet forces evacuate.

May   5 — The national government moves back to Nanking.

23 — Government troops recapture Ch'angch'un.

June   6 — Chiang Kai-shek accepts General Marshall's proposal to issue a second cease-fire order during the 15-day armistice.

July   3 — The Supreme National Defense Council votes to convene the National Assembly on November 12, 1946.

Aug.   17 — Yenan issues a second mobilization order instructing all communist forces to launch full-scale war against the government.

Sept.   3 — Chiang Kai-shek agrees to create a committee of five headed by US Ambassador J. Leighton Stuart to pave the way for a coalition government.

Oct.   16 — Chiang Kai-shek presents the communists with eight conditions for a nation-wide cease-fire.

     18 — The communists reject the government's latest peace offer.

Nov.   4 — China and the United States sign a five-year *Treaty of Friendship, Commerce, and Navigation.*

     8 — Chiang Kai-shek issues a third cease-fire.

     15 — The National Assembly officially opens. Chiang Kai-shek announces termination of Kuomintang tutelage.

Dec.   25 — The National Assembly completes drafting the new Constitution.

1947

Jan.   1 — The government promulgates the Constitution.

     29 — The US State Department announces abandonment of efforts to mediate between the national government and the communists.

Feb.   28 — Rioting breaks out in Taipei, following an incident between police and a peddler who violated the tobacco monopoly.

Mar.   19 — Government troops capture Yenan.

May   26 — The third plenary session of the Fourth People's Political Council adopts a resolution to invite communist members to attend.

June   25 — The Ministry of Foreign Affairs reveals repeated Soviet Union attempts to block Chinese troops from entering Dairen and Port Arthur.

July   22 — General Albert C. Wedemeyer, US President Truman's special representative, arrives in Nanking.

Nov.   21 — The first general elections in China are held.

Dec.   25 — The government adopts the Constitution.

1948

Mar.   29 — China's first National Assembly under the Constitution opens with 1,629 delegates attending.

Apr.   18 — The first National Assembly approves, by a two-thirds majority, temporary provisions granting emergency powers to the president during the period of the anti-communist campaign.

     19 — The first National Assembly elects Chiang Kai-shek as China's first president under the new Constitution by 2,430 out of 2,704 votes.

     21 — Government troops evacuate Yenan.

May   20 — President Chiang Kai-shek and Vice President Li Tsung-jen are sworn in.

1949

Jan.   5 — General Chen Cheng is sworn in as governor of Taiwan.

     15 — Tientsin falls.

     21 — President Chiang announces his retirement from the presidency and leaves for Hangchow. Vice President Li Tsung-jen is empowered to exercise presidential powers temporarily.

Apr.   5 — The national government begins talks with the Chinese communists.

     12 — The Farm Rental Reduction Program goes into effect in Taiwan.

     21 — The communists resume their all-out offensive and cross the Yangtze River.

     23 — Government forces evacuate Nanking.

May   15 — Government forces evacuate Hankow and Wuch'ang.

     27 — Shanghai is evacuated.

June   15 — Taiwan adopts a new currency.

July   10 — At the invitation of Philippine President Elpidio Quirino, President Chiang flies to Baguio to discuss formation of a Far Eastern anti-communist alliance.

Aug.   6 — At the invitation of Korean President Syngman Rhee, President Chiang flies to Chinhae, Korea, to discuss formation of a Pacific alliance.

15 — The Southeast China Governor's Office is established in Taipei, with General Chen Cheng as governor.

Sept. 27 — China files a complaint with the UN General Assembly against the Soviet Union's aid to the Chinese communists and violation of the *Sino-Soviet Treaty* of 1945 and the *UN Charter*.

Oct.   1 — The communists set up a regime in Peking with Mao Tse-tung as "chairman," which is recognized by the Soviet Union the next day.

3 — The ROC severs diplomatic relations with the USSR.

— The US State Department reaffirms US recognition of the national government as the only legal government of China.

13 — Government troops evacuate Canton.

25 — Government troops win a victory at Kinmen (Quemoy) against a communist attack.

Dec.   7 — The government moves its seat to Taipei.

10 — President Chiang flies from Chengtu to Taipei.

15 — The Executive Yuan names Wu Kuo-chen governor of Taiwan.

1950

Jan.   6 — The Republic of China severs diplomatic relations with Britain following Britain's recognition of the communist regime.

11 — The UN Security Council rejects a Soviet proposal for the immediate expulsion of the ROC delegation.

28 — The Ministry of Foreign Affairs declares that the Republic of China will not be bound by any agreement signed between the Chinese communist regime and the Soviet Union.

Mar.   1 — President Chiang Kai-shek resumes office in Taipei.

7 — President Chiang nominates General Chen Cheng as president of the Executive Yuan (premier).

Apr.   5 — The Executive Yuan grants Taiwan authority to carry out self-government by popular election in counties and cities within two months.

June   27 — US President Truman orders the US Seventh Fleet to prevent a communist attack on Taiwan and asks the ROC government to cease air and sea operations against the mainland.

July   2 — A popular election for a Hualien county council is held, marking the beginning of self-government in Taiwan.

31 — General Douglas MacArthur arrives in Taipei to confer with President Chiang.

Aug.   10 — Karl L. Rankin arrives in Taipei as chargé d'affaires of the US embassy.

16 — Taiwan, formerly consisting of eight counties and nine cities, is redivided into 16 counties and five cities.

Nov.   1 — The Chinese communists announce aid to the Korean communists in the fight against UN forces in Korea.

30 — The UN Security Council orders the Chinese communist forces to leave Korea.

1951

Feb.   1 — The UN General Assembly condemns the Chinese communists as aggressors in Korea.

May   1 — US Major General William C. Chase arrives in Taipei as the first chief of the Military Assistance Advisory Group (MAAG) in Taiwan.

18 — The UN General Assembly approves a global embargo on shipments of arms and war material to the Chinese and North Korean communists.

25 — The Legislative Yuan adopts the *37.5 Percent Farm Rental Reduction Act.*

30 — The government announces plans to sell

arable public land to tenant farmers on easy payment terms.

Dec. 11 — The Taiwan Provincial Assembly is established.

1952

Feb. 1 — The UN General Assembly finds the Soviet Union guilty of violation of the 1945 *Sino-Soviet Treaty of Friendship and Alliance*.

Apr. 28 — The *Treaty of Peace between the Republic of China and Japan* is signed in Taipei.

Oct. 22 — The first worldwide Overseas Chinese Conference opens in Taipei.

31 — The China Youth Corps is organized.

1953

Jan. 10 — The Legislative Yuan adopts the *Land-to-the-Tiller Act*.

25 — President Chiang announces abrogation of the *Sino-Soviet Treaty of Friendship and Alliance* of 1945 and its related documents.

Apr. 2 — Karl L. Rankin becomes the American ambassador to the ROC.

12 — The Legislative Yuan passes a bill submitted by President Chiang, extending the term of office for legislators another year, i.e., to May 7, 1954.

July 17 — Guerrillas on Kinmen conduct a successful raid against the communist-held Tungshan Island off the southern coast of Fukien.

Sept. 27 — President Chiang recommends an extension of the term of office of the delegates to the first National Assembly, elected in 1947, until the second National Assembly can be elected.

Nov. 24 — The government protests to the United States against the proposed American transfer of the Amami Oshima Islands to Japan.

27 — Korean President Syngman Rhee arrives in Taipei.

1954

Jan. 23 — More than 14,000 Chinese communist

POW's in Korea, who refused to return to the Chinese mainland, arrive in Taiwan.

Mar. 11 — The second session of the first National Assembly approves indefinite extension of the *Temporary Provisions Effective During the Period of Communist Rebellion*.

22 — Chiang Kai-shek is reelected president for a second six-year term.

24 — Chen Cheng is elected vice president.

May 20 — President Chiang nominates O.K. Yu to be president of the Executive Yuan (premier).

June 4 — President Chiang appoints Yen Chia-kan governor of Taiwan.

Dec. 3 — The *Sino-American Mutual Defense Treaty* is signed in Washington.

1955

Jan. 26 — The US House of Representatives approves a resolution authorizing President Eisenhower to employ American armed forces to defend Taiwan, the Pescadores, and "related positions and territories."

Feb. 7 — Government troops begin to evacuate the Tachen Islands.

Mar. 3 — Foreign Minister George K.C. Yeh and US Secretary of State John Foster Dulles exchange instruments of ratification of the *Sino-American Mutual Defense Treaty* in Taipei.

1956

Jan. 12 — The Taiwan Provincial Government promulgates the *Rules for the Enforcement of the Statute on Urban Land Reform*.

May 28 — Foreign Minister George K.C. Yeh informs Philippine Ambassador Narciso Ramos that the ROC has full sovereignty over the Nansha Islands.

July 7 — Ground is broken for the construction of the East-West Cross-Island Highway.

1957

Apr. 21 — Taiwan voters go to the polls for the third time to elect county magistrates, city mayors, and provincial assemblymen.

May   3 — The Council of Grand Justices of the
Judicial Yuan rules that the nation's three
top representative organs—the Legislative Yuan, the Control Yuan, and the
National Assembly—shall collectively
represent the Chinese parliament in all
international parliamentary organizations.

Aug.   8 — General Chow Chih-jou is appointed governor of Taiwan, succeeding C.K. Yen.

Sept. 26 — The first council meeting of the Asian
Peoples' Anti-Communist League opens
in Taipei.

Oct. 20 — President Chiang is reelected Tsungtsai
(director-general) of the Kuomintang.

1958

May   14 — Mohammed Reza Pahlevi, the Shah of
Iran, arrives in Taipei for a five-day
state visit. ˙

Aug.   1 — An insurance program covering 180,000
government employees is put into effect.

      23 — The Battle of the Taiwan Straits begins
with the Chinese communists firing on
the Kinmen Islands.

Oct. 23 — President Chiang and US Secretary of
State John Foster Dulles issue a joint
communiqué reaffirming solidarity between the two countries and stating that
Quemoy and the Matsu Islands are
"closely related" to the defense of Taiwan and the Pescadores under present
conditions.

1959

Mar.   6 — The Faith (36,000 tons), the first tanker
built in the ROC, is launched at Keelung.

       9 — King Hussein of Jordan arrives in Taipei
for an eight-day state visit.

      13 — Some 300,000 Tibetans revolt against
the communists.

July 21 — The Legislative Yuan revises the Conscription Law, stipulating that 19-year-
old men are to be drafted for two years'
service in the army or three years in the
navy or air force.

Aug. 15 — The ROC Army receives Nike-Hercules

ground-to-air guided missiles from the
United States under a military aid program.

Sept. 1 — The Law on Compensation for Wrongful
Detentions and Convictions, designed to
compensate people in cases of miscar-
riages of justice, goes into effect.

1960

Feb.   2 — The Council of Grand Justices of the
Judicial Yuan announces that the total
membership of the National Assembly,
under the present period of national emergency, shall be 1,576.

      23 — The ROC establishes diplomatic rela-
tions with Cameroon.

Mar. 11 — The third session of the first National Assembly adopts an amendment to the Tem-
porary Provisions Effective During the
Period of Communist Rebellion.

      19 — The third session of the first National
Assembly decides to set up a committee
to study the exercise of initiative and
referendum by the National Assembly.

      22 — Chiang Kai-shek is reelected to a third
term as president, and Chen Cheng, to a
second term as vice president.

May   2 — Philippine President and Mrs. Carlos
Garcia arrive in Taipei for a six-day
state visit.

       9 — The East-West Cross-Island Highway is
opened to traffic.

June 18 — US President Eisenhower arrives in Taipei for a state visit.

      19 — President Chiang and US President Ei-
senhower issue a joint communiqué
pledging that their governments will continue to stand solidly behind the Sino-US
Mutual Defense Treaty against the Chinese communists in this area.

       — The Chinese communists hit Kinmen,
and the ROC artillery units retaliated.

Aug. 15 — The Council of Grand Justices of the
Judicial Yuan rules that, courts of all
levels shall be placed under the jurisdiction of the Judicial Yuan.

— The ROC recognizes the Congo (Brazzaville) Republic.

25 — The ROC Olympic Team in the opening procession of the Olympic Games in Rome protests the International Olympic Committee's ruling compelling ROC athletes to compete under the name of "Taiwan" instead of the "Republic of China."

Sept.   6 — Yang Chuan-kuang, the ROC's decathlon champion, wins the ROC's first Olympic silver medal.

1961

May   14 — US Vice President and Mrs. Lyndon B. Johnson visit the ROC.

Oct.   7 — Two defecting Chinese communist pilots, Shao Hsi-yen and Kao Yu-tsung, arrive in Taipei from South Korea.

27 — The 16th UN General Assembly votes for the admission of Outer Mongolia. The Republic of China abstains.

Dec.   1 — The first nuclear reactor in the ROC, installed by Chinese scientists at the National Tsinghua University campus in Hsinchu, is put into operation.

18 — The ROC establishes diplomatic ties with Upper Volta.

1962

Mar.   14 — Foreign Minister Shen Chang-huan declares that the ROC does not recognize Japan's so-called "residual sovereignty" over the Ryukyu Islands.

Apr.   3 — President and Mme. Philbert Tsiranana of the Malagasy Republic arrive for a six-day state visit.

Oct.   30 — The ROC rejects the McMahon Line as the boundary between China and India.

Nov.   22 — General Huang Chieh is appointed governor of Taiwan, succeeding General Chow Chih-jou.

Dec.   28 — The Ministry of Foreign Affairs declares border agreements signed between the Peking regime and Outer Mongolia and Pakistan illegal and not binding on the ROC.

1963

June   5 — King Bhumibol Adulyadej and Queen Sirikit of Thailand arrive in the ROC for a state visit.

Aug.   4 — The Ministry of Foreign Affairs declares that the ROC does not recognize the border treaty signed between the Peking regime and Afghanistan.

23 — Ambassador to the United States Tsiang Ting-fu signs the nuclear test ban treaty on behalf of the ROC.

Sept.   1 — The Council for International Economic Cooperation and Development is inaugurated to replace the Council for US Aid.

Oct.   6 — Dahomey President and Mme. Hubert Maga arrive for a six-day state visit.

Nov.   16 — The new premier, Yen Chia-kan, assumes office.

1964

Feb.   12 — Japanese Premier Shigeru Yoshida arrives in the ROC to confer with President Chiang Kai-shek.

June   14 — The NT$3,200 million multipurpose Shihmen Dam is dedicated.

Oct.   27 — The ROC and Korea sign a treaty of amity in Seoul.

1965

Apr.   9 — The ROC and the United States conclude in Taipei an accord to establish a Sino-American fund for economic and social development in Taiwan.

May   14 — Thomas Wen-yi Liao returns from Tokyo after renouncing his "Taiwan Independence movement."

25 — The ROC and the United States sign in Taipei an inventory of atomic equipment and materials to be reported to the International Atomic Energy Agency.

July   1 — The United States phases out economic aid to the ROC.

31 — The ROC and the United States sign an agreement in Taipei on the status of US forces in China.

Nov. 11 — Malagasy President Tsiranana arrives for a four-day visit.

23 — US warships return to the ROC 102 cases of rare books that were sent to the United States for safekeeping during World War II.

1966

Jan. 1 — US Vice President Hubert H. Humphrey arrives in the ROC to confer with Chinese leaders.

Feb. 15 — Korean President Park Chung Hee arrives for a four-day state visit.

Mar. 21 — The National Assembly elects President Chiang Kai-shek to a fourth term as president of the Republic.

22 — The National Assembly elects Premier Yen Chia-kan the third vice president of the Republic.

26 — The Ministry of Foreign Affairs announces the ROC's opposition to US recognition of Outer Mongolia.

July 3 — US Secretary of State Dean Rusk arrives in Taipei to confer with Chinese leaders.

6 — The Legislative Yuan approves the *Sino-Haitian Treaty of Amity* signed in Port-au-Prince on Feb. 15, 1966.

1967

Feb. 1 — The National Security Council is established by President Chiang Kai-shek with Vice Premier Huang Shao-ku as secretary-general and Ku Shu-tung as his deputy.

Apr. 4 — Australian Prime Minister Harold E. Holt arrives for a three-day visit.

July 1 — Taipei becomes a special municipality, with Kao Yu-shu as its mayor.

28 — The Chinese Cultural Renaissance Movement is officially organized, with President Chiang Kai-shek as its head.

Aug. 3 — The Executive Yuan decides to extend the period of compulsory education from six to nine years beginning in 1968.

4 — Malawi President Dr. H. Kamuzu Banda arrives for an eight-day state visit.

Sept. 25 — The first conference of the World Anti-Communist League opens in Taipei, with more than 200 leaders from 72 nations and areas attending.

Nov. 24 — The Chinese Economic Development Research Institute is inaugurated in Taipei.

1968

Aug. 24 — Taichung's Golden Dragons baseball team wins the 23rd Little League World Championship.

25 — Lesotho Premier Leabua Jonathan arrives in the ROC for an official visit.

Oct. 23 — Nigerian President Hamani Diori arrives in the ROC for an official visit.

Dec. 17 — The Chinese National Committee of the International Press Institute is established in Taipei.

20 — The nation chooses 26 new members to the National Assembly and the Legislative Yuan from among 52 candidates.

1969

May 26 — Sierra Leone Premier Siaka P. Stevens arrives in Taipei to confer with ROC leaders.

1970

July 12 — ROC athlete Chi Cheng breaks the women's 200-meter record in West Germany, with a time of 22.44 seconds.

1971

Aug. 14 — Ground for the construction of the North-South Freeway is broken near Linkou.

Oct. 25 — The Republic of China withdraws from the United Nations.

1972

Mar. 21 — President Chiang Kai-shek is reelected to a fifth six-year term.

May 26 — Former Vice Premier Chiang Ching-kuo becomes premier after approval by the Legislative Yuan.

Aug. 20 — The ROC Mei Ho baseball team wins the Senior League world title.

27 — The Taipei Little League baseball team wins the world title.

Sept. 29 — The Republic of China severs diplomatic relations with Japan.

Oct.   16 — President Dawda Kairba Jawara of Gambia arrives for an eight-day visit.

Nov.   12 — The Republic of China wins the World Cup Golf Championship in Melbourne.

Dec.   23 — An election of additional members to the National Assembly, Legislative Yuan, the Taiwan Provincial Assembly, and of new mayors and county magistrates is held in Taiwan, Kinmen, and Matsu.

1973

Jan.   22 — H.R.H. Prince Tuipelehake, C.B.E., prime minister of the Kingdom of Tonga, arrives for a one-week visit.

Oct.   30 — Tsengwen Dam and Reservoir, the largest in Taiwan, are completed.

Dec.   25 — Construction of the Suao-Hualien railroad is launched.

1974

Jan.   26 — Premier Chiang Ching-kuo announces an across-the-board price adjustment to help stabilize the economy.

Apr.   20 — The ROC announces the termination of Taiwan-Japan flights by China Airlines and Japan Airlines.

May   14 — Chen Te-nien, director of the Taiwan Railway Administration, and Peter Godwin, representing Lazard Brothers Co., sign an agreement under which a British consortium will loan £575 million to TRA's railway electrification project.

July   29 — The Sanch'ung-Chungli section of the North-South Freeway is opened to traffic.

Oct.   30 — The first F5E Freedom jet fighter made in the Republic of China rolls off the assembly line.

1975

Feb.   17 — The China Steel Corp., the Continental Illinois National Bank, and the Trust Company of Chicago sign a US$200 million loan contract to help finance construction of a steel mill in Kaohsiung.

Mar.   21 — Chinese officials stationed in Phnom Penh return to Taipei.

Apr.   5 — President Chiang Kai-shek passes away.

        6 — Yen Chia-kan, vice president of the Republic of China since 1966, takes the oath of office as the nation's second constitutional president.

       26 — The Embassy of the Republic of China in Saigon suspends operations.

       28 — Premier Chiang Ching-kuo is elected chairman of the Central Committee of the ruling Kuomintang.

June   9 — The Republic of China terminates diplomatic relations with the Republic of the Philippines.

July   1 — The ROC terminates diplomatic relations with Thailand.

        9 — The Republic of China and Japan sign a private aviation agreement that restores the Taiwan-Japan services of China Airline and a Japanese airline.

       26 — The newly built southern portion of the Suao-Hualien railroad is opened to traffic.

Aug.   29 — A nova in the Cugnus constellation is discovered by the Taipei observatory.

Oct.   21 — The second naphtha cracking plant of the Chinese Petroleum Corp. begins production.

1976

Mar.   26 — Dr. Lin Yu-tang, 81, one of the best known Chinese writers in English, dies in Hong Kong.

July   17 — The ROC team withdraws from the Montreal Games to protest competing under the name of "Taiwan."

Aug.   21 — Prince Maphevu Harry Dlamini, prime minister of the Kingdom of Swaziland, accompanied by Madame Dlamini and a party of eight, arrives for a seven-day visit.

Oct.   31 — Taichung Port in west central Taiwan is formally opened.

1977

Mar.   26 — The Chinese research vessel Hai Kung returns to Keelung after a 115-day exploratory expedition to the Antarctic.

May   18 — China Airlines' new Boeing 747SP begins nonstop service between Taipei and
the US West Coast.

June   3 — The 445,000-ton tanker Burmah En-
deavour, built by the China Shipbuilding Corp. for US Gatx Oswego, is
launched at Kaohsiung. It is the world's
third largest vessel.

July   9 — President Yen Chia-kan leaves for a three-
day state visit to Saudi Arabia, at the
invitation of King Khaled Bib Abdul
Aziz Al-Saud.

Sept.   19 — King Taufa'ahau Tupou IV and Queen
Halaevalu Mata'aho of the Kingdom of
Tonga arrive for a week's state visit at the
invitation of President and Madame Yen
Chia-kan.

Oct.   17 — Akira Nishiyama, former Japanese ambassador to South Korea, arrives to assume his duties as director of the Japan
Interchange Association's Taipei office.

1978
Mar.   21 — Premier Chiang Ching-kuo is elected by
the National Assembly as president for
the sixth constitutional presidential term
of the Republic of China.

30 — The first generator of Taiwan's first nuclear power plant begins its full capacity
operation of 636,000 kilowatts.

May   26 — The Legislative Yuan endorses President
Chiang's appointment of Sun Yun-suan,
former minister of economic affairs, as
the new premier.

June   20 — The Republic of China is listed the 25th
largest trading country in the world by
the International Monetary Fund.

Oct.   31 — The Taiwan Area Freeway, with a total
length of 377 km, is opened to traffic.

Dec.   8 — The Legislative Yuan passes the revised *Foreign Exchange Management
Regulations* under which the New Taiwan dollar is no longer pegged to the
US dollar.

16 — President Chiang Ching-kuo strongly
condemns the US decision to sever diplomatic relations with the Republic of
China in favor of the Peking regime.

1979
Mar.   1 — The US embassy in Taipei formally
closes, to be succeeded by the American
Institute in Taiwan.

— The Washington Office of the Coordination Council for North American Affairs
of the Republic of China opens.

Apr.   10 — US President Jimmy Carter signs legislation permitting continued commercial and
cultural relations between the US government and the ROC following the break
in diplomatic ties.

July   1 — The electrification of Taiwan's 1,153-
km-long west coast trunk line railway
between Keelung and Kaohsiung is completed.

— Kaohsiung becomes a special municipality under the direct jurisdiction of the
Executive Yuan.

Sept.   6 — The Cabinet announces the extension of
the ROC's territorial waters to 12 nautical miles, and the establishment of a 200-
mile economic zone.

Nov.   16 — The Republic of China and the United
States conclude 40 days of talks on the
revision of their air transportation agreement. Under the memorandum issued
by the two parties, the ROC will open
civil air services to four new US stops:
Guam, Seattle, New York, and Dallas-
Fort Worth.

1980
Jan.   3 — The US government informs the ROC
government that it will resume arms
sales to the ROC after a one-year suspension.

Dec.   27 — Twenty-two supplementary members
are elected to the Control Yuan from
among 54 candidates by members of
the Taiwan Provincial Assembly, the
Taipei City Council, and the Kaohsiung
City Council.

1981

Apr.   2 — President Chiang Ching-kuo is reelected chairman of the Kuomintang by acclamation at the 12th National Congress in Taipei.

May   4 — The first European Trade Fair in the Republic of China is held at the Taipei World Trade Center with some 293 companies from 13 Western European countries participating.

1982

May 12 — The Council for Agricultural Planning and Development (CAPD) reveals the second phase of the land reform program.

      20 — The Cabinet approves the draft of a *Genetic Health Law* to legalize abortion and prevent couples with known genetic diseases from having children.

June 20 — The Directorate General of Telecommunications (DGT) opens the first public data switching service in the ROC.

Oct. 16 — Aleksandr I. Solzhenitsyn, 1970 Nobel Literature Prize winner, arrives in Taiwan from Tokyo at the invitation of Wu San-lien of the Literary Foundation of the ROC.

1983

Jan. 14 — The Legislative Yuan passes a revision of the *Trademark Law* to impose prison terms for infringement of trademarks.

Feb. 16 — The Dutch airline Martinair inaugurates flight service to Taiwan, marking the opening of air service between the Netherlands and the Republic of China.

Apr. 12 — China Airlines inaugurates regular flight service to Amsterdam as the first step toward establishing a world-girdling commercial air service.

June   7 — The Legislative Yuan passes the *Firearms Control Law*, placing the manufacture, possession, and use of firearms and other weapons under stricter control.

July 12 — A groundbreaking ceremony is held to mark the start of Taipei's underground railway project.

Oct. 31 — Taipei's 809-meter long Kuantu Bridge, the first multi-arch steel bridge in East Asia, is opened to traffic.

1984

Jan. 12 — The Cabinet approves a plan to build a synchrotron research center within five years.

Mar.   1 — The Republic of China's first domestically developed jet trainer AT-3 rolls off the assembly line. The twin-seat trainer, fitted with two Garrett TFE 731-2-2L engines, each with a thrust of 1,590 kg, was developed by the Aeronautical Institute of Science and Technology.

      21 — President Chiang Ching-kuo is reelected for a second six-year term.

May 20 — President Chiang Ching-kuo nominates Yu Kuo-hwa, chairman of the Council for Economic Planning and Development and governor of the Central Bank of China, as the new premier.

June 29 — The Legislative Yuan approves the long-awaited and controversial *Genetic Health Law*.

July 20 — The Legislative Yuan passes the *Labor Standards Law*.

Aug.   1 — ROC athlete Tsai Wen-yee wins a bronze medal in the weightlifting events of the 1984 Olympic Games.

Sept. 20 — The ROC Council of Agriculture is formally established.

Oct. 12 — The ROC-Australia Trade Association and the Chinese-New Zealand Business Council are formally inaugurated in Taipei.

1985

Jan.   8 — The Hong Kong Affairs Task Force under the Executive Yuan decides to simplify exit and entry application procedures, relax controls on foreign exchange, and adopt incentive measures to encourage large enterprises and monetary institutions in Hong Kong to move to Taiwan.

Apr. 16 — The first test tube baby in the Republic of

China is born at Veterans General Hospital in Taipei.

22 — The Industrial Technology Research Institute successfully develops an amorphous-silicon solar battery of high commercial value.

July   9 — The last part of a transoceanic telecommunication cable system, which will link Taiwan, Hong Kong, and Singapore, is hauled ashore in Toucheng, Ilan.

19 — The Ministry of National Defense announces that a domestically developed surface-to-air missile named "Sky Bow" made a successful debut in a test firing.

Sept.   29 — ROC decathlon athletes Ku Chin-shui and Li Fu-en win a gold and silver medal respectively in the sixth Asian Track and Field Championships in Jakarta, Indonesia.

1986

Apr.   23 — National Taiwan University Hospital separates a pair of 14-day-old Siamese twins, saving one of the baby girls' life and setting a world record for separating the youngest Siamese twins.

24 — ROC Minister of Foreign Affairs Chu Fu-sung and Paraguayan Foreign Minister Carlos Augusto Saldivar sign an extradition treaty in Taipei on behalf of their respective governments.

May   18 — The Ministry of National Defense announces that an air-to-air "Sky Sword" missile has been successfully tested by shooting down a Hawk missile.

Aug.   3 — Construction of the Synchronous Radiation Research Center is started at the Hsinchu Science-Based Industrial Park.

Sept.   25 — The Republic of China, after withdrawing 13 years ago, is readmitted to the Olympic Council of Asia (OCA).

Oct.   6 — The Ministry of Economic Affairs decides to invest NT$1.2 billion in developing anti-pollution technology over the next three years.

15 — Lee Yuan-tseh, a member of the Academia Sinica, wins the 1986 Nobel Prize in chemistry.

Nov.   6 — The Democratic Progressive Party (DPP) holds its first Representative Assembly and releases a draft of its charter and platform.

1987

June   23 — The Legislative Yuan passes the *National Security Law during the Period of National Mobilization for Suppression of the Communist Rebellion*. After the law becomes effective, the *Emergency Decree* in Taiwan and the Pescadores (Penghu) will be lifted.

July   15 — The *Emergency Decree* is lifted in the Taiwan area, the *National Security Law* is promulgated, and foreign exchange controls are relaxed.

Aug.   1 — The Council of Labor Affairs is formally established under the Executive Yuan.

Nov.   2 — The ROC Red Cross Society begins accepting applications from local residents wishing to visit relatives in mainland China.

10 — ROC-US talks on intellectual property rights begin in Taipei.

1988

Jan.   1 — Registrations for new newspapers are opened, and restrictions on the number of pages per issue are relaxed.

11 — The Legislative Yuan passes the *Law on Assembly and Parades during the Period of National Mobilization for Suppression of the Communist Rebellion*, which outlines three fundamental principles and specifies areas that will be off-limits to demonstrators.

13 — President Chiang Ching-kuo passes away of heart failure and hemorrhage at 3:50 p.m.

— Vice President Lee Teng-hui is sworn in as president of the Republic of China to complete the late President Chiang's second six-year term, which runs from 1984 to 1990.

Mar.   3 — The Council for Economic Planning and Development approves the establishment of an US$11 billion International Economic Cooperation and Development Fund to assist developing countries.

24 — The Government Information Office and the Ministry of National Defense reiterate that the ROC has never engaged in the development of nuclear weapons. This is confirmed by the US government.

Apr.   18 — The ROC Red Cross Society begins forwarding mail from Taiwan residents to mainland China.

28 — An ROC delegation attends the annual convention of the Asian Development Bank (ADB) in Manila.

July   8 — Acting Chairman Lee Teng-hui is elected chairman of the Kuomintang at the ruling party's 13th National Congress.

28 — The Executive Yuan approves regulations governing the import of publications, films, and radio and television programs from communist-controlled areas.

Aug.   18 — The Mainland Affairs Task Force is established under the Executive Yuan.

30 — ROC-US talks on finance and banking open in Washington. The ROC negotiators agree to open the Taiwan market to credit card companies and to expand credit for foreign banks.

Sept.   5 — The Executive Yuan announces that the long-range Hsiung Feng II missile has been successfully developed and will soon be added to the ROC arsenal.

Oct.   25 — A comprehensive farmer health insurance is initiated.

Nov.   3 — The Mainland Affairs Task Force revises regulations to allow mainland compatriots to visit sick relatives or attend their funerals in Taiwan.

17 — The Executive Yuan approves the private installation of small satellite dish antennas, which will allow viewers to tune into the KU-band and receive television programming from Japan's NHK station.

Dec.   1 — The Executive Yuan announces guidelines governing unofficial participation in international academic conferences and cultural and athletic activities held on the mainland, as well as regulations governing visits to Taiwan by overseas mainland scholars and students.

1989

Jan.   10 — The ROC and the Commonwealth of the Bahamas establish diplomatic relations.

20 — The Legislative Yuan passes the *Law on Civic Organizations*.

26 — The Legislative Yuan passes the *Law on the Voluntary Retirement of Senior Parliamentarians*.

Mar.   6 — President and Madam Lee Teng-hui arrive in Singapore for a four-day visit.

27 — The Central Bank of China announces the cancellation of limits on the daily fluctuation of the NT dollar against the US greenback, to be effective April 3.

Apr.   7 — The Chinese Taipei Olympic Committee announces that ROC athletic teams and organizations will participate in international sports events held on the mainland under the name "Chinese Taipei."

17 — The Mainland Affairs Task Force passes the proposal to allow teachers and staff of public schools to travel to the Chinese mainland for family visits. On the 18th, the council decides to permit newsgathering and filmmaking on the mainland.

30 — Finance Minister Shirley Kuo leads an ROC delegation to the 22nd annual Asian Development Bank meeting in Peking.

May   28 — Ching Kuo, the first ROC-developed and manufactured indigenous defense fighter, successfully completes its first test flight.

31 — One million students participate in a Hand in Hand, Heart to Heart rally in support of the mainland democracy movement.

June   1 — Lee Huan is sworn in as premier of the ROC.

4 — President Lee Teng-hui issues a statement condemning the Tienanmen Massacre.

10 — Direct telephone links are opened between the two sides of the Taiwan Straits.

19 — The Hong Kong and Macau Affairs Task Force announces the government's plan to simplify procedures for the relocation of Hong Kong and Macao compatriots in Taiwan and to provide assistance for their emigration to a third country.

July   11 — The Legislative Yuan approves a partial revision of the *Banking Law* which completely abolishes interest rate controls and deregulates entry into the banking system. The law goes into effect on July 19.

20 — The ROC establishes formal diplomatic ties with Grenada.

Aug.   1 — A foreign currency call loan market is established in Taipei, designed to make the metropolis an international financial center.

Sept.   4 — Guatemalan President Marco Vincicio Cerezo Arevalo and President Lee Teng-hui sign a joint communiqué in Taipei calling for closer bilateral relations.

15 — Prime Minister Mary Eugenia Charles of the Commonwealth of Dominica arrives in Taipei for a six-day visit.

25 — The Sky-bow Weapons System, developed and manufactured by the ROC, is added to the nation's military defense system.

26 — The Executive Yuan permits pro-democracy supporters from the mainland to settle in Taiwan.

Oct.   2 — The ROC and Liberia re-establish diplomatic relations. Peking severs formal ties with Liberia in protest.

12 — The ROC and Belize announce the establishment of diplomatic relations.

— King Mswati III of Swaziland arrives for a five-day visit.

Dec.   2 — Elections for the Legislative Yuan, Taiwan Provincial Assembly, Taipei and Kaohsiung city councils, county magis-

trates, and provincial-level city mayors are held.

1990

Jan.   14 — President Lee Teng-hui and President Prosper Avril of Haiti sign a joint communiqué calling for stronger bilateral cooperation.

16 — Low-ranking government employees are permitted to visit relatives across the Straits, and native Taiwanese who moved to the mainland before 1949 are allowed to visit relatives in Taiwan.

Feb.   13 — The Mainland Affairs Task Force permits Taiwan's performing artists to stage commercial performances on the mainland and to participate in activities sponsored by the Chinese communists.

26 — President Lee Teng-hui and El Salvadoran President Alfredo Felix Cristiani Burkard sign a joint communiqué for closer bilateral cooperation.

Mar.   1 — The Executive Yuan approves direct trade between the ROC and the Soviet Union and Albania.

17 — Thousands of university students stage a sit-down protest at the Chiang Kai-shek Memorial Hall Plaza to express opposition to the National Assembly's attempt to expand its authority.

21 — Lee Teng-hui is elected the eighth-term president of the ROC.

22 — Li Yuan-zu is elected vice president of the ROC.

27 — The eighth plenum of the National Assembly approves

Apr.   5 — The ROC reestablishes diplomatic relations with the Kingdom of Lesotho. Peking severs ties with Lesotho two days later.

8 — Economics Minister Chen Li-an and Singaporean Minister of Trade and Industries, Lee Hsien Loong, preside over the first ministerial-level conference between the two countries on economic cooperation.

30 — Elected officials of all levels are permit-

ted to make private visits to the mainland during recesses. Veterans who were stranded on the mainland after the national government moved to Taiwan in 1949 are allowed to apply for resettlement in Taiwan.

May   16 — The KMT Central Standing Committee accepts the resignation of Premier Lee Huan and his Cabinet ministers.

20 — Lee Teng-hui and Li Yuan-zu are inaugurated as president and vice president of the ROC.

— President Lee Teng-hui announces a special amnesty, which includes the pardoning of dissidents Hsu Hsin-liang and Shih Ming-teh.

26 — The ROC establishes diplomatic relations with Guinea Bissau.

29 — Premier nominee Hau Pei-tsun is approved by the Legislative Yuan, and is immediately appointed premier by President Lee Teng-hui.

June   17 — President Andres Rodriguez of Paraguay arrives in Taipei to sign a joint communiqué calling for closer bilateral relations with the ROC.

21 — The Council of Grand Justices announces that senior parliamentarians should terminate their responsibilities by December 31, 1991.

25 — Reporters from the mainland are permitted to visit Taiwan for newsgathering purposes, and government employees from Taiwan are allowed to visit sick relatives or attend funerals across the Straits.

July   4 — The National Affairs Conference concludes in Taipei, after six days of discussions on parliamentary reforms, the central and local government systems, the Constitution, and mainland policy.

22 — The ROC severs diplomatic relations with Saudi Arabia, after the latter switches formal recognition to communist China.

Aug.   10 — The ROC government declares its support of a United Nations call for world

sanctions against Iraq over its invasion of Kuwait.

31 — Premier Hau Pei-tsun advises the Legislative Yuan that ROC relations with the mainland will operate under the concept of "one country, two areas."

Sept.   1 — Premier Hau Pei-tsun announces the objectives of the Six-Year National Development Plan, which includes public construction projects affecting economics, culture, education, and medicine.

17 — A team of 200 athletes and coaches flies to the Chinese mainland for the ROC's first attendance of the Asian Games in 20 years.

19 — The Red Cross societies of the ROC and the mainland reach agreement on procedures for the repatriation of illegal mainland entrants to Taiwan.

Oct.   7 — The National Unification Council is established under the Office of the President to help plan the policy framework for national unification, and to integrate various opinions about the issue at all levels of society.

11 — The Ministry of the Interior reiterates that the Tiaoyutai island group belongs to the ROC. The chain of eight uninhabited islets, located in the East China Sea, also is claimed by Japan and communist China.

18 — The Mainland Affairs Council is established under the Executive Yuan to formulate and implement mainland policy.

27 — Moscow City Mayor Gavriil H. Popov arrives for a formal visit to the ROC to discuss the strengthening of ROC-Soviet trade relations.

Nov.   1 — President Lee Teng-hui receives an Outstanding International Alumnus Citation from Cornell University.

15 — The Ministry of Foreign Affairs announces the ROC-Canadian agreement to exchange aviation rights and establish Taipei economic and cultural offices in major Canadian cities.

20 — The first ROC-USSR fishery coopera-

tion conference is held in Tokyo for discussions on technological exchanges and expansion of fishing zones.

21 — The Straits Exchange Foundation, a private intermediary organization financially supported by the government, is established to handle technical affairs arising from people-to-people contacts between Taiwan and the mainland.

1991

Jan.   6 — A memorandum is signed between the ROC and Saudi Arabia for the mutual establishment of representative offices in their capital cities.

7 — French Minister of Industry and Territorial Development Roger Fauroux participates in the seventh ROC-France Economic Cooperation Conference in Taipei.

31 — The Executive Yuan approves a budget of about US$303 billion for the Six-Year National Development Plan.

Mar. 14 — The Executive Yuan passes the *Guidelines for National Unification*, which are now the highest directives governing ROC mainland policy. Its long-term goal is to establish a democratic, free, and equitably prosperous China.

Apr. 22 — The second extraordinary session of the First National Assembly passes, at its sixth plenary meeting, the *Additional Articles of the Constitution of the ROC* and approves the abolishment of the *Temporary Provisions Effective During the Period of Communist Rebellion.*

30 — President Lee Teng-hui declares the termination of the Period of National Mobilization for Suppression of the Communist Rebellion, effective on May 1. He abolishes the *Temporary Provisions* and promulgates the *Additional Articles of the Constitution*, also effective on May 1.

May   9 — Visa application restrictions for USSR nationals are relaxed, and visa applications for purposes other than business are permitted.

24 — The Legislative Yuan approves the abolishment of the *Statutes for the Purging of Communist Agents.*

June 26 — Approval is given to 15 of the 19 applications to set up private commercial banks.

27 — Government Spokesman Shaw Yu-ming announces that mainland journalists will no longer have to renounce their membership in the Chinese Communist Party when applying to visit Taiwan.

July   4 — The ROC and Czechoslovakia agree to exchange representative offices.

8 — The ROC and the Central African Republic resume diplomatic relations.

Aug.   5 — President Lee Teng-hui receives Fijian Prime Minister Ratu Sir Kamisese Mara; an ROC-Fiji technological cooperation agreement is signed on August 6.

12 — Two mainland journalists arrive in Taipei, marking the first-ever visit by the mainland Chinese press.

18 — Vice President Li Yuan-zu leaves for a state visit to Costa Rica, Nicaragua, and Honduras, and to attend the 23rd Plenary Meeting of the World League for Freedom and Democracy at San José, Costa Rica.

Sept. 25 — The Mainland Affairs Council announces the establishment of a task force to combat crime across the Taiwan Straits.

Oct.   11 — Direct air service begins between Australia and the ROC.

Nov.   6 — The ROC and Latvia sign memoranda for economic cooperation and the exchange of trade offices.

13 — The ROC joins the Asia-Pacific Economic Cooperation (APEC) along with Hong Kong and mainland China.

15 — South African President Frederik Willem de Klerk signs a joint communiqué with President Lee Teng-hui for closer relations between the two countries.

Dec.   21 — The ruling Kuomintang wins 71 percent of the vote and 254 of the 325 seats in the election for the Second National Assembly.

22 — Dissident mainland Chinese astrophysicist Fang Li-chih visits Taipei.

31 — All senior delegates to the First National Assembly, Control Yuan, and Legislative Yuan retire from office.

1992

Jan.   20 — The French Secretary of State for Foreign Trade Jean-Noël Jeanneney visits Taipei to discuss participation in the Six-Year National Development Plan and further economic cooperation between the ROC and France.

27 — The Fair Trade Commission is established under the Executive Yuan.

29 — The ROC and Latvia announce the establishment of relations at the consulate-general level.

Feb.   4 — The *Fair Trade Law* goes into effect.

18 — A delegation from the US President's Export Council arrives to promote ROC-US trade.

28 — The ROC and the Philippines sign an official investment guarantee agreement to protect investments by Taiwan businessmen.

Mar.   7 — Nicaraguan President Violeta Barrios de Chamorro and President Lee Teng-hui sign a joint communiqué in Taipei for stronger bilateral relations.

23 — The first-ever meeting convenes in Peking between the SEF and the mainland's Association for Relations Across the Taiwan Straits, to discuss issues related to document verification and indirect registered mail services.

27 — The ROC and Bulgaria agree to establish direct air links between Taipei and Sofia.

Apr.   17 — Legislative proceedings are completed for the *National Employment Act*, which will serve as the basis for the employment of foreign nationals in the ROC.

19 — Minister of Foreign Trade Yvonne C.M.T. van Rooy of the Netherlands visits Taipei to seek stronger bilateral relations.

29 — Bolivian Vice President Luis Ossio Sanjines officiates the inauguration of the Bolivian Commercial and Financial Representative Office in Taipei.

May   10 — Swedish Minister of Transport and Communications, Mats Odell, visits Taipei to discuss closer cooperation and future exchanges with the ROC.

11 — President Andre Kolingba of the Central African Republic visits Taipei.

17 — Wu Ta-you, president of Academia Sinica, attends academic conferences in Peking and Tientsin.

30 — The *Additional Articles* 11 through 18 of the Constitution go into effect.

31 — The Mainland Affairs Council allows Chinese mainlanders to come to Taiwan and care for their old or sick relatives.

June   10 — A revised *Copyright Law* goes into effect, providing explicit legal protection for intellectual property rights and imposing heavier penalties for infringement of copyright.

14 — Ronald Freeman, Vice President of the European Bank for Reconstruction and Development, visits the ROC to discuss Sino-European trade and financial relations.

19 — The ROC resumes diplomatic relations with Niger.

— The Legislative Yuan approves the *Law on Foreign Futures Contracts*, which will take effect in January 1993.

July   3 — The Legislative Yuan passes a revision of the *Law on Civic Organizations*, which calls for a Political Party Review Committee be formed under the Ministry of the Interior.

7 — The Legislative Yuan passes a revision of the *National Security Law*, which would reduce the number of black-listed persona non grata from 282 to five.

9 — The Argentine Trade and Cultural Office is opened in Taipei after a 20-year break in diplomatic relations.

16 — The Legislative Yuan passes the *Statute Governing Relations Between People of the Taiwan Area and the Mainland Area*.

19 — The ROC's five-year lease of three Knox-class frigates from the United States is approved by US President George Bush.

23 — Former French Premier Michel Rocard visits the ROC to strengthen friendship between the two countries.

Aug.   1 — The National Unification Council defines "one China" as "one country and two areas separately ruled by two political entities."

— Taiwan Garrison General Headquarters, the ROC's highest security institution in the Taiwan area, is disbanded; and the Coastal Patrol General Headquarters is established under the Ministry of National Defense.

18 — The Department of Anti-Corruption is established under the Ministry of Justice.

23 — The ROC severs diplomatic relations with South Korea.

25 — Niger's Prime Minister Amadou Cheiffou arrives in Taipei to advance mutual understanding between the two countries.

30 — Former British Prime Minister Margaret Thatcher expresses support for the ROC's entry into the GATT during her visit to Taipei.

Sept.   2 — President Lee Teng-hui and Guatemalan President Jorge Antonio Serrano sign a joint communiqué calling for closer bilateral cooperation in Taipei.

— Canadian International Trade Minister Michael Wilson visits Taipei to boost ROC-Canada trade ties; he is the first ministerial official to visit the ROC since bilateral ties were severed in 1970.

— The Bureau of Entry and Exit announces that members of the Chinese People's Political Consultative Conference in mainland China may apply to visit Taiwan for cultural and academic exchanges.

6 — Direct air service between the ROC and Vietnam resumes for the second time in 13 months.

13 — Latvian Prime Minister Ivars Godmanis visits Taipei to seek mutually beneficial cooperation; an ROC-Latvia investment guarantee agreement is signed on September 17.

21 — The US Department of Defense decides to sell 12 SH-2F light airborne multipurpose system helicopters to the ROC.

22 — Political Vice Foreign Minister John Chang and Oleg Lobov, Chairman of the Export Council to the Russian President Boris Yeltsin, sign two diplomatic memoranda and a document of state protocol pledging the promotion of trade, tourism, investment, cultural, and scientific and technological exchanges.

24 — Foreign Minister Fredrick Chien and his Vanuatu counterpart Serge Vohor sign a joint communiqué pledging reciprocal recognition.

29 — The ROC is granted observer status in the GATT, which also resolves to accept the ROC's application into GATT under the name, the "Separate Customs Territory of Taiwan, P'enghu, Kinmen and Matsu".

Oct.   11 — President Lee Teng-hui and Panamanian President Guillermo Endara sign a joint communiqué to expand bilateral cooperation.

12 — Premier Hau Pei-tsun receives Austrian Minister for Economic Affairs Wolfgang Schüssel.

22 — Belgian Foreign Trade Minister Robert Urbain visits Taipei to relay a message of welcome to Taiwan businessmen intending to invest in Belgium and pledges support for the ROC's bid to join GATT.

27 — Australian Tourism and Resources Minister Alan Griffiths visits Taipei to promote closer bilateral trade relations. Mr. Griffiths is the first Australian Minister visiting Taipei since 1972.

Nov.   3 — Indonesian Minister of Research and Technology Bacharuddin Habibie leads a 30-member delegation to Taiwan.

4 — Vice Minister of Economic Affairs Chiang Pin-kung heads an observer delegation to the Geneva meeting of GATT

Council of Representatives after the ROC's absence of 21 years.

7 — After more than three decades of military administration, Quemoy (Kinmen) and Matsu revert to civilian rule as the *Statute Governing the Security and Guidance of the Kinmen, Matsu, Tungsha, and Nansha Areas* goes into effect.

9 — Saint Lucia's Prime Minister John George Melvin Compton visits Taipei.

10 — The Nigerian Trade Office is set up in Taipei to promote economic relations with the ROC.

12 — ROC and US defense representatives sign a letter of offer and acceptance for the ROC's purchase of 150 F-16A and F-16B jet fighters from the United States.

18 — German Vice Chancellor Jürgen Möllemann and Economics Minister Vincent C. Siew reach an agreement on the establishment of direct air links and channels of communication on trade between the ROC and Germany.

19 — The Council of Agriculture bans all import, export, and trade of rhino-horn products.

30 — United States Trade Representative Carla A. Hills visits Taipei.

Dec.   19 — The Kuomintang wins 53.02 percent and the Democratic Progressive Party 31.03 percent of the popular vote in the election for the Second Legislative Yuan.

1993

Jan.   14 — The Legislative Yuan approves a US$12.47 billion budget for the purchase of 150 F-16 jet fighters from the United States and 60 Mirage 2000-5s from France.

15 — ROC and Philippine officials sign an agreement in Manila, setting the guidelines for transforming the former US naval facility at Subic Bay into an industrial complex.

Feb.   22 — Taiwan-made film *The Wedding Ban-*

quet wins a Golden Bear Award for Best Picture at the 43rd annual Berlin International Film Festival.

26 — Two China mainland basketball teams arrive in Taiwan to play exhibition matches against local teams; this marks the first time in four decades that athletes from Taiwan and the mainland will compete in Taiwan.

27 — Taiwan Provincial Governor Lien Chan succeeds Hau Pei-tsun as premier of the ROC following his confirmation by the Legislative Yuan.

Mar.   21 — Republic of Nauru President Bernard Dowiyogo visits Taipei.

26 — In an interview with the US Cable News Network, President Lee Teng-hui stresses the ROC's willingness to form a regional collective security system with Asia-Pacific countries.

29 — Direct air service between the ROC and the United Kingdom begins.

— New Zealand's Minister of Customs and Associate Minister of Tourism, Murray McCully leads a nine-member delegation to Taipei. Mr. McCully is the first New Zealand's Minister visiting Taipei since 1972.

Apr.   22 — The Legislative Yuan ratifies the 1989 ROC-US copyright agreement and passes amendments to the *Copyright Law*, which go into effect on April 26.

— Tonga's Prime Minister Vaea and Madame Vaea visit the ROC.

29 — Representatives of the Straits Exchange Foundation and its mainland counterpart, the Association for Relations Across the Taiwan Straits, sign three agreements and a joint accord at a historic meeting in Singapore; the agreements and accord go into effect on May 29.

May   1 — The Taipei Economic and Trade Office in Tel Aviv begins operation.

7 — The first ROC-made PFG-2 missile frigate, the Cheng-kung, goes into service.

8 — A 186-member team from the ROC par-

ticipates in the first East Asian Games in Shanghai.

13 — Former US Secretary of Defense Dick Cheney visits Taipei.

15 — Tuvalu's Prime Minister Bikenibeu Paeniu and Madame Paeniu visit the ROC.

June   11 — President Lee Teng-hui receives former Philippine President Corazon Aquino.

21 — An ROC-US agreement for technical cooperation in the field of environmental protection is signed in Washington, D.C.

29 — President Lee Teng-hui receives former US Vice President Dan Quayle.

30 — The Executive Yuan approves an Economic Stimulus Package to accelerate industrial upgrading and to develop Taiwan into an Asia-Pacific Regional Operations Center.

July   2 — The *Public Functionary Assets Disclosure Law* goes into effect.

8 — The ROC and Nicaragua sign a joint communiqué pledging bilateral cooperation.

10 — Vietnam's Economic and Cultural Office in Taipei opens.

12 — The Taipei-Moscow Economic and Cultural Coordination Commission begins operation in Moscow.

Aug.   10 — The New KMT Alliance breaks with the ruling Kuomintang and forms the New Party.

11 — The *Cable Television Law* goes into effect.

16 — The 14th National Congress of the KMT opens. President Lee Teng-hui is re-elected chairman of the KMT; while Vice President Li Yuan-zu, former Premier Hau Pei-tsun, Judicial Yuan President Lin Yang-kang, and Premier Lien Chan are elected vice chairmen on August 18.

17 — The ROC and Australia sign two memoranda on the protection of industrial property rights and on investment promotion and technical cooperation.

Sept.   2 — The Executive Yuan passes an adminis-

trative reform package to eradicate corruption and inefficiency in the government.

23 — The ROC and Belgium sign three investment cooperation agreements to boost economic and technological ties.

Oct.   26 — The ROC and Mexico sign a pact to promote investment and technology transfer.

Nov.   19 — Vincent C. Siew, chairman of the Council for Economic Planning and Development, represents President Lee Teng-hui at the APEC leaders economic conference in Seattle.

25 — South Korea opens its Korean Mission in Taipei to replace the embassy closed after South Korea and the ROC broke off diplomatic relations.

30 — The ROC signs an investment promotion and protection pact with Argentina to strengthen economic ties with South America.

Dec.   9 — The Government Information Office lifts the ban on radio stations and approves the applications of 13 broadcasting companies for operation licenses.

15 — The Legislative Yuan approves a revision of the *University Law*, which gives more autonomy to colleges and allows students to participate in meetings related to school affairs.

1994

Jan.   11 — The *Consumer Protection Law* goes into effect; manufacturers are held responsible for harming consumers even when negligence or intent to do harm are not found to be factors.

12 — The ROC and Lesotho sever diplomatic relations.

15 — Lee Yuan-tseh succeeds Wu Ta-you as president of Academia Sinica.

Feb.   9 — President Lee leaves for the Philippines, Indonesia, and Thailand on an eight-day visit.

Mar.   2 — The ROC and Belize sign a joint communiqué pledging bilateral cooperation.

23 — The Legislative Yuan increases the annual number of permanent residency permits for mainland spouses from 300 to 600.

25 — The SEF and the ARATS hold talks in Peking on fishery disputes and the repatriation of illegal entrants and hijackers.

28 — The ROC and the Central African Republic sign a joint communiqué pledging further cooperation.

Apr.   12 — The Mainland Affairs Council decides to suspend all cultural and educational exchanges with the mainland before the Chinese communists provide reasonable and satisfactory explanations of the Qiandao Lake tragedy on Mar. 31 in which 24 Taiwan tourists are killed.

May   2 — The ROC and Grenada sign a joint communiqué pledging bilateral cooperation.

4 — President Lee Teng-hui leaves for Nicaragua, Costa Rica, South Africa, and Swaziland on a 13-day official visit.

June   6 — Premier Lien Chan pays the first visit of a high-ranking ROC official to Mexico in 23 years after the two severed diplomatic ties.

29 — The Peruvian Trade Office opens in Taipei.

July   7 — The Legislative Yuan passes the *Self-governance Law for Provinces and Counties*, explicitly stipulating that provincial governors be chosen by direct election. The *Self-governance Law for Special Municipalities* is passed the next day.

13 — Seven foreign ministers and representatives from Central American countries come to Taiwan to participate in the Third Mixed Commission Conference of Central American Nations, and sign a joint declaration with the ROC supporting the ROC's bid for UN participation.

30 — The SEF and the ARATS start talks in Taipei. This is the first high-level dialogue between the two organizations since the Qiandao Lake incident on Mar. 31, 1994.

Aug.   8 — The SEF and the ARATS sign and make public a joint press release confirming the results of the second round of Chiao-Tang talks.

9 — The US government announces trade sanctions against the ROC under the Pelly Amendment, placing a ban on imports of Taiwan wildlife products effective from August 19, 1994.

Sept. 7 — US Assistant Secretary of State Winston Lord formally notifies the ROC representative in Washington, Ding Mou-shih, of the result from the Clinton administration's policy discussions about Taiwan: The US agrees to the ROC representative office changing its name to the Taipei Economic and Cultural Representative Office in the United States, and to ROC officials visiting all US government offices except the White House and the Department of State on official business.

19 — On behalf of their respective governments, the ROC representative in Washington, Ding Mou-shih, and the chairman of the American Institute in Taiwan, Natale Bellocchi, sign a *Trade and Investment Framework Agreement*.

22 — The chairman of the UN General Committee drops the proposal on the ROC's UN membership from the agenda after a 90-minute debate in which seven nations support the ROC and 20 oppose the proposal.

Oct.   27 — The Legislative Yuan passes revisions to the *Wildlife Conservation Law*, greatly toughening penalties against violators and stipulating that the breeding in captivity of endangered animals must cease within three years.

Dec.   3 — The first popular elections for the governor of Taiwan Province and mayors of Taipei and Kaohsiung municipalities are held. James C.Y. Soong is elected governor of Taiwan. Chen Shui-bian and Wu Den-yih win the mayor seats of Taipei and Kaohsiung, respectively.

4 — US Secretary of Transportation Federico Pena visits the ROC, becoming the first US cabinet member to carry out the new US policy governing high-ranking official visits to Taipei.

12 — The Lien cabinet is re-organized and new cabinet members are sworn in on December 15.

29 — The first squadron of Ching-kuo indigenous defense fighters is officially commissioned, upgrading the combat ability of the ROC Air Force and demonstrating initial results of research and development.

1995

Jan.   5 — The Executive Yuan Council approves the plan for developing Taiwan into an Asia-Pacific Regional Operations Center.

30 — Mainland Chinese President Jiang Zemin offers an eight-point proposal, urging Taiwan to hold talks with the mainland to officially end the hostile standoff between the two sides.

Feb.   28 — President Lee expresses an apology to families of the victims of the Feb. 28, 1947 Incident at the Taipei New Park, where a monument commemorating the tragedy was built with government sponsorship.

Mar.   1 — The National Health Insurance program is formally inaugurated.

6 — A Coordination and Service Office for the Asia-Pacific Regional Operations Center (also known as the APROC Window) is established in the Council for Economic Planning and Development to ensure that the Asia-Pacific Regional Operations Center plan is faithfully implemented.

20 — Sheu Yuan-dong replaces Liang Kuo-shu as governor of the Central Bank of China.

23 — *Regulations Governing the Management and Compensation for Victims of the Feb. 28, 1947 Incident* passes the Legislative Yuan. According to the regulations, a foundation will be established to manage affairs concerned, and Feb. 28 will be designated a national commemoration day.

— The two-day convention of secretaries-general of the Olympic Council of Asia member nations opens in Kaohsiung. Following international practice, the convention hoists the flags of all OCA members—including the five-star flag of mainland China.

Apr.   1 — President Lee starts his four-day visit to the United Arab Emirates and Jordan.

8 — At the meeting of the National Unification Council, President Lee offers a six-point proposal for Taiwan-mainland relations.

19 — Malawi President Bakili Muluzi pays a state visit to Taipei.

May   19 — The Legislative Yuan approves the temporary statute on welfare payments for elderly farmers, granting them a monthly stipend of NT$3,000.

22 — The ROC and Papua New Guinea sign a joint communiqué in Taipei and establish mutual recognition in order to improve cooperation on the basis of reciprocal benefits.

June   7 — President Lee arrives in the United States for a reunion at his alma mater, Cornell University.

15 — Premier Lien Chan launches a six-day visit to three European countries: Austria, Hungary, and Czechoslovakia. He is the highest ROC official to visit Europe since the ROC government moved to Taipei in 1949.

30 — The US government officially announces cancellation of the sanctions against Taiwan issued under the Pelly Amendment.

July   1 — The ROC resumes full diplomatic relations with Gambia after a 21-year hiatus.

19 — The Legislature approves the *Presidential and Vice Presidential Election and Recall Law*, setting ground rules for the

March 23, 1996, popular election of the ROC president and vice president.

21 — The Chinese mainland begins eight days of firing surface-to-surface missiles into the East China Sea about 140 kilometers north of Taiwan.

26 — The US Congress honors Madame Chiang Kai-shek at a Capitol Hill reception in recognition of her contribution to Allied efforts during World War II.

Aug. 15 — The Chinese mainland begins eleven days of firing tactical guided missiles and live artillery shells into the sea 136 kilometers north of Taiwan.

17 — Control Yuan President Chen Li-an announces his candidacy for president and, on the following day, renounces his 42-year KMT membership.

19 — The Foreign Ministry issues a position paper entitled "Why the UN Resolution No. 2758 Adopted in 1971 Should Be Reexamined Today." The paper stresses that UN Resolution 2758, which excludes the ROC from the UN system and its activities, is obsolete and unjust and ought to be reexamined.

22 — The KMT convenes the second plenary session of its 14th National Congress and Lee Teng-hui, party chairman, announces he will seek the party's presidential nomination. Lin Yang-kang, a KMT vice chairman, declares his intention not to seek the nomination but to run as an independent.

24 — President Juan Carlos Wasmosy of Paraguay leads a delegation to Taipei for a 4-day visit.

31 — The KMT nominates incumbent President Lee as its presidential candidate; the next day President Lee names Premier Lien as his running mate.

Sept. 7 — The ROC and Singapore initial an agreement to cooperate on a project to launch a telecommunications satellite.

17 — An exhibition of 71 landscape paintings from the collection of the Louvre in Paris opens at the National Palace Museum in Taipei. The exhibition runs through Jan. 15.

21 — Economic Minister Chiang Pin-kung leads a delegation to the 19th Joint Conference of ROC-USA and USA-ROC Economic Councils in Anchorage, Alaska.

25 — The DPP nominates Peng Ming-min, a former political science professor and a long-time dissident in exile, as its presidential candidate after a 15-week primary; Peng later names Legislator Frank Hsieh as his running mate.

— Rodrigo Oreamuno, vice president of Costa Rica, arrives in Taipei for a weeklong visit.

27 — Jeffrey Koo, chairman of the Chinese National Association of Industry and Commerce, leads a delegation to the Pacific Economic Cooperation Council meeting in Peking.

Oct. 3 — Manuel Saturnino da Costa, prime minister of Guinea-Bissau, arrives in Taipei for a six-day visit.

17 — The ROC and Macau establish a five-year renewable air pact allowing Eva Airways, Transasia Airways, and Air Macau to fly routes between Taiwan and Macau.

21 — Independent presidential candidate Chen Li-an names Wang Ching-feng, a Control Yuan member, as his running mate.

Nov. 15 — Independent presidential hopeful Lin Yang-kang names former Premier Hau Pei-tsun as his running mate.

17 — Koo Chen-fu, a senior adviser to the ROC president, arrives in Osaka, Japan, to attend the Asia-Pacific Economic Cooperation forum summit in place of President Lee.

21 — The ROC and Australia sign a memorandum of understanding to permit temporary duty-free entry of certain goods as a means of increasing two-way trade.

25 — The ROC and Poland, to boost economic ties, initial an agreement to avoid double taxation and prevent tax evasion by investors.

Dec.   2 — The Republic of China elects 164 lawmakers to the Third Legislative Yuan.

1996

Jan.   3 — The ROC and the Republic of Senegal resume full diplomatic relations, increasing to 31 the number of nations with which the ROC maintains such relations.

11 — Vice President Li Yuan-zu leaves for the Republic of Guatemala to attend the inaugural ceremony of President Alvaro Enrique Arzu Irigoyen, traveling via Los Angeles, USA.

16 — The Legislature passes three telecommunications laws—the *Telecommunications Act*, the *Organizational Statute of the Directorate General of Telecommunications, Ministry of Transportation and Communications*, and the *Statute of Chunghwa Telecom Co., Ltd.* These laws relieve the DGT of the function of providing telecommunications services, making it a regulatory agency only; open the telecommunications sector to private and foreign investment; and strengthen controls on transmission frequencies.

23 — An ROC Ministry of Education ad hoc committee decides that 452 works of art from the National Palace Museum in Taipei will be allowed to go on a 13-month exhibition trip to the United States. This is one of the largest bodies of national treasures ever to tour overseas.

Feb.   12 — Faced with threatening military maneuvers undertaken by Peking, the Executive Yuan sets up a temporary policy-making task force to closely follow developments and coordinate the actions of various agencies to respond to the situation.

Mar.   8 — The Chinese mainland begins eight days of test-firing surface-to-surface missiles in waters close to major ports in north-eastern and southwestern Taiwan.

12 — The Chinese mainland commences nine days of naval and air military exercises in an area of the Taiwan Straits only 53 kilometers from Kinmen and 70 kilometers from the Penghu Islands.

18 — The Chinese mainland begins eight days of war games involving ground, air, and naval forces in an area of sea 85 kilometers northwest of Taiwan proper.

23 — Four pairs of candidates compete in the first-ever direct election of the ROC president and vice president. The Lee-Lien ticket wins, garnering 54 percent of the vote. At the same time, 334 members of the Third National Assembly are also elected.

28 — After eight years of construction, the Mucha Line of the Taipei Mass Rapid Transit Systems officially commences operations.

Apr.   29 — On the third anniversary of the Koo-Wang talks, Koo Chen-fu, chairman of the ROC's Straits Exchange Foundation, appeals to the Chinese mainland not to postpone the second Koo-Wang talks so that both sides can resume their pursuit of reunification.

28 — The Ministry of Economic Affairs announces that starting July 1, 1996, imports of another 1,609 categories of industrial commodities will be allowed from the Chinese mainland, marking the ROC government's largest-scale relaxation of restrictions on mainland imports.

May   20 — Lee Teng-hui and Lien Chan are sworn in as ROC president and vice president, respectively.
In his inaugural address, President Lee emphasizes that it is neither necessary nor possible to adopt a so-called "Taiwan independence" line. He expresses his hope that the two sides will counter animosity with peace and forgiveness and turn to the important task of ending the enmity across the Straits. President Lee also indicates his willingness to make a

"journey of peace" to the Chinese mainland. He says that in order to bring forth a new era of communication and cooperation between the two sides, he is willing to meet and directly exchange opinions with the top mainland leadership.

June   5 — President Lee Teng-hui appoints Vice President Lien Chan to serve concurrently as ROC premier. A cabinet reshuffle is passed three days later.

7 — At his first press conference as Vice President/Premier, Lien Chan indicates that the ROC has not ruled out the possibility of the two sides exchanging visits by high-ranking officials. He also emphasizes the need to reopen channels for cross-Straits talks.

28 — The ROC exchanges economic and trade representative office with the Republic of Belarus. Belarus is the second (Russia being the first) member of the Commonwealth of Independent States to establish such a level of relations with the ROC.

30 — South African Foreign Minister Alfred Nzo arrives for a three-day visit. On July 2, South African President Nelson Mandela, speaking in South Africa, states that before the Chinese "domestic problem" is solved, he will not establish diplomatic ties with the Chinese mainland at the cost of relations with the Republic of China.

Appendix II
The Constitution of the Republic of China and the Additional Articles

(Adopted by the National Assembly on December 25, 1946, promulgated by the national government on January 1, 1947, and effective from December 25, 1947)

The National Assembly of the Republic of China, by virtue of the mandate received from the whole body of citizens, in accordance with the teachings bequeathed by Dr. Sun Yat-sen in founding the Republic of China, and in order to consolidate the authority of the State, safeguard the rights of the people, ensure social tranquillity, and promote the welfare of the people, do hereby establish this Constitution, to be promulgated throughout the country for faithful and perpetual observance by all.

Chapter I. General Provisions

Article 1. The Republic of China, founded on the Three Principles of the People, shall be a democratic republic of the people, to be governed by the people and for the people.

Article 2. The sovereignty of the Republic of China shall reside in the whole body of citizens.

Article 3. Persons possessing the nationality of the Republic of China shall be citizens of the Republic of China.

Article 4. The territory of the Republic of China according to its existing national boundaries shall not be altered except by resolution of the National Assembly.

Article 5. There shall be equality among the various racial groups in the Republic of China.

Article 6. The national flag of the Republic of China shall be of red ground with a blue sky and a white sun in the upper left corner.

Chapter II. Rights and Duties of the People

Article 7. All citizens of the Republic of China, irrespective of sex, religion, race, class, or party affiliation, shall be equal before the law.

Article 8. Personal freedom shall be guaranteed to the people. Except in case of *flagrante delicto* as provided by law, no person shall be arrested or detained otherwise than by a judicial or a police organ in accordance with the procedure prescribed by law. No person shall be tried or punished otherwise than by a law court in accordance with the procedure prescribed by law. Any arrest, detention, trial, or punishment which is not in accordance with the procedure prescribed by law may be resisted.

When a person is arrested or detained on suspicion of having committed a crime, the organ making the arrest or detention shall in writing inform the said person, and his designated relative or friend, of the grounds for his arrest or detention, and shall, within 24 hours, turn him over to a competent court for trial. The said person, or any other person, may petition the competent court that a writ be served within 24 hours on the organ making the arrest for the surrender of the said person for trial.

The court shall not reject the petition mentioned in the preceding paragraph, nor shall it order the organ concerned to make an investigation and report first. The organ concerned shall not refuse to execute, or delay in executing, the writ of the court for the surrender of the said person for trial.

When a person is unlawfully arrested or detained by any organ, he or any other person may petition the court for an investigation. The court shall not reject such a petition, and shall, within 24 hours, investigate the action of the organ concerned and deal with the matter in accordance with law.

Article 9. Except those in active military service, no person shall be subject to trial by a military tribunal.

Article 10. The people shall have freedom of residence and of change of residence.

Article 11. The people shall have freedom of speech, teaching, writing and publication.

Article 12. The people shall have freedom of privacy of correspondence.

Article 13. The people shall have freedom of religious belief.

Article 14. The people shall have freedom of assembly and association.

Article 15. The right of existence, the right of work and the right of property shall be guaranteed to the people.

Article 16. The people shall have the right of presenting petitions, lodging complaints, or instituting legal proceedings.

Article 17. The people shall have the right of election, recall, initiative and referendum.

Article 18. The people shall have the right of taking public examinations and of holding public offices.

Article 19. The people shall have the duty of paying taxes in accordance with law.

Article 20. The people shall have the duty of performing military service in accordance with law.

Article 21. The people shall have the right and the duty of receiving citizens' education.

Article 22. All other freedoms and rights of the people that are not detrimental to social order or public welfare shall be guaranteed under the Constitution.

Article 23. All the freedoms and rights enumerated in the preceding Article shall not be restricted by law except by such as may be necessary to prevent infringement upon the freedoms of other persons, to avert an imminent crisis, to maintain social order or to advance public welfare.

Article 24. Any public functionary who, in violation of law, infringes upon the freedom or right of any person shall, in addition to being subject to disciplinary measures in accordance with law, be held responsible under criminal and civil laws. The injured person may, in accordance with law, claim compensation from the State for damage sustained.

Chapter III. The National Assembly

Article 25. The National Assembly shall, in accordance with the provisions of this Constitution, exercise political powers on behalf of the whole body of citizens.

Article 26. The National Assembly shall be composed of the following delegates:

1. One delegate shall be elected from each hsien, municipality, or area of equivalent status. In case its population exceeds 500,000, one additional delegate shall be elected for each additional 500,000. Areas equivalent to hsien or municipalities shall be prescribed by law;

2. Delegates to represent Mongolia shall be elected on the basis of four for each league and one for each special banner;

3. The number of delegates to be elected from Tibet shall be prescribed by law;

4. The number of delegates to be elected by various racial groups in frontier regions shall be prescribed by law;

5. The number of delegates to be elected by Chinese citizens residing abroad shall be prescribed by law;

6. The number of delegates to be elected by occupational groups shall be prescribed by law;

7. The number of delegates to be elected by women's organizations shall be prescribed by law.

Article 27. The function of the National Assembly shall be as follows:

1. To elect the President and the Vice President;

2. To recall the President and the Vice President;

3. To amend the Constitution; and

4. To vote on proposed Constitutional amendments submitted by the Legislative Yuan by way of referendum.

With respect to the rights of initiative and referendum, except as is provided in Items 3 and 4 of the preceding paragraph, the National Assembly shall make regulations pertaining thereto and put them into effect, after the above-mentioned two political rights shall have been exercised in one half of the hsien and municipalities of the whole country.

Article 28. Delegates to the National Assembly shall be elected every six years.

The term of office of the delegates to each National Assembly shall terminate on the day on which the next National Assembly convenes.

No incumbent government official shall, in the electoral area where he holds office, be elected delegate to the National Assembly.

Article 29. The National Assembly shall be convoked by the President to meet 90 days prior to the date of expiration of each presidential term.

Article 30. An extraordinary session of the National Assembly shall be convoked in any of the following circumstances:

1. When, in accordance with the provisions of Article 49 of this Constitution, a new President and a new Vice President are to be elected;

2. When, by resolution of the Control Yuan, an impeachment of the President or the Vice President is instituted;

3. When, by resolution of the Legislative Yuan, an amendment to the Constitution is proposed; and

4. When a meeting is requested by not less than two-fifths of the delegates to the National Assembly.

When an extraordinary session is to be convoked in accordance with Item 1 or Item 2 of the preceding paragraph, the President of the Legislative Yuan shall issue the notice of convocation; when it is to be convoked in accordance with Item 3 or Item 4, it shall be convoked by the President of the Republic.

Article 31. The National Assembly shall meet at the seat of the Central Government.

Article 32. No delegate to the National Assembly shall be held responsible outside the Assembly for opinions expressed or votes cast at meetings of the Assembly.

Article 33. While the Assembly is in session, no delegate to the National Assembly shall, except in case of *flagrante delicto,* be arrested or detained without the permission of the National Assembly.

Article 34. The organization of the National Assembly, the election and recall of delegates to the National Assembly, and the procedure whereby the National Assembly is to carry out its functions, shall be prescribed by law.

Chapter IV. The President

Article 35. The President shall be the head of the State and shall represent the Republic of China in foreign relations.

Article 36. The President shall have supreme command of the land, sea and air forces of the whole country.

Article 37. The President shall, in accordance with law, promulgate laws and issue mandates with the counter-signature of the President of the Executive Yuan or with the counter-signatures of both the President of Executive Yuan and the Ministers or Chairmen of Commissions concerned.

Article 38. The President shall, in accordance with the provisions of this Constitution, exercise the powers of concluding treaties, declaring war and making peace.

Article 39. The President may, in accordance with law, declare martial law with the approval of, or subject to confirmation by, the Legislative Yuan. When the Legislative Yuan deems it necessary, it may by resolution request the President to terminate martial law.

Article 40. The President shall, in accordance with law, exercise the power of granting amnesties, pardons, remission of sentences and restitution of civil rights.

Article 41. The President shall, in accordance with law, appoint and remove civil and military officials.

Article 42. The President may, in accordance with law, confer honors and decorations.

Article 43. In case of a natural calamity, an epidemic, or a national financial or economic crisis that calls for emergency measures, the President, during the recess of the Legislative Yuan, may, by resolution of the Executive Yuan Council, and in accordance with the *Law on Emergency Orders,* issue emergency orders, proclaiming such measures as may be necessary to cope with the situation. Such orders shall, within one month after issuance, be presented to the Legislative Yuan for confirmation; in case the Legislative Yuan withholds confirmation, the said orders shall forthwith cease to be valid.

Article 44. In case of disputes between two or more Yuan other than those concerning which there are relevant provisions in this Constitution, the President may call a meeting of the Presidents of the Yuan concerned for consultation with a view to reaching a solution.

Article 45. Any citizen of the Republic of China who has attained the age of 40 years may be elected President or Vice President.

Article 46. The election of the President and the Vice President shall be prescribed by law.

Article 47. The President and the Vice President shall serve a term of six years. They may be re-elected for a second term.

Article 48. The President shall, at the time of assuming office, take the following oath:

"I do solemnly and sincerely swear before the people of the whole country that I will observe the Constitution, faithfully perform my duties, promote the welfare of the people, safeguard the security of the State, and will in no way betray the people's trust. Should I break my oath, I shall be willing to submit myself to severe punishment by the State. This is my solemn oath."

Article 49. In case the office of the President should become vacant, the Vice President shall succeed until the expiration of the original presidential term. In case the office of both the President and the Vice President should become vacant, the President of the Executive Yuan shall act for the President; and, in accordance with the provisions of Article 30 of this Constitution, an extraordinary session of the National Assembly shall be convoked for the election of a new President and a new Vice President, who shall hold office until the completion of the term left unfinished by the preceding President. In case the President should be unable to attend to office due to any cause, the Vice President shall act for the President. In case both the President and Vice President should be unable to attend to office, the President of the Executive Yuan shall act for the President.

Article 50. The President shall be relieved of his functions on the day on which his term of office expires. If by that time the succeeding President has not yet been elected, or if the President-elect and the Vice-President-elect have not yet assumed office, the President of the Executive Yuan shall act for the President.

Article 51. The period during which the President of the Executive Yuan may act for the President shall not exceed three months.

Article 52. The President shall not, without having been recalled, or having been relieved of his functions, be liable to criminal prosecution unless he is charged with having committed an act of rebellion or treason.

Chapter V. Administration

Article 53. The Executive Yuan shall be the highest administrative organ of the State.

Article 54. The Executive Yuan shall have a President, a Vice President, a certain number of Ministers and Chairmen of Commissions, and a certain number of Ministers without Portfolio.

Article 55. The President of the Executive Yuan shall be nominated and, with the consent of the Legislative Yuan, appointed by the President of the Republic.

If, during the recess of the Legislative Yuan, the President of the Executive Yuan should resign or if his office should become vacant, his functions shall be exercised by the Vice President of the Yuan, acting on his behalf, but the President of the Republic shall, within 40 days, request a meeting of the Legislative Yuan to confirm his nominee for the vacancy. Pending such confirmation, the Vice President of the Executive Yuan shall temporarily exercise the functions of the President of the said Yuan.

Article 56. The Vice President of the Executive Yuan, Ministers and Chairmen of Commissions, and Ministers without Portfolio shall be appointed by the President of the Republic upon the recommendation of the President of the Executive Yuan.

Article 57. The Executive Yuan shall be responsible to the Legislative Yuan in accordance with the following provisions:

1. The Executive Yuan has the duty to present to the Legislative Yuan a statement of its administrative policies and a report on its administration. While the Legislative Yuan is in session, Members of the Legislative Yuan shall have the right to question the President and the Ministers and Chairmen of Commissions of the Executive Yuan.

2. If the Legislative Yuan does not concur in any important policy of the Executive Yuan, it may, by resolution, request the Executive Yuan to alter such a policy. With respect to such resolution, the Executive Yuan may, with the approval of the President of the Republic, request the Legislative Yuan for reconsideration. If, after reconsideration, two-thirds of the Members of the Legislative Yuan present at the meeting uphold the original resolution, the President of the Executive Yuan shall either abide by the same or resign from office.

3. If the Executive Yuan deems a resolution on a statutory, budgetary, or treaty bill passed by the Legislative Yuan difficult of execution, it may, with the approval of the President of the Republic and within ten days after its transmission to the Executive Yuan, request the Legislative Yuan to reconsider the said resolution. If after reconsideration, two-thirds of the Members of the Legislative Yuan present at the meeting uphold the original resolution, the President of the Executive Yuan shall either abide by the same or resign from office.

Article 58. The Executive Yuan shall have an Executive Yuan Council, to be composed of its President, Vice President, various Ministers and Chairmen of Commissions, and Ministers without Portfolio, with its President as Chairman.

Statutory or budgetary bills or bills concerning martial law, amnesty, declaration of war, conclusion of peace or treaties, and other important affairs, all of which are to be submitted to the Legislative Yuan, as well as matters that are of common concern to the various Ministries and Commissions, shall be presented by the President and various Ministers and Chairmen of Commissions of the Executive Yuan to the Executive Yuan Council for decision.

Article 59. The Executive Yuan shall, three months before the beginning of each fiscal year, present to the Legislative Yuan the budgetary bill for the following fiscal year.

Article 60. The Executive Yuan shall, within four months after the end of each fiscal year, present final accounts of revenues and expenditures to the Control Yuan.

Article 61. The organization of the Executive Yuan shall be prescribed by law.

Chapter VI. Legislation

Article 62. The Legislative Yuan shall be the highest legislative organ of the State, to be constituted of members elected by the people. It shall exercise legislative power on behalf of the people.

Article 63. The Legislative Yuan shall have the power to decide by resolution upon statutory or budgetary bills or bills concerning martial law, amnesty, declaration of war, conclusion of peace or treaties, and other important affairs of the State.

Article 64. Members of the Legislative Yuan shall be elected in accordance with the following provisions:

1. Those to be elected from the provinces and by the municipalities under the direct jurisdiction of the Executive Yuan shall be five for each province or municipality with a population of not more than 3,000,000, one additional member shall be elected for each additional 1,000,000 in a province or municipality whose population is over 3,000,000;

2. Those to be elected from Mongolian Leagues and Banners;

3. Those to be elected from Tibet;

4. Those to be elected by various racial groups in frontier regions;

5. Those to be elected by Chinese citizens residing abroad; and

6. Those to be elected by occupational groups.

The election of members of the Legislative Yuan and the number of those to be elected in accordance with Items 2 to 6 of the preceding paragraph shall be prescribed by law. The number of women to be elected under the various items enumerated in the first paragraph shall be prescribed by law.

Article 65. Members of the Legislative Yuan shall serve a term of three years, and shall be re-eligible. The election of Members of the Legislative Yuan shall be completed within three months prior to the expiration of each term.

Article 66. The Legislative Yuan shall have a President and a Vice President, who shall be elected by and from among its Members.

Article 67. The Legislative Yuan may set up various committees.

Such committees may invite government officials and private persons concerned to be present at their meetings to answer questions.

Article 68. The Legislative Yuan shall hold two sessions each year, and shall convene of its own accord. The first session shall last from February to the end of May, and the second session from September to the end of December. Whenever necessary a session may be prolonged.

Article 69. In any of the following circumstances, the Legislative Yuan may hold an extraordinary session:

1. At the request of the President of the Republic;

2. Upon the request of not less than one-fourth of its members.

Article 70. The Legislative Yuan shall not make proposals for an increase in the expenditures in the budgetary bill presented by the Executive Yuan.

Article 71. At the meetings of the Legislative Yuan, the Presidents of the various Yuan concerned and the various Ministers and Chairmen of Commissions concerned may be present to give their views.

Article 72. Statutory bills passed by the Legislative Yuan shall be transmitted to the President of the Republic and to the Executive Yuan. The President shall, within ten days after receipt thereof, promulgate them; or he may deal with them in accordance with the provisions of Article 57 of this Constitution.

Article 73. No Member of the Legislative Yuan shall be held responsible outside the Yuan for opinions expressed or votes cast in the Yuan.

Article 74. No Member of the Legislative Yuan shall, except in case of *flagrante delicto,* be arrested or detained without the permission of the Legislative Yuan.

Article 75. No Member of the Legislative Yuan shall concurrently hold a government post.

Article 76. The organization of the Legislative Yuan shall be prescribed by law.

Chapter VII. Judiciary

Article 77. The Judicial Yuan shall be the highest judicial organ of the State and shall have charge of civil, criminal, and administrative cases, and over cases concerning disciplinary measures against public functionaries.

Article 78. The Judicial Yuan shall interpret the Constitution and shall have the power to unify the interpretation of laws and orders.

Article 79. The Judicial Yuan shall have a President and a Vice President, who shall be nominated and, with the consent of the Control Yuan, appointed by the President of the Republic.

The Judicial Yuan shall have a certain number of Grand Justices to take charge of matters specified in article 78 of this Constitution, who shall be nominated and, with the consent of the Control Yuan, appointed by the President of the Republic.

Article 80. Judges shall be above partisanship and shall, in accordance with law, hold trials independently, free from any interference.

Article 81. Judges shall hold office for life. No judge shall be removed from office unless he has been found guilty of a criminal offense or subjected to disciplinary measure, or declared to be under interdiction. No judge shall, except in accordance with law, be suspended or transferred or have his salary reduced.

Article 82. The organization of the Judicial Yuan and of the law courts of various grades shall be prescribed by law.

Chapter VIII. Examination

Article 83. The Examination Yuan shall be the highest examination organ of the State and shall have charge of matters relating to examination, employment, registration, service rating, scale of salaries, promotion and transfer, security of tenure, commendation, pecuniary aid in case of death, retirement and old age pension.

Article 84. The Examination Yuan shall have a President and a Vice President and a certain number of Members, all of whom shall be nominated and, with the consent of the Control Yuan, appointed by the President of the Republic.

Article 85. In the selection of public functionaries, a system of open competitive examination shall be put into operation, and examinations shall be held in different areas, with prescribed numbers of persons to be selected according to various provinces and areas. No person shall be appointed to a public office unless he is qualified through examination.

Article 86. The following qualifications shall be determined and registered through examination by the Examination Yuan in accordance with law:

1. Qualification for appointment as public functionaries; and

2. Qualification for practice in specialized professions or as technicians.

Article 87. The Examination Yuan may, with respect to matters under its charge, present statutory bills to the Legislative Yuan.

Article 88. Members of the Examination Yuan shall be above partisanship and shall independently exercise their functions in accordance with law.

Article 89. The organization of the Examination Yuan shall be prescribed by law.

Chapter IX. Control

Article 90. The Control Yuan shall be the highest control organ of the State and shall exercise the powers of consent, impeachment, censure and auditing.

Article 91. The Control Yuan shall be composed of Members who shall be elected by Provincial and Municipal Councils, the local Councils of Mongolia and Tibet, and Chinese citizens residing abroad. Their numbers shall be determined in accordance with the following provisions:

1. Five Members from each province;

2. Two Members from each municipality under the direct jurisdiction of the Executive Yuan;

3. Eight Members from Mongolian Leagues and Banners;

4. Eight Members from Tibet; and

5. Eight Members from Chinese citizens residing abroad.

Article 92. The Control Yuan shall have a President and a Vice President, who shall be elected by and from among its Members.

Article 93. Members of the Control Yuan shall serve a term of six years and shall be re-eligible.

Article 94. When the Control Yuan exercises the power of consent in accordance with this Constitution, it shall do so by resolution of a majority of the Members present at the meeting.

Article 95. The Control Yuan may, in the exercise of its powers of control, request the Executive Yuan and its Ministries and Commissions to submit to it for perusal the original orders issued by them and all other relevant documents.

Article 96. The Control Yuan may, taking into account the work of the Executive Yuan and its various Ministries and Commissions, set up a certain number of committees to investigate their activities with a view to ascertaining whether or not they are guilty of violation of law or neglect of duty.

Article 97. The Control Yuan may, on the basis of the investigations and resolutions of its committees, propose corrective measures and forward them to the Executive Yuan and the Ministries and Commissions concerned, directing their attention to effecting improvements.

When the Control Yuan deems a public functionary in the Central Government or in a local government guilty of neglect of duty or violation of law, it may propose corrective measures or institute an impeachment. If it involves a criminal offense, the case shall be turned over to a law court.

Article 98. Impeachment by the Control Yuan of a public functionary in the Central Government or in a local government shall be instituted upon the proposal of one or more than one Member of the Control Yuan and the decision, after due consideration, by a committee composed of not less than nine Members.

Article 99. In case of impeachment by the Control Yuan of the personnel of the Judicial Yuan or of the Examination Yuan for neglect of duty or violation of law, the provisions of Articles 95, 97 and 98 of this Constitution shall be applicable.

Article 100. Impeachment by the Control Yuan of the President or the Vice President of the Republic shall be instituted upon the proposal of not less than one-fourth of the whole body of Members of the Control Yuan, and the resolution, after due consideration, by the majority of the whole body of members of the Control Yuan, and the same shall be presented to the National Assembly.

Article 101. No Member of the Control Yuan shall be held responsible outside the Yuan for opinions expressed or votes cast in the Yuan.

Article 102. No Member of the Control Yuan shall, except in case of *flagrante delicto,* be arrested or detained without the permission of the Control Yuan.

Article 103. No Member of the Control Yuan shall concurrently hold a public office or engage in any profession.

Article 104. In the Control Yuan, there shall be an Auditor General who shall be nominated and, with the consent of the Legislative Yuan, appointed by the President of the Republic.

Article 105. The Auditor General shall within three months after presentation by the Executive Yuan of the final accounts of revenues and expenditures, complete the auditing thereof in accordance with law, and submit an auditing report to the Legislative Yuan.

Article 106. The organization of the Control Yuan shall be prescribed by law.

Chapter X. Powers of the Central and Local Governments

Article 107. In the following matters, the Central Government shall have the power of legislation and administration:

1. Foreign affairs;

2. National defense and military affairs concerning national defense;

3. Nationality law and criminal, civil and commercial law;

4. Judicial system;

5. Aviation, national highways, state-owned railways, navigation, postal and telegraph service;

6. Central Government finance and national revenues;

7. Demarcation of national, provincial and hsien revenues;

8. State-operated economic enterprises;

9. Currency system and state banks;

10. Weights and measures;

11. Foreign trade policies;

12. Financial and economic matters affecting foreigners or foreign countries; and

13. Other matters relating to the Central Government as provided by this Constitution.

Article 108. In the following matters, the Central Government shall have the power of legislation and administration, but the Central Government may delegate the power of Administration to the provincial and hsien governments:

1. General principles of provincial and hsien self-government;

2. Division of administrative areas;

3. Forestry, industry, mining and commerce;

4. Educational system;

5. Banking and exchange system;

6. Shipping and deep-sea fishery;

7. Public utilities;

8. Cooperative enterprises;

9. Water and land communication and transportation covering two or more provinces;

10. Water conservancy, waterways, agriculture and pastoral enterprises covering two or more provinces;

11. Registration, employment, supervision, and security of tenure of officials in Central and local governments;

12. Land legislation;

13. Labor legislation and other social legislation;

14. Eminent domain;

15. Census-taking and compilation of population statistics for the whole country;

16. Immigration and land reclamation;

17. Police system;

18. Public health;

19. Relief, pecuniary aid in case of death and aid in case of unemployment; and

20. Preservation of ancient books and articles and sites of cultural value.

With respect to the various items enumerated in the preceding paragraph, the provinces may enact separate rules and regulations, provided these are not in conflict with national laws.

Article 109. In the following matters, the provinces shall have the power of legislation and administration, but the provinces may delegate the power of administration to the hsien;

1. Provincial education, public health, industries and communications;

2. Management and disposal of provincial property;

3. Administration of municipalities under provincial jurisdiction;

4. Province-operated enterprises;

5. Provincial cooperative enterprises;

6. Provincial agriculture, forestry, water conservancy, fishery, animal husbandry and public works;

7. Provincial finance and revenues;

8. Provincial debts;

9. Provincial banks;

10. Provincial police administration;

11. Provincial charitable and public welfare works; and

12. Other matters delegated to the provinces in accordance with national laws.

Except as otherwise provided by law, any of the matters enumerated in the various items of the preceding paragraph, in so far as it covers two or more provinces, may be undertaken jointly by the provinces concerned.

When any province, in undertaking matters listed in any of the items of the first paragraph, finds its funds insufficient, it may, by resolution of the Legislative Yuan, obtain subsidies from the National Treasury.

Article 110. In the following matters, the hsien shall have the power of legislation and administration:

1. Hsien education, public health, industries and communications;

2. Management and disposal of hsien property;

3. Hsien-operated enterprises;

4. Hsien cooperative enterprises;

5. Hsien agriculture and forestry, water conservancy, fishery, animal husbandry and public works;

6. Hsien finance and revenues;

7. Hsien debts;

8. Hsien banks;

9. Administration of hsien police and defense;

10. Hsien charitable and public welfare works; and

11. Other matters delegated to the hsien in accordance with national laws and provincial Self-Government Regulations.

Except as otherwise provided by law, any of the matters enumerated in the various items of the preceding paragraph, in so far as it covers two or more hsien, may be undertaken jointly by the hsien concerned.

Article 111. Any matter not enumerated in Articles 107, 108, 109 and 110 shall fall within the jurisdiction of the Central Government, if it is national in nature; of the province, if it is provincial in nature; and of the hsien, if it concerns the hsien. In case of dispute, it shall be settled by the Legislative Yuan.

Chapter XI. System of Local Government
Section 1. The Province

Article 112. A Province may convoke a Provincial Assembly to enact, in accordance with the General Principles of Provincial and Hsien Self-Government, regulations, provided the said regulations are not in conflict with the Constitution.

The organization of the provincial assembly and the election of the delegates shall be prescribed by law.

Article 113. The Provincial Self-Government Regulations shall include the following provisions:

1. In the province, there shall be a provincial council. Members of the provincial council shall be elected by the people of the province.

2. In the province, there shall be a provincial government with a provincial governor who shall be elected by the people of the province.

3. Relationship between the province and the hsien.

The legislative power of the province shall be exercised by the Provincial Council.

Article 114. The Provincial Self-Government Regulations shall, after enactment, be forthwith submitted to the Judicial Yuan. The Judicial Yuan, if it deems any part thereof unconstitutional, shall declare null and void the articles repugnant to the Constitution.

Article 115. If, during the enforcement of the Provincial Self-Government Regulations, there should arise any serious obstacle in the application of any of the articles contained therein, the Judicial Yuan shall first summon the various parties concerned to present their views; and thereupon the Presidents of the Executive Yuan, Legislative Yuan, Judicial Yuan, Examination Yuan and Control Yuan shall form a Committee, with the President of the Judicial Yuan as Chairman, to propose a formula for solution.

Article 116. Provincial rules and regulations that are in conflict with national laws shall be null and void.

Article 117. When doubt arises as to whether or not there is a conflict between provincial rules or regulations and national laws, interpretation thereon shall be made by the Judicial Yuan.

Article 118. The self-government of municipalities under the direct jurisdiction of the Executive Yuan shall be prescribed by law.

Article 119. The local self-government system of the Mongolian Leagues and Banners shall be prescribed by law.

Article 120. The self-government system of Tibet shall be safeguarded.

Section 2. The Hsien

Article 121. The hsien shall enforce hsien self-government.

Article 122. A hsien may convoke a hsien assembly to enact, in accordance with the General Principles of Provincial and Hsien Self-Government, hsien self-government regulations, provided the said regulations are not in conflict with the Constitution or with provincial self-government regulations.

Article 123. The people of the hsien shall, in accordance with law, exercise the rights of initiative and referendum in matters within the sphere of hsien self-government, and shall, in accordance with law, exercise the rights of election and recall of the magistrate and other hsien self-government officials.

Article 124. In the hsien, there shall be a hsien council. Members of the hsien council shall be elected by the people of the hsien.

The legislative power of the hsien shall be exercised by the hsien council.

Article 125. Hsien rules and regulations that are in conflict with national laws, or with provincial rules and regulations, shall be null and void.

Article 126. In the hsien, there shall be a hsien government with a hsien magistrate who shall be elected by the people of the hsien.

Article 127. The hsien magistrate shall have charge of hsien self-government and shall administer matters delegated to the hsien by the central or provincial government.

Article 128. The provisions governing the hsien shall apply *mutatis mutandis* to the municipality.

Chapter XII. Election, Recall, Initiative and Referendum

Article 129. The various kinds of elections prescribed in this Constitution, except as otherwise provided by this Constitution, shall be by universal, equal, and direct suffrage and by secret ballot.

Article 130. Any citizen of the Republic of China who has attained the age of 20 years shall have the right of election in accordance with law. Except as otherwise provided by this Constitution or by law, any citizen who has attained the age of 23 years shall have the right of being elected in accordance with law.

Article 131. All candidates in the various kinds of elections prescribed in this Constitution shall openly campaign for their election.

Article 132. Intimidation or inducement shall be strictly forbidden in elections. Suits arising in connection with elections shall be tried by the courts.

Article 133. A person elected may, in accordance with law, be recalled by his constituency.

Article 134. In the various kinds of elections, the number of women to be elected shall be fixed, and measures pertaining thereto shall be prescribed by law.

Article 135. The number of delegates to the National Assembly and the manner of their election from people in interior areas, who have their own conditions of living and habits, shall be prescribed by law.

Article 136. The exercise of the rights of initiative and referendum shall be prescribed by law.

Chapter XIII. Fundamental National Policies
Section 1. National Defense

Article 137. The national defense of the Republic of China shall have as its objective the safeguarding of national security and the preservation of world peace.

The organization of national defense shall be prescribed by law.

Article 138. The land, sea and air forces of the whole country shall be above personal, regional, or party affiliations, shall be loyal to the state and shall protect the people.

Article 139. No political party and no individual shall make use of armed forces as an instrument in a struggle for political powers.

Article 140. No military man in active service may concurrently hold a civil office.

Section 2. Foreign Policy

Article 141. The foreign policy of the Republic of China shall, in a spirit of independence and initiative and on the basis of the principles of equality and reciprocity, cultivate good-neighborliness with other nations, and respect treaties and the Charter of the United Nations, in order to protect the rights and interests of Chinese citizens residing abroad, promote international cooperation, advance international justice and ensure world peace.

Section 3. National Economy

Article 142. National economy shall be based on the Principle of the People's Livelihood and shall seek to effect equalization of land ownership and restriction of private capital in order to attain a well-balanced sufficiency in national wealth and people's livelihood.

Article 143. All land within the territory of the Republic of China shall belong to the whole body of citizens. Private ownership of land, acquired by the people in accordance with law, shall be protected and restricted by law. Privately-owned land shall be liable to taxation according to its value, and the Government may buy such land according to its value.

Mineral deposits which are embedded in the land, and natural power which may, for economic purposes, be utilized for the public benefit shall belong to the state, regardless of the fact that private individuals may have acquired ownership over such land.

If the value of a piece of land has increased, not through the exertion of labor or the employment of capital, the State shall levy thereon an increment tax, the proceeds of which shall be enjoyed by the people in common.

In the distribution and readjustment of land, the state shall in principle assist self-farming land-owners and persons who make use of the land by themselves, and shall also regulate their appropriate areas of operation.

Article 144. Public utilities and other enterprises of a monopolistic nature shall, in principle, be under public operation. In cases permitted by law, they may be operated by private citizens.

Article 145. With respect to private wealth and privately-operated enterprises, the State shall restrict them by law if they are deemed detrimental to a balanced development of national wealth and people's livelihood.

Cooperative enterprises shall receive encouragement and assistance from the State.

Private citizens' productive enterprises and foreign trade shall receive encouragement, guidance and protection from the State.

Article 146. The State shall, by the use of scientific techniques, develop water conservancy, increase the productivity of land, improve agricultural conditions, plan for the utilization of land, develop agricultural resources and hasten the industrialization of agriculture.

Article 147. The Central Government, in order to attain a balanced economic development among the provinces, shall give appropriate aid to poor or unproductive provinces.

The provinces, in order to attain a balanced economic development among the hsien, shall give appropriate aid to poor or unproductive hsien.

Article 148. Within the territory of the Republic of China, all goods shall be permitted to move freely from place to place.

Article 149. Financial institutions shall, in accordance with law, be subject to State control.

Article 150. The State shall extensively establish financial institutions for the common people, with a view to relieving unemployment .

Article 151. With respect to Chinese citizens residing abroad, the State shall foster and protect the development of their economic enterprises.

Section 4. Social Security

Article 152. The State shall provide suitable opportunity for work to people who are able to work.

Article 153. The State, in order to improve the livelihood of laborers and farmers and to improve their productive skill, shall enact laws and carry out policies for their protection.

Women and children engaged in labor shall, according to their age and physical condition, be accorded special protection.

Article 154. Capital and labor shall, in accordance with the principle of harmony and cooperation, promote productive enterprises. Conciliation and arbitration of disputes between capital and labor shall be prescribed by law.

Article 155. The State, in order to promote social welfare, shall establish a social insurance system. To the aged and the infirm who are unable to earn a living, and to victims of unusual calamities, the State shall give appropriate assistance and relief.

Article 156. The State, in order to consolidate the foundation of national existence and development, shall protect motherhood and carry out the policy of promoting the welfare of women and children.

Article 157. The State, in order to improve national health, shall establish extensive services for sanitation and health protection, and a system of public medical service.

Section 5. Education and Culture

Article 158. Education and culture shall aim at the development among the citizens of the national spirit, the spirit of self-government, national morality, good physique, scientific knowledge and the ability to earn a living.

Article 159. All citizens shall have equal opportunity to receive an education.

Article 160. All children of school age from 6 to 12 years shall receive free primary education. Those from poor families shall be supplied with books by the Government.

All citizens above school age who have not received primary education shall receive supplementary education free of charge and shall also be supplied with books by the Government.

Article 161. The national, provincial, and local governments shall extensively establish scholarships to assist students of good scholastic standing and exemplary conduct who lack the means to continue their school education.

Article 162. All public and private educational and cultural institutions in the country shall, in accordance with law, be subject to State supervision.

Article 163. The State shall pay due attention to the balanced development of education in different regions, and shall promote social education in order to raise the cultural standard of the citizens in general. Grants from the National Treasury shall be made to frontier regions and economically poor areas to help them meet their educational and cultural expenses. The Central Government may either itself undertake the more important educational and cultural enterprises in such regions or give them financial assistance.

Article 164. Expenditures of educational programs, scientific studies and cultural services shall not be, in respect of the Central Government, less than 15 per cent of the total national budget; in respect of each province, less than 25 percent of the total provincial budgets; and in respect of each municipality or hsien, less than 35 percent of the total municipal or hsien budget. Educational and cultural foundations established in accordance with law shall, together with their property, be protected.

Article 165. The State shall safeguard the livelihood of those who work in the fields of education, sciences and arts, and shall, in accordance with the development of national economy, increase their remuneration from time to time.

Article 166. The State shall encourage scientific discoveries and inventions, and shall protect ancient sites and articles of historical, cultural or artistic value.

Article 167. The State shall give encouragement or subsidies to the following enterprises or individuals:

1. Educational enterprises in the country which have been operated with good record by private individuals;

2. Educational enterprises which have been operated with good record by Chinese citizens residing abroad;

3. Persons who have made discoveries or inventions in the fields of learning and technology; and

4. Persons who have rendered long and meritorious services in the field of education.

Section 6. Frontier Regions

Article 168. The State shall accord to the various racial groups in the frontier regions legal protection of their status and shall give them special assistance in their local self-government undertakings.

Article 169. The State shall, in a positive manner, undertake and foster the development of education, culture, communications, water conservancy, public health and other economic and social enterprises of the various racial groups in the frontier regions. With respect to the utilization of land, the State shall, after taking into account the climatic conditions, the nature of the soil and the life and habits of the people, adopt measures to protect the land and to assist in its development.

Chapter XIV. Enforcement and Amendment of the Constitution

Article 170. The term "law," as used in this Constitution, shall denote any legislative bill that shall have been passed by the Legislative Yuan and promulgated by the President of the Republic.

Article 171. Laws that are in conflict with the Constitution shall be null and void.

When doubt arises as to whether or not a law is in conflict with the Constitution, interpretation thereon shall be made by the Judicial Yuan.

Article 172. Ordinances that are in conflict with the Constitution or with laws shall be null and void.

Article 173. The Constitution shall be interpreted by the Judicial Yuan.

Article 174. Amendments to the Constitution shall be made in accordance with one of the following procedures:

1. Upon the proposal of one-fifth of the total number of the delegates to the National Assembly and by a resolution of three-fourths of the delegates present at a meeting having a quorum of two-thirds of the entire Assembly, the Constitution may be amended.

2. Upon the proposal of one-fourth of the Members of the Legislative Yuan and by a resolution of three-fourths of the Members present at a meeting having a quorum of three-fourths of the Members of the Yuan, an amendment may be drawn up and submitted to the National Assembly by way of referendum. Such a proposed amendment to the Constitution shall be publicly published half a year before the National Assembly convenes.

Article 175. Whenever necessary, enforcement procedures in regard to any matters prescribed in this Constitution shall be separately provided by law.

The preparatory procedures for the enforcement of this Constitution shall be decided upon by the same National Assembly which shall have adopted this Constitution.

Additional Articles of the Constitution of the Republic of China

(Articles One through Ten were adopted by the fourth extraordinary session of the Second National Assembly at its 32nd plenary meeting on July 28, 1994, and promulgated by the President on August 1, 1994.)

To meet the requisites of national unification, the following additional articles are added to the ROC Constitution in accordance with Article 27, Paragraph 1, Item 3, and Article 174, Item 1:

Article 1. Members of the National Assembly shall be elected according to the following provisions without being subject to the restrictions in Articles 26 and 135 of the Constitution:

1. Two members shall be elected from each Special Municipality, each county or city in the free area. However, where the population exceeds 100,000, one member shall be added for each additional 100,000 persons.

2. Three members each shall be elected from the lowland and highland aborigines in the free area.

3. Twenty members shall be elected from the Chinese citizens who reside abroad.

4. Eighty members shall be elected from one nationwide constituency.

Members for the seats set forth in Items 3 and 4 of the preceding paragraph shall be elected according to a formula for proportional representation among political parties. If the number of seats allotted to a Special Municipality, county or city covered under Item 1, or if the number of seats won by a political party under Item 3 or 4 of the preceding paragraph is between five and ten, then one of the seats stipulated in the pertaining item shall be reserved for a female candidate. Where the number exceeds ten, one seat out of each additional ten shall be reserved for a female candidate.

The powers of the National Assembly shall be as follows notwithstanding the provisions in Article 27, Paragraph 1, Items 1 and 2 of the Constitution:

1. To elect the Vice President in accordance with Article 2, Paragraph 7 of the Additional Articles when said office becomes vacant.

2. To recall the President and Vice President in accordance with Article 2, Paragraph 9 of the Additional Articles.

3. To pass a resolution on the impeachment of the President or Vice President instituted by the Control Yuan in accordance with Article 2, Paragraph 10 of the Additional Articles.

4. To amend the Constitution in accordance with Article 27, Paragraph 1, Item 3 and Article 174, Item 1 of the Constitution.

5. To vote on proposed Constitutional amendments submitted by the Legislative Yuan by way of referendum in accordance with Article 27, Paragraph 1, Item 4 and Article 174, Item 2 of the Constitution.

6. To confirm the appointment of personnel nominated by the President in accordance with Article 4, Paragraph 1; Article 5, Paragraph 2; and Article 6, Paragraph 2 of the Additional Articles.

The National Assembly meets to exercise the powers prescribed in Item 1 or Items 4 through 6 of the preceding paragraph, or when requested by no less than two-fifths of its members, the session shall be convoked by the President. When it meets to exercise the powers prescribed in Item 2 or 3 of the preceding paragraph, the session shall be convoked by the speaker of the National Assembly or by the President of the Legislative Yuan prior to the establishment of the office of the speaker. The provisions in Articles 29 and 30 of the Constitution shall not apply.

When the National Assembly convenes, it shall hear a report on state of the nation by the President, discuss national affairs, and offer counsel. In the event that the National Assembly has not convened for over a year, the President shall convoke an extraordinary session for the aforementioned purpose notwithstanding the restrictions in Article 30 of the Constitution.

Beginning with the Third National Assembly, delegates to the National Assembly shall be elected every four years and the provisions in Article 28, Paragraph 1 of the Constitution shall not apply.

The term of office for the members of the Second National Assembly shall expire on May 19, 1996, and the term of office for the members of the Third

National Assembly shall begin on May 20, 1996. The provisions in Article 28, Paragraph 2 of the Constitution shall not apply.

Beginning with the Third National Assembly, the Assembly shall have a speaker and a deputy speaker who shall be elected by the members of the Assembly from amongst themselves. The speaker shall represent the National Assembly and preside over its meetings.

The procedure for the exercise of powers by the National Assembly shall be determined by the Assembly itself. The provisions in Article 34 of the Constitution shall not apply.

Article 2. The President and Vice President shall be directly elected by the entire populace of the free area of the Republic of China. This shall be effective from the election for the ninth-term President and Vice President in 1996. The presidential and vice presidential candidates shall register jointly and be slated as a pair on the ballot. The pair that receive the highest number of votes shall be the winners of the election. Citizens of the free area of the Republic of China residing abroad may return to the ROC to exercise their electoral rights and this shall be stipulated by law.

Presidential orders to appoint or remove from office personnel appointed with the confirmation of the National Assembly or Legislative Yuan in accordance with the Constitution do not require the counter-signature of the President of the Executive Yuan. The provisions in Article 37 of the Constitution shall not apply.

Orders to remove the President of the Executive Yuan from office shall take effect after the new nominee to this office has been confirmed by the Legislative Yuan.

The President may, by resolution of a council of the Executive Yuan, issue emergency orders and take all necessary measures to avert an imminent danger to the security of the State or of the people or to cope with any serious financial or economic crisis, without being subject to the restrictions prescribed in Article 43 of the Constitution. However, such orders shall, within 10 days of issuance, be presented to the Legislative Yuan for confirmation. Should the Legislative Yuan withhold confirmation, the said emergency orders shall forthwith cease to be valid.

To determine major policies for national security, the President may establish the National Security Council and its subsidiary organ, the National Security Bureau. The organization of the said organs shall be stipulated by law.

Beginning with the ninth presidential term, the term of office for both the President and the Vice President shall be four years. The President and the Vice President may be re-elected for a second term; and the provisions in Article 47 of the Constitution shall not apply.

Should the office of the Vice President become vacant, the President shall nominate a candidate within three months and convoke the National Assembly to elect a new Vice President, who shall serve out the original term until its expiration.

Should the offices of both the President and the Vice President become vacant, the President of the Executive Yuan shall exercise the official powers of the President and the Vice President. A new President and a new Vice President shall be elected in accordance with Paragraph 1 of this Article and shall serve out each respective original term until its expiration. Article 49 of the Constitution shall not apply.

Recall of the President and the Vice President shall be motioned by one-fourth of all delegates to the National Assembly, proposed with the concurrence of two-thirds of such delegates, and passed by more than half of the valid ballots to recall cast by more than half of all voters in the free area.

The President and the Vice President shall be dismissed from office should an impeachment proposal by the Control Yuan submitted to the National Assembly be passed by two-thirds of all delegates in the National Assembly.

Article 3. Members of the Legislative Yuan shall be elected according to the following provisions without being subject to the restrictions in Article 64 of the Constitution:

1. Two members shall be elected from each province and each Special Municipality in the free area. Where the population exceeds 200,000, however, one member will be added for each additional 100,000 persons; and where the population exceeds one million, one member will be added for each additional 200,000 persons.

2. Three members shall be elected from the lowland and highland aborigines in the free area.

3. Six members shall be elected from the Chinese citizens who reside abroad.

4. Thirty members shall be elected from one nationwide constituency.

The members set forth in Items 3 and 4 above shall be elected in accordance with the formula for proportional representation among political parties. If the number of seats allotted to a province or Special Municipality set forth in Item 1 above; or if the number of seats won by a political party under Item 3 or 4 above is between five and ten, then one of the seats stipulated in the pertaining paragraph shall be reserved for a female candidate. Where the number exceeds ten, one seat out of each additional ten shall be reserved for a female candidate.

Article 4. The Judicial Yuan shall have a president, a vice president, and a certain number of Grand Justices, all of whom shall be nominated and, with the consent of the National Assembly, appointed by the President; and the pertinent provisions in Article 79 of the Constitution shall not apply.

The Grand Justices of the Judicial Yuan shall, in addition to discharging their duties according to Article 78 of the Constitution, also form a Constitutional Court to adjudicate matters relating to the dissolution of unconstitutional political parties.

A political party shall be unconstitutional if its goals or activities jeopardize the existence of the Republic of China or free, democratic constitutional order.

Article 5. The Examination Yuan shall be the highest examination body of the State, and shall be responsible for the following matters; and the provisions in Article 83 of the Constitution shall not apply:

1. All examination-related matters;

2. All matters relating to the qualification screening, security of tenure, pecuniary aid in case of death, and retirement of civil servants; and

3. All legal matters relating to the employment, discharge, performance evaluation, scale of salaries, promotion, transfer, commendation and award for civil servants.

The Examination Yuan shall have a president, a vice president, and several members, all of whom shall be nominated and, with the consent of the National Assembly, appointed by the President; and the provisions in Article 84 of the Constitution shall not apply.

The provisions in Article 85 of the Constitution concerning holding examinations in different areas, with prescribed numbers of persons to be selected according to various provinces and areas, shall cease to apply.

Article 6. The Control Yuan shall be the highest control body of the State and shall exercise the powers of impeachment, censure and audit; and the provisions in Articles 90 and 94 of the Constitution concerning exercising the power of consent shall not apply.

The Control Yuan shall have 29 members, including a president and a vice president, all of whom shall serve a term of six years and shall be nominated and, with the consent of the National Assembly, appointed by the President. The provisions from Article 91 through Article 93 of the Constitution shall not apply.

Impeachment proceedings by the Control Yuan against a public functionary in the central government, any local government, or against personnel of the Judicial Yuan or the Examination Yuan shall be initiated by two or more members of the Control Yuan, and be investigated and voted upon by a committee of not less than nine of its members notwithstanding the restrictions in Article 98 of the Constitution.

In the case of impeachment by the Control Yuan of Control Yuan personnel for dereliction of duty or violation of the law, the provisions of Article 95 and Article 97, Paragraph 2 of the Constitution, as well as the foregoing paragraph shall apply.

A motion by the Control Yuan impeaching the President or the Vice President must be initiated by more than half of all the members of the Control Yuan and passed by more than two-thirds of all such members for it to be submitted to the National Assembly notwithstanding the restrictions in Article 100 of the Constitution.

Members of the Control Yuan must be beyond party affiliation and independently exercise their powers and discharge their responsibilities in accordance with the law.

The provisions in Articles 101 and 102 of the Constitution shall cease to apply.

Article 7. The remuneration and pay of the members of the National Assembly and the Legislative Yuan shall be regulated by law. In addition to the general case of annual adjustment, regulations on individual increase of remuneration and pay shall go into effect starting with the subsequent National Assembly or Legislative Yuan.

Article 8. The system of local governments in the provinces and counties shall include the following provisions, which shall be established by the enactment of appropriate laws notwithstanding the restrictions in Article 108, Paragraph 1, Item 1; Articles 112 through 115; and Article 122 of the Constitution:

1. There shall be a provincial assembly in each province and a county council in each county. Members of the provincial assembly and the county council shall be elected by the people of the province and the people of the county, respectively.

2. The legislative power of a province and that of a county shall be exercised by the provincial assembly and the county council, respectively.

3. In a province, there shall be a provincial government with a provincial governor. In a county, there shall be a county government with a county magistrate. The provincial governor and the county magistrate shall be elected by the people of the province and the people of the county, respectively.

4. The relationship between the province and the county.

5. The self-governance of province is subject to supervision by the Executive Yuan, while the self-governance of counties is subject to supervision by the provincial government.

Article 9. The State shall encourage development of and investment in science and technology, facilitate the upgrade of industry, promote the modernization of agriculture and fishery, emphasize the exploitation and utilization of water resources, and intensify international economic cooperation.

Environmental and ecological protection shall be given equal consideration with economic and technological development.

The State shall manage government-run financial organizations in line with the principles of business administration. The management, personnel, budgets, final accounts, and audit of the government-run financial organizations shall be specially regulated by law.

The State shall inaugurate universal health insurance coverage and promote the research and development of both modern and traditional medicines.

The State shall protect the dignity of women, safeguard their personal safety, eliminate sexual discrimination, and further substantive equality between the sexes.

The State shall safeguard the rights of the handicapped and disabled to insurance, medical care, education, training, employment assistance, support for daily living needs and relief, so as to help them attain independence and further their careers.

The State shall accord to the aborigines in the free area legal protection of their status and the right to political participation. It shall also provide assistance and encouragement for their education, cultural preservation, social welfare and business undertakings. The same protection and assistance shall be given to the people of Kinmen and Matsu areas.

The State shall accord to Chinese nationals residing overseas protection of their rights to political participation.

Article 10. Rights and obligations between the people of the mainland China area and those of the free area, and the disposition of other related affairs shall be specially regulated by law.

Appendix III
ROC Government Directory

Office of the President 總統府

122 Chungking South Road, Section 1, Taipei
Phone: (02) 311-3731
Fax: (02) 314-0746 (The First Bureau)
    (02) 311-5877 (Protocol Section)
    (02) 331-1604 (Spokesman's Office)
President: LEE, Teng-hui 李登輝
Vice President: LIEN, Chan 連戰
Secretary-General: HUANG Kun-huei 黃昆輝
Deputy Secretary-General & Spokesman:
CHEN, Stephen S.F. 陳錫蕃

Academia Sinica 中央研究院
128 Yen Chiu Yuan Road, Section 2, Taipei
Phone: (02) 782-2120
Fax: (02) 785-3847
President: LEE, Yuan-che 李遠哲

Academia Historica 國史館
406 Pei Yi Road, Section 2, Hsintien, Taipei County
Phone: (02) 217-4540
Fax: (02) 217-0415
President: PAN, Chen-chew 潘振球

National Security Council 國家安全會議
122 Chungking South Road, Section 1, Taipei
Phone: (02) 361-6132
Fax: (02) 361-1214
Chairman: LEE, Teng-hui 李登輝
Secretary-General: DING, Mou-shih 丁懋時

National Unification Council 國家統一委員會
122 Chungking South Road, Section 1, Taipei
Phone: (02) 314-6561
Fax: (02) 389-9462
Chairman: LEE, Teng-hui 李登輝

National Assembly 國民大會

53 Chung Hwa Road, Section 1, Taipei
Phone: (02) 331-1312
Fax: (02) 314-2056
Speaker: CHIEN, Fredrick F. 錢復
Deputy Speaker: HSIEH Lung-sheng 謝隆盛
Secretary-General: CHEN, Chuan 陳川

Executive Yuan 行政院

1 Chung Hsiao East Road, Section 1, Taipei
Phone: (02) 356-1500
Fax: (02) 394-8727
Premier: LIEN, Chan 連戰
Vice Premier: HSU, Li-teh 徐立德
Secretary-General: CHAO, Shou-po 趙守博
Deputy Secretary-General:
CHANG, Che-shen 張哲琛

Ministers of State 政務委員
KUO, Shirley W.Y. 郭婉容
LIN, Chen-kuo 林振國
MA, Ying-jeou 馬英九
TU, Teh-chi 涂德錡
YANG, Shih-chien 楊世緘
YEH, Chin-fong 葉金鳳
TSAI, Cheng-wen 蔡政文

Ministry of the Interior 內政部
5 Hsuchow Road, Taipei
Phone: (02) 356-5005
Fax: (02) 356-6201
Minister: LIN, Fong-cheng 林豐正

Ministry of Foreign Affairs 外交部
2 Kaitagelan Boulevard, Taipei
Phone: (02) 311-9292
Fax: (02) 314-4972
Minister: John H. CHANG 章孝嚴

Ministry of National Defense 國防部
2nd Floor, 164 Po Ai Road, Taipei

Phone: (02) 314-3272
Fax: (02) 314-4221
Minister: CHIANG, Chung-ling 蔣仲苓
Chief of the General Staff: LO, Pen-li 羅本立

Ministry of Finance 財政部
2 Ai Kuo West Road, Taipei
Phone: (02) 322-8000
Fax: (02) 396-5829
Minister: Paul CHIU 邱正雄

Ministry of Education 教育部
5 Chung Shan South Road, Taipei
Phone: (02) 356-6051
Fax: (02) 397-6949
Minister: WU, Jin 吳京

Ministry of Justice 法務部
130 Chungking South Road, Section 1, Taipei
Phone: (02) 314-6871
Fax: (02) 389-6274
Minister: LIAO, Cheng-hao 廖正豪

Ministry of Economic Affairs 經濟部
15 Foochow Street, Taipei
Phone: (02) 321-2200
Fax: (02) 391-9398
Minister: WANG, Chih-kang 王志剛

Ministry of Transportation and Communications
交 通 部
2 Changsha Street, Section 1, Taipei
Phone: (02) 349-2900
Fax: (02) 311-8587
Minister: TSAY, Jaw-yang 蔡兆陽

Mongolian & Tibetan Affairs Commission
蒙 藏 委 員 會
4th Floor, 5 Hsuchow Road, Taipei
Phone: (02) 356-6166
Fax: (02) 356-6419
Chairman: LEE, Harry H.K. 李厚高

Overseas Chinese Affairs Commission
僑 務 委 員 會
15th-17th Floor, 5 Hsuchow Road, Taipei

Phone: (02) 356-6133
Fax: (02) 356-6323
Chairman: James C.Y. CHU 祝基瀅

The Central Bank of China 中央銀行
2 Roosevelt Road, Section 1, Taipei
Phone: (02) 393-6161
Fax: (02) 322-3223
Governor: SHEU, Yuan-dong 許遠東

Directorate General of Budget,
Accounting and Statistics, Executive Yuan
行 政 院 主 計 處
1 Chung Hsiao East Road, Section 1, Taipei
Phone: (02) 356-1500
Fax: (02) 397-0196
Director-General: WEI, Duan 韋端

Government Information Office, Executive Yuan
行 政 院 新 聞 局
2 Tientsin Street, Taipei
Phone: (02) 322-8888
Fax: (02) 356-8733
Administrator: SU, Chi 蘇起

Central Personnel Administration,
Executive Yuan 行政院人事行政局
9-11th, 2-2 Chinan Road, Section 2,
Taipei,
Phone: (02) 397-9298
Fax: (02) 397-5565
Director-General: CHEN, Keng-chin 陳庚金

Department of Health, Executive Yuan
行 政 院 衛 生 署
100 Ai Kuo East Road, Taipei
Phone: (02) 321-0151
Fax: (02) 322-3877
Director-General: CHANG, Po-ya 張博雅

Environmental Protection Administration,
Executive Yuan 行政院環境保護署
41 Chung Hua Road, Section 1, Taipei
Phone: (02) 311-7722
Fax: (02) 311-6071
Administrator: TSAI, Hsung-hsiung 蔡勳雄

Council for Economic Planning and Development, Executive Yuan 行政院經濟建設委員會
9th Floor.87 Nanking East Road, Section 2, Taipei
Phone: (02) 522-5300
Fax: (02) 568-2439
Chairman: CHIANG, Pin-kung 江丙坤

Veterans Affairs Commission, Executive Yuan
行政院國軍退除役官兵輔導委員會
222 Chung Hsiao East Road, Section 5, Taipei
Phone: (02) 725-5700
Fax: (02) 723-7610
Chairman: YANG, Ting-yun 楊亭雲

National Youth Commission, Executive Yuan
行政院青年輔導委員會
14th Floor, 5 Hsuchow Road, Taipei
Phone: (02) 356-6232
Fax: (02) 356-6307
Chairman: WU, Wan-lan 吳挽瀾

National Palace Museum 國立故宮博物院
221 Chih Shan Road, Section 2, Wai-shuang-hsi, Shihlin, Taipei
Phone: (02) 881-2021
Fax: (02) 882-1440
Director: CHIN, Hsiao-yi 秦孝儀

Atomic Energy Council, Executive Yuan
行政院原子能委員會
67 Lane 144, Keelung Road, Section 4, Taipei
Phone: (02) 363-4180
Fax: (02) 367-6200
Chairman: HU, Ching-piao 胡錦標

National Science Council, Executive Yuan
行政院國家科學委員會
17th-22nd Floor, 106 Ho Ping East Road, Section 2, Taipei
Phone: (02) 737-7501
Fax: (02) 737-7668
Chairman: LIU, Chao-shiuan 劉兆玄

Research, Development and Evaluation Commission, Executive Yuan
行政院研究發展考核委員會

6-8th Floor, 2-2 Chinan Road, Section 2, Taipei
Phone: (02) 341-9066
Fax: (02) 396-9444
Chairman: HUANG, Ta-chou 黃大洲

Council of Agriculture, Executive Yuan
行政院農業委員會
37 Nan Hai Road, Taipei
Phone: (02) 381-2991
Fax: (02) 331-0341
Chairman: TJIU, Mau-ying 邱茂英

Council for Cultural Affairs, Executive Yuan
行政院文化建設委員會
102 Ai Kuo East Road, Taipei
Phone: (02) 351-8030
Fax: (02) 322-2937
Chairwoman: LIN, Cheng-chih 林澄枝

Council of Labor Affairs, Executive Yuan
行政院勞工委員會
5th-15th Floor, 132 Min Sheng East Road, Section 3, Taipei
Phone: (02) 718-2512
Fax: (02) 514-9240
Chairman: SHIEH, Shen-san 謝深山

Mainland Affairs Council, Executive Yuan
行政院大陸委員會
15th-18th Floor, 2-2 Chinan Road, Section 2, Taipei
Phone: (02) 397-5589
Fax: (02) 397-5300
Chairman: CHANG, King-yuh 張京育

Fair Trade Commission, Executive Yuan
行政院公平交易委員會
12-14th Floor, 2-2 Chinan Road, Section 2, Taipei
Phone: (02) 351-7588
Fax: (02) 397-4997
Chairwoman: CHAO, Yang-ching 趙揚清

Counicl of Aboriginal Affairs, Executive Yuan 行政院原住民委員會
3rd Floor, 6 Chung Hsiao West Road, Section 1, Taipei

Phone: (02) 388-2122
Fax:(02)389-1967
Chairman: HUA, Chia-chih   華加志

**Public Construction Commission,
Executive Yuan** 行政院公共工程委員會
9th Floor, 4 Chung Hsiao West Road, Section 1
Taipei
Phone: (02) 361-8611
Fax: (02) 331-5808
Chairman: OU, Chin-der 歐晉德

**Consumer Protection Commission,
Executive Yuan** 行政院消費者保護委員會
1 Chung Hsiao East Road, Secton1
Taipei
Phone:(02) 356-6600
Fax:(02) 321-4538
Chairman: HSU, Li-teh 徐立德

Central Election Commission
中 央 選 舉 委 員 會
5 Hsuchow Road, Taipei
Phone: (02) 356-5484
Fax: (02) 397-6901
Chairman: LIN, Fong-cheng 林豐正

Legislative Yuan 立法院

1 Chung Shan South Road, Taipei
Phone: (02) 321-1531
Fax: (02) 322-3557
President: LIU, Sung-pan 劉松藩
Vice President: WANG, Chin-ping 王金平
Secretary-General: LIU, Pi-liang 劉碧良

Judicial Yuan 司法院

124 Chungking South Road, Section 1, Taipei
Phone: (02) 361-8577
Fax: (02) 371-5583
President: SHIH, Chi-yang 施啟揚
Vice President: LU, Yu-wen 呂有文
Secretary-General: CHU, Shih-yen 朱石炎

Supreme Court 最高法院
6 Changsha Street, Section 1, Taipei
Phone: (02) 314-1160
Fax: (02) 311-4246
President: KO, Yih-tsair 葛義才

Administrative Court 行政法院
4th Floor, 124 Chungking South Road, Section 1, Taipei
Phone: (02) 311-3691
Fax: (02) 311-1791
President: LIN, Ming-teh 林明德

**Committee on the Discipline of Public
Functionaries** 公務員懲戒委員會
3rd Floor, 124 Chungking South Road, Section 1
Taipei
Phone: (02) 331-7908
Fax: (02) 331-1934
President: KO, Yih-tsair 葛義才

Examination Yuan 考試院

1 Shih Yuan Road, Taipei
Phone: (02) 236-3081
Fax: (02) 236-5240
President: HSU, Shui-teh 許水德
Vice President: KUAN, John 關中
Secretary-General: WU, Chin-lin 伍錦霖

Ministry of Examination 考選部
1 Shih Yuan Road, Taipei
Phone: (02) 236-3081
Fax: (02) 236-9592
Minister: CHEN, Ching-jang 陳金讓

Ministry of Civil Service 銓敘部
1 Shih Yuan Road, Taipei
Phone: (02) 236-3081
Fax: (02) 236-9207
Minister: CHIU, Cheyne J.Y. 邱進益

Civil Service Protection and Training Commission
公 務 人 員 保 障 暨 培 訓 委 員 會
136 Roosevelt Road, Section 6, Taipei

Phone: (02) 935-9500
Fax:(02) 935-9521
Chairman: LIN, Chi-yuan 林基源

Control Yuan 監察院

2 Chung Hsiao East Road, Section 1
Taipei
Phone: (02) 341-3183
Fax: (02) 356-6570
President: WANG, Tso-yung 王作榮

National Audit Office 審計部
1 Hangchow North Road, Taipei
Phone: (02) 397-1366
Fax: (02) 397-7889
Auditor-General: SU, Chen-ping 蘇振平

Taiwan Provincial Government
臺灣省政府

1 Kuang Hua Road, Chung Hsing New Village
Nantou
Phone: (049) 33-2201
Fax: (049) 31-6560
Governor: SOONG, James C.Y. 宋楚瑜

Secretariat 秘書處
1 Sheng Fu Road, Chung Hsing New Village, Nantou
Phone: (049) 332-569
Fax: (049) 316-560

Department of Civil Affairs 民政廳
1 Kuang Hua Road, Chung Hsing New Village
Nantou
Phone: (049) 33-9111
Fax: (049) 31-5424

Department of Finance 財政廳
3 Kuang Hua First Road, Chung Hsing New Village
Nantou
Phone: (049) 33-2283
Fax: (049) 31-6007

Department of Education 教育廳
738-4 Chung Cheng Road, Wufeng Hsiang
Taichung
Phone: (04) 339-3032
Fax: (04) 339-8053

Department of Reconstruction 建設廳
4 Sheng Fu Road, Chung Hsing New Village
Nantou
Phone: (049) 35-9171
Fax: (049) 31-5637

Department of Agriculture and Forestry 農林廳
8 Kuang Hua Road, Chung Hsing New Village, Nantou
Phone: (049) 33-2360
Fax: (049) 35-1706

Department of Social Affairs 社會處
3 Kuang Hua Road, Chung Hsing New Village, Nantou
Phone: (049) 33-2401
Fax: (049) 31-6863

Department of Labor Affairs 勞工處
501 Li Ming Road, Section 2, Nantun District
Taichung
Phone: (04) 255-0660
Fax: (04) 252-7931

Department of Environmental Protection
環境保護處
497 Li Ming Road, Section 2, Nantun District
Taichung
Phone: (04) 252-1718
Fax: (04) 252-1352

Taiwan Provincial Police Administration
臺灣省警務處
588 Wen Hsin Road, Section 2, Taichung
Phone: (04) 322-7016
Fax: (04) 328-8238

Department of Transportation 交通處
6 Sheng Fu Road, Chung Hsing New Village
Nantou
Phone: (049) 33-2420
Fax: (049) 33-9740

Department of Health 衛生處
15 Kuang Ming Road, Chung Hsing New Village
Nantou
Phone: (049) 33-2161
Fax: (049) 33-2381

Department of Information 新聞處
150 Tzu Yu Road, Section 1, Taichung
Phone: (04) 221-0840
Fax: (04) 223-9109

Department of Land 地政處
503 Li Ming Road, Section 2, Nantun District
Taichung
Phone: (04) 251-5120
Fax: (04) 252-0035

Housing and Urban Development Bureau
住宅及都市發展局
342 Pa Teh Road, Section 2, Taipei
Phone: (02) 773-1212
Fax: (02) 740-0507

Taiwan Provincial Food Bureau 糧食局
15 Hangchow South Road, Section 1, Taipei
Phone: (02) 393-7231
Fax: (02) 394-7309

Conscription Administration 兵役處
21 Kuang Ming Road, Chung Hsing New Village
Nantou
Phone: (049) 33-2611
Fax: (049) 33-2618

Department of Budget, Accounting and Statistics
主計處
1 Kuang Hua First Road, Chung Hsing New Village
Nantou
Phone: (049) 33-2462
Fax: (049) 35-0163

Department of Personnel 人事處
2 Sheng Fu Road, Chung Hsing New Village
Nantou
Phone: (049) 35-9151
Fax: (049) 33-1274

Council For Economic Planning and Mobilization
經濟建設委員會
56 Fu Hsi Road, Chung Hsing New Village, Nantou
Phone: (049) 31-5405
Fax: (049) 35-0791

Administrative Appeal Commission
訴願審議委員會
7th Floor, 503 Li Ming Road, Section 2, Nantun District
Taichung
Phone: (04) 252-8437
Fax: (04) 252-0235

Research, Development and Evaluation Commission
研究發展考核委員會
56 Fu Hsi Road, Chung Hsing New Village, Nantou
Phone: (049) 33-1628
Fax: (049) 35-0441

Commission on Administrative Regulation
法規委員會
56 Fu Hsi Road, Chung Hsing New Village, Nantou
Phone: (049) 35-9483
Fax: (049) 35-9484

Taiwan Supply Bureau 物資局
3 Kai Feng Street, Section 1, Taipei
Phone: (02) 371-3281
Fax: (02) 371-7854

Taiwan Provincial Training Corps 訓練團
1 Kuang Ming Road, Chung Hsing New Village, Nantou
Phone: (049) 33-2571
Fax: (049) 33-9030

Taipei Watersources Management Commission
臺北水源特定區管理委員會
4th Floor, 5 Lane 45, Pei Hsin Road, Section 1, Hsintien
Taipei
Phone: (02) 917-3282
Fax: (02) 912-8539

Urban Planning Commission
都市計畫委員會
4 Sheng Fu Road, Chung Hsing New Village
Nantou

Phone: (049) 35-1311
Fax: (049) 35-1048

Council of Aboriginal Affairs
   原住民事務委員會
27 Kuang Ming Road, Chung Hsing New Village,
Nantou
Phone: (049) 351-203
Fax: (049) 351-202

Foreign Affairs Department 外事室
9th Floor, 15 Hangchow South Road, Section 1,
Taipei
Phone:(02)395-8077
Fax:(02) 393-2724

Taipei City Government
臺 北 市 政 府

1 Shih Fu Road, Taipei
Phone: (02) 720-8889
Fax: (02) 727-8809
Mayor: CHEN, Shui-bian 陳水扁

Secretariat 祕書處
1 Shih Fu Road, Taipei
Phone: (02) 720-8889
Fax: (02) 759-8997

Bureau of Civil Affairs 民政局
1 Shih Fu Road, Taipei
Phone: (02) 720-8889
Fax: (02) 759-8799

Bureau of Finance 財政局
1 Shih Fu Road, Taipei
Phone: (02) 720-8889
Fax: (02) 720-6022

Bureau of Education 教育局
1 Shih Fu Road, Taipei
Phone: (02) 720-8889
Fax: (02) 759-3380

Bureau of Business Management 建設局
1 Shih Fu Road, Taipei
Phone: (02) 720-8889
Fax: (02) 720-5698

Bureau of Public Works 工務局
1 Shih Fu Road, Taipei
Phone: (02) 720-8889
Fax: (02) 720-5817

Bureau of Transportation 交通局
1 Shih Fu Road, Taipei
Phone: (02) 720-8889
Fax: (02) 729-1814

Bureau of Social Affairs 社會局
1 Shih Fu Road, Taipei
Phone: (02) 720-8889
Fax: (02) 720-6552

Bureau of Labor Affairs 勞工局
1 Shih Fu Road, Taipei
Phone: (02) 720-8889
Fax: (02) 720-9339

Taipei City Police Headquarters 警察局
96 Yen Ping South Road, Taipei
Phone: (02) 331-3561
Fax: (02) 331-8898

Bureau of Health 衛生局
1 Shih Fu Road, Taipei
Phone: (02) 720-8889
Fax: (02) 759-3002

Bureau of Environmental Protection
環 境 保 護 局
1 Shih Fu Road, Taipei
Phone: (02) 720-8889
Fax: (02) 759-7986

Bureau of Urban Development 都市發展局
1 Shih Fu Road, Taipei
Phone: (02) 720-8889
Fax: (02) 759-3321

Fire Department of Taipei 消防局
1 Sung Jen Road, Taipei
Phone: (02) 729-7668
Fax: (02) 758-7743

Department of Land Administration 地政處
1 Shih Fu Road, Taipei
Phone: (02) 720-8889
Fax: (02) 720-1802

Department of Public Housing 國民住宅處
9th Floor, 8 Roosevelt Road, Section 1, Taipei
Phone: (02) 381-3892
Fax: (02) 392-1645

Department of Information 新聞處
1 Shih Fu Road, Taipei
Phone: (02) 720-8889
Fax: (02) 720-5789

Department of Military Service 兵役處
9th Floor, 92 Roosevelt Road, Section 4, Taipei
Phone: (02) 368-4360
Fax: (02) 367-3072

Department of Budget, Accounting and Statistics
主計處
1 Shih Fu Road, Taipei
Phone: (02) 720-8889
Fax: (02) 759-5109

Department of Personnel 人事處
1 Shih Fu Road, Taipei
Phone: (02) 720-8889
Fax: (02) 720-9111

Department of Anti-Corruption 政風處
1 Shih Fu Road., Taipei
Phone:(02) 720-8889
Fax:(02) 759-5690

**Commission of Research, Development
and Evaluation** 研究發展考核委員會
1 Shih Fu Road, Taipei

Phone: (02) 720-8889
Fax: (02) 759-3593

Commission for Examining Petitions and Appeals
訴願審議委員會
1 Shih Fu Road, Taipei
Phone: (02) 720-8889
Fax: (02) 759-3266

Rules and Regulations Commission
法規委員會
1 Shih Fu Road, Taipei
Phone: (02) 720-8889
Fax: (02) 759-6695

Commission for Native Taiwanese Affairs
原住民事務委員會
1 Shih Fu Road, Taipei
Phone:(02) 720-8889
Fax:(02) 720-5996

Department of Rapid Transit Systems
捷運工程局
7, Lane 48, Chungshan North Road, Section 2, Taipei
Phone: (02) 521-5550
Fax: (02) 521-7639

**Bureau of Taipei Feitsui Reservoir
Administration** 台北翡翠水庫管理局
43 Hsin Wu Road, Section 3, Hsintien, Taipei
Phone: (02) 666-7811
Fax: (02) 666-7341

Taipei Water Department 臺北自來水事業處
131 Chang Hsing Street, Taipei
Phone: (02) 735-2140
Fax: (02) 732-3432

Taipei Bank 台北銀行
50 Chungshan North Road, Section 2, Taipei
Phone: (02) 542-5656
Fax: (02) 542-4396

Civilian Employees Training Center
公務人員訓練中心
20, Lane 21, Wanmei Street, Section 2, Taipei

Phone: (02) 932-0210
Fax: (02) 931-2348

Taipei Rapid Transit Co., Ltd.
臺 北 大 眾 捷 運 股 份 有 限 公 司
7 Peiping East Road, Taipei
Phone: (02) 396-2231
Fax: (02) 395-6054

Kaohsiung City Government
高 雄 市 政 府

2 Ssu Wei Third Road, Kaohsiung
Phone: (07) 334-2233
Fax: (07) 333-7633
Mayor: WU, Den-yih 吳敦義

Secretariat 祕書處
2 Ssu Wei Third Road, Kaohsiung
Phone: (07) 335-9566
Fax: (07) 333-7633

Bureau of Civil Affairs 民政局
2 Ssu Wei Third Road, Kaohsiung
Phone: (07) 335-6111
Fax: (07) 331-5944

Bureau of Finance 財政局
2 Ssu Wei Third Road, Kaohsiung
Phone: (07) 334-7866
Fax: (07) 331-8859

Bureau of Education 教育局
2 Ssu Wei Third Road, Kaohsiung
Phone: (07) 337-3110
Fax: (07) 331-4874

Bureau of Reconstruction 建設局
2 Ssu Wei Third Road, Kaohsiung
Phone: (07) 336-6252
Fax: (07) 331-6426

Bureau of Public Works 工務局
2 Ssu Wei Third Road, Kaohsiung

Phone: (07) 333-5386
Fax: (07) 331-5426

Bureau of Social Affairs 社會局
2 Ssu Wei Third Road, Kaohsiung
Phone: (07) 337-3365
Fax: (07) 331-5940

Bureau of Labor Affairs 勞工局
6 Chen Chung Road, Chien Chen District
Kaohsiung
Phone: (07) 812-4612
Fax: (07) 812-4783

Police Headquarters 警察局
260 Chung Cheng Fourth Road
Kaohsiung
Phone: (07) 261-3355
Fax: (07) 241-0973

Fire Department 消防局
3 Chung Cheng 3rd Road
Kaohsiung
Phone:(07) 227-1055
Fax:(07) 227-1058

Health Department 衛生局
261 Chung Cheng Fourth Road,
Kaohsiung
Phone: (07) 261-8387
Fax: (07) 281-4327

Department of Environmental Protection
環 境 保 護 局
2 Ssu Wei Third Road, Kaohsiung
Phone: (07) 337-3395
Fax: (07) 331-6164

Bureau of Rapid Transit Systems 捷運工程局
2 Ssu Wei Third Road, Kaohsiung
Phone: (07) 331-4546
Fax: (07) 331-4366

Department of Land Administration 地政處
2 Ssu Wei Third Road, Kaohsiung

Phone: (07) 337-3445
Fax: (07) 331-4105

Department of Public Housing 國民住宅處
2 Ssu Wei Third Road, Kaohsiung
Phone: (07) 337-3515
Fax: (07) 331-5080

Department of Information 新聞處
2 Ssu Wei Third Road, Kaohsiung
Phone: (07) 333-3269
Fax: (07) 331-5003

Department of Conscription 兵役處
2 Ssu Wei Third Road, Kaohsiung
Phone: (07) 331-6502
Fax: (07) 331-6506

Department of Budget, Accounting and Statistics
主計處
2 Ssu Wei Third Road, Kaohsiung
Phone: (07) 334-1766
Fax: (07) 331-4803

Department of Personnel 人事處
2 Ssu Wei Third Road, Kaohsiung
Phone: (07) 336-0776
Fax: (07) 331-5652

Department of Government Ethics 政風處
2 Ssu Wei Third Road, Kaohsiung

Phone:(07) 330-6816
Fax:(07) 331-3655

Civil Servant Training Center
公務人員訓練中心
801 Chung Te Road, Kaohsiung
Phone: (07) 342-2170
Fax: (07) 342-2142

Research, Development and Evaluation Commission
研究發展考核委員會
2 Ssu Wei Third Road, Kaohsiung
Phone: (07) 337-3675
Fax: (07) 331-3975

Commission for Examining Petitions and Appeals
訴願審議委員會
2 Ssu Wei Third Road, Kaohsiung
Phone: (07) 337-3690
Fax: (07) 330-8971

Commission on Law and Regulations
法規委員會
2 Ssu Wei Third Road, Kaohsiung
Phone: (07) 337-3700
Fax: (07) 333-8191

Bank of Kaohsiung 高雄銀行
21 Wu Fu Third Road, Kaohsiung
Phone: (07) 348-0583
Fax: (07) 348-0524

Appendix IV
Directory of ROC Representatives Abroad

ROC Embassies and Consulates

Asia

Embassy of the Republic of China
Yaren, Republic of Nauru
P.O. Box 294
Republic of Nauru, Central Pacific
Phone: (+674) 4399

Embassy of the Republic of China
Honiara, Solomon Islands
Lengakiki Ridge, Honiara
Solomon Islands
Mailing Address:
P.O. Box 586, Honiara
Solomon Islands
Phone: (+677) 22-590

Embassy of the Republic of China
Nuku'alofa, Kingdom of Tonga
(South Pacific)
Holomui Road, Nuku'alofa
Kingdom of Tonga, South Pacific
Mailing Address:
P.O. Box 842, Nuku'alofa
Kingdom of Tonga, South Pacific
Phone: (+676) 21-766

Embassy of the Republic of China
Funafuti, Tuvalu
P.O. Box 842, Nuku'alofa
Kingdom of Tonga, South Pacific

Africa

Ambassade de la République de Chine
Ouagadougou, Burkina Faso
01 B.P. 5563, Ouagadougou 01
Burkina Faso
Phone: (+226) 316-195

Ambassade de la République de Chine
Bangui, République Centrafricaine
Mailing Address:
B.P. 1058, Bangui
République Centrafricaine
Phone: (+236) 613-628

Embassy of the Republic of China
Banjul, Republic of the Gambia
Mailing Address:
P.O. Box 916, Banjul, The Gambia, West Africa
Phone: (+220) 374-046

Embaixada da República da China
na República da Guiné-Bissau
Mailing Address:
Ambassade de la République de Chine
en République de Guinée-Bissau
Boîte Postale No. 66, Bissau
Guinée-Bissau
Phone: (+245) 201-501

Embassy of the Republic of China
Monrovia, Republic of Liberia
06 B.P. 904, Cidex-1, Abidjan-06, Cote d'Ivoire
Mailing Address:
P.O. Box 5970, Monrovia, Liberia
Phone: (+231) 224-044

Embassy of the Republic of China
Lilongwe, Republic of Malawi
Area 40, Plot No. 9
Capital City, Lilongwe, Malawi
Mailing Address:
P.O. Box 30221
Capital City, Lilongwe 3, Malawi
Phone: (+265) 783-611

Consulate-General of the Republic of China
Calabar, Federal Republic of Nigeria
101 A, Ndidem Usang Iso Road

(Marian Extension)
Calabar, Cross River State, Nigeria
Mailing Address:
P.O. Box 398, State Housing Post Office
Calabar City, Cross River State, Nigeria
Phone: (+234-87) 222-783, 222-835

**Ambassade de la Republique de Chine
en Republique du Senegal**
Mailing Address:
B.P.4164, Dakar
Republique du Senegal
Phone:(+221) 219-819

**Embassy of the Republic of China
Pretoria, Republic of South Africa**
1147 Schoeman Street, Hatfield, Pretoria 0083
Republic of South Africa
Mailing Address:
P.O. Box 649, Pretoria 0001
Republic of South Africa
Phone: (+27-12) 436-071

**Consulate-General of the Republic of China
Cape Town, Republic of South Africa**
1004, 10th Floor, Main Tower
Standard Bank Center, Foreshore, Cape Town
Republic of South Africa
Mailing Address:
P.O. Box 1122, Cape Town 8000
Republic of South Africa
Phone: (+27-21) 418-1188

**Consulate-General of the Republic of China
Durban, Republic of South Africa**
22nd Floor, Embassy Building
199 Smith Street, Durban 4001
Republic of South Africa
Mailing Address:
P.O. Box 3400, Durban 4000
Republic of South Africa
Phone: (+27-31) 378-235

**Consulate-General of the Republic of China
Johannesburg, Republic of South Africa**
10th Floor, Safren House, 19 Ameshoff Street

Braamfontein, Johannesburg 2001
Republic of South Africa
Phone: (+27-11) 403-3281

**Embassy of the Republic of China
Mbabane, Kingdom of Swaziland**
Warner Street, Mbabane
Kingdom of Swaziland
Mailing Address:
P.O. Box 56, Mbabane
Kingdom of Swaziland
Phone: (+268) 44-740

Europe

**Embassy of the Republic of China
Vatican City, Holy See**
Ambasciata Della Republica di Cina
Presso la Santa Sede
Piazza Delle Muse, 7, 00197 Roma, Italia
Phone: (+39-6) 808-3166

Central and South America

**Embassy of the Republic of China
Nassau, Commonwealth of the Bahamas**
P.O. Box N-8325, Nassau
Commonwealth of the Bahamas
Phone: (+1-809) 322-6832

**Embassy of the Republic of China
Belize City, Belize**
P.O. Box 1020, Belize City
Belize
Phone: (+501-2) 78-744

**Embassy of the Republic of China
San José, Republic of Costa Rica**
Del I.C.E. de San Pedro, 700 metros Sur
Carretera lateral izquierda
(Contiguo Bar Zapoticos), San José
Costa Rica, C.A.
Mailing Address:
Apartado 907-1000, San José, Costa Rica
Phone: (+506) 224-8180

Embassy of the Republic of China
Roseau, Commonwealth of Dominica
P.O. Box 56, Roseau
Commonwealth of Dominica
West Indies
Phone: (+1-809) 449-1385

Embassy of the Republic of China
Santo Domingo, Dominican Republic
Edificio Palic-Primer Piso
Ave. Abraham Lincoln, Esq. José
Amado Soler, Santo Domingo
República Dominicana
Mailing Address :
Apartado Postal 4797, Santo Domingo
República Dominicana
Phone: (+1-809) 562-5555

Embassy of the Republic of China
San Salvador, Republic of El Salvador
89 Avenida Norte No. 335
Colonia Escalón, San Salvador
El Salvador, C.A.
Mailing Address:
Apartado Postal (06) 956, San Salvador
El Salvador, C.A.
Phone: (+503)298-3464

Embassy of the Republic of China
St. George's, Grenada
Archibald Avenue, St. George's
Grenada, West Indies
Mailing Address:
P.O. Box 36, St. George's
Grenada West Indies
Phone: (+1-809) 440-3054

Embassy of the Republic of China
Guatemala City, Republic of Guatemala
4a. Avenida "A" 13-25
Zona 9, Guatemala City
Guatemala, C.A.
Mailing Address:
Apartado Postal 1646, Guatemala City
Guatemala, C.A.
Phone: (+502) 339-0711

Embassy of the Republic of China
Port-au-Prince, Republic of Haiti
2 Rue Canape Vert et Ruelle Rivière
Port-au-Prince, Haiti
Mailing Address:
P.O. Box 655, Port-au-Prince, Haiti
Phone: (+509) 450-361

Embassy of the Republic of China
Tegucigalpa, Republic of Honduras
Colonia Lomas del Guijarros
Calle Eucaliptos No. 3750
Tegucigalpa, M.D.C., Honduras, C. A.
Mailing Address:
Apartado Postal 3433
Tegucigalpa, M.D.C., Honduras, C.A.
Phone: (+504) 311-484

Embajada de la República de China
Managua, República de Nicaragua
Planes de Altamira, Lotes #19 y 20
Frente de la Cancha de Tenis, Managua 5
Nicaragua
Mailing Address:
Apartado Postal 4653, Managua 5
Nicaragua
Phone: (+505) 267-4024

Embassy of the Republic of China
Panama City, Republic of Panama
Edificio Torre Banco Union
10ºPiso, Ave. Samuel Lewis, Panama
Republica of Panama
Mailing Address:
Apartado 4285, Panama 5
Republic of Panama
Phone: (+507) 223-3424

Consulate-General of the Republic of China
Colon, Republic of Panama
Apartado 540, No. 9085 Calle 9,
Ave. Roosevelt,
Colón, Republic of Panama
Mailing Address:
Apartado No. 540, Colón

Republic of Panama
Phone: (+507) 441-3403

Embassy of the Republic of China
Asunción, Republic of Paraguay
Avenida Mcal. López 1133, Asunción, Paraguay
Mailing Address:
Casilla de Correos 503, Asunción, Paraguay
Phone: (+595-21) 213-362

Consulate-General of the Republic of China
Eastern City, Republic of Paraguay
No. 1349 Avda. Mcal. Estigarribia
(Ave. Lago de la Republic), Ciudad del Este
Paraguay
Mailing Address:
Casilla Postal No 131
Ciudad del Este, Paraguay
Phone: (+595-061) 500-329

Embassy of the Republic of China
Basseterre, Saint Christopher and Nevis
Taylor's Range, Basseterre
Saint Kitts, West Indies
Mailing Address:
P.O. Box 119, Basseterre
Saint Kitts, West Indies
Phone: (+1-758) 465-2421

Embassy of the Republic of China
Castries, Saint Lucia
Cap Estate Saint Lucia, West Indies
Mailing Address:
P.O. Box 690, Castries
Saint Lucia, West Indies
Phone: (+1-758) 450-0643

Embassy of the Republic of China
Kingstown, Saint Vincent and the Grenadines
Murray's Road
Saint Vincent and the Grenadines
Mailing Address:
P.O. Box 878
Saint Vincent and the Grenadines, West Indies
Phone: (+1-809) 456-2431

ROC Representative Offices

Asia

Taipei Economic and Cultural Office
in Brunei Darussalam
No. 5, Simpang 1006
Jalan Tutong, B.S. Begawan
Brunei Darussalam
Mailing Address:
P.O. Box 2172, B.S. Begawan, 1921
Brunei Darussalam
Phone: (+673-2) 653-410

Taipei Economic and Cultural Representative
Office in Phnom Penh, Cambodia
No.15 bis, Sokun Meanbon Street
Sangkat Phsar Themi 3,
Khan Daun Penh, Phnom Penh,
Kingdom of Cambodia
Phone:(+855-23)725-908

Chung Hwa Travel Service
Hong Kong
4th Floor, Lippo Tower, Lippo Centre
No. 89, Queensway
Hong Kong
Mailing Address:
G.P.O. Box 13485, Hong Kong
Phone: (+852) 2525-8315

Taipei Economic and Cultural Center
in New Delhi
3A Palam Marg Vasant Vihar, New Delhi
India
Phone:(+91-11) 611-6882

Taipei Economic and Trade Office
Jakarta, Indonesia
7th Floor, Wisma Dinarmala, Sakti
J1. Jend Sudirman No. 32, Jakarta 10220
Indonesia
Mailing Address:
P.O. Box 2922, Jakarta Pusat
Indonesia
Phone: (+62-21) 570-3047

Taipei Economic and Cultural Representative Office in Japan
20-2, Shiroganedai 5-chome
Minato-Ku, Tokyo 108
Japan
Phone: (+81-3) 3280-7811

Taipei Economic and Cultural Representative Office in Japan, Yokohama Branch
2nd Floor, Asahiseime Yokohama Building
No. 60, Nihonohdori, Nakaku, Yokohama
Japan
Phone: (+81-45) 641-7730

Taipei Economic and Cultural Office in Osaka
4th Floor, No. 4-8, Nichie Building
Dosabori, 1-chome, Nishi-Ku, Osaka
Japan
Phone: (+81-6) 443-8481

Taipei Economic and Cultural Office in Osaka, Fukuoka Branch
3rd Floor, Sun Life Building III
5-19, 2-chome, Hakataeki Higashi, Hakata-ku
Fukuoka, Japan
Phone: (+81-92) 473-6655

Taipei Mission in Korea
6th Floor, Kwanghwamoon Building
211 Sejong-ro, Chongro-Ku
Seoul, Korea
Phone: (+82-2) 399-2767/70

Taipei Trade and Tourism Office, Macau
Edificio Comercial Central
15 Andar, Avenida Infante D. Henrique No. 60-64
Macau
Mailing Address:
P.O. Box 3072, Macau
Phone: (+853) 306-282

Taipei Economic and Cultural Office in Malaysia
9.01 Level 9, Amoda Building
22 Jalan Imbi, 55100 Kuala Lumpur

Malaysia
Phone: (+60-3) 242-5549

Taipei Economic and Cultural Office in the Philippines
28th Floor, Pacific Star Building
Sen. Gil J. Puyat Avenue
Corner Makati Avenue
Makati, Metro Manila, Philippines
Mailing Address:
P.O. Box 1097
Makati Central Post Office
1250 Makati, Metro Manila, Philippines
Phone: (+63-2) 892-1381

Taipei Representative Office in Singapore
460 Alexandra Road
#23-00, PSA Building
Singapore 119963
Mailing Address:
PSA Building Post Office, P.O. Box 381
Singapore 911143
Phone: (+65) 278-6511

Taipei Economic and Trade Office in Thailand
10th Floor, Kian Gwan Building (1)
140 Witthayu Road, Bangkok
Thailand
Phone: (+66-2) 251-9393

Taipei Economic and Cultural Office Hanoi, Vietnam
2D Van Phuc, Ba dinh distric, Hanoi
Vietnam
Mailing Address:
GPO Box 104, Hanoi, Vietnam
Phone: (+844) 823-4402

Taipei Economic and Cultural Office Ho Chi Minh City, Vietnam
117B Nguyen Dinh Chinh Vietnam
Quan Phu Nhuan, TPHCM Vietnam
Phone: (+84-8) 845-8651

Oceania

Taipei Economic and Cultural office, Australia
Unit 8, Tourism House, 40 Blackall Street
Barton, Canberra ACT 2600
Australia
Phone: (+61-6) 273-3344

Taipei Economic and Cultural Office
Melbourne, Australia
Level 38, 120 Collins Street
Melbourn, Vic. 3000, Australia
Phone: (+61-3) 9650-8611,22,33

Taipei Economic and Cultural Office
Sydney, Australia
Suite 1902, Level 19, M.L.C. Center, King Street
Sydney, N.S.W. 2000, Australia
Phone: (+61-2) 9223-3207

Trade Mission of the Republic of China
Suva, Republic of Fiji
6th Floor, Pacific House, Butt Streets, Suva
Republic of Fiji
Mailing Address:
G.P.O. Box 53, Suva
Republic of Fiji
Phone: (+679) 315-922

Taipei Economic and Cultural Office
Auckland, New Zealand
11th Floor, Norwich Union Building
Cnr. Queen and Durham Streets, Auckland
New Zealand
Mailing Address:
CPO Box 4018, Auckland, New Zealand
Phone: (+64-9) 303-3903

Taipei Economic and Cultural Office
New Zealand
21st Floor, 105 The Terrace, Wellington
New Zealand
Mailing Address:
P.O. Box 10250, The Terrace, Wellington
New Zealand
Phone: (+64-4) 473-6474

Trade Mission of the Republic of China (on Taiwan)
Port Moresby, Papua New Guinea
6th Floor, Defence Haus, Hunter Street
Port Moresby, Papua New Guinea
Mailing Address:
P.O. Box 334, Port Moresby, Papua New Guinea
Phone: (+675) 321-2922

Middle East

Trade Mission of the Republic of China
Manama, State of Bahrain
Flat 1, Abulfatih Building, Bldg.172
Manama Town 319, Al Hoora Area.
State of Bahrain
Mailing Address:
P.O. Box 5806, Manama, State of Bahrain
Phone: (+973) 292-578

Taipei Economic and Cultural Office in Tel Aviv
270 Hayarkon Street, Tel-Aviv 63504
Israel
Mailing Address:
P.O.Box 6115, Tel-Aviv 61060, Israel
Phone: (+972-3) 544-0250

Commercial Office of the Republic of China
(Taiwan), Jordan
Mailing Address:
P.O. Box 2023, Amman 11181, Jordan
Phone: (+962-6) 671-530

Taipei Commercial Representative Office
in the State of Kuwait
House No. 18, Block 6, Street No. 111
Al-Jabriah, State of Kuwait
Mailing Address:
P.O. Box 732-32008, Hawalli-Kuwait
Phone: (+965) 533-9988

Taipei Economic and Cultural Office
Muscat, Oman
Mailing Address:
P.O. Box 1536 Ruwi

Postal Code 112, Muscat
The Sultanate of Oman
Phone: (+968) 605-695

Taipei Economic and Cultural Representative Office in the Kingdom of Saudi Arabia, Jeddah Office
Mailing Address:
P.O. Box 1114, Jeddah 21431
Saudi Arabia
Phone: (+966-2) 660-2264

Taipei Economic and Cultural Representative Office in the Kingdom of Saudi Arabia
Diplomatic Quarter, Riyadh, Saudi Arabia
Mailing Address:
P.O. Box 94393, Riyadh 11693
Saudi Arabia
Phone: (+966-1) 488-1900

Taipei Economic and Cultural Mission in Ankara, Turkey
Resit Galip Cad. No. 97
Gaziosmanpasa, Ankara, Turkey
Phone: (+90-312) 436-7255

Commercial Office of the Republic of China to Dubai, United Arab Emirates
Al Nakheel Building
Office No. 109, Plot No. 273
at Al Hamriyah, Dubai, U. A. E.
Mailing Address:
P.O. Box 3059, Dubai, U. A. E.
Phone: (+971-4) 358-177

Africa

Delegation Especial da Republica da China Luanda, Republica de Angola
Rua Comandante Stona
No. 85/87, Alvalade, Luanda
Republica de Angola
Mailing Address:
Caixa Postal 6051, Luanda
Republica de Angola
Phone: (+244-2) 323-679

Délégation de la République de Chine Brazzaville, République du Congo
Mailing Address:
B.P. 4834 Kinshasa/Gombe
République du Zaire
Phone: (+243-12) 33-626

Commercial Office of the Republic of China Tripoli, Great Socialist People's Libyan Arab Jamahiriya
Mailing Address:
P.O. Box 6604 (or 6694), Tripoli, Libya
Phone: (+218-21) 75-060

Délégation Spéciale de la République de Chine Antananarivo, République de Madagascar
Villa BAKOLY VIII, Lot Pres VR61 B
Ambohimiandra, B.P. 3117, Antananarivo 101
Madagascar
Mailing Address:
B.P. 3117, Antananarivo 101, Madagascar
Phone: (+261-2) 34-838

Trade Mission of the Republic of China Port Louis, Mauritius
5th Floor, British American Insurance Building
25 Pope Hennessy Street, Port Louis
Mauritius
Mailing Address:
P.O. Box 695, Bell Village, Port Louis
Mauritius
Phone: (+230) 212-8534

The Trade Mission of the ROC Lagos, Federal Republic of Nigeria
292E, Ajose Adeogun Street
Victoria Island Annex, Lagos, Nigeria
Mailing Address:
P.O. Box 80035, Victoria Island, Lagos
Nigeria
Phone: (+234-1) 261-6350

Délégation de la République de Chine Kinshasa, République du Zaïre
N 9, Avenue Zongo Ntolo
Kinshasa/Gombe, République du Zaire

Mailing Address:
B.P. 4834 Kinshasa/Gombe
République du Zaire
Phone: (+243-12) 33-626

Europe

**Taipei Economic and Cultural Office
Institute of Chinese Culture
Vienna, Austria**
Praterstr. 31/15 OG, A-1020 Wien
Austria
Phone: (+43-1) 212-4720

**Taipei Economic and Trade Mission
in Minsk, Belarus**
Mailing Address:
P.O. Box 149
220030 Minsk, Republic of Belarus
Phone:(+375-17) 257-4607

**Taipei Representative Office
in Belgium**
Avenue des Arts 41, 1040 Bruxelles
Belgium
Phone: (+32-2) 511-0687

**Taipei Economic and Cultural Office
Prague, Czech Republic**
Revolucní 13, 7P, 110 00, Praha I
Czech Republic
Phone: (+42-2) 2480-3257

**Taipei Representative Office
in Denmark**
Amaliegade 3, 2F
1256 Copenhagen K
Denmark
Phone: (+45) 3393-5152

**Taipei Economic and Cultural Office
Helsinki, Finland**
Aleksanterinkatu 17, 4th Floor
00100, Helsinki, Finland
Phone: (+358-9) 6969-2420

**Bureau de Representation de Taipei
en France**
78 Rue de I'universite, 75007 Paris
France
Phone: (+33-1) 4439-8820

**Taipei Wirtschafts- und Kulturbüro
Berlin, Federal Republic of Germany**
Berliner Str. 55, D-10713 Berlin
Federal Republic of Germany
Phone: (+49-30) 861-2576

**Taipei Wirtschafts- und Kulturbüro
Bonn, Federal Republic of Germany**
Villichgasse 17/IV, 53177 Bonn
Federal Republic of Germany
Phone: (+49-228) 364-014

**Taipei Wirtschafts- und Kulturbüro
Hamburg, Federal Republic of Germany**
Mittelweg 144, 20148 Hamburg
Federal Republic of Germany
Mailing Address:
P.O. Box 323123, 20116 Hamburg
Federal Republic of Germany
Phone: (+49-40) 447-788

**Taipei Wirtschafts- und Kulturbüro
München, Federal Republic of Germany**
Tengstrasse 38/2. Stock
80796 München
Federal Republic of Germany
Phone: (+49-89) 271-6061

**Taipei Economic and Cultural Office
Athens, Greece**
57 Marathonodromon Avenue
154 52 Psychico, Athens
Greece
Phone: (+30-1) 677-6750

**Taipei Representative Office
Budapest, Hungary**
Rakóczi út 1-3/III em., 1088 Budapest
Hungary
Phone: (+361) 266-2884

**Taipei Representative Office
in Ireland**
1st Floor, 10-11 South Leinster Street
Dublin 2, Ireland
Phone: (+353-1) 678-5413

**Ufficio Di Rappresentanza di Taipei
in Italia**
Via Panama 22 PI, Int. 3
00198 Roma, Italia
Phone: (+396) 884-1362

Taipei Mission in the Republic of Latvia
Room 602, World Trade Center
2 Elizabets Street, LV-1340, Riga
Latvia
Phone: (+371) 732-1166

**Taipei Economic and Cultural Office
Luxembourg**
50, route d'Esch, Luxembourg-Ville, L-1470
Grand-Duché de Luxembourg
Phone: (+352) 444-772

**Taipei Representative Office
in The Netherlands**
Javastraat 46-48
2585 AR, The Hague
The Netherlands
Phone: (+31-70) 346-9438

**Taipei Economic and Cultural Office
Oslo, Norway**
P.O. Box 2643 Solli
Riddervolds gate 3, 0203 Oslo, Norway
Phone: (+47) 2255-5471

**Taipei Economic and Cultural Office in
Warsaw, Poland**
4th Floor, Koszykowa Street 54
00-675 Warszawa, Poland
Mailing Address:
P.O. Box 51, ul. Senatorska 40
Urzad. Pocztowo-Telekomunikacyjny
Warszawa 84, Poland
Phone: (+48-22) 630-8438

**Centro Economico e Cultural de Taipei
Lisboa, Portugal**
Rua Castilho 65, 1 Andar Direito, 1200 Lisboa
Portugal
Phone: (+351-1) 386-0617, 386-0763

**Representative Office in Moscow for
the Taipei-Moscow Economic and Cultural
Coordination Commission**
3rd Floor, 24/2 Tverskaya Street, Korpus 1
Gate 4, Moscow 103050
Russian Federation
Phone: (+7-095) 956-3786

**Oficina Económica y Cultural de Taipei
Madrid, España**
C/Rosario Pino 14-16
18 Dcha., 28020 Madrid
Spain
Mailing Address:
Apartado 36016, 28080 Madrid, Spain
Phone: (+34-1) 571-4729

Taipei Mission in Sweden
Wenner-Gren Center, 18tr., Sveavägen 166
S-113 46 Stockholm, Sweden
Phone: (+46-8) 728-8513

**Délégation Culturélle et Economique de
Taïpei
Berne, Suisse**
Monbijoustrasse 30, 3011 Berne, Suisse
Phone: (+41-31) 382-2927

Taipei Representative Office in the UK
50 Grosvenor Gardens, London SW1W OEB
United Kingdom
Phone: (+44-171) 396-9152

North America

Taipei Economic and Cultural Office, Canada
Suite 1960, World Exchange Plaza
45 O'Connor Street, Ottawa, Ontario, K1P 1A4
Canada
Phone: (+1-613) 231-5080

Taipei Economic and Cultural Office, Toronto
151 Yonge Street, Suite 1202, Toronto
Ontario M5C 2W7, Canada
Phone: (+1-416) 369-9030

Taipei Economic and Cultural Office, Vancouver
2008, Cathedral Place, 925 West Georgia Street
Vancouver, B.C. V6C 3L2, Canada
Phone: (+1-604) 689-4111

Taipei Economic and Cultural Representative Office in the United States
4201 Wisconsin Avenue, NW
Washington, DC 20016-2137, U.S.A.
Phone: (+1-202) 895-1800 (20 lines)

Taipei Economic and Cultural Office in Atlanta
Suite 1290, Two Midtown Plaza
1349 West Peachtree Street, NE
Atlanta, Georgia 30309, U.S.A.
Phone: (+1-404) 872-0123

Taipei Economic and Cultural Office in Boston
99 Summer Street, Suite 801
Boston, MA 02110, U.S.A.
Mailing Address:
P.O. Box 120529, Boston, MA 02110, U.S.A.
Phone: (+1-617) 737-2050

Taipei Economic and Cultural Office in Chicago
Two Prudential Plaza, 57th & 58th Floor
180 N. Stetson Avenue, Chicago, Illinois 60601
U.S.A.
Phone: (+1-312) 616-0100

Taipei Economic and Cultural Office in Guam
Suite 505, Bank of Guam Building
111 Chalan Santo Papa Road
Agana, Guam 96932, U.S.A.
Mailing Address:
P.O. Box 3416, Agana, Guam 96932
U.S.A.
Phone: (+671) 472-5865

Taipei Economic and Cultural Office in Honolulu
2746 Pali Highway, Honolulu, Hawaii 96817
U.S.A.
Phone: (+1-808) 595-6347

Taipei Economic and Cultural Office in Houston
Eleven Greenway Plaza, Suite 2006
Houston, Texas 77046, U.S.A.
Phone: (+1-713) 626-7445

Taipei Economic and Cultural Office in Kansas City, Missouri
3100 Broadway, Suite 800
Kansas City, MO 64111, U.S.A.
Mailing Address:
P.O. Box 413617, Kansas City, MO 64141
U.S.A.
Phone: (+1-816) 531-1298

Taipei Economic and Cultural Office in Los Angeles
3731 Wilshire Boulevard, Suite 700
Los Angeles, CA 90010, U.S.A.
Phone: (+1-213) 389-1215

Taipei Economic and Cultural Office in Miami
2333 Ponce de Leon Boulevard, Suite 610
Coral Gables, Florida 33134, U.S.A.
Phone: (+1-305) 443-8917

Taipei Economic and Cultural Office in New York
885 Second Avenue, 47th Floor
New York, NY 10017, U.S.A.
Phone: (+1-212) 754-7100

Taipei Economic and Cultural Office in San Francisco
555 Montgomery Street, Suite 501
San Francisco, CA 94111, U.S.A.
Phone: (+1-415) 362-7680

Taipei Economic and Cultural Office in Seattle
Westin Building, Suite 2410

2001 Sixth Avenue, Seattle, WA 98121, U.S.A.
Phone: (+1-206) 441-4586

Central and South America

**Oficina Comercial y Cultura de Taipei
en la Republica Argentina**
Av. de Mayo 654, 4 piso, 1084 Capital Federal
Argentina
Mailing Address:
Casilla de Correos No. 196
1041 Capital Federal, Buenos Aires, Argentina
Phone: (+54-1) 334-0653

**Oficina Comercial-Consular De La República
de China, La Paz, Bolivia**
Calacoto, Calle 12, No. 7978, La Paz
Republica de Bolivia
Mailing Address:
Casilla No. 13680, La Paz, Bolivia
Phone: (+591-2) 797-307

**Escritório Econômico e Cultural de Taipei
Brasil**
SEPN W3/Norte-Quadra 513-Bloco D-N 30
Edificio Imperador-1, Andar-Salas 121/131
70760-545 Brasilia-DF-Brasil
Phone: (+55-61) 349-1218

**Escritório Econômico e Cultural de Taipei
Rio de Janeiro, Brasil**
Rua Voluntârios da Pátria
45 Sala 405, CEP
270-000 Rio de Janeiro-RJ, Brasil
Mailing Address:
P.O.Box 9200, Rua Sao Clemente 24 Loja B
Cep 22260-000-Rio de Janeiro-Rj, Brasil
Phone: (+55-21) 286-0039

**Escritório Econômico e Cultural de Taipei
São Paulo, Brasil**
Av. Paulista, 2073-Ed. Horsa II
Conj. 1023 e 1204-12 andar
01311-840-São Paulo, SP, Brasil
Phone: (+55-11) 285-6194

**Oficina Económica y Cultural de Taipei
Santiago, República de Chile**
Burgos 345, Las Condes, Santiago, Chile
Mailing Address:
Casilla 175-Santiago 34, Santiago, Chile
Phone: (+56-2) 228-2919, 228-3185

**Oficina Comercial de Taipei
Bogotá, D.E., República de Colombia**
Carrera 7, No. 79-75, Of. 501
Santafe de Bogotá D.E., Colombia, S.A.
Mailing Address:
Apartado Aéreo No. 51620 (Chapinero)
Santafe de Bogotá, D.E., Colombia, S.A.
Phone: (+57-1) 235-4713

**Oficina Comercial de la República de China
Quito, Ecuador**
Av. República de El Salvador 733 y
Portugal, 2do. Piso, Quito, Ecuador
Mailing Address:
P.O. Box 17-17-1788, Quito, Ecuador
Phone: (+593-2) 242-829

**Sucursal de la Oficina Comercial
de la República de China
Guayaquil, Ecuador**
Circunvalacion Norte 301
y Calle Primera, Guayaquil, Ecuador
Mailing Address:
Casilla No. 09-01-9245, Guayaquil, Ecuador
Phone: (+593-4) 886-046

**Oficina Económica y Cultural de Taipei en
México**
Paseo de la Reforma 905
Lomas de, Chapultepec, CP11000
México D.F., México
Phone: (+525) 520-7851

**Oficina Económica y Cultural de Taipei
Lima, República del Perú**
Av. Benavides No. 1780
Miraflores, Lima 18, Perú
Mailing Address:

Casilla: 18-1052, Lima 18, Perú
Phone: (+51-1) 242-1817

Oficina Económica de Taipei
República Oriental del Uruguay
Echevarriarza 3478, Montevideo, Uruguay
Mailing Address:
Casilla de Correo N 16042
Distrito 6 C.P. 11600, Montevideo
Uruguay

Phone: (+598-2) 680-201

Oficina Económica y Cultural de Taipei
Caracas, República de Venezuela
Avenida Francisco de Miranda
Torre Delta, Piso 4, Altamira, Caracas
Venezuela
Mailing Address:
Apartado 68717, Altamira 1062-A, Caracas
Venezuela

Appendix V
Directory of Foreign Embassies and Representatives in the ROC

Foreign Embassies in the ROC

Embassy of Burkina Faso
3rd Floor, 5 Chung Cheng Road, Section 2
Tienmou, Taipei
Phone: (+886-2) 838-3776
Fax: (+886-2) 834-2701

Embassy of the Central African Republic
1th Floor, 7 Lane, 69 Tienmou East Road
Tiemou, Taipei
Phone: (+886-2) 876-1008
Fax: (+886-2) 876-1009

Embassy of the Republic of Costa Rica
6th Floor, 16 Lane 189, Cheng Tai Road, Section 1
Wuku Hsiang, Taipei County
Phone: (+886-2) 293-3446
Fax: (+886-2) 293-3548

Embassy of the Dominican Republic
6th Floor, 76 Tun Hua South Road, Section 2, Taipei
Phone: (+886-2) 707-9006/9
Fax: (+886-2) 709-1429

Embassy of the Republic of El Salvador
15 Lane 34, Ku Kung Road
Shihlin, Taipei
Phone: (+886-2) 881-7995
Fax: (+886-2) 881-9887

Embassy of the Republic of the Gambia
3rd Floor, 92 Huanghsi Street
Shihlin, Taipei
Phone:(+886-2) 833-2434
Fax:(+886-2) 832-4336

Embassy of the Republic of Guatemala
12 Lane 88, Chien Kuo North Road, Section 1
Taipei

Phone: (+886-2) 507-7043
Fax: (+886-2) 506-0577

Embassy of the Republic of Guinea Bissau
6-1 Lane 77, Sungkiang Road
Taipei
Phone: (+886-2) 509-9052
Fax: (+886-2) 507-3111

Embassy of the Republic of Haiti
3rd Floor, 246 Chung Shan North Road, Section 6
Taipei
Phone: (+886-2) 838-4945
Fax: (+886-2) 831-7086

Embassy of the Holy See (Apostolic Nunciature)
87 Ai Kuo East Road, Taipei
Phone: (+886-2) 321-6847
Fax: (+886-2) 391-1926

Embassy of the Republic of Honduras
Room B, 10th Floor, 167 Tun Hua North Road
Taipei
Phone: (+886-2) 712-0743
Fax: (+886-2) 712-0743

Embassy of the Republic of Nicaragua
1st Floor, 110 Chung Cheng Road, Section 2
Tienmou, Taipei
Phone: (+886-2) 874-0234/5
Fax: (+886-2) 874-0265

Embassy of the Republic of Panama
6th Floor, 111 Sungkiang Road, Taipei
Phone: (+886-2) 509-9189
Fax: (+886-2) 509-9801

Embassy of the Republic of Paraguay
1st Floor, 1 Alley 52, Lane 117, Tien Mou West
Road Tienmou, Taipei

Phone: (+886-2) 873-6310
Fax: (+886-2) 873-6312

Embassy of the Republic of South Africa
13th Floor, 205 Tun Hua North Road, Taipei
Phone: (+886-2) 715-3250
Fax: (+886-2) 712-5109

Foreign Representatives in the ROC

American Institute in Taiwan, Taipei Office
7 Lane 134, Hsin Yi Road, Section 3, Taipei
Phone: (+886-2) 709-2000
Fax: (+886-2) 702-7675

American Institute in Taiwan, Kaohsiung Office
3rd Floor, Chung Cheng Building, 2 Chung Cheng
Third Road, Kaohsiung
Phone: (+886-7) 251-2444

Argentina Trade and Cultural Office
Room 1003, 333 Keelung Road, Section 1
Taipei
Phone: (+886-2) 757-6556
Fax: (+886-2) 757-6445

Australian Commerce and Industry Office
Room 2605, 333 Keelung Road, Section 1
Taipei
Phone: (+886-2) 720-2833
Fax: (+886-2) 757-6707

Austrian Trade Delegation, Taipei Office
Suite 608, Bank Tower, 205 Tun Hua North Road
Taipei
Phone: (+886-2) 715-5220
Fax: (+886-2) 717-3242

Belgian Trade Association, Taipei
Suite 901, World Wide House
131 Min Sheng East Road, Section 3, Taipei
Phone: (+886-2) 715-1215
Fax: (+886-2) 712-6258

Bolivian Commercial and Financial Representation
Room 7E-13, 5 Hsin Yi Road, Section 5 , Taipei
Phone: (+886-2) 723-8721
Fax: (+886-2) 723-8764

Brazil Business Center
2th Floor, 3 Chung Cheng Road, Section 2
Tienmou, Taipei
Phone: (+886-2) 835-7388
Fax: (+886-2) 835-7121

British Trade and Cultural Office
9th Floor, 99 Jen Ai Road, Section 2 , Taipei
Phone: (+886-2) 322-4242
Fax: (+886-2) 393-1985

Canadian Trade Office in Taipei
13th Floor, 365 Fu Hsin North Road, Taipei
Phone: (+886-2) 547-9500
Fax: (+886-2) 712-7244

Chilean Trade Office, Taipei
Room 7B-07, 5 Hsin Yi Road, Section 5, Taipei
Phone: (+886-2) 723-0329
Fax: (+886-2) 723-0318

Colombian Trade Office
Room 1005, 333 Keelung Road, Section 1
Taipei
Phone:(+886-2) 757-6055
Fax:(+886-2) 757-6304

Czech Economic and Cultural Office
Room A3, 8th Floor, 51 Keelung Road, Section 2
Taipei
Phone: (+886-2) 738-9768
Fax: (+886-2) 733-3843

Danish Trade Organizations, Taipei Office
Room 1207, 12th Floor, 205 Tun Hua North Road
Taipei
Phone: (+886-2) 718-2101
Fax: (+886-2) 718-2141

Finland Trade Center
Room 7E-04, 5 Hsin Yi Road, Section 5, Taipei
Phone: (+886-2) 725-1516
Fax: (+886-2) 725-1517

French Institute in Taipei
Room 1003, 10th Floor, 205 Tun Hua North Road
Taipei
Phone: (+886-2) 545-6061
Fax: (+886-2) 545-0994

German Cultural Centre
11th Floor, 24 Hsin Hai Road, Section 1, Taipei
Phone: (+886-2) 365-7294
Fax: (+886-2) 368-7542

German Trade Office, Taipei
4th Floor, 4 Min Sheng East Road, Section 3
Taipei
Phone: (+886-2) 506-9028
Fax: (+886-2) 506-8182

**Office of Representative A.H. Hellenic
Organization for the Promotion of Exports
(Greece)**
6th Floor-2, 125 Roosevelt Road, Section 3
Taipei
Phone: (+886-2) 363-5597
Fax: (+886-2) 362-6140

India-Taipei Association
Room 2010, 333 Keelung Road, Section 1, Taipei
Phone: (+886-2) 757-6112
Fax: (+886-2) 757-6117

Indonesian Economic and Trade office to Taipei
16th Floor, 49 Min Sheng East Road, Section 3
Taipei
Phone: (+886-2) 516-9050
Fax: (+886-2) 516-9056

**The Institute for Trade and Investment of
Ireland**
Room 7B-09, 5 Hsin Yi Road, Section 5, Taipei
Phone: (+886-2) 725-1691
Fax: (+886-2) 725-1653

Israel Economic and Cultural Office
Room 2408, 333 Keelung Road, Section 1, Taipei
Phone: (+886-2) 757-7222
Fax: (+886-2) 757-7197

**Italian Economic, Trade and Cultural
Promotion Office**
Room 1808, 333 Keelung Road, Section 1
Taipei
Phone: (+886-2) 345-0320
Fax: (+886-2) 757-6260

Interchange Association (Japan), Taipei Office
10th Floor, 245 Tun Hua South Road, Section 1
Taipei
Phone: (+886-2) 741-2116
Fax: (+886-2) 731-1757

**Interchange Association (Japan),
Kaohsiung Office**
4th Floor, 174 San Duo First Road, Kaohsiung
Phone: (+886-7) 771-4008
Fax: (+886-7) 771-2734

The Jordanian Commercial Office
3rd Floor, 425-1 Chung Shan North Road, Section
6
Taipei
Phone: (+886-2) 871-7712
Fax: (+886-2) 872-1176

Korean Mission in Taipei
Room 1506, 333 Keelung Road, Section 1
Taipei
Phone: (+886-2) 758-8320
Fax: (+886-2) 757-7006

**Malaysian Friendship and Trade Centre
Taipei**
8th Floor, 102 Tun Hua North Road, Taipei
Phone: (+886-2) 713-2626
Fax: (+886-2) 514-9864

Manila Economic and Cultural Office
4th Floor, 107 Chung Hsiao East Road, Section 4
Taipei

Phone: (+886-2) 778-6511
Fax: (+886-2) 778-4969

**Manila Economic and Cultural Office
Extension Office in Kaohsiung**
2nd Floor, 146 Ssu Wei Second Road
Kaohsiung
Phone: (+886-7) 331-7752

Mexican Trade Services
Room 2905, 333 Keelung Road, Section 1
Taipei
Phone: (+886-2) 757-6526
Fax: (+886-2) 757-6180

Netherlands Trade and Investment office
Room B, 5th Floor, 133 Min Sheng East Road
Section 3, Taipei
Phone: (+886-2) 713-5760
Fax: (+886-2) 713-0194

New Zealand Commerce and Industry Office
Room 2501, 333 Keelung Road, Section 1
Taipei
Phone: (+886-2) 757-6725
Fax: (+886-2) 757-6973

Nigeria Trade Office in Taiwan, R.O.C.
Room 1706, 333 Keelung Road, Section 1, Taipei
Phone: (+886-2) 757-6987
Fax: (+886-2) 757-7111

Norwegian Trade Council
11th Floor, 148 Sungkiang Road, Taipei
Phone: (+886-2) 543-5484
Fax: (+886-2) 581-1878

Oman Commercial Office, Taipei
Room 7G-05, 5 Hsin Yi Road, Section 5
Taipei
Phone: (+886-2) 722-0684
Fax: (+886-2) 722-0645

Commercial Office of Peru in Taipei
Room 2411, 333 Keelung Road, Section 1
Taipei

Phone: (+886-2) 757-7017
Fax: (+886-2) 757-6480

**Phnom Penh Economic and Cultural
Representative Office in Taipei**
5th Floor, 400 Keelung Road, Section 1
Taipei
Phone:(+886-2) 729-7789

Saudi Arabian Trade Office
3rd Floor, 726 Chung Shan North Road, Section 6
Taipei
Phone: (+886-2) 872-2060
Fax: (+886-2) 872-1976

Singapore Trade Office in Taipei
9th Floor, 85 Jen Ai Road, Section 4, Taipei
Phone: (+886-2) 772-1940
Fax: (+886-2) 772-1943

Spanish Chamber of Commerce
10th Floor-2, 76 Tun Hua South Road, Section 2
Taipei
Phone: (+886-2) 325-6234
Fax: (+886-2) 754-2572

Exportradet Taipei, Swedish Trade Council
Room 812, 333 Keelung Road, Section 1, Taipei
Phone: (+886-2) 757-6573
Fax: (+886-2) 757-6723

Trade Office of Swiss Industries
Room 3101, 333 Keelung Road, Section 1, Taipei
Phone: (+886-2) 720-1001
Fax: (+886-2) 757-6984

Thailand Trade and Economic Office
7th Floor, 150 Fu Hsing North Road, Taipei
Phone: (+886-2) 712-1882
Fax: (+886-2) 713-0042

Turkish Trade Office in Taipei
Room 1905, 333 Keelung Road, Section 1, Taipei
Phone: (+886-2) 757-7318
Fax: (+886-2) 757-9432

Vietnam Economic and Cultural Office in Taipei
3rd Floor, 333 Keelung Road, Section 1, Taipei
Phone: (+886-2) 516-6626
Fax: (+886-2) 516-6625

Warsaw Trade Office
Room 3111, 16 Min Tsu East Road, Taipei
Phone: (+886-2) 757-6325
Fax: (+886-2) 757-6086

U.S. State Trade Offices in the ROC
Located in the Taipei World Trade Center
5 Hsin Yi Road, Section 5, Taipei

State of Arizona, Asian-Pacific Trade Office
Room 7D17
Phone: (+886-2) 725-ll34
Fax: (+886-2) 725-1146

State of California, Taipei Trade Office
Room 7C04
Phone: (+886-2) 758-6223
Fax: (+886-2) 723-9973

State of Florida, Taipei/Pacific Rim office
Room 7E01
Phone: (+886-2) 758-5181
Fax: (+886-2) 723-5892

State of Hawaii, U.S.A. Office in Taipei
Room 7G07
Phone: (+886-2) 723-0017
Fax: (+886-2) 723-0229

State of Idaho-Asia Trade Office
Room 7D15
Phone: (+886-2) 725-2922
Fax: (+886-2) 725-1248

Indiana Department of Commerce,
Taipei Office
Room 7D16
Phone: (+886-2) 725-2060
Fax: (+886-2) 725-2062

State of Louisiana, Taipei Office
Room 7D13
Phone: (+886-2) 723-1921
Fax: (+886-2) 723-1862

Maryland Trade Office in Taipei
Room 7C03
Phone: (+886-2) 725-1553
Fax: (+886-2) 725-1557

Missouri International Business,
Office in Taipei
Room 7D09
Phone: (+886-2) 725-1622
Fax: (+886-2) 723-2731

Montana Department of Commerce
Taipei Office
Room 7D21
Phone: (+886-2) 723-1762
Fax: (+886-2) 723-1763

Oregon Department of Commerce
Taipei Office
Room 7C14
Phone: (+886-2) 723-2311
Fax: (+886-2) 723-2312

Utah Department of Commerce Taipei Offfice
Room 7C16
Phone: (+886-2) 725-2522
Fax: (+886-2) 725-2459

Washington State Trade Development
Office in Taipei
Room 7G01
Phone: (+886-2) 725-2499
Fax: (+886-2) 723-2545

Located elsewhere:
Massachusetts Office of International Trade
5th Floor, 52 Lane 2, Chung Shan North Road,
Section 6, Taipei
Phone: (+886-2) 835-9080
Fax: (+886-2) 833-8644

Appendix VI
Weights and Measures in Use in the ROC

The metric system is the official system of weights and measures in the ROC, and it is used for nearly all purposes. Certain things, however, continue to be measured according to various other systems. Real estate property, for example, is usually measured in p'ing (tsubo), or the size of a six-by-six-foot tatami mat, a remnant from Taiwan's period of Japanese occupation. There are measures for gold, Chinese herbal medicine, and other specialized commodities (the market system). The following tables give equivalents in the diverse systems in use in Taiwan: the market system, the metric system, and the English system.

Length

Taiwan System	Market System	Metric System	English System
1 ts'un 寸 (inch)	0.90909 ts'un	3.0303 cm	1.193 in.
1 ch'ih 尺 (foot) (=10 ts'un)	0.90909 ch'ih	0.30303 m	0.99419 ft.
1.1 ts'un	1 ts'un (inch) (=10 fen 分)	3.3333 cm	1.3123 in.
1.1 ch'ih	1 ch'ih (=10 ts'un)	0.33333 m	1.0936 ft.
11 ch'ih	1 chang 丈 (=10 ch'ih)	3.3333 m	3.6453 yd.
1,650 ch'ih	1 li 里 (=150 chang)	0.5 km	0.3107 mi.

Area

Taiwan System	Market System	Metric System	English System
1 p'ing 坪 (tsubo)	0.00496 mu	3.30579 sq. m	35.5896 sq. ft.
1 mu 畝 (=30 p'ing)	0.14876 mu	0.99174 are	0.02451 acre
1 chia 甲 (=2,934 p'ing)	14.5488 mu	96.9917 ares	2.39672 acres
—	1 sq. ch'ih 尺 (=100 sq. ts'un 寸)	0.1111 sq. m	1.196 sq. ft.
3.361 p'ing	1 sq. chang 丈 (=100 sq. ch'ih)	11.1111 sq. m	13.28888 sq. yd.
25.7753 chia	1 sq. li 里 (=22,500 sq. chang)	25 hectares	61.776 acres
20.1666 p'ing	1 fen 分 (=6 sq. chang)	66.6666 sq. m	79.7328 sq. yd.
6.72222 mu	1 mu (=10 fen)	6.66667 ares	0.16441 acre
6.8736 chia	1 ch'ing 頃 (=100 mu)	6.66667 hectares	16.441 acres

Weights

Taiwan System	Market System	Metric System	English System
1 ch'ien 錢	0.75 ch'ien	3.75 g	0.12056 oz.
1 liang 兩 (tael) (=10 ch'ien)	0.75 liang	37.5 g	1.2056 oz.
1 chin 斤 (catty) (=16 liang)	1.2 chin	0.6 kg	1.3228 lb.
1 tan 石 (picul) (=100 chin)	1.2 tan	60 kg	132.277 lb.
1.3333 ch'ien	1 ch'ien	5 g	0.1764 oz.
1.3333 liang	1 liang (tael) (=10 ch'ien)	50 g	1.7637 oz.
0.8333 chin	1 chin (catty) (=10 liang)	0.5 kg	1.1023 lb.
0.8333 tan	1 tan (picul) (=100 chin)	50 kg	110.231 lb.

Appendix VII
National and Popular Holidays

Founding Day of the Republic of China *
中華民國開國紀念日
January 1

The president presides over a ceremony commemorating the January 1, 1912, founding of the Republic, which is attended by the presidents of each of the five Yuan (branches) of the central government, heads of the ministries, and other high-level officials.

Government offices are closed on January 1 and 2.

Farmer's Day 農民節
February 4, 1997

The start of spring 立春 has been traditionally marked by Farmer's Day, honoring the most important activity in traditional Chinese agrarian society. It falls at the beginning of one of the 24 seasonal periods of the year, on either February 4 or 5.

Chinese New Year 春節 *
February 7, 1997 (1st day, 1st moon)

Chinese New Year, also known as the Spring Festival, is the biggest festival celebrated in Taiwan. Chinese New Year's Day falls on the second new moon of the lunar calendar after the winter solstice. Thus, the first day of the lunar new year falls between January 21 and February 19 on the Gregorian calendar.

According to the Chinese lunar calendar, an ordinary year contains 12 lunar months of 29 or 30 days. A leap year occurs once every three years, when a 13th intercalary month is added to reestablish agreement with the solar year. The Chinese lunar calendar follows a 60-year cycle.

Festivities begin on the eighth day of the last lunar month of the old year and continue until the 15th day of the first month of the new year. On the eighth day of the last moon, commonly known as *la-pa* 臘八, people eat hot sweet congee, believed to bring good luck during the New Year season.

Families clean out their homes and offer sacrifices to the earth god on the 16th day of the last moon, commonly known as *wei-ya* 尾牙. Employers hold banquets for their employees to show their appreciation.

Offerings are made to propitiate the God of the Hearth 灶神 on the 24th day of the last moon. According to legend, the deity returns to heaven on this day to report to the Jade Emperor 玉皇大帝 the doings and misdoings of every member of the household he guards.

The climax of the festivities is on New Year's Eve 除夕, when every member of the family returns home to partake in a sumptuous family dinner, the last meal of the year, which includes fish and dumplings and other foods with symbolic meaning. Children receive *hung-pao* 紅包, or money placed in red envelopes, as the new year is ushered in with firecrackers.

On New Year's Day, ceremonial candles are lit and incense and sacrificial paper money burned. Endless strings of firecrackers are exploded and spring couplets are pasted on doors or at either side of the doorways to scare away the legendary *nien* 年 monster and evil spirits. People visit temples to pay respects to the gods before calling on their friends and relatives.

On the second day of the New Year 初二, firecrackers sound again as sacrifices are offered to the gods. Married daughters return to visit their parents' homes.

People usually stay at home on the third day, which is believed to be a time for bad luck. Accrding to legend, field mice hold their weddings on this day. Some families place rice outdoors for the occasion.

On the fourth day, the deities, including the God of the Hearth, are welcomed back to earth with sacrificial offerings and firecrackers.

Most people return to work on the fifth day, when businessmen make offerings to the God of Wealth 財神.

On the seventh day, families light seven candles and prepare dinners of seven dishes to mark the anniversary of the creation of man.

The eighth day marks the resumption of normal schedules for those not yet back at work, usually factory workers.

The birthday of the Jade Emperor, the supreme Taoist deity and ruler of heaven, is celebrated on the ninth day.

The New Year season draws to a close with the Lantern Festival (see below) on the 15th day of the first lunar month.

Government offices are closed for five days starting on New Year's Eve.

Lantern Festival 元宵節
February 21, 1997 (15th day, lst moon)

Most temples are illuminated by colorful lanterns of all shapes and sizes in the evening. Riddle-solving contests are held at temples, parks, and public places, with members of the public invited to find answers to clues written in couplets. Glutinous rice dumplings called *yuan hsiao* 元宵 are eaten.

Tourism Day 觀光節
February 21, 1997 (15th day, lst moon)

Tourism Day coincides with the Lantern Festival, the last day of Tourism Week, which begins on the ninth day of the first lunar month. Since the inception of Tourism Week in 1978, the Tourism Bureau has organized a series of events for visitors to Taiwan, including folk arts presentations and folk dance performances.

Peace Memorial Day 和平紀念日*
February 28

In remembrance of those lost in the unrest and aftermath of the February 28 Incident of 1947, and in hopes of healing the wounds and closing the divisions left by the episode, February 28 is observed as a national memorial day. In 1997, Peace Memorial Day was elevated to the status of a national holiday after the Legislative Yuan amended the *February 28 Incident Management and Compensation Act* 二二八事件處理及補償條例 on February 25 and the president promulgated the revised legislation on the same day.

Government offices are closed.

Women's Day 婦女節
March 8

Women's Day has been observed in the ROC since 1924, following the introduction of the women's movement from the West.

Earth God's Birthday 土地公誕辰
March 10, 1997 (2nd day, 2nd moon)

The birthday of the Earth God 土地公 is celebrated with great pomp, and temples are packed with worshippers from early morning till noon. Followers also make simpler offerings to the deity at temples and in front of their homes or stores on the first and 15th day of each lunar month. Every community and home is believed to be guarded by its own Earth God. According to legend, the Earth God was a tax collector who won popular acclaim for his kindness, and was deified after his death.

Arbor Day 植樹節
March 12

Trees are planted by school children in remembrance of Dr. Sun Yat-sen's encouragement of afforestation. The ROC government designated the day of Dr. Sun's passing as Arbor Day four years after his death in 1925.

Kuan Yin's Birthday 觀音誕辰
March 27, 1997 (19th day, 2nd moon)

Kuan Yin's birthday is celebrated with offerings of fruit and vegetables. A patron goddess of both Taoists and Buddhists, she is worshipped by seafarers, farmers, travellers, merchants, and women hoping for offspring.

Youth Day 青年節 *
March 29

Youth Day was initially observed on May 4 in commemoration of student participation in the May Fourth Movement in 1919. It was changed to March 29 in 1943 in remembrance of the young revolutionary fighters' role in the tenth uprising against the Manchus in Canton in 1912.

Government offices are closed.

Children's Day 兒童節 *
April 4

Activities are held at schools and by educational institutions to mark Children's Day, which has been observed since 1932.

Children have the day off from school. Government offices are closed, one day before Tomb-sweeping Day for celebrating Children's Day and Women's Day.

Tomb-Sweeping Day 清明節 *
Passing of President Chiang Kai-shek
蔣公逝世紀念日
April 5, 1997

Family graves are swept, and meats, fruits, and wine are arranged before the tombs. Services for President Chiang Kai-shek, who passed away on April 5, 1975, are held on this day.

Government offices are closed.

Festival of the God of Medicine 保生大帝誕辰
April 21, 1997 (15th day, 3rd moon)

Performing groups, including stilt walkers and musical bands, draw crowds to one of the most elaborate processions in Taiwan, held in Hsüehchia 學甲, Tainan County 台南縣, in honor of the tenth century healer, Wu Pen 吳本. Wu was later immortalized as the Great Emperor Pao Sheng 保生大帝.

Matsu's Birthday 媽祖誕辰
April 29, 1997 (23rd day, 3rd moon)

The birthday of Matsu, the goddess of the sea and patron saint of Chinese fishermen, is celebrated islandwide on this day. According to legend, Matsu saved her brother from drowning while she physically remained at home; she failed, however, to save her father. She is believed to have ascended to heaven at the age of 28.

Labor Day 勞動節 *
May 1

Following the inception of Labor Day by an international alliance in 1889, five years after an "eight-hour movement" was initiated by American workers for better treatment, Chinese workers in Canton began to observe the occasion in 1920. Labor Day was not celebrated nationwide, however, until after the conclusion of the Northern Expedition in 1928.

Workers have the day off.

Literary Day 文藝節
May 4

Awards for outstanding literary achievements are presented on this day. Literary Day has been observed since 1968 in commemoration of the role played by university students in the May Fourth Movement 五四

運動, and their call for democracy, scientific development, and the promotion of literature.

Mother's Day 母親節
May 11, 1997

Awards are presented to model mothers by municipal governments and women's organizations on the second Sunday of May.

Buddha's Birthday 佛誕日
May 14, 1997 (8th day, 4th moon)

Believers attend ceremonies at Buddhist shrines and chant sutras in celebration of the birthday of Siddhartha Gautama, founder of the religion. Images of the Buddha are bathed on this day.

Opium Suppression Movement Day 禁煙節
June 3

This day has been observed since 1930 in commemoration of the burning of imported opium in 1839 during the Opium War against the British.

Dragon Boat Festival 端午節 / 詩人節 *
June 9, 1997 (5th day, 5th moon)

Dragon boat races are held and glutinous rice dumplings wrapped in bamboo leaves are eaten in remembrance of Ch'ü Yüan 屈原, a famous scholar-statesman of the Warring States Period. Ch'ü drowned himself after failing to convince the king of Ch'u 楚王 to guard the kingdom against the enemy.

Government offices are closed.

Kuan Kung's Birthday 關公誕辰
June 17, 1997 (13th day, 5th moon)

Sacrificial offerings are made to Kuan Kung, the god of war and righteousness. Kuan Kung was a mighty warrior during the period of the Three Kingdoms.

Ch'eng Huang's Birthday 城隍誕辰
June 17, 1997 (13th day, 5th moon)

The largest procession honoring Ch'eng Huang, the city god, takes place at Taipei's Ch'eng Huang Temple 城隍廟. The deity is believed to protect the city from danger and guard it from enemies. According to legend, Ch'eng Huang was a river ghost whose harmlessness so impressed the ruler of Hades that he was later elevated to the status of city god.

Father's Day 父親節
August 8

This day was designated Father's Day in 1945. The Chinese characters for "eight" 八 (eighth day of the eighth month of the solar year) and "father" 爸 are both pronounced *pa*.

Ch'i Hsi Festival 七夕
August 9, 1997 (7th day, 7th moon)

On this Chinese version of Valentine's Day, lovers visit the Lovers' Temple 情人廟 in Peit'ou 北投, Taipei, where the Cowherd 牛郎 and Weaving Maid 織女 are enshrined. Legend has it that the Weaving Maid abandoned her work at the spinning wheel after she fell in love with the Cowherd. The Mother Goddess of Heaven 王母娘娘 was so angry that she separated the couple and allowed them to meet only once a year, on the seventh day of the seventh moon, when magpies come together to form a bridge over the Milky Way, which divides the two.

Ghost Festival 中元節
August 17, 1997 (15th day, 7th moon)

On the first day of the seventh moon, the gates of Hades are opened and the spirits are allowed a month of feasting and revelry in the land of the living. The climax is reached on the Ghost Festival, the 15th day of Ghost Month 鬼月, when great sacrificial feasts are set out in temples and in front of homes to appease wandering souls. Paper money is burned and lanterns floated on lakes and streams to deliver the dead.

Ami Initiation Festival 阿美族成年禮
End of August or beginning of September

The initiation ceremony of Ami boys at the age of 17 is preceded by performances of tribal dancers dressed in red and black. The festival is celebrated by the Ami tribes in Hualien.

Armed Forces Day 軍人節 *
September 3

Armed Forces Day was first observed in 1955 in memory of the contributions of military service men during the eight-year Sino-Japanese War, which ended with the Japanese surrender on September 3, 1945.

Servicemen are given leave in accordance with Ministry of National Defense directives.

Mid-Autumn Festival 中秋節 *
September 16, 1997 (15th day, 8th moon)

Families reunite in the evening to eat moon cakes 月餅 and gaze at the full moon. Legend has it that Ch'ang O 嫦娥 was swept to the moon after swallowing a pill of immortality. She later came to be known as the moon goddess.

Government offices are closed.

Teachers' Day 教師節 *
Confucius' Birthday 孔子誕辰紀念日
September 28

Teachers' Day is observed on the birthday anniversary of Confucius, the great sage and teacher who has had far reaching influence on Chinese philosophy and culture. Ceremonies are held at all Confucian temples, the largest one being at Taipei's Confucian Temple 台北孔廟, where a special dance in honor of the great teacher is performed each year. Awards are presented by the government to distinguished teachers.

Government offices are closed.

Double Tenth National Day 雙十節 / 國慶日 *
October 10

The Double Tenth National Day is observed in commemoration of the Wuch'ang Uprising 武昌起義 on October 10, 1911, which led to the establishment of the ROC on January 1, 1912. The president gives a public address in front of the Presidential Office Building, followed by a parade of armed forces academies, representatives of different professions, folk dancers, and dragon dancers. A massive fireworks display lights up the sky over the Tamsui River 淡水河 in the evening.

Government offices are closed.

Double Ninth Festival 九九重陽節
October 10, 1997 (9th day, 9th moon);

Also known as the Ch'ung Yang Festival 重陽節, this day has been set aside to honor senior citizens since 1966. Senior Citizens' Week is observed from the ninth to the 15th day of the ninth lunar month. According to legend, on the ninth day of the ninth lunar month, Matsu 媽祖, goddess of the sea, decided to climb a mountain overlooking the sea in search of her father, who drowned when he was out fishing. Senior Citizens' Day is observed on this day in remembrance of Matsu's filial piety.

Overseas Chinese Day 華僑節
October 21

The ROC government shows its appreciation for the support and contributions of overseas Chinese on this day.

Taiwan's Retrocession Day 光復節 *
October 25

This day marks the restoration of Taiwan to Chinese rule in 1945 after half a century of Japanese occupation.

Government offices are closed.

Chiang Kai-shek's Birthday 蔣公誕辰紀念日 *
October 31

Memorial services are held islandwide and government leaders pay their respects to late President Chiang Kai-shek at his temporary resting place on Tz'uhu 慈湖.

Government offices are closed.

Dr. Sun Yat-sen's Birthday 國父誕辰紀念日 *
November 12

Respects are paid to the Founding Father of the nation at the Sun Yat-sen Memorial Hall 國父紀念館 on this day. Doctors' Day 醫師節 and Cultural Renaissance Day 中華文化復興節 are also observed on this day.

Government offices are closed.

Saisiat Festival 賽夏節
November 14, 1997 (15th day, 10th moon)

The five-day *Pas-taai* Festival 矮靈祭 of the Saisiat tribe is celebrated with aborigines dancing to the ringing of bells, and an exhibition of huge "dance hats" carried by teams of men. These ceremonies in Nanchuang 南庄, Miaoli County 苗栗縣 are held once every two years to seek the forgiveness of a long-gone tribe of pygmies who were double-crossed by the Saisiats more than 500 years ago.

Winter Festival 冬至節
December 22, 1997

Glutinous rice dumplings are eaten to mark the beginning of the winter season. The Winter Festival falls on or around the winter solstice (December 21, 22, or 23) every year. The festival's lunar calendar date varies from year to year.

Constitution Day 行憲紀念日 *
December 25

The Constitution of the ROC was promulgated on January 1, 1947, and went into effect on December 25 of the same year.

Government offices are closed.

* Denotes a national holiday.

Appendix VIII
A Comparison of Various Chinese Romanization Systems

The Mandarin Phonetic Symbols (MPS) are used in ROC schools to teach children how to read Chinese (see Chapter 4, Language). Accordingly, MPS is the most widely known and used system in Taiwan for rendering the Mandarin 國語 pronunciation of Chinese characters into phonetic form. It is, however, much less well known in the West.

Wade-Giles is the Romanization system generally employed in the ROC today and has traditionally been the most frequently used system in Western scholarship. A drawback of this system is the use of apostrophes (') to indicate aspirated consonant sounds. Thus what English speakers hear as a *d*- is written *t*-, and what they know as *t*- is written *t'*-. The original idea was to indicate that Mandarin has no voiced/unvoiced consonant distinctions (like the English *d/t* contrast), but rather differentiates between aspirated and unaspirated consonant initials. While linguistically sound as a transcription system for the Mandarin language of its era, it is confusing for speakers of English. To make things worse, the apostrophes are often left out of some publications due to aesthetic or other concerns, leaving no way to distinguish aspirated from unaspirated consonant sounds.

Another problem is that, while tones can be indicated in the Wade-Giles system with numeral superscripts (e.g. *jen*[2]), they are usually omitted out of convenience. The umlaut in the front rounded vowel sound (*ü*) also tends to be left out due to difficulties in typesetting. With these omissions, it becomes impossible to know the exact pronunciation of any given word without checking the original Chinese. These disadvantages aside, the system does give a general idea of how to pronounce a word.

The Yale system is a relatively consistent and efficient one that is fairly easy for native speakers of American English to master. Its use, however, has never spread beyond a small number of Chinese language teaching texts.

The Pinyin system is the one adopted by the Chinese communists in mainland China, and by the Western news media. It corresponds closely to the MPS system. Its main potential drawback is its use of "leftover" letters like c, q, and x to represent Mandarin sounds that lack a handy equivalent in the Latin alphabet. These letters often confound those uninitiated in the Pinyin system, news broadcasters in particular. The Yale and Pinyin systems both add marks over the main vowel of a syllable to indicate tone. But again, the marks are often omitted as an expedient.

The Gwoyeu Romatzyh (GR) system was the ROC's official (since 1932) system of Romanizing Chinese, but was little known and seldom used. It had the unique feature of incorporating the tone of a word into its Romanized spelling, which was admittedly a convenience in typesetting.

The rules for "spelling" the tones, however, were highly complicated; they varied according to the phonetic composition of the syllable in question. The difficulties in popularizing this system were obvious.

In order to find a solution to such problems, the Ministry of Education held a meeting in January, 1984. A resolution was reached that the Gwoyeu Romatzyh should be revised and a working committee should be established. After extensive and intensive study and comparison of all existing transcription systems for Mandarin, the committee proposed a revised system which was officially called Mandarin Phonetic Symbols II (MPS II).

On May 10, 1984 the Ministry of Education announced that MPS II would be subject to trial use for a period of one year. On January 28, 1986, upon the completion of all relevant revisions after the trial use period, the Ministry of Education formally announced the final official version of MPS II.

The following comparison table of Romanization systems is intended to clear up some of the confusion caused by the simultaneous use of the different systems. It is also a convenient reference when reading Chinese with the aid of the Mandarin Phonetic Symbols.

A hyphen after a symbol or symbols (e.g. *p*-) means it is used as an initial; a hyphen before a symbol or symbols (e.g. *-ung*) signals a syllabic final. For the MPS symbols ㄅ and ㄥ, the vowel *e* is given in parentheses. This is to be transcribed into the other systems only when no other vowel is indicated in the MPS spelling. Multiple spellings for certain sounds in the Wade-Giles system indicate equally correct alternatives unless otherwise noted.

Ultimately, none of the systems has proven better than the others; each has its strengths and shortcomings. Romanization system preferences seem to be strongly tied to which system one learns first and is most accustomed to.

MPS	Wade-Giles	Yale	Pinyin	MPS II
ㄅ	p-	b-	b-	b-
ㄆ	p'-	p-	p-	p-
ㄇ	m-	m-	m-	m-
ㄈ	f-	f-	f-	f-
ㄉ	t-	d-	d-	d-
ㄊ	t'-	t-	t-	t-
ㄋ	n-	n-	n-	n-
ㄌ	l-	l-	l-	l-
ㄍ	k-	g-	g-	g-
ㄎ	k'-	k-	k-	k-
ㄏ	h-	h-	h-	h-
ㄐ	ch-	j-	j-	j(i)-
ㄑ	ch'-	ch-	q-	ch(i)-
ㄒ	hs-	sh-	x-	sh(i)-
ㄓ	chih, ch-	jr, j-	zhi, zh-	jr, j-
ㄔ	ch'ih, ch'-	chr, ch-	chi, ch-	chr, ch-
ㄕ	shih, sh-	shr, sh-	shi, sh-	shr, sh-
ㄖ	jih, j-	r	ri, r-	r, r-
ㄗ	tzu, ts-	dz	zi, z-	tz, tz-

MPS	Wade-Giles	Yale	Pinyin	MPS II
ㄘ	tz'u, ts'-	ts	ci, c-	tsz, ts-
ㄙ	szu, ssu s-	sz	si s-	sz, s-
ㄚ	a	a	a	a
ㄛ	-o	-o	-o	-o
ㄜ	-o, -e	-e	-e	-e
ㄝ	-(i)eh	-(y)e	-(i)e	-(i)e
ㄞ	ai	ai	ai	ai
ㄟ	-ei	-ei	-ei	-ei
ㄠ	ao	au	ao	au
ㄡ	ou	ou	ou	ou
ㄢ	an	an	an	an
ㄣ	(e)n	(e)n	(e)n	en
ㄤ	ang	ang	ang	ang
ㄥ	-(e)ng	-(e)ng	-(e)ng	-(e)ng
ㄦ	(e)rh	(e)r	(e)r	er
一	i, (y)i	yi, -i	yi, -i	yi, -i
ㄨ	wu, -u	wu, -u	wu, -u	wu, -u
ㄩ	yü, -ü	yu	yu, -u, -ü*	yu, -iu
一ㄚ	ya, -ia	ya	ya, -ia	ya, -ia
一ㄝ	yeh, -ieh	ye	ye, -ie	ye, -ie

MPS	Wade-Giles	Yale	Pinyin	MPS II
一ㄞ	yai	yai	yai	yai
一ㄠ	yao, -iao	yau	yao, -iao	yau, -iau
一ㄡ	yu, -iu	you	you, -iu	you, -iou
一ㄢ	yen, -ien	yan	yan, -ian	yan, -ian
一ㄣ	yin, -in	yin, -in	yin, -in	yin, -in
一ㄤ	yang, -iang	yang	yang, -iang	yang, -iang
一ㄥ	ying, -ing	ying, -ing	ying, -ing	ying, -ing
ㄨㄚ	wa, -ua	wa	wa, -ua	wa, -ua
ㄨㄛ	wo, -o, -uo**	wo,	wo, -uo	wo, -uo
ㄨㄞ	wai, -uai	wai	wai, -uai	wai, -uai
ㄨㄟ	wei, -ui, -uei***	wei	wei, -ui	wei, -uei
ㄨㄢ	wan, -uan	wan	wan, -uan	wan, -uan
ㄨㄣ	wen, -un	wen, -wun	wen, -un	wen, -uen

MPS	Wade-Giles	Yale	Pinyin	MPS II
ㄨㄤ	wang, -uang	wang	wang, -uang	wang, -uang
ㄨㄥ	weng, -ung	weng, -ung	weng, -ong	weng, -ung
ㄩㄝ	yüeh, -üeh	ywe,	yue, -ue -üe*	yue, -iue
ㄩㄢ	yüan, -üan	ywan	yuan, -uan	yuan, -iuan
ㄩㄣ	yün, -ün	yun	yun, -un	yun, -iun
ㄩㄥ	yung, -iung	yung	yong, -iong	yung, -iung

*   Used after l- and n-.
**   Used with the initials k-, k'-, h-, n-, l-, and sh-.
*** Used with the initials k- and k'-.

The tone marks for the MPS system are: first tone, no mark; second tone, ´; third tone, ˇ; fourth tone, ˋ; and neutral tone, ˙. The Yale, Pinyin and MPS II systems use the same tone marks, but add a first tone mark, ˉ.

Appendix IX
Internet Addresses of ROC Government Agencies

Government Agencies	World Wide Web	E-mail Address
Office of the President 總統府	http://www.oop.gov.tw	webmaster@www.oop.gov.tw
Academia Sinica 中央研究院	http://www.sinica.edu.tw	service@sinica.edu.tw
Academia Historica 國史館	gopher://gopher.drnh.gov.tw	gopher@sun1.drnh.gov.tw
Executive Yuan 行政院		
Ministry of the Interior 內政部	http://www.moi.gov.tw	gethics@mail.moi.gov.tw
Ministry of Foreign Affairs 外交部	http://www.mofa.gov.tw	
Ministry of National Defense 國防部	http://www.ndmc.edu.tw	
Ministry of Finance 財政部	http://www.mof.gov.tw	root@www.mof.gov.tw
Ministry of Education 教育部	http://www.moe.gov.tw	
Ministry of Justice 法務部	gopher://serv.hinet.net/11 /government /department/EY/moj	
Ministry of Economic Affairs 經濟部	http://www.moea.gov.tw	service@moea.gov.tw
Ministry of Transportation and Communications 交通部	http://www.motc.gov.tw	motceyes@motc.gov.tw
Mongolian & Tibetan Affairs Commission 蒙藏委員會	gopher://serv.hinet.net/11 /government/department/EY/mtac	
Overseas Chinese Affairs Commission 僑務委員會	http://www.ocac.gov.tw	ocacinfo@mail.ocac.gov.tw
The Central Bank of China 中央銀行	http://www.cbc.gov.tw	admirol@cbciso.cbc.gov.tw
Directorate General of Budget, Accounting and Statistics 主計處	http://www.dgbasey.gov.tw	edp@emc.dgbasey.gov.tw
Central Personnel Administration 人事行政局	http://www.cpa.gov.tw	
Government Information Office 新聞局	http://www.gio.gov.tw	service@mail.gio.gov.tw
Department of Health 衛生署	http://www.doh.gov.tw	
Environmental Protection Administration 環境保護署	http://www.epa.gov.tw	www@sun.epa.gov.tw

Government Agencies	World Wide Web	E-mail Address
National Palace Museum 國立故宮博物院	http://www.npm.gov.tw	webmaster@ss20.npm.gov.tw
Mainland Affairs Council 大陸委員會	http://www.mac.gov.tw	macst@mac.gov.tw
Council for Economic Planning and Development 經濟建設委員會	http://www.cepd.gov.tw	
Veterans Affairs Commission 國軍退除役官兵輔導委員會	http://www.vacrs.gov.tw	hsc@www.vacrs.gov.tw
National Youth Commission 青年輔導委員會	http://www.nyc.gov.tw	
Atomic Energy Council 原子能委員會	http://www.aec.gov.tw	
National Science Council 國家科學委員會	http://www.nsc.gov.tw	nsc@nsc.gov.tw
Research, Development and Evaluation Commission 研究發展考核委員會	http://rdec.gov.tw	service@rdec.gov.tw
Council of Agriculture 農業委員會	http://www.coa.gov.tw	webmaster@www.coa.gov.tw
Council for Cultural Affairs 文化建設委員會	http://expo96.org.tw/cca/welcome_c.html	wwwadm@ccpdunx.ccpd.gov.tw
Council of Labor Affairs 勞工委員會	gopher://192.192.46.131	
Fair Trade Commission 公平交易委員會	http://www.ftc.gov.tw	ftcpd@ftc.gov.tw
Public Construction Commission 公共工程委員會	http://www.pcc.gov.tw	
Consumer Protection Commission 消費者保護委員會	gopher://serv.hinet.net/11 /government/department/EY/cpc	
Central Election Commission 中央選舉委員會	gopher://serv.hinet.net/11 /government/department/EY/cec	
Judicial Yuan 司法院	http://www.judicial.gov.tw	
Examination Yuan 考試院	gopher://serv.hinet.net/11 /government/department/exam	
Ministry of Examination 考選部	http://www.moex.gov.tw	

Government Agencies	World Wide Web	E-mail Address
Ministry of Civil Service 銓敍部	gopher://serv.hinet.net/11 /government/department/mop	
Control Yuan 監察院	http://www.cy.gov.tw	
National Audit Office 審計部	http://www.audit.gov.tw	
Taiwan Provincial Government 台灣省政府	http://www.tpg.gov.tw	
Taipei City Government 台北市政府	http://www.tcg.gov.tw	webmaster@serv2.tcg.gov.tw
Kaohsiung City Government 高雄市政府	http://kcg.gov.tw	

Index

H

O